The Oxford Guide to Film Studies

The Oxford Guide to Film Studies

Edited by

JOHN HILL and **PAMELA CHURCH GIBSON**

Consultant Editors

Richard Dyer   E. Ann Kaplan   Paul Willemen

Oxford University Press
1998

Oxford University Press, Great Clarendon Street, Oxford OX2 6DP
Oxford New York
Athens Auckland Bangkok Bogota Bombay Buenos Aires
Calcutta Cape Town Dar es Salaam Delhi Florence Hong Kong Istanbul
Karachi Kuala Lumpar Madras Madrid Melbourne Mexico City
Nairobi Paris Singapore Taipei Tokyo Toronto Warsaw
and associated companies in
Berlin Ibadan

Oxford is a trade mark of Oxford University Press

Published in the United States
by Oxford University Press Inc., New York

British Library Cataloguing in Publication Data
Data available

Library of Congress Cataloging in Publication Data
Data available
ISBN 0–19–871115–8
ISBN 0–19–871124–7 (pbk)

10 9 8 7 6 5 4 3 2 1

Typeset by J&L Composition Ltd, Filey, North Yorkshire
Printed in Great Britain
on acid-free paper by
Alden Press, Osney Mead, Oxford

Acknowledgements

We would like to thank a number of people who have helped in the preparation of this book. We are, of course, grateful to all our contributors, some of whom worked to particularly tight deadlines. We would also like to thank our consultant editors—Richard Dyer, Ann Kaplan, and Paul Willemen—for their assistance and advice. Ginette Vincendeau acted as consultant on the section on European cinema and provided invaluable help; Geoffrey Nowell-Smith also provided good advice and suggestions at an early stage.

At Oxford University Press, we would particularly like to thank our editor Andrew Lockett for his constant support and enthusiasm for the book, Tania Pickering for her invaluable assistance, and Mick Belson for his help and efficiency in preparing the manuscript for publication.

We are also grateful to Roma Gibson, Celia Britton, Stella Bruzzi, and Teresa de Lauretis for their help. John Hill is also indebted to his colleagues David Butler, Dan Fleming, and Martin McLoone at the University of Ulster for their support for the project and to the Faculty of Humanities for a well-timed period of leave of absence.

Thanks also to the staff at BFI Stills and to Timothy Seaton for his translation of the essay by Armand Mattelart (Part 3, Chapter 12) and the British Academy for support/assistance to Murray Smith in the completion of his chapter.

J. H. and P. C. G.

Contents

CONTENTS

Contributors

EDITORS

John Hill is a Senior Lecturer in Media Studies at the University of Ulster. He is the author of *Sex, Class and Realism: British Cinema 1956–63* (1986), co-author of *Cinema in Ireland* (1987), and co-editor of *Border Crossing: Film in Ireland, Britain and Europe* (1994), and *Big Picture, Small Screen: The Relations Between Film and Television* (1996). His book on British cinema in the 1980s is soon to be published by Oxford University Press.

Pamela Church Gibson is a Senior Lecturer in Contextual and Cultural Studies at the London College of Fashion, a constituent college of the London Institute. She is the co-editor of *Dirty Looks: Women, Pornography, Power* (1993) and is currently working on a collection of essays on fashion and film.

CONSULTANT EDITORS

Richard Dyer is Professor of Film Studies at the University of Warwick. He is the author of a number of books including *Stars* (1979), *Heavenly Bodies* (1986), *The Matter of Images* (1993), *Now You See It* (1990), and *White: Essays on Race and Culture* (1997).

E. Ann Kaplan teaches at the Department of English at the Humanities Institute at Stony Brook, New York. She is the author of a number of books including *Women and Film: Both Sides of the Camera* (1983), *Motherhood and Representation: The Mother in Popular Culture and Melodrama* (1992), and *Looking For the Other: Feminism, Film, and the Imperial Gaze* (1997).

Paul Willemen is Professor of Critical Studies at Napier University, Edinburgh. He has published widely on film theory and is the author of *Looks and Frictions: Essays in Cultural Studies and Film Theory* (1994) and co-editor of *Questions of Third Cinema* (1989) and the *Encyclopaedia of Indian Cinema* (1994).

CONTRIBUTORS

Dudley Andrew is a Professor at the Institute for Cinema and Culture at the University of Iowa and is the author of *Major Film Theories* (1976), *Concepts in Film Theory* (1984), and *Mists of Regret: Culture and Sensibility in Classic French Film* (1995).

José Arroyo is Lecturer in Film Studies at the University of Warwick and has written on Spanish and Canadian cinema.

John Belton teaches film at the English Department at Rutgers University and is author of *Widescreen Cinema* (1992) and *American Cinema/American Culture* (1994).

Peter Brunette teaches in the Department of English at George Mason University, Fairfax, Virginia, and is author of *Roberto Rossellini* (1987) and co-author of *Screen/Play: Derrida and Film Theory* (1989).

Julianne Burton-Carvajal teaches at the University of California, Santa Cruz. Her publications include *Cinema and Social Change in Latin America* (1986) and *The Social Documentary in Latin America* (1990).

Jeremy G. Butler is an Associate Professor in the Telecommunication and Film Department of the University of Alabama. He is the editor of *Star Texts: Image and Performance in Film and Television* (1991) and the author of *Television: Critical Methods and Applications*. He also created *Screensite*, a World Wide Web site devoted to film studies: http://www.sa.ua.edu/ScreenSite.

CONTRIBUTORS

Kuan-Hsing Cheng teaches at the Center for Cultural Studies in the College of Humanities and Social Sciences at the National Tsing Hua University in Taiwan. He is the author of *Intellectual Moods and Geo-Colonial Sites* (Taipei, 1996) and co-editor of *Stuart Hall: Critical Dialogues in Cultural Studies* (1996).

Rey Chow is Professor of English and Comparative Literature at the University of California, Irvine. Her publications in English include *Woman and Chinese Modernity: The Politics of Reading between East and West* (1990), *Writing Diaspora: Tactics of Intervention in Contemporary Cultural Studies* (1993), and *Primitive Passions: Visuality, Sexuality, Ethnography, and Contemporary Chinese Cinema* (1995).

Ian Christie is Professor of Film Studies at the University of Kent. He has published widely on Russian and British cinema, on early film, and on the avant-garde, and is author of *Arrows of Desire: The Films of Michael Powell and the Emeric Pressburger* (1994).

Barbara Creed is a Senior Lecturer in the Department of Fine Arts at Melbourne University, Australia. She has published widely on feminism psychoanalysis, and the horror film and is author of *Monstrous-Feminine* (1993).

Stephen Crofts is a Senior Lecturer in Film and Media Studies at Griffith University, Brisbane, Australia, and the author of a forthcoming study on Australian film.

Chris Darke is a freelance writer and part-time lecturer at the University of Warwick and has contributed to *Sight and Sound*, *Screen*, and other publications.

Wimal Dissanayake is a Senior Fellow at the East–West Center, Hawaii, and editor of *Melodrama and Asian Cinema* (1993), *Colonialism and Nationalism in Asian Cinema* (1994), and the *East West Journal*.

Alexander Doty is an Associate Professor in the English Department at Lehigh University, Bethlehem, USA. He is the author of *Making Things Perfectly Queer: Interpreting Mass Culture* (1993) and co-editor of *Out in Culture: Gay, Lesbian and Queer Essays on Popular Culture* (1995) and is currently working on a collection of queer readings of classic films.

Anthony Easthope is Professor of English and Cultural Studies at the Metropolitan University, Manchester, and author of a number of books including *Poetry as Discourse* (1983), *British Post-Structuralism* (1988), *What a Man's Gotta Do: Masculine Myth in Popular Culture* (1986) and *Literary into Cultural Studies* (1991).

Jill Forbes is Ashley Watkins Professor of French at the University of Bristol and author of *The Cinema in France after the New Wave* (1992), *Contemporary France* (1994), *Les Enfants du paradis* (1997), and co-editor of *French Cultural Studies* (1995). She is at present working on a study of Marcel Carné as well as a monograph on French popular culture in the 1940s and 1950s.

Cathy Fowler is a Lecturer in Film Studies at the Southampton Institute of Higher Education and is finishing a Ph.D. on Chantal Akerman at the University of Warwick. She is the main contributor for the 'Belgium' section of the *Encyclopedia of European Cinema* (1995).

Freda Frieberg teaches at Monash University, Melbourne, and is author of *Women in Mizoguchi Films* (1981) and editor of *Don't Shoot Darling! Women's Independent Film making in Australia* (1987).

Douglas Gomery is a Professor in the Department of Radio–Television–Film at the University of Maryland. He has published widely on the film industry and is author of *The Hollywood Studio System* (1986) and *Shared Pleasures: A History of Movie Presentation in the United States* (1992).

Claudia Gorbman is a Professor of Liberal Studies at the University of Washington, Tacoma, USA where she teaches film, media studies, and literature. Her work on film music includes *Unheard Melodies: Narrative Film Music* (1987). Among her translations are Michel Chion's *Audio-Vision: Sound on Screen* (1994).

Daniel J. Goulding is a Professor of Film Studies and Theatre Arts at Oberlin College, Ohio. He is author of *Liberated Cinema: The Yugoslav Experience* (1985) and contributing editor of *Post New*

Wave Cinema in the Soviet Union and Eastern Europe (1989) and *Five Filmmakers: Tarkovsky, Forman, Polanski, Szabó, Makavejev* (1993).

Jostein Gripsrud is a Professor in the Department of Media Studies at the University of Bergen, Norway. He is author of *The Dynasty Years: Hollywood Television and Critical Media Studies* (1995). He was on the Board of the Moving Images in Norway Project 1990–3, and co-authored a book in Norwegian on the recent history of film in Norway (1996).

Tom Gunning teaches in the Art Department at the University of Chicago. He has published widely on early cinema and is author of *D. W. Griffith and the Origins of Narrative Film* (1991).

Susan Hayward is Professor of French at the University of Exeter and author of *French National Cinema* (1993) and co-editor of *French Film: Texts and Contexts* (1990).

Andrew Higson is a Senior Lecturer in Film Studies at the University of East Anglia in England. His publications include *Waving the Flag: Constructing a National Cinema in Britain* (1995), and, as contributing editor, *Dissolving Views: Key Writings on British Cinema* (1996).

John Izod is Dean of the Faculty of Arts and a Senior Lecturer in Film and Media Studies at the University of Stirling in Scotland. He is author of *Reading the Screen* (1984), *Hollywood and the Box Office* (1988), *The Films of Nicolas Roeg* (1992), and, with Richard Kilborn, *An Introduction to Television Documentary* (1997). He is currently working on a theoretical book adapting Jungian theory to the analysis of film and television

Elizabeth Jacka is Professor of Communication Studies and Dean of the Faculty of Humanities and Social Sciences at the University of Technology, Sydney. She is co-author of *The Screening of Australia* (2 vols.) (1987/8), *The Imaginary Industry* (1988), and *Australian Television and International Mediascapes* (1996) as well as co-editor of *New Patterns in Global Television* (1996).

Douglas Kellner is Professor of Philosophy at the University of Texas at Austin. He is the author and co-author of numerous books on social theory, politics, history, and culture, including *Camera Politica: The Politics and Ideology of Contemporary Hollywood Film* (with Michael Ryan) (1988), *Jean Baudrillard* (1989), and *Critical Theory, Marxism and Modernity* (1989). He is currently working on the impact of new information and entertainment technologies on society and culture.

Richard Kilborn is a Senior Lecturer in the Department of Film and Media Studies at the University of Stirling in Scotland. He is the author of *The Multi-Media Melting Pot* (1986), *Television Soaps* (1992) and, with John Izod, *An Introduction to Television Documentary* (1997).

Noel King teaches in the School of Humanities at the University of Technology, Sydney and has written widely on film theory.

Laura Kipnis is an Associate Professor of Radio–Television–Film at Northwestern University, Chicago. Her most recent book is *Bound and Gagged: Pornography and the Politics of Fantasy in America* (1983). She is also an independent videomaker whose work is exhibited and broadcast internationally.

Chuck Kleinhans is a Professor in the Department of Radio, Television, and Film at Northwestern University, Chicago and co-editor of *Jump Cut: A Review of Contemporary Media*.

Robert Phillip Kolker teaches in the Department of English at the University of Maryland and is the author of *The Altering Eye: Contemporary International Cinema* (1983) and *A Cinema of Loneliness* (1988).

Peter Kramer is Lecturer in American Film in the American Studies Department at Keele University. His work on aspects of American film history has been published in *Screen*, *The Velvet Light Trap*, and a number of edited collections.

N. K. Leung works for Satellite Asian Region Ltd in Hong Kong.

Paul McDonald is a Senior Lecturer in Media Studies at South Bank University, London. He is completing a Ph.D. on film acting and has contributed a chapter on 'Star studies' to *Approaches to Popular Film* (1995).

Martin McLoone is a Senior Lecturer in Media Studies at the University of Ulster. He is co-editor of a number of publications including *Television and Irish Society* (1984), *Culture, Identity and Broad-*

casting in Ireland (1991), *Border Crossing: Film in Europe, Britain and Ireland* (1994), and *Big Picture, Small Screen: The Relations Between Film and Television* (1996).

Armand Mattelart is a Belgian sociologist who worked in Chile from 1962 to 1973 and is now Professor of Sociology at the University of Paris. His publications include *Mapping World Communication: War, Progress, Culture* (1994) and *The Invention of Communication* (1996), and with Michele Mattelart, *The Carnival of Images: Brazilian Television Fiction* (1990) and *Rethinking Media Theory: Signposts and New Directions* (1992).

Toby Miller is an Associate Professor in the Department of Cinema Studies at the Tisch School of the Arts, New York University. He is author of *The Well-Tempered Self: Citizenship, Culture, and the Postmodern Subject* (1993), *Contemporary Australian Television* (with Stuart Cunningham) (1994), *The Avengers* (1997), and *Technologies of Truth: Cultural Citizenship and the Popular Media* (1997).

Simona Monticelli completed an M.Phil. thesis on gender and national identity in Italian Neo-Realist cinema at the University of Warwick where she has also been a part-time lecturer in film.

Albert Moran is a Senior Research Fellow in the Faculty of Humanities at Griffith University, Brisbane. He is author of *Projecting Australia* (1991) and *Moran's Guide to Australian TV Series* (1993) and editor of *Film Policy: International, National and Regional Perspectives* (1996).

Michael O'Pray is a Reader in Visual Theories at the School of Art and Design at the University of East London and has written widely on film, the avant-garde, and animation. He is editor of *Andy Warhol: Film Factory* and *Into the Pleasure Dome: the Films of Kenneth Anger* (1989) and author of *Derek Jarman: Dreams of England* (1997). He is currently writing a book on Adrian Stokes and film aesthetics.

Duncan Petrie teaches at the School of English and American Studies at the University of Exeter and is author of *Creativity and Constraint in the British Film Industry* (1991) and *The British Cinematographer* (1996).

Ashish Rajadhyaksha is a freelance writer and researcher and co-editor of the *Encyclopaedia of Indian Cinema* (1994).

Robert Ray is Professor of English and the Director of Film and Media Studies at the University of Florida, Gainesville, and author of *A Certain Tendency of the Hollywood Cinema 1930–1980* (1985) and *The Avant-Garde Finds Andy Hardy* (1995).

Keith Reader is Professor of French at the University of Newcastle. His books include *Cultures on Celluloid* (1981), *The May 1968 Events in France* (1993), and *Regis Debray* (1995).

Bérénice Reynaud teaches film at the California Institute of Arts and has written on Chinese cinema for *Cahiers du Cinema*, *Liberation*, and *Sight and Sound*. She is currently writing a book on the last twelve years of Chinese cinema entitled *New Visions/New China*.

Tom Ryall is a Reader in Film Studies at the School of Cultural Studies at Sheffield Hallam University. He is author of *Alfred Hitchcock and the British Cinema* (1986) and is currently working on a study of the interrelationships between the British and American cinemas.

Ulrike Sieglohr is a Senior Lecturer in Media Studies at Staffordshire University. She has published on aspects of New German Cinema and has completed a Ph.D. on the German filmmaker Werner Schroeter.

Anneke Smelik is a researcher with the Department of Women's Studies at the Utrecht University in The Netherlands. She is author of *And the Mirror Cracked: Feminist Cinema and Film Theory* (1997) and co-editor of *Women's Studies: A Feminist Introduction* (1995).

Murray Smith is a Lecturer in Film Studies at the University of Kent at Canterbury. He is the author of *Engaging Characters: Fiction, Emotion and the Cinema* (1995) and co-editor of *Film Theory and Philosophy: Aesthetics and the Analytical Tradition* (1997).

Will Straw is an Associate Professor in the Centre for Research on Canadian Cultural Industries and Institutions at McGill University, Montreal. He has published widely on popular music, film, and cultural studies and is co-editor of *Theory Rules: Art as Theory/Theory and Art* (1996).

Stephen Teo, originally from Malaysia, works as a critic and filmmaker in Hong Kong and lives part of the year in Australia. For a number of years, he has been the editor of the Hong Kong Cinema Retrospective catalogues published annually by the Hong Kong International Film Festival and is the author of *Hong Kong Cinema* (1997).

Andrew Tudor is a Reader in Sociology at the University of York. He was the film critic of *New Society* for several years and is the author of *Theories of Film* (1974), *Image and Influence: Studies in the Sociology of Film* (1974), and *Monsters and Mad Scientists: A Cultural History of the Horror Movie* (1989).

Graeme Turner is Professor of Cultural Studies in the Department of English at the University of Queensland, Australia. He has published widely on topics in cultural studies and film, and on Australian media and popular culture. He is currently researching the function of celebrity in Australian television news and current affairs programming. He is author of *Film as Social Practice* (1990) and *British Cultural Studies* (1990).

N. Frank Ukadike teaches film and cultural studies at the University of Michigan, Ann Arbor. He is the author of *Black African Cinema* (1994) and *A Questioning of Cinema: Conversations with Black African Filmmakers* (1997).

Ginette Vincendeau is a Professor of Film Studies at the University of Warwick. She has written extensively on French cinema and is the editor of *The Encyclopedia of European Film* (1995). She is currently completing a book on *Pépé le Moko* and a study of 1930s French cinema, entitled *The Art of Spectacle: Popular French Cinema in the 1930s*.

Patricia White is an Assistant Professor of English and Film Studies at Swarthmore College, USA. She has published on feminist film studies and lesbian representation in a number of collections and is author of the forthcoming book *The Uninvited: Cinema and the Conditions of Lesbian Representability*.

Robyn Wiegman is Director of Women's Studies at the University of California, Irvine. She is author of *American Anatomies: Theorizing Race and Gender* (1995) and editor of *Feminism Beside Itself* (1995) and *Who Can Speak? Authority and Critical Identity* (1995).

List of illustrations

LIST OF ILLUSTRATIONS

General Introduction

John Hill

In 1995 the cinema celebrated the centenary of the first public film screening. Since 1895 it has grown and spread globally and, despite a decline in attendances world-wide, filmwatching is now more popular than ever, thanks to television and video. New communication technologies and forms of entertainment have undoubtedly affected the social and cultural role of cinema, but it none the less retains a huge importance as an economic and cultural activity. As such, film continues to attract enormous critical attention, in both popular discourses and academic fields of study, and the ways in which film has been studied and accounted for are the central concern of this book.

The aim of *The Oxford Guide to Film Studies* is to provide the reader, through the eyes of a wide variety of contributors, with a critical overview of the various ways in which film has been understood and made sense of by writers and academics. It looks at the main disciplinary approaches and theoretical frameworks which have been employed in the study of film, the main concepts and methods involved in film analysis, and the main issues involved in the discussion of specific areas (such as national cinemas). As such, the emphasis of the Guide is primarily on *critical concepts*, *methods*, and *debates* in film study rather than on the provision of detailed information. In this respect it is intended to complement rather than duplicate *The Oxford History of World Cinema* (1996), which has already undertaken an ambitious mapping of the historical development of 'world cinema'.

There are several ways in which this book provides a guide to the study of film. First, it looks at film 'in the round'. A distinction is sometimes drawn between 'film' (the actual 'film texts' shown in cinemas or on television and video) and 'cinema' (the array of activities involved in the production and reception of films). In this regard, the Guide is more accurately viewed as a guide to 'cinema studies'. For while the film text is central to the book (and provides film studies with much of its distinctive focus), there is also a clear concern to address the variety of ways in which the film text is intermeshed with a whole set of economic, technological, social, and cultural practices. Thus, the Guide certainly focuses upon film texts, but also examines the development of film as an industry and technology, the role which government and state have played in relation to film production and exhibition, the behaviour of film audiences, as well the larger socio-cultural context in which films are made and received. Accordingly, the Guide not only pays close attention to the techniques and conventions specific to film, and their analysis by film scholars, but also scrutinizes the critical issues involved in explaining how films come to be made and distributed, how they are responded to by audiences, and how the meanings 'spoken' by films—and the various 'readings' which audiences make of them—may be seen to connect to larger patterns of social and cultural identities.

With these aims in mind, the Guide explores not only the various aspects of film production and consumption but also the historical and geographical variety of filmmaking. So, while it gives considerable attention to popular forms of narrative filmmaking (especially those associated with Hollywood), it also examines forms outside this tradition, such as documentary, animation, modernism, and the avant-garde. The Guide also reviews the diversity of filmmaking traditions outside the United States and the critical issues to which differing regional, national, and continental filmmaking traditions have given rise. In consequence, it familiarizes readers with the debates concerning non-mainstream cinemas and also puts to the test some of the theories and critical approaches that have been adopted in relation to mainstream films. As the different contributors to the Guide indicate, the study of Indian, Chinese, Japanese, and African cinemas has rendered problematic many of the assumptions (about filmic conventions or spectator-ship, for example) that have traditionally governed the study of film in the West and has therefore entailed the need for more appropriate alternative perspectives.

A key aim of the Guide therefore, is to represent the diversity of theoretical, critical, and cultural perspectives that have been a feature of film study, which since the 1960s has been so fertile. During this time film studies has borrowed heavily from other areas (importing ideas from semiotics, structuralism, psychoanalysis, Marxism, feminism, post-structuralism, and deconstruction, and, more recently, cultural studies and postmodernism), but has also fed back into more general debates within the humanities and social sciences where the insights of film theory have often been particularly influential. At the same time the study of film has been characterized by intense debate so that while certain theoretical frameworks may have achieved pre-eminence at certain junctures—such as authorship study in the early 1960s or 'psycho-semiotic' approaches in the 1970s—there have always been alternative traditions which have sought to challenge these perspectives and provide alternative means for explaining the workings of film. So while the Guide clearly reflects that certain traditions (such as psychoanalytic feminism) have been especially influential in shaping the study of film, it also acknowledges less well-known perspectives (such as those of Impressionism and hermeneutics) and addresses issues that dominant strands of film study may often have neglected (such as political economy or questions of cultural identity).

The result is a book which, it is hoped, successfully conveys the variety of ways in which film has been studied and the genuine debate that has characterized the field. The Guide does not adopt one 'line' or advocate one critical approach above others (even though individual authors may often argue for particular theoretical frameworks or critical preferences), but seeks instead to suggest the issues that have been a feature of film study and what is at stake in relation to them. It makes no attempt to iron out the differences between these approaches: readers are left to make their own intellectual, and in some cases political, choices concerning the critical approaches and methods of most relevance to their own enthusiasms.

The structure of the book is as follows. Part 1 introduces the field of film studies and the variety of ways in which the study of film has been undertaken. Individual chapters outline the main theoretical frameworks that have been employed in the study of film and assess the strengths and weaknesses of different approaches. Thus they examine not only the various critical approaches to the study of film texts but also the study of film texts within a range of social, historical, and ideological contexts. This part of the Guide, therefore, begins with an examination of methods of textual analysis and the issues involved in studying film texts before opening out into questions concerned with the relationship of films to ideologies (of class, gender, sexual orientation, race, and ethnicity), cultural identities, and the range of social and historical circumstances in which films are made and consumed.

Part 2 focuses on American cinema and Hollywood. Since the end of the First World War the US film industry has been dominant in world cinema and, as many of the chapters in

Part 3 make clear, it has often been in relation to Hollywood that other cinemas have had to define themselves (through competition, differentiation, or opposition). It is therefore unsurprising that American cinema has enjoyed a pre-eminent position within film studies, and this is acknowledged in the space devoted to it. Part 2 looks at the various approaches which have been adopted in relation to the study of American cinema and Hollywood (including the film industry and the uses of technology as well as actual films), the ways in which its historical development has been periodized (as in the concepts of 'classical' and 'post-classical' cinema), and the main concepts and methods (such as authorship study, genre study, star study, and ideology critique) which have been involved in its analysis.

Part 3 is devoted to non-Hollywood cinemas in the sense of films that are both made outside Hollywood and have adopted different aesthetic models of filmmaking. However, although 'other' cinemas are often identified by their difference from Hollywood models, it would of course be a mistake to see them as constituting some kind of homogeneous filmmaking practice. On the contrary, non-Hollywood cinemas have been characterized by aesthetic, cultural, and ideological diversity and its is this diversity that Part 3 explores. In doing so, it reviews the debates that have characterized the study of these cinemas (across Europe, Asia, Africa, and South America), the concepts (such as 'national cinema' and 'art cinema') that have been employed, and the economic, political, and artistic questions that have marked such debates.

Although the Guide aspires to comprehensiveness, it is not exhaustive in its coverage either of critical positions or of topics. There is naturally a degree of selection and readers will find more on certain areas, less on others, than they might have expected. This is particularly the case with Part 3, where use has been made of case-studies of particular cinemas and filmmakers rather than a full coverage of debates concerning 'world' cinema. Thus, while certain countries and filmmakers are omitted, it is expected that the critical concepts and issues raised in this section will be seen to have purchase beyond the circumstances of their immediate application (just as there is clear evidence of overlapping concerns in the study of different national cinemas in the chapters already contained in the book).

In each case, the chapters lay out and assess the history and meanings of key critical terms, issues, and debates in relation to a particular topic. In some chapters, there are also additional 'readings' of individual films which are intended to illustrate how different theories or perspectives have been applied to particular examples. In this respect, the chapters and extracts are also a guide to further reading and viewing, identifying the books, articles, and films that have figured most prominently in debates. The bibliographies which accompany each chapter include not only full details of the material referred to in each chapter but also relevant texts that may not actually be cited but are none the less significant. Particularly useful texts, recommended for further reading, are accompanied by an asterisk.

Chapters follow on from one another to provide a cumulative overview of the field, although they are sufficiently self-contained to be read separately. Cross-references indicate useful connections between chapters, for example between feminism and psychoanalysis or between feminism and gay and lesbian criticism.

The authors of individual chapters have been asked not only to survey their particular area but also to identify some of the questions that still remain unresolved in relation to it. In this way, it is planned that the reader should gain some sense of the field (and individual areas within it), not simply as a body of agreed knowledge but as a site of continuing debate and discussion concerning critical approaches and methods. It is ultimately in this spirit that the Guide is presented: to provoke thought and encourage debate, and to stimulate further research. The excitement of film studies is that, despite a growing institutionalization, it remains a field in which a variety of approaches coalesce and compete and in which basic questions remain unsettled. If the Guide communicates some of that excitement amongst its readers (be they students, teachers, or those with a general interest in the serious study of film), then it can be judged a success.

PART 1

Critical approaches

1

Introduction to film studies

Richard Dyer

Anything that exists can be studied, and in these last years of the twentieth century it may well seem that virtually everything is. Yet only some things become organized into disciplines and institutionalized into departments and conferences; if everything has its web site, only some things have their boards of examiners, refereed journals, and employed enthusiasts, or possess the (often insecure) cultural capital of being understood to be 'studies'. Nor is the form that studies take wholly determined by the object of study—the history of film studies, as of any other discipline, makes clear that there are many different ways of deciding what it is you attend to, and how you attend to it, when you 'study' something.

All manner of factors, including chance, determine why something gets taken up as worthy of 'study' and what form that takes, but cutting across them all is the conviction, one that must be or be made widespread, that the object of study is important, that it matters. It is the terms of such mattering that then characterize the changing forms of study.

In principle, there could be film studies based upon the science and techniques of film, its physics and chemistry, the practices and possibilities of the camera and the other apparatuses of filmmaking. Yet these have not constituted a discrete branch of film studies, nor even very often been seen as indispensable to the study of film. This is despite not only a handful of academic studies, but also the in fact rather wide-spread discourse of film science and technique in the culture at large, from the journals of professional cinematography all the way through to the lively market in special effects (how they are done) fandom.

> All manner of factors, including chance, determine why something gets taken up as worthy of 'study' and what form that takes, but cutting across them all is the conviction, one that must be or be made widespread, that the object of study is important, that it matters.

An interest in the physics and chemistry of film has made some impact within film studies in work on what are seen as the three decisive innovations in the history of film: its very invention and the introductions of sound and colour. (To these we might add wide screen—though this is generally seen as less transformative of the medium—and television, video, and digitization, which sometimes seem to open out onto the vista of the end, or at any rate acute marginalization, of our object of study, film.) Here such matters as the phenomenon of persistence of vision, the chemistry of photographic stock and celluloid, or the subtractive versus additive methods for colour production do form part of many curricula, reference books, and histories. Yet the study of such things, the very basic means and possibility of film, for their own sake, as central to the discipline, is not established. Similarly, although students of film do sometimes know something about technique—know, for instance, what a fresnel does, or the merits of one Eastman Kodak stock over another—such knowledge has remained at best an optional extra to the constitution of film studies.

This has in part to do with the scientific illiteracy of most of those who constructed the field. It has also to do with a divide in conceptions of science and technology, between what I shall call—and polarize as—objectivists and historicists. The former see the truths of science as facts discovered in the natural world and technical practices as things imposed upon practitioners by apparatuses; the latter, the historicists, see scientific knowledge constructed according to cultural paradigms and see practices as routinized uses of apparatuses, apparatuses that were themselves constructed according to cultural norms and could be used differently. Though many scientists and technicians are much more profoundly aware of the relative nature of their knowledge and practices than film scholars are ever likely to be, the wider scientific, technical culture remains wedded to objectivism. Film scholars are far more likely to be on the historicist side, sometimes to the point of refusing altogether to acknowledge—and therefore to know anything about—the stubborn resistance of matter, of apparatuses, of physical and chemical givens.

Yet the reason for the absence, or at any rate extreme marginalization, of scientific and technical discourses in film studies is not so much this epistemological mismatch as those discourses' perceived value in relation to what matters about film. On the one hand, to pure science, film is not important enough of itself to constitute a field of study, but is only an instance in a wider field, optics and acoustics, say, or even physics and chemistry *tout court*. Meanwhile, technical discourse has not yet established for itself the place in scholarship that would enable it to found a field (even though, probably, more people teach and want to learn technical discourse than film studies). On the other hand, scientific and technical discourses don't tell film scholars what they want to know about film or films, that is, why they are fascinating or valuable. Knowledge of the chemistry of Kodak stocks in given periods, or of how a fresnel affects the focus and fall of lighting, tells us how a given image or characteristic filmic quality takes the form it does, and probably enables us to refine our description of it, but it still doesn't tell us why, or even if, it matters.

Mattering has tended to be affirmed in one of two ways: the formal–aesthetic and the social–ideological. The first argues for, or assumes, the importance of film in terms of its intrinsic worth, whereas the latter focuses on film's position as symptom or influence in social processes.

The formal–aesthetic value of film study

For formal and aesthetic discourse, film matters for its artistic merits. In this, it shares a concern with newspaper and magazine film reviewing, even if this common cause is sometimes obscured by antagonism of both journalists and academics towards one another. Both groups are concerned with championing film in general and with debating the merits of particular films. Film journalism long anticipated and made possible academic film study, and it has continued rather more whole-heartedly to concern itself with the questions that won't go away (is this film any good? is film in general any good?). At its best, journalism's readiness to mix a well-expressed, honest response with a fine, accurate, and evocative description of a film is of great methodological importance. There is value in the freshness and immediacy of the reviewer's response, just as there is in the distance and mulled-over character of academic work. And if academics may be rightly wary of the implications of the pressure on journalists to entertain (not least by imposing their personality between the reader and the film), it is regrettable that more film academics do not seem to share the journalistic concern with communication.

> **For formal and aesthetic discourse, film matters for its artistic merits.**

Both reviewing and film studies concern themselves with film as art. The notion of art is notoriously loaded—it carries an inextinguishable overtone of value, so that we may say that the term 'art' in practice designates art that is approved of. For much of its brief life film studies has mobilized just this overtone in its defence, usually quite explicitly. The most famous instance of this—and in terms of widespread, long-term influence, probably film studies' greatest hit—is the auteur theory (see Crofts, Part 2, Chapter 7). This made the case for taking film seriously by seeking to show that a film could be just as profound, beautiful, or important as any other kind of art, provided, following a dominant model of value in art, it was demonstrably the work of a highly individual artist. Especially audacious in this argument was the move to identify such artistry in Hollywood, which figured as the last word in non-individualized creativity (in other words, non-art) in wider cultural discourses in the period. The power of auteurism resided in its ability to mobilize a familiar argument about artistic worth and, importantly, to show that this could be used to discriminate between films. Thus, at a stroke, it both proclaimed that film could be an art (with all the cultural capital that this implies) and that there could be a form of criticism—indeed, study—of it.

Auteurism is the particular form that the argument from art took in the 1960s, the crucial moment for the establishment of film as a discipline. But film scholarship long before this had concerned itself with film as art, including, but not only, in terms of individual creativity. The terms may differ, but the form of the argument remains the same. Film is worth studying because art itself is worth studying and film is art. Why art itself should be deemed to have worth, leave alone to merit study, are not matters to be gone into here: suffice it to say that film as art discourse leans on this wider art-as-a-good discourse, or rather, its many variations (e.g. individual creativity, formal coherence, moral depth, sublime or dionysiac experience).

One particularly productive strand of such discourse can be linked back at least to the German philosopher Lessing and his insistence (in *Laokoon*, 1766) on the importance of establishing what is intrinsic and essential to each artistic medium: only by being true to this can real art emerge. Thus painting should not try to be like sculpture, and much less should either try to be like music or literature. It is some such conviction, whether explicitly acknowledged or not, that informs work that has sought to specify the particularity of film. What is it about the medium itself that makes it distinctive and that therefore properly forms the basis for an account of what is potentially best about it?

Many answers have been proposed. One is film's particular relationship to reality, the fact that it is reality itself that makes an impression on film stock—a sunset is put on a canvas by means of a hand applying paint, but it gets onto film by the chemical reaction of film stock to a real sunset. Theorists and practitioners alike have not naïvely supposed that film unproblematically captures or reflects reality, but they have argued that the fundamental way in which the film image is produced is in some sense by means of reality itself, that this process is unique to the photographic arts and that it is in maximizing the formal implications of this (e.g. shooting on location with available light, using long takes) that the art of film is realized. A second tradition takes film's temporal combination of shots in the act of editing (or 'montage') as most characteristic of it and thus, again, the foundation of film art (see Kolker, Part 1, Chapter 2). Realism and/versus montage long held sway as paradigms in film studies, but more recently there has been a renewed interest in other, obscured conceptualizations: 'photogénie', for instance, the particular *transformation* of recorded reality effected by the camera and its auxiliaries (lighting, movement, editing), or 'Zerstreuung', the delirious, dazzling, profoundly irrational quality of the film experience (bright light flickering on a huge surface in a darkened room, with vertiginous illusions of impossible realities).

The argument from essence remains an argument for film as (approvable) art, but there have developed formalist approaches more equivocal with regard to value. These have sought to establish the forms in practice of cinema—not what they must or should be, as in essentialist arguments, but what, as a matter of fact, they are. Most notoriously, these were developed under the sign of the 'language of cinema'. This is an often unhelpful term. Language is a sign system characterized by arbitrary signs (there is no reason for the word 'cow' to designate the animal 'cow'), discrete elements (the sounds are clearly distinguished from one another, the written elements even more so), and constraining grammar (with only some latitude, you have to follow the rules of grammar if you wish to be understood). Film's signs, on the other hand, are motivated (by the 'special relation' to reality or by virtue of resemblance—an image of a cow looks like a cow), cannot be neatly separated out (for instance, how long does a take have to be to be long?), and their combination knows only the rather particular rules of certain traditions (notably 'classical cinema'). Yet the ambition of linguistics, or more broadly semiotics, to be an objective description, a 'science', of the forms and procedures of a medium of signing has continued to haunt film studies (see Easthope, Part 1, Chapter 6).

The strongest such work has sought to overcome the weaknesses of the language model by identifying formal elements of film which correspond to norms of human perception. Among such work we may note—despite the huge divergence in the paradigms at work—three tendencies. Phenomenological work, which has come and gone and re-emerged as a presence in the field, focuses on the experience of the film image, drawing explicitly upon philosophical understandings of the nature of perception and consciousness. Here the unfolding of the film, the succession of images, and the image repertoire itself are all understood to work, probably in an unusually immediate way, with the habitual processes of the human mind. Psychoanalytic work, developing in the 1970s, links formal elements to unconscious psychic processes, most influentially in the feminist treatment of the point-of-view shot, whose organization is seen to privilege the male look at women in ways which either sadistically punish or satisfyingly fetishize the always threatening image of women to the male psyche (see Creed, Part 1, Chapter 9). Thirdly, most recently, what we might call the Wisconsin School, building on its highly influential work on 'classical Hollywood cinema', has started working on correspondences between film form and norms of perception posited in cognitive psychology, notably those between the film forms and mental processes required in order that a film may be 'followed' (see Christie, Part 1, Chapter 7).

By this stage, though, the need for there to be a point to studying film is in danger of being lost. In part, the yearning for science includes the shibboleth that things are studied because they are there and that there should be no tendentious point. In part, the very success of film studies in establishing itself as a discipline may mean that the reasons for establishing it no longer need asserting or even addressing. This may be short-sighted—funding realities mean that disciplines still have to be defended in terms of why they should be pursued. (The popular-with-students argument is not enough: for one thing, film studies is only popular with students relative to classics or chemistry, not to media or business studies, and for another, those who fund study may be more interested in what government and business want than in what students want.) The scientific stance may also be self-deluding, since in practice a sense of what matters is always present in scholarship at the level of the choice of what instances and aspects get studied and what don't. In any event, it should be stressed that there is a risk of loss of point, not that this has occurred. The study of filmic language or formal–perceptual correspondences consistently provides a ground for understanding how film and films work, even if leaving out of account why we should want to know about this.

The social–ideological value of film

Film-as-art discourses argue, or assume, that film is intrinsically worth studying. If they lean on wider discourses of art, of aesthetics or sometimes erotics, then this is only because film itself is an art and therefore valuable in the terms of art. There is no appeal to something outside film art. Social–ideological arguments, on the other hand, do make such an appeal.

One kind of social argument sees film as the exemplary or symptomatic art form of the category 'modernity'. This itself is conceived of as a structure of feeling characterizing an epoch in Western (and subsequently world) society from, say, the late eighteenth century onwards, based in capitalism, industrialism, urban and large-scale, centralized, 'mass' societies. To what extent we are still in this epoch, or whether there has been a qualitative change so profound that a new epoch must be recognized, one that may be designated 'postmodern', is part of this debate (see Hill, Part 1, Chapter 11). One consequence of considering that we are in transition out of modernity, or perhaps are already in postmodernity, is that film may come to be seen as an archaic and marginal cultural form. Postmodernity may rob film's modernity of the sense of the new and the now.

Film's modernity may be located first in its industrial character. Cameras and projectors are machines. Films are endlessly reproducible, as in all mass commodity production. They are made, for the most part, in conditions akin to factory production, which involves large numbers of people, a highly differentiated division of labour, and a temporally linear organization (e.g., at its most rudimentary, scriptwriting followed by filming, then processing, then editing). The numerical and geographical scale of distribution and marketing are comparable with other major commodities in modern societies. Production and distribution are centralized, a relatively small number of people putting out products consumed by millions upon millions (and, in the case of Hollywood, throughout the world).

The director confronts the studio logo in Guru Dutt's *Kaagaz Ke Phool/Paper Flowers* (1959)

The modernity of film at the level of production and consumption has been seen as of a piece with film form. The camera's mechanical reproduction creates a new, perhaps rather strange relationship between image and reality, just as the experience of modernity is said to distance people from nature and an immediately graspable, localized social reality. Editing is founded in fragments, a characteristic which has produced a variety of analyses in terms of modernity. One is that an art of fragments is analogous to the common experience of fragmentation in modernity, as rapid mobility, mechanical and long-distance communications, the mixing of classes and other social groups in cities, as all these break up the fixed, holistic bonds of traditional communities. A second view of the modernity of editing sees combining fragments as akin to the dynamic of Marxist dialectical thought, itself understood as the mode of thinking and feeling appropriate to modernity and to what modernity makes possible, the construction of a new, post-capitalist society. A third view sees continuity editing as an attempt to cover over the cracks between film fragments in just the same way that mass culture seeks to weld a unity out of the fragmentation of modern societies.

Other aspects of film form have also been seen as distinctly modern. Both editing and the flicker of film (to say nothing of the importance of action and suspense genres in popular cinema) may be of a piece with the restless, febrile quality of modern life, or may, in another version, provide the intensity and excitement lacking in lives essentially drab and anomic. Camera movement, elaborate lighting, and special effects all display the advanced technology at film's disposal. Finally, the conditions under which film is viewed—vast assemblies of strangers gathered together in the dark to see flickering, rapidly changing, fabulous images that they know are being seen in identical form across the world—locate both film's industrial mode of production and its formal properties in the actual experience of being at the movies.

Accounts of film's modernity have in principle simply been attempts to characterize and understand what contemporary life is about, what it feels like; but they have also usually been fuelled by an anxiety about this (see Gripsrud, Part 1, Chapter 22). Is not fragmentation a bad thing for human kind, and does not film either exacerbate it or seek to disguise the reality of it (and thus put it beyond critique and change)? Is there not a danger in the hypnotic quality of the film image, an inherent danger because it is a lure to passivity? Is not passivity dangerous, partly because, *quel horreur*, it is feminine, partly because passivity at the movies is coterminous with political passivity in life (a wholly dubious assumption)? Hasn't film demonstrably been used to manipulate people to acquiesce in totalitarian regimes? In short, is not film inherently political?

It is a concern with the politics of film that has underpinned the emergence of what we may call a cultural studies perspective in recent years. Its central proposition is that culture of all kinds and brows produces, reproduces, and/or legitimizes forms of thought and feeling in society and that the well-being of people in society is crucially affected and shaped by this. Who we think we are, how we feel about this, who we believe others to be, how we think society works, all of this is seen to be shaped, decisively, perhaps exclusively, by culture and to have the most profound social, physical, and individual consequences. Importantly, cultural studies has a differentiated model of society. Rather than treating cultural products as part of a mass, uniform, and homogeneously modern society, it has focused on the particularities of cultures founded on social divisions of class, gender, race, nation, sexuality, and so on. Within this perspective, cultural studies stresses the importance of power, the different statuses of different kinds of social group and cultural product, the significance of control over the means of cultural production. Equally, cultural studies does not assume that cultural products are unified expressions of sections of society, but may often treat them as products of contestation within such sections or else of struggles of such sec-tions against other social groups.

Film is something of a minor player in this. Cultural studies emerged with television and has gone on to privilege popular music and new technologies among the media it analyses. None the less, the cultural studies perspective is widespread in film studies. Its most familiar form is ideological textual analysis. At worst this can be a reductive seeking out of politically incor-rect narrative structures and stereotypical characters or an impossibly elusive, wordplaying, obfuscatory 'deconstruction' (a word often used to mean little more than taking something to bits as brilliantly as possible). At best it seeks to show the way that the textual facts of a film itself, its narrative organization, its address to the viewer, its visual and aural rhetoric, construct, not necessarily coherently or without contra-diction, a perception of social reality (even and espe-cially in films not apparently about social reality at all).

The chief problem for ideological analysis is the methodological weakness of the claims it seems to want to make about the social significance of the ideological operations it uncovers. Wary of claims of the effects of the media, claims associated with right-wing moral panics and unimaginative social-scientific empirical investigation, ideological analysis still assumes that it matters what ideology a film carries. Yet it only matters if it can be shown that the ideology is believed, or acted upon as if believed—in other words, if it cannot be shown to be effective. This is a move cultural studies has often been reluctant to make. Awareness of the problem has, however, led to an opening out of interest in cultural studies into areas that had hitherto been largely left to the social scien-tists but are now beginning to be more centrally dis-cussed within film studies: production and consumption.

At a level of relative abstraction, modes of produc-

> It is a concern with the politics of film that has underpinned the emergence of what we may call a cultural studies perspective in recent years. Its central proposition is that culture of all kinds and brows produces, reproduces, and/ or legitimizes forms of thought and feeling in society and that the well-being of people in society is crucially affected and shaped by this.

tion have been talked about in film studies in the past. There have been moments too of guilty conscience, when it has been felt that students of film 'ought to talk about the industry', often resulting in surprisingly unsophisticated empirical accounts—surprising both because being given house room beside the most arcane textual discussions and because there was no lack of theoretical sophistication about the study of industry and business available in social science. Recently, however, film studies has woken up to the unanticipated impact that cultural studies has had in management, business, and other 'hard' social sciences, where talk of the culture of an enterprise is widely accepted as a key explanatory concept. We are now seeing the beginnings of work on the culture of the production of film. At the other end of the process, and even more developed, we may note the influence in cultural studies of conceptualizations of consumption in terms of active, interpreting, differentiated audiences and an interest in what kinds of sense social groupings make of films, genres, stars, and so on.

At times, films may get rather lost in this process, dissolved into the cultures of producers or the multiplicity of audience readings. This seems a pity, since without a sense of film itself, producers and audiences alike become just one instance of production and consumption among thousands. If this is the case, there is no particular reason to study them any more than producers or users of wheat or cars—perfectly good and important subjects, but neither seems set to define a discrete discipline. Moreover, there remains the problem of how one understands the relation between the culture of producers and the culture they actually produce, or the relation between readings and the detail of what is being read. Why does a given set of personnel, organized like this, with this set of shared and contested understandings of what they are doing, why does all this produce this kind of film? What exactly is it that this given set of readers is latching onto in a film to make this interpretation, to have this feeling about it? And in either case, so what? Why does it matter what kind of film is produced, what kind of reading is made, unless the film itself matters? Cultural studies approaches to production and consumption may show us why films matter to producers and readers, which is good for them but not in itself reason to pursue and fund a discipline. We have to go back to considering the aesthetic or social reasons for thinking why film matters, reasons not themselves entirely vouchsafed by the cultures of production and consumption.

Films studies should include physics and chemistry, technology, aesthetics, psychology (of some sort), the sociology of organizations and consumption, empirical study of producers and audiences, textual study of films themselves, and no doubt much else that we cannot yet envisage. On the other hand, it is never possible to do everything. Most of the time one has to put on hold crucial aspects of a phenomenon that one has not time (or perhaps inclination) to address. This means that one has to operate with a 'closed system, open mind' mental orientation, focusing on a particular neck of the woods but being ready to take on board findings and perceptions from those labouring away in other parts. (The phrase is borrowed from the title of a collection of essays by Max Gluckman published in 1964.) I do not say this in a spirit of tolerating everything—there are substantial intellectual reasons for wishing to dispute particular paradigms at work within all the many modes of film study I have tried to characterize. Rather, I want to insist that in particular, the aesthetic and the cultural cannot stand in opposition. The aesthetic dimension of a film never exists apart from how it is conceptualized, how it is socially practised, how it is received; it never exists floating free of historical and cultural particularity. Equally, the cultural study of film must always understand that it is studying film, which has its own specificity, its own pleasures, its own way of doing things that cannot be reduced to ideological formulations or what people (producers,

> The aesthetic and the cultural cannot stand in opposition. The aesthetic dimension of a film never exists apart from how it is conceptualized, how it is socially practised, how it is received; it never exists floating free of historical and cultural particularity. Equally, the cultural study of film must always understand that it is studying film, which has its own specificity, its own pleasures, its own way of doing things that cannot be reduced to ideological formulations or what people (producers, audiences) think and feel about it.

audiences) think and feel about it. The first cultural fact about film is that it is film. Quite what 'film' then is we must go on debating, but that debate must always be at the heart of a cultural understanding, just as any conclusions we come to will always be cultural as well as aesthetic ones.

BIBLIOGRAPHY

Gluckman, Max (1964), *Closed Systems and Open Minds* (Chicago: Aldine).

Studying the film text

2

The film text and film form

Robert P. Kolker

Defining the film text

What do we mean when we talk about a film? The answers to this apparently straightforward question are not simple, not at all based in common sense, and go to the heart of the complexities of the institutions, the practices, and the viewing of movies.

The terms themselves suggest our uncertainties. Cinema, as Christian Metz (1977/1982: 5–9) suggests, implies the entire institution of filmmaking, film distribution, film exhibition, and film viewing. In England, the cinema usually refers to the place where a film is shown. In the United States, 'movies' replaces 'cinema', and the word 'film' is reserved for serious intent. In Hollywood, the people who make films sometimes call them 'pictures', and once referred to them (some still do) as 'shows'.

Is everyone talking about the same thing? And what is the 'thing'? As we try to untangle a definition of the film text, I will use 'film' instead of 'movie' (reserving my right to be serious) and will try to restrict the term 'cinema' to Metz's definition of the encompassing institution of production, distribution, exhibition, and reception. But that will be the easiest part of the untangling process. Film and the cinema are such a regular part of our lives, that defining, differentiating, and analysing them are not only difficult, but also difficult for many people to accept. Indeed, there are some things we would rather were left alone, and the movies are one of them. The preference to think of a film as a kind of self-constructed presence, full of story, characters, and emotion, is strong. A film is there, complete, full, and waiting for our gaze. Why make it more difficult than it appears? Precisely because it appears so simple and because the influence of film on our lives is so great.

Our first response to the question 'What is a film?' might be: 'A film is what we see when we go to the cinema (or the movies) or watch a videocassette or a television broadcast of a film'. A direct enough response, but one that actually responds to different things. Or, more appropriately, different, but closely related, texts. We can define a text as a coherent, delimited, comprehensible structure of meaning. A text is something that contains a complex of events (images, words, sounds) that are related to each other within a context, which can be a story or narrative. All of the parts of a text cohere, work together towards a common goal of telling us something. In ordinary parlance, a text is also something physical, like a novel or a book of poems. We all know about a textbook. But a painting is also a text. So is a television show, and the entire process of watching television. In fact, any event that makes meaning can be called a text if we can isolate and define its outside boundaries and its internal structure—and our responses to it (for a text to be completed, it must be seen, read, heard by someone). If we think of this in relation to a film, we begin to see how hard it is to define the film text—or texts—which are physical, narrative, economic, and cultural, and which include production, distribution, exhibition, and viewing.

The physical presence of a film constitutes one aspect of film's textuality: the five or six reels of 35mm plastic ribbon containing photographic images that are projected onto the screen in the theatre, or the videocassette we rent from the video store with its hundreds of feet of magnetized plastic coating contained in the cassette. A videocassette shown on a television set is not the same as the theatrical screening of a 35mm print. On the most obvious level, the conditions of its viewing are not the same. The kind of concentration made possible in a darkened cinema where a high-resolution image is projected on the screen is not the same as the bright busy living-room, or the comfort of the bedroom, where a small, low-resolution image is projected from behind onto a cathode ray tube. The image and the ways in which we attend to it are different. The television or videotaped image are not only smaller, but also more square. The sides of the image are lost on most transfers of film to video (almost two-thirds of the image if the original was filmed in anamorphic wide screen and then 'pan and scanned' for videotape). The difference in size, resolution, and response creates a different textual construction for televisual as opposed to theatrical viewing.

We can extend these differences further. In theatrical exhibition the size, proportion, and resolution of the film image are no longer under the control of the filmmakers or the audience. They are controlled by the physical circumstances, resources, and commitment of the exhibitor. For a number of years the size of the

screen in any given theatre has been determined by the size of the theatre, not by a standard ratio for recording and projecting the image. While a standard ratio did exist from the early 1930s to the early 1950s, the advent of different widescreen formats, the small shopping-mall theatre, the need to compose the image ultimately to fit on television, makes image size and composition inexact and undependable for any given film. The film text, in its physical, visible sense, is therefore subject to architecture, to theatre management, to the exigencies of broadcast and videotape conventions. Almost every videotape released in the United States comes with two warnings: one from the FBI, warning us about copyright restrictions; the other telling us that 'this film has been formatted to fit your television'. Physical textuality, like so much else in the creation and reception of film, is subject to external forces that make it difficult for us to define it as some essential, unchanging thing.

Ultimately, the physicality of film, even the forms of its projection, are less important than the effect it has when we view it. Watching a film is more than any of its physical parts: it is an event that occurs when the physical thing becomes activated by human perception through some kind of projection or broadcast. As soon as a thinking, feeling person is present—viewing the film—that person's experience is brought to bear on the film's images, sounds, and narrative. The viewer's experience is itself informed by the culture in which he or she lives. A person's beliefs, understandings, and values are all activated within the context of film viewing. That is true for the people who created the film as well. They, too, are a major part of the text. Their beliefs, their understanding of what a film should or should not be, the economic constraints that allow them to say and do only so much in any given film— these become textualized.

Is this any different from our contact with other works of the imagination? The German critic Walter Benjamin, wrote in his 1936 essay 'The Work of Art in the Age of Mechanical Reproduction' that film is unique among the arts because of the fact that it is not unique. Of all the arts, Benjamin wrote, film is without 'aura', without the singularity of the immediate experience of an artefact uniquely connected with a singular human creative imagination. Film seems to have no origin; it is there, whole and complete, ready for our enjoyment or the enjoyment of anyone else with the price of admission, a monthly cable fee, or money for rental. For Benjamin, film's lack of aura, lack of forbidding uniqueness, and its ease of access makes it the most social and communal of the arts. Film addresses the world, pierces through the realities of daily life like a surgeon's knife (1936/1969: 233) and, by opening perceptions of the ordinary to the many, holds the possibility of engaging an audience in a social and cultural discourse, a mass engagement of the imagination unlike any other art form. (Benjamin also made it clear that film runs the risk of forging an authoritarian assent to the dominant ideology.)

The textuality of film is therefore different from a novel or a painting. Less personal, but more accessible. Neither unique nor intimate, yet closer to the world most of us live in, engaged in its dailiness, and powerfully in touch with the social. The text without aura becomes the text that resonates across many fields and many consciousnesses. In any film we are witness to a rich and often conflicting structure of imaginative, cultural, economic, and ideological events. Because most films are made for profit, they attempt to speak to the largest number of people, and by so doing have to appeal to what their makers believe are the most common and acceptable beliefs of a potential audience. But audiences often respond in ways the filmmakers don't expect. The result is that the film text often lies at a nexus of expectation and response, of cultural belief and individual resistance. It is available and legible to many interpreters, whose responses are themselves part of its very textuality and form.

The film text and authenticity

Textuality and form include questions about 'authenticity'. Benjamin's concept of the work without aura suggests that film removes authenticity from its text. However, despite Benjamin's argument about the loss of aura, actual people do make films. But given the collaborative and commercial basis of filmmaking—so different from the individual creativity attributed to the traditional arts—the creative authority of the filmic text has been at the core of theoretical and historical debate.

One part of the debate involves the ability to find and identify authoritative texts for early cinema that would enable us to create a reliable history of early film. It is estimated that almost 75 per cent of the films made before and just after the turn of the century no longer exist. Those that do exist, from the early twentieth century up to the teens, are in questionable, often inauthentic forms. For example, Edward S. Porter's *The Life of an American Fireman* (1903) has been regarded as one of the earliest films to intercut different scenes for the sake of narrative complexity.

One of the first films to intercut different scenes— Porter's *The Life of an American Fireman* (1903)

13

Recently, it was discovered that the print with the inter-cut scenes (we will discuss intercutting and cross-cutting a bit further on) may have been put together years later by distributors. The speculation is that the original version of *The Life of an American Fireman* may have been constructed with less cross-cutting, depending more on a succession of shots, which was the norm of the period (Gaudreault 1990). We do know that Porter's other famous film, *The Great Train Robbery* (1903), went out to distributors with a shot that showed one of the train robbers pointing his gun at the camera and firing. The film exhibitor was given the choice whether to put that shot at the beginning or the end of the film. This ability of the distributor and exhibitor to alter a film parallels the contemporary problem we spoke of earlier, in which the size of the theatre or television screen determines the look of the film.

As we move forward in film history, the authenticity of the early film text becomes closely related to the personality of the filmmaker. Eric von Stroheim's *Greed* (1925) was brutally cut by MGM. Stroheim's authority over his production was compromised when Irving Thalberg, head of production at MGM, refused to distribute Stroheim's original ten-hour cut. Thalberg caused *Greed* to be trimmed to two hours and destroyed the rest. Stroheim's film, and his career as director, were all but destroyed as well. Orson Welles's *The Magnificent Ambersons* (1942), perhaps the most infamous example of an inauthentic text, was removed from Welles's control before it was edited. The studio, RKO, reshot portions of it, changed the ending, and—as MGM did with *Greed*—destroyed the deleted footage. In both cases studio policy, personal dissension, and economic determinants conflicted sharply with the artistic endeavours of the filmmaker.

What is the authoritative text of *Greed* or *The Magnificent Ambersons*: the films Stroheim and Welles made, or the films released by their studios? These are egregious examples of a perpetual problem, which is intimately connected to the question of authorship. The assumption of auteur theory, for example, has been that we can identify the text with a person—the director. In doing so, it is argued, we can not only discover the authoritative boundaries that give a personal, textual legitimacy to a film, but authorize our reading of the film as well. But the auteur theory—especially as applied to American film—has been based more on desire than fact. The reality is that the texts of classical American studio cinema were and are only rarely the products of an individual imagination,

and the director's job was primarily to transfer the script to film: to make the shots and to coach the actors. In the end, the producer and studio head had the final say on how the film looked.

Because it is so intensely a public, commercial art, film is authorized—or textualized—from a number of directions. No one person or event determines it. During the studio period, a film emerged from the collective work of a large staff under contract. Today a film is often conceived by a scriptwriter who, with the help of an agent, sells his or her idea to a studio. The agent plays a key role, brokering actors and director. During these initial periods of conception and selling, many decisions about narrative, characterization, and commercial appeal are made. Also during this period intense economic negotiations are carried on in an attempt to sell the film to a studio. The shooting of the film by the director may involve some cinematic experiment, but, more often than not, because of budgetary and scheduling restrictions, standard, conventional storytelling techniques predominate, as they will have during the scriptwriting process.

A film is made for an audience and will survive only as far as an audience finds it acceptable. Therefore, the creation of a film is, in part, a structure of educated guesswork and creative repetition. If audiences responded well to certain structures, stories, and characters in the past, they should be (most filmmakers believe) repeated, with some variation, in the new work. When that work is finished, the audience is put into negotiation with it. (During the studio days that negotiation process was fairly immediate, as studio executives and the filmmakers went to suburban Los Angeles theatres to watch a pre-release screening of their current film, and would then make changes to it, depending upon the audience's response.) The negotiation process includes film reviews, familiarity with and responsiveness to the film's stars, resonance with the narrative content of the film, willingness to accept the inevitable exploitation of sexuality and violence that are the major components of most films.

The textuality of a film therefore becomes part of a resonant field of creation and response. It is a field that radiates from the film or videotape back to its making and forward into the environs of movie theatre or living-room. It confuses the safe categories of authentic and inauthentic versions, and calls upon the entire cultural surround of the viewer and its creators. It is encapsulated within other textual forms: the forms of production that drive the economy of a given culture which is as responsible for the way a film is made, marketed, and received as is the work of any individual. In short, the ribbon of plastic that holds the images is only a part of a large structure of imagination, economics, politics, and ideology and of individuals and the culture as a whole.

Analysing the film text: the shot and the cut

The diverse critical approaches to the study of film reflect this complexity. But, no matter what the approach, it is now generally accepted that the film text is a plural, complex, simultaneously static and changing event, produced by the filmmakers who put it together and the audience members who view it. It is unified by certain established ways in which shots are made and edited together. These structures are as conventionalized as the stories they create. By examining the internal structure of film narrative, the way images are made and put together in order to tell us stories, we can discover a great deal of information about what films expect of us and we of them.

Analysis of the form of the cinematic text concentrates on the two basic building-blocks of film, the shot and the cut, and on the structure that comes into being when the film is assembled, the combination of shot and cut that is the finished film. The first element, the shot, is the photographic record made when film is exposed to light. The second comes into being when the shot is interrupted, when the camera is shut off, or when one piece of film is cut and then fastened to another piece of film during the editing process. The third element is the completed structure of image and editing that communicates the narrative (or overall shape of the film). It is the initializing constituent of the text as we have defined it: the complex interaction of film and audience, structure, content, context, and culture.

None of these formal elements are simple or uncontested. Controversy over the structure and importance of the shot and the cut, of the shot versus the cut, forms the bedrock of film theory. In the writings of Sergei Eisenstein and André Bazin, especially, and the work of a variety of filmmakers, belief in the priority of one element over the other has determined the way films are made and understood, at least outside of Hollywood.

Sergei Eisenstein was the great Soviet director of films such as *Battleship Potemkin* (1925), *October* (1928), and *Ivan the Terrible* (1943). He theorized that the shot was only the raw material that the filmmaker used to construct the edifice of his film. For Eisenstein, a shot has no meaning until it is put in contention with another shot in a montage structure. Montage—a specific kind of editing—is constructed out of shots that affect one another in particular ways. One shot takes on meaning in relation to the shot that precedes and follows it. Spatial dynamics of the shot's composition, the length of the shot, the rhythm achieved when different shots of varying visual and thematic content are juxtaposed, all contribute to a carefully calculated 'montage of attractions'. For Eisenstein, montage was not merely the filmmaker's most important tool, but the sign of his aesthetic and political control. The shot, by itself, is inert, he believed. Making the shot (and, with the help of his cinematographer Edward Tisse, Eisenstein filmed powerful and dynamic compositions) was only craft. Turning the shot into a temporal structure of rhythmic, conflicting, kinetic montage was the director's art.

For Eisenstein, editing not only created a visual dynamism of conflicting forms, but it had the potential of being a cinematic equivalent of Karl Marx's theory of dialectical materialism. Through the interaction of form and content between shots, by the way one shot determined the meaning of the preceding or following shot, Eisenstein believed he could create a third thing, a dialectical synthesis of idea, emotion, perception, that would, in turn, create an intellectual perception of revolutionary history for the viewer. Montage, in short, was a tool that allowed the filmmaker to address history, as well as art, in a dialectical way.

Eisenstein believed so profoundly in the basic, driving aesthetic and ideological force of montage that he saw it developing in literature and the arts before film. Montage was an aesthetic event waiting to be politicized with the invention of cinema.

> **Analysis of the form of the cinematic text concentrates on the two basic building-blocks of film, the shot and the cut, and on the structure that comes into being when the film is assembled, the combination of shot and cut that is the finished film.**

André Bazin was not a filmmaker. A critic and film theorist who was active from the end of the Second World War until his death in 1958, he influenced a generation of directors and is considered to be the father of the French New Wave. Bazin's film aesthetic is directly opposed to Eisenstein's. For Bazin, editing was the destruction of cinematic form, indeed the destruction of the essence of cinema. For him, it is the shot, the unedited gaze of the camera onto the world before its lens, that constitutes cinema's aesthetic core. If Eisenstein's aesthetic was political at its root, Bazin's was religious and founded in the faith that the cinematic image could reveal the world in fact and spirit and confirm the temporal and spatial thereness of the world with the camera's meditative eye.

Editing, according to Bazin, denies that faith, because it cuts off the filmmaker's and the film viewer's opportunity to see into the wholeness and continuity of time and space. Editing is manipulative; it forces us to see what the filmmaker wants us to see. The shot is reverential. Political, too. An uninterrupted shot, preferably in deep focus (an effect of lens and lighting that makes everything in the composition, from the closest object in the frame to the farthest, appear to be equally clear) might create a kind of democracy of perception. The viewer would be free to pick and choose what to look at within the frame, rather than have the filmmaker pick out what he or she considers important by cutting and foregrounding specific faces or objects.

Bazin's cinema is painterly. It depends upon composition, lighting, and the profound revelatory effect of the camera's gaze. The construction of mise-en-scène—the complex articulation of space through composition, light, and movement—is pre-eminent

Does 'the long take reveal the world to the viewer', as Bazin suggests? Wyler's *The Best Years of our Lives* (1946)

in Bazin's theory. In fact, Bazin uses the example of painting to describe the prehistory of cinema, the early and ongoing urge of the imagination to preserve images of the world. In a sense, Eisenstein's is a painterly cinema too, a dynamic kinetic form analogous to Cubism and Russian Constructivism (an art movement contemporary with Eisenstein's filmmaking). The difference is that, for Bazin, the image and its complex construction is primary; so is the spectator's gaze, liberated to roam the image and connect its internal parts. Bazin asks the spectator to look and put the parts of the image together, to achieve understanding through contemplation. For Eisenstein, the viewer must respond to the invisible space that is created by images in conflict. The spectator responds to the dialectic of montage and the revolutionary history it articulates.

Eisenstein's concept of montage dominated film theory and some film practice for a brief period (the French avant-garde movement of the 1920s and the American documentarists of the 1930s) and then waned. Its only appearance in Hollywood cinema was through the work of an editor named Slavko Vorkapich, who created 'montage sequences' for such 1930s films as San Francisco (1936) and Mr Smith Goes to Washington (1939). The Bazinian aesthetic of the long take had a broader history and a powerful influence. Bazin looked to the work of Erich von Stroheim, F. W. Murnau, Jean Renoir, Orson Welles, William Wyler, and the films of the post-war Italian Neo-Realists (Roberto Rossellini, Vittorio De Sica, especially) as examples of the cinema of the long take. The followers of Bazin, from Jean-Luc Godard and François Truffaut to Michelangelo Antonioni, Bernardo Bertolucci, the Greek director Theo Angelopoulos, and the British filmmaker Terence Davies (to name only a few), depend upon the complex gaze of the camera rather than editing to construct their mise-en-scène and, from it, their narrative. It can be said, with strong empirical evidence, that any filmmaker who sets out to make a film that is counter to the structure of the dominant Hollywood cinema turns not to Eisenstein, but to the cinema that Bazin applauded and championed, the cinema of the long take, of coherent mise-en-scène.

The concept of mise-en-scène attracted the attention of critics as well. *Cahiers du cinéma* (the French journal Bazin helped found), as well as the British journal *Movie*, along with writers such as V. F. Perkins and Raymond Durgnat, pursued the idea of the shot and its constituent parts as the defining elements of a film. In France, England, and the United States, study of mise-en-scène, hand in hand with the auteur theory, helped to found the field of cinema studies. A focus on mise-en-scène permitted an emphasis upon the elements of film that made it distinct from other narrative forms and was used to explain how images, through composition, camera movement, lighting, focus, and colour, generate narrative event and guide our perception through a film. Mise-en-scène analysis was also a way to connect personality, style, and meaning.

Mise-en-scène and auteur criticism were closely intertwined within the analysis of style, and style was often implicitly defined as the personal expression of mise-en-scène. When V. F. Perkins (1972: 84–5) for example, analyses the use of colour in Nicholas Ray's *Bigger than Life* (1956), or Terry Comito (1971) talks about the vertiginous horizon in Welles's *Touch of Evil* (1958); when any number of critics define F. W. Murnau's use of moving camera, Otto Preminger's long takes, or Hitchcock's use of framing to describe his characters' states of mind, they are speaking of the ways in which the imagination of the auteur visualized their world in distinctly cinematic ways. Mise-en-scène criticism served many purposes: it helped concentrate the critical gaze on the formal structures of film; it explored the significance of style in a medium that few had ever considered capable of manifesting style; and it helped to determine a field—cinema studies— by proving that both artistic personality and style could exist in a mass art.

Like auteurism, mise-en-scène criticism was a useful construct, a way of building a critical discourse. Even as it helped define film form and structure, it was something of an evasion, for it tended to repress the realities of the dominant Hollywood cinema, whose forms construct most of the films we see. Because of its place of origin, this form has come to be known as the classical form of Hollywood cinema or, more simply, the continuity style. It is a remarkable form because of its persistence, its invisibility, and because we learn how to read it easily and without any more instruction than seeing the films themselves.

The continuity style

Eisensteinian montage and the long-take–deep-focus aesthetic advocated by Bazin are attention-drawing forms. They foreground cinematic structure and make them part of the narrative movement. They are intrusive in the sense that they make the viewer aware of the meaning-making apparatus; they ask the viewer to look at the way the world is being observed and constructed cinematically. Despite Bazin's insistence that the long take reveals the world to the viewer, what more often happens is that it reveals the cinematic apparatus and its ways of looking. Montage, of course, is dynamic, intrusive: Eisenstein meant his moviemaking to have a shock effect, to raise the blood pressure and the intellectual temperature. He called it the 'kino fist'. The classical Hollywood style, on the other hand, asks that form be rendered invisible; that the viewer see only the presence of actors in an unfolding story that seems to be existing on its own; that the audience be embraced by that story, identify with it and its participants. Unlike montage and the long take, the continuity style was neither theorized nor analysed (not by the people who developed and used it, at least); its rules were developed intuitively and pragmatically through the early years of filmmaking. The continuity style developed because it worked, and its working was measured by the fact that it allowed filmmakers to make stories that audiences responded to with ease and with desire. They liked what they saw and wanted more. We want more still.

On the level of ideology, the classical Hollywood style is a capitalist version of Eisensteinian montage and a secular version of Bazin's deep-focus, long-take style. (Eisenstein recognized this, and in his essay 'Dickens, Griffith, and the Film Today', wrote about how the Hollywood style spoke the ideology of Western capitalism.) It is the form that placates its audience, foregrounds story and characters, satisfies and creates a desire in the audience to see (and pay for) more of the same. It is also a form that is economical to reproduce. Once the basic methodology of shooting and editing a film became institutionalized—quite early in the twentieth century—it was easy to keep doing it that way. Although every studio during the classical period of Hollywood production (roughly between the late 1910s to the early 1950s) performed slight variations on the continuity style, its basics were constant and used by everyone. What this means is, when we talk about the classical style of Hollywood filmmaking, we are talking about more than aesthetics, but about a larger text of economics, politics, ideology, and stories—an economics of narrative. The Hollywood studio system, which was the central manufacturing arm of the continuity style, developed as many other manufacturing institutions did by rationalizing production, creating a division of labour, and discovering methods by means of which all production parts and personnel would be on hand and easily put into place in order to create a product attractive to the greatest number of people.

> Eisensteinian montage and the long-take–deep-focus aesthetic advocated by Bazin are attention-drawing forms. They are intrusive in the sense that they make the viewer aware of the meaning-making apparatus.

Given the fact that the classical style developed prior to the studio system, we can speculate that the structures of narrative may have contributed to the rise of the economies of studio production. In other words, the development of a means to deliver narrative meaning through an economical visual construction created templates for the formation of an industrial mass production of narratives (Burch 1990). Early film consisted of a presentation of shots in series, each one of which showed something happening (as in the Lumière brothers' early film in which a train pulls into the station, or Edison's first efforts in which a shot showed a man sneezing or a couple kissing). Within a few years, during the turn of the century, such shots became edited together in the service of expressing stories. Georges Méliès made primitive narratives of a trip to the moon or a voyage under the sea in which different shots succeeded one another. Porter's *The Great Train Robbery* reflects a more complex process in which parts of the narrative that are occurring simultaneously, but in different spatial locations, are placed one after the other (Gaudreault 1983). One site where the process of establishing the continuity style can be observed is the series of films made by D. W. Griffith for the Biograph Company from 1908 to 1913. Griffith made more than 400 short films during that period, and in them we can see the development of what would become the basic principles of continuity: an apparent seamlessness of storytelling; the movement of characters and story that appear to be flowing in an orderly, logical, linear progression, with the camera positioned in just the right place to capture the action without being obtrusive; and, perhaps most important of all, an authority of presentation and expression that elicits precisely the correct emotional response at precisely the right moment, without showing the means by which the response is elicited.

The key to the continuity style is its self-effacement, its ability to show without showing itself, tell a story and make the storytelling disappear so that the story seems to be telling itself. This legerdemain was not a natural occurrence. The elements that came together to make it possible began as arbitrary, imaginative, and usually intuitive choices. In early cinema there were no rules and no groups that set the standards that would develop into the classical style. The only arbiters were directors like Porter and Griffith who tried things out, and audiences, who responded favourably to the experiments and their refinements.

> **The key to the continuity style is its self-effacement, its ability to show without showing itself, tell a story and make the storytelling disappear so that the story seems to be telling itself.**

There are a few basic formal components that were developed by Griffith and others in the early 1910s that established the classical style. Narrative flow is pieced together out of small fragments of action in such a way that the piecing together goes unnoticed and the action appears continuous. Sequences that occur at the same time but in different places are intercut to create narrative tension. Dialogue sequences are constructed by a series of over-the-shoulder shots from one participant in the dialogue to the other. The gaze of the viewer is linked to the gaze of the main characters through a series of shots that show a character and then show what the character is looking at. The result of these constructions is that narrative proceeds in a straight trajectory through time. Any transitions that break linearity (flashbacks, for example) are carefully prepared for and all narrative threads are sewn together at the end. The spectator is called into the narrative and becomes part of the story's space (cf. Althusser 1977).

Griffith was instrumental in establishing cross- or intercutting as a primary narrative device. The literary equivalent of this device is the simple narrative transition—'meanwhile' or 'in another part of town' or 'later the same day'—and some films borrow these verbal clues through intertitles or voice-over narration. But

implying such transitions visually is more difficult. In early cinema there lurked the continual concern that such things would be misunderstood. Too much cutting would confuse or trouble the viewer. But these fears were rarely realized, and filmmakers as early as Edward Porter found that, as long as they contained some kind of narrative glue, scenes placed side by side would be understood as occurring either simultaneously, earlier, or later than one another. Shots of a woman held captive by a menacing male (or caught in some other dangerous situation) are intercut with shots of an heroic male figure purposefully moving in a direction that has been established as that of the menaced woman. The result is quite legible: the man is coming to save the threatened woman. The pattern comes from nineteenth-century stage melodrama, but Griffith was imaginative enough to realize that film could stretch its spatial and temporal boundaries (Fell 1974). His audience was imaginative enough to accept the illusion and substitute the emotional reality (suspenseful expectation that the hero will conquer space and reach the heroine in time) for the formal reality (two sequences actually occurring one after the other on the film strip, each sequence constructed in the studio at different times). The pattern stretches out time and narrows space, providing the viewer with a way to enter the narrative and be affected by it. Gender is clearly marked as the woman—like the viewer—becomes the passive figure, waiting for salvation, and the male the active figure, redeemed by his heroism. (Griffith did reverse the roles in contemporary sequences of *Intolerance* (1916), in which a mother moves to save her imprisoned son awaiting execution.) Even less complicated *manœuvres* than the traversal of large areas of physical and narrative space required thought and practice. Take something as simple as getting a character out of a chair, on her feet, and out of the door. In the Biograph films, Griffith worked through the structuring of this movement until it became invisible.

What was the drive to develop such constructions? For one thing, they allow for a great manipulation of space and narrative rhythm. Much of very early cinema consisted of a kind of proscenium arch shot, the camera located at a point at which an imaginary spectator in an imaginary theatre would best see an overall gaze at the space in which events were taking place. This is a restrictive, monocular perspective, static and inflexible. But why create complex editing only to generate the illusion of a continuous movement? Eisenstein didn't. He cut into temporal linearity and restructured it. He would return to a shot of a person falling, for example, at a slighty earlier point than when he left it, so that the inevitable action is retarded, time manipulated. In the famous plate-smashing sequence in *Potemkin*, the single act of an enraged sailor is broken into eight separate shots, each less than a second long, which extends the act and emphasizes the fury behind it. Even Griffith wasn't absolute in his own construction of linearity. In films during the Biograph period, and sometimes later, there are occasional sequences of people rising from chairs in which the second shot is earlier in the trajectory of action than the first, and the person appears as if he were getting up twice.

Despite Griffith's 'lapses' in the continuity cutting he helped develop, the development of continuity in the early 1910s continued to privilege an illusion of linearity and of unbroken movement across a series of edits. We can, finally, only speculate on the reasons after the fact. The continuity style developed as a way to present a story in forward progression, not as a way to look at how the story was created. It generated its own economy, in narrative as well as physical production. Filmmakers developed formal methods that made shooting relatively quick and easy: shoot whatever scenes are most economical to shoot at a given time (shoot out of sequence when necessary); cover any given sequence from as many different angles as possible and with multiple takes of each angle to give the producer and editor a lot of material to choose from; edit the material to create linear continuity, cut on movement, keep eyelines matched (maintaining the direction a person is gazing from one shot to the other). Make the story appear to tell itself as inexpensively and quickly as possible.

No more interesting and enduring examples of the continuity style can be found than in the cutting of basic dialogue sequences. Even before dialogue could be recorded on a soundtrack, the following pattern emerged: the dialogue begins with a two-shot of the participants in the scene. The cutting pattern then starts as a series of over-the-shoulder shots from one participant to the other. The pattern may be slightly altered. For example, shots of just one of the participants listening or talking may appear in the course of the sequence. But the main series of shots are over-the-shoulder cuts, back and forth, that conclude with a return to the original two-shot. A simple dialogue has, therefore, to be filmed many different times with numerous takes of the two-shot and the over-the-

shoulder set-ups. It sounds complicated, but the economies are clear. As a normative process, everyone concerned with the making of a film knows how to do it with dispatch. The use of over-the-shoulder shots means that one of the high-priced actors in the sequence does not have to be present all the time. A shot from behind the shoulder of a stand-in can be made to look just like a shot from behind the shoulder of the primary actor. The reverse shots of the over-the-shoulder sequence do not even have to be done in the same place! Cut together, keeping the eyelines matched, two spaces will look the same as one. The process results in many shots—many choices—available for the producer and the film editor to work with in a much less expensive environment than the studio floor. The result is standard patterns of narrative information, comprehensible to everyone from a technician in the studio to a member of the audience in the theatre.

And the process provides a unifying structure. This is its great paradox. The fragments of over-the-shoulder dialogue cutting, or any other part of the continuity style, create unity out of plurality, focus our gaze, suture us into the narrative flow and the space between the glances of the characters. Theories have been set forth that the constant cutting across the gazes of the characters slips us into their narrative space because we are continually asked by the cutting to expect something more. Someone looks, and we are primed to respond, 'What is the character looking at?' And the next shot inevitably tells us, by showing the person (or object) being looked at. This play of intercut gazes creates an irresistible imaginary world that seems to surround us with character and actions. It is as if the viewer becomes part of the text, reading the film and being read into it (Dayan 1992). It is this element of the irresistible, of desire and its satisfaction, that most clearly demonstrates the staying-power of the classical continuity style.

Alfred Hitchcock—to take one example—can create overwhelming emotions simply by cutting between a character looking and what the character is looking at. Early in *Vertigo* (1958), James Stewart's Scottie drives through the streets of San Francisco, following a woman he has been told is obsessed by someone long dead. The sequence is made up by a relatively simple series of shots and reverse shots. We see Scottie in his car driving, we see from his car window, as if from his point of view, Madeleine's car. She arrives at a museum. Scottie looks at her, Hitchcock cuts to a point-of-view shot of her, looking at a painting, and being looked at by Scottie. She goes into a dark alley. Scottie follows, his gaze pursuing her to a door. As the door opens, and Scottie's gaze penetrates it, the darkness changes to a riot of colourful flowers in a flower shop. Throughout the sequence we see with Scottie, but see (as he does) only a mystery, which, we learn later, is not a mystery but a lie. The woman he follows is not the person he thinks she is: both he and the audience are fooled. The director uses elements of the classical style to manipulate our responses, to place us close to the gaze of the central character, which turns out to be seriously compromised. We identify with an illusion.

And as we identify with it, some of us want to discover how it has been constructed and perpetuated. Some of the most important work in recent film criticism has developed in the process of discovering the working of the classical Hollywood style. Bordwell, Staiger, and Thompson's *The Classical Hollywood Cinema* (1985) is a massively detailed catalogue of the attributes of what its authors call 'an excessively obvious cinema'. Other writers have discovered that beneath or within this obviousness lies a complex form and structure, and a rich interplay between a film and the culture that spawns and nurtures it with its attention. Films speak to us and we respond with the price of admission or the rental of a video. Its articulateness is created through a narrative economy in which narrative, gesture, composition, lighting, and cutting are tightly coded so that we understand the intended meaning immediately.

But immediate comprehension often means simple assenting to the reproduction of gender and racial stereotypes. It is necessary, therefore, to analyse why we assent, to what we assent, and why we keep coming back for more. Theories of subject placement—how the viewer is fashioned by a film into a kind of ideal spectator who desires to see what is shown him or her on the screen—attempt to answer questions of how form creates attention, and attention fashions perception. Critics such as Dana Polan (1986) have investigated the tight links between culture and film, indicating how history and our responses to it make of film an ideological mirror and an engine of affirmation. Others, like Mary Ann Doane (1987), have probed in detail the interplay between the American style and our given ideas of gender; or they have read against the grain to point out how films can question the con-

ventional wisdom if we look carefully and decode them with a knowing eye.

Much has been done and much remains. Attention needs to be paid to the minute particulars of the classical Hollywood style; more needs to be said about the way a gesture with a coffee cup, how a cut between two characters glancing at or away from each other, generate meaning. The economy of style of the classical form may present apparent obviousnesses, but it is in fact a structural shorthand, a code book that keeps critics and viewers attentive and attracted. In its very invisibility lie the structures of desire that make us want to see more and more.

Contesting the Hollywood style

The Hollywood style was and is the dominant style the world over. But there have been periods when some filmmakers consciously worked against its structures, rethinking its structural and semantic codes. These filmmakers favoured long takes (in the Bazinian manner), atemporal or non-linear narratives, and subject-matter that differed from the usual Hollywood stories of violence and melodrama. They called attention to their methods, exploited the possibilities of mise en scène, and asked viewers to become aware that form creates content; that stories don't exist without the telling of them.

One great period of such experimentation occurred during the 1960s and 1970s. Spawned by the French New Wave, extending to Italy, England, the United States, and then, in the 1970s, to Germany, the movement produced a body of work, and a series of imaginative filmmakers who, briefly, changed some basic assumptions of cinematic form. The results were a series of films that reconsidered American genre films in a form that stressed the long take and oblique cutting, an avoidance of classical continuity rules, and, in the case of French director Jean-Luc Godard, a cinema that questioned the form and content of the cinematic image itself. Godard and his contemporaries and followers—Alain Resnais in France; Michelangelo Antonioni, Pier Paolo Pasolini, the early Bertolucci in Italy; Rainer Werner Fassbinder and the early Wim Wenders in Germany; Glauber Rocha in Brazil; the filmmakers of ICAIC (the Cuban film Institute) (to name only a few)—made films that took their own textuality as one of their subjects. They asked their viewers to think about the images they produced, the stories they told. Their films questioned whether other images might be used, other stories be told. Many of these filmmakers worked in the tradition of the German playwright and theorist Bertolt Brecht, who demanded that a work of art put the spectator in a speculative position, reveal its internal mechanisms, and show how the power of the imagination can work with or against the power of a culture's dominant ideology. Many of their films were passionately political, speaking the inquisitive and corrective voice of the left.

> **The Hollywood style was and is the dominant style the world over. But there have been periods when some filmmakers consciously worked against its structures, rethinking its structural and semantic codes.**

The structural principle of this modernist, reflexive movement was complexity and mediation, a recognition that the film image and its editorial structure are not givens, certainly not natural, but the constructions of convention. And what is made by convention can be questioned and altered. The over-the-shoulder cutting pattern, naturalized in the classical American style, is not necessary; and most of the filmmakers of this movement avoided it, using instead the Bazinian long take, which permitted the image to be interrogated, found false or adequate, but always only a representation. 'This is not a just image,' Godard says. 'It is just an image.'

Yet, no matter how much they used film as medium of exploration, these filmmakers kept referring to their base of American cinema. Alain Resnais's *Last Year at Marienbad* (1961) is a radical meditation on the conventions of past and present tense in film editing, and a remake of Hitchcock's *Vertigo*. Antonioni, whose *L'avventura* (1960), *La notte* (1961), *L'Éclisse* (1962), *Red Desert* (1964), and *Blow-up* (1966) show an extraordinary commitment to the idea that filmic composition is an architectural form obeying its own rules of narrative logic, keeps playing his work off against the conventions of 1940s American melodrama. Rainer Werner Fassbinder, the most Brechtian filmmaker after Godard, and the one director most committed to exploring the

working class, bases his interrogations of form on the 1950s American melodrama of Douglas Sirk. Through these approaches they take the classical style into account, respond to it, and, finally, honour it by recognizing it as their base. For better or for worse, the classical style has survived, and absorbed, all of the responses to it. Everything else stands, finally, in dialectical relationship to it. This static, dynamic, dominant, and absorptive textuality embraces the cultural surround and articulates the complexities of ideology. The film text becomes a rich and a complex event, reticent and boisterous, asking passivity from its viewers while provoking their desire, hiding itself while announcing its power in film after film.

BIBLIOGRAPHY

Althusser, Louis (1977), 'Ideology and the Ideological State Apparatuses', in *Lenin and Philosophy*, trans. Ben Brewster (New York: Monthly Review Press).

*****Bazin, André** (1967), *What is Cinema?*, 2 vols., trans. Hugh Gray, i (Berkeley and Los Angeles: University of California Press).

Benjamin, Walter (1936/1969), 'The Work of Art in the Age of Mechanical Reproduction', in *Illuminations*, ed. Hannah Arendt and trans. Harry Zohn (New York: Schocken Books).

Bordwell, David, Janet Staiger, and **Kristin Thompson** (1985), *The Classical Hollywood Cinema: Film Style and Mode of Production to 1960* (New York: Columbia University Press).

*****Burch, Noël** (1990), *Life to those Shadows* (Berkeley: University of California Press).

*****Cameron, Ian** (1972), *Movie Reader* (New York: Praeger).

Comito, Terry (1971), 'Touch of Evil', *Film Comment*, 7/2 (Summer), *Three Masters of Mise-en-Scène: Murnau, Welles, Ophuls.*

Dayan, Daniel (1992), 'The Tudor-Code of Classical Cinema', in Gerald Mast, Marshall Cohen, and Leo Braudy (eds.), *Film theory and Criticism* (New York: Oxford University Press).

Doane, Mary Anne (1987), *The Desire to Desire* (Bloomington: Indiana University Press).

*****Eisenstein, Sergei** (1949), 'Dickens, Griffith, and Film Today', in *Film Form: Essays in Film Theory*, ed. and trans. Jay Leyda (New York: Harcourt, Brace, & World).

—— (1943), *The Film Sense*, ed. and trans. Jay Leyda (London: Faber & Faber).

Fell, John (1974), *Film and the Narrative Tradition* (Norman: University of Oklahoma Press).

Gaudreault, André (1983), 'Temporality and Narrativity in Early Cinema 1895–1908', in John Fell (ed.), *Film before Griffith* (Berkeley: University of California Press).

—— (1990), 'Detours in Film Narrative: The Development of Cross-Cutting', in Thomas Elsaesser and Adam Barker (eds.), *Early Cinema: Space, Frame, Narrative* (London: British Film Institute).

*Kolker, Robert Phillip (1983), *The Altering Eye* (New York: Oxford University Press).

—— (1988), *A Cinema of Loneliness*, 2nd edn. (New York: Oxford University Press).

Metz, Christian (1977/1982), *The Imaginary Signifier*, trans. Celia Britton, Annwyl Williams, Ben Brewster, and Alfred Guzzetti (Bloomington: Indiana University Press).

*Perkins, V. F. (1972), *Film as Film: Understanding and Judging Movies* (Harmondsworth: Penguin).

Polan, Dana (1986), *Power and Paranoia* (New York: Columbia University Press).

Written on the Wind

Robin Wood from Robin Wood: Film Studies at Warwick University Vision, 12 (Dec. 1974), 27–36.

One might talk about *Written on the Wind* (1957) in terms of fundamental American myth, the myth of lost innocence and purity: the characters of the film repeatedly look back to their collective childhood. Universal myth, perhaps, but deriving a particular meaning from the Virgin Land that has so rapidly become one of the most technologically advanced countries of the world. The nostalgic yearning for innocence has a markedly pastoral flavour: the characters, among their oil pumps and scarlet sports cars, long to return to 'the river', where they were happy (or think they were). The same myth, in the form of 'Rosebud', animates *Citizen Kane* (1941).

This might prove a useful starting-point for an exploration of more than *Written on the Wind*. One might develop an investigation of the film itself further by considering the genre within which it is situated: the Hollywood melodrama. Melodrama has proved a very difficult word to define (like so many such shifting, complex, dangerous terms— 'tragedy', 'sentimentality', 'classical', 'Romantic', etc.). It implies in this context, I take it, characters divided fairly markedly into 'good' and 'bad'; simplified issues; violent or extreme emotions; a reliance on rhetoric. '*Crude* melodrama': the words often go together. One can ask— *Written on the Wind* might well prompt one to ask— whether crudeness is a necessary feature of melodrama. Certainly the forceful projection of violent feelings is, though that is also a feature common to many tragedies. One can see the simplification of issues and the powerful projection of emotion as a matter of cliché or vulgarity; one might also see it, in certain cases, as a reduction of things to essentials, the stripping away of the intricacies of personal psychology (though Sirk's film is not exactly lacking in that quarter) to reveal fundamental human drives in the most intense way possible.

Which set of terms should be applied to *Written on the Wind* can only be argued, I would claim, through close attention to the level of realization, or of style: the level at which the personal artist supervenes, the level at which, for the critic, considerations of national myth and genre must give place to a consideration of personal authorship. Certain elementary features of style belong more to the studio than to Sirk: notably the set design. Connoisseurs of Universal films will, for example, probably find the hallway and staircase somewhat familiar: they will have seen them in *Marnie* (1964), and perhaps in other Universal movies. But the extract we have seen contains striking stylistic features which can't be explained in this way; features that are not just functional, like the staircase, but determine our response and

aspire to the creation of the film's meaning. Certain of these features some might again want to label 'crude', though again they are capable of another description. Douglas Sirk was originally Danish, but settled for a time in Germany and made films there before he went to Hollywood. It can be argued that he inherited something of the tradition of German Expressionism (a tradition that other directors also— Lang, Hitchcock, Murnau—have found readily compatible with the Hollywood melodrama in one form or another), of which the central aim was the projection of emotional states by means of imagery: the use of the colour scarlet in *Written on the Wind* might be seen as having Expressionist derivation. Sirk also admired, and collaborated with, Bertolt Brecht, a writer who seems at first sight very far removed from the Hollywood melodrama. There is no room in the Hollywood genre movie for Brechtian alienation devices: the central aims are obviously incompatible, the tendency of the genre movie being to enclose the spectator in an emotional experience, the function of alienation devices being to detach him by means of interruptions. Alienation effects, one might say, can be sneaked into Hollywood movies only on condition that they cease to alienate (unless we bring to the films prior expectations of being 'alienated'). One can, however, see the extremeness of some of Sirk's effects as the result of a desire to break the audience's absorption in the narrative and force it to conscious awareness. In the drugstore at the start of the extract, there are not just one or two signs saying 'Drugs', they are suspended all over the shop to an extent that *almost* oversteps the bounds of the Hollywood demand for plausibility. How does one see this?—as part of the excesses of Hollywood melodrama?—as the legacy of Expressionism?—as derived from Brechtian alienation? The idea of a society drowning its awareness in alcohol (like the Stack character) or in drugs is central to the film.

Then there is the very loaded, obtrusive shot with the camera tracking out of the drugstore in front of Stack to reveal the boy on the wooden horse in the foreground. One can say many things about that: the decision to do it as a tracking shot instead of cutting to a close-up of the boy—the effect is to stress the connection (both psychological and symbolic) between Stack and the boy by uniting them in the frame, without loss of impact. There is then the question of what the boy signifies; and a device that may at first sight seem crude takes on surprising complexity. First, most obviously, the boy represents the son Stack has just learnt he will probably never have; second, the violent rocking–riding motion carries strong sexual overtones, and in Stack's mind the idea of sterility is clearly not distinct from that of impotence;

Written on the Wind continued

third, the child takes up the recurrent idea of the characters' yearning for lost innocence—and for the unreflecting spontaneity and vitality that went with it—a central theme in the film. The child's expression and actions are very precisely judged: we see him as enjoying himself, yet we also see how, to Stack, his smile appears malicious, taunting. The obtrusiveness of the device is perhaps justifiable in terms of density of meaning.

It is impossible to leave this topic without reference to the use of colour. The film is built partly on colour contrasts: the strident scarlet associated with Dorothy Malone against the 'natural' greens and browns of Lauren Bacall. The use of scarlet is a beautiful example of the integration of 'Expressionist' effect within Hollywood's 'psychological realism': the glaring red of Dorothy Malone's phone, toenails, flowers, and car is explainable in psychological

terms as her rebellious assertion of herself in a drab world. The effect is again not simple: the red carries the simple traditional sense of the 'scarlet woman', certainly, but it also expresses vitality and powerful, if perverted, drives; it has positive as well as negative connotations within the world the film creates. I should like to single out two moments where colour is used particularly forcefully and expressively. One is the moment when the camera tracks forward towards Dorothy Malone's car, the whole screen fills with red, and the image dissolves to the *green* car in which Lauren Bacall is arriving for the arranged meeting with her already drunken husband. The use of the colour contrast combines with the technical device of the dissolve to create a complex significance (a significance *felt*, perhaps, rather than consciously apprehended, as we might experience effects in music): it contrasts the two women through the colours with which they are associated; it evokes the idea of

The curved staircase forms an integral part of the mise-en-scène in Douglas Sirk's *Written on the Wind* (1957)

Written on the Wind continued

simultaneity, suggesting the convergence of forces (which will culminate in the father's death); hence it links Dorothy Malone with her brother, underlining the parallels between them—his alcoholism, her nymphomania, the common cause (or complex of causes, at the centre of which is the Rock Hudson character, the film's apparent 'hero'). The second example is the dance, which employs not only scarlet but a particularly strident colour clash involving Dorothy Malone's cerise negligée. The dance itself is an extraordinary device for suggesting all those things that couldn't be shown on the screen in 1956, and which perhaps gain greater force from the partial suppression: sexual exhibitionism and masturbation (the use of Rock Hudson's photograph as a substitute for his physical presence being crucial to this scene and an indication of themes central to Sirk's cinema).

From the use of colour (and with this photograph still in mind), we might pass to another feature of Sirk's style that has elicited the word 'baroque': the use of mirrors and other glass surfaces. One might argue that this is merely decorative, but not that it is accidental: there are three striking shots involving mirrors. First, at the bar, when the camera swings left to show the characters reflected in the bar mirror. Second, when Robert Stack is brought home. Third, when Dorothy Malone is brought home (the parallel between her and her brother again 'musically' underlined), and, as she

passes, Rock Hudson is shown reflected in the hall mirror, watching her. There is also, related to this, the use of windows: repeatedly, Sirk shows characters as seen through glass. One can see this in various ways: the 'framing' of people who are trapped; the inability of people to help each other, each reduced to a glass surface that can't be penetrated; the unreality of the characters, who, trapped in their own fantasies, have become mere 'reflections' of human beings (Sirk's last film was called *Imitation of Life*, 1959).

Finally, I should talk briefly about what is the most difficult aspect of film to analyse. I suggested earlier an analogy with poetry; I hope to make this clearer rather than more obscure by adding to it the analogy with music. Sirk himself has said that his conscious model for *Written on the Wind* was Bach fugue. He talked about the acting as pared down to clean intersecting lines, like counterpoint. If *Written on the Wind* is a fugue for four voices, the sequence of the father's death is clearly the *stretto*. What I want to indicate is the obvious fact that film, like music, has a fixed duration. Hence the appropriateness to it of musical terms like 'tempo' and 'rhythm'. We still haven't found a way of talking satisfactorily about this 'musical' dimension, the direct effect of the *movement* of film on the senses, except in dangerously impressionistic terms. There is a lot of work to be done.

Citizen Kane

Peter Wollen from 'Introduction to *Citizen Kane*', *Film Reader*, no. 1 (1975), 9–15.

To write about *Citizen Kane* (1941) is to write about the cinema. It is impossible to think about this film without thinking about its place in film history. Most critics, despite Welles's own unhappy relations with Hollywood, have seen him primarily, implicitly within the framework of the American narrative cinema. Pauline Kael talks about the 1930s newspaper picture and builds up the role of Mankiewicz, a hard-core Hollywood scribe if ever there was one. Charles Higham talks of a 'wholly American work', Andrew Sarris of 'the American baroque', and they leave no doubt, I think, that, where the cinema is concerned, for them America = Hollywood. And, from the other side, an enemy

of Hollywood such as Noël Burch puts Welles in relation to Elia Kazan, Robert Aldrich, Joseph Losey, and Arthur Penn, and condemns *Kane* for simply displaying an amplification of traditional narrative codes which it does nothing to subvert.

Against this mainstream trend, of course, we have to set the massive influence of André Bazin. For Bazin, *Kane* and *The Magnificent Ambersons* (1942) were crucial moments in the unfolding of the cinema's vocation of realism. Together with the work of Jean Renoir and William Wyler, *Kane* represented a rediscovery of the tradition of realism, lost since the

Citizen Kane continued

silent epoch (Louis Feuillade, Erich von Stroheim, F. W. Murnau). *Kane* looked forward to Italian Neo-Realism and, had Bazin lived longer, his interest would surely have turned to cinéma verité and the new developments in documentary which followed the invention of magnetic tape, lightweight recorder and camera, and the tape join. (Indeed the strain of 'technological messianism' in Bazin's thought must surely have taken him in this direction).

For Bazin, of course, the crucial feature of *Citizen Kane* was its use of deep focus and the sequence shot. Yet one senses all the time, in Bazin's writings on Welles, an uneasy feeling that Welles was far from sharing the spiritual humility and self-effacement, or even the democratic mentality, which marked for Bazin the 'style without style', the abnegation of the artist before a reality whose meaning outruns that of any artefact. It is easy to forget that, on occasion, Bazin talked about the 'sadism' of Welles, of his *rubbery* space, stretched and distended, rebounding like a catapult in the face of the spectator. He compared Welles to El Greco (as well as the Flemish masters of deep focus) and commented on his 'infernal vision' and 'tyrannical objectivity'. But this awareness of Welles the stylist and manipulator did not deflect Bazin from his main point. Fundamentally, his enthusiasm was for the deep-focus cinematography which Welles and Gregg Toland introduced with such virtuosity. It was on this that Welles's place in film history would depend.

Yet a third current has been felt recently, again often more implicit than explicit. Putting together some remarks of Alain Robbe-Grillet, the article by Marie-Claire Ropars-Wuilleumier in *Poétique* and that by William van Wert in *Sub-Stance*, we can see how it is possible to place *Kane* as a forerunner of *Last Year at Marienbad* (1961), a film which pointed the way towards the breakdown of unilinear narration and a Nietzschean denial of truth. It is in this sense too that we can understand Borges's praise of *Kane* as a 'labyrinth without a centre'. *Kane*'s perspectivism (leading so easily to nihilism), its complex pattern of nesting, overlapping, and conflicting narratives, put it in a particular tendency within the modern movement, which has its origins perhaps in Conrad or Faulkner and its most radical exponents in Pirandello and the further reaches of the French new novel.

And of course, this tendency, whose origins are in literature, has begun to spread into the cinema, especially in France, through the influence of writers—Marguerite Duras, Jean Cayrol, Robbe-Grillet—who have worked on films, even become filmmakers.

The oddest of these three versions of *Kane* is undoubtedly

Bazin's. So flexible, so generous in many respects, Bazin was nevertheless able at times to restrict and concentrate his vision to an amazing degree. Obviously he felt the influence of Expressionism (which he hated) on *Kane*, but he simply discounted it—or tried to justify it by pointing to the exaggeration and tension in the character of Kane, a kind of psychological realism, similar to the way in which he defended the expressionist style of a film about concentration camps. (In the same vein, Christian Metz remarks how the formal flamboyance of *Kane*, the film, parallels the flamboyant personality of Kane, the man.) In general, however, Bazin simply hurried on to his favourite theme—the importance of deep focus and the sequence shot.

The key concepts here for Bazin were those of spatial and temporal homogeneity and dramatic unity. It is almost as if the theatrical scene was the model for Bazin's theory of the cinema. Of course, he believed that filmed theatre should respect the scene and the stage. Beyond that, it seems he believed in a *theatrum mundi*, which it was the calling of the cinema to capture and record—there is a sense in which all cinema was for him filmed theatre, only in Neo-Realism, for instance, the world was a stage, the players were living their lives, and the dramatist, who gave meaning to the action, was God himself. No wonder then that, for him, the artist, in Annette Michelson's phrase, was 'artist as witness' and the whole of reality the offering of an 'Ultimate Spectacle'. Indeed, Bazin writes that in Italy daily life was a perpetual *commedia dell'arte* and describes the architecture of Italian towns and cities as being like a theatre set.

Bazin always laid great stress on the theatricality of Orson Welles. He saw Welles as a man of the theatre and talked about the sequence shot as a device for maintaining the primacy of the actor. 'An actor's performance loses its meaning, is drained of its dramatic blood like a severed limb, if it ceases to be kept in living, sensory contact with the other characters, and the setting. Moreover, as it lasts, the scene charges itself like a battery . . .'.

Basically Bazin justifies the sequence shot and deep focus for three reasons: it maintains the dramatic unity of a scene, it permits objects to have a residual being beyond the pure instrumentality demanded of them by the plot, and it allows the spectator a certain freedom of choice following the action. In *Kane* it was the first which was uppermost. The second was important to Bazin—he talks about the door-handle of Susan Alexander's bedroom, in the sequence after the suicide attempt, and goes on to describe the cold feel of copper, the copper or indented enamel of a door-handle,

Citizen Kane continued

yet we must feel that this is his own projection, reverie almost (in the Bachelardian sense), which has little relevance to *Kane*. As for the third reason, Bazin recognizes that Welles directs the spectator's attention through lighting and movement as imperiously as any editor at times, but he remains aware of the potential ambiguity of the sequence shot and, of course, links this to the ambiguous portrayal of Kane's character.

Yet, with the advantage of hindsight, we can see that Bazin's love of the sequence shot has been strangely betrayed by the filmmakers who have subsequently used it. Who do we think of? Andy Warhol, Michael Snow, Jean-Luc Godard, Jean-Marie Straub, Miklós Jancsó. There are links of course—Straub reveres Bazin's hero, Bresson; Godard was deeply marked by Roberto Rossellini—but clearly the sequence shot has been used for purposes quite different from those which Bazin foresaw. Some of these filmmakers have stressed the autonomy of the camera and its own movement, rather than the primacy of the actors or the drama (Jancsó, Snow), others have used the sense of duration to de-realize the imaginary world of the film (Godard), others have been interested in duration as a formal feature in itself (Warhol). Straub, probably the closest to Bazin in his insistence on authenticity, on a refusal of guidance for the spectator's eye, has none the less put his Bazinian style to purposes very different from those Bazin himself could have envisaged.

It is worth noting that most of the sequence shots in *Citizen Kane* are, in fact, used in the framing story rather than the flashbacks, in the scenes in which Thompson talks to each of the interior narrators. The average length of a shot in *Citizen Kane* is not particularly long because of the number of short shots that exist both in the newsreel sequence and in the numerous montage sequences which Welles uses, mostly as transitions. The decision to use sequence shots in the framing story is clearly a decision not to use classical field reverse-field cutting, and thus to de-emphasize the role of Thompson, the narratee. Thompson only appears as a shadowy figure with his back to the camera. It is hard to separate decisions on length of shot and editing from decisions on narrative structure. By shooting Thompson in this way Welles precludes any spectator identification with the character who, from the point of view of information and focalization, is the spectator's representative in the film.

In the last analysis, what concerned Bazin was dramaturgy (even if, as with the Neo-Realists, he could speak of a 'dramaturgy of everyday life'), and he tended to assume the need for characters and a continuous narrative line. He simply thought that psychological truth and dramatic configurations would reveal themselves more fully if there was a minimum of artistic intervention. He remained hostile throughout to experimental film (for him Stroheim was the great experimentalist and Welles, of course, can easily be perceived as an avatar of Stroheim) and thought of theatre and the novel as the models with which cinema should be compared. There too he tended to have conventional tastes—he aligns himself with Sartre's condemnation of Mauriac, but seems also to accept without question Sartre's positive tastes—Dos Passos, Faulkner, Hemingway—and clearly was not interested in the literary revolution inaugurated by Gertrude Stein and James Joyce.

Yet the example of contemporary filmmakers has shown that the long take and the sequence shot tend to undermine the primacy of the dramaturgy: duration becomes a stylistic feature in itself and, far from suppressing the filmmaking process, the sequence shot tends to foreground it. At most, the sequence shot can be associated with a Brechtian type of dramaturgy, based on tableaux. In fact this tendency can be seen even in *Citizen Kane*, where it is disguised by the movement in and out of the framing story and the complex character of the transition. Bazin thought that the principal function of the cut should be that of ellipsis, but, within the kind of rhythm built up by a series of long sequence shots, the cut automatically takes on a role as caesura rather than ellipsis alone.

Truffaut, always fundamentally a conservative critic—as he has shown himself to be a conservative filmmaker—has said that 'if *Citizen Kane* has aged, it is in its experimental aspects'. It seems to me that it is precisely the opposite which is true. All Welles's 'tricks', as they are often contemptuously called—the lightning mixes, the stills which come to life, the complex montages, the elasticity of perspective, the protracted dissolves, the low-angle camera movements, etc.—are what still gives the film any interest. Nobody, after all, has ever made high claims for its 'novelistic' content, its portrayal of Kane's psychology, its depiction of American society and politics in the first half of the twentieth century, its anatomy of love or power or wealth. Or, at any rate, there is no need to take such claims very seriously. It seems quite disproportionate for Noël Burch to submit them to his acute dissection and attack, as he himself seems to half-acknowledge.

Indeed, the 'pro-Hollywood' defence of *Kane* is quite pathetic in its lack of ambition (*Kane* after all, is widely held to be the greatest film ever made). Pauline Kael begins with hyperbole 'the one American talking picture that seems as

Citizen Kane continued

fresh now as the day it opened', but soon descends to dub *Kane*, in a famous phrase, 'a shallow work, a *shallow* masterpiece'. The shallowness does not worry her, however, because it is what makes *Kane* 'such an American triumph', and then we discover its triumph lies in 'the way it gets its laughs and makes its points'. Basically, she assimilates *Kane* to the tradition of the well-made Broadway play, translated into the 1930s comedy film, with all its astringency and sense of pace and fun. Other critics do not really claim much more: Charles Higham talks of a 'masterpiece', but also 'epic journalism'; once again, we get the insistence on the 'American' quality of Welles and *Kane*, ironic in the light of the original intention to call the film *The American*. Energy, grandeur, and emptiness.

The truth is that the 'content' of *Citizen Kane* cannot be taken too seriously. Yet it had an enormous impact—largely because of its virtuosity, its variety of formal devices and technical innovations and inventions. In themselves, of course, these are purely ornamental, and the dominant aesthetic of our age is one that rejects the concept of ornament—the ruling aesthetic of our day is one of expressionism or functionalism or symbolism or formalism, seen as a complex process of problem-solving rather than wit or decoration. Welles is usually described in terms of baroque or expressionism, sometimes the Gothic, but this seems to reflect the ponderousness of his themes. His interest in formal devices and technical ingenuity puts him closer to mannerism, to a conscious appreciation of virtuosity and the desire to astonish.

It is this 'mannerist' aspect of Welles which still lives—not the dramatic unity which deep focus and the long take make possible, but the long take and deep focus as formal features in themselves. Similarly, it is not the theme of time, youth, memory, age, etc. which is of any interest, but the devices used to organize time within the film. Many of these point the way towards a quite different kind of use—contemporary filmmakers' variations on the long take, Robbe-Grillet's variations on the freeze frame-still. *Kane* remains an important film historically, not within the terms it set itself, or those within which it has been mainly seen by critics, but because, by a kind of retroactive causality, it is now possible to read there an entirely different film, one which Welles probably never intended. *Citizen Kane*, we can now say, was a milestone along the road which led, not to a reinvigoration of Hollywood, or a novelistic complication of narrative, or the unfolding of the realistic essence of film, but towards the expansion and elaboration of a formal poetic which would transform our concept of cinema entirely, towards film as a text which is a play with meaning rather than a vehicle for it.

3

Film acting

Paul McDonald

Acting is the form of performance specifically involved with the construction of dramatic character. Actors construct characters by using their voices and bodies. For an audience, the activity of reading a performance involves the bringing together of actor and character, and the interpretation and evaluation of acting has tended to assess whether or not the actor has 'become' the character. This has produced a familiar language of interpretation, in which judgements about acting are articulated in terms of whether a performance is more or less 'believable', 'truthful', or 'realistic'.

Although acting remains a major component of narrative cinema, film studies has yet to provide any sustained inquiry into film acting. If it is to examine acting further, it should not discard such terms as 'believable', 'truthful', and 'realistic', but rather question what they mean and how those meanings are constructed as the effects of film acting. Part of the agenda of film studies has been to develop critical frameworks for analysing and contesting how film reproduces ideological beliefs and 'truths'. Questions of the believable, the truthful, and the realistic in film acting may therefore provide the basis for assessing how, and with what effect, screen performance is a socially meaningful act.

Any study of film acting needs first and foremost to be aware of the medium. Film acting is as much a product of camera angles, camera movements, lighting, editing, and music as it is of the actor's voice and body. Barry King (1985: 28) has discussed how, for

actors working both on stage and screen, film presents a problem of professional power, for the actor loses part of his or her creative control to the camera and the cutting-room. Conversely, in a labour market where work is scarce, some actors criticize film and television because camera-work and editing can made 'bad' actors appear 'good' (1985: 33). What is at stake in this conflict between the film actor and film technology is a debate concerning whether it is the actor or the film technology which is the primary source of meaning. In a famous case of experimentation, the Soviet film-maker Lev Kuleshov took shots of an open prison door and a bowl of soup, along with two reaction shots of an actor longing for freedom and feeling hunger. Although the reaction shots showed different expressions on the actor's face, Kuleshov (1929: 54) reported that, when the shots were juxtaposed, their meaning changed, and concluded that it was the editing and not the actor that determined the meaning of the performance.

Walter Benjamin (1936) saw the impact of film technology on the actor as part of a wider cultural change. For Benjamin, reproduction defined a new phase in cultural production, as the technology of reproduction had the effect of separating the art object from its creator. Benjamin believed this diminished the 'aura' attached to works of art, as the object no longer carried with it the mystical 'presence' of the person who made them. In this context 'presence' should be taken to mean both that the creator was present at the making of the object and that this original contact with the creator left the object with a special 'charisma'. It was this effect of reproduction which led Benjamin to argue that, in contrast to acting for the stage, film acting loses the presence of the performer and, in doing so, diminishes the aura, or charisma, of the individual.

In John Ellis's (1982) view, the overall effect of film reproduction lies in how it forms an illusion of presence in absence. In other words, film constructs the illusion that there is something or somebody present, when that spectacle is in fact recorded, reproduced, and absent. The separation of actor and image is then part of this effect. Using psychoanalytic concepts, Ellis argues that the film actor is placed in relation to the narcissistic, voyeuristic, and fetishistic looks of moviegoers. Through the construction of point of view, moviegoers will adopt various narcissistic identifications with the actors playing characters who control the narrative. By the convention of not looking at the camera, actors become part of the voyeuristic spectacle which the audience spies on. And, as the presence in absence of the film actor divides the moviegoer between relief and disbelief, actors also become part of the fetishistic attraction of cinema (see Creed, Part 1, Chapter 9).

Benjamin and Ellis emphasize the film apparatus as more meaningful than the work of the actor. Both discuss what film does, and what film does to actors, but they do not address what film actors are doing. This type of approach has led to the tendency for film studies to discuss 'performance' as the performance of the medium rather than of the actor (e.g. Heath 1977). This neglect of actors in film studies has left them, instead of a presence in absence, simply absent. Any critical study of film acting would benefit from not merely dismissing 'aura' or 'presence' as metaphysical and mystical qualities, but from asking how such effects are constructed from the material elements of the film actor's voice and body. Benjamin's conclusion that reproduction removes the aura of presence from film acting is debatable, not just because the film image still makes the actor appear to be present, but also because the work and signification of acting may at one level be read as constructing the performer as a special focus of attention. While it is always the case that the film actor is absent, it should not be ignored that the use of camera, lighting, and editing, but more importantly the actor's voice and body, also work at trying to construct a charismatic spectacle. Rather, it should be asked how film acting constructs presence to compensate for the actual absence of the actor?

One way of understanding the film actor's position in the play of presence and absence is suggested by what James Naremore (1988) calls the 'performance frame'. At one level, this frame is to be understood as the limits of the film frame. When projected in the cinema, this frame is equivalent to the proscenium arch in theatre, marking the boundary between the world of the audience and the dramatic world of the actors. As any observation of film acting makes immediately clear, the realistic in acting does not arise from exact imitation of everyday behaviour. This difference between film acting and the everyday world is further distinguished by the performance frame. Whatever appears in the frame may be more or less similar to everyday life, but simply by appearing on screen the actor is immediately framed as apart from the everyday. When turned into public spectacle, the contents of the frame become more significant and meaningful than the experiences of everyday life. At this further level, the frame therefore constructs a context for meaning. Although the film actor only appears as a recorded image, that actor may still have a presence entirely because his or her actions are contextualized as meaningful. This effect is described by Barry King (1985: 41) as the 'hypersemiotisation' of the film actor. The film actor obtains an aura because the frame invests every action of the voice and body with meaning.

> **Any critical study of film acting would benefit from not merely dismissing 'aura' or 'presence' as metaphysical and mystical qualities, but from asking how such effects are constructed from the material elements of the film actor's voice and body.**

The performance frame only provides a context for the meaning of film acting; it does not account for how the acting voice and body actually construct meanings. Stephen Heath (1979: 179–82) proposes that film acting combines different sources or forms of meaning. The role played by the actor can be divided between the 'agent', or narrative function, and the 'character' formed from a set of individuating traits and peculiarities. The 'person' or actor may already be a source of meanings known from previous performances. Each of these sources is visualized in the 'image', but at some points the image may also stand apart from these other forms to present the performer only as spectacle. For Heath, these sources are never integrated to form a closed, coherent construction, but are various points of meaning which remain in continuous circulation to form what he calls a 'figure'.

Heath's model would suggest that the actor never 'disappears' into a role. From this view, believability in film acting is never the effect of how an actor has 'become' a role, but is the effect of how the actor is involved with becoming the role. Therefore, believable acting can in part be understood as the effect of making something which is absent and does not exist, i.e. the dramatic role, into something which is present and which appears to exist. The separation of actor and role makes the voice and body of the actor particularly significant, for these are the means for bringing together agent, character, actor, and image in a believable configuration. The actor's voice and body provide hypersemiotized fragments burdened with meaning. Heath's description of such fragments as 'intensities' (1979: 183) usefully identifies that it is through the small details of the actor's speech and movement that interpretations and judgements about film acting are formed.

Different effects are produced in acting depending on the extent to which the actor or the role is foregrounded. Barry King (1985: 41) describes as 'impersonation' acting in which the actor undergoes significant transformations to 'become' his or her role. Where actors do not impersonate their role but appear across a series of performances always to 'be themselves', acting is described by King as 'personification' (42). Impersonation, constructed through significant transformations, is based on difference, while personification connects similarities between performances. While some actors will produce performances that are more different than similar, and some the reverse, the two categories are not exclusive, and any performance should be seen for how it combines impersonation and personification.

Critical judgements about 'good' or 'bad' film acting can also be understood in terms of impersonation versus personification. Respected performers are often evaluated for what is read as their ability to transform themselves into different roles. This critical judgement is premissed on a realist aesthetic which values the actor's skills employed in attempting to close the gap between actor and role in order to form a figure integrated into the narrative fiction. Personification disrupts this closure, emphasizing the actor's identity against the single role. The importance given to the actor's identity carries distinctive meanings between films, and personification has tended to be integral to the acting of film stars. It is because star acting is usually based on personification rather than impersonation that stars are so often criticized for not 'really' acting but for always 'playing themselves'.

While Heath and King offer terms for understanding the levels at which the relationship of actor to role is formed, they do not provide the means for understanding the detail in how the voices and bodies of film actors construct characters. Richard Dyer (1979: 121) identifies the appearance, speech, gestures, and actions of actors as elements in the construction of character in film. By their physical appearance, actors already represent a set of meanings. The use of costume, make-up, hairstyle, or posture becomes the means for impersonatory transformations. With speech, it is necessary to distinguish what is said from how it is said. Apart from cases where actors improvise, dialogue is usually produced by the writer. It is in how the writer's dialogue is spoken that the work of the actor is identified. The 'paralinguistic' features of volume, tone, and rhythm are the elements by which the actor's voice inflects the script. Dyer divides the signification of the body between gestures, which indicate the personality and temperament of the character, and actions, which are movements produced for the purpose of effecting a change in the narrative (1979: 126–8). In their various ways, it is these 'bits' of voices and bodies from which the relationship between actor, agent, character, and image is constructed.

Both the vocal and bodily significations of acting present a difficulty for the detailed analysis of film acting. Despite references to body language, physical movements and the paralinguistic dimensions of speech do not divide up into units similar to the letters and words of written and spoken language. It is difficult therefore to break down film acting performances into component signs. For this reason, Roberta Pearson (1992) employs the semiotic concept of 'code' as an alternative to the study of discrete acting signs. A code is formed when a set of signs, or signifying features, are deployed in familiar ways to signify a conventionalized set of meanings. Using codes, the analysis of acting

Towards verisimilitude—
Blanche Sweet in an early
Griffith film for Biograph/
The Lonedale Operator
(1911)

shifts from the sign to questions of style. In her analysis of film acting in the early Biograph films of D. W. Griffith, Pearson traces a transformation between 1907 and 1912 from what she calls the 'histrionic code' to the 'verisimilar code'. In the former, the actor represented emotions through large gestures, and Pearson refers to this style as 'histrionic' because of the way in which it used conventions which did not imitate a sense of the everyday but belonged to the stage or screen drama only. In contrast, the verisimilar code was judged to be more 'realistic' because it was not so clearly conventionalized and gave more of a sense of everyday behaviour.

Despite the dominance of the verisimilar in screen acting, it should be noted that the histrionic component of screen acting never entirely disappears. Film acting remains distinguishable from everyday behaviour and so is always to a degree obviously acting. This difference between acting and everyday behaviour indicates that the 'realistic' in film acting has to be examined as a set of coded conventions. Where film acting is closer to approximating to the everyday, then a critical difficulty arises as it becomes less obvious that the actor is acting. This is an important problem, for it is precisely in this 'invisible' acting that the con-

struction of believability, truthfulness, or the realistic is most active. Judgements about 'bad' acting are often formed on the basis that the performer 'was obviously acting' and was therefore unbelievable. Analysis of film acting therefore has to make acting obvious if it is to examine the basis on which such judgements are made.

> **Film acting remains distinguishable from everyday behaviour and so is always to a degree obviously acting. This difference between acting and everyday behaviour indicates that the 'realistic' in film acting has to be examined as a set of coded conventions.**

One way of making acting obvious is suggested by John O. Thompson's (1978) use of the semiotic exercise the 'commutation test'. This test works by substituting actors to see what effect the substitution has on the meaning of a performance. Changes in meaning can then be analysed for the significant features which produced that difference. While the problems of breaking acting down into its constitutive signs prevent this method of analysis from being scientifically precise, it can draw attention to how a change of meaning is read from impressions formed about the colour of the eyes, the length of the nose, or the angle of the fingers, for example. Additionally, the test does not need to work just by substituting actors but can substitute ways of acting, so that the movement of the body becomes evident from substituting fast for slow, or the tone of the voice by changing high for low.

While Pearson's category of the verisimilar is useful, because the realistic in acting has taken several forms it is necessary to appreciate the many styles that the verisimilar has taken. Readings of acting style can be directed at different levels, looking at changes in style across historical periods, the relation of genre to performance style (de Cordova 1986), schools of acting such as the Method (Vineburg 1991), and how actors combine codes to form a personal style, or idiolect. As different ways of acting have served to define at particular times what is believable, truthful, or realistic in film acting, readings of film performances have to be seen in their historical contexts. Grahame F. Thompson (1985) has suggested that acting performances form a discourse which is only meaningful in a context of other discourses. From such a perspective, it is necessary to see how other forms of knowledge will influence what will be regarded as believable or truthful in acting. At the same time, it should be recognized that acting does not just reflect those other discourses, but that it is necessary to examine how an actor's voice and body construct believability and truth in their own terms.

The question of believability in acting is only at issue where film performers are placed in the formal conventions of realist narrative cinema. Alternative or oppositional cinema cultures have often developed through the transformation or rejection of realist and narrative conventions. In such movements the role of the film actor has been used in various ways to counter the illusion of narrative cinema, precisely in order that the actor's work will cease to be believable. The influence of Brechtian theories of acting (Brecht 1940) on filmmakers such as Jean-Luc Godard has resulted in some acting strategies where the film actor works at signifying their distance from a character (Higson 1986). Acting in this way attempts to make the fiction unbelievable as a means of questioning how believ-

ability in representation reproduces familiar and accepted truths. The distance between actor and character therefore opens up a perspective on how meaning is constructed. Other experimentations in film acting occurred as part of the post-revolution Soviet avant-garde. Vsevolod Meyerhold developed a system of training actors called 'bio-mechanics', in which actors used the body in ways which imitated the regular and repetitive actions of machines. Lez Cooke (1986) reads the use of this technique by the director Dziga Vertov as constructing, not a believable character, but a metaphor between the machine and the human body, which, in its historical context, produced a symbol of hope for the future. As these counter-strategies begin to problematize or depart from the actor–character relationship which is fundamental to acting, it could be questioned whether 'acting' is a suitable way of describing these ways of performing.

A considerable amount of current work in film studies is concerned with how cinematic forms produce and reproduce social categories of gender, race, and sexuality. As yet, these critical concerns have not significantly influenced the study of film acting. The concept of 'masquerade' is a useful point from which to establish such connections (see White, Part 1, Chapter 13). According to this concept, social identities such as 'masculinity' or 'femininity' are not the effect of internal and ahistorical essences. Instead, these categories have to be continually constructed and reproduced, so that gender categories are understood as ways of 'acting' or 'performance'. In film studies, some uses of this concept (e.g. Holmlund 1993) have discussed how costuming and narrative situations construct gender. There is a problem with this view though, for it suspends the performance at the level of an artificial 'surface' behind which a 'real' identity is hidden. The fuller implications of the concept of masquerade will only become apparent when gendered, racial, and sexual meanings are seen to be acted in the uses of speaking voices and moving bodies.

BIBLIOGRAPHY

Benjamin, Walter (1936/1977), 'The Work of Art in the Age of Mechanical Reproduction', in J. Curran, M. Gurevitch, and J. Woollacott (eds.), *Mass Communication and Society* (London: Edward Arnold and the Open University).

Brecht, Bertolt (1940/1978), 'Short Description of a New Technique of Acting which Produces an Alienation

Effect', in J. Willet (ed.), *Brecht on Theatre* (London: Methuen).

*Butler, J. (ed.) (1991), *Star Texts: Image and Performance in Film and Television* (Detroit: Wayne State University Press).

Clark, D. (1990), 'Acting in Hollywood's Best Interest: Representations of Actors' Labour during the National Recovery Administration', *Journal of Film and Video*, 42/4.

Comolli, J. (1978), 'Historical Fiction—A Body too Much', *Screen*, 19/2: 41–53.

Cooke, Lez (1986), *Acting in the Cinema: Notes on the 'Acting Tapes'* (London: British Film Institute Education).

de Cordova, R. (1986), 'Genre and Performance: An Overview', in B. K. Grant (ed.), *Film Genre Reader* (Austin: University of Texas Press).

—— (1990), *Picture Personalities: The Emergence of the Star System in America* (Urbana: University of Illinois Press).

Dyer, Richard (1979), *Stars* (London: British Film Institute).

Ellis, John (1982), *Visible Fictions: Cinema, Television, Video* (London: Routledge & Kegan Paul).

Heath, Stephen (1977/1981), 'Film Performance', in *Questions of Cinema* (London: Macmillan).

—— (1979), 'Body, Voice', in *Questions of Cinema* (London: Macmillan).

Higson, A. (1986), 'Film Acting and Independent Cinema', *Screen*, 27/3–4: 110–32.

Holmlund, C. (1993), 'Masculinity as Multiple Masquerade: The "Mature" Stallone and the Stallone Clone', in S. Cohan and I. Hark (eds.), *Screening the Male: Exploring Masculinities in Hollywood Cinema* (London: Routledge).

King, Barry (1985), 'Articulating Stardom', *Screen* 26/5: 27–50.

Kuleshov, Lev (1929/1974), 'Art of the Cinema', in R. Levaco (ed.), *Kuleshov on Film: Writings of Lev Kuleshov* (Berkeley: University of California Press).

*Naremore, James (1988), *Acting in the Cinema* (Berkeley: University of California Press).

Nash, M., and J. Swinson (1985), 'Acting Tapes', *Framework*, 29: 76–85.

Pearson, Roberta (1992), *Eloquent Gestures: The Transformation of Performance Style in the Griffith Biograph Films* (Berkeley: University of California Press).

Peters, A., and M. Cantor (1982), 'Screen Acting as Work', in J. Ettema and D. Whitney (eds.), *Individuals in Mass Communication Organisations* (Beverly Hills: Sage).

Prindle, D. (1988), *The Politics of Glamour: Ideology and Democracy in the Screen Actors Guild* (Madison: University of Wisconsin Press).

Pudovkin, V. (1958), *Film Technique and Film Acting* (London: Vision Press).

Thompson, Grahame F. (1985), 'Approaches to "Performance" ', *Screen*, 26/5: 78–90.

Thompson, John O. (1978), 'Screen Acting and the Commutation Test', *Screen*, 19/2: 55–69.

—— (1985), 'Beyond Commutation: A Reconsideration of Screen Acting', *Screen*, 26/5: 64–76.

Vineburg, S. (1991), *Method Actors: Three Generations of an American Acting Style* (New York: Schirmer).

Wexman, V. (1993), *Creating the Couple: Love, Marriage and Hollywood Performance* (Princeton: Princeton University Press).

Zucker, C. (ed.) (1990), *Making Visible the Invisible: An Anthology of Original Essays on Film Acting* (Metuchen, NJ: Scarecrow Press).

4

Film costume

Pamela Church Gibson

Most students of film and media will probably complete their course without having studied film costume in any detail, if at all. Why this should be the case, when it is arguably such an important component of the way in which a film or television programme functions, needs consideration. It is, after all, one of the aspects of film most frequently mentioned by 'the audience', particularly by women, as is evident from *Star Gazing*, Jackie Stacey's (1994) work on the female spectator. Costume is undeniably an important site of filmic pleasure, and why this source should be so often disregarded as an area of serious academic study must be addressed. This is not to say that there is no literature on the subject—in fact there are a number of books and articles, anecdotal, factual, descriptive, and sometimes lavishly illustrated. What has been missing until quite recently is a body of work which attempts to provide some theoretical framework for the study of film costume. However, things are changing, and it is to be hoped that in five years time an overview such as this will begin by acknowledging the existence of a large number of significant texts and a plurality of critical approaches.

Here some contextualization might seem appropriate. Film costume—and for the purposes of this chapter, 'costume' will be used to mean, quite simply, the clothes worn in films, whether period or contemporary dress—has been slighted in the same way as fashion itself. Only in the last decade or so has fashion really established itself as a serious academic discipline and as an important area of theoretical debate. The reasons, of course, are well documented: the centuries-old belief in the inherent frivolity of fashion, reinforced by the puritanism of many on the left, for whom fashion is the most obvious and the most objectionable form of commodity fetishism, and the conviction of the majority of second-wave feminists that fashion is an arena in which women present and display themselves in order to gratify male desire. As anyone following the progress of Anglo-American feminism over the past thirty years will know, opposition to fashion in the 1970s was both a rallying-point and a seeming consensus. This intransigent attitude to personal adornment persisted until sustained critical interest in consumer culture, particularly within cultural studies, opened up different perspectives. The publication of Elizabeth Wilson's radical text *Adorned in Dreams* (1985) was perhaps the most significant move in a feminist reclamation of fashion. Now, with recent developments in third-wave feminism, all this hostility might yet become history. As Valerie Steele writes in her introduction to the first issue of *Fashion Theory*:

Several years ago I wrote an article entitled 'The F-Word', which described the place of fashion within academia. It was not a pretty picture: Fashion was regarded as frivolous, sexist, bourgeois, 'material' [not intellectual] and, therefore, beneath contempt. Today, it is said, fashion is no longer the 'F-word' in intellectual circles. Certainly, scholars across the disciplines have begun to explore the relationship between body, clothing and cultural identity. . . . The trend began, as many fashions do, in Paris. Thanks to the influence of French theorists, intellectuals around the world recognized the importance of studying the body as a site for the deployment of discourses. Eventually, the subject of clothing also began to receive attention from artists and intellectuals alike. (1997: 1)

If fashion is now a legitimate area of study, what are the implications, if any, for the student of film? Students of fashion design have been denied until recently a body of informing theory other than that specifically concerned with their area of expertise, such as the work of Veblen, Flugel, and Laver (which, unfortunately, *can* be utilized to reinforce the notion of fashion as the provenance of the feeble-minded) and that of later fashion historians, such as Hollander and McDowell. Now there is a proliferation of cultural studies work focused on the field and, following Elizabeth Wilson, concerted efforts to open up specifically feminist studies of fashion (Ash, Craik, Thornton, and Evans, to cite but a few).

It is students of fashion who have traditionally been most interested in, and enthusiastic about, film costume. Many of them can write with authority on the designs of Adrian and Edith Head, can list and describe each outfit worn by Audrey Hepburn in *Sabrina Fair* (1954) (and most, if not all, of her other films) and can make informed observations about mass market spin-offs and tie-ins from the 1930s onwards. Does this devalue costume in the eyes of some 'film scholars'? Is there some sort of élitism at work which suggests that this sort of interest is, indeed, the proper concern of the fashion student or historian? The fact that fashion journalists frequently fill their pages with photographs of their favourite cinematic icons, often accompanied by text that verges on the hagiographic, does not help to establish the study of film costume as a legitimate field of academic discourse.

Charles Eckert's seminal article on the close links between cinema and merchandising in the late 1920s and 1930s, 'The Carole Lombard in Macy's Window' (1978), provoked much debate. Eckert concludes 'Hollywood gave consumerism a distinctive bent . . .'. It 'did as much or more than any other force in capitalist culture to smooth the operation of the production-consumption cycle' (1978/1990: 120–1). Further investigations of the processes he described followed, including articles by Jane Gaines and Mary Ann Doane in a special issue of the *Quarterly Review of Film and Video* (1989) on 'Female Representation and Consumer Culture'. Gaines's article is a fascinating account of the way in which *Queen Christina* (1933)—of all films—was used by retailers across the United States to promote everything from hostess gowns to flatware. However, mass market response to, and use of, cinematic influence is perceived by many involved within the field of film study as of little interest, and more suited to those involved in retail studies, marketing, and visual merchandising.

A final barrier to the study of film costume is the lack of homogeneity within the subject-area itself. It is difficult to write about film costume as a unified subject in the way that acting and music are discussed elsewhere in this volume, given the variety of ways in which costuming is effected within different categories of film. There is, for example, the classic Hollywood film with its studio designer. There are those films where a designer from the world of *haute couture* is involved—an increasingly complex phenomenon in recent years with the on- and off-screen involvement of designers such as Cerruti. There are films set in period—and latterly the European heritage film—where the clothes are of paramount importance in establishing visual style and overall effect. There are European independent, low-budget films where the clothes will probably be sourced, rather than designed and made, so that they do not obtrude and have the appearance of 'authenticity'. There are films, *Orlando* (1992) and *The Sheltering Sky* (1990) for example, where the clothes *do* obtrude, to the extent that they not only dominate the film but interfere in some way with its operation. There are, finally, non-Western cinemas where the semiotics of dress may be impenetrable to Western critics and where costume, in consequence, has not been given the attention it merits. After this contextualization and these observations, it is now time to look at the literature that does exist to date, to attempt some categorization of the texts available, and to ask, where there are omissions, what directions future studies might take.

References to costume are found, firstly, within discussions of mise-en-scène—the visual organization or composition of what is in front of the camera (the 'profilmic' event). Traditionally a concern with mise-en-scène has focused upon a film's use of setting, props, lighting, colour, positioning of figures, and, of course, costume. Mise-en-scène analysis has conventionally been associated with the study of the narrative film and how mise-en-scène may be seen to reinforce,

Updated gangster chic—*Reservoir Dogs* (1993)

complement, or, in some cases, subvert the meanings suggested by plot, dialogue, and character. Costume, in this respect, is read as a signifying element which carries meanings or creates emotional effects, particularly in relation to character. However, although traditional mise-en-scène analysis encourages attention to costume, it is not interested in dress or costume *per se*. Costume is seen as the vehicle for meanings about narrative or character and thus simply as one of a number of signifying elements within a film. Thus, David Bordwell and Kristin Thompson link the analysis of costume to that of props and argue that 'In cinema any portion of a costume may become a prop; a pince-nez (*Battleship Potemkin*), a pair of shoes (*Strangers on a Train*, *The Wizard of Oz*), a cross pendant (*Ivan the Terrible*), a jacket (*Le Million*)' (1980: 81). Similarly, in his article 'Costuming and the Color System of *Leave her to Heaven*', Marshall Deutelbaum provides an intricate analysis of the way in which 'the film constructs a system of relational meaning through consistent oppositions encoded in the colors of the

characters' costumes' (1987: 17). The colours of the women's clothes in the film, he argues, are selected in order to structure and segment the complexities of the narrative. This is in contrast to the more usual narrative readings of colour in costume where the colours are seen to possess symbolic functions seemingly drawn from those that operate within a dominant Western cultural tradition and, in particular, from the language of painting (e.g. Victor Perkins on *Elmer Gantry*, 1960).

An interest in costume as a part of mise-en-scène analysis may be linked to an interest in genres where costuming is often regarded as a defining element. In the 1960s genre theorists turned to the idea of iconography as a way of distinguishing different genres in visual terms. Iconography—recurring patterns of images associated with different genres—is usually subdivided into settings, objects, and dress (McArthur 1972). Thus, in the case of the gangster film, specific settings (the city, saloons), specific objects (cars, machine-guns), and specific kinds of dress (the dark topcoat, the sharp suit, the white shirt and obtrusive tie, the fedora and gloves) have become characteristic icons of the genre, which are used to cue many of the audience's responses. Conventional genre analysis has examined dress in the western, the gangster film, and the horror film; but it is seen only as one of a number of defining elements together with plot, characterization, and setting. The relevant clothes—or 'costume props', to quote again from Bordwell and Thompson (1980)—are nevertheless a vital part of genre recognition.

However, in the case of costume drama, it is costume and setting which are the key generic features. 'Costume drama' is not, of course, an entirely straightforward term, but here it is used to refer to films set in a perceived 'historical' past and includes 'heritage' films. The particular interest of this genre is the emphasis it gives to costume and the way it is linked to traditional 'feminine' genres, such as the 'woman's film'. Thus, whereas feminist film criticism has often read costume in classical cinema, if at all, in terms of a reinforcement of the 'male gaze', feminist analysis of costume drama focuses upon the pleasures of dress for a female audience (and the different kinds of pleasure, other than voyeurism, which it provides). Thus, Richard Dyer identifies the particular appeal of the heritage film for a female audience in terms of the 'sensuousness' of the 'fixtures and fittings', which, he argues, require 'the skilled reading of the female spectator' (1995: 205). Sue Harper, in her comprehensive book *Picturing the Past*, adopts a similar position with regard to costuming in the Gainsborough melodramas: 'The Gainsborough film-makers and their publicists clearly intended that their films would usher women into a realm of pleasure where the female stars would function as the source of the female gaze, and where the males, gorgeously arrayed, would be the unabashed objects of female desire' (1994: 122). She suggests that Elizabeth Haffenden, the costume designer, created in these films a 'costume narrative' working against the moralistic drives within the main narrative 'whose provenance was sexual desire' (30), and she describes in some detail the clothes worn by Margaret Lockwood in *The Wicked Lady* (1944), with the 'vulval symbolism' of some. She contrasts the sumptuous garments Lockwood wears throughout the film with the 'severe tailored blouse, similar to severe 1940s fashion' (like those doubtless worn by many sitting in the audience) seen in her adulterous tryst with James Mason on the moonlit riverbank. This suggests quite graphically the way in which these films give free rein to female desires.

Harper also discusses the way in which Haffenden's designs can be seen as prefiguring the New Look; her costumes, she argues, 'could be seen as a debate, on a symbolic level, on female sexuality and the contemporary crisis of permission'. Pam Cook continues the scrutiny of Gainsborough films—and of their contribution to discourses on national identity—in *Fashioning the Nation* (1996). In the third chapter she explicitly addresses the 'marginalisation of costume design by film theorists', which she argues is 'marked enough to be diagnosed as a symptom' (1996: 41). She examines the links between fashion and fetishism, and the place of fetishism in feminist film theory following the debates initiated by Laura Mulvey's (1975) article 'Visual Pleasure in Narrative Cinema' (see Creed, Part 1, Chapter 9, and White, Part 1, Chapter 13). She continues: 'the concept of fetishism . . . traditionally used to condemn fashion and costume for their impurity . . . can instead be employed to illuminate the ways in which our erotic obsessions with clothes are also transgressive in their play with identity and identification. Identification is another area which has been perceived in a limiting manner by film theory, with consequences for discussion of screen costume' (Cook 1996: 46).

Three of the essays discussed by Cook in this chapter are to be found in *Fabrications: Costume and the Female Body*, edited by Jane Gaines and Charlotte Herzog. Published in 1990, this book arguably made it possible for film costume finally to be recognized as an area for serious and sustained feminist analysis. It includes an account of the conditions under which those clothes were made and another of the ways in which similar garments, and other products featured in films, were widely and successfully marketed. The main thrust of the book, however, is to examine—and reassess—the function of costume in classical Hollywood narrative, and its place within theories of voyeurism, fetishism, and masquerade. These theories, again, are discussed elsewhere in this book, but it is important to understand the way in which they are dependent upon dress. Gaylyn Studlar points out in her article 'Masochism, Masquerade, and the Erotic Metamorphoses of Marlene Dietrich' that 'the role of costuming in forming the pleasures of viewing remain undertheorised within current psychoanalytic discourse on film' (1990: 229). Jane Gaines's essay 'Costume and Narrative: How Dress Tells the Woman's Story' suggests that within melodrama, where 'the work on costume . . . lags behind the work on musical scoring', the 'vestural code' and costume plot can organize an 'idiolect with

Copies of this fringed dress
designed by Givenchy for
Audrey Hepburn (*Breakfast
at Tiffany's*, 1961) soon
appeared in the high street

its own motifs . . . which unfold in a temporality which
does not correspond with key developments' (1990:
205).

She also mentions costume design and its use in the
creation of the 'star persona'—which is where this survey
of costume might have started. The collaborations
between top Hollywood designers and certain female
stars have been extensively documented, as have their
visual solutions to the perceived physical shortcomings
of these stars. The famous full-sleeved dress that
Adrian designed for Joan Crawford in *Letty Lynton*
(1932) was his first obvious gambit to shift the viewer's

gaze upwards, and so away from her wide hips. (Later
he was to use the padded shoulders and the narrow
skirts now synonymous with 1980s power-dressing to
create a similar illusion—that of an inverted triangle.)
Gaines and Herzog, in their article 'Puffed Sleeves
before Tea-Time', show how the Letty Lynton dress
acqired 'far more significance than the film in which it
was showcased', introducing 'a fashion that lingered
until the end of the Thirties' (1985: 25).

Perhaps there is a tendency to devalue the contribution of the stars themselves. Mae West's control over
her own image is well known—but other stars were not

merely passive mannequins, to be draped, disguised, and accoutred. Edith Head describes her work, throughout her career, as involving close collaboration between designer and star. For instance, when starting to work with Dietrich on *Witness for the Prosecution* (1957), she found that the actress had already decided that, for a particular flashback scene, the character should have 'some platform shoes with ankle straps, very hussy, red'. Since no such shoes were to be found in any studio wardrobe in her size, Dietrich arranged a shopping-trip to Main Street the following morning: 'Tomorrow, Edith, you and I will go into town early . . . we'll wear scarfs over our heads' (Head and Ardmore 1959/1960: 15). In the same book, *The Dress Doctor*, Head tells how Cary Grant planned the colour scheme for his clothes in *To Catch a Thief* (1955), asking her exactly what Grace Kelly would be wearing in each scene and then selecting his own outfits in order to complement hers (156).

This might remind the reader of this piece that, so far, men have not been discussed, except by implication as directors, designers, and potential voyeurs. Men as consumers of their own, masculine, dress are not included in the texts discussed—nor are films that have a contemporary setting, or, indeed, a woman director. These last two categories form the basis of an article by Renée Béart, 'Skirting the Issue' (1994), where she examines three films by feminist directors and the ways in which they use clothing. She wishes 'to draw attention to a further approach to costume in women's film, one which also shifts the denotative dimensions of feminine dress onto a second register, doubled over the first', thus establishing 'two interacting positions, feminine and feminist' (1994: 360).

But what of the masculine? Some male film stars are now involved within the world of high fashion in a way reminiscent of the female stars in the heyday of Hollywood. They feature in fashion spreads and designer advertising, they sit in privileged positions at couture shows—some even make it onto the catwalk—and they consort with supermodels. Couturiers fight to dress them, on screen, off screen, and on the night of the Oscars. But critical studies have largely ignored the contemporary and the masculine. Stella Bruzzi's book *Undressing Cinema: Clothing and Identities in the Movies* (1997) seeks to address this particular omission, among others; her intention is 'to reassess and challenge some of the assumptions and truisms that have dominated the study of dress, gender and sexuality, and to recontextualise others by applying them to

cinema'. She discusses not only masculine attire but subcultural style, usually ignored, and argues that in all cinema 'clothing can be seen to construct an independent discursive strategy'. Finally, and significantly, she refutes the assumption that 'fashion is produced for consumption by the opposite sex'. This suggests a programme for the study of film costume which attends to the specificities of the 'language' of dress and the variety of pleasures which costuming affords.

This indicates the way forward, and should widen the debates around costume still further. More interdisciplinary approaches of the type here deployed by Stella Bruzzi are needed, as is more investigation of the relationship between costume, fashion, and industry. Lynn Spigel and Denise Mann have provided a bibliography of texts on 'Women and Consumer Culture' taken, as they explain, 'from what have traditionally been disparate academic fields and interests in order to facilitate research into areas relatively unexplored by film studies' (1989: 85). More in-depth case-studies of fashion 'spin-offs' from film—rather than the intentional tie-ins—would be helpful. Lastly, it is to be hoped that this work will not remain forever focused on Western cultural production. Given critical interest in the re-creation of a recognizable and supposedly 'authentic' past in the heritage film, an interesting comparison could potentially be made with Indian historical films, where the costumes are used to create an ahistorical past, a conglomeration of periods and consequently a mythological realm. A close scrutiny of dress in non-Western cinemas is long overdue.

To conclude: clothing is a part of our daily discourse—and a source of personal pleasures in a way that, say, camera angles and cinematography are not. Yet, for too long film costume has been granted only grudging attention and there has been little informed discussion. While it is pleasant to think that things are finally changing, a current news item seems ominous. In January 1997, exactly fifty years after the unveiling of Dior's New Look and the outraged response it provoked from members of the British government, Labour MP Tony Banks sponsored a motion in the House of Commons to deplore the publicity given to two Paris couture collections. Both were created by British designers—John Galliano for the house of Dior, though Banks seemed unaware of the irony, and Alexander McQueen for Givenchy. 'It is vulgar and obscene', the motion proposed, 'that so much significance should be attached to overpriced and grotesque flights of fancy for hanging on the limbs of the super-rich.' *Plus ça change* . . .

BIBLIOGRAPHY

Ash, Juliet, and Lee Wright (1987), *Components of Dress* (London: Routledge).

Beart, Renée (1994), 'Skirting the Issue', *Screen*, 35/4 (Winter), 354–73.

Bordwell, David, and Kristin Thompson (1980), *Film Art: An Introduction* (Reading, Mass.: Addison-Wesley).

*Bruzzi, Stella (1997), *Undressing Cinema: Clothing and Identities in the Movies* (London: Routledge).

*Cook, Pam (1996), *Fashioning the Nation: Costume and Identity in British Cinema* (London: British Film Institute).

Craik, Jennifer (1994), *The Face of Fashion: Cultural Studies in Fashion* (London: Routledge).

Deutelbaum, Marshall (1987), 'Costuming and the Color System of *Leave her to Heaven*', *Film Criticism*, 11/3 (Spring), 11–20.

Doane, Mary Ann (1989a), 'The Economy of Desire: The Commodity Form in/of the Cinema', *Quarterly Review of Film and Video*, 11/1: 23–35.

—— (1989b) 'Female Representation and Consumer Culture', *Quarterly Review of Film and Video*, 1/11.

Dyer, Richard (1995), 'Heritage Cinema in Europe', in Ginette Vincendeau (ed.) *Encyclopedia of European Cinema* (London: Cassell and British Film Institute).

*Eckert, Charles (1978/1990), 'The Carole Lombard in Macy's Window', in Gaines and Herzog (1990).

Evans, Caroline, and Minna Thornton (1989), *Women and Fashion: A New Look* (London: Quartet Books).

Flugel, J. C. (1930), *The Psychology of Clothes* (London: Hogarth Press).

*Gaines, Jane (1989), 'The *Queen Christina* Tie-Ups: Convergence of Show Window and Screen', *Quarterly Review of Film and Video* 11/1: 35–60.

*—— (1990), 'Costume and Narrative: How Dress Tells the Woman's Story', in Gaines and Herzog (1990).

*—— and Charlotte Herzog (1985), 'Puffed Sleeves before Tea-Time: Joan Crawford and Women Audiences', *Wide Angle*, 6/4: 24–33.

*—— —— (eds.) (1990), *Fabrications: Costume and the Female Body* (London: Routledge).

*Harper, Sue (1994), *Picturing the Past: The Rise and Fall of the Costume Film* (London: British Film Institute).

Head, Edith, and Jane Kesner Ardmore (1959/60), *The Dress Doctor* (Kingswood: World's Work).

Hollander, Anne (1975), *Seeing through Clothes* (New York: Avon Books).

Laver, James (1969), *Modesty in Dress: An Enquiry into the Fundamentals of Fashion* (London: Heinemann).

McArthur, Colin (1972), *Underworld USA* (London: Secker & Warburg).

McDowell, Colin (1991), *Dressed to Kill: Sex, Power and Clothes* (London: Hutchinson).

Perkins, V. F. (1972), *Film as Film: Understanding and Judging Movies* (Harmondsworth: Penguin).

Spigal, Lynn, and Denise Mann (1989), 'Women and Consumer Culture: A Selective Bibliography', *Quarterly Review of Film and Video*, 11/1: 85–105.

Stacey, Jackie (1994), *Star Gazing: Hollywood Cinema and Female Spectatorship* (London: Routledge).

Steele, Valerie (1997), Letter from the Editor, *Fashion Theory: The Journal of Dress, Body and Culture*, 1/1: 1–2.

*Studlar, Gaylyn (1990), 'Masochism, Masquerade, and the Erotic Metamorphoses of Marlene Dietrich', in Gaines and Herzog (1990).

Veblen, Thorstein (1899/1957), *The Theory of the Leisure Class* (London: Allen & Unwin).

Wilson, Elizabeth (1985), *Adorned in Dreams: Fashion and Modernity* (London: Virago).

5 Film music

Claudia Gorbman

Any attentive filmgoer is aware of the enormous power music holds in shaping the film experience, manipulating emotions and point of view, and guiding perceptions of characters, moods, and narrative events. It therefore comes as something of a surprise that, aside from a smattering of isolated writings since the 1940s, the serious, theoretically informed study of film music has come of age only in the last ten years. Film scholars, hailing chiefly from literature and communications backgrounds, have lacked the training and/or interest, while music departments inherit a high-art prejudice; although the latter may have incorporated ethnomusicology and even popular music, they apparently relegate film music to the ranks of the middle-brow, that least worthy category of all. Even now that disciplinary brakes to the academic study of film music have eased, members of the two fields have come to film music with such widely divergent training and scholarly goals that substantial dialogue between them has proven rare. For those trained as musicologists, the music itself, with the film as its context, invariably emerges as the focus of attention. Film scholars tend to examine film music and the conditions of its production primarily in order to understand films and the economic and psychic institution of cinema.

Some framing questions in the current study of film music are as follows. Why do films have music? What constitutes good film music? How should the evolution of film music be historicized, and what can a theoreti-

cally informed history of film music reveal? What are the narrative functions of music in films? To what extent is music in films explicitly heard by the moviegoer, and what are the implications of the spectator attending or not attending to a film's music? What formal and aesthetic relations obtain between film and music? What are the aesthetic and ideological consequences of the foregrounding of popular music on film soundtracks of the last twenty years? How does music work in television, and in film genres such as animated, documentary, and experimental film? How have musical idioms other than those of the European orchestral tradition functioned in Hollywood cinema and other cinemas?

Aesthetics

Auteurism

Within the general field of film studies, the study of film music might well represent the last bastion of film aesthetics. A number of factors help to explain why discussion of film music remains immersed in aesthetic discourses, even when, in film studies at large, aesthetics has been jettisoned in the tidal waves of psychoanalysis, Marxism, and cultural studies over the last twenty years. What might be considered a felt lack of musical competency among many film scholars has created a vacuum; and this vacuum has been filled not only by musicologists, influenced to a much lesser extent by post-structuralism, but also by film music fans and by composers themselves.

Since movie music is now routinely marketed as a commodity apart from the films for which it is composed or compiled, it has its own thriving ancillary audience. Film scores have taken on a musical life of their own especially since the proliferation of the compact disc in the early 1980s. Concerned relatively little with the narrative, visual, or ideological intricacies of the films from which favourite soundtrack discs come, fans and collectors focus rather on canon-formation for film composers. Serious fans have held an unusually prominent place in discussions of film music, often contributing insightful criticism, original research, and analysis.

Another unusually strong presence is the composers themselves. Successful film composers spend their lives analysing the dramatic workings of films in order to score them, and their special knowledge of music and dramatic structure gives them a well-deserved authority. Such articulate individuals as David Raskin and Elmer Bernstein have provided bridges from the classical Hollywood era to the present for students and scholars of film. A number of composers have written important texts on film music, of which Hanns Eisler's book *Composing for the Films* is a classic. More recently Fred Karlin has written two illuminating volumes: *On the Track* (1989), co-authored with Rayburn Wright, for aspiring film composers; and *Listening to Movies* (1994), for film music appreciation. George Burt, both a composer and an academic, offers an insightful examination of the practical and aesthetic aspects of film scoring in his book *The Art of Film Music* (1994).

One conspicuous result of these developments is an auteurism of the Romantic sort. Post-structuralism's dethronement of the individual artist has simply not occurred for film composers, since much academic discussion of film music occurs in contexts such as film music festivals of the Society for the Preservation of Film Music in Los Angeles, where there is a certain pressure to see and appreciate the music through the composer's eye and ear. The canon of film composers is a subject of lively debate. There has developed a virtual industry of Bernard Herrmann criticisms, for example, in the form of a stream of books and articles, and passionate partisanship in Internet forums, fed by new CD releases of Herrmann scores, new concert editions and performances, and an hour-long documentary film about Herrmann (directed by Joshua Waletzky, 1994) shown on public television across the United States.

Aesthetic theory

Among the newest in a long tradition of theorizing relations among the arts and 'compound' arts, scholars of cinema have examined the marriage between the representational art of cinema and the generally non-representational art of music (see e.g. Brown 1994: 12–37; Gorbman 1987: 11–33; Kassabian 1993: 1–23). Thus far they have shown a predilection for studying non-diegetic orchestral film music in its interaction with images and narrative structures in narrative feature films. (Diegetic music, or source music, is music whose apparent source is the narrative world of the film. Non-diegetic music, or 'scoring', is music on the soundtrack which could presumably not be heard by characters in the film.) Areas of concern are the ways in which music inflects scenes with emotional and dramatic resonance, suggests character, setting, and mood, influences perceptions of narrative time and space, creates formal unity and a sense of continuity, interacts with human speech and other sounds, and compensates for the loss of 'liveness' and spatial depth that characterize the cinema's elder sibling, the theatre.

Most recently, Royal Brown (1994) has attempted to elucidate the effects of music as a non-iconic and non-representational medium when it is co-present with the narrative, iconic, representational system of feature films. He argues that music can *generalize* a film event—that is, it encourages the spectator to receive the event not in its particularity but on a mythic level. Thus, when the Western hero rides over a ridge and looks out on the vast landscape before him, or when the heroine of a melodrama embraces her child for the last time, the almost certain presence of orchestral music on the soundtrack in each case—music that is virtually assured to channel a certain field of readings—helps to foster emotional identification.

Brown attempts to account for the very marriage of film and music—why they got together at all. He suggests that because of the cinema's iconicity and its essentially prosaic realism, it 'needed something . . . to justify its very existence as an art form . . . to escape from the trap of referentiality in order to impose perception of its artistic structure and content' (1994: 19–20). Though he cites such artists as Abel Gance and Sergei Eisenstein for support, this position curiously endows the cinema with intention, and hardly explains the ubiquity of pianos in the nickelodeons, where music and the movies enjoyed their mass audience from the beginning.

Brown offers another formulation that is indisputable: music provides a foundation in affect for narrative cinema. To describe how music provides affect, he cites Suzanne Langer to claim that a given piece of music carries no *specific* inherent emotional signification; it is rather that the dialectical interaction of music and images–sounds produces a specific affect (Brown 1994: 26–7). (Philip Tagg (1989) provides an important counterpoint to this idea. Drawing on years of empirical research on musical connotation, he demonstrates that aspects of musical style and melody, as deployed in television and film, carry a surprising degree of semantic precision even when heard outside their audiovisual context.)

An issue central to film music aesthetics is the question of the music's place in the hierarchy of the spectator's attention. Critics and composers in the classical studio era maintained that film music should be unobtrusive. The French composer Maurice Jaubert's dictum that people do not go to the movies to hear music (with obvious exceptions for musical films) is emblematic of this aesthetic position, which dominated theory and practice of film music throughout the period. Kalinak (1992) and Gorbman (1987) cite numerous examples of the principle of inaudibility at work in classical scoring. Conventions of both composition and placement of non-diegetic music prioritize narrative exposition (Kalinak 1992: 79). The classical score features a high degree of synchronization between music and narrative action, and thus commonly relies on such devices as *ostinati*, 'stingers', and mickey-mousing. (An *ostinato* is a repeated melodic or rhythmic figure, to propel scenes which lack dynamic visual action; a stinger is a musical sforzando to emphasize dramatically an action or a character's sudden strong emotion; mickey-mousing is the musical 'imitation', through pitch and/or rhythm, of visual action.) Practices of composing, mixing, and editing privilege dialogue over music, and dictate the entrances and exits of musical cues so as not to distract attention from the narrative action. George Burt (1994) demonstrates that this aesthetic is alive and well in contemporary orchestral scoring.

The breakdown of the studio sytem began to modify the aesthetic (an aesthetic which, it must be said, was always flexible, for music routinely moved from background to foreground in the case of diegetic produc-

tion numbers, narrative moments of spectacle, comedy, beginning and end credits, and so forth). Popular idioms such as jazz and rock 'n' roll, and occasionally even atonal and electronic experiments, joined film music's stylistic arsenal. Many of the newer composers were trained in television or popular music rather than in the European late Romantic tradition.

Now, two generations later, two developments demonstrate that unobtrusiveness is no longer the rule, but rather remains as one among a number of possibilities. Brown identifies the first development as 'postmodern' scoring. This is a tendency toward prominent and self-conscious use of music, such that the music seems to occupy a 'parallel universe' to the film's visual narrative rather than function illustratively and subordinately in the manner of the classical score (Brown 1994: 235–63). To be sure, one may find isolated examples of scoring techniques and effects of this kind in scores of decades past. But in such films as *Diva* (Jean-Jacques Beineix, 1982), *The Hunger* (Tony Scott, 1983), and *Heavenly Creatures* (Peter Jackson, 1994), one senses that the focused deployment of music for irony and excess, using music to disturb rather than contain the hierarchies of subjectivity, high and low musical culture, and diegetic and non-diegetic narration, has resulted in a genuinely new paradigm of interaction between music and film.

The second development shattering the aesthetic of unobtrusiveness is pop scoring, the use of recorded popular songs on the non-diegetic soundtrack. As with 'postmodern' scoring, pop scoring has a considerable history. But the massive cross-marketing of recorded music and films which has become the rule since the 1980s has made at least some pop scoring common place in virtually all commercial feature films. Film music scholarship is beginning to address the aesthetic dimensions of non-diegetic songs accompanying film narrative. The stanzaic form of popular song, the presence of lyrics to 'compete' with the viewer's reception of film narrative and dialogue, and the cultural weight and significance of the stars performing the songs all work directly against classical Hollywood's conception of film music as an 'inaudible' accompaniment, relying on the anonymous yet familiar idioms of symphonic Romanticism, its elastic form dictated by the film's narrative form.

The new pop aesthetic scandalizes film music auteurists. Many critics point accusing fingers at the crass commercialism that drives decisions to insert pop songs into soundtracks and thereby spoil the integrity

'Focused deployment of music for irony and excess'—*Heavenly Creatures* (1994)

of composed scores. Others, primarily critics grounded in film and cultural studies, and also those in the growing field of popular music studies, are enthusiastically investigating the range of possibilities inherent in this new paradigm.

Critics have investigated to a lesser extent the forms and functions of music in animation, documentary, and experimental film—genres which often give music pre-eminence. Eliminating realist fictional narrative from the equation, however, allows one to focus more purely on certain relationships between music and the moving image. Serious study of the virtuousic cartoon music of Carl Stallings, and analyses of work by Virgil Thompson and Philip Glass for documentaries, for example, shed new light on music–film relationships.

Psychology

The psychological dimensions of film music have subtended much writing in the field. What effects does music have on the film's spectator-auditor? What psychological factors motivate the presence of music in movies?

In my book *Unheard Melodies* (1987), I begin to address these questions by summarizing historical,

psychological, and aesthetic arguments explaining the presence of music to accompany the silent film. For one thing, music had accompanied a number of nineteenth-century theatrical forms, and it persisted for numerous practical reasons in the evolution of film exhibition. For another, music covered the distracting noise of the movie projector. It served to explicate and advance the narrative; it provided historical, geographical, and atmospheric setting; it identified characters and qualified actions. Along with intertitles, its semiotic functions compensated for the characters' lack of speech. It provided a rhythmic 'beat' to complement, or impel, the rhythms of editing and movement on the screen. It served as an antidote to the technologically derived 'ghostliness' of the images. And, as music, it bonded spectators together in the three-dimensional space of the theatre.

The book then explores reasons why music persisted in films after the coming of sound—when the movies' new realism would seem to make music an unwelcome guest. One compelling line of thought, which has elicited considerable elaboration and debate, draws on psychoanalytic theory to explain the psychic 'pay-off' of having music on the soundtrack. Psychoanalysis was a dominant discourse of film studies in the 1970s, providing a way to understand the cinema's mechanisms of pleasure and spectator identification (see

Creed, Part 1, Chapter 9). It was particularly well suited to describing the workings of classical Hollywood cinema; in film music studies a decade later, the primary testing ground for the psychoanalytic perspective has also been the classical cinema.

According to French psychoanalytic theorists Guy Rosolato (1974) and Didier Anzieu (1976), sound plays a crucial role in the constitution of the subject. The infant exists in a 'sonorous envelope' consisting of the sounds of the child's body and maternal environment; in this primordial sonic space the child is as yet unaware of distinctions between self and other, inside and outside the body. Rosolato suggests that the pleasure of listening to music—organized, wordless sound—inheres in its invocation of the subject's auditory imaginary in conjunction with the pre-Oedipal language of sounds.

In applying this idea to cinema, critics argue that background music recaptures the pleasure of the sonorous envelope, evoking the psychic traces of the subject's bodily fusion with the mother. Classical cinema capitalizes on music's special relation to the spectator's psyche to lower the threshold of belief in the fiction. Thus film music works in the perceptual background to attack the subject's resistance to being absorbed in the narrative.

Like Muzak, which acts to make consumers into untroublesome social subjects (relieving anxiety in airports and medical waiting-rooms, greasing the wheels of consumer desire in shopping-malls), film music lulls the spectator into being an untroublesome (less critical, less wary) viewing subject. Music aids the process of turning enunciation into fiction. In doing so, film music helps fend off two potential displeasures which threaten the spectator's experience. The first is the threat of ambiguity: film music deploys its cultural codes to anchor the image in meaning. Second, film music fends off the potential displeasure of the spectator's awareness of the technological basis of cinematic discourse—the frame, editing, and so on. Like the sonorous envelope, music's bath of affect can smooth over discontinuities and rough spots, and mask the recognition of the apparatus through its own melodic and harmonic continuity. Film music thereby acts as a hypnotist inducing a trance: it focuses and binds the spectator into the narrative world.

Jeff Smith (1996) has challenged psychoanalytic film music theory by problematizing the basic premise of film music's inaudibility. He quotes my formulation:

'were the subject to be aware (fully conscious) of [music's] presence as part of the film's discourse, the game would be all over' (Gorbman 1987: 64). Although many of the questions Smith raises about my writing on soundtrack audibility are already answered in my book, his critique points aptly to further areas of investigation. If music is crucial to the creation of a 'subject-effect' but also has more foregrounded functions of narrative cueing (such as establishing historical and geographical setting, and conveying information through leitmotifs), then the spectator must be aware of the music at least some of the time. The spectator must be slipping in and out of the trance created by the music-as-hypnotist. There must be a complex fluctuation between the state of unawareness crucial to the psychoanalytic account, and levels that permit cognition of musical cues.

Smith counters the psychoanalytic model with perspectives from cognitive theory, drawing from the work of David Bordwell (1985: 29–47) and Noël Carroll (1988: 213–25) as well as from psychologists of music such as McAdams (1987) and Sloboda (1985). He argues that, like other music, film music is apprehended through a variety of different listening modes and competencies. He calls for an account of film-musical cognition that directly addresses the spectator's mental activities in processing film music's narrative cues. This focus on the competencies of film spectator-auditors is promising.

Kassabian (1993) also emphasizes the issue of competence: 'like any other language, [music] is acquired, learned, in a specific sociohistorical context' (36). Focusing on such categories of filmgoers gender and ethnicity, she lays the groundwork for an understanding of ways in which individuals identify with films. Depending on 'differences in perceivers' relations to the music', they will 'interpret cues' differently in the cues' filmic settings (69).

History

The question of how film music is perceived eludes definitive answers because of its enormous historical variation. Not only is film music more explicitly foregrounded in many scores of the 1990s than it used to be, but today's filmgoers have different competencies and 'reading formations' than those of, say, 1950. Although it seems difficult *not* to notice pop scoring

At the foreground of perception: Max Steiner's score for *Gone with the Wind* (1939)

in contemporary soundtracks, we may imagine that for some moviegoers pop scoring has become so customary that it recedes into the background of perception. Likewise, Erich Korngold's score for *Robin Hood* (USA, 1939), or Max Steiner's for *Gone with the Wind* (USA, 1939), can hardly be termed unobtrusive to today's ears.

The theoretically informed writing of film music history is quite young. Martin Mark's revealing new book *Music in the Silent Film* (1996) documents practices of composing or fitting pre-existing music to films, as well as performance practices, at various stages from the early cinema into the 1920s. (The sheer variety of such practices suggests that the current pop compilation score may have more in common with silent film music than with its more immediate predecessor, the classical film score.) Another musicologist, David Neumeyer (1996), has elucidated scoring practices of Hollywood in the 1930s through often brilliant, methodical research and close readings of film scores. His study of diegetic tunes heard in a scene in *Casablanca* (Michael Curtiz, 1943) reveals the care with which popular music was chosen for the film, and the semantic richness made available to 'competent' listeners. The study of *Casablanca*'s score receives further treatment in an essay by Marks (1996), which demonstrates the wide range of variation in classical scoring by contrasting Max Steiner's scoring techniques in *Casablanca* with Adolph Deutsch's in *The Maltese Falcon*. Krin Gabbard (1996) draws on contemporary theories of culture not so much to outline a history of jazz in the movies as to gain a historical understanding of its significations.

Finally, Jeff Smith's pathfinding dissertation 'The Sounds of Commerce' (1995) brings careful musical analysis and archival research to a study of the economic and institutional factors that led to the pop sounds of such composers as Mancini and Morricone in the 1960s. Smith chronicles the studios' financial restructuring following the 1948 Paramount decree, focusing on the decision of several major studios to acquire recording companies and to cross-market films and film music. His work forcefully demonstrates the intimate relationships among finance, marketing, and ultimately film music style itself in a key historical period. The scholarship of these and other historians bodes well for the study of film music both as art and as mass culture.

BIBLIOGRAPHY

Anzieu, Didier (1976), 'L'enveloppe sonore du soi', *Nouvelle revue de psychanalyse*, 13: 161–79.

Bordwell, David (1985), *Narration in the Fiction Film* (Madison: University of Wisconsin Press).

*****Brown, Royal S.** (1994), *Overtones and Undertones: Reading Film Music* (Berkeley: University of California Press).

Buhler, James, and **David Neumeyer** (1994), 'Film Studies/Film Music', *Journal of the American Musicological Society*, 47/2: 364–85.

Burt, George (1994), *The Art of Film Music* (Boston: Northeastern University Press).

Carroll, Noël (1988), *Mystifying Movies: Fads and Fallacies in Contemporary Film Theory* (New York: Columbia University Press).

Eisler, Hanns (1947), *Comparing for the Films* (New York: Oxford University Press).

Gabbard, Krin (1996), *Jammin' at the Margins: Jazz and the American Cinema* (Chicago: University of Chicago Press).

*****Gorbman, Claudia** (1987), *Unheard Melodies: Narrative Film Music* (Bloomington: Indiana University Press; London: British Film Institute).

*****Kalinak, Kathryn** (1992), *Settling the Score: Music and the Classical Hollywood Film* (Madison: University of Wisconsin Press).

Karlin, Fred (1994) *Listening to Movies: The Film Lover's Guide to Film Music* (New York: Schirmer).

—— and **Rayburn Wright** (1989), *On the Track: A Guide to Contemporary Film Scoring* (New York: Schirmer).

Kassabian, Anahid (1993), 'Songs of Subjectivities: Theorizing Hollywood Film Music of the 1980s and 1990s', dissertation, Stanford University.

McAdams, Stephen (1987), 'Music: A Science of the Mind', *Contemporary Music Review*, 2: 1–61.

Marks, Martin (1996), 'Music, Drama, Warner Brothers. The Cases of *Casablanca* and *The Maltese Falcon*', *Michigan Quarterly Review*, 35/1: 112–42.

—— (1997), *Music and the Silent Film: Contexts and Case Stuies 1895–1924* (New York: Oxford University Press).

Neumeyer, David (1996), 'Performances in Early Hollywood Sound Films: Source Music, Background Music, and the Integrated Sound Track', *Contemporary Music Review*.

Romney, Jonathan, and **Adrian Wootton** (eds.) (1995), *Celluloid Jukebox: Popular Music and the Movies since the Fifties* (London: British Film Institute).

Rosolato, Guy (1974) 'La Voix: entre corps et langage', *Revue fraçaise de psychanalyse*, 38/1: 75–94.

Sloboda, J. (1985), *The Cognitive Psychology of Music* (Oxford: Clarendon Press).

Smith, Jeff (1995), 'The Sounds of Commerce: Popular Film Music 1960–1973', dissertation, University of Wisconsin.

Smith, Jeff (1996), 'Unheard Melodies? A Critique of Psychoanalytic Theories of Film Music', in David Bordwell and Noel Carroll (eds.), *Post-Theory* (Madison: University of Wisconsin Press).

Tagg, Philip (1989), 'An Anthropology of Stereotypes in TV Music?', *Svensk Tidskrift för Musikvetenskap*, 19–39.

6

Classic film theory and semiotics

Anthony Easthope

Film theory had to struggle a surprisingly long time before it could become a proper theory of film. Difficulty arose from the very feature which ensured cinema its universality. ever since the earliest audiences flung themselves out of the way of an oncoming screen locomotive, film has stunned us by its seeming capacity to reproduce reality transparently, immediately, directly. Because of this realism, serious analysis of film was confronted from the first by antagonism from the smothering inheritance of Kantian aesthetics.

In *The Critique of Judgement* (1790) Kant contrasts sensation and contemplation, singular and universal, interested and disinterested (useful and useless). Aesthetic experience is opposed to merely sensuous gratification (eating, for example) because it combines sensation—through hearing and vision—with contemplation. The aesthetic object is focused on as a singularity, not as an instance of a general concept, for its own sake and not for any kind of usefulness or social purpose. All this kicks against what cinema appears to do best; its rendering of the real seems just too obviously contaminated with unprocessed sensation, too liable to documentary appropriation, too easily turned to useful social purposes.

Classic film theory

As Aaron Scharf (1969) shows in convincing detail, the early impact of photography on painting and notions of art was enormous. Although encouraging some artists into innovation and experiment, photography also served to strengthen and substantiate the opposition between art and craft, the aesthetic and the useful. As 'moving pictures', produced when light is projected through strips of celluloid onto a screen, cinematic images have a double intimacy with reality since they are both caused by it (light from these objects marked photosensitive film) and also resemble it. It was only too tempting to deny cinema a status as art.

In the face of a seemingly incontestable naturalism, the labour of classic film theory was to designate the specific value of cinema—what has allowed it to provide such a compelling representation of modernity. For this two main strategies emerged. The creationists (or formalists), including Rudolf Arnheim, Sergei Eisenstein, and Béla Balázs, defend cinema as an art form which goes beyond realism, while the realists, particularly Siegfried Kracauer and André Bazin, appreciate cinema just because it does provide such an exact representation of reality.

Creationism is well represented by Rudolf Arnheim's book *Film* (1933), which sets out 'to refute the assertion that film is nothing but the feeble mechanical reproduction of real life' (1958: 37). Arnheim points out first of all how the experience of sitting in the cinema differs from our empirical perception of the everyday world. In everyday experience the world is three-dimensional, while in the cinema all we get is a flat screen; our life is lived colour with sound, while cinema is black and white, and silent (or was, up to 1929); in our ordinary world we can look wherever we want within our field of vision, while cinema limits what we see within the masked frame of the screen.

> **Formalist theory (Arnheim) and realist theory (Bazin) appear to oppose each other. But *both* positions suppose that cinema, based as it is in the photographic process, must be assessed as in part a mechanical reproduction, whether feeble or convincing.**

Arnheim celebrates the many effects through which cinema transforms and constructs a reality, including camera angles and movement, focus, lighting effects, framing, altered motion, superimposition, special lenses. And, in addition to these features pertaining mainly to the single shot, cinema works through sequences of shots edited together, producing dazzling and significant effects of contrast and repetition, metonymy and metaphor. Editing makes something available to someone in the cinema that could never be seen by any empirical viewer of what was originally filmed.

Arnheim is one of the first to codify the specific resources of cinema and the many ways it produces meanings beyond anything present in the reality from which the photographed image originates. Yet though he argues that film exceeds reality, Arnheim does not challenge the view that film is powerfully influenced by its photographic resemblance to reality. The realists, led by André Bazin, make that relation the essential virtue of the medium, as, for example, in this passage:

The objective nature of photography confers on it a quality of credibility absent from all other picture-making. In spite of any objections our critical spirit may offer, we are forced to accept as real the existence of the object reproduced, actually *re*-presented, set before us, that is to say, in time and space. Photography enjoys a certain advantage in virtue of this transference of reality from the thing to its reproduction. (Bazin 1967: 13–14)

This passage makes it clear that Bazin is aware that in cinema filmed objects are not presented but '*re*-presented'. And elsewhere he explains how he values cinematic reality because it has an almost Brechtian effect in leaving the viewer free to criticize, when more obviously constructed cinema (Eisenstein, for instance) aims to manipulate the viewer's understanding.

Formalist theory (Arnheim) and realist theory (Bazin) appear to oppose each other. But what is crucial, and what marks off classic film theory, is the assumption they share. Formalist theory values cinema to the extent that it is, in Arnheim's phrase, more than 'the feeble mechanical reproduction of real life': realist theory values cinema to the extent that it adheres to 'a mechanical reproduction in the making of which man plays no part', as Bazin says (1967: 12). *Both* positions suppose that cinema, based as it is in the photographic process, must be assessed as in part a mechanical reproduction, whether feeble or convincing. It was not until the 1960s that this view—the naturalist, or reflectionist, fallacy—began to be finally overthrown in film theory.

1968 and after

Film theory was able to develop into a fully fledged account of cinema because it staged what Stephen Heath refers to as 'the encounter of Marxism and psychoanalysis on the terrain of semiotics' (1976: 11). Of these three theoretical interventions, semiotics (or semiology) arrived first. In a posthumous work, *Course in General Linguistics*, published in 1916, Saussure introduced into the study of language a number of theoretical distinctions, of which two in particular proved fruitful when carried over into film theory.

From ancient rhetoric, Saussure revived the distinction between signifier and signified to analyse the naïve concept of 'words'. In any utterance the level of the signifier is made up from the sounds (phonemes) selected for use by a particular language, arranged in a temporal order, while that of the signified consists of the meanings assigned to any group of signifiers. Signifiers consist of entirely arbitrary sounds related only to each other in an internally self-consistent system, and it is purely a matter of convention what set of signifiers give rise to a certain meaning. In modern English, for example, the sounds represented by 'mare' can open onto the meaning 'female horse' or possibly 'municipal leader' (mayor), while a very similar group of signifiers in French ('mer'/'mère') open onto the meanings 'sea' and 'mother'.

A principle is implied by Saussure's distinction, that the material organization of a language is ontologically prior to any meaning it produces. During the 1960s semiotics had a decisive impact upon film theory by concentrating attention on the question what were the specific properties of film, its *specifica differentia*, distinguishing it from other forms of signification (novels and drama, for example).

There are certain problems in detail, however. For while Saussure's distinction between signifier and signified applies perfectly to a language, it is much harder to get it to work for a visual medium such as film. In any famous sequence, such as that at the end of Ford's *The Searchers* (USA, 1956) when the John Wayne figure is left outside the door, what exactly takes the place of the signifier and the signified? This is a question addressed by the work of Christian Metz, as we shall see.

A second distinction put forward by Saussure was also expanded in film semiotics. Language works by moving forward in time so that in English (as in Chinese) syntax can draw simply on word order to make 'Dog bites man' mean something different from 'Man bites dog'. Naming this linear axis of discourse as 'syntagmatic', Saussure pointed out that at every point along this horizontal axis terms were selected and rejected from a potential corpus lying in a vertical dimension (the 'associative' or 'paradigmatic'). Thus, 'Snake' is a possible paradigmatic substitution for 'Dog' or 'Man' in either of the previous examples but 'Yesterday' is not,

since 'Yesterday bites man' is not a meaningful sentence.

In other words, it was possible to think of the syntagmatic axis as a consistent structure which would remain the same even when different paradigmatic terms were substituted along it. In 1928 Vladimir Propp applied this principle to the analysis of narrative, discerning across 115 Russian folk stories a common structure consisting of thirty-one 'functions'. Thus, function (Propp 1968: 11), 'The hero leaves home', can be realized as easily by 'Ivan is sent to kill the dragon' as by 'Dmitri goes in search of the princess'.

A semiotic analysis of film narrative was initiated with enthusiasm and some effect, notably by Raymond Bellour (1972) in his study of *The Birds* (USA, 1963) and by Peter Wollen (1982), also discussing Hitchcock, in his account of *North by Northwest* (USA, 1959). Bellour discusses the Bodega Bay sequence shot by shot, while Wollen aims for a Proppian analysis of the whole movie. Both examinations, plausible as they are in detail, suffer from what are now recognized as the inevitable assumptions of formal narrative analysis— that there is only a single narrative and not a number of simultaneous narrative meanings, that the narrative is fixed once and for all 'out there' in the text and not constructed in a relation between text and reader.

Narrative analysis of film on the precedent of Propp had the definite benefit of shifting argument away from any question of the relation or correspondence between a film and some real it might be supposed to reflect. It focused on film as *text* but did so only by incurring a concomitant limitation. Narrative is an effect which runs across many different kinds of text, so detailing it in films does not advance understanding of what is specific to film. Nevertheless, the overall consequence of semiotic attention to cinema was to weaken concern with the issue of realism and strengthen attention to the cinema as a particular kind of textuality. After 1968 these tendencies were reinforced from a somewhat unanticipated quarter.

Classic Marxism theorized that the economic base and mode of production determines the political and ideological 'superstructure'. However, during the 1960s the French Marxist thinker Louis Althusser had argued that notions of base and superstructure should be rethought in terms of practices—economic, political, ideological—each of which was 'relatively autonomous', each with its own 'specific effectivity'. Carried over to the analysis of cinema after the revolutionary events of 1968 (by, for example, the journal *Cahiers du cinéma*), Althusserian Marxism was as rigorous in excluding apparently non-political approaches to cinema as it was in rejecting film theory which began from literary or theatrical models. As Jean-Louis Comolli and Jean Narboni assert in *Cahiers du cinéma* in 1969, it is the case that 'every film is political' and that 'cinema is one of the languages through which the world communicates itself to itself' (1993: 45, 46). To understand cinema is to understand film as film, not something else.

Christian Metz

The intervention of both semiotics and Althusserian film criticism brought the narrative of the developing discussion of film to a point where it was ready for the cavalry to ride over the hill with a more or less complete theory. This role was taken by someone whose work is characterized less by brilliant insights than by a dogged willingness in a series of essays written over nearly twenty years to try, fail, and try again: Christian Metz (1974*a*, *b*, 1982). Although the conscientious, overlapping, and exploratory nature of his project is thus compromised, it is convenient to divide Metz's writings into three main attempts.

The first, today perhaps better known through refutations than in the original (see Cook 1985: 229–31; Lapsley and Westlake 1988: 38–46), was the theory of the *grande syntagmatique*. In the search for a notion of film language, it became obvious that cinema had no equivalent to the unit of sound (phoneme) which combined to make up the particular signifiers of a language. Images in the cinema are as infinite as photographable reality. Metz therefore decided to concentrate on the single shot and treat it as a primitive sentence, a statement, on this basis considering how effects were built up syntagmatically by organizing segments, beginning with the autonomous shot, into a hierarchy (he discriminates eight levels within this hierarchy) (Metz 1974*a*: 108–46).

To some extent Metz Mark I was following Arnheim, because he looked for the specificity of cinema in its narrativization of what is photographed—the fact that 'reality does not tell stories'. But objections pile up against his account—not only the difficulties faced by semiotic narratology in general (its formalism, its belief that there is always only one narrative), but crucially the

problem of deciding in the first place what constituted an autonomous shot or segment.

From the wreckage of the *grande syntagmatique*, Metz Mark II turned to the concept of codes, describing some as shared between cinema and other kinds of representation (characterization and dialogue, for example) and others as specific to cinema (editing, framing, lighting, and so on). Metz Mark III is already partly anticipated in his previous projects, for he had made the point, a little enigmatically and without properly developing it, that in a film 'the image of a house does not signify "house", but rather "Here is a house"' (1974*a*: 116).

The radical implications of this distinction do not become apparent until Metz Mark III pulls Lacanian psychoanalysis into the orbit of his effort to theorize cinema, notably in his essay 'The Imaginary Signifier', first published in 1975. Lacan distinguishes between the orders of the Imaginary and of the Symbolic, the Imaginary being the world as the individual ego envisages it, the Symbolic being the organization of signifiers which makes this possible (for this, see especially Lacan's 1964 account of vision; 1977: 67–119). Lacan's account enables Metz to argue that imaginary presence in the cinematic image must be thought of as resulting from a signifier that stands for something which is absent. Cinema provides 'unaccustomed perceptual wealth, but unusually profoundly stamped with unreality': the more vividly present the cinematic image appears to make its object, the more it insists that object is actually lacking, was once there but is there no more, 'made present', as Metz says, 'in the mode of absence' (1982: 44).

That the cinematic image is an active making-present clarifies retrospectively the view that in the cinema 'the image of a house does not signify "house", but rather "Here is a house"'. What this affirms, of course, is the ontological disjunction between perceived reality and *anything* that is supposed to be a representation of it. Representation, regardless of whether that representation derives by a photographic process from reality, is an intervention, an act of signifying which reality itself can never make. Although obviously you have to know about houses in order to recognize a shot as a shot of a house (just as you have to know about houses to follow a poem about a house), photographic derivation is neither here nor there in relation to the status of the cinematic image as utterance, statement, a meaning introduced in a semantic context in which it is always saying 'Here is a . . .'.

> Representation, regardless of whether that representation derives by a photographic process from reality, is an intervention, an act of signifying which reality itself can never make.

At the end of his famous 'Concluding Statement: Linguistics and Poetics' (1960), Roman Jakobson tells the story of a missionary complaining about nakedness among his flock, who in turn asked him why he did not wear clothes on his face and then told him they were face everywhere. Similarly, Jakobson argues, 'in poetry any verbal element is converted into a figure of poetic speech' (1960: 377). On a comparable basis, breaking with reflectionism, the achievement of film theory to Metz is to establish the principle that in cinema any visual element may be turned to expressive purpose, converted into 'poetic speech'. This renders the whole visual, aural, and narrative effect of cinema available to inspection for its significance, the meaning it produces.

The critique of realism

An immediate consequence of this theoretical breakthrough was to reopen in a much more suggestive and radical way the whole question of realism in the cinema. While film theory was committed to a reflectionist view that the text was to be assessed against some prior notion of the real, comprehensive analysis of realism was blocked. The moment reflectionism goes, the way is open to consider cinematic realism essentially as an effect produced by certain kinds of the text.

Roland Barthes had already pointed in this direction. And so also, back in the 1930s, had Bertolt Brecht. Dismissing conventional naturalist or realist theatre as Aristotelian, as finished, easily consumed commodity, Brecht promoted his own version of modernist, anti-illusionist 'epic' drama, on the grounds that this form was politically radical because it forced the audience to confront the text and think for itself.

Drawing on both Barthes and Brecht, Colin MacCabe, in a wonderfully compact essay, 'Realism and the Cinema: Notes on Some Brechtian Theses' (1974), put forward an analysis of realism which was wholly 'internal': realism was explained not with reference to

external reality but as an effect the text produced through a specific signifying organization. MacCabe's first move is to concentrate on classic realism, excluding from his account such texts as the novels of Dickens or the Hollywood musical. His next two moves specify realism in terms of a discursive hierarchy and empiricism: 'A classic realist text may be defined as one in which there is a hierarchy amongst the discourses which compose the text and this hierarchy is defined in terms of an empirical notion of truth' (1993: 54).

All texts consist of a bundle of different kinds of discourse: realism, MacCabe argues, arranges these into two categories corresponding to the relation between metalanguage and object language. Introduced by Alfred Tarski, this philosophic distinction refers to what happens when one language discusses another, as, for example, in a book written in modern English called *Teach yourself Japanese*. Japanese is placed as the object language and modern English as the metalanguage, situated outside, as it were, and able to take Japanese as an object of study. In the classic realist text, the words held in inverted commas (what the characters say to each other) become an object language which the narrative prose (what is not marked off as cited) promises to explain as it cannot explain itself.

> 'A classic realist text may be defined as one in which there is a hierarchy amongst the discourses which compose the text and this hierarchy is defined in terms of an empirical notion of truth'

The relation between the two modes of discourse is said to be empiricist because while the object language is seen to be rhetorically constructed—the partiality of the points of view of the represented characters is all too apparent—the metalanguage can pass itself off as though it were simply transparent, the voice of Truth: 'The unquestioned nature of the narrative discourse entails that the only problem that reality poses is to go and see what *Things* are there' (1993: 58). In realist cinema, MacCabe concludes, dialogue becomes the object language, and what we see via the camera takes the place of the metalanguage by showing what 'really' happened. This effect invited the spectator to overlook the fact that film is constructed (through script, photography, editing, sets, and so on) and treat the visual narrative as though it revealed what was inevitably *there*. Realism for MacCabe (as for Brecht) is conservative in that this givenness necessarily cannot deal with contradiction, which contains the possibility of change.

Stephen Heath's (1976) discussion of realism as 'narrative space' follows on from MacCabe's theory. Heath begins with the system of visual representation on which cinema, as photography, depends, that is, the Quattrocentro tradition developed to depict three-dimensional objects on a flat surface in such a way that the image affects the viewer much as the natural objects would have done (for a brilliant development of this thesis, see Bryson 1983). Quattrocento space relies not only on linear perspective but on various strategies for placing the viewer at the centre of an apparently all-embracing view.

Cinema, however, is 'moving pictures', a process which constantly threatens the fixity and centring aimed for by the Western tradition of the still image. Figures and objects constantly move, moving in and out of frame, likely therefore to remind the spectator of the blank absence which actually surrounds the screen. Mainstream cinema seeks to make good this dangerous instability through narrative, a narrativization which 'contains the mobility that could threaten the clarity of vision' (1993: 76) by constantly renewing a centred perspective for the spectator. Heath cites in detail the procedures advised by the film manuals—use of master shot, the 180-degree rule, matching on action, eyeline matching, avoidance of 'impossible angles', and so on—and affirms that all of this is designed to ensure that 'the spectator's illusion of seeing a continuous piece of action is not interrupted' (Heath 1993: 80, quoting Reisz and Millar 1968: 216).

A perfect example is the beginning of *Jaws* (USA, 1975): 'a beach party with the camera tracking slowly right along the line of faces of the participants until it stops on a young man looking off; eyeline cut to a young woman who is thus revealed as the object of his gaze; cut to a high-angle shot onto the party that shows its general space, its situation before the start of the action with the run down to the ocean and the first shark attack' (1993: 80). Through such narrativization, Heath maintains, conventional cinema seeks to transform fixity into process and absence into presence by promoting (in Lacanian terms) the Imaginary over the Symbolic. An alternative or radical cinema would refuse this kind of coherence; it would open its textuality, compelling the viewer to experience the process

they are always part of, a process implying change and which is the condition for any sense of coherence and stability.

In these ways MacCabe and Heath intend to fulfil the promise of bringing together semiology and ideology, a close analysis of the fundamental operation of cinema as a signifying effect with an understanding that cinema is always political. There is, however, one important difference between the two accounts.

Heath's argument is that realism and the effect of narrative space try to *contain* the process of signification, while for MacCabe realism effaces the signifier to achieve *transparency*. It is arguable that MacCabe is still writing from an essentially structuralist conception in which realism is an organization of the signifier which necessarily produces certain effects on the viewer. Heath, in contrast, asserts that transparency is 'impossible' (1993: 82) and assumes from the start a conception of process as a process of the *subject*. Subjectivity does appear in MacCabe's account but is not integral to it as it is to Heath's. Heath, then, looks beyond structuralism to a post-structuralism which draws on psychoanalysis to discuss cinema in relation to subjectivity, including, in the work of Laura Mulvey, *gendered* subjectivity. After Metz, after the redefinition of realism as a textual effect, that is where film theory goes next.

BIBLIOGRAPHY

Arnheim, Rudolf (1933/1958), *Film*; repr. corr. as *Film as Art* (London: Faber).

Barthes, Roland (1953/1968), *Writing Degree Zero*, trans. Annette Lavers and Colin Smith (New York: Hill & Wong).

*****Bazin, André** (1967), *What is Cinema?*, 2 vols., trans. Hugh Gray, i (Berkeley: University of California Press).

Bellour, Raymond (1969/1972), 'The Birds: Analysis of a Sequence', trans. Ben Brewster (London: British Film Institute).

Brecht, Bertolt (1964), *Brecht on Theatre*, ed. and trans. John Willett (London: Eyre Methuen).

Bryson, Norman (1983), *Vision and Painting: the Logic of the Gaze* (London: Macmillan).

Comolli, Jean-Louis, and **Jean Narboni** (1969/1993), 'Cinema/Ideology/Criticism (1)', trans. Susan Bennett, in Antony Easthope (ed.), *Contemporary Film Theory* (London: Longman).

Cook, Pam (ed.) (1985), *The Cinema Book* (London: British Film Institute).

Heath, Stephen (1976a), 'Jaws, Ideology and Film Theory', *Times Higher Education Supplement*, 26 Mar.

—— (1976b, 1993), 'Narrative Space', in Antony Easthope (ed.), *Contemporary Film Theory* (London: Longman).

Jakobson, Roman (1960), 'Concluding Statement: Linguistics and Poetics', in T. A. Sebeok (ed.), *Style in Language* (Cambridge: Mass.: MIT Press).

Kant, Immanuel (1790/1952), *The Critique of Judgement*, trans. James Meredith (Oxford: Oxford University Press).

Lacan, Jacques (1964/1977), *The Four Fundamental Concepts of Psycho-Analysis*, trans. Alan Sheridan (London: Hogarth).

*Lapsley, Rob, and Mike Westlake (1988), *Film Theory: An Introduction* (Manchester: Manchester University Press).

*MacCabe, Colin (1974/1993), 'Realism and the Cinema: Notes on Some Brechtian Theses', in Antony Easthope (ed.), *Contemporary Film Theory* (London: Longman).

*Metz, Christian (1971a/1974a), *Film Language: A Semiotics of Cinema*, trans. Michael Taylor (New York: Oxford University Press).

—— (1971a/1974b), *Language and Cinema*, trans. D. J. Umiker-Sebeok (The Hague: Mouton).

—— (1977/1982), *Psychoanalysis and Cinema: The Imaginary Signifier*, trans. Celia Britton (London: Macmillan).

Propp, Vladimir (1928/1968), *The Morphology of the Folktale*, trans. Laurence Scott (Austin: University of Texas Press).

Reisz, Karel, and Gavin Millar (1968), *The Technique of Film Editing* (New York: Hastings House).

Saussure, Ferdinand de (1916/1959), *Course in General Linguistics*, trans. Wade Baskin (New York: Philosophical Library).

Scharf, Aaron (1968), *Art and Photography* (London: Allen Lane).

Wollen, Peter (1976/1982), '*North by North-West*: A Morphological Analysis', *Film Form*, 1/1: 19–34; repr. in *Readings and Writings* (London: Verso).

7

Formalism and neo-formalism

Ian Christie

Formalism is the usual, if somewhat misleading, name of a critical tendency which has survived for over eighty years, despite misunderstanding and even persecution. First used by opponents, the label was reluctantly adopted by Russian exponents of 'the formal method'—although they protested that it was neither a single method, nor confined to what is normally considered 'form'. But aside from these local disputes, the tradition of Formalism could well be considered the twentieth century's distinctive contribution to aesthetics. For it was born, historically, of the desire to find an objective or scientific basis for literary criticism, partly in order to respond to the novelty of modern art—specifically Futurist poetry—and at the same time to revitalize appreciation of the classics. In short, it was a critical position which uniquely responded to the peculiar challenge of the modern era; and one that would later be echoed by the American 'new critics' of the 1930s, as well as by structuralists and semioticians.

But if its focus was literature, how did Formalism first become involved with film? This is largely explained by the peculiar status that cinema acquired during the early years of the Soviet regime in Russia. With filmmakers like Dziga Vertov and Sergei Eisenstein making large ideological claims for their work, film aesthetics became a subject of intense public debate, and eventually a political issue. In this heady climate of polemic and innovation, leading Formalist critics such as Viktor

Shklovsky and Yuri Tynyanov found themselves not only theorizing the new forms of Soviet cinema, but actually working as scriptwriters and advisers. The scene had been set for a dangerous slippage between critical and political disagreement. When the Soviet leadership began to regiment cultural life at the end of the 1920s, 'Formalism'—now meaning any commitment to artistic experiment, or resistance to an authoritarian 'socialist realism'—became an all-purpose term of abuse, and during the purges of the 1930s it could carry a death sentence.

Unsurprisingly, surviving Russian Formalists fell silent or recanted, and it was not unlike the 1960s, amid renewed Western interest in the early Soviet era, that many key Formalist texts were translated for the first time and began to exert a wide cultural influence. Once again, the links between Formalist criticism and cinema were revived, as semiotics became the basis for a new theorization of film—and for a revival of avant-garde filmmaking, which partly drew on Soviet Formalist models. The Russian structural or cultural semiotic movement which emerged in the late 1960s counted the Formalist school as one of the influences on its wide-ranging analysis of different cultural and artistic texts; and this continues to produce valuable work on cinema. Formalist critical tools are also still used, under the banner of 'Neo-Formalism', by film theorists concerned with analysing the structure of narration and by critics wishing to sharpen our percep-

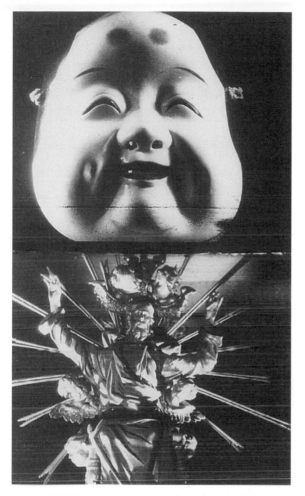

October (1928) undermines the Tsarist invocation of 'God and country' by showing an otherwise unmotivated montage sequence of increasingly bizarre folk-gods

tion of—or in Formalist terms 'defamiliarize'—mainstream cinema.

The birth of a poetics

Formalist poetics developed rapidly in the highly charged atmosphere of Russian avant-garde art in the years immediately before and after the revolutions of 1917. Futurist poets were experimenting with invented language in an effort to return to the very roots of speech in sound and gesture, and Viktor Shklovsky took this as a particularly vivid example of how artists play a vital part in sharpening our habitual

perception by a deliberate 'roughening' of normal language. For Shklovsky and his fellow members of the St Petersburg Society for the Study of Poetic Language (OPOYAZ), the poetic use of language involved a whole range of techniques or 'devices' which are not confined to poetry as such, but may also be found in literary prose. He traces an inexorable movement from poetry to prose, from novelty to routine, as language becomes automatic, and compares this with the way old art is 'covered with the glassy armour of familiarity' as we cease to experience it in a truly artistic way.

What is lost in this transition is art's characteristic purpose of making the familiar screen strange (*ostranenie*), or of 'defamiliarizing' what is normally taken for granted—an influential idea which would later be echoed in Bertolt Brecht's 'alienation effect' in theatre. For the Formalists, art is less an object or a body of work than a *process* by which perception is slowed down, or even obstructed. Hence what the critic studies are the forms and devices which achieve this effect. As Shklovsky put it, provocatively; 'I know how a car is made; I know how *Don Quixote* is made.'

> For the Formalists, art is less an object or a body of work than a *process* by which perception is slowed down, or even obstructed. Hence what the critic studies are the forms and devices which achieve this effect.

Although the Formalists drew much of their inspiration from the contemporary energy of Russian Futurist art, which they saw as typically 'laying bare the device' in its radical new forms, many of their most influential analyses were of the classics seen from a revealing new angle. Shklovsky, in particular, delighted in drawing examples from a wide range of sources, and his 1925 essays on Sterne's *Tristram Shandy* and Cervantes' *Don Quixote* (Shklovsky 1990) established the basic formalist approach to fictional narrative. The crucial distinction to be made in narrative is between what Formalists call *fabula* and *syuzhet*, usually translated as 'story' and 'plot' (Bordwell 1985: 49–50 provides the clearest modern definition of these as applicable to cinema). However, these translations can be misleading (and indeed contradict some uses of these terms in English). For *fabula*, in the Formalist sense, is an imaginary sequence of events narrated by the *syuzhet*, which provides the actual narrative pattern of the work, or 'story-as-told'. Thus, in literature, Cervantes' and Sterne's numerous digressions, abrupt shifts forward and backward in time, repetitions, and withholding of information are all *devices* which constitute the *syuzhet*, or plot; and the Formalists regarded the relationship between the *syuzhet* and *fabula*, rather than one or the other, as the essence of literary art.

Such an analysis of the 'literariness' of literature clearly could be developed for other arts, and Shklovsky led the way in applying formalist analysis to cinema (Shklovsky 1923). His discussion of Chaplin noted that the same basic character, 'Charlie', appears in many films, and that these all use similar cinematic devices, which are 'stunts' such as the fall, the chase, and the fight. In each film some of these devices are 'motivated', in that they appear to arise plausibly from the specific plot's characters or props, while others are 'unmotivated'—the typical 'Charlie' gestures and actions whose familiarity had made Chaplin a star. The critical issue for Shklovsky was whether Chaplin would succeed in going beyond the self-referential parody that was already evident by 1921–2; and he predicted that Chaplin might move toward the 'heroic comic' genre—which, in fact, he did in later films such as *The Gold Rush* (1925) and *The Great Dictator* (1940).

The Formalist insistence that poetic and prosaic language are not confined to the literary genres of poetry and prose could also be applied to cinema, with interesting consequences. Amid the passionate debates of the early Soviet era between advocates of polemical fiction and those who opposed all film drama as intrinsically false, Formalists were able to argue that the use of 'factual' documentary material by Dziga Vertov did not in itself make his films factual. Having rejected the fictional structures of the novel and drama, he had effectively fallen into those of poetry, the lyric, and the epic: 'red verse with the rhythms of cinema'. Similarly, a Formalist comparison between Chaplin's drama *A Woman of Paris* (1923), Vertov's *One Sixth of the World* (1926), and Pudovkin's *The Mother* (1926), based on the idea that poetry uses more arbitrary formal devices than the semantic ones of prose, suggests that Chaplin is here working in cinematic 'prose' and Vertov in poetry, but that Pudovkin had created a hybrid form which moves between prose and poetry (Shklovsky 1927).

This hybrid quality, making full use of the 'poetic' devices that appeared in early cinema, was also what

attracted the Leningrad Formalist critic Yuri Tynyanov to the irreverent Factory of the Eccentric Actor (FEKS) group. Having already worked on the use of parody by such writers as Gogol and Dostoevsky, he adapted Gogol's *The Overcoat* for FEKS in 1926 as a polemical intervention, to pose 'anew the question of "the classics" in cinema'. The film functions as a radical commentary on the original text and its conventional accretions. And in the FEKS's subsequent historical films, *SVD* and *New Babylon* (1929), Tynyanov saw a welcome challenge to the merely picturesque in the elaborate use of metaphorical devices to produce irony and pathos.

The culmination of Russian Formalist engagement with cinema came in 1927, with the publication of an anthology, *The Poetics of the Cinema*, which included Boris Eikhenbaum's major essay 'Problems of Film Stylistics' (Taylor 1982). Amid many shrewd observations which make this one of the most sophisticated early texts in film aesthetics, Eikhenbaum focuses on two key features which can perhaps be considered the filmic equivalents of *fabula* and *syuzhet*. From the French critic Louis Delluc he borrowed the concept of 'photogeny' to describe the photographic raw material of cinema—what makes filmed images of people and things intrinsically attractive—and from the Soviet avant-garde he takes 'montage' as the fundamental principle of syntax for combining these images (plot construction). Filmic utterance then depends on the creation of film phrases, which require the construction of an illusory, yet convincing, impression of continuity in space and time.

Eikhenbaum's most original contribution is his answer to the question: what links film phrases? Or, in Formalist terms, how do transitions appear motivated, rather than arbitrary? He suggests that the viewer is prompted to supply links through internal speech, by completing or articulating what is implied by the sequence of (silent) screen images. This idea is most easily illustrated by examples of visual metaphor. Eikhenbaum quotes the sailor in *The Devil's Wheel* (Chёrtovo koleso', FEKS, 1926), who has decided to stay on shore with his girl and enters a tavern, where we see a billiard-ball *fall* into a pocket, thus triggering the idea of his *fall* from duty. Another example would be the famous 'gods' montage sequence in Eisenstein's *October* (1928), in which a series of images of increasingly bizarre statues of folk-gods are intended to undermine the Tsarist invocation of 'God' by showing this to be a heterogeneous concept.

Boris Eikhenbaum linked the fall of a billiard-ball in the tavern scene in *The Devil's Wheel* (1926) with the sailor's 'fall' from duty as an example of 'inner speech' reinforcing filmic metaphor

Appearing as it did on the even of the sound revolution in cinema, Eikhenbaum's concept of internal speech attracted little interest until the 1970s. In the wake of Christian Metz's (1982) combination of semiology and psychoanalysis, it was then taken up again, notably by Paul Willemen (1974–5, 1994a), who argued that it need not be confined to silent cinema or to examples of 'literalizing' metaphor as in the *Devil's Wheel* example. Might not this discourse of 'thought work' accompany *all* filmmaking and viewing, he asked, and be subject to the same processes of abbreviation, condensation, distortion, and the like that Freud identified in dreams, so that it could function as both a constituent and a product of the filmic text—a kind of unconscious of the filmic system?

Another branch of Russian Formalist research also had to wait nearly forty years before it began to be applied to cinema, although Vladimir Propp's (1968) *Morphology of the Folktale* was already becoming known in the early 1960s through the anthropologist

Claude Lévi-Strauss's use of it in his study of myth, and consequently became a corner-stone of the emergent structuralist movement. In line with the Formalists' ahistorical, scientific spirit, Propp's analysis of a body of Russian fairy-tales took as its model the biological idea of morphology, or the study of a plant's component parts in relation to the whole. By identifying the full range of fairy-tale characters and their narrative functions, and determining the 'moves' which constitute each story, Propp was able to show how these could all be reduced to variations on a single basic formula.

In adapting this structural approach to the study of a filmmaker's body of work, Peter Wollen (1972: 93) noted that there is a danger in mapping resemblances of reducing all the texts in question 'to one, abstract and impoverished'. He draws a distinction between this result, as 'formalist', and the 'truly structuralist' aim of comprehending 'a system of differences and oppositions'. Thus, for Wollen and other structuralist film critics, a measure of success is to bring works which may at first seem eccentric or deviant within an enlarged system of recurrent motifs or 'oppositions'.

Despite this rejection of morphology as a goal, the terms of Propp's narrative analysis have proved valuable in other ways too. Laura Mulvey (1981) recalls the function of marriage as a means of narrative closure in all the tales studied by Propp in her discussion of Oedipal patterns in the western. But unlike the Russian folk-hero who *must* marry to conclude the tale satisfactorily, the western hero may choose not to marry for a different, though no less common, closure. Mulvey's exploration of these alternatives, discussed in terms of *The Man who Shot Liberty Valance* (1962) and *Duel in the Sun* (1947), again points away from Propp's essentially descriptive enterprise, but none the less draws upon its characteristic Formalist clarity.

Neo-formalism

The most substantial and influential modern use of Formalism in the film study has been that of David Bordwell and Kristin Thompson, notably in the former's *Narration in the Fiction Film* (Bordwell 1985) and the latter's 'essays in neoformalist film analysis', *Breaking the Glass Armour* (Thompson 1988). In defending Formalism against claims that it is 'merely' formal, seeking to isolate theory from either detailed textual criticism or social and historical interpretation, Bordwell and Thompson argue that, on the contrary, only its basic tools can contribute to building an adequate historical poetics of cinema.

Formalism, they believe, unlike some structuralist and psychoanalytic methodologies, crucially implies an active spectator, and to supply this important subject Bordwell proposes a 'constructivist' theory which links perception and cognition. Drawing on cognitive psychology, he identifies a hierarchy of schemata by which the individual's perception is organized. Thus, following a film—like many other everyday yet complex activities—routinely involves the use of already learned prototype and template schemata to identify basic situations, characters, and events. Individual films then involve mobilizing (or learning) procedural schemata, at the level of narrative, and stylistic schemata. These art- or film-specific schemata correspond in part to the Formalists' concept of motivations as compositional, realistic, or

artistic (this last expanded to cover 'transtextual' allusion to other texts).

Bordwell's many detailed examples of this enhanced and systematized Formalism at work show how, for example, the typical operations of film noir and melodrama can be distinguished in terms of different patterns of *syuzhet* and stylistic construction—gaps and retardation, the deliberate withholding of information, different motivations—and how a broad sampling of films made within certain production regimes can lead towards a 'formalist' historical classification. Thus 'classical Hollywood' (the subject of Bordwell *et al.* 1985) can be described in more dynamic terms than usual, as having 'normalised options for representing the fabula and for manipulating the possibilities of syuzhet and style'. Art cinema, by contrast, can be defined by a particular set of procedural schemata which underlie widely differing narrational strategies.

Both Thompson and Bordwell make use of the term 'parametric cinema', adapted from Burch (1973) to take their neo-formalist analyses into more challenging terrain. This is defined as the foregrounding of an artistic motivation in a systematic, structuring fashion. Examples discussed range from Jacques Tati's *Play Time* (1968), and Michael Snow's *Wavelength* (1967) (where style completely dominates *syuzhet* as the film's vestigial narrative is subordinated to an overriding continuous zoom structure), and also include films by Robert Bresson and Jean-Luc Godard.

Like Shklovsky's famous comparison of literary history to the knight's move in chess, Formalism's influence outside its Slavic homeland has largely depended on the erratic progress of translation and, indeed, fashion. Thus, it was not until the 1980s that translations began to appear of the long-neglected work of Mikhail Bakhtin and his colleagues, who were critical of the Formalists in the late 1920s but can now perhaps be seen as extending Formalism's range through their critique of its ahistoricism and dogmatism.

Bakhtin's most influential concept is probably that of 'dialogism', which emerged particularly from his study of Dostoevsky's novels. Put at its simplest, in a 1929 paper (Matejka and Pomorska 1978), this involves distinguishing between an author's direct speech and that of his characters, which can 'approach the relationship between two sides in a dialogue'. Bakhtin's wide-ranging analysis of novels from many periods and cultures reveals degrees of 'polyphony' among the discourses present and, by implication, validates such dialogism for its complexity and richness. From his work on Rabelais comes another key concept, 'carnivalism', denoting the persistence of a 'folk tradition of laughter' and parody characteristic of the carnival.

If 'dialogism' and 'carnivalistic' have become quite widely used terms of critical approbation in film as well as literary and cultural criticism, two of Bakhtin's other contributions seem even more pertinent to cinema. In tackling the variety of 'speech genres' encountered in everyday as well as artistic discourse, Bakhtin showed how these interact with literary genres to define a 'genre memory' which sets limits to each genre. Ivanov (1981) suggest that this is directly applicable to cinema, as is Bakhtin's concept of the 'chronotype'. This term, taken from mathematics, is used by Bakhtin (1981) to refer to the specific interrelationship of time and space in differnt forms of narrative. Thus, he identifies 'adventure time' and 'romance time' in the Greek novel, with their characteristic elisions and transitions; and Ivanov proposes that similar distinctions may be made within the main film genres.

Despite the promise of Bakhtin's ideas, it must be admitted that relatively little has been done by non-Russian critics to apply them widely or systematically. Exceptions, however, are Robert Stam's (1989) survey of the tradition of reflexive, carnivalesque works from a specifically Bakhtinian perspective, and the use Paul Willemen (1994) makes of Bakhtin's concepts of dialogue, otherness, and genre as 'a fragment of collective memory' in his work on Third Cinema. Within the Russian tradition, Maya Turovskaya (1989) has used the concept of the chronotope to illuminate Andrei Tarkovsky's idea of cinema as 'imprinted time', and a Bakhtinian influence is discernible in the work of Yuri Lotman and his circle in cultural semiotics (Lotman and Uspenskij 1984).

One of Lotman's followers, Yuri Tsivian (1994), defines cultural semiotics as studying 'texts as they are processed "through" people', so that faulty transmission is as much its focus as 'successful' communication without interference. Tsivian's pioneering study of the early reception of cinema in Russia ranges from consideration of the architecture of cinemas and the practice of projection (including mishaps), to the social reception of films as coloured by prevailing cultural assumptions. Most radically, he argues that the boundary of the 'cinema text' is inherently unstable, since non-filmic elements could, and often did, prove culturally more significant for spectators than the films themselves.

Tsivian's evidence is drawn from journalism, literature, and memoirs, and its extent shows how widely the forms and devices of cinema had permeated Russian culture by the 1920s. Although this was also the culture that produced Formalism, his work has wider methodological implications. And together with that of other contemporary cultural semioticians, Neo-Formalists, and assorted fellow travellers, it proves that the Formalist impulse continues to provide sharp, versatile tools for both critical and historical analysis.

BIBLIOGRAPHY

Bakhtin, Mikhail (1929/1978), 'Discourse Typology in Prose', in *Problems of Dostoevsky's Art* (Leningrad); trans. Richard Balthazar and I. R. Titunik in Ladislav Matejka and Krystyna Pomorska (eds.), *Readings in Russian Poetics* (Ann Arbor: Michigan Slavic Publications).
—— (1981), *The Dialogic Imagination* (Austin: University of Texas Press).
—— (1986), *Speech Genres and Other Late Essays* (Austin: University of Texas Press).
*Bordwell, David (1985), *Narration in the Fiction Film* (London: Methuen).
—— **Janet Staiger,** and **Kristin Thompson** (1985), *The Classical Hollywood Cinema: Film Style and Mode of Production to 1960* (London: Routledge).
Burch, Noël (1973), *Theory of Film Practice* (London: Secker & Warburg).
Ivanov, Vyacheslav (1981), 'Functions and Categories of Film Language', in L. M. O'Toole and Ann Shukman (eds.), *Russian Poetics in Translation*, viii (Oxford 1976).
Lotman, Yuri (1976), *Semiotics of Cinema* (Ann Arbor: Michigan Slavic Contributions).
—— and **Boris Uspenskij** (1984), *The Semiotics of Russian Culture* (Ann Arbor: Michigan Slavic Contributions).
Metz, Christian (1977/1982), *Psychoanalysis and Cinema: The Imaginary Signifier*, trans. Celia Britton (Bloomington Indiana University Press).
Mulvey, Laura (1981/1989), 'Afterthoughts on "Visual Pleasure and Narrative Cinema"', in *Visual and Other Pleasures* (London: Macmillan).
Propp, Vladimir (1968), *Morphology of the Folktale* (Austin: University of Texas Press).
Shklovsky, Viktor (1923/1988), 'Literature and Cinema', extracts in Taylor and Christie 1988.
—— (1925/1990), *Theory of Prose* (Elmwood Park, Ill: Dalkey Archive Press).
—— (1927), 'Poetry and Prose in the Cinema', in Taylor and Christie 1988.
Stam, Robert (1989), *Subversive Pleasures: Bakhtin, Cultural Criticism and Film* (Baltimore: Johns Hopkins University Press).

*Taylor, Richard (ed.) (1927/1982), *The Poetics of Cinema, Russian Poetics in Translation*, ix (Oxford Complete trans. of the original Russian anthology, with essays by Eikhenbaum, Shklovsky, Tynyanov, and other Formalists).

—— and **Ian Christie** (eds.) (1994), *The Film Factory: Russian and Soviet Cinema in Documents 1896–1939* (2nd edn. London: Routledge).

Thompson, Kristin (1988), *Breaking the Glass Armor: Neoformalist Film Analysis* (Princeton, NJ: Princeton University Press).

Tsivian, Yuri (1994) *Early Cinema in Russia and its Cultural Reception* (London: Routledge).

Turovskaya, Maya (1989), *Tarkovsky: Cinema as Poetry* (London: Faber).

Willemen, Paul (1974–5), 'Reflections on Eikhenbaum's Concept of Inner Speech in the Cinema', in *Screen*, 15/4 (Winter), 59–70.

—— (1994a), 'Cinematic Discourse: The Problem of Inner Speech', in *Looks and Frictions* (London: British Film Institute).

—— (1994b), 'The Third Cinema Question', in *Looks and Frictions* (London: British Film Institute).

Wollen, Peter (1972), *Signs and Meaning in the Cinema* (3rd edn. London: Secker & Warburg).

Poetry and prose in cinema

Viktor Shklovsky from Viktor Shklovsky, 'Poetry and Prose in Cinema', in Richard Taylor and Ian Christie (eds.), *The Film Factory: Russian and Soviet Cinema in Documents* (revised edition London and New York, Routledge 1994).

In literary art poetry and prose are not sharply differentiated from one another. On more than one occasion students of prose language have discovered rhythmic segments, the recurrence of the same phrase construction, in a prose work. Tadeusz Zieliński has produced interesting studies of rhythm in oratorical speech and Boris Eichenbaum has done a great deal of work on rhythm in pure prose that is intended to be read rather than recited, although it is true that he has not pursued this work systematically. But, as problems of rhythm have been analysed, the boundary between poetry and prose has, it seems been confused rather than clarified. It is possible that the distinction between poetry and prose does not lie in rhythm alone. The more we study a work of art, the more deeply we penetrate the fundamental unity of its laws. The individual constructional aspects of an artistic phenomenon are distinguished qualitatively, but this qualitativeness rests on a quantitative base, and we can pass imperceptibly from one level to another. The basic construction of plot is reduced to a schema of semantic constants. We take two contrasting everyday situations and resolve them with a third; or we take two semantic constants and create a parallel between them; or, lastly, we take several semantic constants and arrange them in ranking order. But the usual basis of plot (*syuzhet*) is story (*fabula*), i.e. an everyday situation. Yet this everyday situation is merely a particular instance of semantic construction and we can create from one novel a 'mystery novel', not by changing the story but simply by transposing the constituent parts: by putting the ending at the beginning or by a more complex rearrangement of the parts. This is how Pushkin's *The Blizzard* and *The Shot* were produced. Hence what we may call everyday constants, the semantic constants, the situational constants, and the purely formal features may be interchanged with, and merge into, one another.

A prose work is, in its plot construction and its semantic composition, based principally on a combination of everyday situations. This means that we resolve a given situation in the following way: a man must speak, but he cannot, and so a third person speaks on his behalf. In *The Captain's Daughter*, for instance, Grinev cannot speak and yet he must in order to clear his name from Shvabrin's slanders. He cannot speak because he would compromise the captain's daughter, so she herself offers Ekaterina an explanation on his behalf. In another example a man must vindicate himself, but he cannot do so because he has taken a vow of silence: the solution lies in the fact that he manages to extend the deadline of his vow. This is the basis

for one of Grimm's fairy-tales, *The Twelve Swans*, and the story *The Seven Viziers*. But there may be another way to resolve a work, and this resolution is brought about not by semantic means but by purely compositional ones whereby the effect of the compositional constant compares with that of the semantic.

We find this kind of resolution to a work in Fet's verse: after four stanzas in a particular metre with caesura (a constant word division in the middle of each line), the poem is resolved not by its plot but by the fact that the fifth stanza, although in the same metre, has no caesura, and this produces a sense of closure.

The fundamental distinction between poetry and prose lies possibly in a greater geometricality of devices, in the fact that a whole series of arbitrary semantic resolutions is replaced by a formal geometric resolution. It is as if a geometricization of devices is taking place. Thus the stanza in *Eugene Onegin* is resolved by the fact that the final rhyming couplet provides formal compositional resolution while disrupting the rhyme system. Pushkin supports this semantically by altering the vocabulary in these last two lines and giving them a slightly parodic character.

I am writing here in very generalized terms because I want to point out the most common landmarks, particularly in cinema. I have more than once heard film professionals express the curious view that, as far as literature is concerned, verse is closer to film than is prose. All sorts of people say this and large numbers of films strive towards a resolution which, by distant analogy, we may call poetic. There is no doubt that Dziga Vertov's *A Sixth Part of the World* (USSR, 1926) is constructed on the principle of poetic formal resolution: it has a pronounced parallelism and a recurrence of images at the end of the film where they convey a different meaning and thus vaguely recall the form of a triolet.

When we examine Vsevolod Pudovkin's film *The Mother* (USSR, 1926), in which the director has taken great pains to create a rhythmical construction, we observe a gradual displacement of everyday situations by purely formal elements. The parallelism of the nature scenes at the beginning prepares us for the acceleration of movements, the montage, and the departure from everyday life that intensifies towards the end. The ambiguity of the poetic image and its characteristically indistinct aura, together with the capacity for simultaneous generation of meaning by

Poetry and prose in cinema continued

different methods, are achieved by a rapid change of frames that never manage to become real. The very device that resolves the film—the double-exposure angle shot of the Kremlin walls moving—exploits the formal rather than the semantic features: it is a poetic device.

In cinema at present we are children. We have barely begun to consider the subjects of our work, but already we can speak of the existence of two poles of cinema, each of which will have its own laws.

Charlie Chaplin's *A Woman of Paris* (USA, 1923), is obviously prose based on semantic constants, on things that are accepted.

A Sixth Part of the World, in spite of its government sponsorship, is a poem of pathos.

The Mother is a unique centaur, an altogether strange beast. The film starts out as prose, using emphatic intertitles which fit the frame rather badly, and ends up as purely formal poetry. Recurring frames and images and the transformation of images into symbols support my conviction that this film is poetic by nature.

I repeat once more: there exist both prose and poetry in cinema, and this is the basic division between the genres: they are distinguished from one another not by rhythm, or not by rhythm alone, but by the prevalence in poetic cinema of technical and formal over semantic features, where formal features displace semantic and resolve the composition. Plotless cinema is 'verse' cinema.

8

Impressionism, surrealism, and film theory: path dependence, or how a tradition in film theory gets lost

Robert B. Ray

Film theory's two traditions

In the fall of 1938, when the movies were only 40 years old, Walter Benjamin received a rejection letter. Inspired by Louis Aragon's Surrealist narrative *Le Paysan de Paris* (1927) and by Soviet experiments with cinematic montage, Benjamin had conceived what has come to be known as *The Arcades Project*, a history of nineteenth-century Paris constructed primarily from found material—texts, documents, images—whose juxtaposition would reveal the buried origins of modern life. Benjamin had been receiving financial support from Frankfurt's Institute for Social Research, relocated in New York, and he had submitted three chapters of a book on Baudelaire, designed as a prologue to the more experimental work ahead. But speaking for the Institute, Benjamin's friend Theodor Adorno said no. 'Your study', Adorno wrote, in the now famous passage, 'is located at the crossroads of magic and positivism. That spot is bewitched. Only theory could break the spell' (Adorno 1938/1980: 129).

Although Adorno came to regret this decision, his formulation of it defines the history of film theory. For what could be a more exact definition of the cinema than 'the crossroads of magic and positivism'? Or a more succinct definition of film theory's traditional project than to 'break the spell'?

> What could be a more exact definition of the cinema than 'the crossroads of magic and positivism'?

As a technologically based, capital-intensive medium, the movies quickly developed into an industry keenly attracted by positivism's applications: the Taylorist–Fordist models of rationalized production. Indeed, as Thomas Schatz (1988) has described, the Hollywood studios set the tone by explicitly imitating the organizational system developed in large-scale manufacturing. Mass production, standardized designs, concentration of the whole production cycle in a single place, a radical division of labour, the routinizing of workers' tasks, even the after-hours surveillance of employees—all of these Fordist practices became Hollywood's own. Thus, at the peak of its early 1930s power, MGM could produce one feature film per week, a quota enabled by its standardized genres, enormous physical plant, strict definition of roles, and a star system whose performers remained as alienated from their tasks as any factory worker. And to guarantee this system's reliability, L. B. Mayer kept watch on his personnel's every move.

And yet, for all of its commitment to the positivism which Taylor and Ford had perfected, Hollywood was not making Model Ts. That ascetic vehicle, a triumph of functionalism, had succeeded by avoiding any traces of the irrational decoration that Ford portrayed as wasteful, inefficient, 'feminine'. Strikingly, however, the Model T's decline (Ford abandoned the car in 1927) coincided with Hollywood's ascendancy, as Ford's increasingly successful rival General Motors' Alfred Sloan began to demonstrate the enormous seductive power of style (Wollen 1993; Batchelor 1994). In doing so, Sloan was deriving an explicit business practice from the crucial discovery intuited by Hollywood's moguls: the movies succeeded commercially to the extent that they *enchanted*.

Hence the inevitable question: could enchantment be mass-produced? The movies' most influential form, Hollywood cinema (what Noël Burch (1990) calls the Institutional Mode of Representation), arose as an attempt to address this problem. The calculus has always been a delicate one: the temptations of rationalization on the one hand, the requirements of seduction on the other. As a result, any commercial filmmaking represents a site of negotiation between these conflicting positions. 'The cinema', Jean-Luc Godard once told Colin MacCabe, 'is all money' (MacCabe 1980: 27), but at any moment it can also become, as Godard once wrote of Renoir's *La Nuit du carrefour* (France, 1932) 'the air of confusion . . . the smell of rain and of fields bathed in mist' (Godard 1972: 63).

Developed as the means for balancing filmmaking's competing demands, Hollywood's protocols became the norm of cinema. Increasingly, film history has suggested that the key figure in their development was less D. W. Griffith than MGM's Irving Thalberg. Far more than the independent Griffith, Thalberg spent his days negotiating between L. B. Mayer's insistence on thrift and the popular audience's demand for glamour. In effect, he occupied Adorno's crossroads, embracing both positivism and magic. Working at the origins of the cinema's dominant mode, a rationalist longing to be enthralled by his own productions, Thalberg, in fact, embodied the two tendencies of all subsequent film theory.

Film history's conceptual neatness depends on its dual provenance in those great opposites, Lumière and Méliès, documentary and fiction. 'Cinema', Godard famously summed up, 'is spectacle—Méliès—and research—Lumière,' adding (impatient with the forced choice) that 'I have always wanted, basically, to do research in the form of a spectacle' (Godard 1972: 181). Inevitably, film theory took longer to appear, but after the First World War it quickly developed into two analogous positions, only one of which was attached so neatly to a single name.

That name, of course, was Eisenstein. With his insistence that filmmaking-as-an-art depended on repudiating the camera's automatic recording capacity, Eisenstein aligned himself not only with Méliès, but also with pictoralism, the movement that sought to legitimize photography by disguising its images as paintings. Eisenstein avoided that retrograde move while nevertheless sharing its fundamental premise: that a medium's aesthetic value is a direct function of its ability to transform the reality serving as its raw material. For Eisenstein, the means of such transformation was montage, the ideal tool for deriving significance (chiefly political) from the real details swarming in his footage (see Kolker, Part 1, Chapter 2).

As his theoretical essays appeared in the 1920s, Eisenstein assumed the role simultaneously perfected by T. S. Eliot—the artist-critic whose writings create the taste by which his own aesthetic practice is judged. Eisenstein's sensational films enhanced the prestige of his theoretical positions, which quickly triumphed over the alternative proposed by the French Impressionists and Surrealists. If Eisenstein saw the cinema as a means of argument, the French regarded it as the vehicle of revelation, and the knowledge revealed was not always expressible in words. 'Explanations here are out of place,' Louis Delluc wrote about the 'phenomenon' of Sessue Hayakawa's screen presence, an example of what the Impressionists called *photogénie*. 'I wish there to be no words,' Jean Epstein declared, refusing to translate the concept that he posited as 'the purest expression of cinema' (Abel 1988: 138–9, 243, 315).

The concept of *photogénie*, especially in the Surrealists' hands, emphasized precisely what Eisenstein wished to escape: the cinema's automatism. 'For the first time', André Bazin would later elaborate, 'an image of the world is formed automatically, without the creative invention of man' (Bazin 1967: 13). Moreover, for reasons which the French could not define, the camera rendered some otherwise ordinary objects, landscapes, and even people luminous and spellbinding. Lumière's simple, mesmerizing films had proved that fact. Eisenstein anticipated Brecht's proposition that 'less than ever does the mere reflection of reality reveal anything about reality . . . something must in fact be *built up*, something artificial, posed' (Benjamin 1979: 255). The French who followed Lumière, however, insisted that just turning on the camera would do the trick: in René Clair's words, 'There is no detail of reality which is not immediately extended here [the cinema] into the domain of the wondrous' (Willemen 1994: 125). And in his first published essay, Louis Aragon suggested that this effect did not result from 'art' films alone:

All our emotion exists for those dear old American adventure films that speak of daily life and manage to raise to a dramatic level a banknote on which our attention is riveted, a table with a revolver on it, a bottle that on occasion becomes a weapon, a handkerchief that reveals a crime, a typewriter that's the horizon of a desk, the terrible unfolding telegraphic tape with magic ciphers that enrich or ruin bankers. (Hammond 1978: 29)

This response seems, in retrospect, an acute description of the way movies are often experienced—as intermittent intensities (a face, a landscape, the fall of light across a room) that break free from the sometimes indifferent narratives which contain them. Why, then, was the Impressionist–Surrealist approach so rapidly eclipsed by Eisenstein's? First, its emphasis on fragmentation poorly suited the rapidly consolidating commercial cinema whose hard-earned basis lay precisely in its continuity system. Both the Impressionists and the Surrealists, in fact, often regarded narrative as an obstacle to be overcome. ('The telephone rings,' Epstein complained, pointing to the event that so often initiates a plot. 'All is lost'; Abel 1988: 242.) Surrealist filmwatching tactics, for example, were designed to reassert the autonomy and ambiguity of images: think, for example, of Man Ray's habit of watching the screen through his fingers, spread to isolate certain parts of the screen. Lyrical, contemplative, enraptured by the camera's automatism, the Impressionist attitude derived more from Lumière's way of working than from that of Méliès. The latter's commitment to fiction, and his willingness to construct a narrative world out of discontinuous fragments, proved

the premise of all subsequent commercial filmmaking, including Eisenstein's which quickly attracted the attention of the Hollywood studios. (Samuel Goldwyn: 'I've seen your film *Potemkin* and admire it very much. What I would like is for you to do something of the same kind, but a little cheaper, for Ronald Colman.') Although Méliès had begun as a magician, the filmmaking tradition he inspired lent itself readily to the Taylorist procedures adopted by the American moguls. It was Lumière who had discovered the cinema's alchemy.

> **Surrealist filmwatching tactics, for example, were designed to reassert the autonomy and ambiguity of images: think, for example, of Man Ray's habit of watching the screen through his fingers, spread to isolate certain parts of the screen.**

Second, by insisting that film's essence lay beyond words, the *photogénie* movement left even its would-be followers with nowhere to go. As Paul Willemen (1994: 131) has suggested, 'mysticism was indeed the swamp in which most of the theoretical statements of the Impressionists eventually drowned'. By contrast, Eisenstein had a thoroughly linguistic view of filmmaking, with shots amounting to ideograms, which, when artfully combined, could communicate the equivalent of sentences. As the hedonistic 1920s yielded to the intensely politicized 1930s, Eisenstein's propositions seemed a far more useful way of thinking about the cinema.

In fact, however, while *photogénie*'s elusiveness caused the term to disappear gradually from film theory, other people were thinking about it—people like Irving Thalberg. Having perfected its continuity system by the mid-1920s, the Hollywood studios turned to the great remaining problem. MGM's constant screen tests; its commitment to having the best cameramen, costume designers, and lighting technicians; its regular resort to previews—these practices indicated Thalberg's obsessive quest for the photogenic actor, location, or moment. MGM's pre-eminence during this period suggests that Thalberg achieved, however intuitively, what the Impressionist theoreticians did not: a formula for *photogénie*.

Current film theory has often discredited Impressionist–Surrealist film theory by pointing to *photogénie*'s obvious connection to fetishism. Aragon's own explanation of the cinematic marvellous, amounting to a precise definition of the fetishist's gaze, confirms this diagnosis: 'To endow with a poetic value that which does not yet possess it, to wilfully restrict the field of vision so as to intensify expression: these are two properties that help make cinematic *décor* the adequate expression of modern beauty' (Hammond 1978: 29).

In its history, fetishism has appeared most prominently as knowledge's opposite, as a means of false consciousness and disavowal. Marx, for example, argued that the 'fetishism of commodities' encourages us to ignore the exploitative social relations that such objects simultaneously embody and conceal. The commodity is a 'hieroglyph', all right, but not one meant to be read. It substitutes the lure of things for a curiosity about their production. Similarly, Freud posited fetishism as the result of an investigation's *arrest*. Fearing the sight of the mother's genitals, misunderstood as 'castrated', the male infant stops at another place (a foot, an ankle, a skirt's hem), investing this replacement with libidinal energy, but denying the sexual difference his gaze has discovered.

What film theory discredited, however, Hollywood skilfully employed. In fact, the development of classical narrative cinema finds its exact parallel in the etymology of the word 'fetish'. As William Pietz (1985) has shown, the problem of fetishism first arose in a specific historical context: the trading conducted by Portuguese merchants along the coast of West Africa in the sixteenth and seventeenth centuries. Renaissance businessmen, the Portuguese were looking for straightforward economic transactions. Almost immediately, they were frustrated by what Pietz (1985: 7–9) evocatively calls 'the mystery of value'. For the Africans, material objects could embody—'simultaneously and sequentially—religious, commercial, aesthetic, and sexual' worth, and the balance among these categories seemed, at least to the Europeans, a matter of caprice. Especially troubling was the Africans' unpredictable estimate of not only their own objects, but also those of the European traders, which the merchants themselves regarded as 'trifles'.

Like the Portuguese traders, commercial filmmakers began naïvely by proposing an uncomplicated deal: a story in exchange for the price of a ticket. But they were quickly surprised by their viewers' fascination with individual players. For a brief moment, the industry resisted this unintended consequence of the movies, this admiration for actors which seemed an 'overestimation of value', a fetishism. Preserving the players' anonymity, after all, had minimized their power and kept them cheap. Inevitably, however, Hollywood came to recognize this fetishism as a means of making money, and the star system deliberately set out to encourage it (see Butler, Part 2, Chapter 9). In fact, although continuity cinema's insistence on story often reduced the immediate attraction of its components ('while an image could be beautiful,' one cameraman recalls, 'it wasn't to be so beautiful as to draw attention to itself'), inadvertently, as the Impressionists and Surrealists saw, the movies glamorized everything: faces, clothes, furniture, trains. A dining-car's white, starched linen (*North by Northwest*, USA, 1959), a woman's voice (Margaret Sullavan's in *Three Comrades*, USA, 1938), a cigarette lighter (*The Maltese Falcon*, USA, 1941)—even the most ordinary objects could become, as Sam Spade put it in a rare literary allusion, 'the stuff that dreams are made of' (Ray 1995).

It is hard to know whether this effect was always intended. Constant economic pressures, the conversion to sound, and the absolute pre-eminence of narrative all encouraged Hollywood's tendency towards Fordist procedures and laconic filmmaking. The American cinema's functionalism, in other words, abetted the rationalist theoretical tradition descending from Eisenstein. In this context, Thalberg's more complicated approach seems especially significant. For

An impressionist moment, Greta Garbo in *Grand Hotel* (1932)

despite MGM's production quotas, strict regimentation, and highly developed division of labour, Thalberg often encouraged, or at least allowed, moments of the kind so admired by the Impressionists and Surrealists. In *Grand Hotel* (USA, 1932), for example, whose production he closely supervised, the camera cut suddenly to an unmotivated overhead shot of Garbo in her ballerina costume, alone for the first time, opening like a flower as she settled wearily to the floor. The narrative idled, enabling this instance of *photogénie* to unfold because, as Thalberg knew, the movie would be the better for it. The plot could wait.

Path dependence

One of the most decisive moments in the history of film theory occurred during a span of twelve months from late 1952 to early 1953. Having emerged from the Second World War alive, but with the teaching career for which he had trained foreclosed to him because of a stammar and poor health, André Bazin (Andrew 1978) confirmed his commitment to film criticism with 'The Evolution of the Language of Cinema' and 'The Virtues and Limitations of Montage' (Bazin 1967, 1971), essays in which, for the first time, someone suggested that the two most prestigious schools of filmmaking (Soviet montage and German Expressionism) were wrong. The movies' possibilities, Bazin insisted, were more radical than those ways of working had suggested.

Bazin, of course, is famous for arguing that film's true destiny is the objective representation of reality. 'The guiding myth . . . inspiring the invention of cinema', he had argued a few years earlier, 'is the accomplishment of that which dominated in a more or less vague fashion all the techniques of the mechanical reproduction of reality in the nineteenth century, from photography to the phonograph, namely an integral realism, a recreation of the world in its own image, an image unburdened by the freedom of interpretation of the artist or the irreversibility of time' (Bazin 1967: 21). The Soviets and Germans, according to Bazin (24), had betrayed this sacred purpose by 'putting their faith in the image' instead of in reality, convulsing the camera's objectivity with abstracting montages and grotesque *mise-en-scène*.

Since about 1970 this position has been represented as fantastically naïve, another version of Wes-

tern culture's longing for what philosopher Jacques Derrida calls 'unmediated presence'. In a passage often singled out for critique, Bazin (1971: 60), had apparently earned this attack praising *Bicycle Thieves* (Italy, 1948) as 'one of the first examples of pure cinema': 'No more actors, no more story, no more sets, which is to say that in the perfect aesthetic illusion of reality there is no more cinema.' In fact, however, behind Bazin's realist aesthetic lay an intuition about the cinema's most profoundly radical aspect: its automatism. With photography, Bazin kept insisting, an absolutely accurate representation of the world could be produced, for the first time in history, *by accident*. This miraculous revelatory power made the Soviet or Expressionist imposition of subjective meanings seem a kind of misguided vanity.

This argument, of course, amounted to a displacement of Bazin's unrequited religious impulse. But it also involved a revival of the Impressionists' *photogénie* and the Surrealists' automatism. In his own proposed dictionary entry, Breton (1972: 26) had designated this feature of modern technology as Surrealism's defining activity:

SURREALISM, n. Psychic automatism in its pure state, by which one proposes to express—verbally, by means of the written word, or in any other manner—the actual functioning of thought. Dictated by thought, in the absence of any control by reason, exempt from any aesthetic or moral concern.

Breton had also made explicit the metaphoric connection between technology and the Surrealists' favourite game, describing automatic writing as 'a true photography of thought' (Ernst 1948: 177). For the Impressionists, *photogénie* was untranslatable but intentional, the product of particularly talented filmmakers. For the Surrealists, on the other hand, it was often accidental, and thus capable of appearing anywhere. Man Ray made the point provocatively: 'The worst films I've ever seen, the ones that send me to sleep, contain ten or fifteen marvelous minutes. The best films I've ever seen only contain 10 or 15 valid minutes' (Hammond 1978: 84).

Like the Surrealists, Bazin could occasionally find what he valued in forgettable movies. He devoted, for example, a page-long footnote in 'The Virtues and Limitations of Montage' to what he called 'an otherwise mediocre English film', *Where no Vultures Fly* (GB, 1951), praising a single moment that abandoned a 'tricky' and 'banal montage' to show parents, child, and a stalking lioness 'all in the same full shot' (1967: 49–50). In general, however, Bazin preferred to associate his cinematic ideal with a particular set of strategies deliberately employed by an elect group of filmmakers. Jean Renoir, Vittorio De Sica, F. W. Murnau, Robert Flaherty, William Wyler, and Orson Welles were great because in relying on long takes and deep focus, they had modestly permitted reality to speak for itself.

> **At the heart of the *Cahiers* position lay a privileged term that evoked both *photogénie*'s ineffability and the Surrealists' 'objective chance'. That term was 'mise-en-scène'.**

With this argument, Bazin was retreating from his thought's most radical implication, his sense of the fundamental difference between previous representational technologies and the new 'random generators' like the camera. In the hands of his followers, the *Cahiers* critics, Bazin's attitude towards intentionality became even more ambivalent. *La politique des auteurs* seemed to renounce altogether the Surrealist faith in chance, celebrating even Bazin's beloved 'reality' less than the filmmaking geniuses who could consciously summon its charms. But at the heart of the *Cahiers* position lay a privileged term that evoked both *photogénie*'s ineffability and the Surrealists' 'objective chance'.

That term was 'mise-en-scène'. As the *Cahiers* critics used it, mise-en-scène' quickly left behind its conventional meaning ('setting') to become a sacred word, shared by friends who could invoke it knowing the others would understand. (This point, and other important contributions to this chapter, come from Christian Keathley.) At first, it appeared to be simply another version of *photogénie*, a way of talking again about the untranslatable 'essence of the cinema'. Hence, Jacques Rivette on Otto Preminger's *Angel Face* (USA, 1953): 'What tempts [Preminger] if not . . . the rendering audible of particular chords unheard and rare, in which the inexplicable beauty of the modulation suddenly justifies the ensemble of the phrase? This is probably the definition of something precious . . . its enigma—the door to something beyond intellect, opening out onto the unknown. Such are the

contingencies of *mise-en-scène*' (Hiller 1985: 134). Auteurism's basic problem, however, involved just this kind of attribution. More than even most theoretical groups, the *Cahiers* critics had a sense of themselves as a visionary, well-educated, sensitive elect. As long as they were associating the delights of mise-en-scène with filmmakers like Jean Renoir, they could continue to insist on the conscious aspect of a director's decisions. Renoir, after all, was aesthetically well-bred, politically liberal, and personally sympathetic. But the auteurist position increasingly prompted them to celebrate directors who had often made bad films, and who sometimes seemed neither particularly smart nor especially nice. Directors, for example, like Otto Preminger. Faced with this situation, the *Cahiers* writers revised their praise, directing it less at individual filmmakers than at the medium itself. Thus, the *Cahiers*'s American operative Andrew Sarris (1965: 13) could explicitly modulate *la politique des auteurs* into a revival of Surrealism's praise of automatism:

> For me, *mise-en-scène* is not merely the gap between what we see and feel on the screen and what we can express in words, but is also the gap between the intention of the director and his effect upon the spectator. . . . To read all sorts of poignant profundities in Preminger's inscrutable urbanity would seem to be the last word in idiocy, and yet there are moments in his films when the evidence on the screen is inconsistent with one's deepest instincts about the director as a man. It is during those moments that one feels the magical powers of *mise-en-scène* to get more out of a picture than is put there by a director.

The roots of this move lay in Bazin's tacit renewal of the Impressionist–Surrealist branch of film theory. This achievement usually goes unnoticed, since Bazin, after all, remains famous for so many other things: his championing of realism and the Italian post-war cinema, his editorship of the *Cahiers*, his spiritual fathering of the *Nouvelle Vague*. Nevertheless, Bazin's ability to reroute film theory, at least temporarily, amounted to a rare instance of a discipline escaping from what economic historians call 'path dependence' (David 1985; Passell 1996).

Path dependence developed as a way of explaining why the free market's invisible hand does not always choose the best products. Beta and Macintosh lose to inferior alternatives, while a clumsy arrangement of keyboard symbols (known as QWERTY, for the first six letters on a typewriter's upper left) becomes the international standard. Although an initial choice often occurs for reasons whose triviality eventually becomes evident (momentary production convenience, fleeting cost advantages), that decision establishes a path dependence almost impossible to break. Superior keyboard layouts have repeatedly been designed, but with every typist in the world using QWERTY, they have no chance.

Bazin recognized that film theory was especially prone to path dependence. The vagaries of film preservation, the industry's encouragement of amnesia (before television, only a handful of films were regularly and widely revived), the small size of the intellectual film community—these factors all encouraged theoretical consensus. While the Impressionist and Surrealist films, with a few exceptions, had disappeared from sight, Eisenstein's had remained in wide circulation, serving as advertisements for his position. (And vice versa: Jean-Marie Straub once observed that everyone thinks that Eisenstein was great at editing because he had so many *theories* about it; Rosenbaum 1982.) As a result, Eisenstein's rationalist, critical branch of film theory had triumphed, establishing a path dependence that Bazin challenged with all his energy.

Bazin attacked on two fronts. First, he challenged the Eisenstein tradition's basic equation of art with anti-realism. Second, he encouraged, without practising himself, a different kind of film criticism: the lyrical, discontinuous, epigrammatic flashes of subjectivity-cum-analysis that appeared in the *Cahiers du cinéma*. A few now famous examples from Godard (1972: 64, 66) suggest this form's tone:

There was theatre (Griffith), poetry (Murnau), painting (Rossellini), dance (Eisenstein), music (Renoir). Henceforth there is cinema. And the cinema is Nicholas Ray.

Never before have the characters in a film [Ray's *Bitter Victory*, France, 1957] seemed so close and yet so far away. Faced by the deserted streets of Benghazi or the sand-dunes, we suddenly think for the space of a second of something else—the snack-bars on the Champs-Elysées, a girl one liked, everything and anything, lies, the treachery of women, the shallowness, of men, playing the slot-machines. . . .

How can one talk of such a film? What is the point of saying that the meeting between Richard Burton and Ruth Roman while Curt Jurgens watches is edited with fantastic

brio? Maybe this was a scene during which we had closed our eyes.

In many cases, this different critical strategy evolved into filmmaking itself, with Godard (1972: 171) again providing the explanation:

As a critic, I thought of myself as a filmmaker. Today, I still think of myself as a critic, and in a sense I am, more than before. Instead of writing criticism, I make a film, but the critical dimension is subsumed. I think of myself as an essayist, producing essays in novel form or novels in essay form: only instead of writing, I film them.

The film theory sponsored by Bazin would receive its best explanation only after its own moment had passed. Writing in 1973, Roland Barthes (1973/1981: 44) proclaimed, '*Let the commentary be itself a text. . . . There are no more critics, only writers.*'

Bazin's moment lasted only fifteen years. The events of May 1968 discredited both his ideas and the critical practice he had fostered, stimulating different questions about the cinema's relationship to ideology and power. The post-1968 period coincided with the development of academic film study, and although auteurism briefly persisted as a way of doing film criticism (aided by its explicit analogy to literary authorship), its apolitical concern with aesthetics suddenly seemed reactionary. Comolli and Narboni's 1969 *Cahiers* editorial 'Cinema/Ideology/Criticism' (Nichols, 1976) represented the transition, an attempt to preserve the old auteurist heroes (Ford, Capra, et al.) in terms of the new political criteria. But as film studies spread through the universities, it organized itself around a theoretical approach having more to do with Eisenstein than with Bazin.

That approach has come to be known as 'semiotic', using that term as a shorthand way of summarizing the structuralist, ideological, psychoanalytic, and gender theory it encompassed. Committed largely to a species of critique defined by the Frankfurt School, this paradigm accomplished wonderful things, above all alerting us to popular culture's complicities with the most destructive, enslaving, and ignoble myths. It taught us to see the implications of those invisible operations that Brecht had called 'the apparatus', the relation, for example, between Hollywood's continuity system, apparently only a set of filmmaking protocols, and a world-view eager to conceal the necessity of choice (see Ray 1985).

These gains did not come free of charge. The Impressionist–Surrealist half of film theory fell into obscurity, banished for its political irrelevance. Indeed, 'impressionistic' became one of the new paradigm's most frequently evoked pejoratives, designating a theoretical position that was either 'untheorized' or too interested in the wrong questions. The wrong questions, however, frequently turned on the reasons why people went to the movies in the first place, the problem so vital to the Impressionists. In 1921 Jean Epstein had announced that 'The cinema is essentially supernatural. Everything is transformed. . . . The universe is on edge. The philosopher's light. The atmosphere is heavy with love. I am looking' (Abel 1988: 246). In the new dispensation, occasional film theoretician Fredric Jameson (Jameson and Kavanagh 1984: 3–4) would acknowledge that the appeal of beautiful and exciting storytelling is precisely the problem: 'Nothing can be more satisfying to a Marxist teacher', he admitted, 'than to "break" this fascination for students'. Also rendered suspect was formally experimental criticism, deemed irresponsible by rationalist critique. The *Cahiers*-inspired auteurist essay receded, as did the New Wave film, that hybrid of research and spectacle, Lumière and Méliès.

Can the rational, politically sensitive Eisenstein tradition reunite with the Impressionist–Surrealist interest in *photogénie* and automatism?

Twenty-five years ago, Roland Barthes recognized what was happening to criticism. The semiotic paradigm that he himself had done so much to establish— 'it too', Barthes (1977: 166) lamented, 'has become in some sort mythical: any student can and does denounce the bourgeois or petit-bourgeois character of such and such a form (of life, of thought, of consumption). In other words, a mythological doxa has been created: denunciation, demystification (or demythification), has itself become discourse, stock of phrases, catechistic declaration.' The problem, Barthes (1977a: 71) wrote four years later, is 'Where to go next?' In the next decade, the most important debates in film theory will turn on the extreme path dependence Barthes saw constraining the humanities. At stake will be our disciplines' ability to pro-

duce information, defined by information theory as a function of *unpredictability*. (The more predictable the message, the less information it contains; Ray 1995: 10–12). Film studies, in particular, should ask these questions: (1) Can the rational, politically sensitive Eisenstein tradition reunite with the Impressionist–Surrealist interest in *photogénie* and automatism? Can film theory, in other words, imitate filmmaking and recognize that, at its best, the cinema requires, as Thalberg understood, a subtle mixture of logical structure and untranslatable allure? (2) Can film theory revive the *Cahiers*–Nouvelle Vague experiment, learning to write differently, to stage its research in the form of a spectacle? American theoretician Gregory Ulmer (1994) has specified that this new writing practice would provide a complement to critique. It will not be hermeneutics, the science of interpretation. It will look to photography, the cinema, television, and the computer as the source of ideas about invention. It is called 'heuretics'.

A heuretic film studies might begin where *photogénie*, third meanings, and fetishism intersect: with the cinematic detail whose insistent appeal eludes precise explanation. Barthes maintained that third meanings, while resisting obvious connotations, compel 'an interrogative reading'. In doing so, he was implicitly suggesting how Impressionist reverie could prompt an active research method resembling the Surrealists' 'Irrational Enlargement', a game in which players generate chains of associations from a given object (Jean 1980: 298–301; Hammond 1978: 74–80). Here would be the instructions for such a project: *Select a detail from a movie, one that interests you without your knowing why. Follow this detail wherever it leads and report your findings.*

Here is an example of what this Impressionist–Surrealist model might produce. Studying MGM's Andy Hardy movies, I was struck by the occasional presence of a Yale pennant on Andy's wall. Following Barthes's 'instructions', I 'interrogated' this object, producing the following response:

In Andy's bedroom, only two pennants appear: *Carvel High* and *Yale*. In the 1930s, when the best of the Hardy films were made, Yale's two most famous alumni were probably Cole Porter (author of the college's football cheer) and Rudy Vallee (popularizer of 'The Whiffenpoof Song'). *Andy Hardy's Private Secretary* [USA, 1941] gives Porter's 'I've Got My Eyes on You' to Kathryn Grayson, who uses it to satisfy Andy's request (and the audience's) for something besides opera. But with his urbanity, dandyism, aristocratic wit, and cosmopolitan allusiveness, Porter is the Hardy series's antonym. Vallee's deportment, on the other hand—a studied juvenescence deployed to conceal a prima donna's ego—seems more like Rooney's own. In bursts of manic exuberance, Andy is given to expressions of self-satisfaction addressed to his bedroom mirror, pep talks descended from Franklin's *Autobiography*. Although the Hardy films unquestioningly accept Poor Richard's vulgarized legacy (chambers of commerce, boosterism, faith in 'Progress'), those values will eventually be satirized by even popular culture, especially in 1961's *How to Succeed in Business Without Really Trying*, whose hero-on-the-make serenades his own mirror image with the show's hit, 'I Believe in You.' Making a Mickey-Rooney style comeback, that play's costar, in the part of corporation president J. B. Biggley, was Rudy Vallee.

And yet: with the series making no other mention of it, the choice of the Yale pennant seems particularly arbitrary. Andy, after all, eventually follows his father's footsteps to 'Wainwright College,' whose plentiful coeds, accessible teachers, and intimate size represent the Ivy League's opposite. Obvious answers, of course, present themselves. 'Yale' as the best known college name, 'Yale' as a signifier of 'class.' Then why not 'Harvard' or 'Princeton'? If we acknowledge instead another logic (more visual, more cinematic), we might begin to see 'Yale' as an unusually valuable *design*—bold (the rare capital Y), concise (the shortest college name), memorable (the locks), available for multiple rhymes (including *hale*, the inevitable companion of *Hardy*'s near-homonym 'hearty'). From this perspective, the Yale pennant signals a relaxation of filmmaking's referential drive, a turn toward the possibilities inherent in shapes, movements, and sounds. In the Hardy series, 'Yale' suggests the cinema's revision of Mallarmé's famous warning to Degas—movies are not made with words, but with *images*. (Ray 1995: 173–4)

BIBLIOGRAPHY

*****Abel, Richard** (ed.) (1988), *French Film Theory and Criticism, i: 1907–1929* (Princeton: Princeton University Press).

Adorno, Theodor (1938/1980), Letter to Walter Benjamin, trans. Harry Zohn, in Fredric Jameson (ed.), *Aesthetics and Politics* (London: Verso).

Andrew, Dudley (1978), *André Bazin* (New York: Oxford University Press).

Barthes, Roland (1973/1981), 'Theory of the Text', trans. Geoff Bennington, in Robert Young (ed.), *Untying the Text: A Post-Structuralist Reader* (Boston: Routledge & Kegan Paul).

—— (1977*a*), *Image–Music–Text*, trans. Stephen Heath (New York: Hill & Wang).

—— (1977*b*), *Roland Barthes*, trans. Richard Howard (New York: Hill & Wang).

Batchelor, Ray (1994), *Henry Ford: Mass Production, Modernism and Design* (Manchester: Manchester University Press).

*****Bazin, André** (1967), *What is Cinema?*, 2 vols., trans. Hugh Gray, i (Berkeley, Calif.: University of California Press).

*—— (1971), *What is Cinema?*, 2 vols., trans. Hugh Gray, ii (Berkeley: University of California Press).

Benjamin, Walter (1979), *One-Way Street*, trans. Edmund Jephcott and Kingsley Shorter (London: New Left Books).

Breton, André (1972), *Manifestos of Surrealism*, trans. Richard Seaver and Helen R. Lane (Ann Arbor: University of Michigan Press).

Burch, Noël (1990), *Life to those Shadows* (Berkeley: University of California Press).

David, Paul A. (1985), 'Clio and the Economics of QWERTY', *American Economic Review*, 75/2: 332–7.

Ernst, Max (1948), *Beyond Painting and Other Writings by the Artist and his Friends* (New York: Wittenborn Schultz).

Godard, Jean-Luc (1972), *Godard on Godard*, trans. Tom Milne (New York: Viking Press).

*****Hammond, Paul** (ed.) (1978), *The Shadow and its Shadow: Surrealist Writings on the Cinema* (London: British Film Institute).

Hillier, Jim (ed.) (1985), *Cahiers du Cinéma. The 1950s: Neo-Realism, Hollywood, New Wave* (Cambridge, Mass.: Harvard University Press).

Jameson, Fredric, and **James Kavanagh** (1984), 'The Weakest Link: Marxism in Literary Studies', in *The Left Academy II* (New York: Praeger).

Jean, Marcel (ed.) (1980), *The Autobiography of Surrealism* (New York: Viking).

MacCabe, Colin (1980), *Godard: Image, Sounds, Politics* (Bloomington: Indiana University Press).

Nichols, Bill (ed.) (1976), *Movies and Methods* (Berkeley: University of California Press).

Passell, Peter (1996), 'Why the Best doesn't always Win', *New York Times Magazine*, 5 May: 60–1.

Pietz, William (1985), 'The Problem of the Fetish', part 1, *Res*, 9: 5–17.

—— (1987), 'The Problem of the Fetish', part 2, *Res*, 13: 23–45.

—— (1988), 'The Problem of the Fetish', part 3, *Res*, 16: 105–23.

*****Ray, Robert B.** (1985), *A Certain Tendency of the Hollywood Cinema 1930–1980* (Princeton: Princeton University Press).

—— (1995), *The Avant-Garde Finds Andy Hardy* (Cambridge, Mass.: Harvard University Press).

Rosenbaum, Jonathan (1982), 'The Films of Jean-Marie Straub and Danielle Huillet', in *Film at the Public*, Programme for a film series (New York: Public Theater).

Sarris, Andrew (1965), 'Preminger's Two Periods: Studio and Solo', *Film Comment*, 3/3: 12–17.

Schatz, Thomas (1988), *The Genius of the System: Hollywood Filmmaking in the Studio Era* (New York: Pantheon Books).

Ulmer, Gregory L. (1994), *Heuretics: The Logic of Invention* (Baltimore: Johns Hopkins University Press).

Willemen, Paul (1994), *Looks and Frictions: Essays in Cultural Studies and Film Theory* (Bloomington: Indiana University Press; London: British Film Institute).

Wollen, Peter (1993), *Raiding the Icebox: Reflections on Twentieth-Century Culture* (Bloomington: Indiana University Press).

9

Film and psychoanalysis

Barbara Creed

Psychoanalysis and the cinema were born at the end of the nineteenth century. They share a common historical, social, and cultural background shaped by the forces of modernity. Theorists commonly explore how psychoanalysis, with its emphasis on the importance of desire in the life of the individual, has influenced the cinema. But the reverse is also true—the cinema may well have influenced psychoanalysis. Not only did Freud draw on cinematic terms to describe his theories, as in 'screen memories', but a number of his key ideas were developed in visual terms—particularly the theory of castration, which is dependent upon the shock registered by a close-up image of the female genitals. Further, as Freud (who loved Sherlock Holmes) was aware, his case histories unfold very much like popular mystery novels of the kind that were also adopted by the cinema from its inception.

The history of psychoanalytic film criticism is extremely complex—partly because it is long and uneven, partly because the theories are difficult, and partly because the evolution of psychoanalytic film theory after the 1970s cannot be understood without recourse to developments in separate, but related areas, such as Althusser's theory of ideology, semiotics, and feminist film theory. In the 1970s psychoanalysis became the key discipline called upon to explain a series of diverse concepts, from the way the cinema functioned as an apparatus to the nature of the screen–

spectator relationship. Despite a critical reaction against psychoanalysis, in some quarters, in the 1980s and 1990s, it exerted such a profound influence that the nature and direction of film theory and criticism has been changed in irrevocable and fundamental ways.

Pre-1970s psychoanalytic film theory

One of the first artistic movements to draw on psychoanalysis was the Surrealist movement of the 1920s and 1930s. In their quest for new modes of experience that transgressed the boundaries between dream and reality, the Surrealists extolled the potential of the cinema. They were deeply influenced by Freud's theory of dreams and his concept of the unconscious. To them, the cinema, with its special techniques such as the dissolve, superimposition, and slow motion, correspond to the nature of dreaming.

André Breton, the founder of the movement, saw cinema as a way of entering the marvellous, that realm of love and liberation. Recent studies by writers such as Hal Foster (1993) argue that Surrealism was also bound up with darker forces—explicated by Freud—such as the death drive, the compulsion to repeat, and the uncanny. Certainly, the films of the greatest exponent of cinematic Surrealism, Luis Buñel (*Un chien andalou*, France, 1928; *The Exterminating Angel*, Mexico, 1962; and *That Obscure Object of Desire*, France, 1977), explore the unconscious from this perspective.

Not all theorists used Freud. Others drew on the ideas of Carl Gustav Jung, and particularly his theory of archetypes, to understand film. The archetype is an idea or image that has been central to human existence and inherited psychically from the species by the individual. Archetypes include: the shadow or the underside of consciousness; the anima, that is the feminine aspect in men; and the animus, or the masculine aspect in women. But generally, Jungian theory has never been widely applied to the cinema. Apart from Clark Branson's *Howard Hawks: A Jungian Study* (1987) and John Izod's *The Films of Nicolas Roeg: Myth and Mind* (1992), critical works consist mainly of articles, by authors such as Albert Benderson (1979), Royal S. Brown (1980), and Don Fredericksen (1980), which analyse archetypes in the film text. Writers of the 1970s who turned to Freud and Lacan—the two most influential psychoanalysts—were critical, however, of what they perceived to be an underlying essentialism in Jungian theory, that is a tendency to explain subjectivity in unchanging, universal terms.

Many of Freud's theories have been used in film theory: the unconscious; the return of the repressed; Oedipal drama; narcissism; castration; and hysteria. Possibly his most important contributions were his accounts of the unconscious, subjectivity, and sexuality. According to Freud, large parts of human thought remain unconscious; that is, the subject does not know about the content of certain troubling ideas and often much effort is needed to make them conscious. Undesirable thoughts will be repressed or kept from consciousness by the ego under the command of the super-ego, or conscience. In Freud's view, repression is the key to understanding the neuroses. Repressed thoughts can manifest themselves in dreams, nightmares, slips of the tongue, and forms of artistic activity. These ideas have also influenced film study and some psychoanalytic critics explore the 'unconscious' of the film text—referred to as the 'subtext'—analysing it for repressed contents, perverse utterances, and evidence of the workings of desire.

Freud's notion of the formation of subjectivity is more complex. Two concepts are central: division and sexuality. The infantile ego is a divided entity. The ego refers to the child's sense of self; however, because the child, in its narcissistic phase, also takes itself, invests in itself, as the object of its own libidinal drives, the ego is both subject and object. The narcis-

sistic ego is formed in its relationship to others. One of the earliest works influenced by Freud's theory of the double was Otto's Rank's 1925 classic *The Double* which was directly influenced by a famous movie of the day, *The Student of Prague* (Germany, 1913). In his later rewriting of Freud, Lacan took Freud's notion of the divided self as the basis of his theory of the formation of subjectivity in the mirror phase (see below), which was to exert a profound influence on film theory in the 1970s.

Sexuality becomes crucial during the child's Oedipus complex. Initially, the child exists in a two-way, or dyadic, relationship with the mother. But eventually, the child must leave the maternal haven and enter the domain of law and language. As a result of the appearance of a third figure—the father—in the child's life, the child gives up its love–desire for the mother. The dyadic relationship becomes triadic. This is the moment of the Oedipal crisis. The boy represses his feelings for the mother because he fears the father will punish him, possibly even castrate him—that is, make him like his mother, whom he now realizes is not phallic. Prior to this moment the boy imagined the mother was just like himself. On the understanding that one day he will inherit a woman of his own, the boy represses his desire for the mother. This is what Freud describes as the moment of 'primal repression'; it ushers in the formation of the unconscious.

The girl gives up her love for the mother, not because she fears castration (she has nothing to lose) but because she blames the mother for not giving her a penis–phallus. She realizes that only those who possess the phallus have power. Henceforth, she transfers her love to her father, and later to the man she will marry. But, as with the boy, her repressed desire can, at any time, surface, bringing with it a problematic relationship with the mother. The individual who is unable to come to terms with his or her proper gender role (activity for boys, passivity for girls) may become an hysteric; that is, repressed desires will manifest themselves as bodily or mental symptoms such as paralysis or amnesia. Alfred Hitchcock's *Psycho* (USA, 1960) and *Marnie* (USA, 1964) present powerful examples of what might happen to the boy and girl respectively if they fail to resolve the Oedipus complex.

Freud's theories were discussed most systematically in relation to the cinema after the post-structuralist revolution in theory during the 1970s. In particular, writers applied the Oedipal trajectory to the narrative structures of classical film texts. They pointed to the fact that all narratives appeared to exhibit an Oedipal trajectory; that is, the (male) hero was confronted with a crisis in which he had to assert himself over another man (often a father figure) in order to achieve social recognition and win the woman. In this way, film was seen to represent the workings of patriarchal ideology.

In an early two-part article, 'Monsters from the ID' (1970, 1971), which pre-dates the influences of post-structuralist criticism, Margaret Tarratt analysed the science fiction film. She argued that previous writers, apart from French critics, all view science fiction films as 'reflections of society's anxiety about its increasing technological prowess and its responsibility to control the gigantic forces of destruction it possesses' (Tarratt 1970: 38). Her aim was to demonstrate that the genre was 'deeply involved with concepts of Freudian psychoanalysis and seen in many cases to derive their structure from it' (38). In particular, science fiction explores the individual's repressed sexual desires, viewed as incompatible with civilized morality. Utilizing Freud's argument that whatever is repressed will return, Tarratt discusses Oedipal desire, castration anxiety, and violent sadistic male desire.

1970s psychoanalytic theory and after

One of the major differences between pre- and post-1970s psychoanalytic theory was that the latter saw the cinema as an institution or an apparatus. Whereas early approaches, such as those of Tarratt, concentrated on the film text in relation to its hidden or repressed meanings, 1970s theory, as formulated by Jean-Louis Baudry, Christian Metz, and Laura Mulvey, emphasized the crucial importance of the cinema as an apparatus and as a signifying practice of ideology, the viewer–screen relationship, and the way in which the viewer was 'constructed' as transcendental during the spectatorial process.

Psychoanalytic film theory from the 1970s to the 1990s has travelled in at least four different, but related, directions. These should not be seen as linear progressions as they frequently overlap:

The first stage was influenced by apparatus theory as proposed by Baudry and Metz. In an attempt to avoid the totalizing imperative of the structuralist approach, they drew on psychoanalysis as a way of widening their theoretical base.

The second development was instituted by the feminist film theorist Laura Mulvey, who contested aspects of the work of Baudry and Metz by rebutting the naturalization of the filmic protagonist as an Oedipal hero, and the view of the screen–spectator relationship as a one-way process.

The third stage involved a number of feminist responses to Mulvey's work. These did not all follow the same direction. In general, they included critical studies of the female Oedipal trajectory, masculinity and masochism, fantasy theory and spectatorship, and woman as active, sadistic monster.

The fourth stage involves theorists who use psychoanalytic theory in conjunction with other critical approaches to the cinema as in post-colonial theory, queer theory, and body theory.

Apparatus theory: Baudry and Metz

The notion of the cinema as an institution or apparatus is central to 1970s theory. However, it is crucial to understand that Baudry, Metz, and Mulvey did not simply mean that the cinema was like a machine. As Metz explained, 'The cinematic institution is not just the cinema industry . . . it is also the mental machinery—another industry—which spectators "accustomed to the cinema" have internalized historically and which has adapted them to the consumption of films' (1975/1982: 2). Thus the term 'cinematic apparatus' refers to both an industrial machine as well as a mental or psychic apparatus.

Jean-Louis Baudry was the first to draw on psychoanalytic theory to analyse the cinema as an institution. According to D. N. Rodowick, one 'cannot overestimate the impact of Baudry's work in this period' (1988: 89). Baudry's pioneering ideas were later developed by Metz, who, although critical of aspects of Baudry's theories, was in agreement with his main arguments.

Baudry explored his ideas about the cinematic apparatus in two key essays. In the first, 'Ideological Effects of the Basic Cinematographic Apparatus' (1970), he argued that the cinema is ideological in that it creates an ideal, transcendental viewing subject. By this he meant that the cinema places the spectator, the 'eye-subject' (1986a: 290), at the centre of vision. Identification with the camera–projector, the seamless flow of images, narratives which restore equilibrium—all of these things give the spectator a sense of unity and control. The apparatus ensures 'the setting up of the "subject" as the active centre and origin of meaning'

(1986a: 286). Further, according to Baudry, by hiding the way in which it creates an impression of realism, the cinema enables the viewer to feel that events are simply unfolding—effortlessly—before his eyes. The 'reality effect' also helps to create a viewer who is at the centre of representation.

To explain the processes of identification at work in the viewing context, Baudry turned increasingly to the theories of Jacques Lacan. Baudry argued that the screen–spectator relationship activates a return to the Lacanian Imaginary, the period when the child experiences its first sense of a unified self during the mirror stage. 'The arrangement of the different elements—projector, darkened hall, screen—in addition to reproducing in a striking way the mise-en-scène of Plato's cave . . . reconstructs the situation necessary to the release of the "mirror stage" discovered by Lacan' (1986a: 294).

According to Lacan, there are three orders in the history of human development: the Imaginary, the Symbolic, and the Real. It is this area of Lacanian theory, particularly the Imaginary and the Symbolic, that is central to 1970s film theory. Drawing on Freud's theories of narcissism and the divided subject, Lacan proposed his theory of subjectivity. The mirror stage, which occurs during the period of the Imaginary, refers to that moment when the infant first experiences the joy of seeing itself as complete, and imagines itself to be more adult, more fully formed, perfect, than it really is. The self is constructed in a moment of recognition and misrecognition. Thus, the self is split.

Similarly, the spectator in the cinema identifies with the larger-than-life, or idealized, characters on the screen. Thus, as Mulvey (1975) later argued, the viewing experience, in which the spectator identifies with the glamorous star, is not unlike a re-enactment of the moment when the child acquires its first sense of selfhood or subjectivity through identificaton with an ideal self. But, as Lacan pointed out, this is also a moment of misrecognition—the child is not really a fully formed subject. He will only see himself in this idealized way when his image is reflected back through the eyes of others. Thus, identity is always dependent on mediation.

For the moment, the spectator in the cinema is transported back to a time when he or she experienced a sense of transcendence. But in reality, the spectator is not the point of origin, the centre of representation. Baudry argued that the comforting sense of a unified self which the viewing experience re-enacts does not emanate from the spectator but is constructed by the apparatus. Thus, the cinematic institution is complicit with ideology—and other institutions such as State and Church—whose aim is to instil in the subject a misrecognition of itself as transcendental.

In his 1975 essay 'The Apparatus', Baudry drew further parallels between Plato's cave and the cinematic apparatus. The spectators in both are in a state of 'immobility', 'shackled to the screen', staring at 'images and shadows of reality' that are not real but 'a simulacrum of it' (1986b: 303–4). Like spectators in the cinema, they mistake the shadowy figures for the real thing. According to Baudry, what Plato's prisoners–human beings desire—and what the cinema offers—is a return to a kind of psychic unity in which the boundary between subject and object is obliterated.

Baudry then drew connections between Plato's cave, the cinematic apparatus, and the 'maternal womb' (1986b: 306). He argued that 'the cinematographic apparatus brings about a state of artificial regression' which leads the spectator 'back to an anterior phase of his development'. The subject's desire to return to this phase is 'an early state of development with its own forms of satisfaction which may play a determining role in his desire for cinema and the pleasure he finds in it' (1986b: 313). What Baudry had in mind by this 'anterior phase' was an 'archaic moment of fusion' prior to the Lacanian mirror stage, 'a mode of identification, which has to do with the lack of differentiation between the subject and his environment, a dream-scene model which we find in the baby/breast relationship' (1986b: 313).

After discussing the actual differences between dream and the cinema, Baudry suggested that another wish lies behind the cinema—complementary to the one at work in Plato's cave. Without necessarily being aware of it, the subject is led to construct machines like the cinema which 'represent his own overall functioning to him . . . unaware of the fact that he is representing to himself the very scene of the unconscious where he is' (1986b: 316–17).

In 1975 Christian Metz published *Psychoanalysis and Cinema: The Imaginary Signifier* (translated in 1982), which was the first systematic book-length attempt to apply psychoanalytic theory to the cinema. Like Baudry, Metz also supported the analogy between screen and mirror and held that the spectator was positioned by the cinema machine in a moment that reactivated the pre-Oedipal moment of identification—that is, the moment of imaginary unity in which the infant first perceives itself as complete.

However, Metz also argued that the cinema–mirror analogy was flawed. Whereas a mirror reflects back the spectator's own image, the cinema does not. Metz also pointed out that, whereas the cinema is essentially a symbolic system, a signifying practice that mediates between the spectator and the outside world, the theory of the mirror stage refers to the pre-symbolic, the period when the infant is without language.

Nevertheless, Metz advocated the crucial importance of Lacanian psychoanalytic theory for the cinema and stressed the need to theorize the screen–spectator relationship—not just in the context of the Imaginary, but also in relation to the Symbolic. To address this issue, Metz introduced the notion of voyeurism. He argued that the viewing process is voyeuristic in that there is always a distance maintained, in the cinema, between the viewing subject and its object. The cinematic scene cannot return the spectator's gaze.

Metz also introduced a further notion which became the subtitle of his book: the imaginary signifier. The cinema, he argued, makes present what is absent. The screen might offer images that suggest completeness, but this is purely imaginary. Because the spectator is aware that the offer of unity is only imaginary, he is forced to deal with a sense of lack that is an inescapable part of the viewing process.

Metz drew an analogy between this process and the experience of the (male) child in the mirror phase. (Metz assumes the spectator is male.) When the boy looks in the mirror and identifies for the first time with himself as a unified being he is also made aware of his difference from the mother. She lacks the penis he once thought she possessed. Entry into the Symbolic also involves repression of desire for the mother and the constitution of the unconscious in response to that repression. (Here, Lacan reworks Freud's theories of the phallus and castration.) Along with repression of desire for the mother comes the birth of desire: for the speaking subject now begins a lifelong search for the lost object—the other, the little 'o' of the Imaginary, the mother he relinquished in order to acquire a social identity.

As the child enters the Symbolic it acquires language. However, it must also succumb to the 'law of the father' (the laws of society) which governs the Symbolic order. Entry into the Symbolic is entry into law, language, and loss—concepts which are inextricably bound together. Thus, entry into the Symbolic entails an awareness of sexual difference and of the 'self' as fragmented. The very concept of 'I' entails lack and loss.

When the boy mistakenly imagines his mother (sisters, woman) is castrated, his immediate response is to disavow what he has seen; he thinks she has been castrated, but he simultaneously knows that this is not true. Two courses of action are open to the boy. He can accept her difference and repress his desire for unification with the mother on the understanding that one day he will inherit a woman of his own. He can refuse to accept her difference and continue to believe that the mother is phallic. Rather than think of her lack, the fetishist will conjure up a reassuring image of another part of her body such as her breasts or her legs. He will also phallicize her body, imagining it in conjunction with phallic images such as long spiky high heels. Hence, film theorists have drawn on the theory of the phallic woman to explain the femme fatale of film noir (*Double Indemnity*, USA, 1944; *Body Heat*, USA, 1981; *The Last Seduction*, USA, 1994), who is depicted as dangerously phallic. E. Anne Kaplan's edited collection *Women in Film Noir* (1978) proved extremely influential in this context.

The Oedipal trajectory, Metz argued, is re-enacted in the cinema in relation not only to the Oedipal nature of narrative, but, most importantly, within the spectator–screen relationship. Narrative is characteristically Oedipal in that it almost always contains a male protagonist who, after resolving a crisis and overcoming a 'lack', then comes to identify with the law of the father, while successfully containing or controlling the female figure, demystifying her threat, or achieving union with her.

The concept of 'lack' is crucial to narrative in another context. According to the Russian Formalist Tzvetan Todorov, the aim of all narratives is to solve a riddle, to find an answer to an enigma, to fill a lack. All stories begin with a situation in which the status quo is upset and the hero or heroine must—in general terms—solve a problem in order for equilibrium to be restored. This approach sees the structures of narrative as being in the service of the subject's desire to overcome lack.

Furthermore, the processes of disavowal and fetishism which mark the Oedipal crisis are—according to Metz—also replayed in the cinema. In terms of disavowal, the spectator both believes in the existence of what was represented on the screen yet also knows

CRITICAL APPROACHES

that it does not actually exist. Conscious that the cinema only signifies what is absent, the (male) spectator is aware that his sense of identification with the image is only an illusion and that his sense of self is based on lack. Knowing full well that the original events, the profilmic diegetic drama, is missing, the spectator makes up for this absence by fetishizing his love of the cinema itself. Metz sees this structure of disavowal and fetishism as crucial to the cinema's representation of reality.

> **Apparatus theory emphasizes the way the cinema compensates for what the viewing subject lacks; the cinema offers an imaginary unity to smooth over the fragmentation at the heart of subjectivity. Narrative structures take up this process in the way they construct stories in which the 'lost object' (almost always represented by union with a woman) is recovered by the male protagonist.**

Thus, apparatus theory emphasizes the way the cinema compensates for what the viewing subject lacks; the cinema offers an imaginary unity to smooth over the fragmentation at the heart of subjectivity. Narrative structures take up this process in the way they construct stories in which the 'lost object' (almost always represented by union with a woman) is recovered by the male protagonist. In her 1985 essay 'Feminism, Film Theory and the Bachelor Machines', in which she critically assessed apparatus theory as theorized by Baudry and Metz, Constance Penley made the telling point that Metz's 'imaginary signifier' is itself a 'bachelor apparatus'—a compensatory structure designed for male pleasure.

As *The Imaginary Signifier* began to exert a profound influence on film studies in many American and British universities, problems emerged. Critics attacked on a number of fronts: they argued that apparatus theory was profoundly ahistorical; that, in its valorization of the image, it ignored the non-visual aspects of the viewing experience such as sound; and that the application of Lacanian psychoanalytic theory was not always accurate. The most sustained

criticism came from feminist critics, who argued correctly that apparatus theory completely ignored gender.

Psychoanalysis, feminism, and film: Mulvey

Psychoanalytic film theorists, particularly feminists, were interested in the construction of the viewer in relation to questions of gender and sexual desire. Apparatus theory did not address gender at all. In assuming that the spectator was male, Metz examined desire in the context of the male Oedipal trajectory.

In 1975 Laura Mulvey published a daring essay, 'Visual Pleasure and Narrative Cinema', which put female spectatorship on the agenda for all time. As Mulvey later admitted, the essay was deliberately and provocatively polemical. It established the psychoanalytic basis for a feminist theory of spectatorship which is still being debated. What Mulvey did was to redefine, in terms of gender, Metz's account of the cinema as an activity of disavowal and fetishization. Drawing on Freudian theories of scopophilia, castration, and fetishism, and Lacanian theories of the formation of subjectivity, Mulvey introduced gender into apparatus theory.

In her essay, Mulvey argued that in a world ordered by sexual imbalance the role of making things happen usually fell to the male protagonist, while the female star occupied a more passive position, functioning as an erotic object for the desiring look of the male. Woman signified image, a figure to be looked at, while man controlled the look. In other words, cinematic spectatorship is divided along gender lines. The cinema addressed itself to an ideal male spectator, and pleasure in looking was split in terms of an active male gaze and a passive female image.

> **Mulvey argued that in a world ordered by sexual imbalance the role of making things happen usually fell to the male protagonist, while the female star occupied a more passive position, functioning as an erotic object for the desiring look of the male. Woman signified image, a figure to be looked at, while man controlled the look.**

Marlene Dietrich (here admired by Cary Grant) as fetishised spectacle (*Blonde Venus*, 1932)

She argued that, although the form and figure of woman was displayed for the enjoyment of the male protagonist, and, by extension, the male spectator in the cinema, the female form was also threatening because it invoked man's unconscious anxieties about sexual difference and castration. Either the male protagonist could deal with this threat (as in the films of Hitchcock) by subjecting woman to his sadistic gaze and punishing her for being different or he could deny her difference (as in the films of Joseph von Sternberg and Marlene Dietrich) and fetishize her body by overvaluing a part of her body such as her legs or breasts. The narrative endings of films, which almost always punished the threatening woman, reinforced Mulvey's argument about the voyeuristic gaze, while the deployment of the close-up shot, which almost always fragmented parts of the female form for erotic contem-

plation, reinforced Mulvey's argument about the fetishistic look.

Whereas Freudian and Lacanian theory argued that the castration complex was a universal formation that explained the origins and perpetuation of patriarchy, Mulvey demonstrated in specific terms how the unconscious of patriarchal society organized its own signifying practices, such as film, to reinforce myths about women and to offer the male viewer pleasure. Within this system there is no place for woman. Her difference represents—to use what was fast becoming a notorious term—'lack'. However, Mulvey did not hold up this system as universal and unchangeable. If, in order to represent a new language of desire, the filmmaker found it necessary to destroy pleasure, then this was the price that must be paid.

What of the female spectator? In a second article,

'Afterthoughts on "Visual Pleasure and Narrative Cinema" Inspired by King Vidor's *Duel in the Sun* (1946)' (1981), Mulvey took up the issue of the female spectator. Since the classic Hollywood text is so dependent upon the male Oedipal trajectory and male fantasies about woman to generate pleasure, how does the female spectator experience visual pleasure? To answer this question, Mulvey drew on Freud's theory of the libido, in which he asserted that 'there is only one libido, which performs both the masculine and feminine functions' (1981: 13). Thus, when the heroine on the screen is strong, resourceful, and phallic, it is because she has reverted to the pre-Oedipal phase. According to Freud, in the lives of some women, 'there is a repeated alternation between periods in which femininity and masculinity gain the upper hand' (quoted in Mulvey 1971: 15). Mulvey concluded that the female spectator either identifies with woman as object of the narrative and (male) gaze or may adopt a 'masculine' position. But, the female spectator's 'phantasy of masculinisation is always to some extent at cross-purposes with itself, restless in its transvestite clothes' (in Mulvey 1981: 15).

It is this aspect of her work that became most controversial amongst critics, such as D. N. Rodowick (1982), who argued that her approach was too reductive and that her analysis of the female character on the screen and female spectator in the auditorium did not allow for the possibility of female desire outside a phallocentric context.

Developments in psychoanalysis, feminism, and film

Mulvey's use of psychoanalytic theory to examine the way in which the patriarchal unconscious influenced film form led to heated debates and a plethora of articles from post-structuralist feminists. Theorists such as Joan Copjec (1982), Jacqueline Rose (1980), and Constance Penley (1985) argued that apparatus theory, regardless of whether or not it took questions of gender into account, was part of a long tradition in Western thought whereby masculinity is positioned as the norm, thus denying the possibility of a place for woman. They argued that there was no space for the discussion of female spectatorship in apparatus-based theories of the cinema. Responses to Mulvey's theory of spectatorship followed four main lines: one approach was to examine the female Oedipal trajectory; another approach, known as fantasy theory, drew

on Freud's theory of the primal scene to explore the possibility of a fluid, mobile or bisexual gaze; a third concentrated on the representation of masculinity and masochism; and a fourth approach, based on Julia Kristeva's (1986) theory of the 'abject maternal figure' and on Freud's theory of castration, argued that the image of the terrifying, overpowering woman in the horror film and suspense thriller unsettles prior notions of woman as the passive object of a castrating male gaze.

The Oedipal heroine

Drawing on Freud's theory of the libido and the female Oedipal trajectory, feminists extended Mulvey's application of the theory to argue for a bisexual gaze. Perhaps the spectator did not identify in a monolithic, rigid manner with his or her gender counterpart, but actually alternated between masculine–active and feminine–passive positions, depending on the codes of identification at work in the film text.

In a reading of Hitchcock's *Rebecca* (USA, 1940), Tania Modleski (1982) argued that when the daughter goes through the Oedipus complex—although she gives up her original desire for her mother, whom she blames for not giving her a penis, and turns to the father as her love object—she never fully relinquishes her first love. Freud also argued that the girl child, unlike the boy, is predisposed towards bisexuality. The girl's love for the mother, although repressed, still exists. In *Rebecca* the unnamed heroine experiences great difficulty in moulding herself to appeal to the man's desire. When she most imagines she has achieved this aim, the narrative reveals that she is 'still attached to the "mother", still acting out the desire for the mother's approbation' (1982: 38). Recently, the notion of the female Oedipal trajectory has been invoked in a series of articles published in *Screen* (1995) on Jane Campion's *The Piano* (New Zealand, 1993), which suggests that these debates are still of great relevance to film theory.

Other work raised related issues. In *The Desire to Desire* (1987), Mary Ann Doane turned her attention to the 'woman's film' and the issue of female spectatorship. Janet Bergstrom, in 'Enunciation and Sexual Difference' (1979), questioned the premise that the spectator was male, while Annette Kuhn, in *The Power of the Image* (1985), explored cross-dressing, bisexuality, and the spectator in relation to the film *Some Like it Hot* (USA, 1959).

Fantasy theory and the mobile gaze

The concept of a more mobile gaze was explored by Elizabeth Cowie in her article 'Fantasia' (1984), in which she drew on Laplanche and Pontalis's influential essay of 1964, 'Fantasy and the Origins of Sexuality'. Laplanche and Pontalis established three original fantasies—original in that each fantasy explains an aspect of the 'origin' of the subject. The 'primal scene pictures the origin of the individual; fantasies of seduction, the origin and upsurge of sexuality; fantasies of castration, the origin of the difference between the sexes' (1964/1986: 19). These fantasies—entertained by the child—explain or provide answers to three crucial questions: 'Who am I?' 'Why do I desire?' 'Why am I different?' The concept of primal fantasies is also much more fluid than the notion of fantasy permitted by apparatus theory, which inevitably and mechanistically returns to the Oedipal fantasy. The primal fantasies run through the individual's waking and sleeping life, through conscious and unconscious desires. Laplanche and Pontalis also argued that fantasy is a staging of desire, a form of mise-en-scène. Further, the position of the subject is not static in that positions of sexual identification are not fixed. The subject engaged in the activity of fantasizing can adopt multiple positions, identifying across gender, time, and space.

Cowie argued that the importance of fantasy as a setting, a scene, is crucial because it enables film to be viewed as fantasy, as representing the mise-en-scène of desire. Similarly, the film spectator is free to assume mobile, shifting modes of identification—as Cowie demonstrated in her analysis of *Now Voyager* (USA, 1942) and *The Reckless Moment* (USA, 1949). Fantasy theory has also been used productively in relation to science fiction and horror—genres in which evidence of the fantastic is particularly strong.

Masculinity and masochism

Richard Dyer (1982) and Steve Neale (1983) both wrote articles in which they argued against Mulvey's assertion that the male body could not 'bear the burden of sexual objectification' (1975: 28). Both examined the conditions under which the eroticization of the male body is permitted and the conditions under which the female spectator is encouraged to look. Neale explored three main structures examined by Mulvey: identification, voyeurism, and fetishism. He concluded that, while the male body is eroticized and objectified, the viewer is denied a look of direct access. The male is objectified, but only in scenes of action such as boxing. Mainstream cinema cannot afford to acknowledge the possibility that the male spectator might take the male protagonist as an object of his erotic desire.

In her book *In The Realm of Pleasure* (1988), Gaylyn Studlar, however, offers a completely different interpretation of spectatorship and pleasure from the voyeuristic–sadistic model. In a revision of existing feminist psychoanalytic theories, she argues for a (male) masochistic aesthetic in film. Studlar's original study was extremely important as it was one of the first sustained attempts to break with Lacanian and Freudian theory. Instead, Studlar drew on the psychoanalytic-literary work of Gilles Deleuze, and the object-relations school of psychoanalytic theory.

Object-relations theory, derived from the work of Melanie Klein and, more recently, D. W. Winnicott, is a post-Freudian branch of psychoanalysis that places crucial importance on the relationship between the infant and its mother in the first year. Klein placed the mother at the centre of the Oedipal drama and argued for a primary phase in which both sexes identified with the feminine. She argued for womb-envy in boys as a counterpart to Freud's penis envy in girls. In particular, she explored destructive impulses the infant might experience in its relationship with the mother and other objects (parts of the body) in the environment. During this early formative phase, the father is virtually absent.

Focusing on the pre-Oedipal and the close relationship formed during the oral phase between the infant and the dominant maternal figure, Studlar demonstrates the relevance of her theory in relation to the films of Marlene Dietrich and Joseph von Sternberg. In these Dietrich plays a dominant woman, a beautiful, often cold tyrant, with whom men fall hopelessly and helplessly in love. Titles such as *The Devil is a Woman* (USA, 1935) indicate the kinds of pleasure on offer. Studlar argues that the masochistic aesthetic has so many structures in common with the Baudry–Metz concept of the cinematic apparatus, in its archaic dimension, that it cannot be ignored and constitutes a central form of cinematic pleasure which had been previously overlooked.

Kaja Silverman also developed a theory of male masochism in *Male Subjectivity at the Margins* (1992). Silverman's aim was to explore what she describes as 'deviant' masculinities, which she sees as representing 'perverse' alternatives to phallic masculinity. Drawing on Freudian and Lacanian theory, and concentrating on the films of Rainer Werner Fassbinder, she examined the misleading alignment of the penis with the phallus and the inadequate theorization of male subjectivity in film studies. Silverman explored a number of different forms of male masochism, from passive to active. Her analysis of 'male lack' is particularly powerful, and her book, in which she argued that the spectator can derive pleasure through passivity and submission, made an important contribution to growing debates around psychoanalytic interpretations of spectatorial pleasure.

The monstrous woman

Perhaps it was inevitable, given analyses of the masochistic male, that attention would turn towards the monstrous, castrating woman. Feminist theorists argued that the representation of woman in film does not necessarily position her as a passive object of the narrative or of viewing structures. Mary Russo's essay 'Female Grotesques' (1986), which drew on the Freudian notion of repression, was very influential. So, too, was the Kristevan notion of the abject as a structure which precedes the subject–object split. Drawing on psychoanalytic theories of woman—particularly the mother—as an abject monster, writers such as Modleski (1988), Lurie (1981–2), and Creed (1993) adopted a very different approach to the representation of woman in film, by arguing that woman could be represented as an active, terrifying fury, a powerfully abject figure, and a castrating monster. This was a far cry from Freud's image of woman as 'castrated other'.

Criticisms of psychoanalytic film theory

Psychoanalysis exerted a powerful influence on models of spectatorship theory that emerged during the 1970s and early 1980s. One of the dominant criticisms of the apparatus theory was that, in all of its forms, it invariably constructed a monolithic spectator. In the Baudry model the spectator is male and passive; in the Mulvey model the spectator is male and active. Psychoanalytic criticism was accused of becoming totalizing and repetitive. Film after film was seen as always representing the male character as in control of the gaze, and woman as its object. Or woman was invariably described as 'without a voice', or as standing outside the Symbolic order.

Rejecting the role of ideology in the formation of subjectivity, some critics were more interested in the actual details of how viewers responded to what they saw on the screen. Given that 1970s theory developed partly in reaction to this kind of empiricism, it is significant that, in recent years, there has been a renewal of interest in the area. This is evident in the work of David Bordwell and Noel Carroll, whose edited volume *Post-Theory* (1996) sets out to challenge the dominance of 1970s theory and to provide alternative approaches to spectatorship based on the use of cognitive psychology. Their interest is the role played by knowledge and viewing practices in relation to spectatorship. According to Carroll, 'Cognitivism is not a unified theory. Its name derives from its tendency to look for alternative answers to many of the questions addressed by or raised by psychoanalytic film theories, especially with respect to film reception, in terms of cognitive and rational processes rather than irrational or unconscious ones' (1996: 62). Judith Mayne argues that, while cognitivists have formulated a number of important criticisms of psychoanalytic film theory, 'the "spectator" envisaged by cognitivism is entirely different from the one conceptualized by 1970s film theory' (1993: 7). The latter addressed itself to the 'ideal spectator' of the cinematic process, while cognitivism speaks to the 'real viewer', the individual in the cinema. Mayne argues that all too often cognitivists, such as Bordwell, ignore the 'attempts that have been made to separate the subject and the viewer' (1993: 56) and recommends the writings of Teresa de Lauretis in *Alice Doesn't* (1984) as 'illustrating that the appeal to perception studies and cognitivism is not necessarily in radical contradistinction from the theories of the apparatus (as in the case with Bordwell and others), but can be instead a revision of them' (1993: 57).

Second, psychoanalytic theory was charged with ahistoricality. As early as 1975 Claire Johnston warned that 'there is a real danger that psychoanalysis can be used to blur any serious engagement with political–cultural issues'. The grand narratives of psychoanalysis, such as the Oedipus complex and castration anxiety, dominated critical activity in the 1970s and early 1980s, running the real danger of sacrificing historical issues in favour of those related to the formation of subjectivity and its relation to ideology. These critics proposed the importance, not of the grand narratives of subjectivity, but of 'micro-narratives' of social change such as those moments when cultural conflict might reveal weaknesses in the dominant culture. They argued that film should be studied more in its relationship to history and society than to the unconscious and subjectivity.

Third, some attacked the centrality of spectatorship theory and its apparently exclusive interest in the ideal spectator rather than the actual viewer. Spectatorship theory did not take into account other factors such as class, colour, race, age, or sexual preference. Nor did it consider the possibility that some viewers might be more resistant to the film's ideological workings than others. Political activists argued that psychoanalytic criticism did not provide any guide-lines on how the individual might resist the workings of an ideology that appeared to dictate completely the formation of subjectivity as split and fractured. Furthermore, they argued, not all individuals are locked into roles determined by the way subjectivity is formed.

Cultural studies has developed partly in response to these problems. It sees culture as a site of struggle. It places emphasis, not on unconscious processes, but on the history of the spectator (as shaped by class, colour, ethnicity, and so on) as well as on examining ways in which the viewer might struggle against the dominant ideology. Whereas the cognitivists have clearly rejected psychoanalysis, the latter's status within cultural studies is not so clear as cultural critics frequently utilize areas of psychoanalytic theory.

Fourth, empirical researchers argue that the major problem with psychoanalysis is that it is not a science, that psychoanalytic theories are not based on reliable data which can be scientifically measured, and that other researchers do not have access to the information pertaining to the case-studies on which the theories have been formulated.

Psychoanalytic theories reply that by its very nature theoretical abstraction cannot be verified by 'proof'. Furthermore, the entire thrust of 1970s psychoanalytic film theory was based on the fact that there is no clear or straightforward relation between the conscious and the unconscious, that what is manifested on the surface may bear no direct relation to what lies beneath, that there is no cause-and-effect relation, which manifests itself in appearance, between what the subject desires to achieve and what takes place in reality. Only via psychoanalytic readings can one explore such things as displacement, disguise, and transformation.

The entire thrust of 1970s psychoanalytic film theory was based on the fact that there is no clear or straightforward relation between the conscious and the unconscious, that what is manifested on the surface may bear no direct relation to what lies beneath, that there is no cause-and-effect relation, which manifests itself in appearance, between what the subject desires to achieve and what takes place in reality. Only via psychoanalytic readings can one explore such things as displacement, disguise, and transformation.

Recent developments

Although psychoanalytic film theory has been subject to many forms of criticism over the past twenty years, it continues to expand both within and outside the academy. This is evident, not only in the work of cultural theorists such as Stuart Hall, but also in the relatively new areas of post-colonialism and queer theory, and in writings on the body. Scholars working in these areas do not use psychoanalytic theory in the totalizing way in which it was invoked in the 1970s. Rather, they draw on aspects of psychoanalytic theory to illuminate areas of their own special study. The aim in doing so is often to bring together the social and the psychic.

Post-colonial theorists such as Homi K. Bhabha and Rey Chow have drawn on psychoanalytic theories in their work. Whereas earlier writers on racism in the cinema tended to concentrate on questions of stereotyping, narrative credibility, and positive images, the focus of post-colonial theorists is on the process of subjectification, the representation of 'otherness', spectatorship, and the deployment of cinematic codes. In short, the shift is away from a study of 'flawed' or 'negative' images ('positive' images can be as demeaning as negative ones) to an understanding of the filmic construction of the relationship between colonizer and colonized, the flow of power between the two, the part played by gender differences and the positioning of the spectator in relation to such representations. In order to facilitate such analyses, theorists frequently draw on aspects of psychoanalytic theory.

In 'The Other Question', Homi K. Bhabha uses Freud's theory of castration and fetishism to analyse the stereotypes of black and white which are crucial to the colonial discourse. He argues that the fetishized stereotype in film and other cultural practices works to reactivate in the colonial subject the imaginary fantasy of 'an ideal ego that is white and whole' (1992: 322). Drawing on these concepts, he presents a new interpretation of Orson Welles's *A Touch of Evil* (USA, 1958). In his writings on the nation, Bhabha draws on Freud's 1919 essay 'The Uncanny', in which Freud refers to the 'cultural' unconscious as a state in which archaic forms find expression in the margins of modernity. Bhabha also uses Freud's theory of doubling, as elaborated in 'The Uncanny', to examine the way in which colonial cultures have been coerced by their colonizers to mimic 'white' culture—but only up to a point. Difference—and hence oppression—must always be maintained. Throughout his writings, Bhabha uses many of Freud's key theories, reinterpreting them in order to theorize the colonial discourse.

This approach has been adopted by other critics. In *Romance and the 'Yellow Peril'* (1993), Gina Marchetti focuses on Hollywood films about Asians and interracial sexuality. Adopting a position informed by postcolonial theory, Marchetti draws on psychoanalytic theories of spectatorship and feminine masquerade, refiguring these concepts for her own work on race.

In a similar vein, film critics, drawing on queer reading strategies, have carefully selected aspects of psychoanalytic theory to analyse film texts 'against the grain'. As in post-colonial theory, queer theory represents a methodological shift. It, too, rejects an earlier critical emphasis on praising 'positive' and decrying 'negative' images of homosexual men and lesbians in film. Instead, queer theory sees sexual practices—whether heterosexual, homosexual, bisexual, autosexual, transsexual—as fluid, diverse, and heterogeneous. For instance, the practices of masochism, sadism, or coprophilia may be adopted by homosexual and heterosexual alike: the belief that only heterosexual relationships (or any other type of relationship, for that matter) are somehow 'normal' is patently incorrect.

As a critical practice, queer theory seeks to analyse film texts in order to determine the way in which desire, in its many diverse forms, is constructed, and how cinematic pleasures are instituted and offered to the spectator. Previously reviled films such as *The Killing of*

Sister George (GB, 1968), have been re-examined, and the history of the representation of gays and lesbians in film is being rewritten. In some films the homosexual and/or lesbian subtext, previously ignored, has been reinscribed.

Judith Butler's *Gender Trouble* (1990), which presents a queer critique of the psychoanalytic concept of fixed gender identities, has exerted a strong influence on film theorists seeking to analyse the representation of gays and lesbians in film. Wary of the 1970s approach to psychoanalytic theory, because it largely ignored the question of the gay and lesbian spectatorship, film theorists have turned to the work of writers such as Butler, Diane Fuss, Teresa de Lauretis, and Lee Edelman (see Smelik and Doty, Part 1, Chapters 14 and 15).

A number of essays in *How do I Look? Queer Film and Video* (Bad Object-Choices 1991) discuss the fact that psychoanalytic approaches to the cinema have avoided discussions of lesbian sexual desire. In her article 'Lesbian Looks' Judith Mayne criticizes the way in which feminist film theory has employed psychoanalysis while also drawing on, and reinterpreting, aspects of psychoanalytic theory in her own analysis. Valerie Traub's article 'The Ambiguities of "Lesbian" Viewing Pleasure' (1991), on lesbian spectatorship and the film *Black Widow* (USA, 1987), provides a good example of a queer reading.

Another area in which film theorists have drawn on a rereading of psychoanalytic theory is that of the body. Contemporary interpretations of the horror film have generally favoured a psychoanalytic reading with emphasis on the workings of repression. Since the mid-1980s writers have paid particular attention to the representation of the body in horror—the grotesque body of the monster. Based on psychoanalytic theories of abjection, hysteria, castration, and the uncanny, such an approach sees the monstrous body as intended partly to horrify the spectator and partly to make meaning at a more general level, pointing to the abject state of the social, political, and familial body.

Other approaches to the body take up the issue of the actual body as well as the cinematic body. Steven Shaviro's *The Cinematic Body* (1993) presents a thorough attack on apparatus theory, arguing instead for 'an active and affirmative reading of the masochism of cinematic experience' (1993: 60). Drawing on the early work of Gilles Deleuze, he suggests that what 'inspires the cinematic spectator is a passion for that very loss of control, that abjection, fragmentation and subversion of self-identity that psychoanalytic theory so dubiously classifies under the rubrics of lack and castration' (1993: 57). Shaviro is highly critical of what he sees as the conventional use of psychoanalysis to construct a distance between spectator and image; he wants to use psychoanalysis to affirm and celebrate the power of the image, and of the visceral, to move and affect the viewer.

I have referred briefly to aspects of post-colonial, queer, and body theory to demonstrate that film theory, in its current use of psychoanalysis, has become more selective and nuanced. While no one would suggest a return to the totalizing approach of the 1970s, it would be misleading to argue that application of psychoanalysis to the cinema is a thing of the past. If anything, the interest in psychoanalytic film theory is as strong as ever. And the debates continue.

BIBLIOGRAPHY

Bad Object-Choices (ed.) (1991), How do I Look? Queer Film and Video (Seattle: Bay Press).

*Baudry, Jean-Louis (1970/1986a), 'Ideological Effects of the Basic Cinematographic Apparatus', in P. Rosen (ed.), Narrative, Apparatus, Ideology (New York: Columbia University Press).

—— (1975/1986b), 'The Apparatus: Metaphysical Approaches to Ideology', in P. Rosen (ed.), Narrative, Apparatus, Ideology, (New York: Columbia University Press).

Benderson, Albert (1979), 'An Archetypal Reading of Juliet of the Spirits', Quarterly Review of Film Studies, 4/2: 193–206.

Bergstrom, Janet (1979), 'Enunciation and Sexual Difference', Camera Obscura, 3–4: 33–70.

Bhabha, Homi K. (1992), 'The Other Question: The Stereotype and the Colonial Discourse', in The Sexual Subject: A Screen Reader In Sexuality (London: Routledge).

Bordwell, David, and Noel Caroll (eds.) (1996), Post-Theory: Reconstructing Film Studies (Wisconsin: University of Wisconsin Press).

Branson, Clark (1987), Howard Hawks: A Jungian Study (Santa Barbara, Calif.: Capra Press).

Brown, Royal S. (1980), 'Hitchcock's Spellbound: Jung versus Freud', Film/Psychology Review, 4/1: 35–58.

Butler, Judith (1990), Gender Trouble: Feminism and the Subversion of Identity (New York: Routledge).

Copjec, Joan (1982), 'The Anxiety of the Influencing Machine', October, 23.

Cowie, Elizabeth (1984), 'Fantasia', m/f, 9: 71–105.

Creed, Barbara (1993), The Monstrous-Feminine: Film, Feminism and Psychoanalysis (New York: Routledge).

de Lauretis, Teresa (1984), Alice Doesn't: Feminism, Semiotics, Cinema (Bloomington: Indiana University Press).

Doane, Mary Ann (1987), The Desire to Desire: The Woman's Film of the 1940s (Bloomington: Indiana University Press).

Donald, James (ed.) (1990), Psychoanalysis and Cultural Theory: Thresholds (London: Macmillan).

Dyer, Richard (1982), 'Don't Look Now: The Male Pin-Up', Screen, 23/3–4: 61–73.

Foster, Hal (1993), Compulsive Beauty (London: MIT Press).

Fredericksen, Don (1980), 'Jung/Sign/Symbol/Film', Quarterly Review of Film Studies, 5/4: 459–79.

Freud, Sigmund (1919/1953–66), 'The Uncanny', in The Standard Edition of the Complete Psychological Works of Sigmund Freud, 24 vols., trans. James Strachey (London: Hogarth), xxi.

Izod, John (1992), The Films of Nicholas Roeg: Myth and Mind (London: St Martin's Press).

Johnston, C. (1975), 'Femininity and Masquerade: Anne of the Indies', in Claire Johnston and Paul Willemen (eds.), Jacques Tourneur (Edinburgh: Edinburgh Film Festival).

Kaplan, E. Ann (ed.) (1978), Women in Film Noir (London: British Film Institute).

*—— (ed.) (1990), Psychoanalysis and the Cinema (New York: Routledge).

Kristeva, Julia (1986), Powers of Horror: An Essay in Abjection, trans. Leon S. Roudiez (New York: Columbia University Press).

Kuhn, Annette (1985), The Power of the Image: Essays on Representation and Sexuality (London: Routledge & Kegan Paul).

Laplanche, J., and J.-B. Pontalis (1964/1986), 'Fantasy and the Origins of Sexuality', in Victor Burgin, James Donald, and Cora Kaplan (eds.), Formations of Fantasy (London: Methuen).

Lebeau, Vicky (1995), Lost Angels: Psychoanalysis and the Cinema (New York: Routledge).

Lurie, Susan (1981–2), 'The Construction of the "Castrated Woman" in Psychoanalysis and Cinema', Discourse, 4: 52–74.

Marchetti, Gina (1993), Romance and the 'Yellow Peril': Race, Sex and Discursive Strategies in Hollywood Fiction (Berkeley and Los Angeles: University of California Press).

Mayne, Judith (1991), 'Lesbian Looks: Dorothy Arzner and Female Authorship', in Bad Object-Choices (1991).

—— (1993), Cinema and Spectatorship (London: Routledge).

*Metz, Christian (1975/1982), Psychoanalysis and Cinema: The Imaginary Signifier (London: Macmillan).

Modleski, Tania (1982), 'Never to be Thirty-Six Years Old', Wide Angle, 5/1: 34–41.

CRITICAL APPROACHES

Modelski, Tania (1988), *The Women who Knew too Much: Hitchcock and Feminist Theory* (New York: Methuen).

*****Mulvey, Laura** (1975), 'Visual Pleasure and Narrative Cinema', *Screen*, 16/3: 6–18.

—— (1981), 'Afterthoughts on "Visual Pleasure and Narrative Cinema" inspired by *Duel in the Sun*', *Framework*, 15–17: 12–15.

Neale, Steve (1983), 'Masculinity as Spectacle', *Screen*, 24/6: 2–16.

Penley, Constance (1985), 'Feminism, Film Theory and the Bachelor Machines', *m/f*, 10: 39–59.

Rank, Otto (1925/1971), *The Double: A Psychoanalytic Study* (Chapel Hill: University of North Carolina Press).

Rodowick, D. N. (1982), 'The Difficulty of Difference', *Wide Angle*, 5/1: 4–15.

—— (1988), *The Crisis of Political Modernism: Criticism and Ideology on Contemporary Film Theory* (Berkeley: University of California Press).

Rose, Jacqueline (1980), 'The Cinematic Apparatus: Problems in Current Theory', in Teresa de Lauretis and Stephen Heath (eds.), *The Cinematic Apparatus* (New York: St Martin's Press).

Russo, Mary (1986), 'Female Grotesques: Carnival and Theory', in Teresa de Lauretis (ed.), *Feminist Studies/ Critical Studies* (Bloomington: Indiana University Press).

Screen (1995), 36/3: 257–87. Articles on *The Piano*.

Shaviro, Steven (1993), *The Cinematic Body* (Minneapolis: University of Minnesota Press).

Silverman, Kaja (1981), 'Masochism and Subjectivity', *Framework*, 12: 2–9.

—— (1992), *Male Subjectivity at the Margins* (New York: Routledge).

Sobchack, Vivian (1992), *The Address of the Eye: A Phenomenology of Film Experience* (Princeton: Princeton University Press).

Studlar, Gaylyn (1988), *In the Realm of Pleasure: Von Sternberg, Dietrich, and the Masochistic Aesthetic* (Urbana: University of Illinois Press).

Tarratt, Margaret (1970), 'Monsters from the Id', part 1, *Films and Filming* (Nov.–Dec.), 38–42.

—— (1971), 'Monsters from the Id', part 2, *Films and Filming* (Jan.–Feb), 40–2.

Traub, Valerie (1991), 'The Ambiguities of "Lesbian" Viewing Pleasure: The (Dis)articulations of *Black Widow*', in Julia Epstein and Kristina Straub (eds.), *BodyGuards: The Cultural Politics of Gender Ambiguity* (New York: Routledge).

Williams, Linda (ed.) (1995), *Viewing Positions: Ways of Seeing Film* (New Brunswick, NJ: Rutgers University Press).

10

Post-structuralism and deconstruction

Peter Brunette

Post-structuralism is a rather vague generic name for a host of disparate theoretical developments that have followed in the wake of structuralism and semiotics. The term has been applied occasionally to the work of Michel Foucault and the later Roland Barthes, but most especially to the challenging and innovative revision of Freud propounded by the French psychoanalyst Jacques Lacan, and to the work of Jacques Derrida, a kind of 'anti-philosophy' that has come to be known as deconstruction. Since the Guide contains a separate article (by Barbara Creed, Part 1, Chapter 9) detailing the crucial influence of Lacanian psychoanalysis on film studies, this chapter will concentrate on the application of Derridean thought to the cinema.

> **Deconstruction is not a discipline or, even less, a methodology, but rather a questioning stance taken towards the most basic aspects of the production of knowledge. Like Lacanian psychoanalysis, it tends to concentrate on the slippages in meaning, the gaps and inconsistencies, that inevitably mark all understanding.**

If the mission and focus of film studies is seen as the formal and thematic interpretation of individual films, deconstruction has little to offer. Deconstruction is not a discipline or, even less, a methodology, but rather a questioning stance taken towards the most basic aspects of the production of knowledge. Like Lacanian psychoanalysis, it tends to concentrate on the slippages in meaning, the gaps and inconsistencies, that inevitably mark all understanding. As such, deconstruction has been seen by its critics as part of the 'hermeneutics of suspicion' that has developed out of the anti-foundationalist investigations of Freud and Nietzsche.

The specific application of deconstruction to film has been far less evident than that of Lacanian psychoanalysis, but Derrida's influence on such thinkers as (to name but two) Judith Butler, a gender theorist, and Homi Bhabha, a specialist in post-colonial studies, has been profound. These theorists have in turn had a tremendous impact on recent writing on film, and thus, in this sense, it is probably correct to say that the application of Derridean thought to film has been important but largely indirect. A further complication is that some on the left have denounced deconstruction because it tends to call *all* thinking into question, even that which presents itself as progressive and liberatory. In fact, Derrida's writings can be seen as thoroughly political in nature when they are properly understood as a critique of the outmoded 'logocentric' thinking that has led to numerous political impasses now and in the past.

Nevertheless, several key deconstructive notions have been applied directly to film by a number of theorists in France and elsewhere. For example, a deconstructive perspective can challenge the historiographical assumptions that allow us conveniently to divide film history into specific, self-identical movements such as German Expressionism, Italian Neo-Realism, and so on. The notion of film genre as well is vulnerable to a deconstructive analysis, as is auteurism, and authorial intentionality, already much challenged anyway (see Crofts, Part 2, Chapter 7). Most importantly, perhaps, deconstruction challenges the very basis of interpretation itself, revealing the institutional and contextual constraints that necessarily accompany all attempts at reading.

Deconstruction can be approached from any number of different directions, but perhaps it can be most easily seen as a radicalization of the basic insights, developed around the turn of the century, of Swiss linguist Ferdinand de Saussure. Saussure, considered the father of structuralism and semiotics, argued that there are 'no positive terms' in language; in other words, that meanings do not stem from something inherent in the words and sounds themselves, but rather from their *difference* from other words and sounds. Thus, all alone, the sound 'p' could never be functional, nor could the word 'truth' carry any meaning, but only in so far as they differed from 't' or 'r' or 's' on the one hand, or 'error', say, on the other. If this is the case, it becomes clear that 'error' is, in some strange way that defies traditional Western logic (which, Derrida claims, is based upon a 'metaphysics of presence'), part and parcel of the meaning of its supposed opposite, truth. Paradoxically, in other words, truth cannot be thought, and thus cannot even exist, without error. Error is thus both there and not there 'within' truth, both present and absent, thus casting doubt upon the principle of non-contradiction (the very basis of Western logic), that a thing cannot be A and not-A at the same time.

It can easily be seen that Western thought has, since the beginning, relied upon a set of self-identical concepts that align themselves as binary oppositions, such as truth–error, good–evil, spirit–body, nature–culture, man–woman, and so on. In each case, one term is favoured or seen as primary or original; the second term is regarded as a (later) perversion of the first, or in some way inferior to it. The principal work of decon-

struction has been to reverse and—since a mere reversal would not disturb the underlying binary logic—to displace these ostensible oppositions as well.

Since deconstruction builds upon the insights and terminology of semiotics, one of the first binary oppositions that is called into question is that founding distinction between signifier and signified. From a poststructuralist perspective, it is easy to see the latter as a transcendent, almost spiritual entity that is privileged over the 'merely' material signifier, which is usually seen as a dispensable container with no effect on the contained. Derridean thought tends rather to focus on the 'free play' between signifier and signified that constitutes all meaning, and to show that the marks of the material signifier never really disappear in the face of the signified.

> **Derridean thought tends rather to focus on the 'free play' between signifier and signified that constitutes all meaning, and to show that the marks of the material signifier never really disappear in the face of the signified.**

Furthermore, deconstruction, like Lacanian psychoanalysis, points out that meaning effects occur as a result of the sliding within chains of signifiers, rather than because a signifier leads inevitably to a signified. After all, when one looks up a word in the dictionary, what is found is not a fixed signified, but rather more signifiers, which must be looked up in turn. Despite this similarity in viewpoint, Derrida has criticized Lacan for the impermissible originary grounding that he seems to offer in his founding triad of the Imaginary, the Symbolic, and the Real. (For deconstructionists, there can be no fixed ground or origin, since such concepts, once again, are symptoms of the metaphysics of presence.) For the same reason, deconstructive theorists have also tended to agree with the feminist critique of Lacanian film theory concerning its privileging of the phallus as the primary signifier from which all meaning arises.

In his early work, especially in *Of Grammatology* (1967), Derrida concentrates on deconstructing the symptomatic binary opposition that privileges, throughout the history of Western philosophy, speech over writing. In this book, Derrida shows that as far back as Plato and as recently as Saussure and Claude Lévi-Strauss, speech has been associated with the living breath and the speaker's 'true' meaning, guaranteed by her presence, whereas writing has been seen as dead, misleading, always the sign of an absence. This is largely the result of the curious biological fact that when we speak (and listen), meaning seems to be an unproblematic, 'natural' event with no intermediary. Signifier and signified merge effortlessly, whereas in writing their relationshiop is always more problematic. Naïvely we seem to feel that if we could only have a writer speaking to us in person, in other words, *present*, we would know exactly what she meant. Derrida shows in this book that the supposed immediacy and direct-ness of speech is a fiction, and that all the negative features associated with writing are characteristic of speech as well. In a familiar move, he reverses the hierarchy, putting writing before speech, and then displaces the hierarchy altogether by rewriting the term 'writing', as 'Writing', with an expanded, purposely contradictory meaning that encompasses both writing (in the conventional sense) and speech. As such, the term joins a host of other key terms that Derrida has developed over the last thirty years, including trace, hinge, hymen, supplement, and *différance* (he purposely misspells this French word to highlight its difference from itself, a difference that is reflected in writing but not in speech)—terms which attempt to name an impossible 'space', to express presence and absence simultaneously, without, however, becoming a new ground. In a (to some extent quixotic) attempt to circumvent the metaphysics of presence, Derrida declares that these terms are neither 'words nor concepts'.

This newly expanded sense of Writing can be easily applied to film, since, after all, the word *cinematography* clearly points to its 'written' nature. Like written words, whose meanings, according to Derrida, are always 'disseminated' in multiple directions rather than being strictly linear, the image can never be constrained to a single set of meanings. In fact, meanings that are located/constructed will inevitably be contradictory. Nor can authorial intentionality, already notoriously weak in film, be said to anchor meaning, for intention will always be divided, never a unity. In fact, film itself is fundamentally split between a visual track and an audio track, which actually occupy different physical locations on the strip of celluloid, but which are artificially brought together to achieve an effect of wholeness and presence. In all these senses, it can be

said that the image is thus fundamentally 'incoherent', since any attempt to make it cohere will always necessitate a more or less violent epistemological effort of repression of 'secondary' meanings.

Thinking of film as a kind of writing also complements the anti-realist bias of recent film theory, for it works against the idea that film can ever be a 'copy' of its referent. André Bazin and other realist theorists insisted upon the intrinsic relationship or similarity between reality and its filmic representation, but from a deconstructive perspective, once it is admitted that reality and its representation must always be *different* from each other (as well as similar), then difference has just as much a claim as similarity to being the 'essential' relation between the two.

More generally, deconstructive thinking can lead us away from a conventional idea of cinema, and its relation to reality, as an *analogical* one based on similarity, to an idea of cinema, as Brunette and Wills (1989: 88) have put it, as 'an *anagram* of the real', a place of writing filled with non-natural conventions that allow us to understand it as a representation of reality.

Broadly speaking, cinema itself is, as a medium, clearly produced through negation, contradiction, and absence. It depends for its effect on the absence of what it represents, which is also paradoxically present at the same time in the form of a 'trace' (which in the original French also means 'footprint', thus carrying the simultaneous sense of absence and presence). Similarly, the photographic process is based on a negation which is reversed in a positive print. And through the application of the (now partially discredited) notion of the persistence of vision, we can understand that we literally could not even see the cinematic image unless it were, through the operation of the shutter, just as often *not* there. (One film theorist has pointed out that the screen is completely dark about half the time we are watching a film.) The screen itself, as a material of support of the image, must also be there and not there at the same time, for if we can actually see it, we can see nothing else.

Deconstruction also calls into question the 'natural' relation between original and copy (for example, we never speak of an 'original' of a document, unless there is also a 'copy' in question; thus, in a sense, the copy can be said to create the original), and this has a profound effect on a mimetic or imitative theory of artistic representation. It is clear, for example, that a documentary, though it ostensibly 'copies' the reality it focuses upon, also helps to individuate that aspect of reality, to bring it specifically to our attention, and thus to 'create' it.

This is closely related to another idea that Derrida has explored at great length, the notion of iterability (repeatability). Here, he has pointed out that each repetition of the 'same' must, by definition, also be different (otherwise, it could not be individuated). Similarly, each time something is quoted, it has a different meaning depending on its context, something that Derrida has shown is never fully specifiable. Here the idea of the 'graft', which is closely related to Roland Barthes's notion of intertextuality, is also important. All texts are seen as being made up of innumerable grafts of other texts in ways that are never ultimately traceable. For example, when we see an actor in a film, our response is inevitably conditioned by his or her appearances in other films; yet in a conventional, logocentric form of criticism such meanings would not be considered part of the film, properly speaking, and thus 'improper'.

This leads to another crucial binary distinction that deconstruction challenges, that between the inside and the outside. During the heyday of formalist literary analysis, Marxist and Freudian critics were chastised for 'importing' discourses that were seen as 'extrinsic' into a poem or novel. In regard to film, we might ask, for example, whether the opening or closing credits are 'in' the film, thus a part of it, or 'outside' the film proper, external to it. (Is a book's preface—usually written last—part of the book proper or not?) Similarly, one wonders whether Alfred Hitchcock's famous cameo appearances in his films mean that he is a character in them. Our inability to answer these questions points precisely to a problem in the logic of inside–outside binary thinking itself.

The larger question here, one that is explored at great length in Derrida's book *The Truth in Painting* (1978), is the question of the *frame*. In Derrida's famous formulation in that book, 'there is framing, but the frame does not exist' (1978/1987 81; translation modified). This means that the location of the frame (both a physical frame, say, of a painting, or an interpretive frame or context, or any sort of boundary marker) can never be precisely determined, though its effects can be seen. In film, the cut is similarly a function with clear effects, but no physical existence. Because it is a kind of relational absence rather than an explicitly present entity, it too serves to call into question the metaphysics of presence. With this ambiguity in mind, some deconstructive film theorists have suggested that, in

fact, it makes as much sense to base a film aesthetics on the cut (absence) as on the individual image (presence).

In any case, this idea of the frame is obviously paramount in film as well, and, though focused in a somewhat different manner, just as ambiguous. What is curious about this word in its cinematic usage is that it means two opposite things at the same time (and thus can be added to Derrida's list of key words): it is both the 'outside' boundary (one speaks of the 'frameline'), and the entire *inside* of the image as well (Godard said that cinema is 'truth twenty-four frames per second'). More widely, the film frame can also be seen as that set of understandings of genre, or of the so-called 'real world', or of cinematic conventions, and so on, that we bring to a film—in other words, that *context*, ever changeable, that both allows and constrains meaning.

This frame, this image that is framed, can, furthermore, be seen both as heterogenous (think of how many discrete elements within it must be repressed in order to 'interpret' it) and graphic (again, in the sense that it is *written*), as well as pictorial. Much of Derrida's later work has been involved with exploring the pictorial nature of writing (in the conventional sense) and, conversely, the graphic nature of the image, and these investigations are directly applicable to a study of how meaning is created in film. (See especially *The Truth in Painting* and Ulmer 1985, 1989).

The most important work done thus far in relating Derrida and film has been that undertaken by the French theoretician Marie-Claire Ropars-Wuilleumier, notably in her book *Le Texte divisé* (1981). There, *inter alia*, she brilliantly compares Derrida's discussion of the hybrid form of the hieroglyph (which is made up of phonetic, that is, graphic marks that represent speech, as well as pictorial elements) with Eisenstein's development of montage theory. In both, meaning is seen as a complicated operation that comes about partially through representation, but also through the very disruption of the image itself in the form of juxtaposition. (For a provocative application of Derrida to television, see Dienst 1994.)

Perhaps the most far-reaching consequence of a deconstructive perspective on film concerns the act of interpretation. Ultimately, deconstruction shows that it is, strictly speaking, impossible to specify what a 'valid' interpretation would look like. (See Conley 1991 for the most adventurous application of this principle to the interpretation of individual films.) In this sense, it might be said that deconstruction's most important work has been the investigation of the institutions that both allow and restrict reading, or meaning-making of any sort. It is important to note, however, that Derrida himself is no propounder of an 'anything goes' theory of reading, despite the impression given by his detractors and some of his more enthusiastic followers. Instead, he has always insisted upon the double nature of his work: to push beyond the bounds of conventional logic, all the while remaining rigorously logical.

> It might be said that deconstruction's most important work has been the investigation of the institutions that both allow and restrict reading, or meaning-making of any sort.

As film studies evolves more fully into cultural studies, deconstruction will provide a corrective by revealing the ultimately metaphoric nature of much of the terminology that surrounds the relating of cultural artefacts to an economic or social 'base'. As such, its influence will continue to be powerful, if subterranean.

BIBLIOGRAPHY

*Brunette, Peter, and David Wills (1989), Screen/Play: Derrida and Film Theory (Princeton: Princeton University Press).

Conley, Tom (1991), Film Hieroglyphs: Ruptures in Classical Cinema (Minneapolis: University of Minnesota Press).

Derrida, Jacques (1967/1976), Of Grammatology, trans. Gayatri Spivak (Baltimore: Johns Hopkins University Press).

—— (1978/1987), The Truth in Painting, trans. Geoff Bennington and Ian McLeod (Chicago: University of Chicago Press).

Dienst, Richard (1994), Still Life in Real Time: Theory after Television (Durham, NC: Duke University Press).

Ropars-Wuilleumier, Marie-Claire (1981), Le Texte divisé (Paris: Presses Universitaires de France).

Ulmer, Gregory (1985), Applied Grammatology (Baltimore: Johns Hopkins University Press).

—— (1989), Teletheory: Grammatology in the Age of Video (London: Routledge).

11

Film and postmodernism

John Hill

The concept of 'postmodernism' is a notoriously problematic one, given the diverse ways (in both academia and popular discourse) in which it has been used. The term itself has been applied to an almost bewilderingly wide range of economic, social, and cultural phenomena, with the result that many commentators on postmodernism are not necessarily referring to, or focusing upon, the same things. Moreover, the epithet 'postmodern' is used not only to identify particular socio-cultural and aesthetic features of contemporary life, but also to designate new forms of theorization which are held to be appropriate to making sense of the new 'postmodern' condition. So, while postmodern theory and the analysis of postmodernism may go hand in hand, it is not necessary that they do so. Fredric Jameson, for example, is one of the most influential analysts of postmodernism; but he himself is not a postmodern theorist, given his commitment to conventional forms of social analysis and explanation (especially Marxism).

It is also fair to say that in relation to film, postmodernism has not led to a theoretical approach or body of critical writings in the way that other theoretical perspectives, such as psychoanalysis of feminism, may be seen to have. This is because it is in the character of postmodernism to be suspicious of unified theoretical frameworks and, if postmodern ideas have had an influence on film study, it has often been through unsettling the knowledge claims or ontological assumptions of earlier theory (as in the theory of 'the subject' which has underpinned much psychoanalytic and feminist film theory). Moreover, the interest in postmodernism as an object of study has often been directed towards cultural shifts which go beyond a narrow attention to film, and if film has commonly been linked with the experience of modernity, then it is generally television, rather than film, which is seen to embody the postmodern.

In order to locate some of the ways in which ideas about the postmodern have influenced the study of film, it is therefore helpful to distinguish three main strands of thinking about postmodernism. Hence, the term can be seen to have been used in philosophical debates concerned with the scope and groundings of knowledge; in socio-cultural debates concerned to assess the significance of economic and social shifts in contemporary life; and in aesthetic debates concerned with the changing character of artistic practices in the wake of the 'decline' of modernism. These three sets of debates are not, of course, unconnected, but they are sufficiently distinct to make it useful to consider them separately.

Philosophical debates

In philosophy, debates about postmodernism may be seen to demonstrate a growing suspicion towards 'universal' or all-embracing systems of thought and explanation. An influential source, in this respect, has been Jean-François Lyotard's *The Postmodern Condition* (1979). For Lyotard 'the postmodern condition' may be defined in terms of a growing 'incredulity' towards what he calls 'les grands récits' or 'metanarratives' of Western thought (1979/1984, p. xxiv). In this respect, the 'modern' which the 'postmodern' is seen to be superseding is not the artistic modernism of the late nineteenth and early twentieth century but the 'modern' system of thought associated with the Enlightenment (and philosophers such as Voltaire, Locke, and Hume) and its association with a project of 'scientific' explanation and mastery of the natural and social world. For Lyotard, the idea of progress characteristic of Enlightenment thought is no longer tenable, and he argues that it is now impossible to believe in either the progressive advancement of thought—the emancipation of reason—or the social and political emancipation to which it was once believed such reason might contribute. 'What kind of thought', Lyotard asks, 'is able to sublate Auschwitz in a general . . . process towards a universal emancipation?' (1986: 6).

Lyotard's work, in this respect, may be linked to more general strains of post-structuralist thinking and to share with them a number of features. In general terms, these may be seen to include a suspicion of totalizing theories and explanations which attempt to offer comprehensive and all-embracing accounts of social and cultural phenomena; an anti-foundationalism that rejects claims to 'absolute' or 'universal' foundations for knowledge; a rejection of the 'false universalism' of ethnocentric or Eurocentric systems of thought; and an anti-essentialism that rejects both 'depth' epistemologies which seek to lay bare 'hidden' or 'essential' realities as well as ideas of a fixed notion of identity or human 'essence'. In this last respect, a critique of Enlightenment reason is likened to a critique of the unified self which was assumed to underpin it and provide it with its foundations. Thus Stuart Hall draws a distinction between 'the Enlightenment subject', which is based upon 'a conception of the human person as a fully centred, unified individual, endowed with the capacities of reason, consciousness and action', and 'the postmodern subject', which is conceptualized as having 'no fixed, essential or permanent identity' but rather as assuming 'different identities at different times' (Hall 1992: 277).

Postmodern theory, in this regard, lays stresss on the heterogeneity and fragmented character of social and

cultural 'realities' and identities as well as the impossibility of any unified, or comprehensive, account of them. As such, postmodernism is often seen as, and criticized for, embracing both a relativism which accepts the impossibility of adjudicating amongst different accounts of, or knowledge claims about, reality and an 'idealism' or 'conventionalism' which accepts the impossibility of gaining access to 'reality' other than via the 'discourses' through which 'realities' are constructed. Moreover, it has also been a tendency of many postmodern arguments apparently to belie their own precepts and 'universalize' their claims concerning the 'postmodern condition' or erect precisely the 'grand narratives' of the transition from 'modernity' to 'postmodernity' which it is otherwise argued are no longer possible. As Gregor McLennan suggests, 'the progressive decline of the grand narratives' is itself 'an alternative grand narrative' (1989: 177). In this respect, it may be helpful to distinguish the scepticism towards grand theory which is a feature of postmodern philosophy from the more substantive sociological and cultural claims which have been made concerning the character of postmodernity and postmodern culture, even though these are often interlinked (as in Lyotard's work, which is both an investigation into the status of knowledge in post-industrial society and a polemic against totalizing theory).

Socio-cultural debates

Thus, in sociological debates, postmodernism has been used to identify the emergence of what is often believed to be a new economic and social order. This is sometimes linked to the idea of 'post-industrialism' (Rose 1991) and designated as either 'postmodernity' (Lyon 1994) or 'postmodernization' (Crook *et al.* 1992). 'Postmodernism' (or 'postmodernity') is, in this respect, seen to be following a period of 'modernity'. However, this is a term which is itself disputed and whose periodization is not always agreed. Thus, while 'modernity' may be seen to have emerged with the break with 'tradition' (and feudalism) represented by the advent of capitalism in the fifteenth and sixteenth centuries, it is more commonly identified with the economic and social changes characteristic of the nineteenth and early twentieth centuries, and especially those ushered in by industrialization, urbanization, and the emergence of mass social movements. Accordingly, the main features of the emerging 'postmodern' social order are usually identified in terms of a transition from an old industrial order to a new 'post-industrial' one which is, in turn, characterized by a number of features: a decline in manufacturing and the increased importance of service industries (be they business and financial or heritage and tourism); the replacement of old models of standardized, or 'Fordist', mass production by new flexible and geographically mobile forms of 'post-Fordist' production involving batch production and the targeting of specific consumer groups, or market segments; a decline in the traditional working class and the growth of white-collar workers and a 'service class' (whose attitudes and tastes, some accounts claim, postmodernist culture expresses); and therefore a diminution of the significance of class identities and divisions and an increased importance of other forms of social identity such as those related to age, gender, sexual orientation, ethnicity, and region. In this respect, the shift away from the politics of mass movements towards a 'politics of difference' may be seen to link with postmodern arguments concerning the increasing contingency and fluidity of social identities in the contemporary era.

Such shifts are also identified with the growing importance (and convergence) of the new computing and communications technologies to the changing economic and social order. Media output and information services not only provide a major 'force of production' of the 'post-industrial' economy, but also increasingly exemplify 'post-Fordist' economic practices (Lash and Urry 1994). Even more importantly, the media and the new technologies are seen to be significantly reshaping social experience and subjectivity. Two main themes can be identified. First, the speeding up of the circulation of information and images through computer-linked systems and satellites, for example, has been seen as responsible for an increasing compression of time and space, a 'deterritorialization' of culture and the construction of forms of identity which are no longer strongly identified with place (Harvey 1989; Meyrowitz 1985). These processes may in turn be linked to arguments about 'globalization' and the mixing, and pluralization, of cultural perspectives and influences which the accelerated flow of people, goods, services, images, ideas, and information is presumed to permit (albeit that this is still characterized by acute imbalances of power). A second theme emerging from the analysis of postmodernism concerns how the media, and media images and signs, are increasingly identified as a key, if not *the*

key, reality for the modern citizen. The controversial French theorist Jean Baudrillard is particularly associated with this position.

In common with post-industrial theorists, Baudrillard identifies a transition from an old industrial order based upon labour and the production of goods to a new social reproductive order based upon communication and the circulation of signs (Baudrillard 1975). However, for Baudrillard, this change also provides the basis of a new cultural condition. It is not simply that we live in a world increasingly dominated by images and signs, but that these have become our primary reality. We now live, he suggests, in a world of *simulations*, or hyperreality, which has no reality beyond itself. Indeed, for Baudrillard (1983: 41), it is 'now impossible to isolate the process of the real, or to prove the real': all that we have access to are signs and simulations. This provocative line of argument was pushed to extremes when, in 1991, Baudrillard examined the representation of the Gulf War as a 'virtual' event and declared that 'the Gulf War did not take place'. Although it is possible to read this as an argument about the changed character of contemporary warfare in the postmodern era, it also suggests some of the weaknesses of a postmodern perspective that both displays an indifference to the actuality of events beyond the 'simulacrum' and, under the guise of radicalism, simply joins a lengthy tradition of social commentary in attributing an exaggerated power and effectivity to media imagery.

Although the Baudrillardian vision of a media world of simulations is undoubtedly overstated, it does none the less direct our attention to the omnipresence within contemporary culture of media signs and images and their increasing detachment from exterior realities. However, it is television—given its continuous availability and presence within contemporary culture—that is most commonly associated with the postmodern condition rather than film. Thus, for Kroker and Cook it is television that is 'in a very literal sense, the real world . . . of *postmodern* culture, society and economy' (1986/1988: 268). This is not, of course, to say that arguments about film have not been informed by postmodern ideas. However, they have tended to be applied to individual films rather than, in the case of television, to the medium as a whole (albeit that this has then led to gross generalizations about the functioning of television 'in general'). At this point, it is therefore appropriate to look at the artistic context in which debates about postmodern film have occurred.

Aesthetic debates

If postmodern philosophy may be linked to a failing confidence in 'universal reason' and ideas of progress, it is also possible to see certain kinds of cultural practice—designated as 'postmodern'—emerging as a response to a growing lack of confidence in the value or progressiveness of modernism in the arts and design. Much of the early debate about postmodernism was linked to a consideration of architecture, and it is in relation to architecture that some of these ideas emerge most clearly.

Putting it in general terms, modernism in architecture (as, for example, in the work of Le Corbusier, the Bauhaus group, Mies van der Rohe, and the International Style) has placed a particular emphasis on function and social utility. Modern architecture, in this respect, may be seen to have demanded a 'truth to function', involving a rejection of ornament and decoration in favour of a laying bare of the materials employed and clear display of their purpose. These architectural principles were also linked to 'modern' social objectives such as the provision of mass housing (even if they were not always implemented by politicians and planners with the appropriate degree of financial investment) and seen, as in the International Style, to be 'universal' in application. For Charles Jencks, postmodernist architecture should be seen as a response to the failure of this modernist project. Indeed, he associates the 'death' of modern architecture with such events as the collapse of the Ronan Point tower block in 1969 and the blowing up of high-rise blocks in St Louis in 1972. Such events, he argues, not only signalled the failure of modern architecture as 'mass housing', but also its failure to appeal to, or communicate with, its inhabitants (Jencks 1986: 19). Thus, for Jencks, postmodernist architecture seeks to reconnect with its occupants by rejecting the functionalism of modernism, making use of decoration and ornamentation and mixing styles from different periods and places (including the vernacular). As such, Jencks defines postmodernism in terms of the concept of 'double coding', involving 'the combination of modern techniques with something else (usually traditional building) in order to communicate with the public and a concerned minority, usually other architects' (14).

Jencks acknowledges that while 'double coding' may be a feature of postmodern culture more generally, the 'failure' of modern architecture is not directly analogous to other arts. Andreas Huyssen (1986), however, suggests that the emergence of postmodern art, especially in the United States, may be linked to a certain kind of failure, or 'exhaustion', of modernism (or, more specifically, the version of modernism which became institutionalized in the United States in the 1950s). Postmodernism in this regard may be seen as a response to what Russell Berman (1984–5: 41) describes as the 'obsolescence of shock' and the corresponding loss of modernism's transgressive power. Due to its incorporation into the art market and its institutionalization as 'high art', modern art, it is argued, has lost its capacity to challenge and provoke as well as its capacity to communicate to a public beyond a small élite.

For Huyssen, the origins of this challenge may be found in pop art of the 1960s with its reaction against the dominant aesthetic of abstract expressionism and challenging of conventional notions of art through the incorporation of elements from popular culture. As such, pop art may be seen to embody a number of features which are now commonly associated with postmodern cultural practice. These may, loosely, be identified as eclecticism, an erosion of aesthetic boundaries, and a declining emphasis upon originality. Thus, just as postmodern philosophy and postmodern culture have been associated with pluralism, so the most commonly identified feature of postmodernism has been its eclecticism—its drawing upon and mixing of different styles, genres, and artistic conventions, including those of modernism. Postmodernism, in this regard, is to be understood as a movement beyond modernism which is none the less able to make use of modernist techniques and conventions as one set of stylistic choices amongst others. It is in this sense that Featherstone describes postmodernism as demonstrating 'a stylistic promiscuity' (1988: 203), while other critics have placed an emphasis upon its strategies of 'appropriation' and 'hybridization' (e.g. Wollen 1981: 168; Hassan 1986: 505).

A central component of this process has been a mixing of elements from both 'high' and 'low' culture (which may in turn be seen as an example of 'de-differentiation', or the breaking down of boundaries, which has been identified as a feature of postmodernism more generally). As Jameson has argued, artists of the 'postmodern' period have displayed a fascination with popular forms of culture such as advertising, the B movie, science fiction, and crime-writing. He suggests, however, that postmodern art does not simply 'quote' popular culture in the way that modernist art once did, but that this quotation is incorporated into the works to the point where older distinctions between 'modernist and mass culture' no longer seem to apply (Jameson 1988: 113). It is worth noting, again, that the 'break' between modernism and postmodernism is in this sense relative rather than absolute. Thus, as a number of commentators have noted, many of the features associated with postmodernism (such as the appropriation and juxtaposition of diverse materials) were also a characteristic of modernism even if they did not possess quite the same significance for the work as a whole (e.g. Callinicos 1989: 12–16; Wolff 1990: 98–9).

Finally, the borrowing of styles and techniques characteristic of postmodern art may be linked to a declining premium upon originality and the personal imprint of the 'author' (who, in parallel with the 'Enlightenment subject', is seen to have undergone something of a 'death'). Thus, for Dick Hebdige, the postmodern use of 'parody, simulation, pastiche and allegory' may be seen 'to deny the primacy or originary power of the "author"', who is no longer required to 'invent' but simply 'rework the antecedent' or rearrange the 'already-said' (Hebdige 1988: 191). However, the opposition between modernist originality and post-modernist appropriation and replication is not as clear-cut as it is sometimes argued and, even in popular culture, the 'author' has remained curiously resilient. Thus, while a film like *Blue Velvet* (USA 1986) clearly exemplifies such postmodern features as eclecticism, the mixing of avant-garde and popular conventions, and an ironic play with surface signifiers, it has still been very much in terms of the presumed 'author', David Lynch, that the film has been put into circulation, discussed, and interpreted.

Postmodernism and film

However, while individual films such as *Blue Velvet* and *Blade Runner* (Ridley Scott, 1982) have figured prominently in debates about postmodernism and film, the identification of what constitutes postmodern cinema has not been straightforward. Three main kinds of concern have been in evidence. First, the organization of the film industry itself has often been taken to exemplify 'postmodern' features. Thus, it has been argued that Hollywood has undergone a transition from 'For-dist' mass production (the studio system) to the more 'flexible' forms of independent production (the 'New Hollywood' and after) characteristic of 'postmodern' economies, while the incorporation of Hollywood into media conglomerates with multiple entertainment interests has been seen to exemplify a 'postmodern' blurring of boundaries between (or 'de-differentiation' of) industrial practices, technologies, and cultural forms (Storper and Christopherson 1987; Tasker 1996). Second, films have, in various ways, been seen to exemplify postmodern themes or to offer 'images of postmodern society' (Harvey 1989: 308–23; Denzin 1991). Thus, the dystopian character of the contemporary science fiction film might be seen to be connected with a 'postmodern' loss of faith in the idea of progress or the changing film representations of men with a breakdown of confidence in the 'grand narratives' surrounding masculinity and patriarchal authority (Kuhn 1990; Modleski 1991). Finally, films have been seen to display the aesthetic features (such as eclecticism and the collapse of traditional artistic hierarchies) that are characteristically associated with postmodernist cultural practice. However, the identification and assessment of such aesthetic features has not been without its complications.

This is partly to do with the diversity of films to which the label has been attached (including both mainstream Hollywood films as well as 'independent' or 'experimental' film and video) and partly to do with the difficulty of clearly differentiating a 'postmodern' filmmaking practice in relation to an earlier 'modern' one (especially in the case of Hollywood). These problems have been further compounded by the differing interests that have conventionally underpinned the concern to identify postmodernist film. On the one hand, the idea of postmodernism has been used to carry on a tradition of ideological criticism which has sought to identify the social conservatism of the aesthetic conventions employed by postmodern cinema. On the other, it has been used to discuss films which may be seen to continue the 'oppositional' or 'trans-gressive' tradition of 'political modernism' but through a deployment of what is regarded as more culturally appropriate (i.e. postmodern) means. In this respect, discussion of postmodern cinema may be seen to follow in the wake of earlier distinctions between a 'reactionary postmodernism' and a 'postmodernism of resistance' (Foster 1983: p. xii) or between a socially conservative 'affirmative postmodernism' and an 'alternative postmodernism in which resistance, critique and negation of the status quo were redefined in non-modernist and non-avantgardist terms' (Huyssen 1984: 16).

These tensions can be seen at work in the ways in which Hollywood films since the 1970s have been addressed. Since the emergence of the New Hollywood in the late 1960s it has been common to note in Hollywood films an increasing stylistic self-consciousness, use of references to film history, and quotation from other styles (e.g. Carroll 1982). The significance of this development is, however, contested. For Fredric Jameson, in his ground-breaking essay 'Postmodernism; or, The Cultural Logic of Late Capitalism' (1984), it is clearly to be read negatively. Jameson defines postmodern culture in terms of a 'depthlessness' representative of 'a new culture of the image or the simulacrum'; a new kind of spatialized temporality and consequent 'weakening of historicity'; and the creation of a 'new type of emotional ground tone' which he describes as 'a waning of affect' (1984: 58–61). In seeking to substantiate these points, Jameson points to the 'nostalgia film' of the 1970s (such as *Chinatown* (USA, 1974) and *Body Heat* (USA, 1981)). He argues that, as a result of their use of pastiche and 'intertextual' reference, such films may be seen to exemplify a characteristically postmodern loss of historical depth. Such films, he claims, are unable to re-create a 'real' past but only a simulation of the past based upon pre-existing representations and styles (67).

In this respect, Jameson's analysis links with other critiques of recent Hollywood cinema for both its 'emptiness' and ideological conservatism. Thus, it has been common to see the formal invention and social questioning of the New Hollywood films of the late 1960s and 1970s as giving way to a more conventional and conservative Hollywood cinema from the mid-1970s onwards, especially in the wake of the success of *Star Wars* (USA, 1977) (e.g. Ryan and Kellner 1988). This has in turn been associated with a decline in what Kolker has referred to as 'the modernist project' of New Hollywood filmmaking and its replacement by the 'postmodern American film' which 'has done its best to erase the traces of sixties and seventies experimentation' (Kolker 1988: pp. x–xi). In this respect, Kolker may be seen to link postmodernism with a kind of anti-modernism (or 'reactionary postmodernism') involving a return to the 'classical' conventions or 'a linear illusionist style' (p. xi). However, it is not entirely clear whether the distinction he draws is so clear-cut. For, clearly, the New Hollywood films may themselves be plausibly identified as 'postmodern', given their self-consciousness about film history and film technique, extensive use of reference and quotation, and mixing of 'high' and 'low' art conventions (such as those of the European 'art' film and the Hollywood genre film). Similarly, although there has been an undoubted return to the 'classical' conventions of narrative and character in many post-New Hollywood films, this has also been accompanied by a continued (and, indeed, growing) use of quotation and mixing of genre elements.

Fredric Jameson's distinction between parody and pastiche may be helpful in this regard. Although both parody and pastiche are conventionally associated with postmodernism, Jameson argues that, within postmodern culture, it is pastiche which is dominant. For Jameson, while parody involves a sense of criticism or mockery of the text or texts which are being parodied, pastiche simply consists of 'blank parody': a 'neutral mimicry without parody's ulterior motives' (1984: 64–5). Although it is not an unproblematic distinction, it does have some heuristic value in discriminating between the films of the New Hollywood and after. Thus, while a New Hollywood film such as Robert Altman's *The Long Goodbye* (1973) quotes from film history and reworks genre conventions with obvious parodic intent—to debunk the myth of the private eye and the values he represents—the use of film quotations and references in a 1980s 'event' film such as *The Untouchables* (Brian De Palma, 1987) is largely characterized by the use of pastiche (as in the clever, but politically and emotionally 'blank', reconstruction of the Odessa steps sequence from the revolutionary Russian film *Battleship Potemkin*, 1925). As such, the film's use of pastiche offers less a critique of the male hero (as *the Long Goodbye* does) than an 'alibi' for the film's ideological conservatism by inoculating the film against being read too straight (in much the same way as the more recent *Independence Day* (1996) also invests its conservative militarism with a measure of tongue-in-cheek knowingness).

What this suggests is that the use of 'postmodern' conventions in Hollywood cannot simply be read off as ideologically uniform (or, indeed, that Hollywood films are *all* usefully labelled as 'postmodern' given the degree of aesthetic diversity which characterizes contemporary Hollywood filmmaking). Thus, for Linda Hutcheon, Jameson's 'blanket condemnation of Hollywood' is overstated and fails to take into account the 'oppositional and contestatory' potential of postmod-

**Hollywood postmodernism—
David Lynch's *Blue Velvet*
(1986)**

ernism which may be found in certain Hollywood films (Hutcheon 1989: 114). Unlike Jameson, she holds out the possibility of Hollywood films making use of irony and parody both to address history (as in Woody Allen's *Zelig*, 1983) and to 'subvert' Hollywood from within by their challenge to audience expectations concerning narrative and visual representation (even in such a 'light' film as De Palma's *Phantom of the Paradise*, 1974). Nevertheless, Hutcheon also acknowledges that postmodernist films are not always 'challenging in mode', that they are often likely to be 'compromised', and that, as a result of their reliance upon irony, they may also be 'ideologically ambivalent or contradictory' (1989: 107). Hence, most of her examples are actually films which are outside the mainstream of Hollywood production (*Zelig*, *The Purple Rose of Cairo*, (1985), *The French Lieutenant's Woman* (1981)) or not Hollywood films at all (Suzanne Osten's *The Mozart Brothers*, Sweden, 1986), Maximilian Schell's *Marlene* (West Germany, 1983), and Peter Greenaway's *A Zed and Two Noughts* (UK/Netherlands, 1985)). Indeed, more generally it is typical of writing concerned to identify a 'critical' strain of postmodernism within Hollywood that it focuses on films which tend to be unusual in Hollywood's terms (e.g. *Bladerunner*, *Blue Velvet*, *Thelma and Louise* (1991)) rather than ones which can be seen as typical.

Accordingly, it has often been outside of Hollywood that the 'adversarial' qualities of postmodern cinema

have been most firmly located. Despite its extensive use of 'allusion', Noel Carroll (1982) argues against the application of the 'postmodern' label to Hollywood filmmaking and, in a subsequent essay, identifies 'postmodern' film with the avant-garde, and specifically with various reactions against structural filmmaking, such as 'deconstructionism, the new talkie, punk film the new psychodrama, and the new symbolism' (1985: 103). In this 'alternative' tradition of filmmaking, the reworking of old materials and representations by postmodernism is interpreted not simply as a kind of surface play (or 'depthlessness'), but as part of a critical project to 'deconstruct' and subvert old meanings as well as 'construct' new ones through the repositioning of artistic and cultural discourses. Thus, Laura Kipnis explains postmodernism in terms of a cultural practice of 're-functioning' (1986: 34), while Jim Collins argues it involves the use of 'juxtaposition' as a mode of 'interrogation' (1989: 138). Thus, for Collins, the bringing together of different discursive modes in a film such as Hans-Jurgen Syberberg's *Parsifal* (1984) consists of more than just pastiche, or the aimless plundering of past styles, but both a questioning of earlier traditions of representation and 'a way of making sense of life in decentered cultures' (1989: 140).

In this respect, the critical engagement with prior representations has been seen as especially attractive to filmmakers who wish to challenge the traditional ways in which particular social groups or 'others' (such as blacks, indigenous peoples, women, and gays) have been represented and to do justice to the complexities of identity in the postmodern era. Thus, for Janet Wolff, the 'promise of postmodernism' for feminism is that, by employing the tactics of 'pastiche, irony, quotation, and juxtaposition', feminist cultural practice may engage directly with 'current images, forms, and ideas, subverting their intent and (re)appropriating their meanings' (1990: 88). Similarly, Kobena Mercer identifies the work of black British filmmakers in the 1980s as constituting 'a kind of counter-practice that contests and critiques the predominant forms in which black subjects become socially visible in different forms of cultural representation' (1988: 8). Despite the use of the term 'counter-practice' by Mercer, such filmmaking should, nevertheless, be differentiated from the Godardian model of 'counter-cinema' (or 'political modernism') and its apparent prescription of one 'correct' way of making political cinema which is universally applicable. Rather, Mercer argues that such films as *Territories* (1984) and *Handsworth Songs* (1987) employ a postmodern strategy of 'appropriation' which, through a reworking of pre-existing documentary footage, found sound, quotations, and the like, involves both a 'dis-articulation' and a 're-articulation' of 'given signifying elements of hegemonic racial discourse' (1988: 11). In doing so, he also indicates how such work represents a 'syncretism' or 'hybridity' which, he argues, is appropriate to the 'diasporean conditions' of the black communities in Britain (11).

In this respect, Mercer's work interlinks with postmodern and post-colonial emphases on the 'anti-essentialist' nature of social and cultural identities and what Ella Shohat describes as 'the mutual imbrication of "central" and "peripheral" cultures' in both the 'First' and 'Third Worlds' (1992/1996: 329). Although Shohat warns against any simple celebration of post-colonial hybridity, which she argues assumes diverse and ideological varied forms, she also suggests how hybridity can be used as 'a part of resistant critique' (331). Thus, she and her collaborator Robert Stam echo a number of postmodern themes (such as the breakdown of confidence in 'grand narratives' and the problemization of representation) in their discussion of how the 'post-Third Worldist' films has moved 'beyond' the anti-colonial nationalism and political modernism of films such as *Battle of Algiers* (Algeria/Italy, 1966) and *Hour of the Furnaces* (Argentina, 1968) to interrogate nationalist discourse from the perspectives of class, gender, sex-

ual orientation, and diasporic identity, and embrace what they call 'anthropophagic, parodic-carnivalesque, and media-jujitsu strategies' (Shohat and Stam 1994: 10). In all of these cases, filmmakers in the Third World are seen to make use of First World techniques and conventions but for politically subversive ends. Thus, it is argued that, 'in their respect for difference and plurality, and in their self-consciousness about their own status as simulacra, and as texts that engage with a contemporary, mass-mediated sensibility without losing their sense of activism', the 'jujitsu' strategies of such films as the Aboriginal *Babakiueria* (Don Featherstone, Australia, 1988) and the Philippine *Mababangong Bangungot* ('Perfumed Nightmare', Kidlat Tahimik, 1977) exemplify Foster's notion of a 'resistance postmodernism' (1994: 332). However, the appropriateness of the conceptualization and periodization of postmodernism in relation to non-Western cultures remains controversial, as does its relationship to the concept of the 'post-colonial', the debate around which has now effectively overshadowed earlier arguments about the postmodern.

Conclusion: postmodernism and film studies

Although the debates about postmodernism have led to various discussions about the usefulness of the term in relation to film, it is less easy to identify a distinctive postmodern film theory. Postmodern ideas, in this respect, have tended to inform other film theories, rather than develop as a body of theory in their own right. In this respect, postmodern polemicizing against 'universalizing' and 'totalizing' theory has led to a certain refocusing of interest on the local and the specific which may be detected in the turn away from '*Screen* theory' of the 1970s towards historical research, cultural studies, and an interest in the social and cultural specificities of non-Euro-American cinemas (and a more 'multicultural' and 'dialogistic' approach to their study). One illustration of this may be found in feminist film theory.

Although feminist film theory was crucially important in the mid-1970s in introducing questions of gender into the previously sex-blind 'apparatus theory' (see Creed, Part 1, Chapter 9), it itself became criticized for an 'essentializing' conceptualization of the 'female spectator' which failed to do justice to 'the multiple and fluid nature' of the female spectator who 'may be, and/or be constructed as, simultaneously female and black and gay' (Kuhn 1994: 202). As a result, Kuhn argues that 'the future for feminist work on film would appear to lie in micronarratives and microhistories of the fragmented female spectator rather than in any totalizing metapsychology of the subject of the cinematic apparatus' (202). In this respect, the convergence of feminism and cultural studies around the question of audiences has already moved in that direction. However, as Nancy Fraser and Linda Nicholson (1988) have argued in their discussion of the relations between feminism and postmodernism, while postmodern feminism may share a 'postmodernist incredulity towards metanarratives', it 'must remain theoretical' and hold on to some 'large narratives' if 'the social-critical power of feminism' is to be maintained. In this respect, their recommendation that postmodern feminist theory should be 'explicitly historical' and 'attuned to the cultural specificity of different societies and periods and to that of different groups within societies and periods' (1988/1990: 34) would seem to be a good recipe for 'postmodern' analysis more generally.

BIBLIOGRAPHY

Baudrillard, Jean (1975), *The Mirror of Production* (St Louis: Telos Press).

—— (1983), *Simulations*, trans. Paul Foss, Paul Patton, and Philip Beitchman (New York: Semiotext(e)).

—— (1991/1995), *The Gulf War did not Take Place*, trans. Paul Patton (Sydney: Power).

Berman, Russell A. (1984–5), 'Modern Art and Desublimation', *Telos*, 62: 31–57.

Callinicos, Alex (1989), *Against Postmodernism: A Marxist Critique* (Cambridge: Polity Press).

Carroll, Noel (1982), 'The Future of Allusion: Hollywood in the Seventies (and Beyond)', *October*, 20: 51–81.

—— (1985), 'Film', in Stanley Trachtenberg (ed.), *The Postmodern Moment* (Westport, Conn.: Greenwood Press).

*Collins, Jim (1989), *Uncommon Cultures: Popular Culture and Post-Modernism* (London: Routledge).

Connor, Steven (1989), *Postmodernist Culture: An Introduction to Theories of the Contemporary* (Oxford: Blackwell).

Crook, Stephen, Jan Pakulski, and Malcolm Waters (1992), *Postmodernization* (London: Routledge).

Denzin, Norman (1991), *Images of Postmodern Society: Social Theory and Contemporary Cinema* (London: Sage).

*Featherstone, Mike (1988), 'In Pursuit of the Postmodern: An Introduction', *Theory, Culture and Society*, 5/2–3: 195–215.

*Foster, Hal (1983/1985), 'Postmodernism: A Preface', in Foster (ed.), *The Anti-Aesthetic: Essays on Postmodern Culture* (Port Townshend: Bay Press); repr. as *Postmodern Culture* (London: Pluto).

Fraser, Nancy, and Linda J. Nicholson (1988/1990), 'Social Criticism without Philosophy: An Encounter between Feminism and Postmodernism', in Nicholson (ed.) *Feminism/Postmodernism* (London: Routledge).

Hall, Stuart (1992), 'The Question of Cultural Identity', in Stuart Hall and Tony McGrew (eds.), *Modernity and its Futures* (Cambridge: Polity Press).

Harvey, David (1989), *The Condition of Postmodernity* (Oxford: Blackwell).

Hassan, Ihab (1986/1987), 'Pluralism in Postmodern Perspective', *Critical Inquiry*, 12/3 (Spring), 503–20; repr. in *The Postmodern Turn: Essays in Postmodern Theory and Culture* (Ohio: Ohio State University Press).

Hebdige, Dick (1988), *Hiding in the Light: On Images and Things* (London: Routledge).

Hutcheon, Linda (1989), *The Politics of Postmodernism* (London: Routledge).

Huyssen, Andreas (1984), 'Mapping the Postmodern', *New German Critique*, 33: 5–52; repr. in *After the Great Divide: Modernism, Mass Culture and Postmodernism* (London: Macmillan).

*Jameson, Fredric (1984/1991), 'Postmodernism; or, The Cultural Logic of Late Capitalism', *New Left Review*, 146: 53–92; repr. in *Postmodernism: Of the Cultural Logic of Late Capitalism* (London: Verso).

—— (1988), 'The Politics of Theory: Ideological Positions in the Postmodernism Debate', in *The Ideologies of Theory, ii: The Syntax of History* (London: Routledge).

Jencks, Charles (1986), *What is Post-Modernism* (London: St Martin's Press).

Kipnis, Laura (1986), '"Refunctioning" Reconsidered: Towards a Left Popular Culture', in Colin MacCabe (ed.), *High Theory/Low Culture: Analysing Popular Film and Television* (Manchester: Manchester University Press).

Kolker, Robert Phillip (1988), *A Cinema of Loneliness: Penn, Kubrick, Scorsese, Spielberg, Altman*, 2nd edn. (Oxford: Oxford University Press).

Kroker, Arthur, and David Cook (1986/1988), *The Postmodern Scene: Excremental Culture and Hyper-Aesthetics* (New York: St Martin's Press; Basingstoke: Macmillan).

Kuhn, Annette (ed.) (1990), *Alien Zone: Cultural Theory and Contemporary Science Fiction Cinema* (London: Verso).

—— (1994), *Women's Pictures: Feminism and Cinema*, 2nd edn. (London: Verso).

Lash, Scott, and John Urry (1994), *Economics of Signs and Space* (London: Sage).

Lyon, David (1994), *Postmodernity* (Buckingham: Open University Press).

Lyotard, Jean-François (1979/1984), *The Postmodern Condition: A Report on Knowledge*, trans. Geoff Bennington and Brian Massumi (Minneapolis: University of Minnesota Press).

—— (1986), 'Defining the Postmodern', in Lisa Appignanesi (ed.), *Postmodernism* (London: ICA).

McClennan, Gregor (1989), *Marxism, Pluralism and Beyond: Classic Debates and New Departures* (Cambridge: Polity Press).

Mercer, Kobena (1988), 'Recoding Narratives of Race and Nation', in Mercer (ed.), *Black Film British Cinema* (London: ICA).

Meyrowitz, Joshua (1985), *No Sense of Place: The Impact of Electronic Media on Social Behavior* (Oxford: Oxford University Press).

Modleski, Tania (1991), *Feminism without Women: Culture and Criticism in a 'Postfeminist' Age* (London: Routledge).

Rodowick, D. N. (1988), *The Crisis of Political Modernism: Criticism and Ideology in Contemporary Film Theory* (Urbana: University of Illinois Press).

Rose, Margaret A. (1991), *The Post-Modern and the Post-Industrial* (Cambridge: Cambridge University Press).

Ryan, Michael, and Douglas Kellner (1988), *Camera Politica: The Politics and Ideology of Contemporary Hollywood Film* (Bloomington, Indiana University Press).

Shohat, Ella (1992/1996), 'Notes on the "Post-Colonial"', in Padmini Monga (ed.), *Contemporary Postcolonial Theory* (London: Arnold).

*—— and Robert Stam (1994), *Unthinking Eurocentrism: Multiculturalism and the Media* (London: Routledge).

Storper, Michael, and Susan Christopherson (1987), 'Flexible Specialization and Regional Industrial Agglomerations: The Case of the US Picture Industry', *Annals of the Association of American Geographers*, 77/1: 104–17.

Tasker, Yvonne (1996), 'Approaches to the New Hollywood', in James Curran, David Morley, and Valerie Walkerdine (eds.), *Cultural Studies and Communications* (London: Arnold).

Wolff, Janet (1990), *Feminine Sentences: Essays on Women and Culture* (Cambridge: Polity Press).

Wollen, Peter (1972), 'Counter Cinema: *Vent d'est*', *Afterimage*, 4: 6–16.

—— (1981), 'Ways of Thinking about Music Video (and Post-Modernism), *Critical Quarterly*, 28/1–2: 167–70.

Film text and context: gender, ideology, and identities

12

Marxism and film

Chuck Kleinhans

Although Marx never went to the movies, Marxism has significantly affected filmmaking by politically committed directors such as Sergei Eisenstein and Tomás Gutiérrez Alea, as well as shaped the critical and historical analysis of film in aesthetic, institutional, social, and political terms. Fundamental Marxist concepts such as ideology profoundly inform most contemporary theories of and approaches to the analysis of individual films as well as to cinema as a social institution.

Marxism fuses several different sources and types of concern. From English political economy, Marx developed his understanding of the economic foundation as fundamentally shaping (though not immutably determining) the social superstructure. From German philosophy, by inverting Hegelian idealism into a materialism that saw the world as historical and dynamically changing, Marx studied capitalism and capitalist societies as always in process. From French socialism, Marx drew his analysis of class-divided society with an active working class struggling for economic and social justice against the ruling capitalist class. Although internally divided by different movements, schools, and tendencies, and sometimes deformed into dogmatism in theory and dictatorship in practice, in its comprehensiveness, and at its best, Marxism provides a remarkably supple method for analysis. It combines practical progressive and democratic political goals with a social examination that centres on historical development and the dialectical potential for change. For this reason, Marxist analysis is an essential part of much contemporary gender, race–ethnicity, and post-colonial thinking in film studies, even when not explicitly underlined.

Marx and Engels did not write a full-fledged aesthetics, but their comments on art (almost exclusively on literature) can be synthesized into a view which validates the Western classics and upholds a broadly construed realism in representation and narration (Morawski 1973; Solomon 1973). Marx recognized Balzac as personally a royalist in politics, but viewed his novels as narratives that accurately portrayed the complex social fabric of their time. Similarly, Lenin saw Tolstoy as a political reactionary but the author of novels which mirrored the social–political tensions of Russia. Such was the orthodoxy until the Bolshevik revolution, when Marxism shaped cinema and the other arts. With Marxists holding state power, questions of entertainment versus instruction, traditional versus radical form, drama versus documentary, literary versus visual communication, native versus foreign (especially Hollywood) models, ethnic nationalisms versus national culture, religious versus secular culture, urban versus rural, and popular audience versus intellectual creators, were raised as practical as well as theoretical matters. Intellectuals experienced and vigorously argued over both the economics of constructing a socialist film industry relying on box-office receipts and the relation of creative output to party doctrines and priorities. Sergei Eisenstein, Dziga Vertov, Lev Kuleshov, Vsevolod Pudovkin, and others wrote as filmmakers while intellectuals from different tendencies participated in the highly political and polemical debates (Taylor and Christie 1988).

The crucible of the Soviet Union of the 1920s first played out issues still important in later times and other places. In the USSR a national mass culture emerged, itself industrialized in production and partly responsive to market conditions in consumption. The state–party took control of information and journalism, as radio, the newsreel, and educational film developed. And, given limited print literacy, print journalism was complemented and, in many cases, superseded by audio and visual journalism. A comprehensive understanding of Soviet film demands an understanding of this larger context. Within the narrower realm of film aesthetics, the period dramatized several key issues. Because many artistic innovators joined the early years of the revolution, film experimentalism appeared in radical forms ranging from Alexander Dovzhenko's lyrical poeticism to Vertov's rigorous montage of images (and later sound–image) and Eisenstein's epic and operatic work. The intellectual studies of the Russian Formalists contributed to the question of innovative forms matching a revolutionary content (see Christie, Part 1, Chapter 7). Traditional forms were viewed as compromised, and the possibility of developing intellectual content through the means of film form and expressive stylistics was asserted.

At the same time in the West, particularly Germany, a heightened awareness of capitalism's encroachment on the fields of culture and leisure developed with the rise of an urban mass culture audience and new means of mass-produced and disseminated culture and journalism: cinema, recorded music, the radio, the picture newspaper, and so on. Kracauer (1995), Brecht (1964), and Benjamin (1936) witnessed the expansion of the mass audience, fearing for its passivity but also identifying the liberating potential of the new media. As with the Russians, these thinkers saw cinema as changing perception and cognition as society moved from a written literacy to a visual dominance. New understandings of space and time, heralded in Cubist painting, seemed inherent to film. Informed by Freudian psychology, left-wing intellectuals hoped that new art forms could stimulate new forms of politicized thinking. Bertolt Brecht argued against the narcotic effects of dominant dramatic forms, seeing the realist–naturalist tradition since Ibsen as conforming to the Aristotelian model of catharsis: raising political issues only to send the audience away purged of any fervour for change. He championed disruptive forms which provoked viewers to new thought.

The rise of German fascism offered a new challenge to Marxist theories, and produced a series of exchanges that marked important differences within Marxist analysis of mass culture. These differences continued in the debate after the Second World War, and in film studies after 1968. The philosopher Georg Lukács advocated what amounted to a continuation of nineteenth-century realism in literature, while Brecht argued for modernist artistic innovation. Walter Benjamin agreed with Brecht and optimistically projected an inherently radical nature to film, while Marxist influenced Frankfurt School thinkers Theodor Adorno and Max Horkheimer pessimistically concluded that fascist and US capitalist media were fundamentally alike in producing a passive public (Horkheimer and Adorno 1947).

While Soviet creative innovation and theoretical variety declined in the 1930s with Stalin's prescriptive doctrine of socialist realism in all the arts, in the West some new activities expanded the field of issues for Marxist aesthetics: examples include the development of partisan documentary and grass-roots newsreel in the United States with the Film and Photo League (Alexander 1981; Campbell 1982) and propaganda films for the Spanish Civil War. In the mid-1930s the abrupt shift in international communist politics to build a broad anti-fascist Popular Front raised new issues of producing films with and for sympathizers and liberals, such as Jean Renior's *La Vie est à nous* 'Life is Ours', (1936) (see Buchsbaum 1988). Western communist parties encouraged working with and recruiting people in the dominant capitalist media industries, including Hollywood (which created a pretext for the notorious post-war Red scare and blacklist).

The post-Second World War era saw the development of new aspects of Marxism and film. Hollywood emerged stronger than ever, dominating more of the world market (see Miller, Part 2, Chapter 12). New socialist nations were established in Eastern Europe and China with attendant national cinemas, and Marxists were active in many national liberation movements in the developing world. Italian Neo-Realism provided a model of a humanistic socially committed film practice that eschewed the expensive entertainment and star system of Hollywood while validating matters of social justice, a sympathetic depiction of the lower classes, and vernacular expression in a thrifty mode (see Monticelli, Part 3, Chapter 8). Neo-Realism influenced independent efforts in the capitalist world, and inspired directors in the developing world, particularly in Latin America and India. Critics, too, validated Neo-Realism. André Bazin, as a liberal Catholic, could find moral seriousness, while Siegfried Kracauer, from a critique of mass culture and German Expressionist film, found an alternative to frivolity and emotional manipulation (Kracauer 1947, 1960). Both posited an ontological basis for film in the replication of the physical world (see Easthope, Part 1, Chapter 6). In general, in the post-war era, Marxists favoured an aesthetic of progressive realism which stood against the superficiality of entertainment and allowed for social criticism. Auteurists with progressive credentials such as Luchino Visconti and Jean Renoir, Bimal Roy and Mrinal Sen, Stanley Kubrick and Orson Welles, were esteemed. After Stalin, alternatives to Soviet models gained attention, and new militancy provoked new thinking. In Poland, Hungary, Czechoslovakia, Yugoslavia, and Cuba, significant directors and films appeared veering away from socialist realist orthodoxy.

In the 1960s a complex set of changes brought about a new stage in Marxist film analysis. Most of the intellectuals involved in developing this stage of film studies were outside, or on the border of, academia, coming from journalism, publishing, and arts and education administration, or they were students and junior faculty in higher education, often in interdisciplinary or marginalized fields since academic film studies was still being established. Thus many were self-taught in the pertinent issues, and living through the process of discovering what a New Left could be, or learning Marxist concepts after beginning political activism. At the same time, local conditions and traditions heavily inflected the reception and diffusion of these ideas. What 'Marxist' meant in each place was distinctly different because of these contexts. And the local situation uniquely shaped the fusion of Marxism with other intellectual trends as well as the emergence of radical cultural analysis. This history played out in diverse radical film magazines. In France *Positif*, *Cinéthique*, and *Cahiers du cinéma*; in the UK *Screen* and *Framework*; in Canada *Ciné-Tracts* and *CineAction*; and in the United States *Cinéaste* and *Jump Cut*.

By the early 1970s the centre of gravity of Marxist film analysis shifted. Concepts of ideology and realism were drastically reoriented. The analysis of the dominant Hollywood cinema and European art film as 'illusionist', and that illusion having an ideological effect, evolved from several developments. The optimism of nineteenth-century Marxism in assuming that revolution would take place in the most industrialized nations as trade union and electoral politics heightened workers' consciousness and capacity for revolutionary change was severely damaged by the nationalist division during the First World War, the appearance of revolution in Russia (the most backward of the capitalist nations with an overwhelming peasant base), and the acceptance of fascism by much of the masses in Italy and Germany. As a result, Western Marxists sought deeper explanations. For some, insights from Freudian psychology showed the persistence of deep patterns in the conscious–unconscious mind. For others, the insights of Lenin's contemporary, the Italian Antonio Gramsci were helpful, particularly in his emphasis that people were not simply coercively forced by the state's police authority, but also manipulated by the hegemony or dominance of ruling-class cultural and social structures to stay in place, and to accept the existing order as 'natural'.

In classical Marxism, ideology was generally understood as the propagation of false ideas by the capitalist class, producing a 'false consciousness' in the masses which could then be countered by revolutionary 'correct ideas'. In the 1960s ideology was increasingly understood as a structural condition operating like myth in traditional societies described by Claude Lévi-Strauss: fairly complex patterns which embodied narratives and contradictions, which functioned to

'Shallow and glossy
melodramas' or a
'fundamental critique of
social institutions'? The
films of Douglas Sirk—
here, *Imitations of Life*
(1959)

maintain order. In modern cultures the mass media could be seen as promulgating similar myths (Barthes 1957). French philosopher Louis Althusser drew from Mao, Gramsci, and Lacanian psychoanalysis to posit a concept of ideology which stressed that people are socially positioned in power relationships and internalize this in their unconscious: a concept given further elaboration by Foucault, who emphasized the social basis of ideology by considering institutions and history. Such an understanding of ideology meshed well with developments in semiotics and long-standing analogies between film and dreams, daydreams, and hypnotic and other liminal mental states, although it tended to produce a pessimistic, deterministic view of the potential for change. Althusser argued that revolutionary theory could move beyond ideology: a notion that (few noticed) reproduced the Leninist model with Marxist theories occupying the position formerly held by vanguard party activists in relation to the proletariat (Althusser 1965, 1970).

This view led in one direction to a position virtually identical with the Frankfurt School's pessimistic denunciation of mainstream film as narcotic, or circus-like distraction, validating only rigorous high modernist art (Arnold Schoenberg, James Joyce) as truly revolutionary. Althusser also inspired arguments that, by resisting the illusionary cinema of 'bourgeois' realism, a radical modernist form could be wedded to a politically radical content, leading some critics to validate directors such as Nagisa Oshima and Jean-Marie Straub. With translations and new critical attention, Benjamin's 'work of art' essay and other writings gained new attention, while the revived Brecht–Lukács debate became the theoretical ground for an endorsement of formal innovation and explicit politics over traditional realism. Simultaneously, Eisenstein's films and writings were recast as aesthetic experiments, and Vertov's self-reflexive *Chelovek s kinoapparatom* ('Man with the Movie Camera', USSR, 1929) was rediscovered as an avant-garde work which explored the epistemology of film. Meanwhile, in the developing world, Solanas and Getino (1969) called for a militant Third Cinema poised apart from Hollywood and auteurist art cinema and García Espinosa (1967) defended Cuban cinema as necessarily 'imperfect' compared to high production value Hollywood, but to be valued for its political content. Complemented by a wave of militant and innovative films in Latin America (and later Africa and South Asia), such arguments strengthened the case for a militant aesthetics.

It is a truism that around 1970 contemporary film studies came into being through the weaving together of Marxism, structuralism, Saussurean linguistics, psychoanalysis, and semiotics, and then was further elaborated in post-structuralist terms. In some cases, the changes amounted to complete reversals. The tradition of social documentary was called into question because of its unreflective realism. A European auteur such as Ingmar Bergman, previously praised for his high moral seriousness, was critiqued for being too theatrical by an increasingly cinematically sophisticated audience, while *Persona* (Sweden, 1966) was validated for its complex self-referentiality (see Darke, Part 3, Chapter 13*b*). But the biggest change came in a shift in the left analysis of commercial entertainment cinema as Hollywood film was reinterpreted as fundamentally realist. Thus a normative realism, understood as identical with Hollywood's practice of illusionism, was seen as producing a coherent imaginary subject position. Audience pleasure was seen as originating in the cinematic apparatus (the ensemble of physical and social conventions that govern the cinema institution, including the subject's psychology) and its illusionism, rather than contingent narrative practices, performance, and spectacle (see Creed, Part 1, Chapter 9). In contrast, a self-reflexive modernism and avant-garde practices can be read as themselves producing a dispersal of meaning and deconstructing the subject position, thus calling into question both illusionism and the dominant ideology. As a result, some interpreted an extreme formalism as sufficient to establish a work as politically radical, irrespective of content, as, for example, with *Cahiers du cinéma*'s validation of Jerry Lewis's *The Bellboy* (USA, 1960), and in Gidal's advocacy of 'structural–materialist' films, while others critiqued the idea that self-reflexivity alone was political (Gidal 1978; Polan 1985).

While the overall change can be summed up as the 'politicizing of form', the precise working out varied from individual to individual, by nation, and with uneven access to ideas and films in translation. It also produced logical inconsistencies. For example, in line with their then Maoist politics, *Cahiers du cinéma* in 1972 enthusiastically validated the Godard–Gorin 'Groupe Dziga Vertov' films (1968–72)—intensely radical in form and content—as well as formally conventional Chinese documentaries. Given the investment in auteurist approaches to Hollywood prevalent in the 1960s, French and anglophone critics who were pushed in the direction of Marxist thought and politics by the heated political climate of the times tended to justify the auteurist canon using the new insights of Marxist thought. *Cahiers du cinéma* put forth a broad agenda for criticism in 1969, Comolli and Narboni's 'Cinema/Ideology/Criticism', which granted considerably leeway for considering films which appeared to be under the dominant ideology, but which escaped through formal 'cracks and fissures'. The classic demonstration was their analysis of John Ford's *Young Mr Lincoln* (USA, 1939), which argued that the director's 'inscription' of a unique 'writing' opened gaps in the text which were evidence of an escape from ideology (*Cahiers du cinéma* 1976). Left authorship analysis promoted various figures such as Nicholas Ray and Douglas Sirk who could be read as offering a fundamental critique of social institutions. The critics' motivation can be understood as stemming both from a desire to validate popular film and from the persistence of an aesthetic centred on creators (see Crofts, Part 2, Chapter 7). Following Bazin's dictum that 'style creates meaning', and repeating the argument of conservative auteurist Andrew Sarris, left critics asserted that Sirk's formal manipulations called his ostensibly shallow and glossy melodramas into question. Paul Willemen, for example, concluded that, 'by altering the rhetoric of bourgeois melodrama, through stylization and parody, Sirk's films distanciate themselves from the bourgeois ideology' (Willemen 1971: 67). Essentially these positions attributed class politics to cinema style. In the same vein, Jean-Luc Godard's *Week-end* (France, 1967) was interpreted by Henderson (1972, 1976) as having 'a non-bourgeois camera style' without further specifying whether that was then a working-class style.

The problems of this type of analysis derived from two false assumptions: that ideology directly reflects class identity, and that the film was the sole source of meaning. As further consideration (including critiques of some ludicrous case-studies) occurred, positions were modified and ideology was understood in a much more flexible way. While the critique of simple reflectionist concepts of 'realism' in cinematography and as an aesthetic was maintained, and the ideological nature of the apparatus was understood, increasingly theory turned to examining the meaning of a film as produced by an interaction between a text and a spectator who was understood not as an ahistorical 'subject' but as a historical person with social attributes of gender, race, class, age, nationality, and so on—all of which shaped the interpretive context. With history readmitted to the analytic frame, institutional analyses, including economic issues, were considered.

Marxism contributes to contemporary film studies in the form of historical, economic, and ideological analysis, as well as media activism. Drawing on its founders' own interests and methods, Marxism emphasizes historical analysis which aims at providing a broad context stressing multiple interacting factors including social, economic, and political connections. The revival of historical analysis reminds us that in an earlier period many film historians were Marxists: Georges Sadoul, Siegfried Kracauer, Jay Leyda, and Lewis Jacobs. Contemporary counterparts include Noël Burch, Michael Chanan, Thomas Elsaesser, David James, Klaus Kreimeier, and Janet Staiger. Studies of the class composition of cinema's past audiences, the representation of class in film, and the labour history of the cinema industry obviously interest Marxists. Wary of simple reflectionist models of film and society, Marxists remain committed to understanding the relation of film art and social–political activity. Two persistent themes are the historical film (a staple of Marxist film-making) and the analysis of current history in terms of the proliferation and combination of new media technologies.

Because of its inherent interest in industrial and global economics, Marxism is the primary methodology of most economic analysis of film and mass communications in general. Such studies involve not only questions of finance, production, and marketing, but also state policies (Pendakur 1990; Wasko 1982). In the past such analyses have often made sweeping generalizations about actual films and their reception, but a younger generation of researchers combines political economy with textual and reception analysis and avoids simplistic assertions of economic determination of cultural production. Increasingly issues of transnational capital, globalization of the market, capitalist ownership and control of national film cultures, and intellectual property rights focus the analysis (Mattelart and Mattelart 1992, see also Miller, Part 2, Chapter 12).

Marxism has had a long-standing relation to questions of political action and media. This has tended to be expressed in terms of films for propaganda and agitation, and especially in terms of a class or anti-imperialist analysis. The validation of new films and videos and the promotion of documentary has been at stake (Waugh 1984; Steven 1993). The development of a more sophisticated Marxist media theory has affected makers since the 1960s, especially with the postmodernist increase in self-conscious analytical–expository strategies combined with the social documentary tradition. Such work often discusses social–political issues such as race, nationalism, and AIDS, and critiques the dominant media representation of those concerns.

Today Marxism seems most dynamic when it combines its analysis of class with an analysis of gender, race, national, post-colonial, and other issues raised by progressive social–political movements. Some claim that the fall of the Soviet Union made Marxism obsolete. However, as a critical analysis of capitalist societies, at a time when the gap between rich and poor nations and between capitalist and working classes within those nations is growing, its relevance is assured.

BIBLIOGRAPHY

Adorno, Theodor, and **Walter Benjamin, Ernst Bloch, Bertolt Brecht, Georg Lukács,** and **Fredric Jameson** (1977), *Aesthetics and Politics*, trans. Ronald Taylor (London: New Left Books).

Alexander, William (1981), *Film on the Left: American Documentary Film from 1931 to 1942* (Princeton: Princeton University Press).

Althusser, Louis (1965/1970), *For Marx*, trans. Ben Brewster (New York: Monthly Review Press).

—— (1970/1972), *Lenin and Philosophy, and Other Essays*, trans. Ben Brewster (New York: Monthly Review Press).

Barthes, Roland (1957/1972), *Mythologies*, trans. Annette Lavers (New York: Hill & Wang).

Benjamin, Walter (1936/1968), *Illuminations*, ed. Hannah Arendt and trans. Harry Zohn (New York: Harcourt, Brace, & World).

Brecht, Bertolt (1964), *Brecht on Theatre*, ed. and trans. John Willett (New York: Hill & Wang).

Browne, Nick (ed.) (1990), *Cahiers du Cinéma 1969–1972: The Politics of Representation* (Cambridge, Mass.: Harvard University Press).

Buchsbaum, Jonathan (1988), *Cinéma Engagé: Film in the Popular Front* (Urbana: University of Illinois Press).

Burch, Noël (1990), *Life to those Shadows*, trans. Ben Brewster (Berkeley: University of California Press).

Cahiers du cinéma (1976), 'John Ford's *Young Mr Lincoln*', in Bill Nichols (ed.), *Movies and Methods*, i (Berkeley: University of California Press).

Campbell, Russell (1982), *Cinema Strikes Back: Radical Filmmaking in the United States 1930–1942* (Ann Arbor: UMI Research Press).

Chanan, Michael (1996), *The Dream that Kicks: The Prehistory and Early Years of Cinema in Britain*, 2nd edn. (London: Routledge).

*****Comolli, Jean-Louis,** and **Jean Narboni** (1969/1990), 'Cinema/Ideology/Criticism', trans. Susan Bennett in Browne (1990).

Elsaesser, Thomas (1989), *New German Cinema: A History* (New Brunswick, NJ: Rutgers University Press).

García Espinosa, Julio (1967/1979), 'For an Imperfect Cinema', *Jump Cut*, 20: 24–6.

Gidal, Peter (1978), 'Theory and Definition of Structural/ Materialist Film', in Gidal (ed.), *Structural Film Anthology* (London: British Film Institute).

Gramsci, Antonio (1929–35/1971), *Selections from 'The Prison Notebooks'*, ed. and trans. Quintin Hoare and Geoffrey Nowell-Smith (New York: International).

Gutiérrez, Alea Tomás (1989), 'The Viewer's Dialectic', trans. Julia Lesage (Havana: Casa de las Americas).

*****Harvey, Sylvia** (1978), *May '68 and Film Culture* (London: British Film Institute).

Henderson, Brian (1972), '*Weekend* and History', *Socialist Review*, 2/6 (no. 12): 57–92.

—— (1976), 'Toward a Non-Bourgeois Camera Style', in Bill Nichols (ed.), *Movies and Methods* (Berkeley: University of California Press).

Horkheimer, Max, and **Theodor Adorno** (1947/1972), 'The Culture Industry', trans. John Cumming in *The Dialectic of Enlightenment* (New York: Herder & Herder).

Jacobs, Lewis (1940), *The Rise of the American Film: A Critical History* (New York: Teacher's College Press).

James, David E. (1989), *Allegories of Cinema: American Film in the Sixties* (Princeton, NJ: Princeton University Press).

—— and **Rick Berg** (eds.), (1996), *The Hidden Foundation: Cinema and the Question of Class* (Minneapolis: University of Minnesota Press).

Kracauer, Siegfried (1947), *From Caligari to Hitler: A Psychological History of the German Film* (Princeton, NJ: Princeton University Press).

—— (1960), *Theory of Film: The Redemption of Physical Reality* (New York: Oxford University Press).

—— (1995), *The Mass Ornament: Weimar Essays*, ed. and trans. Thomas Y. Levin (Cambridge, Mass.: Harvard University Press).

Kreimeier, Klaus (1992), *Die Ufa-Story: Geschichte eines Filmkonzerns* (Munich: C. Hanser).

Leyda, Jay (1960), *Kino: A History of the Russian and Soviet Film* (London: George Allen & Unwin).

MacBean, James Roy (1975), *Film and Revolution* (Bloomington: Indiana University Press).

Mattelart, Armand, and **Michèle Mattelart** (1992), *Rethinking Media Theory*, trans. James A. Cohen and Urquidi (Minneapolis: University of Minnesota Press).

Morawski, Stefan (1973), 'Introduction', in Lee Baxandall and Stefan Morawski (eds.), *Marx and Engels on Literature and Art: A Selection of Writings* (St Louis: Telos Press).

Pendakur, Manjunath (1990), *Canadian Dreams and American Control: The Political Economy of the Canadian Film Industry* (Detroit: Wayne State University Press).

—— (1997), *Indian Cinema: Industry, Ideology, Consciousness* (Chicago: Lakeview Press).

Polan, Dana (1985), 'A Brechtian Cinema? Towards a Politics of Self-Reflexive Film', in Bill Nichols (ed.), *Movies and Methods* (Berkeley: University of California Press).

Richter, Hans (1986), *The Struggle for Film: Towards a Socially Responsible Cinema*, trans. Ben Brewster (Aldershot: Wildwood House).

Sadoul, Georges (1946–54), *Histoire générale du cinéma*, 5 vols. (Paris: Éditions Denoël).

Shohat, Ella, and **Robert Stam** (1994), *Unthinking Eurocentrism: Multiculturalism and the Media* (London: Routledge).

Solanas, Fernando, and **Octavio Getino** (1969/1976), 'Towards a Third Cinema', in Bill Nichols (ed.), *Movies and Methods* (Berkeley: University of California Press).

Solomon, Maynard (ed.) (1973), *Marxism and Art: Essays Classic and Contemporary* (New York: Vintage).

Staiger, Janet (1992), *Interpreting Films: Studies in the Historical Reception of American Cinema* (Princeton, NJ: Princeton University Press).

*Steven, Peter (ed.) (1985), *Jump Cut: Hollywood, Politics, and Counter-Cinema* (New York: Praeger).

—— (1993), *Brink of Reality: New Canadian Documentary Film and Video* (Toronto: Between the Lines).

Taylor, Richard, and Ian Christie (eds.) (1988), *The Film Factory: Russian and Soviet Cinema in Documents 1896–1939* (Cambridge, Mass.: Harvard University Press).

Walsh, Martin (1981), *The Brechtian Aspect of Radical Cinema* (London: British Film Institute).

Wasko, Janet (1982), *Movies and Money: Financing the American Film Industry* (Norwood, NJ: Ablex).

Waugh, Thomas (ed.) (1984), *'Show Us Life!': Toward a History and Aesthetics of the Committed Documentary* (Metuchen, NJ: Scarecrow Press).

Willemen, Paul (1971), 'Distanciation and Douglas Sirk', *Screen*, 12/2: 63–7.

The political thriller debate

John Hill from John Hill, 'Finding a Form: Politics and Aesthetics in *Fatherland, Hidden Agenda* and *Riff-Raff'*, in George McKnight (ed.), *Agent of Challenge and Defiance: The Films of Ken Loach* (Trowbridge: Flicks Books, 1997).

The background to 'the Costa-Gavras debate' was the world-wide social and political upheavals of the 1960s, when it was only to be expected that questions regarding what political role films could perform would come to the forefront. In common with the realism debate with which it was associated, the central issue concerned the possibility of making a radical film employing conventional cinematic forms. Two directors, in particular, seemed to crystallize the choices at hand. On the one hand, the films of Jean-Luc Godard, especially from *La Chinoise* (1967) onwards, demonstrated an insistence on the need for revolutionary messages (or content) to be accompanied by an appropriate revolutionary form, and were characterized by a deliberate abandonment of the traditional Hollywood conventions of linear narrative, individual, psychologically rounded characters, and a convincing dramatic illusion (or 'classic realism'). On the other hand, the films of Costa-Gavras, beginning with his exposé of political assassination, *Z* (1968), exemplified a model of political filmmaking which sought to bend mainstream Hollywood conventions to radical political ends. In doing so, they attempted to sugar the pill of radical politics with the 'entertainment' provided by the conventions of the thriller. For supporters of political thrillers, their great strength was their ability both to reach and to maintain the interest of an audience who would normally be turned off by politics; for their detractors, the weakness of such films was that their use of popular forms inevitably diluted or compromised their capacity to be genuinely politically radical and to stimulate active political thought. From this point of view, radical political purposes were more likely to be bent to the ends of mainstream Hollywood than vice versa.

What critics of political thrillers highlighted was how the use of the general conventions of narrative and realism characteristic of classical Hollywood, and of the specific conventions characteristic of the crime story or thriller, would, by their nature, encourage certain types of political perspective and discourage others. Hollywood's narrative conventions characteristically encourage explanations of social realities in individual and psychological terms, rather than economic and political ones, while the conventions of realism, with their requirement of a convincing (or 'realistic') dramatic illusion, not only highlight observable, surface realities at the expense of possibly more fundamental underlying ones, but also attach a greater significance to interpersonal relations than to social, economic, and political structures. Moreover, it is because of these tendencies, implicit in the conventions of Hollywood's narrative realism,

that political thrillers so often gravitate towards conspiracy theory or, as Kim Newman drolly observes of US thrillers of the 1970s, the view that society and government are run according to 'the same principles as the coven in *Rosemary's Baby'* (USA, 1968). Conspiratorial actions can be seen and dramatized (as in *Hidden Agenda*, GB, 1990 when a senior Tory politician and senior member of MI5 are brought together to admit what they have done) in a way that underlying social and economic forces cannot within the conventions of narrative and realism. As a result, conspiracy becomes the preferred form of explanation for how power is exercised in society, and how events are to be accounted for. In *Days of Hope* (GB, 1975). Ken Loach and Jim Allen presented the failure of the British 1926 General Strike as simply the result of individual treachery on the part of Labour and trade union leaders; in *Hidden Agenda* no less than two conspiracies are unveiled—both the conspiracy to pervert the course of justice by the security services in Northern Ireland in the early 1980s, and the conspiracy on the part of a small group of businessmen, security personnel, and politicians (led by a thinly disguised Airey Neave) to overthrow a Labour government and replace Edward Heath with Margaret Thatcher as leader of the Conservatives in Britain in the 1970s.

To be fair to the makers of the film, they appear to be convinced of the evidence for conspiracy in 1970s Britain. Moreover, there is undoubtedly a case to be answered. Conspiracy, nevertheless, provides a singularly problematic basis for political analysis and explanation, and is certainly of little value in helping us to understand the crisis of social democracy and labourism which occurred during the 1970s, and the subsequent rise to power of the New Right. The rise of the New Right was not simply willed or manufactured, but grew out of a complex set of economic, political, and ideological circumstances. Conspiracy would, at most, have been a response to these circumstances, just as the likelihood of its success would have depended upon them. In this respect, conspiracy theory has the virtue of neatness, but its cost is the loss of genuine social and political complexity.

The tendency towards personalization which is encouraged by the conventions of narrative realism is reinforced by the specific properties of the crime thriller, especially when it is structured around the investigation of an individual detective and his quest to reveal, or make visible, the truth behind a crime or enigma. Moreover, as a number of critics have suggested, the detective story formula is also characteristic-

The political thriller debate continued

ally a conservative one. It depends upon the superior powers (either intellectual or physical) of an individual investigator (who is often a loner) and, in doing so, tends to prefer the values of individualism to those of the community. In addition, the conventional narrative movement towards a solution of the crime will encourage both an identification with the forces of 'law and order' (even when the investigator is not actually a member of the police), and a general confidence in the ability of the current social set-up to triumph over injustice and right wrongs (which are then characteristically identified as the responsibility of an isolated or atypical individual, rather than of social institutions or political regimes). It is partly in recognition of these problems that political thrillers have attempted to blunt the affirmative and socially conservative impulses of the crime story by stressing the limitations of the individual detective hero and the difficulties of actually getting to the truth. Thus, the investigator may prove unable to solve the crime due to the complexity and deviousness of the forces confronting him, or he may indeed succeed in solving the mystery but then find himself unable to do anything about it—the most paranoid example of which is undoubtedly *The Parallax View* (USA, 1974), in which Warren Beatty's reporter uncovers the inevitable political conspiracy, but is then himself assassinated. *Hidden Agenda* adopts a similar, if less dramatic, strategy. CID inspector Kerrigan (Brian Cox), loosely modelled on John Stalker, is brought from England to Northern Ireland to investigate the murder of Paul Sullivan (Brad Dourit), an American lawyer who had been working for the League of Civil Liberties. He uncovers evidence of both a shoot-to-kill policy and a conspiracy to overthrow a democratically elected Labour government, but is unable to do anything about it, having been effectively silenced by the military and political forces arraigned against him. Admittedly, Ingrid (Frances McDormand), Paul's widow, is still in possession, at the film's end, of an incriminating tape which Harris (Maurice Roëves), the renegade Special Branch officer, has provided. However, given that the film has already made clear that the tape will lack credibility without Harris (whom we now know to be dead at the hands of the security services), the film's ending remains resolutely pessimistic.

While such an ending avoids glib optimism about the prospect of social reform, the film's negative inflexion of the thriller format has its limitations, not only projecting the paranoia characteristic of the political thriller genre, but also engendering a sense of powerlessness about the possibilities for social and political changes ('You can't win against these people', Kerrigan informs Ingrid).

Concern about the absence of any perspective for political

change is linked to the final criticism which has traditionally been directed at the political thriller. For, whatever the strengths and weaknesses of the actual message which the political thriller succeeds in communicating, it is still one that is, so to speak, 'pre-digested'. That is to say, opponents of the political thriller have argued that, by virtue of a reliance upon individual characters and stars with whom we identify, and upon the tightly structured patterns of narrative suspense which engage us emotionally rather than intellectually, the political thriller 'makes up our minds for us'. It may challenge, as *Hidden Agenda* does, the prevailing ideologies of society, but it does so by employing the same emotional patterns of involvement as films which offer the contrary view, and hence fails to encourage audiences to engage critically with political ideas.

In revisiting some of the criticisms of realism and the political thriller, it should be clear that I am doing so from a changed political context, and that I am not therefore advocating any return to the Godardian or 'counter-cinema' model of political filmmaking. Indeed, two major shortcomings of the traditional critique of realism was its characteristic reliance on crude binary oppositions (*either* narrative realism or the revolutionary avant-garde; *either* Costa-Gavras *or* Godard) and general tendency to assume that certain aesthetic strategies (primarily Brechtian) would almost necessarily deliver a radical politics. It is evident that the unitary model of political cinema which underpinned such formulations is inadequate, and that changed political circumstances now require more diverse forms of political filmmaking. It is for this reason that the revival of the concept of 'Third Cinema' has also been helpful.

The concept of Third Cinema was initially employed by the Argentinian filmmakers Fernando Solanas and Octavio Getino, to identify an emergent political cinema which was distinct from both mainstream Hollywood (First Cinema) and European 'art' cinema (Second Cinema). Current usage of the term has continued to emphasize Third Cinema's original commitment to political explanation and dialogue, but has also recognized that this commitment cannot be fulfilled by any pre-given artistic recipes. As Paul Willemen has stated, Third Cinema is not only engaged in the creation of 'new, politically . . . and cinematically illuminating types of filmic discourse', but also is aware of 'the historical variability of the necessary aesthetic strategies to be adopted'. What artistic means are appropriate to Third Cinema, therefore, will vary according to the social, political, and cultural contexts in which it is produced and to which it is addressed. The virtue of Third Cinema in this respect, is that, unlike models of counter-cinema, it does not prescribe one 'correct' way of making political cinema which is universally applicable, but

The political thriller debate continued

recognizes the need for aesthetic diversity and a sensitivity to place, and to social and cultural specifics. In doing so, it also insists upon the importance of constantly rethinking and reworking (but not necessarily overthrowing) traditional artistic models (including those of both Hollywood and the avant-garde) if cinema is to continue to be critically lucid and politically relevant.

13 Feminism and film

Patricia White

Feminism is among the social movements and cultural–critical discourses that most definitively shaped the rise of Anglo-American film studies in the 1970s. In turn, film studies, a relatively young and politicized field, provided fertile ground for feminist theory to take root in the academy. Feminist film studies, emerging from this juncture, has been both highly specialized in its theoretical debates on representation, spectatorship, and sexual difference, and broad in its cultural reach and influence. It has also involved a dual focus on critique and cultural production.

As a critical methodology, feminism makes salient the category of gender and gender hierarchy in all forms of knowledge and areas of inquiry. The female image—the female as image—has been a central feature of film and related visual media; in film criticism and theory, making gender the axis of analysis has entailed a thoroughgoing reconsideration of films for, by, and about women, and a consequent transformation of the canons of film studies. Bringing into focus the overlooked contributions of women to film history has been a key objective of feminist film studies as well as an organizing principle of women's film festivals and journalism. A concern with representation, in both a political sense (of giving voice to or speaking on behalf of women) and an aesthetic sense, has also united the activist and theoretical projects of women's film culture.

Over the past two decades, in the context of feminist politics and women's studies in the academy, feminist film studies has extended its analysis of gender in film to interrogate the representation of race, class, sexuality, and nation; encompassed media such as television and video into its paradigms; and contributed to the rethinking of film historiography, most notably in relation to consumer culture. The feminist interest in popular culture's relation to the socially disenfranchised has influenced film studies' shift from textual analysis and subject positioning to broader cultural studies of institutions and audiences. A postmodern, globalized, technologically saturated social reality has set new questions for feminist theory and methodology as for the whole of film studies.

> **In film criticism and theory, making gender the axis of analysis has entailed a thoroughgoing reconsideration of films for, by, and about women, and a consequent transformation of the canons of film studies.**

An account of principal issues, texts, and debates that have established feminist critical studies of film as a unique area of inquiry will be followed by a discussion of some of the diverse women's film production practices with which the field has engaged.

Feminist film criticism and theory

Most histories of the field of feminist film studies find a starting-point in the appearance of several book-length popular studies of women in film in the United States in the early 1970s (e.g. Rosen 1973; Haskell 1974; Mellen 1974). Their focus on 'images of women' was immediately critiqued by 'cinefeminists' interested in theorizing the structure of representation. As a result, an opposition—rhetorical in part—arose between 'American' sociological approaches and 'British' theory, of 'cinefeminism', which was based upon a critique of realism.

Reflection theory

Molly Haskell and Marjorie Rosen's studies are usually considered exemplars of 'reflection theories' of women and film: they assume that film 'reflects' social reality, that depictions of women in film mirror how society treats women, that these depictions are distortions of how women 'really are' and what they 'really want', and that 'progress' can be made (see Petro 1994). Such accounts are related to powerful feminist critiques of the effects of mainstream media, pornography, and advertising on body-image, sex roles, and violence against women, which, in turn, fuelled advocacy for women's intervention in image-making. Typically, such studies present and critique a typology of images of women—an array of virgins, vamps, victims, suffering mothers, child women, and sex kittens. The emerging film criticism of lesbians, as well as African American and Asian American women, and other women of colour, also tends to identify and reject stereotypes—such as the homicidal, man-hating lesbian, the African American mammy, the tragic mulatto, and the Asian dragon lady—and advocates more complex representations. These are categories, however, which tend to limit consideration of the social function of stereotypes and frequently lead to simplistic 'good'–'bad' readings of individual films. The identification of types and generic conventions is an important step, but simply replacing stereotypes with positive images does not transform the system that produced them.

Haskell narrativizes the history of film as an arc from 'reverence' (the silent era) to 'rape' (Hollywood in the 1960s and 1970s); the high point is represented by the strong, independent heroines of the 1940s, which reached its apotheosis in stars such as Katharine Hepburn. Presenting herself as a maverick critic, Haskell frequently distances herself from feminism, neglects to consider non-white women, and betrays a profound heterosexism (Hepburn and Tracy are for her the romantic ideal of complementarity of the sexes). Yet she makes several useful contributions, and criticism of the reductionism of her study can itself be reductive. She diagnoses violence against, and marginalization of, women in acclaimed 'New Hollywood' films, as reactions to the emergence of feminism and the threat posed by women's autonomy, and she is wary of the mystifications of European art cinema, which would appear to place women and their sexuality more centrally in their stories, while offering only a new version of the 'eternal feminine'. Finally, Haskell's comments on the woman's picture, or 'weepie'—a production category denigrated by the industry and most critics—suggest that such films actually did represent the contradictions of women's lives in patriarchal capitalism and inaugurated one of the most fruitful areas of feminist film studies.

Semiotics and ideology critique

Reviewing Haskell and Rosen's books, Claire Johnston (1975b) notes the inadequacies of the 'images of women' approach: while it grasps the ideological implications of cinema, images are seen as too easily detached from the texts and psychic structures through which they function, as well as the institutional and historical contexts that determine their form and their reception. For Johnston, film must be seen as a language and woman as a sign—not simply a transparent rendering of the real (see also Pollock 1992). In perhaps the most influential statement of this position, 'Women's Cinema as Counter Cinema', Johnston (1973) combines Roland Barthes's concept of myth as the rendering natural of ideology with auteur theory to decode the function of women in Hollywood films by Howard Hawks and John Ford, as well as women auteurs Dorothy Arzner and Ida Lupino. This, in turn, set a pattern for subsequent feminist studies of Hollywood genres such as film noir, the musical, and the western, which showed how woman as signifier performed precise iconographic and ideological functions, either constituting a genre's structural dimensions (woman = home in the western) or exposing its ideological contradictions (the femme fatale figure in film noir; see Kaplan 1978).

In this latter case, as Janet Bergstrom (1979) points out, Johnston and others were influenced by the concept of the 'progressive text' derived from the French journal *Cahiers du cinéma*. Indeed, the progressive text, or popular film which 'displayed the ideology to which it belonged' (Comolli and Narboni 1969), was the chief inheritance of feminist film studies from Marxist cultural theory (through the Russian Formalist notion of 'making strange', to Brechtian 'distanciation' and Althusserian 'contradiction') and shaped the ongoing interest in Hollywood film. *Cahiers'* methodology was also assimilated by the British journal *Screen*, which emerged as the dominant venue of work combining structuralism, semiotics, Marxism, and psychoanalysis and the touchstone for developments in feminist film theory.

Psychoanalysis

The most thoroughgoing and explicit introduction of neo-Freudian psychoanalytic theory to feminist film studies, and the single most inescapable reference in the field (and arguably in contemporary English-language film theory as a whole), is Laura Mulvey's 'Visual Pleasure and Narrative Cinema', published in *Screen* in 1975. Recommending 'a political use of psychoanalysis', this essay, like Johnston's 'Women's Cinema as Counter Cinema', was polemical both in tone and in its advocacy of theoretical rigour and a new, materialist feminist cinematic practice. However, whereas Johnston had argued that 'in order to counter our objectification in the cinema, women's collective fantasy must be released . . . [and] demands the use of the entertainment film', Mulvey insisted on a break with dominant cinema (in the form of a modernist cinematic practices which would provoke conscious reflection on the part of the spectator) and the 'rejection of pleasure as a radial weapon'. This position derived from her account of the gendered processes of spectatorial desire and identification orchestrated by classical narrative cinema and is summed up in one of her piece's headings: 'woman as image/man as bearer of the look'.

Mulvey argued that the institution of cinema is characterized by a sexual imbalance of power, and psychoanalysis may be used to explain this. Because psychoanalysis makes sexual difference its central category, feminist thinking can use it to understand women's exclusion from the realms of language, law,

and desire—from, in short, what Jacques Lacan called the symbolic register. Freud's description of scopophilia—pleasure in looking—was Mulvey's starting-point. Dominant cinema deploys unconscious mechanisms in which the image of woman functions as signifier of sexual difference, confirming man as subject and maker of meaning. These mechanisms are built into the structure of the gaze and narrative itself through the manipulation of time and space by point of view, framing, editing, and other codes.

> **This position derived from her account of the gendered processes of spectatorial desire and identification orchestrated by classical narrative cinema and is summed up in one of her piece's headings: 'woman as image/ man as bearer of the look'.**

Centred around the spectator's and the camera's look, cinema offers identificatory pleasure with one's on-screen likeness, or ego ideal (understood in terms of the Lacanian mirror stage), and libidinal gratification from the object of the gaze. The male *spectator* is doubly supported by these mechanisms of visual gratification as the gaze is relayed from the male surrogate within the diegesis to the male spectator in the audience. The woman, on the other hand, is defined in terms of *spectacle*, or what Mulvey described as 'to-be-looked-at-ness'. As Mulvey observed, 'In a world ordered by sexual imbalance, pleasure in looking has been split between active/male and passive/female'. Mulvey excluded from consideration the possible pleasures afforded a female spectator by narrative cinema through her provocative use of the male pronoun to designate the spectator. As she explained later, her essay explored 'the relationship between the image of woman on screen and the "masculinization" of the spectator position, regardless of actual sex (or possible deviance) of any real live movie-goer' (Mulvey 1981/1988: 69).

Yet if the image of woman is to be 'looked at', it also, according to the Freudian account, connotes sexual difference and a threat of castration that must be contained. According to Mulvey, narrative cinema has developed two ways to neutralize this threat, which she correlates with the filmic practices of two of film theory's most privileged auteurs: Josef von Sternberg and Alfred Hitchcock. Von Sternberg's baroque compositions, centred around the impossibly stylized image of Marlene Dietrich, are seen as exemplary of a fetishistic disavowal of the threat of sexual difference. In the Freudian scenario, the fetish stands in for the missing penis, and the fetishist disavows his knowledge of lack with belief in the compensatory object. The oblique narratives and iconic, layered compositions in von Sternberg's films exemplify, therefore, what Mulvey called fetishistic scopophilia.

In another oft-quoted formula, Mulvey described the second avenue of mastering castration anxiety as voyeurism gratified by investigation and punishment or redemption of the 'guilty' (that is, different, female) object: 'sadism demands a story', she wrote. For example, the angst-ridden, illogical world of film noir is stabilized by pinning guilt on the femme fatale. Mulvey argued that Alfred Hitchcock's films (*Vertigo* USA, 1958; and *Rear Window* USA, 1954) brilliantly fuse the fetishistic and voyeuristic–sadistic solutions to the threat posed by the image of women, and her reading inaugurated a rich strain of feminist work on the director.

Prior to Mulvey, psychoanalytic film theory had tended to confirm the hegemony and homogeneity of the patriarchal unconscious in cinema. Christian Metz extrapolated the mechanism of fetishism (considered an exclusively male perversion) to define the spectator's belief in the cinematic illusion itself; Jean-Louis Baudry argued that the 'cinematic apparatus' (defined technologically, institutionally, and ideologically) extended Western representation systems to position an ideal, transcendental subject; and the theory of suture demonstrated how cinematic syntax, for example the point-of-view construction so often used in establishing the woman as image, confirmed the coherence of the viewing subject over and against lack (see Creed, Part 1, Chapter 9, for a fuller exposition of these arguments).

Feminist work in the wake of Mulvey's essay highlighted how all of these metapsychological accounts implicitly posited a male viewer—however illusory his mastery and unity might prove to be—and went on to elaborate the effects of the cinema's seemingly necessary and massive exclusion of the female subject position. However, in articulating the problem of dominant cinema so very exactly, the feminist psychoanalytic paradigm risked being trapped within the monolith. As Raymond Bellour, whose meticulous textual analyses traced and confirmed the male Oedipal trajectory

of Hollywood films from the micro-codes of editing to the macro-codes of narrative structure, candidly stated in an interview with *Camera Obscura*: 'To put it a bit hastily . . . I think a woman can love, accept, and give a positive value to these films only from her own masochism' (quoted in Bergstrom 1988: 195).

Needless to say, Bellour's was not the last word on the subject, and a number of responses to the totalization of the apparatus model soon evolved. For some theorists, if the woman's 'visual presence tends to work against the development of a story line' (Mulvey 1975: 33), then it could be argued that spectacle itself could be understood as a weak link in the totalizing patriarchal regime Mulvey delineated and used as a way of interrupting narrative closure and its presumed confirmation of spectatorial mastery. The spectacularized woman—for example, the female star, whose iconicity is also constructed intertextually and thus may exceed narrative placement—can demonstrate or defy the logic of the system that would subordinate her to the gaze of the male. Similarly, the musical genre's subordination of narrative codes to performance and spectacle might resist ideological containment, and this is possibly one source of its appeal to female and gay audiences. Other responses to and extensions of Mulvey's paradigm suggested that the male spectator's relation to the image signifying sexual difference might be masochistic, rather than necessarily sadistic. Gaylyn Studlar (1988), for example, argues that this is the effect—and the subversiveness—of the von Sternberg–Dietrich films, and Carol Clover (1992) suggests that contemporary horror films encourage their young male spectators to identify with the female victim. Finally, it was argued that cases of the spectacularization of masculinity or ethnicity, while not contradicting the association of femininity with to-be-looked-atness, permitted an interrogation of the wider cultural logic determining the power and hierarchy of the gaze.

Mulvey herself addressed two key omissions in her argument in her own 'Afterthoughts' on the issue: what she called 'the "woman in the audience" issue' and 'the "melodrama" issue' (Mulvey 1981/1988: 69). Both concerns stemmed from her 'own love of Hollywood melodrama' and demonstrated the irony of her earlier essay's conclusion that 'Women . . . cannot view the decline of the traditional film form with anything much more than sentimental regret' (1975: 39). Much like the choice faced by the melodrama's heroine between pursuing her desire or accepting 'correct femininity',

Mulvey argued that female spectatorship entails a tension or oscillation between psychical positions of masculinity and femininity which are legacies of the female Oedipal complex and socialization under patriarchy confirmed in dominant narrative patterns. Making a 'trans-sex identification' with the agent of desire and narrative is habitual for women. Mulvey's account of female spectatorship as it is engaged in narrativity suggests that gender identification, and hence identity, is a *process*, and this point has been picked up by Teresa de Lauretis. 'The real task', she argued, 'is to enact the contradiction of female desire, and of women as social subjects, in the terms of narrative; to perform its figures of movement and closure, image and gaze, with the constant awareness that spectators are historically engendered in social practices, in the real world, and in cinema too' (1984: 156).

In other words, the 'woman in the audience' cannot be reduced to that single term in the polarity: 'woman as image'. Her identification with that position must continually be solicited by narrative, visual, and wider cultural codes. Moreover, not every 'woman in the audience' is the same. The idea that formalist intervention is the only way of interrupting mimetic spectator–text relations ignores the fact that the socio-historical location of many audience members presents a difficult 'fit' with the textually ordained position. Lesbian spectatorship has posed a particularly revealing challenge to psychoanalytic theory's seeming equation of 'sexual difference' with heterosexual complementarity—the presumption that women cannot desire the image because they *are* the image (Doane 1982). As Jackie Stacey points out: 'psychoanalytic accounts which theorize identification and object choice within a framework of linked binary oppositions (masculinity/femininity: activity/passivity) necessarily masculinize female homosexuality' (1987: 370). She then goes on to stress the inherent homoerotic components of female spectatorship. Attempts to address lesbians precisely as social subjects, as viewers, have therefore side-stepped the psychoanalytic paradigm to consider how lesbian viewers might appropriate dominant, heterosexist representations (Ellsworth 1990). Other challenges to Mulvey's paradigm from within psychoanalysis, such as the theory of film's homology with fantasy as the 'mise-en-scène of desire' (Cowie 1984), suggest that spectators do not necessarily take up predetermined or unitary positions of identification. However, while making room for identifications across gender and sexuality, such accounts tend to overestimate fantasmatic mobility, downplaying the constraints of social–sexual identity on spectatorship.

Critiques of the field's largely unexamined ethnocentrism also became more and more insistent (see Gaines 1990). In so far as sexual difference is the organizing axis of subjectivity in psychoanalysis, Lacanian feminist film theory was ill equipped to theorize the intersection of gender with racial, ethnic, class, national, or other differences—whether in visual and narrative codes or in spectatorial response. The institutionalization of the field reinforced this structuring omission. Although psychoanalytic concepts of the gaze, disavowal, and fetishism have been used to account for the racialized image (notably in work drawing on the writings of Frantz Fanon), the discourse is generally seen as too ahistorical and individualistic to be useful to an anti-racist film theory. In 'The Oppositional Gaze' (1992), bell hooks argues that black female spectators cannot help but view Hollywood films from an oppositional standpoint as the fetishized woman in film is white. Such glaring blind spots in feminist film theory called for concrete readings and new methodologies—drawn from feminist and anti-racist politics, and historical and cultural studies—to explicate the relationships of diverse women in the audience to dominant representations of femininity.

The woman's film

Mulvey's own linkage of 'the woman in the audience issue' with 'the melodrama issue' sets up an important contest of textual and contextual models. Cinema has inherited a great deal from theatrical and literary melodrama; however, the association of melodrama with femininity can be detected in the pejorative attitude with which it is often regarded. Studies of silent melodrama in various national contexts, the Hollywood 'family melodrama' of the 1950s, television genres such as soap operas, and particularly that subset of melodrama known as 'the woman's film' offer the opportunity to compare feminist methodologies and epistemologies concerned with historical context and actual viewers with those focused on textually constructed spectator positions.

The woman's film flourished in Hollywood in the 1930s, 1940s, and 1950s, but is found in most industries and survives today, notably in the made-for-TV movie. It is centred around a female star–heroine, frequently written by or adapted from the work of women, often fairly inexpensively made, and explicitly marketed to and consumed by female audiences. Typically, such films are concerned with evoking emotional responses to such 'women's issues' as heterosexual romance, domesticity, and motherhood. While some feminists have rejected such traditional associations, particularly their survival in contemporary popular culture, others have found in them an expression, however mediated, of women's contradictory experience in the patriarchal family. Indeed, the films have seemed to offer the opportunity to decode the mother as an ideological construct and to come to terms with the pre-feminist generation of 'mothers'. From the perspective of genre theory, the woman's film could be seen as performing 'cultural work'—speaking to, if displacing, genuine social conflicts—between women's economic dependence and desire for autonomy, between heterosexual and maternal ideology and sexual self-definition. The woman's film thus links the focus on 'depictions of women' in sociological criticism with cinefeminists' concern with 'the figure of the woman'. Their methodologies and evaluations, even their organizing questions, differ, however.

> **The woman's film could be seen as performing 'cultural work'—speaking to, if displacing, genuine social conflicts—between women's economic dependence and desire for autonomy, between heterosexual and maternal ideology and sexual self-definition.**

In her influential study *The Desire to Desire* (1987), Mary Ann Doane develops a theory of female spectatorship through intricate textual analyses of films produced for a female audience in wartime Hollywood. Identifying 'maternal', 'medical', and 'paranoid' subgenres of the woman's film, Doane demonstrates the frequency of overt thematizations of psychoanalysis in their depictions of family, romantic, and doctor–patient relationships; and her readings uncover scenarios of masochism and hysteria that confirm Lacanian psychoanalysis's definition of femininity as deficiency or lack. Analysing the designation 'woman's film' in terms of both possession and address, Doane con-

cludes that such films ultimately position the women they address as subject *to*, rather than *of*, the discourse of desire. Like the Joan Crawford character in the woman's film *Possessed* (USA, 1947), the female spectator is dispossessed of what appears to be her own story.

In a crucial contribution to spectatorship theory, 'Film and the Masquerade' (1982), Doane argues that the visual economy and affective intensity of the woman's film encourages the female spectator to over-identify with the image. According to the psychoanalytic model of sexual difference, the distance upon which fetishism, desire, and even criticism depend is simply not available to her: the woman is deficient in relation to the gaze. The title and plot conceit of *Dark Victory* (USA, 1939), in which the heroine must mime being able to see so that the hero (but not the audience) will leave her to suffer and die alone, serves as a hyperbolic illustration. When Doane acknowledges that it is 'quite tempting to foreclose entirely the possibility of female spectatorship', her statement must be seen in the context of feminist anti-essentialism: 'the woman' of 'the woman's film' does not exist—she is a discursive category produced within a phallocentric representational regime. Doane proposes a new trope for female spectatorship: masquerade, defined by Freudian analyst Joan Rivière as indistinguishable from 'genuine womanliness', and which can provide a means of 'flaunting' femininity's lack.

Unwilling to reject films that historically have given women solace and pleasure, other feminist theorists argue that female spectatorship encompasses more than narcissism or masochism. Although, as Ann Kaplan argues (1983a), *Stella Dallas* (USA, 1937) does indeed end with an extravagant scene of female abjection (anonymous among the crowd, the title character watches from afar the wedding of the daughter she gave up), Linda Williams argues that in it women recognize contradictory points of view: that they engage their 'multiple identificatory power' and their critical reading skills (1984/1990: 154). Not simply glorifying female sacrifice, such films allow women to mourn loss and reject its necessity.

These contrasting emphases in feminist film theory can be illustrated by two strikingly different interpretations of Alfred Hitchcock's 'woman's picture' *Rebecca* (USA, 1940), based on the 1938 novel by Daphne du Maurier. While Doane (1987) sees the anonymity of the film's heroine and the absence of the eponymous character (the hero's dead first wife Rebecca) as a negation of female subjectivity, Tania Modleski (1988) sees a compelling version of the female Oedipal drama in which the object of desire and identification is another woman—a drama all the more compelling because the power that that woman exerts over the heroine (and in turn the spectator) comes from outside the visual field (indeed from beyond the grave). Relating the woman's film to traditions in women's fiction and to popular genres such as soap operas and Gothic and romance fiction, Modleski views such highly codified narratives as responses to women's social and psychological conditions, utopian 'resolutions' of real conflicts through aesthetic means, fantasies of omnipotence and outlets for rage and desire.

If Doane is careful to specify that she speaks only of the discursively constructed female subject, who is not to be conflated with actual members of the audience, and Modleski seeks to *theorize* the position and pleasure of real women, still other feminist film scholars have challenged psychoanalytic explanations by emphasizing historical and audience studies in their work on the woman's film (see Stacey 1987). This is part of a wider movement in film studies away from the homogeneity of the cinematic institution presumed in apparatus theory, and from the centrality and determinism of the film text, towards the heterogeneity of what Stuart Hall (1980) calls encoding and decoding practices. Many signifying systems intersect in any given spectatorial situation, and spectators bring diverse identities, histories, cultural competences, and responses—both conscious and unconscious—to the movies. The tension between the plurality and diversity of actual viewers and responses and that textual and theoretical construction conceived in the singular as 'the female spectator' can be related to what Teresa de Lauretis (1984) identifies as one of the central, necessary contradictions in feminism—between woman, a philosophical or aesthetic construct, and women, materially and historically located beings who are gendered female. Work on the woman's film seeks not to resolve this tension but to explore its productivity.

Stars, reception studies, and consumer culture

It is a defining feature of the 'woman's film' that it showcases popular female stars as its suffering or transgressive heroines. Despite its central tenet that woman is a constructed image, psychoanalytically informed

feminist analyses had little to say about the signifying effects of a star image in a particular textual system—let alone about how the interaction between text and spectator might be determined by foreknowledge and anticipation of the star; by, in short, intertextuality. This careful avoidance was in part a reaction to work such as Haskell's which followed journalistic conventions of writing about characters and stars, and in part a logical extension of the theory of the image of woman as male fetish and its identification with ideological complicity.

The increasing influence of cultural studies (identified with the work of the Birmingham Centre for Contemporary Cultural Studies), which looks beyond the film text for the social meaning of cinematic practices, as well as of approaches in film history that include institutional and promotional discourses and reception studies, invigorated work on film stars. As Judith Mayne (1993: 124) notes, the consequences of this shift in perspective are immediate: taking stars into account makes it hard to accept that the fascination of the movies inheres in the regressive pleasure of the projection situation, as apparatus theory argued. This approach is of particular interest to feminists, not only because female stars are the most powerful women in the film industry and represent ideologically significant versions of femininity throughout the culture, but because it is as 'fans' that women are addressed as the prototypical moviegoers. This demands reconsideration of the pronouncement that women are excluded from the spectator position and from the articulation of desire. At the very least, stars, like genre films, are offered as particular imaginary solutions to women's unfulfilled desires.

Following the methodology set out in Richard Dyer's book *Stars* (1979), critics read the inflexions of particular star images across the body of films in which the star appears as well as in promotional, publicity, and critical texts such as fan magazines and testimonials, commodity tie-ins, public appearances, tributes, and cultural citations. Dyer sees 'independent women stars' such as Katharine Hepburn and Bette Davis, or, to give a contemporary example, Susan Sarandon, as potentially oppositional types—at least at the basic level of embodying the category of the individual *as female*. Maria Laplace (1987) traces the roots of Davis's public persona and her roles in her star vehicles to the heroines of women's fiction, and reads her association with work, as well as with consumption, as particularly appealing to female spectators. Dyer also analyses Davis's restless performance style, her 'bitch' and camp roles and their reception and imitation in gay male culture. This 'structured polysemy' of a star image allows the figure to be claimed by diverse audiences and generates unpredictable effects in a range of reception contexts over time.

For example, the 'mystery' and self-sufficiency of Dietrich and Garbo (evident in their visual presentation as well as the plots of their films), the former's cruelty to men and the latter's tragic relation to love, as well as costuming codes and their on-screen flirtations with women, have been understood not only as open to appropriation by lesbian spectators today, but as drawing on the visual codes of lesbian self-representation in the 1930s. Black or ethnically coded star-images, such as those of Lena Horne or Carmen Miranda, have been decoded in relation to fantasies of racialized sexuality and the construction of American national identity and as figures of oppositional identification for non-white spectators (see Roberts 1993), and studies of national cinemas have increasingly mined the semiotic riches of popular star images.

The analysis of stars entails both sociological and psychoanalytic approaches and touches on several important directions in contemporary feminist film studies: placing the cinema within consumer culture, historicizing film exhibition and reception, and understanding active spectatorship as a process of 'negotiation'. Historically, cinema emerges within the culture of consumption. Once again it is not unreasonable to suggest that women are not marginalized as spectators, with no access except through disempowering identification with femininity-as-commodity in the figure of the star, but energetically addressed as consumers. Miriam Hansen (1991) looks at the Valentino craze in the 1920s as a definitive moment in locating female sexuality in modernity and the public sphere. Fan culture involves a range of concrete practices of consumption, purveyed by magazines, fashions, and commodity tie-ins. Jane Gaines and Charlotte Herzog (1987) demonstrate that costuming is a crucial dimension of the personae of 'women's' stars such as Joan Crawford. Consumerist discourse works *in* as well as through the woman's film, often as a potent allegory of women's attempt to define herself or satisfy her desire. Consumer goods and the surfaces of costume, skin, and hair also offer non-narrative, tactile, and visual pleasures to women. Television, which addresses consumers in the home, extends such dimensions of women's viewing practice; arguably, the television 'apparatus' itself is feminized. Television

audience studies, and feminist television scholarship in general, have been increasingly important to developments in film studies. Finally, work on consumerism can restore the question of gender to the now dominant concept of postmodernism. Many of the characteristics of postmodern society—fragmentation over coherence, style over history, surface over depth, and consumption over production—have traditionally been associated with women's condition, as Anne Friedberg (1994) demonstrates by linking the visual culture of modernity to contemporary spectatorial practices of the shopping-mall, cineplex, and home video. Friedberg suggests that there is at least some potential for mobilizing such associations on women's behalf—even as postmodernism threatens identity categories upon which feminism and other oppositional politics would seem to depend.

Indeed the traditional left's rejection of popular culture as capitalist manipulation, a position commonly associated with the Frankfurt School, frequently betrays the equation of consumption with feminine passivity. On the other hand, an unproblematic celebration of consumerism in the name of women's pleasure does not constitute 'resistance'. Generally speaking, feminist cultural studies rejects the view of female viewers as victims of 'false consciousness', but without then attributing inherently subversive powers to them. Stuart Hall's (1980) term 'negotiation' (itself a market-place metaphor, as Mayne (1993) points out) describes viewers' strategies of decoding media messages—from television news to film endings—as not wholly in conformity with, nor in complete opposition to, dominant ideology. A negotiated reading is inflected by viewers' socio-historical location and the discourses available to them. Jacqueline Bobo, in *Black Women as Cultural Readers* (1995), analyses her ethnographic research among black women viewers of Steven Spielberg's film *The Color Purple* (USA, 1985). She finds that their familiarity with Alice Walker's novel, the opportunity to see a high-budget film with a black female protagonist, and the community in which they viewed and discussed the film contributed to a more nuanced and positive reception of the film than that of many liberal reviewers, both black and white.

As the preceding account demonstrates, after more than twenty years feminist film studies has become an established academic discipline, with the critique of dominant media a primary preoccupation. But while recent work stressing the agency of the film or television viewer is an important challenge to the hierarchies

> It has been women's film *production*, rather than reception, that has been the most prominent model of resistance and opposition to the status quo.

presumed in Laura Mulvey's influential model, it has been women's film *production*, rather than reception, that has been the most prominent model of resistance and opposition to the status quo. Not simply an important parallel sector of 'feminism in film', women's film-making practice has been a constant reference and dynamic ground for theoretical work. Reclaiming women filmmakers' work within mainstream industries and in national and alternative film movements entails the re-evaluation of concepts of film authorship and criteria of film historiography and raises interesting methodological questions, such as the role of the critic in the definition of a 'feminist' film and the problem of essentialism (the notion that all women or all women's films share inherent qualities). The next sections look at areas of women's production that have raised particularly generative issues for feminist film studies.

Women's filmmaking

One of the most important discoveries of women's film festivals was of the pioneering role women played in the emergence of film. Alice Guy-Blaché is widely credited with directing the very first fiction film in 1896. She made hundreds of short films in France and later in the United States, and more than twenty feature films through her film company, Solax. The work of another prolific early woman writer-director-producer, Lois Weber, helps illuminate links between early twentieth-century middle-class feminism and the emerging cultural role of cinema. Her 'quality' dramas depicted women's agency and their favourable moral influence, addressing social issues, such as birth control (*The Hand that Rocks the Cradle*, 1917) and abortion (*Where are my Children?*, 1916), within the framework of melodrama. Well known at the time, Weber, like Guy-Blaché, was all but forgotten until feminist rediscovery in the 1970s made possible an acknowledgement of the role her work played in the contest for the respectability of cinema in the United States, and its place in hierarchies of class and taste. Film

preservation movements and new interpretations of early film history emerging in the 1980s have assisted feminist efforts to restore women's contributions to silent cinema. The role of women in the public sphere—in political and social movements, labour, leisure, and the culture of consumption—and in the formation of national identities in the first decades of the twentieth century, have been illuminated by recent studies of Neapolitan filmmaker Elvira Notari (Bruno 1995) and of Nell Shipman, the Canadian-born director of outdoor adventure films (Armatage 1995).

Feminist film scholars' questioning of established film canons draws on the retrieval of women authors and influences in feminist literary criticism. But cinema not only presents a much more limited history and scope than literature; it raises the difficulty of *defining* authorship, given the capital and technology-intensive, commercial and collaborative nature of film production, especially in Hollywood.

Women in Hollywood

Independent women directors and producers who flourished in the first decades of filmmaking were quickly marginalized by the entrenchment of the Hollywood studio system and its eventual dominance of world-wide markets. Studies of women who exercised creative control in sound-era Hollywood such as screenwriters (see Francke, 1994) or stars represent a challenge to the conflation of the idea of cinematic authorship with the figure of the director. But the few women who did work as directors in the heyday of Hollywood—Dorothy Arzner, who directed her first feature at Paramount, where she had been an editor, in 1927, and made sixteen more films before retiring from the movies in 1943, and Ida Lupino, a leading actress at Warners who turned independent producer-director in 1949 and later directed for television—have played a central role in feminist film historiography and criticism.

Claire Johnston's and Pam Cook's contributions to *The Work of Dorothy Arzner* (Johnston 1975a) combined the work of recovery with the critical model developed in Johnston's 'Women's Cinema as Counter Cinema'. The authors looked not for coherent feminist expression in Arzner's work, but for traces of 'the woman's discourse', readable in the 'gaps and fissures' of the classic text. One such moment in Arzner's 1940 film *Dance, Girl, Dance*, in which the female character 'returns the look' of the burlesque audience that would objectify her, has become a canonical example of a textual 'rupture' within patriarchal ideology. In *Directed by Dorothy Arzner* (1994), Judith Mayne reintroduced biographical information and evaluated the significance of the director's lesbianism—not only to readings of her films (her 'authorial signature' decipherable in the highlighting of relationships between women and marginal women characters in her films) but to her public profile when she was an active woman director and to her status and stature in feminist film studies as a figure of fascination.

Contemporary with the emergence of such feminist criticism, women directors were finding greater opportunities in the New Hollywood. The genre-film work of such directors as Stephanie Rothman (*Student Nurses*, 1970) or Amy Heckerling (*Fast Times at Ridgemont High*, 1982) were similarly read 'against the grain' for their feminist inflexions. The cross-over successes of a number of women first active in feminist documentary, such as Claudia Weill's *Girlfriends* (1978), Joyce Chopra's *Smooth Talk* (1985), and Donna Deitch's lesbian romance *Desert Hearts* (1985), received particular scrutiny and anticipated the emergence of contemporary figures such as Mira Nair (*Mississippi Masala*, 1992) and Kathryn Bigelow (*Strange Days*, 1995) from feminist production sectors to Hollywood.

Art film, new national cinemas, third cinema

The European 'art film' has produced a number of indisputable female 'auteurs'. Although they might make fewer compromises to commerce or popular taste than women working within the mainstream industries, their work is even less easily assimilable to the feminist rubric. This does not, however, make them uninteresting to feminist critics. The paradigmatic case is Leni Riefenstahl, documentarian to the Third Reich. Susan Sontag's influential study (1972) of a consistent fascist aesthetic in Riefenstahl's work from *Triumph of the Will* (Germany, 1935) and *Olympia* (Germany, 1938) to her African photography of the 1960s, also lays the groundwork for decoding the Riefenstahl persona. Her celebration as 'female artist' works to place her outside history (and politics), subjecting her to the same codes governing the representation of woman in film. Johnston (1973) critiqued the films of French New Wave director Agnes Varda for perpetuating the

mythology of woman as essentially unknowable and childlike, signifier of nature and sexuality *for men*. The male protagonists and fraught sexual politics of the Italian director Liliana Cavani, initially regarded as evidence that women directors could indeed make anti-feminist films, have been read more subtly by Kaja Silverman (1988) as authorial projections that unsettle patriarchal power hierarchies. Hungarian director Márta Mészáros in Hungary has built up a body of feature films unusual for a woman director, permitting auteurist analysis while expanding West European concepts of feminism and film. However, these directors' achievements must be seen not as exceptional, but inside history, politics, and national contexts. Thus, feminist critical interest has foregrounded the work of women within the New German Cinema, too often identified only with its male proponents (see Sieglohr, Part 3, Chapter 10) and in Australian cinema (see Jacka, Part 3, Chapter 16).

In the case of 'Third Cinema' (see Dissanayake, Part 3, Chapter 18) which explicitly opposed commercially controlled 'First' cinemas and auteurist 'art', or 'Second', cinema, several women's films have been seen as definitive. The single feature Afro-Cuban director Sara Gomez completed before her untimely death, *One Way or Another* ('De cierta manera', Cuba, 1977) has been widely hailed as Brechtian post-colonial feminist cinema. Its dialectical structure of romance plot and 'documentary' analysis of economic conditions stresses the necessity of consciousness-raising around sexual politics as an essential part of the transformation of the social order. Caribbean-born Sarah Maldoror depicted revolutionary women's struggle in Angola in *Sambizanga*, (1972) and women's film collectives formed in Columbia, Brazil, and Peru, and on the Indian subcontinent. The introduction of the films of Third-world women into the canon of Eurocentric feminist criticism, however, should not homogenize the struggles and conditions within which they intervened: feminist, Marxist, and anti-imperialist paradigms have not always overlapped.

Avant-Garde and counter-cinema

Despite vast disparities in resources, conditions of production, and audience, most of the work discussed so far shares the general qualities of feature-length, narrative form, produced with some division of labour, and aimed for theatrical exhibition. Avant-garde work conceived outside that model has historically been an important venue for women; the various avant-garde movements offer feminist critics examples of 'auteurs' in the truest sense, as well as grounding for theories of alternative film language. Germaine Dulac claims the title of first feminist filmmaker; she played a prominent role in the French avant-garde as an educator and theorist, as well as the maker of abstract, narrative, and documentary films. In her most important film, *The Smiling Mme Beudet* (France, 1923), Dulac infused the conventional narrative about a provincial wife with experimental techniques rendering the protagonist's frustration and fantasy. For Sandy Flitterman-Lewis (1989), Dulac's career exemplified 'a search for a new cinematic language capable of expressing female desire'.

> **While feminist film theory has consistently championed formal experimentation, the avant-garde's ethos of personal expression can be seen to foreclose consistent socio-political critique and, frequently, significant engagement with audiences.**

In the poetically rendered subjective space of *Meshes of the Afternoon* (USA, 1943) and subsequent works, Russian-born Maya Deren could be said to be conducting a similar search. Beyond the general influence that earned her the rather dubious appellation 'mother of the American avant-garde', Deren's aesthetic innovations were paid homage in the explicitly feminist work of experimental filmmakers in the 1970s such as Joyce Wieland in Canada and lesbian feminist Barbara Hammer in the United States. Economically accessible and institutionally alternative, avant-garde film has given a significant place to American women since at least the 1950s; yet the movement has been pervaded by a male heroic modernism. In an article arguing for the political importance of *naming* women's media practices, B. Ruby Rich calls the avant-garde 'the Cinema of the Sons', a cinema of rebellion against the dominant 'Cinema of the Fathers' (Rich 1990: 269). While feminist film theory has consistently championed formal experimentation, the avant-garde's ethos of personal expression can be seen to foreclose consistent socio-political critique and, frequently, significant engagement with audiences.

The women's films most privileged in the corpus of feminist film theory have tended to be forms of 'counter-cinema' (see Smith, Part 3, Chapter 2) which question the centrality of the image of women to representational regimes: cinematic signifying systems such as editing or the synchronization of sound and image, narrative logic, the structure of the look, processes of voyeurism and identification. These films have also been linked to the concerns of writers such as Hélène Cixous, Julia Kristeva, and Luce Irigaray with the concept of feminine writing (*écriture feminine*). Perhaps the most commented-upon text was Belgian director Chantal Akerman's minimalist three-hour portrait of a middle-class housewife-prostitute: *Jeanne Dielmann: 23 Quai du Commerce, 1080 Bruxelles* (Belgium and France, 1975) which depicted traditional femininity from a feminist stance (see Fowler, Part 3, Chapter 13c). Laura Mulvey and Peter Wollen's exploration of Lacanian and Freudian theory from the mother's point of view in *Riddles of the Sphinx* (GB, 1975), Sally Potter's experimental short *Thriller* (GB, 1979), and American dancer-choreographer-filmmaker Yvonne Rainer's *Film about a Woman Who . . .* (USA, 1974) and *The Man who Envied Women* (USA, 1985) have also generated considerable debate (see Kuhn 1994; Kaplan 1983). For Mary Ann Doane, these filmmakers have attempted 'the elaboration of a special syntax for the female body' (1988: 227) and their concerns with language, desire, and identity have found an important critical venue in the US feminist film journal *Camera Obscura*.

Documentary

Although generally under represented in academic criticism, the mode of filmmaking in which women's intervention has been most extensive and influential, which feminists first entered, and which remains most accessible to emerging artists, including women and people of colour, is documentary. In 1974 the National Film Board of Canada set up Studio D, a women's documentary unit, and more than 100 films, of whose style Bonnie Klein's indictment of the sex industry *Not a Love Story* (1981) is characteristic, have been made and distributed within that favourable institutional climate. Cinema verité and 'talking heads', interview-based formats allowed women to speak for themselves and to narrate history—exemplifying the feminist slogan 'the personal is the political'. Such films were meant to raise consciousness and to effect social

Unexpected framings and discontinuous editing in Trinh T. Min-ha's *Reassemblage* (1982)

New subject positions—Sian Martin in Ngozi Onwurah's *The Body Beautiful* (1991)

change, addressing viewers in an accessible style and encouraging an active response. Hence, the form is particularly effective in constructing a community. In the heyday of 'ideological criticism', these documentary practices tended to be charged with a 'naïve realism'. Barbara Kopple's important feature-length documentary *Harlan County USA* (1976), for example, was critiqued for effacing the choices made in filming and editing that built narrative suspense. However, Julia Lesage makes a convincing case for 'the political aesthetics of feminist documentary film' in her essay of that title (1990)—arguing that such films construct, among other things, an iconography of everyday women completely absent from mainstream media—and the radical film magazine *Jump Cut*, of which Lesage is a founding editor, maintains a critical and aesthetic engagement with political films.

In the influential film *Daughter Rite* (1978), Michelle Citron, a contributor to *Jump Cut*, drew upon the immediacy and identificatory appeal of documentary while questioning its form. The film juxtaposed a cinéma verité interview with a pair of sisters with journal entries and home movie footage in order to explore the fraught connection between mother and daughter. Only by reading the credits does the viewer learn that the 'interviews' are scripted, but the film's emotional resonance, achieved through the autobiographical voice and the shared experience of being a daughter, is not diminished thereby. More recent work such as Mona Hatoum's *Measures of Distance* (1988) and Ngozi Onwurah's *The Body Beautiful* (1991) inscribe new subject positions—those of the diasporan daughter, the black daughter, and the mother herself—within the hybrid documentary 'genre' *Daughter Rite* might be credited with founding (see Kuhn 1994).

Such polyphony—of voices, points of view, and filmic idioms—increasingly characterizes feminist documentaries, particularly the self-representations of women of colour. This has, in turn, revitalized critical approaches to the form. In particular, an emerging body of theory takes on ethnographic film's traditional gaze at the 'Other', foregrounding questions of authenticity, authority, and testimony in the work of indigenous media-makers and critical anthropologists. No figure has been more crucial to this revision in feminist film studies than Vietnamese American filmmaker and theorist Trinh T. Min-ha (1991). In *Reassemblage* (1982) the filmmaker's voice-over states her intention not to speak about the Senegalese women the image track depicts in unexpected framings and discontinuous editing, but to 'speak nearby'.

With the widespread availability of the relatively inexpensive medium of video, women's media genres, exhibition venues, and critical paradigms have also proliferated. Lightweight and unobtrusive, the camcorder rejuvenated activist documentary, enabled the production of erotic videos by and for women, and reflected the 'identity politics' of the 1980s in an expanding body of independent work by women of colour and lesbians. Television commissions, women's film festivals, and the institutionalization of women's studies and film studies ensure that women's media culture remains a meeting-place of makers, users, and critics, although the symbiotic relationship that existed in the early 1980s between a certain kind of filmmaking practice and feminist film theory seems to have passed. This is due in part to the fact that the corpus is so much larger, in part to the maturation and hence diversification of feminist film studies as a discipline, and in part to larger cultural fragmentation of various kinds. Feminist filmmakers' interventions in cinematic language fit well with the 1970s and early 1980s focus in film theory on textual analysis—whether of dominant or modernist films. However, postmodernism, multiculturalism, and cultural studies has demanded a shift to contextual and local analysis, in which the boundaries between dominant and alternative, resistance and appropriation, production and reception, are significantly remapped. 'Diasporan', black, gay and lesbian, and other independent cinemas, and the cultural contexts in which they have circulated, have all required the refashioning of critical frameworks. As Teresa de Lauretis writes: 'If we rethink the problem of a specificity of women's cinema and aesthetic forms . . . in terms of address—who is making films for whom, who is looking and speaking, how, where, and to whom—then what has been seen as . . . an ideological split within feminist film culture between theory and practice, or between formalism and activism, may appear to be the very strength, the drive and productive heterogeneity of feminism' (de Lauretis 1985/1990: 296).

Conclusion

Pam Cook wrote in 1975 that 'from the outset, the Women's Movement has assumed without question the importance of mobilizing the media for women's struggle, at the same time subjecting them to a process of interrogation' (1975: 36). While carrying out that two-pronged strategy, feminist film studies has established itself as an academic field. If the terms of once-heated arguments—around the usefulness of psychoanalysis, the privileged status of Hollywood, the primacy of sexual difference—appear to have been superseded, contemporary debates are clearly founded upon them. Feminist cultural studies of popular cinema understand 'progressive texts' in social contexts: films such as *Fatal Attraction* (USA, 1987), *Aliens* (USA, 1986), and *Thelma and Louise* (USA, 1991) have therefore been analysed in terms of social anxieties about feminism, genre-mixing, popular reviews, and feminist appropriations. Queer theory has introduced the concept of gender performativity to studies of filmic representation and spectatorial response, drawing on psychoanalytic feminist theory's understanding of sexual identity as unstable, while critiquing heterosexist presumptions and giving voice to a new cultural politics. Transnational exhibition practices confirm that hypotheses of the film text as a bounded object and the spectator as fixed and unitary (Western and male) are untenable. Viewers, critics, and media practitioners mobilize 'the politics of location' to counter new forms of Hollywood hegemony with strategic new voices (see Shohat and Stam 1994). Such diverse and often contradictory methods, objects, and affiliations constitute the productive heterogeneity of contemporary feminist film culture.

BIBLIOGRAPHY

Armatage, Kay (1995), 'Nell Shipman: A Case of Heroic Femininity', in Pietropaolo and Testaferri (1995).
Bergstrom, Janet (1979), 'Rereading the Work of Claire Johnston', in Penley 1988.
—— (1988), 'Alternation, Segmentation, Hypnosis: Interview with Raymond Bellour', in Penley (1988).
Bobo, Jacqueline (1995), *Black Women as Cultural Readers* (New York: Columbia University Press).
Bruno, Giuliana (1995), 'Streetwalking around Plato's Cave', in Pietropaolo and Testaferri (1995).
*Carson, Diane, Linda Dittmar, and Janice Welsch (eds.) (1994), *Multiple Voices in Feminist Film Criticism* (Minneapolis: University of Minnesota Press).
Clover, Carol J. (1992), *Men, Women, and Chain Saws* (Princeton: Princeton University Press).
Comolli, Jean-Louis, and Jean Narboni (1969/1971), 'Cinema/Criticism/Ideology', *Screen*, 12/1: 27–35.

Cook, Pam (1975), 'Dorothy Arzner: Critical Strategies', in Johnston (1975b).
Cowie, Elizabeth (1984), 'Fantasia', *m/f*, 9: 76–105.
de Lauretis, Teresa (1984), *Alice Doesn't: Feminism, Semiotics, Cinema* (Bloomington: Indiana University Press).
—— (1985/1990), 'Rethinking Women's Cinema: Aesthetic and Feminist Theory', in Erens (1990).
Doane, Mary Ann (1982/1990), 'Film and the Masquerade: Theorizing the Female Spectator', in Erens (1990).
—— (1987), *The Desire to Desire: The Woman's Film of the 1940s* (Bloomington: Indiana University Press).
—— (1988), 'Woman's Stake: Filming the Female Body', in Penley (1988).
Dyer, Richard (1979) *Stars* (London: British Film Institute).
Ellsworth, Elizabeth (1990), 'Illicit Pleasures: Feminist Spectators and Personal Best', in Erens (1990).
*Erens, Patricia (ed.) (1990), *Issues in Feminist Film Criticism* (Bloomington: Indiana University Press).
Flitterman-Lewis, Sandy (1989), *To Desire Differently: Feminism and the French Cinema* (Urbana: University of Illinois Press).
Francke, Lizzie (1994), *Script Girls: Women Screenwriters in Hollywood* (London: British Film Institute).
Friedberg, Anne (1994), *Window Shopping: Cinema and the Postmodern* (Berkeley: University of California Press).
Gaines, Jane (1990), 'White Privilege and Looking Relations: Race and Gender in Feminist Film Theory', in Erens (1990).
—— and Charlotte Herzog (eds.) (1990), *Fabrications: Costume and the Female Body* (New York: Routledge).
Gledhill, Christine (1987), *Home is where the Heart Is: Studies in Melodrama and the Woman's Film* (London: British Film Institute).
Hall, Stuart (1980), 'Encoding/Decoding', in Stuart Hall *et al.* (eds.), *Culture, Media, Language* (London: Hutchinson).
Hansen, Miriam (1991), *Babel and Babylon: Spectatorship in American Silent Film* (Cambridge, Mass.: Harvard University Press).
Haskell, Molly (1974/1987), *From Reverence to Rape: The Treatment of Women in the Movies* (New York: Holt, Rinehart & Winston; 2nd edn. Chicago: University of Chicago Press).
hooks, bell (1992), 'The Oppositional Gaze', in *Black Looks* (Boston: South End Press).
Johnston, Claire (1973), 'Women's Cinema as Counter Cinema', in Claire Johnston (ed.), *Notes on Women's Cinema* (London: Society for Education in Film and Television); in Bill Nichols (ed.), *Movies and Methods*, ii (Berkeley: University of California Press).
—— (1975a), *The Work of Dorothy Arzner: Towards a Feminist Cinema* (London: British Film Institute).
—— (1975b), 'Feminist Politics and Film History', *Screen*, 16/3: 115–24.

*Kaplan, E. Ann (ed.) (1978), *Women in Film Noir* (London: British Film Institute).

—— (1983a), 'The Case of the Missing Mother: Maternal Issues in Vidor's *Stella Dallas*', *Heresies*, 16: 81–5.

—— (1983b), *Women and Film* (New York: Methuen).

*Kuhn, Annette (1994), *Women's Pictures: Feminism and Cinema*, 2nd edn. (London: Verso).

Laplace, Maria (1987), 'Producing and Consuming the Woman's Film: Discursive Struggle in *Now, Voyager*', in Gledhill (1987).

Lesage, Julia (1990), 'The Political Aesthetics of the Feminist Documentary Film', in Erens (1990).

Mayne, Judith (1990), *Woman at the Keyhole: Feminism and Women's Cinema* (Bloomington: Indiana University Press).

—— (1993), *Cinema and Spectatorship* (London: Routledge).

—— (1995), *Directed by Dorothy Arzner* (Bloomington: Indiana University Press).

Mellen, Joan (1974), *Women and their Sexuality in the New Film* (New York: Dell).

Modleski, Tania (1988), *The Women who Knew too Much: Hitchcock and Feminist Theory* (New York: Methuen).

Mulvey, Laura (1975/1990), 'Visual Pleasure and Narrative Cinema' in Erens (1990).

—— (1981/1988), 'Afterthoughts on "Visual Pleasure and Narrative Cinema" Inspired by *Duel in the Sun*' (1947) in Penley (1988).

Penley, Constance (ed.) (1988), *Feminism and Film Theory* (New York: Routledge; London: British Film Institute).

Petro, Patrice (1994), 'Feminism and Film History', in Carson *et al.* (1994)

Pietropaolo, Laura, and Ada Testaferri (eds.) (1995), *Feminisms in the Cinema* (Bloomington: Indiana University Press).

Pollock, Griselda (1992), 'What's Wrong with "Images of Women"?', in *The Sexual Subject: A 'Screen' Reader in Sexuality* (London: Routledge).

Rich, B. Ruby (1984), 'From Repressive Tolerance to Erotic Liberation: *Maedchen in Uniform*', in Mary Ann Doane, Patricia Mellencamp, and Linda Williams (eds.), *Re-Visions: Essays in Feminist Film Criticism* (Frederick, Md.: University Publications of America and American Film Institute).

—— (1990), 'In the Name of Feminist Film Criticism', in Erens (1990).

Roberts, Shari (1993), 'The Lady in the Tutti Frutti Hat: Carmen Miranda, a Spectacle of Ethnicity', *Cinema Journal*, 32/3: 3–23.

Rosen, Marjorie (1973), *Popcorn Venus: Women, Movies and the American Dream* (New York: Coward McCann & Geoghegan).

Shohat, Ella, and Robert Stam (1994), *Unthinking Eurocentrism: Multiculturalism and the Media* (New York: Routledge).

Silverman, Kaja (1988), 'The Female Authorial Voice', in *The Acoustic Mirror* (Bloomington: Indiana University Press).

Sontag, Susan (1972), 'Fascinating Fascism', in *Under the Sign of Saturn* (New York: Doubleday).

Stacey, Jackie (1987/1990), 'Desperately Seeking Difference', in Erens (1990).

Studlar, Gaylyn (1988), *In the Realm of Pleasure: Von Sternberg, Dietrich and the Masochistic Aesthetic* (Urbana: University of Illinois).

Trinh T. Min-Ha (1991), *When the Moon Waxes Red: Representation, Gender and Cultural Politics* (New York: Routledge).

Williams, Linda (1984/1990), '"Something Else besides a Mother": *Stella Dallas* and the Maternal Melodrama', in Erens (1990).

Rebecca

Mary Ann Doane, from Mary Ann Doane, *The Desire to Desire: The Woman's Film of the 1940s* (Bloomington: Indiana University Press/Basingstoke: MacMillan, 1987).

Rebecca (USA, 1940) belongs to that group of films which are infused by the Gothic and defined by a plot in which the wife fears her husband is a murderer. In films like *Rebecca, Dragonwyck* (USA, 1946), and *Undercurrent* (USA, 1946), the woman marries, often hastily, *into* the upper class; her husband has money and a social position which she cannot match. The marriage thus constitutes a type of transgression (of class barriers) which does not remain unpunished. The woman often feels dwarfed or threatened by the house itself (*Rebecca, Dragonwyck*). A frequent reversal of the hierarchy of mistress and servant is symptomatic of the fact that the woman is 'out of place' in her rich surroundings. Nevertheless, in films of the same genre, such as *Suspicion* (USA, 1941), *Secret beyond the Door . . .* (USA, 1948), and *Gaslight* (USA, 1944), the economic–sexual relationship is reversed. In each of these, there is at least a hint that the man marries the woman in order to obtain her money. Hence, it is not always the case that a woman from a lower class is punished for attempting to change her social and economic standing. Rather, the mixture effected by a marriage between two different classes produces horror and paranoia.

By making sexuality extremely difficult in a rich environment, both films—*Caught* (USA, 1949) and *Rebecca*—promote the illusion of separating the issue of sexuality from that of economics. What is really repressed in this scenario is the economics of sexual exchange. This repression is most evident in *Caught*, whose explicit moral—'Don't marry for money'—constitutes a negation of the economic factor in marriage. But negation, as Freud points out, is also affirmation; in *Caught* there is an unconscious acknowledgment of the economics of marriage as an institution. In the course of the film, the woman becomes the object of exchange, from Smith Ohlrig to Dr Quinada. A by-product of this exchange is the relinquishing of the posited object of her desire—the expensive mink coat.

There is a sense, then, in which both films begin with a hypothesis of female subjectivity which is subsequently disproven by the textual project. The narrative of *Caught* is introduced by the attribution of the look at the image (the 'I' of seeing) to Leonora and her friend. The film ends by positioning Leonora as the helpless, bedridden object of the medical gaze. In the beginning of *Rebecca*, the presence of a female subjectivity as the source of the enunciation is marked. A female voice-over (belonging to the Fontaine character) accompanies a hazy, dreamlike image: 'Last night I dreamed I went to Manderley again. It seems to me I stood by the iron gate leading to the drive. For a while I could not enter.' The voice goes on to relate how, like all dreamers, she was suddenly possessed by a supernatural power and passed through the gate. This statement is accompanied by a shot in which the camera assumes the position of the 'I' and, in a sustained subjective movement, tracks forward through the gate and along the path. Yet the voice-over subsequently disappears entirely—it is not even resuscitated at the end of the film in order to provide closure through a symmetrical frame. Nevertheless, there *is* an extremely disconcerting re-emergence of a feminine 'I' later in the film. In the cottage scene in which Maxim narrates the 'unnarratable' story of the absent Rebecca to Joan Fontaine, he insists on a continual use of direct quotes and hence the first-person pronoun referring to Rebecca. His narrative is laced with these quotes from Rebecca which parallel on the soundtrack the moving image, itself adhering to the traces of an absent Rebecca. Maxim is therefore the one who pronounces the following statements: 'I'll play the part of a devoted wife'; 'When I have a child, Max, no one will be able to say that it's not yours'; 'I'll be the perfect mother just as I've been the perfect wife'; 'Well, Max, what are you going to do about it? Aren't you going to kill me?' Just as the tracking subjective shot guarantees that the story of the woman literally culminates as the image of the man, the construction of the dialogue allows Maxim to appropriate Rebecca's 'I'.

The films thus chronicle the emergence and disappearance of female subjectivity, the articulation of an 'I' which is subsequently negated. The pressure of the demand in the woman's film for the depiction of female subjectivity is so strong, and often so contradictory, that it is not at all surprising that sections such as the projection scenes in *Caught* and *Rebecca* should dwell on the problem of female spectatorship. These scenes internalize the difficulties of the genre and, in their concentration on the issue of the woman's relation to the gaze, occupy an important place in the narrative. Paranoia is here the appropriate and logical obsession. For it effects a confusion between subjectivity and objectivity, between the internal and the external, thus disallowing the gap which separates the spectator from the image of his or her desire.

In many respects, the most disturbing images of the two films are those which evoke the absence of the woman. In both films these images follow projection scenes which delineate the impossibility of female spectatorship. It is as though each film adhered to the logic which characterizes dreamwork—establishing the image of an absent woman as the delayed mirror image of a female spectator who is herself only virtual.

Rebecca

Tania Modleski, from Tania Modleski, *The Women who Knew Too Much: Hitchcock and Feminist Theory* (New York: Methuen, 1988).

As is well known by now, Laura Mulvey considers two options open to the male for warding off castration anxiety: in the course of the film the man gains control over the woman both by subjecting her to the power of the look and by investigating and demystifying her in the narrative. In *Rebecca* (USA, 1940), however, the sexual woman is never *seen*, although her presence is strongly evoked throughout the film, and so it is impossible for any man to gain control over her in the usual classical narrative fashion. I have discussed how, in the first shot of Maxim, the system of suture is reversed. This is of utmost importance. In her discussion of the system, Kaja Silverman notes, 'Classic cinema abounds in shot/reverse shot formations in which men look at women.' Typically, a shot of a woman is followed by a shot of a man—a surrogate for the male spectator—looking at her. This editing alleviates castration anxiety in two ways: first, the threat posed by the woman is allayed because the man seems to possess her; secondly, the 'gaze within the fiction' conceals 'the controlling gaze outside the fiction'—that of the castrating Other who lurks beyond the field of vision. But in *Rebecca* the beautiful, desirable woman is not only never sutured in as object of the look, not only never made a part of the film's field of vision, she is actually posited within the diegesis as all-seeing—as for example when Mrs Danvers asks

the terrified heroine if she thinks the dead come back to watch the living and says that she sometimes thinks Rebecca comes back to watch the new couple together.

In 'Film and the Labyrinth', Pascal Bonitzer equates the labyrinth with suspense and notes the power of off-screen space or 'blind space' to terrorize the viewer:

Specular space is on-screen space; it is everything we see on the screen. Off-screen space, blind space, is everything that moves (or wriggles) outside or under the surface of things, like the shark in *Jaws*. If such films 'work,' it is because we are more or less held in the sway of these two spaces. If the shark were always on screen it would quickly become a domesticated animal. What is frightening is that it is not there! The point of horror resides in the blind space.

Similarly, Rebecca herself lurks in the blind space of the film, with the result that, like the shark and unlike the second Mrs de Winter, she never becomes 'domesticated'. Rebecca is the Ariadne in this film's labyrinth, but since she does not relinquish the thread to any Theseus, her space, Manderley, remains unconquered by man.

In one of the film's most extraordinary moments the camera pointedly dynamizes Rebecca's absence. When Maxim tells

A negation of female subjectivity or a variant on the Oedipal drama? *Rebecca* (1940)

Rebecca continued

the heroine about what happened on the night of Rebecca's death ('She got up, came towards me', etc.), the camera follows Rebecca's movements in a lengthy tracking shot. Most films, of course, would have resorted to a flashback at this moment, allaying our anxiety over an empty screen by filling the 'lack'. Here, not only is Rebecca's absence stressed, but we are made to experience it as an active force. For those under the sway of Mulvey's analysis of narrative cinema, *Rebecca* may be seen as a spoof of the system, an elaborate sort of castration joke, with its flaunting of absence and lack.

It is true, however, that in the film's *narrative*, Rebecca is subjected to a brutal devaluation and punishment. Whereas the heroine, throughout most of the film, believes Rebecca to have been loved and admired by everyone, especially by Maxim, she ultimately learns that Maxim hated his first wife. 'She was', he says, 'incapable of love or tenderness or decency.' Moreover, the film punishes her for her sexuality by substituting a cancer for the baby she thought she was expecting, cancer being that peculiar disease which, according to popular myth, preys on spinster and nymphomaniac alike. In addition, Mrs Danvers receives the usual punishment inflicted on the bad mother–witch: she is burned alive when she sets fire to the Manderley mansion.

The latter part of *Rebecca*, concerned with the investigation, can be seen as yet another version of the myth of the overthrow of matriarchy by a patriarchal order. After all, Rebecca's great crime, we learn, was her challenge to patriarchal laws of succession. The night of her death she goaded Maxim into hitting her when she told him that she was carrying a child which was not his but which would one day inherit his possessions. Even more importantly, after Rebecca's death her 'spirit' presides and its power passes chiefly down the *female* line (through Mrs Danvers). Rebecca's name itself (as well as that of the house associated with her) overshadows not only the name of the 'second Mrs de Winter' but even the formidable one of the patriarch: George Fortesquieu Maximillian de Winter.

Ultimately the male authorities must step in and lay the ghost of Rebecca to rest once and for all (and true to Hollywood form, the point of view is eventually given over to Maxim while the heroine is mostly out of the picture altogether).

Nevertheless, despite this apparent closure, the film has managed in the course of its unfolding to hint at what feminine desire might be like were it allowed greater scope. First, it points to women's playfulness, granting them the power and threat of laughter. Over and over Rebecca's refusal to take men seriously is stressed, as when Mrs Danvers tells Maxim, Jack Favell, and Frank Crawley (another victim of Rebecca's seductive arts) that 'she used to sit on her bed and rock with laughter at the lot of you'. Even after the investigation, Maxim becomes upset all over again at the memory of Rebecca on the night of her death as she 'stood there laughing', taunting him with the details of her infidelity.

Moreover, Rebecca takes malicious pleasure in her own plurality. Luce Irigaray remarks, 'the force and continuity of [woman's] desire are capable of nurturing all the "feminine" masquerades for a long time'. And further, 'a woman's (re)discovery of herself can only signify the possibility of not sacrificing any of her pleasures to another, of not identifying with any one in particular, of never being simply one'. Rebecca is an intolerable figure precisely because she revels in her own multiplicity—her remarkable capacity to play the model wife and mistress of Manderley while conducting various love affairs on the side. Even after Rebecca's death, the 'force of her desire' makes itself felt, and, most appropriately, in light of Irigaray's comments, during a *masquerade* ball, in which the heroine dresses up like Rebecca, who had dressed up as Caroline de Winter, an ancestor whose portrait hangs on the wall. And all this occurs at the instigation of Mrs Danvers, another character who is identified with Rebecca, but to whom Rebecca is not limited. The eponymous and invisible villainess, then, is far from being the typical femme fatale of Hollywood cinema brought at last into the possession of men in order to secure for them a strong sense of their identity. Occupant of patriarchy's 'blind space', Rebecca is, rather, she who appears to subvert the very notion of identity—and of the visual economy which supports it.

It is no wonder that the film is (overly) determined to get rid of Rebecca, and that the task requires massive destruction. Yet there is reason to suppose that we cannot rest secure in the film's 'happy ending'. For if death by drowning did not extinguish the woman's desire, can we be certain that death by fire has reduced it utterly to ashes?

Gay and lesbian criticism

Anneke Smelik

Histories

Homosexuality in cinema has been there since the movies began. Homosexual characters could be glimpsed in films—as they still can today. However, their presence has characteristically been coded while homosexual characters have been taunted, ridiculed, silenced, pathologized, and more often than not killed off in the last reel. It is this rather sad history of homosexuality in cinema that Vito Russo wittily wrote down in his pioneering study *The Celluloid Closet* (1981) and which was subsequently turned into the film *The Celluloid Closet* (Rob Epstein and Jeffrey Friedman, USA, 1996), in which the filmmakers loyally adhere to Russo's project. *The Celluloid Closet* was closely linked to the rise of the gay and lesbian movement, which prompted lesbians and gay men to look differently at film and film history. This 're-visionary' look resulted in the rediscovery of forgotten films, directors, scriptwriters, producers, and actors and actresses; precious findings which would often be shown on the gay and lesbian film festivals that came into existence at the time, first starting in San Francisco in 1976. Russo's book, therefore, was a timely historical survey that politicized an emerging field of film studies: gay and lesbian criticism.

Until the publication of *The Celluloid Closet* in 1981, only one other book had been dedicated to this field: Parker Tyler's *Screening the Sexes* (1973), a camp clas-

sic that makes curious reading because of its delirious language, streak of misogyny, and penchant for the avant-garde and art cinema at the expense of Hollywood films. However, its wit and unabashed lack of 'political correctness' are quite refreshing, while its pagan-Greek relish of the libidinal pleasures of the sexed body put it peculiarly close to the interests in perverse sexualities of today's queer theory. Whereas Tyler's book is written in a highly individualistic mode, *The Celluloid Closet* is invaluable not only for the political dimension that it gives to films, but also for writing a history of a hitherto oppressed group. The key term for Russo is 'visibility'. His project is to unveil the 'big lie' that lesbians and gay men do not exist and to expose the rampant homophobia that kept homosexuality in the closet both on and off the screen. His project is, therefore, an archaeological one of uncovering and exposing those moments where homosexuality becomes visible on the screen.

The Celluloid Closet has, however, been criticized for its unproblematic view of history (Medhurst 1977/1984). While Russo's book provided the gay and lesbian movement with a necessary history of cinema from the gay point of view, it could only do so by projecting a linear story of the representation of homosexuality in Hollywood cinema. Such a linear story presupposes a smooth history of progression, from taboo, censorship, and stereotypes to liberation, freedom, and positive images, only to be (temporarily?) disturbed by the backlash that the AIDS crisis has induced. This progressive narrative denies the twists and turns as well as the ambivalences and contradictions of history. It also presupposes an undifferentiated notion of homosexuality, regardless of differences of gender, race, or class; Russo, indeed, has been reproached for his neglect of lesbians, and even for his 'bitchy misogyny' (Rich 1981/1984: 129 n. 30).

Stereotypes

Russo's historical approach is akin to early feminist studies of the 1970s that describe the position of women in the movies. The feminist movement and the gay and lesbian movement share a concern with questions of gender and sexuality and both are committed to the linking of the personal and the political; indeed, most of the essays and books that I discuss in this chapter are marked by a distinctly personal tone in which the writer's homosexuality is brought to bear on cinema and theory. Like early feminist and black film criticism, early gay and lesbian criticism was mostly directed at stereotyping. Films, and especially those from Hollywood, were criticized for reproducing dominant stereotypes of homosexuals—such as the sissy, the sad young man, the gay psychopath, the seductive androgyne, the unnatural woman, or the lesbian vampire—and failing to represent 'real' gays and lesbians. For straight spectators, such stereotypes could confirm prejudice, while for gay and lesbian spectators they might encourage self-hatred. However, while anger at the unfavourable representation of homosexuality (and at the reduction of homosexuals to sexuality as the defining aspect of their character) is fully justified, a simple call for positive images is not the solution as images of gays and lesbians cannot simply be seen as 'true' or 'false'. Rather, it is necessary to understand how stereotypes function in both ideological and cinematic terms.

Richard Dyer was among the first to offer a more theoretical critique of stereotypes (1977a). Dyer argues that stereotypes have the function of ordering the world around us. Stereotyping works in society both to establish and to maintain the hegemony of the dominant group (heterosexual white men) and to marginalize and exclude other social groups (homosexuals, blacks, women, the working class). Stereotypes, then, produce sharp oppositions between social groups in order to maintain clear boundaries between them. They are also normative. Stereotypes of gays and lesbians such as the queen and the dyke reproduce norms of gendered heterosexuality because they indicate that the homosexual man or woman falls short of the heterosexual norm: that they can never be a 'real' man or woman. The fashion queen Madame Lucy in *Irene* (USA, 1926), the dresser Diggs in *It's Love I'm After* (1937), the homosexual men in *La dolce vita* (Italy,1960) or the black queen Lindy in *Car Wash* (USA, 1976) are just a few examples of 'sissies' who fail the norm of masculinity. If the queen is characteristically a source of comedy (*La Cage aux folles*, France, 1978), the dyke is mostly associated with violence. The lesbian Nazi in *Roma, città aperta* ('Rome, Open City' Italy, 1945), the communist butch in *From Russia with Love* (GB, 1963), or George–June in *The Killing of Sister George* (GB, 1969) are all examples of the dyke stereotyped as a predatory, sadistic, castrating bitch–butch (Sheldon 1977; Hetze 1986).

> **Stereotypes of gays and lesbians such as the queen and the dyke reproduce norms of gendered heterosexuality because they indicate that the homosexual man or woman falls short of the heterosexual norm: that they can never be a 'real' man or woman.**

The stereotypes of the queen as the effeminate man and the dyke as the mannish woman are, therefore, informed by the structuring opposition of sexual difference. Within semiotics, narrative is also understood to be structured through oppositions (de Lauretis 1984), and it is easy to see how stereotypes contribute to this process. For example, stereotypes of decadent homosexuals can be used to contrast with the uncorrupted heterosexual male hero, as is the case with Peter Lorre and Humphrey Bogart respectively in *The Maltese Falcon* (USA, 1941). The implication of this is that a hero can rarely be other than heterosexual (and white) in Hollywood. Thus, in spite of biographical and historical evidence of his homosexuality, the hero Lawrence is made staunchly heterosexual in *Lawrence of Arabia* (USA, 1962), while homosexuality is delegated to the evil Turkish boy.

Stereotypes can also be introduced through iconography. Visual and aural details can be used to typify homosexuality immediately. For example, codes in dressing, certain gestures, stylistic decor, or extended looks can at a glance invoke the homosexuality of a character. As Dyer (1977a) points out, such stereotypical imagery makes homosexuality visible. In contrast to gender or ethnicity, homosexuality is not after all visible at first sight. Therefore, it has to be established visually, especially in the many films in which homosexuality remains closeted. Stereotyping through iconography, therefore, categorizes the gay or lesbian character as distinct from straight characters and maintains the boundaries between them.

The main problem with stereotypes is that they appear to be inevitable and 'natural'. Here, Barthes's notion of 'myth', introduced into film studies by Claire Johnston (1973), may explain how stereotypes become naturalized. The stereotype of the homosexual character functions as a structure, a code or convention. The sign 'homosexual' represents the ideological meaning that the homosexual has for heterosexuality, as the negative or the failure of the heterosexual norm. The realist conventions of classical cinema veil the ideological representation of the sign 'homosexual', (re)presenting the constructed images, the stereotypes, of gay men and lesbians as natural and realistic. Such a theoretical critique of stereotypes helps to explain the normative and normalizing effects of heterosexual hegemony. The question is therefore not how to get rid of stereotypes (as they are both efficient and resilient), nor how to replace them with positive images (which leave the heterosexist imperative intact), but how to achieve complexity, diversity, and self-definition (see Dyer 1977a). This has been the quest of gay and lesbian cinema, which I will discuss later.

Authorship

The shift away from a sociological examination of the ways in which homosexuals have been represented on the screen to issues of ideology and sexual politics opens up a much wider and more complex field of inquiry for lesbian and gay film criticism, including a reassessment of theoretical frameworks from a gay perspective. Thus, Robin Wood (1977) returns to his earlier auteur criticism to bring questions of ideology and sexual politics to bear on the cinema of such

'auteurs' as Jean Renoir, Ingmar Bergman, and Howard Hawks. In doing so, he now finds an ambiguity in their films which indicate both a repression of homosexuality as well as the inevitable cracks in bourgeois heterosexuality.

With the advent of post-structuralist theory, however, the notion of the auteur more or less disappeared from the theoretical agenda (see Crofts Part 2, Chapter 7). Neither feminists nor homosexuals deplored this 'death of the author', who was invariably a white, heterosexual male, and a genius at that. Such heroes were better buried. Yet, for feminists it mattered a great deal whether an author was female or not, and similarly for lesbians and gay men it was of paramount importance whether a text was the work of a homosexual. Medhurst (1991a: 198) reveals a double standard at work, in this respect: 'Authorship was bad, Gay Authorship was good.' The death of the author also signified a more general death of the subject, and hence of subjectivity and identity, which was now seen to be forever dispersed and disrupted. Many feminists, however, have been suspicious of the time loop involved in the death of the subject (Braidotti 1991; hooks 1990). At the historical moment when marginalized subjects—blacks, people of colour, post-colonial subjects, women, lesbians, and gay men—claim their subjectivity, the white, middle-class, heterosexual male declares that very subject to be over and out.

> **For feminists it mattered a great deal whether an author was female or not, and similarly for lesbians and gay men it was of paramount importance whether a text was the work of a homosexual.**

Medhurst (1991a) reintroduces the question of authorship in relation to homosexuality in an article on the film *Brief Encounter* (GB, 1941). While he is aware of the pitfalls of an essentialist claim to homosexual identity in the case of a gay rereading of *Brief Encounter* (attributing that gay sensibility to the playwright Noel Coward), he still wants to maintain that marginal groups like gay people should hold on to authorship for political reasons. This does not mean a regression to a simplistic reading of authorial intentions in texts, but a construction of a

Dorothy Arzner, 'the great exception'

contradictory history of homosexual identity in a heterosexual culture.

Judith Mayne (1990) tackles the difficulties of female and lesbian authorship in classical cinema in a case-study of director Dorothy Arzner, who is generally considered as the great exception—the only woman director who made a career in Hollywood. Feminist attempts to theorize Arzner's authorship have claimed her as an auteur in the male pantheon and identified her films as a progressive critique of patriarchal cinema.

However, for Mayne, Arzner's authorial inscriptions can be situated in the problematization of (lesbian) pleasure: in the relations between and among women and in marginal lesbian gestures. She suggests that 'female authorship acquires its most significant contours in Arzner's work through relations between and among women', recognizing in the representations of those relations a complex form of irony (1990: 101). In dedicating a book to the life and work of Dorothy Arzner, Mayne (1994) therefore focuses on the issues of secrecy, visibility, and lesbian representation involved in the writing of a history of a closeted lesbian film-maker in Hollywood.

Rereadings of Hollywood and spectatorship

The lesbian appeal of female Hollywood stars has also been commonly recognized. Weiss (1992) discusses the attraction of Hollywood stars like Marlene Dietrich, Greta Garbo, and Katharine Hepburn for lesbian spectators in the 1930s. Because the silver screen was often a place where dreams could be fulfilled at a time when gays were still socially isolated, she argues that the powerful image of these stars helped to shape the white urban lesbian subculture of the time. The androgynous appearances of Dietrich in *Morocco* (USA, 1930), Garbo in *Queen Christina* (USA, 1933), and Hepburn in *Sylvia Scarlett* (USA, 1935), in particular, were embraced as an image of sexual ambiguity which served as a point of identification outside conventional gender positions.

Gay male spectators performed similar kinds of oppositional reading. The homoerotic appeal of male stars like the young Marlon Brando and James Dean has been widely commented upon. Russo discovered a gay subtext in many a Hollywood film, from the display of male bodies and competition in *Ben Hur* (USA, 1926 and the 1959 remake) to the ritualized fights in westerns, such as that between Montgomery Clift and John Wayne in *Red River* (USA, 1948). The loving looks between Richard Barthelmess and Cary Grant in *Only Angels have Wings* (USA, 1939) or Dewey Martin and Kirk Douglas in *The Big Sky* (USA, 1952) also alerted the homosexual spectator to a gay subtext in the films of Howard Hawks (Russo 1981). But as Russo never tires of pointing out, homosexuality was still very much silenced and closeted in classical Hollywood films and a gay subtext was never more than a hidden text which could only be discovered by the spectator who was sensitized to the coded messages of homosexuality.

Such rereadings of Hollywood cinema have inevitably raised the issue of gay and lesbian spectatorship. Gay and lesbian criticism took most of its lead from feminist film studies and, until at least the mid-1980s, the dominant paradigm remained focused upon the organization of the look, the male gaze and the female spectacle. Although productive for feminism, the heterosexual bias of this exclusive focus on sexual difference proved difficult for gay and lesbian studies. Indeed, feminist film theory—not unlike the Hollywood cinema it criticized so fiercely—seemed unable to conceive of representation outside heterosexuality. As Patricia White (1991) aptly remarks, the 'ghostly presence of lesbianism' haunts not only Hollywood Gothics but also feminist film theory. In its special issue *Lesbians and Film* (1981, 24–5: 17), the journal *Jump Cut* also claimed that: 'It sometimes seems to us that lesbianism is the hole in the heart of feminist film criticism.' Almost ten years later matters had apparently improved very little. Mayne (1990) complains that the denial of Arzner's lesbian identity points to a curious gap in feminist film theory, indeed to the 'structuring absence' of lesbianism (1990: 107).

The indictment that Hollywood cinema was tailored to the pleasures of the male spectator raised questions about the position of the female spectator. In spite of the increasing focus on female spectatorship in feminist scholarship, the homosexual pleasures of the female spectator were largely ignored. The difficulties in theorizing the female spectator have led Jackie Stacey (1987) to exclaim that feminist film critics have written the darkest scenario possible for the female look as being male, masochistic, or marginal. In breaking open the restrictive dichotomies of feminist film theory, Stacey tries to create a space for the homosexual pleasures of spectatorship. A more complex model of cinematic spectatorship is needed in order to avoid a facile binarism that maps homosexuality onto an opposition of masculinity and femininity. Stacey suggests the need 'to separate gender identification from sexuality' which are 'too often conflated in the name of sexual difference' (1987: 53). When difference is no longer reduced to sexual difference but is also understood as difference among women, representation of an active female desire becomes possible, even in Hollywood films. In films like *All about Eve* (USA, 1950) or *Desperately Seeking Susan* (USA, 1984), narrative desire is produced by the difference between two women; by women wanting to become the idealized other. An interplay of difference and otherness prevents the collapse of that desire into identification, prompting Stacey to conclude that the rigid psychoanalytic distinction between desire and identification fails to address different constructions of desire.

De Lauretis (1988) has also drawn attention to the difficulties of imagining lesbian desire within a psychoanalytic discourse that predicates sexual difference on sexual *in*difference. She here follows Luce Irigaray's notion of the symbolic law representing only one and not two sexes: patriarchy is deeply 'hommo-sexual' as it erects the masculine to the one and only norm. Discussing the same problematic in a later essay, de Lauretis (1991: 252) observes that the institution of heterosexuality defines all sexuality to such an extent that 'the effort to represent a homosexual–lesbian desire is a subtle and difficult one'. She criticizes Stacey for conceiving of desire between women as 'woman-identified female bonding' and failing to see it as sexual. Here, and more extensively in her later book *The Practice of Love* (1994), de Lauretis returns to Freudian theory to account for the specificity of lesbian desire in terms of fetishism.

In answer to de Lauretis's criticism, Stacey (1994) argues in her study of female spectatorship that she is not concerned with a specifically lesbian audience but with a possible homoeroticism for all women in the audience. Her aim is to eroticize identification rather than de-eroticize desire. The female spectator is quite likely to encompass erotic components in her desiring look, while at the same time identifying with the woman-as-spectacle.

While these discussions of lesbian spectatorship are part of a wider movement in film studies to include the heterogeneity of the spectatorial situation, most discussions of spectatorship have been about white audiences. De Lauretis was criticized for not taking into account racial dynamics in the lesbian film *She must be Seeing Things* (USA, 1987) (see the discussion following de Lauretis's 1991 article). Little research is available about black audiences, although some critics have examined black female spectatorship in popular culture (e.g. Bobo 1995). The issue of black lesbian spectatorship, however, has hardly been raised.

On masculinity

Male gay criticism has also been concerned to assess the implications of the binary ideology of sexual difference which gay and lesbian criticism inherited from feminist film theory. Just as the dominant paradigm of feminist film theory raised questions about the male look and the female spectacle, it also raised questions about the eroticization of the male body. What, it was asked, if the male body is the object of the female gaze or of another male gaze; and how exactly does the male body become the signifier of the phallus? (*Screen* 1992). The discussion of the representation of masculinity in cinema took off in the early 1980s and almost immediately raised the issue of homosexual desire in two programmatic articles (Dyer 1982; Neale 1983).

The image of the male body as object of a look is fraught with ambivalences, repressions, and denials. Like the masquerade, the notion of spectacle has such strong feminine connotations that for a male performer to be put on display or to don a mask threatens his very masculinity. Because the phallus is a symbol and a signifier, no man can fully symbolize it. Although the patriarchal male subject has a privileged relation to the phallus, he will always fall short of the phallic ideal. Lacan notices this effect in his essay on the meaning of the phallus: 'the curious consequence of making virile display in the human being itself seems feminine' (1977: 291). Male spectacle, then, entails being put in a feminine position. The immanent feminization of male spectacle then brings about two possible dangers for the performing male: functioning as an object of desire he can easily become the object of ridicule, and within a heterosexist culture accusations of homosexuality can be launched against him (Neale 1983; Tasker 1993).

Most critics agree that the spectatorial look in mainstream cinema is implicitly male. While for Dyer this means that images of men do not automatically 'work' for women, according to Neale the erotic element in looking at the male body has to be repressed and disavowed so as to avoid any implications of male homosexuality. Yet, male homosexuality is always present as an undercurrent; it is Hollywood's symptom. The denial of the homoeroticism of looking at images of men constantly involves sado-masochistic themes, scenes, and fantasies; hence the highly ritualized scenes of male struggle which deflect the look away from the male body to the scene of the spectacular fight. Richard Meyer (1991) explores the more homely representations of Rock Hudson's body, which made him available as an object of erotic contemplation. Meyer argues that Hudson's image was produced for the female spectator, which was only possible as long as his homosexuality remained unspoken. With the public disclosure of Hudson as an AIDS victim in 1985, his now homosexualized body was imaged as the signifier of illness and death.

Kobena Mercer (1991a) problematizes the gay male look in his exploration of aesthetic ambivalence in visual representations of the black male nude. While Robert Mapplethorpe's photographs of black males can be seen as an objectification and fetishization of the nude male body, Mercer also sees a homoerotic subversive dimension to the pictures. The identification and involvement of Mapplethorpe with his models undermine a voyeuristic gaze. Here Mercer argues that the gay identity of the author and of the spectator are important to the process of interpretation. The context of a homosexual subculture enables Mercer to read the pictures as humorous and sensitive deconstructions of race and sexuality. By replacing the object of the conventional nude in Western culture, the white woman, by the black gay male, Mapplethorpe creates a subversive ambivalence. For Mercer, Mapplethorpe problematizes the white male subject in his visual work and he ends his essay with a call for a study of the construction of whiteness within gay and lesbian criticism.

Many studies on visual representations of masculinity refer to the homoeroticism of popular figures like Batman (Medhurst 1991b) or Pee-Wee Herman (Camera Obscura 1988; Doty 1993). Most studies of masculinity point to the crisis in which the white male heterosexual subject finds himself, a crisis in which his masculinity is fragmented and denaturalized, in which the signifiers of 'man' and 'manly' seem to have lost all of their meaning and which makes Hollywood desperate to find a 'few good white men' (Easthope 1986; Kirkham and Thumin 1993; Tasker 1993; Jeffords 1994). Yet, what is a crisis to one (the dominant subject) may well mean a liberation, or at least an opening, to the other (the marginalized subjects). Therefore, the crisis in masculinity is welcomed by gay critics. In his book on male impersonators, Mark Simpson takes great pleasure in celebrating the deconstruction of 'masculinity's claim to authenticity, to naturalness, to coherence—to dominate' (1994: 7). He hopes that the crisis of masculinity signifies a desegregation of homosexuality and heterosexuality in popular culture, transforming both in the process.

Camp

Gay studies of masculinity often border on camp readings of the male spectacle (Medhurst 1991b; Simpson 1994). Dyer (1986) addresses a different kind of homo-

sexual spectator identification in his discussion of Judy Garland's appeal for gay men. He suggests that the star image of Garland played a role in white urban male subculture because of two of her qualities: authenticity and theatricality. Garland embodied an intensity of emotional life which was recognized as truthful by gay men who themselves lived a life on the edge as homosexuals in a straight world. Yet, Garland's deep passion was inflected with an equally deep irony, which can be seen as a characteristic of gay sensibility. Like Garland, gay sensibility holds together the antithetical qualities of authenticity and theatricality, or, in the words of Dyer, 'a fierce assertion of extreme feeling with a deprecating sense of its absurdity' (1986: 154). Of course, we enter here the notion of camp and its relation to male gay subculture. Garland was experienced as being camp. She was over-the-top, ironic, excessive, and thus a grateful object of drag acts (for example, Craig Russell in Outrageous!, Canada, 1977). Camp, however, is not merely humour but also inflected with pathos. Dyer draws attention to the 'knife edge between camp and hurt' (1986: 180) in Garland's public pain and suffering, an edge that resonated deeply with her male gay audience.

> **Camp can be seen as an oppositional reading of popular culture which offers identifications and pleasures that dominant culture denies to homosexuals.**

I do not want to discuss camp here as a phenomenon in itself. Rather than running the risk of being dead serious about something as quixotic as camp, I propose to discuss camp as a reading strategy for gay people. Camp can be seen as an oppositional reading of popular culture which offers identifications and pleasures that dominant culture denies to homosexuals. Jack Babuscio (1977) discusses camp as an expression of gay sensibility, by which he means a heightened awareness of one's social condition outside the mainstream. In this sense, camp is experiential and resists analytical discourse (Medhurst 1991b). According to Babuscio, the 'bitter-wit' of camp points to the transformation of pain into laughter, the chosen way of dealing with the incongruous situation of gays in society.

As an oppositional reading, camp can be subversive for bringing out the cultural ambiguities and contradictions that usually remain sealed over by dominant ideology. This characteristic brings camp into the realm of postmodernism, which also celebrates ambivalence and heterogeneity. Subcultural camp and postmodern theory share a penchant for irony, play, and parody, for artificiality and performance, as well as for transgressing conventional meanings of gender. This queer alliance between camp and postmodernism has often been noted. Medhurst even claims provocatively that 'postmodernism is only heterosexuals catching up with camp' (1991a: 206). It is indeed an easy leap from Babuscio's understanding of camp as signifying performance rather than existence, to Judith Butler's notion of gender signifying performance rather than identity. Just as Babuscio claims that the emphasis on style, surface, and the spectacle results in incongruities between 'what a thing or person *is* to what it *looks* like' (1977/1984: 44), Butler (1990) asserts that the stress on performativity allows us to see gender as enacting a set of discontinuous if not parodic performances. In the context of gay and lesbian criticism, it is important to realize that both camp and postmodernism denaturalize feminity and masculinity.

Camp is very much the prerogative of gay male, mostly white, subculture (although Mercer (1991b) points to the camp element in the soul tradition of black musicians, long before white pop stars began to exploit such imagery). In its deconstruction of heterosexual male authority and its expression of a displaced subjectivity within dominant culture, camp might be considered an attractive framework for lesbians. Paula Graham (1995), however, expresses her doubts about camp as a possible paradigm for lesbian readings. She argues that camp allows gay men to identify with feminine excess, that is with the phallic female star, precisely as a threat to or parody of male authority (Judy Garland, Joan Crawford, Bette Davis). For lesbians, such an identification with femininity would 'mark a subordination to masculine authority, and not a form of resistance to it' (1995: 178). This does not mean that lesbians do not enjoy camp films or the spectacle of sexual excess, but rather that gay men and lesbians do not share the same 'canon' of camp. Lesbians characteristically prefer a display of strong, masculinized, active female stars such as

Sigourney Weaver as Ripley in the first *Alien* movie (USA, 1979), Linda Hamilton in *Terminator 2: Judgement Day* (USA, 1991), and, yes, even Sharon Stone in *Basic Instinct* (USA, 1991). Such a lesbian appropriation of subject positions may be disruptive and transgressive, but not camp.

It is significant that in the 1990s the notion of 'camp' is often replaced by the term 'queer'. Camp is historically more associated with the closeted homosexuality of the 1950s and only came to the surface in the 1960s and 1970s. Postmodernism of the 1980s and 1990s brought campy strategies into the mainstream. Now, lesbians and gay men identify their oppositional reading strategies as 'queer'. Away from the notions of oppression and liberation of earlier gay and lesbian criticism, queerness is associated with the playful self-definition of a homosexuality in non-essentialist terms. Not unlike camp, but more self-assertive, queer readings are fully inflected with irony, transgressive gender parody, and deconstructed subjectivities.

Gay and lesbian filmmaking

Alongside rereadings of Hollywood films, gay and lesbian criticism has also turned to the few films made by lesbians and gay men and with gay subject-matter, although these critical explorations are relatively few and did not appear until the late 1980s (see Gever *et al.* 1993). European art cinema has provided a tradition in which the representation of gay and lesbian subject-matter is not a priori foreclosed. *Mädchen in Uniform* ('Girls in Uniform', Germany, 1931) was one of the earliest films to be rediscovered from a lesbian perspective. The film had always been praised for its stylistic qualities, as well as for its anti-fascism, but its explicit theme of lesbianism was long subject to silence and censorship. Rich (1981) argues that the anti-fascist politics of *Mädchen in Uniform* is interconnected with its lesbian theme and its struggle against authoritarian structures and sexual repression. Rich places the film in the historical context of Weimar with its vibrant lesbian subculture, especially in Berlin. Dyer (1990) too discusses the film within the German context of Weimar culture, its general openness about sexuality, and its public discussions of the notion of a third sex as introduced by Max Hirschfeld and his Institute of Sexual Science. The open lesbianism, the plea for sexual freedom, and the revolt against patriarchy have made

Mädchen in Uniform (1931) — 'open lesbianism' and a 'plea for sexual freedom'

Mädchen in Uniform a popular classic that still moves and delights lesbian audiences today.

Mädchen in Uniform, however, does not stand alone, but is part of a tradition of gay and lesbian filmmaking within early cinema (see Dyer 1990; Weiss 1992). Some films are explicitly gay, like *Anders als die Andern* ('Different from the Others', Germany, 1919), an ambivalent film in which the gay main character commits suicide despite the affirmative lectures given by Hirschfeld himself within the film. Other films were made by gay or lesbian filmmakers, like the surrealist shorts of Germaine Dulac which have been read as critiques of heterosexuality. Fantasy plays an important role in these experimental films. In *La Souriante Madame Beudet* ('The Smiling Mme Beudet', France, 1923) a woman fantasizes murdering her bully of a husband and escaping from her bourgeois marriage, and *La Coquille et le clergyman* ('The Seashell and the Clergyman', France, 1927) exposes Oedipal male fantasies about the mystery of 'woman'. Yet other films featured lesbian or gay characters, like the Countess Geschwitz in *Die Büchse der Pandora* ('Pandora's Box', Germany, 1928) or the male prisoner in *Geslecht in Fesseln* ('Sex in Bondage', Germany, 1928).

Jean Genet's prison film *Un chant d'amour* ('A Song of Love', France, 1950) is another classic which has become enormously popular with gay audiences until today and which also has influenced gay film-makers. Dyer (1990) places this short erotic fantasy in the prestigious tradition of French literature by the 'poétes maudits', the 'accursed poets' like de Sade, Baudelaire, Rimbaud, Verlaine, and Cocteau; a literature which intertwines the elements of evil, criminality, and (homo)sexuality. In his detailed analysis of the narrative structure, imagery, and ways of looking in *Un chant d'amour*, Dyer discusses the film's eroticism in terms of the tension between politics and pleasure. While some gay critics have reprimanded the film for its 'oppression' of gay men or were disturbed by its 'homophobic' representation of erotic pleasures, others took a more permissive or even celebratory attitude to the sado-masochism of the film. Dyer argues that the renewed political interest in perverse sexualities opened a Foucauldian reading of the film's eroticism in terms of the social and historical relation between sexuality and power.

The play of power and desire has become the theme of some gay and lesbian films in the 1980s, which Dyer calls a 'Genetesque' tradition. The high artificiality of Fassbinder's last film, *Querelle* (Germany, 1982, based on Genet's 1947 novel), places the story firmly within the realm of fantasy and desire. For Dyer (1990: 91), the film is 'an abstraction of the erotics of power'. The same ritualization of desire and power can be found in the sadean theatre of *Verführung: Die grausame Frau* ('Seduction: The Cruel Woman', Germany, 1985) by Elfi Mikesch and Monika Treut. This highly formalized and aestheticized exploration of sado-masochism was one of the first films to bring female desire and lesbian sexuality within the domain of power and violence. Similarly, the fantasmatic films of Ulrike Ottinger—from *Madame X—eine absolute Herrscherin* ('Madame X—an Absolute Ruler', Germany, 1977) to *Johanna D'Arc of Mongolia* (Germany, 1989)—humorously deconstruct traditional femininity and celebrate nomadic lesbian subjectivities (White 1987; Longfellow 1993).

Gay activism and identity politics

The art-house tradition of filmmaking, with its investment in fantasy as well as in the exploration of 'perverse' sexualities, is obviously related to gay and lesbian subcultures, but could not be further removed from the activist movies which came out of the gay and lesbian movement. The difference lies not so much in style (some activist movies have also used experimental forms, like the films of Barbara Hammer) as in the emphasis on the affirmation of gay identity. This kind of identity politics is quite adverse to the subversion and deconstruction of gay identity found in art-house films. Diana Fuss describes identity politics as 'the tendency to base one's politics on a sense of personal identity—as gay, as Jewish, as Black, as female' (1989: 97). In order to be able to build a political community, gay men and lesbians felt the need to consolidate a unified and visible identity. Strategies of consciousness-raising and coming out helped them to stimulate personal awareness and political action. Film was an excellent medium to lend visibility to gays and lesbians. Between 1970 and 1980 alone, the movement produced over forty affirmative documentaries, of which *Word is Out* (USA, 1977) is no doubt the most famous (see Dyer 1990). Documentary was the privileged genre, because it was considered to record reality, i.e. to document the so far unwritten and invisible history of gays and lesbians.

Identity politics, however, runs the risk of essentialism: of seeing identity as the hidden essence of one's being. Although gay activism needed this view of iden-

tity for its organization and politics, this very notion of sexual identity as eternal, ahistorical, and unchanging is paradoxically at odds with the demands for political transformation. The debate here is between essentialism and constructionism. In this respect, the influence of Foucault's discourse theory on gay and lesbian studies cannot be overestimated (although Foucault was more influential in gay studies than in lesbian studies; see Fuss 1989). His efforts to de-essentialize sexuality and to historicize homosexuality dealt a blow to any simplistic notion of homosexuality as a unified, coherent, and fixed category as well as to any claim to an unproblematic authenticity and truth. From a constructionist point of view, sexuality is not a given of nature but a construct of culture. Thus, the debate shifts from realizing a shared essence to understanding homosexuality as a product of social forces. (Dyer 1990: 275). The question then becomes how homosexuality has been shaped, defined, and regulated by dominant culture throughout history.

> From a constructionist point of view, sexuality is not a given of nature but a construct of culture. Thus, the debate shifts from realizing a shared essence to understanding homosexuality as a product of social forces.

Psychoanalytic theories have also added to a more complex understanding of identity. Especially within Lacanian psychoanalysis, identity is seen as fundamentally unstable and fictitious. The unconscious workings of the psyche constantly destabilize a coherent identity. Identity is therefore never a finished product, but rather always in process (see de Lauretis 1984, 1994). Such an understanding of identity does not mean that there is no identity at all; as Fuss points out 'fictions of identity, importantly, are no less powerful for being fictions' (1989: 104). Nevertheless, the Foucauldian and psychoanalytic views of identity and sexuality have together created a post-structuralist climate in which assertions of an uncomplicated gay and lesbian identity have become rather suspect.

Essentialist identity politics seeks to smooth over differences. If homosexual identity is understood as a homogeneous and shared essence, both differences *within* identity as well as differences *between* identities are ignored. As a result, gay activism had difficulties dealing with differences between gay men and lesbians, let alone accounting for differences of class and ethnicity. However, if post-structuralist theory opened up questions of identity and difference within gay and lesbian criticism (Doan 1994), it presented the problem of how different kinds of social identity relate to one another. Adding age to class to sexuality to ethnicity and so on simply results in divisive and mutually exclusive categories which fight for a position within a hierarchy of oppressions. As Kobena Mercer has argued, the rhetorical invocation of the 'race, class, gender mantra' obscures the way in which these social categories intersect (1993: 239). Mercer pleads for a hybridized understanding of identity. A hybrid identity negotiates between a plurality of different positions, which opens up the recognition of 'unity-in-diversity' (240).

The films *Looking for Langston* by Isaac Julien (GB, 1989) and *Tongues Untied* by Marlon Riggs (USA, 1990) are examples of hybridized cultural practice by black gay filmmakers. For Mercer, the foregrounding of autobiographical voices in *Tongues Untied* produces a multilayered 'dialogic voicing', which is fully aware of the multidimensional character of politics. The dialogic strategy becomes subversive in its use of playfulness and parody. These two elements, the dialogic voicing and the humour, are embedded in the oral tradition of African American culture.

Mercer reads the stylistic formalism of *Looking for Langston* as a deconstructive appropriation and re-articulation of dominant signifiers of racial and sexual representation. While the film offers an archaeology of black modernism in its 'promiscuous intertextuality' (1993: 251), it is also an allegory of black gay desire. Through the key motif of looks and looking the film explores the role of fantasy within desire. Mercer concludes his analysis of the two films with a brief discussion of authorship. The notion of hybridized identity does not foreclose the importance of an authorial signature. As Mercer argues, in so far as 'identity is not what you are so much as what you do' (240), he can claim that 'these rich, provocative, and important works do indeed "make a difference" not because of who or what the filmmakers are, but because of what they do, and above all because of the freaky way they do it' (255). It is also this proliferation of multiple voices within gay and lesbian filmmaking and criticism which testifies to the liveliness of this political field within the study of film and popular culture.

BIBLIOGRAPHY

Babuscio, Jack (1977/1984), 'Camp and Gay Sensibility', in Richard Dyer (ed.), *Gays and Film* (rev. edn. New York: Zoetrope).

Bobo, Jacqueline (1995), *Black Women as Cultural Readers* (New York: Columbia University Press).

Braidotti, Rosi (1991), *Patterns of Dissonance: A Study of Women in Contemporary Philosophy* (Cambridge: Polity Press).

Butler, Judith (1990), *Gender Trouble: Feminism and the Subversion of Identity* (New York: Routledge).

Camera Obscura (1988), Special Issue: *Male Trouble*, 17 May.

de Lauretis, Teresa (1984), *Alice Doesn't: Feminism, Semiotics, Cinema* (Bloomington: Indiana University Press).

—— (1988), 'Sexual Indifference and Lesbian Representation', *Theatre Journal*, 40/2: 155–77.

—— (1991), 'Film and the Visible', in Bad Object-Choices (eds.), *How do I Look? Queer Film and Video* (Washington: Bay Press).

—— (1994), *The Practice of Love: Lesbian Sexuality and Perverse Desire* (Bloomington: Indiana University Press).

Doan, Laura (1994), *The Lesbian Postmodern* (New York: Columbia University Press).

Doty, Alexander (1993), *Making Things Perfectly Queer: Interpreting Mass Culture* (Minneapolis: University of Minnesota Press).

*Dyer, Richard (1977a/1984), 'Stereotyping', in Richard Dyer (ed.), *Gays and Film* (rev. edn. New York: Zoetrope).

—— (1977b/1993), 'Homosexuality and Film Noir', in *The Matter of Images: Essays on Representations* (London: Routledge).

—— (1980), 'Reading Fassbinder's Sexual Politics', in Tony Rayns (ed.), *Fassbinder* (London: British Film Institute).

—— (1982/1992), 'Don't Look Now: The Male Pin-Up', in *The Sexual Subject: A 'Screen' Reader in Sexuality* (London: Routledge).

—— (1983/1993), 'Seen to be Believed: Some Problems in the Representation of Gay People as Typical', in *The Matter of Images: Essays on Representations* (London: Routledge).

—— (1986), *Heavenly Bodies: Film Stars and Society* (New York: St Martin's Press).

*—— (1990), *Now you See It: Studies on Lesbian and Gay Film* (London: Routledge).

Easthope, Anthony (1986), *What a Man's Gotta Do: The Masculine Myth in Popular Culture* (London: Paladin).

Ellsworth, Elizabeth (1990), 'Feminist Spectators and *Personal Best*', in Patricia Erens (ed.), *Issues in Feminist Film Criticism* (Bloomington: Indiana University Press).

Fuss, Diana (1989), *Essentially Speaking: Feminism, Nature and Difference* (New York: Routledge).

Galvin, Angela (1994), '*Basic Instinct*: Damning Dykes', in Diane Hamer and Belinda Budge (eds.), *The Good, the Bad and the Gorgeous: Popular Culture's Romance with Lesbianism* (London: Pandora).

Gever, Martha, John Greyson, and Pratibha Parmar (1993), *Queer Looks: Perspectives on Lesbian and Gay Film and Video* (New York: Routledge).

Graham, Paula (1995), 'Girl's Camp? The Politics of Parody', in Tamsin Wilton (ed.), *Immortal, Invisible: Lesbians and the Moving Image* (London: Routledge).

Hetze, Stefanie (1986), *Happy-End für wen? Kino und lesbische Frauen* (Frankfurt: Tende Verlag).

hooks, bell (1990), *Yearning: Race, Gender, and Cultural Politics* (Boston: South End Press).

Jeffords, Susan (1994), *Hard Bodies: Hollywood Masculinity in the Reagan Era* (New Brunswick, NJ: Rutgers University Press).

Johnston, Claire (1973/1977), 'Women's Cinema as Counter Cinema', in Claire Johnston (ed.), *Notes on Women's Cinema* (London: Society for Education in Film and Television); reprinted in Bill Nichols (ed.), *Movies and Methods*, 2 vols., ii (Berkeley: University of California Press).

Kirkham, Pat, and Janet Thumin (eds.) (1993), *You Tarzan: Masculinity, Movies and Men* (London: Lawrence & Wishart).

Lacan, Jacques (1977), 'The Signification of the Phallus', in *Écrits: A Selection* (New York: W. W. Norton).

Longfellow, Brenda (1993), 'Lesbian Phantasy and the Other Woman in Ottinger's *Johanna d'Arc of Mongolia*', *Screen*, 34/2: 124–36.

Mayne, Judith (1990), *The Woman at the Keyhole: Feminism and Women's Cinema* (Bloomington: Indiana University Press).

—— (1994), *Directed by Dorothy Arzner* (Bloomington: Indiana University Press).

Medhurst, Andy (1977/1984), 'Notes on Recent Gay Film Criticism', in Richard Dyer (ed.), *Gays and Film* (New York: Zoetrope).

—— (1991a), 'That Special Thrill: *Brief Encounter*, Homosexuality and Authorship', *Screen*, 32/2: 197–208.

—— (1991b), 'Batman, Deviance and Camp', in Roberta E. Pearson and William Uricchio (eds.), *The Many Lives of the Batman: Critical Approaches to a Superhero and his Media* (London: British Film Institute; New York: Routledge).

Mercer, Kobena (1991a), 'Skin Head Sex Thing: Racial Difference and the Homoerotic Imaginary', in Bad Object-Choices (eds.), *How do I Look? Queer Film and Video* (Seattle: Bay Press).

—— (1991b), 'Monster Metaphors: Notes on Michael Jackson's Thriller', in Christine Gledhill (ed.), *Stardom: Industry of Desire* (London: Routledge).

—— (1993), 'Dark and Lovely Too: Black Gay Men in Independent Film', in Gever et al. (1993).

Merck, Mandy (1993), *Perversions: Deviant Readings* (London: Virago).

Meyer, Richard (1991), 'Rock Hudson's Body', in Diana Fuss (ed.), *Inside/Out: Lesbian Theories, Gay Theories* (New York: Routledge).

Neale, Steve (1983/1992), 'Masculinity as Spectacle', *The Sexual Subject: A 'Screen' Reader in Sexuality* (London: Routledge).

Rich, Ruby (1981/1984), 'From Repressive Tolerance to Erotic Liberation: *Maedchen in Uniform*', in Mary Ann Doane, Patricia Mellencamp, and Linda Williams (eds.), *Re-Vision: Essays in Feminist Film Criticism* (Los Angeles: American Film Institute and University Publications of America).

*Russo, Vito (1981/1987), *The Celluloid Closet: Homosexuality in the Closet* (New York: Harper & Row).

Screen (1992), *The Sexual Subject: A 'Screen' Reader in Sexuality* (London: Routledge).

Sheldon, Caroline (1977/1984), 'Lesbians and Film: Some Thoughts', in Richard Dyer (ed.), *Gays and Film* (rev. edn. New York: Zoetrope).

Simpson, Mark (1994), *Male Impersonators: Men Performing Masculinity* (London: Cassell).

Stacey, Jackie (1987), 'Desperately Seeking Difference', *Screen* 28/1: 48–61.

—— (1994), *Star Gazing: Hollywood Cinema and Female Spectatorship* (London: Routledge).

—— (1995), '"If You Don't Play You Can't Win": *Desert Hearts* and the Lesbian Romance Film', in Tamsin Wilton (ed.), *Immortal, Invisible: Lesbians and the Moving Image* (London: Routledge).

Tasker, Yvonne (1993), *Spectacular Bodies: Gender, Genre and the Action Cinema* (London: Routledge).

Tyler, Parker (1973/1993), *Screening the Sexes: Homosexuality in the Movies* (New York: Da Capo Press).

Weiss, Andrea (1992), *Vampires and Violets: Lesbians in the Cinema* (London: Jonathan Cape).

White, Patricia (1987), 'Madam X of the China Seas', *Screen*, 28/4: 80–95.

—— (1991), 'Female Spectator, Lesbian Specter: The Haunting', in Diana Fuss (ed.), *Inside/Out: Lesbian Theories, Gay Theories* (New York: Routledge).

Williams, Linda (1986), ' "Personal Best": Women in Love', in Charlotte Brunsdon (ed.), *Films for Women* (London: British Film Institute).

Wood, Robin (1977), 'Responsibilities of a Gay Film Critic', in Bill Nichols (ed.), *Movies and Methods* 2 vols., ii (Berkeley: University of California Press).

—— (1986), *Hollywood from Vietnam to Reagan* (New York: Columbia University Press).

Zimmerman, Bonnie (1981), 'Lesbian Vampires', *Jump Cut*, 24–5: 23–4.

15 Queer Theory

Alexander Doty

Queer theory shares with feminism an interest in non-normative expressions of gender and with lesbian, gay, and bisexual studies a concern with non-straight expressions of sexuality and gender. However, queer film and popular culture theory and criticism has developed as much as a reaction to feminism and to lesbian and gay work as it has been an expansion of this work.

The questioning of essentialist identity politics, the rise of AIDS activism, and the debates surrounding 'political correctness' laid the groundwork for reappropriating the term 'queer' inside and outside the academy beginning in the mid-1980s. However, in the decade that followed, 'queer' and 'queerness' has been used and understood a number of ways in film and popular culture theory, criticism, and practice. Some use 'queer' as a hipper synonym for 'gay male', or, less frequently, 'lesbian', or as a new umbrella term for gay and lesbian (and bisexual sometimes). In relation to film and popular culture theory and criticism, perhaps this use of 'queer' can be connected to the beginning of what has been called 'New Queer Cinema' or the 'Queer New Wave'. As a result of certain high-profile screenings and awards at the Sundance and Toronto film festivals of 1991 and 1992, critics and distributors heralded a new film movement that included such works as *Paris is Burning* (Jennie Livingstone, 1990), *Tongues Untied* (Marlon Riggs, 1990), *Poison* (Todd Haynes, 1991), *My Own Private Idaho* (Gus van Sant, 1991), *Young Soul Rebels*

(Isaac Julien, 1991), *Edward II* (Derek Jarman, 1991), *The Hour and the Times* (Christopher Munch, 1992), *The Living End* (Gregg Araki, 1992), and *Swoon* (Tom Kalin, 1992). For many critics, what tied these films and videos together and set them apart from others, aside from their independent production status, was how they directly addressed a non-straight audience, as well as how they presented material that was sexually explicit, unconcerned with 'positive images', and more generally 'politically incorrect'. Some saw these characteristics, in part, as responses to the AIDS crisis, pornography, and anti-censorship debates, and in-your-face AIDS and gay and lesbian activism (ACT UP!, Outrage, Queer Nation).

However, a number of commentators at the time, including B. Ruby Rich (1993), Cherry Smyth (1992), and Pratibha Parmar (Gever *et al.* 1993), noted that 'New Queer Cinema' was used most often to describe and market independent films and videos by or about gay men, and largely white middle-class gay men at that. But adding work by women to the roll-call of New Queer Cinema—Pratibha Parmar (*Kush*, 1991), Sadie Benning (*It wasn't Love*, 1992), Su Friedrich, (*First Comes Love*, 1991), Cecilia Dougherty (*Coal Miner's Granddaughter*, 1991, *Flaming Ears* 1991) still wasn't enough to justify the use of 'queer' for some. Smyth (1992) was among those who felt that most of what was called New Queer Cinema (and video) in the early 1990s was really only repackaged lesbian, gay, or 'les-

The Queer New Wave, Gus van Sant's *My Own Private Idaho* (1991)

bian and gay' work, because these films and videos do not seriously challenge or transgress established straight *or* gay and lesbian understandings of gender and sexuality. Beyond this, some commentators and film- and videomakers feel that expressing and representing queerness—as opposed to gayness, lesbianism, and bisexuality—is most (or only) possible within non-mainstream production and formal contexts, that is within avant-garde, documentary, and other independently produced alternative-to-traditional narrative forms.

Much of the queer film and popular culture theory and criticism developed in the 1990s was fuelled by the examples of New Queer Cinema, its critics, and the work of cultural critics like Judith Butler (*Gender Trouble*, 1990), Eve Kosofsky Sedgwick (*Between Men*, 1985; *Epistemology of the Closet*, 1991), Michael Warner (*Fear of a Queer Planet*, 1993), Diana Fuss (*Essentially Speaking*, 1989), Teresa de Lauretis ('Queer Theory' issue of *differences*, 1991), Sue-Ellen Case ('Tracking the Vampire', 1991), and Smyth (*Lesbians*

Talk Queer Notions, 1992). Of course, as suggested earlier, queer film and popular culture theory and criticism has also developed in relation or in response to earlier lesbian and gay film and popular culture theory and criticism, represented by the work of Richard Dyer, Robin Wood, B. Ruby Rich, Teresa de Lauretis, Jack Babuscio, and special sections in *Jump Cut* (1977, 1981) (see also Smelik, Part 1, Chapter 14). But just how, or even if, queer theory and criticism is connected to lesbian and gay approaches is an issue that is still being negotiated and debated.

Aside from its uses as a synonym for gay or lesbian or bisexual, certain uses of 'queer' and 'queerness' as new umbrella terms have most strongly suggested how it might work with(in) established lesbian, gay, and bisexual film and popular culture theory and criticism. In these uses, 'queer' might be used to describe the intersection or combination of more than one established 'non-straight' sexuality or gender position in a spectator, a text, or a personality. For example, when a text like *Gentlemen Prefer Blondes* (1953) or *All about Eve* (1950) accumulates lesbian, gay, and bisexual cultural readings, it could be deemed a queer text, rather than, say, only a gay or a lesbian or a bisexual text. In a similar way, Marlene Dietrich and Bette Davis could be said to have queer star images as they have inspired lesbian, gay, and bisexual cultural appreciations. By this meaning, the text or the performer's star image does not have to have obvious (so-called 'denotative') non-straight elements to be termed 'queer'; it just needs to have gathered about it a number of non-straight cultural readings. Indeed, some queer critics contend that many popular culture texts that do contain visible gay, lesbian, bisexual, or otherwise non-straight characters and content—like *Silence of the Lambs* (1991)—aren't necessarily queer texts as they work to oppress and eliminate queerness rather than to express it. The uses of 'queer' outlined above are generally careful not to replace specifically lesbian, gay, and bisexual critical positions, readings, and pleasures. The goal here is to collect and juxtapose these positions, readings, and pleasures in order to construct a range of 'non-straight' (that is, queer) approaches to film and popular culture.

A slight variation on the approaches described above would be using queer to describe the non-straight work, positions, pleasures, and readings of people who don't share the same 'sexual orientation' as that articulated in the text they are producing or responding to. A gay man would take queer pleasure in a lesbian film, for example. Or a lesbian or straight women might be said to do queer work when she directs a film with gay content, or writes an essay discussing the erotics of, say, Kenneth Anger's films. Certain feminist critics and theorists have also begun using the term 'queer' to describe any non-normative expressions of gender by or about straight women (and, sometimes, straight men) in film and popular culture production and representation. But whether connected to feminism or not, this understanding of 'queer' can describe any work by straight-identifying film and popular culture theorists, critics, or producers that is concerned with non-normative straightness.

As with many of the films and videos of the New Queer Cinema movement, the critical and theoretical uses of 'queer' outlined above largely maintain gender difference and the orthodoxies about sexuality developed within liberal feminist theories and gay and lesbian 'identity politics' approaches. However, another variety of queer film theory and criticism has followed the more radical programmes outlined by Smyth,

Case, and others as it concentrates upon those aspects of spectatorship, cultural readership, and textual codes that suggest or establish spaces that are not quite contained within established gender and sexuality categories. By this definition, 'queer' would be reserved for those films and popular culture texts, spectator positions, pleasures, and readings that articulate spaces outside gender binaries and sexuality categories, whether these are outside normative straight understandings of gender and sexuality or outside orthodox lesbian and gay understandings of these things. This type of queer film and popular culture theory and criticism is concerned with that which does not seem to fall within either current definitions of straightness, nor within those of lesbianism or gayness—and perhaps even those of bisexuality, although this area has been given precious little attention thus far in film and popular culture theory and criticism (but see below).

> **Ultimately, the theories, criticism, and film and popular culture texts produced within this definition of 'queer' would seek to examine, challenge, and confuse sexual and gender categories.**

Ultimately, the theories, criticism, and film and popular culture texts produced within this definition of 'queer' would seek to examine, challenge, and confuse sexual and gender categories. Some film and popular culture work in this area seeks to bring established sexuality and gender categories to a crisis point by exposing their limitations as accurate descriptive terms for what happens in a lot of film and popular culture production and consumption and reading practices. For example, together or separately, 'masculine', 'feminine', 'straight', 'lesbian', and 'gay' (or, to use a term more in keeping with the period, 'homosexual') don't quite describe the image of, or the spectator responses to, Katharine Hepburn dressed as a young man within the narrative of *Sylvia Scarlett* (1936). I have deliberately left the terms 'bisexual' and 'androgynous' off the list above, as some theorists and critics working with queer–queerness feel that among established gender and sexuality concepts bisexuality and androgyny offer two of the best starting-points from which to develop theoretical and critical positions that

Katharine Hepburn dressed
as a young man in *Sylvia
Scarlett* (1936)

will move film and popular culture criticism and theory beyond gender difference and orthodox sexual categories. Perhaps this is because bisexuality and androgyny are often understood as being positioned both 'between' and outside gender and sexuality binaries. In a similar manner, some writers are examining transvestism and transsexuality–transgenderism as potential sites for developing queer theoretical and critical approaches to film and popular culture that are founded upon potentially more radical transgressions of gender and sexuality orthodoxies.

Given the existing range of understandings, uses, and approaches to queerness in film and popular culture theory and criticism, it is not possible to establish one 'politics' of queerness. While some would like to reserve the term 'queer' only for those films, videos, articles, and books that take up progressive or radical political positions on gender and sexuality, the fact remains that at present 'queer' and 'queerness' have been, and are being, used in film and popular culture theory and criticism in relation to a wide range of political and ideological positions, from conservative to radical.

But in one or another of their many definitional and political forms, there are signs that established theoretical and critical areas in film and popular culture are being queered. Take, for example, textual coding and

spectatorship. Certain queer film and popular culture theorists have already profoundly challenged what has come before by asserting that the concepts of subtexting and connotation are most often used as heterocentrist paradigms to undermine, subordinate, or deny a range of non- (normative) straight readings that are as 'denotative' as any others. So queer readings (decodings) of texts are not 'alternative readings' or 'subcultural readings', but readings to stand alongside normatively straight ones. Taking up certain feminist work with spectatorship and gender, queer work with spectatorship has suggested that viewers, no matter what their stated gender and sexuality identities, often position themselves 'queerly'—that is, position themselves within gender and sexuality spaces other than those with which they publicly identify. Most radically, this ever-shifting gender and sexuality positioning in relation to film and popular culture would obliterate for the spectator the sense of functioning within any particular gender and sexuality categories.

Historical studies, semiotics and structuralism, Marxist and ideological criticism, auteurism, genre studies, reception theory, and psychoanalytic, feminist, gay, lesbian, and bisexual approaches have all begun to be scrutinized, critiqued, supplemented, revised, or, in certain cases, rejected by queer film and popular culture theorists and critics. They are either seeking ways to form 'coalitions' between non- (normative) straight approaches, or wanting to examine more accurately and complexly those spaces and places in film and popular culture that fall outside existing gender and sexuality categories.

BIBLIOGRAPHY

*Bad Object-Choices (ed.) (1991), *How do I Look?: Queer Film and Video* (Seattle: Bay Press).

Bornstein, Kate (1994), *Gender Outlaw: Of Men, Women, and the Rest of Us* (New York: Routledge).

Butler, Judith (1993), 'Critically Queer', *GLQ: Journal of Lesbian and Gay Studies*, 1/1: 17–32; repr. in *Bodies that Matter: On the Discursive Limits of 'Sex'* (New York: Routledge.

—— (1990), *Gender Trouble: Feminism and the Subversion of Identity* (New York: Routledge).

Case, Sue-Ellen (1991), 'Tracking the Vampire', *differences: A Journal of Feminist Cultural Studies*, 3/2 (Summer), 1–20.

*Creekmur, Corey, K., and Alexander Doty (eds.) (1995), *Out in Culture: Gay, Lesbian and Queer Essays on Popular Culture* (Durham, NC: Duke University Press).

de Lauretis, Teresa (1991), Introduction, *differences: A Journal of Feminist Cultural Studies*, 3/2 (Summer), Special Issue: *Queer Theory*, pp. iii–xviii.

Doty, Alexander (1993), *Making Things Perfectly Queer: Interpreting Mass Culture* (Minneapolis: University of Minnesota Press).

Fuss, Diana (1989), *Essentially Speaking: Feminism, Nature and Difference* (New York: Routledge).

Garber, Marjorie (1992), *Vested Interests: Cross-Dressing and Cultural Anxiety* (New York: Routledge).

*Gever, Martha, John Greyson, and Pratibha Parmar (eds.) (1993), *Queer Looks: Perspectives on Gay and Lesbian Film and Video* (New York: Routledge).

The Independent Film and Video Monthly (1995), 18/5 (June), Special Issue: *Queer Media*.

Jump Cut (1977), 16, Special Section: *Gays and Film* 13–28.

—— (1981), 24–5, Special Section: *Lesbians and Film* 17–51.

Martin, Biddy (1994), 'Sexuality without Gender and Other Queer Utopias', *Diacritics*, 24/2–3: 104–21.

—— and Judith Butler (eds.) (1994), *differences: A Journal of Feminist Cultural Studies* 6/2–3 (Summer–Fall), Special Issue: *Feminism Meets Queer Theory*.

'New Queer Cinema' (1992), *Sight and Sound*, 2/5 (Sept.), 30–41.

Pramaggiore, Maria, and Donald E. Hall (1995), *Representing Bisexualities: Subjects and Cultures of Fluid Desire* (New York: New York University Press).

Rich, B. Ruby (1993), 'Reflections on a Queer Screen', *GLQ: A Journal of Lesbian and Gay Studies*, 1/1: 83–91.

Sedgwick, Eve Kosofsky (1985), *Between Men: English Literature and Male Homosocial Desire* (New York: Columbia University Press).

—— (1991), *Epistemology of the Closet* (Hemel Hempstead: Harvester Wheatsheaf).

—— (1993), 'Queer and Now', in *Tendencies* (Durham: Duke University Press).

Smyth, Cherry (1992), *Lesbians Talk Queer Notions* (London: Scarlet Press).

Straayer, Chris (1990), 'The She-Man: Postmodern Bi-Sexed Performance in Film and Video', *Screen*, 31/3 (Autumn), 262–80.

—— (1992), 'Redressing the "Natural": The Temporary Transvestite Film', *Wide Angle*, 14/1 (Jan.), 36–55.

Warner, Michael (1993), Introduction, in *Fear of a Queer Planet: Queer Politics and Social Theory* (Minneapolis: University of Minnesota Press).

Wilton, Tamsin (1995), *Immortal Invisible: Lesbians and the Moving Image* (New York: Routledge).

16

Pornography

Laura Kipnis

Pornography doesn't appear to be going away any-time soon, so I suggest we take this opportunity to study it. However, the question of pornography as an area of academic study or as an aspect of a film studies curriculum is invariably political and controversial. Feminism—of both popular and academic varieties—has successfully overhauled the previously prevailing definition of pornography and brought about something of an epistemic shift in thinking on the subject. Whereas pornography was once viewed as a medium simply devoted to sexual explicitness (and to whatever corresponding feelings of sexual arousal such explicitness might occasion in the—typically male—viewer), feminists have largely redefined and complicated the genre as one whose concern is not simply sex and sexual expression, but rather gender relations and power: specifically, patriarchal power and the continuing disempowerment and oppression of women.

Pornography has become a rallying-point for many feminists, the most onerous form of the 'objectification of women'—a phrase that has achieved wide currency both in and outside the academy. It has been widely seen as something of a model for degrading treatment of women in other media, from album covers to advertising to mainstream film and television. But pornography has also been regarded by some feminists as the dominant cause of female oppression, and held responsible for a vast range of effects in the world. The case against it begins with the personal discomfort it causes some (but certainly not all) women, creating a 'hostile environment' for women encountering pornographic explicitness on news-stands or in the workplace. This charge begs a question that goes largely unasked in these discussions: *why* is pornography more offensive to women than to the men who buy it or display it? If displaying pornography is considered a hostile act to women at large, what guarantees its success in achieving that aim? In other words, why don't women have the choice of being indifferent to pornography? It might seem that the question of comfort or discomfort around sexual explicitness is central to the very constitution of gendered subjectivity, a point that Freud makes about the acquisition of femininity: originally girls and boys are equally interested in sexual facts, but Oedipalization for the female entails an increasing inhibition about sexuality (Freud 1965).

The focus for anti-porn feminists, however, is not on sexual difference or on the intrapsychic realm, but on the effects it is charged pornography has in the world—from 'keeping women in their place' to violence, rape, and murder. Anti-porn feminists have charged that men are incited to re-enact the scenes that they view in pornography, that pornography is not merely fantasy, or speech, but a call to action (see Mackinnon 1993; Dworkin 1981, 1987; Gubar and Hoff 1989). Anti-porn feminists often cite controversial effects research in which men are shown pornography and pornographic films in experimental settings, and then queried about their feelings towards women and sex. In some of these studies it appears that men self-report increased violent or callous feelings toward women after viewing pornography, or increased cavalier attitudes about rape. But at the same time, much of this research suffers from quite simplistic assumptions about the nature of its content. Edward Donnerstein and Daniel Linz, leading pornography effects researchers, routinely screen the notorious sexploitation movie *I Spit on your Grave* (Meir Zarchi, USA, 1977) as an example of sexual violence against women, then measure male audiences for mood, hostility, and desensitization to rape (Donnerstein and Linz 1986). But as anyone who's actually seen this movie knows, it's no simple testimonial to rape. This is a rape-*revenge* film, in which a woman rape victim wreaks violent reprisal against her rapists, systematically and imaginatively killing all three—and one mentally challenged onlooker—by decapitation, hanging, shooting, and castration. Film theorist Carol Clover points out that even during the rape sequence, the camera angles force the viewer into identification with the female victim (1992: 139). If male college students are hostile after watching this movie (with its grisly castration scene), it's far from clear what it is they're actually reacting to.

Feminists who have desired to contest the anti-porn movement's positions have often returned to a pre-feminist position that pornography really is about sex, but that with feminism under their belts, so to speak, now women too can enjoy its forbidden fruits. The insistence by anti-porn feminists that there is no distinction between thought and deed in the pornography viewer, and that the image dictates the viewer's

Whereas pornography was once viewed as a medium simply devoted to sexual explicitness (and to whatever corresponding feelings of sexual arousal such explicitness might occasion in the—typically male—viewer), feminists have largely redefined and complicated the genre as one whose concern is not simply sex and sexual expression, but rather gender relations and power.

position—that a violent act by a male character automatically decrees a male viewer's identification with that act—has also incited pro-porn or anti-censorship feminists into a mini-stampede back to the gates of psychoanalytic theory for a more complicated model of fantasy, one which reanimates these sticky questions of identification (see Stern 1982 for an early example of this move). Aren't there gaps between identity (sexual or gendered) and identification in the film viewing experience? Is that, perhaps, what pornography is good for? This is a position also suggested by Carol Clover's (1992) work on horror—a study with much relevance to pornography studies—which maintains that male horror film viewers identify with character functions rather than character genders, and that these functions (victim, hero, monster, sadist) resonate with competing parts of the viewer's psyche. Cross-gender identification offers male viewers a chance to experience a range of emotions, fears, and conflicts, with female characters functioning as 'fronts' for those more culturally forbidden affects. Other theorists have pointed out that the implication of Laura Mulvey's work ('Sadism demands a story . . .') has been to repress the issue of masochism in the male viewing experience, and that film theory in general has had a lopsided focus on male mastery and aggressivity, excluding the 'feminine', along with the complexities of cross-gender identifications (see Mulvey 1975; Rodowick 1982; Studlar 1985).

Introducing more complicated theories of identification also counterbalances a determinist tendency in feminist film theory often known by its codename: 'the gaze'. In following Mulvey's assertion that the cinematic code is based on positioning the woman as objects of either a sadistic-voyeurism or a fetishizing scopophilia, feminist theorists have often unwittingly collapsed the 'male gaze' into something resembling the Foucauldian panoptic gaze of *Discipline* and *Punish*. The unfortunate result is the theoretical invention of a new, all-powerful male viewing subject: not one caught in the abject dialectic of castration and futile compensatory exercises of mastery, but one for whom 'the gaze' actually accomplishes its mission. For this monolithic male gaze, fetishization *works*: male power *can* be 'natural', and the female body *can* be contained—psychically, socially, and politically. In Joan Copjec's view, the mutually constitutive interrelationship posed between gaze, subject, and apparatus in much feminist film theory results from a tendency to misread Lacan as assimilable to Foucault, and thus to

Accessible, soft Europorn of the 1970s *Emmanuelle* (1973)

miss the misrecognition and radical indeterminacy that constitute the subject for Lacan, instead smuggling back in a stable self and along with it a theoretical tendency to 'court determinism' (Copjec 1989; see also Kipnis 1993: 8–11). However, for other writers who have taken up Foucault's work as a tool in approaching pornography, notably Linda Williams (1989), the inherent contradictions in pornography itself—constituted as a genre by the quest for a truth which can't be represented, namely, female sexual pleasure—undermine the stability of both the form and the positions from which it can be viewed.

More recently, the rise of gay and queer studies within the academy, as well as the use of pornography in AIDS education, have introduced other questions—and other bodies—into the equation, also contesting the feminist anti-porn monopoly on the discourse. As activist-theorist Cindy Patton writes, 'The special vernacular of porn can be used in efforts to reconstruct a language of sex to go along with the reconstructed sexualities that resist both potentially HIV-transmitting activities and the destructive effects of attempts to silence, once again, the eloquent voice of homo-sexualities' (1991: 378).

These debates don't, however, exhaust the topic, and I would like to suggest another area of focus for the academic study of pornography, and suggest another reason that pornography is an invariably political issue. This has to do with pornography's position at the very bottom of the very lowest rungs of the cultural hierarchy. It would be difficult to argue that the academy is not still, to a large degree, structured by an Arnoldian relation to culture, in which the very term 'culture' signifies elevation and gentility: 'higher learning'. The study of 'lower' varieties of culture—even in the form of film and television studies, established academic disciplines at this point—can still provoke a certain degree of *frisson* within the humanities.

Studying something in the humanities necessitates taking it seriously, inventing complexity for it, building some form of intimate relationship with it. It involves proximity, and thus contamination. In contrast, the social sciences can, and, indeed by definition, do safely take on all variety of deviance and abnormality—low culture, criminality, violence, sex as object of study—because social science methodologies entail a quite different set of relations from their objects of study. The social sciences are not in danger from their low objects, because their claim to the status of 'science' gives them sufficient mastery and distance.

Yet, by contrast, there is no end of cultural fretting that the humanities are 'brought down' by the study of popular culture, and this 'lowering of standards' is blamed by conservative social critics for all manner of social ills (see e.g. Bloom 1987). The energy behind the recent canon wars, the call for a return to 'traditional values'—not only for families, but in curricula—all signal a certain anxiety about the social effects that 'low' forms of culture pose to the orderly operation of social reproduction, when the low manages to infiltrate 'higher' venues, such as college campuses. It may be that this is not an unreasonable fear, given that the social world we inhabit is certainly organized along a hierarchy that runs from high to low in terms of class, and that despite whatever movement towards democratization in higher education has taken place in the post-war years, university education is still a primary instrument of class reproduction, a mechanism for ensuring the proper distinctions and segregations between classes. My argument is that none of this is unrelated to curricular issues, to the question of what gets taught and studied on campuses. Because if the social world is organized hierarchically, it is also the case that culture is organized hierarchically, along a spectrum that also runs from high to low. That is, culture too is classed, with the lower forms of culture in something of an analogous relation to the lower tiers of the class structure. Note that this is not an argument about the demographics of viewership or cultural consumption—I'm not arguing that the upper classes consume 'higher' forms of culture, and the lower classes consume strictly 'low' culture—although given that the price of a pair of opera tickets these days runs to roughly a week's salary for a minimum-wage worker, certain forms of high culture are presumably cordoned off from the lower-paid masses.

> **The feminist anti-porn argument is that pornography is a special case, with special powers to cause effects in viewers; that unlike other genres, porn viewers are seized by overwhelming urges to act out what they see on screen, whereas no one seems to think that viewers of musicals are suddenly, irresistibly compelled to start tap-dancing.**

Rather, this is an argument about the semiotics of culture, and the symbolic valences of the study of 'lower' forms of culture within institutions of 'higher' education. Given the way that cultural forms map onto class forms, with pornography implicitly in an analogy with the bottom tiers of the social, its introduction into the academy opens onto a welter of issues around class, value, and their overstructured relation to scholarship. Thus it is no accident that film studies earned a place in the academy by fashioning itself along the lines predominant in the established academic disciplines: film as 'art', auteurs as their emanating consciousness—even if the realities of industrial production contra-indicated that model of authorship (see Crofts, Part 2, Chapter 7). The relationship

between a discipline and its object of study is an intricate one, and there are material realities governing the institutional contexts in which these disciplines operate and their objects are studied: decisions about hiring, promotion and tenure, granting and funding, also affect whether and how pornography gets studied by academics—not to mention that the study of pornography in academic settings invariably sexualizes the setting and complicates the codes of the classroom in quite unpredictable ways (Kleinhans 1996).

Dwelling on the issue of cultural value postpones another obvious issue: that pornography's manifest content is sex. Does that change how film studies should approach it as an object of analysis? Is pornography simply another film genre—like comedy, melodrama, the western—to which film studies can bring familiar analytical tools to bear, or is pornography a special case? As indicated above, the feminist anti-porn argument is that pornography is a special case, with special powers to cause effects in viewers; that unlike other genres, porn viewers are seized by overwhelming urges to act out what they see on screen, whereas no one seems to think that viewers of musicals are suddenly, irresistibly compelled to start tap-dancing. So, for these feminists, there's no distance between representation and reality, between 'realism' and documentary, between image and 'propaganda'. For these feminists, pornography *advertises*: as if any film about divorce, say, were automatically seen as advocating broken homes, or as though all war films were incitements to bomb things.

It may be that this confusion between representation and the real is something inherent to the genre, because in pornography, or at least, in hard-core pornography in which sex acts such as penetration actually *do* take place, the act is *real*. One might argue that, at those moments, the film slips—transgresses—genre boundaries; it suddenly becomes documentary. Part of the *frisson* of pornography is the power of direct cinema: we witness actors crossing a line between performing and 'being', which may complicate the identifications and pleasures of viewing. We slip from viewers into witnesses. Of course, the question of what precisely is being witnessed is a complicated one, given the way sex functions as a vehicle for so *many* meanings and affects, not just for pleasure, but also for experiences of transgression, utopian aspirations, sadness, optimism, loss, and the most primary longings for love and plenitude. If sex can be this multivalent in its meanings—and this brief list certainly doesn't exhaust the possibilities, which are as numerous as there are humans—then pornography, too, is vast in the kinds of contents and messages it opens onto.

> The question of what precisely is being witnessed is a complicated one, given the way sex functions as a vehicle for so *many* meanings and affects, not just for pleasure, but also for experiences of transgression, utopian aspirations, sadness, optimism, loss, and the most primary longings for love and plenitude.

Whether the pornography experience is seen as pleasurable or profoundly displeasurable, it holds a mirror up to the culture, mapping its borders and boundaries through strategic acts of transgression. Pornography is dedicated to propriety violations of every shape, manner, and form, and proprieties have deep links to the maintenance of social order and to who we are as social subjects (see Kipnis 1996). The links between the culture, proprieties, and the deep structure of the psyche are evident in how very transfixed we are, as viewers and as a culture, before the pornographic scene, whether with pleasure or disgust, intellectually or viscerally. The intensity of the debates it has spawned are some testament to this fascination, and to the work pornography does as a genre: it distils the issues that are central to our culture and to the constitution of the self, and reiterates them through the code of sex. Unlikely as it may seem, I'd suggest that pornography contains a vast amount of social knowledge, which is another reason it demands study.

Now go do your homework.

BIBLIOGRAPHY

Bloom, Allan (1987), *The Closing of the American Mind* (New York: Simon & Schuster).

*Church Gibson, Pamela, and **Roma Gibson** (eds.) (1993), *Dirty looks: Women, Pornography, Power* (London: British Film Institute).

Clover, Carol (1992), *Men, Women and Chain Saws: Gender in the Modern Horror Film* (Princeton: Princeton University Press).

Copjec, Joan (1989), 'The Orthopsychic Subject', *October* (Summer), 53–71.

Donnerstein, Edward, and **Daniel Linz** (1986), 'Mass Media, Sexual Violence and Male Viewers: Current Theory and Research', *American Behavioral Scientist* 29 (May–June), 601–18.

Dworkin, Andrea (1981), *Pornography: Men Possessing Women* (New York: Perigee).

—— (1987), *Intercourse* (New York: Free Press).

Freud, Sigmund (1965), 'Femininity', in *New Introductory Lectures on Psychoanalysis* (New York: Norton).

Gubar, Susan, and **Joan Hoff** (eds.) (1989), *For Adult Users Only: The Dilemma of Violent Pornography* (Bloomington: Indiana University Press).

Kipnis, Laura (1993), *Ecstasy Unlimited: On Sex, Capital, Gender and Aesthetics* (Minneapolis: Minnesota University Press).

*—— (1996), *Bound and Gagged: Pornography and the Politics of Fantasy in America* (New York: Grove).

Kleinhans, Chuck (1996), 'Some Pragmatics in Teaching Sexual Images', *Jump Cut*, 40, Special Section: *Teaching Sexual Images*, 119–22.

MacKinnon, Catharine (1993), *Only Words* (Cambridge, Mass.: Harvard University Press).

Mulvey, Laura (1975), 'Visual Pleasure and Narrative Cinema', *Screen*, 16/3: 6–18.

Patton, Cindy (1991), 'Visualizing Safe Sex: When Pedagogy and Pornography Collide', in Diana Fuss (ed.), *Inside/Out: Lesbian Theories, Gay Theories* (New York: Routledge).

Rodowick, D. N. (1982), 'The Difficulty of Difference', *Wide Angle*, 5/1: 4–15.

Stern, Lesley (1982), 'The Body as Evidence', *Screen*, 23/5: 38–60.

Studlar, Gaylyn (1985), 'Masochism and the Perverse Pleasures of the Cinema', in Bill Nichols (ed.), *Movies and Methods* (Berkeley: California University Press).

*Williams, Linda (1989), *Hard Core: Power, Pleasure, and the Frenzy of the Visible* (Berkeley: California University Press).

17

Race, ethnicity, and film

Robyn Wiegman

It is rare to find a film studies scholar today who would assert that the study of race and ethnicity has little or no bearing on the discipline. Who can talk about the western, for instance, without some attention to the ideological construction of a mythic American past predicated on the wholesale binary arrangement of good white men and bad, bloodthirsty Indians? What account of the silent film era can proceed without commentary on its language of stereotype, from the Italian American gangster to the Latino greaser to the African American rapist? And how can we discuss the Hollywood industry without analysis of its workplace segregations or Motion Picture morality codes? From genre to spectator, from directorship to narration, in the ideological as well as the material realm, race and ethnicity have a foundational effect on the study of Hollywood film industry, representational practices, and spectatorial cultures.

And yet, it is difficult to speak of the study of race and ethnicity as constituting a fully formed field within film studies, at least not one definable along the lines set forth by Patricia White in 'Feminism and Film' for this volume. In that chapter, White convincingly offers a history and theoretical agenda that constitutes feminist film criticism as a coherent field within the broader disciplinary area of Anglo-American film studies. Citing the women's movement as genesis for investigations into images of women, White surveys several decades of feminist scholarship which have fundamentally

altered the way film is studied and, arguably, produced. No such overarching narrative or shared body of primary scholarship exists for the study of race and ethnicity in film.

This does not mean that political activism has not been crucial to the development of race and ethnicity in film criticism, or that the diverse categories of analysis and production organized under the rubrics of race and ethnicity bear no political or critical affinities to one another. Chicano film history, for instance, cannot be adequately discussed apart from Chicano political activity in the 1960s (Fregoso 1993), and much of the new black cinema is formed in the context of the political complexities of diasporic identities (Martin 1995). The point is simply that the study of race and ethnicity in film has taken shape according to the formation of race and ethnicity in US culture more widely, reflecting not a cross-ethnic political agenda geared to white supremacy's massive deployment, but the discrete histories and political projects of specific identity sites: African American, Asian American, Chicano–Latino, Native American, Jewish American, Italian American, and Irish American (see, respectively, Bogle 1989; Wong 1978; Garcia Berumen 1995; Bataille and Silet 1980; Friedman 1982; Lourdeaux 1990; and Curran 1989).

Focused on specific identities, and the characters, actors, writers, or directors who embody them, the large majority of film studies scholarship traces the history of representation (the images' school) and documents the discriminatory employment practices of the industry. While such analyses have been important, critics in the late 1980s began to question the implicit segregation of race and ethnicity to non-white and non-WASP others. What would it mean to think of race and ethnicity in ways that both critique and exceed the 'minority' rubric? What aspects of formal cinematic analysis might be affected by considering race and ethnicity as critical categories irreducible to bodies? And what theoretical frameworks best articulate the historical differences and schematic overlap between the two terms? These are only some of the questions being posed by film studies scholars as the twentieth century draws to a close.

In such a context, the task of defining race and ethnicity as key themes in film studies is rather daunting. Not only must we account for the cinematic histories of specific groups, but we must also address how and why the thematic approach is an inadequate critical framework for understanding the relationships of power embedded in race and ethnicity as both socio-political and critical terms. To begin to meet these needs, this chapter examines the way the study of race and ethnicity has taken shape, first as a critical concern with the stereotype and later as a conversation about the stereotype's production in the context of post-structuralism and global image cultures. The final section looks to cross-ethnic and interethnic analysis, alongside an interrogation into the racialization of whiteness, as the new directions through which race and ethnicity might coalesce as a collective critical endeavour and organized field. But first, what do scholars mean when we talk about race and ethnicity?

Defining terms

The answer to this question varies, in part because the definitions of terms are historically mobile. As Lester Friedman points out in *Unspeakable Images* (1991), 'ethnicity' is a derivative of the Greek *ethnos*, meaning nation or race. In its earliest usage, ethnicity referred to pagans, those who were not Christian or Jewish, and only later became attached to political, national, linguistic and/or physical differences. To contemporary race theorists, this mobility demonstrates that race and ethnicity are social constructions linked to the specific discursive spheres within which they are used (Goldberg 1990). In the transformation of natural history into

the human sciences, for instance, race undergoes a radical rearticulation, losing its primary tie to national identity to become a biological distinction evinced by skin, hair, and cranial shape (Wiegman 1995). In the United States, these changes were crucial to white supremacy in the aftermath of the Civil War, making possible a continued subjugation of African Americans as racially different in the context of their official entrance into a shared national identity. So powerful has the racialization of 'blackness' been in the United States that film scholarship today concerning African Americans overwhelmingly uses race and not ethnicity as its central term (see Bobo 1995; Boyd 1996; Reid 1993; Snead 1994).

> **To contemporary race theorists, this mobility demonstrates that race and ethnicity are social constructions linked to the specific discursive spheres within which they are used.**

Scholarship examining Jewish American filmic representation and industry participation, on the other hand, is decidedly organized under the rubric of ethnicity (Erens 1984; Friedman 1982). This is the case even though early cinematic representations of Jews were predicated on nineteenth-century racialized notions of Jewish identity, notions which culminated in the genocidal catastrophe of the Second World War. In the cinematic classic, *The Jazz Singer* (USA, 1927), in which a cantor's son seeks assimilation into the American 'mainstream' through vaudeville, Jakie Rabinowitz erases his Jewishness only to put on blackface and participate in the miming of African American musical traditions (Rogin 1996). In blackface, the protagonist demonstrates his assimilable whiteness, and it is this demonstration that inaugurates the necessary compromise between a racialized difference and ethnic life in a new world.

The transformation of Jewish identity from a primarily racial to ethnic discourse is the most extreme example of a process that, in far more subtle ways, has affected other European immigrant groups, most notably the Italian and Irish. In silent film and the early talkies, images of these groups relied on certain characteristics of race discourse, featuring—through the representation of the body, its skin, hair, and facial shape—physiognomic assertions of innate and inferior differences. Edward G. Robinson's stereotype-setting role of an Italian gangster in *Little Caesar* (USA, 1930), for instance, indexes ethnic identity via the characteristics of racial physical deficiencies such as his 'swarthy' skin, and it does so in the context of an emergent generic form, the gangster film, that would criminalize Italian American identity (see Golden 1980). But while race discourse influenced the early images of immigrants from Europe and promoted certain essentializing notions of difference, their representation throughout the twentieth century has been part of an expanding whiteness. Ethnic variations within white racial identity reference, often stereotypically (but without the institutional force of national discrimination and exclusion), customs, languages, and artefacts drawn from a group's past cultural or national milieu.

Other immigrant groups in the United States have not fared as well in the popular imaginary as have those of European descent. Asians, for instance, have long sought the kind of differentiation within race categorization which would recognize specific ethnicities, but instead the popular conception melds together the disparate histories, cultures, and languages of those from East Asia (Korea, China, and Japan) and Southeast Asia (Vietnam, Cambodia, Laos, Thailand, the Philippines, and the Indonesian archipelago). In Charlie Chan, Kung Fu, the Dragon Lady, and other staple Asian figures of US film (such as the Vietcong), ethnicity is powerfully overridden by an emphasis on physical difference. Richard Feng's 'In Search of Asian American Cinema' reads the lack of specificity informing the film industry's approach to, and conversation about, Asian American ethnicities in the context of the contemporary commodification of identity. As he puts it, 'there is a market for Asian American Cinema—the problem is, it's a market that looks for Asian faces and looks no further' (Feng 1995: 34).

The illegibility of ethnic differentiations is the norm as well for those groups pre-existing the arrival of European colonialists in the Americas. Film scholarship on Native Americans, like the movies themselves, have rarely paid attention to the specificities of tribal cultures (Friar and Friar 1972). Instead the 'Indian' is represented as a homogenized figure whose cultural and highly racialized physical differences serve as background for the ideological production of the 'American' as of white European descent. Rarely are tribal languages part of the Hollywood text. *Little Big Man* (USA, 1970)

begins with Cheyenne but fails to carry it through; *Windwalker* (USA, 1980) and *Dances with Wolves* (USA, 1990) both use Lakota, but the former stars Trevor Howard in redface while the latter continues to centre the sensitive white man (Castillo 1991).

In a similar way, but with a somewhat more complicated political genealogy, scholarship on what Allen Woll (1980) first called the 'Latin image' in cinema foregrounds the complexities of immigration and colonization as the primary ways (in addition to slavery) that we organize groups within the critical terrain of race and ethnicity. While contemporary debates about immigration often highlight a 'crisis' at the Mexican–American border, the history of this border is inextricable from US colonialism, making Mexican Americans the products of two overlapping historical formations: colonialism (in the US military acquisition of the South-west and California in the mid-nineteenth century) and immigration (in the economic exploitation of Mexico in the twentieth). It is no doubt because of this tense and lengthy relationship that Hollywood films have been far more interested in Mexicans and their US descendants (Chicanos) than in any other group from the whole of Latin America. It is also the case that some of the most politicized counter-cinema in the United States has been produced under the banner of Chicano–Latino (Noriega 1992; Noriega and Lopez 1996), and much of this film production and its critical analysis stresses ethnic and not racial difference. Edward James Olmos's *American Me* (USA, 1992), for instance, makes this point through its representation of the white Chicano JD (William Forsythe).

> **Where ethnicity provides the means for differentiations based on culture, language, and national origins, race renders the reduction of human differences to innate, biological phenomena, phenomena that circulate culturally as the visible ledger for defining and justifying economic and political hierarchies between white and non-white groups.**

What this brief, and albeit condensed, history of the deployment of race and ethnicity as critical terms in the study of US cinema indicates is twofold. First, the terms are differentially mobile. Where ethnicity provides the means for differentiations based on culture, language, and national origins, race renders the reduction of human differences to innate, biological phenomena, phenomena that circulate culturally as the visible ledger for defining and justifying economic and political hierarchies between white and non-white groups. Only when we are dealing with European immigrants and their descendants does ethnicity become the sole operative term, whether in the complex language of specific films or the critical archive. In all other instances, a racial fetishism of the corporeal is at least covertly, if not overtly, staged. Therefore (and this is the second point), race and ethnicity as terms in film criticism are themselves products of a broader and highly political discourse about power and privilege in the United States.

The stereotype

To the extent that all stereotypes of human groups are predicated on the reduction of complex cultural codes to easily consumable visual and verbal cues, the film stereotype is paradigmatically linked to racial discourse. This does not mean that all stereotypes are raced, but rather that the logic of race as visually discernible underwrites the production and circulation of the stereotype. For film studies scholars concerned with the way cinema shapes the cultural imaginary, this 'fact' has generated a large body of scholarship dedicated to cataloguing and critiquing stereotypical images (Hilger 1986; Leab 1975; Miller 1980; Pettit 1980; O'Connor 1980; Richard 1992, 1993, 1994; Woll and Miller 1987). Across the three decades that now constitute the history of the study of stereotypes, we can trace the emergence of important issues about representation and difference, the political economy of the industry, spectatorship and identification, and, most importantly, the relationship between film and culture.

Eugene Franklin Wong's *On Visual Media Racism* (1978) remains one of the earliest and best studies of the function and production of the stereotype in Hollywood film. In his specific concern with the reduction of the diverse histories and cultures of Asians in US media, Wong's analysis exemplifies the way the stereotype has been critically approached for other racialized cultural identities (African American, Chicano–Latino, and Native American) by focusing on the stereotype's rela-

tionship to (1) broad historical and political processes, (2) labour practices in the industry, (3) ideologies concerning race, sexuality, and gender, and (4) film characterization, narrative, setting, costume, and cosmetics. He thus provides a materialist analysis of the stereotype, its ideological production, and its function as an element of the symbolic structure of the filmic text.

For Wong, the stereotype is a form of representation in film that produces non-white cultures and characters as static and one-dimensional. Acting is therefore more gestural than performatively complex; more about the cliché than emotional range. For this reason, a group's stereotyped image tends to oscillate between two simple poles: good and bad, noble and savage, loyal and traitorous, kind-hearted and villainous. It is by virtue of this condensation that an image becomes a stereotype; its racialization is achieved by an implicit or explicit moral assessment concerning the group's inherent 'essence'. Silent-film images of Asians, for instance, relied on a small range of signifiers to evoke Asian difference, such as the pigtail, the slanted eye, nodding, and laundry work. The titles alone tell the story of subordinate difference: *Heathen Chinese and the Sunday School Teachers* (USA, 1904), *The Chinese Rubbernecks* (USA, 1903), and *The Yellow Peril* (USA, 1908).

> It is by virtue of this condensation that an image becomes a stereotype; its racialization is achieved by an implicit or explicit moral assessment concerning the group's inherent 'essence'.

Many of the stereotypes of non-white men that film critics have analysed—the Mexican 'greaser', the Native savage, the African American beast—can be found in the silent era, which coincides historically with widespread political conversation about immigration, racial equality, and the meaning of being 'American'. These stereotypes most often functioned to shape popular memory about slavery, the Civil War, and Anglo-American acquisition of both Native and Mexican land. The violent Mexican, for instance, justified US aggression and spawned a series of films whose titles foreground their type: *The Greaser's Gauntlet* (USA, 1908), *Tony the Greaser* (USA, 1911), *Bronco*

The Ku Klux Klan mete out their version of justice in Griffith's controversial *Birth of a Nation* (1915)

Billy and the Greaser (USA, 1914), *The Greaser's Revenge* (USA, 1914), *Guns and Greasers* (USA, 1918). When the Mexican government threatened to ban all Hollywood imports in the 1920s (Delpar 1984), the 'greaser' disappeared from the screen, only to return with a vengeance in the second half of the century in *The Wild Bunch* (USA, 1969) and *Bring me the Head of Alfredo García* (USA, 1974). A new genre form, what critics call 'gang exploitation', is the latest rendition of the theme: *Boulevard Nights* (USA, 1979), *Walk Proud* (USA, 1979), *Defiance* (USA, 1980), and *Bound by Honor* (USA, 1993).

Violent Native Americans are likewise a long-running stereotype, making their 'savage' debut in such films as *The Massacre* (USA, 1912) and D. W. Griffith's *The Battle of Elderbush Gulch* (USA, 1913), before

becoming enshrined in the western. The narrative formula is now familiar: Native tribal cultures are homogenized as bloodthirsty hordes that attack, rape, and mercilessly pillage well-meaning Anglos who are trying to bring civilization to the continent. Late-century updates of the battle for territory have fared well at the box-office with *Dances with Wolves* (USA, 1990) and *Last of the Mohicans* (USA, 1992) (Edgerton 1994).

No single film in the silent era is more important to the critical history of the stereotype than is D. W. Griffith's *The Birth of a Nation* (USA, 1915). Here, the late nineteenth-century image of the African American male as rapist turns to pure spectacle in the ideologically weighted aesthetics of black-and-white film. In Gus, played in blackface by Walter Long, we have the filmic birth of what Donald Bogle

(1989) calls the 'brutal black buck', a sexually uncontrollable figure who lusts after white women. As the repository for a host of white anger and fear in the aftermath of the Civil War, the rapist image was part of a public discourse that 'explained' lynching; it is this replication of the justification of hate crimes against blacks that spurred the National Association for the Advancement of Colored People (NAACP) to seek complete censorship of the film. It was banned in five states and nineteen cities (Bogle 1989), but, according to Cripps (1977), white liberals were so overpowered by the film's aesthetic splendour that on the whole they failed to protest against the film's rendition of black equality as a national crisis (just as film scholarship has often seen the film's discourse on race as a surface aspect of narrative and not central to its aesthetic success; see Rogin 1985).

The African American male is not the only figure for whom racial difference becomes sexualized in the repetitive logic of the stereotype, nor is violence the only formulation of racialized sexuality in the cinema. As Wong (1978) discusses in his analysis of the industry's institutional forms of racism, a double standard governs sexuality, affecting both narrative structures and casting practices. This standard, which enables white men alone to transgress the social injunction against miscegenation and all interracial sexual desire, has produced two gendered sets of stereotypes, each one containing an opposed symbolic pair. For non-white males, the image is either of a sexually aggressive masculinity that threatens white womanhood or of an effeminate and symbolically castrated male—the difference between, say, Gus and Mr Bojangles from the Shirley Temple films—or, in terms of Asian representation, Tori of The Cheat (USA, 1915) and Song Liling of M Butterfly (USA, 1993). For non-white females, the stereotype oscillates between a nurturing, de-sexualized, loyal figure and a woman of exotic, loose, and dangerous sexuality: from O-Lan in The Good Earth (USA, 1937) to Hue Fei in Shanghai Express (USA, 1932) or from Mammy in Gone With the Wind (USA, 1939) to Epiphany Proudfoot in Angel Heart (USA, 1987).

Film studies scholars have interpreted the sexualization of race in Hollywood film as evidence of a much larger anxiety in American culture concerning interracial sexuality. After all, the democratic ideal of the 'melting-pot' brings into crisis the relationship between separatist cultures, languages, and sexual activity and the full force of integration which would

reconfigure the family and romance along with national identity. Since their beginning, film narratives have been obsessively drawn to this crisis, rehearsing a variety of interracial configurations and concluding, almost always, that the cost of interracial sex is much too high (The Savage, USA, 1953; Imitation of Life, USA, 1959; A Man Called Horse, USA, 1970; West Side Story, USA, 1961; and Jungle Fever, USA, 1991) or likely to result in tragedy. Thus, in The Indian Squaw's Sacrifice (USA, 1910), the title character, Noweeta, nurses a wounded white man back to health and marries him. Later he meets a white woman he had loved before, so Noweeta kills herself to allow her husband to return to the woman he loves. The same pattern occurs with minor variations in other films representing Native Americans as in The Kentuckian (USA, 1908) and Cecil DeMille's The Squaw Man (USA, 1914). Often, one of the lovers is killed at the end, thereby undoing the interracial liaison, as in Broken Arrow (USA, 1950) and A Man Called Horse.

> Film studies scholars have interpreted the sexualization of race in Hollywood film as evidence of a much larger anxiety in American culture concerning interracial sexuality.

Reflected in many of these narratives are industry labour practices, or what Wong (1978) calls role segregation and role stratification. Role segregation refers to the ways in which non-white actors are, by virtue of their race, ineligible for certain kinds of roles, while white actors are able to move 'horizontally' into even those roles racially defined as black, Asian, Native American, or Chicano. In the study of stereotypes, 'breakthrough' films are those in which lead roles designated as non-white are actually played by non-white actors, as in Salt of the Earth (USA, 1954), The World of Suzie Wong (USA, 1960), and Uncle Tom's Cabin (USA, 1927). Until the mid-1960s role segregation facilitated the anxiety around miscegenation by enabling white actors to play roles of non-white characters in stories of interracial sexuality, thereby skirting the Motion Picture Production Code (called the Hays Code), which forbade representations of miscegenation (Cortés 1993). In Pinky (USA, 1949), for instance, the title character, who has been passing for white, returns home, where she comes to terms with her 'blackness' and rejects the white man who loves her. Here, the scenes between Pinky and her beau, while narratively interracial, are none the less white, thereby avoiding a realist depiction of black and white sexual desire. The larger the role, the more likely it is—think of *Bordertown* (USA, 1935), *Down Argentine Way* (USA, 1940), *Viva Zapata!* (USA, 1952), *The Searchers* (USA, 1956), *Windwalker* (USA, 1980), and *Evita* (USA, 1996)—that a white actor will get the part, especially if the story entails an interracial sexual encounter (Wong 1978).

The industry's use of role segregation is part of the history of the stereotype for a number of reasons. First, it enables white actors to occupy and signify the full range of humanity in film as a body of cultural representation, which has the powerful effect of locking non-white actors into minor roles, or what Wong (1987) calls role stratification. In minor roles, character development and complexity are even harder to achieve as narrative combines with the ideology of the camera to reiterate the secondary or background nature of non-white groups and cultures. In the western, for instance, most Native Americans will be confined to minor roles, often shot in groups from long distance, and rarely individualized through spoken lines (Hilger 1995). Other genres, such as the war story, assemble groups of non-white actors as the enemy, thereby reiterating stereotyped notions of a group's inherent violence (*Full Metal Jacket*, USA, 1987; *Sands of Iwo Jima*, USA, 1949). Second, the practice of horizontal movement of whites into non-white roles has necessitated certain kinds of development in film cosmetology that are part of the stereotype's performance. In *My Geisha* (USA, 1962), make-up artists created a new procedure for actress Shirley MacLaine's transformation from Anglo to Asian by using dental plaster, clay, and wax to fashion rubber eyepieces as her epicanthic fold. This, combined with dark brown contact lenses, a black wig, and certain habits of halting speech, perform Asian racial difference for the big screen (Wong, 1978).

What scholarly analysis of the stereotype most powerfully reveals, then, is the pervasiveness of racism as an institutionalized element of Hollywood film. In filmic structure and forms of visual pleasure (narrative, setting, cosmetology, and camera technique) as well as in industry labour practices and 'morality' codes, we witness the full arsenal of the stereotype's production. Add to this other elements—the ethnicity of directors and producers, or the specificities of English-language

use—and one can begin to explore how the seeming simplicity of stereotypes is the effect of complex histories and representational forms. This is not to say, however, that the scholarly archive on the stereotype has gone uncritiqued. In light of independent cinematic production and post-structuralist theorizations of both 'representation' and subjectivity, critical understandings of the stereotype have been transformed.

Textuality, spectatorship, and the 'real'

Perhaps the most important early critique of the stereotype is Steve Neale's 'The Same Old Story: Stereotypes and Difference' (1979). Neale defines four primary critical problems. First, the emphasis on stereotypes constrains critical analysis by remaining too tied to the level of character and characterization, thereby obscuring other features of a text or ignoring altogether the textual specificities of individual films. Second, the identification of a stereotype does not illuminate racism as either a representational or a social practice; it merely points to it. In doing so it relies, third, on an empirically based notion of the 'real' that both precedes and measures the accuracy of the image. And, fourth, such an approach promotes the idea that artistic production is inherently progressive when it offers positive images to counter the negativity of the stereotype. Because of these critical fallacies, Neale proposes a shift in attention from repetition (the citing of the 'same old story' in text after text) to difference (a focus on how texts construct racial meanings).

In defining what he understands as the weakness of ideological criticism, Neale draws on the theoretical traditions of formalism, psychoanalysis, and post-structuralism to foreground the text as a specific and discrete cultural production, question the forms of identification involved in spectatorship, and retrieve representation from its reduction to the 'real'. All these issues have remained central to critical conversations in the 1980s and 1990s, but Neale's emphasis on the stereotype as inherently problematic, perhaps even useless, has not been retained (Snead 1994; Shohat and Stam 1994). Instead, the impulse has been to deepen the theorization of the stereotype by elaborating its textual production—its circulation as a sign—and by exploring its function in the construction of social subjectivities and psychic identifications and disavowals.

In their editorial introduction to *Screen*'s first special issue devoted to questions of race, Robert Stam and

Louise Spence (1983) begin to elaborate a comprehensive methodology to account for the textual practices and intertextual contexts through which 'difference is transformed into "other"-ness and exploited or penalized by and for power' (1983: 3). This emphasis on power directs attention both to the use of the camera as a representational practice and to cinema as an economic and political apparatus that circulates ways of interpreting and consuming the world. Framing the concept of voyeurism around race, and tying it both to the diegesis and to the political economy of cinema (i.e. the international market), Stam and Spence cite the camera as a crucial element in the global construction of the First World as 'subject'.

In the western's repeated motif of the encircled wagon, for instance, the camera transforms Native American difference into hierarchical otherness by locating the primary point of view behind or at the level of the wagon, with sound in the ensuing battle isolating Anglo pain and death (and most often collectivizing Indian utterance in the war 'whoop'). Shot scale and duration—close-ups focusing down upon white women and children, for instance, or the wide angle long shot taking in a horizon filled by hostile figures—wed the technical features of filmic production to ideologies of race. The racism of a text is thus an effect of its aesthetic language and formal features of production and not simply a matter of narrative or characterization. As such, 'positive images' can be as pernicious as degrading ones, depending on the comprehensive racial discourse of a text (as in *Guess Who's Coming to Dinner*, USA, 1968).

> **The racism of a text is thus an effect of its aesthetic language and formal features of production and not simply a matter of narrative or characterization.**

In demonstrating that racial discourse is more than a citation of historically racialized bodies, Stam and Spence theoretically identify a 'structuring absence' fundamental to the segregationist logic of much pre-1960s Hollywood film. For instance, Alfred Hitchcock's *The Wrong Man* (USA, 1957), in which scenes of New York City are devoid of people of colour, offers a racial discourse keyed to white visual pleasure. Critically to analyse the structuring absence of this film does not mean decrying its lack of realism in depicting New York City, but examining instead how its racial fantasy and visual pleasure are connected. In doing so, the critic will locate the question of realism within (and not outside) the text by explicating the film's mechanisms of suture—its construction of an internal 'reality'. For Stam and Spence, a comprehensive methodology for studying the stereotype thus entails an analysis of the narrative structures, genre conventions, and cinematic styles through which a discourse of race achieves its reality effect in a given film. In the analysis of dominant Hollywood cinema, this critical move has shifted the burden of the charge of racism from individuals (e.g. Hitchcock) to the broader practices of filmic production.

But what about the spectator? For Stam and Spence, the audience is not fully constituted by the film text, nor is the filmic experience limited to its individualized visual consumption. Spectators are shaped simultaneously by the ideologies of the wider culture and their specific gender, race, and class locations. Because of this, 'aberrant readings' are both possible and plausible. 'Black Americans, presumably, never took Stepin Fetchit to be an accurate representation of their race as a whole' (Stam and Spence 1983: 19). Note 'presumably'. Here, the stereotype that fixes the black image on the screen is transparent in its distortion, thereby enabling black audiences to reject and rewrite the stereotype. Homi Bhabha's essay on the stereotype, published later in the same year, begins to complicate this picture of resistant readers and their identifications, and on two counts. One, knowledge of the inaccuracy of the stereotype, he argues, does not forestall the political effect of the stereotype; indeed, the stereotype is effective on a colonialized subject precisely through its distortion. Two, spectator identifications are far more complex and ambivalent than their reduction to social identity asserts; therefore, 'the' black audience takes shape in contradictory and disparate ways (Bhabha 1983). More recently, Stuart Hall captures these issues in his title 'What is this "Black" in Black Popular Culture?' (1992).

In film studies, the critique of identity that is now nearly synonymous with post-structuralist analysis owes a great deal to the conversations about realism in the early 1980s. From these conversations the assumption that one 'reads' a film according to one's social identity, which is itself produced by one's positioning in hierarchies of power, is reframed; identity is rather an effect of discursive and material practices, not the essentialist ground for their explanations (Lubiano 1991; Snead 1994). And further, counter-reading is about historical and political oppositionality, and not essentialized difference (Fregoso 1993). This last point is forcefully made in a 1988 *Screen* volume titled *The Last 'Special Issue' on Race*. Here, guest editors Isaac Julien and Kobena Mercer assert that '*Screen* theory' has marginalized race and ethnicity not only through the 'special', segregated volume, but in its popularization of the notion of difference as 'Otherness'. Declaring this the 'last special issue', they hope to move the conversation of race and ethnicity from margin to centre by foregrounding the politics of both critical discourse and cinematic practices. In doing so, the volume sets the stage for three of the most important critical emphases in the 1990s: independent film, whiteness, and ethnicity in the context of global media culture.

The present tense

The issue of independent cinema has always gone hand in hand with the analysis of the stereotype, leading to a general assumption in the 1960s and 1970s that once those from stereotyped groups controlled the means of production, new film cultures would be born. *Zoot Suit* (USA, 1981), *Chan is Missing* (USA, 1982), *El Norte* (USA, 1983), *She's Gotta Have It* (USA, 1986), *Born in East LA* (USA, 1987), and *Pow Wow Highway* (USA, 1988) each gained recognition for their self-conscious counter to Hollywood formulations. A number of these directors—Luis Valdez, Wayne Wang, and Spike Lee—have made the 'crossover' move, with big budgets and mainstream critical acclaim (*La Bamba*, USA, 1987; *The Joy Luck Club*, USA, 1993; *Do the Right Thing*, USA, 1989).

With Hollywood seemingly willing to cash in on 'ethnic' markets, media critics and activists find themselves in the 1990s debating the 'burden of representation' that attends such widely circulated texts (Diawara 1993; Leong 1991). In a complicated analysis of Spike Lee's own claims to tell the truth of African American culture and experience, Wahneema Lubiano, for instance, emphasizes the scarcity of diverse representations within ethnic groups as part of her broader critique of Lee's political retreat into homophobic and sexist interpretations of black masculinity (Lubiano 1991). At issue in Lubiano's analysis is

the relationship between representative blackness and the proliferate whiteness of US image industries.

Whiteness, of course, has long been the context and subtext of the study of stereotypes, but until Richard Dyer's 'White' in the 'last special' *Screen* issue (1988), it has lacked any careful critical analysis. Dyer's essay begins by noting how whiteness as an ethnic category seems to lack specificity, coming into focus only as emptiness, absence, denial, or death, as is the case in *Night of the Living Dead* (USA, 1968, 1990). The resistance of whiteness to specification is an effect of its construction as the unmarked category in US racial discourse. For this reason, new work in the field is geared toward explicating both the socio-historical relationship between white identity forms and cinema and the representational practices within specific films that produce and circulate whiteness as sign (Bernardi 1996). The critical project of rendering whiteness tangible in the filmic text as one of film's most powerful and reliable narrative, characterological, and signifying systems entails a methodology that attends to textuality, on the one hand, and to Hollywood film's pedagogic function in the construction of a national imaginary, on the other (Carby 1993).

> *Unthinking Eurocentrism* elaborates an interethnic and cross-ethnic critical agenda for the study of film, one that situates difference not in a paradigm of margin and centre, but as a de-centred, polyvocal multiculturalism.

It is this emphasis on the pedagogic that underwrites Ella Shohat and Robert Stam's important book *Unthinking Eurocentrism* (1994). Situating filmic production in the histories and formations of nations, and paying attention to the international economy of film, this text implicitly argues against the Eurocentric formulation of difference as physiological and racial. Instead, the authors want a critical analysis that examines 'ethnicities-in-relation', which means rethinking official national histories in order to link communities, histories, and identities formed across the borders of formalized nation-states. They read film culture in the context of the 'Americas' and not simply the United States, in the regions of Britain's imperial reach and not simply Europe, in the Third World, and not simply the First. In so doing, *Unthinking Eurocentrism* elaborates an interethnic and cross-ethnic critical agenda for the study of film, one that situates difference not in a paradigm of margin and centre, but as a de-centred, polyvocal multiculturalism. This text thus offers a model for the study of race, ethnicity, and film in contemporary transnational economies of production and consumption. But more than this, it stakes out a comprehensive theoretical agenda that links diverse US populations—African Americans, Asian Americans, Chicano–Latinos, Native Americans, Jews, and Anglo-Americans—to global image cultures, independent cinemas, and Third World productions. In short, it defines a new disciplinary agenda for the study of race, ethnicity, and film.

BIBLIOGRAPHY

Aleiss, Angela (1995), 'Native Americans: The Surprising Silents', *Cineaste* 21/3: 34–5.

Balibar, Étienne, and **Immanuel Wallerstein** (1991), *Race, Nation, Class: Ambiguous Identities* (London: Verso).

Bataille, Gretchen M., and **Charles L. P. Silet** (1980), *The Pretend Indians: Images of Native Americans in the Movies* (Ames: Iowa State University Press).

Bernardi, Daniel (ed.) (1996), *The Birth of Whiteness: Race and the Emergence of US Cinema* (New Brunswick, NJ: Rutgers University Press).

Bernstein, Matthew, and **Gaylyn Studlar** (eds.) (1996), *Visions of the East: Orientalism in Film* (New Brunswick, NJ: Rutgers University Press).

Bhabha, Homi (1983), 'The Other Question . . . The Stereotype and Colonial Discourse', *Screen*, 24/6: 18–36.

Bobo, Jacqueline (1995), *Black Women as Cultural Readers* (New York: Columbia University Press).

*Bogle, Donald (1989), *Toms, Coons, Mulattoes, Mammies, and Bucks: An Interpretive History of Blacks in American Films* (New York: Continuum).

Boyd, Todd (1996), *Am I Black enough for You? Popular Culture from the Hood and Beyond* (Berkeley: University of California Press).

Carby, Hazel (1993), 'Encoding White Resentment. Grand Canyon: A Narrative for our Times', in Cameron McCarthy and Warren Crichlow (eds.), *Race, Identity, and Representation in Education* (New York: Routledge).

Castillo, Edward (1991), Review of *Dances with Wolves*, *Film Quarterly*, 44/4: 14–23.

Churchill, Ward (1992), *Fantasies of the Master Race: Literature, Cinema, and the Colonization of American Indians* (Monroe, Me.: Common Courage Press).

Cortés, Carlos E. (1993), 'Them and Us: Immigration as Societal Barometer and Social Education in American Film', in Robert Brent Toplin (ed.), *Hollywood as Mirror: Changing Views of Outsiders and Enemies in American Movies* (Westport, Conn.: Greenwood Press).

Cripps, Thomas (1977), *Slow Fade to Black: The Negro in American Film 1900–1942* (New York: Oxford University Press).

—— (1993), *Making Movies Black: The Hollywood Message Movie from World War II to the Civil Rights Era* (New York: Oxford University Press).

Curran, Joseph M. (1989), *Hibernian Green on the Silver Screen: The Irish and American Movies* (Westport, Conn.: Greenwood Press).

Delpar, Helen (1984), 'Goodbye to the Greaser': Mexico, the MPPDA, and Derogatory Films', *Journal of Popular Film and Television*, 12: 34–41.

Diawara, Manthia (ed.) (1993), *Black American Cinema* (New York: Routledge).

Dyer, Richard (1977), 'Stereotyping', in Dyer (ed.), *Gays and Film* (London: British Film Institute).

—— (1988), 'White', *Screen*, 29/4: 44–65.

Edgerton, Gary (1994), '"A Breed Apart": Hollywood, Racial Stereotyping and the Promise of Revisionism in *The Last of the Mohicans*' *Journal of American Culture*, 17/2: 1–20.

Erens, Patricia (1984), *The Jew in American Cinema* (Bloomington: Indiana University Press).

Feng, Richard (1995), 'In Search of Asian American Cinema', *Cineaste*, 21/3: 32–5.

Fregoso, Rosa Linda (1993), *The Bronze Screen: Chicana and Chicano Film Culture* (Minneapolis: University of Minnesota Press).

Friar, Ralph E., and **Natasha A. Friar** (1972), *The Only Good Indian: The Hollywood Gospel* (New York: Drama Book Specialist).

Friedman, Lester D. (1982), *Hollywood's Image of the Jew* (New York: Ungar).

—— (ed.) (1991), *Unspeakable Images: Ethnicity and the American Cinema* (Urbana: University of Illinois Press).

Gaines, Jane (1988), 'White Privilege and Looking Relations: Race and Gender in Feminist Film Theory', *Screen*, 29/4: 12–27.

Garcia Berumen, Frank Javier (1995), *The Chicano/Hispanic Image in American Film* (New York: Vantage Press).

Goldberg, Theo (ed.) (1990), *Anatomy of Racism* (Minneapolis: University of Minnesota.

Golden, Daniel Sembroff (1980), 'The Fate of La Famiglia: Italian Images in American Film', in Randall M. Miller (ed.) *The Kaleidoscopic Lens: How Hollywood Views Ethnic Groups* (Englewood, NJ: Jerome S. Ozer).

Hall, Stuart (1992), 'What is this "Black" in Black Popular Culture?', in Gina Dent (ed.), *Black Popular Culture* (Seattle: Bay Press).

Hilger, Michael (1986), *The American Indian in Film* (Metuchen, NJ: Scarecrow Press).

—— (1995), *From Savage to Nobleman: Images of Native Americans in Film* (Lanham, Md.: Scarecrow Press).

Julien, Isaac, and Kobena Mercer (1988), 'De Margin and De Centre', *Screen*, 29/4: 2–10.

King, John, Ana M. Lopez, and Manuel Alvarado (eds.) (1993), *Mediating Two Worlds: Cinematic Encounters in the Americas* (London: British Film Institute).

Leab, Daniel (1975), *From Sambo to Superspade: The Black Experience in Motion Pictures* (Boston: Houghton Mifflin).

Leong, Russell (ed.) (1991), *Moving the Image: Independent Asian Pacific American Media Arts* (Los Angeles: UCLA Asian American Studies Center and Visual Communications Publications).

Lourdeaux, Lee (1990), *Italian and Irish Filmmakers in America: Ford, Capra, Coppola, and Scorsese* (Philadelphia: Temple University Press).

Lubiano, Wahneema (1991), '"But Compared to What? Etc.": Reading Realism, Representation, and Essentialism in *School Daze*, *Do the Right Thing* and the Spike Lee Discourse', *Black American Literature Forum*, 25/2: 253–82.

Lund, Karen C. (1994), *American Indians in Silent Film: Motion Pictures in the Library of Congress* (Washington: Library of Congress).

Martin, Michael T. (ed.) (1995), *Cinemas of the Black Diaspora: Diversity, Dependence, and Oppositionality* (Detroit: Wayne State University Press).

Miller, Randall (ed.) (1980), *The Kaleidoscopic Lens: How Hollywood Views Ethnic Groups* (Englewood, NJ: Jerome S. Ozer).

Neale, Steve (1979), 'The Same Old Story: Stereotypes and Difference', *Screen Education*, 32–3: 33–7.

Noriega, Chon A. (ed.) (1992), *Chicanos and Film: Representation and Resistance* (Minneapolis: University of Minnesota Press).

—— and Ana M. Lopez (eds.) (1996), *The Ethnic Eye: Latino Media Arts* (Minneapolis: University of Minnesota Press).

O'Connor, John E. (1980), *The Hollywood Indian: Stereotypes of Native Americans in Films* (Trenton, NJ: New Jersey State Museum).

Pettit, Arthur G. (1980), *Images of the Mexican American in Fiction and Film* (College Station: Texas A & M University Press).

Reid, Mark (1993), *Redefining Black Film* (Berkeley: University of California Press).

Richard, Alfred Charles (1992), *The Hispanic Image on the Silver Screen: An Interpretive Filmography from Silents into Sound 1898–1935* (Westport, Conn.: Greenwood Press).

—— (1993), *Contemporary Hollywood's Negative Hispanic Image: An Interpretive Filmography 1936–1955* (Westport, Conn.: Greenwood Press).

—— (1994), *Contemporary Hollywood's Negative Hispanic Image: An Interpretive Filmography 1956–1993* (Westport, Conn.: Greenwood Press).

Rogin, Michael (1985), '"The Sword became a Flashing Vision": D. W. Griffith's *The Birth of a Nation*', *Representations*, 9/1: 150–95.

—— (1996), *Blackface, White Noise: Jewish Immigrants in the Hollywood Melting Pot* (Berkeley: University of California Press).

*Shohat, Ella, and Robert Stam (1994), *Unthinking Eurocentrism: Multiculturalism and the Media* (New York: Routledge).

Snead, James A. (1994), *White Screens, Black Images: Hollywood from the Dark Side*, ed. Colin MacCabe and Cornel West (New York: Routledge).

Sollors, Werner (1986), *Beyond Ethnicity* (New York: Oxford University Press).

Stam, Robert, and Louise Spence (1983), 'Colonialism, Racism and Representation', *Screen*, 24/2: 2–20.

Thi Thanh Nga (1995), 'The Long March from Wong to Woo: Asians in Hollywood', *Cineaste*, 21/4: 38–40.

Trinh T. Min-ha (1991), *When the Moon Waxes Red: Representation, Gender and Cultural Politics* (New York: Routledge).

Wiegman, Robyn (1995), *American Anatomies: Theorizing Race and Gender* (Durham, NC: Duke University Press).

Woll, Allen L. (1980), *The Latin Image in American Film* (Los Angeles: UCLA Latin American Center Publications).

—— and Randall M. Miller (eds.) (1987), *Ethnic and Racial Images in American Film and Television* (New York: Garland).

Wong, Eugene Franklin (1978), *On Visual Media Racism: Asians in American Motion Pictures* (New York: Arno Press).

18

Film and cultural identity

Rey Chow

A film about how film was first invented in Germany, Wim Wenders's *Die Brüder Skladanowsky* ('The Brothers Skladanowsky' Part I, 1994) offers important clues to the contentious relationship between film and cultural identity. Using the style and the shooting and editing skills of the silent era, and filming with an antique, hand-cranked camera, Wenders and students from the Munich Academy for Television and Film recast this originary moment in cinematic history as the tale of a loved one lost and found.

Disturbed by her Uncle Eugen's imminent departure on a long journey, Max Skladanowsky's 5-year-old daughter implores her father and his other brother, Emil, to bring Eugen back into her life. She gets her wish: as she waves goodbye to Uncle Eugen, the little girl is told that he is still with them, inside the box containing the film they had made of him before he left. Soon she is overjoyed to see, through the 'Bioscop' invented by her father, a life-size Uncle Eugen flickering on the screen, making funny expressions and performing acrobatic feats just as when he was still with them. Uncle Eugen has disappeared in person, but has reappeared on film—and he will be there for ever.

Elegant and moving, Wenders's film about the beginning of film reminds us of the key features of the medium of signification that was novel in the 1890s. First, film (and here I intend photography as well as cinema) is, structurally, a story about the relationship between absence and presence, between dis-

appearance and reappearance. Filmic representation reproduces the world with a resemblance unknown to artists before its arrival. Whether what is captured is a human face, a body, an object, or a place, the illusion of presence generated is such that a new kind of realism, one that vies with life itself, aggressively asserts itself. If cultural identity is something that always finds an anchor in specific media of representation, it is easy to see why the modes of illusory presence made possible by film have become such strong contenders in the controversial negotiations for cultural identity. Second, in a manner that summarizes the essence of many early silent films, Wenders's work draws attention to the agile movements of the human body as they are captured by the equipment built by Max Skladanowsky. Because sound and dialogue were not yet available, the filmmaker had to turn the ingredients he had into so many spatial inscriptions on the screen. What could have better conveyed the liveliness of this new illusory world than the exaggerated hieroglyphic movements of the human body, coming across as a series of images-in-motion? The compelling sense of photographic realism in film is thus punctuated with an equally compelling sense of melodrama—of technologically magnified movements that highlight the presences unfolding on the screen as artificial and constructed experiments. Melodrama here is not so much the result of sentimental narration as it is the effect of a caricatured defamiliarization of a familiar form (the human body). Made possible by the innovative manœuvres of light and temporality, of exposure and speed, such defamiliarization has a direct bearing on the new modes of seeing and showing.

The coexistence of an unprecedented realism and a novel melodramatization means that, from the very earliest moments, the modes of identity construction offered by film were modes of *relativity* and *relations* rather than essences and fixities. Film techniques such as montage, close-ups, panoramic shots, long shots, jump cuts, slow motion, flashback, and so forth, which result in processes of introjection, projection, or rejection that take place between the images and narratives shown on the screen, on the one hand, and audiences' sense of self, place, history, and pleasure, on the other, confirm the predominance of such modes of relativity and relations. With film, people's identification of who they are can no longer be regarded as a mere ontological or phenomenological event. Such identification is now profoundly enmeshed with technological intervention, which ensures that even (or especially) when the camera seems the least intrusive, the permeation of the film spectacle by the apparatus is complete and unquestionable. And it is the completeness of the effect of illusion that makes the reception of film controversial.

> **With film, people's identification of who they are can no longer be regarded as a mere ontological or phenomenological event. Such identification is now profoundly enmeshed with technological intervention.**

It was the understanding of this fundamentally manipulable constitution of film—this open-ended relation between spectacle and audience due, paradoxically, to the completeness of technological permeation—that led Walter Benjamin to associate film with revolutionary production and political change (Benjamin 1936, 1969, 1986). For, as Benjamin speculated in the 1930s, film's throughly *mediated* nature makes it a cultural opportunity to be seized for political purposes. Just as for the film actor performing in front of the camera is a kind of exile from his own body because it demands the simulation of emotional con-

tinuity in what is technically a disjointed process of production, so for the audience, Benjamin writes, the new attitude of reception is distraction and manipulation. As opposed to the absorption and concentration required by the traditional novel, which has to be read in solitude and in private, film requires a mode of interaction that is public and collective, and that allows audiences to take control of their situation by adopting changing, rather than stable, positions. Film, in other words, turns the recipient potentially into a producer who plays an active rather than passive role in the shaping of his or her cultural environment.

Whereas Benjamin in his Marxist, Brechtian moments was willing to grant to a movie audience the significance of an organized mob, later generations of film critics, notably feminist critics with a training in psychoanalysis, would elaborate the agency of the viewer with much greater complexity by way of processes of subjectivity formation. Such critics would argue that fantasies, memories, and other unconscious experiences, as well as the gender roles imposed by the dominant culture at large, play important roles in mediating the impact of the spectacle (see Creed and White, Part 1, Chapters 9 and 13).

The crucial theoretical concept informing psychoanalytic interpretations of identity is 'suture'. In the context of cinema, 'suture' refers to the interactions between the enunciation of the filmic apparatus, the spectacle, and the viewing subject—interactions which, by soliciting or 'interpellating' (see Althusser 1971) the viewing subject in a series of shifting positions, allow it to gain access to coherent meaning (see Heath 1981). As Kaja Silverman writes, 'The operation of suture is successful at the moment that the viewing subject says, "Yes, that's me," or "That's what I see"' (Silverman 1983: 205). As expressed through suture— literally a 'sewing-up' of gaps—cinematic identification is an eminently ideological process: subjectivity is imagined primarily as a lack, which is then exploited, through its desire to know, by the visual field enunciated by the omnipotent filmic apparatus, which withholds more than it reveals. In order to have access to the plenitude that is the basis for identity, the subject must give up something of its own in order to be 'hooked up' with the Other, the visual field, which is, none the less, for ever beyond its grasp. No matter how successful, therefore, the subject's possession of meaning is by definition compensatory and incomplete. (This process of subject formation through suture is comparable to an individual's attempt to acquire identity in certain social situations. For instance, in order to gain acceptance into a particular social group, an individual must be willing to sacrifice, to part with certain things to which he or she feels personally attached but which are not socially acceptable; such personal sacrifices, however, are not guarantees that the social identity acquired is complete or permanent because, as is often the case, the social group is capricious and arbitrary in its demands.)

Because it foregrounds processes of identification through relations of visuality, cinema is one of the most explicit systems of suturing, the operations of which can be explained effectively through the simple acts of seeing. Meanwhile, cinema also offers a homology with the dominant culture at large, in that the latter, too, may be seen as a repressive system in which individual subjects gain access to their identities only by forsaking parts of themselves, parts that are, moreover, never fully found again.

Using suture, ideology, and other related psychoanalytic concepts, feminist critics concerned with identitarian politics have, since Laura Mulvey's groundbreaking work in 1975, been steadily exposing the masculinism of mainstream cinema as well as of the dominant, heterosexist culture of the West. As a means of countering the repressive effects of dominant modes of visuality and identification, some go on to analyse in detail the ambiguities of the visual representations of women (see, for instance, Mayne 1989; Doane et al. 1984; Penley 1989), while others make use of the problematic of spectatorship, notably the spectatorship of women audiences, to theorize alternative ways of seeing, of constructing subjectivities and identities (see e.g. Silverman 1988; de Lauretis 1984, 1987).

Once identity is linked to spectatorship, a new spectrum of theoretical possibilities opens up. For instance, critics who have been influenced by Edward Said's *Orientalism* (1978) can now make the connection that orientalism, as the system of signification that represents non-Western cultures to Western recipients in the course of Western imperialism, operates visually as well as narratologically to subject 'the Orient' to ideological manipulation. They point out that, much like representations of women in classical narrative cinema, representations of 'the Orient' are often fetishized objects manufactured for the satiation of the masculinist gaze of the West. As a means to expose the culturally imperialist assumptions behind Euro-pean and American cinemas, the spectatorship of non-Western audiences thus also takes on vital significance (see e.g. Chow 1991: 3–33).

Because it conceptualizes identity non-negotiably as the effect of a repressive but necessary closure, suture has been theoretically pre-emptive. This can be seen in the two major ways in which the relationship between film and identity is usually investigated. For both, an acceptance of the idea of suture is indispensable.

This acceptance may function negatively, when the understanding of suture is used as a way to debunk and criticize certain kinds of identity—as ideologically conditioned by patriarchy and imperialism, for instance. Or, this acceptance may function positively and *implicitly*, in the counter-critical practice of demonstrating that some types of film may serve as places for the construction of other (usually marginalized) types of identity. It is important to remember, however, that even when critics who are intent on subverting mainstream culture assert that 'alternative' cinemas give rise to 'alternative' identities, as long as they imagine identities exclusively by way of the classic interpellation of subjectivities, they are not departing theoretically from the fundamental operations of suture. In fact, one may go so far as to say that it is when critics attempt to idealize the 'other' identities claimed for 'other' cinemas that they tend to run the greatest risk of reinscribing the ideologically coercive processes of identification through suturing.

For these reasons, I would propose that any attempt to theorize film and cultural identity should try to move beyond both the criticism and the implicit reinscription of the effects of suture. In this light, it might be productive to return to aspects of film which may not immediately seem to be concerned with identity as such but which, arguably, offer alternatives to the impasses created by suture.

Let us think more closely about the implications of the modes of visuality opened up by film. To go back to the story of the Skladanowsky brothers, what does it mean for Uncle Eugen to 'appear' when he is physically absent? From an anthropocentric perspective, we would probably say that the person Eugen was the 'origin', the 'reality' that gave rise to the film which then became a document, a record of him. From the perspective of the filmic images, however, this assumption of 'origin' is no longer essential, for Eugen is now a movie which has taken on an independent, mechanically reproducible existence of its own. With

New and undreamt-of possibilities of experimentation—Ruttman's *Berlin, Symphony of a City* (1927)

the passage of time, more and more reprints can be made and every one of them will be the same. The 'original' Uncle Eugen will no longer be of relevance.

Film, precisely because it signifies the thorough permeation of reality by the mechanical apparatus and thus the production of a seamless resemblance to reality itself, displaces once and for all the sovereignty of the so-called original, which is now often an imperfect and less permanent copy of itself: Uncle Eugen's image remains long after he is dead. This obvious aspect of filmic reproduction is what underlies Benjamin's argument about the decline of the aura, the term he uses to describe the irreplaceable sense of presence that was unique to traditional works of art when such works of art were rooted in specific times and spaces (Benjamin 1969). What was alarming about the arrival of film (as it was for many poets and artists) was precisely the destruction of the aura, a destruction that is programmed into film's mode of reproduction and is part of film's 'nature' as a medium. This essential *iconoclasm* of filmic reproduction is encapsulated in Wenders's story by the phantasmagorically alive and replayable image of Uncle Eugen in his own absence. This image signifies the end of the aura and the sacredness that used to be attached to the original human figure, to the human figure as the original. It also signifies a change in terms of the agency of seeing: the realist accuracy of the image announces that a mechanical eye, the eye of the camera, has replaced the human eye altogether in its capacity to capture and reproduce the world with precision (see Comolli 1978). As the effects of mechanicity, filmic images carry with them an inhuman quality even as they are filled with human contents. This is the reason why film has been compared to a process of embalming (Bazin 1967: 9–16), to fossilization, and to death.

But what film destroys in terms of the aura, it gains in portability and transmissibility. With 'death' come new, previously undreamt-of possibilities of experimentation, as the mechanically reproduced images become sites of the elaboration of what Benedict Anderson, in a study of the emergence of nationalism in modern history, calls 'imagined communities' (Anderson 1983). We see this, for instance, in the mundane, anonymous sights of the big city that are typical of early silent films such as Walther Ruttmann's *Berlin—Die Sinfonie der Großstadt* ('Berlin: Symphony of a City', Germany 1927) and Dziga Vertov's *Man with the Movie Camera* (USSR, 1929). Scenes of workers going to work, housewives shopping, schoolchildren assembling for school,

passengers travelling by train; scenes of carriages, engines, automobiles, railway stations, typewriters, phones, gutters, street lamps, shop fronts—all such scenes testify to a certain fascination with the potentialities of seeing, of what can be made visible. The mechanically reproduced image has brought about a perception of the world as an infinite collection of objects and people permanently on display in their humdrum existence. At the same time, because film is not only reproducible but also transportable, it can be shown in different places, usually remote from the ones where they are originally made. Coinciding with upheavals of traditional populations bound to the land and with massive migrations from the countryside to metropolitan areas around the world, film ubiquitously assumes the significance of the monumental: the cinema auditorium, as Paul Virilio writes, puts order into visual chaos like a cenotaph. As the activity of moviegoing gratifies 'the wish of migrant workers for a lasting and even eternal homeland', cinema becomes the site of 'a new aboriginality in the midst of demographic anarchy' (Virilio 1989: 39).

The iconoclastic, portable imprints of filmic images and the metropolitan, migratory constitution of their audiences mean that film is always a rich means of exploring cultural crisis—of exploring culture itself as a crisis. We have seen many examples of such uses of film in various cinemas in the period following the Second World War: the suffocating existentialist portrayals of the breakdown of human communication in Italian and French avant-garde films; the sentimental middle-class family melodramas of Hollywood; the aesthetic experiments with vision and narration in Japanese cinema; the self-conscious parodies of fascism in the New German Cinema; the explosive renderings of diaspora and 'otherness' in what is called 'Third Cinema' (see Hall 1990; Pines and Willemen 1989). By the 1980s and early 1990s, with the films of the mainland Chinese Fifth Generation directors, it becomes clear that film can be used for the exploration of crises, especially in cultures whose experience of modernity is marked, as it were, by conflicts between an indigenous tradition and foreign influences, between the demands of nationalism and the demands of Westernization.

For mainland Chinese directors such as Chen Kaige, Zhang Yimou, Tian Zhuangzhuang, and Zhang Nuanxin, reflecting on 'culture' inevitably involves the rethinking of origins—the 'pasts' that give rise to the present moment; the narratives, myths, rituals, customs, and practices that account for how a people becomes what it is. Because such rethinking plays on the historical relation between what is absent and what is present, film becomes, for these directors and their counterparts elsewhere in Asia (see Dissanayake 1988), an ideal medium: its projectional mechanism means that the elaboration of the past as what is bygone, what is behind us, can simultaneously take the form of images moving, in their vivid luminosity, in front of us. The simple dialectical relationship between visual absence and visual presence that was dramatized by film from the very first thus lends itself appropriately to an articulation of the dilemmas and contradictions, the nostalgias and hopes, that characterize struggles towards modernity. In such struggles, as we see in films such as *Yellow Earth* (1984), *Sacrifice Youth* (1985), *Judou* (1990), and *Raise the Red Lantern* (1991), the definitively modernist effort to reconceptualize origins typically attributes to indigenous traditions the significance of a primitive past in all the ambiguous senses of 'primitivism'. This special intersection between film and primitivism has been described in terms of 'primitive passions' (Chow 1995).

As the viewing of film does not require literacy in the traditional sense of knowing how to read and write, film signals the transformation of word-based cultures into cultures that are increasingly dominated by the visual image, a transformation that may be understood as a special kind of translation in the postmodern, postcolonial world. Intersemiotic in nature, film-as-translation involves histories and populations hitherto excluded by the restricted sense of literacy, and challenges the class hierarchies long established by such literacy in societies, West and East (Chow 1995). And, in so far as its images are permanently inscribed, film also functions as an immense visual archive, assimilating literature, popular culture, architecture, fashion, memorabilia, and the contents of junk shops, waiting to be properly inspected for its meanings and uses (Elsaesser 1989: 322–3).

Any attempt to discuss film and cultural identity would therefore need to take into account the multiple significance of filmic visuality in modernity. This is especially so when modernity is part of post-coloniality, as in the case of many non-Western cultures, in which to become 'modern' signifies an ongoing revisioning of indigenous cultural traditions alongside the obligatory turns towards the West or 'the world at large'. In this light, it is worth remembering that film has always been, since its inception, a *transcultural* phe-

nomenon, having as it does the capacity to transcend 'culture'—to create modes of fascination which are readily accessible and which engage audiences in ways independent of their linguistic and cultural specificities. Consider, for instance, the greatly popular versions of fairy-tale romance, sex, kitsch, and violence from Hollywood; alternatively, consider the greatly popular slapstick humour and action films of Jackie Chan from Hong Kong. To be sure, such popular films can inevitably be read as so many constructions of national, sexual, cultural identities; as so many impositions of Western, American, or other types of ideology upon the rest of the world. While I would not for a moment deny that to be the case, it seems to me equally noteworthy that the world-wide appeal of many such films has something to do, rather, with their *not* being bound by well-defined identities, so that it is their specifically *filmic*, indeed phantasmagoric, significations of masculinism, moral righteousness, love, loyalty, family, and horror that speak to audiences across the globe, regardless of their own languages and cultures. (Hitchcock is reputed to have commented while making *Psycho* (USA, 1960) that he wanted Japanese audiences to scream at the same places as Hollywood audiences.)

> **Film has always been, since its inception, a *transcultural* phenomenon, having as it does the capacity to transcend 'culture'—to create modes of fascination which are readily accessible and which engage audiences in ways independent of their linguistic and cultural specificities.**

The phantasmagoric effects of illusion on the movie screen are reminders once again of the iconoclasm, the fundamental replacement of human perception by the machine that is film's very constitution. This originary iconoclasm, this power of the technologized visual image to communicate beyond verbal language, should perhaps be beheld as a useful enigma, one that serves to unsettle any easy assumption we may have of the processes of identification generated by film as a medium, be such identification in relation to

subjectivity or to differing cultural contexts. In a theoretical climate in which identities are usually imagined—far too hastily I think—as being 'sutured' with
specific times, places, practices, and cultures, thinking
through this problematic of film's transcultural appeal
should prove to be an instructive exercise.

BIBLIOGRAPHY

Althusser, Louis (1971), 'Ideology and Ideology State
Apparatuses (Notes towards an Investigation)', in *Lenin
and Philosophy and Other Essays*, trans. Ben Brewster
(New York: Monthly Review Press).

Anderson, Benedict (1983), *Imagined Communities:
Reflections on the Origin and Spread of Nationalism*
(London: Verso).

Bazin, André (1967), *What is Cinema?*, ed. and trans. Hugh
Gray, i (Berkeley and Los Angeles: University of California Press).

Benjamin, Walter (1936/1969), 'The Work of Art in the
Age of Mechanical Reproduction', in *Illuminations*, ed.
Hannah Arendt and trans. Harry Zohn (New York:
Schocken Books).

—— (1986), 'The Author as Producer', in *Reflections:
Essays, Aphorisms, Autobiographical Writings*, ed. Peter
Demetz and trans. Edmund Jephcott (New York:
Schocken).

Chow, Rey (1991), *Woman and Chinese Modernity: The
Politics of Reading between West and East* (Minneapolis:
University of Minnesota Press).

—— (1995), *Primitive Passions: Visuality, Sexuality, Ethnography, and Contemporary Chinese Cinema* (New York:
Columbia University Press).

Comolli, Jean-Louis (1978), 'Machines of the Visible', in
Teresa de Lauretis and Stephen Heath (eds.), *The Cinematic Apparatus* (London: Macmillan).

de Lauretis, Teresa (1984), *Alice Doesn't: Feminism,
Semiotics, Cinema* (Bloomington: Indiana University
Press).

—— (1987), *Technologies of Gender: Essays on Theory,
Film, and Fiction* (Bloomington: Indiana University Press).

*****Dissanayake, Wimal** (ed.) (1988), *Cinema and Cultural
Identity: Reflections on Films from Japan, India, and
China* (Lanham, Md.: University Press of America).

Doane, Mary Ann, Patricia Mellencamp, and **Linda Wil-
liams** (eds.) (1984), *Re-Vision: Essays in Feminist Film
Criticism* (Frederick, Md.: University Publications of
America).

Elsaesser, Thomas (1989), *New German Cinema: A History* (New Brunswick, NJ: Rutgers University Press).

Hall, Stuart (1990), 'Cultural Identity and Diaspora', in J.
Rutherford (ed.), *Identity: Community, Culture, Difference* (London: Lawrence & Wishart).

Heath, Stephen (1981), *Questions of Cinema* (Bloomington: Indiana University Press).

Mayne, Judith (1989), *Kino and the Woman Question:
Feminism and Soviet Silent Film* (Columbus: Ohio State
University Press).

Mulvey, Laura (1975), 'Visual Pleasure and Narrative
Cinema', *Screen*, 16/3: 6–18; repr. in Penley (1989).

Penley, Constance (ed.) (1989), *Feminism and Film Theory*
(New York: Routledge; London: British Film Institute).

—— and **Sharon Willis** (eds.) (1993), *Male Trouble* (Minneapolis: University of Minnesota Press).

Pines, Jim, and **Paul Willemen** (eds.) (1989), *Questions of
Third Cinema* (London: British Film Institute).

Said, Edward (1978), *Orientalism* (London: Routledge &
Kegan Paul).

Silverman, Kaja (1983), *The Subject of Semiotics* (New
York: Oxford University Press).

—— (1988), *The Acoustic Mirror: The Female Voice in Psychoanalysis and Cinema* (Bloomington: Indiana University Press).

Virilio, Paul (1989), *War and Cinema: The Logistics of
Perception*, trans. Patrick Camiller (London: Verso).

19

Film and history

Dudley Andrew

Attitudes

We are concerned here with film and with history; so let's begin by calling up a film that nearly half a century ago abruptly burrowed into the past so unforgettably that it was said to inaugurate the modern cinema, thus constituting itself an event of history. *Viaggio in Italia* ('Voyage to Italy', Italy, 1953) 'burst open a breach, and all cinema on pain of death must pass through it', wrote Jacques Rivette in a famous declaration of faith. 'With the appearance of *Viaggio in Italia* all films have suddenly aged ten years', he continued (Rivette 1955/1985: 192). Like James Joyce's *Ulysses*, Rossellini's film was controversial in its own day and remains recalcitrant even now, because it minutely records a contemporary civilization that appears at once diminished and sacred in the light of its ancient counterpart. Rossellini's film defines the modern by clinically analysing post-war European values and by inventing a form to do so. A meandering essay, a sort of 'ba(l)ade', in Deleuze's term (1983: 280), it ignores the classicism of narrative cinema and the hermeticism of the avant-garde to thrust cinematography up against a reality that is both material and spiritual. Rossellini had the audacity to name his main character Joyce and to send him and his wife Katherine (Ingrid Bergman) on a journey as full of the ordinary and the extraordinary as that of Leopold Bloom.

This voyage of a couple in domestic crisis across strange and ancient landscapes becomes a descent into a past that is both personal and public, where private ethical choices are equivalent to decisive historiographic options. Mr Joyce (George Sanders), acerbic, sceptical, and practical, will sell Uncle Homer's(!) estate, eager to convert the 'strangeness' of what he has inherited into the familiarity of negoti-

Ingrid Bergman overwhelmed by her feelings—the Pompeii sequence in *Voyage to Italy* (1953)

able currency that he can take back with him to England. His wife, by contrast, gradually allows the features of the landscape and the people she sees to break through her preoccupations and her diffidence. Slowly she opens herself to the stunning world that she is drawn to visit. We see her looking, available, though she averts her gaze when confronted by those of a pregnant woman and then of an immense Roman statue.

Two magnificent sequences analogize the historian's encounter with the past. In the first of these Katherine visits the phosphorous fields around Vesuvius guided by an old and garrulous caretaker. Annoyed by his patter of arcane lore, she is about to return to her car when he demonstrates the effect of holding a torch near any of the volcanic openings on this torn-up crust of earth. Even the warmth of a cigarette produces a startling release of smoke far across the field, an immense exhalation from inside this ancient but living and explosive mountain. Later, at Pompeii, the couple assist at the exhumation of what turns out to be another couple buried by the volcano 2000 years ago. As the archaeologists dextrously bring out the outline of a man and woman caught by sudden death in bed

together, Katherine finds herself overwhelmed. She runs from the spot, followed by her estranged husband. 'I was pretty moved myself,' he confesses. She is more than moved. She recognizes to her fullest capacity the tedium and insignificance of her own existence measured against this unmistakable sign of the holiness and the brevity of life. This is the epiphany she had earlier avoided when, at the art museum, she ran from the statue of Apollo, whose gaze accused her small-mindedness.

Viaggio in Italia alerts her and us to the possibilities of exchange between past and present, through the manner by which we look and through our response to being looked at, that is, being measured by a living past. When we take time to locate the fissures on their surfaces—their breathing-holes—we allow films to exhale, to release a fine mist that is evidence of an immense power they still retain while locked away in archives or in the pages of history books. Like any history, that of the cinema is an account—even an accounting—of a former state of affairs. But as *Viaggio in Italia* continues to prove, this is a history of living matter, whose inestimable power to affect us should be found and released by our probing.

In what follows, I aim to track the tension between the sheer existence of films and our ways of making sense of their appearance and effects, that is, the tension between *films* as moments of experience and the *cinema* as a tradition and an institution. The discipline of film history tends to leave the moments of experience alone, since these are singular, whereas it strives instead to explain the system that holds them suspended.

Traditionally the primary task of the film historian has been to unearth unknown films or unknown facts and connections relating to known films, in an effort to establish, maintain, or adjust the value system by which cultures care about a cinematic past. Not long ago this seemed a simple thing, unproblematic compared to theory or criticism. Done well or badly, film history was in essence a chronicle of inventors, businessmen, directors, and, most particularly, films. Not all films naturally, just as not all directors or inventors, but the worthy ones, those that made a difference, from *A Trip to the Moon* (France, 1902) to *Wings of Desire* (West Germany and France, 1987) or *Jurassic Park* (USA, 1993). The early accounts by American Terry Ramsaye (1926) or by Frenchmen Maurice Bardèche and Robert Brasillach (1938), interrogate 'worth' hardly at all; instead they directly attribute worth to this or that movie or personality.

> **Traditionally the primary task of the film historian has been to unearth unknown films or unknown facts and connections relating to known films, in an effort to establish, maintain, or adjust the value system by which cultures care about a cinematic past.**

This attitude paved the way for the auteurism of the 1960s and 1970s, when the critic Andrew Sarris (1969) could claim to be providing film history by delivering his notorious seven-tiered ranking of film directors. Of course such a canon answers to values which are of purely aesthetic, not historical, interest. This is confirmed by the auteurist's attraction to masterpieces, films that, by definition, escape history and speak timelessly.

Lists of significant films, directors, and events may not constitute good history, but they do form the basis for the overviews of the development of film art written after the Second World War and that spawned the many histories of film available as textbooks today. Multi-volume treatises by Georges Sadoul (1975) and Jean Mitry (1968–80) in French, Ulrich Gregor and Enno Patalas (1962) in German, and Jerzy Toeplitz (1979) in Polish and German have had single-volume counterparts in English (by Arthur Knight (1957), David Robinson (1973/1981), and many others) that trace what might be thought of as the biography of cinema, from its birth through a clumsy adolescence to an increasing maturity after the Second World War. Maturity is measured less by the growth of the industry than by the subtlety and variety of techniques of expression, by the extension of themes and subjects, and by the respect accorded the medium by the culture at large.

Aesthetic film histories strive to account for all significant developments that cinema has undergone, but therein lies the problem, for a single conception of significance constrains them to think of difference in terms of the formation of identity. This is clearest in Mitry's monumental project, which traces only those cinematic rivulets and streams that feed into the current of the present. If a source dried out or went permanently underground, it was deemed unfit for study, because demonstrably unfit for life. This was the case, for instance, with the Shanghai melodramas of the early 1930s and with Brazilian *cangaços* of the 1950s, neither of which show up in Mitry or in other aesthetic overviews. Mitry's volumes can be read as a Darwinian tale of survival, that is, as the tale of 'ourselves' and 'our' cinema, since 'we' are the ones who have survived and have commanded a history. This explains his dismissal (and not his alone) of other forms of film (animated, educational, and home movies), of other peoples making films (the massive output of Egypt and Turkey, scarcely ever mentioned), and of 'others' represented in film (women and minorities in particular). The force of these less visible 'phenomena' surely carved out underground galleries and waterways, or seeped into swamps and bogs, but canonical historians abandon them there without much thought, until recently when one can note an effort to give them a place in textbooks.

Confidence in a grand, singular story of film art began to erode in the 1970s even before news of the general crisis in historiography reached the ears of film scholars. It was in order to dig beneath taste and to interlink isolated observations and judgements that 'professional' history came to insist on a more positivist approach to the study of cinema's past. All along there have been devoted individual archival researchers who know what it is to establish evidence and advance defensible (and refutable) claims about this or that aspect of film history, but only towards the end of the 1970s can one sense the emergence of an entire positivist ethos among film scholars concerned with, or suddenly turning to, historical matters. Robert Allen and Douglas Gomery in their important *Film History* (1985) coupled good film historiography with standard social history, thereby giving to film history maturity and a method its earlier phases completely lacked.

> **Confidence in a grand, singular story of film art began to erode in the 1970s even before news of the general crisis in historiography reached the ears of film scholars.**

Under positivism one can group every disciplinary approach to film, including the discipline of history itself with its tradition of balances and counterbalances. Those writing on film from historical perspectives no longer can exempt themselves from the burdens of exhaustive research and the ethics of corroboration. They have also felt the responsibility of incorporating within their historical research the gains made possible by the disciplines of sociology, anthropology, economics, and even psychology, all of which have been called upon to make cinema studies responsible to modern criteria of plausibility and of appropriate academic discourse. And, more recently, they have sought to apply these rationalized approaches to an indefinitely large corpus, recognizing that all films, not just the canonical, participate in broader systems that require systematic understanding.

The priority now accorded to discipline and system obliterates the concept of intrinsic value. The laws and rules by which events occur or by which names emerge into history are far more significant to the positivist than those events or names themselves. Most historians today are out to show the forces and conditions that produced the past and thus indicate the present, whether in a strict (determinist) or loose (conjunctural) manner.

A recent essay by one of the most prominent of such scholars, David Bordwell (1994), bears an indicative title: 'The Power of a Research Tradition: Prospects for Progress in the Study of Film Style'. Tradition and progress are precisely terms that can anchor a notion of 'positivism', since they implement regulated research protocols complete with systems of checks and balances. In this way history can become less idiosyncratic, apparently less dependent on taste, rhetoric, or ideology. And in this way scholars from utterly different perspectives and background can contribute to the project of increased understanding of the various factors at play in the cinema complex. Particular topics or problems (the emergence of film noir during and after the Second World War, the growth of the blockbuster style along with its attendant marketing strategy, the anomaly of *Viaggio in Italia* and the dispersal of neo-realism) are analysed less through attention to their own properties than by a calculus of determination which brings to bear from the full complex those factors that are pertinent to the case at hand.

Bordwell's essay generously credits work from various historiographic paradigms, including those who gave us 'the standard version of the basic story'. According to Bordwell, André Bazin countered the standard version of film as a standard art by emphasizing not the development of cinema's signifying prowess but the tension between stylization and realism. Bazin's 'dialectical' view accounted for many more types of film that grew up once the sound era had overturned many original conceptions about the medium. Bordwell completes his survey of histories of film style by isolating the 'revolutionary' views of Noël Burch, the first scholar to scour the back alleys of film production for those neglected films and movements that, by the fact of their neglect, provide a particularly apt index to the technical, stylistic, and social range of possibilities for the medium. Burch studied the special cases of primitive cinema, Japanese pre-war works, and the avant-garde, isolating for analysis types of film that are seldom mentioned in either the standard version or its dialectical Bazinian counterpart.

These three versions of history, along with Bordwell's compendium that includes them all, are themselves largely determined by the moment of their own composition. All help form the zigzag pattern of knowledge about film style to which we in the university today should feel urged to contribute. The excesses of one version call for the correctives of the next. In this way, a more and more refined view takes shape under successive rhetorics and with increasingly subtle research strategies. Positivism would let nothing be lost. It was born in the university and flourishes there.

And yet in its sober procedures academic film history, history as autopsy, gives up the surprising life the movies may still retain for those who adopt the attitude of revelatory history Walter Benjamin wanted to foster. For Benjamin the past can catch up with and overwhelm the future in sudden bursts. If lived vigilantly and in high expectation, the present may suddenly illuminate shards of the broken mirror of the past scattered throughout the rubble of that catastrophe we call history. Benjamin—fetishistic book collector yet visionary Marxist—married the sacred to what he understood to be the post-historical. The cinema precociously serves both functions, for films exist not just in archives but in ciné-clubs and on video, where they can still release their power. *Viaggio in Italia* certifies this. The most modern of films, abjuring tradition, beauty, and premeditation to grasp its subject with unprecedented swiftness and immediacy, it nevertheless stands in awe of something quite ancient: the Neopolitans who coexist with statues, legends, icons, and a landscape that speaks to them incessantly and to which they respond in prayer and patter. Like Ingrid Bergman's eye, Rossellini's darting camera, indiscreet on the streets of Naples, probing caves, museums, holes in the crust of the earth, is an opening into which pours something at once ancient and of the moment, something that struck André Bazin forcefully in 1953 and can strike us anew today. We should not have been surprised when Rossellini later took up his grand project to film the history of civilization. It was meant to be a living history.

Though he claims professional allegiance to the positivist line, Pierre Sorlin recognizes the persistence of an unprofessional, unruly, and revelatory history of exceptional moments when he patronizingly observes: 'The pre-positivist attitude remains widespread, is unlikely to disappear, and if it is not taken too seriously this baroque—or even surrealist—encounter with mystical moments (Expressionism, film noir, the nouvelle vague . . .) and madonnas (Marilyn Monroe, Brigitte Bardot) . . . is not without its charm' (Sorlin 1992: 5).

Sorlin's characterization, and even his vocabulary, play into a dichotomy Robert Ray (1988) laid out some years ago in reviewing David Bordwell's work: on the one side lies the progressive, disciplined, impersonal, verifiable, classical paradigm of knowledge; on the other, the haphazard, personal, baroque, surrealist, form (see

also Ray, Part 1, Chapter 8). Think of scholarship as travel. One may move into cinema's past in several different fashions. The positivist approach I have characterized as a military march that conquers ground under the direction of a general (who surveys the field from on high, plotting strategic approaches). In utter contrast, the baroque, surrealist approach remains personal, whimsical, effectively unrepeatable and nontransferable. Though best exemplified by the *flâneur*, if one sought a military model to oppose to the general it would be the 'knight errant', for this historian works by chance encounters, by erring, by finding order in error.

These two extremes, the one fully public and accountable, the other private and creatively irresponsible, do not exhaust the approaches open to anyone interested in going into the past. There lies a third approach, what Claude Lévi-Strauss in the introduction of his *Tristes tropiques* (1955) termed the 'excursion'. The historian intent on an excursion—preparing to write an 'excursus'—sets off with a goal vaguely in mind but is prepared to let the event of the journey itself and the landscape it traverses help steer or even dictate the inquiry. Such a historiography is patently hermeneutic, for it opens the vision of the historian to a different vision altogether. In our field that different vision may be provided by a powerful film or by a different culture indexed by a host of films. We may despair of understanding these in the way they were first understood, but we can 'comprehend' their significance for ourselves as well as for others (see Andrew 1984: 180–7 for an elaboration on this distinction). Let us keep this array of research attitudes in mind as we turn to historical methods in film scholarship.

Methods

The archives of films

Cinema grew to its majority just in time to participate in a serious shift in historiography towards an account of existence and away from the recounting of the triumphs and defeats of the powerful. Goaded on in the latter half of the nineteenth century by the emergence of sociology and anthropology—nascent disciplines eager to understand the micro-operations of everyday life among seldom heard 'other peoples'—a new breed of historian began to question the utility of the age-old historical enterprise of providing the pedigree for, and singing the exploits of, some ruler, ruling class, or nation. Before this century, even the most measured 'story of civilization' was inevitably one of princes and the vicissitudes of their political and military struggles. While the legacy of this tradition persists, particularly in more popular books, professional historiography since 1900 looks more often and more closely at the complex weave of the tapestry that makes up civilization rather than reading the colourful patterns that stand out as its dramatic picture.

Unquestionably, this lowering of historical goals suggests an evolution of a discipline as old as Herodotus, an evolution visible in literary mimesis as well, whereby the means of representation have increasingly taken sustenance from the everyday, the heterogeneous, the facticity of teeming life. History, like fiction, and like cinema, involves a ratio of brute material to intelligible organization. At the turn of this century, the coefficient of the material side of this ratio grew dramatically as historians took account of new sorts of archive telling of different sorts of life, telling in effect a different history.

Cinema constitutes a crucial historical archive of this sort, and in two senses. First, all films preserve visual information gathered through the lens, some parading this function, others oblivious to it. Of all film types, home movies would seem most intent to gather and preserve; next would come newsreels, since these claim merely to capture and catalogue the events they purport to address. Distant relatives of newsreels are documentaries, which rely on the veracity of the images they steal from newsreels or capture themselves, organizing these to some purpose or argument whose intent interacts with this material. Fiction films would seem to be at the far end of the archive, made to tease the imagination; nevertheless, such films can occasionally be caught napping, as they reveal to the vigilant historian (seldom to the paying customer) some raw matter undigested by the stories they tell (Ferro 1988: 30).

Cinema's second archival function derives from fiction films once again, only this time when they operate alertly, and quite properly, as fiction. Movies, especially popular ones, comprise a record of the aspirations, obsessions, and frustrations of those who spend time and money making or viewing them. Such investment guarantees and measures the value attached to fiction—value which it is the job of the historian to calculate, explain, or extend. Marc Ferro, perhaps the most notable historian to have devoted full attention to the cinematic archive, puts it thus: 'Every film has a value as

a document, whatever its seeming nature. This is true even if it has been shot in the studio . . . Besides, if it is true that the not-said and the imaginary have as much historical value as History, then the cinema, and especially the fictional film, open a royal way to psycho-socio-historical zones never reached by the analysis of "documents"' (Ferro 1988: 82–3).

Given its double archival existence, films have sustained two quite different types of historical investigation: social historians raid films for the direct (audio)visual evidence they supply about social existence at a precise moment, while film historians interest themselves in the indirect testimony fiction films deliver concerning fads, prejudices, obsessions, moods, neuroses. Generally the former consult the fullest archive available for their topic (several years of a newsreel, for example, or all the home movies taken by a particular family), while the latter may focus on a few fiction films, selected as the richest examples, the most indicative source, of indirect evidence.

> **Social historians raid films for the direct (audio)visual evidence they supply about social existence at a precise moment, while film historians interest themselves in the indirect testimony fiction films deliver concerning fads, prejudices, obsessions, moods, neuroses.**

It must be said immediately that the social historian maintains no special relation to 'historical films' (*La Marseillaise*, France, 1938; *Scipione l'Africano* Italy, 1937; *October*, USSR, 1928) since these constitute merely one genre among others that may attract certain historians personally but that offer no intrinsically privileged site for professional historical investigation. On the other hand, the aesthetic and rhetorical elements and patterns of all films must at some level and at some point concern all historians. This is the case even in the most straightforward newsreels where camera placement or movement and shot juxtaposition contribute to defining the event under consideration. Ferro (1988: 30–44) proved this point by giving equal analytical attention to a series of quite different films from the Soviet silent period: newsreels, propaganda efforts by both Reds and Whites, commissioned historical fictions made by Eisenstein and Pudovkin, and a purportedly neutral fiction by Kuleshov (*Dura Lex*, 'By the Law', USSR, 1926). Each film can be read for its inclusions and exclusions, for its structure, and for what French historians have called the 'mentalité' it expresses. Ferro entitles another brief article 'Dissolves in *Jud Süss*', to signal that even when dealing with explicitly social effects (anti-Semitism in the case of this notorious piece of Nazi propaganda art) the historian can (and often must) work directly with the language of cinema (Ferro 1988: 139–41). Whether or not the historian claims aptitude in this regard, it is assumed by all that cinematic techniques reveal patterns and intentions of organization as the medium shapes to some extent (depending on the genre) the material in the chosen archive.

By conducting minute analyses of aspects of little-known films, Ferro edged close to another sort of film history, that coming from buffs, collectors, and critics. Such people are unashamed to be concerned with something much smaller than social history: with films, their makers, their mutual influences, and their processes of production and reception. Film historians, as we commonly know them and as opposed to social historians, descend from this family tree of 'amateurs', often those who have laboured within the cinema community and feel authorized to report upon its workings. Today's more conscientious film students riffle through archives of movies, studio records, private papers of famous personalities, and journalistic criticism just to step into the footprints of their predecessors who sauntered nonchalantly alongside the film industry and culture of some earlier epoch. They understand that they must break out of the bubble of lore and engage the social and cultural reach of a favourite movie or personality just to explain properly its particular resonance and fascination.

And so both types of historian, those primarily concerned with movies and those concerned with society, find that they need to enter the other's domain simply to do justice to their topic. The latter now must adopt a disciplinary vocabulary and learn techniques of analysis seldom employed in the days when films were raided unproblematically as an open archive to be moved wholesale into the historian's discourse. And the former must read widely in the records of a bygone era so as to place a prized or fascinating phenomenon in a context where it becomes significant, not just iridescent.

The social historian and film

Partisans of one or another tradition of social science discourse may want to claim for some forebear the role of first pioneer to enter the unexplored domain of films. German scholars mark the date 1914, when a stunning dissertation on patterns of film spectatorship appeared seemingly from nowhere (Altenloh 1914). For a long time it had been felt that the earliest serious writing on cinema concerned artistic issues alone, with Hugo Munsterberg and Vachel Lindsay generally cited in front of a phalanx of French aestheticians led by Louis Delluc and Riccioto Canudo, all of whom were intent to distinguish the remarkable properties of this new medium. This dissertation, however, inaugurates a different tradition of writing about film, a social analysis that takes account of cinema's sharp intervention in modern history (see Gripsrud, Part 1, Chapter 22).

The most common sociological studies consider cinema a mirror to society, and in two senses. First, one can tabulate the frequency with which various social types crop up in the movies of a particular time and place. This quantitative study is usually preliminary to an interpretation of the way groups are depicted and therefore valued. The very effect of interpretation makes cinema a mirror in a second sense, for it displays the face not just of those whom the movies are about but of those who make and watch the movies. It may be shocking for us today to see how a social group has been misrepresented (see e.g. the studies of Jews (Sorlin 1981), women (Flitterman-Lewis 1989), and North Africans (Slavin 1996) in French pre-war movies), but the greater shock comes from recognizing the face of those by whom and for whom such misrepresentations were exactly what fit.

German sociology of cinema has unquestioanbly produced the most profound work of this sort, primarily through the Frankfurt School, which was a product of the Weimer culture it learned to analyse. Arguably the most celebrated of all social film histories was written by Siegfried Kracauer, who eventually consolidated his daily reflections on the portentous movies he watched during the Weimar years into the magisterial *From Caligari to Hitler* (1947). This full-blown psycho-social analysis makes the ugly visage of a nascent Nazism emerge from the several-score films under consideration. While his audacious thesis has inspired countless other social historians to enlarge their ambitions *vis-à-vis* cinema, Kracauer has been reproached for having set up his conclusions in the very choice of films that guide his vision. That choice rests on the conviction that the cinema gives privileged access to a national unconscious and its predispositions, equally in films whose ambitions do and don't go beyond that of simple entertainment. Kracauer here encounters a perpetual conundrum, for at one and the same time he relies on the instinctive, unthought relation of film images to the culture that produces them while he also gives priority to the most complex, resonant, and sophisticated examples—examples that have behind them a good deal of thought as well as the prestige of art. In fact, his corpus consists of the export cinema of the Weimar period, from the Expressionist masterpiece mentioned in his title to *M* (1931) and *The Blue Angel* (1930), films, it is fair to say, that extend and transmit certain literary obsessions from the Romantic era right up through the Weimar period.

Kracauer was certainly not alone in believing that the cinema had in fact become the mechanism for the massive dissemination of significant cultural values. Moreover, he paid scant attention to the popular sources of popular genres (comedies, for example, other than those of Lubitsch, or Tyrolian films). Paul Monaco (1976), on the other hand, investigating the same Weimar period, explicitly restricts himself to the films with the highest box-office success so as to exclude his own judgements, letting the audience decide what is important through their attendance. While box-office performance still serves as an important indicator of the social influence of films, clearly television has taken over cinema's mass entertainment function. Hence films engender numerous competing criteria for their importance, whereas in our day statistical head-counts (Nielsen ratings) are justified as the prime research protocol in the study of television's impact.

In short, most film histories accept the role interpretation plays from the outset, including the selection of those films that promise to respond most fully to a certain social interrogation. In his influential articles, ostensibly written to correct Kracauer, Thomas Elsaesser (1982, 1983) doesn't hesitate to name and work with a limited number of Weimar films that entwine an intricate cinematic discourse with a deeply psychoanalytic one. He argues that these privileged examples foster a particularly trenchant understanding of German culture applicable to the hundreds of films he chooses to leave by the wayside, including those where attendance may have been highest.

No matter how consistent Elsaesser's arguments

may be, by openly adopting an interpretive stance he will leave unsatisfied those historians intent on emphasizing different values. Exactly this dissatisfaction is visible in still another book on German films of the 1920s, Patrice Petro's *Joyless Streets* (1989). Petro forthrightly admires the work accomplished by Kracauer and Elsaesser, yet she senses something more to be said, another interpretation of the period accessed not by a statistical selection à la Monaco, but by a different—in this case feminist—critical insight. Petro's corpus includes only films that rather openly appeal to women, specifically melodramas of the street. Hers is not—or not yet—a reception study, although she has obviously divided national psychology into male and female subjectivity, implying that further subdivisions (according to social class, education, urbanization, profession) might provide a more refined understanding of the specific attractions and psycho-social 'work' cinema performed in this epoch. Petro remains on the side of textual analysis, however, because her impressive contextual research doesn't displace cinema, but assists her in choosing the films worth analysing and the terms of analysis that seem most warranted. The street films, she discovers, directly solicited a female audience that was larger than the male one that Kracauer inevitably speaks about. Producers must have had women in mind for these melodramas and for other genres as well. The burgeoning magazine trade aimed at women supports this supposition, especially when one learns of the business ties between the press and the cinema in late Weimar.

As Petro among others makes clear, cinema never exists in a sphere by itself but is supported by other cultural phenomena that it draws on, transforms, or transmits. And so one might categorize film histories less on the basis of the films chosen for discussion than on that of the intertexts (explicit or implied) from which those films derive their power for the historian. Petro's interest in contemporaneous journalism and fashion sets her directly against Lotte Eisner, for instance, whose influential version of Weimar cinema, *The Haunted Screen* (1969), bears its context in its subtitle: *Expressionism in the German Cinema and the Influence of Max Reinhardt*.

Having reached Eisner, we have drifted beyond social historiography and into the history of film as art, where interpretation unapologetically establishes both the corpus to be investigated and the pertinent contexts within which to read the films. But even

Eisner's comparatively rarefied art-historical attitude illustrates that all film histories bear a social dimension. When she details the persistence in key films of nightmarish metaphors or when she places Weimar masterworks alongside theatre productions of inhuman scale on the one side and of private anguish on the other, she characterizes the troubled era she writes about and the spiritual key of its social dysfunctionalism. Petro, meanwhile, though anxious to contribute to a precise understanding of a broader spectrum of society, happily makes her case through the astute analysis of films that take on importance in their difference from other films we know about, that is, in a film-historical context.

Only the pure sociologist, hoping to avoid interpretation, escapes this hermeneutic situation, but thereby risks escaping film history as well, making films no different from other cultural phenomena that could equally have been chosen as indices (or mirrors) of peoples at a given place and moment. The interests of film history lie beyond the purely social.

The film historian and culture

It has already been argued that the primary task of the film historian has traditionally been to unearth unknown films or unknown facts and connections relating to known films. First of all this has meant refining the map that displays these films and relations. Spatially, historians, after having so regularly mined Hollywood and Europe, look to other centres of production, discovering archives in distant locations. In the United States alternative production practices such as the New York avant-garde, black film companies, and studios based in Chicago have been excavated. Small in scale though these may be, they point to a cinematic potential that the dominant paradigm denies or suppresses. As for the temporal map, our lazy reliance on decades has always been questioned by historians who measure rhythms of change on more intrinsic criteria: on changes in technology, for instance, or artistic and cultural movements.

As for the content of the map, film historians are ever goaded to startle us, to upset or adjust our picture of how things have been. They do this most patently through discoveries of lost films (Oscar Micheaux's *œuvre*) or misunderstood practices (the *benshi* in Japan, the *bonimenteur* in Quebec). We are also startled by new configurations of things already known, or new ideas about the significance of these.

The surge of interest in early cinema, for instance, measures the strength of the 'cinema of attractions', a comparatively recent idea that rescued—for attention and for preservation—hundreds of films and techniques from the dustbin to which they had been assigned, a dustbin labelled 'false starts' or 'primitive' (see Gunning, Part 2, Chapter 4).

> **Film historians are ever goaded to startle us, to upset or adjust our picture of how things have been.**

Still another way historians upset the historical horizon that surrounds us is by changing scale. Zooming in to snoop on the minutiae of a film or a studio or a distribution agency can reverse received opinions about the standard operations of something presumably as well known as the classical Hollywood cinema. This was the case with the standard assumption that Hollywood studios of the 1930s were hothouses of self-engendered fictions. Intense examination of daily trade journals has now shown that all studios employed personnel to ferret out news stories that might be capitalized upon in both production and distribution. Far from this being an era of pure fiction, the documentary impulse was systematically exploited at all levels (Benelli 1992). Baseball movies, films about current events like the birth of the Dion quintuplets, and of course the entire gangster genre were part of a strategy that became visible when historians zeroed in on micro-operations of studios.

At the other extreme are relations exposed for the first time when a historian gambles on a very distant perspective. Jacques Aumont (1989) has studied cinema in relation to the long history of painting. Cinema participates in a relatively new function of the image that ever since the French Revolution has addressed what he dubs 'the mutable eye'. With the modern spectator in mind, he links cinema to various nineteenth-century optical phenomena (the diorama, the railroad car) and ties techniques satisfying this spectator that originated in silent movies to the most recent of Godard's inventions.

Each of these disruptions of the historical horizon provides a contrary view of the past through the assertion of a new perspective. Even more disruptive, however, and therefore in some senses more genuinely in line with critical historiography, are the efforts—increasing in recent years—to invalidate any single perspective whatever. In cinema studies, historians now take pride in describing situations wherein more than one temporal framework is at play (African cinema's laconic pace, both tied to indigenous life and to the European art film), more than one audience function (the appeal to gays and to straights of Judy Garland), more than one idea of the national (the self-conflicted Irish cinema, or the œuvre of Juzo Itami in relation to a Japan he references but scarcely believes in), and so on. The acknowledgement, and often the celebration, of subcultures and fragmented nations goes hand in hand with the description of hybrid genres and films. This assertion of the power of specific elements over unity and order comes at a high price. Historians risk occupying a position from which they can understand only singularities, which are by definition unrepeatable, and from which no generalizations can be drawn. Historical detail can stand in the way of the story of history.

In fact every history that treats the cinema must calculate the importance of films within a world larger than film. Culture can be said to surround each film like an atmosphere comprised of numerous layers or spheres, as numerous as we want. One may identify these as though they successively encompass one another moving from the centre (the individual film) out towards the stratosphere of national and international politics and events. Intermediate layers might include the film industry, traditions of genres, the biographies of filmmakers, the status of the other arts, the institutions of culture, and the organization of social classes. The further out from the centre the historian navigates, the more difficult it is to steer research in a way that is powered by the medium and not by some other agenda or discipline. Thus a political history of Hollywood in the 1950s needs to articulate the links that connect decadent film noir, self-conscious musicals, and budding docu-dramas to the concerns of Capitol Hill and of voters comfortable with Dwight Eisenhower at their helm but uncomfortable about their own security. Of course the blacklistings and the McCarthy hearings have provided precisely this type of linkage, as do biographies of the Hollywood Ten, the agenda of the Legion of Decency, and other such factors.

The permeability of these spheres permits an event at one layer to affect elements in another layer, producing interactions that can bring individual movies or the cinema as a whole into prominence. The direction

of this interactive flow is reversible, although it is usually tracked from the top down. For example, a change of government may bring in a new minister of education who promotes the expansion of literary journals. These journals may, in turn, promote an aesthetic that works its views on the legitimate theatre. Ultimately film acting, including the kinds of roles created for, or chosen by, key actors, may encourage a specific cinematic style, amounting to a significant alteration in the way the culture represents itself on the screen (see Andrew 1995, chapter 1, for an exemplification of this process).

Cultural interaction of this sort—a trickle-down process from government to popular expression—may be rare in a country like France, but occurs regularly in states exercising rigid political control. But the pervasiveness of censorship, even in democratic societies, reminds us that governments themselves can be disturbed by images bubbling up from beneath the cultural surface. Censorship bears witness to the power that films evidently deploy beyond the sphere of the strictly cinematic.

No history with aspirations of thickly representing an era's cinema can ignore this traffic among spheres. Yet every history needs to identify the most pertinent spheres within which to track the (shifting) values of cinema. Pertinence depends both on the researcher and on the topic under scrutiny. In my study of French films of the 1930s (Andrew 1995), for example, I was at pains to establish the special relevance of a particular cultural sphere containing subgroups such as the Surrealists and the novelists published by Gallimard Press. This choice challenged an earlier study, Francis Courtade's *Les Malédictions du cinéma français* (1977), which examines French films within the atmosphere of official history (political proclamations, censorship rulings) and official events in the film world (technological innovations like sound, economic developments like the fall of Gaumont). In certain revolutionary eras such as that of the Soviet Union of the 1920s, Courtade's focus seems apt; one would expect the Soviet film historian to follow very closely the major events of public life, since cinema explicitly participated in a national reawakening. But in the inter-war period of France, cinematic values were forged and debated less in the political sphere than in the cultural sphere, or rather in the nebulous zones where transactions between high and popular culture were possible. Here the effect on cinema of personalities from the established arts outweighed, from my perspective, all governmental and most economic pressures. And so the involvement in cinema of novelists and publishing houses, classical composers, painters, architects, and playwrights serve as more than anecdotes and do more than validate a popular art. Their involvement testifies to changes in the function of cinema and helps specify the direction such changes took. This cultural sphere is pertinent precisely because it identifies the site of development in a cinema that, from the perspective of the political or economic spheres, can hardly be said to have changed at all.

> **A cultural history of cinema proceeds neither through the direct appreciation of films, nor through the direct amassing of 'relevant facts' associated with the movies, but through an indirect reconstruction of the conditions of representation that permitted such films to be made, to be understood, even to be misunderstood.**

In brief, a cultural history of cinema proceeds neither through the direct appreciation of films, nor through the direct amassing of 'relevant facts' associated with the movies, but through an indirect reconstruction of the conditions of representation that permitted such films to be made, to be understood, even to be misunderstood (see King, Part 1, Chapter 23). This is a doubly hermeneutic venture, for it puts into play the reading of films for their cultural consequence and the reading of culture for the values or moods conveyed in films. Deciding which films are appropriate in relation to which spheres constitutes a founding act of interpretation.

Against interpretation: history without the historian

Aware how blind official culture has been to the presence (and the history) of women, minorities, the disfranchised, and the unrepresented, how can a film historian guard against simply repeating or varying the tastes she or he has inherited? Since interpretation selects and values, some historians work to dispense with it altogether by refusing to discriminate amongst the objects brought in for examination. This applies to a certain sociological film history that avoids the pre-judgement involved in selecting material, through a protocol of inclusion that chooses automatically. In *The Classical Hollywood Cinema* (1985), for example, Bordwell and his co-authors developed an algorithm to select films for analysis so as to avoid the vagaries of personal or cultural preference.

In current terminology, 'histoire sérielle' counters standard interpretive history, where a 'series' is any set of homogeneous elements (such as films, or studio contracts) that can be ordered into chronological sequence and counted. Originally developed to help map the history of slow-moving factors (prices of corn across decades, for example, as opposed to a peasant rebellion cropping up in one concentrated moment), serial history has been adopted by certain film historians, who have begun to treat films as elements in a series (see Burguière 1984: 631–3). Michèle Lagny, arguing for this new form of history, reminds us that, no matter what their quality, films are produced regularly and under conditions that apply equally to neighbouring films (Lagny 1994). Instead of singling out one film or making an intelligent selection, serial history submits all films in a given corpus to an unchanging inquiry. Trends can thus be measured statistically.

Serial methods seem ideally suited to documentaries, where the distinctiveness of the individual text or auteur is seldom a significant factor. But nothing prohibits a historian from employing this method for the fiction films of a period, measuring their length, for example, or their cost, or the number of dissolves, or the number of actors they employ. In this sort of history individual films lose their 'centrality' in favour of the extended lateral series. Moreover, the series constituted by a chronology of films is not surrounded by decreasingly relevant spheres, as in the model put forth above, but coexists with other series that can be called into play by the intuition (or whim) of the historian. On the other hand, just as in the concentric model, any series becomes significant only when significantly related to something outside it, usually to other series that are parallel or that intersect it at some nodal point. Thus a series of wartime documentaries might be placed alongside a series of newspaper editorials or against the number of troops conscripted. In short, statistics never really speak for themselves. They must be articulated, that is, put into relations that form a discourse and eventually an argument.

The significance of a group of simultaneous series

suggests the existence of a pervasive and distinct approach to experience obtaining in a given culture, a *mentalité*, linked to what is often discussed as the 'sensibility', 'ideology', or 'mood' of a substantial period of time. A *mentalité* is, like a climate, something that humans have no control over, and something that usually exists before and after them; yet to establish such an entity would seem to require far more interpretation than statistics. One might track the *mentalité* of a nation by analysing the kinds of material set for baccalaureate examinations or the fields of research of professors promoted to national chairs. In our period, the vocabulary of top-forty songs over a couple of decades might be examined in conjunction with dialogue in top-grossing films, and these two series could be placed alongside various demographic studies (teenage pregnancy, suburbanism, and so on).

Few film histories have rigorously employed the methods of the history of *mentalités*. Most studies of films written in this vein aim for global characterizations of national mood. For the period of 1940s America, for example, Dana Polan's book *Power and Paranoia* (1985) samples a number of genres and styles in characterizing the prevalent mood and dominant aesthetic of the time. Obvious social conditions are mentioned as fostering this attitude (the war and its aftermath with attendant shifts in work, status, and values). Yet to what specific institutions, policies, or events can films be tied? Segregation? The bomb? Communism? These are constant sources of irritation that undoubtedly affected, or directly motivated, films from the end of the war into the 1950s, yet the terms themselves are unruly, requiring detailed analysis before we can see the issues actually affecting a specific arena such as the cinema. We are led to ask what sort of historical, as opposed to thematic, examination might reveal the connections between films and these weighty concerns. And once again interpretation seems inevitable, perhaps not at the initial point of selecting material, but at the later stage of putting it into significant relation with other material.

Participating in a gnawing debate between objectivity and interpretation, the most sophisticated kinds of historical examination (in cinema studies as elsewhere) share much with the discipline of anthropology, conceived as a dialogue between self and other, a dialogue whose rules are constantly being renegotiated. In our case, this means maintaining a dialogue between films and culture that remains open and under constant revision. Rather than becoming

trapped inside a closed field of movies, yet before giving the movies over to laws that sociologists and economists have already arrived at, the film historian may interact with movies on behalf of culture. This is the middle road located somewhere between the highway of socio-economic history and the folk path of personal biography. Along this road lies the varied landscape of culture, a landscape whose ecology features the complex and contradictory interplay of institutions, expressions, and repressions, all subject to the force fields of power. The cultural historian bears, to the limit, the burden of the contested middle, by insisting on a stance between the already hermeneutic enterprises of the critic and the historian. Refusing to stop where most critics do, at the boundaries of texts, refusing as well the comfort of a direct pipeline to an era's 'imaginary' held out by certain brands of socio-economics, the cultural historian reads and weighs culture in texts and texts in culture. In this way the logic of changing values can be understood as felt.

It is no coincidence that this section on method should conclude with an affirmation of hermeneutics, exactly as did the first section, on attitude. History, as Siegfried Kracauer observed in his book on the subject, *The Last Things before the Last* (1969), hovers above the particulars of life, but not so high as theory, whose obsession with regularities and design blinds it to the contours of the landscape below. Historians can drop down low for detail, then rise to gain the perspective that seems to suit them or gives them densest significance. If those 'details' be movies playing, we might imagine, at some drive-in theatre below, the film historian can home in to watch something projected on a social landscape. Fascinated, the historian may momentarily cease thinking of the past as past, but directly view his or her own world as touched by what is shown; this is when history is projected straight through our present and into an open future.

*Allen, Robert, and **Douglas Gomery** (1985), *Film History: Theory and Practice* (New York: Knopf).
Altenloh, Emilie (1914/1977), *Zur Sociologie des Kinos* (Jena: Eugen Diedrichs; Hamburg: Medienladen)
Andrew, Dudley (1984), *Concepts in Film Theory* (New York: Oxford University Press).
—— (1989), 'Response to Robert Ray: The Limits of Delight', *Strategies*, 2: 157–65.

187

CRITICAL APPROACHES

Andrew, Dudley (1995), *Mists of Regret: Culture and Sensibility in Classic French Film* (Princeton: Princeton University Press).

Aumont, Jacques (1989), *L'Œil interminable* (Paris: Librarie Séguier).

—— **André Gaudreault,** and **Michel Marie** (1989), *Histoire du cinéma: nouvelles approches* (Paris: Publications de la Sorbonne).

Bardèche, Maurice, and **Robert Brasillach** (1938), *History of the Moving Pictures*, trans. Iris Barry (New York: Museum of Modern Art).

Bazin, André (1967/1970), *What is Cinema?*, 2 vols., trans. Hugh Gray (Berkeley: University of California Press).

Benelli, Dana (1992), 'Jungles and National Landscapes: Documentary and Hollywood Film in the 1930s' (doctoral dissertation, University of Iowa).

Benjamin, Walter (1930/1968), 'Theses on the Philosophy of History', in *Illuminations* (New York: Schocken Books).

Bordwell, David (1994), 'The Power of a Research Tradition: Prospects for Progress in the Study of Film Style', *Film History*, 6/1: (Spring), 59–79.

—— **Kristin Thompson,** and **Janet Staiger** (1985), *The Classical Hollywood Cinema* (New York: Columbia University Press).

Burch, Noël (1979), *To the Distant Observer: Form and Meaning in the Japanese Cinema* (Berkeley: University of California Press).

—— (1991), *Life to those Shadows* (London: British Film Institute).

Burguière, André (ed.) (1984), *Dictionnaire des sciences historiques* (Paris: Presses Universitaires de France).

Cinémaction (1992), no. 65, Special Issue: *Cinéma et histoire: autour de Marc Ferro.*

Courtade, Francis (1978), *Les Malédictions du cinéma français* (Paris: Alain Moreau).

Deleuze, Gilles (1983), *L'Image-Mouvement* (Paris: Éditions de Minuit).

Dyer, Richard, and **Ginette Vincendeau** (eds.) (1992), *Popular European Cinema* (London: Routledge).

Eisner, Lotte (1969), *The Haunted Screen: Expressionism in the German Cinema and the Influence of Max Reinhardt* (Berkeley: University of California Press).

Elsaesser, Thomas (1982), 'Social Mobility and the Fantastic: German Silent Cinema', 5/2, 14–25.

—— (1983), 'Lulu and the Meter Man: Louise Brooks, Pabst and Pandora's Box', *Screen*, 4–5 (July–Oct.), 4–36.

—— (1984), 'Film History and Visual Pleasure: Weimar Cinema' in Patricia Mellencamp and Philip Rosen (eds.), *Cinema Histories/Cinema Practices* (Frederick, Md.: University Publications of America).

*****Ferro, Marc** (1988), *Cinema and History*, trans. Naomi Greene (Detroit: Wayne State University Press).

Film History: An International Journal (1994), 6/1, Special Issue: *Philosophy of Film History* (Spring).

Flitterman-Lewis, Sandy (1989), *To Desire Differently: Feminism and the French Cinema* (Urbana: University of Illinois Press).

Godard, Jean-Luc (1980), *Introduction une véritable histoire du cinéma* (Paris: Albatros).

Gregor, Ulrich, and **Enno Patalas** (1962), *Geschichte des Films* (Gütersloh: S. Mohn).

Iris (1984), 2/2, Special Issue: *Toward a Theory of Film History.*

Knight, Arthur (1957), *The Liveliest Art* (New York: Macmillan).

Kracauer, Siegfried (1947), *From Caligari to Hitler* (Princeton: Princeton University Press).

—— (1969), *History: The Last Things before the Last* (New York: Oxford).

Lagny, Michèle (1992), *De l'histoire du cinéma* (Paris: Armand Colin).

—— (1994), 'Film History, or History Expropriated', *Film History*, 6/1 (Spring), 26–44.

Mitry, Jean (1968–80), *Histoire du cinéma*, 5 vols. (Paris: Éditions Universitaires).

Monaco, Paul (1976), *Cinema and Society* (New York: Elsevier).

Petro, Patrice (1989), *Joyless Streets: Women and Melodramatic Representation in Weimar Germany* (Princeton: Princeton University Press).

Polan, Dana (1986), *Power and Paranoia: History, Narrative and the American Cinema 1940–1950* (New York: Columbia University Press).

Prédal, René, *La Société française à travers le cinéma* (Paris: Armand Colin).

Ramsaye, Terry (1926), *A Million and One Nights* (New York: Simon & Schuster).

Ray, Robert (1988), 'The Bordwell Regime and the Stakes of Knowledge', *Strategies*, 1 (Fall), 143–81.

—— (1995), *The Avant-Garde Finds Andy Hardy* (Cambridge, Mass.: Harvard University Press).

Rivette, Jacques (1955/1985), 'Letter on Rossellini', in Jim Hillier (ed.), *Cahiers du Cinéma. The 1950s: Neo-Realism, Hollywood, New Wave* (Cambridge, Mass.: Harvard University Press).

*****Robinson, David** (1973/1981), *The History of World Cinema* (New York: Stein & Day).

Rotha, Paul (1949), *The Film till Now* (London: Vision Press).

Sadoul, Georges (1975), *Histoire générale du cinéma* (Paris: Denoel).

Sarris, Andrew (1969), *the American Cinema: Directors and Directions* (New York: Dutton).

Schefer, Jean-Louis (1980), *L'Homme ordinaire du cinéma* (Paris: Gallimard).

Slavin, David (1996), 'Native Sons? White Blindspots, Male Fantasies, and Imperial Myths in French *Cinéma Colonial* of the 1930s', in S. Ungar and T. Conley (eds.), *Identity Papers* (Minneapolis: University of Minnesota Press).

*Sorlin, Pierre (1980), *The Film in History: Restaging the Past* (NJ: Barnes Noble).

—— (1981), 'Jewish Images in French Cinema of the 1930s', *Historical Journal of Film, Radio and TV*, 1/2: 140–9.

—— (1991), *European Cinemas, European Societies* (London: Routledge).

—— (1992), 'Cinema, an Undiscoverable History?', *Paragraphs*, 14/1 (Mar.), 1–18.

Toeplitz, Jerzy (1979), *Geschichte des Films*, 4 vols., trans. Lilli Kaufman from Polish (Munich: Rogner & Bernhard).

Weinberg, Herman G. (1970), *Saint Cinema* (New York: Dover).

20 Sociology and film

Andrew Tudor

The rise of sociology as an academic discipline is one of the more striking intellectual success stories of the twentieth century. From its roots in the attempt to comprehend properly the enormous changes that came with industrial capitalism, sociology has grown into a richly diverse assembly of theories, methods, and substantive studies which, however else they may differ, share a desire to examine the emergent patterns of social organization that characterize human activity. At first sight, then, it is both surprising and disappointing to discover how little the discipline has contributed to our understanding of film. After all, before the advent of television the cinema was perhaps *the* institution of large-scale cultural production, exemplifying much of what was distinctive about the twentieth century's new forms of communication. Surely such a remarkable social development should have been of vital sociological interest.

For a brief period, of course, it was, though now more than sixty years ago. Fuelled by public concern in the United States at the end of the 1920s, the Payne Fund financed a series of ambitious research projects, conducted between 1929 and 1932, exploring the impact of motion pictures upon youth: 'our movie made children' as the popularization of the Payne Fund Studies called them. The studies brought together sociologists and social psychologists to investigate a range of topics, the flavour of which may be inferred from some of the titles under which the

research was published: *Movies, Delinquency and Crime* (Blumer and Hauser 1933); *The Content of Motion Pictures* (Dale 1933); *The Social Conduct and Attitude of Movie Fans* (May and Shuttleworth 1933); *Motion Pictures and the Social Attitudes of Children* (Peterson and Thurstone 1936). These volumes shared a forthright concern about the capacity of this new and powerful medium to have an impact on the attitudes, emotions, and behaviour of the young people who, then as now, formed the majority of its audience. They also shared a commitment to the newly emergent methodologies of the social sciences, using experimental studies, survey research techniques, extended interviews, and early forms of content analysis in their attempt to demonstrate that the movies were indeed having significant effects. Summarizing their findings, Charters (1935: 43) claimed that the motion picture 'has unusual power to impart information, to influence specific attitudes toward objects of social value, to affect emotions either in gross or microscopic proportions, to affect health in minor degree through sleep disturbance, and to affect profoundly the patterns of conduct of children'.

The Payne Fund Studies, then, set the tone for subsequent sociological approaches to film. First and foremost they were concerned with the *effects* of film, and, more specifically, with the possibility of deleterious effects on those (the young) presumed to be least able to fend for themselves. Having once focused on effects, they were inevitably much concerned with method and measurement. How to measure attitude before and after exposure to a film? How to analyse content scientifically, so as to assess a film's distinctive impact? They sought variously ingenious answers to these methodological questions, and in so doing they, and their academic descendants in the mass communications research of the 1930s and 1940s, made a remarkable contribution to the general development of social research methodology. So much so, indeed, that in retrospect it is possible to see in the Payne Fund Studies an outline of methodologies of precisely the kind that would much later attract critical charges of empiricism and scientism and that, as we shall see, were important in modern film theory's distrust of sociology. In fairness, however, it should be noted that not all the studies were equally open to the charge of restrictive empiricism. Herbert Blumer's contributions, for example (Blumer 1933; Blumer and Hauser 1935), are marked by the more ethnographic concerns of his Chicago School background, and in the 1950s he was himself to campaign against widespread scientist use of the language of 'variables' in social research. But for the most part the Payne Fund Studies did begin a tradition in the sociology of film that was to focus primarily upon the measurable effects of film on particular social categories of audience. In so doing they not only limited the kinds of question that sociology might pose about film; they also ensured that the distinctive character of cinema itself was lost within the more general rubric of 'mass communications'.

Thus it was that the dominant framework within which sociologists came to consider the cinema—if they considered it at all—was that of mass communications research. Not exclusively, of course. There were one or two social portraits of the movie industry in its heyday (e.g. Rosten 1941; Powdermaker 1950) and there was always the industry-fostered enterprise of audience research, whether predominantly statistical (Handel 1950) or more concerned with qualitative accounts of the moviegoing experience as volunteered by audience members (Mayer 1946, 1948). But these were minor tributaries to the mainstream of communications research where, in the 1950s especially, widespread concern to measure media effects dovetailed neatly into the frequent claim that modern society was typically a 'mass society'.

This is not the place to examine the detail of the mass society thesis. Sufficient here to enumerate only those elements of the thesis which were to have a formative impact on the way sociology approached the study of film. We have already seen something of that in the emphasis on effects of mass communications research. To this mass society theory added a profoundly negative evaluation of so-called 'mass culture', employing the category as something of a conceptual dustbin into which cultural critics of otherwise quite diverse persuasions could cast all the distinctive cultural products of modern society (for a useful account of the origin and development of these mass culture arguments, see Swingewood 1977). The unreflective élitism of this view is well known, whether its proponents were conventionally of the left (the Frankfurt School) or of the right (Leavis, Eliot). What is perhaps less apparent is its impact on sociological approaches to the media, film included, which often took as given the characteristic evaluations espoused by mass society theorists and led researchers to conduct their work on the assumption that mass culture was inevitably crude and unsubtle, while its consumers were little more than undiscriminating dupes. The mass society thesis, then, served to legitimize a framework for sociological analysis which effectively denied both the variability of audiences and the richness of many popular cultural texts, thereby neglecting the complexity of the cinematic institution as well as the polysemic potential of its products. Much cinema, in this view, was no more than a commercially motivated means of pandering to the lowest common denominator, its inherent crudity ensuring that little or no theoretical or methodological sophistication was necessary for its proper sociological comprehension. Any intelligent observer, it was implied, could easily see popular film for the restricted form that it was.

Of course this view is unsustainable. Yet for many years something quite like it was sustained in the received wisdom of sociological approaches to the mass media. Only a tiny proportion of sociological work resisted the mass culture argument and examined film with any commitment to the idea that processes of meaning construction might be more complex than was suggested by the traditional 'hypodermic model' of mass communication. Some of that work simply bypassed the mass culture tradition by examining those rarer forms of cinema which were by then widely recognized as approximating to 'high art' and therefore could be seen to invite and merit more elaborate treatment. One such instance was Huaco's (1965) analysis of three 'film movements' (German Expressionism, Soviet Expressive Realism, and Italian

Neo-Realism) employing a curious combination of Smelser's functionalist theory of collective behaviour and a somewhat unsophisticated base–superstructure metaphor. Revealingly, this volume claimed to deal with 'film art' rather than just film. However, as mass culture orthodoxy came under sustained attack during the course of the 1960s, sociological work developed on more than just 'film art', a process driven especially by the re-evaluation of Hollywood film by critics first in France and then in Britain, although also fed by growing dissent within sociology itself. When, later in the decade, the ideas of French structuralism began to have an impact in a range of subject areas (including both sociology and the nascent discipline of film studies) there was promise of a common framework of analysis through which a new, interdisciplinary understanding of film might be forged. By the late 1960s this had advanced to the point where the interests of the semiology and the sociology of film appeared to be converging, so much so that when the British Film Institute's Education Department published a collection of working papers emerging from its influential seminar series, four of the five contributors were academic sociologists (Wollen 1969).

Yet this positive concern with sociology was to prove short-lived, and as film theory became a central intellectual focus in English-language film studies its emergent orthodoxy systematically sidelined sociology's potential contribution. The charge most commonly made was that sociology suffered from precisely the kind of unreflective empiricism which film theory sought to combat in its own field of study. Ten years earlier that might have been true. By the late 1960s, however, such an allegation was, at best, questionable and, at worst, uninformed misrepresentation. The mass communications tradition was already under severe critical attack from within the discipline, and sociology more generally was in some ferment, shifting away from the apparent methodological and theoretical consensus that had characterized the post-war years. Whatever else it might have been, the sociology of this period was not empiricist in the traditional sense. Indeed, as a discipline it was arguably more theoretically reflexive and sophisticated than anything then envisaged in film theory.

In the event, the marginal role played by the sociology of film in the flowering of film theory in the 1970s had less to do with sociology's intrinsic empiricist failings than with the characteristic assumptions within which film theory itself developed. Here the position that came to be associated with the journal *Screen* was extremely influential, dictating terms within which debate was conducted and hence moulding the concerns of film theory even for those who did not subscribe to the *Screen* group's position. What was it about this perspective that had the effect of excluding sociology? The answer is not straightforward. After the first wave of enthusiasm for structuralist and semiotic approaches to film, it rapidly became apparent that the very formalism of such theories, in some ways a virtue, also extracted a price. Analysis tended to focus excessively on the film text (and film language) at the expense of any systematic understanding of the context within which texts were produced and understood. In consequence, neither individual spectators nor social structures featured satisfactorily in early semiotic analyses of cinema. On the face of it, this perceived failing opened up conceptual space for a distinctive sociological contribution. Unfortunately, however, film theory developed in a different direction, undeniably seeking to incorporate a social dimension into analysis, but not by application of sociological theories or methods. Instead, it was through the concept of ideology as that had been developed in Althusser's work that film theory sought to progress, borrowing particularly from his Lacan-influenced account of the ways in which subjects are constructed by systems of discourse. In this account the subject is constituted by and through the film text and is thereby caught within ideology.

Why this particular theoretical emphasis came to the fore is a complex question of intellectual and political history which cannot be dealt with here. The net effect, though, was to turn the film-theoretical enterprise towards analyses of the textual constitution of subjects and to a method based in structural psychoanalysis, rather than towards the kind of contextual concerns which would have necessitated a more directly sociological approach (see Creed, Part 1, Chapter 9). To make matters worse, the Althusserian framework offered an especially distinctive reading of the role of theory itself, a form of conventionalism within which theory was seen to constitute its object without reference to an independent 'reality'. Accordingly, any attempt to promote empirical work not cast in these terms— necessarily the case for a sociology of film—was condemned with the catch-all label 'empiricism', an allegation which was applied as indiscriminately as it was empty of intellectual force (see Lovell 1980 for an excellent critique). Thus was sociology marginalized in subsequent film theory.

In claiming that the Althusserian and Lacanian turn in film theory effectively excluded sociological considerations I do not mean to suggest that this was a matter of wilful intellectual conspiracy. It was, rather, that the terms of film-theoretical discourse which became commonplace during the 1970s and 1980s relegated sociological considerations to the periphery. The irony is that this was precisely when sociology could have best played a positive role in contributing to an interdisciplinary understanding of film, and subsequent film theory has been less than adequate in this respect, largely persisting with a radically unsociological view of cinema. Even those later scholars dissatisfied with the prevailing dependence on psychoanalytically influenced film theory have resorted to alternative psychological approaches—for example, drawing upon cognitive psychology—rather than to sociological frameworks (e.g. Bordwell 1985; Branigan 1992). Such authors have done much to expand the concerns of modern film theory, but without making a great deal of progress in understanding the sociological workings of the cinematic apparatus.

Accordingly, sociological analyses of film have been sporadic rather than sustained over the past quarter of a century, moving from the naïve optimism of general framing texts (Jarvie 1970; Tudor 1974) to qualified applications of the sociological perspective, often in the context of other theoretical and substantive interests. In this respect the rise of cultural and media studies as legitimate academic 'disciplines' has been crucial, providing a framework within which sociologically informed researchers have contributed to further understanding of film. Although rarely explicitly labelled sociology, the work of Dyer (1979, 1986), Hill (1986), and Wright (1975), among others, will serve to suggest the variety of such indirect sociological influences. It is this kind of work that offers the constructive blurring of disciplinary boundaries that was once promised by the temporary alliance between the sociology and the semiotics of film. Today, however, the energy and promise of such interdisciplinary alliances is not to be found in film studies at all, but more generally in cultural studies, where television is understandably the single most prominent focus. And in spite of the recent efforts of, for example, Norman Denzin (1991, 1995), a sustained sociology of film is still something of a pipe-dream.

But why should we need any such enterprise? One line of argument is to suggest that during the twentieth century sociology has accumulated a good deal of empirical knowledge about the workings of the social world, as well as establishing a not inconsiderable repertoire of research methods, and that both resources could contribute significantly to our stock of knowledge about film. In this respect we have no less need now than we have ever had for specific sociological studies of particular genres, of systems of film production, or of the social character of film spectatorship. Ironically, however, in the present circumstance of film studies it is perhaps in the area of general theory and method that sociology is most immediately relevant. This is especially apparent once we recognize that the future of film studies is inextricably bound up with the fate of cultural studies, which, deeply influenced by film theory in its formative days, has now outgrown its ailing film-theoretical parent. But contemporary cultural studies, it is widely believed, is faced with what various authors have called a 'paradigm crisis'. Formerly committed to a deterministic analysis which largely equated culture with ideology and which gave analytic primacy to texts and to systems of discourse, in recent years cultural studies has retreated from this 'strong programme', turning instead to much more localized, ethnographically inclined researches into processes of cultural consumption.

In many ways this has been a welcome development, especially where it has led to detailed empirical research into people's diverse and inventive 'reading practices'. But it has also bred dissatisfaction. For all the virtues apparent in recent work, there is a growing belief that cultural studies is losing its critical and analytic edge by retreating into forms of analysis which neglect the larger social context within which culture is utilized and reproduced, or by theorizing that context only in the grossest terms. Interestingly, sociology too has experienced just such conceptual polarization, at different times expressing itself in conflicting concerns with micro- versus macro-theorizing, with social determinism versus social phenomenology, and with society versus the individual. The difference is that sociology faced these divisions significantly earlier than cultural studies and has in the course of the 1980s generated a body of new theory oriented to concepts appropriate for understanding the crucial interaction between social structure and social agency.

It is here, surely, that sociology could play a positive part in renewing theory and method in cultural studies and, thereby, foster a more sophisticated understanding of the social institution of cinema. Film, after all, is more than mere celluloid. It is socially constructed within a three-cornered association between film-makers, film spectators, and the film texts themselves, and at every point in that nexus of relationships we encounter negotiation and interaction involving active social beings and institutionalized social practices. Sociology is the intellectual resource best suited to probing that particular complex of social activity. Note, however, that this is not to propose an academically imperialist project, a sociology *of* cinema in a strongly reductive sense. It is, rather, to suggest that in its recent theoretical and methodological concerns sociology has begun to forge an analytic position which could help to reconcile the potentially warring opposites of modern cultural studies. In so doing, it could still contribute centrally to a multidisciplinary understanding of twentieth-century culture, a culture within which film itself played a historically crucial formative role.

BIBLIOGRAPHY

Blumer, Herbert (1933), *Movies and Conduct* (New York: Macmillan).
—— and P. M. Hauser (1935), *Movies, Delinquency and Crime* (New York: Macmillan).
Bordwell, David (1985), *Narration in the Fiction Film* (Madison: University of Wisconsin Press).
Branigan, Edward (1992), *Narrative Comprehension and Film* (London: Routledge).
Charters, W. W. (1935), *Motion Pictures and Youth* (New York: Macmillan).
Dale, Edgar (1933), *The Content of Motion Pictures* (New York: Macmillan).
Denzin, Norman K. (1991), *Images of the Postmodern: Social Theory and Contemporary Cinema* (London: Sage).
*—— (1995), *The Cinematic Society: The Voyeur's Gaze* (London: Sage).
Dyer, Richard (1979), *Stars* (London: British Film Institute).
—— (1986), *Heavenly Bodies: Film Stars and Society* (London: British Film Institute and Macmillan).
Handel, Leo A. (1950), *Hollywood Looks at its Audience* (Urbana: University of Illinois Press).
Hill, John (1986), *Sex, Class and Realism: British Cinema 1956–1963* (London: British Film Institute).
Huaco, George A. (1965), *The Sociology of Film Art* (New York: Basic Books).
Jarvie, I. C. (1970), *Towards a Sociology of the Cinema: A Comparative Essay on the Structure and Functioning of a Major Entertainment Industry* (London: Routledge & Kegan Paul).
Lovell, Terry (1980), *Pictures of Reality: Aesthetics, Politics, Pleasure* (London: British Film Institute).
May, Mark A., and Frank K. Shuttleworth (1933), *The Social Conduct and Attitudes of Movie Fans* (New York: Macmillan).
Mayer, J. P. (1946), *Sociology of Film* (London: Faber & Faber).
—— (1948), *British Cinemas and their Audiences* (London: Dobson).
Peterson, Ruth C., and L. I. Thurstone (1933), *Motion Pictures and the Social Attitudes of Children* (New York: Macmillan).
Powdermaker, Hortense (1950), *Hollywood: The Dream Factory* (Boston: Little Brown).
Rosten, Leo C. (1941), *Hollywood: The Movie Colony, the Movie Makers* (New York: Harcourt Brace).
Swingewood, Alan (1977), *The Myth of Mass Culture* (London: Macmillan).
*Tudor, Andrew (1974), *Images and Influence: Studies in the Sociology of Film* (London: George Allen & Unwin).
Wollen, Peter (ed.) (1969), *Working Papers on the Cinema: Sociology and Semiology* (London: British Film Institute).
Wright, Will (1975), *Six Guns and Society: A Structural Study of the Western* (Berkeley: University of California Press).

21

Cultural studies and film

Graeme Turner

The development of film studies and its establishment within the academy precedes that of cultural studies, but over the last two decades there have been close parallels between the two intellectual and analytical projects. Both traditions are implicated in the turn towards the analysis of popular culture that commenced during the 1950s and 1960s in most Western countries. The spread of mass media culture, the installation of the teenager as an identifiable market category, and the various expressions of anxiety about the 'Americanization' of Western cultures as a consequence of the large-scale export of the products of the American mass entertainment industries, all assisted in raising the level of seriousness with which popular culture came to be regarded over the post-war decades. This change in the kind of attention directed towards popular culture in both the academic and the broader community resulted in significant modifications in the way popular cultural forms were examined and understood. Film studies and cultural studies have been among the participants in, and beneficiaries of, these shifts.

Film studies and cultural studies share a common interest in the textual analysis of popular forms and in the history of the cultural and industrial systems which produce these forms. However, there are limits to the commonality this might imply. Film studies is intensely interested in the individual text and retains a fundamental acknowledgement of aesthetic value; cultural studies disavowed the notion of aesthetic value from the beginning and is only now returning to see just how it might come to grips with such a fundamental gap in its account of the operation of culture (Frow 1995). Film studies is an academic discipline, with all the institutional and political considerations that entails. Cultural studies likes to think of itself as an 'undiscipline' (Clarke 1991) and, despite its galloping institutionalization, operates in an interdisciplinary fashion as a mode of critique and interrogation. The project of film studies in the academy is still primarily an interpretive one—of textual analysis—while the history of cultural studies has seen it move from a focus on the text to the analysis of the audience, and from there to mapping the discursive, economic, and regulatory contexts within which the two come together. Notwithstanding these rather fundamental differences, one can still trace important historical links between the two traditions and suggest ways in which trade between them has been, and might continue to be, useful.

These links are not uniformly distributed across the various national academies and intellectual traditions, however. Departments of film are most numerous in the United States, and the discipline is perhaps the most established and secure there. Cultural studies is, alternatively, a relatively recent addition to the humanities in the United States and is still at the very early stages of establishing its territory and its relation to cognate disciplines such as film, English, or communications. Further, and in constrast to the situation in Britain or in Australia, cultural studies in the United States seems intent on becoming a discipline itself and thus implicitly challenges film and English in ways that encourage the elaboration of points of difference rather than the pursuit of common goals. In Australia, and to a lesser extent in Canada, film studies, media studies, and cultural studies all move across similar interdisciplinary terrain, thus discouraging the kind of close identification with any single disciplinary tradition that would make comparisons especially meaningful. It is in Britain where the most explicit and productive 'trade' has occurred, and so this chapter will concentrate on the British situation.

The beginnings of cultural studies in Britain have been traced to such events as the conference of the National Union of Teachers in 1960 (Laing 1986; Turner 1990), itself embedded in the gradual development of public debates about the problem of 'discrimination' in popular culture (Hoggart 1958; Hall and Whannel 1964; Thompson 1964). Popularly framed as a problem highlighted by school pupils' enthusiastic consumption of mass culture products their teachers regarded as meretricious, its discussion led to the view that popular culture could no longer be dismissed without closer analysis. Indeed, if teachers expected their students to discriminate between 'good' and 'bad' cultural forms, they should start to exercise some discrimination themselves by resisting the temptation to see all popular culture as uniformly worthless.

At this time, most popular cultural forms were a long way from benefiting from such a view, but film was actually quite well positioned. The work of the French journal Cahiers du cinéma during the 1950s had recovered previously denigrated examples of mainstream Hollywood cinema for serious analysis, thus blurring the distinctions between commercial and art cinema. The development of theories of 'auteurism' in the United States during the 1960s, which appropriated the literary notion of authorship and bestowed it upon directors of (even Hollywood) films, legitimized the critical reassessment of such mainstream commercial filmmakers as John Ford and Alfred Hitchcock (Caughie 1981; Sarris 1969, 1970; Wollen 1972; see also Crofts, Part 2, Chapter 7). A further associated enabling strategy was the renovation of conventional understandings of film genres which dispelled some of their pejorative connotations—those which placed them as merely the markers of an industrial or formula-driven system of production (Braudy 1976;

Cawelti 1976; Schatz 1981; Feuer 1982; see also Ryall, Part 2, Chapter 8). This revised understanding of genre more realistically acknowledged the conditions within which mainstream feature films were produced, as well as the expressive or artistic potential of films produced within such conditions. Consequently, film studies established a form of analysis for a broad range of film texts which was not dissimilar to that already familiar within literary studies. It focused on the evaluation of the single film text, interested itself in the signatures of individual auteurs, and charted the trajectories of genres and film movements through variations in the patterns of their textual properties. Film, then, was probably the first of the mass communication forms to achieve respectability among critics of mass culture by establishing its validity as a textual system and as an aesthetic object—in spite, and in the full understanding, of its industrial conditions of production.

Film studies responded to this opportunity by developing a very sophisticated body of analysis of individual film texts, of individual directors, of film movements, and of film's formal signifying systems. By the middle of the 1970s, when cultural studies was still at a very early stage of development, film studies' analytical protocols were falling into place. Significantly, its interest in the workings of film 'language' had moved it towards more linguistic and systemic models of analysis: the influence of semiotics had begun to be felt, and the explanatory promise of psychoanalysis was also being explored (Metz 1974; Wollen 1972; Dayan 1974; see also Creed, Part 1, Chapter 9). As a consequence of such interests, the relation between film and other signifying systems—language, dreams, culture itself—became more important (Metz 1982). Film ceased to be regarded solely as an aesthetic object and was increasingly the subject of exploration as a signifying system which had cultural, psychological, technological, even physiological, bases (Neale 1985). Into the 1980s the importance of also understanding the industrial systems of production and the principles of economic organization became a prominent consideration as well (Bordwell et al. 1985; Kerr 1986; Gomery 1986).

By the mid-1970s cultural studies, too, was developing systemic models to enable the close analysis of a wide range of textual forms. Cultural studies' objective was slightly different, however: its target was the nature of the political interests served by the patterns of meaning or strategies of representation such analyses uncovered (Hall 1977, 1980a, 1982). Initially moti-

Cultural studies' target was the nature of the political interests served by the patterns of meaning or strategies of representation such analyses uncovered.

vated by its conviction of the importance and complexity of mass cultural forms, cultural studies from the mid-1970s to the mid-1980s was dominated by an assessment of the political function of these forms in practice—usually approached through the nomination of the ideologies they revealed and enacted through media texts (Fiske and Hartley 1978; Williamson 1978; Hall 1982). While far from celebratory of mass culture at this point in its history, cultural studies nevertheless took it very seriously as a system for making meaning.

While one might have expected the parallels between this cultural studies project and that of film studies to have encouraged some convergence of the two traditions, for most of this period they were in vigorous disputation. The form and function of the textual systems produced by mass culture became the primary subject of dispute between cultural studies and the body of film theory identified with the British journal *Screen*. What came to be known through this debate as '*Screen* theory' was, of course, a simplified and perhaps unfairly homogenized digest of what had actually appeared in the pages of the journal. Nevertheless, there were certain prevailing influences on the content of *Screen* at this time: the semiotic–pyschoanalytic cinema theory of Christian Metz and Althusserian explanations of ideology (Metz 1974, 1982; Althusser 1971). While these influences were also powerful in cultural studies, the shared interest did not produce much co-operation, however. When the Birmingham Centre for Contemporary Cultural Studies (BCCCS) began to investigate *Screen* theory, it was largely to contest what it regarded as *Screen*'s deterministic view of the power of the text (Hall 1980*b*; Morley 1980). In *Screen* theory, it was argued, texts were discussed in terms of their capacity to 'position' the viewer, telling the viewer how to 'read' the text and thus inserting him or her into a particular relationship to the narrative and into a complacent relationship to dominant ideologies. At its most extreme, suggested the BCCCS critiques, such an account saw the text as all-powerful: as if film texts always determined how

they were to be read. Morley (1980) among others, argued for a much greater recognition of 'agency', of the audience's freedom to negotiate quite resistant and even oppositional readings to those apparently structured into by the text. It was wrong, in Morley's view, to suggest that texts were read 'whole and straight' by every reader who encountered them.

This became a lengthy debate between the two theoretical traditions, one which helped shape the definition of the category of the text during the 1980s and still affects discussion of the text–reader relation today. The most celebrated exchange, perhaps, occurred around the critique of the subgenre of documentary realist television drama exemplified by the BBC's series *Days of Hope* (Ken Loach, GB, 1975), a story of British working-class experiences from before the First World War to the late 1920s which was screened in Britain in the mid-1970s. The series had a clearly oppositional agenda, setting out a left critique of contemporary British politics through its detailed and damning re-creation of the past. However, by accusing it of unwittingly offering a complacent view of history, *Screen* theorists seemed to some to be employing the most extreme application of 'textual determinism'. Colin MacCabe (1981) was the most uncompromising proponent of the *Screen* theory line, arguing that realist narratives were doomed by their narrative form and the epistemology which underpinned it. Realist narratives, MacCabe suggested, could never be critical of current political ideologies. This was because realism was a set of representational codes which must offer the viewer a comfortable position from which to see the representation even of bitter political struggles as natural or inevitable, hence defusing any potential for a critical or 'progressive' reading. By implication then, no matter what its intentions were, *Days of Hope* was defeated by its formal and ideological complicity with the politics it set out to attack. While such a critique had largely been accepted when applied to mainstream Hollywood realism, its application to projects that appeared to do something a little more radical was vigorously contested, primarily from within cultural studies but also from within film theory. Paradoxically, even though the battle lines were initially drawn around these competing formulations of the power of textual conventions, the focus on television meant that the debate moved across the boundaries between cultural studies and film studies. Under the heat of this debate, it seemed, firm distinctions between the two disciplinary traditions started to melt away. (A collection of the key essays in this debate can be found in Bennett *et al.* 1981.)

An analogous debate developed around Laura Mulvey's critique of classical Hollywood narrative (1975), which also seemed to argue that the dominant narrative form used in mainstream cinema offered only one position from which it could make sense. In this case, paraphrased crudely, Mulvey argued that if popular texts establish a position from which we find it comfortable to view and identify with them, it should not surprise us to discover that the viewing position constructed within the conventional discourses of Hollywood cinema is that of the male, not the female, viewer. The debates around what Mulvey called 'the male gaze' are of central importance to contemporary film studies and are dealt with elsewhere in this volume (see Creed and White, Part 1, Chapters 9 and 13); however, it is worth noting their implication in the relation between film and cultural studies. Again, cultural studies responses to this argument have questioned the implicit proposition of a single, overly determined, reading of the text (Modleski 1988). While the original idea has been productively developed and elaborated within film studies and has its own history there, within cultural studies Mulvey's argument has been a crucial provocation to the analysis of the popularity of mass media texts aimed particularly at female consumers—soap operas and romance fiction, for instance (Hobson

1982; Radway 1984; Ang 1985). Significantly, it is the revised notion of the 'female spectator', a notion which appropriates and then complicates Mulvey's suggestion of a single, undifferentiated female response to the film text, which has been particularly enabling in cultural studies, where it has been most usefully applied to television and popular fiction (Pribram 1988; Seiter *et al.* 1991). As researchers from both traditions have pursued the shared broad objectives of feminist critiques of represenation, the line dividing the two disciplines is very thin indeed in this analytical territory. Many contemporary analyses of film texts which focus on the representation of women—through discussions of the female hero in *Aliens* (USA, 1986), or *Thelma and Louise* (USA, 1991), for instance—do so through a striking hybrid of film and cultural studies approaches (Collins *et al.* 1993).

Such hybridizing notwithstanding, the above debates emphasize a crucial difference between what cultural studies and *Screen* theory did with their texts. *Screen* theory sought its 'progressive texts', those which were both textually unconventional (anti-realist and ultimately avant-garde) and politically radical in their denial of the 'comfortable' viewing position associated with both MacCabe and Mulvey's critiques. At its most programmatic, this quest looked like an aesthetic preference for the avant-garde which almost automatically wrote off all popular cinema. On the other hand, for cultural studies, it was the popularity

Female heroes—*Thelma and Louise* (1991)

of popular cinema itself that was so interesting. If we were not to believe that this popularity was simply the result of people being duped, then we had to go further than critiques of realism or the more deterministic assessments of the relation between the reader and the text had so far taken us. Crucially, it was the processes which produced texts and audiences, not the experience of the texts themselves, that interested cultural studies.

> **Crucially, it was the processes which produced texts and audiences, not the experience of the texts themselves, that interested cultural studies.**

Such concerns were also percolating through other discussions of film—even in the pages of *Screen*. Richard Dyer's work (1982, 1986) on the social and cultural significance of 'stars' investigated the way popular cinema creates its meanings and maintains its relation with its audience. Examining stars as semiotic 'signs', Dyer explored how particular well-known actors take already encoded meanings onto the screen with them, meanings which are also part of the audience's cultural competencies (see Butler, Part 2, Chapter 9, for a fuller exposition). Dyer's work straddled the two competing traditions; while it was unashamedly evaluative in its description of the film experience, it also insisted upon the cultural origins of the processes through which texts generate their meanings, and through which these meanings circulate and establish themselves. Such work provided a clear acknowledgement of the importance of both text and context, and a respect for the agency of the spectator that has come to be typical of contemporary film studies.

It is possible to discern a number of common directions in film and cultural studies since the mid-1980s. First, the devotion to 'high-theory' (such as that identified with *Screen*) has slackened considerably. Indeed, one recent collection adopted what it clearly regarded as a novel strategy by having well-known film theorists actually write about contemporary popular film texts and place them within current social and political debates; finally, it seemed, 'film theory' could 'go to the movies' (Collins *et al.* 1993). Next, as cultural studies has moved away from texts to audiences, and thence to the social structures which situate people as audiences, so too has film studies returned to exam-

ine its constitutive cultural and economic contexts. Studies of the classical Hollywood cinema today are as likely to be industrial histories of production houses, studios, and the international trade in cinema 'product' as a review of classic film texts (Bordwell *et al.* 1985). The broad debates about globalization that have so dominated discussion of television in recent years have also informed discussions of Hollywood and its relation to other, smaller, 'national' cinemas. To deal with 'national cinema' today is to interrogate closely discourses of nationality, the enclosure of small film industries within the imperatives of international competition, and the rationale and effect of local systems of subsidy, protection, and regulation, and then to place the film texts produced by national cinemas within this complex discursive, economic, and cultural framework (see Crofts, Part 2, Chapter 7). The problematics of regional cinemas such as the Asian cinema (Dissanayake 1994), of small national cinemas such as the Australian cinema (O'Regan 1996), or of the broader cultural politics of representation within Third-World cinema (Chow 1995) are becoming fundamental issues within contemporary film studies. Such problematics situate film within arguments about nation formation, about post-coloniality, and about the regulation of international trade in cultural products, and in many cases will privilege such problematics over the interpretive treatment of individual film texts. At such points, cultural studies and film share common concerns and pursue very similar goals.

Where cultural studies may still have something to offer film studies is in the area of audience research. For cultural studies, the late 1980s were dominated by what came to be called 'audience studies'. Beginning with the *Nationwide* studies by Charlotte Brunsdon and David Morley (1978), and developing in sophistication (Morley 1986, 1992; Buckingham 1987), the history of cultural studies analysis of the audience begins—again—with the text. Initially, these so-called ethnographies of audience readings (primarily) of television programmes were set up as a way of authorizing the researcher's preferred readings of texts. Increasingly, however, the variety and contingency of audience readings became the focus of attention and the

> **Where cultural studies may still have something to offer film studies is in the area of audience research.**

text was left behind. Morley's later work (1986, 1992) turned up rich evidence that certain contextual factors (social determinants such as one's position within the family, whether or not one was employed, one's gender) could dramatically influence audience reading positions and encouraged the view that it was these social determinants and *their* operation that would really repay study. By broadening beyond their textual provocations, the contextualizing rhythms of audience studies have taught us a great deal about how we read television texts and how we integrate these readings with other aspects of our everyday life. So far, there are few parallels to this tradition in film studies, although there is some very interesting historiographical work which does build on feminist appropriations of audience research (Hansen 1991). Indeed, as Janet Staiger (1992) has suggested, research into the reception of film texts can differentiate itself from the cultural studies tradition by a detailed focus on the specific historical conditions within which consumption occurs. In general, however, industry audience research remains the dominant mode of audience analysis in film studies, and the possible benefits of the cultural studies ethnographies—contestable as they admittedly are—have not yet been explored.

Film studies, for its part, has something to offer cultural studies in that it has managed to provide criticism that is socially and culturally informed but which still maintains some notion of value which can help explain what it is (beyond ideology, that is) that attracts audiences over and over again to particular texts. Cultural studies has ducked this issue for most of its history and is only now returning cautiously to it. Film theory may be of some assistance in this task as the boundaries between the approaches become more permeable. There is some prospect of this. It is certainly true that disciplinary disputes between the two traditions seem to be in the past and the capacity for the attributes of each to inform the analyses of the other is very strong. The relation so far has been complicated, but the tensions I have described in this overview—disputes over territory, over the framing protocols of textual analysis, and over the appropriate conception of the culturally constructed relation between text, reader, and context—have proved to be immensely productive.

BIBLIOGRAPHY

Althusser, Louis (1971), *Lenin and Philosophy and Other Essays* (New York: Monthly Review Press).

Ang, Ien (1985), *Watching 'Dallas': Soap Opera and the Melodramatic Imagination* (London: Methuen).

*****Bennett, Tony, Susan Boyd-Bowman, Colin Mercer,** and **Janet Woollacott** (eds.) (1981), *Popular Television and Film* (London: British Film Institute).

Bordwell, David, Janet Staiger, and **Kristin Thompson** (1985), *The Classical Hollywood Cinema: Film Style and Mode of Production to 1960* (London: Routledge).

Braudy, Leo (1976), *The World in a Frame* (New York: Anchor Press).

Brunsdon, Charlotte, and **David Morley** (1978), *Everyday Television: 'Nationwide'* (London: British Film Institute).

Buckingham, David (1987), *Public Secrets: 'EastEnders' and its Audience* (London: British Film Institute).

Caughie, John (1981), *Theories of Authorship* (London: Routledge & Kegan Paul).

Cawelti, John (1976), *Adventure, Mystery and Romance: Formula Stories as Art and Popular Culture* (Chicago: University of Chicago Press).

Chow, Rey (1995), *Consuming Passions: Visuality, Sexuality, Ethnography and Contemporary Chinese Cinema* (New York: Columbia University Press).

Clarke, John (1991), *New Times and Old Enemies: Essays on Cultural Studies and America* (London, HarperCollins).

Collins, Jim, Hilary Radner, and **Ava Preacher Collins** (eds.) (1993), *Film Theory Goes to the Movies* (New York: Routledge).

Dayan, Daniel (1974), 'The Tutor Code of Classical Cinema', *Film Quarterly*, 28/1: 22–31.

Dissanayake, Wimal (ed.) (1994), *Colonialism and Nationalism in Asian Cinema* (Bloomington: Indiana University Press).

Dyer, Richard (1982), *Stars* (London: British Film Institute).

—— (1986), *Heavenly Bodies: Film Stars and Society* (London: British Film Institute).

Feuer, Jane (1982), *The Hollywood Musical* (London: British Film Institute and Macmillan).

Fiske, John, and **John Hartley** (1978), *Reading Television* (London: Methuen).

Frow, John (1995), *Cultural Studies and Cultural Value* (Oxford: Oxford University Press).

Gomery, Douglas (1986), *The Hollywood Studio System* (London: Macmillan).

Hall, Stuart (1977), 'Culture, the Media and the "Ideological Effect"', in James Curran, Michael Gurevitch, and Janet Woollacott (eds.), *Communication and Society* (London: Edward Arnold).

—— (1980a), 'The Determination of News Photography', in Stanley Cohen and Jock Young (eds.), *The Manufacture of News: Social Problems, Deviance and the Mass Media* (London: Constable).

—— (1980b), 'Recent Developments in Theories of Language and Ideology: A Critical Note', in Stuart Hall,

Dorothy Hobson, Andrew Lowe, and Janet Woollacott (eds.), *Culture, Media, Language* (London: Hutchinson).

—— (1982), 'The Rediscovery of "Ideology": The Return of the Repressed in Media Studies', in Michael Gurevitch, Tony Bennett, Andrew Lowe, and Paul Willis (eds.), *Culture, Society and the Media* (Milton Keynes: Open University Press).

—— and **Paddy Whannell** (1964), *The Popular Arts* (London: Hutchinson).

Hansen, Miriam (1991), *Babel and Babylon: Spectatorship in American Silent Film* (Cambridge, Mass.: Harvard University Press).

Hobson, Dorothy (1982), *'Crossroads': The Drama of a Soap Opera* (London: Methuen).

Hoggart, Richard (1958), *The Uses of Literacy* (London: Penguin).

Kerr, Paul (ed.) (1986), *The Hollywood Film Industry* (London: Routledge & Kegan Paul).

Laing, Stuart (1986), *Representations of Working Class Life 1957–1964* (London: Macmillan).

MacCabe, Colin (1981), 'Realism and the Cinema: Notes on Some Brechtian Theses', in Tony Bennett et al. (eds.), *Popular Television and Film* (London):

Metz, Christian (1974), *Film Language: A Semiotics of the Cinema*, trans. Michael Taylor (London: Oxford University Press).

—— (1982), *Psychoanalysis and the Cinema: The Imaginary Signifier*, trans. Celia Britton et al. (Bloomington: Indiana University Press).

Modleski, Tania (1988), *The Women Who Knew Too Much: Hitchcock and Feminist Film Theory* (New York: Methuen).

Morley, David (1980), 'Texts, Readers, Subjects', in Stuart Hall, Dorothy Hobson, Andrew Lowe, and Janet Woollacott (eds.), *Culture, Media, Language* (London: Hutchinson).

—— (1986), *Family Television: Cultural Power and Domestic Leisure* (London: Comedia).

—— (1992), *Television, Audiences and Cultural Studies* (London: Routledge).

Mulvey, Laura (1975), 'Visual Pleasure and Narrative Cinema', *Screen*, 16/3: 6–18.

Neale, Steve (1985), *Cinema and Technology: Image, Sound, Colour* (London: British Film Institute and Macmillan).

O'Regan, Tom (1996), *Australian Cinema* (London: Routledge).

Pribram, Deidre (1988), *Female Spectators: Looking at Film and Television* (London: Verso).

Radway, Janice (1984), *Reading the Romance: Women, Patriarchy and Popular Literature* (Chapel Hill: University of North Carolina Press).

Sarris, Andrew (1969), *The American Cinema: Directors and Directions 1929–1968* (New York: Dutton).

—— (1970), 'Notes on the Auteur Theory in 1970', *Film Comment* 6/3 (Fall), 1–8.

Schatz, Thomas (1981), *Hollywood Genres: Formulas, Filmmaking, and the Studio System* (New York: Random House).

Seiter, Ellen, Hans Borchers, Gabriele Kreutzner, and **Eva-Marie Warth** (eds.) (1991), *Remote Control: Television, Audiences and Cultural Power* (London: Routledge).

Staiger, Janet (1992), 'Film, Reception and Cultural Studies', *Centennial Review*, 36/1: 9–104.

Thompson, Denys (1964), *Discrimination and Popular Culture* (London: Penguin).

*****Turner, Graeme** (1990), *British Cultural Studies: An Introduction* (Boston: Unwin Hyman).

Wollen, Peter (1972), *Signs and Meaning in the Cinema* (Bloomington: Indiana University Press).

Williamson, Judith (1978), *Decoding Advertisements: Ideology and Meaning in Advertising* (London: Marion Boyars).

22 Film audiences

Jostein Gripsrud

Why are audiences interesting?

When the hundredth anniversary of cinema was celebrated in 1995, 'cinema' was defined as the screening of moving images for a paying audience. The presence of an audience is, in other words, an essential part of the very definition of the medium. Very different kinds of film scholarship are concerned with film audiences or relations between film and its audiences. In quantitative terms, scholarly research and writing about film audiences, or some dimension of film–audience relations, clearly outnumber (and outweigh!) publications about any other aspect of the film medium, such as film production or the aesthetics of film.

Film's early status as a paradigmatic mass medium is a major part of the explanation for this. Its colossal popularity with working-class people and women and children of most classes gave various 'responsible' people reasons to worry about the impact of the movies on the minds and behaviour of these social groups. Given the intense and pleasurable experiences that people seemed to get from the cinema, it appeared obvious that the influence on people's minds would also be intense. Modern, social-scientific mass communication research was to a considerable extent developed in response to such fears through projects launched to document and substantiate them (even though these did not necessarily deliver the expected results).

But film's enormous potential for influencing the masses was also central to seminal contributions to theories of film as a textual form. The leader of the Bolshevik revolution in Russia, V. I. Lenin, proclaimed that film was the most important of all the arts since it was the most efficient medium for propaganda, and Soviet film theory (and that of Eisenstein, in particular) was very much concerned with how to move the mass audiences of film to perceive the world in certain ways—and act accordingly. The basis for a long tradition in film theory is precisely a Marxist conception of film as a medium for changing people's way of thinking

> In quantitative terms, scholarly research and writing about film audiences, or some dimension of film–audience relations, clearly outnumber (and outweigh!) publications about any other aspect of the film medium, such as film production or the aesthetics of film. Film's early status as a paradigmatic mass medium is a major part of the explanation for this.

in 'progressive' directions, or, on the contrary, for the reproduction and dissemination of ideology in the sense of 'false consciousness'. The semiotic and psychoanalytic *Screen* theory of the 1970s represented a particular development of this tradition.

A more recent, quite heterogeneous body of work favours a more pragmatic theory of meaning, according to which determinate meaning is not inherent in the filmic signs or texts themselves but is constructed by spectators in accordance with certain context-dependent conventions. This position can take a variety of forms, drawing on diverse theoretical traditions such as hermeneutics, phenomenology, the semiotic theory of C. S. Peirce, or eclectic formations such as British cultural studies. Cognitivist approaches, focusing on the 'processing' of film in the human brain, have also gained some prominence (see King, Part 1, Chapter 23).

All of the above approaches to film audiences and the encounter between audiences and films share the idea that it is through the existence of an audience that film acquires social and cultural importance. The production of a film provides a raw material which regulates the potential range of experiences and meanings to be associated with it, but it is through audiences that films become 'inputs' into larger socio-cultural processes.

> **The production of a film provides a raw material which regulates the potential range of experiences and meanings to be associated with it, but it is through audiences that films become 'inputs' into larger socio-cultural processes.**

The following overview will largely concentrate on the tradition of research on actual film audiences, as it has developed in response to the history of the medium. (For reasons of space, I have had to exclude the otherwise very interesting forms of audience studies conducted by or for the film industry. A good overview is provided in Austin 1989.) This emphasis is chosen partly because other entries in the present volume will cover the other, text-centred approaches, and partly because there has been a revived interest in empirical audience research since the early 1980s, not least in

studies of film history. Much of the prehistory of such work has been little known, however. Empirical audience research has often been regarded antagonistically by scholars in text-oriented film studies—and vice versa. However, creative scholarship can only benefit from a broad knowledge of different traditions.

The movies as a social problem: the first audience studies in context

The first public complaints over the moral standards of films were heard in the 1890s both in the United States (cf. Jowett 1976: 109–10) and the United Kingdom (Kuhn 1988: 15), but public reactions against the medium did not gain momentum until after 1905. It seems reasonable to assume that it was the explosive growth in the number of more or less permanent movie theatres from about 1905 that really brought the cinema to the attention of public authorities and the social groups that actively participate in public debates. Importantly, the repertoire of the cinemas was also beginning to change at about the same time, with fiction formats such as anarchic farces, crime stories, and melodramatic love stories becoming increasingly prominent.

The introduction of censorship which occurred in a number of different forms in most Western countries in the course of just six to seven years around 1910 is an indication of how seriously the 'dangers' of the movies were perceived. All such measures were preceded by public debates which to a greater or lesser extent also involved forms of research on movie theatres and movie audiences. The first film audience research was, in other words, motivated by anxieties about the social consequences of the medium's immense popularity, especially with children and adolescents. Numerous attempts were made in many countries to estimate audience numbers and social patterns of attendance before 1910, often in methodologically crude surveys conducted by teachers' associations, school authorities, social workers, and the like (see e.g. Jowett 1976: 45–6). Such efforts characteristically sought to verify the intuitive feelings of educators, religious leaders, and many social reformers that movies were for the most part detrimental to the psychic, moral, and even physical health of those who regularly went to see them.

The themes and results of these early studies were to be repeated again and again in later, and methodologically more sophisticated, studies. A research tradition was formed in which the medium of film was (is) conceived primarily as a social problem. It was seen as an isolated, primary cause of a number of negative effects. This cause–effect (or, rather, stimulus–response) conception of the relations between movies and audiences was drawn from mechanistic and biologistic psychological theories in vogue in the early decades of this century. Seeing the movies as a social problem was also related to widespread theories of the mass as a characteristic social form in modern societies. Individuals who had moved to rapidly growing cities had been cut off from their traditional bonds, norms, and authorities and were now seen to be basically vulnerable to mass persuasion. Moreover, for the first theorist of the mass, Gustave Le Bon, writing in 1895, the mass or crowd was 'distinguished by feminine characteristics' as it tended to move very easily into emotional extremes (Huyssen 1986: 196). One might suspect, therefore, that the cinema was conceived as a social problem precisely because central parts of its *audiences* were experienced as a problem for teachers and other authorities. That the problem was in part conceived as *feminine* is highly significant: for the threat of the movies was, not least, about a loss of control and a tendency towards self-indulgence and weakness.

The cinema became a privileged sign of social and cultural changes which made élites worried. As such, it played the role of a much-needed scapegoat which rational arguments could hardly do much to change. In 1917 the British National Council of Public Morals undertook an 'independent enquiry into the physical, social, moral and educational influence of the cinema, with special reference to young people' (quoted in Richards 1984: 70). A 400-page report, based on numerous sources of information, was published, in which the general conclusion was that 'no social problem of the day demands more earnest attention', and that the cinema had 'potentialities for evil' which were 'manifold' (even though cinema could also become 'a powerful influence for good'). And on the question of links between movies and juvenile crime, the commission of inquiry concluded 'that while a connection between the cinema and crime has to a limited extent in special cases been shown, yet it certainly has not been proved that the increase in juvenile crime generally has been consequent on the cinema, or has been independent of other factors more conducive to wrongdoing' (Richards 1989: 71). Still, the issue was

not settled, and the same anxieties motivated new inquiries well into the 1930s.

The movies as social force: the Payne Fund Studies

By the 1920s the cinema was well established as the major form of entertainment for the larger part of the population in all Western countries. An 'art' cinema was developed in, for instance, Germany and France, and cinema's increasing respectability could also be seen in many countries from the emergence of film criticism in major newspapers and magazines. However, in the United States, especially, it seems that the earlier moral panics over the influence of the movies were still in evidence. Unlike many other countries, the United States had not established forms of public censorship which would have calmed the nerves of those most worried. Moreover, as the prohibition of alcohol between 1920 and 1933 indicates, the so-called 'roaring twenties' was a period when puritan morality was particularly strong, perhaps in reaction to the number of social and cultural changes then challenging traditional values, such as women's entry into the labour force and new relations between the sexes, and the emergence and spread of consumerism (involving spending rather than saving).

In this situation, the movies were still very much suspected of being a primary source of inspiration for delinquency and general moral decay. This was so even if a 1925 study of 4,000 'juvenile delinquency' cases showed that only 1 per cent of these could in some way be tied to movie influence. (The study was conducted by Healy and Brommer and referred to in Blanchard 1928: 204; cf. Jowett 1976: 216.) Alice Miller Mitchell published the first major scholarly survey entirely devoted to children and the movies in 1929, and concluded that, even if 'the delinquent does have a wider cinema experience than do the other children studied', the survey did not provide any conclusive evidence for a causal link between movies and delinquency (quoted in Jowett 1976: 219). However, such sensible reasoning was not to deter activists who perceived the movie repertoire in much more offensive and threatening terms.

The most comprehensive and also probably most influential of all empirical research projects on film audiences—the so-called Payne Fund Studies—was organized in 1928 by the Reverend William H. Short, who was executive director of something called the Motion Picture Research Council. A group of psychologists, sociologists, and educators from a number of institutions, directed by Dr W. W. Charters from the Bureau of Educational Research, Ohio State University, began work as soon as a grant of $200,000 was secured from the philanthropic foundation the Payne Fund. Investigations took place between 1929 and 1932, and the results were published in at least twelve volumes—eight books in 1933, three in 1935, and one in 1937. In addition, a journalist, Henry James Forman, wrote a popularized summary of the studies, *Our Movie Made Children* (1933). This book focused completely on results which seemed to support the view that movies had detrimental effects, and it became very influential in the public debate which preceded the much stricter enforcement of Hollywood's so-called Production Code from the summer of 1934 on. The actual studies themselves also had an undertone of anxiety or concern, but they were far more nuanced than Forman's outright attack on the movie industry suggested.

The Payne Fund Studies employed all the research methods then available to 'scientific' studies of sociological and psychological phenomena, and developed some of them further. Methods included quantitative 'content analyses', large-scale surveys, laboratory experiments, participant observation, the collection of written 'movie autobiographies' from large numbers of people, and so on. The studies can be grouped in two categories. The first consists of studies which tried to determine the size and composition of movie audiences, and to assess the 'contents' of films. The second category of studies were attempts to assess the various 'effects' of viewing.

One series of studies of this latter sort was conducted by Ruth C. Peterson and L. I. Thurstone (1933). They were interested in whether films influenced the general attitudes of children towards ethnic or racial groups and certain central social issues such as crime, the punishment of criminals, war, capital punishment, and prohibition. The results were very clear: even single films seemed to have considerable influence on children's attitudes, and the cumulative effect of several films with a similar view of groups or issues was even more striking (Lowery and DeFleur 1995). Despite their sophistication, these studies, none the less, displayed a number of severe theoretical and methodological problems. The very term 'attitude' is problematic, the methods for 'measuring' the phe-

nomenon are debatable, no so-called control groups were used—and so forth. Still, the evidence presented could well be seen as quite convincing, particularly since the children had little or no experience of, or insight into, the respective areas under investigation. Very few, if any, of these small-town kids had ever known black or Chinese people, for example. Films portraying these groups positively or negatively, therefore, could be all the more influential. It is similarly unlikely that they had given much thought to the issues of war or the treatment of criminals. What was demonstrated, then, was the impact of films in a situation where other sources of information were more or less lacking and opinions and attitudes were therefore relatively easy to influence.

The most interesting of the Payne Fund Studies, however, was methodologically very different. Herbert Blumer collected 'motion-picture autobiographies' from over 1,100 university and college students, 583 high-school students, 67 office workers, and 58 factory workers, who were instructed to 'write in as natural and truthful manner as possible accounts of their experiences with "movies" as far as they could recall them' (Blumer 1933: 4). In addition, about 150 students and schoolchildren were interviewed, and accounts of conversations ('taken nearly as verbatim as possible', 11) between students at different levels were collected. Finally, questionnaires were distributed to 1,200 children in the fifth and sixth grades of twelve public schools in different areas of Chicago, and the behaviour of children at neighbourhood cinemas and in play after these visits was observed. The voluminous material gathered in these ways was not primarily intended for sophisticated statistical treatment. Rather the point was to explore the ways in which cinema audiences themselves thought and felt about their moviegoing, the films they saw, and how they influenced them. The published report, *Movies and Conduct* (Blumer 1933), is full of vivid descriptions of movie experiences and of how young people picked up tips on anything from play, kissing, fashion, and table manners to attitudes and daydreams. Just one random example from a female high-school student's contribution:

I have imagined playing with a movie hero many times, though; that is while I'm watching the picture. I forget about it when I'm outside the theater. Buddy Rogers and Rudy Valentino have kissed me oodles of times, but they don't know it. God bless 'em!—Yes, love scenes have thrilled me and made me more receptive to love. I was going with a fellow whom I liked as a playmate, so to speak; he was a little younger than me and he liked me a great deal. We went to the movie—Billie Dove in it. Oh, I can't recall the name but Antonio Moreno was the lead, and there were some lovely scenes which just got me all hot 'n' bothered. After the movie we went for a ride 'n' parked along the lake; it was a gorgeous night. Well, I just melted (as it were) in his arms, making him believe I loved him, which I didn't. I sort of came to, but I promised to go steady with him. I went with him 'til I couldn't bear the sight of him. . . . I've wished many times that we'd never seen the movie. (Blumer 1933: 223)

Blumer's conclusions were relatively careful. However, the material had convinced him that 'the forte of motion pictures is in their emotional effect', and that 'their appeal and their success reside ultimately in the emotional agitation which they induce'. A successful production was one which managed to draw 'the observer' into the drama so that 'he loses himself' and, in such a condition, 'the observer becomes malleable to the touch of what is shown' and 'develops a readiness to certain forms of action which are foreign in some degree to his ordinary conduct' (Blumer 1933: 198). Blumer also argued that the movies were so emotionally demanding that the audience could be left 'emotionally exhausted' and, instead of ordinary emotional responses, they would experience an emotional and moral confusion: 'Insofar as one may seek to cover in a single proposition the more abiding effect of motion pictures upon the minds of movie-goers, it would be, in the judgement of the writer, in terms of a medley of vague and variable impressions—a disconnected assemblage of ideas, feelings, vagaries, and impulses' (199). Blumer's conclusion was that films could confuse people morally in various ways: for instance, by presenting immoral behaviour as attractive even if the film's overt moral 'message' was impeccable. In a methodologically similar study of inmates, ex-convicts, and young people in various reform schools and so on, he pointed to the obvious importance of social-background factors both in the choice of films and in reactions to them. But he remained convinced that movies could 'lead . . . to misconduct', and that this inevitably raised the issue of 'social control' (Blumer and Hauser 1933: 202).

The Chicago School sociologist Blumer was thus no simplistic 'hypodermic needle' theorist, even if there are clear traces of the stimulus–response model in his work, and his conclusion is that movies had a powerful influence on young people's lives. His observations of strong emotional experiences, and identification as 'losing oneself', have links to both previous and later scholarship on film (and television). Hugo Münsterberg's *The Photoplay: A Psychological Study* (1916), which Hansen (1983: 154 n. 14) describes as 'the first systematic attempt to theorize spectatorship', provided, for example, a sort of theoretical basis for ideas of film as a 'strong' medium which could be used both for better and for worse. Films could, Münsterberg argues, be an 'incomparable power for remoulding and upbuilding the national soul', even if '[t]he possibilities of psychical infection cannot be overlooked'. 'No psychologist', he continues, 'can determine exactly how much the general spirit of righteous honesty, of sexual cleanliness, may be weakened by the unbridled influence of plays which lower moral standards' (May 1983: 42). With somewhat different, and far more impressive, theoretical underpinnings, the whole theorization of 'the spectator' in cine-psychoanalytic studies from Christian Metz onwards is also centred on the persuasive ideological functions of 'identification' (see Creed, Part 1, Chapter 9). In this respect, Blumer was probably less blind to the importance of contextual factors in determining the 'effects' of cinema than some of the work in the *Screen* tradition appeared to be.

The Payne Fund Studies, however, are all quite insensitive to film as a form of *art*. They chop up filmic texts in so many 'themes' and 'content elements', with total lack of respect for a film's wholeness and the interrelations of a variety of aesthetic means and potential meanings. This provoked the neo-Aristotelian philosopher Mortimer Adler to formulate a fundamental critique of this whole approach to what he considered an art form in his *Art and Prudence* (1937), subsequently popularized in Raymond Moley's *Are we Movie Made?* (1938). Nevertheless, at least some of the Payne Fund Studies were more nuanced and theoretically reflective than much post-war research. Sociologist Paul G. Cressey (1938) summarized the experiences gained in the project as follows:

'Going to the movies' is a unified experience involving always a specific film, a specific personality, a specific social situation and a specific time and mood; therefore, any program of research which does not recognize all essential phases of the motion picture experience can offer little more than conjecture as to the cinema's net 'effect' in actual settings and communities. (Cressey 1938: 518)

It is worth wondering where such insights went in the following decades. Research along similarly intelligent lines had in fact been done almost twenty-five years earlier, in Germany. But for a number of imaginable reasons, it remained unknown to Anglo-Americans until Miriam Hansen referred to it in a 1983 article in English.

The cinema as cultural resource: Emilie Altenloh

The German sociologist Emilie Altenloh's doctoral dissertation, *Zur Soziologie des Kino* (1914), which she wrote at the age of 26, is in fact one of the most interesting contributions to empirical audience studies. This is particularly so because of her general approach. The dissertation is marked by a holistic sociological and historical perspective on the cinema and its audiences. Almost half of its 102 pages are devoted to film production, including the product itself, distribution, and the legal framework. The second half is about the audience, and their attendance at the cinema is understood in relation to both their other cultural preferences (theatre, music, and so on) and their gender, class, profession, and political interests. A historical perspective runs through the whole text; and both social developments (industrialization, modernization) and the changes in the domain of popular culture are brought into her interpretive and explanatory reasoning. What also makes it strikingly different from, say, the Payne Fund Studies is that worries over 'harmful effects' are hardly expressed at all. While the author openly distinguishes between more and less 'primitive' movies and tastes (the genre preferences of many young male workers were expressed in answers that 'smell of blood and dead bodies'; Altenloh 1914: 66), the tone is generally one of sympathy, not moralizing.

Altenloh's primary material for the audience study was movie theatre statistics and 2,400 simple questionnaires which were distributed via professional organizations, trade unions, and schools of various kinds in the city of Mannheim and, in part, in Heidelberg. The study provides a detailed picture not only of the social composition of audiences but also of the differences between various sections of the audience in terms of genre preferences and the overall context of their going to the movies, including their relations to other cultural forms and media. The survey demonstrated, for instance, that male audiences varied quite a lot in their generic preferences and general attitudes

to the cinema, in ways which clearly related to their membership of particular social groups, while female moviegoers seemed to be more homogeneous in their tastes for music, melodrama, and particular kinds of documentary material (waterfalls, waves, ice floes . . .). What was striking in all of the questionnaire material, however, was how little people could say to explain why they were so drawn to the movie experience. The reasons were as many as there were individuals in the audience; they were, however, all out for something their everyday experiences did not provide. Altenloh thought that 'the cinema succeeds in addressing just enough of those individuals' needs to provide a substitute for what could really be "better", thus assuming a powerful reality in relation to which all questions as to whether the cinema is good or evil, or has any right to exist, appear useless' (Hansen 1983: 179).

Altenloh's study suggested that the cinema functioned as a social space for experiences and forms of communication that were largely excluded from other public arenas—not least because central parts of the audience were in practice excluded from these other arenas. It was, to a degree, a public sphere for the unspeakable, where those otherwise spoken *for*, without a voice of their own, felt at least spoken *to*. And whatever else one could say about Altenloh's questionnaire methodology, it did, even if within strict limitations, allow cinema's core audiences to speak for themselves—and through a sympathetic interpreter.

British observations—and two blank decades

In Britain the early 1930s brought a series of local inquiries into the 'effects' of cinema, particularly on children and youth. Most of them sought to justify the hostility towards the movies which motivated their efforts, and were generally deficient in scholarly standards of research and argumentation. While reports like these played an important role in public debates, the more interesting work on cinema audiences was of a different nature. The statistician Simon Rowson conducted the first systematic survey of cinema attendance in 1934 (Rowson 1936), and a number of other surveys were also conducted throughout the decade. But the most fascinating of British studies of film audiences in the 1930s and 1940s were of the kind now referred to as 'ethnographic', i.e. mainly based in various forms of participant observation.

Sociological studies such as E. W. Bakke's *The Unemployed Man* (1933) and H. Llewellyn Smith *et al.*'s *The New Survey of London Life and Labour* (1935) included observations of the role of the cinema in the everyday lives of ordinary people in particular social milieux, as did a number of other books and articles with both scholarly and other kinds of authors (Richards 1989, ch. 1). The interest in an 'anthropological study of our own civilization' also lay behind the establishment of Mass-Observation in 1937. This was a unique organization devoted to the gathering of knowledge about everyday life in British society, and was based on the voluntary observational work of ordinary (if, predominantly, middle-class) people. Mass-Observation grew out of the same intellectual milieu as the documentary film movement associated with John Grierson, and cinemagoing was first studied in what was known as the 'Worktown' project—a study of Bolton, Lancashire—which was obviously inspired by Robert Lynd and Helen Merrell's *Middletown: A Study in American Culture* (1929). Survey methodology, loosely structured interviews, and participant observation were employed in this project, and the material collected provides a richly detailed picture of moviegoing in Bolton. Both before and during the war Mass-Observation continued to collect information from its volunteers all over Britain about cinemagoing (including that of the volunteers themselves), reactions to particular films during screenings (laughs, comments, etc.), favourite stars and films, and so on. Material was also gathered through popular newspapers and the film magazine *Picturegoer*, the readers of which were asked to write letters about their cinema habits and preferences (Richards and Sheridan 1987: 1–18).

This last procedure was also used by the sociologist J. P. Mayer when working on his *British Cinemas and their Audiences* (1948), which includes sixty of the letters Mayer received from readers of *Picturegoer*. This book, however, seems to be the last of its kind to arrive for decades. From the early 1950s on, television largely took over the cinema's role as the major source of popular entertainment and, as a result, became the object of very similar concerns to those previously directed at the movies. Social scientists generally lost interest in film and its 'effects', while an individualistic and consumer-oriented 'uses and gratifications' approach evolved as a new paradigm in mainstream communication research. When film studies became

established as an academic discipline in the 1960s, it was as a purely aesthetic discipline, devoted to studies of films-as-texts, of masterpieces and 'auteurs'. Having film accepted as a worthy object of study entailed a qualification of it as 'Art'. Sociological studies of the audience were regarded as irrelevant—as philistine activities, which were only of interest to aesthetically insensitive social scientists, politicians, bureaucrats, and the movie business. When the audience reappeared in film theory around 1970, it was at first as a generalized textual construct only. But in 1978, at the Centre for Contemporary Cultural Studies, Tom Jeffrey published a paper entitled *Mass-Observation: A Brief History*. Mass-Observation and empirical studies of actual audiences were, in other words, 'rediscovered' in the context of the ethnographic studies of contemporary (youth) culture conducted by the so-called Birmingham School. The 1980s then brought a new wave of interest in film audiences.

From textually derived spectators to actual audiences

The politically inflected theorization of spectatorship in the 1970s can be seen, to use a psychoanalytical metaphor, as a 'return of the repressed' after a period of purely aesthetic approaches. But the political interest in film spectators may also be seen as a kind of 'displacement', in that the central audiovisual medium had for a number of decades been television. From a political point of view, it is also striking that most of the films analysed were made decades before—they were not what contemporary audiences went to the cinema to see. An interest in contemporary movie audiences is still relatively rare in film studies.

This is not at all to say that the theories in question were irrelevant and that all the efforts of *Screen* theory were a waste of time and energy. Ideas about 'spectator positions' suggested by filmic texts are in line with ancient rhetorical theory and also with more recent phenomenological and hermeneutic theories of literature. However problematic it may have been, Laura

An interest in contemporary movie audiences is still relatively rare in film studies.

The position of the spectator—a film audience of the classical era

Mulvey's 1975 article about the structural gendering of mainstream film was a seminal attempt at grounding a feminist theory of film in more fundamental matters than the simple counting of stereotyped sex roles. On the whole, psychoanalytic theory in the tradition of Christian Metz is still the only significant theory which seriously approaches the 'deeper' reasons for our desires for and pleasures in film experiences. It deals with phenomena we cannot expect to explain either through direct observation or through interviews, but which still remain essential. The tradition of empirical studies of actual audiences can only, like Emilie Altenloh in 1914, conclude that people have few and hardly satisfactory answers when asked why they go to the movies again and again.

The problem of *Screen* theory was rather that the issue of *real* audiences was either dismissed as 'empiricist' or postponed indefinitely. This contrasted with developments in literary studies (which film studies for the most part grew out of), where studies of historical, concrete instances of reception were, so to speak, booming in many countries in the 1970s inspired, in part, by German reception theorists. Film studies only took a similar turn after the cultural studies of *television* demonstrated that textual analysis and audience studies could be intelligently and fruitfully combined. Charlotte Brunsdon and Dave Morley's work on the programme *Nationwide* (Brunsdon and Morley 1978; Morley 1980) was seminal here. It was followed later by such work as Ien Ang's influential study of the Dutch reception of *Dallas* (1985), and in the late 1980s the 'ethnographic' study of television audiences was generally recognized as the 'sexiest field within the field' in the increasingly interdisciplinary area where mass communication, communication, media, cultural, and film studies converged. This convergence was also facilitated by a 'ferment in the field' of mass communication research which opened the way for so-called qualitative (as opposed to strictly quantitative and statistical) methods in both textual and audience analyses, and forms of critical theory.

It is characteristic of film studies, though, that work on film audiences is still largely of a historical kind. Present-day, actual film audiences get very little attention. Thus, there has been quite intensive research on the exhibition practices, forms of reception, and social composition of audiences between the 1890s and 1960, and research on early film (before 1917), in particular, has flourished, combining solid historical investigation of primary sources with considerable theoretical sophistication (see Elsaesser 1990 on seminal work here). Ways of theorizing 'spectatorship' in a social context that are new to Anglo-American film studies have also been introduced in this area, specifically through Miriam Hansen's use of the concept of (proletarian) public sphere(s) in her *Babel and Babylon* (1991) (see also Gunning, Part 2, Chapter 4).

The general transition in feminist film studies from an interest only in a textually constructed spectator to studies which are concerned at least as much with actual audiences was marked, for instance, by Annette Kuhn's 1984 *Screen* article 'Women's Genres', which called for a rethinking of interrelations between the two. This demand was linked to other work within feminist film theory which had severely complicated the notion of 'the spectator' by, first, distinguishing between male and female spectator positions, and then further deconstructing the apparent unity or singularity of each of these (see Modleski 1988, introduction). In anthologies such as Deidre Pribram's *Female Spectators* (1988), the relations between textual and socio-historical approaches were discussed in new, more open ways, and Patrice Petro's *Joyless Streets* (1989) took to non-filmic sources (magazines, photojournalism) in an attempt to construct historically specific female spectator positions in Weimar Germany.

The convergence between previously segregated approaches has been particularly striking in studies of film stars, previously a phenomenon reserved for fandom and sociology. Richard Dyer's book *Stars* (1979) introduced this area into academic film studies, and it rapidly became a meeting place between historical, sociological, culturalist, semiotic, and cine-psychoanalytical forms of scholarship (Gledhill 1991). In many respects Jackie Stacey's *Star Gazing* (1994) represents a coming-together of all of these, integrating (among other things) discussions of spectator theories, statistical information, and the written memories of female

moviegoers of the 1940s and 1950s. She draws on Mass-Observation material, and employs methods similar to those of both Herbert Blumer and (particularly) J. P. Mayer, thus acknowledging the value of the historical tradition of empirical, sociological studies of movie audiences (even if, significantly, neither of these two forerunners are mentioned in her book).

Stacey's book thus indicates that film studies may have reached a point where theoretical and methodological orthodoxies have given way to a more productive, critically informed rethinking of theoretical and methodological boundaries. Such reasoned eclecticism is far from unproblematic, however, for there are, in the current conjuncture, many reasons to suggest the importance of film scholarship which goes beyond empirical studies of historical or current film audiences and their experiences of the movies. Still, it seems clear that the theoretical and methodological developments over the last two decades or so have clearly contributed to making film studies a highly vital, central field within the broader area of media studies.

BIBLIOGRAPHY

Adler, Mortimer J. (1937), *Art and Prudence* (New York: Longmans, Green).

Altenloh, Emilie (1914), *Zur Soziologie des Kino: Die Kino-Unternehmung und die sozialen Schichten ihrer Besucher* (Leipzig: Spamerschen Buchdruckerei).

Ang, Ien (1985), *Watching 'Dallas': Soap Opera and the Melodramatic Imagination* (London: Methuen).

*****Austin, Bruce A.** (1989), *Immediate Seating: A Look at Movie Audiences* (Belmont, Calif.: Wadsworth).

Blanchard, Phyllis (1928), *Child and Society* (New York: Longman's, Green).

*****Blumer, Herbert** (1933), *Movies and Conduct* (New York: Macmillan).

—— and **Philip M. Hauser** (1933), *Movies, Delinquency and Crime* (New York: Macmillan).

Brunsdon, Charlotte, and **David Morley** (1978), *Everyday Television: 'Nationwide'* (London: British Film Institute).

Cressey, Paul G. (1938), 'The Motion Picture Industry as Modified by Social Background and Personality', *American Sociological Review*, 3/4: 516–25.

Dyer, Richard (1979), *Stars* (London: British Film Institute).

Elsaesser, Thomas (ed.) (1990), *Early Cinema: Space, Frame, Narrative* (London: British Film Institute).

Forman, Henry James (1933), *Our Movie Made Children* (New York: Macmillan).

Gledhill, Christine (ed.) (1991), *Stardom: Industry of Desire* (London: Routledge).

*Hansen, Miriam (1983), 'Early Silent Cinema: Whose Public Sphere?', *New German Critique*, 29 (Spring–Summer), 147–84.

*—— (1991), *Babel and Babylon: Spectatorship in American Silent Film* (Cambridge, Mass: Harvard University Press).

Huyssen, Andreas (1986), 'Mass Culture as Woman: Modernism's Other', in T. Modleski (ed.), *Studies in Entertainment: Critical Approaches to Mass Culture* (Bloomington: Indiana University Press).

Jeffrey, Tom (1978), *Mass-Observation: A Short History*, Birmingham Centre for Contemporary Cultural Studies Stencilled Occasional Papers, No. 55, (Birmingham: BCCCS).

Jowett, Garth (1976), *Film: The Democratic Art* (Boston: Little, Brown).

Kuhn, Annette (1984), 'Women's Genres', *Screen*, 25/1: 18–28.

—— (1988), *Cinema, Censorship and Sexuality 1909–1925* (London: Routledge).

Le Bon (1895/1981), *The Crowd* (Harmondsworth: Penguin).

Lowery, Shearon A., and Melvin L. DeFleur (1995), *Milestones in Mass Communication Research: Media Effects* (New York: Longman).

Lynd, Robert S., and Helen Merrell (1929), *Middletown: A Study in American Culture* (New York: Harcourt, Brace, & World).

May, Lary (1983), *Screening out the Past: The Birth of Mass Culture and the Motion Picture Industry* (Chicago: University of Chicago Press).

Mayer, J. P. (1948), *British Cinemas and their Audiences* (London: Dennis Dobson).

Mitchell, Alice Miller (1929/1971), *Children and the Movies* (Chicago: University of Chicago Press; repr. New York: Jerome S. Ozer).

Modleski, Tania (1988), *The Women who Knew too Much: Hitchcock and Feminist Theory* (New York: Methuen).

Moley, Raymond (1938), *Are we Movie Made?* (New York: Macy-Masius).

Morley, David (1980), *The 'Nationwide' Audience* (London: British Film Institute).

Mulvey, Laura (1975), 'Visual Pleasure and Narrative Cinema', *Screen*, 16/3: 6–18.

Münsterberg, Hugo (1916/1970), *The Photoplay: A Psychological Study* (New York: Dover).

National Council of Public Morals (1917), *The Cinema: Its Present Position and Future Possibilities* (London: NCPM).

Peterson, Ruth C., and L. I. Thurstone (1933), *Motion Pictures and the Social Attitudes of Children* (New York: Macmillan).

Petro, Patrice (1989), *Joyless Streets: Women and Melodramatic Representation in Weimar Germany* (Princeton: Princeton University Press).

Pribram, E. Deidre (ed.) (1988), *Female Spectators: Looking at Film and Television* (London: Verso).

Richards, Jeffrey (1989), *The Age of the Dream Palace: Cinema and Society in Britain 1930–1939* (London: Routledge).

*—— and Dorothy Sheridan (eds.) (1987), *Mass-Observation at the Movies* (London: Routledge & Kegan Paul).

Rowson, Simon (1936), 'A Statistical Survey of the Cinema Industry in Great Britain in 1934', *Journal of the Royal Statistical Society*, 99(1), 67–129.

Smith, H. Llewellyn, et al. (1935), *The New Survey of London Life and Labour* (London).

*Stacey, Jackie, (1994), *Star Gazing: Hollywood Cinema and Female Spectatorship* (London: Routledge).

23

Hermeneutics, reception aesthetics, and film interpretation

Noel King

> Meaning in cinema is obvious: the average cinema film appears straightforward and can be understood immediately (with subtitles) by virtually everyone on the planet.
> John Ellis 1981: 14

> Very few spectators seek to read texts. They want to raid them for some relevance to their own interests. The study of movies undoubtedly has its place, but very few moviegoers want to study movies. They want to loot them.
> Raymond Durgnat 1981: 77

> Any interpretive practice seeks to show that texts mean more then they seem to say. But one might ask, why does a text not say what it means?
> David Bordwell 1989a: 64–5

Between readerly respect and textual pillage falls the shadow. The gap that opens across these quotation-epigraphs indicates an enduring dilemma for film criticism's way of understanding the act of film viewing: is it to be thought of as a self-evident, communally shared activity of meaning-making ('meaning is obvious') or as an unpredictable activity in which the many individualities present in a specific cinema audience submit a particular film to many different interpretative processings ('raid', 'loot')? Once the traditions of hermeneutics and reception aesthetics are recruited to the area of film studies, they soon confront a double question: what will count as an 'appropriate' reading of a given film and to what extent will the contingencies of the extra-textual determine the form of interpretative processing to which a particular film is subject? The central theoretical issue concerns the extent to which a text can be said to exert determinacy in the face of its many readings and uses. If reading is 'poaching', as Michel de Certeau (1984: 165–76) has suggested, if it is, 'by definition . . . rebellious and vagabond', as Roger Chartier (1994, p. viii) claims, then dispute necessarily centres on whether it is the rights of texts or of readers which are to prevail.

Interpretation

In *Interpretation and Overinterpretation* (1992), Umberto Eco intervenes in these debates on meaning, reading, and interpretation, principally by debating the 'neo-pragmatist' position that says texts have no essential coherence and that there is no difference between interpreting a text and using it. In outlining the 'dialectics between the rights of texts and the rights of their interpreters' (1992: 23), Eco side-steps debates

> **The central theoretical issue concerns the extent to which a text can be said to exert determinacy in the face of its many readings and uses.**

about authors' versus readers' intentions by introducing a third factor, the *'intention of the text'* (25). In the wake of the floating of the signifier, Eco wants to establish some terms upon which interpretation might be grounded. Accordingly, he distances himself from ecstatic notions of the interpretative licence afforded by a belief in unlimited semiosis by talking about the criteria enabling one to put forward an interpretation.

While acknowledging that interpretations sometimes work by generating 'associations', Eco would prefer these associations to be at least partially evoked by the text. When Wordsworth used the word 'gay' it did not possess the meaning it would later carry, and so an interpretation of Wordsworth should respect the 'cultural and liguistic background' (69) against which his writing was produced. Concerned, as he is, to establish the interpretative criteria by which one could specify a degree of textual facticity rather than infinite elasticity or malleability, Eco argues that some version of 'the text-in-itself' exists 'between the mysterious history of a textual production' (e.g. medieval practices of textual composition) and 'the uncontrollable drift of its future readings' (e.g. what a contemporary critic 'reads into' Wordsworth). A degree of determinacy is to be found in the fact that 'the text qua text still represents a comfortable presence, the point to which we can stick' (88).

This is a view which is anathema to the neo-pragmatist Richard Rorty (1992: 93), however, who argues that 'all anybody ever does with anything is use it. Interpreting something, knowing it, penetrating to its essence, and so on are all just various ways of describing some process of putting it to work.' Textual coherence, therefore, is not internal but produced by the uses to which a text is put: 'a text just has whatever coherence it happened to acquire during the last roll of the hermeneutic wheel' (97). Rorty's example is a 'set of marks' that could variously be described as English words, hard to read, a Joyce manuscript, an early version of *Ulysses*, or worth a million dollars, and he argues that this coherence 'is neither internal nor external to anything, it is just a function of what has been said so far about those marks' (98).

A similar concern to weigh the relationship between formal(ist) attention to textual structure and phenomenological attention to a reader's subjectivity is also central to the accounts of interpretation provided by hermeneutics and reception aesthetics. In the case of film studies, the turn towards reception theory has been in reaction to the perceived limitations of 'textual

analysis' (and the forms of text–subject relationship which this seems to imply). Patrice Petro (1986: 11) suggests that the interest in reception has grown out of 'a general dissatisfaction with prevailing theories of subject-formation in film and literary studies', while Janet Staiger (1992: 8) argues that 'reception studies' is preferable to 'textual studies', because of its emphasis on 'the history of the interactions between real readers and texts, actual spectators and films'. According to Staiger, 'textual studies' explains an object by generating an interpretation of it, whereas 'reception studies' seeks to understand acts of interpretation as so many historically and culturally situated events: 'Reception studies is not textual interpretation but a historical explanation of the activities of interpretation' (212).

Arguing in this way, Staiger is not only distancing herself from textual analysis but questioning the whole value of 'interpretation'. As such she is a part of a debate over whether or not academic writing on film should continue to generate 'new' interpretations of texts or whether it should perform some other, non-interpretative function. From the late 1970s on, an increasing exasperation has been expressed in relation to the proliferation of acts of interpretation in film and literary studies. In 1981 Jonathan Culler claimed that the 'one thing we do not need is more interpretations of literary works' (1981: 6). David Bordwell (1989a: 18, 261) echoed Culler's sentiment. Arguing that film studies had followed 'the interpretive path . . . already laid down in the humanistic disciplines', he goes on, 'We need no more diagnoses of the subversive moment in a slasher movie, or celebrations of a "theoretical" film for its critique of mainstream cinema, or treatments of the most recent art film as a meditation on cinema and subjectivity.' The show of exasperation from these two critics in the face of ever-proliferating interpretative manœuvres testifies to the triumph of criticism-as-interpretation within university humanities courses and to its broader reach into the domains of book, journal, and magazine publication. However, for Bordwell, one particularly baleful consequence of the institutionalization of intepretation-as-criticism has been the production of a person who 'look[s] for *interpretability*' in relation to the films he or she encounters (32), according to a 'dominant framework' of 'revealing' 'hidden' 'levels' of meaning (2).

It is this interpretative tradition of which Bordwell is heavily critical. Echoing Wittgenstein, he argues that 'we must look beneath what critics say and examine what they—concretely, practically—do' (1989a: 144).

For him, the production of an interpretation is 'a skill, like throwing a pot' and because 'its primary product is a piece of language, it is also a rhetorical art' (251). He therefore describes the critic as:

a person who can perform particular tasks: conceive the possibility of ascribing implicit or repressed meanings to films, invoke acceptable semantic fields, map them onto texts by using conventional schemata and procedures, and produce a 'model film' that embodies the interpretation. Though acquired by each individual, these skills and knowledge structures are institutionally defined and transmitted. And though it is possible to abstract a critical 'theory' or 'method' from individual 'readings', and thus to reify that theory or method as a self-sufficient procedure of discovery or validation, employing such an apparatus will not carry any critic all the way through an interpretation. Decisions about cues, patterns, and mapping must still be made by 'just going on' as Wittgenstein puts it, and following the tacit logic of craft tradition. (202, 204)

In this respect, Bordwell's account of the institution of—and academic institutionalization of—film criticism connects him, however loosely, with such things as Stanley Fish's notion of 'interpretive communities' (presented in *Is there a Text in this Class?*, 1980) and with Fish's subsequent work on 'professionalism' and 'the literary community' (now collected in *Doing what Comes Naturally*, 1990). At the same time, Bordwell's book has similarities with some other writing that seeks to show the specific institutional limits of interpretation (Culler 1988; Frow 1986; Weber 1985). Bordwell's characterization of this situation is to say: 'To use Todorov's term, film interpretation has become almost wholly "finalistic", based upon an a priori codification of what a film must ultimately mean. "It is foreknowledge of the meaning to be discovered that guides the interpretation." Many of the film's nuances now go unremarked because the interpretive optic in force has virtually no way to register them' (1989a: 260). The critical manœuvre of deciding that the 'the driven male protagonist' and 'overall style' of Anthony Mann's *Raw Deal* (1947) would 'put it into the class of *film noir*' is an example of such an 'optic' in action. Making such an interpretative move 'will recast the film along certain lines, throwing particular cues into relief and downplaying others' (142).

In presenting this account of the dominant practices of film criticism, and in stressing that 'meanings are not found, but made', Bordwell none the less insists that film criticism is not a place where total relativism or an infinite diversity of interpretation operate. For Bordwell, meaning is constructed out of textual cues (a composition, a camera movement, a line of dialogue), and the play between the individual and the institutional is evident in the fact that 'each individual' acquires those 'skills and knowledge structures' (3) courtesy of the institution. Critics, he claims, 'typically agree upon what textual cues are "there", even if they interpret the cues in differing ways' (3). However, a stronger distinction needs to be made between applying a grid of reading—or activating a regime of reading—and producing an interpretation. One could, for example, produce very different 'interpretations' of the imagistic significance of tattoos in Charles Laughton's *The Night of the Hunter* (1946), Jonathan Demme's *The Silence of the Lambs* (1991), and Martin Scorsese's 1992 version of J. Lee Thompson's *Cape Fear* (1962) while working within an agreed system of image, motif, or theme-based reading. To ask the significance of a motif in a text is to invite a series of declarations of interpretative difference which are all generated within a shared system constituted by the act of asking about the significance of a particular motif.

One of the main strengths (and provocations) of Bordwell's position lies in his claim that the institution of film criticism encourages a drive to produce innovative acts of critical exegesis at the same time as it operates certain limits and constraints in order to determine what will count as 'innovative'. The academic institution, he suggests, regulates the production of novelty in interpretation, and a broad rule for the interpreter is said to be: 'Quit when the interpretation starts to sound like those that we supplant' (1989a: 247). The film scholar's principal authority derives from 'knowing how to make movies mean', and this is done by applying a series of rhetorical strategies. Bordwell mentions one such interpretative strategy, that of '*domestication*, the taming of the new', an activity which 'subsumes the unfamiliar to the familiar'. This is said to be an 'institutionally necessary function' since 'the unschematised film is the uninterpretable film' (256). Given the drive to produce new interpretations, and given the potential endlessness of interpretation, the question inevitably arises of when and how to stop the pursuit of interpretative novelty. Initially, says Bordwell, one finds the threshold of interpretative termination only 'by positing a meaning that is more subtle, pervasive, remote, or elusive than other meaninings, particularly those already constructed by other critics' (246).

Historical poetics and cultural poetics

If Bordwell is sceptical of the value of 'interpretation', his counter-bid for a more productive form of film criticism promotes the twin notions of a 'historical poetics' and a 'neoformalism' (1989a: 263–74; 1989b: 369–98). According to Bordwell, 'neoformalist poetics' is not a methodology but 'an angle of heuristic approach, a way of asking questions' (1989b: 379). The neo-formalist critic's task is to provide a descriptive reconstruction of the options facing a filmmaker within a given historical conjuncture: 'Neoformalist poetics has been especially interested in how, against a background of conventions, a film or a director's work stands out' (1989b: 382). Bordwell says that the two main questions film criticism should ask are: 'how are particular films put together? Call this the problem of films' *composition*', and, 'what *effects* and *functions* do particular films have?' (1989a: 263). The principal virtue of a 'historical poetics' of cinema, therefore, rests in its attempt to reconstruct earlier acts of film comprehension (see e.g. Gunning 1991). Bordwell contends that a 'self-conscious historical poetics of cinema' (1989a: 266) is best placed to produce studies of particular cinematic forms, genres, and styles in such a way as would demonstrate 'how, in determinate circumstances, films are put together, serve specific functions and achieve specific effects' (266–7). The beginnings of such a critical practice are said to reside in the work of Arnheim, Russian Formalism, the early Soviet filmmakers, Bazin's (1967) writing on the evolution of cinematic language, and Noël Burch's (1979) work on the history of style in Japanese cinema. An 'open-textured historical poetics of film' would display, Bordwell argues, an 'awareness of historically existent options' (268) in cinema. The poetician's task is to analyse the 'norms, traditions, habits . . . that govern a practice and its products' (269). Such a historical poetics would study practices of reception as well as those of production, seeking to establish particular viewing conventions, 'the inferential protocols of certain historical modes of viewing' (272) or historically specific 'norms of comprehension' (274).

The neo-formalist perspective, therefore, escapes the cycle of interpretative one-upmanship described above by setting itself a different critical task, describing how innovation is achieved within a received and enabling system: 'Neoformalism balances a concern for revealing the tacit conventions governing the ordinary film with a keen interest in the bizarre film that subtly, or flagrantly, challenges them' (1989b: 382). This formulation also overlaps with points Stephen Greenblatt has been making since he invented the term 'new historicism' in the early 1980s to describe a particular orientation towards textuality and interpretation (1982: 3–6). Greenblatt uses the term interchangeably with 'cultural poetics' or a 'poetics of culture', and has recently added to his definition of what is involved (1994: 114–27). He does so, characteristically, by relating an anecdote concerning his visit to the Uffizi, in Florence, to attend an exhibition called 'A School for Piero', on the occasion of Piero's 500th anniversary. Although the exhibition sought to place Piero in context, the 'school' of the exhibition's title, Greenblatt was none the less struck by the strangeness of the Piero painting when displayed in this context:

I think the intention of the exhibit was, in a sense, the intention of the 'old historicism'. That is, to give you a sense of the context out of which Piero's work came. It would explain and help you to understand the remarkable achievement of Piero, indicating how he learned to do these things with perspective and how he learned to achieve certain effects of light and so on. But actually the effect of the exhibit on me was *exactly* the opposite of this. I was staggered by how *weird* Piero's double-portrait [of Federico de Montefeltro and his wife, Battista Sforza] was. . . . Not that the radical achievement of Piero had been normalised but rather that its true peculiarity, its unexpected, unforeseeable, surprising power, suddenly welled up. And I would say that one long-term commitment of any cultural poetics or new historicism—which is always, to some extent, an anti-historicism—would be to *intensify* and not to lose that sense of surprise. One of the problems with Marxist aesthetics was that it tended so easily to round up the usual suspects, and tended so much to collapse what looked remarkable into the predictable, the familiar, the same. But in fact one's experience of life is *precisely* of things that you can't possibly have predicted. *Afterwards* they may look inevitable or you may project back.

The anecdote demonstrates the importance of two key words for Greenblatt's formulations, 'resonance' and 'wonder'. The play between these two terms indicates the difference of the 'new historicism' from an 'old(er) historicism' and also from the 'new criticism' that was so dominant in American English departments from the 1950s to the late 1970s. Greenblatt's new historicism is not a stunningly sharp break with these earlier interpretative traditions, but it is a significant reorientation of them. Respectful of the deep historical contextualizing knowledge of the older historicism (for example, the work of Louis Martz and Stephen Orgel) new historicism is also mindful of the intense formal attention to detail contained in the new criticism. The particular reorientation contained in the new historicism rests in the extent to which it seeks to relate the 'wonder' of a particular textual artefact—the capacity for an artwork to astonish or surprise its viewer or reader in a moment of ravishing *arrest*—to a sense of the artwork's 'resonance'—the broader cultural-discursive framework which enabled it to be composed in the first place. The notion of 'resonance' directs our attention to those larger systems of cultural meaning which enable someone to write, paint, create an artistic work of some kind within the artistic or cultural conventions of a given historical period. The notion of 'wonder' describes those occasions on which the artwork escapes, exceeds, or somehow breaks away from the larger system which made it possible in the first place.

For Greenblatt, cultural poetics designates the play between the available discourses enabling cultural production in a particular time together with an acknowledgement of those occasions on which an artwork seems to move beyond the discursive or representational systems that obtain in a particular historical moment. In this respect, the parallel with Bordwell's neo-formalist interest in the 'bizarre' film is evident. However, just as Bordwell expresses an interest in 'historical modes of viewing', so Greenblatt's concern is as much with the habitual critical-theoretical ways of knowing about cultural objects as it is with the historically available representational systems enabling the composition of particular cultural artefacts in particular historical periods. In this sense, there is a double temporality to be placed on the concepts of 'resonance' and 'wonder'.

Cultural hermeneutics

Similar issues are also explored in Dudley Andrew's two books *Film in the Aura of Art* (1984) and *Mists of Regret* (1995). In *Film in the Aura of Art*, Andrew generates readings of seven film classics and offers a reconsideration of the work of Orson Welles and Kenji Mizoguchi. Discussing the relation of particular films to the systems in which they were produced, Andrew says, 'these films would be unreadable without the system whose sameness they hope to escape' (1984: 13). For Andrew, meaning 'is formed in the give and take between tradi-

tion and the encounter of the new' (14), and he later suggests, 'every film struggles to stand on its own apart from the system that confers intelligibility on it. Hollywood is only one name for the regularity of this process of differentiation endemic to the culture industry of every nation and art form' (193–4).

Andrew's critical practice unites formalism with phenomenology, and if it displays a closeness to Bordwell's position (on the side of formalism) it is also close to the phenomenological film criticism of Stanley Cavell (1981). Both Andrew and Cavell regard their film criticism as a kind of cultural conversation, and each claims to have been selected by the films they discuss rather then the other way about. So Andrew's 'close study of fertile films' is one in which 'the films have the first word and, frequently, the last' (1984, p. xi), while Cavell claims, 'I am always saying that we must let the films themselves teach us how to look at them and how to think about them' (1981: 25). Andrew's critical practice is in part calculated to discover 'what sort of films command the kind of respect I am according them?' (1984, p. xi) since, 'like all interpretation, my essays are a conversation within culture, not an argument about culture' (p. xiii).

By the time of *Mists of Regret*, Andrew has consolidated his critical stance into what he calls a 'cultural hermeneutics' (1995: 3), explaining that a cultural history of cinema seeks to establish 'an indirect reconstruction of the conditions of representation that permitted such films to be made, to be understood, even to be misunderstood, controversial, or trivial' (22). Inspired by Barthes's (1967) notion of *écriture* as outlined in *Writing Degree Zero* (rather than the different understanding later given to that term by Derrida and Kristeva), he coins the term 'optique' to designate 'the limited plurality of (cinematic) options available in any epoch' (1995: 19). 'Optique', he argues, carries 'an echo of option, of a limited set of possibilities alive at a given moment in a specific cinematic situation' and also 'involves the specification of audience expectations, needs and uses' (19).

The phenomenological side of Andrew's writing is evident when he suggests that the films with which he is concerned 'are entrances to a different way of being a spectator, not totally different . . . but different enough to tempt us to reconstruct the spectator to which they were addressed . . . As a historian, I am a spectator ready to become another spectator' (22–3). This is an argument anticipated in an earlier piece when he describes hermeneutics as 'a theory which entertains the relationship between a text worthy of respect and a consequential, historically grounded reading of that text . . . It seeks in the body of the text the significance which only that body has for it' (1982: 60). He goes on, 'The point of departure for hermeneutics couldn't be more evident: what do we have to do when we don't understand what we read?' (62). The apparent straightforwardness of his statement, however, belies the fact that 'not understanding' can take a number of quite different forms.

'Not understanding'

For example, it could indicate our lack of familiarity with the representational-compositional system within which the text was produced, thereby requiring a task of historical familiarizing. As Roger Chartier (8–9) has warned, 'A history of reading must not limit itself to the genealogy of our own contemporary manner of reading, in silence and using only our eyes; it must also (and perhaps above all) take on the task of retracing forgotten gestures and habits that have not existed for some time.' He argues against 'a purely semantic definition of the text (which inhabits not only structuralist criticism in all its variants but also the literary theories most attuned to a reconstruction of the reception of works)' in favour of a recognition of how 'a text . . . is invested with a new meaning and status when the mechanisms that make it available to interpretation change' and when 'its form is apprehended by new readers who read it in other ways than did previous readers' (3, 16). In saying this, Chartier has in mind the fact that while a text retains a certain textual structure, it also changes as the social circumstances and modes of reading that surround it undergo change. Chartier's point is the same as de Certeau's: namely, that the more distant a text becomes from the institutions that participated in its initial socio-cultural visibility, the

> **The more distant a text becomes from the institutions that participated in its initial socio-cultural visibility, the more likely it is that readers will exercise their capacities for forms of reading that depart from the terms within which the text initially counted on being read.**

more likely it is that readers will exercise their capacities for forms of reading that depart from the terms within which the text initially counted on being read.

A second instance of 'not understanding' could involve a clash of representational systems, thereby requiring a task of cross-cultural familiarizing. Umberto Eco's discussion of the reception of Michelangelo Antonioni's China film *Chung Kuo Cina* (1972), provides evidence of this form of misunderstanding (1986: 281–8). The differences between the encoding and decoding of Antonioni's film led to a clash of representational systems which in turn generated highly politically charged encounters. Eco reports that Antonioni wanted to present a 'tender, docile picture' of China and the Chinese because 'for us, gentleness is opposed to neurotic competition'. Unfortunately, 'for the Chinese that docility decodes as resignation' (285), and so the representation was taken to be an insulting one. Eco describes a specific sequence in the film, one involving the representation of the Nanking Bridge, as a way of indicating a clash of representational systems: 'Thus we see how the now famous criticism in *Renmin Ribao* could regard the shot of the Nanking bridge as an attempt to make it appear distorted and unstable, because a culture that prizes frontal representation and symmetrical distance shots cannot accept the language of Western cinema, which, to suggest impressiveness, foreshortens and frames from below, prizing asymmetry and tension over balance.' Consequently the Chinese critic 'sees another logic . . . and becomes indignant' (287).

Finally, 'not understanding' could be the positive consequence of our familiarity with a particular *dispositif*, whereby a state of incomprehension or unknowingness is the calculatedly produced relation of reader to textual artefact. As Schlegel (quoted in Hunter 1988: 164) observed, 'A classical text must never be entirely comprehensible. But those who are cultivated and who cultivate themselves must always seem to learn more from it.' This would seem to be a good description of the kinds of things art cinema viewers do when they consume art films. Ian Hunter has used the Schlegel quotation to argue that a reader's self-doubt and a text's inscrutability are the twin outcomes of a post-Romantic aesthetic system in which the notion of the unfathomable, aesthetically inexhaustible text, far from being an essential textual attribute, is purely the artefact of the critical machinery that is put to work on a text in order to produce a sense of 'aesthetic unfathomability'. When activated in this way it produces a sense of 'ethical incompletion' in the interpreter, as one who can only ever 'imperfectly' understand the text (1988: 159–84). Tony Bennett's gloss on the system Hunter is describing refers to it as involving the 'conception of the literary text as unfathomable—as the site for an endless practice of reading which can never be wrong yet never be right' (1990: 280).

For example, Bordwell (1989: 268) responds to Teresa de Lauretis's (1984) interpretation of *Bad Timing* (Nicolas Roeg, 1980) as a film which 'undercuts the spectator's pleasure by preventing both visual and narrative identification, by making it literally as difficult to see as to understand events and their succession, their timing: and our sense of time becomes uncertain in the film, as its vision for us is blurry'. Bordwell's comment on this is: 'On the contrary: such problems of identification and such temporal uncertainties constitute fundamental art cinema conventions, and they have shaped viewing skills ever since *Hiroshima mon amour* [Alain Resnais, 1959], *The Red Desert* ['Deserto rosso', Michelangelo Antonioni, 1964], *Persona* [Ingmar Bergman, 1966] and similar films became models for ambitious directors' (1989a: 268). To stay with the example of *Bad Timing*, one can see how Bordwell's point can be linked to some aspect of Hunter's arguments. First, if we contrast the editing technique used to introduce a flashback to the techniques used in classical Hollywood cinema, we can notice the way an interpretation is produced by the viewer's knowledge of or familiarity with a particular textual technique (here a mode of editing) *in tandem with* that viewer's performing of some ethical work on the self of the kind described by Hunter.

For a neo-formalist poetics, the flashback would be a device whose different renderings across the history of Hollywood could become the object of scrutiny (see Turim 1989). To recall some signallings of flashbacks in classical Hollywood cinema: wind blows through an open window as the camera moves in close on a table-top calendar whose leaves are 'blown' backwards until we reach the date it is necessary to reach for that point in the fiction (Douglas Sirk's *Written on the Wind*, 1957). A character has to tell another character what *really* happened in a gunfight that occurred some time earlier. He drags on a cigarette, says, 'Think back, Pilgrim,' and exhales the smoke, which momentarily defocuses the screen to enable us to make the transition back to that time (John Wayne to Jimmy Stewart in John Ford's 1962 film *The Man who Shot Liberty Valance*, although, to be more precise, this is a flashback within a flashback structure). An intense light fixes around the eyes of a character as the camera moves into close-up (typical film noir flashback).

Bad Timing, on the other hand, cuts directly, taking its viewer abruptly across different times and locations. And the controversial scenes depicting Alex's (Art Garfunkel) rape or 'ravishment' of the comatose Milena (Theresa Russell)—scenes which have provoked

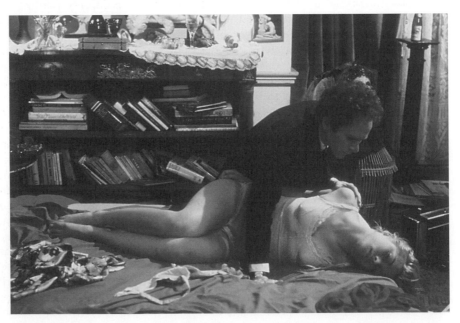

Structured ambiguity—*Bad Timing* (1980)

much writing on this film—are given to the viewer by way of a cut on the look of the investigator, Netusil (Harvey Keitel). This is one of the film's modernist gestures (or, as Bordwell would put it, 'art cinema conventions')—albeit one used to troubling sexual-political effect. Its consequence is to prompt the viewer to ask him- or herself whether this event really happened or whether it is Netusil's fantasy. And this viewer also knows that the film will not provide a definitive answer (no John Wayne here). So we encounter a film which employs some of the techniques of a modernist, art-cinema practice to produce structured ambiguity or the 'ambiguity effect'. Its viewer can never know for sure, although of course many viewers might decide one way or another and have conversations and arguments accordingly.

But one of the textual points of the film is to insist on the ambiguity and undecidability of this moment. There is no equivalent of third-person omniscient narration and no first-person character confession. All we have to go on is our capacity to interpret a textual device calculated to help produce an ambiguity effect. The 'correct' reading-position to take up is one in which we are content *not* to be able to decide. Consequently, these features of textual openness, ambiguity, and undecidability are achieved under definite conditions. The technique of editing constitutes a formal textual convention or condition, but it is one which needs to be accompanied by the ethical-interpretive work the viewer has to do on him- or herself. For example, the viewer has to inhabit a mode of reading which says: 'Read for maximum ambiguity; interpret knowing that there will be no definite resolution and take pleasure in this circumstance.' And one of the main points to be derived from a reading of Bordwell and Hunter is that particular critical protocols need to be in place in order for a film to be said to be ineffable. This ability to entertain ineffability constitutes a specific reading competence.

Reading formation

This discussion of the relations between texts and readings returns us to the central questions concerning text–reading–context relations. What is to count as a text and a reading, and to what extent is a text to be explained in terms of the conditions of its production, its first appearance and initial social circulation, as opposed to its subsequent insertion into a range of historically varying social–cultural contexts? In recent film studies, there has been an adoption of Tony Bennett's notion of a 'reading formation' (1983a, 1984) as one way of answering these questions and rethinking what historically situated viewers and/or commentators have done with specific films (Staiger 1992; Klinger 1994). Since Bennett's notion of a 'reading formation' has become a favoured way of rethinking the idea of 'reception' in relation to popular media texts, it seems appropriate to outline the reading formation that allowed Bennett to generate his notion.

The conception most immediately derives from Bennett's reading of Brecht (on 'rewriting'), Macherey (1977, on 'textual encrustations'), Carlo Ginzburg's suggestive account in *The Cheese and the Worms* (1978) of Menocchio as a reader, and the then-developing notion of intertextuality. But a broader context for the development of the term was the late 1970s reconsideration of Marxist aesthetics (to which Bennett's *Formalism and Marxism* (1979) was a strong contribution), principally in relation to literary texts as English literary critics became more familiar with the work of Brecht, Althusser, and Pierre Macherey. A revitalized Marxism focused on the notion of 'rewriting' and 'consumptional production' by advocating critical analysis of the historically variable existence and activities of texts. It was a mode of analysis that started from the proposition that 'what the entire history of discourse on literature shows is how much, in how many different circumstances, a text can be made to signify' (Mulhern 1978: 102). For this perspective 'text' means 'not only the works themselves but all the interpretations which have been attached to them and which finally are incorporated into them' (Macherey 1977: 7).

Bennett's conception of a 'reading formation' was meant to show that meaning is always transitive rather than inherent: 'It is not a *thing* which texts can *have*, but is something that can only be produced, and always differently, within the reading formations that regulate the encounters between texts and readers' (1983a: 218). It was also calculated to help rethink questions of popular reading, where reading was understood to refer to 'the means and mechanisms whereby all texts . . . may be "productively activated" during what is traditionally, and inadequately, thought of as the process of their consumption or reception'. The conception of reading formation was thus meant to attend to the actual history of a text's social functioning rather than privileging the originating conditions of a given text's production. The notion of a productive activation was meant to replace or displace the notion of textual interpretation: it provided a means of targeting the procedures whereby 'in the course of its history, a text is constantly re-written into a variety of different material, social, institutional and ideological contexts' (223). Bennett sought to 'imply a process in which texts, readers and the relations between them are all subject to variable determinations' (223). Any notion of an autotelically secure text-in-itself as a stable object-to-be-read, or even as a fixed unit able to be ranged alongside the many readings done of it, is dissolved into 'the reading relations and, within those, the reading formations which concretely and historically structure the interaction between texts and readers' (223). Rather than conceiving of an encounter between the polarized entities of 'the text' (open to a formal description) and 'the reading subject' (open to a reader-response perspective) Bennett proposed an investigation of the 'interaction between the *culturally activated* text and the *culturally activated* reader, an interaction that is structured by the material, social, ideological and institutional relationship in which both texts and readers are inescapably inscribed' (22).

In this way the conception of a 'reading formation' seeks to avoid both a textual formalism and an extra-textual notion of a social context that finds a particular textual expression. Texts, readers, and contexts are not conceived as 'separable elements, fixed in their relation to one another' because 'different reading formations . . . produce their own texts, their own readers and their own contexts' (8). Thus texts are studied 'as constituted as objects-to-be-read within the different reading formations which have modulated their existence as historically active, culturally received texts' (8). The study is simultaneously of texts in the light of their readings, readings in the light of their texts. The theoretical consequence of this, applied to 'the Bond phenomenon', and expressed in *Bond and Beyond* (Bennett and Woollacott 1987), is that the text that is read 'is an always-already culturally activated object', just as 'the reader is an always-already culturally activated subject . . . text and reader are conceived as being co-produced within a reading formation, gridded onto one another in a determinate compact unity' (64).

Barbara Klinger's (1994) book on Douglas Sirk uses Bennett's theoretical emphases to chart the way in which Sirk's films, over the years, have been characterized as 'subversive, adult, trash, classic, camp, and vehicles of gender definition' (p. xv). Her case-study of the reception of Sirk's films outlines 'how different historical, cultural, and institutional contexts produced meaning and ideological significance for Douglas Sirk melodramas from the 1950s to the 1990s' (157). By examining 'the institutional, cultural, and historical conditions that enabled these different identities to emerge' the book becomes a study of how some 'habitats of meaning operate', and by surrendering the idea that 'a film or novel has an essence that can be captured once and for all by the proper critical method' Klinger's analysis is able to attend to textual forms conceived as 'historical chameleons with shifting identities' (pp. xv, xvi). Thus Klinger is able to pursue the social destiny of a filmmaker's critical reputation and explore the various interpretive grids that were activated in order to make Sirk's films mean differently in different social-historical contexts. By presenting a picture of 'a text continually in the throes of transformation' (161), her book indicates 'the social conditions and institutions that help constitute contingent meanings for texts as they circulate publicly' (p. xvi). In doing this Klinger elaborates Janet Staiger's notion of a criticism that avoids textual interpretation in favour of a historical explanation of the event of interpreting a text.

> **Klinger is able to pursue the social destiny of a filmmaker's critical reputation and explore the various interpretive grids that were activated in order to make Sirk's films mean differently in different social-historical contexts.**

Historical case-studies of particular films 'show how, under different circumstances, films assume different identities and cultural functions' (1994, p. xvii). Klinger's analysis explores the way diverse regions of commentary seek to define the Hollywood film over a long period of time. 'Historical research helps reconstruct the semiotic environment in which the text/viewer interaction took place, showing us discourses at work in the process of reception' (p. xx). Such a theoretical orientation eschews textual interpretation, any analysis of the text's internal strategies, in favour of seeking to describe the institutions underpinning the text's social reception at various points in its social life. In a similar critical gesture, Paul Smith (1993), analysing the cultural presence of Clint Eastwood, uses the phrase 'cotextual histories' to refer to 'the ensemble of ever-shifting discursive possibilities that cohabit with any particular text in a given culture at a specific moment . . . cotextual histories implicate the processes of both the production and reception of a text or utterance' (p. xv).

'Rereading' and the category of queer

Once things take root, it is sometimes hard to remember how historically contingent, how adventitious, their emergence was. The emergence and rapid consolidation and institutionalization of 'queer theory' in the United States, United Kingdom, and Australia throughout the 1990s is a case in point. There has been an explosion of books, articles, and conferences as queer theory widens from being a localized rethinking of what to do in the already (in the United States) firmly established field of gay–lesbian studies, to engage the critical attention of other literary–film–cultural domains. A measure of the success of queer as a cultural category and an intellectual–academic commodity is evident in the way it exists both as a means of rereading cultural texts produced before the emergence of the category of queer (it enables an interpretive remapping of earlier cultural terrain) *and* it becomes an umbrella term used by current cultural producers to describe their products and activities (films, novels, plays, installations). Queer theory performs a double cultural-hermeneutic operation by rereading earlier texts and providing a self-understanding for current cultural production, whereas, say, the new historicism seems confined to the first activity of providing new ways of reading cultural texts from earlier historical periods. New historicism licenses interpretation in a new way, as does neo-pragmatism. And from a neo-pragmatist perspective two questions present themselves in relation to the category of queer: is the 'queer voice' *really* there or is it produced by an act of theoretical invention–intervention? Does this difference matter? Does queer theory become further evidence of the claims of neo-pragmatism? As a mode of reading, is it, to recall Rorty's remarks on *Ulysses*, simply something we currently are able to 'say about the marks'? Or, as Durgnat might put it, is it one more way we have of 'looting' texts?

For example, Alfred Hitchcock's film *Marnie* (1964) is found to contain a 'queer voice' (Knapp 1993). This reading was not available in 1964 because the ability to perform a queer theory analysis only became possible twenty-five years later as a result of a specific reorganization of critical protocols conducted in relation to film and literary texts. (And here it would be necessary to establish the relation of queer theory to the category of camp which had been around for thirty years (at least since Manny Farber's 1940s and 1950s film criticism) and which had attracted more concentrated critical attention from the 1960s (Sontag) on to 1970s and 1980s (Russo, Dyer, Britton) and 1990s (Ross, Robertson).)

Conclusion

The brief discussion of some issues attaching to the highly productive category of queer returns us to some of the points made at the beginning. If we accede to the notion that an appropriate interpretation is one which respects and, where necessary, reconstructs the meaning-making context into which the film first emerged, then Bordwell's 'historical poetics', Andrew's 'optique' and 'cultural hermeneutics', Greenblatt's 'cultural poetics', and Eco's respecting of lexical historicity all share a surprising amount of common ground. And yet the work of people like Bennett and Klinger alert us to the need to be aware of the many different contexts within which meanings can be produced for texts (something also supported by that aspect of Greenblatt's 'cultural poetics' which places an obligation on current acts of critical analysis to grasp and explain the 'difference' of an 'astonishing' artwork).

It is not, finally, a matter of opting for neo-pragmatism over cultural poetics or historical poetics over cultural hermeneutics. The different critical orientations explored throughout this chapter would, I think, agree with the following observation from Chartier: 'to be sure, the creators . . . always aspire to pin down their meaning and proclaim the correct interpretation, the interpretation that sets out to constrain reading (or viewing). But without fail, reception invents, shifts about, distorts' (1994, p. x). And, equally without fail, there will be generated an ongoing set of critical perspectives seeking to explain the gap that opens between textual composition and origin and textual peregrination and appropriation.

BIBLIOGRAPHY

Andrew, Dudley (1982) 'Interpretation, the Spirit in the Body', *Bulletin of the Midwest Modern Language Association*, 15/1: 57–70.

—— (1984), *Film in the Aura of Art* (Princeton: Princeton University Press).

—— (1995), *Mists of Regret: Culture and Sensibility in Classic French Film* (Princeton: Princeton University Press).

Barthes, Roland (1967) *Writing Degree Zero*, trans. Annette Lavers and Colin Smith (New York: Hill & Wang).

Bazin, André (1967), 'Evolution of the Language of Cinema', in *What is Cinema?* ed. and trans. Hugh Gray (Berkeley: University of California Press).

Bellour, Raymond (1975), 'The Unattainable Text', *Screen*, 16/3: 19–28.

Bennett, Tony (1979), *Formalism and Marxism* (London: Methuen)

—— (1983*a*), 'Texts, Readers and Reading Formations', *Literature and History*, 9/2: 214–27.

—— (1983*b*) 'The Bond Phenomenon: Theorising a Popular Hero', *Southern Review*, 16/2: 195–225.

—— (1984), 'Texts in History: The Determination of Readings and their Texts', *Australian Journal of Communication*, 5/6: 3–11.

—— (1990), *Outside Literature* (London: Routledge).

—— and **Janet Woollacott** (1987), *Bond and Beyond: The Political Career of a Popular Hero* (London: Macmillan).

*****Bordwell, David** (1989*a*) *Making Meaning: Inference and Rhetoric in the Interpretation of Cinema* (Cambridge, Mass.: Harvard University Press).

—— (1989*b*) 'Historical Poetics of Cinema', in R. Barton Palmer (ed.), *The Cinematic Text: Methods and Approaches* (New York: AMS Press).

Burch, Noël (1979), *To the Distant Observer: Form and Meaning in the Japanese Cinema* (Berkeley: University of California Press).

Cavell, Stanley (1981), *Pursuits of Happiness: Hollywood's Comedies of Remarriage* (Cambridge, Mass.: Harvard University Press).

Chartier, Roger (1994), *The Order of Books: Readers, Authors, and Libraries in Europe between the Fourteenth and Eighteenth Centuries*, trans. Lydia G. Cochrane (Stanford, Calif.: Stanford University Press).

Culler, Jonathan (1981), *The Pursuit of Signs: Semiotics, Literature, Deconstruction* (London: Routledge & Kegan Paul).

—— (1988), *Framing the Sign: Criticism and its Institutions* (Oxford: Basil Blackwell).

de Certeau, Michel (1984), *The Practice of Everyday Life*, trans. Steven F. Rendall (Berkeley: University of California Press).

de Lauretis, Teresa (1984), *Alice Doesn't: Feminism, Semiotics, Cinema* (Bloomington: Indiana University Press).

Durgnat, Raymond (1981), 'Nostalgia: Code and Anticode: A Review of Jonathan Rosenbaum's *Moving Places: A Life at the Movies*', *Wide Angle*, 4/4: 76–8.

Eco, Umberto (1986), 'De Interpretatione: The Difficulty of Being Marco Polo (On the Occasion of Antonioni's China Film)', in *Faith in Fakes: Essays*, trans. William Weaver (London: Secker & Warburg).

—— (1992), with **Richard Rorty, Jonathan Culler,** and **Christine Brooke-Rose** *Interpretation and Overinterpretation*, ed. Stefan Collini (Cambridge: Cambridge University Press).

Ellis, John (1981), 'Notes on the Obvious', in M. A. Abbas and Tak-Wai Wong (eds.), *Literary Theory Today* (Hong Kong: Hong Kong University Press).

Fish, Stanley (1980), *Is there a Text in this Class?: The Authority of Interpretive Communities* (Cambridge, Mass.: Harvard University Press).

—— (1990), *Doing what Comes Naturally: Change, Rhetoric, and the Practice of Theory in Literary and Legal Studies* (Durham, NC: Duke University Press).

Frow, John (1986), *Marxism and Literary History* (Oxford: Basil Blackwell).

Ginzburg, Carlo (1978), *The Cheese and the Worms: The Cosmos of a Sixteenth Century Miller*, trans. John and Ann Tedeschi (London: Routledge & Kegan Paul).

Greenblatt, Stephen J. (1982), 'Introduction', *Genre*, 13: 3–6.

—— (1990), *Learning to Curse: Essays in Early Modern Culture* (London: Routledge).

—— (1994), 'Intensifying the Surprise as well as the School', Interview with Noel King, *Textual Practice*, 8/1: 114–27.

Gunning, Tom (1991), *D. W. Griffith and the Origins of American Narrative Film: The Early Years at Biograph* (Chicago: University of Illinois Press).

Hansen, Miriam (1991), *Babel and Babylon: Spectatorship in American Silent Film* (Cambridge, Mass.: Harvard University Press).

Hunter, Ian (1988), 'The Occasion of Criticism', *Poetics*, 17/1–2: 159–84.

*****Klinger, Barbara** (1990), 'Digressions at the Cinema: Commodification and Reception in Mass Culture,' in James Naremore and Patrick Brantlinger (eds.), *Modernity and Mass Culture* (Bloomington: Indiana University Press).

—— (1994), *Melodrama and Meaning: History, Culture and the Films of Douglas Sirk* (Bloomington: Indiana University Press).

Knapp, Lucretia (1993/1995), 'The Queer Voice in *Marnie*', *Cinema Journal*, 32/4 (Summer), 6–23; repr. in Corey K. Creekmur and Alexander Doty (eds.), *Out in Culture: Gay, Lesbian and Queer Essays in Popular Culture* (London: Cassell).

Macherey, Pierre (1977), 'An Interview', ed. and trans. Colin Mercer and Jean Redford, *Red Letters*, 5: 3–9.

Mulhern, Francis (1978), 'Marxism in Literary Criticism', *New Left Review*, 108.

Palmer, R. Barton (ed.), *The Cinematic Text: Methods and Approaches* (New York: AMS Press).

Petro, Patrice (1986), 'Reception Theories and the Avant-Garde', *Wide-Angle*, 8/1: 11–17.

Rorty, Richard (1992), 'The Pragmatist's Progress', in Eco (1992).

Smith, Paul (1993), *Clint Eastwood: A Cultural Production* (Minneapolis: University of Minnesota Press).

*Staiger, Janet (1992), *Interpreting films: Studies in the Historical Reception of American Cinema* (Princeton: Princeton University Press).

Turim, Maureen (1989), *Flashbacks in Film: Memory and History* (New York: Routledge).

Weber, Samuel (1985), 'The Limits of Professionalism', *Oxford Literary Review*, 5/1–2: 59–79.

American cinema: history, industry, and interpretation

| 1 | American cinema and film history |

American cinema and film history

John Belton

Early film history

Between 1975 and 1985 the writing of film history underwent a modest revolution. Before this period, the standard texts on America (and world) film history tended to construct history according to nineteenth-century models of historiography which were grounded in theories of knowledge that were positivist and empiricist in nature. Events were understood as the consequences of the acts of individual agents, such as inventors, producers, directors, performers exhibitors, and others. There was little or no consideration of the cinema as a *systemic* phenomenon: as an institution determined by overlapping, contradictory, and/or mutually exclusive economic, technological, ideological, and socio-cultural demands.

These pioneering texts provided a linear account of film history, based on first-hand observation of the film industry and on data furnished by film industry personnel, trade magazines, newspaper articles and reviews, and other primary sources. Film historians were themselves often part of the very industry about which they were writing.

The first 'histories' were, in fact, written by and for the film industry. The writing of the history of the American cinema began with descriptions of its invention in the late 1880s and early 1890s. These took the form of patent applications, various articles in scientific journals (such as *Scientific American*), and accounts of the demonstrations of various motion picture cameras, projectors, and viewing mechanisms in newspapers. One of the first deliberate 'histories' of American film was written by an inventor, W. K. L. Dickson. Published in 1895, Dickson's *History of the Kinetograph, Kinetoscope, and Kineto-Phonograph* (co-authored with his sister, Antonia Dickson) recounted his development of the Kinetograph (a camera) and the Kinetoscope (a peepshow viewing device) for Thomas Edison. Published by Raff & Gammon, the distributor of Edison's Kinetoscope, the book served to promote sales of the Kinetoscope to potential customers.

The next major history was Robert Grau's *Theatre of Science* (1914). Grau was a theatrical agent and (later) a writer for the *Moving Picture World*. Grau's work celebrated the achievements of major American exhibitors, producers, directors, actors, screenwriters, and other creative talents. As Robert Allen and Douglas Gomery (1985: 59–60) have noted, Grau's history was published by subscription; the author raised money to publish the book by selling subscriptions to it to members of the film industry, offering them coverage in exchange for advance orders for the book. Like the Dicksons' earlier work, the book was part-history and part-advertisement. In both instances, history was 'in-house': it was written by (and for) the very individuals who were credited with creating it.

The objectivity of subsequent historians was never as severely compromised as that of Dickson and Grau, but the major works of history that followed were none the less products of individuals whose livelihood once (or still) depended upon the film industry. A former jounalist, Terry Ramsaye began work in the motion picture industry in 1915, serving as a publicist for the Mutual Film Corporation, where he launched a newsreel series, *Screen Telegram*. During the First World War he produced and edited films for the United States Treasury Department; after the war he was a publicist for Samuel Rothafel's Rialto and Rivoli Theatres in New York City. In 1920 he began writing *A Million and One Nights* (1926), a two-volume history of the motion picture. A considerable portion of this history was commissioned and published in the early 1920s by *Photoplay* magazine, a trade journal that also enjoyed a general readership. At the same time, he wrote and produced films for the Associated Screen News of Canada and edited ethnographic feature films, including *Grass* (1925) and *Simba* (1928). From 1931 to 1949 he was the editor of the trade magazine *Motion Picture Herald*.

Prominent figures within the next few generations of film historians were also personally involved with the film industry, including Benjamin Hampton (1931), Lewis Jacobs (1939), Paul Rotha (1930), Arthur Knight (1957), Kenneth Macgowan (1965), and David Robinson (1973). For these early historians, the writing of film history became an act of affirmation of the cinema's importance as a social, economic, cultural, and/or aesthetic form. These historians were, in effect, too close to the cinema—too much a part of it themselves—to hold it up to a more critical and distanced scrutiny.

Rewriting the history of the American cinema

During the 1970s a new generation of film scholars began to correct the errors of the standard histories and to present new research. A number of these scholars, including Thomas Cripps, Garth Jowett, Daniel Leab, Robert Sklar, and others, had been trained as historians. Others, such as Tino Balio, had extensive prior experience as scholars working with primary source material in the field of English literature. Most of this new generation were academics. The exceptions—independent scholars such as Kevin Brownlow (1968, 1990) and Anthony Slide (1970, 1976, 1978)—played a crucial role in gathering together primary research collections and in rewriting the history of silent American cinema; academics, however, tended to ignore their work because it lacked a clearly articulated theoretical base.

In his discussion of film historiography, Robert Sklar (1990) identifies three generations of film scholars: the self-taught non-academics (journalists, archivists, filmmakers); the academically trained humanists (himself included); and cinema studies doctorates. For Sklar, revisionist historiography is the product of the third generation—cinema studies doctorates, such as Robert Allen and Douglas Gomery (1985) and David Bordwell, Janet Staiger, and Kristin Thompson (1985). Taking issue with these scholars' theoretical and ideological conservativism (i.e. their non-radical, non-Marxist social vision), Sklar complains that revisionists tend to 'emphasize institutions and processes' rather than 'the lived experiences of people' (1990: 28).

The rewriting of traditional history by this second and third generation of historians was indebted, in part, to the recent deposits of primary research materials in American and European archives. Wisconsin-based activities, such as the publication of *The Velvet Light Trap* (1971) and Tino Balio's first two books (1975, 1976), relied extensively on the United Artists Collection, which contained films and production information for United Artists films, as well as for pre-1948 Warner Bros., RKO, and Monogram films. This collection, of which Balio was the curator, was donated to the Wisconsin Center for Film and Theater Research in 1969. Rarely seen archival prints also launched revisionist interest in early cinema ten years later. In 1978, at a film conference held by the International Federation of Film Archives (FIAF) at Brighton, film archivists and film scholars met, watched rare early films made between 1900 and 1906, and began to rethink standard histories of early cinema.

The publication in 1975 of Robert Sklar's *Movie-Made American* led a challenge to the traditional narrative of American film history as told by Ramsaye and others. At the very beginning of his history, Sklar reviews the standard account of factors leading to the film industry's movement from New York to Hollywood in the 1910s. Hampton (1931/1970: 77, 79), Ramsaye (1926: 533–4), and others had insisted that independent filmmakers using unlicensed cameras in violation of exclusive rights held by the Motion Picture Patents Company (MPPC, the Trust) had moved to southern California in order to escape the watchful eye of the MPPC and, when necessary, to flee the Trust's detectives by crossing the border into Mexico. Sklar points out that the Mexican border was not close; it was at least five hours away by car. He also notes that the Trust's subpoenas could just as easily have been served on the New York sales offices of these independent companies. He suggests that the move to California was driven, instead, by climate, which permitted year-round filmmaking, by the terrain, which featured a variety of potential settings (mountains, the desert, the city, the sea); by cheap land for studio space; and by an inexpensive, non-unionized labour force (Sklar 1975: 67–8).

An example of New Left historiography, Sklar's book sought 'to reconstruct a past in which common people struggled to determine their own lives and institutions' (Sklar 1990: 20). The standard film histories, such as those by Hampton and Ramsaye, had described the audiences for early (pre-1914) cinema as composed of lower-class immigrants and blue-collar workers (Ramsaye 1926: 431; Hampton 1931/1970: 47). Sklar reaffirms this argument, linking the rise of the movies to the emergence of a 'new social order' and identifying early audiences as members of 'the lowest and most invisible classes in American society' (1975: 3). However, in the late 1970s revisionist film historians such as Russell Merritt (1973) and Robert C. Allen (1979) used business directories and other demographic data to identify the location of urban nickelodeons in Boston and New York City. Both Merritt and Allen discovered

that most nickelodeons were, in fact, located in middle-class, as well as in lower-class, neighbourhoods. These findings were used to support an argument that the motion picture was, from its beginning, a middle-class amusement and to trace the growing use of the cinema by the middle class to express and reinforce its own bourgeois values.

The 1970s revisionism of Merritt and Allen has recently been subject to yet another revision which Allen (1996) has subsequently dubbed 'postrevisionism'. Using additional primary sources that list more New York City nickelodeons and give more detailed census data, Ben Singer (1995) concludes that immigrants and the working-class population did indeed constitute the majority of moviegoers as late as 1908–10 and that the standard histories 'may not have been as far off the mark as revisionist historians maintain' (28).

New methodologies

Revisionist history is characterized, in part, by its response to attacks, by comtemporary theorists on the methodology employed in traditional film history. These attacks begin to appear in the early 1970s, most notably in Jean-Louis Comolli's multi-part essay 'Technique et idéologie' (1971–2). Comolli argued that traditional film history was both empiricist in method and idealist in concept.

Employing Marxist theories of historical determination, Comolli called, instead, for a 'materialist' historiography. In part, materialist historiography was simply a repudiation of the methods of standard historiography. Traditional histories were regarded as teleological and reliant upon cause-and-effect reasoning. Thus, as André Bazin suggests in 'The Myth of Total Cinema' (1967), silent black-and-white cinema gave way to sound, colour, and widescreen cinema, and the cinema evolved, in Darwinian fashion, towards greater and greater realism. Comolli rejected the concept of linear causality, arguing instead for a non-linear, uneven development in which events are the results of a field of different, often opposing, determinations; change is not continuous but rather is characterized by gaps and delays. Comolli also rejected the notion that the cinema evolves autonomously, independent of technological, economic, and ideological forces. He insisted that its evolution was highly *mediated*; cinematic forms were determined by the often contradictory demands of technology, economics, and ideology. Comolli's 'materialism' thus views history as a non-linear series of ruptures whose uneven process reflects underlying contradictions within the existing social, economic, and cultural institutions that inform it.

Comolli's call for materialist historiography has not yet been fully answered, but the influence of his essays can be seen in the work of Edward Buscombe (1977, 1978), Edward Branigan (1979), James Spellerberg (1979), Kristin Thompson and David Bordwell (1983), Allen and Gomery (1985), and John Belton (1992).

Much as film theory and criticism sought to systematize its study of the cinema by drawing upon the 'sciences' of structural anthropology (Claude Lévi-Strauss), Marxism (Louis Althusser), and psychoanalysis (Sigmund Freud, Jacques Lacan), the new historians also brought scientific method to bear upon historical methodology. Ed Buscombe (1977) invoked Thomas Kuhn's *The Structure of Scientific Revolutions* (1962). At the same time, Allen (1977) and Allen and Gomery (1985) expressed their concern with issues of historio-

graphy and the development of a methodology for conducting film history by referring to E. H. Carr's *What is History?* (1961). While Kuhn pointed out the quasi-subjective nature of scientific observation, Carr noted the role that interpretation played in reading events yet rejected a relativism that would insist that one interpretation of an event was therefore as good as another. Carr viewed history as a 'continuous process of interaction' between events and their interpreters.

Following Kuhn, film historians began to view historiography as a subclass of epistemology. Kuhn problematized empiricist observation, arguing that scientific observation occurs through models, paradigms, and frames of reference, which shape those observations. Science does not explain phenomena; instead, it *constructs* phenomena, filtering it through pre-existing assumptions or conventions. Film historians, ranging from Allen and Gomery to Charles Musser, read Terry Lovell's *Pictures of Reality* (1980) and began to weigh the relative merits of empiricism and conventionalism. As a theory of knowledge, empiricism 'posits a real world which is independent of consciousness and theory, and which is accessible through sense-experience' (Lovell 1980: 10). Empiricism argues that the subjectivity of the observer does not invalidate the knowledge gained from observation. Conventionalism, on the other hand, insists that observation is always subjective, that knowledge is socially produced, and that, because events are necessarily perceived through frames of reference or systems of knowledge that transform them, these events cannot be known or observed.

Robert Allen and Douglas Gomery's book *Film History* (1985) has proved to be one of the seminal texts in the shaping of contemporary film historiography. In it, the authors draw extensively on Kuhn, Carr, and Roy Bhaskar's *A Realist Theory of Science* (1978), from whom (and Rom Harré) they appropriate the concepts of 'generative mechanisms' and 'realism'. Realism, a philosophy of science and history, is empiricist in so far as it acknowledges a world 'out there' that exists independently of the scientist and that can be known. But unlike the empiricist, the realist views observable phenomena as the effects of non-observable processes; though not observable, these processes do exist and are not simply constructions posited by the scientist or historian. It is these processes, or generative mechanisms, that produce observable events. Against this background, Allen and Gomery seek to negotiate the two extremes of empiricism and conventionalism by

> **Comolli rejected the concept of linear causality, arguing instead for a non-linear, uneven development in which events are the results of a field of different, often opposing, determinations; change is not continuous but rather is characterized by gaps and delays. Comolli also rejected the notion that the cinema evolves autonomously, independent of technological, economic, and ideological forces. He insisted that its evolution was highly *mediated*; cinematic forms were determined by the often contradictory demands of technology, economics, and ideology. Comolli's 'materialism' thus views history as a non-linear series of ruptures whose uneven process reflects underlying contradictions within the existing social, economic, and cultural institutions that inform it.**

combining empirical observation with theories of knowledge to identify generative mechanisms that determine historical events.

First, they discuss the approaches which structured traditional histories, breaking them down into aesthetic, technological economic, and social categories. Each of these approaches is seen, in turn, as driven by a single notion of historical change—the agency of the individual (the director, the inventor, etc.). For example, for Allen and Gomery, aesthetic film history can be understood as the history of film masterpieces which had been created by the individual genius of a director, writer, producer, or star. It involves the study of the cinema as an art form and of filmmakers as individual artists whose visions determine the thematic and aesthetic significance of their films.

Allen and Gomery note several problems with this approach. In celebrating the cinema as an art form, historians tended to neglect other aspects of the cinema, such as its identity as an economic, technological, and/or cultural product. Furthermore, the masterpiece tradition dealt with only a small percentage of films, concentrating on a handful of art films and ignoring the great majority of ordinary films produced by the industry. More importantly, this tradition understood the value, meaning, and significance of individual works to be determined by the degree to which they transcended their historical or industrial context. Finally, what determined a masterpiece's uniqueness was the genius of the individual artist whose vision it reflected.

In response to the limited nature of the explanation of historical events found in traditional approaches such as the masterpiece tradition, Allen and Gomery propose that historians consider instead a network of causal elements that determine events. They refer to this system of determinations as generative mechanisms, i.e. forces which can be seen to have a certain explanatory value in accounting for the production of observable events. These mechanisms are, in effect, systemic rather than isolated occurrences. History is the result of specific modes of production, determined by various economic, technological, and ideological demands.

The masterpiece tradition relied extensively on the critical evaluation of films, on the analysis of visual style, and on the identificaton of authorial vision. In their discussion of *Sunrise* (1927), Allen and Gomery barely mention the film itself, concentrating instead on the film's 'background'. They explore director F. W. Mur-

nau's 'biographical legend', producer William Fox's interest in Murnau and the film in terms of his promotional strategies for elevating the status of his studio, and various public discourses surrounding Murnau and the production and reception of the film. Thus the historical significance of *Sunrise* is seen to reside not so much in its aesthetic qualities as in its exemplary status as a product of a complex background set of various economic, technological, and social forces.

Historicizing classical Hollywood

The same year that witnessed the publication of Allen and Gomery's book also saw the appearance of David Bordwell, Janet Staiger, and Kristin Thompson's monumental effort *The Classical Hollywood Cinema* (1985). During the 1970s film theorists, ranging from the editors of *Cahiers du cinéma* and *Screen* to individual authors such as Laura Mulvey (1975) and Colin MacCabe (1974), repeatedly referred to a phenomenon called 'classical Hollywood cinema'. But the exact nature of this 'dominant cinema', which they somewhat vaguely characterized as 'illusionistic', 'transparent-invisible', and/or 'patriarchal', was never clearly defined. In their book, Bordwell, Staiger, and Thompson set out to provide a film historian's definition of this phenomenon.

The approach taken by the authors to classical Hollywood cinema is multifaceted. Classical Hollywood cinema is understood, in part, as a 'style' of filmmaking. Its stylistic (and narrative) features are explored in terms of the relationship of those features to sets of other dterminants, chiefly to developments in film technology and changes in the economic structure of the film industry. However, the development of classical Hollywood cinema is not directly driven by the forces of technology and economics; rather these forces are mediated by the entire system (mode of production) of industrial practices, including those of various professional organizations such as the Academy of Motion Picture Arts and Sciences, the American Society of Cinematographers, and the Society of Motion Picture (and Television) Engineers.

The most prominent features of their history illustrate the revisionist nature of their project. Unlike traditional histories, theirs draws not only on films, but on other, previously neglected, bodies of evidence such as manuals for screenwriters and cinematographers, publications of craft guilds and unions, and technical

A silent masterpiece *and* product of complex background forces—Murnau's *Sunrise* (1927)

and trade journals. Their focus is not on a handful of masterpieces but on 'typical' films. Thus their work draws on an 'unbiased sample' of 100 films made during the period 1915–60. Conclusions made from this study were then tested by analysing them against a background set of 200 additional films from the same period. At the same time, while traditional histories focused their discussion of style on first usages of specific devices, Bordwell et al. looked instead at usages when a stylistic device had become a norm.

> **The most prominent features of their history illustrate the revisionist nature of their project. Unlike traditional histories, theirs draws not only on films, but on other, previously neglected, bodies of evidence such as manuals for screenwriters and cinematographers, publications of craft guilds and unions, and technical and trade journals. Their focus is not on a handful of masterpieces but on 'typical' films. At the same time, while traditional histories focused their discussion of style on first usages of specific devices, Bordwell et al. looked instead at usages when a stylistic device had become a norm.**

For Bordwell, Staiger, and Thompson (1985), classical Hollywood cinema constituted a 'group style' or norm of stylistic practices that had evolved by (roughly) 1917. Prior to 1917 the modes of production and stylistic practices within Hollywood continued to change—from the cameraman system (1896–1907), in which films were made by cameramen; to the director system (1907–9); the director–unit system (1909–14), in which a director, like Griffith, developed and paid his own stock company; to the producer–unit system (1914 on) within which an individual producer co-ordinated the production process. However, once the system had maximized its efficiency as a mode of production, the basic features of the film style that had evolved remained 'constant across decades, genres, studios, and personnel' (1985: 10).

Their history viewed this group style or norm as more or less static from 1917 to 1960. Disruptions of that norm occurred in the form of individual directors, whose work occasionally violated dominant practice, and in the form of film noir, which deviated in terms of stylistic and narrative conventions from earlier Hollywood cinema. Bordwell argued that neither film noir nor auteur films resulted in the creation of a radically new norm. Indeed, even with the advent of sound, colour, and widescreen, the system of classical Hollywood cinema remained more or less constant.

For example, in one of his more elegant arguments, Bordwell notes that the coming of sound posed a threat to the classical paradigm developed during the silent era. The classical mode of narration depended upon a careful breakdown of shots, through editing, to analyse the action of a scene. Yet early sound technology, which was based on the exact synchronization of sound and image (on the same strip of film in two of the three major sound systems), encouraged the use of a single camera filming a scene without interruption. In order to maintain the classical paradigm, the studios introduced the practice of filming with multiple cameras. This gave them different views (in precise sound synchronization) of the same scene, which could then be edited together in the conventional manner (1985: 304–5). Thus stylistic continuity was maintained across the breach created by the new technology.

The chief flaw of the book lies in its insistence upon the resilience and constancy of the classical paradigm to the exclusion of any sense of the significance of the variations within that paradigm from period to period. Thus the disruptive nature of the transitions to sound, colour, and widescreen and the dramatic violation of classical norms by film noir tend to be softened and viewed as moments of continuity rather than discontinuity. In other words, the book pursues the systemic nature of classical Hollywood cinema to a fault. Yet, given the extensive time period under investigation (1917–60), classical Hollywood cinema ultimately does enjoy a certain constancy and coherence as a system, especially in comparison to other modes of film practice, such as European art cinema.

Recent developments

In the 1990s the macroscopic perspective of Bordwell, Staiger, and Thompson's *Classical Hollywood Cinema* gives way to more microscopic histories, and the interest in classical Hollywood cinema seen in that work gives way to an interest in early, pre-classical cinema, exemplified in the work of Charles Musser (1990, 1991), Eileen Bowser (1990), Richard Koszarski (1990), Tom Gunning (1991), Miriam Hansen (1991), Gregory Waller (1995), Janet Staiger (1995), David Robinson (1996), and others. Pioneering this approach was Scribner's History of the American Cinema series, which appeared in 1990 with three separate volumes devoted to the silent American cinema. Musser's book dealt with 1895–1907; Bowser's with 1907–15; Koszarski's with 1915–28.

Like *The Classical Hollywood Cinema*, these books draw on primary research conducted by the authors, using trade periodicals, daily and weekly (local) newspapers, national and local archives, Supreme Court and local circuit court records, and various special collections, ranging from scrapbooks to personal and corporate papers housed at regional libraries, museums, and universities. These diverse historical materials are used to provide a technological, economic, and cultural context within which early cinema takes its place as an entertainment practice alongside other contemporary forms of commercial entertainment.

Thus Musser explores the relation of pre-1907 cinema to illustrated lectures, magic-lantern and photographic slide shows, amusement park and fairground attractions, vaudeville, theatre, newspapers, cartoon strips, popular songs, fairy-tales, and other cultural forms. As a result, Musser's history is not 'the history of a product (the films) or of an industry (Hollywood and its precursors) but of a practice' (1990: 495). For Musser, the 'presentational' techniques of pre-existing entertainment practices (such as those of illustrated lectures or lantern slide shows) determined the way an event is presented or a story is told. For example, in turn-of-the-century cinema it was the exhibitor rather than the producer who assembled discrete shots into a coherent entertainment experience and who, thus, maintained editorial control over the narrative.

In a similar manner, Eileen Bowser focuses on general 'practices' rather than on individual pictures. Traditional histories covering her period (1907–15) celebrate film directors, such as D. W. Griffith, and film masterpieces, such as *The Birth of a Nation* (1915). Although 'the names of the director and the film appear in almost every chapter' (1990, p. xii), Bowser's chief interest lies with normative practices of the period rather than with individual artists or works.

Though Richard Koszarski necessarily foregrounds the emergence of the star system and the feature-length film in examining the period 1915–28, his book also emphasizes industrial context over individual achievement. Like the other books in the series, Koszarski's volume provides a portrait of American cinema as an *institution*, as an industrial (i.e. economic and technological) and socio-cultural entity.

Recent work on American film history follows the institutional approach taken by Bordwell, Staiger, and Thompson and the Scribner series. These books do not construct their histories around individual films, filmmakers, or stars, but around institutional practices. They explore the cinema's status as a mode of production and its significance as a new form of mass consumption, drawing less upon films themselves than upon primary, print-based research materials such as trade journals, studio files, court testimony, censorship records, screenwriting manuals, and other forms of evidence.

Douglas Gomery provides economic analyses of film production (*The Hollywood Studio System*, 1986) and exhibition (*Shared Pleasures*, 1992). Janet Staiger contributes a history of film reception (*Interpreting Films*, 1992) and a cultural study of the representation of female sexuality on the screen between 1907 and 1915 (*Bad Women*, 1995). Using Hays Office memos, Lea Jacobs examines 'fallen woman' films of the 1930s in *The Wages of Sin* (1991). In a similar effort, communications historian Gregory Black consulted studio production records and Production Code Administration files to construct a history of motion picture censorship in the 1930s in *Hollywood Censored* (1994). Tino Balio added another volume and decade (the 1930s) to Scribner's series of institutional histories with *Grand Design* (1993). Columbia University Press has recently published a number of books that examine various aspects of the American cinema. These books integrate recent work in cultural theory, such as the construction of national identity and the representation of race, class, gender, and other forms of social identification, with issues of film historiography. This series looks back to earlier works of cultural history, such as those of Charles Eckert (1978) and Lary May (1980). Yet it also responds to more recent models, integrating Eckert's and May's approach with the institutional model pioneered by Bordwell *et al.* through studies of directors (Sikov 1994), stars (Studlar 1996), genres (Jenkins

1992; Rubin 1993; Doherty 1993; Berenstein 1995; and Paul 1995), and individual films (Bobo 1995).

The writing of American film history reflects the changing landscape of contemporary film studies. As Bowser notes, 'every generation needs its own history, rewritten with a different emphasis and from new viewpoints' (1990, p. xi). Traditional histories, such as Ramsaye's, convey contemporary—or rather, nineteenth-century—attitudes towards the writing of history. Traditional histories attempt to read the twentieth-century reality of rapid industrialization, urbanization, mass production, and the advent of consumer culture in nineteenth-century terms. Historians romanticize history, rewriting the anonymity of mass culture as a saga of individual achievements. Thus, for them, history consists of the individual accomplishments of heroic inventors, showmen, producers, directors, stars, and others.

Prompted by the academicization of film studies, revisionist film history reflects the theoretical turmoil of the 1970s. Influenced by linguistics and structural anthropology, film theorists attempt to view the cinema not in terms of its individual elements but as a 'system'. Events are the products, not of isolatable features of observable reality, but of underlying structures that exist in a complex system of interconnectedness with one other. Allen and Gomery's 'scientific' approach to film history thus seeks to identify the underlying structures, or generative mechanisms, that determine historical events. This notion of 'system' informs subsequent film historiography, which attempts to explore American cinema as a coherent mode of production that results in the creation of a classical paradigm—classical Hollywood cinema—which can be seen to possess a group style. The interest of contemporary historians in classical Hollywood cinema as a mode of production and as a group of stylistic, economic, and industrial practices culminates in the institutional approach to American cinema that has characterized the most recent phase of American film historiography. The relationship of Hollywood as an institution to its role within the larger phenomenon of American culture has emerged as the latest site for the rewriting of film history. In this way, the history of film history reflects the history of film studies and documents our ever-changing understanding of what it means to do film history

BIBLIOGRAPHY

Allen, Robert (1977), 'Film History: The Narrow Discourse', in Lawton and Staiger (1977).

—— (1979), 'Motion Picture Exhibition in Manhattan, 1906–1912: Beyond the Nickelodeon', *Cinema Journal*, 18/2 (Spring), 2–15.

—— (1996), 'Manhattan Myopia; or, Oh! Iowa!', *Cinema Journal*, 35/3 (Spring), 75–103.

*—— and **Douglas Gomery** (1985), *Film History: Theory and Practice* (New York: Knopf).

Altman, Charles F. (1977), 'Towards a Historiography of American Film', *Cinema Journal*, 16/2 (Spring), 1–25.

Balio, Tino (1975), *United Artists: The Company Built by the Stars* (Madison: University of Wisconsin).

—— (ed.) (1976), *The American Film Industry* (Madison: University of Wisconsin).

—— (1993), *Grand Design: Hollywood as a Modern Business Enterprise 1930–1939* (New York: Scribner's).

Bazin, André (1967), 'The Myth of Total Cinema', in *What is Cinema?*, i (Berkeley: University of California Press).

Belton, John (1992), *Widescreen Cinema* (Cambridge, Mass.: Harvard University Press).

—— (1994), *American Cinema/American Culture* (New York: McGraw-Hill).

Berenstein, Rhona (1995), *Attack of the Leading Ladies: Gender, Sexuality, and Spectatorship in Classic Horror Cinema* (New York: Columbia University Press).

Bhaskar, Roy (1978), *A Realist Theory of Science* (Atlantic Highlands, NJ: Humanities Press).

Black, Gregory (1994), *Hollywood Censored: Morality Codes, Catholics, and the Movies* (New York: Cambridge University Press).

Bobo, Jacqueline (1995), *Black Women as Cultural Readers* (New York: Columbia University Press).

***Bordwell, David, Janet Staiger,** and **Kristin Thompson** (1985), *The Classical Hollywood Cinema: Film Style and Mode of Production to 1960* (New York: Columbia University Press).

Bowser, Eileen (1990), *The Transformation of Cinema 1907–1915* (New York: Scribner's).

Branigan, Edward (1979), 'Color and Cinema: Problems in the Writing of History', *Film Reader*, 4: 16–34.

Brownlow, Kevin (1968), *The Parade's Gone By* (New York: Ballantine).

—— (1990), *Behind the Mask of Innocence: Sex, Violence, Prejudice, Crime: Films of Social Conscience in the Silent Era* (London: Jonathan Cape).

Buscombe, Ed (1977), 'A New Approach to Film History', in Lawton and Staiger (1977).

—— (1978), 'Sound and Color', *Jump Cut*, 17 (Apr.), 48–52.

Carr, E. H. (1961), *What is History?* (New York: Vintage Books).

Comolli, Jean-Louis (1971–2), 'Technique et idéologie',

Cahiers du cinéma, no. 229 (May–June 1971), 4–21; no. 230 (July 1971), 51–7; no. 231 (Aug.–Sept. 1971), 42–9; nos. 234–5 (Dec.–Jan. 1971–2), 94–100; no. 241 (Sept.–Oct. 1972), 20–4; part 1 trans. Diana Matias in Bill Nichols (ed.), *Movies and Methods*, ii (Berkeley: University of California Press, 1985); parts 3 and 4 trans. Diana Matias in Philip Rosen (ed.), *Narrative, Apparatus, Ideology: A Film Reader* (New York: Columbia University Press, 1985).

Dickson, W. K. L., and Antonia (1895/1970), *History of the Kinetograph, Kinetoscope, and Kineto-Phonograph* (Raff & Gammon; repr. New York: Arno Press).

Doherty, Thomas (1993), *Projections of War: Hollywood, American Culture, and World War II* (New York: Columbia University Press).

Eckert, Charles (1978), 'The Carole Lombard in Macy's Window', *Quarterly Review of Film Studies*, 3/1 (Winter) 1–21.

Gomery, Douglas (1986), *The Hollywood Studio System* (New York: St Martin's).

—— (1992), *Shared Pleasures: A History of Movie Presentation in the United States* (Madison: University of Wisconsin Press).

Grau, Robert (1914), *Theatre of Science: A Volume of Progress and Achievement in the Motion Picture Industry* (New York: Broadway).

Gunning, Tom (1991), *D. W. Griffith and the Origins of American Narrative Film: The Years at Biograph* (Urbana: University of Illinois Press).

Hampton, Benjamin (1931/1970), *History of the American Film Industry From its Beginnings to 1931* (repr. New York: Dover).

Hansen, Miriam (1991), *Babel and Babylon: Spectatorship in American Silent Film* (Cambridge: Harvard University Press).

Jacobs, Lea (1991), *The Wages of Sin: Censorship and the Fallen Woman Film 1928–1942* (Madison: University of Wisconsin Press).

Jacobs, Lewis (1939), *The Rise of the American Film* (New York: Columbia University's Teachers College).

Jenkins, Henry (1992), *What Made Pistachio Nuts? Early Sound Comedy and the Vaudeville Aesthetic* (New York: Columbia University Press).

Knight, Arthur (1957), *The Liveliest Art* (New York: New American Library).

Koszarski, Richard (1990), *An Evening's Entertainment: The Age of the Silent Feature Picture 1915–1928* (New York: Scribner's).

Kuhn, Thomas S. (1962), *The Structure of Scientific Revolutions* (Chicago: University of Chicago Press).

Lawton, Ben, and Janet Staiger (eds.) (1977), *Film: Historical–Theoretical Speculations, The 1977 Film Studies Annual*, part 2 (New York: Redgrave).

Lovell, Terry (1980), *Pictures of Reality: Aesthetics, Politics, and Pleasure* (London: British Film Institute).

MacCabe, Colin (1974), 'Realism and the Cinema: Notes on some Brechtian Theses', *Screen*, 15/2 (Summer), 7–27.

MacGowan, Kenneth (1965), *Behind the Screen* (New York: Delta).

May, Lary (1980), *Screening Out the Past: The Birth of Mass Culture and the Motion Picture Industry* (New York: Oxford).

Merritt, Russell (1973), 'Nickelodeon Theaters: Building an Audience for the Movies', *AFI Report*, 4/2 (May), 4–8.

Mulvey, Laura (1975), 'Visual Pleasure and Narrative Cinema', *Screen*, 16/3: 6–18.

Musser, Charles (1990), *The Emergence of Cinema: The American Screen to 1907* (New York: Scribner's).

—— (1991), *Before the Nickelodeon: Edwin S. Porter and the Edison Manufacturing Company* (Berkeley: University of California Press).

Paul, William (1995), *Laughing Screaming: Modern Hollywood Horror and Comedy* (New York: Columbia University Press).

Ramsaye, Terry (1926), *A Million and One Nights*, 2 vols. (New York: Simon & Schuster).

Robinson, David (1973), *The History of World Cinema* (New York: Stein & Day).

—— (1996), *From Peepshow to Palace: The Birth of American Film* (New York: Columbia University Press).

Rotha, Paul (1930/1960), *The Film till Now* (London: Spring); rev. with Richard Griffith (New York: Twayne).

Rubin, Martin (1993), *Showstoppers: Busby Berkeley and the Tradition of Spectacle* (New York: Columbia University Press).

Sikov, Ed (1994), *Laughing Hysterically: American Screen Comedy of the 1950s* (New York: Columbia University Press).

Singer, Ben (1995), 'Manhattan Nickelodeons: New Data on Audiences and Exhibitors', *Cinema Journal*, 34/3 5–35.

*Sklar, Robert (1975), *Movie-Made America: A Cultural History of American Movies* (New York: Random House).

—— (1990), 'Oh! Althusser: Historiography and the Rise of Cinema Studies', in Robert Sklar and Charles Musser (eds.), *Resisting Images: Essays on Cinema and History* (Philadelphia: Temple University Press).

Slide, Anthony (1970), *Early American Cinema* (London: A. S. Barnes).

—— (1976), *Early Women Directors* (London: A. S. Barnes).

—— (1978), *Aspects of American Film History Prior to 1920* (Metuchen, NJ: Scarecrow Press).

Spellerberg, James (1979), 'Technology and Ideology in the Cinema', *Quarterly Review of Film Studies*, 2/3 (Aug.), 288–301.

Staiger, Janet (1992), *Interpreting Films: Studies in the Historical Reception of American Cinema* (Princeton: Princeton University Press).

—— (1995), *Bad Women: Regulating Sexuality in Early American Cinema* (Minneapolis: University of Minnesota Press).

Studlar, Gaylyn (1996), *This Mad Masquerade: Stardom and Masculinity in the Jazz Age* (New York: Columbia University Press).

Thompson, Kristin, and David Bordwell (1983), 'Linearity, Materialism and the Study of Early American Cinema', *Wide Angle*, 5/3: 4–15.

Waller, Gregory (1995), *Main Street Amusements: Movies and Commercial Entertainment in a Southern City* (Washington: Smithsonian Press).

2

History and cinema technology

Duncan Petrie

The cinema is predicated on machines. Indeed in the early days of the fledgling medium the audience was attracted by the technology rather than the actual material being exhibited. As Stephen Heath notes, 'what is promoted and sold is the experience of the machine, the "apparatus". The Grand Café programme is headed with the announcement of "Le Cinématographe" and is continued with its description . . . only after that description is there mention of the titles of the films to be shown . . . relegated to the bottom of the programme sheet' (Heath 1980: 1).

Raymond Williams makes a useful distinction between two categories frequently treated as interchangeable in discussions of cinema technology. He defines *technical invention* as 'a specific device, developed from practical experience or scientific knowledge and their interaction'. These include pre-cinema devices associated with the development of still photography, and others concerned with the display of moving images including magic lanterns, zoetropes, and other optical entertainments. Such inventions are subsequently 'selected, improved and developed into a *systematic technology* of "film" or "cinema" ' (Williams 1983: 12–13). This implies that technology is necessarily directed towards particular goals or uses. Indeed, the interest most film scholars have in technology is very much in how it relates to aesthetic practice. Their task, therefore, is not only to describe and identify particular inventions, technolo

gies, and techniques, but to account for them within a dynamic perspective grasping the processes of development and change.

> **Technology is necessarily directed towards particular goals or uses. Indeed, the interest most film scholars have in technology is very much in how it relates to aesthetic practice. Their task, therefore, is not only to describe and identify particular inventions, technologies, and techniques, but to account for them within a dynamic perspective grasping the processes of development and change.**

Idealist technological history

Since the formative years of film theory, many discussions of technology have been underpinned by an idealist, evolutionary perspective, characterized by a romantic conception of the autonomous individual subject and a teleological view of historical process. Robert Allen and Douglas Gomery (1985) have identi-

238

fied two strands of such evolutionary history. The 'great man' theory is grounded upon an assumption of the autonomous agency of human subjects, regarding technological development as dependent upon the activities of a handful of individual inventors and pioneers. This theoretical perspective underpins such pioneering works of film history as Gordon Hendricks's painstaking investigations (1961, 1964, 1966) into the origins of the cinema in America and John Barnes's similar endeavours (1976, 1983, 1988, 1992) in relation to Britain.

A second evolutionary approach shifts the focus from the creative individual to the technology and its relationship to aesthetic consequences. Raymond Williams describes this approach as involving 'technological determinism': 'new technologies are discovered by an essentially internal process of research and development, which then sets the conditions for social change and progress. The effects of the technologies, whether direct or indirect, foreseen or unforeseen, are, as it were, the rest of history' (Williams 1974: 13).

Such an approach informs the work of the technological historian Raymond Fielding, for whom each technological advance contains within it the seeds of subsequent aesthetic uses by filmmakers. Technology sets the parameters and determines the space within which innovative techniques can occur: 'Just as the painter's art has changed with the introduction of different media and processes, just as the forms of symphonic music have developed with the appearance of new kinds of instruments, so has the elaboration and refinement of film style followed from the introduction of more sophisticated machinery' (Fielding 1967).

But however detailed and compelling as narrative, the shortcomings of such approaches lie in their inability to account adequately for why the cinema developed at the times, in the places, and in the forms it did; and why certain technologies and techniques were adopted and others rejected in the emergence of the new medium. For example, technological determinism cannot explain why the same basic film technology was utilized for widely divergent kinds of filmmaking in the early days of cinema, yet by the mid-1910s the narrative feature film had emerged as the dominant form of filmmaking practice.

The most influential analysis of the development of the cinema within idealist film theory may be found in the seminal writing of André Bazin. More theoretical than empirical in his project, Bazin locates what he terms 'the myth of total cinema' in the minds of the individuals who invented the medium: 'In their imaginations they saw the cinema as a total and complete representation of reality; they saw in a trice the reconstruction of a perfect illusion of the outside world in sound, colour and relief' (Bazin 1967: 20). The evolution of cinema is viewed as moving towards an ever-increasing verisimilitude, a re-creation of the world in its own image, with each subsequent innovation—from still images, to movement, to sound, to colour—marking a more advanced stage in the process. (This was subsequently extended by Charles Barr (1963) to the introduction of widescreen cinema. Processes like CinemaScope open out the frame, presenting a greater impression of depth which, following Bazin's own discussion of deep focus, preserved the essential ambiguity of the real within the image.) This also gives rise to a history based on 'firsts' or 'founding moments', signposted by such 'innovations' as the first 'projected' film programmes by the Lumière brothers in Paris in 1895; the first 'talkie', *The Jazz Singer*, in 1927 and the first three-colour Technicolor feature, *Becky Sharp*, in 1935; and the first CinemaScope film, *The Robe*, in 1953. Others might include the first use of Dolby stereo sound, *Star Wars*, in 1977, and the first animated feature to be entirely generated by computer, *Toy Story*, in 1996.

The first steps away from evolutionary models of technological development began to emerge in the 1970s. In his examination of the development of deep-focus cinematography in Hollywood in the 1940s, Patrick Ogle (1972) challenges conventional understandings which associated this with innovative 'auteurs' such as Orson Welles and William Wyler. Drawing upon primary source material, including technical journals such as *American Cinematographer*, he identifies a historical lag between the technical possibility of deep focus and its adoption, a gap accounted for by the resistance of Hollywood cinematographers to deviations from the established visual style of soft tonal qualities and shallow depth of field. Unfortunately Ogle does not offer any explanation as to why Hollywood cameramen were so conservative. Moreover, his assertion of the centrality of cinematographer Gregg Toland in the exploitation of the technical possibility of deep focus in films like *The Grapes of Wrath* (1940), *The Long Voyage Home* (1940), and *Citizen Kane* (1941) resurrects an idealist perspective by merely shifting the focus from the director to the technician as creative individual.

Barry Salt's copious writings on the history of film

technology and style (1976, 1983/1992) represent a similar move away from overtly linear models. Salt constructs an avowedly empirical analysis based on detailed examination of primary sources coupled with close viewings of numerous films. Highly critical of deterministic theories, he regards technology as at best a loose pressure on film practice and cites instances where technology can be seen to respond to aesthetic demands such as the trend towards longer shots in 1940s Hollywood, which led to the development of more sophisticated camera dollies. Despite an impressive grasp of historical detail, Salt's unashamed empiricism, a method he terms 'scientific realism', set him increasingly at odds with the major currents of contemporary theoretical development.

Anti-idealist technological history

Under the influence of the twin discourses of Marxism and psychoanalysis, film theory in the 1970s began to shift the focus away from idealistic perspectives towards more materially based analyses concerned with the operation of the various factors underpinning and determining the nature of the cinematic process, including the question of technology. The most obvious 'external' factor, given the highly capitalistic nature of the film business, was the role of economics. Douglas Gomery's (1976) analysis of the coming of sound in Hollywood utilizes neo-classical economic theory to explain technological change via a three-stage model incorporating invention, innovation, and diffusion. The first is dominated by the research and development activities of two corporate giants, the American Telephone and Telegraph Corporation (AT&T) and the Radio Corporation of America (RCA) aimed at developing telephone and radio technology respectively. One side-effect common to both was the perfected capability for sound recording and reproduction. The innovation stage was subsequently driven by the activities of two Hollywood film companies, Warner Bros. and Fox, who adapted the basic technology for practical use in the production and exhibition of sound films. The third and final phase involved the diffusion of such new techniques throughout the industry, with all the other studios embracing sound. At each stage, the overriding concern of the companies concerned was the maximization of long-term profitability.

Edward Buscombe (1977) comments that Gomery's model is very persuasive, but since it does not explain the need for a particular innovation, it suggests the operation of ideological rather than economic concerns. Buscombe proceeds to apply this theory to the development of colour in cinema. According to 'the myth of total cinema', colour would appear to signify a greater realism than black and white, the ideology of realism 'has never been a question of what *is* real but of what is *accepted* as real' (Buscombe 1977: 24). When colour was first introduced it tended to be restricted to 'unreal' genres such as cartoons, musicals, fantasies, and comedies, while the more 'realistic' genres—crime films, war films, documentaries, and newsreels—were predominantly in black and white. The ideological appeal of colour, it seems, was both as a signifier of spectacle and as a self-conscious celebration of the technology itself. Of course, this cannot be divorced from economic considerations, since the association of colour with particular genres aided Hollywood's need for product differentiation.

The role of ideology was given centre-stage even more in subsequent materialist theory. Stephen Heath criticizes historians like Barry Salt for their belief in technology as a self-autonomous instance:

Cinema does not exist in the technological and then become this or that practice in the social; its history is a history of the technological and the social together, a history in which the determinations are not simple but multiple, interacting, in which the ideological is there from the start. (Heath 1980: 6)

In a similar vein, the influential French Marxist critic Jean-Louis Comolli criticizes perspectives which consider technology to be ideologically neutral by attempting to show how the cinematic apparatus is necessarily rooted in ideology—'the machine is always social before it is technical'. Comolli writes:

the historical variation of cinematic techniques, their appearance–disappearance, their phases of convergence, their periods of dominance and decline, seem to me to depend not on a rational-linear order of technological perfectibility nor an autonomous instance of scientific 'progress' but much rather on the offsettings, adjustments, arrangements carried out by a social configuration in order to represent itself, identify itself, and itself produce itself in its representation. (Comolli 1980: 121)

This particular mode of representation, which presents itself as 'natural' rather than ideologically determined, previously underpinned Renaissance painting and photography and is rooted in the invention of artificial perspective, which centres space around the eye. This in turn designates the perceiving subject as the origin of meaning, and hence transcendentally separated from the material world—the autonomous subject of idealist theory. Comolli may share with Bazin a fascination with the relationship between representation and the real, but he regards 'realism' as ideologically constructed, suppressing difference and promoting identity in the interests of the dominant bourgeois order.

While materialist arguments have proved persuasive, Comolli's conception of ideology has been criticized as somewhat monolithic, tending towards the abstract and the ahistorical. John Belton suggests that he 'reduces the complex interaction of various (often conflicting) ideologies to the uniform operation of a single unchanging ideology' (Belton 1988), while James Spellerberg notes: 'Dominant ideology is dominant, not total, and the technology as well as the signifying practice of the cinema is created in the field of ideology and is subject to the stresses and contradictions of that field' (Spellerberg 1977: 296).

The materialist idea of technological development has informed less abstract commentaries such as those of Peter Wollen (1980) and Steve Neale (1985). Wollen stresses both the heterogeneity of technology—citing various examples of the interplay of developments in the fields of mechanics, optics, chemistry, and electronics—and the uneven process of technological development, in which innovations in one area can produce conservatism or even retreat in another. The introduction of sound, for example, created obstacles in the fields of lighting and film stocks, enforced a shift from location to studio filming, altered shooting techniques, and led to the automation of the studio laboratory process.

John Belton similarly applies a materialist method to his historical analysis of the introduction of Cinema-Scope. He poses the question why, given the invention of the anamorphic Hypergonar lens in the late 1920s, it was a further twenty-five years before the introduction of CinemaScope as a viable widescreen process. His answer is that while technological and ideological determinants existed in the 1920s to support the introduction of anamorphic cinema, there was no economic interest from either lens manufacturers or the studios. By the 1950s all the economic factors had been reversed, with a declining film industry desperate to find ways to reinvest the cinema with new appeal as a spectacle distinct from the experience offered by television. Belton is at pains to note that this is not an instance of a delayed take-up of an already existing

Wollen stresses both the heterogeneity of technology—citing various examples of the interplay of developments in the fields of mechanics, optics, chemistry, and electronics—and the uneven process of technological development, in which innovations in one area can produce conservatism or even retreat in another. The introduction of sound, for example, created obstacles in the fields of lighting and film stocks, enforced a shift from location to studio filming, altered shooting techniques, and led to the automation of the studio laboratory process.

technology, as empiricist historians would have it. Rather, recent technical developments in the fields of optics, stock design, colour, sound, and screen fabric were crucial to the emergence of anamorphic cinema in the 1950s. Ideology also played a part in how the experience of CinemaScope was differentiated not only from conventional cinema but also from other new formats such as 3-D and Cinerama.

Equally rich in historical data is the consideration by David Bordwell and Janet Staiger of the role of technology within Hollywood cinema, which they regard as 'a distinct mode of film practice with its own cinematic style and industrial conditions of existence' (Bordwell and Staiger 1985, p. xiii). Technological development can be explained by the operation of one or more of three basic factors—production efficiency (economy), product differentiation (novelty), and adherence to standards of quality (aesthetic norms)—with the classical Hollywood stylistic paradigm being constructed in relation to specific ideologies governing narrative, realism, and spectacle. These factors can either complement or collide with one another: for example, change to effect product differentiation may be costly at least in the short run. Differentiation also takes place within defined limits of stylistic standardization.

Within their analysis, Bordwell and Staiger (1985) identify certain historical agents of change, including institutions such as the manufacturing and supply firms Eastman Kodak, Western Electric, and Bell & Howell

The delights of
CinemaScope as advertised
in publicity for *The Ten
Commandments* (1956)

and professional associations like the American Society of Cinematographers, the Society of Motion Picture Engineers, and the Academy of Motion Picture Arts and Sciences. Cumulatively these served to transfer the industry's economic structures and aesthetic precepts to the spheres of technological innovation and film form, ensuring that the latter developed within the constraints set by the former. For example, the professional associations played a major role in regulating technical change and linking the production sector with the service industries.

Multideterminate approaches also opened up interesting questions of the diffusion of technological development outside Hollywood. Gomery (1980) extends his discussion of the economics of sound technology to the complex process of Europe's conversion to sound via a consideration of the economic relations between the advanced capitalist countries at the time. Against the historical backdrop of post-Second World War multinational expansion, particularly in the new technological industries such as automobiles and motion pictures, Gomery proceeds to chart a process of economic struggle between the American studios and equipment manufacturers and their European competitors, the latter determined to resist the seemingly overwhelming tide of Hollywood imperialism.

This struggle resulted in the formation of a loose cartel between Western Electric, RCA, and the mainly German-backed conglomerate Tobis-Klanffilm to divide up the world for patent rights. While this cartel was only partially successful, it provides a tangible example of the central role of capitalist expansion and competition in the process of technological diffusion.

Dudley Andrew (1980) examines a similar process of struggle with regard to the introduction of colour in France after the Second World War. His intentions are to demonstrate the role played by self-conscious (as opposed to invisible) ideological discourse in relation to technological and economic determinants in a particular historical context characterized by suspicion and mistrust. He describes the relevant material circumstances of the time: the hegemony of Technicolor, the (limited) potential of new processes derived from the German Agfacolor system, and the hostility towards America felt in France—particularly in the wake of the Blum–Byrnes accord, which limited the extent to which the French cinema industry could resist Hollywood domination, effectively restricting a regeneration of indigenous production. As it transpired, colour was barely used in French production until the mid-1950s owing to a combination of factors including the influence of contradictory ideological discourses. On the one hand, there was an appreciation of the artistic potential of Technicolor, displayed in some British films like *Henry V* (1944). But, because of certain technical and economic factors, Technicolor could not meet the increase in demand, and after the failure of indigenous experiments the French industry adopted the Belgian Geva system. At the same time the strategy adopted by the French industry to resist American domination was the pursuit of a 'quality' aesthetic which, as Andrew puts it, 'would unquestionably have preferred the formal and saturated look of Technicolor to the more casual and documentary look of Agfa processes' (1980: 73). He concludes that these contradictory discourses of a desire and loathing for American technology served to paralyse the development of colour in France until 1953, when, unsettled by rumours of a new danger posed to their industry by television, French producers began to put up the extra finance necessary for colour production.

Perhaps one of the major differences between recent historical accounts and earlier writing is a certain degree of self-reflexivity with regard to theoretical approaches and methods, including the processes of selection and interpretation of data. As Edward Branigan notes, 'categories arranged in a scheme are not just a way of looking at the world but in some sense determine what we see' (Branigan 1979: 16). And, as John Belton argues, materialist histories are as prone to this as idealist histories: 'Idealist methodologies will reveal only the essential linearity of history, while materialist methodology will only reveal the essential contradictions and discontinuities that underlie historical change' (Belton 1988: 23). While this contingency might seem to negate any claims to 'truth', it does underline the importance of clarity of purpose and method, of defining terms and categories, and of making the implicit explicit. It has also guided scholars back towards the treasure-trove of historical data, refining our understanding of the complexities of the technologies of cinema and their use in concrete, historically specific contexts.

BIBLIOGRAPHY

Allen, Robert, and **Douglas Gomery** (1985), *Film History: Theory and Practice* (New York: Kopt).

Andrew, Dudley (1980), 'The Post War Struggle for Colour', in Teresa de Lauretis and Stephen Heath (eds.), *The Cinematic Apparatus* (London: Macmillan).

Barnes, John (1976), *The Beginnings of the Cinema in England* (Newton Abbot: David & Charles).

—— (1983), *The Rise of the Cinema in Great Britain* (London: Bishopsgate).

—— (1988), *Pioneers of the British Film* (London: Bishopsgate).

—— (1992), *Filming the Boer War* (London: Bishopsgate).

Barr, Charles (1963/1974), 'CinemaScope: Before and After', in Gerald Mast and Marshall Cohen (eds.), *Film Theory and Criticism* (Oxford: Oxford University Press).

Bazin, André (1967), 'The Myth of Total Cinema', in *What is Cinema?*, 2 vols., ed. and trans. Hugh Gray, i (Berkeley and Los Angeles: University of California Press).

Belton, John (1988), 'CinemaScope and Historical Methodology', *Cinema Journal*, 28/1: 22–44.

Bordwell, David, and **Janet Staiger** (1985), 'Technology, Style and Mode of Production', in David Bordwell, Janet Staiger, and Kristin Thompson, *The Classical Hollywood Cinema: Film Style and Mode of Production to 1960* (London: Routledge).

Branigan, Edward (1979), 'Colour and Cinema: Problems in the Writing of History', *Film Reader*, 4: 16–34.

Buscombe, Edward (1977), 'Sound and Colour', *Jump Cut*, 17: 23–5.

Comolli, Jean-Louis (1980), 'Machines of the Visible', in Teresa de Lauretis and Stephen Heath (eds.), *The Cinematic Apparatus* (London: Macmillan)

Fielding, Raymond (ed.) (1967), Introduction, in *A Technological History of Motion Pictures and Television* (Berkeley and Los Angeles: University of California Press).

Gomery, Douglas (1976), 'The Coming of the Talkies: Invention, Innovation Diffusion', in Tino Balio (ed.), *The American Film Industry* (Madison: University of Wisconsin Press).

—— (1980/1985), 'Economic Struggle and Hollywood Imperialism: Europe Converts to Sound', in Elisabeth Weis and John Belton (eds.), *Film Sound: Theory and Practice* (New York: Columbia University Press).

Heath, Stephen (1980), 'The Cinematic Apparatus: Technology as Historical and Cultural Form', in Teresa de Lauretis and Stephen Heath (eds.), *The Cinematic Apparatus* (London: Macmillan).

Hendricks, Gordon (1961), *The Edison Motion Picture Myth* (Berkeley and Los Angeles: University of California Press).

—— (1964), *The Beginnings of the Biograph* (New York: privately published).

—— (1966), *The Kinetoscope* (New York: privately published).

*****Neale, Steve** (1985), *Cinema and Technology: Image, Sound, Colour* (London: British Film Institute).

Ogle, Patrick (1972), 'Technological and Aesthetic Influences on the Development of Deep Focus Cinematography in the United States', *Screen*, 13/1: 45–72.

Salt, Barry (1976), 'The Evolution of Sound Technology', *Film Quarterly*, 30/1: (Fall), 19–32.

—— (1983/1992), *Film Style and Technology: History and Analysis* (London: Starword).

Spellerberg, James (1977), 'Technology and Ideology in the Cinema', *Quarterly Review of Film Studies*, 2/3: 288–301.

Williams, Raymond (1974), Television: Technology and Cultural Form (London: Fontana).

—— (1983), 'British Film History: New Perspectives', in James Curran and Vincent Porter (eds.), *British Cinema History* (London: Weidenfeld & Nicolson).

Wollen, Peter (1980), 'Cinema and Technology: A Historical Overview', in Teresa de Lauretis and Stephen Heath (eds.), *The Cinematic Apparatus* (London: Macmillan).

3

Hollywood as industry

Douglas Gomery

While the study of film may involve a concern with aesthetics, technology, ideology, and audience, it is the study of film as an industry which remains central and is basic to all other cinema studies. For in most of the world cinema is first of all organized as an industry, that is as a collection of businesses seeking profits through film production, film distribution, and the presentation of movies to audiences (whether in theatres, on television, through video, or by some new method). So, although we may wish that cinema was not a business, we none the less need to study the industrial character of film in order to understand fully the impact and influence of motion pictures.

A central question which most scholars characteristically face is: how does the study of the organization and control of the film industry help to explain the aesthetics, ideology, and reception of film? There is no simple answer to this, but I side with the argument that, while the film industry does not straightforwardly determine the aesthetic and ideological characteristics of film, it none the less sets the constraints within which aesthetics, ideology, and reception must operate. However, the theory linking the study of film as an industry to concerns of aesthetics, ideology, and reception remains to be worked out and will constitute one of the central tasks for film historians.

The study of the film industry itself is complex, but it is simplified by one key historical fact. Since the 1920s—that is, for most of the history of cinema—

one industry, that based in the United States and known as Hollywood, has dominated the world. Thus the locus of study for the history of the film industry properly begins with Hollywood, not because the cinema industry based in the United States has produced the best films (by some criteria) but because it has forced all other national cinemas to begin by dealing with the power of Hollywood as an industry.

First principles

Hollywood is first of all an industry, a collection of profit-maximizing corporations operated from studio headquarters in the United States, and so, like all film industries, it consists of three fundamental components: production, distribution, and presentation of feature films.

Production. Films must be created. Since the early 1910s this has been done in studios in and around Los Angeles in an area generically known as Hollywood. However, it encompasses more than that city section: the Universal Studios, for example, are in Universal City, Warner Bros. in Burbank.

Distribution. Once films are made, Hollywood companies then peddle their films around the world. World-wide distribution has long been the basis of Hollywood's power and no other film industry has been as far-reaching for as long as Hollywood.

Presentation. Finally, movies are watched in theatres and cinemas, and on television at home. Prior to the television age, films were shown principally in theatres which were sometimes vast 6,000-seat movie palaces. Since the 1960s most people see most movies at home on television.

The key question then is: how did a collection of major studio corporations (Hollywood) come to dominate the production, distribution, and exhibition of movies and continue to maintain its control through the coming of sound, the innovation of colour and widescreen images, and the diffusion of television and home video? I shall explore the answers to this question by examining the history of Hollywood as an industry, identifying four key periods:

- the rise of Hollywood, from the late nineteenth century to the coming of sound;
- the studio era of the 1930s and 1940s;
- the television broadcasting age beginning with the rise of television in the 1950s;
- and the era inaugurated by the coming of the feature film blockbuster in the mid-1970s.

> **The key question then is: how did a collection of major studio corporations (Hollywood) come to dominate the production, distribution, and exhibition of movies and continue to maintain its control through the coming of sound, the innovation of colour and widescreen images, and the diffusion of television and home video?**

The rise of Hollywood

The motion picture industry in the United States grew from its origins during the final years of the nineteenth century to consolidation into an oligopoly (that is, control by a few corporations) in 1930, amidst the coming of sound. This initial period of Hollywood history is tainted by an overlay of sadness in that Hollywood has been seen as preventing what might have been—a group of progressive filmmakers serving a working-class audience—adopting instead an overt

profit-maximizing structure (Wasko 1982; Guback 1969). Nevertheless, we need to continue to look at how the remarkable institution of Hollywood came to be.

In the beginning, cinema was just another technology. Through the decade of the 1890s into the early days of the twentieth century inventors worked with the first filmmakers and exhibitors to persuade a sceptical public to embrace the movie show. The study of the introduction of this new technology focuses on a set of businesses formed to exploit the new knowledge in the United States and around the world.

The early inventors and entrepreneurs were not operating in a vacuum, seeking to create some ideal new enterprise, but rather sought to sell their discoveries through the existing entertainment industries. Robert Allen (1985) shows that the vaudeville (or variety) hall provided the first business outlet. However, as Allen (1982) demonstrates for Manhattan, and I have shown for other cities in the United States (Gomery 1992), this model of exhibition soon gave way to the nickelodeons—the thousands of converted store-front theatres—that from 1905 to 1910 presented hour-long all-movie shows; and it was the nickelodeon that formed the basis of the film industry that within a decade became Hollywood.

However, more than a locus for presenting was needed; a system of producing films also had to develop, and Hollywood established a flexible system for regularly producing and distributing feature-length motion pictures, along with short subjects and newsreels (Staiger 1982). It is this process of learning to make movies that would sell on a year-round basis that constitutes part of the analysis of David Bordwell, Janet Staiger, and Kristin Thompson in their highly influential book *The Classical Hollywood Cinema* (1985).

Finally, Hollywood came to stand for world distribution and presentation. The diffusion of the Hollywood cinema throughout the world was successfully completed by the early 1920s, but the achievement of world hegemony was not straightforward. Robert Anderson (1985) shows that a monopoly based on patents was formed by Thomas Edison and others, but then quickly failed, and it was to take flexibility of a different kind to gain long-term control.

This initial period ended with a sudden technical change—the coming of sound. The popularity of the talkies enabled new companies such as Warner Bros. to rise to power and join the small list of major studios including Paramount, Loew's, and other powerful corporations of the silent era, which not only retained but increased their power (Gomery 1980, 1982a).

The studio system

The coming of sound consolidated Hollywood's control over the world market and moved the United States into the studio era in which filmmaking, distribution, and exhibition were dominated by five theatre corporations: Paramount, Loew's (parent company to the more famous MGM), Fox Film (later Twentieth Century-Fox), Warner Bros., and RKO. They ruled Hollywood during the 1930s and 1940s and operated around the world as fully integrated business enterprises.

Historians have struggled to deal with the studio system. We have a number of 'insider' studio histories best exemplified by Bosley Crowther's (1957) authorized history of Loew's Inc. and MGM. Although this is rich in data, it is almost wholly lacking in perspective and method; Lillian Ross's (1952) history of the same studio is far more critical. In recent years a few histories of individual studios and powerful producers have appeared, such as Tino Balio's (1976) history of United Artists and Mathew Bernstein's (1994) study of Walter Wanger. But fine as these two studies are, United Artists and Walter Wanger hardly stood at the centre of the Hollywood industry. In-depth studies of the operations of key studios such as Twentieth Century-Fox and Paramount remain to be done. Gomery (1986) is a general study covering the studio system as a whole, including its major participants. Some of the detail it omits is provided by Kathy Klaprat's (1985) analysis of a single star, Bette Davis, and how she struggled to work within the studio system, and by Ida Jeter's (1986) examination of the attempts to unionize workers with less fame and fortune. More basic building-block studies such as these two are needed.

However, it was theatre ownership rather than studio production which defined the status of Hollywood in this era. By controlling picture palaces in all of the downtown areas across the United States, the major studios took three-quarters of the average box-office receipts. Only after their own theatres had soaked up as much as possible of the initial wave of box-office grosses through first and exclusive runs did the 'Big Five' permit smaller, independent theatres to scramble

for the remaining bookings, sometimes months, or even years, after a film's première.

Universal Pictures, Columbia Pictures, and United Artists constituted the studio era's 'Little Three' and led the scramble for these left-over film revenues. While always considered part of the Hollywood studio colossus, these three corporations could never match the economic muscle of the Big Five because they did not own the top (exclusively first-run) theatres. Even less powerful were Monogram and Republic Pictures, the inhabitants of 'Poverty Row', which created low-budget fare for marginal theatres. This type of production was partly fuelled by changes in exhibition practice brought on by the Great Depression. Borrowing techniques from the dime stores, marginal neighbourhood movie houses began regularly to offer two films for the price of one—the double feature—and thus stimulated the demand for the B movie.

The television broadcasting age

The decline of the studio era was the result of three main factors: the Paramount antitrust decrees, the social transformation of the United States with suburbanization and the baby boom, and the emergence of a moving-image rival, television. In 1948, as a consequence of what became known as the Paramount case, the federal government of the United States forced the Big Five to sell their movie palaces, and suddenly Hollywood lost direct control of and access to the movie market. This legal antitrust case against the Big Five and the Little Three had its origins in the second administration of President Franklin D. Roosevelt (1936–40) which, as Conant (1960, 1985) has shown, turned to enforcement of existing antitrust laws to help bring the nation out of the Great Depression.

This action against the major studios also occurred at a time when cinema audiences were falling. Weekly attendance in movie theatres in the United States peaked in 1946 and then began to drop, so that by the early 1960s it was half of what it had been in the glory days of the Second World War. The causes of this decline have been much debated and television is conventionally identified as the central villain. The common argument is this: once television programming commenced in the United States after the Second World War, movie fans stayed at home, attracted by 'free' (i.e. funded by advertising) television enter-

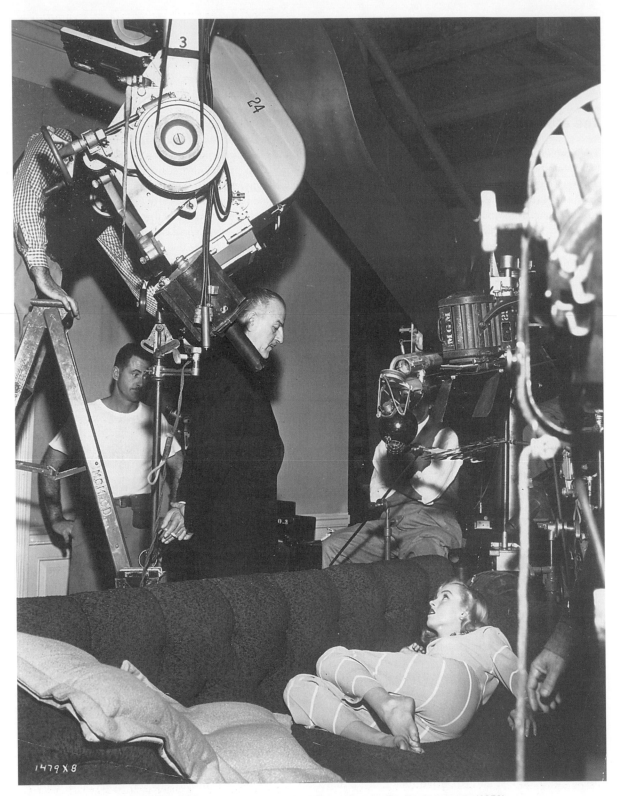

Struggles within the studio system—Marilyn Monroe and Louis Calhern rehearse *The Asphalt Jungle* (1950)

tainment. Going out to the movies suddenly became a relatively expensive night out, requiring a long journey downtown. Television entertainment was so much cheaper that millions of citizens of the United States simply stayed at home.

However, this 'analysis of substitution' ignores that, in most parts of the United States, television signals did not become available until long after the decline in moviegoing had commenced (see Gomery 1992). During the late 1940s and early 1950s only one-third of the nation had sets, but it was precisely then that millions stopped going to the movies. After the Second World War, formerly loyal film fans in the United States began to look for other things to do: starting families, finding nicer homes in the suburbs, buying cars, refrigerators, or the elusive pair of nylons not available during the war. It was therefore suburbanization and the baby boom (and the costs to a family involved) that were probably most responsible for the initial decline in movie attendance in the United States.

During the 1950s and 1960s the film industry adjusted to these new circumstances, first with auto theatres (drive-ins) and then with cinemas in shopping-malls, the long-term solution. In this completely new network of venues Hollywood also differentiated its product from black-and-white television with the development of widescreen and colour images. These and the introduction of Panavision lenses and Eastman Color film stock ought to be judged as important in their day as the coming of sound had been a generation earlier.

The arrival of television transformed Hollywood in expected and unexpected ways. Ever since the 1950s, when citizens of the United States stuffed their homes with television sets, Hollywood has been predicted to lose its power. This, however, has not been the case as the industry has adapted to, and taken advantage of, its changed circumstances. There are too few studies of this era of change. Concerning the corporate level there is Tino Balio's (1987) history of United Artists in the television age, from 1952 to the late 1970s. This company, Balio argues, demonstrated the importance of independent production for future Hollywood filmmaking; but unlike its rivals of the 1950s, the pioneering United Artists did not benefit from its innovations and by the 1980s had been reduced to a minor player in Hollywood.

Balio and others argue that these moves towards independent filmmaking represented a new mode of Hollywood production. Gone were the studios as fac-

tories turning out regular product for their theatre chains. Instead, independent producers put together packages of stars, a story, and production values which they turned into feature films that were distributed by a studio. In this formulation, the studio boss is seen to lose his former power, while that of the director as auteur is seen to increase.

This, however, was not the case. Independent production simply provided the studios with a more flexible, less costly way to fill their quotas of releases. No production was made without the green light from a studio head, whether the director was an auteur or a hired hand from a talent agency. Packagers came and went, but the studios remained all-powerful. Without studio approval, no blockbuster was made.

And while Hollywood may have used the blockbuster to distinguish the cinematic experience from that of television, the film industry also made its peace with broadcast television. This began with the movie made for television and then expanded into the mini-series and novel adapted for television. While these low-budget made-for-television dramas have often been attacked by critics, they are really the successors to Hollywood's B movies of yesteryear and have helped to boost ratings—which is why mini-series such as *Hollywood Wives* (1985) and *The Thorn Birds* (1983) have arrived like clockwork at key ratings-measurement periods.

Today and into the future

By the mid-1970s Hollywood as an industry had adjusted to a new world of flexible film production and the new suburban audiences captured by television. However, as the work of Mayer (1978), Gomery (1993), and Vogel (1995) suggests, a new era for Hollywood as a film industry began in the mid-1970s following the innovation of the blockbuster, exemplified by such films as *Jaws* (1975) and *Star Wars* (1977). Despite the heralded 'end' of moviegoing, theatrical attendance in the United States has remained steady at 1 billion admissions per year. Millions of fans still journey in the summer high season to nearby multiplex cinemas in the shopping-mall to relish Hollywood blockbusters. Indeed Hollywood corporate stock market prices rise and fall with the weekend figures for such films.

Hollywood as an industry has also continued to redefine itself, principally by adding to its technological bag of tricks. Computers in particular have enabled filmmakers to craft special effects to live action and animation in a way which was simply not possible before, and major hits such as *Who Framed Roger Rabbit?* (1988) and *Jurassic Park* (1993) have achieved near-miraculous interaction of live and animated figures. Yet, despite these technological innovations, the process of moviemaking has stayed remarkably constant because the underlying ideology of narrative production has remained unchanged.

This position differs from that of Janet Staiger, who has argued for various periods of production in Hollywood and their key differences (Staiger 1982). Staiger's meticulous work identifies a mutation from independent production to a package system. Yet, looking over the history of production in Hollywood, I find a consistent pattern—with studios always selecting films for production and groups under studio control making them—rather than some fundamental set of transformations. My view, however, is a minority one, and the debate about understanding the history of modes of production in Hollywood is destined to continue.

For me, it is the new ways and places to watch movies—especially cable, satellite, and video—that have defined the era of contemporary cinema. In the mid-1970s Time Inc. changed the world of cable television in the United States for ever with its Home Box Office (HBO), which, for a monthly fee of about $10, offered cable television subscribers recent Hollywood motion pictures—uncut, uninterrupted by commercials, and not sanitized to please network censors. For the first time in the television age a way had been found to make viewers pay for what they watched in their living-rooms. As 'pay television', HBO also lured back the older movie fan who did not want to go out to a theatre but loved watching second-run films on television at home.

But cable television offers the film fan much more than HBO. The entrepreneur Ted Turner took a typical independent television station, complete with its sports, reruns, and old movies, and beamed it to all America via the satellite to create his famous Superstation with half of the schedule filled with old films. By 1995 there were also American Movie Classics and a number of other repertory cable television cinemas in the home, where old Hollywood films, the best and worst, run all day long.

The post-1975 video age achieved its greatest change in the mid-1980s with the home video revolu-tion. Sony introduced its Betamax half-inch home video cassette recorder in 1975. Originally priced at more tha $1,000, the cost of the Beta machines and their newer rivals from VHS dropped to just over $300 by the mid-1980s. An enthusiastic American public (plus millions in other nations) snapped up so many machines that by 1989 fully two-thirds of American households were equipped to tape off the air or run pre-recorded tapes.

At first the Hollywood moguls loathed the new machine. Jack Valenti, President of the Motion Picture Association of America, declared that the VCR was a parasitical instrument robbing Hollywood's take at the box-office. But quickly enough, during the 1980s, Hollywood found a way to capitalize on the innovation. In 1986 the returns from ancillary video sidelines exceeded the take at the box-office in the United States. During the mid-1980s about 400 new pre-recorded cassettes were being released each month, 70 per cent of which were Hollywood feature films. In the 1990s came 'sell through', by which Hollywood studios, led by Disney with *Aladdin* (1992) and *The Lion King* (1994), sold tapes at prices between $10 and $20 directly to the public, bypassing rental altogether. As Hollywood moved towards the end of the twentieth century, it had fully absorbed the impact of the VCR and had begun to look forward to the next technological change.

This adaptation to the new delivery systems has been accompanied by a change of ownership of the major Hollywood corporations and their emergence as media conglomerates. This process of conglomeratization may be seen to have begun during the television age, as the example of the rise of the Disney operation shows (Gomery 1994). As the age of television began after the Second World War, Disney was a minor player in corporate Hollywood, and indeed nearly went out of business during the early 1950s. But the studio entered television production early on, pioneered theme parks, and later skilfully exploited cable television, home video, and merchandising. Disney became a major Hollywood operation and then a major producer of feature films. Since the mid-1980s this process of conglomeratization has intensified. The owners and operators of the Hollywood of the television era, led by Lew Wasserman at Universal, cashed in, while outsiders—recognizing the advent of a new industrial era characterized by video, multiplying cable television channels, and movies on demand—bought in.

This process began in 1985–6, when Rupert Murdoch took over Twentieth Century Fox (and dropped the hyphen). At the same moment Michael Eisner began to transform and rebuild the Walt Disney Corporation. At the end of the 1980s Japan entered the fray; Sony took over Columbia Pictures, and Matsushita acquired MCA. Time and Warner merged. Viacom took over Paramount, and in 1995 Seagrams bought MCA from Matsushita. As a result, the Hollywood industry today consists of but six multinational media conglomerates: Disney, Murdoch's Twentieth Century Fox, Seagram's Universal, Viacom's Paramount, Sony's Columbia, and Time Warner's Warner Bros.

A key feature of these conglomerates is their involvement in nearly all forms of mass media. Viacom's Paramount division, with its Simon & Schuster division leading the way, is one of the leading book publishers in the world. MCA, Warner, and Sony are all top makers and distributors of recorded music—in cassettes and compact discs and whatever new forms will come. Time Warner is the world's leader in magazines. Disney pioneered theme parks; MCA and Viacom's Paramount are key theme park operators as well. Fox, as part of Rupert Murdoch's News Inc. empire, is allied with leading newspapers around the world. And more media convergence is on the way. The Hollywood media conglomerates presently stand at the centre of the new world of video, computers, and interactive media. Within a decade our homes and workplaces will be wired with fibre optics and will make use of even more of Hollywood's products. As a result, the six media conglomerates are destined to become even more diversified and powerful.

Thus, a handful of companies formed more than a half century ago still have hegemony over the creation of the movies and the distribution of them throughout the world. Since the end of the Second World War the Hollywood major studios have survived the enforced selling of their theatre chains, the rise of network television, the advent of cable and pay television, the video cassette revolution, and the arrival of digitization. These companies may have new owners, but they show no signs of weakening—if anything, they are getting stronger. During the past decade, a number of enterprises have challenged the major studios only to lose millions of dollars and declare bankruptcy. The corporate shells of Orion and New World were always marginal at best; even the once-powerful United Artists is poised to go out of business.

> A handful of companies formed more than a half century ago still have hegemony over the creation of the movies and the distribution of them throughout the world. Since the end of the Second World War the Hollywood major studios have survived the enforced selling of their theatre chains, the rise of network television, the advent of cable and pay television, the video cassette revolution, and the arrival of digitization. These companies may have new owners, but they show no signs of weakening—if anything, they are getting stronger.

Critical debates

As this survey suggests, historians continue to tackle the vexing problems of how best to understand the development of Hollywood as an industry. While historians need to work to find better accounts of changes in finance, ownership structure, corporate actions, modes of production, international distribution, and new technologies of presentation, they also need to challenge past 'certainties'. Three areas of debate may be seen to be of particular importance: the significance of the studio system, the explanation of the control of Hollywood, and the identification of the appropriate analytical focus for the study of 'Hollywood'.

The significance of the studio system

It is commonplace to identify the studio system of the 1930s and 1940s as the most important—and interesting—era for film industry study. At that time, it is believed, Hollywood filmmaking was somehow purer and uncompromised by that 'evil of all evils', television. Yet, while the studio era was important, it also represents only one of four fundamental eras in the history of Hollywood as industry.

We like the studio era because it had a defined beginning, middle, and end. The industry was logically organized, transformed only by intrusions from the outside. This studio era began with the invention of sound, which created a peak in attendance. This high point was followed by a decline in demand caused by the Great Depression. The studio era came to a close, transformed by the Paramount antitrust decrees, sub-urbanization, and the advent of television.

> **The six media conglomerates which dominate contemporary Hollywood now possess a power and cohesion against which the oligopoly of the Hollywood studios during the 1930s and 1940s simply pales in comparison.**

However, we have to be careful not to overestimate the typicality of this one epoch, or to exaggerate its importance. Indeed, in comparison with the contemporary industry, the operations of the studio era, as explained by Bordwell, Staiger, and Thomspon (1985), seem positively quaint. Moreover, the six media conglomerates which dominate contemporary Hollywood now possess a power and cohesion against which the oligopoly of the Hollywood studios during the 1930s and 1940s simply pales in comparison.

The explanation of the control of Hollywood

This second issue is concerned with the question of the control of Hollywood. Historians of Hollywood as industry such as Janet Wasko (1982, 1995) and her mentor Thomas Guback (1969) have argued that the Hollywood industry is controlled by financial institutions. Under this type of Marxist-influenced economics there is no reason to do any further analysis. For, as with all aspects of capitalism in the United States, the mass media industries are shaped by forces found in the investment banking community, commonly known as Wall Street.

This analysis of finance capitalism, as it is known, can be found in its purest form in the argument that Hollywood in the 1930s was controlled by J. P. Morgan and John D. Rockefeller, who, it is suggested, held the balance of power within the eight major studios and their affiliated theatre and distribution channels and thus controlled Hollywood as an indus-

try. In 1937 Klingender and Legg popularized the Morgan and Rockefeller hypothesis, and since then it has served as a corner-stone of the history of Hollywood as an industry.

New work suggests that the Morgan and Rockefeller hypothesis is misleading and that the Great Depression signalled the close, not the continuation, of the epoch of finance capitalism (Gomery 1982). Bankers helped Hollywood studios get started in the 1920s, but were jettisoned as major players with the coming of the studio era, when corporate hegemony replaced control by Wall Street. It is therefore corporations, rather than bankers, that hold the key to power and control in the US motion picture industry. To consider Wall Street as other than an investor since the 1930s is to focus on the wrong issue.

One can best appreciate the power of the corporations by pushing aside corporate propaganda about how tough a competitive environment these companies face and focus instead on how the major studios and their corporate owners co-operate. They have long done this through one of the least-appreciated institutions in Hollywood industry history—the Motion Picture Association of America.

Too often Hollywood historians tell us only about the Motion Picture Association of America as an agent of restraint, first through the Hays Code and today with movie ratings. But the Association is better understood as a co-operative agency, or trade association, set up to maintain corporate power. This has meant lobbying for favourable rules in its own market of the United States and the elimination of all regulations in foreign markets.

The Motion Picture Association of America was the agent that the major studios used to work for an open US market in negotiations required by the National Recovery Act in the 1930s and for an open Europe through the General Agreement on Tariffs and Trade (GATT) talks in the 1990s (Gomery 1982). In both cases—and most times in between—the Association has skilfully protected its corporate owners. Indeed, protected by the Association, the Hollywood industry has demonstrated remarkable continuity. The corporations that controlled Hollywood in 1930, as the Great Depression commenced, have remained as the top corporations to the end of the century—and will probably continue to do so. No new corporation as a major studio has been created, although many have tried. Hollywood as an industry is thus best analysed and understood as one of the most enduring and powerful corporate oligopolies in the history of world business.

The analytical focus of Hollywood

Although this seems a straightforward issue, it is not. Generally, the US film industry has been seen to have a simple analytical focus, the Detroit of the movie business—Hollywood. However, this argument reduces the film industry from three functions (production, distribution, and presentation) to one, filmmaking.

To take Hollywood as a single industrial centre therefore is misleading. The centre of power of the film industry based in Hollywood has, since the close of the First World War, rested with its control over international distribution. The Hollywood industry has long dominated bookings around the globe, and film box-office figures in the United States, even with blockbusters, are small in comparison with the total take from all sources around the world. By taking advantage of sizeable economies of scale, Hollywood corporations have been able to spread production over dozens of films and amortize the costs of multi-million-dollar production budgets and a global network of offices. This has also meant that their distribution costs per film have been far lower than competitors. Moreover, unlike in the United States, Hollywood companies have been able to work together abroad to ensure the distribution of their films. Through various alliances, individual foreign film companies have not simply faced a Warner Bros. or Twentieth Century Fox, but the two companies (sometimes three or more) working in tandem: if films are not booked from the major Hollywood companies, under their terms, the chance of any Hollywood blockbuster may be lost (Thompson 1985; Guback 1969)

> To take Hollywood as a single industrial centre is misleading. The centre of power of the film industry based in Hollywood has, since the close of the First World War, rested with its control over international distribution. The Hollywood industry has long dominated bookings around the globe, and film box-office figures in the United States, even with blockbusters, are small in comparison with the total take from all sources around the world.

However, if the core of Hollywood's power has been its international control of distribution, this has inspired proportionally little scholarly research. Distribution, sadly, is the least analysed part of the industry; there are no fascinating movies to consider, only dry, dull figures, both numerical and executive, defining and producing raw power. This is why Thompson and Guback ought to be praised for the path-breaking character of their work.

Conclusion: Hollywood and economic power

If the economic power of Hollywood derives from control of not just the production of feature films but their distribution and exhibition, it would still be wrong to exaggerate their economic might. For, despite the size of these vast empires, they generate revenue figures that pale beside a truly big business such as Exxon or General Motors. As poorly as IBM has done in the 1990s, it could absorb all of Hollywood and these mighty media conglomerates would remain but a small division.

This is, perhaps, not recognized because Hollywood's products have always taken up large portions of people's leisure time. People in the United States watch a lot of television and film, and once we pile up all those minutes, the time commitment comes to 250 billion hours per year. If we take the average hourly wage in the United States to be about $10, we come to a couple of trillion dollars of time invested. However, since this is not the actual amount paid for the pleasure, Hollywood as industry must ultimately be understood as a medium-sized, though highly profitable, and very influential, set of business enterprises.

BIBLIOGRAPHY

Allen, Robert C. (1982), 'Motion Picture Exhibition in Manhattan 1906–1912', in Gorham Kindem (ed.), *American Film Industry: A Case Studies Approach* (Carbondale: Southern Illinois University Press.

—— (1985), 'The Movies in Vaudeville: Historical Context of the Movies as Popular Entertainment', in Tino Balio (ed.), *The American Film Industry: An Anthology of Readings* (Madison: University of Wisconsin Press.

Anderson, Robert (1985), 'The Motion Picture Patents Company: A Reevaluation', in Tino Balio (ed.), *The*

American Film Industry: An Anthology of Readings (Madison: University of Wisconsin Press).

Balio, Tino (1976), *United Artists: The Company Built by the Stars* (Madison: University of Wisconsin Press).

—— (1987), *United Artists: The Company that Changed the Film Industry* (Madison: University of Wisconsin Press).

Bernstein, Mathew (1994), *Walter Wanger: Hollywood Independent* (Berkeley: University of California Press).

Bordwell, David, Janet Staiger, and Kristin Thompson (1985), *The Classical Hollywood Cinema* (New York: Columbia University Press).

Conant, Michael (1960), *Antitrust in the Motion Picture Industry* (Berkeley: University of California Press).

—— (1985), 'The Paramount Decrees Reconsidered', in Tino Balio (ed.), *The American Film Industry: An Anthology of Readings* (Madison: University of Wisconsin Press).

Crowther, Bosley (1957), *The Lion's Share: The Story of an Entertainment Empire* (New York: Dutton).

Gomery, Douglas (1980), 'Hollywood Converts to Sound: Chaos or Order?', in Evan William Cameron (ed.), *Sound and the Cinema* (Pleasantville, NY: Redgrave).

—— (1982a), 'Hollywood, the National Recovery Administration, and the Question of Monopoly Power', in Gorham Kindem (ed.), *American Film Industry: A Case Studies Approach* (Carbondale: Southern Illinois University Press).

—— (1982b), 'Warner Bros. Innovates Sound: A Business History', in Gerald Mast (ed.), *The Movies in our Midst* (Chicago: University of Chicago Press).

*—— (1986), *The Hollywood Studio System* (New York: St Martin's Press).

*—— (1992), *Shared Pleasures: A History of Motion Picture Presentation* (Madison: University of Wisconsin Press).

—— (1993), 'The Contemporary Movie Industry', in Alison Alexander, James Owers, and Rodney Carveth (eds.), *Media Economics* (Hillsdale, NJ: Lawrence Erlbaum Associates).

—— (1994), 'Disney's Business History: A Re-interpretation', in Eric Smoodin (ed.), *Disney Discourse: Producing the Magic Kingdom* (New York: Routledge).

Guback, Thomas H. (1969), *The International Film Industry* (Bloomington: Indiana University Press).

Jeter, Ida (1986), 'The Collapse of the Federated Motion Picture Crafts: A Case Class Collaboration', in Paul Kerr (ed.), *The Hollywood Film Industry: A Reader* (London: Routledge & Kegan Paul).

Klaprat, Cathy (1985), 'The Star as Market Strategy: Bette Davis in Another Light', in Tino Balio (ed.), *The American Film Industry: An Anthology of Readings* (Madison: University of Wisconsin Press).

Klingender, F. D., and Stuart Legg (1937), *Money behind the Screen* (London: Lawrence & Wishart).

Mayer, Michael (1978), *The Film Industries*, 2nd edn. (New York: Hastings House).

Ross, Lillian (1952), *Picture* (New York: Rinehart).

Staiger, Janet (1982), 'Dividing Labor for Production Control: Thomas Ince and the Rise of the Studio System', in Gorham Kindem (ed.), *American Film Industry: A Case Studies Approach* (Carbondale: Southern Illinois University Press).

Thompson, Kristin (1985), *Exporting Entertainment: America in the World Film Market 1907–1934* (London: British Film Institute).

Vogel, Harold L. (1995), *Entertainment Industry Economics* (New York: Cambridge Unviersity Press).

Wasko, Janet (1982), *Movies and Money* (Norwood, NJ: Ablex).

*—— (1995), *Hollywood in the Information Age* (Austin: University of Texas Press).

4

Early American film

Tom Gunning

Early cinema as a challenge to film history and theory

Since the early 1970s the study of early American cinema (from its origins until about 1916) has transformed conceptions of film history and of the relation between theory and history. When this research began in the late 1970s film history was a neglected field. Previous film historians had only limited access to films or other primary materials from the early period, and usually operated under implicit teleological assumptions, chronicling film's gradual technical and aesthetic maturation. Cinema's beginnings were viewed as immature babblings, followed by precocious discoveries and a growing mastery of editing and storytelling. Historians who began working in the 1970s questioned this teleological approach, benefiting from increased access to archival collections of films and other primary materials. These scholars abandoned the pejorative connotations of describing early film as 'primitive', maintaining that this era possessed a different approach to filmmaking than that of later cinema, so often considered the norm.

Under the dominance of apparatus theory (see Creed, Part 1, Chapter 9), which marked film studies in the decade of the 1970s, film theorists tended to view history with suspicion. From an amalgam of Lacanian psychoanalysis and Althusserian critique of ideology, a systematic model of the way cinema operated had been fashioned that owed little to historical research. Film history as it had been practised was viewed as an empirical gathering of facts that could hardly shed light on the deep structures of the way the cinematic apparatus constructed its spectator as subject—a process, theorists claimed, which embodied ideologies endemic to Western thought at least since Plato. How could chronicling changes in industrial practices reveal anything of deep significance?

New approaches to early cinema emerged, however, not so much in opposition to film theory as in dialogue with it, and from a desire to test some of its propositions. Apparatus theory constructed a model of cinema based on a number of assumptions about cinematic form and text–spectator relations: the centring of the film spectator as master of a visual field and decoder of narrative puzzles, and a viewing process in which the spectator remains immobile and loses all sense of surroundings, in thrall to an illusion of reality deriving from psychological regression (Baudry 1986). Investigating early cinema, historians could ask whether these assumptions functioned during cinema's first decades.

Early cinema as a different sort of cinema

Work on early cinema took on historical and theoretical tasks. As models of new research methods and increased rigour, Gordon Hendricks, George C. Pratt, and Jay Leyda provided inspiration for the systematic use of archives, drawing on contemporary documents and looking more thoroughly at archival films. The event which many scholars see as the origin of the rethinking of early cinema, the conference *Cinema 1900–1906* (Holmann 1982), held by the International Federation of Film Archives (FIAF) in Brighton in 1978, was devised by a group of forward-looking archivists (particularly Eileen Bowser, David Francis, and Paul Spehr) to pull early films out of the vault and have them examined by scholars. In many ways the renaissance of early-film studies was begun by film archivists (Cherchi Usai 1994). Around the same time seminal works, such as Robert C. Allen's (1980) dissertation on the interrelation between vaudeville and early film, exemplified new carefully focused research projects.

Realizing that early cinema could offer new theoretical insights was primarily the inspiration of Noël Burch, whose interest in oppositional film practices led him to approach early films in a radical manner (Burch 1990). Burch located the significance of early film in its differences from the way films were made and understood within the dominant mode of filmmaking, which he termed the IMR, the institutional mode of representation, exemplified by Hollywood film, but international in scope. He described early cinema as an alternative approach, a PMR, or primitive mode of representation. The PMR consisted of a number of unfamiliar structures: a spatial approach combining frontality with non-centred composition and distant camera placement to create a 'primitive externality'; a lack of narrative coherence, linearity, and closure; and an underdevelopment of character.

Burch's view of the relation of this PMR to the later IMR was complex and ambivalent. At points, he related the different approaches of early films to the working-class background of early cinema's audience and of at least some of its showmen producers. The IMR, in contrast, introduced bourgeois values of coherence and subjectivity into this originally primitive and popular mode of entertainment. Burch raised what has remained a vexed issue in the history of early cinema: the role of class in its development and the class make-up of its audiences. However, he stressed that his interest in the PMR lay primarily in the light it could shed on the IMR, the dominant cinema as it was described by apparatus theory. As a contrast to IMR, PMR allowed Burch to denaturalize this dominant mode, revealing it as the product of historical development rather than the discovery of the natural language of cinema, as teleological film history had assumed. In this respect, Burch launched a strong critique of linear teleological film history. But he also resisted any conception of early cinema as a 'lost paradise', claiming (particularly in his later work) that early cinema was less rich and complex than IMR. For Burch an assumption of progressive development remained, and he retained the term 'primitive' partly to indicate that in his view this early mode remained underdeveloped. Burch's analysis of early film often does not stress its difference from the IMR as much as the way early film techniques anticipate many of IMR's basic assumptions in a primitive fashion. He therefore saw early cinema as rehearsing a variety of elements essential to IMR and the apparatus theory of the cinema. Thus, the evolution of early cinema strove to *overcome* the primitive externality that marks the PMR. The centred masterful spectator of apparatus theory appeared in the PMR in a number of precocious yet underdeveloped ways. This classical spectator acted as a goal which impelled the development of centred compositions and continuity editing strategies, but it also appeared in a number of seemingly deviant features, as later practices appeared in 'infantile' versions. For instance, Burch claimed that the frequent theme in trick films of a body that explodes into fragments (as in Cecil Hepworth's *Explosion of a Motor Car*, 1900) anticipated the later schema of fragmentation through editing. Following from the assumptions of the apparatus theory that the cinema in its basic apparatuses (the camera, the projector, and the movie theatre) reproduces the Western ideology of subject formation, Burch found that early cinema already held the seeds for these later structures. Although he added a historical dimension to his analysis, the determination of theoretical structures provided the ultimate significance of early cinema.

Burch's approach to early cinema received swift criticism from David Bordwell and Kristin Thompson (1983). The authors offered a critique of the linear and teleological assumptions of traditional film history, inspired by Jean-Louis Comolli's call for a materialist history of film, based on discontinuities and ruptures rather than a schema of evolution. While Comolli never supplied an example of materialist history, the authors found that Burch attempted one, but, in their view, failed. Much of their criticism targeted a cavalier attitude towards research and verification in Burch's work, but they also criticized his theoretical assumptions. The authors questioned the role of working-class culture in early cinema's formal difference from traditonal bourgeois forms, pointing out that the first audiences for film in the United States were in vaudeville theatres, a basically middle-class form, while the working-class nickelodeon appeared only as the codes of the IMR were emerging. In addition, Bordwell and Thompson noted Burch's return to linearity in his belief that the basic assumptions of the IMR are present in embryonic form in early film.

In a key work in revisionist film history *The Classical Hollywood Cinema* (1985), written jointly by David Bordwell, Janet Staiger, and Kristin Thompson, Thompson developed a view of early film which also accentuated its difference from later filmmaking practice. Maintaining that from 1917 until the 1960s American mainstream commercial cinema shows a remarkable stability in its style and mode of production (the 'classical Hollywood cinema' of the title), Thompson saw the age of early cinema as a time when films were 'so fundamentally different as to be incomprehensible' (Bordwell *et al.* 1985: 157). Early cinema can be understood as 'pre-classical', standing in varying degrees outside the codes of spatial and temporal relations that define the stability of the classical Hollywood film. The authors' definition of the classical system, although in some ways parallel to (and possibly inspired by) Burch's IMR, made little use of the apparatus theory of subject construction. Instead, Thompson placed storytelling at the centre of the classical system and saw primitive cinema struggling to harness cinematic space and time to this dominant function. Thompson's emphasis on narrative allowed the difference between early cinema and classical cinema to gain more clarity. Since the basic apparatus, the camera, the projector, the darkened room, was the same in both periods, an approach founded in the ideological effect of the basic apparatus would be hard-pressed to discover significant differences between periods.

Thompson applied the principles articulated in Bordwell and Thompson (1983), and investigated the transformation between primitive cinema (she retained this term, although with misgivings) and classical Hollywood forms by investigating the economic and cultural determinants of this change. Retaining

Burch's description of the exteriority of early cinema, she related this to the dominant influence of vaudeville on early cinema both economically and as a model. Thompson claims primitive cinema transformed itself by taking up the task of storytelling, overcoming the exteriority of the vaudeville spectator and replacing it by a spectator immersed in the narrative space of the film.

My own work also defined the difference between early cinema and the later classical mode in terms of its relation to narrative. The work of my colleague and collaborator André Gaudreault, analysing the structures of early cinema through structuralist narrative theory, differentiated cinematic *narrators* (cinematic devices which narrated a story) and *monstrators* who, instead of telling a story, displayed or showed things (Gaudreault 1988, 1990). For Gaudreault, these two different functions in cinema corresponded to the narrating function of an edited sequence and the monstrative display of the single shot. Early cinema, particularly in its very earliest period in which films most often consisted of a single shot (before 1904), related more to monstration than to narration. In my work, this contrast between formal devices of storytelling and display became less a matter of a contrast between the single shot and the edited sequence than a broadly based address to the spectator in early cinema, which I termed the cinema of attractions (Gunning 1990).

While Thompson had shown that early cinema differed from the classical model primarily through its lack of narrative dominance, there remained the question of how to describe what early cinema *was*, rather than what it *wasn't*. Burch's ideas about exteriority and Gaudreault's concept of monstration were useful guides. Taking a cue from Sergei Eisenstein's theatrical work in the 1920s, I felt that the essential gesture of early cinema (which could not be described simply as an incomplete mastery of the task of storytelling) lay in its aggressive address to the spectator's attention. The spectator addressed by early cinema was very different from the spectator of classical cinema, absorbed in a coherent fictional world, attentive to character cues and immersed in following a story. The exteriority noted by Burch and Thompson corresponded to an outward address of the films themselves, a sort of hailing of the viewer, most obvious in the look at the camera and the bows and gestures directed at the audience so common in early cinema (as in such films as *From Show Girl to Burlesque Queen*, Biograph,

1903, or nearly any Méliès films, e.g. *The Man with the Rubber Head*, 1902) but taboo in most genres in classical cinema.

The exteriority of early cinema expresses the basis of the cinema of attractions: the act of display of something to a viewer. The attraction itself is aware of the viewer's gaze, is constructed to attract it. Rather than narrative development based on active characters within detailed fictional environments, the cinema of attractions presented a series of curious or novel views to a spectator. These views could be non-fictional actualities (current events, human oddities, natural wonders), vaudeville acts (dances, acrobatics, gags), famous fragments (peak moments from famous plays, realizations of well-known paintings), or trick films (magical transformations and illusions). In contrast to the temporal development inherent in narrative, the cinema of attractions presented bursts of interest, such as the rapid transformations in a magic film, or the succession of sights in a scenic film (Gunning 1995a). In this cinema, characterization was unimportant and the spatial and temporal relations essential to narrative development were basically irrelevant.

> **The exteriority of early cinema expresses the basis of the cinema of attractions: the act of display of something to a viewer. The attraction itself is aware of the viewer's gaze, is constructed to attract it. Rather than narrative development based on active characters within detailed fictional environments, the cinema of attractions presented a series of curious or novel views to a spectator. These views could be non-fictional actualities (current events, human oddities, natural wonders), vaudeville acts (dances, acrobatics, gags), famous fragments (peak moments from famous plays, realizations of well-known paintings), or trick films (magical transformations and illusions).**

Although there are differences and even contradictions between these models of early cinema, they all emphasize the difference between the early period of film history and the cinema which eventually became dominant. These models were primarily focused on the formal aspects of early films. Further discoveries came as historians broadened the focus from films to the contexts in which they were shown.

From early film to early cinema: exhibitors, audiences, and the public sphere

The new generation of historians of early film investigated not only the films themselves, but also the way they were shown and understood. This involved a shift, to use the terms suggested by Christian Metz, from early *films* to early *cinema*, the culture surrounding films, including their industry, their theatres, and their audiences. Of course, cinema culture and actual films are inseparable, the one implying and enlightening the other. Charles Musser's (1991) work on Edwin Porter and other early American filmmakers emphasized that simply looking at archival prints of early films, while essential, was not sufficient for a full understanding of early cinema. Not only editing, compositional techniques, and narrative strategies differed in early cinema; classical cinema had also transformed the ways films were presented and the means audiences used for understanding them.

Research into primary sources about the presentation of early film led Musser to stress the role of the exhibitor. In cinema's first decade, particularly before 1903, the person showing the film took over important roles in what is now termed post-production, which would later be under the control of film producers. Since many films consisted of a single shot, the exhibitor assembled them into a programme. This could be done with great ingenuity, joining individual films together to stress similarity or contrast; interspersing other material, such as lantern slides or recitations; adding music or other sound effects; and frequently narrating the whole with a spoken commentary or lecture. The exhibitor therefore endowed each film with aesthetic effects and meanings, becoming the author of the film programme (Musser 1991; Musser and Nelson 1991). Buttressed by research into the importance in this era of the film lecturer (the performer who spoke a commentary as the film was projected) by Gaudreault

(1988), Burch (1990), Martin Sopocy (1978), and others, Musser showed that formal analysis of films alone was not sufficient for understanding the meanings and pleasures derived from them by early audiences.

In contrast to classical films, early film had a more open form. As Burch had indicated, their narratives were not as complete and finalized as the films of the IMR. However, this openness was not an avant-garde love of ambiguity. Narrative coherence was supplied in the act of reception, rather than inherent in the film itself. Filmmakers frequently relied on familiar stories or current events well known to their audiences, who could fill in gaps in the narrative or supply significance. These cultural contexts outside film—like the magic-lantern narratives of fire rescues discussed by Musser (1991) which influenced Porter's *Life of an American Fireman* (1903), or the theatrical performances of the novel *Uncle Tom's Cabin* cited by Janet Staiger (1992) which contextualize Porter's 1903 film *Uncle Tom's Cabin*—could explain some formal differences in early films. Staiger claims that early film narratives were less divergent from classical practices than they may seem—they simply used other means to make themselves comprehensible. However, if audience foreknowledge or other extrafilmic aids did supply narrative coherence, the means of achieving it remained different from classical cinema, which supplies the necessary narrative information within the film itself. Early films seem less aberrant and irrational when foreknowledge or other aids are factored in, but their difference from later practice also becomes highlighted.

The investigation of early cinema must consider the broader cultural context in which films were made, exhibited, and understood. The importance of vaudeville for early cinema, both as an exhibition outlet and as a model, had received renewed attention. But what about the nickelodeon, the theatre of the masses, which traditional histories saw as defining the early American cinematic experience? How did the nickelodeon appear, who was its audience, and how did it relate to changes in early films? The nickelodeon era (which began in 1905, became widespread in 1906, and was ending by 1912) began with the rise of story films, while the end of that era saw the first development of classical traits such as characterization and narrative closure. Did the nickelodeon encourage the growth of story films, or, as Musser (1991) claims, were they a pre-condition for it?

The nickelodeon remains an area of controversy.

Musser has pointed out that, even before the nickelodeon, a range of contexts existed in which films were shown, including not only the middle-class vaudeville palaces, but also fairground exhibitors, travelling tent shows, sponsored entertainments in local opera-houses or other public halls, educational exhibitions in schools and even churches (Musser, 1990). As Robert C. Allen (1980) found, vaudeville possessed a range of levels, moving from palaces to purveyors of 'cheap vaudeville', which also offered motion pictures at a price considerably below that of high-class vaudeville. While the audiences for motion pictures when they premièred as the latest novelties were undoubtedly middle class, patrons of all classes had seen films before 1905. But the nickelodeon, with its low admission price of 5 cents, specifically targeted new entertainment seekers, the working class, whose gains in the early twentieth century of a bit more leisure time and disposable income provided an opportunity for small-time entertainment entrepreneurs. But were the working class the main patrons of the nickelodeon?

Doubt was cast on this traditional thesis by a number of scholars. Russell Merritt (1976), Douglas Gomery (1982), and Robert C. Allen (1983) investigated Boston and New York City and decided that the location of nickelodeons in those cities actually avoided working-class neighbourhoods in favour of more central commercial districts, areas frequented by middle-class shoppers as well as working-class patrons. The patrons of these cheap theatres might well have been more frequently middle class than traditional histories had assumed. Further, as Merritt in particular emphasized, the nickelodeon operators wooed middle-class patrons, seeming uncomfortable with their identity as 'democracy's theatre', and anxious for middle-class respectability. But scholars have also rushed to revise these revisionists. Robert Sklar objected to Allen's and Merritt's thesis, maintaining the importance of working-class culture to the development of the nickelodeon and to our understanding of the role of film in working-class experience (Sklar 1990). Recently Ben Singer (1995b) has returned to the site of Allen's research, New York City, and found that nickelodeons were more prevalent in working-class neighbourhoods than Allen had indicated. Clearly this is an area of continuing debate, as recent exchanges between Allen and Singer indicate (Allen 1996; Singer 1996).

At issue, however, is more than the accurate description of the class make-up of New York neighbourhoods or the number of film theatres. The effect of class

The theatre of the masses—
the nickelodeon

antagonism and class definition on early American cinema remains a vital issue. The work of social historian Roy Rosenzweig showed that the relation between film theatres and working-class culture cannot simply be dismissed as a sentimental myth of traditional historians. It is not necessary to attribute early American cinema to the domain of a single class. Rather, the most valuable approach sees cinema as one of the areas in which turn-of-the-century America defined class relations, culture, and dominance. Preliminary work by

J. A. Lindstrom (1996) on nickelodeons in Chicago has centred less on attributing theatres to specific classes than on the way film theatres inspired new systems of zoning and regulation, as leisure time and entertainment became an aspect of municipal control and class struggle.

The history of film exhibition has become one of the liveliest areas of film scholarship. It occupies important sections of the carefully researched and conceived volumes in the History of American Cinema series by

Musser (1990) and Eileen Bowser (1990) and is exemplified by the fine work of Douglas Gomery (1992), showing early cinema's vanguard position in framing and pursuing innovative questions in film history. Gregory Waller's (1995) work on exhibition in a smaller city, Lexington, Kentucky, demonstrated the value in investigating exhibition contexts beyond the metropolis. His work also investigates African-American exhibition and audience patterns, an area all too often ignored in favour of immigrant populations. Waller places early cinema within pre-existing patterns of entertainment, including not only vaudeville, but the multi-purpose opera-house, the amusement park, and local fairs. Robert Allen (1996) has theorized that such viewing situations in small-town and rural America were different from the urban nickelodeon in tems of class and surroundings.

The most broadly conceived attempt to theorize the class basis of the nickelodeon came in Miriam Hansen's (1991a) conception of the nickelodeon as a working-class public sphere. The concept of the public sphere was introduced by Jurgen Habermas's (1991) consideration of the rise of bourgeois democracy, in which certain contexts of public discussion—coffee-houses, newspapers, literary discussion groups—formed an ideal of equitable exchange and reasonable debate. The public sphere provided Hansen with a historical model of the manner in which institutions and discourse created new forms of subjectivity quite different from the ahistorical model of subject formation offered by apparatus theory. However, for Habermas, the classical public sphere was almost immediately compromised by the rise of capitalism, which undermined the claim of a realm of free discussion divorced from economic power. Further, for Habermas, the modern commercialized technological forms of media have seriously undermined the classical terms of debate and participation through techniques of manipulation and opinion management.

Hansen draws on critical reformulations of Habermas's concept. Emphasizing that the classical public sphere had always excluded certain groups (obviously the working class, but also women), critics such as Negt and Kluge (1993) developed the idea of oppositional or proletarian public spheres. The key issue here is less public discussion or overt political action than what Hansen describes as the 'experience' of the participants, 'that which mediates individual perception with social meaning, conscious with unconscious processes, loss of self with self reflexivity' (Hansen 1991a:

12). Negt and Kluge claim the collective viewing of films, the way they could speak to viewers' experience, opened the possibility of cinema as an oppositional public sphere.

For Hansen this possibility became a historical tool for approaching not only the stylistic alterity of early films (as in her analysis of Porter's 1907 film The 'Teddy' Bears), but also its specific modes of exhibition and relation to its audience. Hansen theorized that early cinema may have provided 'an alternative horizon of experience' for groups excluded from the classical public sphere, such as working-class and immigrant audiences and women. Following the research of social historian Kathy Peiss (1986), Hansen showed that the nickelodeon moved away from a homosocial, gender-specific world of male entertainment which excluded women, to a heterosocial world of commercial entertainment where women not only attended, but frequently made up the majority.

The importance of cinema as a new public sphere for women has become a key issue in early cinema research, with such scholars as Lauren Rabinovitz (1990), Janet Staiger (1995), Judith Mayne (1990), Constance Balides (1993), and Shelley Stamp Lindsey (1996) exploring the role of female spectators and at points testing the feminist understanding of apparatus theory which saw the cinema as embodying a male gaze. While the patriarchal and even sexist content of early cinema is unquestionable (see such films as Thomas Edison's 1901 Trapeze Disrobing Act, or Porter's 1903 film The Gay Shoe Clerk), women patrons attending this new medium could transform these male-oriented films in unexpected ways, as in Hansen's famous example of the women who flocked to early boxing films, breaching a former male bastion.

For Hansen, early cinema's difference from classical cinema reflects its role as an oppositional public sphere, allowing viewer relationships that would become suppressed in the classical paradigm. The diversity of display evident in the cinema of attractions did not entice viewers to lose their sense of being present in a public space. The direct address of the cinema of attractions encouraged a recognition of the viewer as part of an audience, rather than as an atomized consumer absorbed into the coherent fictional world of the classical paradigm. The lack of devices channelling spectator attention into following a narrative meant that the cinema of attractions allowed its viewer more imaginative freedom. Further, the less controlled modes of nickelodeon exhibition, with live music, occasional use of a lecturer, egalitarian seating, variety format, and continuous admission, gave it 'a margin of participation and unpredictability' (Hansen 1991: 43) lacking in classical cinema. The alternative public sphere of the nickelodeon gave way to the domesticating of audience behaviour within the elaborate picture palaces which became the premier show-place for films in the middle to late 1910s. This change in exhibition, along with the adoption of the classical paradigm in the feature film, eliminated most elements of earlier film culture in favour of a universal address to a film spectator unspecific in class or gender.

> **For Hansen, early cinema's difference from classical cinema reflects its role as an oppositional public sphere, allowing viewer relationships that would become suppressed in the classical paradigm. The diversity of display evident in the cinema of attractions did not entice viewers to lose their sense of being present in a public space. The direct address of the cinema of attractions encouraged a recognition of the viewer as part of an audience, rather than as an atomized consumer absorbed into the coherent fictional world of the classical paradigm. The lack of devices channelling spectator attention into following a narrative meant that the cinema of attractions allowed its viewer more imaginative freedom.**

Periodization and transitional stages

However they might differ in dividing them up, scholars of early cinema agree that in a relatively short amount of time (two decades or so) so much change occurs that several distinct periods exist. This stands in stark contrast to the classical Hollywood cinema, which for Bordwell, Staiger, and Thompson (1985) remained stable for more than four decades. The period of early cinema stretches from the origins of motion pictures in the late nineteenth century to around 1916. The year given by Bordwell, Staiger, and Thompson for the consolidation of the classical Hollywood cinema is 1917, so this end-date marks early cinema as pre-classical. Around 1913 to 1915 the American film industry moved definitively to the production of longer feature films (from one to several hours) as the new basis of the industry, exiling one- or two-reel films to marginal theatres, or to 'added attractions' in a feature programme. The middle 1910s witnessed new institutions (feature films, the star system, the picture palace, new studios, and systems of distribution) essential to the classical Hollywood cinema.

Exhibition, production, and distribution underwent a series of reorganizations in the two decades of 'early cinema'. Originally films and projection machines were produced by the same company, and these were offered to vaudeville theatres as a complete package. By the turn of the century, both films and machines were sold publicly, and entrepreneurs acquired them and became exhibitors, marking the first differentiation within the industry. Around 1905 the next essential differentiation occurred as exchanges appeared: middlemen who purchased films from production companies and rented them to exhibitors. This increased the availability of films to an exhibitor and led to the nickelodeon explosion. The multiplication of cheap theatres showing new films on a daily basis created a demand for films the American producers could not initially fulfil, and the French company Pathé took up much of the slack. Around 1909 American producers attempted to seize control of the industry again, and submit the exchanges and exhibitors to a series of regulations. The organ for this was the Motion Picture Patents Company (MPPC), in which Edison and Biograph tried to exert control through their ownership of patents. Opposition to the MPPC arose with 'independent' producers, but even they soon adopted its methods of control over distribution through regulation of release dates and price schedules. By 1913 the power of the MPPC had waned, as well as the popularity of the one-reel film, replaced by longer feature films and the rise of new 'independent' companies, such as Universal, Famous Players in Famous Plays, and Mutual. Exhibition became dominated by large urban picture palaces, some of which were already owned by production studios, paving the way for the later vertical integration of the industry. While changes in film style cannot be neatly tied to all these changes, the volatile nature of the industry explains why there is probably more transformation in the way films were made and conceived (both by producers and audiences) in this period than in the rest of film history.

Changes in film style can be divided into periods partly in terms of the opposition between the cinema of attractions and narrative form. Like all binary oppositions, the contrast between attractions and narrative can lead to unfortunate simplification. These aspects should never be seen as mutually exclusive, but need to be dialectically interrelated. While there are films (particularly in the first decade of cinema) which function purely as attractions with no narrative structure, many early films (especially after 1902) show an interaction between the two aspects. I claim that the cinema of attraction works as a 'dominant' up to about 1905, employing forms of direct address, punctual temporality, and surprise rather than narrative development.

The concept of the dominant comes from the literary analysis of the Russian Formalists and has been applied to film by Kristin Thompson (1988). It recognizes that, though various elements might coexist in a work, one element may organize the others. In the classical style, narrative structures act as the dominant, so that, even though attractions persist (such as special effects, the physical attraction of stars, spectacular sets, or musical numbers), they are subordinated to a narrative structure. Likewise, although certain fairy films of Méliès or Pathé, such as *A Trip to the Moon* (1902) or *The Red Spectre* (1907) have stories, they basically serve as show-cases for the dominant attractions of camera tricks, costumes, elaborate sets, and stencil colouring. Certain early films, particularly from the years around 1903 to 1907 (such as Pathé's *A Policeman's Tour of the World* from 1906), appear as almost equal contests between the claims of attractions and narrative, veering from one logic to the other. One basic arc of stylistic transformation traces the increasing dominance of narrative structures, leading to structures that are clear harbingers of later classical forms. From 1906 more films were made with narrative structures as their dominant. By 1908 films became increasing narrativized and were provided with volitional characters. However, 'narrative' is an expansive term, including many styles of storytelling. The difference that early films show when compared to films of the classical style should not be reduced simply to a contrast between narrative and non-narrative forms. Even the narrative films of this early period tell stories differently from the classical paradigm.

The non-classical narrative forms of early cinema make up a series of genres. Closest to the form of attractions are fragment narratives. This minimally narrative genre consisted of a single fragment or series of fragments, often famous moments from a play or famous events, to be completed by the viewer's understanding of previous (non-film) versions. Biograph's 1903 production of the famous temperance play *Ten Nights in a Barroom* consisted simply of five key scenes (or rather moments from the well-known play: *Death of Little Mary*; *Death of Slade*; *The Fatal Blow*; *Murder of Willie*; and *Vision of Mary*)—to someone unfamiliar with the play these brief films would be incomprehensible. Such fragments could be more or less incomplete. The versions of the Passion play produced both in the United States and France showed the range of possibilities, from early discontinuous and highly fragmented films to later, nearly narratively coherent, versions. In their lack of temporal development the fragment narratives are close to attractions.

Perhaps the earliest complete narrative form was the gag, the brief visual joke, often centred around physical pranks, which had a minimum essential narrative development: a set-up for the gag and a pay-off as the gag (usually some minor disaster) takes place, creating the fundamental narrative roles of prankster and victim. Early American companies produced scores of such films, and a few titles from American Mutoscope and Biograph in 1903 give some sense of their flavour: *How Buttons Got Even with the Butler*; *Pulling off the Bed Clothes*; *You will Send me to Bed, Eh?* Their disaster structure gives them a brief and punctual temporality—like an exploding cigar—as well as an often highly visual pay-off which makes them resemble attractions. In the period of multi-shot films, Edison

> **Perhaps the earliest complete narrative form was the gag, the brief visual joke, often centred around physical pranks, which had a minimum essential narrative development: a set-up for the gag and a pay-off as the gag (usually some minor disaster) takes place, creating the fundamental narrative roles of prankster and victim.**

and Biograph reworked such gags into longer films, as a bad boy or other trickster carried out a series of practical jokes (*The Truants*, Biograph, 1907; *The Terrible Kids*, Edison, 1906). This form of concatenation led to another simple narrative form, which I have called 'linked vignettes', consisting of a series of brief gags linked by a common character (Gunning 1994*b*).

As Burch and others have pointed out, the first extended self-contained narrative form in film was the chase. Burch (1990) saw the linearity of the chase as an anticipation of later classical narratives. In its earliest examples (*The Escaped Lunatic*, 1903; *Personal*, 1904, both Biograph) the chase created a continuous fictional space, rendered coherent by its methodical following of a single physical action. While chases often included attractions (such as dogs leaping fences and swimming streams, or ladies revealing legs as they slid down a hill), a single-minded focus on a pursuit through several shots created a new narrative dominance. However, unlike later classical films, the chase remained dependent entirely on physical action for its narrative structure. Figures running through various locales created the continuous geography of the film. The initiation of a pursuit provided the inciting incident of the film and capture marked its completion. This picks out a decidedly non-classical aspect of early film narrative, its lack of characterization or motivation behind action.

Around 1906 a number of films attempted stories with a greater degree of character and less physical action (such as Edison's *The Miller's Daughter*, 1905, or *Fireside Reminiscences*, 1908). Contemporary comments leave no doubt that many character-based films of this era were obscure to their contemporaneous audiences. Basic codes for conveying thoughts and emotions had not yet been devised by filmmakers, nor were they understood by audiences. Perhaps the greatest transformation of early film style came with the adoption of new narrative codes which conveyed character motives and organized storytelling devices. To some extent, this shift in narrative style parallels the attempts to regulate and rationalize the film industry which culminated in the formation of the MPPC in 1908 (Gunning 1991*a*). This large-scale transformation of American filmmaking has frequently been referred to as the 'transitional' period, marking its mediation between the radically different earlier cinema and the establishment of the classical paradigm. Narrative in the transitional period obeyed new rules: interior coherence (lack of reliance on audience foreknow-

ledge or other extra-filmic aids); a strong narrative closure; and, especially, an emphasis on characterization, frequently building stories around changes in character or key decisions whose motivations are indicated within the film. Many of the Griffith one-reel dramas produced for the Biograph company display these qualities (such as *The Drunkard's Reformation*, 1909), as do the films produced by the Vitagraph Company (such as *An Official Appointment*, 1912, so well analysed by Ben Brewster (1991*a*)). This form differs sharply from the earlier forms based primarily in physical action, although many films united the two forms (including Griffith's Biograph melodramas, such as *The Lonedale Operator*, 1911).

However, this transitional period remained volatile and ambivalent, as the term suggests. While new narrative structures were evident in many films (particularly dramas from the Vitagraph, Biograph, and Edison studios), and were praised by trade journals devoted to the film industry (which began to appear around this time), variation occurs. Research by both Ben Singer (1993) and Charles Keil (1995) has stressed that the most advanced films by Griffith are not typical of the period. Films even as late as 1913 sometimes show uncertainty in conveying character psychology or even a coherent plot. Singer (1993) cites an episode from the Thanhouser Company's 1913 serial *Zudora* as an example of pure incoherence.

While actual achievements varied from studio to studio (or film to film), organizing films around clear stories and motivated, volitional characters was, none the less, an acknowledged value in this period. Of course, action genres like westerns and other sensational films still showed the importance of non-narrative attractions, but these were largely absorbed into character-driven plots. At the same time, while the narrative integration of the transitional period certainly looks forward to the later classical style, it maintained a unique style. Ben Brewster (1991*b*) and Charles Keil (1995) have stressed that the one-reel film standard of this period demanded narrative compression and encouraged patterns of recurrence. While these aspects are not contradictory to the classical style, they seem more endemic to short films than to features. Brewster (1991*b*) has pointed out that early features, such as the scandalous *Traffic in Souls* from 1913, often reflected the patterns of individual reels in their structure (partly due to the fact that many theatres owned only one projector, necessitating a pause between reels). Indeed, one of the earliest long film formats, the serial (appearing around 1912–13 with Edison's *What Happened to Mary*), literally spun out its narrative reel by reel, as single-reel instalments were screened every week. The serial, with its strong emphasis on thrilling attractions, its often rather incoherent plotting, and its compromise between the single reel and the feature structure, may, as Singer (1993) claims, stand as an emblem of the often contradictory impulses of the transitional period.

If the transitional period corresponds to an attempt to bring order and regularity to film production and distribution (often through legally dubious practices, as the US courts decided when they ruled against the MPPC in an antitrust action in 1914), how does this new narratively integrated film structure relate to changes in exhibition and audience? A number of scholars, myself included (Gunning 1990), see the cinema of narrative integration as an element in a concerted attempt to attract a middle-class audience and gain respectability for the cinema. Production companies adapted literary classics, while filmmakers devised cinematic codes to tell stories of the type familiar from middle-class forms like the short-story magazine, apparently with such audiences in view.

However, this view of the bourgeoisification of cinema during the transitional period can be exaggerated, particularly if one relies on trade journals, whose desire for the imprimatur of respectability led them to exaggerate the number of middle-class patrons attending movies or the comfort and order of theatres. Careful reading of trade journals and industry publicity reveals a strong desire to retain working-class patrons, while the emphasis on signs of middle-class approval partly served to allay the attacks of reformers suspicious of the new form, rather than indicated real conditions. The only existing survey of film audiences indicates that in New York City the working class still made up nearly three-quarters of the audience in 1910, while a category called 'clerical', referring most likely to office workers (i.e. a newly emerging lower middle class), constituted most of the other quarter (Davis 1911; Singer 1996). However, small-town audiences may have had a different composition, as Allen (1996) stresses.

William Uricchio and Roberta Pearson's (1993) investigation of Vitagraph's 'quality films'—adaptations from Dante or Shakespeare (*Francesca di Rimini, Julius Caesar,* both 1908), or films on cultural figures such as Napoleon or Moses (*Napoleon, the Man of Destiny,* 1909; *The Life of Moses,* 1910)—found that while such films aimed at attracting an audience who might scorn typical nickelodeon fare, they were also carefully designed to be accessible to the working-class audience most exhibitors relied upon. This 'dual address' seems typical of this period and should alert us to the dangers of seeing the bourgeoisification of the cinema

A model for future westerns—*The Great Train Robbery* (1903)

at the end of early cinema as an established fact without complexity or resistance. The transitional period appears to be less a gradual fade into the classical paradigm than a period of ambivalence and contestation.

Early cinema and modernity

The study of early cinema has consistently expanded its area of investigation. Research into the exhibition of early films extended into a consideration of audiences and the role the nickelodeon played in American society. Uricchio and Pearson (1993) found that determining what audience producers aimed for, or how widely films were comprehensible to different classes, called for an investigation of the intertextual framework in which images of Napoleon or scenes from Shakespeare circulated outside cinema, from school textbooks to advertising cards.

Perhaps the most far-reaching (and possibly most controversial) extension of the study of early cinema relates techniques of early film, particularly the cinema of attractions, to large-scale transformations of daily experience in the era of urbanization and modernization. This approach draws inspiration from Walter Benjamin (1969) and Siegfried Kracauer (1995) as well as Miriam Hansen's (1987, 1991b, 1993, 1995) discussion of these authors' writings on the cinema. Benjamin, writing in the 1930s, related the shock of the rapidly changing experience of the urban environment and new technology to cinematic techniques, such as rapid montage, slow or fast motion, and huge close-ups. Kracauer, writing in the later 1920s, found that the visual stimulus of the picture palace captured the mechanization and surface character of the modern life as the pursuit of distraction. In my writings (Gunning 1994a, c, 1995b), I have claimed that Benjamin's and Kracauer's analyses could be used to describe the cinema of attractions with its aggressive viewer-confronting address and discontinuous structures.

Early films dealing with the railroad provide a powerful intersection of the aggressive address of the cinema of attractions and the technological transformations of modern life. The many early films taken from trains of the passing landscape (e.g. Biograph's *Into the Heart of the Catskills*, 1906) and the Hales Tours exhibition of films in theatres designed to imitate railroad cars (including sound effects and ticket takers) reveal early cinema's affinity with the railroad. Lynne Kirby's (1996)

work on this subject, as well as works by Mary Ann Doane (1985) and myself (Gunning 1994a, 1995c) drew on the work of a contemporary Benjaminian, Wolfgang Schivelbusch, whose book *The Railway Journey* (1977) claimed that the experience of railway travel, with its speed and potential danger, was emblematic of modern perception. In films shot from moving trains Kirby found a fascination with what Schivelbusch calls 'panoramic perception', a view of the world in motion through a window or other framing device. The shocklike structure of the abrupt transitions and often aggressive imagery of the cinema of attractions also reflected for Kirby the sense of hysteria which the fear of the railway accident brought to modern consciousness. Eileen Bowser (1995), Yuri Tsivian (1994), and Gunning (1991b) have made a similar case for the telephone in early cinema, knitting together distant spaces and creating new dramatic situations.

Following Walter Benjamin's example, writers on early cinema have isolated a number of emblematic instances of modernity besides the railway and the telephone: the World Expositions, the department store, the city streets, the diorama and panorama, urban billboards. Anne Friedberg (1993) has related a number of these to the 'mobilized virtual gaze', the heightened involvement of a viewer in a visual illusion combined with motion which she sees as essential not only to the pre-history of cinema (in devices like the diorama and panorama), but also to the subjectivity of modernity. My writings (Gunning 1994a, b) have emphasized that such relations are embedded in the way early films embraced modern technology or new environments (such as the World Expositions or the amusement park) as subjects for films (Porter's *Coney Island at Night*, 1905; Biograph's *Panorama St Louis Exposition*, 1904). Ben Singer (1995b) has detailed how the most aggressive aspects of the cinema of attractions reflected both the experience of urban life with its threats and danger, and its portrayal in the sensationalist press. Lauren Rabinovitz's (1990) research on Chicago amusement parks sees these mechanized forms of amusement as another example of accelerated modern experience with a stong relation to early cinema, focusing as well on the way amusement parks shed light on female subjectivity, an issue central to many investigations of modernity, including the work of Hansen (1991a), Friedberg (1993), Bruno (1993), and Singer's (1995a) work on the serial queen, the powerful woman protagonist of the films of the serial genre, such as Pathé's *The Perils of Pauline*, from 1914.

Feminist theory has provided a key motive for these investigations on multiple levels, not only as part of the vitally important project of bringing to light the neglected and often suppressed role of women in American history. One could claim that feminist film theory in the late 1970s both adopted the subjectivity of the apparatus theory of cinema and supplied its most radical critique. Laura Mulvey (1975) pointed out that the apparatus as constructed within this theory and as exemplified by classical Hollywood cinema embodied a male gaze. If this were so, not only did it marginalize and problematize female subjectivity, but it also traced a basic fissure in the theory's universal claims if one had to conceive the subject, not as a Platonic entity, but as a gendered being. This introduction of gender difference opened the flood gates for a reconceptualization of the film spectator open to history and the play of gender and ethnic difference. While an attempt to reconcile this historical and cultural investigation of spectatorship with the assumptions of apparatus theory may encounter contradictions in method, the historical investigation of early cinema and modernity has sketched a model of a more fluid concept of subjectivity, along the lines of Hansen's (1991a) treatment of the public sphere of early cinema as providing a ground for processing new experiences.

Art historian Jonathan Crary provides one of the most far-reaching theories of the relation between modernity and historical subjectivities. Crary (1990) investigates psychological theories and accounts of the physiology of perception of the nineteenth century (such as those of Helmholtz and Fechner), claiming that these new models of perception switched focus from the accurate reflection of exterior phenomena to the physiology of the senses. This view found support in the perceptional illusions that optical devices, such as the phenakistiscope and the stereoscope (which are often seen as precursors to the cinema), make visible, but which do not actually exist other than in the observer's sensorium. Crary claims that the breakdown of representation in painting associated with modernism has its roots in this earlier technological and philosophical modernization of vision. Closer to Foucault than to apparatus theory, Crary sees subject formation as a historical process inscribed in techniques and institutions specific to different periods. He locates a major shift in the conception of visuality in the modern period. Although Crary discusses early cinema only in passing, his insights provide a basis for the historicization of perception and visual experience.

What has been termed the 'modernity thesis' has recently been subjected to serious criticism, particularly by David Bordwell (1996a, b). As a cognitivist, Bordwell finds a 'history' of vision, perception, or experience a dubious concept, vague at best and absurd at its most extreme. 'It is highly unlikely that visual perception has changed over recorded human history,' he claims (1996: 23). Bordwell finds that the ultimate failure of the modernity thesis lies in its dubious attempt to tie stylistic aspects of early cinema to modern experience. Developing an objection also raised by Charles Keil (1995), Bordwell asks how one can relate the fragmentary, aggressive form of the cinema of attractions to abrasive modern experience in the street or to new modes of transportation, since these aspects of modernity continued, or even increased during the transitional period, which subordinated the more aggressive aspects of attractions to the coherence of narrative integration.

In many respects such criticism is well taken, but it may reflect irreconcilable positions about the nature of history and experience. Bordwell is aware that no theorist of modernity could responsibly claim a transformation in the perceptual hard wiring of human beings, so some of his objections seem to be based on a disingenuous *reductio ad absurdum*. However, there is no question that terms such as 'experience' or even the use of the word 'perception' remain in need of greater precision and discussion. Crary (1990: 6) states: 'Whether perception or vision actually change is ir-

> **While an attempt to reconcile this historical and cultural investigation of spectatorship with the assumptions of apparatus theory may encounter contradictions in method, the historical investigation of early cinema and modernity has sketched a model of a more fluid concept of subjectivity, along the lines of Hansen's treatment of the public sphere of early cinema as providing a ground for processing new experiences.**

relevant, for they have no autonomous history. What changes are the plural forces and rules composing the field in which perception occurs.' Thus what needs to be made more precise are the social mediations of experience, observable not only in works of art, but in the scientific and political discourse of the period.

Bordwell's contention that the experience of modernity remains irrelevant to the history of film style is more complex. There is no question that the relations drawn between the structures of modernity and those of early film frequently lack specificity and remain on the level of vague analogies. However, in tying the pace and abruptness of early films to modern experience, contemporary critics are not so much inventing an analogy as rediscovering one. Such connections were frequently made by the first commentators on the cinema, who recognized in the new media an experience related to modern city life. As a fact of discourse this is an important element of the history of film reception, one worth careful research and consideration. Bordwell's and Keil's claim that the modernity thesis cannot explain stylistic change is probably correct, but seems to defeat a claim that no scholar of early cinema ever made. The relations between modernity and early film need not be limited to the cinema of attractions. The thrill melodramas of the transitional period, such as Griffith's last-minute rescues in such films as *The Lonely Villa*, 1909, and *The Lonedale Operator*, 1911 (with their use of modern technology such as the telephone, the railway, and the telegraph to convey a new sense of urgency and danger), are prime examples of early film's relation to modernity. Reference to the broader contexts of modernity cannot, and does not desire to, explain everything. Changes in film style derive from many immanent causes: changes in technology, industry realignment, cycles of innovation and canonization, as well as transformations in film's relation to society—relations, I should add, that are fully mediated and traceable in contemporary discourse, and not a matter of a mystical reflection of a *Zeitgeist*.

Topics for further research

While the history of early cinema in the last two decades has seen a sudden growth that almost recalls the nickelodeon explosion, with many more scholars making important contributions than can be included in this summary, there are still many issues to explore. Many of these, such as the relation between social class

and the nickelodeon, or the validity of the relation of early cinema to modernity, have already been discussed. I want briefly to add some others. Since this chapter treats early *American* cinema, I have not dealt with scholarship on early cinema in other countries. While the United States has served as a key area of investigation, it is hard to conceive of early cinema history without the work done on early French cinema by a large number of scholars in France as well as the United States, and increasingly in Italy, Germany, Britain, Denmark, Sweden, and Russia, as well as work on film production and exhibition outside Europe and the United States. The period of early cinema marks a time when films circulated freely across borders and in which the concept of a national cinema was largely unarticulated. Richard Abel's recent research (1995b) on the effect of the French production company Pathé on American cinema shows that to examine even American cinema within a narrowly national context leads to distortion. Since Pathé films were the most widely shown and most successful films exhibited in the United States at the beginning of the transitional period (1906–9), Abel's claim that they had a definitive effect on the development of American film seems unquestionable. Pathé's early experiments in parallel editing certainly influenced Griffith's development of this technique at Biograph, as the comparison of Pathé's *Physician of the Castle* (1908) and Griffith's *The Lonely Villa* (1909) undertaken by both myself (Gunning 1991b) and Barry Salt (1985) demonstrates. In the transitional period the American film industry tried to define and produce an 'American film' in opposition to Europe, a goal that matched the MPPC's attempt to marginalize European producers. The construction of national cinema cultures began in early cinema and calls for more research.

An area of relative neglect in the study of the early cinema is non-fiction filmmaking. While this has gained more attention from European scholars such as Stephen Bottomore (1988) and the archivists at the Nederlands Filmmuseum (Hertogs and De Klerck 1994), it remains in need of more research and theorization from a US perspective. Until about 1905 the bulk of American production was non-fiction films, but these have not received the investigation that reflects their importance in this period.

The transitional period needs more research. Because of its limited focus my work on Griffith at Biograph during this period, while setting up issues of broad concern, cannot serve as an account of this period in the US generally. Charles Keil's (1995) broader-based survey of the transitional period should answer a number of questions about the techniques of narrative integration. Even more neglected is the end of the transitional period, the era of early features. Perhaps the most important work being produced about this era comes from Ben Brewster and Lea Jacobs's (1997) thorough discussion of early cinema's relation to theatrical practice. Although not restricted to the United States, this work traces the often surprising degree to which theatrical practice (including performance style, lighting techniques, and sensation scenes) inspired early feature films, while also undergoing strong transformations. Rather than repeating the simple account promulgated by Nicholas Vardac (1949), of cinema taking up the visual tradition of nineteenth-century theatre, Brewster and Jacobs tell a much more nuanced and detailed story of cross-media influence. The date that Bordwell, Staiger, and Thompson selected for the beginning of the classical Hollywood cinema—1917—still seems a reasonable one for the period in which most American films show a mastery of the basic codes and conventions of fiction filmmaking. However, the selection of this date, several years after feature films had become the basic product of the American film industry, acknowledges that the early feature period itself saw a gradual spread of the codes of classical narration as well as competing alternatives. Further research on early features will undoubtedly find a number of stylistic approaches in terms of reliance on editing versus deep staging and the relative importance of intra-scene editing versus parallel editing. But by the end of the teens a basic narrative vocabulary is in place meriting Bordwell, Staiger, and Thompson's term 'classical Hollywood cinema'.

Early cinema remains an area which grapples with crucial issues of film study. Besides providing a clearer picture of the earliest era of our medium through new research and historical models, the investigation of early cinema continues to explore and redefine encounters between spectator and screen, audience and film, cinema and social context. From the energy generated by such debates, early cinema has demonstrated that film studies still engages vital issues, and that cinema stands at the core of our understanding of the modern world.

BIBLIOGRAPHY

Abel, Richard (ed.) (1995a), *Silent Cinema* (New Brunswick, NJ: Rutgers University Press).

—— (1995b), 'The Perils of Pathé; or, The Americanization of the American Cinema', in Charney and Schwartz (1995).

Allen, Robert C. (1980), *Vaudeville and Film 1895–1915: A Study in Media Interaction* (New York: Arno Press).

—— (1983), 'Motion Picture Exhibition in Manhattan 1906–1912: Beyond the Nickelodeon', in Fell (1993).

—— (1996), 'Manhattan Myopia; or, Oh! Iowa!', *Cinema Journal*, 35/3: 75–103.

Balides, Constance (1993), 'Scenarios of Exposure in Everyday Life: Women in the Cinema of Attractions', *Screen*, 34/1: 19–31 (Spring).

Baudry, Jean-Louis (1986), 'Ideological Effects of the Basic Cinematographic Apparatus', in Rosen, 'Narrative, Apparatus, Ideology' (New York: Columbia University Press).

Benjamin, Walter (1969), *Illuminations: Essays and Reflections*, ed. Hannah Arendt and trans. Harry Zohn (New York: Schocken Books).

Bordwell, David, (1996a), 'La Nouvelle Mission de Feuillade; or, What was Mise en Scène?', *The Velvet Light Trap*, 37: 10–29.

—— (1996b), *Visions of Cinema: On the History of Film Style* (Cambridge, Mass.: Harvard University Press).

—— and **Kristin Thompson** (1983), 'Linearity, Materialism and the Study of Early American Cinema', *Wide Angle*, 5/3: 4–15.

—— **Janet Staiger,** and **Kristin Thompson** (1985), *The Classical Hollywood Cinema: Film Style and Mode of Production to 1960* (New York: Columbia University Press).

Bottomore, Stephen (1988), 'Shots in the Dark: The Real Origins of Film Editing', *Sight and Sound*, 57/3 (Summer), 200–4.

Bowser, Eileen (1990), *The Transformation of Cinema: History of the American Cinema, II: 1907–1915* (New York: Scribner's).

—— (1995), 'The Telephone Thriller; or, The Terrors of Modern Technology', lecture given at the British Film Institute.

Brewster, Ben (1991a), 'A Bunch of Violets', paper presented to the Society for Cinema Studies Conference, Washington, June.

—— (1991b), '*Traffic in Souls*: An Experiment in Feature Length Narrative Construction', *Cinema Journal*, 31 (Fall).

*—— and **Lea Jacobs** (1997), *Theatre to Cinema: Stage Pictorialism and the Early Feature Film* (Oxford: Oxford University Press).

Bruno, Giuliana (1993), *Streetwalking On a Ruined Map: Cultural Theory and the City Films of Elvira Notari* (Princeton: Princeton University Press).

Burch, **Noël** (1990), *Life to those Shadows* (Berkeley: University of California Press).

Charney, **Leo,** and **Vanessa R. Schwartz** (eds.) (1995), *Cinema and the Invention of Modern Life* (Berkeley: University of California Press).

Cherchi Usai, **Paolo** (1994), *Burning Passions: An Introduction to the Study of Silent Cinema* (London: British Film Institute).

Crary, **Jonathan** (1990), *Techniques of the Observer: On Vision and Modernity in the Nineteenth Century* (Cambridge, Mass.: MIT Press).

Davis, **Michael** (1911), *The Exploitation of Pleasure: A Study of Commerical Recreations in New York City* (New York: Russell Sage Foundation).

Doane, **Mary Ann** (1985), 'When the Direction of the Force Acting on the Body is Changed: The Moving Image', *Wide Angle,* 7/2.

*Elsaesser, **Thomas** (ed.) (1990), *Early Cinema: Space Frame Narrative* (London: British Film Institute).

Fell, **John** (ed.) (1993), *Film before Griffith* (Berkeley: University of California Press).

Friedberg, **Anne** (1993), *Window Shopping: Cinema and the Postmodern* (Berkeley: University of California Press).

Gaudreault, **André** (1988) *Du littéraire au filmique: système du récit* (Paris: Meridians Klincksieck).

—— (1990), 'Film, Narrative, Narration: The Cinema of the Lumière Brothers', in Elsaesser (1990).

Gomery, **Douglas** (1982), 'Movie Audiences, Urban Geography and the History of American Film', *The Velvet Light Trap,* 19: 23–9.

—— (1992), *Shared Pleasures: A History of Movie Presentation in the United States* (Madison: University of Wisconsin Press).

*Gunning, **Tom** (1990), 'The Cinema of Attractions: Early Film, its Specator and the Avant-Garde', in Elsaesser (1990).

—— (1991a), *D. W. Griffith and the Origins of American Narrative Film* (Champaign: University of Illinois Press).

—— (1991b), 'Heard over the Phone: *The Lonely Villa* and the De Lorde Tradition of Terrified Communication', *Screen,* 32/2 (Summer), 184–96.

—— (1994a), 'The Whole Town's Gawking: Early Cinema and the Visual Experience of Modernity', *Yale Journal of Criticism,* 7/2 (Fall).

—— (1994b), 'Crazy Machines in the Garden of Forking Paths: Mischief Gags and the Origins of American Film Comedy', in Kristine Karnick and Henry Jenkins (eds.), *Classical Hollywood Comedy* (London: Routledge).

—— (1994c), 'The World as Object Lesson: Cinema Audiences, Visual Culture and the St Louis World's Fair', *Film History* 5/4 (Winter), 422–44.

—— (1995a), 'Now you See it, now you Don't: The Temporality of the Cinema of Attractions', in Richard Abel (ed.), *Silent Cinema* (New Brunswick, NJ: Rutgers University Press).

—— (1995b), 'An Aesthetic of Astonishment: Early Film and the [In]Credulous Spectator', in Linda Williams (ed.), *Viewing Positions: Ways of Seeing Films* (New Brunswick, NJ: Rutgers University Press).

Habermas, **Jurgen** (1962/1991), *The Structural Transformation of the Public Sphere: An Inquiry into a Category of Bourgeois Society,* trans. Thomas Burger and Frederick Lawrence (Cambridge, Mass.: MIT Press).

Hansen, **Miriam** (1987), 'Benjamin, Cinema and Experience: The Blue Flower in the Land of Technology', *New German Critique,* 40 (Winter), 179–224.

*—— (1991a), *Babel and Babylon: Spectatorship in American Silent Film* (Cambridge: Mass.: Harvard University Press).

—— (1991b), 'Decentric Perspectives: Kracauer's Early Writings on Film and Mass Culture', *New German Critique,* 54 (Fall), 47–76.

—— (1993), 'Of Mice and Ducks: Benjamin and Adorno on Disney', *South Atlantic Quarterly,* 92/1 (Winter), 27–61.

—— (1995) 'America, Paris, the Alps: Kracauer (and Benjamin) on Cinema and Modernity', in Leo Charney and Vanessa R. Schwartz (eds.), *Cinema and the Invention of Modern Life* (Berkeley: University of California Press).

Hertogs, **Daan,** and **Nico De Klerck** (eds.) (1994), *Non-Fiction from the Teens* (Amsterdam: Nederlands Filmmuseum).

Holman, **Roger** (ed.) (1982), *Cinema 1900–1906: An Analytical Study* (Brussels: FIAF).

*Keil, **Charles** (1995), 'American Cinema 1907–1913: The Nature of Transition', dissertation, University of Wisconsin at Madison.

*—— (1996), paper presented to the Society for Cinema Studies Conference, New York City, May.

Kirby, **Lynne** (1996), *Parallel Tracks: The Railroad and Silent Cinema* (Durham, NC: Duke University Press).

Kracauer, **Siegfried** (1963/1995), *The Mass Ornament: Weimar Essays,* ed. and trans. Thomas Y. Levin (Cambridge, Mass.: Harvard University Press).

Lindsey, **Shelley Stamp** (1996), *Ladies' Night: Women and Movie Culture in America during the Transitional Era* (Princeton: Princeton University Press).

Lindstrom, **J. A.** (1996), ' "Class Hatred Seeds Sown": Zoning the Debate about Class and Early Film Exhibition in Chicago', paper presented to the Society for Cinema Studies Conference, New York City, May.

Mayne, **Judith** (1990) *The Woman at the Keyhole: Feminism and Woman's Cinema* (Bloomington: University of Indiana Press).

Merritt, **Russell** (1976), 'Nickelodeon Theaters 1905–1914: Building an Audience for the Movies' in Tino Balio (ed.), *The American Film Industry* (Madison: University of Wisconsin Press).

Mulvey, **Laura** (1975), 'Visual Pleasure and Narrative Cinema', *Screen,* 16/3: 6–27.

*Musser, Charles (1990), *The Emergence of Cinema: The American Screen to 1907*, History of the American Cinema, i (New York: Scribner's).

—— (1991), *Before the Nickelodeon: Edwin S. Porter and the Edison Manufacturing Company* (Berkeley: University of California Press).

—— and **Carol Nelson** (1991), *High Class Motion Pictures: Lyman Howe and the Forgotten Era of Traveling Exhibition 1880–1920* (Princeton: Princeton University Press).

—— (1994), 'Rethinking Early Cinema: Cinema of Attractions and Narrativity', *Yale Journal of Criticism*, 7/2 (Fall), 203–32.

Negt, Oskar, and **Alexander Kluge** (1993), *Public Sphere and Experience: Towards an Analysis of the Bourgeois and Proletarian Public Sphere* (Minneapolis: University of Minnesota Press).

Peiss, Kathy (1986), *Cheap Amusements: Working Women and Leisure in Turn-of-the-Century New York* (Philadelphia: Temple University Press).

Rabinovitz, Lauren (1990), 'Temptations of Pleasure: Nickelodeons, Amusement Parks and the Sights of Female Pleasure', *Camera Obscura*, 23: 71–90.

Rosenzweig, Roy (1983), *Eight Hours for what we Will: Workers and Leisure in an Industrial City 1870–1920* (Cambridge: Cambridge University Press).

Salt, Barry (1985), '*The Physician of the Castle*', *Sight and Sound*, 54/4 (Autumn), 284–5.

Schivelbusch, Wolfgang (1977), *The Railway Journey* (New York: Urizen Press).

Singer, Ben (1993), 'Fiction Tie-ins and Narrative Intelligibility 1911–1918', *Film History*, 5/4: 489–504.

—— (1995a), 'Female Power in the Serial Queen Melodrama: The Etiology of an Anomaly', in Richard Abel (ed.), *Silent Cinema* (New Brunswick, NJ: Rutgers University Press).

—— (1995b), 'Manhattan Nickelodeons: New Data on Audiences and Exhibition', *Cinema Journal*, 34/3 (Spring), 5–35.

—— (1995c), 'Modernity, Hyperstimulus and the Rise of Popular Sensationalism', in Charney and Schwartz, (1995).

—— (1996), 'New York, just like I Pictured It . . .', *Cinema Journal*, 35/3: 104–28.

Sklar, Robert (1990), 'Oh! Althusser!: Historiography and the Rise of Cinema Studies', in Robert Sklar and Charles Musser (eds.), *Resisting Images: Essays on Cinema and History* (Philadelphia: Temple University Press).

Sopocy, Martin (1978), 'A Narrated Cinema: The Pioneer Story of James A. Williamson', *Cinema Journal*, 18/1 (Fall), 1–28.

Staiger, Janet (1992), *Interpeting Films: Studies in the Historical Reception of American Cinema* (Princeton: Princeton University Press).

—— (1995), *Bad Women: Controlling Sexuality in Early American Cinema* (Minneapolis: University of Minnesota Press).

Thompson, Kristin (1988), *Breaking the Glass Armour: Neoformalist Film Analysis* (Princeton: Princeton University Press).

Tsivian, Yuri (1994), 'Speeding the Bullet Message: Images of "Elsewheres" in the Age of Electronic Media', paper presented to the Domitor Conference, New York City, June.

Uricchio, William, and **Roberta Pearson** (1993), *Reframing Culture: The Case of the Vitagraph Quality Films* (Princeton: Princeton University Press).

Vardac, Nicholas (1949), *Stage to Screen: Theatrical Method from Garrick to Griffith* (Cambridge, Mass.: Harvard University Press).

Waller, Gregory A. (1995), *Main Street Amusements: Movies and Commerical Entertainment in a Southern City 1896–1930* (Washington: Smithsonian Institution Press).

5

Classical Hollywood film and melodrama

E. Ann Kaplan

In the first half of the twentieth century the classical Hollywood film was the dominant popular form through which the bourgeoisie increasingly represented itself, its values, and the working classes—to whom cinema was earlier largely addressed. This dominant popular form developed out of, and existed alongside, the popular and classical novel and their corollaries—the melodrama and the 'well-made' play—that preceded film and with which it had most affinity (Altman 1992). Indeed, as will be clear in what follows, Hollywood film becomes the site in which notions of the 'classical', developed in relation to drama and the novel as transparent forms reflecting social reality, find themselves in tension with the sensationalism and spectacle of the melodrama.

Geoffrey Nowell-Smith (1977) has argued that theatrical melodrama arose in the late eighteenth century as a form that specifically addressed the new bourgeoisie. As Nowell-Smith puts it, 'Author, audience and subject matter are put on a place of equality,' as against the hierarchical relations implied in the earlier epic and tragic forms. 'Mystified though it may be,' Nowell-Smith notes, 'the address is from one bourgeois to another bourgeois, and the subject matter is the life of the bourgeoisie' (Nowell-Smith 1975: 71). The Greek melodrama, while anticipating some of the modes of hysteria and excess of late eighteenth-century melodrama, is situated in a very different relation to its audience. The characters are far from mimicking the lives and status of those watching, retaining their mythic and ritualistic dimensions. It is when the monarchic paradigm is overthrown by democratic urges that, first, the melodrama arises and leads, once the camera is invented, to the Hollywood film.

Given these origins of Hollywood cinema, about which theorists of the classical cinema do not basically disagree, it is somewhat paradoxical that such theorists coined the term 'classical cinema' in the first place. As will be clear, the term arose because links were forged (somewhat misleadingly) between cinema and the classical novel rather than with popular theatre. It is precisely this tension between a paradoxical 'classical' (melodramatic) cinematic form and feminist theories of a less 'classical', and therefore possibly subversive, melodramatic mode that I explore below.

Film theorists, then, differ first in their understanding of the 'classical' in cinema, and second in the degree to which they are willing to distinguish classicism from the possibly subversive aspects of the sensationalism and spectacle of melodrama. I first outline differing theories of classical cinema. I will then show how feminist film theorists' interventions in turning to the woman's melodrama (building on the research of Nowell-Smith, Peter Brooks, and Thomas Elsaesser) unwittingly exposed the limitations and blindnesses of both conceptions of classical cinema outlined earlier. I end by offering a position that seems pertinent to the current moment.

Classical cinema

Two main theorizations of classical cinema were developed by film scholars between 1950 and 1980. The first evolved out of French 1950s film criticism—largely through André Bazin, but also, later, through Christian Metz. Bazin's theories were extended in the 1960s in the context of French left politics and under the influence of Althusserian Marxism. The resistances of May 1968 and their aftermath also contributed to the *Cahiers du cinéma* positions outlined below, especially in the work of Jean-Louis Comolli and Jean Narboni. British film scholars in and around the journal *Screen* further developed French theories (e.g. Noël Burch, Stephen Heath, Ben Brewster, and Colin MacCabe). Both the British and the French ideas about classical cinema became part of American scholars' research (see Rosen 1986).

The second conception of classical cinema emerged in reaction to, but still governed by and strangely similar to, these prior theories, mainly through the work on Hollywood narrative by David Bordwell, Janet Staiger, and Kristin Thompson in the 1980s. These theories have become increasingly influential in the 1990s in the wake of students trained in them. In what follows, I detail briefly the development of these two main conceptions of classical cinema from Bazin to Bordwell.

The concept of classical cinema emerged in France through the influence of André Bazin's lectures in the 1950s (collected in Bazin 1967, 1971). Particularly in his essay 'The Evolution of the Language of Cinema', Bazin began to outline the practices of camera-work, editing, and sound that he appreciated in both selected Hollywood and French directors—practices which he claimed as representing cinema at its height (or 'in its essence'). In Bazin's words, seeing films by William Wyler, John Ford, or Marcel Carné, 'one has the feeling that in them an art has found its perfect balance, its ideal form of expression' (Bazin 1967: 29). The necessary practice of montage, which Bazin believed Soviet and German directors fetishized, must be combined with 'the sequence of shots "in depth"'. Citing particularly the films of William Wyler and Orson Welles as exemplary, Bazin argues that 'depth of focus brings the spectator into a relation with the image closer to that which he enjoys with reality' (35). Here, Bazin establishes that narrative coherence and the unity of filmic elements (a kind of classicism in the sense of the French neo-classicism of Racine, for example) define the best in Hollywood cinema.

Although he does not mention the classical novel explicitly, it seems that Bazin has this form in mind as he tries to argue for the kind of cinema that represents its 'highest' mode. Bazin's ideas influenced the *Cahiers du cinéma* collective in the 1960s, but in developing Bazin's ideas in the context of May 1968, the group moved from the concept of Hollywood's aesthetic representing cinema's 'maturity' to a focus on the ideological investment underlying the aesthetic forms Bazin had described. Comolli and Narboni's 1969 *Cahiers du cinéma* editorial, which was to shape dramatically Euro-American research on Hollywood cinema in the 1970s, started from the proposition that since films (like books and magazines) are 'produced and distributed by the capitalist economic system and within the dominant ideology' then they must ask 'which films, books and magazines allow the ideology a free, unhampered passage, transmit it with crystal clarity, serve as its chosen language? And which attempt to make it turn back and reflect itself, intercept it, make it visible by revealing its mechanisms, by blocking them?' (Comolli and Narboni 1969/1989: 23–4). They are not interested in whether or not cinema is a high or low form: for them, what is important (and what defines specific Hollywood films) is the *class* address of its aesthetic forms.

> **Bazin establishes that narrative coherence and the unity of filmic elements (a kind of classicism in the sense of the French neo-classicism of Racine, for example) define the best in Hollywood cinema.**

Comolli and Narboni claim that, while ideology says that 'cinema "reproduces" reality', in fact this idea of reality is 'nothing but an expression of the prevailing ideology'. Here they challenge Bazin's classical notion that the camera 'is an impartial instrument which grasps, or rather is impregnated by, the world in its "concrete reality"' (25). They proceed to distinguish five basically different types of film considered in relation to prevailing ideology. The types range from those completely complicit with prevailing ideology; to those which can be read on two levels, one of which

Touch of Evil (1958)—Orson Welles as a corrupt detective checks out Janet Leigh, pawn in the struggle between Welles and Leigh's husband, Charlton Heston

critiques prevailing ideology; to those which take politics as their subject-matter but do not challenge governing cinematic codes; to, finally, those which 'point out the gap produced between film and ideology by the way the films work, and show how they work' (28).

It was this famous formulation that resulted in the pervasive 1970s binary of a 'classical realist' and a 'counter' cinema perhaps most clearly articulated in Peter Wollen's essay on Godard's *Vent d'est* (1982). This in a way combined Bazin's notion of classicism from classical drama and novel and the ideological schematics of Comolli and Narboni. The ordering and coherence devices of classical Hollywood realism are seen to cover over ideological contradictions and to position the spectator through editing practices within dominant ideology.

Christian Metz's bold attempt to establish an over-arching 'language of film' with his semiotic model of classical Hollywood (he called it 'la grande syntagmatique') was an important attempt to make a science out of filmic narrative patterns (Metz 1974). His in-depth analysis of *Adieu Philippine* (1962) provided a model that others—such as Stephen Heath (1975) in his brilliant study of Welles's *Touch of Evil* (1958)—strove to follow. In doing so, he revealed how diverse and multifaceted these narratives were. While Metz failed to develop a set of codes that would apply to all films, his schema has been useful in determining how far a film fits, or departs from, classical narrative modes. His work helped in understanding film as a 'discourse', and the multiple ways time and space could be ordered in film. But, even within the 'classical' group, fitting a film into Metz's language of film—into the codes he had defined—exposed segments that could not be labelled according to the choices which Metz had described. It was also not always clear how charting the film's narrative segments helped in understanding its meanings (but see Stam *et al.* 1992: 37–56 for positive claims).

Metz's (1975) later psychoanalytically based research on the 'Imaginary Signifier' was influential in introducing *subjectivity* into theories seeking to establish fixed systems on which Hollywood worked. Metz combined Lacan's linguistic extensions of Freud's psychoanalytic theories and his distinction between an 'Imaginary' and a 'Symbolic' psychic arena with Metz's own semiotics to produce an important application of psychoanalytic theories to film and its reception. His most important contributions here were finding a correspondence between Lacan's mirror phase and the spectator's identification with the screen; and his distinction of two main kinds of cinematic identification, which he called 'primary' and 'secondary'.

In Britain and then the United States, the scholar who took up and developed Comolli and Narboni's ideas in the 1970s was Noël Burch. Burch's research developed their notions of five kinds of cinema ranging out from the classical to the avant-garde. This had a great impact on the *Screen* group as well as on the United States' burgeoning cinema studies. However, these scholars, coming as many did out of literary training, returned to Bazin's implicit linking of cinema with the classical *novel* instead of with the popular melodrama, and to the centrality of realism to the form.

Colin MacCabe's (1974) essay 'Realism and Cinema: Notes on Some Brechtian Theses' is a case in point. The essay succinctly summarized and furthered many of the *Cahiers* ideas, only now with specific reference to the classical novel, to Brechtian theatre, and Rossellini films. MacCabe shares with Bazin the idea that classical Hollywood cinema relies on realism, but he is concerned to show that this is only one construction of a 'real', not *the* reality that Bazin claimed cinema could capture. For MacCabe, 'The detour through literature is necessary because, in many ways, the structure is much more obvious there and also because of the historical dominance of the classic realist novel over much film production' (1974: 8). MacCabe argues that classical realism is characterized by a hierarchy of discourses 'defined in terms of an empirical notion of truth', which means that the 'metalanguage is not regarded as material: it is dematerialised to achieve perfect representation—to let the identity of things shine through the window of words' (8). As will be clear

below, the conception of 'classical cinema' produced from this analogy was ultimately insufficient to account for the complex traditions on which 'classical' cinema actually relied.

Noël Burch's 1979 film *Correction, Please!* provided an amusing and informative demonstration of how Hollywood's classical narrative style was historically produced as a method for engaging the spectator's identification and permitting the evolution of a profitable film production *system* not that different from factory modes of production. His film cleverly satirized Hollywood realism and suggested strategies for reversing and revealing its ideological codes.

It is important that this post-Bazin notion of the classical cinema was primarily ideological. It was designed to show how the Hollywood system worked to produce its formidable realist illusionism with its individualist, materialist, and inherently capitalist ideology, repeated from genre to genre through the repetition of similar cinematic codes and conventions.

> **This post-Bazin notion of the classical cinema was primarily ideological. It was designed to show how the Hollywood system worked to produce its formidable realist illusionism with its individualist, materialist, and inherently capitalist ideology, repeated from genre to genre through the repetition of similar cinematic codes and conventions.**

While the broad outlines of the first conception of classical cinema as an *ideological* institution that serves specific class needs and whose values never stray far from mainstream US perspectives still seems valid, clearly there were problems with the rigidity of some formulations and with the absence of empirical research to back up broad claims about the ideological construction of the classical cinema. In much of the discussion, 'Hollywood' is both essentialized and homogenized and analysed with insufficient historical specificity.

It is precisely such lacks that David Bordwell, Janet Staiger, and Kristin Thompson began (and continue) to address, attacking certain broad claims made by ideologial scholars of cinema through the accumulation of data on Hollywood and other films from the silent era onwards (Bordwell *et al.* 1985). Like Metz's 'language of cinema', what has become known as 'the Wisconsin project' aims to return cinema analysis to 'science' and away from thematic modes, although their method differs from that of Metz. They refuse the psychoanalytic argument about an ideological appeal to an unconscious and pursue a cognitive psychology approach. Viewers are seen as predisposed to look for the cues a film's narrative provides, and then to organize the sensory data into patterns for processing information already available to the viewers. The method was first worked out in relation to early Soviet directors and Carl Dreyer's films, as well as with Japanese cinema. A 'hypothetical entity', the viewer 'executes operations based on inferences and assumptions to generate the *fabula* from the *syuzhet*, which provides cues as to the order, frequency, and duration of events' (Nichols 1992: 59). For Bordwell, 'the classical Hollywood film . . . presents psychologically defined individuals as its principal causal agents, struggling to solve a clear-cut problem or to attain specific goals, the story ending either with a resolution of the problem, or a clear achievement or non-achievement of the goals. Causality revolving around character provides the prime unifying principle, while spatial configurations are motivated by realism as well as compositional necessity' (Stam *et al.* 1992: 189). Bill Nichols notes the many strengths of Bordwell's analysis of narrational process, including 'its supple blend of theory, criticism and, to a more limited extent, history' (Nichols 1992: 55).

But ironically the structure of Bordwell's overall system is not so dissimilar from that of the ideological notion of classical cinema: Bordwell's formalism results in a highly condensed and somewhat mechanical theory in which he isolates in all texts a 'dominant' to which all other elements are subordinated (Altman 1992). However, for Bordwell, this structure emerged for reasons of narrative coherence rather than (as with MacCabe) to impose as 'truth' a limited and class-based concept of reality. Bordwell, Staiger, and Thompson (1985) offer empirical studies to support claims *vis-à-vis* how film narrative evolved historically, and show that things were in fact more varied and less ideologically driven by bourgeois economic motives than the French-influenced proponents of classical cinema had argued.

I do not here aim to debate in depth the relative merits of these two broad positions on classical cinema—positions that remain pretty much in circulation and that, as indicated, strangely mimic each other in their would-be scientism and would-be 'objectivity'. While I value the empirical research of scholars like Bordwell, I am not convinced by the substitution of a 'formalist poetics' for a governing system of ideology (see *Film Criticism* 1993, esp. Kaplan 1993, Wood 1993). Bordwell's poetics usefully involves close attention to the surface of a film, which means giving perception a bigger role and attending carefully to any one film's unique functions and effects. Important also is the detailed attention to historical development in analysing film narrative. But this begs the question of what Bordwell, Staiger, and Thompson mean by 'history' just as the question was begged by the ideological group. As Nichols points out, Bordwell's notion of history is very limited, not including reference to television, the other arts, or to non-Western films. Further, while Bordwell claims that feminist analyses and concern with minority discourse in film are simply new ideological orientations, telling us nothing about a film *per se*, I would note that there cannot be a 'poetics of film' which is not already deeply implicated in Western issues of race and gender. Bordwell's 'science' excludes feminist theory and also, as Nichols notes, 'regards the viewer as a sexless, genderless, classless, stateless "hypothetical entity"' (Nichols 1992: 64). Only cyborgs—that is, imaginary entities that combine human and machine—Nichols ironically concludes, fit the kind of decoder of cues, or executer of operations that Bordwell's poetics requires.

Thus, we have the irony of a similarity between Bordwell's position and that of Comolli and Narboni. Both claim to outline a specific classical *system*, but their concerns with the system are quite opposite: the French position focuses on cinema's ideological inscription, Bordwell's on the way it functions cognitively to transfer meaning regarding narrative codes and plots. He is not interested in any film's ideology; the French are not interested in any film's 'poetics'. And neither can deal with historically positioned subjects for whom much is at stake in cinematic identification.

Both these conceptions of the 'classical' minimize, if they do not ignore, the other powerful influences—those of popular stage melodrama and consumer culture—feeding the developments in Hollywood and producing the film industry as a site of tension and contradictions. In regard to the melodramatic aspects of sensationalism and the spectacle, the invention of film at the turn of the century was part of a crucial change taking place in the late nineteenth century with the advent of modern consumer culture and advertising. As Allon White has argued, this change 'involved the displacement of pleasure into the realm of the signifier (form, style, association) and its dissociation from the "real" world of work and dreary production'. White notes that this 'dissociation was a necessary correlative to the unfettering of commodity-centered, consumer capitalism' and that 'the creaming off of the signifier from the signified marked a new phase in the production of Western subjectivity in its long march from Feudalism to a bureaucratic society of controlled consumption' (White 1983).

Consumer culture hooks onto the subject's inevitable desiring mode, re-enforcing and exploiting it by constant stimulation. Beginning with the department store and the stage melodrama, the culture of the spectacle is fully inscribed in society with the development of the cinema as an apparatus. Film becomes the form that replaces the popular theatre melodrama in the way it addresses desires invoked by the new consumer culture and, while the popular stage melodrama continues, it is also affected by the culture of the spectacle. The popular novel begins to use description in a self-consciously 'cinematic' style, while some theatre leaves spectacle to the cinema and becomes minimalist.

Film's mode as spectacle dovetails with modes of consumer culture in a circular fashion. That is, film emerges at a certain stage of consumer culture, its modes increasing consumerism and encouraging upward class-striving through accumulation of consumer products. Cinema stimulates new desires and signifying of status through objects. With the invention of cinema, a new self-consciousness is built into the subject's constitution. If Lacan's mirror phase had always been a necessary part of the subject's entry into the Symbolic, it now becomes an inherent part of cultural experience. The other self offered by the mirror becomes part of society's cultural mechanisms, transforming the subject's ways of perceiving and desiring.

Many of the theories of classical cinema I have outlined tended to omit these aspects of sensationalism and spectacle, along with attention to the subject in general, let alone the subject as gendered. Paradoxically, the new culture of the spectacle (mainly used to reinscribe oppressive female modes) as it emerged in women's melodrama could be used to *destabilize* and subvert the unifying and ordering aspects of classicism, especially *vis-à-vis* the female subject, the female spectator.

> **Paradoxically, the new culture of the spectacle (mainly used to reinscribe oppressive female modes) as it emerged in women's melodrama could be used to *destabilize* and subvert the unifying and ordering aspects of classicism, especially *vis-à-vis* the female subject, the female spectator.**

Male theorists of classical cinema basically had in mind a male spectator and male unconscious processes. While still working within the limits of French male theory of the classical cinema (and not yet theorizing women's melodrama), Laura Mulvey's well-known 1975 essay 'Visual Pleasure and Narrative Cinema' set up the terms for the first round of feminist discussion of classical cinema in illuminating how that cinema basically was constructed for the male spectator which theorists had assumed without question. Constructing a model of the cinematic gaze as it embodied Freud's twin mechanisms of voyeurism and fetishism, Mulvey showed how, in classical cinema, woman was situated as bearer of meaning rather than maker of meaning (see Creed and White, Part 1, Chapters 9 and 13 for an exposition of this argument). This insight about the main classical male genres led Mulvey to claim that Hollywood could not offer anything to women, and that women must free the camera from its realist oppressions.

Melodrama

It was in response to Mulvey's essay and in an effort to see what Hollywood might offer women that feminist film theorists turned to study the melodrama form that explicitly addresses woman, that is, to what has been called 'the weepie' or 'the woman's film'. The most constructive and challenging work on the classical cinema, then, emerged almost by default in this new attention to the women's melodrama form. The 1970s concept of classical cinema is qualified in this research, or repositioned in different ways depending on theorists' concerns. In critiquing the male bias of classical film theory, feminist film theorists (perhaps unintentionally) opened classical film up to far different perspectives, issues, and concerns.

Earlier (largely male) historians and literary theorists had been concerned to chart the history of melodrama as a specific theatre and film genre. Peter Brooks (1972) and Thomas Elsaesser (1972) expanded the concept of melodrama beyond the confines of a specific theatrical genre to focus on a generalized type of aesthetic experience that produces specific emotional effects in the specator. Brooks's main thesis is that melodrama is a response to the 'loss of tragic vision' exacerbated by the Industrial Revolution and the creation of a society deprived of an organic and hierarchical order. The ensuing solidification of the bourgeois class, with its specific form of nuclear family, was accompanied by an ethical vacuum in the public sphere. Melodrama, then, is a type of sense-making characterized by 'indulgence of strong emotionalism; moral polarization and schematization; extreme states of being, situations, actions; overt villainy, persecution of the good and final reward of virtue; inflated and extravagant expression; dark plottings, suspense, breathtaking peripety' (Brooks 1976: 4).

If one accepts Peter Brooks's general definition of the melodramatic, then all the main Hollywood genres are melodrama in attempting an ethical recentring, a 'search for a new plenitude in reaction to the decentering of modern consciousness' (Brooks 1976). This produces some confusion in relation to theories of the classical cinema which originally did not *per se* include the term 'melodrama', nor distinguish amongst the main forms of Hollywood genres within an overall category of 'melodrama'.

A further distinction needs to be made between the melodrama form (including those addressed to male spectators) and the Bazinian and Bordwellian concepts of the 'classical'. For, as Brooks and Elsaesser had already pointed out, melodrama conventions often disrupt or work against the ordering and unifying tendencies which the concept of the 'classical' implies. In Rick Altman's words, melodrama permits excess not to be positioned outside the system but to have a system of its own—a system that complicates and puts pressure on the dominant (Altman 1992: 34). But the early male critics engaged in this work focused more on broadly defined bourgeois ideology about the family in general than on the films' specifically *female* address.

But it was feminist film critics who discovered a need to distinguish the films specifically geared for female audiences (women's melodramas) from those aimed at both male and female spectators generally. Films focused on in this research include the series of films made from the notorious stage melodrama *East Lynne* (see Kaplan 1992); King Vidor's *Stella Dallas* (1937); the two versions of *Imitation of Life* (Jonathan Stahl, 1934, Douglas Sirk, 1959); and Dorothy Arzner's films. The focus on women's melodrama—as against the implicit category of melodrama for all Hollywood films—included giving attention to film and television melodrama forms seen as explicitly addressing female spectators, and as dealing with issues pertinent to women. There is, then, a 'politics' of melodrama structures that feminist theorists exposed and (sometimes building on work by Stephen Heath) linked to the psychoanalytic processes at work in melodrama. The fact that melodrama is the genre which, in its recent form, arises with modernization—that is, at the intersection of absolutist (or premodern) social forms and later specifically capitalist forms—makes it particularly pertinent to the study of maternal (and other) images in the modern period (Kaplan 1992: 21–6). For feminists, melodramas open space prohibited by the so-called classical realist film text, which is restricted to oppressive patriarchal norms.

> **For feminists, melodramas open space prohibited by the so-called classical realist film text, which is restricted to oppressive patriarchal norms.**

In remedying the gap in male discussion of melodrama, feminist critics brought renewed interest in melodrama, and asked new questions of the form while building on Brooks's and Elsaesser's theories. In a first wave of work, critics like Laura Mulvey (who saw the possibilities of the woman's film) and Mary Ann Doane (to take two important examples) began to explore the important difference between films addressed to a male and to a female spectator. Mulvey, writing in 1977, defined the family melodrama as explicitly a form with female address, one that deliberately functioned to counter-balance the dominant male genres. For her, 'a dramatic rendering of women's frustrations, publicly acting out an adjustment of balance

Duel In the Sun (1946)—
Gregory Peck and Jennifer
Jones in a combination of
classical western and
melodrama

in the male ego is socially and ideologically beneficial'
(1977/1989: 40). But she goes on to assume that the
melodrama involves 'reaffirmation of the Oedipus
complex'. That is, although in the family melodrama
'[t]he phallocentric, castration-based, more misogynist
fantasies of patriarchal culture' are 'sacrificed in the
interest of civilization', Mulvey reads 'civilization' in
terms of how man comes to be man. Adapting Freud
and Kristeva, for Mulvey 'civilization' is produced
through male rejection of the mother, and the insistence on the mother's serving patriarchy. Nevertheless.

Mulvey finds something important for women in these
films about female victims. First, the mother may try to
keep her son with her, down in the Imaginary and in this
way resist the mother's position as a patriarchal function. As Mulvey puts it: 'In the absence of any coherent
culture of oppression, the simple fact of recognition
has aesthetic importance: there is a dizzy satisfaction in
witnessing the way that sexual difference under patriarchy is fraught, explosive, and erupts dramatically into
violence within its own stomping ground, the family'
(39).

Building on this work, Mary Ann Doane has shown that most women's films construct a heroine who is a victim, entailing a masochistic identification for the female viewer. These repeated masochistic scenarios effectively immobilize the female spectator, refusing her the imaginary identification which in the male forms produces a sense of mastery and control.

Mary Ann Doane's work has been central in theorizing the female spectator in the woman's film. In a 1984 essay, she uses Freud's work on femininity to build on Mulvey's essay, arguing that woman is constructed differently in relation to the processes of looking (Doane 1984). Doane goes to French feminist theory to show how woman cannot assume the fetishistic position because 'the lack of distance between seeing and understanding, the mode of judging "in a flash" (a reference to Freud's theory of the girl's sudden reaction to seeing the penis for the first time) is conducive to what might be termed as "over identification" with the image' (69).

Doane views this over-identification with the image as necessarily entailing a passive, masochistic position because of the position woman is assigned in cinematic narrative. On the other hand, woman may also identify with the active hero, in which case, as Mulvey had already argued, woman took up a masculine spectator position. Doane moves from here to discussion of woman's more natural transvestism resulting from her apparently greater inherent bisexuality. As Juliet Mitchell has noted (in contrast to some recent feminist Freudian revisionists), male sexual identity is more sure than feminine identity because of the greater compulsion (via the castration complex) to turn away from the first feminine identification with the mother. While the girl also must reject this early feminine identification (as Mitchell put it, the shadow of the phallus falls over the girl's ego as also over the boy's, creating a masculine 'I' born out of the baby's desiring what the mother desires), this identification, albeit much reduced, nevertheless remains. The girl is then more naturally bisexual than the boy, slipping easily over into masculine identification.

But for Doane this transvestism is not recuperable, and woman is left with only two alternatives: the masochism of over-identification or the narcissism entailed in becoming one's own object of desire' (Doane 1987: 18–22). A third possibility, that of the masquerade (i.e. exaggerating the accoutrements of the patriarchal feminine in order to create a distance from the image, to reveal femininity as precisely a mask covering a non-

identity and thus to disrupt patriarchal systems), is not really a solution. But in this later work, Doane sees possibilities of dislocating the position assigned woman through understanding the various spectatorship places (176–83).

Doane's formulation tends to generalize the mechanisms she explores to the entire genre of the woman's film, including its subgroupings. Elsewhere, I have differentiated those films addressing women that involve such despecularization of the female spectator from others which function to allow the female spectator certain kinds of pleasure in the struggle to resist patriarchal definitions and positionings (Kaplan 1992).

Another problem with psychoanalytic film theory in general, pointed out by Teresa de Lauretis, is the focus on the gaze—on woman as spectacle, to the detriment of considering types of identification other than with the camera. De Lauretis (1985) argues that narrative identificationn and closure are equally important and may afford the female spectator more space. These arguments gain force through linking the woman's melodrama to the nineteenth-century popular woman's novel, since obviously issues of the gaze are less central in fiction.

In a second wave of work on the family melodrama, critics like Linda Williams (1984) and Tania Modleski (1983) (to take again just two examples) have used spectatorship theory to argue that women are not merely offered identification with victims in these films. Referring to *Stella Dallas*, for example, Williams showed that female victims are situated in relation to other female figures with whom the female spectator identifies as well and that, out of this multiple and shifting series of identifications, the spectator learns about victimization, about woman's deprivations, and glimpses other female ways of being (Williams 1984), while Modleski's (1993) study of Hitchcock argued that they included female address. Stimulating debates followed these interventions (Kaplan 1985a, b, 1986).

Conclusion

Mulvey's early work exposed the oppressive aspects of the classical cinema outlined for women, but did not critique the theory *per se*. It offered an understanding of the sexist bias of classical cinema without questioning its premises. But the study of melodrama and the address of the genre of the woman's film as summarized above did implicitly begin to critique the male assumptions and obsessions of prior formulations of classical cinema. Feminist film criticism of women's melodramas thus opened up new avenues of discussion *vis-à-vis* classical cinema. It complicated the rigid totalizing tendencies in both conceptions of classical cinema with which I began. It allowed for multiple identifications, not just a blind adherence to a proposed 'dominant' (Bordwell *et al.* 1985: 41–84) or a capitalist bourgeois ideology (Burch 1969; Comolli and Narboni 1989).

Certainly, the overall values that Hollywood cinema still promotes are those of individualism, materialism, heterosexuality (despite the increasing interest in gay and lesbian couples and issues), and the nuclear family. And it promotes these values through a specific set of cinematic codes, prime among which is illusory realism. Hollywood illusionism masks the actual operations of power and patriarchal hierarchies. As long as it does this, it is an ideological cinema whose strategies promote unconscious identification with protagonists through appeals to erotic aims.

Yet the breakdown of the Hollywood studio system has allowed variations of the classical cinema to become more mainstream. Arguably, since 1960 the large Hollywood studios that provided the institutional basis for the cinema that film theorists named 'classical' have become less monolithic and, in the course of this process, the distribution and exhibition systems have changed significantly. If the needs of the American middle classes continue to find expression in Hollywood film even today, it is in a form modified to fit existing social formations.

BIBLIOGRAPHY

*Altman, Rick (1992), 'Dickens, Griffith, and Film Theory Today', in Jane Gaines (ed.), *Classical Hollywood Narrative: The Paradigm Wars* (Durham, NC: Duke University Press).

Bazin, André (1967/1971), *What is Cinema?*, 2 vols., trans. Hugh Gray (Berkeley: University of California Press).

*Bordwell, David, Janet Staiger, and Kristin Thompson (1985), *The Classical Hollywood Cinema: Film Style and Mode of Production to 1960* (New York: Columbia University Press).

Brooks, Peter (1976), *The Melodramatic Imagination* (New Haven: Yale University Press).

Burch, Noël (1969), *Theory of Film Practice* (Princeton, NJ: Princeton University Press).

Comolli, Jean-Louis, and Jean Narboni (1969/1989), 'Cinema/Ideology/Criticism', in Bill Nichols (ed.), *Movies and Methods*, 2 vols., i (Berkeley: University of California Press).

de Lauretis, Teresa (1985), 'Oedipus Interruptus', *Wide Angle*, 7/1–2: 34–40.

Doane, Mary Ann (1981), 'Film and the Masquerade: Filming the Female Body', *October*, 17 (Summer), 25–32.

—— (1984), 'The Woman's Film: Possession and Address', in *Re-Vision: Essays in Feminist Criticism* (Frederick, Md.: University Publications of America, with the American Film Institute).

—— (1987), *The Desire to Desire* (Bloomington: Indiana University Press).

Elsaesser, Thomas (1972), 'Tales of Sound and Fury: Observations on the Family Melodrama', *Monogram*, 4: 2–15.

Film Criticism (1993), 17/2–3 (Winter–Spring), Special Issue: *Interpretation Inc.: Issues in Contemporary Film Studies*.

Heath, Stephen (1975), 'Film and System: Terms of Analysis, Part I', *Screen*, 16/1 (Spring), 7–77.

Kaplan, E. Ann (1985a), 'Dialogue: Ann Kaplan Replies to Linda Williams' "Something else besides a Mother": *Stella Dallas* and the Maternal Melodrama', *Cinema Journal*, 24/2: 40–3.

—— (1985b), 'Dialogue: E. Ann Kaplan Replies to Petro and Flinn' (continuing *Stella Dallas* debate), *Cinema Journal*, 25/1: 51–4.

—— (1986), 'Dialogue: Thoughts on Melodrama': Reply to Christine Gledhill' (continuing *Stella Dallas* debate), *Cinema Journal*, 25/4: 49–53.

—— (1992), *Motherhood and Representation: The Mother in Popular Culture and Melodrama* (New York: Routledge).

—— (1993), 'Disorderly Disciplines', *Film Criticism*, 17/2–3 (Winter–Spring), Special Issue: *Interpretation Inc.: Issues in Contemporary Film Studies*, 48–52.

MacCabe, Colin (1974), 'Realism and Cinema: Notes on Some Brechtian Theses', *Screen*, 15/2 (Autumn), 7–32.

Metz, Christian (1974), *Film Language: A Semiotics of the Cinema* (New York: Oxford University Press).

—— (1975), 'The Imaginary Signifier', *Screen*, 16/2 (Summer), 14–76.

Mitchell, Juliet (1975), *Psychoanalysis and Feminism* (New York: Vintage Books).

Modleski, Tania (1983), 'The Rhythms of Reception: Daytime Television and Women's Work', in E. Ann Kaplan (ed.), *Regarding Television. Critical Approaches: An Anthology* (Frederick, Md.: University Publications of America).

Mulvey, Laura (1975/1989), 'Visual Pleasure and Narrative Cinema', in *Visual and Other Pleasures* (London: Macmillan).

—— (1977/1989), 'Notes on Sirk and Melodrama', in *Visual and Other Pleasures* (London: Macmillan).

Nichols, Bill (1992), 'Form Wars: The Political Unconscious of Formalist Theory', in Jane Gaines (ed.), *Classical Hollywood Narrative: The Paradigm Wars* (Durham, NC: Duke University Press).

Nowell-Smith, Geoffrey (1977), 'Minnelli and Melodrama', *Screen*, 18/2: 113–18.

Rosen, Philip (ed.) (1986), *Narrative, Apparatus, Ideology: A Film Theory Reader* (New York: Columbia University Press).

Stam, Robert, Robert Burgoyne, and **Sandy Flitterman-Lewis** (1992), *New Vocabularies in Film Semiotics: Structuralism, Post-Structuralism and Beyond* (New York: Routledge).

White, Allon (1983), 'Why did the Signifiers Come out to Play?', MS.

Williams, Linda (1984), '"Something else besides a Mother": *Stella Dallas* and the Maternal Melodrama', *Cinema Journal*, 24/1: 2–27.

Wollen, Peter (1982), *Readings and Writings: Semiotics and Counter-Strategies* (London: Verso).

Wood, Robin (1993), 'Critical Positions and the End of Civilization; or, A Refusal to Join the Club', *Film Criticism*, 17/2–3 (Winter–Spring), Special Issue: *Interpretation Inc.: Issues in Contemporary Film Studies*, 79–92.

Casablanca

Richard Maltby from Richard Maltby, *Harmless Entertainment: Hollywood and the Ideology of Consensus* (Metuchen, NJ: Scarecrow Press, 1983)

The primary fiction that the Hollywood cinema of the consensus—to whose aesthetic strategies *The Green Berets* (1968) and *Guess who's Coming to Dinner* (1967) both adhere—requires its audience to accept is that they should think of the story a film is telling them as if it were a real event. That is not to say that they are intended to regard, say, the story of *The Wizard of Oz* (1939) as having actually taken place in front of a fortuitously placed camera. But they are expected to operate a particular suspension of disbelief in which the mimesis of the photographic image reinforces the circumstantial and psychological 'realism' of the events those images contain, so that they can presume upon those normative rules of spatial perception, human behaviour, and causality which govern their conduct in the world outside the cinema. Thus they may respond to the characters as if they were real people, and regard the story that is told through the characters as if it were unfolding before them without the mediation of cameras or narrative devices.

Hollywood's realism operated at two levels. Perfect reproduction effaced the techniques by which it produced a seamless flow, and concentrated the audience's attention on the contents of that flow, the narrative. The spatial construction of narrative placed the spectator in the film, while the ordering of events attached the spectator emotionally to its characters as benevolent sources of meaning and significance. Despite the opportunism of its techniques, the cinema of the consensus was committed absolutely to the maintenance of continuity as the primary ingredient of its realism. As a result it was firmly attached to the articulation of a coherent narrative structure.

The narrative of *Casablanca* (Michael Curtiz, 1943)—which may indisputably be regarded as a 'classic Hollywood text' of the consensus—is constructed to support and clarify the story of the film, aiming at a coherence in the revelation of the plot in order to concentrate attention on the story as it is revealed. The audience is attached to the film by the process of the revealing of the story, not by the facts of the story's revelations. One example among many is the introduction of Ingrid Bergman, and the establishment of her previous relationship with Bogart. Up to this point the film has concentrated on establishing its locale, Bogart's cynical isolationism ('I stick my neck out for nobody'), and the apparent major plot device of the theft of the letters of transit and the arrival of Resistance leader Victor Laszlo (Paul Henreid). Henreid and Bergman first appear entering Rick's Café in a long medium tracking shot, which takes them past Sam (Dooley Wilson) at the piano. Wilson and Bergman seem to recognize each other, and Wilson looks worried and shakes his head. A signal to the audience's attention has been provided, but it is not immediately pursued. Henreid and Bergman are joined first by Berger (John Qualen), a member of the Resistance, and then by Captain Renault (Claude Rains), in conversations about Henreid's situation. Bergman asks Rains about Wilson—'somewhere I've seen him'—a remark whose significance is signalled by its delivery in extreme close-up. Rains supplies an enigmatic description of Bogart, and its impact on Bergman is again shown in close-up when the group is joined by Major Strasser (Conrad Veidt). However, the subject is not pursued and conversation returns to Henreid's politics and future. But the disruptive influence of Bogart's presence is registered by the repetition of close shots of Bergman, detaching her from the men's conversation. When Rains and Veidt return to their table, a female guitarist begins a song, during which Bergman and Wilson exchange looks of recognition, and Wilson repeats his concerned expression. Once more, the cue is left hanging while Henreid joins Qualen at the bar. Bergman calls Wilson over to her table. Wilson tries to convince her Bogart has another girl, but she tells him 'You used to be a much better liar, Sam.' He replies, 'Leave him alone, Miss Ilsa, you're bad luck to him. In its ordering, her next line encapsulates in microcosm the mechanism of the narrative: 'Play it once, Sam, for old times' sake . . . play it, Sam, play, "As Time Goes By".' The audience are inveigled into a process of revelation, without discovering, until the end, what the object of that revelation is. The spectator is cued to anticipate an event, the content and meaning of which has not been disclosed. Wilson's playing of a song whose significance is never explained is made important by its presentation over an extreme, melancholic, close-up of Bergman that lasts for twenty seconds, much longer than any previous shot. The song brings Bogart to the table, and the existence of a mutual bond is again established by the intercutting of extreme close-ups of their faces (the first close-up of Bogart in the film), reinforced by the sudden introduction of violins on the soundtrack. At this point, with the nature of their involvement completely unstated by the same means that it has been declared central to the narrative, Rains and Henreid appear once again to change the subject, and the couple spend the rest of the scene exchanging looks and reminiscences of their last meeting ('The Germans wore grey, you wore blue') which provide the spectator with no more explicit information.

The process of revelation is continued, at a broader level, throughout the narrative. The audience witness Bogart's

Casablanca continued

The classical narrative text 'speaking with two voices'—*Casablanca* (1942)

Casablanca continued

remembering his time with Bergman in Paris, while her marriage to Henreid, her intention to leave Henreid for Bogart, and Bogart's final decision to send her to America with Henreid are all revealed by similar constructions to that of her introduction. The plot is presented as a linear causal chain, each event located by a relationship of cause and effect to those which precede and follow it, but it only functions if it is correctly placed in the chain. Bogart's memory of Paris is, obviously, chronologically misplaced—it happened before all the other events of the film. But it is, more importantly, placed at the point in the plot when its partial vision of events (Bergman's explanations will qualify it later) is most emotionally affective.

The linear causal chain of the plot leads inevitably to a point of resolution, but because the spectator is engaged in the process by which the story is revealed, he or she can ignore the determinist causality of such a structure and the restrictions it places on possible interpretations of an event. There is, inevitably, a tension between the plot's determinist pressure towards a resolution of events, and the 'realist' objections to an idealist simplicity in the tidy end-stopping of events at the film's conclusion. This structurally insoluble tension in narrative realism (the force that draws realism towards melodrama) is dissipated by the consensus cinema's mode of construction. Guided through the plot by the revelatory narrative, the audience is encouraged to feel unconcerned about the conflict between determinism and normative, unresolved reality by the coherence of what they see and hear. Their acceptance of the story comes not from what they are told, but from the way it is told to them. They can accommodate the contradictions of realist narrative by seeing the events of the film as amounting to a crisis which determines the course of the lives of the characters in it. The typical film of the consensus ends at the point at which another film might begin: in *Casablanca*, for example, Bogart's adventures with the Free French in Tangiers, or Bergman and Henreid in America.

What holds for narrative structure also holds for scene construction. Because the coherent narrative locates an individual scene at one point in its causal chain, an element of the scene must be reserved for the elucidation and justification of that process of causal linkage. Each scene in *Casablanca* advances the plot by confirming the knowledge the audience have derived from previous scenes, and adding further information to it. The process of confirmation is enacted through the consistency with which the scenes are presented, a consistency which can be regarded as a form of psychological and circumstantial realism. Consistency of character motivation projects a believable psychology: when Bogart rejects Bergman on her first night-time visit to the

café the audience recognize that his drinking has exposed the sentimentality beneath the cynical exterior. When he meets her in the market the next morning and asks for the explanation he turned down the night before, the audience understand that the cynicism ('after all, I got stuck with a railway ticket, I think I'm entitled to know') is only a defensive veneer. Bogart's psychology, along with that of the other characters, is being gradually revealed to the audience, who have to construct it from the information the film provides. Circumstantial realism, similarly, is provided by the consistency with which the film describes and relates its locations and the creation of the seamless illusion hinges, at a level more basic than psychological characterization, on the two fundamental areas of perception most immediately available to cinematic manipulation: the depiction of time and space.

A cinematic narrative is temporally composed of a set of ellipses; it is a distillation of a series of significant events. The presentation of time within a narrative is more immediately apparent than the presentation of space, since the periods not included in the narrative are evident by their omission. We may, for example, see a man getting into his car and driving off, and then cut to his arriving at his destination. The coherent narrative, however, attempts to disguise the elliptical nature of its temporal construction by subordinating both the actual time of a depicted event and the real time experienced by the spectator in the cinema to the artificial, perceived time presented by the narrative. For this purpose, it uses a number of devices to create continuity in perception of two narratively linked discontinuous events. The most simple device is a passage of 'linking' music, which, by its rhythmic or patterned management of the passage of time, provides a suitable vehicle for the presentation of the narrative's temporal continuum. Appropriately enough, the opening bars of 'As Time Goes By' have this function in *Casablanca*. The same purpose, the subordination of external time to the narrative continuum, may be served by the use of 'linking' shots, the content of which is unimportant save for their function of relating two consecutive scenes by an association of ideas. For example, one scene may end up with a tilt up off the characters onto blue sky, followed by a cut, perhaps imperceptible, to blue sky, which tilts down to the same characters in a different location, different characters, or whatever. The plane to Lisbon serves this purpose on more than one occasion in *Casablanca*, transferring attention from one group of people looking at it to another, or to the scene of its arrival. The same effect can be achieved by the use of fades or dissolves, which have their own connotations as accounts of elapsed time, or, in the extreme assertion of narrative control over plot events, by a montage sequence. In each case the linkage device

Casablanca continued

establishes a chain of causality which is stylistically asserted by the film, subordinating other perceptions of time to that of the narrative. The arbitrariness of all these devices is contained by their conventionality. The attribution of a distinctive connotation to each of them (a fade implies a longer ellipsis than a dissolve, while a wipe suggests spatial rather than temporal alteration) covers their presence as techniques by emphasizing their function as meaning. The coherent narrative cinema requires that the scene-to-scene linkage should be as unobtrusive as possible, since the main intention is to persuade the audience to assume the connections of linear causality, in order that they focus their attention on the plot or theme. The technical devices of the cinema of coherence aim to divert the spectator's attention away from themselves as mechanisms of the illusion, and to concentrate it more on the illusion they create—that is, to divert the spectator's attention away from the film as object to the subject of the film.

A similar argument may be advanced in relation to the depiction of space within the scene. A coherent narrative aims to present space in terms which are immediately recognizable to its audience. This requirement encourages the construction of images which do not distort conventional perspective relations, implying that most images will be recorded by lenses in a relativey narrow range of focal lengths. Equally, it encourages the development of

conventional patterns for the juxtaposition of shots: the pattern of establishing long shot, medium shot, close-up is one example; angle–reverse angle cutting is another. When these conventions of the image are disrupted, the audience is being signalled: for example, the close-up of Bogart when he first sees Bergman not only takes the camera closer to him than it has been before, breaking a convention of distance, but is also shot with a wider-angle lens than is used for other close-ups, and taken from an angle above, rather than level with, Bogart's eyeline. All this communicates surprise and discomfort without articulating them explicitly, or markedly disrupting the image stream. Unless aiming for a particular extraordinary effect such as shock, the coherent narrative requires the audience to understand the way the space in a scene works (e.g. the area in which a character can move), in the same way that it aims for an unconscious awareness of the temporal ellipses in the narrative. They share the same purpose of convincing the audience of the film's stylistic benevolence in presenting the most readily comprehensible depiction of events. We understand by a simple time ellipsis that nothing important has happened in it, and this process is made easier by a stylistic device that is self-effacing and allows us to ignore it. The normal perception of spatial relationships similarly allows us to take them for granted as comprehensible. Thus it is possible for us to divert our energies towards comprehending the events of the plot, rather than the manner of their presentation.

Casablanca

Rick Altman 'Dickens, Griffith and Film Theory Today' in Jane Gaines (ed.), *Classical Hollywood Narrative: The Paradigm Wars* (Durham, NC: Duke University Press, 1992)

For years the classical text was seen as opposed to the modernism of the Brechtian, the reflexive, and the dialogic. Then, in the wake of Barthes's *S/Z*, study after study attempted to champion this or that novel or style of filmmaking by demonstrating its relative modernity. Perhaps we now have reached the point where we acknowledge the short-sightedness of both enterprises. If so many apparently classical texts have modernist leanings, then maybe the classical text is not as unitary as was once thought. It operates as a dialogic text precisely because its single-focus linearity presupposes an embedded dual-focus context. With one foot in history and the other still in myth, the classical narrative text must always speak with two voices, each using its own logic.

Take the case of the quintessential Hollywood, Warner's 1942 *Casablanca*. The film's linear narrative stretches from Rick and Ilsa's idyll in Paris, through their reunion in Casablanca, to Rick's final heroic decision to send Ilsa off with her husband, while he and the French captain Renault walk off into the distance towards a career in the Resistance. Like *Le Père Goriot*, however, *Casablanca* does not owe its longevity to this familiar linear story. If *Casablanca* continues to enjoy success, it is not so much because of the ability of Bogie and Bergman to express the changing state of their emotions (in fact, in this film they are better at hiding emotions than expressing them), but because of the stakes for which they are playing. The secret of this film lies in its apocalyptic intensity. With the stereotypically sinister German major Strasser and the archetypically pure Resistance hero Victor Laszlo embodying the values of Good and Evil, as represented by the Nazis and their victims, the atmosphere of *Casablanca* provides a melodramatic backdrop to the personal actions that capture our more immediate attention.

While character psychology appears to advance the film through a chain of cause-and-effect relationships, the major moments are either coincidental or only minimally motivated. What brings Ilsa to the very café run by the man she jilted in Paris? (Little more than coincidence.) How does Rick gain possession of the visas apparently needed to liberate Ilsa and her husband? (Through the minimally motivated activities of the Peter Lorre character Ugarte, who is killed off as soon as the function has been fulfilled.) What motivates Rick's decision to send Ilsa off to freedom with her husband? (The overall melodramatic set-up much more than any clearly developed line of psychological reasoning.) How do Ilsa and her husband actually escape from Casablanca? (Not through the use of the much-touted visas which turn out

to be nothing more than a plot-unifying Macguffin, but by an armed confrontation between the Nazi commander and his liberty-loving American opponent.) What leads Captain Renault, ever the self-serving neutral womanizer, to break his bottle of Vichy water and march towards a life of bravery and moral rectitude? (Congenial hatred of the Hun? Embodiment of audience desires? No explanation is offered except to recognize that Renault is making the right decision within the film's melodramatic framework, even if the decision is not clearly motivated by the film's psychological progression.)

Nearly every character, every glance, serves to heighten the air of impending doom—or freedom. With the exception of *Casablanca*'s profiteers (and even profiteering has long been recognized as a common symptom of apocalyptic intensity), every character is directly defined by the conflict between national allegiance and personal independence. An aroused soldier, a sad woman, an expectant old man—all embody the hope and freedom represented by the United States in opposition to the cruelty and imprisonment threatened by the Nazis. Even the paradigms of money, clothing, and linguistic accent contribute to this opposition. Indeed, this effect has been heightened by the fact that one of the film's descriptive terms—concentration camp—has since taken on such strong connotations of inhuman cruelty.

We should not conclude, though, that the entire power of the film's melodrama is spent of the local and historical. By its very nature melodrama carries eternal mythic qualities, like those that make Major Strasser embody not just Nazism, but Evil itself, and those that make Bogie and Bergman an archetypal couple. The film's theme song further reinforces this sense that we are witnessing more than just an episode in the life of some guy named Rick.

Whenever the film moves towards psychology and time it is wrenched back towards myth and eternity. It is the very conflict between the two that leads to the bitter-sweet conclusion.

Why does *Casablanca* continue to enchant audiences around the world? Because of its linear causality? Yes, without a doubt. The film's suspense and expectation are carefully used to focus our attention on the future. As we dutifully fill all the plot's little gaps, we settle comfortably into the spectator position allotted to us. Because of the film's melodramatic underpinnings? Yes again. *Casablanca* is a film about human allegiance to things of eternal beauty and value. The one pushes us towards a temporal solution, the

Casablanca continued

union of Bogie and Bergman, the beautiful couple, while the other pulls us towards the eternal apotheosis of Good. That the melodramatic reasoning holds sway in the end does not mean that we should accept mythic causality as the film's dominant, overwhelming classical narrative causality. Instead we should retain from this analysis the importance of reading the text—even at this schematic level—as an amalgam of deformed, embedded melodramatic material and carefully elaborated narrative classicism. To the personal identification that pushes us forward along a suspenseful linear hermeneutic corresponds a process of cultural identification that keeps us ever-mindful of a broader set of oppositions compared to which the problems of three people don't amount to a hill of beans.

6 Post-classical Hollywood

Peter Kramer

Since the 1980s critical debates within film studies and related disciplines such as cultural studies have increasingly been concerned with the identification, description, explanation, and evaluation of epochal shifts. The proliferation of the prefix 'post' is the most visible sign of this widespread concern with a set of fundamental transformations in the socio-economic organization and forms of cultural expression prevalent in the United States and Western Europe. Post-feminism and postmodernism have featured prominently in discussions of contemporary American cinema (Modleski 1991; Denzin 1991; Corrigan 1991). In recent years 'post-classicism' has emerged as a closely linked third term signalling an epochal shift in Hollywood cinema (Jenkins 1995; Rowe 1995; Neale and Smith, forthcoming). At the most basic level, this critical term is used to mark the end of the classical period in American film history, that is the disintegration or displacement of classical narration and of the studio system as the dominant forms of aesthetic and institutional organization within mainstream American cinema. Post-classicism does not refer to a complete break in American film history; rather the term is meant to highlight the fact that, despite overriding stylistic and institutional continuities, Hollywood has undergone a set of fundamental changes which deserve critical attention. In contrast to the relative aesthetic and institutional homogeneity and stability of classical Hollywood which has been described most authoritatively by

David Bordwell, Janet Staiger, and Kristin Thompson (1985) and Thomas Schatz (1988), the post-classical period is seen to be characterized by differing and frequently changing approaches to the unchanging main objective of the American film industry, which is to make money by telling entertaining stories to paying audiences (Jenkins 1995).

This basic description of post-classicism raises a number of important questions. When does the classical period end and the post-classical era begin? What are the most important stylistic and thematic innovations introduced during the post-classical period? What is their relationship to changes in the organization of the film industry? And why did these changes occur in the first place? By necessity, the concept of post-classicism also gives rise to concerns about the notion of classical Hollywood cinema. What are the characteristic features and the historical boundaries of this dominant mode of film practice? The critical debate about most of these issues is still in its early stages, as the concept of post-classicism is not yet established as an obligatory reference-point in discussions of contemporary American cinema. However, some of these questions about the conceptualization of historical developments in American cinema have been discussed extensively with reference to other periodizing terms, such as 'postmodernism' (Corrigan 1991; Denzin 1991), New Hollywood (Tasker 1996; Schatz 1983, 1993; Hillier 1993; Neale 1976), and, most generally, the era following the Second World War. In fact, while the 1960s are usually regarded as the decade which saw the rise of the New Hollywood and the beginning of post-classicism, most accounts of these developments explain them with reference to a series of crucial events in the immediate post-war period (between 1946 and 1953) such as the antitrust action against the major Hollywood studios, the decline of cinema attendances, and the rise of television. Furthermore, it was during this same period that the concept of classicism was first introduced into film criticism in a sustained and rigorous fashion. Arguably, the very act of identifying Hollywood classicism already implied a certain historical distance from it, a vantage-point from which classicism could be seen as a stage in the development of American cinema. The first decade after the end of the Second World War, then, provides an appropriate starting-point for a historical investigation of the various attempts which film critics and film scholars have made to conceptualize the history of Hollywood beyond its classical period.

André Bazin, classicism, and changes in the Hollywood aesthetic

Schatz (1988: 8) and Bordwell, Staiger, and Thompson (1985: 3) point to André Bazin as the most important source for the basic assumptions underpinning their respective projects: that the Hollywood aesthetic can be understood as a form of 'classicism', and that this classical film aesthetic is in turn dependent on a particular 'system' of production. Bazin developed this approach to American cinema between 1945 and 1958, in the context of a massive influx of Hollywood films into France and of new trends in European film-making, most notably neo-realism (Andrew 1978, chs. 4–7). Bazin's use of the term 'classical' was double-edged. On the one hand, it derived from his enthusiasm for American cinema, which contrasted sharply with the disdain for Hollywood shown by many of his contemporaries amongst established French critics. By labelling Hollywood cinema a 'classical art', he elevated it, setting it up as an artistic practice worthy of serious consideration. On the other hand, right from the start, Bazin rejected the limitations that the rules of classicism imposed on filmmaking, in particular on the more 'realistic' practices that he championed, such as long takes, deep-focus cinematography, and staging

in depth. Both his admiration and his critique of classical Hollywood are brought into sharp focus in an oft-quoted passage from his 1957 essay 'On the *politique des auteurs*': 'Paradoxically, the supporters of the *politique des auteurs* admire the American cinema, where the restrictions of production are heavier than anywhere else. . . . The American cinema is a classical art, but why not then admire in it what is most admirable, i.e. not only the talent of this or that film-maker, but the genius of the system, the richness of its ever-vigorous tradition, and its fertility when it comes into contact with new elements' (Bazin 1985: 257–8).

A closer look at Bazin's writing reveals that the classicism of American cinema provided him with a backdrop against which he could define and promote the qualities of a new kind of realist cinema which was emerging in Europe and in the United States in the 1940s, exemplified most strikingly by *Paisa* (Italy, 1946) and *Citizen Kane* (USA, 1941). 'The Evolution of the Language of Cinema' is arguably Bazin's most famous and influential essay, an early version of which appeared in the first issue of *Cahiers du cinéma* in April 1951. In this essay, Bazin proposed a periodization of the history of cinema. Despite the gap between silent cinema and talking film, the years from 1920 to 1939 constituted a unified period characterized by the world-wide diffusion of 'a common form of cinematic language . . . originating largely in the United States' and based on the principles of continuity editing (1967: 28–31). By 1939 this cinema 'had reached a level of classical perfection' in Hollywood and elsewhere, yet it was also on the verge of a 'revolution in the language of the screen' (30, 37). In Hollywood, directors such as Orson Welles and William Wyler participated in the international 'regeneration of realism in storyteling' which insisted on 'bringing together real time, in which things exist, along with the duration of the action, for which classical editing had insidiously substituted mental and abstract time' (39). This would seem to suggest that Hollywood's classicism of the 1930s was superseded, or at least partially displaced, by a new aesthetic in the 1940s, which could be called 'post-classical'.

In the essay 'The Evolution of the Western' Bazin discussed this epochal shift with respect to what he had called 'the American film par excellence' (1971: 140). Again the years 1939–40 marked 'a point beyond which some new development seemed inevitable' because with *Stagecoach* (USA, 1939) the western had achieved 'the maturity of a style brought to classi-

> In effect, Bazin again presented the outlines of a 'post-classical' American cinema which is described as an impure, less rigorous, highly flexible cinema, characterized by the coexistence of contradictory aesthetic strategies (classical editing, expressionism, realism) rather than a strict and exclusive adherence to the continuity system; by the extension, embellishment, playfulness, and mixing of its genres rather than by generic purity; and by an engagement with topical issues and controversial subject-matter even in its most conventional generic offerings.

cal perfection' (149). Referring to 'the famous law of successive aesthetic periods', which posits the inevitable displacement of classicism by 'the baroque', Bazin observed the emergence of a new kind of western in the 1940s: 'The superwestern is a western that would be ashamed to be just itself, and looks for some additional interest to justify its existence—an aesthetic, sociological, moral, psychological, political, or erotic interest' (150–1). In effect, Bazin again presented the outlines of a 'post-classical' American cinema which is described as an impure, less rigorous, highly flexible cinema, characterized by the coexistence of contradictory aesthetic strategies (classical editing, expressionism, realism) rather than a strict and exclusive adherence to the continuity system; by the extension, embellishment, playfulness, and mixing of its genres rather than by generic purity; and by an engagement with topical issues and controversial subject-matter even in its most conventional generic offerings.

American critical responses to post-war changes in the Hollywood aesthetic and the end of the studio system

Bazin explained changes in the Hollywood aesthetic in the 1940s and 1950s in terms of an internal logic of artistic developments inevitably moving through a series of stages. In his teleological view, the result of such developments in the medium of film was an ever more realistic representation of the world. When American critics considered changes in Hollywood filmmaking in the post-war period, they also addressed questions of realism, yet they were more likely to focus these questions on the issue of Hollywood's 'maturity' or lack thereof, and to draw on a wide range of social, cultural, and industrial determinants to explain the complex developments they observed. While the terms 'classical cinema' and 'studio system' were not used, what critics engaged with was in fact the dismantling of the system of production, distribution, and exhibition and of the classical aesthetic which had underpinned Hollywood's operations in preceding decades. In sharp contrast with Bazin's belief in the 'genius' of the Hollywood system, American critics took a largely negative view of American film culture, and responded to its fundamental transformation in the late 1940s and the 1950s with more scepticism than hope.

In the aftermath of the Second World War critics looked for signs of Hollywood's social and artistic maturation. In his bi-weekly column in *The Nation*, James Agee identified and welcomed an important trend towards 'journalistic, semi-documentary, and "social-minded"' films in Hollywood in 1946 and 1947 (1963: 289). Celebrating *The Best Years of our Lives* (USA, 1946) as an outstanding example of this trend, Agee related Hollywood's 'new maturity' to the war experiences of filmmakers such as Wyler and John Huston (237). He also noted the increasing influence of European imports, most notably *Roma, città aperta* (Italy, 1945), which exemplified 'the best general direction movies might take' with its passionate commitment to, and intimate understanding of, a topical and realistic story 'worthy of such knowledge and passion . . . made on relatively little money, as much at least by gifted amateurs as by professionals, in actual rather than imitated places' (236). In 1949 Parker Tyler discussed Hollywood's move, particularly in crime films such as *The Naked City* (USA, 1948), towards 'quasi-documentary', that is the employment of 'documentary devices' such as location shooting and references to a wealth of factual material (1949/1960: 29–35). He also pointed out that Hollywood had produced a series of commercially successful 'problem pictures', most notably *Gentleman's Agreement* (USA, 1947) and *Pinky* (USA, 1949), which dealt with 'such large issues as social prejudices against Negroes and Jews' (107).

However, in the light of Hollywood's commercialism and political conservatism, Agee and Tyler did not expect that these mature trends could make a lasting impact on American film culture.

In 1950 Gilbert Seldes linked the issue of Hollywood's continuing immaturity to the decline of cinema attendances in his comprehensive analysis of mass media in post-war America, *The Great Audience*. Unlike other American critics, Seldes did not object to the profit motive guiding the operations of the film and broadcast industries, but he argued that instead of 'creating genuinely democratic entertainment', they catered only 'to a sizable minority which they pretend is the mass of the people' (1950: 6). Making use of audience statistics, Seldes demonstrated not only that cinema attendance had been declining dramatically since 1946, but also that this decline reinforced Hollywood's tendency to cater primarily to young audiences, most notably adolescents. By the late 1940s it was clear that people over 30 largely stopped going to the cinema, while people in their twenties went regularly but infrequently, so that '[t]he movies live on children from the ages of ten to nineteen, who go steadily and frequently and almost automatically to the pictures' (12). Seldes argued that in the context of recent developments such as the end of block-booking, the divorce of the major producer-distributors from their theatre chains, the temporary closing-off of important foreign markets, and the competition provided by the free domestic entertainment of television, 'the recapture of the adult audience will be an absolute necessity for survival' (22). Unlike European films, however, Hollywood's output had concentrated on 'a small group of myths' concerning heroism, passion, and success that were appropriate for adolescents, especially during courtship, but lost their relevance and appeal when these young people started their working lives, married, and set up their own households (22–4). Seldes urged the film industry to bring its products more in line with mature audiences' everyday experiences by ensuring that story-lines were 'logical', situations and actions 'credible', characters individualized, and their motivations 'understandable' (37).

Seldes warned against a misconception of 'mature' filmmaking which was shared by 'both Hollywood producers and intellectual critics': 'Maturity does not necessarily imply either a tragic sense of life or an excessive sophistication' (36). With reference to the socially conscious films discussed by Agee and Tyler, Seldes demonstrated that Hollywood was able to produce mature films which were entertaining and commercially successful. He expected that the newly fragmented theatrical market and the growing ability of television to deliver 'routine' entertainment free of charge would encourage studios to reduce their output and concentrate on 'making fewer pictures for longer runs', 'attracting fresh audiences' to the movie theatres rather than merely catering for the regulars (41–2). Seldes hoped that studios would take their cue from the rapidly increasing number of so-called 'art theatres', which provided further evidence that there was an audience for mature films (42). The growing number of 'independent producing companies' set up by 'men of talent [who] wished to produce movies without interference from the front office' were particularly suited to deliver such films (48). Despite these possibilities, Seldes's analysis of post-war Hollywood ended on a cautious note. Political pressures, best exemplified by the Hollywood hearings of the House Committee on Un-American Activities, in combination with the rigid Production Code regulating the content of Hollywood's output, prevented studios from producing films which dealt with the realities of contemporary life. In conclusion, Seldes reiterated the social relevance of Hollywood's influence on 'popular emotion' in a 'postwar world [which] has not yet built its foundations' (102).

The remainder of the decade saw a reorientation of critical debates about Hollywood, away from the sense of urgency and the position of high-minded seriousness exemplified by Seldes's study and towards an acknowledgement of the very limited role moviegoing was going to play in American life from then on. With films being ever more explicitly addressed to minority interests rather than to the American public as a whole, the cinema lost its centrality in debates about mass media and American society. Questions of Hollywood's maturity or lack thereof were now discussed with specific reference to the two groups singled out by critics as the most influential target audiences for the post-war film industry—educated people and male youth. Hollywood's attempts to cater to these audiences were received with considerable criticism.

In 1952 Manny Farber launched a sustained critique of the pretensions of the film industry's current output, highlighting in particular its foregrounding of style and message ('overacting, overscoring, overlighting, overmoralizing') and its emphasis on the specialness and artistic merit of individual films (1971: 54–7). Farber contrasted 'smartly tooled art works' such as *Sunset*

Boulevard (USA, 1950) with 'the unspectacular, unpolished "B" (movies)' which 'capture the unworked-over immediacy of life before it has been cooled by "Art"' (55). Drawing on the thematic concerns and stylistic richness of sophisticaed and 'highbrow' works in the American cinema (such as *Citizen Kane*) and, more importantly, in other arts, a number of post-war films departed from the basic objectives of traditional Hollywood filmmaking, which were 'to present some intelligible, structured image of reality . . . to tell a story and to entertain' (72). Instead they presented themselves as symbolic acts of communication between 'a brave, intransigent artist' and a discerning audience, in which story, character, and the reproduction of the sounds and images of reality merely served as vehicles for 'hidden content', and film viewing turned into an act of interpretation (73–5). Farber linked the rise of this kind of 'New Movie' to the emergence of a new generation of filmmakers, such as Elia Kazan (director of *Gentleman's Agreement* and *Pinky*), who had been shaped by the political activism of the Depression years and by their 'higher . . . education' in the New York theatre (82).

By 1957 Farber had broadened his attack by situating a second wave of artistically minded and socially conscious writers and directors, most of whom had previously worked in live television drama and who started to make an impact on the film industry with the release of *Marty* (USA, 1955), in the context of a 'revolution' in American arts (1971: 113–24). In the cinema, music, painting, and literature, Farber saw 'the whole idea of "felt", committed art' under attack from an intellectualized, heavily rhetorical, and excessively technical approach to creative production 'known as advanced, radical, experimental, progressive, or, simply, avant-garde art' (113). The films arising from this movement were characterized by the foregrounding of meaningful detail and a despairing mood, by staginess, unsympathetic characterization, and 'masochistic acting, which is usually in the hands of Strasberg-influenced performers' (118). Farber rejected these films as exercises in self-promotion for their makers appealing to the snobbishness of their educated audiences, and again contrasted the new 'hard-sell cinema' with the transparency of traditional Hollywood entertainment: 'it differs from old-fashioned Hollywood direction in that the style parades in front of the film instead of tunneling under a seminaturalistic surface' (120). Farber argued that the 'male action film', which best exemplified the virtues of traditional Hollywood entertainment, was rapidly disappearing: 'the action directors are in decline, many of them having abandoned the dry, economic, life-worn movie style that made their observations of the American he-man so rewarding' (12). Directors such as Howard Hawks had flourished in 'a factory of unpretentious picture-making', that is a production system geared towards 'continuous flow of quality' rather than 'momentary novelties' (12–14). With the disappearance of this production system and the closing of action-oriented neighbourhood theatres in the 1950s, these filmmakers and their preferred genres such as the western were pushed towards artistic self-consciousness, thematic seriousness, and big-budget spectacle, creating what Bazin had called the 'super-western'.

At the same time, Hollywood abandoned the traditional image of the American male as mature, active, efficient, graceful, and stoic, and instead concentrated on a new type of masculinity, represented by Montgomery Clift, Marlon Brando, and James Dean. Writing in the mid-1950s, both Parker Tyler (1960: 127–8) and Pauline Kael (1966b: 44–62) linked the rise of these new male stars to a generational shift in post-war American culture. Dissatisfied with the political and material achievements of the parent generation, young people, who clearly dominated the cinema audience in the 1950s, began to question traditional values and lifestyles and through their actions gave rise to 'the social problem of juvenile delinquency', which was quickly taken up by Hollywood, with Brando and Dean being 'selected to illustrate the neurotic types that make up rebellion in the young' (Tyler 1960: 127). In sharp contrast to traditional images of masculinity, Tyler described these stars as 'naturally infantile types', intuitive, undisciplined, and heavily reliant on their 'babyish' good looks (128). Kael noted their ability to provoke 'violent audience reactions' in movie theatres and described the new character type as 'a complete negation of previous conceptions of heroism: the hero is not responsible for his actions—the crazy, mixed-up kid becomes a romantic hero by being treated on an infantile level' (1966b: 57, 60).

While Hollywood's new heroes were targeted specifically at a young male audience, and its artistic 'New Movies' appealed primarily to educated audiences, the film industry also continued to pursue an undifferentiated mass audience with big-budget widescreen spectacles. These films attempted to redefine and revitalize the cinematic experience itself by turning it into an innovative and unique technological and cultural event for a mass audience which had grown out of the moviegoing habit and had transferred its habitual consumption of audiovisual entertainment to television. Reviewing a wide range of widescreen and 3-D processes (typically supported by stereophonic sound and colour), Tyler argued in 1953 that the film industry was effectively relaunching the cinema itself by foregrounding its technological basis and its ability to transform the audience's experience of themselves and their surroundings: 'Television is centripetal in relation to its spectator, drawing the world into his domestic space, while 3-D movies are centrifugal in relation to their spectator's axis, drawing him out, collectively, into the world's space' (1960: 121).

In his second study of mass media in post-war America, Gilbert Seldes described the widescreen revolution in equally epochal terms, referring to the temptation 'to write a second obituary for the movies' in 1952–3, so as to register the death of a certain kind of 'flat' cinema in the same way that twenty-five years earlier 'silent' cinema had died with the coming of sound (1956: 17). Seldes was considerably more optimistic than in his earlier book about the possibility that American cinema might be revitalized: 'we have the exciting prospect of experiencing, for the third time in our lives, a new art of the movies' (60). This new art would combine the power of widescreen technologies to envelop, overwhelm, astonish, and unsettle the cinema audience with Hollywood's traditional storylines and characterization and its careful guiding of viewer attention through shot composition and continuity editing. In contrast to his earlier condemnation of Hollywood's immaturity, Seldes now argued that, despite the cinema's 'appeal to our most infantile desires' and its avoidance of 'the realities of existence', the formal and stylistic rigour and elegance of filmic storytelling constituted 'a separate gratification, as legitimate in its essence as that of any other art' (13). Seldes was willing to accept the mythical structure of Hollywood movies precisely because movies had been displaced from the centre of American culture by television's provision of entertainment as 'a free and continuous and integrated part of the daily home life of an entire nation' (1).

Also writing in 1956, Pauline Kael judged Hollywood's increasing reliance on 'big' pictures much more negatively (1966a). She argued that the inflated budgets, epic length, and wide screens of Hollywood's big pictures allowed them to become a massive 'compendium' of exotic locations, stock situations, realistic details, recognizable characters, and spectacular views that were not fused into a coherent whole but served mainly to celebrate the 'glamour' and 'magic' of 'bloated production methods' and thus of Hollywood's apparently limitless resources (52, 54). Kael predicted that this approach to filmmaking, which displaced the delineation of story events with the attempt to turn the production and release of the film into a major event, would soon lose its appeal and Hollywood would thus again lose favour with the general public: 'Spectacles will cease to be events, and audiences can be more comfortably bored at home' (64).

Building on these critical interventions in the 1950s, the early 1960s saw the appearance of book-length studies offering a broad historical evaluation of the fundamental changes in Hollywood's theatrical market and its production strategies in the immediate post-war period. In 1961 Ezra Goodman announced 'the end of Hollywood' (1961: 438). With television now serving as the primary outlet for audiovisual entertainment, the major studios' traditional concern with the production of films for the theatrical market was no longer economically viable. The major studios sold off their back catalogues of movies to television and their real estate to development companies, they transferred the efficiency and tight control characteristic of traditional studio operations to telefilm production, or they merged with television companies. The studios' reduced output of theatrical films had to compete with 'the good Hollywood movies, mostly those made up to the latish Thirties', which were available to audiences free of charge on the domestic television screen (447). Thus, theatrical production had effectively become an anachronism: 'Today, in the television ice age, the motion picture has already taken on an archaeological tinge' (p. x).

Richard Dyer MacCann saw the future of American cinema more optimistically, as is indicated by the title of his 1962 study *Hollywood in Transition*. MacCann argued that, far from being obsolete, films made for theatrical release had been given 'a new position' (p. x). Liberated from the 'tyranny' of self-censored, studio-controlled, assembly-line-like film production (p. xii), the production of a major theatrical feature had turned into a complex, infinitely variable, and highly volatile enterprise, a time-consuming, labour- and capital-intensive high-risk business venture whose only certainty was 'sudden change' and whose main aim was to create 'a special event' (3, 108). Apart from encouraging technological innovation, adaptations of Broadway hits and bestselling novels, and sensationalist films dealing with taboo subject-matter, this new situation also created opportunities for innovative, realistic, and socially conscious filmmaking. MacCann suggested that a new generation of filmmakers might be able to realize this potential, and that an increased emphasis on the preservation, study, and revival of the classics of American cinema, and on the training and promotion of young creative personnel and executives, would provide a good basis for the regeneration of American film culture. The model for such a more 'intellectual' approach to filmmaking could be found in France, where 'thirty or forty new young directors . . . have been fortified by a decade of talk and criticism [and] . . . fed with motion picture history at the film showings of the Cinématèque in Paris', resulting in an explosion of cinematic creativity (64).

Thus, between the late 1940s and early 1960s critics debated the disappearance of many of the certainties of American film culture of preceding decades. The stability and continuity of the studio system, the undifferentiated mass audience, the dominance of traditional storytelling and transparent entertainment, and the centrality of cinema in American life were all things of the past. Critics agreed that in the 1950s American cinema in its traditional form had come to an end, and the widescreen revolution and Hollywood's big pictures had failed to restore the movies to their previous key position in American popular culture. It was not clear what shape Hollywood might take in the future, nor was there a lot of confidence that an improvement on the old studio system could be expected. It was understood, however, that European film culture would have an important influence on the 'new' Hollywood that was eventually going to emerge from this period of transition.

New waves, new schools of Anglo-American film criticism, and the New Hollywood

In the early 1960s it became a critical commonplace to celebrate an artistic renaissance in world cinema, which was said to have begun in 1956 and to include the work of individual directors such as Michelangelo Antonioni and of movements and schools such as the French Nouvelle Vague (Houston 1963: 182–95).

Anglo-American critics tended to agree that Hollywood's contribution to this renaissance was minimal. Hollis Alpert declared in 1960 that in sharp contrast with the traditional 'belief that Americans were preeminent in the motion picture field', Hollywood was now 'losing such world-wide respect as it once had' (1960/1971a: 253), and in 1966 Dwight MacDonald stated categorically: 'None of the important postwar schools or directors have been American' (1966/1969: 38). In this critical climate, 'newness' became an important category in discussions of American cinema. At the low-budget and experimental end of American film production, critics engaged with a self-declared 'New American Cinema' exemplified by the work of writers and directors such as Jonas Mekas, Kenneth Anger, and John Cassavetes, certain aspects of which constituted, according to David Bordwell, a conscious 'modernist' break with Hollywood classicism (Houston 1963: 185–8; MacDonald 1966/1969: 39; Bordwell 1989: 54–8). Even at the centre of Hollywood production, a group of former television directors including Sidney Lumet and Arthur Penn, who had been much vilified by Manny Farber in the 1950s, could now be celebrated as a 'new breed', combining 'greater interest in social questions' with stylistic experimentation and improvisation, thus arguably constituting 'America's "new wave"' (Hart 1965; Jenkins 1995: 115).

However, this concern with, and positive evaluation of, newness was not characteristic of the bulk of Hollywood criticism in the 1960s, which concentrated on the systematic critical re-evaluation and close analysis of the work of a small group of Hollywood directors, most of whom had received their training and directed many of their important films during the studio era of the 1930s and 1940s, working mainly in well-established genres such as the western. Following on from Manny Farber's celebration of Hawks and the 'male action film' and from the *politique des auteurs* of *Cahiers du cinéma* with its similar emphasis on Hollywood directors such as Hawks and Alfred Hitchcock, Anglo-American 'auteurist' criticism in the 1960s elevated the films of certain genre directors to the status of art (Bordwell 1989: 42–53; Caughie 1981: 9–67). These critics rejected the self-consciously artistic and socially relevant films of the new generation of theatre- and television-trained directors joining Hollywood in the 1950s, and engaged with contemporary cinema mostly in terms of the latest works of old masters (Gillet 1971; Sarris 1963/1968).

The general critical shift towards a re-evaluation of

the studio era provided the context for one of the earliest uses of the term 'new Hollywood'. In a 1959 *Esquire* article entitled 'Elegy for Wonderland' veteran screenwriter Ben Hecht wrote that while 'the good old Hollywood' in which writers had been used and abused by powerful producers was 'dead', the 'new Hollywood . . . has in a measure solved the writer problem . . . [by] making movies so full of horses, bonfires, collapsing temples, Indian uprisings, wild beasts and uncovered breasts . . . that a writer would actually be in the way' (1971: 356, 362). Unlike his outright condemnation of contemporary Hollywood, Hecht's attitude towards the 'old' Hollywood was a mixture of contempt and nostalgia, a grudging acknowledgement that an industrial system inimical to art could nevertheless produce 'beauty and fine drama': 'The great Hollywood factories were interested only in turning out a standard product for mass consumption. But talent, brought to heel, did speak in this mass product' (363).

In Andrew Sarris's polemical reformulation of these ideas, the very restrictons imposed on directors working in Hollywood studios, especially in the 1930s and 1940s, were a pre-condition for the kind of qualities auteurist critics looked for: 'The auteur theory values the personality of a director precisely because of the barriers to its expression' (1968: 31). The 'modern' cinema of the post-war period, mainly in Europe but also in the United States, tended to elevate the director, giving him more control over the production process, valuing his personal experience and originality, and thus encouraging him to depart from traditional modes of filmic communication and indulge his idiosyncrasies: 'Paradoxically, however, the personalities of modern directors are often more obscure than those of classical directors who were encumbered with all sorts of narrative and dramatic machinery' (32). In Sarris's view, the art of cinema was based on the precarious balance of, on the one hand, commercial imperatives, collaborative work procedures, and stylistic and generic conventions, and, on the other hand, the unique vision and powerful personality of a director, capable of 'a sublimity of expression almost miraculously extracted from his money-oriented environment' (37). Idiosyncratic self-expression was thus kept in check by the overriding objective to tell meaningful and entertaining stories to a mass audience: 'The classical cinema was more functional than the modern cinema. It knew its audience and their expectations' (32).

Although Pauline Kael attacked Sarris and other auteurist critics for what she perceived as their logical inconsistencies, their 'narcissistic male fantasies', and their critical elevation of 'trash' films to the status of 'true film art' (1966: 319), she shared their concern with coherent storytelling as the basis for successful filmmaking. In her 1964 survey of contemporary filmmaking, she stated that 'processes of structural disintegration are at work in all types of movies', ranging from the experimental works of the New American Cinema and recent art-house favourites such as *Last Year at Marienbad* (France, 1961) to Hollywood's big pictures such as *Cleopatra* (USA, 1963) which included 'incomprehensible sections' or were simply 'incoherent' (1966: 8–9, 14). Echoing Manny Farber's critical outbursts in the 1950s, Kael saw the disintegration of filmic narrative as a symptom of the disintegration of traditional film culture in general. She lamented the rejection of 'craftsmanship as well as meaning' and 'critical standards' in the films and manifestos of the New American Cinema (18–19). Similarly, an emphasis on 'technique', 'purely visual content', and the possibility of open-ended 'elaborate interpretations' meant that '[t]he art-house audience accepts lack of clarity as complexity, accepts clumsiness and confusion as "ambiguity" and as style' (15, 20–1). While experimental filmmaking and art cinema were thus tranforming film into an élitist and excessively intellectual cultural form, Kael was equally critical of the experiences facilitated by Hollywood's mainstream releases. The lack of concern for coherent storytelling on the part of producers and directors in charge of the volatile and overblown process of filmmaking was matched by the audience's enthusiastic response to spectacular attractions and shock effects, irrespective of their degree of narrative motivation.

Kael tentatively explained the change in audience expectations with reference to 'modern life and the sense of urgency it produces', which was exemplified by television: 'It's possible that television viewing, with all its breaks and cuts, and the inattention, except for action, and spinning the dial to find some action, is partly responsible for the destruction of narrative sense . . . it may be that audiences don't have much more than a TV span of attention left' (9–10). Kael contrasted this set of expectations with the audience response characteristic of an earlier period (the 'classical cinema' in Sarris's terminology): 'audiences used to have an almost rational passion for getting the story straight . . . A movie had to tell some kind of story that held together: a plot to parse' (9). On the basis of this plot, traditional Hollywood films could develop the simple qualities that Kael, much like Farber and Sarris, was holding up as the foundation of a truly popular American cinema, now that this cinema largely seemed to have disappeared: 'energy', 'excitement', 'honest vulgarity', 'vitality' (24, 26).

For Kael and other critics, Hollywood's long-awaited renaissance finally occurred when the traditional qualities of American filmmaking were combined with the intellectual sophistication and stylistic innovations of the new directors and new waves of European cinema in films addressing contemporary and specifically American subject-matter. It is clear, both from critical responses at the time and from later retrospective accounts, that the film which most clearly marked the beginning of this renaissance was *Bonnie and Clyde* (USA, 1967). The film was a substantial hit, establishing the commercial viability of a new kind of Hollywood movie, and it was also the subject of enormous critical controversy (Cawelti 1973). In her review Pauline Kael declared *Bonnie and Clyde* to be 'the most excitingly American American movie' in half a decade, making 'a different kind of contact with an American audience from the kind that is made by European films, however contemporary' (1967/1970: 47). Kael argued that the film, which had originally been developed by scriptwriters Robert Benton and David Newman for François Truffaut and had then been offered to Jean-Luc Godard before it was finally directed by Arthur Penn, echoed the enthusiasm of French film critics and film-makers for 'the poetry of crime in American life' and the 'fast action, laconic speech, plain gestures' of traditional Hollywood entertainment (54). In line with the 'romanticism' of the Hollywood tradition, *Bonnie and Clyde* celebrated 'the cynical tough guy's independence', yet it did so in a 'specifically modern' fashion (47–9). It kept an ironic distance from its protagonists and their story and created 'a kind of eager, nervous imbalance' in the spectators, who oscillated between a serious engagement with the events on the screen and comic distanciation from it (49). The film offered neither a 'secure basis for identification' with the protagonists, nor a clear-cut moral framework for judging their behaviour, and it articulated contemporary concerns, especially with the role of violence in American society, through a 'nostalgia for the thirties' (51, 53).

In December 1967 *Time* magazine officially announced a 'renaissance' in American film culture exemplified by *Bonnie and Clyde* (1967/1971: 333). Echoing many of the critical debates of the 1950s and early 1960s, the magazine's cover story outlined a 'new cinema', which had originated in Europe and which 'Hollywood has at long last become part of' (323). This new cinema was characterized by narrative complexity, the foregrounding of cinematic devices, generic hybrids, and taboo subject-matter. According to the article, American audiences had been 'prepared for change and experiment both by life and art', in particular by 'the questioning of moral traditions, the demythologizing of ideals, the pulverizing of esthetic principles' in painting, music, and literature, and also by the familiarity with complex forms of audiovisual communication engendered by television (325). Reversing earlier negative judgements on the influence of television, Hollis Alpert argued that 'the visual training and orientation the young viewers received' through televison had created a cinema audience seeking out 'the visually dynamic film, the more "cinematic" kind of film experience' that was 'principally espoused by younger directors, many of them trained in television' (1968a/1971b: 337). In the wake of the excitement about *Bonnie and Clyde* and the spectacular box office returns of Mike Nichols's *The Graduate* (USA, 1967), Alpert declared an end to the 'star system', with its emphasis on the personalities of performers on and off the screen (336). Instead of an interest in stars, the response of young movie audiences was more likely to be informed by an intense identification with characters and by a close attention to stylistic devices, symbolic messages, and thematic

> For Kael and other critics, Hollywood's long-awaited renaissance finally occurred when the traditional qualities of American filmmaking were combined with the intellectual sophistication and stylistic innovations of the new directors and new waves of European cinema in films addressing contemporary and specifically American subject-matter. It is clear, both from critical responses at the time and from later retrospective accounts, that the film which most clearly marked the beginning of this renaissance was *Bonnie and Clyde* (1967).

The Hollywood renaissance—Warren Beatty and Faye Dunaway in *Bonnie and Clyde* (1967)

ambiguities in the film: the viewers returning to see *The Graduate* several times 'cultishly attach all sorts of significance to the most minor of details' (1968b/1971c: 405). For Steven Farber, the most significant aspect of Hollywood's new youth-oriented films was their frequent display of spectacular violence, which best expressed the films' fundamental 'antagonism toward authority', their 'anti-social bias', and their 'disillusionment with the normal life choices and life styles of American cinema' (1968/1971: 287).

The fundamental reorientation of the American film industry in the late 1960s, which was further solidified by the explicit counter-cultural concerns of popular films such as *Easy Rider* (USA, 1969), led to a more sustained engagement with contemporary Hollywood by auteurist critics. Unlike previous Anglo-American critics publishing books and articles in newspapers and magazines addressed to a general audience, many auteurist writers now addressed themselves to a much more specialized academic readership in film magazines such as *Movie* and *Monogram*, rearticulating key issues and observations in previous debates about Hollywood cinema in increasingly theoretical language (Maltby with Craven 1995: 421–4). *Monogram* writers highlighted the concept of a 'new Hollywood' to describe the transformation of mainstream American cinema in the late 1960s, and they also gave the concept of 'classic' or 'classical' Hollywood a new meaning, which was both broader in its historical application and more specifically tied to a particular type of narrative than earlier usage had suggested (Lloyd 1971; Elsaesser 1971, 1975).

In Bazin's periodization, the year 1939 had been both a high point and a turning-point for Hollywood classicism, marking the beginning of the Hollywood 'baroque' in the 1940s. Anglo-American critics from Seldes to Sarris had used the studio era of the 1930s and 1940s (which Sarris was mainly referring to when he used the label 'classical') as the main reference-point in their discussions of American film history, characterizing the following decades as a period of transition. For *Monogram* writers Thomas Elsaesser and Peter Lloyd, however, Hollywood's classical period lasted from the 1910s to the mid-1960s. During this period 'the filmic language evolved by Griffith, Stroheim and Murnau . . . retained its validity as the syntactical basis, whatever its modifications in terms of sound-effects, montage and camera-movements' (Elsaesser 1971: 5), and the long careers of key directors such as John Ford and Raoul Walsh produced 'the

component parts of this essential classicism' (Lloyd 1971: 11). Although both writers acknowledged substantial changes in Hollywood's mode of production and in the cinema's status in American culture during this period, in their view classical Hollywood was unified by a fairly stable system of genre conventions, by the centrality of a basic narrative formula focusing on goal-oriented characters who had to learn to balance individual desire and communal values, and by a particular stylistic approach to filmic storytelling characterized by 'efficiency, formal elegance and lucid simplicity' (Elsaesser 1971: 8).

In the late 1960s television-trained directors, '[o]wing perhaps to the harmful influence of the auteur theory', increasingly departed from these fundamental qualities of classicism to 'indulge in a kind of baroque and ornate elaboration of basically simple plots, without there being so much as a shred of dramatic or thematic necessity for their stylistic grand-guignol' (Elsaesser 1971: 8). The single most important 'aesthetic feature' marking the difference between classical and modern American cinema was 'the increasingly dislocated emotional identity of the central protagonist, and the almost total absence of the central drive and its dramatic mechanisms' (10). Without clearly defined goals and 'clearly identifiable moral and social objectives', the actions of the heroes of modern cinema frequently revolved around 'outbursts of unmotivated and wholly irrational violence' (10). Modern films thus signalled 'the gradual collapse of the efficacy of the heroic individual', and, instead of hinging on decisive action which brought about clear results, the films tended to move towards an 'ambiguous, open-ended situation' (Lloyd 1971: 12).

By 1975 the modern trend in Hollywood cinema had produced a substantial body of work by a group of high-profile directors which Elsaesser referred to as 'the new Hollywood of Altman, Pollack, Boorman, of Rafelson, Hellman, Spielberg or Ashby' (1975: 13). While classical Hollywood cinema expressed 'a fundamentally affirmative attitude to the world it depicts', key films of the new Hollywood had a 'liberal outlook' which led them to 'reject affirmation' and instead to project 'a radical scepticism . . . about the American virtues of ambition, vision, drive' (14–15). This shift had partly been caused by the changing status of cinema and the changing composition of its audiences. While television now catered for the mass audience previously served by classical Hollywood cinema, the new Hollywood had to address itself to 'ideologically less representative' segments of the population, and it did so by reflecting 'stances of dissent typical among minority groups' (14). The 'liberal' response to this challenge, which had become the focus of discussions of the new Hollywood, was exemplified by road movies. These combined 'the unmotivated hero and the motif of the journey', which largely functioned as an end in itself rather than getting the hero anywhere, thus expressing his disillusionment or cynicism (13). However, there was also a 'conservative' response exemplified by the 'cop thriller', which featured 'overdetermined heroes' and 'moralized violence' (15). Further responses included the disaster movie, the critical examination of classical genres in the form of 'pastiche' and 'parody', and the celebration of 'an affirmative, innocent past' in the 'nostalgia movie' (14, 18). Elsaesser noted that even the most radical formal and ideological departures from classical storytelling in the liberal films of the new Hollywood, which reflected the 'fading confidence in being able to tell a story' so characteristic of the work of leading European directors, nevertheless remained true to the basic objective of Hollywood cinema to engage audiences emotionally in its stories (13). Unlike many recent European films, the new Hollywood 'remains an audience-oriented cinema that permits no explicitly intellectual narrative construction' and operates by 'shifting and modifying traditional genres and themes, while never quite shedding their support' (18).

Also in 1975 *Movie* published a discussion amongst its main contributors about contemporary Hollywood which confirmed many of the observations and insights put forward by Elsaesser and Lloyd, although, in more traditional auteurist fashion, the magazine judged recent developments in Hollywood much more negatively (Cameron *et al.* 1975). In response to the persistent claims made by these and other publications (Madsen 1975) about a fundamental shift in Hollywood cinema, in 1976 the leading scholarly film magazine *Screen* finally took note of what was now officially known as the 'New Hollywood Cinema'. Steve Neale listed a variety of 'formal and thematic changes' which had been identified by auteurist critics. These ranged from '[t]he use of devices such as the zoom and telephoto lenses, slow-motion and split-screen [which] destroyed the dramatic and spatio-temporal unity that founded classical mise-en-scène with its economy, density and "subtlety" of signification', to the breakdown of genre conventions (1976: 117–18). Neale also reviewed the various 'socio-cultural factors which have

been seen to some extent as determinants' for the above changes, including 'the breakdown of censorship codes' (which had been finalized when the Production Code was replaced with a ratings system in 1968) and 'the breakdown of confidence in traditional American values' (118). Echoing Elsaesser's argument, Neale argued that in the 1950s television had taken over cinema's role as 'the main vector of ideology in the mass media', being able to fulfil it much more effectively due to its 'presence in the home, continuous transmission, (and) relative cheapness' (118). This allowed cinema 'to diversify its appeal and, therefore, its product', responding in particular to 'the rise of the youth movement and the struggles for liberation of both blacks and women: the growth of counter-cultures and ideologies generally, some of which could be sought and appealed to as a potential audience which was not catered for by television' (1991). For Neale, Hollywood here acted as a safety-valve, giving in to ideological pressure only to recuperate oppositional stances. Despite changes in its mode of production and, in its narrative strategies, Hollywood continued to operate successfully as a capitalist enterprise and did not disrupt the fundamental operations of the 'classical text' with its 'ordering meta-discourse' aimed at eliminating ideological contradictions and thus creating an imaginary 'unity of position' for the spectator (120–1). In Neale's view, contemporary Hollywood continued the hegemonic project of classical cinema.

The theoretically sophisticated discussions of the 1970s about recent developments in Hollywood cinema had two major results. On the one hand, 'New Hollywood' became firmly established as an important concept in critical debates, referring to American mainstream cinema since 1967 and, more specifically, to the stylistic, narrative, and thematic innovations characteristic of the films of certain directors and of certain 'liberal' cycles. On the other hand, the concept of 'classical Hollywood' was applied to a dramatically extended period in American film history which lasted from the 1910s to the 1960s, and the notion of a 'classical text' went even further by also incorporating the films of the New Hollywood. In this way, academic discourse effectively erased previous critical debates about complex changes in the Hollywood aesthetic and about the multiplicity of social, cultural, and industrial factors shaping these changes that had been conducted between the late 1940s and the mid-1960s. Hollywood's 'transitional' post-war period was of interest only in so far as it paved the way for the emergence of the New Hollywood from 1967 onwards.

Critical responses to developments in the New Hollywood: movie brats, neo-classicism, and post-modernism

When 'New Hollywood' became firmly established as a critical term in film studies in the mid-1970s, Hollywood itself was in the midst of an aesthetic, cultural, and industrial reorientation, which was signalled most dramatically by the unprecedented box-office successes of *Jaws* (USA, 1975) and *Star Wars* (USA, 1977). In subsequent years critics described Holly-

wood's reorientation in the second half of the 1970s in terms of the films' increasing emphasis on special effects and cinematic spectacle (Neale 1980), their return to a psychologically and politically regressive outlook (Wood 1985, 1986, ch. 8; Britton 1986) and the film industry's increasingly narrow focus on 'blockbusters', that is heavily promoted big-budget films (Monaco 1979, chs. 1–3). In retrospect, the original New Hollywood of the years 1967–75 came to be seen as a brief and exceptional period in American film history in which artistically ambitious and politically progressive filmmaking had been commercially viable, competing successfully for a while with conservative film cycles (Maltby 1983, ch. 10; Ray 1985, chs. 8–9; Ryan and Kellner 1988, chs. 1–3). Auteurist critics have continued to explore and evaluate the achievements

An unprecedented box-office success—*Star Wars* (1977)

Spielberg's first
blockbuster, *Jaws* (1975)

of the small group of directors who had been at the centre of Hollywood's short-lived artistic renaissance (Pye and Myles 1979; Kolker 1980, 1988). Other critics, however, have concentrated on a general outline and critique of the aesthetic and commercial logic underpinning Hollywood's operations since the 1960s, best exemplified by *Jaws* and subsequent films by George Lucas and Steven Spielberg (Monaco 1979; Thompson 1981; Biskind 1990; Schatz 1993; Wyatt 1994). These critics emphasize the incorporation of Hollywood studios into giant industrial conglomerates since the mid-1960s, the proliferation of delivery systems for films

gaining momentum with the successful introduction of pay-cable and home video in the mid-1970s, and the multi-media marketing of movies, which connects their theatrical release with the launching of a whole product line of popular cultural artefacts (ranging from pop songs to computer games), while also using a film's theatrical exposure as the key to ancillary markets such as video and pay-cable, where the bulk of film revenues have been generated since the mid-1980s. Confusingly, this second group of critics frequently employs the term 'New Hollywood' to refer to the much longer period they are dealing with, and, in particular, to the years after 1975. Thus, in different critical contexts 'New Hollywood' may refer to the period 1967–75 as well as to the post-1975 period, to the aesthetic and political progressivism of the liberal cycles of the earlier period as well as to the regressiveness of the blockbusters of the later period (Tasker 1996).

As if that was not confusing enough, critical discourses about the New Hollywood often revolve around the very same issues that concerned critics writing about Hollywood's transitional period between the late 1940s and the mid-1960s. For example, European influences, stylistic innovations, taboo subject-matter, new cinematic conceptions of heroism and masculinity, and critical awareness of social realities had already been hotly debated with respect to key Hollywood films and cycles of the late 1940s and the 1950s, long before they became identified with the Hollywood renaissance after 1967. Juvenilization, the technological renewal of the cinematic experience, the trend towards big event pictures, and the displacement of narrative by spectacle had all been the subject of critical debates in the 1950s, long before the new breed of blockbusters in the 1970s and 1980s provoked strong critical reactions along these lines. Such continuities in critical debates and in Hollywood's aesthetic and commercial logic often go unacknowledged. Consequently, recent critical discourses about the New Hollywood (in both its restricted and its general meaning) have tended to exaggerate its newness, instead of situating the New Hollywood in relation to long-term trends in the post-war period.

To complicate matters further, since the 1980s critics have made concerted efforts to apply the concepts of modernism and postmodernism to developments in post-war American cinema. These concepts are used both to demarcate historical periods and to characterize particular film cycles. They may be used primarily with reference to aesthetic issues, or more generally with reference to the totality of a cultural formation, comprising cultural artefacts as well as media industries, forms of social organization, and ideologies. In the light of the wide-ranging and varying applications of these concepts in film criticism, it is difficult to map them onto the established periodizations of post-war Hollywood which take the concept of classicism as their starting-point. For example, studies of the emergence and development of postmodern culture in the United States tend to refer broadly to the post-war period, identifying the 1960s as a decade of crucial cultural transformations in the arts, yet locating

key examples of postmodern cinema such as *Blade Runner* (USA, 1982), *Blue Velvet* (USA, 1984), and *Batman* (USA, 1989) in more recent years (Denzin 1991; Jameson 1991; Corrigan 1991). In this view, then, despite the late appearance of exemplary postmodern films, the whole period since the Second World War is overshadowed by postmodernism. In sharp contrast, an analysis using a narrow Bazinian definition of Hollywood classicism, which sees the year 1939 as a crucial historical turning-point, would identify *Citizen Kane* as the beginning of a modernist trend in American cinema which gained momentum with the self-consciously artistic New Movie of the 1950s and the experiments of the New American Cinema in the early 1960s, and culminated in the artistic renaissance of the New Hollywood between 1967 and 1975. Alternatively, using *Monogram*'s definition of classicism as the dominant Hollywood aesthetic betwen the 1910s and the mid-1960s, only the sustained attack on the fundamental principles of Hollywood storytelling in the liberal cycles of the New Hollywood qualifies as a genuinely modernist intervention into mainstream American cinema. In both cases, the post-1975 period may be characterized either as a turn towards postmodernism or as a return to the principles of classicism.

These periodizations intersect with the standard auteurist account of developments in Hollywood since the late 1960s, which concentrates on the impact of the so-called 'film school generation' or 'movie-brats' (Belton 1994, ch. 14; Hillier 1993). In their highly influential 1979 book *The Movie Brats*, Michael Pye and Lynda Myles discussed the work of a closely knit group of filmmakers born in the 1940s (with the exception of Francis Ford Coppola, who was born in 1939). The group, consisting of Coppola, Scorsese, George Lucas, Brian De Palma, John Milius, and Steven Spielberg and also including some of their frequent collaborators such as Gary Kurtz, represented 'a ciné-literate generation of filmmakers' (1979, p: vii). They had become thoroughly familiar with Hollywood's history through television broadcasts of old movies, had learnt about European film movements in art-houses, and had had the opportunity (which many of them took) to learn their profession at film school and to gain practical experience in the exploitation sector, most notably with Roger Corman's New World Pictures, before they moved into regular feature production from the late 1960s onwards, writing scripts and acting as producers as well as working as directors, and often giving support to, or working with, each other.

According to Pye and Myles, this new generation of filmmakers was detached from, and often critical of, the Hollywood establishment, and approached mainstream filmmaking in an analytical and self-conscious fashion, producing a new kind of movie which combined the powerful storytelling of classical Hollywood with the transgressive subject-matter of exploitation cinema and the stylistic innovations of European new waves.

> **According to Pye and Myles, this new generation of filmmakers was detached from, and often critical of, the Hollywood establishment, and approached mainstream filmmaking in an analytical and self-conscious fashion, producing a new kind of movie which combined the powerful storytelling of classical Hollywood with the transgressive subject-matter of exploitation cinema and the stylistic innovations of European new waves.**

Pye and Myles's account of Hollywood cinema since the late 1960s identified a crucial generational shift in the film industry, although it largely ignored the parallels to, and connections with, earlier waves of Hollywood outsiders making a strong impact on the industry (such as the theatre- and television-trained writers and directors of the 1950s and 1960s). Their account emphasized the transformation of the 1960s outsiders into the Hollywood establishment of the 1970s. Due to a string of box-office hits, from Coppola's *The Godfather* (USA, 1972) to Spielberg's *Close Encounters of the Third Kind* (USA, 1977), the six key filmmakers and their associates 'at the end of 1977, stood unchallenged as the powers within a new Hollywood. They inherited the power of the moguls to make films for a mass audience' (7). Thus, in effect Pye and Myles argued that, following three decades of aesthetic and economic crisis and flux, the late 1970s saw a return to the stability, popularity, and high standards of the studio era. In this neo-classical Hollywood, auteurs had taken over the executive role of the moguls.

Robert Phillip Kolker approached the crucial shift in late 1970s Hollywood with reference to the concepts of modernism and postmodernism. In his 1980 study *A Cinema of Loneliness*, Kolker explored 'the growth of modernism' in mainstream American cinema of the 1960s and 1970s (1980: 16), grouping older directors such as Arthur Penn, Robert Altman, and Stanley Kubrick together with movie brats Coppola and Scorsese. In Kolker's view, the work of these filmmakers balanced entertainment values with a critical investigation of 'the nature of their medium, its history, its methods and effects' (p. viii). Their self-conscious approach to filmic storytelling, '*refusing* the classical American approach to film, which is to make the formal structure of a work erase itself as it creates its content', demanded an equally self-conscious spectator: 'These directors delight in making us aware of the fact that it is film we are watching, an artifice, something made in special ways, to be perceived in special ways' (9). In the revised edition of his book, Kolker declares that, as far as mainstream American cinema is concerned, '[t]he modernist project . . . is over', with '[p]ostmodern American film . . . returning with a vengeance to a linear illusionist style' (1988, p. xi). Kolker dates this transition in the second half of the 1970s, and sees Steven Spielberg as its key figure, who best exemplifies contemporary Hollywood's 'increased ability. . . to use images and narratives to manipulate response' and to subject the viewer to 'great imaginary structures of displaced yearning, misplaced heroism, and forced amelioration' (p. xi). Schatz gives a similar account, discussing *Annie Hall* (USA, 1977) as an exemplary modernist film, and situating it in the context of a commercial cinema still 'dominated by classical narratives that are technically more proficient . . . than products of the Old Hollywood but otherwise rely on the same principles of construction and methods of viewer engagement' (1983: 223). He goes as far as saying that in particular the films of Lucas and Spielberg 'are even "more classical" than traditional Hollywood movies because of the narrative and technical expertise of their creators' (223).

Noel Carroll (1982) argues that both Hollywood's modernism and its (postmodern or neo-classical) revisionism participate in a culture of allusion. In the 1970s the outlook of large segments of the cinema audience as well as many directors had been shaped by the comprehensive education in film history they had received through television, art-houses, college courses, film societies, film criticism, and film schools while growing up in the 1950s and 1960s. Film history became an important reference-point in the artistic communcation between filmmakers and their audiences. By alluding to the cinema's past in their films, directors created complex texts which engaged and thus rewarded the audience's film-historical knowledge. Instead of distancing spectators from the textual operations of their films, directors employed allusions as 'expressive devices: they are a means for projecting and reinforcing the themes and the emotive and aesthetic qualities of the new films' (Carroll 1982: 53). The culture of allusion embraced a wide variety of practices, 'including quotations, the memorialization of past genres, the reworking of past genres, homages, and the recreation of "classic" scenes, shots, plot motifs, lines of dialogue, themes, gestures, and so forth from film history' (52). While allusions might be used critically by filmmakers such as Robert Altman in a challenge to the ideas and values underpinning traditional genres and the contemporary social order, they were equally in evidence in the revisionist genre films that gained dominance in the second half of the 1970s, addressing themselves both to an older film-educated audience and to a much less knowledgeable 'adolescent clientele' (56). Filmmakers developed 'a two-tiered system of communication which sends an action/drama/fantasy-packed message to one segment of the audience and an additional hermetic, camouflaged, and recondite one to another' (56).

Since the mid-1970s, then, critical debates about the New Hollywood have been characterized by a confusing proliferation of contradictory and shifting definitions of the term, and by different attempts to conceptualize the development of mainstream American cinema in the post-war era with reference to modernism and postmodernism. Yvonne Tasker's (1996) review of these debates indicates that, while there is still no agreement about proper definitions and mappings, there is perhaps a general direction in which these definitions and mappings develop. The original association of the term 'New Hollywood' with the artistic renaissance of the late 1960s and early 1970s has largely been displaced by its identification with the post-1975 period. Furthermore, the critical analysis of the stylistic and thematic innovations introduced by a new generation of auteurs has given way to a concern with the corporate strategies of media conglomerates, with blockbusters and multi-media marketing, and with new forms of film consumption. Indeed, Tasker suggests that changes in the wider cultural and media

landscape may be the best way to separate New Hollywood from classical American cinema and to situate it in relation to postmodernism: 'The newness of the new Hollywood stems from the rapidly changing entertainment world in which it exists. In this context an analysis of film style in the new Hollywood might be most usefully approached through an awareness of the interaction between film and other media and the proliferation of cultural commodities, rather than exclusively in terms of a relationship to the cinematic past' (1996: 226–7). Hence, New Hollywood may be defined not so much in terms of stylistic and thematic changes in filmmaking, clearly separating the contemporary period from a previous modernist moment in American film history as well as from Hollywood's classicism, but in terms of a postmodern multi-media world which undermines the very notion of 'film as a distinct medium' (Tasker 1996: 226). Postmodern New Hollywood, then, is American filmmaking in the age of a fully integrated multi-media culture which originated in the 1960s and consolidated itself in the 1970s and 1980s.

> Hence, New Hollywood may be defined not so much in terms of stylistic and thematic changes in filmmaking, clearly separating the contemporary period from a previous modernist moment in American film history as well as from Hollywood's classicism, but in terms of a postmodern multi-media world which undermines the very notion of 'film as a distinct medium'. Postmodern New Hollywood, then, is American filmmaking in the age of a fully integrated multi-media culture which originated in the 1960s and consolidated itself in the 1970s and 1980s.

The historical poetics of classicism and post-classicism

In her discussion of the New Hollywood, Yvonne Tasker employs the term 'post-classical' to refer primarily and specifically to stylistic changes in mainstream American filmmaking since the 1960s (1996: 220–1). She refers to Bordwell, Staiger, and Thompson's monumental study *The Classical Hollywood Cinema* (1985) as the most comprehensive account of the normative stylistic system, which the innovations of post-classicism need to be defined against. In doing so, Tasker follows the model of other recent critics such as Justin Wyatt (1994: 7–8, 15–16, 60–4), Henry Jenkins (1995: 113–17), and Richard Maltby and Ian Craven (1995: 217–21), all of whom have identified significant departures from classical storytelling, as described in *The Classical Hollywood Cinema*, in certain film cycles since 1960, although they acknowledge that the majority of American films stay firmly within the classical tradition. While the term 'post-classical' may also be used more loosely to refer to other aspects of contemporary American cinema (Rowe 1995; Neale and Smith, forthcoming), its value as a critical tool would seem to depend on its precise application to the form of stylistic analysis exemplified by Bordwell, Staiger, and Thompson's study.

Bordwell has called this form of analysis 'historical poetics of the cinema', and defined it as 'the study of how, in determinate circumstances, films are put together, serve specific functions, and achieve specific effects' (1989: 266–7). While historical poetics proceeds from the stylistic analysis of individual films and sees any film as 'the result of deliberate and founding choices' made by filmmakers, '[t]he poetician aims to analyze the conceptual and empirical factors—norms, traditions, habits—that govern a practice and its products' (269). To establish the norms and traditions governing a mode of film practice such as classical Hollywood, it is necessary to analyse a large number of films and to ensure that these films constitute a representative sample of the vast corpus they are meant to exemplify. The idiosyncrasies of individual films are thus discussed systematically in relation to the norms embodied in a larger body of texts. Similarly, the use of particular devices in any given film is analysed in relation to the stylistic system of the film as a whole. Furthermore, film analysis is typically complemented by an investigation into the concrete work procedures of filmmaking and the system of production which organizes them. This investigation can make use of a variety of sources ranging from written codifications of rules and norms (e.g. manuals) to interviews with participants. Finally, historical poetics aims to identify stylistic developments within particular film

practices, by tracing the diffusion of new stylistic devices such as, for example, zooms, split screens, and freeze frames across the overall corpus of films, and by identifying changes in the normative stylistic system which, in any given film, assigns individual devices a particular function, in Hollywood usually for the purpose of storytelling.

An example of a systemic stylistic change in classical Hollywood filmmaking would be the introduction of aimless protagonists, the loosening of causal connections between narrative events, the foregrounding of stylistic devices in their own right, which serves to demonstrate the filmmakers' artistic presence and intentions, and the refusal of unambiguous narrative closure, which invites audiences to speculate about the film's significance. According to Bordwell, these are some of the key narrational strategies of European art cinema that were absorbed by the filmmakers of the New Hollywood in the late 1960s. While *Monogram* had argued that this absorption constituted a decisive break in the development of mainstream American filmmaking, Bordwell writes: 'these new films do not constitute a sharply distinct style, but can better be explained by that process of stylistic assimilation we have seen at work throughout Hollywood's history' (Bordwell, Staiger, and Thompson 1985: 373). Bordwell uses the penultimate chapter of *The Classical Hollywood Cinema*, entitled 'Since 1960: The Persistence of a Mode of Film Practice', to argue, in effect, that all stylistic innovations in American filmmaking in recent decades 'remain within classical boundaries' (377), and that the date 1960 is a fairly arbitrary cut-off point for their study, which is by no means meant to indicate the end of the classical epoch. By analysing narrational strategies in a sample of recent Hollywood films and their codification in contemporary scriptwriting manuals in comparison with practices in early American feature filmmaking in the mid-1910s, Kristin Thompson (1995) has also argued forcefully for the overall continuity of the classical Hollywood up to the present.

Bordwell, Staiger, and Thompson's work has been criticized (much like *Screen*'s concept of the classical text) for its tendency to play down or erase the differences between individual Hollywood films and between particular œuvres, cycles, and periods, and to describe the basic tenets of classical Hollywood style in such general terms that any form of mainstream filmmaking would appear to fit into this model (Britton 1988–9; Williams 1994). Henry Jenkins (1995), however, argues that *The Classical Hollywood Cinema* and its underlying methodology allow for a more dynamic account of stylistic differences and developments than they are sometimes given credit for. At the centre of Bordwell, Staiger, and Thompson's study and of the project of historical poetics in general are, after all, processes of stylistic change, brought about, for example, by the introduction of new technologies such as synchronized sound or by the encounter with alternative stylistic systems such as European art cinema. Jenkins finds the description and explanation of such stylistic changes offered by Bordwell, Staiger, and Thompson 'essentially correct', although he would prefer to shift the critical focus of the investigation from the ultimate assimilation of new stylistic elements into the established system, to the early stages of that process, that is the 'periods of transition and experimentation before the system can fully stabilize itself around these changes' (1995: 114, 104). During these usually very brief periods, new stylistic elements are perceived by filmmakers and audiences alike as a disruption of the normative stylistic system or as a welcome novelty. The force of this perception is easily underestimated when such innovations are analysed in retrospect from a position which has already witnessed their complete assimilation.

While numerous examples of the process of defamiliarization and assimilation can be found in Hollywood between the 1910s and the 1940s, Jenkins suggests that the post-war period is characterized by the dramatic intensification of stylistic change: 'Since the breakdown of the studio system, Hollywood has entered a period of prolonged and consistent formal experimentation and institutional flux with a media-savvy audience demanding   aesthetic novelty and difference. As a result, stylistic changes which might have unfolded over several decades under the studio system have occurred in a matter of a few years in contemporary Hollywood' (114). It is this increased speed and intensity of stylistic change which the concept of post-classicism is meant to describe. While Jenkins's examples are mainly from the 1960s, 1970s, and 1980s (the movie brats, 'high-concept' films, MTV aesthetics), his analysis would also seem to apply to the immediate post-war period, during which critics, and presumably American filmmakers and audiences as well, responded very strongly to a wide variety of stylistic developments which included: the increasing use of long takes, deep-focus cinematography and staging in depth; the move towards quasi-documentary; the

self-conscious artistry of the New Movie; the wide-screen revolution; and the big picture.

Some of these developments in the post-war period have been covered in *The Classical Hollywood Cinema*. Yet, in general, critical debates about developments in post-war American cinema have dealt with stylistic change only in a cursory, abstract, and unspecific fashion, quickly moving from observations about individual film examples to claims about fundamental shifts in the overall aesthetic and industrial system. In this situation, the conceptual debate about Old Hollywood and New Hollywood, modernism and postmodernism, classicism and post-classicism, is perhaps less urgent and productive than the kind of careful, systematic, and complex stylistic analysis which historical poetics demands.

BIBLIOGRAPHY

Agee, James (1963), *Agee on Film* (London: Peter Owen).

Alpert, Hollis (1960/1971a), 'Are Foreign Films Better?: Show of Strength Abroad', in Arthur F. McClure (ed.), *The Movies: An American Idiom* (Rutherford: Fairleigh Dickinson University Press).

—— (1968a/1971b), 'The Falling Stars', in Arthur F. McClure (ed.), *The Movies: An American Idiom* (Rutherford: Fairleigh Dickinson University Press).

—— (1968b/1971c), 'The Graduate Makes Out', in Arthur F. McClure (ed.), *The Movies: An American Idiom* (Rutherford: Fairleigh Dickinson University Press).

Andrew, Dudley (1978), *André Bazin* (New York: Oxford University Press).

Bazin, André (1951/1967), trans. Hugh Gray 'The Evolution of the Language of Cinema', in *What is Cinema?*, in 2 vols., i (Berkeley: University of California Press).

—— (1957/1985), 'On the *politique des auteurs*', trans. Peter Graham in Jim Hillier (ed.), *Cahiers du Cinéma*, i: *The 1950s: Neo-Realism, Hollywood, New Wave* (London: Routledge & Kegan Paul).

—— (1971), 'The Evolution of the Western', in *What is Cinema?* trans. Hugh Gray, 2 vols., ii (Berkeley: University of California Press).

Belton, John (1994), *American Cinema/American Culture* (New York: McGraw-Hill).

Biskind, Peter (1990), 'Blockbuster: The Last Crusade', in Mark Crispin Miller (ed.), *Seeing through Movies* (New York: Pantheon).

Bordwell, David (1989), *Making Meaning: Inference and Rhetoric in the Interpretation of Cinema* (Cambridge, Mass.: Harvard University Press).

—— **Janet Staiger,** and **Kristin Thompson** (1985), *The*

Classical Hollywood Cinema: Film Style and Mode of Production to 1960 (London: Routledge & Kegan Paul).

Britton, Andrew (1986), 'Blissing Out: The Politics of Reaganite Entertainment', *Movie*, 31–2: 1–42.

—— (1988–9), 'The Philosophy of the Pigeonhole: Wisconsin Formalism and "The Classical Style"', *CineAction*, 15: 47–63.

Cameron, Ian *et al.* (1975), 'The Return of the Movie', *Movie*, 20: 1–25.

*****Carroll, Noel** (1982), 'The Future of Allusion: Hollywood in the Seventies (and Beyond)', *October*, 20: 51–81.

Caughie, John (ed.) (1981), *Theories of Authorship* (London: Routledge & Kegan Paul).

Cawelti, John G. (ed.) (1973), *Focus on 'Bonnie and Clyde'* (Englewood Cliffs, NJ: Prentice Hall).

Corrigan, Timothy (1991), *A Cinema without Walls: Movies and Culture after Vietnam* (London: Routledge).

Denzin, Norman K. (1991), *Images of Postmodern Society: Social Theory and Contemporary Cinema* (London: Sage).

Elsaesser, Thomas (1971), 'The American Cinema: Why Hollywood?', *Monogram*, 1: 4–10.

*—— (1975), 'The Pathos of Failure. American Films in the 1970s: Notes on the Unmotivated Hero', *Monogram*, 6: 13–19.

Farber, Manny (1952/1971), *Negative Space: Manny Farber on the Movies* (London: Studio Vista).

Farber, Steven (1968/1971), 'The Outlaws', in Arthur F. McClure (ed.), *The Movies: An American Idiom* (Rutherford: Fairleigh Dickinson University Press).

Gillet, John (1959/1971), 'The Survivors', in Arthur F. McClure (ed.), *The Movies: An American Idiom* (Rutherford: Fairleigh Dickinson University Press).

Goodman, Ezra (1961), *The Fifty-Year Decline and Fall of Hollywood* (New York: Simon & Schuster).

Hart, Peter (1965), 'New Breed Scans New Horizons', *New York Times*, 10 Jan. 1965.

Hecht, Ben (1959/1971), 'Elegy for Wonderland', in Arthur F. McClure (ed.), *The Movies: An American Idiom* (Rutherford: Fairleigh Dickinson University Press).

*****Hillier, Jim** (1993), *The New Hollywood* (London: Studio Vista).

Houston, Penelope (1963), *The Contemporary Cinema* (Harmondsworth: Penguin).

Jameson, Fredric (1991), *Postmodernism; or, The Cultural Logic of Late Capitalism* (Durham, NC: Duke University Press).

Jenkins, Henry (1995), 'Historical Poetics', in Joanne Hollows and Mark Jancovich (eds.), *Approaches to Popular Film* (Manchester: Manchester University Press).

Kael, Pauline (1956/1966a), 'Movies, the Desperate Art', in Daniel Talbot (ed.), *Film: An Anthology* (Berkeley: University of California Press).

—— (1966b), *I Lost it at the Movies* (London: Jonathan Cape).

—— (1967/1970), *Kiss Kiss Bang Bang* (London: Calder & Boyars).

Kolker, Robert Phillip (1980), *A Cinema of Loneliness: Penn, Kubrick, Coppola, Scorsese, Altman* (New York: Oxford University Press).

*—— (1988), *A Cinema of Loneliness: Penn, Kubrick, Scorsese, Spielberg, Altman*, 2nd edn. (New York: Oxford University Press).

Lloyd, Peter (1971), 'The American Cinema: An Outlook', *Monogram* 1: 11–13.

MacCann, Richard Dyer (1962), *Hollywood in Transition* (Boston: Houghton Mifflin).

MacDonald, Dwight (1966/1969), *Dwight MacDonald on Movies* (Englewood Cliffs: Prentice Hall).

Madsen, Axel (1975), *The New Hollywood: American Movies in the 1970s* (New York: Thomas Y. Crowell).

Maltby, Richard (1983), *Harmless Entertainment: Hollywood and the Ideology of Consensus* (Metuchen, NJ: Scarecrow).

—— with **Ian Craven** (1995), *Hollywood Cinema: An Introduction* (Oxford: Blackwell).

Modleski, Tania (1991), *Feminism without Women: Culture and Criticism in a Postfeminist Age* (London: Routledge).

Monaco, James (1979), *American Film Now: The People, the Power, the Money, the Movies* (New York: Plume).

Neale, Steve (1976), 'New Hollywood Cinema', *Screen* 17/2: 117–22.

—— (1980), 'Hollywood Strikes Back: Special Effects in Recent American Cinema', *Screen*, 21/3: 101–5.

—— and **Murray Smith** (eds.) (forthcoming), *Contemporary American Cinema* (London: Routledge).

Pye, Michael, and **Lynda Myles** (1979), *The Movie Brats: How the Film Generation Took over Hollywood* (New York: Holt, Rinehart, & Winston).

Ray, Robert B. (1985), *A Certain Tendency of the Hollywood Cinema 1930–1980* (Princeton: Princeton University Press).

Rowe, Kathleen (1995), 'Melodrama and Men in Post-Classical Romantic Comedy', in Pat Kirkham and Janet Thumim (eds.), *Me Jane: Masculinity, Movies and Women* (London: Lawrence & Wishart).

Ryan, Michael, and **Douglas Kellner** (1988), *Camera Politica: The Politics and Ideology of Contemporary Hollywood Film* (Bloomington: Indiana University Press).

Sarris, Andrew (1963/1968), 'The American Cinema', *Film Culture*, 28; repr. rev. as 'Toward a Theory of Film History', in *The American Cinema: Directors and Directions 1929–1968* (New York: Dutton).

*****Schatz, Thomas** (1983), *Old Hollywood/New Hollywood: Ritual, Art, Industry* (Ann Arbor, Mich.: UMI Research Press).

—— (1988), *The Genius of the System* (New York: Pantheon).

—— (1993), 'The New Hollywood', in Jim Collins, Hilary Radner, and Ava Preacher Collins (eds.), *Film Theory Goes to the Movies* (New York: Routledge).

Seldes, Gilbert (1950), *The Great Audience* (New York: Viking).

—— (1956), *The Public Arts* (New York: Simon & Schuster).

*Tasker, Yvonne (1996), 'Approaches to the New Hollywood', in James Curran, David Morley, and Valerie Walkerdine (eds.), *Cultural Studies and Communications* (London: Arnold).

Thompson, Kristin (1995), 'Narrative Structure in Early Classical Cinema', paper presented to Celebrating 1895: An International Conference on Film before 1920, National Museum of Photography, Film, and Television, Bradford, June 1995.

Thomson, David (1981), *Overexposures: The Crisis in American Filmmaking* (New York: William Morrow).

Time (1967/1971), 'The Shock of Freedom in Films', in Arthur F. McClure (ed.), *The Movies: An American Idiom* (Rutherford: Fairleigh Dickinson University Press).

Tyler, Parker (1960), *The Three Faces of the Film* (New York: Thomas Yoseloff).

Williams, Christopher (1994), 'After the Classic, the Classical and Ideology: The Differences of Realism', *Screen*, 35/3: 275–92.

Wood, Robin (1985), '1980s Hollywood: Dominant Tendencies', *CineAction*, 1: 1–5.

*—— (1986), *Hollywood from Vietnam to Reagan* (New York: Columbia University Press).

Wyatt, Justin (1994), *High Concept: Movies and Marketing in Hollywood* (Austin: University of Texas Press).

Critical concepts

<table>
<tr><td>7</td><td></td></tr>
</table>

Authorship and Hollywood

Stephen Crofts

Authorship is by far the best-known 'theory' of cinema, and Hollywood much the best-known national cinema. Many conceptions of authorship have arisen in relation to Hollywood—and other national cinemas—over the last seven decades, and proper consideration of these varied notions requires contextualization in terms of the institutions which support them. For, unlike most other ways of making sense of cinema, discourses of authorship have emerged across the whole gamut of cinematic institutions from film production and circulation through film reviewing, criticism and analysis, and film education, to film history and theory. In doing so, discourses of authorship assert the central significance of individual creativity within the cinema, and usually locate this in the director.

The attachment of authorial discourses to Hollywood warrants some comment. Authorial discourses, after all, find stronger empirical connection to the more artisanal modes of filmmaking practice which characterize art and avant-garde cinemas. Both these modes of filmmaking exhibit greater degrees of individual creativity than were possible within the industrial modes of production characteristic of Hollywood in what David Bordwell, Janet Staiger, and Kristin Thompson (1985) identify as the classical period to 1960, and often subsequently. Classical Hollywood had little use for a discourse of authorship and few outside Walt Disney, Alfred Hitchcock, and Charlie Chaplin attained name status (1985: 96–112, 78), this is not at all to deny the *differentiation* and *innovation* which Bordwell, Staiger, and Thompson note as accompanying the standardization of Hollywood. In the context of its successful marketing of films by star and genre, directorial power could be greater in practice than was acknowledged in promotion: 'Narrative coherence and clarity supported the movement of star personalities to the foreground and their directors toward the top of the pyramid . . . the movement from the 1930s has been increasingly in the direction of assuming that one individual . . . producer, director, writer . . . ought to control almost all aspects of filming so that that individual's personal vision can be created' (Bordwell *et al.* 1985: 335–6). Whereas the mobilization of authorial discourses was crucial to the substantial emergence and circulation of art cinemas in the 1950s, it was not until some while later—and, indeed, partly in response to competition from art cinemas— that Hollywood, under the package-unit system, came to accept the frequent attachment of authorial discourses to its films. Authorship has therefore recently added the promise of certain spectatorial pleasures, the cachet of cultural respectability, or cult status to the labels which traditionally typified classical Hollywood's promotion of its films—genre and star.

Film critics and reviewers have used the principle of authorship to argue for the artistic respectability of cinema and to attribute the status of creative artist to those working within the industrial system of Hollywood. As a polemical principle of film criticism and reviewing, authorship has had massive success and has placed many Hollywood directors in the international pantheon. It has been used to force the cultural and educational recognition of film and is now institutionalized into most Western film reviewing and criticism, film books, film festivals world-wide, and film studies syllabuses. The fact that the discourse of authorship arose in European rather than American critical institutions testifies to the strength of the former's aesthetic discourses. As early as 1959 Jean-Luc Godard could proclaim the success of the principle of authorship in 'having it acknowledged that a film by Hitchcock, for example, is as important as a book by Aragon. Film authors, thanks to us, have finally entered the history of art' (Godard 1959/1972: 147). For Andrew Sarris, transplanting the principle to the less congenial soil of the United States in 1962, authorship was 'primarily a critical device for recording the history of American cinema, the only cinema in the world worth exploring in depth beneath the frosting of a few great directors at the top' (Sarris 1962/1971: 130). The principle attained broad acceptance in Anglo-American reviewing and criticism in the 1970s and 1980s.

Its critical success, however, belies its theoretical bankruptcy. Firstly, Sarris muddied the issue enormously by mistranslating 'la politique des auteurs'— correctly 'the principle of/polemic for authors'—as 'the auteur theory' (124). Furthermore, many commentators have noted the failure of the principle's proponents to theorize or even logically justify their chosen critical tool and it remained less a clearly defined concept than a critical construct which arbitrarily attributed significance to the work of some directors rather than others.

Both the critical success and the theoretical limits of the principle stem from the embedded cultural force of the key Western concept underpinning it: the human individual. But once we recognize with Foucault that 'man is an invention of recent date . . . [a]nd perhaps nearing its end' (1966/1973: 387), it becomes easier to theorize the principle and to analyse the discourses which traverse and constitute it within its various institutional locations. This account seeks to examine the historical development of what I shall abbreviate as Authorship: the critical discourse of authorship on film. It thus acknowledges how some significant recent shifts in Western theories of subjectivity have informed Authorship.

The history of the varying conceptualizations of authorship follows broadly the three principal emphases in Western critical and theoretical writing on film since the 1950s:

1. the aesthetically focused textual analysis characterizing most work until the 1970s;

2. the theoretical turn of the mid-1970s associated with *Screen's* challenge to the impressionism and empiricism of most previous writing on film; and

3. the move dating from the mid-1980s towards film histories encompassing institutions of production and circulation, and sometimes the cultures and societies in which film texts are produced.

Textual analysis

Four modes of Authorship can be associated with the emphasis on textual analysis: forerunners of auteurism, auterism, auteur-structuralism and the author or instance of politics and/or pleasure.

The key relation attended to is that between text and reader. With the exception of the politicized criticism of the fourth mode, questions of social provenance, not to mention industrial production, are bracketed off, usually in the service of an avowedly or implicitly aesthetic critical undertaking. This critical activity routinely disengages certain thematic and stylistic properties from the text(s) concerned and attributes to them the coherence associated with the name of an author—who, as Foucault notes (1969/1979: 18), is a discursive construction independent of any empirical director. Often an evaluative exercise, such criticism uses author-names to mark out film texts by given directors as being aesthetically—or, occasionally, politically—superior to others.

The first two modes treated here are overtly aesthetic in conception, and occur principally within institutions of film reviewing, criticism, and sometimes history. Their guiding assumptions, if not polemic, are of cinema as 'art', and their conceptions of subjectivity are very much those of a transcendental individualism and Romantic sensibility. The last two modes, introducing structuralism, historical materialism, and psychoanalysis, are more analytical in aim, and operate largely in the fields of film criticism and analysis. Their polemic is sometimes political, and partly theoretical, testing the productivity of theoretical discourses in the analysis of film texts. They largely dissent from auteurism's Romantic notions of individual expressivity, and anticipate and bleed over into the two notions of authorship discussed in Modes 5 and 6.

Mode 1: proto-auteurism

This forerunner of auteurism emerges sporadically in European film reviewing and criticism from the 1920s onwards. Not only does it lack the later systematic, polemic thrust of auteurism proper but, more significantly, it restricts itself to directors who empirically possessed more creative freedom than most within Hollywood. This meant a canon centring on Chaplin, D. W. Griffith, Erich von Stroheim, King Vidor, Orson Welles, and John Ford, alongside such European directors as Sergei Eisenstein, Vsevolod Pudovkin, Abel Gance, and Marcel Carné. In general, this was a common-sense transfer of the discourse of authorship from other artistic practices, epitomized in Alexandre Astruc's famous proclamation of the 'camera-pen' (1948).

Proto-auteurism constituted a readily identifiable critical currency in France, the Soviet Union, and Britain from the 1920s until the present. It was made possible in these countries by the substantial art film production and/or exhibition sectors and their often powerful aesthetic discourses. This contrasted with the entertainment imperative of Hollywood, whose central producer and producer-unit modes of production operative between the 1930s and mid-1950s militated against public acknowledgement of directorial creativity.

Four instances from the early 1920s to 1950 plainly demonstrate that auteurism—and indeed some later developments in the history of Authorship—did not emerge unheralded:

1. Among the first authorial criticism on film may well be Louis Delluc's (1922–3) analyses of Griffith, Thomas Ince, Maurice Tourneur, Marcel L'Herbier, and Chaplin (see Tariol 1965: 104–9). In their clear interest in recognizable constants of style and world-view across the works of the directors concerned, these accounts foreshadow auteurism in the style of the *Cahiers du cinéma* of the 1950s.

2. Similarly, Lindsay Anderson's (1950) treatment of Ford adumbrates auteur-structuralism in his argument that *They were Expendable* (1945) 'illuminate[s Ford] films which came before it and reveal[s] qualities in them which may up to now have gone unremarked. In this light recognisable patterns emerge from the rather baffling diversity of Ford's films' (1950: 1).

3. Writing in 1930, Paul Rotha applies authorial principles selectively to Hollywood in order to suggest that certain artists are capable of transcending the anonymous machine:

despite these conditions of manufacture, the mass production, the obstinate committees, the uncreative producers, the horrors of the star system and the corrugated iron environment, there are occasions when a single film, the creation of one man's mind, makes its appearance. There are, in Hollywood, fortunately, men whose very personality overrides the machinery. With wisdom and discretion they use to full advantage the organisation of Hollywood and its excellent technical resources. (1930: 141)

4. Countering this vision of Romantic expressivity in and against Hollywood, a sound empirical recognition of directorial creativity where production circumstances licensed it may also be discovered. The following appeared in 1943 in a French student newspaper: 'The problem of film authorship is not resolved and cannot be so, a priori. The facts of production are just too vari-

able from work to work, for one to be able to accept the director as invariably the unique creator. The cinema is a team art. Each film requires of the critic an individual judgment concerning its authorship' (quoted in Crisp 1993: 238). Written by André Bazin, this prefigures not only his later moderation of the excesses of *Cahiers*' 1950s application of auteurism, but also the empirical approach to authorship in film production taken up by 1980s film historians.

Mode 2: auteurism

This ungainly portmanteau word is the term which regularly describes the best-known conception of authorship. In the early 1950s critics in *La Revue du cinéma* in its second series and *La Gazette du cinéma*, consolidated in their successor, *Cahiers du cinéma*, and in *Positif*, the already established principle of proto-auteurism as a *polemic*, which was strenuously advocatory, evaluative, and canonic. The context in which these critics worked included the huge influx of Hollywood films after the fall of the Vichy government and the thriving ciné-club movement which facilitated 'an unmatched perception of the historical dimensions of Hollywood and the careers of individual directors' (Wollen 1969/1972: 75–7). In the context of contemporaneously available forms of entertainment, these critics adopted a Romantic discourse of creativity as a means of cultural assertion for film as art in the age of the rise of television (Crisp 1993: 73).

Concerned not just with reviewing but also with historicizing cinema, the highly influential *Cahiers* polemicized against the 1950s script-based French cinema of psychological realism; for such French directors as Jean Cocteau, Jean Renoir, Robert Bresson, and Gance; and for Hollywood directors such as Howard Hawks, Hitchcock, Fritz Lang, Douglas Sirk, and Nicholas Ray. This Hollywood canon extended beyond those directors praised by proto-auteurists to embrace many (e.g. Sam Fuller, Vincente Minnelli) whose celebration scandalized some contemporary critics, and others (Don Weis, Edgar G. Ulmer) to whom later, less passionate commentators have been strikingly less kind. Apart from Bazin, Astruc, and Amédée Ayfre, the best known of *Cahiers*'s reviewers in the phase of establishing auteurism as a critical orthodoxy were the so-called 'young Turks'—Jacques Rivette, Godard, Claude Chabrol, François Truffaut, and Rohmer (often under

his real name, Maurice Schérer)—who were later to be central to the world's first film movement led by directors aware of film history, the Nouvelle Vague. Most stridently auteurist, perhaps, was Truffaut, whose article 'Une certaine tendance du cinéma français' (1954) was soon mythologized as inventing auteurism and giving the journal a sense of direction it previously lacked. Bazin consistently served as internal moderator and distanced himself from the excesses of the younger guard (Bazin 1957). The consolidation of auteurism is marked in Éditions Universitaires' starting its film-book series in 1954 with monographs on individual directors.

Given *Cahiers*' extension of the canon to directors who had limited influence over scripts, stylistic criteria of evaluation usually took explicit precedence over thematic ones. Style, 'mise-en'scène, through which everything on the screen is expressed' (Hoveyda 1960: 42), distinguished the 'auteur' from the mere 'metteur-en-scène', the mere manufacturer, whose use of mise-en-scène, it was deemed, did not transform the script material into an original work. Witness Bazin in 1953: 'Huston has no truly personal style. The author of *I Confess* [Hitchcock, 1952] has a personal style. He is the inventor of original cinematic forms, and in this his superiority to Huston is incontestable' (1953: 53). Bordwell, Staiger, and Thompson invaluably clarify how the narrating instance of Hitchcock's films supplies textual evidence supporting such views: 'Hitchcock's authorial persona oscillates between being modest and uncommunicative (i.e. presenting a single character's point of view) and flaunting its omniscience by suppressing crucial information' (1985: 79).

In the auteurist critical enterprise, the author is impressionistically read off from thematic and/or stylistic properties in the film(s). In Foucault's analysis, the purpose of this process is 'to construct the rational entity we call an author. Undoubtedly this construction is assigned a "realistic" dimension as we speak of an individual's "profundity" or "creative" power . . . Nevertheless, these aspects of the individual . . . which comprise an individual as author . . . are projections . . . of our way of handling texts: in the comparisons we make, the traits we extract as pertinent, the continuities we assign, or the exclusions we practise' (1969/1979: 21). Critics thus read certain textual characteristics as signifiers of a particular signified, called the director. Much interpretative latitude is possible here, not least on account of the third-person mode of narration adopted by conventional fictional cinema, or, in Émile Benveniste's terms, its holding of *discours* onto *histoire*

(1975: 237–50). So vertical overhead camera angles may signify Lang, Hitchcock, or Chabrol, tilt frames Hitchcock, eye-level camera Hawks, and simultaneous track and zoom Robert Altman. In thematic terms, male camaraderie marks Hawks, the overreaching hero Anthony Mann, and so on. The shortcomings of such simple ascriptions are evident enough. Can these same features not be found in many different directors' films? By what criteria does the reader select certain features as pertinent? Why do readers routinely construct authors on the basis of continuities, not discontinuities, from work to work? Why is thematic consistency a guarantee of good films (witness Andrew MacLaglen)? What ideological values are masked in the critical promotion of certain authors at the expense of others?

A striking comment on this last issue, of canon formation, is made in Hoveyda's (1960) retrospect on the previous six years of *Cahiers'* polemic for directors such as Hitchcock, Roberto Rossellini, and Lang: 'The evidence was undeniable: our favourite authors, when it came down to it, were all talking about the same things. The "constants" of their particular universes belonged to everybody: solitude, violence, the absurdity of existence, sin, redemption, love and so on. Each epoch has its own themes, which serve as a backdrop against which individuals, artists or not, act out their lives' (1960: 41). As John Hess (1974) has noted, a Catholic metaphysic, tinged with existentialism, structures a film aesthetic. Auteurism, it should be remembered, was polemical and evaluative before it was analytical.

Cahiers debated vigorously with *Positif* about canons. The difference between the two was at bottom political. *Cahiers* favoured directors whose optimism and spirituality drew on contemporary strains of cultural conservatism, an ostrich-like reaction against the Resistance-based left progressivism of the post-war period. *Positif*, conversely, was leftist, Surrealist, and anti-Catholic, favouring, amongst Hollywood directors, liberals like Elia Kazan, Sidney Lumet, and Fred Zinneman, and the less than uplifting world-views of Stanley Kubrick and William Wellman, along with Richard Brooks, Frank Tashlin, and John Huston.

With less polemical thrust as time has proceeded, auteurist criticism remains the dominant mode of Authorship, widely circulated as it now is throughout Western film reviewing and criticism. Hollywood was the prime concern of the Anglo-American criticism which transplanted auteurism, to Britain in 1962 via *Movie*, and to the United States in the same year via *Film Culture* (Sarris 1962/1971). For *Movie*, the principle was mobilized in the service of polemics for Hollywood, and against what was perceived as the uncreative torpor of British cinema. Culturally, *Movie* was reacting against the élitism of Bloomsbury and Leavisite assumptions, and film-culturally, against the dilettantish strain of *Sight and Sound* and its high-cultural protocols. One of the lasting benefits of *Movie*, especially Victor Perkins's work, has been its rich mise-en-scène analyses of Hollywood films, analyses which were remarkably precise given the then non-availability of video (and rarely even Steenbeck editing-tables) for close analysis.

Sarris's cultural context in the United States was scarcely more favourable than that of *Movie*. His concern was to redeem Hollywood from the high-cultural critical dismissal which denigrated it in favour of European art cinema, and from sociological readings which denied its aesthetic values. Hence both the boldly polemic assertiveness of his nine-rank pantheon of Hollywood directors published in *The American Cinema* (1968) and his preparedness to 'wrench . . . directors . . . from their historical environments', a practice common to almost all auteurism, but rarely made so explicit (1962/1971: 128). Distinguishing himself from *Cahiers'* young Turks, he avers that 'the critic can never assume that a bad director will always make a bad film', and acknowledges changes through directors' careers and 'the constant flux' of his pantheon of auteurs (Sarris 1962/1971: 132, 134). Pauline Kael (1963) merits a proverbial footnote for her vigorous, if ill-focused, attack on Sarris, advancing an empiricist suspicion of systematized criticism and a robust faith in the critic's common sense. More substantially, Jonathan Rosenbaum notes not only Sarris's omission of 'two important blacklisted directors' Cy Endfield and Jules Berry, but also how auteurist celebrations of Welles's 'genius' have long obscured his involvement with left politics (1991: 42–3).

Auteurism was to become a major element of a very significant feedback loop from the French Nouvelle Vague to Hollywood with the emergence in the late 1960s of the New Hollywood associated with such names as Altman, Arthur Penn, Martin Scorsese, and Woody Allen (see Kramer, Part 2, Chapter 6). Three factors were laying the groundwork for this: European art-film imports to the United States were beginning to present positive evidence to American critical taste of production practices which were overtly supportive of directors; a growing recognition of auteurist critical practices urged more director-centred practices and promotions; and these were more readily accommodated after Hollywood's 1950s adoption of the package-unit system and its 1960s production crises.

Auteurism habitually maps the critical activity of reading textual characteristics as traces of a director onto the empirical entity who on set calls 'Cut!', the director of the film. For all that this figure sometimes fools obsequious interviewers about his or her 'real intentions', the figure is usually characterized as an individual expressing her- or himself untrammelled by cultural determinants and transcending industrial interference. Against this assumption, as Wollen argues, it is vital to distinguish the structure of 'Ford' from Ford the person (1969/1972: 168). What is elided in the process of mapping auteurism onto the empirical individual is consideration of any potential difference in assumptions between that individual and the reader's construction of an author from the film texts. Readings which ignore the distinction between empirical author and author-name makes a wild leap of faith from the moment of reading to the moment of production. Not only do they disregard a whole semiosis, they also re-create the world in their own ideological image, whether the homogenization is transcultural or transhistorical or both.

Auteurism differently

An immediately obvious variant on this pattern is the assertion that authorial functions other than direction are involved in the collaborative work of most filmmaking. Cases have been made for the producer as author (e.g. Val Lewton, Arthur Freed), performer as author (e.g. the Marx brothers, Clint Eastwood as actor, Mae West), and scriptwriter as author (e.g. Jules Furthman, Ben Hecht, Frank Nugent). It is from the scriptwriters' standpoint that directorial auteurism has been most forcefully debated. Richard Corliss argues for a *politique des collaborateurs*, that scripts have to be considered alongside, if not before, direction, and valuably adumbrates, for instance, the significance of the contributions to Ford's films of Nunally Johnson, Dudley Nichols, and Nugent (Corliss 1972: 20–3; 1974/1975). Such argument has, however, barely troubled the status of the director as author.

With the partial exception of *Cahiers'* category E, described below, all the following modes of Authorship variously challenge the communication model underpinning auteurism, with its assumptions of a transcendental subject in full control of the meanings she or he somehow directly 'communicates' to the reader.

Mode 3: auteur-structuralism

Auteur-structuralism is a kind of shotgun marriage very much of its moment. It grew out of the intellectual left in London in the late 1960s, which was then increasingly receptive to European theoretical discourses, and out of the film-cultural work of the British Film Institute's Education Department, which was urging serious analytical attention to film, and was soon to advance film studies into universities. The speed of development of film study, historically telescoping an array of intellectual influences, may account for the simultaneous circulation of authorial discourses, with their Romantic aesthetics, and ideas of applying to film analysis the structuralist methodology of Lévi-Strauss, belonging to a markedly less individualist paradigm, and promising a rigorously scientific basis from which to counter the predominant impressionism of film reviewing and criticism. Besides drawing on different paradigms, these discourses also inhabited different institutional locations: film reviewing on the one hand, and film criticism and analysis on the other, the latter fast growing with, for instance, the establishment in 1967 of both the Cinema One and Movie paperbacks series of film books.

Auteur-structuralism employed a theoretical sophistication and analytical substance lacking in auteurism. With its emphasis on the importance of systematically analysing a body of texts, auteur-structuralism conceives of the author as a set of structures identifiable within a director's films. In the words of Nowell-Smith, whose book on Luchino Visconti was virtually the first instance of auteur-structuralism, 'The purpose of criticism becomes therefore to uncover behind the superficial contrasts of subject and treatment a structural hard core of basic and often recondite motifs. The pattern formed by these motifs, which may be stylistic or thematic, is what gives an author's work its particular structure, both defining it internally and distinguishing one body of work from another' (1967: 10).

Auteur-structuralism crystallized most famously and influentially in Wollen's *Signs and Meaning in the Cinema* (1969/1972). His structuralist analysis contrasts the relative simplicity of the crazy comedies' inversion of the macho adventure dramas in Hawks's œuvre with 'the richness of the shifting relations between antinomies in Ford's work that makes him a great artist, beyond being simply an undoubted auteur' (1969/ 1972: 102). Marshalled under the cardinal antinomy of nature–culture are overlapping pairs of binary oppositions, with some pairs of binaries in different films 'foregrounded, discarded or even inverted, whereas others remain stable and constant'—garden–wilderness; plough share–sabre; settler–nomad; European–American Indian; civilized–savage; book–gun; married–unmarried; East–West (with this last open to further disaggregation as Boston–Washington); and, in *The Last Hurrah* (1958), Irish immigrants–Plymouth Club; Celtic–Anglo-Saxon; and so on (1969: 104, 94). This structuralist analysis also invaluably illuminates such oddball Ford films as *Donovan's Reef* (1963) and *Wings of Eagles* (1957).

Many regarded such heuristic yields as adequate justification for auteur-structuralism. But there was robust theoretical debate. This arose not just from auteur-structuralism's strange yoking-together of the pre-structuralist with the structuralist, but also from its appearance at a time when post-structuralist theoretical discourses were, in the anglophone world, just beginning to destabilize the empiricist and idealist securities of structuralism. Theoretical problems arising from the auteur–structuralism conjunction include the following. Firstly, the trans-individual origination and currency of myths, the focus of Lévi-Strauss's structuralism, render them less than compatible with a body of works predicated on the individualism of an auteur. Thus in Wollen's assessment of Ford quoted above, there is a clear desire to hold on to the evaluative passion endemic in much auteur criticism, with little sense of embarrassment about retaining the 'great artist' while uncovering the structure. Confusingly, the conclusion to the 1972 edition insists that the auteur be an 'unconscious catalyst', not that 'he has played the role of artist, expressing himself or his vision in the film, but because it is through the force of his preoccupations that an unconscious, unintended meaning can be decoded in the film' (1972: 167–8). After encountering semiotics, such directorial structures became the authorial subcode (Brewster 1973: 41) or the author as a textual system constructed, and susceptible to appropriation, by the critic (Nowell-Smith 1976: 29–30). A second critique of auteur-structuralism points out that many of the structures disentangled by the analysis have a wider than individual currency, such as the garden–wilderness binary which is found in almost all westerns, as well as in most Ford films. In other words, this auteur seems to have the capacity to subsume broadly cultural as well as film-industrial determinants of meaning. Thirdly, this begs the question of the pertinence of the films made by a

given director as the criterion of sample selection. Why not all films from a given genre in a given year? Or even all films, as Wollen himself suggests, made by given directors with or without a given producer?

Auteur-structuralism was also debated from the standpoint of post-structuralist ideas, notably those of the later Barthes, which underpin the later, theoretical deconstruction of authorial principles examined below. One question concerns, in Brian Henderson's words, the auteur-structuralists' 'failure to found their criticism theoretically, the absence of an auteur-structuralist epistemology' (1973: 27). Another critique advanced by Henderson is that structuralism 'is an empiricism' which assumes the object as given, as already fully constituted, and posited as other and unchanged in the process of reading (33). Other charges levelled against auteur-structuralism include the reduction of films to structures alone, and the privileging of themes above all else.

Read symptomatically, almost all of the logical contortions and rhetorical slippages evident in auteur-structuralism in general, and in Wollen's two accounts in particular, find their explanation in the convergence of imported theoretical discourses, vitalizing the empiricist traditions of British philosophy, with the polemical desire to intellectualize film studies. As Rob Lapsley and Mike Westlake argue, Wollen's 1972 conclusion is better read not 'as a resolution of the problem of synthesising auteurism and structuralism, but as transitional text from a pre-structuralist concept of the author as creator of meaning to a post-structuralist concept of the author as a construct of the reader' (1988: 111).

Mode 4: author as instance of politics and/ or pleasure

The demise of the May 1968 'revolution' bequeathed a legacy of intellectual speculation on the reasons for its failure to unseat French capitalism. It gave urgency to work on ideology analysed as a means of assisting dominant groups to retain political power. The renowned political typology of Jean-Louis Comolli and Jean Narboni (1969) categorized films in terms of their perceived political effectivity in circulating or challenging dominant ideologies. Although New Left politics here displaced aesthetic achievements as the criterion of evaluation and canon formation, the aesthetic pleasures associated with some author-names

The complex notion of authorship—John Ford's *Young Mr Lincoln* **(1939)**

rather surreptitiously reappeared in the typology's then fashionable category E.

This embraces

films which at first sight seem to be under the sway of the dominant ideology, but in which . . . there is a disjunction, a dislocation, a distortion between the starting point and the end product. The ideology is not intentionally transmitted by the author . . . but encounters obstacles in the film which throw it off course . . . with the result that it is both exposed and denounced by the filmic structure which seizes the ideology and *plays it back against itself*, allowing its limits to be seen at the same time as transgressing them. . . . An oblique, symptomatic reading will reveal, beyond the film's apparent formal coherence, cracks and faultlines which an ideologically anodyne film does not have. (Comolli and Narboni 1969: 13–14)

Poised like auteur-structuralism between contending paradigms, this category could, perhaps conveni-

ently, combine left political credentials with a reinstatement of the auteurist vision of the (preferably left-wing) artist critiquing, even if only momentarily, the conventions of Hollywood, as in the ostensibly disruptive characteristics of certain favoured directors: the fauvist lighting of the climax of *Some Came Running* (Minnelli, 1959) or the insistently obtrusive grilles, blinds, and paintings of *Imitation of Life* (Sirk, 1959).

The most famous film analysis associated with category E is that of *Young Mr Lincoln* (Ford, 1939) by the editors of *Cahiers du cinéma* (1970). It is more concerned with historical and ideological factors than are most representatives of category E, and in its albeit mechanistic materialism—reading the film in terms of the perceived ideological needs of the Republican Party—anticipates the next section ('Historical Emphases') articulations of the author with culture. It also sets up somewhat anomalous roles for the author. As Lapsley and Westlake note, Lincoln's contradictory positions of both having and being the phallus are not allowed by *Cahiers* to offer multiple reading positions—as in the fantasy model—but are reined in to a limiting auteurist reading such that the 'incompatible functions in the figure of Lincoln . . . set . . . up tensions within the text "which oppose the order of Ford's world"' (1988: 122; *Cahiers du cinéma* 1970/1976: 46). This contradicts *Cahiers*' expressed desire to 'force the text, even to rewrite it' (1970/1976: 44). Such a tension between authorial intentionality and textual productivity recalls Wollen's 1972 conclusion to *Signs and Meaning in the Cinema*, which is similarly positioned on the cusp between pre- and post-structuralist paradigms.

Caughie's (1981) concept of 'the author in the text' extends and reworks *Cahiers*' category E. It dynamizes the reader–text relationship in terms of 'a theory of the subject of enunciation in film which involves an understanding of the shifting relation between enunciating subject and spectating subject' (1981: 201). Caughie distinguishes the author here as a subject position constructed and shifting in the film's performance whereby the reader, identified by means of classical cinema's third-person narration with the film's diegesis and thus finding no first-person authorial source in the text, can nevertheless, at certain points, be pulled back from identification, shifted from the register of *histoire*, in Benveniste's (1975) terms, to that of *discours*, to appreciate 'a moment of pure delight, of visual delight, of an excess of style' (Caughie 1981: 203). Pleasurably dislodged from identification with the fiction by these moments, the viewer constructs 'the figure of the author . . . to fill the subject position of the film's performance. The appearance of this new subject establishes me outside the fiction, but still within the textual space, still within a certain possession of the film (the performance is for me) . . . In those films where the director does not operate as a recognisable figure, the "performer" is as likely to be identified as the actor, the designer, or simply the film itself' (1981: 204–5). While Caughie's examples remain strikingly close to those of category E—Sirk, Minnelli, Max Ophuls, Josef von Sternberg—the instances can be extended to less critically respectable films: James Bond movies, for instance, the bulk of which persistently joke about their implausibilities, or the manifest implausibilities of adventure films like *Raiders of the Lost Ark* (Steven Spielberg, 1981) which the narrative drive delightedly recuperates, or any number of postmodern 'spoof' films.

Theoretically, then, this model advances considerably *Cahier's* category E. It constructs the author as a figure of discourse and takes cognizance of the interaction between subject and text underlined by post-structuralism. Yet its definition of the author potentially embracing actors, cameraperson, set designer, and so on is somewhat promiscuous. And in opening up 'questions of subjects other than the purely textual subject—social subjects, sexual subjects, historical subjects' (1981: 206), Caughie's essay sets up a number of theoretical and historical questions of textual positions and spectator identifications which have not been elaborated until quite recently (Crofts 1993: 68–88; Stacey 1994).

Theoretical emphases

Whereas the conceptions of authorship described above largely see the author as constitutive of the text, the two versions considered here separate empirical author and text, and largely discount the former from consideration. Underlying earlier versions of authorship had been a communication model of language, which Saussure's structural linguistics radically challenged, emphasizing the non-natural, but merely linguistically differential, relationship of signifier and signified, and arguing that meaning was generated within systems of signification, and with no necessary reference to outside phenomena. In these theoretically concerned constructions of authorship, language or discourse therefore take over the role formerly ascribed to authors, and refuse to be instrumentalized by an author. In opposition to the expressive humanism of auteurism, the theories of subjectivity informing this work can be broadly characterized as anti-humanist. The theoretical turn of the mid-1970s built on the post-structuralist ideas mentioned in connection with auteur-structuralism above. It polemicized for theory, against empiricism and impressionism, especially in terms of the (originally British) intellectual and academic discourses and institutions in which it operated.

Mode 5: author as effect of the text

This conception of the author is indissolubly linked with the name of Roland Barthes, whose writings were translated and imported into anglophone film theory by Stephen Heath. Inverting the norm, Barthes pronounces the birth of the reader at the expense of the death of the author (1968). It follows from Saussurean linguistics' focus on the purely differential nature of signifier and signified that meaning arises in the act of reading rather than being author-ized in and by the mind of a creative individual: 'language . . . ceaselessly calls into question all origins . . . a text is [intertextually] made of multiple writings, drawn from many cultures and entering into mutual relations of dialogue, parody, contestation, but there is one place where this multiplicity is focused and that place is in the reader and not . . . the author. The reader is . . . simply that *someone* who holds together in a single field all the traces by which the written text is constituted' (Barthes 1968/1977: 146, 148). For Heath, the old-fashioned 'author is constituted *at the expense of* language, of the orders of discourse (he is what the texts can be stripped away to reveal)' (1973: 88–9). This notion of the author is fundamentally incompatible with the anti-humanism of Althusser's conception of the subject—favoured by Heath—which refused to see subjects as given, unified beings but rather as constructed and positioned by ideology. Therefore authorship becomes an irredeemably ideological construction that forecloses thinking about theories of the subject in ideology. In the face of the text's ceaseless productivity, any author exterior and prior to it appears unthinkable. The author becomes merely an effect of the text, 'a *fiction*, figure—fan of elements—of a certain pleasure which begins to turn the film, or series of films, the ones over the others, into a plurality, a play of assemblage and dispersion' (1973: 91).

Some problems arise from this stance regarding authorship. For all the justified post-structuralist stress on how, in the reading process, the reader enters 'into a process of dispersal and inter-mixture with the film' (Nowell-Smith 1976: 31), the reader does not have to dissolve in the process. Moreover, the author is no more a mere effect of a structure than he or she is a punctual source of meaning. To fly from one old-fashioned, humanist pole to the opposite, anti-humanist pole may be to indulge in extremism. Bordwell critiques a widespread academic consequence of this move: ' "Theory" justifies the object of study, while concentration on the object can be attacked as naïve empiricism' (Bordwell 1989: 97). Later critiques of Althusser, particularly by Hindess and Hirst (1975), allow greater agency to the subject; and such conceptions of subjectivity underpin the first grouping of

historically oriented ideas of authorship examined below.

Mode 6: author as author-name

While sharing Barthes's desire to displace notions of originating subjects, Foucault rejects his relish for the ecstasy of the free-floating signifiers of 'écriture', 'the negative where all identity is lost' (1968/1977: 142). Foucault's attention to the relations between discourse, power, and subjects directs him rather to a concern with the conditions of existence of discourses, including those of authorship (1969/1979: 28). He theorizes the author as a function of the circulation of texts. Institutions of authorship allow an author-name, which labels a given body of texts, to be disengaged from any author as expressive individual. The very existence of pseudonyms epitomizes this separability.

The author-name is one way of regulating the circulation of texts. It serves as a means of distinction of certain texts from unauthored ones. Many texts are unsigned, including many journalistic texts prior to the rise of personality journalism. Among authored texts the author-name serves to classify and evaluate texts differentially: a Campion film, for example, as against a Tarantino film. The history constructed in this chapter already indicates how, even within its relatively brief account of film criticisms, the author-function 'does not operate in a uniform manner in all discourses, at all times, and in any given culture'; and the 'precise and complex procedures' by which texts are attributed to creators include those instanced above with reference to auteurism (Foucault 1969/1979: 23). These principles will be further applied in the historical analysis of author names in Mode 10 below.

Historical emphases

If the preceding focuses on textual analysis and theory can be characterized as involving theories of subjectivity which are respectively constituting and constituted, most of the historically oriented approaches to authorship see the author as both constituting *and* constituted, in other words, as both agent and effect. The historical emphasis emerges after the theoretical concerns which had preoccupied film studies in the 1970s—which had justifiably critiqued most existing film histories as auteurist and empiricist—were themselves running aground on their own theoretical purism. These 1980s historical emphases broadly sought to remedy the aestheticism and theoreticism observed respectively in the two previous tendencies of Authorship. This historical work is found mainly in academic and intellectual institutions. A first grouping of historically oriented approaches to authorship conceives the director variously in relation to three instances: culture and society, film industry, and film texts. This grouping focuses largely on the moment of production of the texts, treating the empirical author. The second analyses consumption or reading, treating the textual author. Drawing on Foucault, it anlayses historically author-names in critical and/or commercial circulation.

Mode 7: author as social subject

This stress on the social subjectivity of the author, usually seen in its inscription in the film text, constitutes a crucial qualification of auteurism's transcendental subject. As long as it was saddled with such assumptions, Authorship, in Nowell-Smith's words, 'continued to ascribe to the author as subject whole sets of categories, concepts, relations, structures, ideological formations and God knows what, enough to blow to pieces any mind that had to contain them' (1973: 96). John Tulloch's genetic structuralism, it might be noted, would assimilate the author's social subjectivity into auteur-structuralism (1977: 553–84).

In recent years (Crofts 1983: 19) it has become easier to see John Ford ('My name's John Ford. I make Westerns') as being *not* wholly responsible (an inference Wollen once permitted) for the western genre, for its transformation of desert into garden, and so on (Wollen 1969: 94). The films labelled by Ford's name can be seen instead to inflect conventions of genre and narrative structure. Auteurist readings of Ford overload his individual psyche when charting the marked shift in attitude towards Indians evinced by *The Searchers* (1956) and *Cheyenne Autumn* (1964). The first represents Indians as subhuman, bestial and vicious, deserving a fair deal of what a vengeful Wayne–Ethan can give them; in the second, harried by the cavalry, they figure as sympathetic, honourable human beings. To ascribe such changes to the 'mellowing' of the ageing individual is a typical auteurist move (e.g. Bogdanovich 1967; Sarris 1976: 161). To see this change as related— by a characteristic generic displacement—to contemporary civil rights movements is to de-centre the author, to conceive of the film credited to Ford as being

historically and culturally shaped. Ford no longer stars as the films' 'onlie begetter'.

Mode 8: author in production institutions

If the preceding mode locates the author in relation to society and culture, this one connects her or him with the production industry. The *locus classicus* of such work is the monumental rewriting of Hollywood by Bordwell, Staiger, and Thompson (1985). Lapsley and Westlake observe rightly that this work

present[s] a model of agents in dialectical interaction with their economic, technological and ideological context. In their version of Hollywood, individuals are not simply bearers of positions, but function in terms of belief, desire and intention. The distinction between, for example, Ford and 'Ford' does not imply the denial of the existence of Ford as an agent in the production process. While the spectator constructs an image of the author on the basis of texts, this in no way rules out the necessity of returning to the concept of the empirical author for an analysis of the film as commodity. Indeed, this was made explicit in the paradigm of Hollywood as a set of norms that the director could choose to follow or, within certain bounds, transgress . . . the authors of the study insisted that the explanation must be in terms of material determinants—economic, technological and ideological . . . The various determinations are irreducible to one another and interact mutually. (1988: 115, 117)

In this broadly historical-materialist conception, the author has of necessity to work within existing industrial and institutional frameworks and dominant aesthetic conventions, and the interrelations between these practices are contingent, not matters of causality *à la* Althusser.

Mode 9: author as gendered

The most influential theoretical discourse affecting film theory in the last two decades, feminism has necessarily impinged on Authorship. It treats the author both in relation to filmmaking institutions and as social subject. As regards access to production, feminist work in film criticism and theory has had more immediate impact on independent cinema production than on Hollywood. Claire Johnston's *The Work of Dorothy Arzner* (1975) represents the first attempt to reconstruct a female and feminist Hollywood, a corrective to Sarris's quaint sneer at Arzner and other Hollywood women directors as 'little more than a ladies' auxiliary' (Sarris 1968: 216). As regards the gendering of representations, feminist work has substantially critiqued the work of male directors (a near-monopoly in Hollywood), with strong emphasis on the patriarchal discourses informing the film director and recirculated by him. Hitchcock's films have understandably been prime candidates for attention (e.g. Mulvey 1975; Modleski 1988; see also White, Part 1, Chapter 13).

Mode 10: historical analysis of Authorship

The concept of the author-name opens up the possibility of thinking of authorship in historical and cultural terms. Once the text has left its producer it is substantially subject to the vicissitudes of different markets and of varied critical assumptions. The circulation and meaning of a given author-name is conditioned historically and culturally. The films named as those of Ford do not sell well in the Soviet Union, nor do those ascribed to Ince do the business in the United States that they used to do. What passes for 'Brecht' in Australia is a far cry from the East German version, while 'Freud' meant something very different to those inside and those outside Lacan's École Freudienne. The meaning of 'Ford' which any given reader brings to a film by that name will vary according to his or her cultural, and particularly film-cultural, formation. It may mark a certain spectatorial pleasure; it may connote a reactionary politics; it may signal the 'father' of the western; it may just be meaningless.

In an earlier essay (1983: 20–1), I outlined two examples of the historical construction of the author-name of Ford in the United Kingdom in the late 1960s and early 1970s (Klinger (1994) has analysed Sirk's critical reputation in similar terms). What film-critical assumptions made it possible in 1969 in the UK to ascribe to Ford, as described in Mode 7 above, responsibility for virtually the entire western genre? First, the fast-growing acceptance of Authorship within journals and weeklies. Secondly, this had its corollary in the then merely embryonic state of genre study: witness the collapsing of intentions of genre analysis into auteurism in Kitses' *Horizons West* (1969) and McArthur's *Underworld USA* (1972). Thirdly, the reputation of Ford's films was then riding high, buoyed up especially by Bogdanovich's worshipful interview book (1967).

Prior to its second coming in the United Kingdom in the early 1970s Ford's name was taken up in 1969 in France as an exemplar of *Cahiers*' category E examined above in Mode 4. While the structures of any subversion of a dominant ideology were often shown to be

unconscious, the names of such directors quickly became the marks of certain supposedly disruptive pleasures, especially once transposed to a UK context. Ford's name, especially as 'evidenced' in such films as *Wings of Eagles*, was amongst those hailed in the early 1970s as 'subverting dominant codes'. The clear right-wing politics of many of these films, it seems, were eclipsed by a few ostensibly leftist formal tinkerings. How else, after all—other than via a fetishized author-name—could any self-respecting left-wing intellectual overlook the politics of the average Ford film?

The explanation for this—as for the similar celebration of other author-names detailed in Mode 4—may well lie in the film-cultural formation of the critics concerned. Many of the names honoured in the 1970s for their 'diegetic ruptures' were the same as those earlier promoted by pre-1968 *Cahiers*, by Sarris, and particularly by *Movie* in its passion for Hollywood directors notable for their rich mise-en-scène: Minnelli, Sirk, Nicholas Ray, Hitchcock, Sternberg. 1970s additions to the pantheon included Ford, Sam Fuller, Roger Corman, Tashlin, Ophuls, and Dreyer, several of whom were the subjects of Edinburgh Film Festival retrospectives. The 1970s celebrators of these names and their spectatorial pleasures were mostly of the generation raised on the pre-1968 *Cahiers*–Sarris–*Movie* passion for certain late classical Hollywood films. Of that generation, many, after the post-1968 *Cahiers*–*Cinéthique*–*Screen* critique of the organicist aesthetics of *Movie* and others remained more or less unreconstructed film buffs, while others might be seen to have rationalized their earlier pleasures in new theoretical clothing.

Since the 1970s Authorship's conditions of existence have undergone significant transformations. Building on the success of auteurism and its partial assimilation by Hollywood, Authorship has increasingly become a commercial as well as a critical strategy, installing the author-name as a cult personality in the 1970s. Witness the title *The Film Director as Superstar* (Gelmis 1970); by the decade's end the names of directorial 'movie brats' Spielberg, George Lucas, and Francis Ford Coppola (though very few others) were being used to market films which they *produced* as well as those they directed. Several factors underlie the changes of the last quarter-century. The broader acceptance of Authorship within diverse, interconnecting media institutions has obliged directors to engage with other, wide forms of media coverage, extending to television reviews and frequent interviews, magazine profiles, advertising and sponsorship appearances. Simultaneously, distribution has grown more powerful and more global, and the commodification of culture has accelerated. Author-names have therefore taken on greater significance as marketing labels than previously under the package-unit system, especially as genres have destabilized, and audiences fragmented beyond the entertainment–art split towards a larger number of relatively unco-ordinated subgroups (Andrew 1993: 80).

Such are the conditions of existence of what Corrigan calls the auteur's reappearance 'in the eighties and nineties as a commercial performance of *the business of being an auteur*' (1991: 104). Where Foucault had neglected the empirical author—maybe she or he figured as the hapless victim of what was done to her/his name—Corrigan reinstates this author in adopting a model of social agency to account for directorial engagement in promoting 'the author as a *commercial strategy* . . . as a critical concept bound to distribution and marketing aims that identify and address the potential cult status of an auteur . . . Auteurs have become increasingly situated along an extratextual path in which their commercial status as authors is their chief function as auteurs: the auteur-star is meaningful primarily as a promotion or recovery of a movie or a group of movies, frequently regardless of the filmic text itself' (103–5). While earlier film-buffery, as with Paris's MacMahon cinema in the late 1950s, operated without the knowledge of the director, she or he could now actively work on trying to promote her/his name. Corrigan accordingly examines how three directors have variously interacted with the media in order to construct their auteur personae: 'Coppola's call for "self-creativity" within the technology of agency or [Alexander] Kluge's eliciting of "self-interpretation" across his own mobile persona [or Raúl Ruiz's strategies of] cultural exercise and intellectual game meant to make all notions of self disappear within a hall of mirrors' (123). Corrigan valuably expands the notion of the author-name to account for the post-1970s roles of directors (the difference from Foucault is symptomatic of disciplinary differences: history attends to the dead more often than does film studies). However, Corrigan's claim that 'the commercial conditioning of this figure has successfully evacuated it of most of its expressive power and textual coherence' (136) is somewhat exaggerated. A further worry lies with his seeming promotion of acceptance of the wholesale commodification of culture.

This might be the place to refer to postmodern conceptions of the author. Corrigan deploys such a notion of the author as potentially disappearing behind intertextuality, pastiche, and parody, certainly as being mixed in with a decentred, postmodern condition. Other postmodern accounts of the author (e.g. Andrew 1993) appear to wish to rescue directors (principally French ones) from such an undesirable condition, in moves reminiscent of Rotha (1930) redeeming authors from the popular culture of Hollywood.

The persistence of Authorship

Why does the notion of authorship persist so strongly? While it is not central to the legal and contractual basis of cinematic production and distribution, it still has enormous influence within cultural discourse. Some reasons have been set out above: the author-name has become a central means of marketing and product differentiation; its publicity is widely distributed across many media forms; and it supports the cultural and cult statuses of cinema. Additionally, with the withering away of the socialist alternative to consumer capitalism, individualist discourses enjoy high status globally. Further, the author can serve as a constructed coherence with which the reader identifies (Lapsley and Westlake 1988: 127–8), the more so in the rapid social changes and uncertainties of post-industrial capitalism. Given the entrenchment of Authorship, it is worth recalling its ideological operations. In sum, it perpetuates the divorce between artistic product and any social determination, both at the moment of production (the syndrome of the creative author) and at the moment of reading (the reader who recirculates individualist discourses while pronouncing 'objective' critical judgement on the text).

This chapter clearly points to the necessity of abandoning any theory of authorship based on a communication model of language. Not only the author and the text but, just as importantly, the reading must be seen as historically and culturally shaped. Time and place will, almost always, divide the moment of production from the moment of reading. The 'meaning' of any text will thus vary, as will that of any author-name which may be attached to it.

BIBLIOGRAPHY

Anderson, Lindsay (1950), 'They were Expendable and John Ford', Sequence, 11: 1–4.

Andrew, Dudley (1993), 'The Unauthorised Auteur Today', in Jim Collins, Hilary Radner, and Ava Preacher Collins (eds.), Film Theory Goes to the Movies (New York: Routledge).

Astruc, Alexandre (1948/1968), 'The Birth of a New Avant-Garde: La Caméra-Stylo', in Peter Graham (ed.), The New Wave (London: Secker & Warburg).

Barthes, Roland (1968/1977), 'The Death of the Author', in Image, Music, Text, ed. and trans. Stephen Heath (London: Fontana).

Bazin, André (1953), 'De l'ambiguïté', Cahiers du cinéma, 27 (Oct.), 137–55.

—— (1957/1968), 'La Politique des auteurs', in Peter Graham (ed.), The New Wave (London: Secker & Warburg).

Benveniste, Émile (1975), Problèmes de linguistique générale (Paris: Seuil).

Bogdanovich, Peter (1967), John Ford (London: Studio Vista).

Bordwell, David (1989), Making Meaning: Inference and Rhetoric in the Interpretation of Cinema (Cambridge, Mass.: Harvard University Press).

—— **Janet Staiger**, and **Kristin Thompson** (1985), The Classical Hollywood Cinema: Film Style and Mode of Production to 1960 (New York: Columbia University Press).

Brewster, Ben (1973), 'Notes on the Text of "John Ford's Young Mr Lincoln" by the Editors of Cahiers du cinéma', Screen, 14/3 (Autumn), 29–43.

Cahiers du cinéma (1970/72), 'Young Mr Lincoln de John Ford', 223 (July–Aug.), trans. Helen Lackner and Diana Matias as 'John Ford's Young Mr Lincoln', Screen, 13/3 (Autumn), 5–44.

*****Caughie, John** (ed.) (1981), Theories of Authorship: A Reader (London: Routledge & Kegan Paul and British Film Institute).

Comolli, Jean-Louis, and **Jean Narboni** (1969), 'Cinéma/idéologie/critique', Cahiers du cinéma, 216 (Oct.), 11–15; repr. in Bill Nichols (ed.), Movies and Methods, i (Berkeley: University of California Press).

Corliss, Richard (1972), The Hollywood Screenwriters (New York: Avon).

—— (1974/1975), Talking Pictures: Screenwriters in the American Cinema (New York: Penguin).

*****Corrigan, Timothy** (1991), Cinema without Walls: Movies and Culture after Vietnam (New Brunswick, NJ: Rutgers University Press).

Crisp, Colin (1993), The Classic French Cinema 1930–1960 (Bloomington: Indiana University Press).

*****Crofts, Stephen** (1983), 'Authorship and Hollywood', Wide Angle, 5/3: 16–22.

—— (1993), Identification, Gender and Genre in Film: The Case of 'Shame', (Melbourne: Australian Film Institute).

Foucault, Michel (1966/1973), The Order of Things (New York: Vintage).

*—— (1969/1979), 'What is an Author?', Screen, 20/1: 13–29.

Gelmis, Joseph (1970), The Film Director as Superstar (Garden City, NY: Doubleday).

Godard, Jean-Luc (1959/1972), 'Debarred Last Year from the Festival, Truffaut will Represent France at Cannes with Les Quatre Cent Coups', in Godard on Godard, ed. Jean Narboni and Tom Milne, trans. Tom Milne (London: Secker & Warburg).

Heath, Stephen (1973), 'Comment on "The Idea of Authorship"', Screen, 14/3 (Autumn), 86–91.

Henderson, Brian (1973), 'Critique of Ciné-Structuralism', part 1, Film Quarterly, 27/1 (Fall), 25–34.

Hess, John (1974), 'La Politique des auteurs', part 1, Jump Cut, 1 (May–June), 19–22.

Hindess, Barry, and **Paul Q. Hirst** (1975), Pre-Capitalist Modes of Production (London: Routledge & Kegan Paul).

Hoveyda, Fereydoun (1960), 'Tâches de Soleil', Cahiers du cinéma, 110 (Aug.), 37–43.

Johnston, Claire (1975), The Work of Dorothy Arzner (London: British Film Institute).

Kael, Pauline (1963/1966), 'Circles and Squares: Joys and Sarris', in I Lost it at the Movies (New York: Bantam).

Kitses, Jim (1969), Horizons West (London: Thames & Hudson).

Klinger, Barbara (1994), Melodrama and Meaning: History, Culture and the Films of Douglas Sirk (Bloomington: Indiana University Press).

*****Lapsley, Rob,** and **Mike Westlake** (1988), Film Theory: An Introduction (Manchester: Manchester University Press).

McArthur, Colin (1972), Underworld USA (London: Secker & Warburg).

Modleski, Tania (1988), The Women who Knew too Much: Hitchcock and Feminist Theory (New York: Methuen).

Mulvey, Laura (1975), 'Visual Pleasure and Narrative Cinema', Screen, 16/3 (Autumn), 6–18.

Nowell-Smith, Geoffrey (1967), Visconti (London: Secker & Warburg).

—— (1973), 'I was a Starstruck Structuralist', Screen, 14/3 (Autumn), 92–9.

*—— (1976), 'Six Authors in Pursuit of The Searchers', Screen, 17/1 (Spring), 26–33.

Rosenbaum, Jonathan (1991), 'Guilty by Omission', Film Comment, 27/5 (Sept.–Oct.), 42–5.

Rotha, Paul (1930), The Film Till Now (London: Cape).

Sarris, Andrew (1968), The American Cinema: Directors and Directions 1929–1968 (New York: Dutton).

—— (1962/1971), 'Notes on the Auteur Theory in 1962', in P. Adams Sitney (ed.), Film Culture Reader (London: Secker & Warburg).

Sarris, Andrew (1976), *The John Ford Movie Mystery* (London: Secker & Warburg).

Stacey, Jackie (1994), *Star gazing: Hollywood Cinema and Female Spectatorship* (London: Routledge).

Tariol, Jean (1965), *Louis Delluc* (Paris: Seghers).

Truffaut, François (1954/1976), 'Une certaine tendance du cinéma français', *Cahiers du cinéma*, 31 (Jan.), 13–17; trans. as 'A Certain Tendency of the French Cinema', in Bill Nichols (ed.), *Movies and Methods*, i (Berkeley: University of California Press).

Tulloch, John (ed.) (1977), *Conflict and Control in the Cinema* (Melbourne: Macmillan).

Wollen, Peter (1969/1972), *Signs and Meaning in the Cinema* (London: Secker & Warburg).

John Ford

Peter Wollen from Peter Wollen, *Signs and Meaning in the Cinema* (London: Secker & Warburg, 1992).

It is instructive to consider three films of John Ford and compare their heroes: Wyatt Earp in *My Darling Clementine* (1946), Ethan Edwards in *The Searchers* (1956), and Tom Doniphon in *The Man who Shot Liberty Valance* (1962). They all act within the recognizable Ford world, governed by a set of oppositions, but their *loci* within that world are very different. The relevant pairs of opposites overlap; different pairs are foregrounded in different movies. The most relevant are garden versus wilderness, ploughshare versus sabre, settler versus nomad, European versus Indian, civilized versus savage, book versus gun, married versus unmarried, East versus West. These antinomies can often be broken down further. The East, for instance, can be defined either as Boston or Washington and, in *The Last Hurrah* (1948), Boston itself is broken down into the antipodes of Irish immigrants versus Plymouth Club, themselves bundles of such differential elements as Celtic versus Anglo-Saxon, poor versus rich, Catholic versus Protestant, Democrat versus Republican, and so on. At first sight, it might seem that the oppositions listed above overlap to the extent that they become practically synonymous, but this is by no means the case. As we shall see, part of the development of Ford's career has been the shift from an identity between civilized versus savage and European versus Indian to their separation and final reversal, so that in *Cheyenne Autumn* (1964) it is the Europeans who are savage, the victims who are heroes.

The master antinomy in Ford's films is that between the wilderness and the garden. As Henry Nash Smith has demonstrated, in his magisterial book *Virgin Land*, the contrast between the image of America as a desert and as a garden is one which has dominated American thought and literature, recurring in countless novels, tracts, political speeches, and magazine stories. In Ford's films it is crystallized in a number of striking images. *The Man who Shot Liberty Valance*, for instance, contains the image of the cactus rose, which encapsulates the antinomy between desert and garden which pervades the whole film. Compare with this the famous scene in *My Darling Clementine*, after Wyatt Earp has gone to the barber (who civilizes the unkempt), where the scent of honeysuckle is twice remarked upon: an artificial perfume, cultural rather than natural. This moment marks the turning-point in Wyatt Earp's transition from wandering cowboy, nomadic, savage, bent on personal revenge, unmarried, to married man, settled, civilized, the sheriff who administers the law.

Earp, in *My Darling Clementine*, is structurally the most simple of the three protagonists I have mentioned: his progress is an uncomplicated passage from nature to culture, from the wilderness left in the past to the garden anticipated in the future. Ethan Edwards, in *The Searchers*, is more complex. He must be defined not in terms of past versus future or wilderness versus garden compounded in himself, but in relation to two other protagonists: Scar, the Indian chief, and the family of homesteaders. Ethan Edwards, unlike Earp, remains a nomad throughout the film. At the start, he rides in from the desert to enter the log house; at the end, with perfect symmetry, he leaves the house again to return to the desert, to vagrancy. In many respects, he is similar to Scar; he is a wanderer, a savage, outside the law: he scalps his enemy. But, like the homesteaders, of course, he is a European, the mortal foe of the Indian. Thus Edwards is ambiguous; the antinomies invade the personality of the protagonist himself. The oppositions tear Edwards in two; he is a tragic hero. His companion, Martin Pawley, however, is able to resolve the duality; for him, the period of nomadism is only an episode, which has meaning as the restitution of the family, a necessary link between his old home and his new home.

Ethan Edwards's wandering is, like that of many other Ford protagonists, a quest, a search. A number of Ford films are built round the theme of the quest for the Promised Land, an American re-enactment of the Biblical exodus, the journey through the desert to the land of milk and honey, the New Jerusalem. This theme is built on the combination of the two pairs: wilderness versus garden and nomad versus settler; the first pair precedes the second in time. Thus, in *Wagon Master* (1950), the Mormons cross the desert in search of their future home; in *How Green was my Valley* (1941) and *The Informer* (1935), the protagonists want to cross the Atlantic to a future home in the United States. But, during Ford's career, the situation of home is reversed in time. In *Cheyenne Autumn* the Indians journey in search of the home they once had in the past; in *The Quiet Man* (1952), the American Sean Thornton returns to his ancestral home in Ireland. Ethan Edwards's journey is a kind of parody of this theme: his object is not constructive, to found a home, but destructive, to find and scalp Scar. Nevertheless, the weight of the film remains orientated to the future: Scar has burned down the home of the settlers, but it is replaced and we are confident that the homesteader's wife, Mrs Jorgensen, is right when she says: 'Some day this country's going to be a fine place to live.' The wilderness will, in the end, be turned into a garden.

The Man who Shot Liberty Valance has many similarities with *The Searchers*. We may note three: the wilderness becomes a garden—this is made quite explicit, for Senator Stoddart

John Ford continued

has wrung from Washington the funds necessary to build a dam which will irrigate the desert and bring real roses, not cactus roses; Tom Doniphon shoots Liberty Valance as Ethan Edwards scalped Scar; a log home is burned to the ground. But the differences are equally clear: the log home is burned after the death of Liberty Valance; it is destroyed by Doniphon himself; it is his own home. The burning marks the realization that he will never enter the Promised Land; that to him it means nothing; that he has doomed himself to be a creature of the past, insignificant in the world of the future. By shooting Liberty Valance he has destroyed the only world in which he himself can exist, the world of the gun rather than the book; it is as though Ethan Edwards had perceived that by scalping Scar, he was in reality committing suicide. It might be mentioned too that, in *The Man who Shot Liberty Valance*, the woman who loves Doniphon marries Senator Stoddart. Doniphon, when he destroys his log house (his last words before doing so are 'Home, sweet home!'), also destroys the possibility of marriage.

The themes of *The Man who Shot Liberty Valance* can be expressed in another way. Ransom Stoddart represents rational-legal authority, Tom Doniphon represents charismatic authority. Doniphon abandons his charisma and cedes it, under what amount to false pretences, to Stoddart. In this way charismatic and rational-legal authority are combined in the person of Stoddart and stability thus assured. In *The Searchers* this transfer does not take place; the two kinds of authority remain separated. In *My Darling Clementine* they are combined naturally in Wyatt Earp, without any transfer being necessary. In many of Ford's late films—*The Quiet Man*, *Cheyenne Autumn*, *Donovan's Reef* (1963)—the accent is placed on traditional authority. The island of Ailakaowa in *Donovan's Reef*, a kind of Valhalla for the homeless heroes of *The Man who Shot Liberty Valance*, is actually a monarchy, though complete with the Boston girl,

wooden church, and saloon made familiar by *My Darling Clementine*. In fact, the character of Chihuahua, Doc Holliday's girl in *My Darling Clementine*, is split into two: Miss Lafleur and Lelani, the native princess. One represents the saloon entertainer, the other the non-American in opposition to the respectable Bostonians Amelia Sarah Dedham and Clementine Carter. In a broad sense, this is a part of a general movement which can be detected in Ford's work to equate the Irish, Indians, and Polynesians as traditional communities, set in the past, counterposed to the march forward to the American future, as it has turned out in reality, but assimilating the values of the American future as it was once dreamed.

It would be possible, I have no doubt, to elaborate on Ford's career, as defined by pairs of contrasts and similarities, in very great detail, though—as always with film criticism—the impossibility of quotation is a severe handicap. My own view is that Ford's work is much richer than that of Howard Hawks and that this is revealed by a structural analysis; it is the richness of the shifting relations between antinomies in Ford's work that makes him a great artist, beyond being simply an undoubted auteur. Moreover, the auteur theory enables us to reveal a whole complex of meaning in films such as *Donovan's Reef*, which a recent filmography sums up as just 'a couple of Navy men who have retired to a South Sea island now spend most of their time raising hell'. Similarly, it throws a completely new light on a film like *Wings of Eagles* (1957), which revolves, like *The Searchers*, round the vagrancy versus home antinomy, with the difference that when the hero does come home, after flying round the world, he trips over a child's toy, falls down the stairs, and is completely paralysed so that he cannot move at all, not even his toes. This is the macabre *reductio ad absurdum* of the settled.

8

Genre and Hollywood

Tom Ryall

It is an irony that the critical acceptance of Hollywood cinema was initially achieved through its extensive mapping, by the critics of *Cahiers du cinéma*, in terms of authorial *œuvres* rather than in terms of the genres that, along with the stars, have defined its image for the moviegoing public. For whatever else it is, Hollywood is surely a cinema of genres, a cinema of westerns, gangster films, musicals, melodramas, and thrillers. Indeed, in early reflections on Hollywood cinema, it was this very quality that generated antagonistic criticism, with generic structures being deemed an impediment to artistic achievement. Thus, Paul Rotha, writing in the late 1920s, attacked Hollywood for its standardized pictures made to type (genre). He regarded this as a debasement of cinema inhibiting the creation and development of film art characteristic of European filmmakers from countries such as France and, especially, Germany (Rotha 1930/1967). While his characterization of the American cinema in terms of its standardized generic basis certainly captures one of its significant features, subsequent generations of writers, especially from the late 1960s onwards, have valued such qualities differently. Some have argued that the genre system was a positive quality in Hollywood, providing a useful disciplined framework within which directors worked, ensuring curbs on creative indulgence and guaranteeing that the cinema kept in touch with its mass public (McArthur 1972). At the very least, most writers have seen genre as a necessary concep-

tual tool in relation to American films, and the body of criticism to be discussed here is predominantly concerned with the understanding of genre as a concept and with the definition of individual genres.

The critical literature of genre is both extensive and multifaceted, reflecting influences from a range of disciplines including literary criticism, art history, linguistics and semiotics, and structural anthropology, as well as from the discourses of the film industry itself and from journalistic film criticism and reviewing. But while some agreement may be found about basic terms such as 'convention', 'iconography', 'recurrent patterns', 'audience expectation', and the typology of generic modes (westerns, gangster films, etc.), it is important to note that different models, different sets of assumptions, and different theories underpin the range of accounts that address the generic system of Hollywood and the individual genres in that system, and, at the micro-level, account for the specificities of individual films. As a further complication, 'genre' itself is sometimes replaced by and sometimes situated in relation to a constellation of cognate terms such as 'type', 'mode', 'cycle', 'series', and 'formula'. Although important accounts of genre in cinema can be traced back to at least the 1950s (Bazin 1953/1971; Warshow 1948/1970, 1954/1970; Alloway 1963, 1971), it was not until the late 1960s that something like a corpus of genre criticism emerged in Britain, principally, though not exclusively, from writers working in, or associated in some way with, the Education Department of the British Film Institute (Lovell 1967; Kitses 1969; McArthur 1972; Buscombe 1970; Ryall 1970). Subsequently, the turn to semiotics meant that more attention was paid to underlying systems, to general explanations of communicative phenomena such as genre films, and to attempts to define genre itself as well as defining individual genres. However, some have seen this as an inherently difficult task because of the medley of ways in which individual genres have been identified, with classifications deriving from a varied list of features embracing subject-matter, mode of address, style, audience effects, and so on. David Bordwell has suggested that '[t]heorists have been unsuccessful in producing a coherent map of the system of genres and no strict definition of a single genre has won widespread acceptance' and that 'no strictly deductive set of principles can explain genre groupings' (1989: 147). He cites the Russian Formalist Boris Tomashevsky, whose view was that '[n]o firm logical classification of genres is possible. Their demarcation is always historical, that is to say, it is correct only for a specific moment of history; apart from this they are demarcated by many features at once, and the markers of one genre may be quite different in kind from the markers of another genre and logically they may not exclude one another' (Bordwell 1989: 147).

Problems of definition notwithstanding, for many critics 'genre' seemed more appropriate than traditional approaches for grasping the historical realities of Hollywood with its factory-like production regimes and the organization of production schedules along generic lines. Creative and technical production personnel were hired on long-term contracts which, in some ways, could determine a generic structure. As Edward Buscombe has suggested, 'stars and genre were, particularly at Warners, mutually reinforcing. Because the studio had Bogart, Cagney and the rest under contract they made a lot of gangster pictures; and because they made a lot of gangster pictures they had stars like this under contract' (1974: 59). Elaborate standing sets—the western townscape, the Chicago street—once constructed, the costume collection once established, reinforced generic tendencies; as Rick Altman has put it, 'Hollywood's economic imperative mandates concerted attempts at economy of scale. Only by producing large quantities of similar films [could] studios justify their enormous investment in real estate, personnel, publicity and technology' (1989: 328). Films were marketed and advertised in ways which highlighted their generic specificity and, in addition to this, the trade press used generic terminology and referred to westerns, gangster pictures, melodramas, and so on in their discussion of Hollywood films. Hollywood studios consciously produced genre cycles, audiences went to see westerns and the like rather than films made by auteurs, and reviewers referred to gangster films and other film types; accordingly, for critics such as Lawrence Alloway (1971), this meant that genre was the pertinent and pre-eminent critical concept for students of the American film.

The auteur approach absorbed cinema into conventional ways of thinking about cultural production and appeared to confer a certain respectability on popular films, permitting their 'creators'—the auteurs—to be discussed as artists along with the poets, painters, composers, and novelists. Genre criticism confronted aspects of popular film—conventionality, formulas, stars, industrial production systems, publicity—which jarred with conventional approaches to artistic production and were often overlooked by auteur critics. It moved against the grain of a criticism dominated both by the individual work valued for its distinctiveness and difference, and by the individual artist valued for the extent to which he or she moved beyond the common to the individual and the personal. The central assumption of genre criticism is that a work of art and communication arises from and is inserted into a specific social context and that its meaning and significance is constrained and limited by this context. Individual artists and filmmakers manipulate signs and meanings, but in contexts which are authorized by communal public consent, and these contexts, in the case of the American cinema, we call genres. The 'rules' of a genre—the body of conventions—specify the ways in which the individual work is to be read and understood, forming the implicit context in which that work acquires significance and meaning. Genres were seen in social terms as institutions implying a bond, or contract, between producers (director, studio) and audience relating to the significance and meaning of what was on the screen. In a different vocabulary, genres constituted systems for the regulation and circulation of meaning which had a public and historical existence and in which the popular American cinema was grounded.

The scope of genre criticism

At the most general of levels, genres have been divided into two kinds—the theoretical and the historical (Todorov 1975: 13–14). Theoretical genres are a priori categories which it is possible to envisage as based upon logical deduction from the basic characteristics of the art form itself rather than the analysis of actual works. For example, the ancient Greeks devised theoretical systems for fictional works which were divided into genres on the basis of mode of delivery, i.e. those in which the narrator speaks, those in which characters speak, and those in which both speak. As can be seen, the intention is exhaustively to predict the gamut of possibilities based upon certain assumptions about the key element of literary activity—in this example, the performance of the speech act (Palmer 1991: 116). In terms of cinema, an equivalent exercise would base itself on the possibilities of cinema in relation to some very general feature such as representation, rather than the familiar divisions of western, gangster film, and musical. Accordingly, films could be divided into the *fictional* (representation of staged events), the *documentary* (representation of actual events), or the *abstract* (non-representational), although even such a broad scheme may have problems with the animated film. Some writers have explicitly proposed theoretical genres for cinema (e.g. Shklovsky 1927; Williams 1984), and others, including V. F. Perkins for example, have implicitly constructed the beginnings of a system of theoretical genres in suggesting that the 'basic genre to inspect is the narrative movie' (*Movie* 1975: 11). Most critical writing, however, has concentrated on historical genres, on groupings of actual films inductively linked on the basis of common themes, styles, and iconography.

In terms of the analysis of historical genres, the scope of genre criticism is broad, and, as a preliminary, it is necessary to distinguish between three levels of analysis to which the concept can refer. The first, and most general, concerns the definition of *generic system*, which relates individual genres to each other in terms of broad shared principles; the second is the analysis of *individual genres*, defining their internal logics and conventions; and the third is the analysis of *individual films* in relation to a genre or genres in the case of the many Hollywood pictures which draw from and relate to more than a single genre. It is also necessary to distinguish between the discussion of generic systems and individual genres as overarching concepts, and the analysis of the individual genre film. Generic systems and genres do not exist in the way in which individual films exist, but rather are abstractions based partly, though not entirely, upon individual films and operating in a different logical universe. Although genre and the individual film are the basic elements of the system, as Fredric Jameson has suggested in relation to literary genres, they

are wholly distinct in nature from each other, the one—the generic system—being a constellation of ideal relationships, but the other—the work itself—being a concrete verbal composition. We must understand the former as constituting something like an environment for the latter, which emerges into a world in which the genres form a given determinate relationship among themselves, and which then seeks to define itself in terms of that relationship. (Jameson 1975: 153)

If 'film' is substituted for 'verbal composition' we have a succinct definition of the circuit in which a genre film is positioned as a historically formed instance of the overarching intertextual entity we refer to as the generic system. From the point of view of the filmmaker, the generic system is the conceptual environment within which the film will be situated, and, from the point of view of the spectator, the conceptual intertextual context, or one of the contexts, within which the individual film makes sense.

There are two further broad dimensions to genre study. The first involves genre history and is concerned with the ways in which genres emerge, develop, and change; the second focuses upon the social and cultural function of genre cinema. Genres change and evolve and, although a western such as *The Searchers* (1956) is recognizably part of a continuum which includes its generic predecessors such as *Stagecoach* (1939) or *The Gunfighter* (1950), the film nevertheless differs from them in certain respects because it was made at a different moment both of the history of the genre itself and, more generally, of the history of the social and political environment. Genres can be studied both in terms of an internal history of forms, themes, and iconography, and in terms of their relationship to broader cultural and social shifts. Thomas Schatz (1981: 38) has proposed an evolutionary model for internal generic development based on a shift from 'straightforward story-telling to self-conscious formalism', from *Gold Diggers of 1933* (1933) to *Singin' in the Rain* (1952) for the musical, from *Stagecoach* to *The*

Searchers for the western. Others, however, have been sceptical about the neatness of such historical patterning and its somewhat segregated view of individual genres. Steve Neale's (1990) brief but suggestive sketch of the historical development of Hollywood's genres, derived from the 'Formalist conception of genre as a historical system of relations', moves away from Schatz's somewhat self-contained account of generic change in favour of a more fluid historical model which links change to a range of factors. Some are internal to cinema such as the state of film technology; some are external and relate film genres to intermedia influences such as vaudeville theatre, popular literature and music, the press and comics, and to changing social patterns of cinema attendance (Neale 1990: 58–62).

Consideration of the social and cultural function of cinema has provided other ways of defining a rationale for the Hollywood genre system (see Kellner, Part 2, Chapter 10). For some, the system is part of the *ideological* network which constrains political perception and regulates attitudes towards social and cultural tensions and conflicts; for others, it is more akin to *mythic* systems of the past, and it has been suggested that 'genre films, television, and literature have to a great extent replaced more formal versions of mythic response to existence such as religion and folk-tale' (Stuart Kaminsky, quoted in Grant 1986: 94). Ideological critiques range from the notion that Hollywood genres are instruments of American capitalist ideology transmitting its beliefs and values in their different ways (Hess Wright 1974) to more nuanced versions which suggest that, while some genres might well be regarded as 'conservative', others, such as horror, film noir, and melodrama, may be seen to question conventional social and political values (Klinger 1984). Writers using the notion of ideology are committed to the idea that the genre system, or, at least, certain genres, impose beliefs and values to some degree; those using notions of myth and ritual posit a more participatory situation in which the audience plays a role in the constitution of the cinema's value systems through box-office acclaim and other interactive mechanisms such as fan magazines and clubs, sneak previews, and so on. Ideological criticism sometimes operates with the model of a passive audience absorbing the appropriate social and political values, and this contrasts with ritual–myth analyses in which the genre system is construed as expressive of deep-seated beliefs and desires 'whose function is the ritualisation of collective ideals, the celebration of temporarily resolved social and cultural conflicts, and the concealment of disturbing cultural conflicts behind the guise of entertainment' (Schatz, in Grant 1986: 97).

Genre systems: some theoretical proposals

A brief examination of the familiar generic categories—westerns, gangster films, musicals, horror films, thrillers, comedies, melodramas, films noirs, women's pictures—indicates the variety of ways in which critics have attempted to define genre systems and individual genres. These range from simple differentiation based on an array of protocols enveloping subject-matter, style, effects, and intended audience; to attention to the ways in which shared elements of subject-matter, theme, or style are handled differently in different genres; to the technical distinctions of semantics and syntactics that can generate a range of combinatory options or genres.

The 'familiar' list above incorporates a variety of differentiating criteria. Understandings of westerns and gangster films derive from the historical subject which is dealt with: the American west and urban America in the 1920s respectively. The musical is recognized in terms of formal qualities such as the presence of musical and dance performance. This can be linked to a range of subject-matters including that of the western—*Seven Brides for Seven Brothers* (1954)—and the gangster film—*Guys and Dolls* (1955). Some genres can be defined in ways which highlight their intended effect on the audience, as in the horror film, the thriller, and the comedy, which elicit fear, suspense, and laughter respectively. Again, these are effects that are realizable across different subject-matters. Melodrama has been defined in terms of a concern with the tensions of domestic life, with intergenerational problems, with heterosexual romance (subject-matter), together with a certain approach to narrative construction and film style and, particularly, an extravagant use of mise-en-scène to embody the emotional highpoints of the drama (formal qualities). In similar fashion, attempts to define the film noir usually range across subject-matter—crime and detection—and the shadow-laden mise-en-scène which is often regarded as the essential generic ingredient. The category of the

A musical with a western setting—*Seven Brides for Seven Brothers* (1954)

women's picture, closely related to the melodrama and sharing its subject-matter to an extent, is based on the nominated target audience of females and their supposed desires and interests.

From the late 1960s onwards there were a number of books and articles which attempted to systematize the varied bases for differentiation, and which sought to construct overall theories of genre, schema for generic definition, and definitions of individual genres (Buscombe 1970; Kitses 1969; McArthur 1972; Ryall 1970). Based primarily on the western and the gangster film, such work isolated two factors in particular. These were, first, the two distinct phases of American history which constituted the basic subject-matter of the two genres, and secondly, the distinctive visual qualities which each possessed. This latter dimension—'iconography', as it was named with a term borrowed from art history—was seen by many critics as the key source of differentiation, providing individual genres with a distinctive evocation of a generic universe by way of a repertoire of established and conventionalized images. In the case of the western, these included the settings (desert and mountain, makeshift townscapes of saloons and gaols); the specificities of costume (the black garb of the hired gun, the tight-bodiced dress of the saloon-girl); the weaponry used by westerners (Colt 45, Bowie knife, bow and arrow); and horses. The gangster genre also lent itself to such analysis with its urban, street-at-night settings, its night-clubs and bootleg liquor factories; the gangster's fedora and well-tailored suit; and the cars and tommy-guns which were the gangster's tools of the trade. However, while this approach appears coherent and plausible when applied to the western and gangster genres, it seems less easy to translate across the generic spectrum. What, for example, would constitute an iconography of the comedy film?

Colin McArthur centred the iconographic description of the gangster film on the physical presence and dress of the leading actors in the genre, thus incorporating the star system into his generic account (McArthur 1972). Such an approach also characterizes Jean-Loup Bourget's account of a particular strand of melodrama variously referred to as 'sentimental melodrama', 'romantic drama', and 'the women's picture' (1971). Such a strand, he suggests, is grounded in the acting presences of an array of female stars including Joan Crawford and Bette Davis, Barbara Stanwyck and Lana Turner. The iconographic approach, couched in terms of stars whose presence shapes and determines the course of the narrative, would be applicable across a range of genres and would at least enable the construction of coherent generic strands (subgenres?) on a consistent basis. Accordingly, James Cagney and Edward G. Robinson may be seen to define a powerful subgenre of the gangster film; John Wayne and Henry Fonda, of the western; Humphrey Bogart and Robert Mitchum, of the film noir; Fred Astaire, Ginger Rogers, and Gene Kelly, of the musical; Chaplin, Keaton, Laurel and Hardy, and the Marx brothers, of the comedy; and so on. In some cases—Cagney and Robinson and the gangster genre, Wayne and the western, Astaire and Kelly and the musical—it can be argued that such stars have defined the generic prototypes which tend to dominate thinking about particular genres. A further point to make is that there are plenty of examples of stars who have worked in particular genres without forging generic identity in the manner of the stars cited above. For example, Gary Cooper and Spencer Tracy both played gangster roles in the early 1930s, but it was Cagney and Robinson whose performances clearly impressed in generic terms. This suggests that other factors play a role in such generic identification and that certain stars are suitable for certain genres rather than others.

The writers cited above differed in their degree of systematicity, but provided models of genre which highlighted certain key dimensions such as iconography and stars which worked as explanations for some genres but not all. This work foregrounded concepts such as 'convention' and 'audience expectation' which are central to any account of genre, and presented persuasive specifications for genres such as the western and the gangster film. However, the work did not provide an easy means of moving from local description of specific genres to general specification of the generic system, and what worked for the gangster film did not necessarily translate easily into an explanation for, say, the musical. This early work on genre emerged from an intellectual climate in Britain which was just beginning to accommodate the structuralist theories that were to have a decisive impact on film studies through the 1970s, and there is a sense in which a number of the issues raised by genre critics were taken up in different ways by the new intellectual-cum-political interests of areas such as semiotics, ideology, psychoanalysis, and feminist theory.

Steve Neale's *Genre* (1980) attempted to redefine genre in the context of such influences and to provide the terms in which the system of genre worked in Hollywood cinema. Previous writers had noted that American genre films belonged 'to the traditions of

the American narrative film' (Pye 1975: 31) and, for Neale, this basic shared feature was the foundation of the genre system in Hollywood. Genres, it was suggested, were best considered as variants of 'the traditions of the American narrative film', or 'classical narrative cinema' as it was increasingly called. Its set of broad formal characteristics such as linear narrative progression, closure, symmetry, its balance of narration and spectacle, as well as its 'characteristic semantic fields' (Bordwell 1989: 150–1), defined very broadly a type of narrative film which was different from other models such as the European 'art' film. Neale's work recognized that the Hollywood genre system deployed a limited number of themes in a restricted stylistic context and the factor which differentiated one genre from another was the weight and function of the form and content of the shared general discourse of the system. For example, as many critics have noted, heterosexual romance and desire are present in most, and maybe all, Hollywood films as a key constitutent of the 'characteristic semantic field'. However, it is not a uniform presence: whereas romance between the leading characters is an essential feature of the musical, providing the crucial motivation for the progress of the narrative, such relationships are often peripheral to the narrative in the western. The musical *Singin' in the Rain* traces the romance which develops between Don Lockwood (Gene Kelly) and Kathy Selden (Debbie Reynolds) within a story about Hollywood and the arrival of the sound film; the western *My Darling Clementine* (1946) traces a story about the bringing of civilization to the west which has, as an aside, an embryonic romantic encounter between Wyatt Earp (Henry Fonda) and Clementine Carter (Cathy Downs). The certain union of Don and Kathy at the end of the musical is a generic requirement; the rather more tentative finale of the western, in which the hero and heroine part with vague promises of reuniting, is also appropriate in the context of a genre where romance is a secondary concern. The generic system, therefore, is a way of differentially deploying the characteristic discourses of Hollywood films, including romance and other forms of human relationships, violence, social order and disorder, the law, community, work and leisure, current affairs and popular history, and so on. None of these, however, are exclusive to any of the genres. A parallel account is offered for matters of style and narrative address in which the balance between narrative (the advancement of the story) and spectacle (the display of action and performance) varies from genre to genre. Neale summarizes thus: 'part of the very function of genres is precisely to display a variety of the possibilities of the semiotic processes of main-stream narrative cinema while simultaneously containing them as genre' (1980: 31).

Rick Altman, also working in the context of structuralism and semiotics, has suggested that genres can be established from two perspectives:

we can as a whole distinguish between generic definitions which depend on a list of common traits, attitudes, characters, shots, locations, sets and the like—thus stressing the semantic elements which make up the genre—and definitions which play up instead certain constitutive relationships between undesignated and variable placeholders—relationships which might be called the genre's fundamental syntax. The semantic approach stresses the genre's building blocks, while the syntactic view privileges the structures into which they are arranged. (Altman 1989: 95)

The same genre—for example, the western—can be analysed into two distinct, though interrelated, dimensions. First, there is the stock of primary elements embracing themes such as the wilderness, the community, law and order, and icons such as cowboys, Indians, deserts, mountains, and half-built towns. These correspond to the thematic and iconographic elements highlighted by previous writers and constitute a semantic field present in some way in any single instance of the western. Secondly, there are particular structural relationships between such elements established over time to constitute a set of syntactical conventions. Jean Mitry's definition of the western as a genre 'whose action, situated in the American West, is consistent with the atmosphere, the values, and the conditions of existence in the Far West between 1840 and 1900' (quoted in Altman 1984: 10) highlights the broad semantic field underpinning the genre. In contrast, Jim Kitses' (1969) analysis of the genre foregrounds the ways in which particular semantic elements, such as individual and community or savagery and civilization, are placed in opposition to each other, and offers a different way of defining the western in terms of the syntactic or relational structures between the elements specified in the broad semantic field. The semantic perspective offers broad inclusive definitions identifying fixed and recurrent elements which cross all instances of the genre, while the syntac-

tic perspective focuses on narrow, exclusive definitions drawing attention to particular distinctive patterns established between semantic elements in subsets of the semantic genre.

Much of the writing on genre from Bazin and Warshow onwards had built effective categories in a local way, separating off the western from the gangster film in quite clear terms (subject-matter, history, iconography). By contrast, the structuralist-influenced work recognized the somewhat unstable nature of the generic system. Subject-matter, style, narrative address and structure, iconography even, were quite fluid, and elements associated with particular genres often cropped up across a range of genres and operated in a number of different ways, sometimes occupying a central position within a genre, sometimes relegated to a peripheral significance. To take a previously noted example, *Seven Brides for Seven Brothers* clearly operates within the semantic field of the western although its title suggests other concerns. It is set in 'Oregon Territory 1850' (the post-credit title) and the opening sequences show a figure in buckskins (Adam–Howard Keel) driving a wagon into a frontier town. However, the film's credits are accompanied by orchestral versions of two of the main songs from the film—'Bless your Beautiful Hide' and 'Wonderful Day'—and, it might be argued, the musical motifs undercut the 'western' images. Similarly, the opening sequence in the store, in which Adam, a farmer in town to buy winter supplies, adds a wife to the shopping-list, foregrounds the 'romantic courtship' theme usually peripheral to the genre though. In this case, clearly announced by the film's title. When Adam leaves the store and launches into song the generic focus is sharpened and the world of the musical is evoked through one of its central conventions, which permits characters to sing about their thoughts and feelings. From the perspective of structuralist versions of genre, it is the musical conventions that dominate and direct spectator comprehension towards the values and assumptions of that genre rather than those of the western, to which it also clearly relates. This is only a problem if we regard genres as pigeon-holes into which films must fit, rather than elements in a flexible conceptual world—the fluid framework for our reading of individual Hollywood films.

Individual genres: inclusive and exclusive definitions

Another way of recognizing the somewhat fluid nature of generic systems rests on the distinction between inclusive and exclusive definition (Altman 1984: 6–7). Semantic definitions of genre tend to be inclusive, incorporating as many films as possible, while syntactic definitions are exclusive and focused on a small number of films. Inclusive definitions, the characteristic province of the large encyclopaedias of the genre (Buscombe 1988; Hardy 1985), also usually reflect the ways in which the terms are used in everyday common-sense discourse and by the studios themselves. Such definitions envelop a range of films with some degree of intertextual relationship to each other but without laying claim that these relationships are strong or especially significant. These might be regarded as involving a 'weak' or 'neutral' use of the generic term. By contrast, other accounts of the western operate what might be called a 'strong' sense of genre and imply precise and significant interrelationships between individual westerns. André Bazin, for example, identified a small corpus of films as embodying the 'essence' of the western and positioned instances of the genre in relation to this core (Bazin 1971: 149). Accordingly, individual films were located in relation to what Bazin called the 'classic' western, exemplified by films such as *Stagecoach*, *Virginia City* (1940), and *Western Union* (1941). Bazin also developed contrasting categories such as the 'superwestern' for films from the 1950s like *High Noon* (1952) and *Shane* (1952) that deviated from the classical norms and imported concerns foreign to the genre, and the 'novelistic' western for films such as *Johnny Guitar* (1954) that represent an enrichment of the traditional themes of the genre.

In fact, although exclusive definitions are rarely proclaimed explicitly, they have proved extremely influential, constituting the effective operative contexts for discussion of individual westerns and dominating accounts of the genre. Thus, 'exclusive' accounts of the western normally include *The Great Train Robbery* (1903), *The Covered Wagon* (1923), and *The Iron Horse* (1924) from the silent years, *Stagecoach*, *Destry Rides Again* (1939), and *Western Union* (1941) from the Bazin classical centre of the late 1930s–early 1940s, and *My Darling Clementine*, *Red River* (1948), *The Gunfighter* (1950), *Broken Arrow* (1950), *High Noon*, *Shane*, *The Searchers*, *Rio Bravo* (1959), and *Ride the High Country/Guns in the Afternoon* (1962) from later

periods. Together these films constitute a canon and frequently figure as reference-points in discussions of the western, establishing the contours of the genre, exemplifying its basic thematic patterns, and defining its iconographical qualities. However, in one sense, the canonic films do not typify the genre. They are drawn mainly from the A feature westerns made by the big studios or by prestigious independents rather than from the modest B pictures and series films which, in quantitative terms, constitute the bulk of the genre. In general, most westerns have come from outside the major studios, apart from certain periods such as 1939–42 and 1950–3, when almost as many came from the majors as from the independents. There is a sense, then, in which the real core of the genre, at least in statistical terms, lies in the B western, the staple series pictures, the Hopalong Cassidy films, the singing-cowboy pictures, and so on. *Pace* Bazin, *Stagecoach* and *My Darling Clementine*, as well as *Shane* and *High Noon*, only occupy a penumbraic position in the genre and (to continue the spatial metaphor) belong to a periphery.

Indeed, this bears upon the discussion of norms and deviations which often underpins analyses of the select canon of A features. For it can be argued that the norms, the basic conventions, the 'pure' versions of the genre, are really to be found only in the relatively self-contained world of the B western, whilst the A features were much more subject to the need to vary the conventions, to break the generic rules, and to conform, in certain respects, with the prevalent narrative and stylistic norms of the period. As Edward Buscombe has suggested, the 'A-Western . . . was always more of a risk financially; production was more erratic since each film had to sell itself on its merits. For this reason the A-Western was more susceptible to changes in fashion, more influenced by developments in other kinds of films and in Hollywood generally' (1988: 40–1). Accordingly, in the 1940s westerns such as *Pursued* (1947), *Blood on the Moon* (1948), *Station West* (1948), *Colorado Territory* (1949), and *The Furies* (1950), amongst others, reflect the Hollywood fashion for introspective psychologically oriented pictures and embody some of the stylistic and narrative features of the film noir. Generic definition, however, is a matter not simply of films themselves but also of the public discursive regimes that mediate between films and the audience and select certain examples for attention and ignore others. As a result, the focus upon the familiar and better-publicized A features—*My Darling*

Clementine, *The Searchers*, and so on—is not surprising. These, rather than the singing-cowboy films, are the ones discussed by critics and reviewers, analysed by film scholars, and used as the foundation-stones for the canonic edifice known as the western genre, which in turn constitutes the environment in which individual instances of the genre circulate and on which they depend for their currency.

The inclusive–exclusive distinction has been expressed in another way by David Bordwell, who claims that generic categories are 'core/periphery schema, with the more "central" members of the category creating a prototype effect' (1989: 148). While there are problems in using a core–periphery model of genre when it underpins an evaluative, rather than a descriptive, critical approach to genre (as is the case with critics such as Bazin), such a model nevertheless provides an opportunity for capturing the diversity of films traditionally rounded up under the familiar generic categories. Even the most sharply delineated genres include considerable variety, and, as Rick Altman has suggested, there is a 'need to recognise that not all genre films relate to their genre in the same way or to the same extent' (1984: 6–18). For example, the gangster film embraces both the urban settings of *Scarface* (1932) and *Little Caesar* (1930) and the rural mountain retreats of *High Sierra* (1941); the musical genre contains both the light touch of *Singin' in the Rain* and the darker themes of *A Star is Born* (1954). It is necessary to take account of such diversity in the defining of particular genres, and, indeed, to go further and acknowledge that part of this diversity reflects the hybrid generic qualities of many American films and a fluidity of generic boundaries which is, perhaps, best embodied in the film noir–women's picture–melodrama *Mildred Pierce* (1945). It might be suggested that both inclusive and exclusive definitions of individual genres are necessary and both, in their distinctive ways, represent particular aspects of the genre system. The notion of the broad, inclusive corpus alerts us to the extensive skein of relationships that encompass most Hollywood films. Although *Seven Brides for Seven Brothers* has many of the attributes of the western—it is set in the west, is about pioneers, has horses and guns, and so on—its syntactic structure, which relates romance to community, is characteristic of the musical. Indeed, with its singing and dancing and its focus upon romance, it is probably easier to relate the film to *Oklahoma!* (1955), another 'folk-musical', to use Altman's (1989) terminology, than to its western

contemporaries such as *The Searchers*. This does not mean that the film is not a western, but rather that it is more likely to be mentioned in inclusive definitions of the genre (as in encyclopaedias) than in focused discussion; also, it is more likely to be positioned on the periphery of the western while simultaneously occupying a place nearer the core of the musical.

Genre and the individual film

The discussion so far has focused upon generic systems and individual genres, abstract conceptual entities generated through a range of discourses and including extrafilmic elements such as advertising, press reviews, journal commentary, television and radio programmes on cinema, and other discourses often referred to as 'secondary' or 'subsidiary' to the films themselves which, of course, are at the centre of the critical project. The enterprise, in some respects, is one of classification: the construction and definition of generic systems and individual genres, the compilation of inventories of their characteristic subject-matter, themes, iconography, narrative syntax, and visual style. Problems occur, however, if the notion of classification is carried through to the ways in which the concept of genre functions in relation to individual films. This is especially the case when films appear not to settle easily into a category or, to put it another way, when a film offers elements which could be claimed by a number of genres, as the example of the 'western–musical' or 'musical–western' *Seven Brides for Seven Brothers* suggests. *Mildred Pierce*, to take another example, is centred on a woman played by one of the leading female stars (Joan Crawford), whose presence signals 'romantic drama' (Bourget 1971/1978); the film also begins with a crime, a murder, and has the investigative flashback structure of the film noir; a further generic strand (family melodrama) is evoked by the themes of female domesticity versus female career, children versus romantic relationships, from which the tensions surrounding the central character arise. In these cases, clear classification is impossible as both films relate in various ways to more than one genre; and this multigeneric quality is not confined to a few odd or unusual films as 'nearly all Hollywood's films were hybrids insofar as they tended to combine one type of generic plot, a romance plot, with others' (Neale 1990: 57).

If genre criticism were simply a matter of constructing taxonomies and allocating films to their places in the system, then the intellectual basis of the exercise would certainly be open to doubt. A shift in emphasis, however, to the activity of *reading* an individual film in the context of a notion of genre is one way of rethinking the entire concept and moving away from the somewhat static idea of genre criticism as taxonomy. Indeed, one of the central critical concerns with the notion of genre could be seen to be its provision of a background aid to the understanding of the individual film. Genre critics, as David Bordwell has suggested, '[f]ar from being concerned with definition or reasoning from genus to species . . . often identify the genre only to aid interpreting the particular work. The identification is transitory and heuristic, like that of nearly all the categories we draw upon in everyday life. Genres, and genre, function as open-ended and corrigible schemata' (1989: 148).

Thus, a notion of a particular genre or genres, sometimes accompanied by a sense of generic system, supervises the critical analysis and definition of the individual film. However, the critical work on that film may well rebound on the initial notion of the genre and/or of the generic system, transforming it and drawing attention to the 'open-endedness', the transitory status, of genres as conceptual entities. Looked at from this perspective, the notion of genre captures a process in which definitions—the western, the gangster film—are provisional, 'corrigible schemata', waiting upon the next instance of the genre which may balance confirmation of existing elements with their transformation, repetition with difference, in various and not entirely predictable ways.

A return to the individual film and its analysis enables us to find an appropriate role for the system-building, the taxonomic and inventory-oriented activity that characterizes genre criticism. Instead of asking the question 'To what genre does *Mildren Pierce* belong?', it is necessary to probe the consequences of positioning the film in relation to the various genres to which it has a family resemblance, and to think about genre in relation to the process of film comprehension, in relation to what literary theorist Jonathan Culler has called the 'operations of reading' (1975: 136). As Culler suggests, the process of reading requires background, context, a general reference-point against which the actual object of reading acquires sense and meaning. For Hollywood films this background is the generic system and its individual genres which constitute a framework for comprehension. The familiar constella-

tion of terms such as 'convention', 'iconography', 'horizon of expectation', 'audience expectation' acquires a specific sense in this context deriving from the 'ideal world' of the generic system which is constructed through a range of discourses including, of course, the individual films which make up the individual generic corpus (particularly as it emerges and definitions in exclusive terms are focused on a handful of films thought to be typical and/or regarded as prototypes). The individual viewer confronted with a genre film has already internalized a number of assumptions about the genre system and will have a perception of the 'world' implied by each genre with its characteristic iconography, situational conventions, and stock of characters. He or she will read the film against a 'horizon of expectations' derived from critical and journalistic discourse in the various media, marketing, and publicity activities, and from the memory of previous viewing of films which are sufficiently similar to act as guides in relation to the formation of the horizon of expectation. The notion of each genre evoking a 'world', a particular configuration of 'fictional reality' with its own rules of behaviour, its particular fictional trajectories, its distinctive visual surface, its overall verisimilitude or structure of plausibility, is useful if regarded as a background mental set which readers of genre cinema bring to the individual film and through which the film sustains at least some of its levels of comprehensibility and maybe its dominant level of comprehensibility.

Looked at in this light, questions of generic membership—'To what genre does this film belong?'—become less relevant. Indeed, alternative questions are required such as: 'What genre or genres constitute an effective and pertinent context for the reading of this film?' or 'What is/are the world/worlds invoked by aspects of this film which will enable it to be situated and understood, its narrative trajectory anticipated, its characters to be constructed, and so on?' If we return to *Mildred Pierce*, we can see that its sense and meaning derive from the ways in which it interweaves different generic strands which are, in many ways, in tension with each other. *Mildren Pierce* is not unique in its multigeneric character and the flexible world of genre identified in the work of Neale and Altman correlates with a flexible approach to the making of genre films in Hollywood itself. This is particularly the case with contemporary, 'postmodern' Hollywood and is exemplified in, for example, *The Silence of the Lambs* (1991), which combines elements of the police-procedural—the mechanics of detection, a focus on forensic detail—with the horror film.

Genre: a summary

The impulses behind the development of genre criticism included a sense of unease with traditional critical approaches which highlighted individuality and distinctiveness, and which were centred on the unconventional in film. It was argued, by Lawrence Alloway (1971) in particular, that popular American cinema required a different critical approach from those adopted for the more traditional art forms, an approach which recognized the positive role of formula and convention, stereotypical characterization, familiar narratives, and their centrality to Hollywood picture-making. It was suggested that audiences for Hollywood pictures read them according to a detailed set of assumptions—an intertextual consciousness—derived from a regular viewing of related films and an awareness of the various secondary discourses; and that their pleasures were derived from such qualities as the ritualistic predictability of the narratives and the nuancing of familiar conventions. The unacknowledged assumption was that other forms of cinema were different, non-generic, and subject to different and less restricted modes of reading.

However, the interplay of semiotics and genre in writers such as Neale and Altman suggests less of a difference between genre films and other forms of cinema at least in terms of the basic processes of communication and reading. All communicative forms, including all films, are underpinned by systems—arguably modelled on language—against which they acquire their significance and meaning. The audience for the films of Michelangelo Antonioni and Ingmar Bergman require a reading-context no less than the audience for the films of John Ford and Sam Peckinpah, and all films have woven into their texture at some level (narrative, style, iconography) signals that indicate the appropriate ways in which they might be understood and appreciated. American genre cinema becomes a special case from this perspective rather than a distinct form, and takes its place in a spectrum of cinematic types.

BIBLIOGRAPHY

Alloway, Lawrence (1963), 'Iconography and the Movies', *Movie*, 7: 4–6.

—— (1971), *Violent America: The Movies 1946–1964* (New York: Museum of Modern Art).

Altman, Rick (1984), 'A Semantic/Syntactic Approach to Film Genre', *Cinema Journal*, 23/3: 6–18; repr. in Grant (1986).

—— (1989), *The American Film Musical* (London: British Film Institute).

Bazin, André (1953/1971), Preface to J.-L. Rieupeyrout, *Le Western ou le cinéma américain par excellence*, in Bazin (1971).

—— (1971), *What is Cinema?*, 2 vols., trans. Hugh Gray, ii (Berkeley: University of California Press).

Bordwell, David (1985), *Narration in the Fiction Film* (London: Methuen).

—— (1989), *Making Meaning* (Cambridge, Mass.: Harvard University Press).

Bourget, Jean-Loup (1971/1978), 'Faces of the American Melodrama: Joan Crawford', in *Film Reader*, 3: 24–34.

Buscombe, Edward (1970), 'The Idea of Genre in the American Cinema', *Screen*, 11/2: 33–45.

—— (1974), 'Walsh and Warner Brothers', in P. Hardy (ed.), *Raoul Walsh* (Edinburgh: Edinburgh Film Festival and British Film Institute).

—— (ed.) (1988), *The BFI Companion to the Western* (London: Andre Deutsch and British Film Institute)

Culler, Jonathan (1975), *Structuralist Poetics* (London: Routledge & Kegan Paul).

*Grant, Barry K. (ed.) (1986), *Film Genre Reader* (Austin, Tex.: University of Texas Press).

Hardy, Phil (ed.) (1985), *The Encyclopedia of Western Movies* (London: Octopus Books).

Hess Wright, Judith (1974/1986), 'Genre Films and the Status Quo', *Jump Cut*, 1 (May–June), 1, 16, 18; repr. in Grant (1986).

Hutchings, Peter (1995), 'Genre Theory and Criticism', in Joanne Hollows and Mark Jancovich (eds.), *Approaches to Popular Film* (Manchester: Manchester University Press).

Jameson, Fredric (1975), 'Magical Narratives: Romance as Genre', *New Literary History*, 7: 135–63.

Kitses, Jim (1969), *Horizons West* (London: Thames & Hudson and British Film Institute).

Klinger, Barbara (1984/1986), '"Cinema/Ideology/Criticism": The Progressive Text', *Screen*, 25/1: 30–44; repr. in Grant (1986).

Lovell, Alan (1967/1976), 'The Western', in B. Nichols (ed.), *Movies and Methods*, 2 vols, (University of California Press).

McArthur, Colin (1972), *Underworld USA* (London: Secker & Warburg).

Maltby, Richard (1995), *Hollywood Cinema* (Oxford: Blackwell).

Movie, (1975), 'The Return of Movie', no. 20 (Spring) 1–25.

*****Neale, Steve** (1980), *Genre* (London: British Film Institute).

—— (1990), 'Questions of Genre', *Screen*, 31/1: 45–66.

Palmer, Jerry (1991), *Potboilers: Methods, Concepts and Case Studies in Popular Fiction* (London: Routledge).

Pye, Douglas (1975), 'Genre and Movies', *Movie*, 20: 29–43.

Rotha, Paul (1930/1967), *The Film Till Now* (London: Spring Books).

Ryall, Tom (1970), 'The Notion of Genre', *Screen*, 11/2: 22-32.

*—— (1975–6), 'Teaching through Genre', *Screen Education*, 17: 27–33.

Schatz, Thomas (1981), *Hollywood Genres* (New York: Random House).

Shklovsky, Victor (1927), 'Poetry and Prose in Cinematography', *Twentieth Century Studies*, 7–8: 128–30.

Todorov, Tzvetan (1975), *The Fantastic* (Ithaca, NY: Cornell University Press).

Warshow, Robert (1948/1970), 'The Gangster as Tragic Hero', in Warshow (1970).

—— (1954/1970), 'Movie Chronicle: The Westerner', in Warshow (1970).

—— (1970), *The Immediate Experience* (New York: Atheneum).

Williams, Alan (1984), 'Is Radical Genre Criticism Possible?', *Quarterly Review of Film Studies*, 9/2: 121–5.

Body genres

Linda Williams excerpted from Linda Williams, 'Film Bodies: Gender, Genre and Excess', *Film Quarterly*, 44/4 (Summer 1991), 2–13.

The repetitive formulas and spectacles of film genres are often defined by their differences from the classical realist style of narrative cinema. These classical films have been characterized as efficient action-centred, goal-oriented, linear narratives driven by the desire of a single protagonist, involving one or two lines of action, and leading to definitive closure. In their influential study *The Classical Hollywood Cinema*, David Bordwell, Janet Staiger, and Kristin Thompson call this the classical Hollywood style.

As Rick Altman has noted in a recent article, both genre study and the study of the somewhat more nebulous category of melodrama has long been hampered by

assumptions about the classical nature of the dominant narrative to which melodrama and some individual genres have been opposed. Altman argues that Bordwell, Staiger, and Thompson, who locate the classical Hollywood style in the linear, progressive form of the Hollywood narrative, cannot accommodate 'melodramatic' attributes like spectacle, episodic presentation, or dependence on coincidence except as limited exceptions or 'play' within the dominant linear causality of the classical.

Altman writes: 'Unmotivated events, rhythmic montage, highlighted parallelism, overlong spectacles—these are the excesses in the classical narrative system that alert us to the

Mildred Pierce (1945)—the fluidity of generic boundaries

Body genres continued

existence of a competing logic, a second voice'. Altman, whose own work on the movie musical has necessarliy relied upon analyses of seemingly 'excessive' spectacles and parallel constructions, thus makes a strong case for the need to recognize the possibility that excess may itself be organized as a system. Yet analyses of systems of excess have been much slower to emerge in the genres whose non-linear spectacles have centred more directly upon the gross display of the human body. Pornography and horror films are two such systems of excess. Pornography is the lowest in cultural esteem, gross-out horror is next to lowest.

Melodrama, however, refers to a much broader category of films and a much larger system of excess. It would not be unreasonable, in fact, to consider all three of these genres under the extended rubric of melodrama, considered as a filmic mode of stylistic and/or emotional excess that stands in contrast to more 'dominant' modes of realistic, goal-oriented narrative. In this extended sense melodrama can encompass a broad range of films marked by 'lapses' in realism, by 'excesses' of spectacle and displays of primal, even infantile, emotions, and by narratives that seem circular and repetitive. Much of the interest of melodrama to film scholars over the last fifteen years originates in the sense that the form exceeds the normative system of much narrative cinema. I shall limit my focus here, however, to a more narrow sense of melodrama, leaving the broader category of the sensational to encompass the three genres I wish to consider. Thus, partly for purposes of contrast with pornography, the melodrama I will consider here will consist of the form that has most interested feminist critics—that of 'the woman's film' or 'weepie'. These are films addressed to women in their traditional status under patriarchy—as wives, mothers, abandoned lovers, or in their traditional status as bodily hysteria or excess, as in the frequent case of the woman 'afflicted' with a deadly or debilitating disease.

What are the pertinent features of bodily excess shared by these three 'gross' genres? First, there is the spectacle of a body caught in the grip of intense sensation or emotion. Carol Clover, speaking primarily of horror films and pornography, has called films which privilege the sensational 'body' genres. I am expanding Clover's notion of low body genres to include the sensation of overwhelming pathos in the 'weepie'. The body spectacle is featured most sensationally in pornography's portrayal of orgasm, in horror's portrayal of violence and terror, and in melodrama's portrayal of weeping. I propose that an investigation of the visual and narrative pleasures found in the portrayal of these three types of excess could be important to a new direction in genre criticism that would take as its point of departure—rather than as an unexamined assumption—questions of gender construction, and gender address in relation to basic sexual fantasies.

Another pertinent feature shared by these body genres is the focus on what could probably best be called a form of ecstasy. While the classical meaning of the original Greek word is insanity and bewilderment, more contemporary meanings suggest components of direct or indirect sexual excitement and rapture, a rapture which informs even the pathos of melodrama.

Visually, each of these ecstatic excesses could be said to share a quality of uncontrollable convulsion or spasm—of the body 'beside itself' with sexual pleasure, fear and terror, or overpowering sadness. Aurally, excess is marked by recourse not to the coded articulations of language but to inarticulate cries of pleasure in porn, screams of fear in horror, sobs of anguish in melodrama.

Looking at, and listening to, these bodily ecstasies, we can also notice something else that these genres seem to share: though quite differently gendered with respect to their targeted audiences, with pornography aimed, presumably, at active men and melodramatic weepies aimed, presumably, at passive women, and with contemporary gross-out horror aimed at adolescents careening wildly between the two masculine and feminine poles, in each of these genres the bodies of women figured on the screen have functioned traditionally as the primary *embodiments* of pleasure, fear, and pain.

In other words, even when the pleasure of viewing has traditionally been constructed for masculine spectators, as is the case in most traditional heterosexual pornography, it is the female body in the grips of an out-of-control ecstasy that has offered the most sensational sight.

There are, of course, other film genres which both portray and affect the sensational body—e.g. thrillers, musicals, comedies. I suggest, however, that the film genres that have had especially low cultural status—which have seemed to exist as excesses to the system of even the popular genres—are not simply those which sensationally display bodies on the screen and register effects in the bodies of spectators. Rather, what may especially mark these body genres as low is the perception that the body of the spectator is caught up in an almost involuntary mimicry of the emotion or sensation of the body on the screen along with the fact that the body displayed is female. Physical clown comedy is another 'body' genre concerned with all manner of gross activities and body functions—eating shoes, slipping on banana skins. None the less, it has not been deemed gratuitously excessive,

Body genres continued

TABLE 1. **AN ANATOMY OF FILM BODIES**

	GENRE		
	Pornography	**Horror**	**Melodrama**
Bodily excess	Sex	Violence	Emotion
Ecstasy—shown by	Ecstatic sex	Ecstatic violence	Ecstatic woe
	Orgasm	Shudder	Sob
	Ejaculation	Blood	Tears
Presumed audience	Men	Adolescent boys	Girls, women
	(active)	(active–passive)	(passive)
Perversion	Sadism	Sadomasochism	Masochism
Originary fantasy	Seduction	Castration	Origin
Temporality of fantasy	On time!	Too early!	Too late!
GENRE CYCLES			
'Classic'	Stag films	'Classic' horror	'Classic' women's films
	(1920s–1940s)	Dracula	Maternal melodrama
	The Casting Couch	Frankenstein	Stella Dallas
		Dr Jekyll and Mr Hyde	Mildred Pierce
		King Kong	romance
			Back Street
			Letter from an Unknown
			Woman
Contemporary	Feature-length hard-core	Post-Psycho	Male and female 'weepies'
	porn	Texas Chainsaw Massacre	Steel Magnolias
	Deep Throat etc.	Halloween	Stella
	The Punishment of Anne	Dressed to Kill	Dad
	Femme Productions	Videodrome	
	Bisexual		
	Trisexual		

probably because the reaction of the audience does not mimic the sensations experienced by the central clown. Indeed, it is almost a rule that the audience's physical reaction of laughter does not coincide with the often dead-pan reactions of the clown.

In the body genres I am isolating here, however, it seems to be the case that the success of these genres is often measured by the degree to which the audience sensation mimics what is seen on the screen. Whether this mimicry is exact, e.g. whether the spectator at the porn film actually orgasms, whether the spectator at the horror film actually

shudders in fear, whether the spectator of the melodrama actually dissolves in tears, the success of these genres seems a self-evident matter of measuring bodily response.

What seems to bracket these particular genres from others is an apparent lack of proper aesthetic distance, a sense of over-involvement in sensation and emotion. We feel manipulated by these texts—an impression that the very colloquialisms of 'tear-jerker' and 'fear-jerker' express—and to which we could add pornography's even cruder sense as texts to which some people might be inclined to 'jerk off'.

9

The star system and Hollywood

Jeremy G. Butler

The human body on screen ignites the desires of moviegoers. The actor's performance provides an essential pleasure in the film-viewing experience. The star's image dominates movie posters and appears on dozens of magazine covers; it is clearly one of the principal commodities that is used to market a film to an audience—equal in importance, in the minds of film producers and film viewers alike, to a compelling story or majestic scenery or a trendy director. And yet until the 1980s the presence of human bodies in motion, the impact of the actor's performance, and significance of the star's image were rarely discussed in film studies. Consequently, in order to understand the study of the star system, one must first ask: Why has the star system been ignored for so long by film studies?

The origins of this neglect lie in the very beginnings of film theory. Early theorists were sensitive to the charge that film, as a mechanical reproduction of reality, was not a true art form. They focused their attention on the aspects of filmmaking that separated it from reality and thereby provided the artist with tools for artistic expression. A particular camera angle could make someone look smaller or larger than he or she does in reality; a lighting style could make an actor appear grotesque; wide-angle lenses could distort perspective; and so on. Film could be justified as an art form, they argued, because the filmmaker did not just mechanically reproduce reality; he or she actually manipulated reality or even fabricated an entirely new

reality. Foremost among these first theorists was Lev Kuleshov (1975), who devised an editing experiment during the early 1920s. In the Kuleshov experiment, a shot of an expressionless actor was intercut with various significant objects—a bowl of soup, a baby in a coffin, and so on. (The actual components of the experiment are in doubt because no copies of it exist today.) Kuleshov maintained that spectators saw emotions in the actor's face (hunger, sorrow, and so on) that were generated through film technique rather than the work of an actor. Meaning did not exist in the actor's performance, but rather in the manipulation of performance through editing.

Thus, Kuleshov, founder of the world's first film school, devalued the significance of the actor's presence in his determination to fix the cinema's essence in editing (montage)—in which the actor's face is no more consequential than a bowl of soup. Other film theorists from the 1920s and 1930s were also uninterested in acting and stars, choosing instead to try and ascertain the components of film art and its impact upon viewers. Stars fared little better in subsequent decades. Film scholars in the 1940s–1960s often came to the cinema with a training in literary criticism. Such individuals were well equipped to analyse narrative forms common to film and literature, but could shed little light on the work of the star. They viewed the actor, instead, as simply the body that held the character's place on screen. It was the character's position within a narrative structure that mattered, not the star's embodiment of that character.

This emphasis on narrative and character over actors and their work also informs two of the major critical approaches to Hollywood cinema that are presented in this volume: genre and authorship studies (see Crofts and Ryall, Part 2, Chapters 7 and 8). Most genres, with the major exception of the musical, are defined mainly by the stories they tell, and this leaves little room for the consideration of performance. And so it is not surprising that most critics have interpreted genre using narrative-based methods borrowed from structural anthropology and ideological criticism. Thus, despite several meaningful intersections of star and genre (as in the case of John Wayne and the western, Lana Turner and the melodrama, Fred Astaire and the musical), the impact of stars on genres has yet to be fully assessed. Britton (1984) and Gledhill (1991*a*), however, have offered some introductory thoughts.

In the case of authorship study (by which is meant, principally, the so-called 'auteur theory'), some concern with the star's impact upon a film might have been expected. After all, in common parlance, moviegoers characteristically identify a film in terms of its star—as if the star were its author. For example, despite the opening credits which declare *Pretty Woman* (1990) to be a 'Garry Marshall film' (referring to its director), most viewers are likely to refer to it as a 'Julia Roberts movie'. In some regard, then, the star is seen to be the central presence, the 'auteur', behind such a film. And, certainly, there are numerous examples of films being designed specifically for particular stars. In such cases, the star's image has determined the overall construction of the film, even if he or she didn't actually write the script or choose the camera angles. Even so, proponents of the auteur theory have seldom discussed the star as auteur, preferring instead to privilege the director as 'author' and to discuss his or her mise-en-scène, narrative structure, and thematics. This emphasis on the director over other members of the production team derives, à la Kuleshov, from a conception of the 'artist' as the man or woman in control of film technique (which is principally the director). Since the actor does not govern film technique—does not, in a sense, speak the language of the cinema—he or she cannot be considered a film artist.

In sum, analysis of the star system has been hampered by early film studies' reliance upon antiquated aesthetic traditions—particularly conventional literary criticism and Romanticism—that are ill-equipped to deal with the work of art in the age of mechanical reproduction (to invoke Walter Benjamin's telling phrase). The attempts in the 1920s–1940s to justify the cinema as an art form according to these traditions blinded theorists to the significance of the star system. More recently, however, analytical methods from semiotics, psychoanalysis, and cultural studies have been brought to bear upon the cinema, resulting in a re-evaluation of the position of stars in the cinematic apparatus. Leading the way in this regard was a slender volume entitled *Stars*, by Richard Dyer (1979). Following Dyer, there has been a growth of writing concerned with stardom and film performance, much of which may be found in two anthologies: *Star Texts* (Butler 1991) and *Stardom* (Gledhill 1991*b*).

The fundamentals of star studies

Central to Dyer's approach, and to that of many subsequent star studies, is the semiotics notion that stars should be studied as clusters of signs, as systems of signifiers or texts that communicate meaning to a spectator. These star texts are, of course, grounded in the lives of real human beings. There is no doubt that Mel Gibson and Demi Moore really exist. But Dyer stresses that these images are highly manipulated texts that have been fabricated, intentionally and unintentionally, through the work of the star, his or her representatives, and other cultural workers (e.g. gossip columnists, talk show hosts, and so on). Moreover, since there is no way to know a star except through media artefacts such as magazine articles and news reports, it is fruitless to search for the star's true identity 'behind' or 'beneath' the media-constructed façade. Few of us will ever meet Gibson or Moore in person, and even if we did there is little chance that we would penetrate their media shells and glimpse their 'true' identities. In so far as the viewer–analyst is concerned, the star's identity is his or her façade—our knowledge of him or her is always filtered through media accounts. Consequently, it is impossible to know the star in any other way. The study of stars, therefore, does not aim to reveal the truth behind a star's image—as is often the false claim of TV and magazine journalists—but rather seeks to bring out the meanings within a star's image and to contextualize them within larger discursive structures.

Having stressed the constructed, fabricated nature of star images—the existence of stars as texts—it is important to recognize that these texts do not exist in a hermetically sealed, nice-and-tidy, semiotic vacuum. Rather, star texts also exist within particular economic, ideological, and psychological contexts. Dyer and others, in this respect, recognize the importance of stars to both the cinema's mode of production and to a film's reception by viewers. To understand the star system fully, therefore, one must consider three interlocking elements:

1. star production: economic and discursive structures;
2. star reception: social structures and the theory of the subject;
3. star semiotics: intertextuality and structured polysemy.

Star production: economic and discursive structures

The star system is such an integral part of today's film and television industries that it is sometimes difficult to remember that this so-called 'system' did not always exist. The early cinema survived quite nicely for over a decade without it. Indeed, actor's names were not even listed in the credits of films at first. Using a star's image to promote a film would have been unthinkable around the turn of the century, but by 1910 the Hollywood mode of production had shifted and the actor had become a marketable commodity. Interestingly, quite a bit of controversy surrounds accounts of the star system's introduction into the Hollywood mode of film production. Examining that controversy can tell us much about the position of the star in the cinematic economic apparatus, as well as illustrating more general problems associated with the writing of film history.

The conventional history of the star system's evolution—a history which has been repeated in decades of film textbooks—constructs a convenient narrative of lone-wolf independent producers initiating the star system in order to outsmart the Motion Picture Patents Company (MPPC). (The MPPC was a protective trade association of the most powerful production companies formed by Thomas Edison in a monopolistic attempt to control film production and exhibition.) As the story is usually told, film producers initially resisted promoting actors' identities because they presumed a well-known actor would demand more money for his or her work. Also it is said that actors were ashamed of appearing in low-prestige 'flickers' and refused to have their names credited. However, the filmgoing public soon came to identify their favourites even without the aid of on-screen credits, lobby posters, or fan magazines. One such favourite was Florence Lawrence, identified by her public as the 'Biograph Girl' for her work in films produced by American Biograph, one of the members of the MPPC. In 1909 Lawrence was lured away from Biograph by an adversary of the MPPC, independent producer Carl Laemmle, of the Independent Motion Picture (IMP) Corporation. The following year, Laemmle mounted what is said to be the first promotional campaign for a film actor. Rumours were circulated—probably by IMP publicists—that Lawrence had been killed in a streetcar accident. Then Laemmle took out an advertisement in *Moving Picture World* declaring, 'We Nail a Lie' (reproduced by Staiger in Gledhill 1991*b*: 4). He heatedly denied these rumours and asserted that Lawrence was not only alive and well, but that, coincidentally, a film of hers was just about to be released. The success of promotions such as this, conventional wisdom maintains, led to the independent producers' triumph over the MPPC, which stodgily refused to promote its actors as stars.

Film historians such as Staiger (1983) and deCordova (1990) have challenged this conventional narrative. Attractive as this story is, it is undermined by several inaccuracies and misconceptions. As deCordova points out, an MPPC company (Kalem) publicized their actors a year before Laemmle and IMP did; and the Edison Company was probably the first (in 1909) to include a cast list in the film credits. Indeed, in 1910 most MPPC companies, with the notable exception of Biograph, began to promote their stars—at the same time as the independent producers did so. Thus, the independents were not alone in using stars as a marketing device. The emergence of the star system was not an instance of the underdog independents battling the bullying MPPC, but rather was the result of a more generalized shift in the mode of production and the discourses surrounding the medium. More significant

> **The star system is such an integral part of today's film and television industries that it is sometimes difficult to remember that this so-called 'system' did not always exist.**

to the emergence of the star system, contemporary historians (Bordwell, Staiger, and Thompson 1985) have argued, are other discursive and economic shifts.

First, in terms of aesthetic discourse, the introduction of major theatrical actors into the films of the Film D'Art and the Famous Players Film Company helped to legitimize film acting and to alter the discourse on film in general. Whereas early promotion of the cinema focused on the technology itself (objects in motion! on a screen!) and the stories presented (will the firemen rescue the endangered child?), a discourse on acting and the lives of actors began to intrude around 1909. When noted theatrical presence Sara Bernhardt appeared in *La Dame aux camélias* (France, 1912; *Camille*) it helped import a long tradition of performance discourse from the theatre into the movies and shifted the promotional spotlight from the technology and the narrative to the actor's body and the actor's life. For example, a 1912 advertisement for *La Dame aux camélias* focuses attention on the actor with some rather astonishing claims: 'Like the Noonday Sun Alone in the Blazing Majesty Giving Light and Life to Art Madame Sarah Bernhardt Illuminates the whole Motion Picture World Through Her Stupendous Genius Revealed in Her First and Only Photo Play "CAMILLE" In which she is taking the nations by storm and making a girdle of her pictured glory around the globe' (reproduced by Staiger in Gledhill 1991*b*: 13).

In deCordova's view, companies such as the Film D'Art and Famous Players changed the way actors were regarded in film. Adding to this were print media that began to publicize the off-screen existence of the performers. Although several film magazines initially slighted actors and stressed instead summaries of film stories—as the titles of *The Motion Picture Story Magazine* and *Photoplay* attest—by 1910 many of these magazines had begun running features on actors' off-screen lives. This journalist discourse was an essential component in the transition of the actor from nameless body on the screen to genuine film star—with a name and an identity that extended beyond the characters he or she played on-screen.

The construction of off-screen star identities, of true star images, had a significant economic impact on the cinema. Since by the time of the First World War actors had a presence larger than their individual characters, they could now be used to distinguish one film from another. The presence of a star such as Mary Pickford, for example, could set a film apart from the dozens of others competing for viewer attention. Thus, the Holly-wood mode of production quickly absorbed the star as commodity, as a source of product differentiation as significant as narrative-based genres and more powerful than studio identities. With the establishment of stars' extra-filmic identities and the arrival of the star as economic commodity, the star system was complete.

Star reception: social structures

Once the star system was in place and formerly anonymous actors had become stars, their images began to have a social presence. This presence became quite clear in the United States in the 1920s, when several scandals illustrated the new-found significance of the motion picture star. The enormous media attention paid to the murder of director William Desmond Taylor (involving actors Mary Miles Minter and Mable Normand), actor Wallace Reid's death from a drug overdose, and comedian Roscoe 'Fatty' Arbuckle's trial for rape and murder indicates the change in position of the film actor from turn-of-the-century anonymity to 1920s notoriety. It also suggests just how forceful the star's off-screen presence had become. It is tempting to read these events, and the images of the stars associated with them, as a reflection of the 'roaring twenties'—of an era of flappers, gangsters, and 'anything goes'. Indeed, it is a common presumption that star images are a reflection of society's values. Contemporary star studies, however, rejects this sort of 'reflectionism' as simplistic and reductive. Instead, the (many) meanings associated with a star are seen to form a part of the meaning system of that star's society, the ideology of that particular time and place.

From ideological criticism, star studies has fastened onto the basic presumption that ideology consists of the taken-for-granted values and concepts that underpin a particular society. Moreover, it is argued that these values exist in a systemic relationship to one another and that they have 'real' social causes and effects. Ideological values are presumed to be generated by a society's economic and social infrastructure and related to the ways that society treats individuals of different classes, races, and gender. As a result, star studies has sought to analyse the meanings of star images in relation to ideologies of class, race, and gender.

Eckert (1974), for example, incorporates Freudian notions of condensation, repression, and displace-

Shirley Temple, child-heroine of the Depression

ment in his consideration of Shirley Temple's position within the class discourse of the United States during the Depression. He argues that the potentially disruptive, class-based topics of work and money are repressed in Temple's films, displaced into charity and love. Capitalist, bourgeois values, he argues, were under assault at the time of these films' production and Temple helps paper over the resulting ideological fissures: by bringing together the classes (Temple's character often romantically unites a wealthy man and a working-class woman, or vice versa) and embodying charity and love. She does not 'reflect'

1930s values so much as process them—repressing, condensing, and displacing.

Star studies often highlights this resolution of ideological conflicts by stars. Dyer adopts this approach when discussing the images of several stars. Marilyn Monroe (Dyer 1986) and Lana Turner (Dyer 1977–8), for example, are both discussed in terms of their reconciliation of conflicting gender values (innocent–sexy, ordinary–glamorous), while Paul Robeson's connections to conflicting racial discourses (African and European) form the basis of Dyer's (1986) analysis of his work. For Dyer and others, ideology is not a monolithic, hegemonic phenomenon that crushes all opposing viewpoints—as it might be for a traditional Marxist. Instead, ideology is explored for its conflicts and contradictions, many of which are inscribed on stars' images. The ideological function that stars such as Monroe, Turner, and Robeson serve is magically to resolve those contradictions. This is an essential allure of the star: the resolution of contradictions that cannot be resolved in the social sphere, in 'real life'. In this regard, stars operate in much the same way as genre narratives, which often relate mythic stories that manage the unmanageable and 'resolve' the unresolvable. Genres and stars, it has been argued, comfort the viewer because they offer fantasy solutions to social problems that cannot be resolved in reality.

> **This is an essential allure of the star: the resolution of contradictions that cannot be resolved in the social sphere, in 'real life'.**

Stars and society: the special case of feminism

Feminism and gender studies hold a special place in star studies. Feminists were among the first film scholars to publish extended considerations of stars—notably, of women stars. Molly Haskell's *From Reverence to Rape* (1974) is filled with analyses of actors, although the consideration of stars is often eclipsed by her overweening auteurism. Haskell discusses stars in terms of socially determined, patriarchal stereotypes that they do or do not fulfil. Mostly, she sees women stars as unique inflections of their society's gender roles. Her comments on Greta Garbo are illustrative: 'As actress, myth, and image of woman, Garbo, like any other star, was neither wholly unique nor wholly representative. She was not like the solitary and self-derived creation of the writer, on the one hand; nor was she a spontaneous eruption of the national "anima", an archetypal heroine as might emerge from a truly "collective" art like television' (Haskell 1974: 106–7). The problem with Haskell's perspective for subsequent feminists is that she does not examine the complicated discursive operations by which the image of woman in film reflects and refracts social realities. As she contrasts

the star with the stereotype, she presumes that that stereotype is a stable, uncomplicated mirror of reality. In short, she does not develop an understanding of the star's and the stereotype's positions within ideological processes.

This 'image-of-woman' approach predominated in feminist film studies during its formative years, the later 1960s and early 1970s. Subsequently, this method of writing about women stars has been criticized for at least two reasons: first, its reliance upon the simple 'reflection' theory of ideology; and second, its naïve understanding of how the cinematic apparatus positions the female image relative to the viewer. Since the publication of Laura Mulvey's seminal 'Visual Pleasure and Narrative Cinema' (1975), feminist film study has veered off into approaches grounded in Lacanian psychoanalysis in an attempt to comprehend the process of film viewing. Informed by psychoanalytic film theory, the cinematic spectator has been renamed the 'subject', who views and interacts with the on-screen human 'object'. This has had important implications for star studies because the 'theory of the subject' attempts to articulate the psychic mechanisms of desire behind the spectator's viewing of the star.

Star reception: the theory of the subject

It would seem self-evident that the relationship of the spectator-subject to the star-object is grounded in some form of visual desire, of pleasure in the image. We look at stars because it pleases us to do so. Nobody forces or coerces us to watch Brad Pitt or Marilyn Monroe. And yet, traditional film theory had little to say about visual pleasure and desire. Voyeurism has been the unspoken pleasure of the cinema. Mulvey's work in the mid-1970s opened the floodgates to analyses of cinematic pleasure based in Freud and the reworking of Freud by French psychoanalyst Jacques Lacan.

Even though Mulvey is less concerned with film stardom *per se* than with the apparatus by which visual pleasure is orchestrated, her analysis does offer some specific thoughts on the star image of Marlene Dietrich and helps clarify (from a feminist psychoanalytic perspective, at least) the star–spectator relationship. Mulvey maintains that there are two aspects of visual pleasure in classical cinema: 'The first, scopophilic, arises from pleasure in using another person as an object of sexual stimulation through sight. The second, developed through narcissism and the constitution of the ego, comes from identification with the image seen' (Mulvey 1975: 10). Scopophilia, or voyeurism, is argued to be the key to understanding the representation of women in film. In this scenario, the viewing subject is specifically male and the viewed object is specifically female (see Creed and White, Part 1, Chapter 9 and 13 for further discussion of this argument). Although the woman connotes 'to-be-looked-at-ness' (Mulvey's phrase), she also threatens to signify castration anxiety, which, according to Lacan, is the foundation upon which all language and signification is constructed. The classical cinema deals with the threatening object, the woman, by either investigating and demystifying her, or turning her into a safe 'fetish object'. By catering to the pleasure of the male spectator-subject, the classical cinema exists as 'an illusion cut to the measure of desire' (Mulvey 1975: 17).

It seems clear that many women stars are fabricated illusions cut to the measure of male desire: from Theda Bara to Jean Harlow to Lena Horne to Rita Hayworth to Kim Novak to Ann-Margret to Julie Christie to Bo Derek to Demi Moore. The castration anxiety that these women pose, in Freudian terms, is ameliorated by turning their bodies into fetish objects. Other, more threatening women are handled through containment or punishment in their story lines. Lana Turner's Cora, in *The Postman always Rings Twice* (1946), gets away with murder, but then perishes in a car crash. Jane Greer's Kathie Moffat, in *Out of the Past* (1947), betrays her lover but is killed at the end of the film. To psychoanalytic film theorists, the classical cinema is a phallocentric, patriarchal machine that has developed devices to check the peril embodied by women. Since stars are the most popular and the most powerful female figures in film, they are also the most capable of instigating both disruption and pleasure.

Recent considerations of women in film have been

It seems clear that many women stars are fabricated illusions cut to the measure of male desire: from Theda Bara to Jean Harlow to Lena Horne to Rita Hayworth to Kim Novak to Ann-Margret to Julie Christie to Bo Derek to Demi Moore.

critical of Mulvey and other psychoanalytic film theorists for their presumption of a male viewer and a masculine viewing position. What if, Hansen (1986) has queried, the viewing subject is female and the viewed object is male? Moreover, what if the viewing position for a film is designed for a feminine perspective? Hansen has written, specifically, on Rudolph Valentino, a star image successfully designed for a female audience. Her essay begins by noting the shifts in women's social position that accompanied the First World War—specifically, their integration into a consumer economy—and the first twentieth-century wave of the women's movement, the suffragettes. However, her central concern is the sexual politics of Valentino's films. She argues that the deep ambivalence of Valentino's sexuality, expressing a 'slippage of gender definitions', provides the opportunity for the taboo expression of female voyeurism. Further, Valentino also disrupts conventional sado-masochistic rituals; his masochistic femininity fissures patriarchal structures of dominance and submission. Hansen, like Mulvey, is concerned with the issue of desire and the movie star, but she inverts the genders of Mulvey's original structure.

Hansen's challenge to Mulvey still exists within the bounds of Freudian psychology, but other contemporary feminists go even further in their contesting of psychoanalytic interpretations of the image of woman in film. Stacey (1994) criticizes the psychoanalytic method for a number of reasons—not the least of which is that theorists such as Mulvey (1975/1989), Doane (1987), de Lauretis (1987), *et al.* seldom deal with actual film viewers. Their theories are developed from psychoanalytical principles, and they are never tested out on viewers in a screening situation. Stacey's approach, in contrast, grows out of ethnography, which uses interviews, surveys, viewers' letters and diaries, and so on, to study the discourse of real viewers. Like Hansen, Stacey is also dissatisfied with psychoanalytic film criticism's emphasis on the male viewer, but her book, *Star Gazing* (1994), does not merely invert the traditional viewing situation by studying female viewers and a male viewed. Instead, she focuses on how women look at women, at images of femininity, on screen. She does so by analysing letters and surveys from British viewers about US film stars from the 1940s and 1950s. This also allows her to study viewer discourse in a specific national and historical context. Another weakness of psychoanalytic theory, she contends, is that it presumes a universal subject, one out-

Rudolf Valentino, a star image successfully designed for a female audience (*The Sheikh*, 1926)

side the determinations of class, nation, and race (for further discussion of feminist interest in stars, see White, Part 1, Chapter 13).

Star semiotics: intertextuality and structured polysemy

As has been noted, Dyer's *Stars* merges the sociological and ideological criticism outlined above with elements of semiotics. (And, although Dyer does occasionally borrow from Freudian psychology, his work skirts the Lacanian revision of Freud.) The semiotic approach that Dyer uses has provided the foundation for the analysis of stars as 'texts', as clusters of analysable signs, that informs much star analysis of the 1980s and 1990s. Dyer's semiotics is grounded in the notion that, at any one particular ideological moment, a star signifies a wealth of meanings, or a 'polysemy'. For Dyer, however, this polysemy is not infinite. It is seen as fabricated through a process involving 'media texts', as limited in its range, and as bearing a certain structure in the way that meanings relate systematically to one another. In his own words, 'From the perspective of ideology, analyses of stars, as images existing in films and other media texts, stress their structured polysemy, that is, the finite multiplicity of meanings and affects they embody and the attempts so to structure them that some meanings and affects are foregrounded and others are masked or displaced' (Dyer 1979: 3). It is worth stressing that Dyer does not see the range of meanings attached to a star as being unbounded. Doubtless it would be possible, for example, to find an individual who believes that Kevin Costner is descended from a race of space aliens, but such an individual exists outside the realm of contemporary ideology. Textual analysis, therefore, concerns itself with articulating the range of possible meanings that may be read in a star's image at a particular ideological moment (even if it does not speak to the actual interpretation of specific stars by real viewers—as is attempted in ethnographic work such as Stacey's).

For semioticians, the star image is constructed through media texts. These texts consist of a variety of phenomena: performances in films, articles in print publications, posters in theatre foyers, and so on. They have been grouped by Dyer into four types:

1. promotion;
2. publicity;
3. film roles/characters;
4. criticism and commentary on those roles.

Dyer seeks to distinguish promotion and publicity, although he recognizes that these two often overlap. Promotional texts consist of materials designed by the star and/or his or her minions in the deliberate attempt to manufacture a favourable image of the star. A poster for *Niagara* (1953), for example, proclaims 'Marilyn Monroe and "Niagara" a raging torrent of emotion that even nature can't control!' (in Dyer 1979: 123)—with an illustration that blends an enormous version of Monroe's body with Niagara Falls itself. Obviously, Twentieth Century-Fox's promotional department is here emphasizing the animal, 'natural' sexuality of Monroe's image.

Publicity texts, in contrast, are those that are uncontrolled by the star. When print media published reports that Roseanne, while a teenager, had given up a child for adoption, the star made public efforts to suppress this information. Despite her efforts, the story was released to the public. When articles about the incident appeared they affected how Roseanne's mothering skills (a central component of the meanings attached to her image) were understood. Though there is little doubt that Roseanne did not plant this piece of publicity, there are many cases in which the line between publicity and promotion are blurred or erased—such as when IMP spread rumours of Florence Lawrence's death.

Roseanne's perceived poor mothering skills ('abandoning' her child, in the parlance of the tabloid press) relate to other media texts: specifically, her role as a mother in a popular television sitcom. Although it might seem initially that, in this case, one element of the star's 'textuality' is conflicting with another, these two components actually fit together quite well. For the type of mother that Roseanne portrays in *Roseanne* is a sharp, sarcastic one who often makes disparaging remarks to her children. On television her maternal sarcasm is vitiated by her overarching ability to solve any domestic crisis and eventually provide each child with the nurturing he or she requires. The publicity about her as a bad mother does not contradict her on-screen role, although it does heighten one anti-nurturing component of it. Roseanne, as with all true stars, possesses an image constructed from interlocking media texts. Or, in other words, her polysemy is generated by the intertextuality of numerous media texts.

Intertextuality is a key component to understanding stars. According to Dyer, stars are separated from non-star actors by their presence in more than one area of the general media textuality. If an actor is only known for his or her character—as with many soap opera actors—then he or she has no intertextuality and is not truly a star. A star must appear in numerous texts, which play off one another. Thus, one could say that a star is defined by his or her intertextuality, by the ability to correlate various media texts.

. The relationship of a star to the characters he or she plays is an interesting and complex one. Few viewers belive that the star actually is the character—even if they do bear the same name, as with Roseanne and her character Roseanne Conner—and yet characteristics of the character do align with characteristics of the star's image, and vice versa. Once a star is well established, the characters that he or she plays may fit the star image in one of three ways, according to Dyer (1979: 142–9):

1. selective use;
2. perfect fit;
3. problematic fit.

In the first instance, the character makes selective use of elements of a star's polysemy. During the 1940s, as Damico (1975) points out, Ingrid Bergman's polysemy contained seemingly contradictory sexual meanings. She was associated with a certain spiritual purity as well as a coarse sexuality. In her role as Joan of Arc (in *Joan of Arc*, 1948) her spirituality was 'selected' while her practically sordid earthiness was disregarded. Later, when her sexual liaison with Roberto Rossellini became public knowledge, other more sexually ambiguous elements of her polysemy were selected in roles such as Isabelle in Rossellini's *Viaggio in Italia* ('Voyage to Italy', Italy, 1953).

Dyer's perfect fit occurs when the character and the star's polysemy appear to be completely matched. It is almost as if the star has become the character. When Hugh Grant appeared in *Nine Months* (1995) he played Samuel Faulkner, an irresponsible playboy who was unable to commit to marriage. This fit closely with media texts describing his arrest with a prostitute just a few months previously. Indeed, in an odd juxtaposition of the fictional and the real, his police mug shot circulated in the media at the same time that previews

for *Nine Months* were featuring a fictional mug shot. The sexual indiscretions of Grant the star perfectly fit the character of Grant in the film. The fit between Grant and Faulkner was often commented upon in various media texts and led to anecdotes such as this one, appearing in *People Online* (24 July 1995): 'Grant [as Faulkner in *Nine Months*] is parked in his car with a sexy woman other than the woman with whom he shares his life. This hot number asks him if he would like to come up for coffee. He declines. "How about for sex, then?" she asks. At the screening I attended, an audience member yelled out, "I'll pay for it".' The implication that the *People* reporter is making is that viewers were finding humour in the blending of the behaviours and identities of the character and the star. Note also the use of Grant's, the actor's, name to refer to the *character's* conduct. Of course, it is common practice for popular magazines to refer to characters with the names of actors, but in this context *People*'s use of 'Grant' to refer to Faulkner further accentuates the perfect fit between star and character.

The problematic fit is the least common instance of character–star relations. In this case, the star is cast against his or her image. The role is the polar opposite of her or his image. One example is comedian Mary Tyler Moore's appearance in *Ordinary People* (1980). Her star image as a perky, upbeat, loving, and lovable woman had been firmly established through television roles in *The Dick Van Dyke Show* (1961–6) and *The Mary Tyler Moore Show* (1970–7), but in *Ordinary People* her character is a cold, remote mother of a troubled teenager. Very little of her star image was selected to construct that role. In Dyer's view, the problematic fit can have distinctive ideological significance as the star is called upon to reconcile social tensions. One could argue, for example, that the position of woman in the family was particularly unstable in 1980 in the United States after more than a decade of feminist activism, shifts in family economics that demanded more women working outside the home, and the landslide election of Ronald Reagan and the presumed endorsement of his conservative agenda. What better image to work through these tensions than a latter-day Mary Pickford, 'America's sweetheart' for the 1980s?

Dyer's use of semiotics contributes key elements to the study of stars, but it is not a systematic, global semiotics of the cinema. In fact, Dyer makes little use of the ground-breaking work of 1960s–1970s film semioticians such as Metz (1974a, b) and Heath (1981). Metz, Heath, and most conventional film semioticians have, in turn, been remarkably mute about the significance of the star. However, a few recent theorists associated with *Screen* and the British Film Institute have attempted to apply the rigour of semiotics to the study of stars. Thompson (1978) introduces the notion of the 'commutation test' to the study of performance. This concept is borrowed from early Barthes, and, although Thompson himself rejects commutation in a later article, we may still find it a useful method for contrasting stars' polysemies. In the commutation test, one alters one component of a text's signifiers and then examines what effect that change has on its signifieds. What if, for example, the character–performance signifiers created for the role of Scarlett O'Hara (*Gone with the Wind*, 1939) by Vivien Leigh had been generated by Bette Davis? Or what if Cary Grant, instead of Dustin Hoffmann, had played Ratso Rizzo (*Midnight Cowboy*, 1969)? The shift in meaning that these hypothetical recastings cause tells us something about the signifying power of those particular stars. This is particularly evident if the commutation test is grounded in actual recastings that can be compared and contrasted. A film and its remake provide such an opportunity. Although a remake frequently makes changes that are too broad for the commutation test, one can usually find individual scenes that are repeated verbatim and can be used to highlight the differences between two actors. For example, if you view the two versions of *Imitation of Life* (1934, 1959), you'll note sharp differences in the performance styles of Claudette Colbert and Lana Turner and you may draw conclusions about their star images based on those differences.

Another notable strain in the 1980s' *Screen*–BFI work is Barry King's (1985) 'cultural materialist' approach to performance and stardom. For King, the star text catalyses certain 'discursive resources' (meaning-generating phenomena) relevant to the cinema: 'the cultural economy of the human body as a sign, the economy of signification in film, and the economy of the labour market for actors' (King 1985: 27). Each of these 'economies' governs the production of meaning by star actors. King, significantly, does not limit himself to the discursive strategies of the film text, but also explores the influence of 'practical' matters (such as the availability of work for actors) upon the meanings associated with stardom.

Star studies: the current situation

Star studies is still in a rather embryonic state. It seems clear that the most productive approaches to stars are ones that will help us comprehend the economic significance, cultural meanings, and psychic pleasures associated with star images, but there is no one clear path to that goal. The ethnographic and ideological, semiotic, and psychoanalytic approaches to stars surveyed here are important attempts to rectify the decades of neglect that stardom has suffered. Until film studies comes to an understanding of the significance of stars and the star system it will have only a partial comprehension of the cinematic apparatus.

BIBLIOGRAPHY

Bordwell, David, Janet Staiger, and **Kristin Thompson** (1985), *The Classical Hollywood Cinema: Film Style and Mode of Production to 1960* (New York: Columbia University Press).

Britton, Andrew (1984/1991), *Katharine Hepburn: The Thirties and After* (Newcastle upon Tyne: Tyneside Cinema) excerpts in Gledhill (1991*b*).

*****Butler, Jeremy G.** (ed). (1991), *Star Texts: Image and Performance Film and Television* (Detroit: Wayne State University Press).

Damico, James (1975/1991), 'Ingrid from Lorraine to Stromboli: Analyzing the Public's Perception of a Film Star', *Journal of Popular Film*, 4/1: 3–19; repr. in Butler (1991).

deCordova, Richard (1990), *Picture Personalities: The Emergence of the Star System in America* (Urbana: University of Illinois Press).

de Lauretis, Teresa (1987), *Technologies of Gender: Essays on Theory, Film and Fiction* (Bloomington: Indiana University Press).

Doane, Mary Ann (1987), *The Desire to Desire: The Woman's Film of the 1940s* (Bloomington: Indiana University Press).

Dyer, Richard (1977–8/1991), 'Four Films of Lana Turner', *Movie*, 25: 30–52; repr. in Butler (1991).

*—— (1979), *Stars* (London: British Film Institute).

—— (1986), *Heavenly Bodies* (New York: St Martin's Press).

Eckert, Charles, (1974/1985/1991) 'Shirley Temple and the House of Rockefeller', *Jump Cut*, 2: 1, 17–20; repr. in Butler (1991), Gledhill (1991*b*); and Peter Steven (ed.), *Jump Cut: Hollywood, Politics and Counter Cinema* (Toronto: Between the Lines).

Gledhill, Christine (1991*a*), 'Signs of Melodrama', in Christine Gledhill (ed.), *Stardom: Industry of Desire* (London: Routledge).

*—— (ed.) (1991*b*), *Stardom: Industry of Desire* (London: Routledge).

Hansen, Miriam (1986/1991), 'Pleasure, Ambivalence, Identification: Valentino and Female Spectatorship', *Cinema Journal*, 25/4: 6–32; repr. in Butler (1991) and Gledhill (1991*b*).

Haskell, Molly (1974), *From Reverence to Rape: The Treatment of Women in the Movies* (Chicago: University of Chicago Press).

Heath, Stephen (1981), *Questions of Cinema* (Bloomington: Indiana University Press).

King, Barry (1985/1991), 'Articulating Stardom', *Screen*, 26/5: 27–50; repr. in Butler (1991) and Gledhill (1991*b*).

Kuleshov, Lev (1974), *Kuleshov on Film*, ed. and trans. Ronald Levaco (Berkeley: University of California Press).

Metz, Christian (1974*a*), *Film Language: A Semiotics of the Cinema*, trans. Michael Taylor (New York: Oxford University Press).

—— (1974*b*), *Language and Cinema*, trans. Donna Jean Umiker-Sebeok (The Hague: Mouton).

Mulvey, Laura (1975/1989), 'Visual Pleasure and Narrative Cinema', *Screen*, 16/3: 6–18; repr. in *Visual and Other Pleasures* (Bloomington: Indiana University Press).

Stacey, Jackie (1994), *Star Gazing: Hollywood Cinema and Female Spectatorship* (London: Routledge).

Staiger, Janet (1983/1991), 'Seeing Stars', *The Velvet Light Trap*, 20: 10–14; repr. in Gledhill (1991*b*).

Thompson, John O. (1978/1991) 'Screen Acting and the Commutation Test', *Screen*, 19/2: 55–69; repr. in Gledhill (1991*b*).

10 Hollywood film and society

Douglas Kellner

Film emerged as one of the first mass-produced cultural forms of the twentieth century. Based on new technologies of mechanical reproduction that made possible simulations of the real and the production of fantasy worlds, film provided a new mode of culture that changed patterns of leisure activity and played an important role in social life. From the beginning, film in the United States was a mode of commercial activity controlled by entertainment industries that attempted to attract audiences to its products. Film production was accordingly organized on an industrial model and manufactured a mass-produced output aimed at capturing a secure audience share and thus realizing a substantial profit. As a commercial enterprise, American film developed as an entertainment industry, rather than as an educational instrument or art form (Horkheimer and Adorno 1972).

Film soon became the most popular and influential form of media culture in the United States (Sklar 1975; Jowett 1976). Indeed, for the first half of the twentieth century—from 1896 to the 1950s—movies were a central focus of leisure activity and deeply influenced how people talked, looked, and acted, becoming a major force of enculturation. The number of theatres grew from about 10,000 store-front nickelodeons with daily attendance of 4 to 5 million in 1910 to around 28,000 movie theatres by 1928 (May 1983). In the 1920s the average audience was between 25 and 30 million customers a week, while by the 1930s from 85 to 110 million people paid to go to the movies each week (Dieterle 1941). Consequently, films were a central form of entertainment and an extremely popular leisure activity.

Moreover, films became a major force of socialization, providing role models and instruction in dress and fashion, in courtship and love, and in marriage and career. Early films were produced largely for working-class, immigrant, and urban audiences and it was believed films could help to 'Americanize' immigrants and teach film audiences how to be good Americans (Ewen and Ewen 1982). Whereas some films from the silent and early sound era presented poverty and social struggle from progressive perspectives sympathetic to the poor and oppressed, many films focused on the rich and celebrated wealth and power, serving as advertisements for the consumer society and the ruling élites. Cecil B. de Mille's comedies and dramas of modern marriage, for example, can be seen as marriage and fashion models, and the romantic films of the 1920s can be read as 'manuals of desire, wishes, dreams' for those wanting to assimilate themselves to mainstream America (Ewen and Ewen 1982: 102). Consequently, films played an important socializing role by mobilizing desires into certain models. In particular, films helped socialize immigrant and working-class cultures into the emerging forms of the consumer society, teaching them how to behave properly and consume with style and abandon.

However, although films for the most part reflected mainstream American values, they also represented modern and urban social values, and as a result conservatives often attacked the alleged 'immorality' and 'subversiveness' of Hollywood films (Jowett 1976). Romantic dramas were attacked by the Legion of Decency for promoting promiscuity, while crime dramas were frequently criticized for fostering juvenile delinquency and crime. Due to pressure from civic groups and the threat of government regulation, a set of censorship boards was established with the co-operation of the film industry which produced a Production Code that was adopted by the film industry by the mid-1930s. Explicit limits were set on the length of allowable kisses and prescribed that no open-mouth kisses could be shown. No nudity or explicit sexuality was allowed, such things as prostitution and drugs could not be portrayed, criminals had to be punished, and religion and the church could not be criticized (the code is reproduced and discussed in Jowett 1976). The Production Code held sway until the 1960s (although it was challenged in the 1950s) and set firm ideological and social parameters to Hollywood films.

But the crucial determinants of the ideological functions of Hollywood film had to do with control of film production by major studios and the production of films primarily for profit. Since films had to attract large audiences, they needed to resonate to audiences'

dreams, fears, and social concerns, and thus inevitably reflected social mores, conflicts, and ideologies. Consequently, some of the first critical analyses of Hollywood film argued that films reflected American society, providing mirror images of its dreams, fears, and mode of life.

Film and society

The writings of Siegfried Kracauer provided one of the first systematic studies of how films articulate social content and was to influence the study of Hollywood. His book *From Caligari to Hitler* (1947) argues that German inter-war films reveal a fear of emerging chaos and disposition to submit to social authority. For Kracauer, German films thus reflect and foster anti-democratic and passive attitudes of the sort that paved the way for Nazism. While his assumption that 'inner' psychological tendencies and conflicts are projected onto the screen opened up a fruitful area of socio-cultural analysis, he frequently ignored the role of mechanisms of representation, such as displacement, inversion, and condensation in the construction of cinematic images and narratives. He posits film society analogies ('Their silent resignation foreshadows the passivity of many people under totalitarian rule'; 1947: 218) that deny the autonomous and contradictory character and effects of film discourse and the multiple ways that audiences process cinematic material.

Against this view, one could argue that the language of film does not find its exact analogue in social events, nor does film discourse exist as a parallel mirror to actual events. Rather, films take the raw material of social history and of social discourses and process them into products which are themselves historical events and social forces. Films, therefore, can provide information about the 'psychology' of an era and its tensions, conflicts, fears, and fantasies, but they do so not as a simple representation or mirroring of an extra-cinematic social reality. Rather, films refract social discourses and content into specifically cinematic forms which engage audiences in an active process of constructing meaning.

Sociological and psychological studies of Hollywood film proliferated in the United States in the post-Second World War era and developed a wide range of critiques of myth, ideology, and meaning in the American cinema. Parker Tyler's studies *The Hollywood Hallucination* (1944) and *Myth and Magic of the*

Movies (1947) applied Freudian and myth–symbol criticism to show how Walt Disney cartoons, romantic melodramas, and other popular films provided insights into social psychology and context, while providing myths suitable for contemporary audiences. In *Movies: A Psychological Study* (1950), Martha Wolfenstein and Nathan Leites applied psychoanalytical methods to film, decoding fears, dreams, and aspirations beneath the surface of 1940s Hollywood movies, arguing that '[t]he common day dreams of a culture are in part the sources, in part the products of its popular myths, stories, plays and films' (1950: 13). In her sociological study *Hollywood: The Dream Factory* (1950), Hortense Powdermaker studied an industry that manufactured dreams and fantasies, while Robert Warshow (*The Immediate Experience*, 1970) related classical Hollywood genres like the western and the gangster film to the social history and ideological concerns of US society.

> **Films can provide information about the 'psychology' of an era and its tensions, conflicts, fears, and fantasies, but they do so not as a simple representation or mirroring of an extra-cinematic social reality.**

Building on these traditions, Barbara Deming demonstrated in *Running away from Myself* (1969) how 1940s Hollywood films provided insights into the social psychology and reality of the period. Deming argued that '[i]t is not as mirrors reflect us but, rather, as our dreams do that movies most truly reveal the times' (1969: 1). She claimed that 1940s Hollywood films provided a collective dream portrait of its era and proposed deciphering 'the dream that all of us have been buying at the box office, to cut through to the real nature of the identification we have experienced there' (1969: 5–6). Her work anticipates later, more sophisticated and university-based film criticism of the post-1960s era by showing how films both reproduce dominant ideologies and also contain proto-deconstructive elements that cut across the grain of the ideology that the films promote. She also undertook a sort of gender reading of Hollywood film that would eventually become a key part of Hollywood film criticism.

Another tradition of film scholarship and criticism in the United States attempted to situate films historically and to describe the interactions between film and society in more overtly political terms. This tradition includes Lewis Jacob's pioneering history of Hollywood film (1939), John Howard Lawson's theoretical and critical works (1953, 1964), Ian Jarvie's sociological inquiries into the relation between film and society (1970, 1978), David M. White and Richard Averson's studies of the relation between film, history, and social comment in film (1972), and the social histories written by Robert Sklar (1975), Garth Jowett (1976), Will Wright (1977), Peter Biskind (1983), and Thomas Schatz (1988). While this tradition has produced useful insights into the relationships between Hollywood film and US society in specific historical eras, it has also tended to neglect the ways in which specific films or genres work to construct meaning and the ways in which audiences themselves interact with film.

More theoretical approaches to Hollywood emerged in the 1960s, including the ideological analyses of *Cahiers du cinéma* and the extremely influential work associated with *Screen* which translated many key *Cahiers* and other works of French film theory (see Metz 1974; Heath 1981). The *Cahiers* group moved from seeing film as the product of creative auteurs, or authors, to focus on the ideological and political content of film and how it transcoded dominant ideologies (see Crofts on auteurism, Part 2, Chapter 7). At the same time, French film theory and *Screen* focused on the specific cinematic mechanisms which helped produce meaning.

During this same period of ferment in film studies during the 1960s and 1970s, the Birmingham Centre for Contemporary Cultural Studies was discovering that gender, race, and subculture were also an important element of analysing the relationships between culture, ideology, and society. Encouraged by feminism to recognize the centrality of gender, it was argued that the construction of dominant ideologies of masculinity and femininity were a central aspect of Hollywood film (Kuhn 1982; Kaplan 1983). Studies of the ways in which Hollywood films constructed race, ethnicity, and sexuality also became a key aspect of film studies, and various post-structuralist-influenced theories studied the role of film and media culture in the social construction of ideologies and identities (see White, Smelik, and Wiegman, Part 1, Chapters 13, 14, and 17).

As the theory wars of the past two decades have proliferated, a tremendous range of new theories have in turn been applied to film. Consequently, structuralism and post-structuralism, psychoanalysis, deconstruction, feminism, postmodernism, and a wealth of other theoretical approaches have generated an often bewildering diversity of approaches to theorizing film which join and add complexity to previous critical stances such as genre theory, auteur theory, and historical–sociological approaches. My own take on the cacophony of contemporary approaches to film is that it is not a question of either/or and that a variety of approaches can be deployed to engage the relations of film to society. Consequently, in the following section I will discuss the genre approach to analysing the intersection of film and society, while in the concluding section I will note the use of auteur criticism and socio-ideological approaches to explain developments in contemporary Hollywood film. These approaches can be combined, I would argue, with the newer theoretical approaches to provide fuller and richer thematizations of the relations of Hollywood film to US society. Thus, analysing the connections between film and society requires a multidimensional film criticism that situates its object within the context of the social milieu within which it is produced and received (Kellner 1995).

Hollywood genres

Although much of the best European art film can be interpreted as a result of the creative vision and talent of individual directors, Hollywood film from the beginning was deeply influenced by the dominant genres in its studio system. The Hollywood mode of cinematic production formed an integrated system whose major studios not only controlled film production, but also distribution. This ensured a guaranteed exhibition site for Hollywood product. The system first emerged in the teens, took its distinctive shape in the 1920s, reached maturity in the 1940s, and began to disintegrate in the 1950s owing to antitrust legislation which caused the studios to divest themselves of their distribution and exhibition channels, and also to competition from other media of entertainment such as television (see Balio 1976; Schatz 1981, 1988; Gomery, Part 2, Chapter 3).

Since the main Hollywood studios repeatedly reproduced the types of film that they thought were the most popular, Hollywood cinema became primarily a genre cinema in which popular formulas are repeated in

cycles of genres that in turn deal with central societal conflicts, problems, and concerns of its audiences (see Ryall, Part 2, Chapter 8). The western, for example, deals with conflicts between civilization and threats to civilization, whereas the gangster film deals with threats to law, order, and social stability within an already established urban society. Melodramas, social comedies, and musicals deal with conflicts and problems within domestic arenas like the family and romance, whereas war films and adventure genres generally deal with conflicts in the public sphere outside the private realm.

In order to resonate to audience fears, fantasies, and experiences, the Hollywood genres had to deal with the central conflicts and problems in US society, and had to offer soothing resolutions, assuring its audiences that all problems could be solved within existing institutions. Western films, for example, assured their audiences that 'civilization' could be maintained in the face of threats from criminals, outsiders, and villains of various sorts, and celebrated individualism, white male authority figures, and violence as a legitimate way of resolving conflicts. In the westerns' mythologized version of American history, it was glossed over that the 'villains' in many westerns were the land's original inhabitants who had their property stolen by the white settlers, presented as being forces of civilization. This in turn generated ideologies of racism and imperialism whereby the 'enemies' of civilization (Indians, Mexicans, villains) were portrayed negatively, thus legitimizing the 'settlement' of the west by (white-male-dominated) forces of 'civilization'. In addition, women were stereotyped as either whores or submissive representatives of the domestic order, thus reproducing patriarchal ideologies.

Gangster films appealed to people's fear of crime and fascination with criminals; the classical Hollywood gangster films inculcated the message that 'crime does not pay' and showed the police and legal system able to contain crime and to deal with criminals. But gangster films also explored cultural conflicts and contradictions central to American capitalism. Gangsters are, in fact, prototypical capitalists who will do anything to make a buck and thus are allegorical stand-ins for capitalist energy and will. Gangster films explore the tensions within American life between making money and morality, between self-interest and legality, and between private and public interests. The gangsters are fantasy characters who act out secret audience desires to get ahead no matter what, although it is still not clear if their

A celebration of maternal sacrifice? Barbara Stanwyck, *Stella Dallas* (1937)

repeated punishment (mandated by the Production Code) actually helped prevent crime through dramatizing what would happen if one broke the rules of the game and stepped outside the law, or promoted crime through making the gangsters—often played by popular figures like James Cagney or Humphrey Bogart—extremely dynamic, attractive, and vital figures.

Melodramas, social comedies, and musicals in turn legitimized male-dominated romance, marriage, family, and moral rectitude as the proper road to happiness and well-being. Musicals followed formulas of boy meets girl, boy loses girl, and boy gets girl to celebrate the desirability of male-dominated romance. Melodramas dramatized what would happen to wayward women or wilful men who failed to conform to dominant gender roles. They celebrated hard-working

mothers who sacrificed their own happiness for their children, thus projecting the proper role for women (as, for example, in *Imitation of Life* (1934/1959), *Stella Dallas* (1937), *Mildred Pierce* (1945), and others), and intimated that life's greatest happiness derived from marriage and family. And social comedies, too, celebrated marriage and family as the proper goals for men and women (Cavell 1982). Indeed, David Bordwell claims that in his random selection of 100 typical Hollywood movies, 95 made romance at least one important line of action while, in 85, heterosexual romantic love was the major focus (Bordwell *et al.* 1985: 16).

Hollywood genre films thus tended to promote the American dream and dominant American myths and ideologies. The Hollywood genres taught that money and success were important values; that heterosexual romance, marriage, and family were the proper social forms; that the state, police, and legal system were legitimate sources of power and authority; that violence was justified to destroy any threats to the system; and that American values and institutions were basically sound, benevolent, and beneficial to society as a whole. In this way, Hollywood film, supported by other forms of media culture, helped establish a certain hegemony or cultural dominance of existing institutions and values to the exclusion of others. As Raymond Williams has argued,

in any society, in any particular period, there is a central system of practices, meanings and values, which we can properly call dominant and effective . . . what I have in mind is the central, effective and dominant system of meanings and values, which are not merely abstract but which are organized and lived. That is why hegemony is not to be understood at the level of mere opinion or mere manipulation. It is a whole body of practices and expectations; our assignments of energy, our ordinary understanding of the nature of man and of his world. It is a set of meanings and values which as they are experienced as practices appear as reciprocally confirming. (Williams 1983: 8–9)

Hollywood film is thus implicitly 'political' in the way it tends to support dominant American values and institutions. The more explicitly political functions of Hollywood cinema generally emerge in times of social crisis.

During both world wars war films and other genres advocated patriotism and presented the 'enemy' in stereotypical terms. During the Cold War period Hollywood produced a genre cycle of anti-communist films that depicted the threat to democracy and the 'American way of life' by the 'communist conspiracy'. Whereas during the Second World War Russians were presented positively as US allies against fascism, from the late 1940s on through *Rambo* (1985) communists are generally presented as the incarnation of evil.

> **Genre films could be used to contest ideological norms as well as reproduce them, and to provide ideology critique as well as legitimization.**

Yet the Hollywood system was flexible enough to allow individual cinematic statements and social critique within the genre system. Hollywood films prized difference and variation within accepted boundaries

and left a limited range open for artistic expression and social commentary. As a result, it is not certain that the genre films always resolved the social contradictions portrayed or successfully served as ideological advertisements for existing social institutions, discourses, and practices. As previously noted, the crime dramas often made the criminal's transgressions of societal norms more appealing and attractive than their punishment, and likewise women's transgressions of bourgeois norms in the melodrama often put in question established patriarchal institutions. The western could also be used to portray the victims of the conquest of the frontier sympathetically and could be used to attack the crimes and barbarism of the 'civilizing' forces. Genre films could thus be used to contest ideological norms as well as reproduce them, and to provide ideology critique as well as legitimization.

Hollywood today and into the future

During the 1950s the studio system, which had produced genre cycles as the mode of production of Hollywood film, began to break up, and the genre system was challenged, opening the way to new types of film. The result was a very fertile period of production in the 1960s, with film becoming more varied, diverse, and socially critical than in previous eras. The rise of new directors like Stanley Kubrick, Arthur Penn, and Robert Altman who had distinctive artistic visions and styles seemed to give credence to the notion of a 'New Hollywood' and provided a boost to auteur criticism that focused on the cinematic style and form of key directors and films (see Kramer, Part 2, Chapter 6). However, a focus simply on the new freedoms granted to 'auteurs' is too one-sided; one also needs insight into the complex interaction of film, the production system, and more general social discourses and social struggles (Kellner and Ryan 1988).

It was widely perceived in the 1960s, for example, that youth constituted a major audience for Hollywood film and so more youth-oriented films and directors emerged, creating new cycles of films which cinematically inscribed the discourses of the New Left student movements, as well as the feminist, black-power, sexual liberationist, and counter-cultural movements, producing a new type of socially critical Hollywood film. These films transcoded (i.e. translated) representations, discourses, and myths of 1960s culture into specifically cinematic terms, as when *Easy Rider* (1969) transcodes the images, practices, and discourses of the 1960s counterculture into a cinematic text. Popular films intervened in the political struggles of the day, as when 1960s films advanced the agenda of the New Left and the counter-culture. Films of the 'New Hollywood' (such as *Bonnie and Clyde*, 1967, *Medium Cool*, 1969, and *Easy Rider*, 1969), however, were contested by a resurgence of right-wing films during the same era (e.g. *Dirty Harry*, 1971, *The French Connection*, 1971, and John Wayne films), leading many to conclude that Hollywood film, like US society, should be seen as a contested terrain and that films could be interpreted as a struggle of representation over how to construct a social world and everyday life.

In 1970s films, intense battles between liberals and conservatives were evident throughout the decade in Hollywood film, with more radical voices—of the sort that occasionally were heard in the late 1960s and early 1970s—becoming increasingly marginalized. As the 1970s progressed, conservative films became more popular (e.g. *Rocky*, 1976, *Star Wars*, 1977, *Close Encounters of the Third Kind*, 1977, *Superman*, 1978, and so on), indicating that conservative sentiments were growing in the public and that Hollywood was nurturing these political currents. This was linked to the growth of the 'blockbuster' syndrome begun by *Jaws* in 1975. Henceforth, 'high-concept' films that could be clearly described and marketed became a major focus of the Hollywood film industry, which sought blockbuster hits that would turn over a high profit (Wyatt 1994).

> **Hollywood film, like US society, should be seen as a contested terrain and films could be interpreted as a struggle of representation over how to construct a social world and everyday life.**

Indeed, during the 1970s even liberal films ultimately helped advance the conservative cause. A cycle of liberal political conspiracy films (e.g. *The Parallax View*, 1974, *All the President's Men*, 1976, *The Domino Principle*, 1977, *Winter Kills*, 1979, and so on) vilified the state and thus played into the hands of the conservative Reaganite argument that government was the source of much existing evil. And even the most socially critical films (such as the Jane Fonda films, *Network*, 1976, and other Sidney Lumet films) posited

individual solutions to social problems, thus reinforcing the conservative appeal to individualism and the attack on statism. Consequently, reading Hollywood films of the decade politically allowed one to anticipate the coming of Reagan and the New Right to power by demonstrating that conservative yearnings were ever more popular within the culture and that film and popular culture were helping to form an ideological matrix more hospitable to Reagan and conservatives than to embattled liberals (Kellner and Ryan 1988).

However, it is also worth noting that even seemingly conservative film genres such as the horror film, or seemingly anti-gay films like *Cruising* (1980), could contain critical moments, problematicizing hegemonic ideologies and putting in question dominant ideologies like the family (Wood 1986). Robin Wood argues that the 'incoherent text' is a dominant cinematic mode of the 1970s, full of ideological contradictions and conflicts that reproduce existing social confusion and turmoil. Thus, film, like society, was very much a contested terrain, with the future of society and culture up for grabs.

With the election of Reagan in 1980, the conservative wave of films continued throughout the decade, with the blockbuster syndrome remaining the predominant trend. Gender struggles were particularly intense with a return to the 'hard-body' masculine hero of an earlier era, replacing the more feminized male heroes of the late 1960s and early 1970s (Jeffords 1994). As part of the backlash against feminism, there was also a cycle of films that villainized independent women, showing single career women without families being driven into pathological behaviour. (*Fatal Attraction*, 1987, *Basic Instinct*, 1992, *The Hand that Rocks the Cradle*, 1992, and so on). On the other hand, conservative ideologies were contested by liberal and radical films like *Missing* (1982), *Reds* (1981), *Salvador* (1986), *Platoon* (1986), and other Oliver Stone films, as well as a wealth of films by independent filmmakers like John Sayles and Spike Lee. A cycle of gay and lesbian films expanded the representations of sexuality, and many films began to provide more complex, varied, and progressive representations of gender and ethnicity.

At the same time, a proliferation of new critical strategies emerged, including the multicultural approach of cultural studies. There was an especially intense focus on audience research, on how audiences produced meanings, on how films mobilized pleasure and influenced audiences, and on how audiences decoded and used the materials of media culture. Consequently, a wide range of positions appeared on the relationship between film, media culture, and its audiences (see the discussion in Staiger, 1991).

During the past decade globalization has made Hollywood film an ever more familiar and popular artefact throughout the world. Whereas Hollywood films have dominated the world market for decades, it is even more the case today with American global corporations playing an important role in distributing its products throughout the world. To some extent globalization equals Americanization, and Hollywood film is an effective arm of media culture to sell the 'American way of life' (see Cvetovich and Kellner 1997). However, the relationships between Hollywood film, US society, and the entire world are complex and require a multiperspectival approach that dissects the political economy of the film industry and the production of film; provides critical and analytical readings of cinematic texts; and studies how audiences appropriate and use film and other cultural artefacts (see Miller, Part 2, Chapter 12).

Finally, we are currently undergoing one of the most dramatic technological revolutions of all time with new entertainment and information technologies emerging, accompanied by unprecedented mergers of the entertainment and information industries (Wasko 1994). These new syntheses are producing novel forms of visual and multi-media culture in which it is anticipated that film will appear in seductive new virtual and interactive forms, accessible through computer, satellite, and other new technologies. There is feverish speculation that the Internet and its assorted technologies will create a new entertainment and information environment, and currently the major corporations and players are envisaging what sort of product and delivery system will be most viable and profitable for films and other entertainment of the future. Thus, one imagines that the relationships between film and society will continue to be highly significant as we approach a new century and perhaps a new era that will supply novel forms of film and new perspectives on the film culture of the past.

BIBLIOGRAPHY

Balio, Tino (ed.) (1976), *The American Film Industry* (Madison: University of Wisconsin Press).

Biskind, Peter (1983), *Seeing is Believing: How Hollywood Movies Taught us to Stop Worrying and Love the 50s* (New York: Pantheon).

Bordwell, David, Janet Staiger, and **Kristin Thompson** (1985), *The Classical Hollywood Cinema* (New York: Columbia University Press).

Cavell, Stanley (1982), *Pursuits of Happiness* (Cambridge, Mass.: Harvard University Press).

Cvetovich, Ann, and **Douglas Kellner** (1997), *Articulating the Global and the Local: Globalization and Cultural Studies* (Boulder, Colo.: Westview).

Deming, Barbara (1969), *Running away from Myself* (New York: Grossman).

Dieterle, William (1941), 'Hollywood and the European Crisis', *Studies in Philosophy and Social Science*, 9: 96–103.

Ewen, Stuart, and **Elizabeth Ewen** (1982), *Channels of Desire* (New York: McGraw-Hill).

Heath, Stephen (1981), *Questions of Cinema* (Bloomington: Indiana University Press).

Horkheimer, Max, and **T. W. Adorno** (1972), *Dialectic of Enlightenment* (New York: Seabury).

Jacobs, Lewis (1939), *The Rise of the American Film* (New York: Harcourt, Brace).

Jarvie, I. C. (1970), *Toward a Sociology of the Cinema* (London: Routledge & Kegan Paul).

—— (1978), *Movies as Social Criticism* (Metuchen, N.J: Scarecrow Press).

Jeffords, Susan (1994), *Hard Bodies* (New Brunswick, NJ: Rutgers University Press).

Jowett, Garth (1976), *Film: The Democratic Art* (New York: William Morrow).

Kaplan, E. Ann (1983), *Women and Film* (New York: Methuen).

Kellner, Douglas (1995), *Media Culture* (New York: Routledge).

*—— and **Michael Ryan** (1988), *Camera Politica: The Politics and Ideology of Hollywood Film* (Bloomington: University of Indian Press).

Kracauer, Siegfried (1974), *From Caligari to Hitler* (Princeton: Princeton University Press).

Kuhn, Annette (1982), *Women's Pictures* (London: Routledge & Kegan Paul).

Lawson, John Howard (1953), *Film in the Battle of Ideas* (New York: Mainstream).

—— (1964), *Film: The Creative Process* (New York: Hill & Wang).

May, Lary (1983), *Screening out the Past* (Chicago: University of Chicago Press).

Metz, Christian (1974), *Language and Cinema* (The Hague: Mouton).

Powdermaker, Hortense (1950), *Hollywood: The Dream Factory* (Boston: Little, Brown).

Schatz, Thomas (1981), *Hollywood Genres* (Philadelphia: Temple University Press).

Schatz, Thomas (1988), *The Genius of the System* (New York: Pantheon).

Sklar, Robert (1975), *Movie-Made America: A Social History of American Film* (New York: Random House).

Staiger, Janet (1991), *Interpreting Films: Studies in the Historical Reception of American Cinema* (Princeton: Princeton University Press).

Tyler, Parker (1944), *The Hollywood Hallucination* (New York: Simon & Schuster).

—— (1947), *Myth and Magic of the Movies* (New York: Simon & Schuster).

Warshow, Robert (1970), *The Immediate Experience* (New York: Atheneum).

Wasko, Janet (1994), *Hollywood in the Information Age* (Austin: University of Texas Press).

White, David M., and Richard Averson (1972), *The Celluloid Weapon: Social Comment in the American Film* (Boston: Beacon Press).

Williams, Raymond (1973), 'Base and Superstructure in Marxist Cultural Theory', *New Left Review*, 82: 6–33.

Wolfenstein, Martha, and Nathan Leites (1950), *Movies: A Psychological Study* (Glencoe, Ill.: Free Press).

Wood, Robin (1986), *Hollywood from Vietnam to Reagan* (New York: Columbia University Press).

*Wright, Will (1977), *Six-Guns and Society: A Structural Study of the Western* (Berkeley: University of California Press).

Wyatt, Justin (1994), *High Concept: Movies and Marketing in Hollywood* (Austin: University of Texas Press).

Hollywood and ideology

Robert B. Ray from Robert B. Ray, *A Certain Tendency of the Hollywood Cinema, 1930–1980* (Princeton: Princeton University Press, 1985).

My work initially proceeded from a naïve reflection theory that sought to explain the evolution of the popular American cinema in terms of the movies' response to changing historical conditions. Eventually I realized that the movies not only reflected but also excluded the world, and that I needed an approach that would account for both a reflection more complicated than I had originally granted and an exclusion more systematic than I had reckoned on. In short, I needed theories of overdetermination and transformation. I found them in three schools of thought that have converged in recent film scholarship: Marxism (especially Althusser's discussions of ideology); myth study (especially Lévi-Strauss's notion that myths are transformations of basic dilemmas or contradictions that in reality cannot be solved); and psychoanalysis (especially Freud's dream work and its notions of condensation and displacement).

Each of these schools entails a particular assumption about film. For Marxism, movies are ideological formations, screened and shaped by political censorship. For myth study, movies are myths whose individual shapes arise from the 'rules of transformation'. For psychoanalysis, movies are dreams, screened and reshaped by a culture's collective psychic censorship.

The merger of these three methodologies (especially in *Screen* and the *Cahiers du cinéma*) derives from their two basic similarities: all three are theories of both overdeterminism and transformation. Althusserian Marxism proposes that any phenomenon at any level of society results from multiple determinations (economic, cultural, political, personal, traditional, aesthetic). Lévi Strauss suggests that each version of a myth results from those multiple determinations that have shaped the rules of transformation—that flexibility which enables a single cultural anxiety to assume different shapes in response to an audience's changing needs. Freud refers to dream images as condensations and displacements resulting from multiple dream thoughts.

All three methodologies attempt to define the rules of transformation or censorship, the system that enables a message to cross a boundary and enter another domain. Thus, analysis in all three cases becomes an attempt to trace the path of that message back to its previous site. Marxism wants to discover the 'cause' of a culture's particular way of representing material conditions (i.e. its ideology)—in the case of Hollywood movies, for example, the material origins of melodrama. Lévi-Strauss asks why a body of myths has appeal for a given culture: what dilemma does it attempt to solve? Freud wants to locate the repressed anxiety or wish behind the overdetermined dream images. Thus, according to these theories, *Casablanca* (1942), for example, becomes, as ideology, a representation of an unsolvable dilemma—the conflicting appeals of intervention and isolationism; as myth, an attempt to resolve that dilemma; as dream, a displaced condensation of the anxiety generated by that contradiction.

Since the beginning, however, film theory's particular preference for the psychoanalytic accounting (the movie-as-dream) has resulted in an impasse. Certainly, Freud's condensation and displacement (and his insistence on the dream's need for concrete representation) offered rules by which latent dream thoughts (wishes, anxieties) get transformed into dream images. But the associative chains by which Freud retraced these images to their unconscious sources were utterly private, available only to the particular dreamer (and, after enormous effort, to Freud himself). Dream images, in other words, are at best *subjective* correlatives whose import typically remains hidden from even the dreamer.

To the extent that movies do work like dreams, Hollywood's challenge lay in developing rules of condensation and displacement that would work for the audience as a whole, or, to put it another way, that would provide immediately (albeit unconsciously) recognizable objective (?) correlatives for the common wishes and fears of the mass audience. Hollywood's enormous commercial success proves that it met this challenge. It did so by becoming intuitively Lévi-Straussian: the American film industry discovered and used the existing body of mythic oppositions provided it by the local culture. In effect, the great Hollywood tsars became naïve, prodigious anthropologists.

The determinedly commercial nature of the American movie business, however, and its financial servitude to the politically powerful eastern banks, insured that Hollywood's elaborations of American mythology would not proceed according to the mathematically indifferent rules of transformation posited by Lévi-Strauss, but rather according to the ideologically censoring standards posited by Marx in a famous passage:

The ideas of the ruling class are in every epoch the ruling ideas, i.e. the class which is the ruling *material* force of society, is at the same time its ruling *intellectual* force. The class which has the means of material production at its disposal has control at the

Hollywood and ideology continued

same time over the means of mental production, so that thereby, generally speaking, the ideas of those who lack the means of mental production are subject to it.

Thus, each variation of what I will call the thematic paradigm (in westerns, musicals, gangster movies, etc.) could pose issues only in terms allowed by the prevailing ideology—or could refuse to acknowledge that ideological disposition only at its own commercial risk. *Casablanca*, as I will argue, could deal with the intervention–isolationism opposition only by displacing it into the ideologically favoured realm of melodrama, where (since such displacements were traditional to American culture) ample mythic types, images, and stories were available.

Have dissident variations (thematic or stylistic) *any* chance of disrupting or subverting a movie's intended ideological effect? This question seems to me the most interesting thing we can ask about the American cinema. Unfortunately, we still have to ask it on a case-by-case basis. I have not been able to develop a general theory that would account in the

abstract for a dissident thematic variation's ability to outfight the context that seeks to subdue it. I do not want to fall back on a lame imitation of Potter Stewart's famous 'I-know-it-when-I-see-it' definition of obscenity, but for the present, I can only suggest the value of a thesis proposed by Charles Eckert in an article that deserves to be far more famous than it is: writing about *Marked Woman* (1937), Eckert argues that truly effective challenges to Hollywood's prevailing ideology surface in those moments within a movie when the emotional quotient is simply excessive in terms of the narrative's needs—emotion, in other words, that remains inadequately motivated.

Significantly, some of the most abidingly interesting American movies display precisely these moments of excess. These same films have proved among the most popular ever made in this country, a fact suggesting that the mass audience in this country likes to live dangerously, likes to see the most privileged elements of its ideology sorely challenged, if not defeated.

11

Film policy: Hollywood and beyond

Albert Moran

Policy is a series of practices engaged in by an agency—whether government, private, or commercial—to achieve a particular set of outcomes. But although commercial agencies may engage in various market strategies such as restricted competition with rivals and price-fixing, they do not have the legislative force that the state can confer on its policy measures. The study of policy must therefore inevitably focus on the role of state apparatuses, even if it also attends to the capacity of private capitalist interests to influence the state in the establishment and maintenance of these mechanisms. The agencies, whether state or private, will follow different policy strategies, such as legislation, regulation, and financial assistance, as well as more general commercial strategies. Their goals may be short-term and specific as well as more long-term and general, and policy also may be at lower or higher level—a single measure or tactic, or an inter-linked group of strategies that merit the name 'policy'. Policy always exists in a complex field affected by factors such as constitutional and legislative arrangements, general economic conditions, the prevailing culture, social awareness, and technological capacities, as well as such human agencies as politicians, business entrepreneurs, white- and blue-collar labour, bureaucrats, and cultural and social workers. International forces have also become increasingly important. Given this variety of elements and players, policy may fall short of realizing its announced objectives, gener-ating other, less anticipated results, and consequently requiring adjustment or major overhaul.

Film policy consists of measures that apply not only to the feature film exhibited in the hard-top cinema but also to several other forms of audiovisual product including television and video. It also applies across a series of areas and institutions including production, distribution, and exhibition, film education, film as visual art, and censorship. Film policy study may involve the investigation of any one or more of these areas. It may be prompted by an immediate practical need to analyse the effectiveness of existing policies, or it may be more removed from the various objects of its investigation and more concerned with gaining broader understanding of the historical and social context that produced particular policies. And film policy study will be undertaken by a range of practitioners, from those sharing pragmatic interests in immediate practical results, such as government officials and private consultants, to more dispassionate analysts, such as critical researchers and historians. Equally, the two groups can overlap.

These background remarks are necessary, not least because many areas of film study can legitimately be regarded as studies of film policy that are frequently denied that kind of recognition. For example, although there are individual entries under topics such as censorship and national cinemas in Richard MacCann and Edward Perry's *New Critical Film Index*, a summational bibliographical source for film scholarship and research published in 1972, there is no entry under the term 'film policy study'. Similarly, many actual studies of film policy pass without name in scholarly accounts of national cinema developments; for example, in the inaugural study of cinema in Ireland by Kevin Rockett, Luke Gibbons, and John Hill (1988), part 1 of the book, entitled 'History, Politics and Irish Cinema', by Rockett, traces the development of film production in Ireland and is in fact a sustained interrogation of the course of the film policies of the Irish state. In other words, although film policy is everywhere studied in its detail and in its operations, as well as in a broader, more historical context, and as such could be said to constitute a sizeable literature, the paradox remains that the field is little recognized. Given this, the aim here is to indicate rather than provide an exhaustive survey of the range of studies in the area of film scholarship that can be bracketed under the term 'policy'.

> **Although film policy is everywhere studied in its detail and in its operations, as well as in a broader, more historical context, and as such could be said to constitute a sizeable literature, the paradox remains that the field is little recognized.**

A good point of departure is the American cinema, for although it appears that Hollywood exists only as a private institution outside the apparatus of the state, this has not, in fact, been the case. The American cinema does not exist in a vacuum, either at the level of international relations or inside the United States itself. National cinemas throughout the rest of the world have long existed in the economic and cultural shadow cast by the American cinema, and state policies in relation to film implicitly address the American cinema as the 'other' of a national cinema. Nor has the American cinema existed autonomously within the United States. Although in private hands, Hollywood has been profoundly affected by legislation and regulation by municipal, state, and federal governments, by the activities of government departments and agencies, and by more general factors to do with the Constitution, labour relations, and moral legislation.

American cinema has also had to adopt policies in relation to other arenas, such as religion and politics, and these relationships, too, have attracted the attention of scholars. Given such an array of film policy areas, some of the more notable studies can be mentioned.

> **Although in private hands, Hollywood has been profoundly affected by legislation and regulation by municipal, state, and federal governments, by the activities of government departments and agencies, and by more general factors to do with the Constitution, labour relations, and moral legislation.**

US film policies

The Hollywood film companies established several mechanisms to control the film industry both in terms of its internal operations, such as controlling the costs of production, as well as in its external relationships with other American institutions. One key instrument was the establishment in 1922 of the Hays Office, which brought an important measure of self-regulation to the industry and which has been analysed both in an early study by Louis Nizer (1935) and more extensively by Raymond Moley (1945). Two other of the industry's own instruments for conferring general prestige on itself, as well as increasing the box-office appeal of individual films, are the Academy of Motion Picture Arts and Science, established in 1927, and, especially, the Oscar awards, whose development has been analysed by Emanuel Levy (1987). But these visible instruments are only the most external evidence of the oligopolistic nature of the motion picture industry. As antitrust action was initiated by the US Justice Department in the 1930s and 1940s, a series of studies analysed in detail the vertically integrated nature of the film industry and the practices pursued by the major studios in dominating it (Cassady 1956; Bertrand et al. 1941; Temporary National Economic Committee 1941; Huettig 1944).

If these studies are primarily concerned with distribution, the business policies of the industry in relation to film audiences have been given more attention elsewhere. Frank Ricketson's (1938) study of the management of film exhibition was an important codification of practices that obtained in film theatres across the country, and more recently the film historian Douglas Gomery (1975, 1978, 1979, 1981) has researched the history of changing exhibition policies and practices in the film industry. This research links with Gomery's earlier analysis (1975) of the coming of sound to the American film industry, a study that emphasized both the deliberate policy of technological innovation pursued by one of the major companies as well as the new policies relating to both production and exhibition that had to be adopted in the face of the innovation of sound. The coming of sound technology was one of the few occasions when oligopolistic arrangements among the film companies were broken. By the early 1930s this control was widely recognized, especially in government circles, and led to antitrust action. Scholars such as Michael Conant (1960), David Daly (1980), Gomery (1981), and, more recently, Asu Aksoy and Kevin Robins (1992) have investigated the distribution and exhibition policies adopted by the dominant groups following the success of this action.

Censorship is another aspect of film policy, and this too has been subjected to extensive analysis. Two important such studies by Ira Carmen and Richard Randall appeared in 1968 and both emphasized that censorship of film exhibition in the United States had been instigated by municipal and city authorities, with prohibitions and regulations being directed initially at exhibition venues and only later at movie content. However, the findings of these studies only echoed earlier work on film censorship such as that of Donald Young (1922). But, as is well known, the major film companies during the studio era also exercised their own form of censorship of film content in the form of a production code, and part of Moley's (1945) study of the Hays Office follows how the companies came to develop this production policy in the face of attack from moral pressure groups such as the Catholic church and as a safeguard against possible intervention in the film industry by the American government. However, if the company owners and executives were willing to accept the Hays Code, those further down the production line, such as producers, writers, and directors, often had a good deal of difficulty in producing films that would secure the seal of approval of the Office. Murray Schumach (1964) has collected a series of often hilarious case-studies of particular productions and the often complex and arcane accommodations

made to ensure films conformed to the letter of the law as far as this instrument of self-regulation was concerned.

In their internal relationships with their own production workers, the motion picture companies were perennially opposed to workers' rights, especially the right to unionize, and many bitter struggles ensued. The labour relations policies of the companies have been traced in detail in several studies, especially Ross (1945), Lovell and Carter (1955), and Jeter (1979). One particular aspect of the union relations between the motion picture companies and both their blue- and white-collar workers had to do with the policy of the blacklist that operated against suspected communists in the 1950s. This was a combined policy of the major and minor companies, another instance of joint action by groups that were in ostensible competition in the market-place. The standard study of this policy is Cogley (1956), but there have been several others, including a more full-length, historically informed book by the film star Robert Vaughan that began life as a Ph.D. dissertation (Vaughan 1972).

Finally we might briefly note some studies of various measures undertaken by the industry in relation to three particular institutions of American society: the Catholic church, the banking sector, and the federal courts. Moley's (1945) study of the pressures for censorship exerted by the Catholic church especially in the 1920s and 1930s and Martin Quigley's (1937) monograph demonstrate how one particular pressure group could marshal a case for censorship and articulate what it saw as appropriate policies by the industry. In turn, Paul Facey (1974) helps put Quigley's polemic in context. Secondly, although there had been much earlier work on the financing of the motion picture, both Edward Buscombe's (1975) study of Columbia's film production financing and, especially, Janet Wasko's (1982) analysis of Hollywood's relationship with American banks have introduced an important new area for consideration under the broad topic of film policy. Finally, the federal courts have been an important arena in which the US state has been involved in setting various aspects of film policy in place, and a full study of this subject would fill many volumes. Two crucial areas in which the courts reached important legal decisions for the industry can be mentioned. The first was a series of decisions concerning patents and copyright in the very early years of the twentieth century, decisions that were crucial to enabling the early cinema to be reorganized as a modern industry (Allen 1980; Bordwell *et al.*

1985). The second set of decisions which were equally profound in their effect were the antitrust actions and court decisions which ultimately resulted in the abandonment of involvement in production and exhibition by the film companies (Donovan and McAllister 1933; Conant 1960).

International film policies

If we turn to nation-states outside the United States, we are struck by the fact that, with the possible exception of national cinemas in India and China, by 1939 all other national cinemas had become directly dependent on state funding. This has led to a large body of studies of film policy in specific national settings.

In the case of Canada, America's closest neighbour, the study of film policy has assumed particular importance. The Canadian state has long been involved in the production and distribution of film through different film policy apparatuses—the Government Motion Picture Bureau, the National Film Board, the Canadian Film Development Corporation, and Telefilm Canada—and there is an impressive body of scholarship on the course of Canadian film policy. Studies by C. W. Gray (1973), Charles Backhouse (1973), David Jones (1980), Gary Evans (1984), and Peter Morris (1986, 1987) have done much to clarify not only the different policies concerning the production and circulation of documentary film but also the wider political and social context of these measures. Historical studies of Canadian cinema written in the past quarter-century, such as those by Pierre Berton (1975), Morris (1978), Manjunath Pendakur (1990), and Ted Magder (1993), have stressed the degree to which Canadian film policy has been contained within parameters set by the American film industry. The nationalist strain usually evident in these accounts of film policy has also been present in general collections on Canadian cinema such as those by Seth Feldman and Joyce Nelson (1977), Pierre Vronneau and Piers Handling (1980), Feldman (1984), Gene Walz (1986), and Douglas Fetherling (1988). Film policy has also been considered in the more general context of what has been called the Canadian culture industries by Susan Crean (1976), Dallas Smythe (1981), Paul Audley (1983), and Michael Dorland (1996). However, recent studies by Magder and Dorland have indicated a significant break with these nationalist accounts with analyses that are sensitive to recent debates in cultural studies and theories of state policy and power.

Of course, the operation, and therefore the study, of state film policy is by no means restricted to any one particular nation-state and further studies and bibliographies can be found in my collection of analyses of film policy (Moran 1996), which contains both national studies and studies of film policy at the regional and the international levels.

Although research on the international dimension of particular national film policies began as early as 1937 with the study by Donald Klingender and Stuart Legg of the economic impact of American film on the British market, itself a parallel to studies by the US Department of Commerce of the international market (Golden 1939), it was not until the end of the Second World War that research began on the international film industry (Bächlin 1945). However, Bächlin's pioneering study was available only in French and German. Another quarter-century passed before there was any English-language study of the international context of national film policies; Thomas Guback's (1969) analysis of the American film industry in Western Europe was the first. Adopting a comparative methodology, Guback analysed film policies instituted by national governments in Britain, France, Germany, and Italy in relation to policies pursued by the American film industry and the US State Department. The research started life as a thesis under the supervision of Dallas Smythe, the 'father' of political economy approaches to mass communications (Wasko et al. 1993). It was part of a wave that examined such areas as the overseas reach of American television and the cultural import of Disney comics and which used the concept of the 'national' in an unproblematic way in discussing the cultural and economic impact of US film and television programmes on national audiovisual systems. Guback's study was a major work of film policy research, whose continuing value lies in the detail and clarity of its analysis.

In 1985 Guback's work was joined by a complementary study by Kristin Thompson which analysed the policies pursued by the American film industry in the period from the turn of the century up to the mid-1930s that enabled it to dominate the international film business. One other major study in this tradition, by Armand Mattelart, Xavier Delacourt, and Michèle Mattelart, was published in France in 1983 and appeared in English in 1984. *International Image Markets* grew out of the report of a French government mission to explore the feasibility of a 'Latin audiovisual space' that would include several European and South

American countries. Like Guback's, the study is of most interest and continuing value in the details it produces about the international film and television industries in the 1980s. Conversely, it is at its weakest in its assumptions about the homogeneity of an audiovisual space, the latter being a modern label for 'national cinema' or 'national television' (Schlesinger 1987).

Summary

Film policy studies has a long lineage and features detailed scholarship and often passionate argument and advocacy. Although a cinema characterized by private ownership, Hollywood has long been aware of the domestic and international politics that underline its existence. National studies of film policy that focused on the key role played by Hollywood began in the 1930s while more dialectical studies of Hollywood and national cinemas date from the 1960s. Many of these studies are animated by cultural imperialist theory, although very recent accounts indicate new approaches based on notions of cultural pluralism rather than cultural nationalism.

BIBLIOGRAPHY

Aksoy, A., and **K. Robins** (1992), 'Hollywood for the Twenty-First Century: Global Competition for Critical Mass in Image Markets', *Cambridge Journal of Economics*, 16/1: 1 22.

Allen, Jeanne Thomas (1979), 'Copyright and Early Theatre: Vaudeville and Film Competition', *Journal of the University Film Association*, 31 (Spring), 5–11.

—— (1980), 'The Industrial Context of Film Technology: Standardisation and Patents', in Teresa de Laurentis and Stephen Heath (eds.), *The Cinematic Apparatus* (London: Macmillan).

Audley, Paul (1983), *Canada's Cultural Industries: Broadcasting, Publishing, Records and Film* (Toronto: James Lorimer).

Bächlin, P. (1945), *Der Film als Ware* (Basel: Burg).

Backhouse, Charles (1973), *Canadian Government Motion Picture Bureau 1917–1940* (Ottawa: Canadian Film Institute).

Berton, Pierre (1975), *Hollywood's Canada: The Americanization of our National Image* (Toronto: McClelland & Stewart).

Bertrand, Daniel, W. Duane Evans, and **E. L. Blanchard** (1941), *Investigation of Concentration of Economic Power*, study for Temporary National Economic Committee.

Bordwell, David, Janet Staiger, and **Kirstin Thompson** (1985), *The Classical Hollywood Cinema: Film Style and Mode of Production to 1960* (New York: Columbia University Press).

Buscombe, Edward (1975), 'Notes on Columbia Pictures Corporation 1926–1941', *Screen*, 16/3 (Autumn), 65–82.

Carmen, Ira H. (1968), *Movies, Censorship and the Law* (Ann Arbor: University of Michigan Press).

Cassady, Ralph, Jr. (1956), 'Impact of the Paramount Decision on Motion Picture Distribution and Price Making', *Southern California Law Review*, 32/4 (Summer), 325–90.

Cogley, John (1956), *Report on Blacklisting*, i: *Movies* (Santa Barbara, Calif.: Fund for the Republic).

Conant, Michael (1960), *Anti-Trust in the Motion Picture Industry* (Berkeley: University of California Press).

Crean, Susan (1976), *Who's Afraid of Canadian Culture?* (Toronto: General Publishing).

Daly, David A. (1980), *A Comparison of Exhibition and Distribution Patterns in Three Recent Feature Motion Pictures* (New York: Arno Press).

Donovan, William, and **Breck P. McAllister** (1933), 'Consent Decrees in the Enforcement of Federal Anti-Trust Laws: The Moving Picture Industry', *Harvard Law Review*, 46 (Apr.), 929–31.

Dorland, Michael (ed.) (1996), *The Culture Industries in Canada* (Toronto: James Lorimer).

Evans, Gary (1984), *John Grierson and the National Film Board: The Politics of Wartime Propaganda* (Toronto: University of Toronto Press).

Facey, Paul W. (1974), *The Legion of Decency: A Sociological Analysis of the Emergence and Development of a Pressure Group* (New York: Arno Press).

Feldman, Seth (ed.) (1984), *Take Two: A Tribute to Film in Canada* (Toronto: Irwin).

—— and **Joyce Nelson** (eds.) (1977), *Canadian Film Reader* (Toronto: Peter Martin).

Fetherling, D. (ed.) (1988), *Documents in Canadian Film* (Toronto: Broadview Press).

Golden, Nathan (1939), *Review of Foreign Film Markets 1938* (Washington: US Dept. of Commerce).

Gomery, Douglas (1975), 'The Coming of Sound to the American Cinema: A History of the Transformation of an Industry', Ph.D. dissertation, University of Wisconsin.

—— (1978), 'The Picture Palace: Economic Sense or Hollywood Nonsense?', *Quarterly Review of Film Studies* 3/1 (Winter), 23–36.

—— (1979), 'The Movies Become Big Business: Public Theatres and the Chain Store Strategy', *Cinema Journal*, 18/2: 315–30.

—— (1981), 'The Economics of US Film Exhibition Policy and Practice', *Cinetracts*, 12 (Winter), 36–40.

Gray, C. W. (1973), *Movies for the People: The Story of the National Film Board of Canada's Unique Distribution System* (Montreal: National Film Board).

Guback, Thomas (1969), *The International Film Industry: Western Europe and America since 1945* (Bloomington: University of Indiana Press).

Huettig, Mae D. (1944), *Economic Control of the Motion Picture Industry* (Philadelphia: University of Pennsylvania Press).

Jeter, Ida (1979), 'The Collapse of the Federated Motion Picture Crafts: A Case Study of Class Collaboration', *Journal of the University Film Association*, 31 (Spring), 37–45.

Jones, David (1980), *Movies and Memoranda: An Interpretive History of the National Film Board of Canada* (Ottawa: Canadian Film Institute).

Klingender, D. F., and Stuart Legg (1937), *Money behind the Screen* (London: Lawrence & Wishart).

Levy, Emanuel (1987), *And the Winner Is: The History and Politics of the Oscar Awards* (New York: Unger).

Lovell, Hugh, and Tasile Carter (1955), *Collective Bargaining in the Motion Picture Industry: A Struggle for Stability* (Berkeley: University of California Institute of Industrial Relations).

MacCann, Richard, and Edward S. Perry (eds.) (1972), *The New Critical Film Index: A Bibliography of Articles in English 1930–1970* (New York: Dutton).

Magder, Ted (1993), *Canada's Hollywood: The Canadian State and Feature Films* (Toronto: University of Toronto Press).

Mattelart, A., C. X. Delcourt, and M. Mattelart (1984), *International Image Markets: In Search of an Alternative Perspective* (London: Comedia).

Moley, Raymond (1945), *The Hays Office* (New York: Bobbs-Merrill).

*Moran, Albert (ed.) (1996), *Film Policy: International, National and Regional Perspectives* (London: Routledge).

Morris, Peter (1986), 'Backwards to the Future: John Grierson's Film Policy for Canada', in Walz (1986).

—— (1987), 'Rethinking Grierson: The Ideology of John Grierson', in P. Vronneau *et al.* (eds.), *Dialogues* (Montreal: Mediatext).

—— (1978), *Embattled Shadows: A History of Canadian Cinema 1895–1936* (Kingston, Ont.: McGill-Queen's University Press).

Nizer, Louis (1935), *New Courts of Industry: Self-Regulation under the Motion Picture Code* (New York: Longacre Press).

Pendakur, Manjunath (1990), *Canadian Dreams and American Control: The Political Economy of the Canadian Film Industry* (Detroit: Wayne State University Press).

Quigley, Martin (1937/1971), *Decency in Motion Pictures* (New York: Macmillan; repr. New York: Jerome S. Ozer).

Randall, Richard S. (1968), *Censorship of the Movies: The Social and Political Control of a Mass Medium* (Madison: University of Wisconsin Press).

Ricketson, Frank H. (1938), *The Management of Motion Picture Theatres* (New York: McGraw-Hill).

Rocket, Kevin, Luke Gibbons, and John Hill (1988), *Cinema and Ireland* (London: Routledge).

Ross, Murray (1945), *Stars and Strikes: Unionization of Hollywood* (New York: Columbia University Press).

Schlesinger, Phillip (1987), 'On National Identity: Some Conceptions and Misconceptions Criticised', *Social Science Information*, 22/2: 219–64.

Schumach, Murray (1964), *The Face on the Cutting Room Floor* (New York: William Morrow).

Smythe, Dallas (1981), *Dependency Road: Communications, Capitalism, Consciousness and Canada* (Norwood, NJ: Ablex).

Temporary National Economic Committee (1941), *Motion Picture Industry: A Pattern of Control*, Monograph 43 (Washington: Government Printing Office).

Thompson, Kristin (1985), *Exporting Entertainment: America in the World Film Market 1907–1934* (London: British Film Institute).

Vaughan, Robert (1972), *Only Victims* (New York: G. P. Putnam's Sons).

Vronneau, Pierre, and Piers Handling (eds.) (1980), *Self Portrait* (Ottawa: Canadian Film Institute).

Walz, Gene (ed.) (1986), *Flashback: People and Institutions in Canadian Film History* (Montreal: Mediatext).

Wasko, Janet (1982), *Movies and Money: Financing the American Film Industry* (Norwood, NJ: Ablex).

—— Vincent Mosco, and Manjunath Pendakur (eds.) (1993), *Illuminating the Blindspot: Essays Honoring Dallas Smythe* (Norwood, NJ: Ablex).

Young, Donald R. (1922/1971), *Moving Pictures: A Study in Social Legislation* (Philadelphia: Westbrook; repr. New York: Jerome S. Ozer).

12

Hollywood and the world

Toby Miller

. . . When Saddam Hussein chose Frank Sinatra's globally recognized 'My Way' as the theme song for his 54th birthday party, it wasn't as a result of American imperialist pressure
(Michael Eisner)

. . . The Americans have colonised our subconscious
(Wim Wenders)

Hollywood history

We are all experts on American film. We have to be, since it comprises between 40 and 90 per cent of the movies shown in most parts of the world. The United States produced eighty-eight of the 100 top-grossing films in 1993, and in 1994 American cinema made more money overseas than at home for the first time (Rockwell 1994, H1). This is not to deny the importance of other screen cultures: people of colour are the majority filmmakers in the world, with much more diverse ideological projects and patterns of distribution than Hollywood (Shohat and Stam 1994: 27). But Los Angeles culture and New York commerce dominate screen entertainment around the globe, either directly or as an implied other, and the dramatic success of US film since the First World War has been a model for the export of North American music, television, advertising, the Internet, and sport. The spread of satellite television and the video cassette recorder, combined with deregulation of national broadcasting, continues to increase the reach of audiovisual technology (Wasko 1994. 233). How did such dominance come about?

Economics has had difficulty theorizing the cinema. Unlike most forms of manufacturing, the production of film drama is dominated by a small number of large companies with limited, individually differentiated output. Most investments are complete failures, a pain that can only be borne by large firms. The absolute significance of story over cost for audiences goes against classical economics' standard assumptions about the role of price in balancing supply and demand and, because of a film's textual meaning, external factors play a crucial role in a film's economic performance.

Conventional economics explains Hollywood's historical success in terms of 'a flexible managerial culture and an open and innovative financial system' that has adapted to changing economic and social conditions. On this account, the silent era saw films made for the big American domestic market that also sold in other English-speaking countries. Because English was an international language, the coming of sound aided the process, whilst the diverse ethnic mix of the US population encouraged a more universal mode of storytelling than those of other cultures. The argument goes that these strengths have been built on since, under the guiding principle of free-enterprise competitiveness (Acheson and Maule 1994: 271–3). In contrast, a political economy approach would propose that this success has been a co-ordinated, if sometimes conflictual and chaotic, attempt by capital and the state to establish and maintain a position of market and ideological dominance in ways that find governments every bit as crucial as audiences and firms.

Indeed, the balance of textual trade was not always as we find it today: France sold a dozen films a week to the United States early in the century and in 1914 most movies and much movie-making technology in North America was imported, while Italy and France dominated exhibition in Latin America (Balio 1993: 32–3). But the Vitagraph Company was producing two negatives for every reel by 1907, one for European and one for domestic use (de Grazia 1989: 57). By 1909 North American companies could rely on the local market to recoup costs and were tailoring export prices to meet other markets (O'Regan 1992: 313). Between 1915 and 1916 US exports rose from 36 million feet of film to 159 million feet, while imports fell from 16 million feet before the First World War to 7 million by the mid-1920s (King 1990: 10, 22). As the feature film took off during those years, Hollywood began to sell to Asia and Latin America, almost wiping out Brazilian production, for example, by purchasing local distributors (Shohat and Stam 1994: 28). From 1919 overseas receipts were factored into Hollywood budgets, and in the 1920s Hollywood's leading export sites were Britain, Australia, Argentina, and Brazil (Armes 1987: 48). By the 1930s foreign sales provided between a third and a half of industry returns. When sound was standardized, non-English speakers were courted by the musical, and studios set up in different countries created foreign-language versions of domestic hits (Tunstall 1977: 91). The industry also achieved horizontal integration by linking the sale of radio and records to the musical film. In 1939 the Department of Commerce estimated that the United States supplied 65 per cent of the films exhibited world-wide (Harley 1940: 21).

Of course, some of this success was the result of textual appeal. In 1920s and 1930s Italy, for example, Hollywood projected fabulous modernity that appealed even to Mussolini. Beauty, youth, and wealth merged under the sign of fun. Local marketing played up the extraordinary pleasures of this world and its difference from traditional Italian life. At the same time, the local industry was held back by the growth of US-owned distribution, new government taxes, and a reliance on importing American technology (Hay 1987: 66–71).

But the two world wars complicate any notion of simple managerial sophistication or global consumer preferences explaining American dominance. The 1914–18 and 1939–45 conflicts left national production across Europe either shut down or at least slowed (Izod 1988: 61–3, 82, 118). A plenitude of unseen US 'inventory' waited to be unleashed (Italy was sent over 2,000 features in the four years from 1945), while the developing US shipping industry improved transport infrastructure. Hollywood's new Motion Picture Export Agency referred to itself as 'the little State Department' in the 1940s, so isomorphic were its methods and contents with US policy and ideology (Guback 1987: 92–3). This was also the era when the industry's self-regulating Production Code appended to its bizarre litany of sexual anxieties something requested by the 'other' State Department: selling the American way of life around the world (Schatz 1988: 160; Powdermaker 1950: 36). The compulsory dismantling of state film-making institutions among the Axis Powers complemented Hollywood profit plans with anti-fascist and anti-communist political agendas. For all its rhetoric of pure competition, therefore, the US film industry has been assisted by decades of tax-credit schemes, film commissions, State and Commerce Department representation, currency assistance, and oligopolistic domestic buying, while the US government has devoted massive resources to generate and sustain its 'private-sector' film industry in the interests of ideology and profits (Harley 1940: 3; Elsaesser 1989: 10–11).

With profits endangered at home by anti-monopoly laws and the arrival of television, the world market grew in importance for Hollywood during the 1950s (Armes 1987: 49). Vertical integration through ownership of production, distribution, and exhibition may have been outlawed at home, but not on a global scale. By the 1960s the United States relied on exports for half its film revenue. Britain and Latin America were Hollywood's most lucrative importers until the 1970s. In both cases, economic downturn and the failure to invest in multiplexes diminished attendances. As a result, Hollywood turned to new forms of internal commercial exploitation (as in the 'discovery' of the African American audience and the emergence of the 'blaxploitation' genre). Following recapitalization and the studios' acquisition by conglomerates, strategies were developed to regain world audiences (Mattelart 1979:

194). US government and industry set up cartels to market films everywhere, with special agencies created for anglophone and francophone Africa. Hollywood's African Motion Picture Export Company has dominated cinema sales to former British colonies since the 1960s, when the continent screened about 350 films a year, perhaps half of them American (Diawara 1992: 106, 1994: 385–6; Ukadike 1994: 63). Today, it is easier to find an African film screened in Europe or the United States than on home territory. Following the hyperinflation of the 1970s and 1980s, with film production in Mexico and Argentina decimated, the percentage of Hollywood films exhibited in Latin America has increased dramatically, while by the mid-1980s Japan was the principal source of foreign profit (Himpele 1996: 52; O'Regan 1992: 304). As we shall see below, shifts towards a neo-liberal, multinational investment climate over the past decade have aided Hollywood further through the privatization of media ownership, a unified West European market, openings in the former Soviet bloc, and the proliferation of video cassette recorders (Elsaesser 1989: 15; Guback 1987: 98–9; Wasko 1994: 220, 224).

However, if the growing economic dominance of world markets by Hollywood is clearly apparent, why has this dominance alarmed so many governments? Why have industrial issues about the balance of trade been matched by cultural concerns about the balance of meaning? What is the 'threat' which such dominance has been sent to represent, and what are the issues at stake?

Cultural imperialism

Countries on the periphery have exchanged ideas and goods for a millennium. Networks of information and trade connected the Pacific, Asia, the Mediterranean, and Africa until the fifteenth century, when the slavery, militarism, and technology of European imperialism began to wipe out these routes. Intracontinental communications came to rely on Europe as a conduit. New ideologies came too: racial supremacy and the conversion mission of Christianity (Hamelink 1990: 223–4). Culture and information were now imperial concerns.

Cinema technology and narrative emerged around the same time as some major transformations in colonial politics: the United States seized the Philippines and Cuba, the European powers agreed on a division of Africa, and Native American resistance was crushed.

While First Peoples' rights were being trampled, commercial cultural export and sovereign authority were synchronizing (with an array of genocidal stories being enacted on-screen). Hollywood exporters were aware as early as 1912 that where their films travelled, demand was created for other US goods. Will Hays told the J. Walter Thompson advertising agency in 1930 that 'every foot of American film sells $1.00 worth of manufactured products some place in the world' (Hays 1931: 15). By the late 1930s stories of heroic merchandising links between the cinema and sales were legion, such as the one that told of the new Javanese market for US sewing-machines following a screening of American factory conditions, Hollywood-style. The producer Walter Wanger even expressed delight at a strike by Paris stenographers in protest at the gap between their conditions and those of office workers in US films, the impact of what he called '120,000 American Ambassadors' (the number of prints exported each year) (Wanger 1939: 50, 45). Such links are encapsulated in two famous scenes involving Clark Gable. *It Started in Naples* (Melville Shavelson, 1960) finds him instructing a local boy on how to make a hamburger. This produced public controversy about compromising Mediterranean cuisine. A quarter of a century earlier a deputation of Argentinian businessmen had protested to the US Embassy about *It Happened One Night* (Frank Capra, 1934) because Gable was seen removing his shirt, revealing no singlet below and creating an inventory surplus in their warehouses (King 1990: 32).

Although an interest in screen stereotypes is often identified with a contemporary liberal sensibility, it has, in fact, been a long-standing concern of conservatives. Since the 1920s Hollywood has monitored how representations affect audiences. Mexico placed embargoes because of this issue in 1922 and official complaints from Germany, Britain, France, Italy, and Spain over cultural slurs also occurred during the same decade (Vasey 1992: 618, 620–1, 624, 627, 631). As different countries became profitable sources of income, their leverage over scripts increased. The industry's 1927 list of 'Don'ts and Be Carefuls' instructed producers to 'avoid picturizing in an unfavorable light another country's religion, history, institutions, prominent people, and citizenry'. The British insisted on the unrepresentability of Christ, so he was absent from *The Last Days of Pompeii* (Ernest B. Schoedsack, 1935), while Samuel Goldwyn complained that 'the only villain we dare show today

Culinary imperialism, or how to make a hamburger—Clark Gable in *It Started in Naples* (1960)

[1936] is a white American' (quoted in Harley 1940: 23). On the other hand, the Japanese were threatened with narrative stereotyping as criminals in the 1930s if they failed to give access to Hollywood films.

American advertising executives were quick to work on commodity tie-ins to film. This produced a negative response from many poorer nations, especially after the Second World War, when such exports were officially legitimized as part of making less-developed countries into modern ones. Widespread reaction against the racist and self-seeking—or at best patronizing—discourses of modernization foregrounded the international capitalist media as crucial components in the formation of public taste in commodities, mass culture, and forms of economic and political organization in the Third World. Examples include the export of US screen products and infrastructure as well as American dominance of international communications tech-

nology. Critics claimed the rhetoric of development through commercialism was responsible for decelerating economic growth and disfranchising local culture, with emergent ruling classes in dependent nations exercising local power only at the cost of relying on foreign capital and ideology.

These theories of dependency spread from Latin America across the globe during the 1960s and 1970s, finding agreeable surrounds in international cultural organizations and Group of Seventy-Seven alliances. But the position has declined politically and intellectually since then. Once adopted by Unesco, it became vulnerable to that agency's complex pluralism, which insisted on the equivalence of all cultures as well as the association of national identity with cultural forms. The United States and United Kingdom withdrew from the Organization in the mid-1980s, draining resources it had allocated towards a new world order of culture and communication. At the same time, the conceptualization of *dependencia* was attacked from the left for an inadequate theorization of capitalism, post-coloniality, internal and international class relations, the role of the state, and the mediation of indigenous culture (Tunstall 1977: 57; Reeves 1993: 30–5; Schlesinger 1991: 145; Mann 1993: 119, 132).

This last concern—the mediation of Hollywood's output by indigenous cultures—has been particularly important in qualifying the cultural imperialism thesis. Michel Foucault's story of a white psychologist visiting Africa is instructive in its detail of differing aesthetic systems: when the academic asks local viewers to recount a narrative he has screened, they focus on 'the passage of light and shadows through the trees' in preference to his interest in character and plot (Foucault 1989: 193). As the *Economist* magazine's 1994 television survey remarked, perhaps cultural politics is always so localized in its first and last instances that the 'electronic bonds' of exported drama are 'threadbare' (Heilemann 1994, Survey 4). In their study of the reception of the television series *Dallas* in Israel, Japan, and the United States, Tamar Liebes and Elihu Katz establish three prerequisites for the successful communication of US ideology: the text contains information designed to assist the US overseas, is decoded as encrypted, and enters the receiving culture as a norm. They 'found only very few innocent minds' across the different cultural groups that discussed the programme; instead, a variety of interpretive frames led to a multiplicity of readings (Liebes and Katz 1990: 3–4, p. v).

Indeed, anxieties about American entertainment are frequently expressed under the guise of concern for 'national cultures' that have themselves been repressive or phantasmatic. The extraordinary puritanism of some cultural protection denies the liberatory aspects of much US entertainment for stifling class structures, as in the case of Britain. Nor have national cinemas necessarily taken a critical distance from Hollywood as some damned other. Many seek to imitate it, notably the 1980s Si Boy cycle in Indonesia, with its youth culture of fast cars (and English-speaking servants) (Sen 1994: 64, 73, 129–30), while some countries have fused imported strands of popular culture with indigenous ones to rework notions of cultural identity, as in Irish cinema (Rockett *et al.* 1988: 147). Others indeed, may import Hollywood texts as buffers against cultural imports that are too close for comfort: Pakistan

may prefer the difference of North America to the similarity of India (O'Regan 1992: 343).

Armand and Michèle Mattelart, leading names in the discourse of cultural imperialism, today see it as an enabling alliance of intellectual engagement rather than a sustainable theory. Cultural imperialism mobilized people to think through the implications of international textuality via local audits of relations between states, especially the nexus between 'new' nations, their former colonizers, and the United States. It is not surprising that a concentration on the inequality of exchange emphasized directions in flow rather than signs and their reception. However, the accusation of cultural imperialism did bring local culture to bear in resistance to the assumptions of neo-classical economics and its heroization of the sovereign consumer (Mattelart and Mattelart 1992: 175–7). Moreover, the spread of such critiques exemplified the export of theory itself from the Third World to the First, contributing to and drawing upon the ideals of Third Cinema along with the Cuban Revolution, Peronism, and Cinema Nôvo (Shohat and Stam 1994: 28). Nor do revisions to the thesis mean film trade is a happily settled matter. The apparent domestication of exported culture sometimes merely offers a few signifiers of localism while the values of practice and genre are imported, as debates about Indian and Philippine cinema over the past twenty years indicate (McAnany 1989; Binford 1987: 146; David 1995: 33). In this sense, difference and a sensitivity to cultural specificity can be one more incorporative means to homogenize cultural production. This then leads us to cultural imperialism's 'successor'—the concept of globalization.

Globalization

I would argue that . . . the entertainment industry of this country is not so much Americanizing the world as planetizing entertainment. (Michael Eisner)

Global exchange has been with us for a long time, but since the 1970s financial and managerial decisions made in one part of the world have taken rapid effect elsewhere. New international currency markets sprang up with the decline of a fixed exchange rate, matching regulated systems with piratical financial institutions that crossed borders. Speculation brought greater rewards than production, as the trade in securities and servicing debt outstripped profits from selling cars or building houses. The world circulation of money created the conditions for imposing international creditworthiness tests on all countries. At a policy level, it meant an end to import substitution industrialization and the very legitimacy of 'national' economies, supplanted by export-oriented industrialization and the idea of an international economy. With productive investment less profitable than financial investment, and companies rationalizing production, marketing, labour, and administration were reconceived on a world-wide scale. The corollary of open markets and critiques of cultural protectionism is that national governments cannot guarantee the economic well-being of their citizens. The loan-granting power of the World Bank and International Monetary Fund has forced a shift away from local provision of basic needs and towards comparative advantage. In the domain of cinema, this means that 'if you aren't doing it profitably already, don't start or you will be punished'. However, we need to beware of interpreting globalization as a structural change that puts an end to centre–periphery inequalities, competition between states, and integrated macro-decision-making by corporations; it just cuts the capacity of the state system to control such transactions (McMichael 1996: 27–9; Marshall 1996; Connelly 1996: 12–13).

Economic, cultural, environmental, and political forces are increasingly world-wide in their scope and effects, dynamically interpenetrating local realities and practices. Theories of globalization put space and speed at the centre of both analytic and business concerns: social theory links commodification critique to advertising practice in a giddy process akin to the experience of watching an action-adventure film's climactic struggle. As capital moves at high velocity, it lights promiscuously on areas and countries, with materials and people exchanged across the globe. If the modern saw everyday life determined by events beyond the horizon in national institutions of the economy and polity, the postmodern sees these determinations across borders, languages, and skies via multiple diasporas, computerized technology, finance capital, media entertainment, international organizations, neo-classical economics, regional blocs, and democratic ideology. Put another way, the experience of empire for First Peoples is now experienced—in milder form—as corporate domination by former colonizers and colonized alike.

Globalization's meanings for screen studies vary between concerns over American-dominated cultural flow (as per cultural imperialism), the international spread of capitalistic production and conglomerates, and the chaotic, splintered circulation of signs across cultures (Jacka 1992: 5, 2). Ownership is concentrated in a diminishing number of increasingly large corporations. What used to be nationally dominated markets for terrestrial television have undergone vast changes. Companies like Disney are in a position to produce films, directly promote them across a variety of subsidiaries, screen them on an owned network, and generate television replicas—not to mention compact discs and reading-material—and all with an eye to external profits (McChesney 1996: 4) (but they may cower in the face of Marguerite Duras's condemnation of EuroDisney as 'cultural Chernobyl'; quoted in Van Maanen 1992: 26). Digital systems cut the cost and quicken the speed of communication and generic transformation. Some components of globalization theory are sanguine about such developments, stressing the skill of audiences in negotiating texts. Certain writers offer 'multicultural' business strategies, themselves a segment of US transnationalism extending its domain. Critics focus on the direction of multinational finance: the Hollywood studios have recently been French-, Japanese-, Canadian-, and Australian-owned and are increasingly beholden to cross-cultural audiences for their success. At the same time as this diversity appears, the means of communication, association, and political representation are seen to be converging (Jameson 1991, pp. xiv–xv; Reeves 1993: 36, 62; Sreberny-Mohammadi 1996: 3–8).

What is interesting about globalization is that all its theorists place culture at the centre. Whereas the phrase 'cultural imperialism' always seemed qualified by the power of the noun to conjure up structural domination, 'globalization' is more processual. It marks new forms of economic life in a decolonized, privatized world system that sees overlapping and mutually determining spheres of influence and flexible specialization in production and consumption. Unlike cultural imperialism, globalization allows for incoherent, multilateral forms and directions of power, celebrating them as market flexibilities or sites of popular resistance, depending on who is speaking (Tomlinson 1991: 175–6; Marshall 1996: 197).

Of course, part of the talent of international cultural commodities is their adaptability to new circumstances: the successes and meanings of Hollywood films need to be charted through numerous spatial, generic, and formatting transformations as they move through US release to Europe and Asia then domestic and international video, cable, and network television (Aksoy and Robins 1992: 14). Because culture is about discrimination as well as exchange, it is simultaneously a key to international textual trade and one of its limiting factors. The Ford Motor Company has long worked with the adage 'To be a multinational group, it is necessary to be national everywhere'. And General Motors translates its 'hot dogs, baseball, apple pie, and Chevrolet' jingle into 'meat pies, football, kangaroos, and Holden cars' in Australia. Each US film is allotted a hundred generic descriptions for individual use in specific markets. Kevin Costner's *Dances with Wolves* was sold to the 1990 French cinemagoer as a documentary-style dramatization of Native American life and *Malcolm X* (Spike Lee, 1992) was promoted there with posters of a burning Stars and Stripes (Wasser 1995: 433; Danan 1995). Such stories indicate the paradigmatic nature of the national in an era of global companies. New forms of rationalization standardize the acknowledgement of difference as part of capital's need for local marketability. What are the implications for the Hollywood film industry of this still-unfolding mode of multinational capitalism?

The new international division of cultural labour

We have created a product that by, say, putting the name of Warner Brothers on it is a stamp of credibility. But that could be an Arnon Milchan film, directed by Paul Verhoeven, starring Gérard Depardieu and Anthony Hopkins, and shot in France and Italy, and made with foreign money.
(John Ptak)

Hollywood is a place you can't geographically define. We don't really know where it is.
(John Ford)

Despite the US government's positive attitude to the movie business as ideology and trade, New Dealers opposed Hollywood's domestic cartels and vertical integration. A combination of antitrust decisions and the advent of television meant that the decade from 1946 saw a decrease of a third in the number of Hollywood-made films and more than a doubling of imports. Films went overseas—'runaway production'—as the world audience grew, while location shooting became a means of differentiating stories. Between 1950 and 1973, just 60 per cent of Hollywood

films began their lives in the United States, as studios purchased facilities across the globe to utilize cheap labour (Christopherson and Storper 1986). In 1949 there were nineteen runaway productions (Guback 1984: 56–7). Twenty years on, the figure was 183, mostly in Europe. Co-productions became a norm, with Dino De Laurentiis a pioneer of today's global pre-sales, which garner funds from distributors around the world in advance of production in Los Angeles. American film institutions are practised at purchasing foreign theatres and distribution companies and sharing risk and profit with local businesses (Izod 1988: 119). The 1990s have seen the emergence of truly global film distribution cartels, such as Warner and United International (Sorlin 1991: 93; Wasko 1994: 226). This may be seen to represent a possible new international division of cultural labour.

The concept of a new international division of cultural labour derives from revisions to the theory of economic dependency that emerged from West Germany in the late 1970s. The shift from the spatial sensitivities of electrics to the spatial insensitivities of electronics had pushed businesses away from treating the Third World as a source of raw materials. Instead, it set the shadow price of work, competing internally and with the First and Second Worlds. Production became split across continents in what Folker Fröbel and his collaborators christened a new international division of labour (Fröbel *et al.* 1980: 2–8, 13–15, 45–8). I am suggesting that, just as we have seen manufacturing flee the First World, which then depended for its employment base on the services sector, much cultural production has relocated around the world and may continue to do so at the level of creativity, marketing, and information. The factors determining this are a complex mix of legal and political frameworks, productivity, and skills. A peripheral group of suppliers can increase the profit margin of a centralized company that retains control of finance, research, and overall direction (Miège 1989: 41–3; Marshall 1996: 202; Mittelman 1995: 278).

Internationalization has quite different effects on stars and 'creative' people from its impact on artisanal workers. Unlike the vertically integrated studio system era, most Hollywood film production is now undertaken by small lighting, studio, and editing companies on behalf of independent producers who contract with major distributors or regional groups to show films around the world, sharing revenue through formulae that include non-recoverable advances to fund the movies (Christopherson and Storper 1986). Since the 1980s overseas firms have invested in Hollywood or lent money against distribution rights in their countries of origin. Joint production arrangements are well-established between US firms and Swedish, French, Italian, and British companies, with connections to video, cable, and theme parks (Buck 1992: 119, 123). So at the top and bottom end of the labour market, Hollywood has internationalized, while its large mid-section remains provincial (Briller 1990: 75–8). New technology problematizes the necessity for the collocation of financing, shooting, and editing, but it also reduces the need for 'authenticity', so filming abroad is mostly about cost. The diversity at production level, however, does not amount to dispersed power. Independents have always been part of the scene, but never sufficiently capitalized or vertically integrated either domestically or overseas to survive costly failures. Finance and distribution remain under the control of major studios (Acheson and Maule 1994: 279–80; Wasko 1994: 33; Miège 1989: 46; Aksoy and Robins 1992: 8–9).

We might consider the way the new international division of cultural labour can affect other countries through a brief case-study of *Kangaroo* (Lewis Milestone, 1952) and *The Return of Captain Invincible* (Philippe Mora, 1983). They provide chronological and conceptual limiting cases of US screen investment in a film industry. *Kangaroo* was the first of several Hollywood features shot in Australia during the 1950s. Twentieth Century-Fox dispatched a crew and most of the cast because its Australian-based capital reserves had been frozen to prevent foreign exchange from leaving the country. Shooting took place in Zanuckville, named to honour the studio head. A formulaic western, the film failed, but then the need to use money lying idle was probably the sole reason for its coming into being. Three decades on, *Captain Invincible* represented another outcome of the state producing conditions for foreign filmmaking. Taxation incentives designed to make the industry less dependent on canon-forming cultural bureaucrats and more attentive to the private sector saw the Australian Treasury subsidizing US producers to make a film set almost 'nowhere'. It concerns a lapsed American superhero, played by Alan Arkin, who migrates to Australia and dipsomania following McCarthyite persecution, reviving his powers and sobriety to thwart a villainous Christopher Lee. Recut by US producers following difficulties obtaining American distribution, the text was disavowed by Mora and denied certification by the Australian government as insufficiently local by comparison with its original script. A court challenge against this ruling succeeded, but the tax haven designed to boost commercial production was politically and culturally compromised from that point.

The present and future

For all its lopsidedness, the contemporary trade in film is far from a unilateral exercise of power. When Congress was inquiring into foreign ownership of Hollywood in the late 1980s, Milos Forman expressed concern that if a German corporation bought Fox, 'all the war films could be "slightly corrected"' (quoted in Briller 1990: 77). The American Film Institute is anxious about the loss of cultural heritage to internationalism, and others ask what will become of US drama now that it is increasingly scripted with an eye to foreign audiences. Internationalization occurs at ancillary levels, as audience targeting becomes increasingly specific: Sean Connery is cast as a Hollywood lead because European audiences love him, while Michael Apted speaks with optimism of a gradual 'European-izing of Hollywood' (quoted in Dawtrey 1994: 75). George Quester laments that expensive British costume-history crowds out indigenous 'quality' fiction on US television, noting that there is more Australian high-end drama than locally produced material (Quester 1990: 57), while Paul Hirsch speaks of globalization displacing American dominance across the culture industries (Wasser 1995: 433; Danan 1995: 131–2, 137; Hirsch 1992: 677).

At the level of distribution and exhibition, the picture is unstable. As Chinese-language groups develop in many parts of the world, sometimes US exports do not even meet quota limits set on them in those territories, while Indonesia has seen a decline in Hollywood popularity since the mid-1980s (Sen 1994: 63–4). America blames this on government intervention but it may have more to do with the popularity of Hong Kong and Taiwanese film. Meanwhile, US government agencies pressure proprietors and politicians around the world to open up the audiovisual sector to additional imports, leading to bizarre acts of resistance such as Korean film industry people releasing snakes into theatres during screenings of *Fatal Attraction* (Adrian Lyne, 1987) to scare audiences away (Buck 1992: 129).

US film revenue from members of the European

Community increased throughout the 1980s, to 90 per cent of cinema receipts there by 1990. If we consolidate television, film, and video texts as at mid-1994, the American industry relied on exports for $8 billion of its annual revenue of $18 billion, with 55 per cent from Western Europe (*Daily Variety* 1994: 16). Europe imported $3.7 billion in 1992, compared to $288 million in reciprocal sales; and the disparity is increasing. Overseas hard-top exhibition is now a more significant source of Hollywood's revenue than domestic receipts, as the new multiplexes have massively increased attendances throughout Europe over the 1990s. US opposition to the single European market as a cultural producer is laughable given how much it benefits from the EC as a cultural consumer (Hill 1994: 2, 7 n. 4; Miller 1993: 102).

The television–film nexus has become increasingly critical. True to the style of the new international division of cultural labour, Turner Broadcasting, Time Warner, Disney, Viacom, NBC, and others are at the centre of the fast-growing West European industry, finding new sites of production as well as dumping-grounds for old material. Meanwhile, the US Department of Commerce offers policy materials on globalization to Congress that converge economic development and ideological influence, problematizing claims that Hollywood is free enterprise and its government uninterested in blending trade with cultural change. Business and the state luxuriate in the industry's 65 per cent share of the world box-office and an immeasurable share in emerging forms of life (Ferguson 1992: 83–4; Eisner, in Costa-Gavras et al. 1995: 9). Students of film need to blend our expertise in watching American films with an understanding of how and why they come before us.

BIBLIOGRAPHY

Acheson, Keith, and Christopher J. Maule (1994), 'Understanding Hollywood's Organization and Continuing Success', *Journal of Cultural Economics*, 18/4: 271–300.

*Aksoy, Asu, and Kevin Robins (1992), 'Hollywood for the Twenty-First Century: Global Competition for Critical Mass in Image Markets', *Cambridge Journal of Economics*, 16/1: 1–22.

Armes, Roy (1987), *Third World Film Making and the West* (Berkeley: University of California Press).

Balio, Tino (1993), *Grand Design: Hollywood as a Modern Business Enterprise 1930–1939* (New York: Scribner's).

Binford, Mira Reym (1987), 'The Two Cinemas of India', in

John D. H. Downing (ed.), *Film and Politics in the Third World* (New York: Autonomedia).

Bordwell, David, Janet Staiger, and Kristin Thompson (1985), *The Classical Hollywood Cinema: Film Style and Mode of Production to 1960* (London: Routledge).

Briller, Bert R. (1990), 'The Globalization of American TV', *Television Quarterly*, 24/3: 71–9.

Buck, Elizabeth B. (1992), 'Asia and the Global Film Industry', *East–West Film Journal*, 6/2: 116–33.

Christopherson, Susan, and Michael Storper (1986), 'The City as Studio; the World as Back Lot: The Impact of Vertical Disintegration on the Location of the Motion Picture Industry', *Environment and Planning D: Society and Space*, 4/3: 305–20.

Connelly, M. Patricia (1996), 'Gender Matters: Global Restructuring and Adjustment', *Social Politics*, 3/1: 12–31.

Costa-Gavras, Michael Eisner, Jack Lang, and Benjamin Barber (1995), 'From Magic Kingdom to Media Empire', *New Perspectives Quarterly*, 12/4: 4–17.

Daily Variety (1994), 'After GATT Pique, Pix Pax Promoted', 8 June, 1, 16.

Danan, Martine (1995), 'Marketing the Hollywood Blockbuster in France', *Journal of Popular Film and Television*, 23/3: 131–40.

David, Joel (1995), *Fields of Vision: Critical Applications in Recent Philippine Cinema* (Quezon City: Ateneo de Manila University Press).

Dawtrey, Adam (1994), 'Playing Hollywood's Game: Eurobucks Back Megabiz', *Variety*, 7–13 (Mar.), 1, 75.

de Grazia, Victoria (1989), 'Mass Culture and Sovereignty: The American Challenge to European Cinemas 1920–1960', *Journal of Modern History*, 61/1: 53–87.

Diawara, Manthia (1992), *African Cinema: Politics and Culture* (Bloomington: Indiana University Press).

—— (1994), 'On Tracking World Cinema: African Cinema at Film Festivals', *Public Culture*, 6/2: 385–96.

Elsaesser, Thomas (1989), *New German Cinema. A History* (Basingstoke: Macmillan; London: British Film Institute).

Ferguson, Marjorie (1992), 'The Mythology about Globalization', *European Journal of Communication*, 7/1: 69–93.

Foucault, Michel (1989), *Foucault Live* (interviews, 1966–84), ed. Sylvère Lotringer, trans. John Johnston (New York: Semiotext(e) Foreign Agents Series).

Fröbel, Folker, Jürgen Heinrichs, and Otto Kreye (1980), *The New International Division of Labour: Structural Unemployment in Industrialised Countries and Industrialisation in Developing Countries*, trans. Pete Burgess (Cambridge: Cambridge University Press; Paris: Éditions de la Maison des Sciences de l'Homme).

Guback, Thomas H. (1984), 'International Circulation of US Theatrical Films and Television Programming', in George Gerbner and Marsha Siefert (eds.), *World Communications: A Handbook* (New York: Longman).

Guback, Thomas H. (1987), 'Government Support to the Film Industry in the United States', in Bruce A. Austin (ed.), *Current Research in Film: Audiences, Economics and Law*, iii (Norwood, NJ: Ablex).

Hamelink, Cees (1990), 'Information Imbalance: Core and Periphery', in John Downing, Ali Mohammadi, and Annabelle Sreberny-Mohammadi (eds.), *Questioning the Media: A Critical Introduction* (Newbury Park, Calif.: Sage).

Harley, John Eugene (1940), *World-Wide Influences of the Cinema: A Study of Official Censorship and the International Cultural Aspects of Motion Pictures* (Los Angeles: University of Southern California Press).

Hay, James (1987), *Popular Film Culture in Fascist Italy: The Passing of the Rex* (Bloomington: Indiana University Press).

Hays, Will (1931), Speech, 12 May, J. Walter Thompson Collection, Duke University, Creative Staff Meeting File, Monday Evening Meetings.

Heilemann, John (1994), 'A Survey of Television: Feeling for the Future', *Economist*, 330/7850, Survey 1–18.

Hill, John (1994), Introduction, in John Hill, Martin McLoone, and Paul Hainsworth (eds.), *Border Crossing: Film in Ireland, Britain and Europe* (Belfast: Institute of Irish Studies; London: British Film Institute).

Himpele, Jeffrey D. (1996), 'Film Distribution as Media: Mapping Difference in the Bolivian Cinemascape', *Visual Anthropology Review*, 12/1: 47–66.

Hirsch, Paul (1992), 'Globalization of Mass Media Ownership', *Communication Research*, 19/6: 677–81.

Izod, John (1988), *Hollywood and the Box Office 1895–1986* (New York: Columbia University Press).

Jacka, Elizabeth (1992), Introduction, in Elizabeth Jacka (ed.), *Continental Shift: Globalisation and Culture* (Sydney: Local Consumption).

Jameson, Fredric (1991), *Postmodernism; or, The Cultural Logic of Late Capitalism* (London: Verso).

King, John (1990), *Magical Reels: A History of Cinema in Latin America* (London: Verso).

Liebes, Tamar, and **Elihu Katz** (1990), *The Export of Meaning: Cross-Cultural Readings of Dallas* (New York: Oxford University Press).

McAnany, Emile G. (1989), 'Television and Cultural Discourses: Latin American and United States Comparisons', *Studies in Latin American Popular Culture*, 8: 1–21.

McChesney, Robert W. (1996), 'The Global Struggle for Democratic Communication', *Monthly Review*, 48/3: 1–20.

McMichael, Philip (1996), 'Globalization: Myths and Realities', *Rural Sociology*, 61/1: 25–55.

Mann, Michael (1993), 'Nation-States in Europe and Other Continents: Diversifying, Developing, not Dying', *Daedalus*, 122/3: 115–40.

Marshall, Don D. (1996), 'Understanding Late-Twentieth-Century Capitalism: Reassessing the Globalization Theme', *Government and Opposition*, 31/2: 193–215.

Marvasti, A. (1994), 'International Trade in Cultural Goods: A Cross-Sectional Analysis', *Journal of Cultural Economics*, 18/2: 135–48.

Mattelart, Armand (1979), *Multinational Corporations and the Control of Culture: The Ideological Apparatuses of Imperialism*, trans. Michael Chanan (Sussex: Harvester Press; Atlantic Heights, NJ: Humanities Press).

—— and **Michèle Mattelart** (1992), *Rethinking Media Theory: Signposts and New Directions*, trans. James A. Cohen and Marina Urquidi (Minneapolis: University of Minnesota Press).

Miège, Bernard (1989), *The Capitalization of Cultural Production*, trans. Josiane Hay, Nicholas Garnham, and Unesco (New York: International General).

Miller, Toby (1993), *The Well-Tempered Self: Citizenship, Culture, and the Postmodern Subject* (Baltimore: Johns Hopkins University Press).

Mittelman, James H. (1995), 'Rethinking the International Division of Labour in the Context of Globalisation', *Third World Quarterly*, 16/2: 273–95.

O'Regan, Tom (1992), 'Too Popular by Far: On Hollywood's International Popularity', *Continuum*, 5/2: 302–51.

Powdermaker, Hortense (1950), *Hollywood the Dream Factory: An Anthropologist Looks at the Movie-Makers* (Boston: Little, Brown).

Quester, George H. (1990), *The International Politics of Television* (Lexington, Mass.: Lexington).

Reeves, Geoffrey (1993), *Communications and the 'Third World'* (London: Routledge).

Rockett, Kevin, Luke Gibbons, and **John Hill** (1988), *Cinema and Ireland* (Syracuse, NY: Syracuse University Press).

Rockwell, John (1994), 'The New Colossus: American Culture as Power Export', *New York Times*, 30 Jan. H1, H30.

Schatz, Thomas (1988), *The Genius of the System: Hollywood Filmmaking in the Studio Era* (New York: Pantheon).

Schlesinger, Phillip (1991), *Media, State and Nation: Political Violence and Collective Identities* (London: Sage).

Sen, Krishna (1994), *Indonesian Cinema: Framing the New Order* (London: Zed).

Shohat, Ella, and **Robert Stam** (1994), *Unthinking Eurocentrism: Multiculturalism and the Media* (London: Routledge).

Sorlin, Pierre (1991), *European Cinemas, European Societies 1939–1990* (London: Routledge).

Sreberny-Mohammadi, Annabelle (1996), 'Globalization, Communication and Transnational Civil Society: Introduction', in Sandra Braman and Annabelle Sreberny-Mohammadi (eds.), *Globalization, Communication and Transnational Civil Society* (Cresskill: Hampton Press).

*Tomlinson, John (1991), *Cultural Imperialism: A Critical Introduction* (London: Pinter).

Tunstall, Jeremy (1977), *The Media are American: Anglo-American Media in the World* (London: Constable).

Ukadike, Nwachukwu Frank (1994), *Black African Cinema* (Berkeley: University of California Press).

Van Maanen, John (1992), 'Displacing Disney: Some Notes on the Flow of Culture', *Qualitative Sociology* 15/1: 5–35.

Vasey, Ruth (1992), 'Foreign Parts: Hollywood's Global Distribution and the Representation of Ethnicity', *American Quarterly*, 44/4: 617–42.

Wanger, Walter (1939), '120,000 American Ambassadors', *Foreign Affairs*, 18/1: 45–59.

*Wasko, Janet (1994), *Hollywood in the Information Age: Beyond the Silver Screen* (Cambridge: Polity Press).

Wasser, Frederick (1995), 'Is Hollywood America? The Trans-Nationalization of the American Film Industry', *Critical Studies in Mass Communication*, 12/4: 423–37.

Weinraub, Bernard (1993), 'Directors Battle over GATT's Final Cut and Print', *New York Times*, 12 Dec., L24.

Wenders, Wim (1991), *The Logic of Images: Essays and Conversations*, trans. Michael Hofmann (London: Faber & Faber).

Redefining cinema: international and avant-garde alternatives

1

Concepts of national cinema

Stephen Crofts

Prior to the 1980s critical writings on cinema adopted common-sense notions of national cinema. The idea of national cinema has long informed the promotion of non-Hollywood cinemas. Along with the name of the director-auteur, it has served as a means by which non-Hollywood films—most commonly art films—have been labelled, distributed, and reviewed. As a marketing strategy, these national labels have promised varieties of 'otherness'—of what is culturally different from both Hollywood and the films of other importing countries. The heyday of art cinema's 'new waves' coincided with the rise of anglophone film-book publishing in the mid-1960s. Later, 1960s radical politics extended the range of territories covered to those engaged in post-colonial struggles. The ideas of a national cinema underpinning most of these studies remained largely unproblematic until the 1980s, since which time they have grown markedly more complex. Prior to this period, ideas of national cinema tended to focus only on film texts produced within the territory concerned while ideas of the nation-state were conceived primarily in essentialist, albeit if in sometimes anti-imperialist, terms.

Problematizing the nation-state

Key publications in the rethinking of the nation-state and nationalism have been Anderson (1983), Gellner (1983), Hobsbawm (1990), Smith (1991), and Hutchinson (1994). These have all advanced non-essentialist conceptions of the nation-state and national identity, arguing for both the constructedness of the 'imagined community' (Anderson) which constitutes the nation-state, and its historical limits as a post-Enlightenment organizer of populations, affected particularly by the huge migrations and diasporas resulting from post-

Second World War processes of decolonization. Such ideas have informed recent accounts of national cinemas which seek to resist the homogenizing fictions of nationalism and to recognize their historical variability and contingency, as well as the cultural hybridity of nation-states (so that US culture, for example, is seen to be a part of most 'national' cultures and to interact with them). In Philip Rosen's words, 'identifying the . . . coherences [of] a "national cinema" [and] of a nation . . . will always require sensitivity to the countervailing, dispersive forces underlying them' (1984: 71).

Historically, the 1980s and 1990s have put further pressure on the national, with the global spread of corporate capital, the victory of finance over industrial capital, the consolidation of global markets, the speed and range of electronic communications, and the further weakening of national cultural and economic boundaries which has followed the disintegration of Soviet communism and Pax Americana. Half a century after 1945 it is difficult to imagine a nation-state retaining the congruence of polity, culture, and economy which characterized most nation-states before then. Arjun Appadurai's (1990) model for accounting for these developments emphasizes the deterritorialized character of the supranational imagined communities which displace those of the nation-state. He pinpoints the accelerating transnational flows of people (tourists, immigrants, exiles, refugees, guest workers), of technology (mechanical and informational), of finance and media images (all moving ever faster through increasingly deregulated markets), and of ideologies (such as the global spread of Western rhetorics of democracy), and the disjunctions amongst these flows: 'people, machinery, money, images and ideas now follow increasingly non-isomorphic paths . . . the sheer speed, scale and volume of each of these flows is now so great that the disjunctures [rather than overlaps] have become central to the politics of global culture' (1990: 297–301).

This conceptualization of the post-national does, however, have weaknesses. Shohat and Stam (1994) note that 'discernible patterns of domination channel the "fluidities" even of a "multipolar" world; the same hegemony[ies] that unifies[y] the world through global networks of circulating goods and information also distribute[s] them according to hierarchical structures of power, even if those hegemonies are now more subtle and dispersed' (1994: 31). Nevertheless, Appa-

durai's model has many implications for the study of national cinemas, some taken up later, some now. One consequence of the disjunctive relationships he identifies 'is that the state and the nation are at each other's throats' (1990: 304). The former Yugoslavia—with its five nations, three religions, four languages, and two alphabets—stands as a grim emblem of the historical role of the state in suppressing ethnic, religious, and cultural differences. In view of the growing lack of congruence between nations and states, I therefore propose to write of states and nation-state cinemas rather than nations and national cinemas, while clearly differentiating states within a *federal* system, and without of course collapsing all into totalitarian states.

Problematizing nation-state cinema studies: categories of analysis

Nation-state (or 'national') cinema studies until the 1980s focused almost exclusively on the film texts produced within the territory, sometimes seeing these—in a reflectionist manner—as expressions of a putative national spirit. Typically, a historical survey would construct its chosen films as aesthetically great works (usually seen as made by great directors) and as great moments (the longest film, most expensive film, and so on). Such studies rarely analysed the industrial factors enabling the films to be produced.

Since the 1980s new categories of analysis have begun to emerge. A number of these are summarized in Andrew Higson's 'The Concept of National Cinema' (1989), one of the first general considerations of nation-state cinema, based on generalizations around the British case. Higson argues that nation-state cinemas should be defined not only in terms of 'the films produced by and within a particular nation state', but also in terms of distribution and exhibition, audiences, and critical and cultural discourses. Textual and generic questions, however, are strange lacunae in his (industrially oriented) account; for texts do, after all, mediate between exhibition and audiences. The factors which analyses of nation-state cinemas involve, therefore, may be identified as follows:

Production. David Bordwell, Janet Staiger, and Kristin Thompson's monumental *The Classical Hollywood Cinema* (1985) redresses the lack of attention to the industrial which has been characteristic of film studies. They reject any simple reflectionist thesis of text–

context relations and argue how the economic, technological, and ideological factors affecting Hollywood production act as mutually interacting determinations which are irreducible to one another (Lapsley and Westlake 1988: 117). Hollywood's mode of film practice, they conclude, 'consists of a set of widely held stylistic norms sustained by and sustaining an integral mode of film production' (Bordwell *et al.* 1985, p. xiv). Most subsequent analyses of production have adopted a similarly post-Althusserian model. Crisp's (1993) account of the production of French cinema between 1930 and 1960, for example, develops the Americans' mode of analysis, breaking down the heading of production into various components: political economy and industrial structure, plant and technology, personnel and their training, discursive endeavours to form audiences, authorial control in relation to the mode of production, and work practices and stylistic change.

Distribution and exhibition (these two are taken together because of their virtual interconnectedness). Higson argues that categories of analysis of nation-state cinemas should include 'the range of films in circulation within a nation-state' (1989: 44). One of the few analyses of imported films and their audiences is Paul Swann's *The Hollywood Feature Film in Postwar Britain* (1987), but attention towards 'imported' cinemas is becoming more common in nation-state cinema studies as in Thomas Elsaesser's *New German Cinema* (1989). Given Higson's concern that nation-state cinemas should not be defined solely in terms of production, it is fair to note that many states actually have no production industry. Poor states, especially in Africa, cannot afford it unless, like Burkina Faso—one of the world's most impoverished states—foreign funding sustains an art cinema offering exotic representations to foreign audiences. Some states principally watch films in a language they share with other states, for instance Tunisia and Uruguay. Other states, such as in South Asia and the South Pacific, have no audiovisual production and no cinemas, but do have flourishing video distribution.

Audiences. This remains an under-researched category. It is arguably to the benefit of film studies that it has not followed media studies in its massive investment in empirical audience research. Film studies has thus largely avoided the latter's effective collusion with global consumerisms since the 1980s (see Willemen 1987*b*). Largely, but not entirely: see John Hill's critique of Higson's willingness to allow Hollywood's popularity in Britain 'to blur the arguments for film *production*

which is specifically British rather than North American' (1992: 13–14). Unlike the approach to the audience in media studies, however, nation-state cinema studies has in the main analysed audiences in terms of box-office statistics. Discussion of audiences has been particularly significant in studies analysing the problems which locally produced cinemas experience when faced with transnational domination by Hollywood (Hill 1994), or in sustaining an indigenous 'art cinema' as in Elsaesser's (1989) analysis of the audience desperately sought by the state-funded practitioners of the New German Cinema.

Discourses. The discourses in circulation about film, as well as wider cultural discourses in the nation-state, clearly affect industry and audiences, and also inform—and are articulated within—film texts. Given cultural hybridity, these will of necessity include foreign-originated ideas. Hence, since the 1980s nation-state cinema studies have less commonly treated films as objects for the exercise of aesthetic judgement than as instances of (national-)cultural discourses. Hill (1986), for example, analyses British cinema's ideological articulations—and repressions—of class, gender, youth, consumerism, and related categories in films from the period 1956–63. Marsha Kinder's (1993) account of Spanish cinema gives central attention to 'its distinctive cultural reinscription of the Oedipal narrative, that is, the way Oedipal conflicts within the family were used to speak about political issues and historical events that were repressed from filmic representation during the Francoist era and the way they continue to be used with even greater flamboyance in the post-Franco period after censorship and repression had been abolished' (1993: 197–8). In a similar vein, some scholars have adopted the idea of a national or social imaginary (Elsaesser 1980; Dermody and Jacka 1988: 15–23).

Textuality. Rather than see nation-state cinemas in terms of 'great works', writers have increasingly identified systems of textual conventions, principally generic ones, as characterizing 'national' cinema. Dermody and Jacka, for example, employ a quasi-generic taxonomy to identify the 'aesthetic force-field' of Australian cinema between 1970 and 1986. Genres, in this respect, are seen less in industrial terms than as codifications of socio-cultural tendencies.

National-cultural specificity. National-cultural specificity may be differentiated from both nationalism, and definitions of national identity. As Paul Willemen argues: 'The specificity of a cultural formation may be

Antonio das mortes (1969)—
Latin American counter-cinema

marked by the presence but also by the absence of preoccupations with national identity . . . the discourses of nationalism and those addressing or comprising national specificity are not identical . . . the construction of national specificity in fact encompasses and governs the articulation of both national identity and nationalist discourses' (1994: 210). Nationally specific cinema, then, is not bound to the homogenizing myths of nationalism and national identity. Hill uses Willemen's example of black British cinema to illustrate the point, arguing how such films display a 'sensitivity to social differences (of ethnicity, class, gender and sexual orientation) within an identifiably and specifically British context' (Hill 1992: 16) and that this is strikingly different from the nationalistically 'successful . . . marketing and packaging [of] the national literary heritage, the war years, the countryside, the upper classes and elite education' noted by Elsaesser (1984: 208) as characterizing dominant British cinema. In contrast, the international co-production can often be seen to erase cultural specificity: as Geoffrey Nowell-Smith observes of *Last Tango in Paris* (Bernardo Bertolucci, 1972), it 'had no nationality in a meaningful sense at all' (1985: 154).

The cultural specificity of genres and nation-state cinema 'movements'. A nation-state cinema's capacity to produce culturally specific genres depends on whether it can sustain production in sufficient volume to support the requisite infrastructures and audience familiarity; on the power of its local cultural traditions; and on how strongly these are articulated by film relative to other artistic practices. The generation and/or survival of local genres has been a gauge of the strength and dynamism of nation-state cinemas, but this may be less so in the 1990s as genres diversify, fragment, and recombine. Local cultural traditions and their articulation through film rather than other artistic practices have likewise underpinned the best-known nation-state cinema 'movements'. These have frequently arisen at historical moments when nationalism connects with genuinely populist movements to produce specifically national films that can claim a cultural authenticity or rootedness (Crofts 1993). Some of these—Italian Neo-Realism, Latin American Third Cinema, and Fifth Generation Chinese Cinema—arose on the crest of waves of national-popular resurgence. The French Nouvelle Vague marked a national intellectual and cultural recovery in the making since the late 1940s. However, cultural hybridity is often a characteristic as well. As Kinder (1993: 6) notes, such movements regularly borrow from elsewhere formal 'conventions to be adapted to the [importers'] own cultural specificity': Italian Neo-Realism from French poetic realism, the Nouvelle Vague from Hollywood and Rossellini, the Fifth Generation from Chinese and foreign painting traditions.

The role of the state. The idea of nation-state cinema needs to be conceptualized in terms not only of the categories above, but also of the state's own involvement. The state retains a pivotal role. For all the much-vaunted 'disintegration' and/or 'supersession' of the state under the forces of globalization and cyber-hype, and alongside the more realistic recognition of its fragmentation under sub- and suprastate pressures, it is still state policies and legislation (or lack of them) which substantially regulate and control film subsidies, tariff constraints, industrial assistance, copyright and licensing arrangements, censorship, training institutions, and so on. Individual states desiring to restrict Hollywood imports, for instance, do at the least have the power to decide whether or not they *want* to risk a trade war, as can be seen in the case of South Korea in 1990, when it battled with the Motion Picture Export Association of America to reduce Hollywood imports to roughly 5 per cent per year (Lent 1990: 122–3).

The global range of nation-state cinemas. In an argument also applicable to film, Geoffrey Hartman argues that every literary theory is 'based on experience of a limited canon or generalised strongly from a particular text/milieu' (1979: 507). In a similar fashion I have argued previously that '[f]ilm scholars' mental maps of world film production are often less than global . . . Sadoul (1962), informed by French colonialism, knows more of African cinema than of Latin American,

while an American scholar, informed by the US imperium and substantial Hispanic immigration, knows more of Latin American cinema than of African cinema' (Crofts 1993: 60–1). Such limited understandings of the cross-cultural have severe implications for canon formation as well as for global politics. Even in 1962 Sadoul took note that Third World production was more plentiful than North American and European combined (1962: 530–1). It is this global range of nation-state cinemas that the following section aims to cover.

Varieties of nation-state cinema production

Table 1 presents a model for differentiating types of nation-state cinema that takes into account the three main industrial categories of production, distribution and exhibition, and audiences as well as those of textuality and national representation (this account distils and substantially reworks Crofts 1993: 50–7). As in most taxonomies, these varieties of nation-state cinema are highly permeable. Individual films can be cross-bred between different varieties. And a given state may host different varieties by sustaining different modes of production, most commonly the industrial and cultural modes. Moreover, the export of a given text may shift its variety, as in the common recy-

TABLE 1. **EIGHT VARIETIES OF NATION-STATE CINEMA PRODUCTION**

	Mode of production as regulated and controlled by the state			
	Minimal ('market economy')	Mixed economy	Maximal, centrally controlled economy	Other or outside state provision
Industrial	1. United States cinemas 2. Asian commercial successes	3. Other entertainment cinemas	4. Totalitarian cinemas	
Cultural	5. Art cinemas:			
	American art	Art 6. International co-productions	Art for socialist export	
Political (anti-state)				7. Third Cinemas 8. Sub-state cinemas

cling of films from Third and totalitarian cinemas as art cinema.

The eight varieties of nation-state cinema shown in the table can be briefly summarized as follows:

1. *United States cinema.* This is covered in Part 2 of this volume. It is so called to include the recent medium-budget 'independent' films associated with, say, the Sundance Institute as well as Hollywood. Hollywood's domination of world film markets since as early as 1919 is so well known (Guback 1976; Thompson 1985) that Western nation-state cinemas are habitually defined against Hollywood. It is hardly ever spoken of as a national cinema, perhaps because of its transnational reach. This has been further consolidated since the 1980s by its increased domination of West European screens, and the substantial inroads it has made into East European and other new markets.

2. *Asian commercial successes.* With large domestic and reliable export markets, Indian and Hong Kong cinemas can afford to ignore Hollywood, while Japanese production sometimes outstrips Hollywood imports at the local box-office (Lent 1990: 47).

3. *Other entertainment cinemas.* These include European and Third World commercial cinemas which adopt genres such as melodrama, thriller, and comedy. They customarily depend more on private than state investment, but mostly fail to dominate their local markets (except in rare cases such as Egypt, which supplies other Arab states). This variety of nation-state cinema includes anglophone (Australian, Canadian) imitations of US cinema and Bangladeshi imitations of Indian cinemas.

4. *Totalitarian cinemas.* These include those of fascist Germany and Italy, communist China, and the Stalinist regimes of the Soviet bloc.

5. *Art cinemas.* These vary somewhat in the sourcing of their finances, and in their textual characteristics. Bordwell (1979, 1985) describes the textual characteristics of art cinema in their heyday and Smith (Part 3, Chapter 2) summarizes its features.

6. *International co-productions.* Like offshore productions, these films exemplify the mobility of capital and personnel, as well as the international merging of media images noted by Appadurai (1990) above.

7. *Third Cinemas.* This term originally referred to the anti-imperialist cinemas of Latin America, but its definition has been expanded, especially by Willemen, to cover films with 'a historically analytic yet culturally specific mode of cinematic discourse' (1987a: 8). Directors such as the Indian Mrinal Sen, the Filipino Kidlat Tahimik, the Africans Ousmane Sembene and Souleymane Cissé, as well as black British filmmakers have been included in this category (Pines and Willemen 1989).

8. *Sub-state cinemas.* These may be defined ethnically in terms of suppressed, indigenous, diasporic, or other populations asserting their civil rights and giving expression to a distinctive religion, language, or regional culture. Catalan, Québecois, Aboriginal, Chicano, and Welsh cinemas are examples.

While the categories of state regulation and control on the horizontal axis of Table 1 are self-explanatory, the three modes of production may require some clarification. The industrial mode is that which characterizes Hollywood and applies similarly to the Hong Kong and Indian industries. The cultural mode of production is distinguished from Hollywood by state legislation overtly supporting production subsidy—increasingly via television—and quotas and/or tariffs on imported films. In its anti-state politics, the political mode of production is characterized by artisanal modes of filmmaking, and in its purest form—for example, *Hour of the Furnaces* (Argentina, 1969)—is conducted clandestinely and at risk to the film workers involved.

Under its two axes, Table 1 subsumes nine categories analysable in nation-state film industries. These allow us to expand upon the categories of analysis described in the preceding section:

(a) Mode of production effectively subsumes:

(b) the mode of audience address targeted through distribution and exhibition of texts of the mode of production involved; and

(c) the kinds of genre which it typically produces. Similarly, state regulation of production and distribution–exhibition comprises the following three categories:

(d) state subvention and regulation or control of production (or not);

(e) state intervention in and regulation or control of distribution and exhibition (or not)—in the case of the 'free market' option, the lack of regulation is nevertheless an active state policy decision; and

(f) the implicitly or explicitly nationalist, or indeed anti-nationalist representations—if any (for, as seen above, there need be none)—encouraged by the mode of production concerned.

Three further categories, concerning audiences, are implicit in the table and will be explicated below:

(g) the success or otherwise of the variety of state cinema within its local market;

(h) its success in exporting to other territories; and

(i) the range of competing entertainment forms available within the state concerned.

Under the industrial mode of production there is an almost complete correlation between categories (a) to (c): between, that is, the industrial mode of production, entertainment modes of address in distribution and exhibition, and entertainment genres, with the inflexion of the entertainment mode of address towards the didactic in the case of totalitarian mode. Similarly, there is a strong correlation between the cultural mode of production, the modes of address of the art film—to the cultured, film-literate viewer—which characterizes art cinemas' distribution and exhibition channels, and art film genres. The bulk of international co-productions also conform to these criteria, with the main exceptions being the higher-budget samples of 'Euro-pudding'. Much as the political mode of original Third Cinema production is clandestine, fugitive, and makeshift, so its politicized mode of address endangers its target audiences, and its typically agit-prop documentary genres serve its anti-state politics. Later versions of Third Cinema are less life-threatening. With variable production levels and degrees of access to mainstream distribution and exhibition, the substate cinemas are also instances of this mode of production but are less co-ordinated in their strategies of production, mode of address, and genre.

The horizontal dimension covers categories (d) to (f): state regulation and intervention in the sectors of production and distribution and exhibition, and the explicit or implicit nationalisms advanced by the cinemas

involved. Most varieties of state film production exhibit a strong correlation between these three categories. The minimal government subsidy to production which characterizes Hollywood, Asian commercial successes, and to a lesser extent other entertainment cinemas finds echoes in the general lack of intervention in the distribution and exhibition sectors in the territories involved, and in the usually implicit forms that any nationalistic representations adopt. This contrasts with totalitarian cinemas, whose states control production—with the exceptions of fascist Italy and pre-1938 Nazi Germany—and which intervene strenuously in distribution and exhibition with censorship scrutiny of local and foreign product, and which urge expressly, and usually explicitly, nationalistic representations.

The most familiar art cinemas (i.e. of the European model) differ again in that while their production depends largely on state subsidy, their distribution and exhibition operates largely *without* state intervention (post-Second World War France being the conspicuous exception) and their representations are aesthetically constructed before they are nationalistic. American art cinema differs in the lack of state production support, while socialist states subsidize their art cinemas in both production and export distribution. International co-productions function in the same way as art cinemas, except that any nationalisms may disappear in the bland mix (while those of the Fifth Generation Chinese Cinema post-Tiananmen seriously *question* the nationalisms of the People's Republic of China). Original Third Cinema enjoys state support for neither production nor distribution, and its practitioners would argue that their states' abuse of freedoms of speech and assembly justify—indeed necessitate—its anti-state representations. Later versions enjoy less brutal, if still less than comfortable, state patronage. Third Cinema representations overlap with substate cinemas' interests in regions, ethnicities, religions, and/or languages which are non-hegemonic within the state. These latter rarely benefit from state support in production or distribution and exhibition unless from states within a federal system such as the Québecois.

Audiences, conceived in box-office terms, figure under headings (g)–(i): the films in predominant circulation in the state concerned, the success or otherwise of its exports, and the range and popularity of competing entertainment forms available within the state concerned. The last of these is a factor for consideration in nation-state cinema studies. As regards the first two, nation-state cinemas can be categorized as net importers and net exporters. Hollywood, Indian, Hong Kong, and big totalitarian cinemas dominate their local markets, through market and/or regulatory means, and garner varying degrees of additional revenue from foreign markets. Smaller totalitarian cinemas (the Soviet Union's European satellite states) and the other five varieties of nation-state cinema production fight over the remainder, their principal enemy being Hollywood, which dominates most anglophone markets and exerts considerable influence through the United States' world-wide strategic, economic, and cultural links. Indian and Hong Kong cinemas export to their ethnic diasporas, Hong Kong also throughout East Asia, and big totalitarian cinemas to their colonized and satellite territories. Art cinemas of all kinds distribute themselves broadly world-wide, but also thinly, within the limits, that is, of art film distribution and exhibition channels. Third and substate cinemas rarely break out in the mainstream (an exception is the Québecois *Jesus of Montreal* (Denys Arcand, 1989) which was in fact a Canadian–French co-production). Given their predominant anti-state politics, circulation is sorely limited, and sometimes wider—because less policed—outside their country of origin.

Recent cultural issues and debates

Politically critical national cinemas

Perched on the edge of Table 1, the space for anti-state cinemas is very limited, emerging from the political underground in the case of the original Third Cinemas, from the interstices of the contradictions of liberal pluralist funding regimes, from the capacity of production units with progressive heads to cross-subsidize funding in the Fifth Generation Chinese case, or, in the case of those same directors post-Tiananmen, from their ability to raise non-PRC international co-production finance on the strength of their names as auteurs. Willemen has noted the growing pressures on politically unorthodox cinema:

The capital-intensive nature of film production, and of its necessary industrial, administrative and technological infrastructures, requires a fairly large market in which to amortise costs, not to mention the generation of surplus for investment or profit. This means that a film industry [other than Third, substate, and poor cinemas] must address either an international market or a very large domestic one. If the

latter is available, then cinema requires large potential audience groups, with the inevitable homogenising effects that follow from this . . . a cinema addressing national specificity will be anti- or at least non-nationalistic, since the more it is complicit with nationalism's homogenising project, the less it will be able to engage critically with the complex, multi-dimensional and multidirectional tensions that characterise and shape a social formation's cultural configurations . . . the marginal and dependent [politically critical] cinema is simultaneously the only form of national cinema available: it is the only cinema that consciously and directly works with and addresses the materials at work within the national cultural constellation. (Willemen 1994: 211–12)

In terms of the table, internationalizing economic interests force their way downwards and to the right; cultural, national ones struggle upwards and to the left!

Arguing for the cultural

While box-office dollars increasingly drive the industry globally, this should not preclude our attending to cultural issues—indeed, it should demand it. Europe in the 1990s provides some key debates. Even French cinema, which has probably been the world's most successful in meshing industrial and economic concerns with cultural discourses, is feeling the pressure of global commodification in the 1990s. In the case of Britain, Hill elegantly advances cultural against economic arguments in seeking to influence policy and practice on nation-state cinemas, critiquing in particular the policy endorsement of 'the operations of the market place (and its domination by transnational conglomerates) and, hence, the restricted range of cultural representations which the market provides' (1992: 18). This returns the argument to the issue of cultural specificity set out above. The Celtic poor cinema for which Colin McArthur campaigns poses acute problems for the realizability of acceptable culturally specific representations. Given centuries of English othering of Celtic Scotland, Ireland, and Wales as 'uncivilized' and 'backward', he offers this 'axiom to Celtic film-makers: the more your films are consciously aimed at an international market, the more their conditions of intelligibility will be bound up with regressive discourses about your own culture' (1994: 118–20). In the context of the much more powerful West German state, Elsaesser still has occasion to urge the importance of commitment to 'the politics of culture, where independent cinema is a protected enclave, indicative of a will to create and preserve a national film and media *ecology* amidst an ever-expanding international film, media and information *economy*' (1989: 3).

Export and cultural difference

As observed above, a given film can shift its variety of nation-state cinema when exported, depending on the distribution and exhibition parameters of the importing state and its political relationships with the exporter. Cross-cultural readings are more of a worry for art and substate cinemas than for Hollywood, the world's biggest producer of largely undifferentiated product for export. Elsewhere I distinguish three levels of critical response to imported films:

(a) blank incomprehension, which is mostly pre-empted by distributors' not importing culturally specific materials such as the films of Werner Schroeter or Alexander Kluge, or most social realist and poor cinemas;

(b) the subsumption of the unfamiliar within depoliticizing art cinema discourses of 'an essentialist humanism ("the human condition"), and complemented by a tokenist culturalism ("very French") or an aestheticizing of the culturally specific ("a poetic account of local life")'; and

(c) ethnocentric readings, such as in US accounts of *Crocodile Dundee* (Peter Faiman, 1986) which use the film to inscribe American frontier myths and to rediscover an age of innocence (Crofts 1992, 1993: 58–9). This last mode of reading Willemen calls a 'projective appropriation' (1994: 212).

Theorizing the culturally specific

Besides 'projective appropriation', which includes the 'imperial and colonising strategy' of universalist humanism (Willemen 1994: 210), Willemen distinguishes two other ways of analysing cultural specificity. 'Ventriloquist identification' has the speaker 'immersed in some ecstatic fusion with the others' voices . . . the monopolist-imperialist's guilty conscience' (213). The move beyond these complicit stances is based on Bakhtin's dialogic mode, and is 'not simply a matter of engaging in a dialogue with some other culture's products, but of using one's understanding of another cultural practice to re-

perceive and rethink one's own cultural constellation at the same time . . . a double-outsideness' whereby the analyst relates both to her or his situation and to the group 'elsewhere' as an other (214, 216–17). Rajadhyaksha and Willemen's (1994) encyclopaedia of Indian cinemas represents a realization of that goal. In a similar vein Chow argues for the relevance of the Western theoretical discourse of psychoanalysis to the examination of Chinese social and cultural repressions (1991, p. xiv). And later positioning herself outside both Western and Eastern readings of China, she challenges the notion of an authentic cultural identity as any more than an ideological construct (Chow 1995).

Future projections

Will the wash of globalization rinse out cultural differences between states? If nation-state cinemas and their marketing constitute a point of resistance to the growing pressures against the state from within and without, many argue that they cannot resist for long: 'the concepts "cinema", "nation" and "national cinema" are increasingly becoming decentred and assimilated within larger transnational systems of entertainment' (Kinder 1993: 440). The accelerating flows of people, technologies, images, and ideas combine with the intensifying search of film producers for multiple international markets to imply growing homogeneity in nation-state film production. And the possibility of distinguishing product with nation-state cinema labels is threatened not just by the increasing number of international co-productions, but also by developments in electronic and fibre-optic delivery systems with their encouragement of indiscriminate channel-zapping and image-mixing. On the other hand, art film sectors world-wide offer new hopes of interest in cultural specificity, even if only in the form of finding new foreign sets on which to inscribe old scenarios of innocence and nostalgia. Growing attendances at film festivals in many parts of the West hold out hopes for raised interest in cultural specificities. And the emergence in the 1990s of 'cross-over' distribution successes and of the American 'independent' production sector holds out some promises for growing consumer discrimination, at least in the West, against the typically Hollywood mainstream fare.

BIBLIOGRAPHY

Anderson, Benedict (1983), *Imagined Communities: Reflections on the Origin and Spread of Nationalism* (London: Verso).

*Appadurai, Arjun (1990), 'Disjuncture and Difference in the Global Cultural Economy', in Mike Featherstone (ed.), *Global Culture: Nationalism, Globalisation and Modernity* (London: Sage).

Bordwell, David (1979), 'Art Film as a Mode of Film Practice', *Film Criticism*, 4/1.

—— (1985), *Narration in the Fiction Film* (London: Methuen).

—— Janet Staiger, and Kristin Thompson (1985), *The Classical Hollywood Cinema: Film Style and Mode of Production to 1960* (New York: Columbia University Press).

Chow, Rey (1991), *Woman and Chinese Modernity: The Politics of Reading between East and West* (Minneapolis: University of Minnesota Press).

*—— (1995), *Primitive Passions: Visuality, Sexuality, Ethnography and Contemporary Chinese Cinema* (New York: Columbia University Press).

*Crisp, Colin (1993), *Classic French Cinema 1930–1960* (Bloomington: Indiana University Press).

Crofts, Stephen (1992), 'Cross-Cultural Reception Studies: Culturally Variant Readings of *Crocodile Dundee*', *Continuum*, 6/1.

*—— (1993), 'Reconceptualising National Cinema/s', *Quarterly Review of Film and Video*, 14/3: 49–67.

Dermody, Susan, and Elizabeth Jacka (1988), *The Screening of Australia*, ii: *Anatomy of a National Cinema* (Sydney: Currency Press).

Elsaesser, Thomas (1980), 'Primary Identification and the Historical Subject: Fassbinder and Germany', *Ciné-Tracts*, 11 (Fall), 43–52.

—— (1984), 'Images for England (and Scotland, Ireland, Wales . . .)', *Monthly Film Bulletin* (Sept.), 267–9.

*—— (1989), *New German Cinema: A History* (London: Macmillan).

Gellner, Ernest (1983), *Nations and Nationalism* (Oxford: Blackwell).

Guback, Thomas (1976), 'Hollywood's International Market', in Tino Balio (ed.), *The American Film Industry* (Madison: University of Wisconsin Press).

Hartman, Geoffrey (1979), 'A Short History of Practical Criticism', *New Literary History*, 10/3.

*Higson, Andrew (1989), 'The Concept of National Cinema', *Screen*, 30/4 (Autumn), 36–46.

Hill, John (1986), *Sex, Class and Realism: British Cinema 1956–1963* (London: British Film Institute).

*—— (1992), 'The Issue of National Cinema and British Film Production', in Duncan Petrie (ed.), *New Questions of British Cinema* (London: British Film Institute).

—— (1994), 'The Future of European Cinema? The Economics and Culture of Pan-European Strategies', in John Hill, Martin McLoone, and Paul Hainsworth (eds.) *Border Crossing: Film in Ireland, Britain and Europe* (Belfast: Institute of Irish Studies; London: British Film Institute).

Hobsbawm, E. J. (1990), *Nations and Nationalism since 1780: Programme, Myth, Reality* (Cambridge: Cambridge University Press).

Hutchinson, John (1994), *Modern Nationalism* (London: Fontana).

Kinder, Marsha (1993), *Blood Cinema: The Reconstruction of National Identity in Spain* (Berkeley: University of California Press).

Lapsley, Rob, and Mike Westlake (1988), *Film Theory: An Introduction* (Manchester: Manchester University Press).

Lent, John (1990), *The Asian Film Industry* (Austin: University of Texas Press).

McArthur, Colin (1994), 'The Cultural Necessity of a Poor Celtic Cinema', in John Hill, Martin McLoone, and Paul Hainsworth (eds.), *Border Crossing: Film in Ireland, Britain and Europe* (Belfast: Institute of Irish Studies; London: British Film Institute).

Nowell-Smith, Geoffrey (1985), 'But do we Need It?', in Martin Auty and Nick Roddick (eds.), *British Cinema Now* (London: British Film Institute).

Pines, Jim, and Paul Willemen (1989), *Questions of Third Cinema* (London: British Film Institute).

Rajadhyaksha, Ashish, and Paul Willemen (1994), *Encyclopaedia of Indian Cinema* (London: British Film Institute and Oxford University Press).

Rosen, Philip (1984), 'History, Textuality, Nation: Kracauer, Burch, and Some Problems in the Study of National Cinemas', *Iris*, 2/2: 69–84.

Sadoul, Georges (1962), *Histoire du Cinéma* (Paris: Flammarion).

Shohat, Ella, and Robert Stam (1994), *Unthinking Eurocentrism: Multiculturalism and the Media* (London: Routledge).

*Smith, Anthony D. (1991), *National Identity* (London: Penguin).

Swann, Paul (1987), *The Hollywood Feature Film in Postwar Britain* (London: Croom Helm).

Thompson, Kristin (1985), *Exporting Entertainment: America in the World Film Market 1907–1934* (London: British Film Institute).

Willemen, Paul (1987a/1994), 'The Third Cinema Question: Notes and Reflections', *Framework*, 34: 4–38; repr. in *Looks and Frictions* (London: British Film Institute).

—— (1987b), Review of John Hill, *Sex, Class and Realism: British Cinema 1956–1963*, *Framework*, 34: 114–20.

*—— (1994), 'The National', in *Looks and Frictions* (London: British Film Institute).

2 Modernism and the avant-gardes

Murray Smith

The avant-garde and other alternatives

The types of cinema that I will be discussing are extremely varied, and it might be argued that the only thing that unites them all is their status as 'other' to orthodox narrative filmmaking. Another index of this heterogeneity is the cluster of distinct, if overlapping, terms denoting the filmic practices to be discussed here: art, avant-garde, experimental, independent, and underground, to name the most widespread. Initially, it is useful to bracket these terms and to frame the discussion more generally in terms of modes of film practice. Such a practice is defined by an integrated set of economic, institutional, and aesthetic norms (Bordwell *et al.* 1985, pp. xiii–xv, 378–5).

From our point of view, the most pertinent modes of film practice are art cinema and the avant-garde, both of which contrast with the classical Hollywood mode of film practice. While the latter is characterized by its commercial imperative, corporate hierarchies, and high degree of specialization and division of labour, the avant-garde is an 'artisanal' or 'personal' mode. Avant-garde films tend to be made by individuals or very small groups of collaborators, financed either by the filmmakers alone or in combination with private patronage and grants from arts institutions. Such films are usually distributed through film co-operatives, and exhibited by film societies, museums, and universities

(consequently, such films can only usually be seen in urban centres—and only in a handful of those with any regularity). Importantly, this alternative system of production, distribution, and exhibition is not driven by profit. Avant-garde films rarely break even, let alone make a profit, through the markets of either the mass commodity or the luxury item. There is no market in the negatives of avant-garde films, and truly famous practitioners of avant-garde film have made their fame and fortune either through other activities (Andy Warhol), or through moving into the realm of the art film (Warhol, Derek Jarman, Peter Greenaway), discussed below. Most avant-garde filmmakers make a living as teachers, technicians within the film industry, or through other day-jobs. In this respect, the filmic avant-garde is markedly different from the avant-garde in music, literature, and especially painting—a fact which is obscured by the tendency of critics to talk of *the* avant-garde, as if its conditions of existence were identical from discipline to discipline.

Within the domain of cinema, the avant-garde differs not only from Hollywood cinema, but from that other mode of film practice known as art cinema (even if there have been many practical and aesthetic cross-overs, from Fernand Léger and Germaine Dulac to Chantal Akerman, Jarman, and Sally Potter). Art films are typically characterized by aesthetic norms that are different from those of classical narrative films; they are made within a somewhat less rationalized

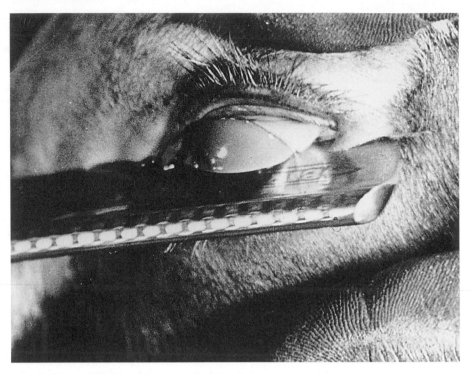

The aggressivity of the avant-garde—the eye-slicing scene in Buñuel's *Un chien andalou* (1928)

system of production; and they are often supported by government policies designed to promote distinctive national cinemas. But art cinema is still a commercial cinema, which depends for its existence on profits, rather than the more ethereal rewards of status and prestige.

So much for the economic and institutional nature of the avant-garde; what of its cultural and aesthetic character? If mainstream cinema is governed by an ethos of entertainment—with all the associations of escapism and leisure implied by that term—the avant-garde, by contrast, aims to challenge and subvert. At its most radical, the avant-garde asks us to rethink fundamentally our preconceptions about cinema. The tone of this challenge may vary widely, from the aggressive stance of *Un chien andalou* (Luis Buñuel and Salvador Dali, France, 1928) (the notorious eye-slicing scene being an apt emblem of its attitude towards the spectator), to the wit and playfulness of Robert Breer's work. An evening of avant-garde films ought to be thought-provoking and stimulating, but offers no guarantee of being pleasurable or beautiful in the conventional senses.

The 'otherness' of the avant-garde has been conceived in two distinct ways—as a *parallel* phenomenon and as a *reactive* phenomenon. P. Adams Sitney argues that the relationship of the avant-garde to commercial cinema is one of 'radical otherness', in which each operates 'in different realms with next to no influence on each other' (Sitney 1974, p. viii). Although Sitney's study is the classic work on the American avant-garde, this has become an unusual perspective. More typical is the view of David James (1989), who sees the avant-garde as a 'reactive' or 'critical' phenomenon, continually challenging and undermining both the established values of mainstream society and the norms of orthodox aesthetic practice. Doubtless there have been individual avant-garde filmmakers who have had little knowledge or interest in commercial cinema, and thus in intentional terms were forging a parallel aesthetic. But looked at from a social perspective, even the work of such filmmakers becomes bound up in the larger rhetoric of the institutions of the avant-garde.

But from where, one might ask, do these cultural and aesthetic attitudes come from? A full sociological exploration of this question is still to be undertaken, and is certainly beyond the scope of this chapter. One widespread view, articulated in different contexts by the art critic Clement Greenberg (1939) and the philosophers Theodor Adorno and Max Horkheimer (1947/1979), is that the subversive strategies of the avant-garde are a reaction to the rise of mass culture. Such 'kitsch' culture—to use Greenberg's term—relentlessly reduces art to stereotyped patterns incapable of arousing active, intelligent responses. The formulaic nature of mass culture offers only a debased sentimentality, providing nothing more than a temporary respite from the regimentation of work. The fundamentally stagnant nature of mass culture is masked, however, by a continual striving for superficial novelty, and to this end the 'culture industry' (Adorno's phrase) co-opts every genuine cultural expression to its own ends. And it is this that gives rise to the avant-garde, the difficulty and obscurity of which is a deliberate act of resistance to such recuperation. The preservation of a sphere of *autonomous* artistic practice—that is, one guided by internal processes of development, not by the demands of the socio-political order—becomes, paradoxically, a political gesture. It functions—or so Adorno and Greenberg, in their different ways, argue—as a form of resistance to a society which attempts to rationalize, commodify, and so degrade every aspect of life; in the words of Adorno, to reduce even the 'purposelessness' of art to the 'purpose' of commerce.

Of the many things that such 'alternative practices' have challenged, narrative and 'realism' have often been prime targets because of their perceived dominance in commercial filmmaking. What counts as 'realism' is an immensely complex issue, but what is objected to is the claim to realism on the basis of an accurate rendering of the perceivable aspects of the world—continuity of time and space, for example—while equally real, if not directly visible, social and psychological processes are either ignored or mystified. Narrative, or more particularly the kind of traditional narrative form associated with the nineteenth-century novel and the Hollywood film, has been blamed for a variety of evils, but once again a constricting realism is central. 'Classic realism', it is argued, presents a contingent view of the world as if it were a necessary, inevitable one, and so inhibits both psychic freedom and any impetus towards progressive social change. Films conforming to such 'realism' are thought to induce a kind of passivity in the spectator, while anti- or non-realist texts demand a much more active response. The German dramatist Bertolt Brecht is one of the most influential sources for the critique of 'surface realism' and the contribution of traditional narrative to it, though kindred attacks can be found in Surrealism, the French *nouveau roman*, and the circle of writers associated with the journal *Tel quel*, all of which have fed into alternative filmmaking at some point. A recurrent motif in the history of avant-garde cinema is the idea that cinema need not have become a narrative form at all, but could rather have modelled itself on other art forms, especially painting and music. In his book *Abstract Film and Beyond* (1977), Malcolm Le Grice constructs a history of avant-garde cinema in just these terms, counterposing the origins of orthodox narrative cinema in literature and theatre with the painterly, poetic, and musical origins of the first avant-garde experiments. In doing this, Le Grice was elaborating a gesture made earlier by, among others, Léger, Dulac, Maya Deren, and the art historian Élie Faure: 'There will some day be an end of the cinema considered as an offshoot of the theater, an end of the sentimental monkey tricks and gesticulations of gentlemen with blue chins and rickety legs' (1923/1967: 4). The most extreme statement of this 'anti-narrative' sentiment may be found in the work of the 'structural-materialist' filmmakers of the 1960s and 1970s (to whom we will return). But surveying the history of the avant-garde as a whole, it would be more accurate to say that narrative has been displaced, deformed, and reformed, rather than simply expunged altogether.

Modernism and the avant-garde

The concept of the avant-garde is intimately related to those of modernity and modernism. 'Modernity' refers to the network of large-scale social, economic, technological, and philosophical changes wrought by the Enlightenment and the Industrial Revolution. 'Modernism' is usually used to denote the period of dramatic innovation in all of the arts, from around the end of the nineteenth century (Symbolism and Aestheticism) up to the Second World War, when the sense of a fundamental break with inherited modes of representation and expression became acute. Modernism is thus above all associated with a pervasive formal self-consciousness, though many would also identify a thematic preoccupation with the modern city and its technologies—with the exhilaration of speed and rapid development, but also the potential for physical, social, and emotional dislocation (the latter erupting amidst the former in Walter Ruttmann's *Berlin: Die Sinfonie der Großstadt* ('Berlin: Symphony of a City', Germany, 1927).

CRITICAL APPROACHES TO WORLD CINEMA

Renato Poggioli has described the avant-garde as a 'culture of negation' (1968: 107–8). This commitment to ceaseless (self-)critique may be seen as a prime instance of the modernist emphasis on the new (although, as we shall see, the relationship between modernism and the avant-garde is a matter of considerable controversy). While Poggioli's study *The Theory of the Avant-Garde* pays little attention to film, it analyses the very notion of the avant-garde and relates its history. The term 'avant-garde' is military in origin, referring to the 'advance party' who interrogate the terrain ahead of the main army. (The military basis of the metaphor is sustained by titles like 'Film: The Front Line' (e.g. Rosenbaum 1983) a series of books on contemporary avant-garde filmmaking begun in the 1980s.) In mid-nineteenth-century France, the term was applied metaphorically to revolutionary political groups (in just the way that one speaks in English of 'vanguardist' politics). Towards the end of the century the term's use was extended so as to encompass the idea of, in Robert Hughes's phrase, 'social renewal through cultural challenge'—rather than overtly political activity. This leads Poggioli to talk of 'two avant-gardes'—a political and a cultural avant-garde, which sometimes walk hand in hand but by no means always do. This phrase was later used by Peter Wollen in a very similar fashion to discriminate what he argued were two rather different currents of 'avant-gardism' within film history (Wollen 1975/1982a). First, there is the apolitical avant-garde, concerned more with developing a purist film aesthetic, running from Léger and others in France in the 1920s through the co-operative movements in post-war Europe and the United States. Second, there is a political avant-garde, running from the Soviet montage directors in the 1920s through to the work of such directors as Jean-Luc Godard and Miklós Jancsó from the 1960s onwards. While Wollen's account has the virtue of giving us a broad perspective on the history of avant-garde practice and in making connections across that history that may not be obvious, its vice lies in its over-simplification of specific phases of avant-garde filmmaking. Some avant-gardists were apolitical, some overtly political, some only implicitly so. Many were members or fellow travellers of the leftist parties, but some avant-gardists, notably in Italy and pre-revolutionary Russia, aligned themselves with the far right. As David James has argued, the positing of a 'single, transhistoric, self-regulating avant-garde' occludes important differences in the economic, cultural, and aesthetic character of superficially similar movements. James argues rather that there is a 'spectrum of alternative practices which develop and decay with historically specific needs and possibilities' (1989: 22).

Moreover, Wollen's use of the phrase 'avant-garde' cuts across the one we began with—that is, as a mode of film practice—in that his two avant-gardes share the 'critical' stance, but otherwise differ dramatically in terms of their institutional and economic foundations. We can see this by comparing the Surrealists (part of what Wollen terms the apolitical avant-garde) with the Soviet montage filmmakers (the first manifestation of an overtly political avant-garde), both active in the 1920s and early 1930s. The Soviets—chiefly Alexander Dovzhenko, Sergei Eisenstein, Lev Kuleshov, V. I. Pudovkin, and Dziga Vertov—began their careers in the early years of the new communist state. Like Soviet artists in other fields—the Constructivist painters, for example—they were concerned to harness radical formal strategies to Bolshevik rhetoric. Until the 1930s such experimentation was supported by the state (though not without controversy). Eisenstein's *Strike* (1925), Pudovkin's *Mother* (1926), and Dovzhenko's *Arsenal* (1929) all relate tales of revolution drawn from Soviet history, organized around either a typical, 'positive' hero, or the 'mass hero' (the proletariat in general), or both. These narratives form the basis of an agitational aesthetic, in which editing—as the label 'montage' implies—plays a crucial role. Whether conceived primarily in terms of architectural construction (Kuleshov), dialectical conflict (Eisenstein), or the musical interval (Vertov), montage aimed to infuse the narrative with a conceptual interplay out of which a revolutionary argument would emerge. The brutal

> **'Modernism'** is usually used to denote the period of dramatic innovation in all of the arts, from around the end of the nineteenth century (Symbolism and Aestheticism) up to the Second World War, when the sense of a fundamental break with inherited modes of representation and expression became acute. Modernism is thus above all associated with a pervasive formal self-consciousness.

The political avant-garde—montage imagery in *Arsenal* (1929)

inequalities of the Tsarist regime, for example, are forcefully rendered in the opening montage of *Arsenal*. Shots of the Tsar writing a stupefyingly dull diary entry ('Today I shot a crow') are intercut with shots of an old woman collapsing from exhaustion as she sows a field, and others depicting frustrated factory workers, hungry children, and a man beating a scrawny horse in desperation.

France provides us with the first example of a fully fledged avant-garde film community in a liberal democracy. Over the course of the 1920s a set of institutions developed through which non-commercial films were made, distributed, exhibited, and discussed critically (Abel 1984). While there were certainly tensions and disputes within the French avant-garde, and many of them centred on political issues, it is not possible to boil them down to a political and an apolitical strain. Ian Christie (1979) has proposed a tripartite division. First, there were the filmmakers associated

with the notion of 'Impressionism: Abel Gance, Louis Delluc, Jean Epstein, Marcel L'Herbier, and the early Germaine Dulac. These filmmakers generally made narrative films which dwelt upon subjective experience, and experimented with the ways in which cinema could render aspects of that experience (e.g. Epstein's *La Glace à trois faces*, France 1927). Many of these films were feature-length and exhibited commercially; in other words, they really constitute an early effort to forge a national art cinema. The second strand Christie picks out is that associated with the notion of 'cinéma pur' (akin to Élie Faure's 'cineplastics'), in which the formal and often abstract exploration of cinematic possibilities dominated. Léger's *Ballet mécanique* (France, 1924) mixes such exploration with other tendencies; later films by Henri Chomette and Germaine Dulac were 'purer' still. The abstract experiments of cinéma pur have come to be thought of as the quintessential modernist aesthetic.

Many authors regard the terms 'avant-garde' and 'modernism' as essentially synonymous. Others, such as Peter Bürger in his *Theory of the Avant-Garde* (1984), Thomas Crow (1981), and (writing specifically on cinema) Paul Willemen (1984), treat them as overlapping but distinct. For them, modernism most appropriately describes a certain kind of formal innovation in the arts (above all, autonomous, reflexive strategies, rooted in the Aestheticism of the late nineteenth century) while avant-gardism implies something more radical, namely an attack on the very institutions and definitions of established practice (including the notion of artistic autonomy, that is, of a complete separation of art from socio-political life). (It should also perhaps, be noted that some commentators, like John Harwood (1995), argue that the term 'modernism', originally nothing more than an umbrella term for the whole range of experimental artistic practices during the period, now carries a spurious explanatory and evaluative force, implying as it does that radically different artists were all in the grip of an underlying, unified *Zeitgeist*. The same could be said of the term 'avant-garde'.)

If we accept the definition argued for by Bürger and Willemen, then the honorific 'avant garde' is most aptly applied to the third grouping of alternative filmmakers in France identified by Christie, the Surrealists—even if, in a rhetorical gesture utterly typical of the avant-garde, the Surrealist poet Robert Desnos lambasted the notion of the 'avant-garde', associated as it was for him with the Impressionists and the Aestheticism of

Jean Cocteau. The dynamic of 'negation' is not restricted to a criticism of mass culture by everything outside it, but operates within the field of avant-garde artistic practice as well. Nothing is more characteristic of the avant-garde than disputes within its ranks about which subgroup is most deserving of the epithet.

Surrealism was born out of the ashes of an earlier movement, Dada. Dada had been founded in 1916 by a group of expatriate artists in Zurich, but the movement became an international one, with practitioners adopting the banner in Berlin, Cologne, and New York. Tristan Tzara, the Romanian poet who became the leader of the movement, moved to Paris, which became the major centre for Dada, as it was later for Surrealism. Dada is a nonsense word, and as such is a clue to the nature of the movement, which was anarchic, violently anti-traditional, and vociferously anti-bourgeois—at least rhetorically. Many of the Dada artists had been involved in the First World War, and the Dada movement has been understood as a reaction of disgust at a society which could sustain such a barbaric war. If the war was the end-product of a society supposedly built on the principles of rationality espoused by Enlightenment philosophers, then the means of protest against this society would have to be irrational. This is the context in which Marcel Duchamp began to exhibit his 'ready-mades'—ordinary objects, like bicycle wheels and the urinal he named 'Fountain', signed 'R. Mutt', and presented as a sculpture. In doing so, Duchamp offended not only the assumption that art involves creative effort, but also the assumption that only certain objects are appropriate subject-matter for art, and this does not include utterly utilitarian ones. In the words of Thomas Elsaesser, Dada sought 'ways of radically short-circuiting the means by which art objects acquire financial, social, and spiritual values' (Elsaesser 1987: 17), thus fulfilling Bürger's definition of the avant-garde as an attack on the foundations of artistic institutions.

Several artists associated with Dada made films, including Hans Richter and Man Ray. The most accomplished Dada films—completed some time after the movement had disintegrated—was René Clair's *Entr'acte* (France, 1924). Two aspects of the film stand out. First, while the outlines of a narrative can be found—involving the shooting of a man and his subsequent funeral—the energies of the film are invested in a variety of non-narrative strategies which cut across and often completely submerge its progress. Since narrative is a form of rationality—we explain ourselves through stories revealing our reasons for doing things—it becomes an object of attack, along with standards of propriety (scattered across the film are 'crotch-shots' of a ballerina, ultimately revealed to be a bearded man in drag). Narrative logic is replaced by an unpredictable mix of associative and abstract links. Second, the film was originally conceived and projected as a part of a larger performance: the film acted as an intermission (the literal meaning of 'entr-acte') within the Dada ballet *Relâche* ('Cancelled'). The scenario for the film was the creation of the painter Francis Picabia, who wrote the ballet with the composer Erik Satie (the two of them also 'star' in the film). Thus, although the film was directed by a figure who was to sustain a career as a film director, it emerged very much out of collaboration with artists working in the plastic and musical arts. This was typical of avant-garde film production in the 1920s, and to a lesser degree continued to be so throughout its history.

Surrealism was a more formal movement, with a dominant leader (André Breton) and a more elaborate theory, but which nevertheless continued the Dada interest in the irrational. This was now buttressed by explicit appeals to Freud's theory of the unconscious. In an article from 1927, Breton identified two 'methods' of Surrealist composition: automatism (the attempt to relinquish conscious control of design in the actual creation of the art object), and the controlled depiction of dream and unconscious imagery. What the two methods share is the depiction of chance and 'marvellous' juxtapositions, creating an impression of randomness and irrationality for the viewer, and thus a rejection of the idea that art must cling to the representation of an everyday visible reality.

Another notable feature of Dada and Surrealism was a fascination with popular culture: the Surrealist canon of filmmakers includes Georges Méliès, Buster Keaton, Charlie Chaplin, and the popular French serial Fantômas. This was a fascination shared by many other modernist and avant-garde artists: an animated 'Charlot' (Charlie Chaplin) figurine introduces Léger's *Ballet mécanique*, while *Entr'acte* juxtaposes its ballerina with a host of references to popular attractions—fairground shooting-ranges, chase films, and rollercoasters. This suggests that the 'culture of negation' is a little more complicated than it at first appears, for what we have here are approving references to the very mass culture which the avant-garde is said to negate. Pierre Bourdieu, in his monumental sociology of culture, class, and taste *Distinction*, provides a clue: 'the avant-garde defin[es] itself in a quasi-negative way, as the sum of the refusals of all socially recognized tastes: refusal of the middle-of-the-road taste of the big shop-keepers . . . refusal of bourgeois taste . . . refusal of the teachers' pedantic taste . . . And so the logic of double negation can lead the artist back, as if in defiance, to some of the preferences characteristic of popular taste' (1979/1984: 294). This attitude is delightfully and succinctly expressed in a slogan used by the German Dadaist Georg Grosz: Chaplin beats Rembrandt!

These textual strategies were echoed by the viewing habits that the Dadaists and Surrealists adopted, at least apocryphally. Breton claims that groups of them would drift in and out of cinemas, disregarding the beginnings and endings of particular films, and break out picnic hampers and champagne while they watched. The effect of such fleeting and broken attention would be to undermine narrative unity and turn fragments of narrative films into prompts for an oneiric, associative spectatorship. Such behaviour also evinced a nostalgia for an earlier era of 'primitive' cinema, when attending the movies shared more with the boisterous atmosphere of the fairground and vaudeville than with bourgeois theatre or opera. The historical accuracy of such an image of early cinema is less at stake here than the fact that such an image was used to upset more 'refined' conventions of spectatorship. What emerges in France of the 1920s is a dialectic, rather than simple negation, of avant-garde and popular culture: the avant-garde may oppose what it takes to be bourgeois taste, but in doing so it frequently embraces and transforms aspects of popular culture.

The Surrealists had been inspired by the Russian Revolution to believe in the possibility of a radically new society, and for a period in the late 1920s they formally allied themselves with the French Communist Party. There was always a tension, though, between Surrealist aesthetics and the demands of direct political agitation. The alliance with the Communist Party eventually broke down in 1935, when 'socialist realism' was adopted as the official aesthetic of the Communist Party, first in the Soviet Union and then in Western Europe. In the Soviet Union itself, Eisenstein, Vertov, and the other montage directors increasingly attracted criticism—for the alleged exclusivity and élitism of their innovative work—in spite of its explicit Bolshevik commitments. Experimental montage was curtailed when socialist realism became mandatory in the Soviet Union in 1934. Thus, for all the differences between the Soviet montage movement and the Surrealists, there is an important parallel between them in their incompatibility with unalloyed and unadorned political agitation, manifest in the events of 1934–5 in both France and the Soviet Union. That said, state repression of the avant-garde was much more obvious under the totalitarian regimes of the Soviet Union and Germany, where avant-garde practice was denigrated as, respectively, 'formalist' and 'degenerate'. In both cases, avant-gardism was stamped out because it conflicted with, or merely failed to serve, official state policy. The dramatic decline of the European avant-garde in the 1930s is thus connected with a paradoxical feature of the avant-garde ethos discussed by Poggioli (1962/1968). Avant-garde artistic practice can only flourish under liberal political regimes, which are willing to tolerate vigorous expressions of dissent against the state and society more generally. In this respect the avant-garde bites the hand that feeds, or, in Poggioli's words, it pays 'involuntary homage' (1968: 106) to the bourgeois liberal democracies it attacks.

Post-war art cinema, political modernism, and Third Cinema

The rise of fascism and the arrival of war definitively broke up the pre-war avant-garde movements in the most literal sense: an entire generation of artists was geographically displaced, politically silenced, or co-opted. After the war, three forms of cinema developed with links to the pre-war experiments. First, within the institutions of the international art cinema, filmmakers like Godard, Jean-Marie Straub and Danièle Huillet, Glauber Rocha, Nagisa Oshima, Gillo Pontecorvo, Jansó, Dušan Makavejev, Rainer Werner Fassbinder, and Raúl Ruiz produced feature-length works which integrated radical-left politics with varying degrees of aesthetic experimentation. Second, in Europe and more visibly in the United States, a new generation of 'artisanal' avant-gardists emerged, whose interests were extremely diverse, ranging from a continuation of the abstract experiments of the 1920s to political satire. In the 1960s a third type of radical cinema emerged, reviving and developing the agitational practices of the Soviet Union in the 1920s. This militant, 'engaged' cinema shared with the artisanal avant-garde small-scale production and co-operative distribution, and the leftist political agenda of some art cinema directors; but it disdained the stress in both art and avant-garde cinema on authorship and aesthetics in favour of agitation and political intervention on specific issues.

Although the notion of an art cinema had existed since at least the formation of the Film d'Art company in France in 1908, it was not until after the Second World War that European art cinema became firmly established, with the succession of movements such as Italian Neo-Realism, the French Nouvelle Vague, and the New German Cinema. A number of factors account for its rise at this point: new legislation in many of the European countries to promote indigenous film cultures, combined with new opportunities for foreign films within the American film market as a result of the dismantling of vertical integration.

The 'art' in 'art cinema' is differentiated from the art of other cinemas in two ways. First, art films are usually expressive of national concerns, even if these concerns are ones that, ironically, make them internationally marketable (for example, it is partly the perceived 'Englishness' of *My Beautiful Laundrette* (Stephen Frears, GB, 1985) that makes it of interest to American audiences). Second, art films attempt to conform with canons of taste established in the existing 'high' arts. That is, art films are generally characterized by the use of self-consciously 'artful' techniques designed to differentiate them from 'merely entertaining', popular cinema, these techniques frequently drawing on nationally specific legacies within the established arts (Expressionist painting in Robert Wiene's *The Cabinet of Dr Caligari* (Germany, 1920), the *nouveau roman* in Alain Resnais's *Hiroshima mon amour* (France, 1959) and *Last Year at Marienbad* (France, 1961), Italian opera in Bernardo Bertolucci's *The Spider's Strategem* (Italy, 1970)). These 'native' cultural markers are often commingled with allusions, critical or affectionate, to American popular culture, this internal contrast further highlighting the national specificity of such films.

This strategy enables the art film to be viewed at home as part of a national culture, and abroad as exotic or sophisticated—or both—and therefore as worthy of the attention of an educated audience. In the United States in particular, simply being European gives a film an edge in this regard, because of the view of Europe as the 'Old World', repository of Art and Wisdom. For this reason, art cinema still tends to be thought of as European art cinema, even though a substantial proportion of art-house material has for some time come from Asia, South America, Australia, and (less fre-

> The 'art' in 'art cinema' is differentiated from the art of other cinemas in two ways. First, art films are usually expressive of national concerns, even if these concerns are ones that, ironically, make them internationally marketable. Second, art films attempt to conform with canons of taste established in the existing 'high' arts.

quently) Africa. 'Art cinema', then, is partly a matter of the marketing and consumption of films outside their countries of production, and the circumstances of *production* of 'art' films varies widely depending on the peculiarities of particular national film industries.

In aesthetic terms, 'art cinema' encompasses a diverse range of options, from the tradition of 'quality', literary adaptations of Merchant–Ivory, to the genre reworkings of Claude Chabrol, to the experiments of Godard. Within this diversity, however, some consistent trends and patterns stand out. David Bordwell (1979) has argued that by the 1960s a distinctive art cinema 'mode of narration' had emerged. Where the Hollywood film typically featured a sympathetic protagonist pursuing his or her goal until an unambiguous conclusion was reached, the art film dwelt upon characters with less clearly defined and singular desires. This produced a narrative less clearly structured by explicit temporal markers like deadlines, and enabled the self-conscious use of style to evoke atmosphere and ambiguity. In general, the art film foregrounds narration (the process of storytelling) as much as narrative (the action itself, assumed to be the locus of attention in the classical film). Distinctive uses of style and idiosyncratic narrational stances in turn become associated with individual directors, around which the marketing of art films centre (a Chabrol film is marketed primarily as a Chabrol film, not as a thriller).

Bordwell sees this form as a modification of classical norms of narration and style, not a radical departure from them. Although the art film director has more freedom to explore stylistic options, a story with recognizable characters must still be told, generally within a screening time of between 80 and 180 minutes, since these are commercial films which must be exhibited in the art-house circuit. For these reasons, Bordwell characterizes art cinema narration as a 'domesticated modernism', and contrasts it with the more radical departures from classical form found within the artisanal avant-garde. The key here, once again, is the freedom of artisanal filmmakers to explore spatial and temporal form in the cinema outside any obligation to tell a story; and to make films—with or without any traces of narrative—of any length, ranging from a few seconds to many hours.

Bordwell's description certainly applies to many art films of the 1960s and 1970s, and captures many of the features of art cinema which differentiate it from straightforward Hollywood-style fare. It is a description, however, only of the typical form of art films during a specific historical phase, and for this reason particular art films and directors will fall outside its ambit. These include not only more conservative filmmakers like Merchant–Ivory, where the 'art' usually amounts to little more than a national picturesque 'gloss' applied to classical narrative form, but also those filmmakers who use the feature-length format for more radical ends—aesthetically, politically, or both.

Chief among these are directors such as Godard, Straub and Huillet, and Oshima, for whom a radical political agenda must be articulated within and by radical, anti-realist form—a trend often identified as political modernism or, in Peter Wollen's terminology, 'counter-cinema'. Wollen sums up the tendencies of such filmmaking through seven contrasts with orthodox narrative filmmaking, such as those between 'identification' and 'estrangement', and 'transparency' and 'foregrounding'. The revolt and protests by French students and workers in May 1968 have come to symbolize this convergence of radical politics and experimental form, but this was the culmination of developments throughout the 1960s. In West Germany in 1963 Jean-Marie Straub and Danièle Huillet made their first film, the short Machorka-Muff. Like their first feature, Nicht versöhnt ('Not Reconciled', West Germany, 1965), it explored the history and legacy of fascist politics in Germany. Not Reconciled—subtitled 'Only Violence Serves where Violence Reigns'—traces the history of a family across three generations, from the First World War to the time of the film's making. The continuity of fascist beliefs and behaviour across the generations is rendered by a patchwork of flashbacks which moves us back and forth between different times without the usual transitional markers (dissolves, music, and so forth). The title thus evokes at least two connotations: the lack of reconcilia-

tion among various social groups in Germany, represented by different members of the family; and the refusal of the film to provide a resolution—a reconciliation—of the conflicts among agents and interests in the film's narrative. The film thus executes Brecht's dramaturgy in its narrative of 'leaps' and 'curves' rather than simple linear development, as it does in its muted performance style, both techniques seeking a 'distanciated' rather than highly emotive, putatively uncritical, response.

Other important instances of the convergence between experimental form and radical left politics were evident outside Europe. Oshima's Nihon no yoru to kiri ('Night and Fog in Japan', Japan, 1960) depicted opposition to the US–Japan Security Treaty, using stylized tableaux and an intricate flashback structure to explore conflict among different generations of protesters. In Brazil the Cinema Nôvo filmmakers—among them Glauber Rocha and Ruy Guerra—exhibited a formal inventiveness and diversity akin to the Nouvelle Vague filmmakers who had inspired them, but used them in treating overtly political narratives. In Cuba Julio García Espinosa published in 1969 his manifesto calling for an 'Imperfect Cinema'—one responsive to popular needs rather than the high production values of either Hollywood or most European art cinema. In the same year in Argentina Fernando Solanas and Octavio Getino argued for a 'Third Cinema'—a cinema of militant and interventionist 'film acts' aimed at undermining the neo-colonial status quo—which would be an alternative to both Hollywood (First) and art (Second) cinema. Developing a model similar to the Soviet agitki (short propaganda films, often disseminated by trains and trucks to rural areas lacking screening facilities), and the similar use of film by the Vietcong in the Vietnam conflict, Third Cinema advocated the exhibition of films on immediate issues by activist, student, and worker groups, to be used as the basis of political discussion. As Solanas and Getino (1969/1976) note, a kindred movement had already developed in the United States, represented by the Newsreel collectives, and the work of such filmmakers as Robert Kramer and Emile de Antonio (a practice sustained and developed in the 1970s by Christine Choy and Third World Newsreel). Although the enthusiasm for such a project has waned or at least mutated in North America and Europe—an issue we will return to in the final section—the notion of a Third Cinema continues to be of relevance to Third World and diasporic filmmakers in Europe and North America.

The connections between European and Third World radicalism were explicitly represented in a scene in Godard's *Weekend* (France, 1967), in which two black immigrant workers declare a programme of militant resistance to economic and political oppression by the West through guerrilla warfare. Within this apocalyptic film, which views European culture and cinema as profoundly decadent—the film ends with the title 'fin du cinéma'—this dialogue represents the only vital political programme. Godard's arrival at this moment was not a straightforward one, however. His films from the beginning were marked by an unparalleled formal playfulness in which Eisenstein and Brecht were both obvious sources of inspiration. But in contrast to these earlier figures, Godard's formal inventiveness in the first phase of his career was only occasionally yoked with political radicalism. From 1964 onwards, however, an interest in socialist politics comes to occupy an ever-more central role in Godard's work. Spurred on by the events of May 1968, Godard pushed the radicalism of *Weekend* still further and formed with Jean-Pierre Gorin the Dziga–Vertov Group—named after an earlier master of political modernism, and one of a number of film cadres which formed in the wake of May 1968. The political 'essays' made by the group represented a synthesis of ideas drawn from European modernism with others derived from the activist and agitational tradition extending from the Soviets to the Vietcong (an influence cited in the black workers' speech in *Weekend*) and the followers of Third Cinema. In the late 1970s, however, Godard again reoriented himself, moving away from the heavily politicized films of the early and mid-1970s, opting for a more poetic—and commercially viable—form. Godard's retreat from an overtly radical political cinema is emblematic of the fate of political modernism in Europe as a whole.

The post-war avant-garde

Along with better-known figures such as Fritz Lang, Bertolt Brecht, and Jean Renoir, Hans Richter was among the leftist intelligentsia who fled Nazi Europe for the United States. The Second World War was a turning-point not only in the individual lives of so many artists and intellectuals, but in the history of the avant-garde as a whole. If the centre of avant-garde activity between the wars had been Europe (with Paris often identified as playing the leading role), this role passed to the United States, or, more particularly, New York, after the war. Just as Abstract Expressionism emerged in the post-war years as the first style of avant-garde painting geographically rooted in the United States, so a vigorous avant-garde film community began to develop. By 1962 a cohesive non-commercial system of production, distribution, exhibition had been created, with its centres in New York and San Francisco; a critical establishment was not long coming.

The presence of *émigrés* like Richter also played a role in these developments. Richter took up a position teaching film at New York's City College Institute of Film Technique in 1943, and in 1947 attempted to bring the aesthetics of the film avant-garde to a wider audience with the feature-length film *Dreams that Money can Buy*. Funded by the art patron Peggy Guggenheim, the film was comprised of a series of episodes, each of which represents a dream being sold by a dream salesman. Obviously enough, the film is a metaphor for commercial cinema—the dream factory. The style of each episode, however, was anything but commercial, since each was made by an established avant-garde artist (e.g. Max Ernst) and accompanied by avant-garde compositions (e.g. John Cage). Many of the episodes were reprises of avant-garde works from the 1920s. However, Richter framed these episodes with a narrated voice-over which motivates each episode as a dream designed for each client and their particular neuroses. Narrative coherence was to be the bridgehead between avant-garde aesthetics and a wider audience. But the film found little favour with the embryonic American avant-garde, perhaps because it was in the process of establishing its own institutions, and in its aesthetics reaffirming that suspicion of narrative so apparent in the pre-war European avant-garde (Maya Deren, for example, complained that 'narrative pattern has come to completely dominate cinematic expression in spite of the fact that it is, basically, a visual form'; 1946: 318). Richter had recognized that the avant-garde was 'blessed in its liberty and cursed in its alienation' (Poggioli 1968: 109) but discovered that the avant-garde community were not at this point interested in trading in any part of their aesthetic liberty for the sake of reaching a broader audience.

Of the indigenous figures in the nascent American film avant-garde, Deren is among the most significant—not just for making one of the most influential films of the tradition, but for her activities as a promoter and proselytizer of the avant-garde. Her first and most well-known film is *Meshes of the Afternoon*, made in 1943 in collaboration with her husband Alexander Hammid (another European *émigré*). The film depicts a series of narrative loops, in which a dreaming woman (played by Deren) sees herself in a number of menacing confrontations with a husband (played by Hammid), a mysteriously cloaked figure, and several *doppelgängers*. Parker Tyler (1960), and later P. Adams Sitney, saw the film as a precursor of a major 'genre' of the American avant-garde: the 'trance' film or 'psychodrama', in which a 'protagonist wanders through a potent environment toward a climactic scene of self-realization' (Sitney 1979: 21).

Sitney situates this concern with 'self-realization' within the Romantic tradition, that is, the dominant intellectual and literary legacy deriving from European philosophers and artists of the eighteenth-century. Expression of feeling and the transformative power of the imagination are the factors which link these twentieth-century filmmakers with earlier artists; Sitney's history is titled *Visionary Film*, stressing the powerful, shaping force of the individual artistic imagination. Other critics have disputed the appropriateness of Romantic thought as the context in which the American avant-garde is examined. While there are limitations to the approach, however, two factors weigh in Sitney's favour. First, it is hard to conceive of avant-garde culture in general without Romanticism. In its stress on innovation and the continual violation of convention over the values of tradition and the observation of rules, the avant-garde is the apotheosis of Romantic thought. Second, Sitney was in part taking his cue from practitioners who cited ideas drawn from the Romantic tradition. Chief among these was the most prolific filmmaker in avant-garde history, Stan Brakhage.

Many of Brakhage's early films, like *Reflections on Black* (USA, 1955), were trance films. As his work developed, though, Brakhage massively expanded the scale and visual vocabulary of such films and intensified their subjective character. The Romantic character of Brakhage's project emerges most clearly in his collection of writings *Metaphors on Vision* (originally published as issue 30 of the journal *Film Culture*). In Brakhage's view, the human subject loses its authentic identity as it learns language, the conventions of pictorial perspective, and narrative—in other words, as it becomes socialized. By 'wrecking' these conventions, as they are embodied in narrative filmmaking, film can render an 'untutored' perception and consciousness. In *Window Water Baby Moving* (USA, 1959), which depicts

his wife Jane giving birth to their first child, Brakhage pursues this effect by counterpointing the sequential development of the birth with repetitive abstract and rhythmic patterns.

By the early 1960s two new notions had entered circulation within this milieu: the New American Cinema and underground cinema. A central figure in these developments was Jonas Mekas. Writing of the 'Cinema of the New Generation' in 1960, Mekas saw promising parallels between the European art cinema. In a fashion somewhat similar to Richter in the late 1940s, Mekas envisaged a cinema reconciling self-conscious aesthetic seriousness with popular accessibility, and incorporated under this rubric everything from Brakhage, Breer, and Marie Menken to early direct cinema and independent feature narratives. In 1960 credence was given to this argument by the formation of the New American Cinema Group, comprised of filmmakers, producers, performers, and the catalyst Mekas himself. In 1961 the group published a statement in the journal *Film Culture* which, in its rejection of the 'product film' and 'official cinema', used that rhetoric of negation so typical of the avant-garde (Mekas 1961). However, the positive strategies which were to replace the 'product film' were too diverse to hold together for very long, resulting in a split between the 'purist' artisanal ethos, and a modified commercial practice. Mekas promoted the former, which, increasingly inflected by the post war youth and counter-cultures, became known as 'underground cinema' (Mekas 1972).

Kenneth Anger's *Scorpio Rising* (USA, 1963) is probably the most well-known icon of the underground cinema—partly because of its early notoriety, partly because it combines superficial accessibility with a formidable density of form. Structured by thirteen contemporaneous pop songs, the film follows the actions of a biker and his associates, dressing and preparing for a climactic race in which one of the bikers is killed. By juxtaposing the songs with the hedonistic and nihilistic activities of the biker gang, the film continually draws out of the pop songs the painful and perverse implications within them, but easily overlooked in their original context.

Another feature of *Scorpio Rising* representative of broader activities within the underground was its use of collage or assemblage—the creation of new works through found or 'quoted' material. Anger's film juxtaposes original footage with rephotographed television and cartoon material (and, of course, the soundtrack, which is also created in collage fashion). The purest form of film collage is the compilation film: a film entirely comprised of footage lifted from other films, as in the work of Bruce Conner (and much earlier, Joseph Cornell's *Rose Hobart*, USA, 1936).

In *Scorpio Rising*, Anger's collage works by a process of 'reverse metaphor', in which the traits and qualities of the counter-cultural bikers are projected onto mainstream figures we would normally regard as virtuous or at least innocuous: children's cartoons and images of Christ (Peterson 1994: 160–1). Bruce Conner's work is similarly subversive and ironic. His film *Report* (USA, 1963–7) explores the Kennedy assassination through a radio broadcast relating the build-up to and aftermath of the event, against which are placed repeated shots of the motorcade, countdown leader, and other filmic detritus, and a furious climactic montage intercutting various shots of Kennedy with (among others) shots of a bullfight, a light bulb being shattered in slow motion, and an advertisement for a fridge. All of this is found footage, re-edited to suggest new meanings: the bulb becomes a metaphor for Kennedy's shattered skull, the bullfight suggesting first Kennedy's status as hero (the matador), then his descent into the role of publicly slaughtered victim (the bull), and finally his status as a commodity to be sold, like the fridge. At the most general level, the film heightens its attention to public spectacles of violence—a theme also explored by Conner's *A Movie* (1958)—by pointedly denying us a direct visual image of the moment of assassination itself.

Films like *Report*, and many other collage films, give the lie to the argument that the avant-garde in America is wholly apolitical. In addition to the artisanal works discussed so far, there also appeared in the United States in the 1960s some politicized narrative films which form a parallel with Wollen's 'political avant-garde'. Some of these were formally conventional features like *Nothing but a Man* (Michael Roemer and Robert Young, USA, 1964), which dealt with black oppression in the American south. The closer parallel is with Jon Jost, who has managed to sustain an idiosyncratic career as a 'guerrilla filmmaker' from the mid-1960s to the present day. Involved early in his career with the founding of a Newsreel office in Chicago, Jost went on to combine familiar art cinema strategies with more unusual ones. *Speaking Directly* (USA, 1974), for example, is an essay on the relations between individual, private existence, political power, and forms of representation. The film combines diary footage of

Jost's everyday existence with staged, almost allegorical demonstrations of the film's main thesis (that all filmmaking is intrinsically political, no matter how 'personal' or 'subjective' it appears to be), and collage sections using in one case documentary footage of Vietnam, and magazine advertisements in another.

A rather pointed absence in my discussion of the American avant-garde so far is the name Andy Warhol. Warhol's early filmmaking (1962–6) can be seen as a kind of hinge between the 1960s underground and the avant-garde movement which was to command critical attention in the late 1960s and early 1970s in both Europe and America: structural filmmaking. The most obvious connection between Warhol's films and the underground is the explicit representation of sexuality—straight, gay, and polymorphous—in films like *Kiss* and *Blow Job* (both 1963), *Couch* (1964), and *My Hustler* (1965). But films like *Sleep* (1963) and *Empire* (1964) (eight hours of footage of the Empire State Building, projected at sixteen frames per second) exhibit a different form of outrageousness: the refusal to provide even the most minimal dramatic or visual development.

It is in this respect that Warhol's early filmmaking adumbrates structural aesthetics. Structural films empty themselves of apparent 'content' in order to draw our attention to the functioning of a particular aspect of film technique. The most famous example is Michael Snow's *Wavelength* (USA, 1967), a film comprised of a gradual zoom shot across a loft apartment, interrupted by coloured frames, and accompanied by the sound of an ever-rising tone. Characters involved in a murder narrative stray into this space, but none of this action deflects the zoom from its continual cropping of the space or the sound from its relentless ascent through the frequencies. In Warhol's *Couch*, the use of fixed camera positions and the overt use of the length of film reels (the flare at the beginning and end of each reel is not edited out) give the film an obvious, minimal structure, and emphasize the material features of filmmaking almost in resistance to the 'scandalous' sexual actions which are depicted.

Sitney viewed Snow's work as a further development within 'visionary' cinema. If Brakhage had produced a cinema of vision, Snow's achievement was to create a cinema of the mind, in which the films metaphorically represent or explore features of human consciousness. This view of Snow's work, first proposed by Annette Michelson (1971/1978), has been lucidly elaborated by Sitney and William Wees (1982). But objections to

Sitney's argument have been more common. The most important of these seek to situate structural filmmaking within modernism rather than Romanticism (where it is assumed that modernism, while evolving from Romanticism, makes a decisive break with it). In *Abstract Film and Beyond* (1977), Malcolm Le Grice presents an alternative history of the avant-garde to that proposed by Sitney. Le Grice situates the avant-garde within modernism, in his case drawing implicitly on the influential account of modernism associated with Clement Greenberg. For Greenberg, modernism represents the phase in the history of an art when it reflects upon its materials and undergoes a kind of purification (Greenberg 1961/1973). Similarly, Le Grice traces efforts through the history of cinema to focus on the peculiar properties of film. To this is added the implication that such work is *politically* radical—an argument more explicitly made by Peter Gidal (1989)—in so far as it demystifies the means by which films are made. Le Grice's own films from this period, like *Berlin Horse* (GB, 1971), exemplify this aesthetic; but one of the purest examples of this form of reflexive filmmaking is David Crosswalte's elegant *Man with the Movie Camera* (GB, 1973), which manipulates mirrors and focus to create a series of enigmatic images of a film camera, explained as the film itself reveals progressively more parts of the apparatus. 'Structural-material' film—as it came to be known in the British context—represented the moment at which these 'specifist' concerns fully realized themselves.

Structural film dominated critical attention, and perhaps practice, for at most ten years, but it seems pivotal for a variety of reasons. It was heralded, particularly in its British manifestation, as an ultimate and pure manifestation of modernism within film. This as accompanied by attacks on other trends within the avant-garde made with even more than the usual vigour. In criticism, one consequence of Le Grice's view is the marginalization of a great deal of avant-garde practice—much of the work of the Surrealists and the underground—on the grounds that the incorporation of 'dramatic' elements undermines a film's radical and oppositional status. In filmmaking practice, this purity consisted of a more rigorous—or, to its detractors, rigid—expulsion of all vestiges of narrative. Consequently, viewers unfamiliar with the avant-garde find structural filmmaking the most puzzling and 'difficult' of its many trends. The structural phase of the avant-garde is also important in institutional terms. Although certain filmmakers had occasionally held teaching positions from the 1940s onwards, the emergence of structural film coincided with a much greater integration of the avant-garde community with art schools, universities, and museums. Structural film, it might be argued, represents at once the apogee and the end of the avant-garde—an idea most usefully discussed in relation to the notion of postmodernism later in this chapter.

Feminism and the avant-garde

The importance attributed to structural film should not obscure other significant developments in the wake of the 1960s underground. One of these is the emergence of a more self-conscious feminist presence within the avant-garde. To some degree, avant-garde filmmaking has always provided opportunities for women's expression denied them in the mainstream, just as it has for gays. Dulac in the 1920s and Deren in the 1940s were important both as theorists and as practitioners, and both made films of proto-feminist import: *La Souriante Madame Beudet* (France, 1923) and *Meshes of the Afternoon*. There have clearly also been other women filmmakers—such as Marie Menken, a major early influence on Stan Brakhage, and later figures such as Shirley Clarke and Joyce Wieland—whose significance has been underestimated in many avant-garde histories (Rabinovitz 1991). But it is only with the emergence of the post-war women's movement in the 1960s that 'woman' as such becomes a major focus within the avant-garde.

Underground cinema embodies the notion of 'Sixties liberation', but as often as not underground films echoed, rather than challenged, the constraining representations of women found in the mainstream. Robert Nelson's exuberant neo-Dada *Oh Dem Watermelons* (USA, 1965) may subject racial stereotypes to parodic distension, but its footage of a naked woman caressing herself with a watermelon hardly subverts the sexual economy of the mainstream film, in which women are usually the object and rarely the subject of the erotic gaze. A number of women filmmakers, however, turned underground aesthetics to feminist ends, including Barbara Rubin, Anne Severson, and Carolee Schneemann. Schneemann's *Fuses* (USA, 1967) is a diary film concerned with the detail of her erotic life with James Tenney, and was made partly out of dissatisfaction with two films made by Brakhage about this relationship. The film breaks with patriarchal conventions of the representation of women not by denying the female body as an object to look at, but by placing it in a fuller context. In addition to love-making, we see unerotic, domestic action. The naked female body is not idealized through soft focus and modelled lighting. Moreover, Schneemann is presented as an initiator in the sexual act, and shots of Tenney are just as frank and frequent as those of her.

This strategy was not welcomed by many in the women's movement at the time, because of the at least superficial resemblance between *Fuses* and pornographic films, which by the early 1970s had become a target for many feminists (as did earlier, apparently liberating representations of women, such as Brakhage's *Window Water Baby Moving*). A very different type of film, drawing heavily on feminist theory, emerged in the 1970s. In 'Visual Pleasure and Narrative Cinema' (1975) British critic and filmmaker Laura Mulvey argued that the narrative and visual construction of orthodox narrative films embodied a patriarchal ideology in which women were either idealized or punished, but either way diminished. Her call for the 'destruction' of the pleasures derived from such cinema—prefigured by Claire Johnston's (1973) discussion of 'women's cinema as counter-cinema'—inspired her own filmic practice (e.g. *Penthesilea*, GB, 1974, and *Riddles of the Sphinx*, GB, 1977, both made with Peter Wollen), as well as influencing that of Yvonne Rainer in the United States. Rainer's *The Man who Envied Women* (USA, 1985), for example, is structured around a female protagonist who is never visible; she is rendered only through voice-over. Her husband, the man in the title, is by contrast doubly visible, in that he is played by two actors. So the film reverses the polarity that, according to Mulvey, structures Hollywood cinema, by exempting the main female character entirely from the look of the camera and spectator. In this, as in her other films, however, Rainer does not simply adopt Mulvey's or anybody else's thesis; rather, the film interweaves a great multitude of theories, and types of footage and imagery, around a narrative core, tending to play them off one another rather than endorsing any one. In addition, the film questions the sexual politics not only of Hollywood, but also of the avant-garde itself. The film 'quotes' the opening of *Un chien andalou* and implies that the slicing of the woman's eye is not merely a provocative 'shock' image, but another manifestation of misogyny.

In their efforts to create a feminist cinema in formal—not merely thematic—terms, the work of Mulvey and

Rainer echoed that of European filmmakers like Marguerite Duras and Chantal Akerman. Such films shared with structural aesthetics a profound suspicion of conventional narrative—Rainer once talked of the 'tyranny' of narrative—but as the influence of structural film waned, narrative returned with a vengeance, becoming a major object of concern for both feminists and others within the avant-garde. Several factors motivated this renewed attention to narrative. Paul Willemen questioned the idea that there was a stable relationship between a particular kind of form (like structural form) and an 'avant-garde' or critical effect. The functioning of different strategies had to be re-addressed in each new context. Willemen argued that the investigation of historical questions was a priority, and that narrative was essential to such a project. Other filmmakers became concerned about the exclusivity of the avant-garde, a problem highlighted by structural filmmaking, and one that both Richter and Mekas had tried to solve. Sally Potter turned to narrative form and familiar narrative types in *Thriller* (GB, 1979)—albeit in a novel way—in order to connect with the pleasures of conventional narrative cinema and so address a potentially larger audience.

Along with this return to narrative came a renewed attention to expressivity in various ways. Some feminists, like Schneemann, had always found themselves out of tune with the detachment of structural filmmaking. Similar remarks were made by younger women filmmakers whose careers began in the 1980s, such as Vivienne Dick and Su Friedrich. Friedrich's *Gently down the Stream* (USA, 1981) constitutes a particularly interesting case because of the way it returns to the highly expressive mode of the trance film, while reshaping it for feminist and lesbian ends. Here, the dreams of the implied protagonist concern anxieties over her lesbian desires and religious allegiances. The gradual and painful passage to a new sexual identity is suggested by a progression of water images, each one suggesting greater control over the water than the last. Like Brakhage, Friedrich scratches words onto the surface of the film, but where Brakhage uses this as a way of underlining the personal nature of the film, in Friedrich's film scratched intertitles vie with images for domination of the film in a most un-Brakhagean manner. Identity, it is implied, will occur partly through language, not by transcending it. And like *Window Water Baby Moving*, the film is filled with birth imagery, but rather than being rendered as a natural process to be experienced in the most 'untutored' fashion possible, here it is presented as a metaphor for the drea-mer's difficulty in attaining selfhood.

The return of interest in narrative and expressivity has been evident in a diverse range of practices since the mid-1970s: New Narrative, New Talkie, Cinema of Transgression, and most recently, New Underground. In contrast to the heyday of the structural films, there is little critical consensus about which mode or style of filmmaking is most important. As in the avant-garde more widely, stylistic pluralism has been a feature of avant-garde film over the last twenty years. There have been moments of such pluralism before—in the 1920s for example—but it is widely held that the contempor-ary situation is qualitatively different from earlier phases of avant-garde and modernist practice. This is the shift denoted by the term 'postmodernism'.

Postmodernism and the paradox of tradition

The term 'postmodernism' has come to assume a bewildering variety of connotations, but for our pur-poses these can be reduced to three. In the first use it refers to the stylistic pluralism noted above. In archi-tecture, where this version of the phrase has been particularly important, it refers to the eclectic mixing of various historical styles in the design of buildings (a dominant trend in post-war architecture). The problem with this definition, at least as it is extended to film history, is that the mixing of radically different styles was already evident in the work of many 1920s avant-gardists (as we have seen). A more sophisticated ver-sion of the postmodern argument claims that it is not the mere presence of eclecticism, but its cultural posi-tion and use, that has changed. Rather than function-ing within an avant-garde ethos in which the gesture of mixing styles constituted a typical attempt to occupy the position of most advanced and subversive trend, in postmodern culture stylistic pluralism marks an exhaustion of the subversive energies and ambitions associated with the avant-garde. In Fredric Jameson's words, 'all that is left is to imitate dead styles, to speak through the masks and with the voices of the styles in the imaginary museum' of the past (1991: 115).

Writing more than a decade before Jameson, and reworking the military metaphor underpinning the notion of avant-gardism, Harold Rosenberg argued that we have entered a period in which the culture of

negation is replaced by a 'demilitarized zone, flanked by avant-garde ghosts on one side and a changing mass culture on the other' (1972: 219). The once sub-versive styles of the avant-garde have been assimilated by mass culture, so that the gap between nominally avant-garde products and popular, mass cultural ones is greatly reduced. Is there such a difference, one might ask, between Sadie Benning's *Jollies* (USA, 1990), which explores the filmmaker's passage into lesbian-ism with hand-held, pixelvision video footage and a soundtrack of rock tunes, and any number of music videos which place imagery ransacked from the avant-garde under the song being marketed? The avant-garde has become nothing more than a posture of aggression and defiance; postmodernism repre-sents a kind of disenchantment with its high ideals. Indeed, in what is perhaps the ultimate indignity, the very phrase 'avant-garde' has now become a market-ing device itself, as the name of a new line of deodorant in 1994.

Parallel with the absorption of once-subversive styles within the lexicon of mass culture, the objects of the avant-garde have become useful commodities for the 'Establishment', in the fullest sense of that sometimes vague word. 'Avant-garde' paintings and sculptures adorn the walls of major corporations and wealthy individual clients. They at once constitute use-ful market investments, and signify a supposed com-mitment to culture, education, and refinement transcending the materialism of the market. If the Cologne Dadaists had once subverted the polite con-ventions of the art gallery by forcing patrons to enter an exhibition through a mock lavatory, the institutions of gallery and museum have had the last laugh by simply continually expanding the objects which could accrue value by being exhibited within them (urinals, bricks, latterly dead sheep and heads sculpted from frozen blood). Peter Bürger writes of the emergence of a 'Neo-avant-garde' in the 1960s—an *institutionalized* avant-garde which, by definition, undercuts its own rhetoric of subversion (Bürger 1984: 58). More bluntly,

> Parallel with the absorption of once-subversive styles within the lexicon of mass culture, the objects of the avant-garde have become useful commodities for the 'Establishment', in the fullest sense of that sometimes vague word.

Christopher Butler states: 'Aesthetic subversion has . . . become revolutionary pantomime' (1980: 122).

The notion of postmodernism has proven to be compelling to many, but a host of questions can be raised about its legitimacy. A common complaint is that it overlooks the presence within modernism of the defining traits of 'postmodernism' (e.g. Crow 1981: 257). One might also question whether the idea of the avant-garde ever had the power which we assume was ascribed to it before the Second World War; perhaps this is merely a symptom of an ongoing nostalgia for an idea which was always regarded as utopian. (Rosenberg notes that doubts about the continued existence of the avant-garde have been voiced almost as long as the avant-garde has existed—not least by members of the avant-garde.) Similarly, one can question the assumption that there was a moment when avant-garde practice stood wholly outside, or successfully challenged, the operations of the art market. This is true even in the case of the filmic avant-garde, in spite of its displaced position in relation to arguments about a general, cross-media avant-garde. Avant-garde filmmaking has never been embraced by corporations and collectors (notwithstanding the support of Peggy Guggenheim in the 1940s and 1950s, and the brief flirtation of the Ford Foundation with grants to Anger, Conner, and ten other filmmakers in the 1960s). But the filmic avant-garde has become an established part of art schools and many museums, and in Britain has increasing ties with television (for which the avant-garde is another supplier of material for its ever-expanding broadcast hours). More generally, many of the stylistic practices of the filmic avant-garde—especially collage—have been adopted by music videos, TV advertising, and credit sequences (think of Michael Moore's TV Nation, USA/GB, 1994–5). If it did once maintain a more authentically avant-garde status—relative to similar practices in the other arts—it surely no longer does.

J. Hoberman argues that the moment of postmodernism can be described as the moment when the 'oxymoronic tradition of the new'—Rosenberg's description of the avant-garde—'had truly become a tradition' (1991: 117). The sceptical view would hold that, paradoxically, the avant-garde has always in practice 'truly' worked as a tradition. In the words of James Peterson, 'The American avant-garde community trumpets the ideal of aesthetic revolution, but lives a reality of refinement and revision' (1994: 186). The rhetoric of negation has always existed alongside the practice of imitation; the dream of a 'total liberation' from all prior conventions is just that—an unattainable fantasy.

Taking all of this into account, it might be argued that reports of the death of the cinematic avant-garde have been premature, at least if we operate with a more realistic perspective regarding the ambitions and achievements of the historical avant-gardes. There are still filmmakers who work outside commercial structures, depending on their own resources and grants, and who see their work as continually challenging the stylistic and attitudinal norms of the mainstream. When we survey the contemporary scene, we can recognize descendants of all the various strains of avant-garde practice I have discussed: collage in Lewis Klahr's *Tales of the Forgotten Future* (USA, 1988–91), for example, or the fusion of Surrealism and the underground in *The Deadman* (Peggy Ahwesh and Keith Sanborn, USA, 1991). Even the goals of political modernism have survived, in the form of a politicized postmodernism in which the role of representation in politics is as central as it was for political modernism. Laura Kipnis (1986), for example, advocates the 'refunctioning' of pre-existent texts in such a way as to realize their oppositional potential, as in the re-editing of popular television shows in Dara Birnbaum's work. Here, however, the focus on politics and ideology is combined with both a suspicion of universal or 'totalizing' claims (e.g. those of Marxist class analysis), as well as the more relaxed attitude to narrative and its pleasures noted above (for example, Potter's *Thriller*, and some of the films associated with the 'New Queer Cinema', such as Todd Haynes's *Poison*, USA, 1990). And so it is that some critics talk of a 'postmodern avant-garde' (e.g. Sayre 1989)—a contradiction in terms for the version of postmodernism I began with—in which the critical, subversive, and utopian aspirations of the historical avant-gardes are sustained. The status and value of the avant-garde thus remains a contested issue, as, in different ways, it has been through most of its history.

BIBLIOGRAPHY

Abel, Richard (1984), *French Cinema: The First Wave, 1915–1929* (Princeton: Princeton University Press).

Adorno, Theodor, and **Max Horkheimer** (1947/1979), 'The Culture Industry', trans. John Cummings in *Dialectic of Enlightenment* (London: Verso).

Arthur, Paul (1986–7), 'The Last of the Machine?: Avant-garde Film since 1966', *Millennium Film Journal*, 16–18 (Fall–Winter), 69–97.

*Bordwell, David (1979/1985), 'The Art Cinema as a Mode of Film Practice', *Film Criticism*, 4/1 (Fall), 56–64; repr. rev. in *Narration in the Fiction Film* (Madison: University of Wisconsin Press).

—— Janet Staiger, and Kristin Thompson (1985), *The Classical Hollywood Cinema: Film Style and Mode of Production to 1960* (New York: Columbia University Press).

Bourdieu, Pierre (1979/1984), *Distinction: A Social Critique of the Judgement of Taste*, trans. Richard Nice (London: Routledge & Kegan Paul).

Bürger, Peter (1984), *Theory of the Avant-Garde*, trans. Michael Shaw (Minneapolis: University of Minnesota Press).

Butler, Christopher (1980), *After the Wake: The Contemporary Avant-Garde* (Oxford: Clarendon Press).

Christie, Ian (1979), 'French Avant-Garde Film in the Twenties: From "Specificity" to Surrealism', in Phillip Drummond, Deke Dusinberre, and A. L. Rees (eds.), *Film as Film: Formal Experiment in Film 1910–1975* (London: Hayward Gallery).

Crow, Thomas (1981), 'Modernism and Mass Culture in the Visual Arts', in Benjamin Buchloh, Serge Guilbaut, and Daniel Solkin (eds.), *Modernism and Modernity* (Halifax: Press of the Nova Scotia College of Art and Design).

Curtis, David (1971), *Experimental Cinema: A Fifty-Year Evolution* (New York: Delta).

Deren, Maya (1946/1988), 'Cinema as an Art Form', in VèVè A. Clark, Millicent Hodson, and Catrina Neiman (eds.), *The Legend of Maya Deren: A Documentary Biography and Collected Works*, vol. i, part 2 (New York: Anthology Film Archives and Film Culture).

Dwoskin, Stephen (1974), *Film is . . . The International Free Cinema* (London: Peter Owen).

Elsaesser, Thomas (1987), 'Dada/Cinema?', in Rudolf E. Kuenzli (ed.), *Dada and Surrealist Film* (New York: Willis Locker & Owens).

Faure, Élie (1923/1967), 'The Art of Cineplastics', in Dan Talbot (ed.), *Film: An Anthology* (Berkeley: University of California Press).

Garcia Espinosa, Julio (1969/1979), 'For an Imperfect Cinema', *Jump Cut*, 20: 24–6.

Gidal, Peter (1989), *Materialist Film* (London: Routledge).

Greenberg, Clement (1939), 'Avant Garde and Kitsch', *Partisan Review*, 6 (Fall), 34–9.

—— (1947), 'Towards a Newer Laocoon', *Partisan Review*, 7 (Fall), 296–310.

—— (1961/1973), 'Modernist Painting', in Gregory Battcock (ed.), *The New Art* (New York: E. P. Dutton).

Harwood, John (1995), *Eliot to Derrida: The Poverty of Interpretation* (London: Macmillan).

Hoberman, J. (1991), *Vulgar Modernism: Writings on Movies and Other Media* (Philadelphia: Temple University Press).

Horak, Jan-Christopher (ed.) (1995), *Lovers of Cinema: The First American Film Avant-Garde 1919–1945* (Madison: University of Wisconsin Press).

Hughes, Robert (1980), *The Shock of the New: Art and the Century of Change* (London: British Broadcasting Corporation).

James, David E. (1989), *Allegories of Cinema: American Film in the Sixties* (Princeton: Princeton University Press).

Jameson, Fredric (1991/1993), 'Postmodernism; or, The Cultural Logic of Late Capitalism', in Thomas Docherty (ed.), *Postmodernism: A Reader* (London: Harvester-Wheatsheaf).

Johnston, Claire (1973), 'Women's Cinema as Counter-Cinema', in Johnston (ed.), *Notes on Women's Cinema* (London: Society for Education in Film and Television).

Kaplan, E. Ann (1983), *Women and Film: Both Sides of the Camera* (London: Macmillan).

Kipnis, Laura (1986), '"Refunctioning" Reconsidered: Towards a Left Popular Culture', in Colin MacCabe (ed.), *High Theory/Low Culture: Analysing Popular Television and Film* (Manchester: Manchester University Press).

*Le Grice, Malcolm (1977), *Abstract Film and Beyond* (Cambridge: Mass.: MIT Press).

MacDonald, Scott (1989), *A Critical Cinema*, i (Berkeley: University of California Press).

—— (1992), *A Critical Cinema*, ii (Berkeley: University of California Press).

Mekas, Jonas (1960), 'Cinema of the New Generation', *Film Culture*, 21: 1–19.

—— (1961), 'First Statement of the Group', *Film Culture*, 22–3: 131–3.

—— (1972), *Movie Journal: The Rise of a New American Cinema 1959–1971* (New York: Collier Books).

Michelson, Annette (1971/1978), 'Toward Snow', in P. Adams Sitney, *The Avant-Garde Film: A Reader of Theory and Criticism* (New York: Anthology Film Archives).

Mulvey, Laura (1975), 'Visual Pleasure and Narrative Cinema', *Screen*, 16/3 (Autumn), 6–18.

Neale, Steve (1981), 'Art Cinema as Institution', in *Screen*, 22/1: 11–39.

Peterson, James (1994), *Dreams of Chaos, Visions of Order: Understanding the American Avant-Garde Cinema* (Detroit: Wayne State University Press).

Poggioli, Renato (1962/1968), *The Theory of the Avant-Garde*, trans. Gerald Fitzgerald (Cambridge, Mass.: Harvard University Press).

Rabinovitz, Lauren (1991), *Points of Resistance: Women, Power and Politics in the New York Avant-Garde Cinema 1943–1971* (Urbana: University of Illinois Press).

Rosenbaum, Jonathan (1983), *Film: The Front Line–1983* (Denver: Arden Press).

411

Rosenberg, Harold (1972), *The De-definition of Art: Action Art to Pop to Earthworks* (New York: Horizon Press).

Sayre, Henry M. (1989), *The Object of Performance: The American Avant-Garde since 1970* (Chicago: University of Chicago Press).

Sitney, P. Adams (1979), *Visionary Film: The American Avant-Garde 1943–1978*, 2nd edn. (New York: Oxford University Press).

Solanas, Fernando, and Octavio Getino (1969/1976), 'Towards a Third Cinema', in Bill Nichols (ed.), *Movies and Methods* (Berkeley: University of California Press).

Tyler, Parker (1960), *The Three Faces of the Film* (New York: Yoseloff).

Wees, William C. (1982), *Light Moving in Time: Studies in the Visual Aesthetics of Avant-Garde Film* (Berkeley: University of California Press).

*Willemen, Paul (1984), 'An Avant Garde for the Eighties', *Framework*, 24: 53–73.

*Wollen, Peter (1975/1982a), 'The Two Avant-Gardes', in *Readings and Writings: Semiotic Counter-Strategies* (London: Verso).

*—— (1982b), 'Godard and Counter Cinema: *Vent d'Est*', in Wollen (1982a).

3

Realism, modernism, and post-colonial theory

Ashish Rajadhyaksha

'When was "the post-colonial"?', asks Stuart Hall. 'What should be included and excluded from its frame? Where is the invisible line between it and its "others"—colonialism, neo-colonialism, Third World, imperialism—in relation to whose termination it ceaselessly, but without final supersession, marks itself?' (Hall 1996). Does 'post-colonial' refer to some people, or some societies, and not others, as something like a 'badge of merit' (Hulme 1995, quoted in Hall 1996)—or does it signal something more abstract? Bill Ashcroft, Gareth Griffiths, and Helen Tiffin effectively include all nations which have once been colonized in order to 'cover all the culture affected by the imperial process from the moment of colonization to the present day' (1989: 2). In doing so, however, they designate as equally 'post-colonial' 'very different national-racial formations—the United States, Australia and Canada, on the one hand, and Nigeria, Jamaica and India, on the other' (Shohat 1992). Ruth Frankenberg and Lata Mani's (1993) rejoinder to this has been to claim that, while these are all indeed post-colonial societies, they are not so 'in the same way'. A further difficulty with the concept of the 'post-colonial' is that it seems to suggest a period that follows the demise of colonialism. As has often been pointed out, this is a misnomer since colonialism certainly does not end with the arrival of national independence in formerly colonized states. This in turn has lead to charges that post-colonial theory has 'managed to obfuscate some of the enduring legacies of colonialism, including the pauperization of the Third World in the age of late capitalism' (Majid 1995–6). Efforts, sometimes acrimonious, have been made, in this context, to bring to light what post-colonialism is 'actually' all about. Thus, Kwame Anthony Appaiah suggests how post-colonial theory may be seen as the political theory of the diasporic Third World intellectual, who is part of 'a relatively small, Western-style, Western-trained, group of writers and thinkers who mediate the trade in cultural commodities of world capitalism at the periphery' (1991: 348) while Arif Dirlik begins an essay on post-colonialism with the—avowedly facetious—statement that the 'post-colonial' begins 'when Third World intellectuals have arrived in First World academe' (1994: 329).

The seeming shambles that is current post-colonial theory is caused partly, as a number of writers have pointed out, through uncertainty as to whether the concept of post-colonialism is a chronological or an epistemological one. Hall goes further and argues that post-colonial theory is faced with a choice of epistemologies: a 'rational and successive logic or a deconstructive one' (Hall 1996: 255). The way out of this, he suggests, is to agree that, whatever our location, post-colonial theory allows us to reconceptualize colonialism itself, in the light of our current knowledge of global capitalism.

Colonization, from this 'post-colonial' perspective, was no local or marginal sub-plot in some larger story (for example the transition from feudalism to capitalism in Western Europe . . .) In the re-staged narrative of the post-colonial, colonization assumes the place and significance of a major, extended and ruptural world-historical event . . . signifying the whole process of expansion, exploration, conquest, colonization and imperial hegemonization which constituted the 'outer face', the constitutive outside, of European and then Western capitalist modernity after 1492. (Hall 1996: 249)

This needs to be said. However, once said, it is worth adding that we cannot simply speak of only one 're-staged narrative of the post-colonial'. First, in the designation of the site of the restaging act: it would be my experience, living and working in India, that the route by which issues such as these arrive on my doorstep constitutes them less as issues with an autonomous import than as a staging-ground of numerous binary oppositions. It is precisely this staging context—rather than the debate—that is in turn replicated and restaged in other, typically 'nationalist' contexts which then appear free to introduce to it their own subject-matter. Second, in the (dominant) deconstructionist version of the role of narrative in the post-colonial, there is an assertion that post-coloniality is not one of the *grands récits* of modernity but a baggage of 'narratives' which, because they are narratives, leave out things, have limits, and do not present themselves as 'solutions for the future' (Spivak, in Harasym 1990: 18–19). When I try to situate this kind of argument in India, in some of the most violent, as well as politically contentious, events that have addressed caste (the Mandal Commission), religion (the rise of a Hindu right), and gender (the Uniform Civil Code debates)—none of which, unfortunately, can feature in a brief survey of this kind—I find myself arguing that 'rational and successive logic' is not an epistemological either–or in relation to deconstructionism. It is, rather, that the two alternatives always live in some kind of negotiated relationship to each other, and this in itself is one of the reasons why the sphere of an objective, 'political' arena is so difficult to designate.

This is perhaps best revealed in the crisis of the cinema itself in relation to post-colonial theory. Until the early 1980s the cinema was at the forefront of post-colonial theory but has now virtually disappeared from recent debates on post-coloniality. The very construction of the filmic image, through editing, sound recording and mixing, and the process of projecting that image to an audience, had a relationship with the structuring of various kinds of modernist 'public-ness' which has, in the relocated status of colonialism, lost out to larger, less controllable impulses and to the range of technologies that mediate such 'autonomous social impulses' (to use Spivak's term). In this context, it is worth looking at the three-decade history of post-colonial relations between national cinemas in the 'Third World' and independent film movements in the West.

> Until the early 1980s the cinema was at the forefront of post-colonial theory but has now virtually disappeared from recent debates on post-coloniality. The very construction of the filmic image, through editing, sound recording and mixing, and the process of projecting that image to an audience, had a relationship with the structuring of various kinds of modernist 'public-ness' which has, in the relocated status of colonialism, lost out to larger, less controllable impulses and to the range of technologies that mediate such 'autonomous social impulses' (to use Spivak's term).

The Western avant-garde

In 1972 Peter Bürger's influential book *Theory of the Avant-Garde* was first published in German, reflecting, as he wrote later, 'a historical constellation of problems that emerged after the events of May 1968 and the failure of the student movement in the early 70s' (1994: 95). That book in many ways launched a series of theoretical interventions to resuscitate the concept of an avant-garde which Bürger saw as challenging bourgeois notions of aesthetic autonomy. Most of the contributors to this debate agreed that the 'historical avant-garde', which Bürger located mainly in Dadaism, Surrealism, and the post-revolutionary Russian avant-garde, had met its demise following the Second World War, with the institutionalization of modernism in the

United States. Thereafter, while the term survived, it was increasingly 'overpowered by conformism' (in Walter Benjamin's (1973/1979) widely quoted phrase). For Rosalind Krauss (1986) this conformism was identified with a valorization of originality, while Andreas Huyssen (1986) sought to find avant-garde impulses (amongst other places) within mass culture. Several of these debates in New York occurred specifically in the context of the rise of a European 'trans-avant-garde', a set of Neo-Expressionist movements mainly in Germany (Georg Baselitz, Markus Lupertz, A. R. Penck) and Italy (Sandro Chia, Clemente), which were extensively debated in Europe and the United States, and attacked (notably by Buchloh 1981) for their aggressive assertion of a neo-nationalist élitism, 'reflect[ing] and dismantl[ing] the ideological impact of growing authoritarianism' (Wallis and Tucker 1984: 108).

It was within this broad context that Peter Wollen in 1975 wrote his classic essay 'The Two Avant-Gardes', which identified two parallel movements in the West (see Smith, Part 3, Chapter 2). The first avant-garde emphasized formal experimentation and was deeply suspicious of 'programmatic' political activism; the second was more aggressively political, but still preoccupied with 'the whole process of signification out of which a world view or an ideology is constructed'. In drawing this distinction, Wollen drew the debate into the ambit of modernism proper, emphasizing the 'critical semiotic shift' represented by the avant-gardes: the 'change of emphasis from the problem of signified and reference, a classic problem of realism, to that of signifier and signified within the sign itself'.

It is perhaps only in retrospect that Wollen's essay reveals just why it proved so influential: it was not the two specific vanguard movements that made the essay significant so much as the virtually global resonances of his paradigm. The paradigm spoke of a modernist model in which two (or more) movements were presented as being on different sides of a divide, with each side in some sense staked onto historical precedents which were reprised, reinvented, or re-enacted in order to address the present.

It was characteristic of the time (the 1970s–1980s) that none of the theorists mentioned above, dealing with theories of the avant-garde, were familiar with, or even seriously interested in, what was going on outside the Euro-American context. Nevertheless, I think the model itself remains useful, even as we include those other contexts here. In doing so, I will revert to the original opposition which preceded the concept of the 'two avant-gardes'—that of realism versus modernism—and add a third term: that of nationalism.

Nationalist realism–modernism

A second history can be inscribed into this battle of two avant-gardes. From the 1950s and the Brazilian Cinema Nôvo, 'new cinema' movements swept through large parts of Latin America, Europe, Africa, and Asia. Many of the filmmakers associated with these movements addressed issues similar to those of the Western avant-garde, and were, indeed, in some kind of dialogue with it: most celebratedly in the meeting between Godard and Glauber Rocha (emblematically presented in *Vent d'est* (1969), where Rocha appears in a brief sequence). Indeed, in this phase many of those active in the 'Third World' were possibly unaware of their counterparts in similar situations, and often came together as a consequence of having common Western referents.

In many countries New Cinema movements were constituted through direct state intervention, and were intended to establish indigenous film infrastructures in the context of political independence. To put it bluntly, in several countries, for example in Africa, there was literally no cinema before the New Cinema. In many of these movements, a commitment to institutionalization went alongside a commitment to the promotion of indigenous realisms. This can be seen in Cinema Nôvo's commitment to GEICINE (the Grupo executivo da indústria cinematográfica, set up by the government to examine the Brazilian film industry in 1961), and later, more significantly, Embrafilme, the Brazilian state organization for funding cinema; the Cuban cinema and ICAIC (the Cuban Institute of Cinematographic Art and Industry, started in 1959, within three months of the success of the revolution); the FEPACI (the Fédération panafricaine des cinéastes) in Africa; the NFDC (National Film Development Corporation) in India; and a host of others (such as the Sri Lankan State Film Corporation and the Royal Nepal Film Corporation).

Thus, it is possible to see several nationalist reconstruction agendas adopting economic programmes based on the principles of scientific rationalism and its aesthetic counterpart of realism. As Fredric Jameson argues, 'realism designates an active, curious,

The Nouvelle Vague meets counter-cinema—Glauber Rocha at the crossroads in Godard's *Vent d'est* (1969)

experimental, subversive—in a word scientific—attitude towards social institutions and the material world; and the "realistic" work of art is therefore one which encourages and disseminates this attitude, yet not merely in a flat or mimetic way or along the lines of imitation alone' (Jameson 1977: 205). Thus, in India the report of the Patil Enquiry (Film Enquiry Committee 1951), the first major state initiative after Independence to address and reform the film industry, embodies several key tenets of this aesthetic of realism, in advocating a cinema of 'social purpose', denigrating the mass-cultural industry as 'gamblers' who work 'often at the cost of both the taste of the public and the prosperity of the industry', and recommending that numerous state institutions be started, including the Film Finance Corporation, the National Film Archive of India, and a film training institute. Between 1945 and 1975, which Aijat Ahmad identifies as the 'high period of decolonization' (1992b: 39–40), indigenous realism played a crucial role in nation-building. In the words of Gyanendra Pandey, realism—or rather, various national realisms—were important in writing up the 'biography of the emerging nation-state' (1991: 560), and creating the authoritative self-image of the nation.

During this same period, one particular strand of 'author cinema' from the 'Third World' also came to critical prominence and was associated with artists whose major virtue, it appeared, was the fact that they 'straddled two cultures'. Roy Armes's (1987) book on the subject is exemplary in its identification of this category. In a chapter entitled 'Cinema Astride Two Cultures', he lists a small number of 'first generation' film-authors—Satyajit Ray, Youssef Chahine, Glauber Rocha, Yilmaz Güney, Ousmane Sembene, and Jorge Sanjinés—who are seen as contributing simultaneously to Western modernism as well as to their 'own native tradition' (Armes 1987: 229–30). (We might also add the names of Lester James Peries, Lino Brocka, Nelson Pereira dos Santos, and maybe even Akira Kurosawa.) Most of these filmmakers have consistently been showcased in Western film festivals as exemplars of modernist 'author cinema'. This has led to the virtual exclusion of all knowledge about the contexts in which the filmmaking practices of these very names occur—as well as the work of others who explicitly aligned themselves to (or opposed) a socialist avant-garde internationalism. Furthermore, it has resulted in the elision of any argument that might assign to the mass-cultural mainstream of newly independent 'Third World' nations their own vanguardist initiatives (for example, in creating audiences, or in shaping their own anti-colonial indigenous mass culture).

The Third Cinema and the avant-garde

In 1969 the famous manifesto of Fernando Solanas and Octavio Getino was published, heralding the new concept of a 'Third Cinema' which, for the first time, allowed a second, more explicitly avant-garde position to emerge in opposition to the one of modernist 'author-cinema'. The manifesto, which was followed by several other texts and films hitherto unknown outside their local contexts (see Chanan 1983), was premissed on a replacement of nationalism with 'the development of a worldwide liberation movement whose force is to be found in Third World countries'. According to Solanas and Getino's typology, First Cinema was represented by Hollywood; the Second Cinema by the 'so-called "author's cinema", "expression cinema", "nouvelle vague", and "cinema novo"'; while Third Cinema was seen as using 'films as a revolutionary tool', and radically relocating the practices of viewing and the industrial–economic designation of cinema itself.

It is worth noting that the Third Cinema manifesto was, among other things, in dialogue with a post-May 1968 European–American film avant-garde, and the work of Jean-Luc Godard in particular (see Godard and Solanas 1987: 82 9). Indications of this engagement include the years of Salvador Allende's Popular Unity government, when European filmmakers as diverse as Chris Marker (who helped complete Patricio Guzmán's *Battle for Chile*, 1973–9) and Roberto Rossellini contributed in their own ways to the Chilean filmmakers' famous call for 'national liberation and the construction of socialism' (quoted in Fusco 1987: 118). Indeed, it is clear that Wollen is indebted, in part at least, to Solanas and Getino for his own manifesto statement written six years later and that there are evident continuities between Solanas and Getino's characterization of 'Second' and 'Third' Cinemas and Wollen's identification of two avant-gardes. It is therefore possible to see in Wollen's (1975) essay a relocating of the two concepts of authorship and political activism into more explicitly semiotic and narrative pratices, not only in this essay itself but more schematically in an earlier essay on 'Godard and Counter-Cinema', where he marks the divide in terms of narrative transitivity versus intransitivity, identification versus estrangement, and fiction versus reality (Wollen 1972).

Among the consequences of this manifesto in film—

which accompanied a literary 'boom' that followed the arrival of Latin Americans Gabriel García Marquez, Mario Vargas Llosa, and Julio Cortazar, and the African Ngũgĩ wa Thiong'o on the Western literary scene of the 1960s–1970s—was the excavation of a vastly more complex history, and existing contemporary practice, than allowed by the modernist engagement with 'Third World' film-authors. Senior 'first-generation' filmmakers—notably Ousmane Sembene and Med Hondo (see Diawara 1992; also Jameson 1986 and Mulvey 1991), Nelson Pereira dos Santos, Ritwik Ghatak, and Lino Brocka—were now seen as involved in a far more complex practice than had been earlier allowed to them, and as refusing to offer in opposition to 'the values of colonial or imperial predators' a simplistic notion of 'national identity or of cultural authenticity' (Willemen 1989: 4). On the other side, younger filmmakers from all three continents emerged, and introduced not just filmmaking practice but theory, with a far more explicitly critical post-colonial awareness of their national histories than had previously been possible. In this respect, we could mention (following Willemen), Amos Gitai (from Israel; see Willemen 1993), Haile Gerima (Ethiopia; see Gerima 1989), Kumar Shahani (India; see Shahani 1986), Edward Yang (Taiwan), Chen Kaige and the 'Fifth Generation' (China), and the remarkable avant-garde movement in the Philippines in the early 1980s, gathered at the Moweltund Film Institute, working mainly in Super-8 and video and involving filmmakers like Raymond Red and Nick Deocampo (see Deocampo 1985).

This phenomenon has gone alongside one in literature: as in Africa, for instance. Appaiah (1991), for example, argues that whereas the first generation of modern African novels (Chinua Achebe's *Things Fall Apart*, Camara Laye's *L'Enfant noir*) were 'written in the context of notions of politics and culture dominant in the French and British university and publishing worlds in the 1950s and 60s' (348) when it was 'held to be obvious both by these writers and by the high culture of Europe of the day . . . that new literatures in new nations should be anti-colonial and nationalist (in the tradition of Sir Walter Scott)' (348–9), a second generation emerged with radically different perceptions.

Ouologuem's novel [*Le Devoir de violence*, 'Bound to Violence'] is typical of novels of this second stage in that it is not written by someone who is comfortable with and accepted by the new elite, the national bourgeoisie. Far from being a celebration of the nation, then, the novels of the second, postcolonial, stage are novels of delegitimation: they reject not only the Western *imperium* but also the nationalist pro-ject of the postcolonial national bourgeoisie. (Appaiah 1991: 353)

As many writers have pointed out, the 'end' of anti-colonial developmentalist nationalism also coincides with the rise of post-structuralism. Ahmad, for instance, writes that

. . . the national-bourgeois state partly basked in the reflected glory of the wars of national liberation, hence in the greater valorization of nationalism as such. . . . Now, as the stagnation of that type of post-colonial state has become more obvious in more recent years, and as the perception of that stagnation coincided chronologically with the ascendency of post-structuralism in literary theory, cultural nationalism itself is currently in the process of being discarded as illusion, myth, totalizing narrative. (Ahmad 1992*b*: 41)

Post-colonial theory and internationalism

It is possible to list a three-way split in the directions that post-colonial theory has broadly taken since the early 1980s—all three differently informed by post-structuralism and the work of Edward Said, especially *Orientalism* (1978). The first, we might broadly charac-terize as an investigation into nationalism itself: the best-known work being, in the West, Benedict Ander-son's remarkable book *Imagined Communities* (see also Gellner 1983) and, outside the West, the influen-tial writings of the Subaltern Studies Collective (see Guha 1982–9), and those of Partha Chatterjee (1986, 1994) in particular. A second track sought mainly to shift erstwhile 'Third World' nationalism into a theory of the 'Third World' itself: effectively transforming the more subtle divides along the fault lines of modern-ism–realism, as these impacted upon the construction of citizenship, into more straightforwardly 'First-World'–'Third World' opposites. While this was intro-duced into film theory by Teshome Gabriel's *Third Cinema in the Third World* (1982), with its prescriptive listing of how 'First World' films differed from those of the 'Third World', later developments have taken place almost entirely outside the ambit of film, and would be, in some respects, the dominant trend in US academia today. The third track, in which cinema did (and still does) feature, albeit on the margins, was a more expli-cit effort to deploy post-colonial theory to address the condition of immigrant minorities in the West, and it is mainly in this area that cultural studies has made its most significant impact on post-colonial theory.

Two seminal essays by Fredric Jameson—'On Magic Realism in Film' and the more controversial 'Third World Literature in the Era of Multinational Capital' (1986*a*, *b*)—attempt to link, on the one side, the Brecht-Lukács debate concerning realism with, on the other, a new literary categorization of the 'Third World' in post-colonial theory that might address all the three alternatives stated above. The trajectory that both essays assume is the one that began with nation-alist 'Third World' efforts to translate the realism–mod-ernism divide into their own terms, and ended with the redesignation of nationalism itself within post-colonial theory. On the way, they make indirect reference to Third Cinema theory, and more pertinently seem to designate the place where that theory came to reside in its post-colonial versions of the 1980s.

Both essays are premised on questions of narra-tive—on structures that seemingly resemble, but do not eventually play the part of, more familiar narrative conventions in the West (as in the resemblance, at times, between magic realism and the American nos-talgia film). The first essay seeks, it seems to me, to address the poignant question of Kwame Anthony Appaiah's (1991) text 'Is the Post- in Postmodernism the Post- in Postcolonial?' Jameson chooses to com-pare a Polish film (Agnieszka Holland's *Fever*, 1981) with a Venezuelan production (Jacobo Penzo's *La casa de agua*, 1984) and a Colombian production (Francisco Norden's *Condores no entierran todos las días*, 1984) to argue that the very location of narra-tive—the 'shock of entry into narrative—departs from the 'consumed . . . visual commodity' of the nostalgia film in the way that the 'permutations of the gaze, which irritate and intensify it, do not . . . as in postmo-dernism and the nostalgia film, transform its objects into images in the stronger sense of that word'. Although both genres deal with history, the magic realist film is a 'history-with-holes', where a 'whole range of subtle or complicated forms of narrative atten-tion, which classical film . . . laboriously acquired and adapted from earlier developments in the novel, are now junked and replaced . . . Narrative here has not been subverted or abandoned, as in the iconoclasm of the experimental film, but rather effectively neutra-lised, to the benefit of a seeing or a looking in the filmic present.' All of this is presented in contrast to the 'enfeebled'—both in terms of history and class—post-modernism of the industrialized West.

The second essay takes this argument further: narrative, in non-canonical 'Third World' literatures, is not only woven in more complex and subtle ways into history and political action than its seeming resemblance to Western conventions would reveal, but plays a different role altogether even in its position in civil society. The key (and intensely controversial, as we shall see) paragraph goes: 'All third world texts are necessarily, I want to argue, allegorical, and in a very specific way: they are to be read as what I will call *national allegories*, even when, or perhaps I should say, particularly when their forms develop out of predominantly Western machineries of representation, such as the novel.' Jameson goes on to argue that whereas 'the culture of the Western realist and modernist novel' involves 'a radical split between the private and the public', Third World texts—'even those which are seemingly private and invested with a properly libidinal dynamic'—'necessarily project a political dimension in the form of national allegory: *the story of the private individual destiny is always an allegory of the embattled situation of the public third world culture and society'*.

Jameson's avowed intention is to 'rethink our [i.e. the US academic] humanities curriculum' and to do so in a way that avoids simply embracing non canonical texts by proving that these are 'as great as those of the canon itself', a self-defeating exercise which 'borrows the weapons of the adversary'.

There is, however, a second history that feeds into this intervention, contributing to Jameson's somewhat deliberately provocative tone. This history constitutes, in one spectacular moment of the 'end of nationalism',

a literal migration of Third Cinema into the 'West', notably into the United States, and thereby also into post-colonialism. In 1973 the Allende government fell in Chile and through the 1970s state repression in several Latin American countries increased massively. Jorge Sanjinés and Mario Arrieta, members of the Ukamau group, went into exile following the *coup d'état* in Bolivia in 1971; the Third World Cinémathèque in Montevideo was ransacked by the police in 1972, who confiscated all films, equipment, and records; while elsewhere organizations like the Argentine Anti-communist Alliance (AAA) were on the rise. The AAA killed Julio Troxler, an actor, while working on a Fernando Solanas production. In 1976, in an epochal statement, Leopoldo Torre Nilsson, when in Spain, vowed never to return to his native Argentina as long as his films were banned there.

To a great extent, this caused the very concept of the Third Cinema, along with its key protagonists, to go into exile (in the United States and in Europe) or turn to Cuba, its only major support in Latin America still to be intact. In 1976 the Emergency Committee to Defend Latin American Filmmakers, based in New York, was supported by Hollywood stars like Candice Bergen, Francis Ford Coppola, Jane Fonda, Jack Nicholson, and Martin Scorsese. A decade later, the Fundación del nuevo cine latinoamericano (New Latin American Film Foundation, FNCI) was founded in 1985, with Marquez as chairman and with major—if radically different from the past—ambitions, including owning movie theatres in every Latin American country and several cities in Europe, and even installing their own satellite. But it was soon forced to resort to a political–aesthetic survival strategy addressed mainly towards garnering support within the 'First World'. In 1986 the FNCI started the Escuela internacional de cine y TV (International School of Cinema and TV), with Fernando Birri as its first director. The school constituted one important statement of this intention with its barely concealed effort to export 'revolutionary film' to the capitalist world. Apart from Latin American connections (the Instituto Nacional de Cinematográfia (INC) Argentina, Embrafilme, the Colombian Ministry of Communication), the only 'exchange link' this school had was with Robert Redford's Sundance Film Institute. Birri, in his inaugural speech, provided a virtual recipe for the by-now vastly broadened concept of the Third Cinema when he debunked 'marginalism' versus 'professionalism' as a false option, promising to provide students with filmmaking that included possibilities

> **Jameson goes on to argue that whereas 'the culture of the Western realist and modernist novel' involves 'a radical split between the private and the public', Third World texts—'even those which are seemingly private and invested with a properly libidinal dynamic'—'necessarily project a political dimension in the form of national allegory'.**

'that go from pure political cinema to pure experimental cinema, taking into account all the possible alternatives: clandestine, militant, denunciation, resistance, social, didactic, independent, vocational, underground, marginal, diverse, off and off-off cinema' (Birri 1986: 5).

During much of this time, the contribution of writers like Julianne Burton and Julia Lesage, as well as journals like *Jump Cut*, was perceived even by people as eminent as Tomás Gutiérrez Alea as providing a virtual lifeline to the Cuban cinema in familiarizing and popularizing their work with US audiences. This issue was for a while extensively debated, notably in an encounter between Burton and Teshome Gabriel in the pages of *Screen* (Gabriel 1983, 1986; Burton 1983, 1985). Fredric Jameson himself saw the three films he discusses in his 'magic realism' essay (1986a) at the Latin American Film Festival in Havana, 1984, and dedicates the essay to the Cuban Revolution. This essay, written at the same time as the Burton–Gabriel debate, suggests that the Western critic, in the current situation, could—indeed, had to be—'critic and interpreter' within certain new terms of globalization requiring new kinds of political responsibility to be addressed.

Aijaz Ahmad's (1987) attack on Jameson's (1986b) 'Third World Literature' essay constitutes a seminal launch of post-colonial theory into one of its current positions. Ahmad begins by questioning Jameson's very intention: in seeking a 'cognitive aesthetics of third world literature', he argues, Jameson suppresses the multiplicity of significant differences to create a simple, binary opposition between 'First' and 'Third World' literatures. Much of Ahmad's critique stems from his argument that the 'Third World' itself consists of several independent nation-states, with developed social formations and with their own well-established literary canons. He therefore recommends the abolition of the 'three worlds' concept, and its replacement by the 'radically different . . . proposition that we live not in three worlds but in one; that this world includes the experience of colonialism and imperialism on both sides of Jameson's global divide . . . that societies in formations of backward capitalism are as much constituted by the division of classes as are societies in advanced capitalist countries' (Ahmad 1992a: 103).

Post-colonial theory: political–deconstructionist

By the 1990s post-colonial theory had clearly carved for itself a distinct disciplinary 'area', as is evident in the appearance of several 'readers' and anthologies (see especially Williams and Christman 1994; Prakash 1995; Chambers and Curti 1996). Virtually all of these, in their choice of authors as well as their category distinctions, embody a new contest between efforts to find political modes of addressing 'Otherness', versus a more deconstructionist initiative featuring, mainly, the writings of Trinh T. Min-ha, Gayatri Chakravorty Spivak, and Homi K. Bhabha.

Homi K. Bhabha's influential work began in the 1980s as a deliberate confrontation with such themes of 'Third Worldist' resistance. At the Edinburgh Third Cinema conference he presented what he saw as a false and disabling opposition.

Between what is represented as the 'larceny' and distortion of European 'metatheorizing' and the radical, engaged, activist experience of Third World creativity, [he argued,] one can see the mirror image (albeit reversed in content and intention) of that ahistorical nineteenth century polarity of Orient and Occident which, in the name of progress, unleashed the exclusionary imperialist ideologies of self and other. This time round, the term 'critical theory', often untheorized and unargued, is definitely the 'other', an otherness that is insistently identified with the vagaries of the depoliticised Eurocentric critic. (Bhabha 1994: 19)

He argued, instead, for theory as negotiation: 'the event of theory becomes the negotiation of contradictory and antagonistic instances that open up hybrid sites and objectives of struggle' (Bhabha 1989/1994: 25). Bhabha's insistence on discovering, within colonial discourse, those spaces where 'hybridity' starts shifting away from strait-jacketed oppositions and into 'a heterogeneity that the existing dichotomies themselves make simultaneously possible and impossible' (Prakash 1992: 17) revitalized the very terrain on which theory could now operate, seemingly overcoming the shambles of 'multiple subjects of fragmented histories' that post-colonial theory had become in the late 1980s. As Gyan Prakash puts it, 'at these moments of indeterminacy, when the discourse can be seen to veer away from the implacable logic of oppositionality, the critic can intervene, and, using historical work as a license for a strategy of critical reading, re-negotiate the terms of discourse' (17).

Crucial to Bhabha's work has been his formulation of 'colonial mimicry', or the 'desire for a reformed, recognisable Other, as a subject of a difference that is almost the same, but not quite . . . the discourse of mimicry is constructed around an ambivalence; in order to be effective, mimicry must continually produce its own slippage, its excess, its difference' (Bhabha 1987). Such terms as 'slippage', 'excess', and the crucial one, 'difference', or the ones that circulate extensively in Trinh T. Min-ha's work—'hybridity, interstices, voids, intervals, in-betweenness' (cited in Chambers and Curti 1996)—opened a new space, veritably a flood, of theory for what still goes broadly under the title 'deconstructionism'.

Perhaps the most significant contribution contextualizing both the political as well as discursive constitution of the 'subject' of theory—including crucially the colonial subject—is Gayatri Spivak's essay 'Can the Subaltern Speak?' (1988). Working with a triangular grid of 'power, interest, desire', Spivak distinguishes between two concepts of representation: representation, in the sense in which the 'people', an absent collective consciousness often dispersed and dislocated as 'subjects', find a category of representatives (who sometimes betray them), versus re-presentation: the space for rhetoric, realism, the 'scene of writing'; radical practice should attend to this 'double session of representations rather than reintroduce the individual subject through totalizing concepts of power and desire'.

It is on this terrain, of the tragic, eternally silenced subaltern figure whose own voice is always lost in the tumult of an invoked subject of oppression, that Spivak seems to bring together two until then incompatible intellectual positions: the Derridean and the explicitly stated anti-élitist historiography of the Subaltern Studies group. Both effectively work on their resistance to the constitution of the undifferentiated, textualized subject.

Gyan Prakash's contribution to this debate has been to suggest, controversially, a need to move beyond 'foundational histories'.

The subaltern is a figure produced by historical discourses of domination, but it nevertheless provides a mode of reading history different from those inscribed in elite account . . . these historians seek to uncover the subaltern's myths, cults, ideologies and revolts that colonial and nationalist elites sought to appropriate and conventional historiography has laid to waste by their deadly weapon of cause and effect. (Prakash: 1992: 9)

The importance of the link between Derridean–Spivakian deconstructionism and Subaltern historiography is, however, less related to its linguistic designation of the subaltern voice (or its absence) than it is to a consequent validation of the status of a new kind of history-writing, which Prakash calls 'Post-Foundational history'. Work by the Subaltern Studies historians 'disrupts . . . the nationalist narrative that considers all colonial revolts as events in the becoming of the . . . nation and contests the older Marxist accounts which see these episodes as preludes to the emergence of full-fledged class-consciousness' (Prakash 1990: 399–400).

The most contentious of Prakash's statements was an apparent dismissal of capitalism itself on the grounds that capitalist narratives, being by definition homogenizing and therefore foundational, cannot therefore thematize post-colonial history, since it is precisely histories emphasizing heterogeneity—rather than mere documentation of how capitalism becomes dominant—that will allow us to contest capitalist homogenization. Two major attacks followed: one by Rosalind O'Hanlon and David Washbrook (1992), who argued that, for Prakash, capitalism becomes a 'disposable fiction', and a second by Dirlik (1994), who argued, effectively, that this entire trend of argumentation (represented by Spivak, Bhabha, Prakash et al.) constitutes a deliberate 'obfuscation of its own relationship to what is but a condition of its emergence, that is, to a global capitalism that, however fragmented in appearance, serves as the structuring principle of global relations' (331).

Post-colonial theory and diaspora: negritude to immigritude

Politically, there is a straightforward problem with the very approach of deconstructionism: a problem that Stuart Hall sums up as the 'fantasy of a powerless utopia of difference. It is only too tempting to fall into the trap of assuming that, because essentialism has been deconstructed theoretically, therefore it has been displaced politically' (1996: 249). There is however a different sense in which one can, perhaps more fruitfully, contextualize Spivak's and Bhabha's work: as an interrogation of the colonial encounter in the context of, and addressing the condition of, immigrant minorities in the West. In his effort to shift the emphasis of identity politics away from its burden upon the slave, the colonized, the immigrant, to the colonial authority itself, Bhabha (and generally deconstructionist politics) intervenes, along with major writers mainly from Africa, the Caribbean, and the black community in Britain and the United States, in the shift away from colonial ethnography and into a new terrain of ethnic cultural politics.

> **There is however a different sense in which one can, perhaps more fruitfully, contextualize Spivak's and Bhabha's work: as an interrogation of the colonial encounter in the context of, and addressing the condition of, immigrant minorities in the West.**

The inversion of ethnography, a colonial discipline to tackle the problems of studying alien cultures, into an assertive politics premissed on identity is a key part of this history. An early inversion of colonial identity was the concept of 'negritude', originating in the work of Aimé Césaire and Leopold Sedar Senghor. In its original form, negritude claimed black culture as 'emotional rather than rational' with 'a distinctive African view . . . separated from the supposedly universal values of European taste and style' (Ashcroft et al. 1989: 21–2). Although extensively critiqued by African writers— most notably by Wole Soyinka, who declared 'a tiger does not proclaim its tigritude'—negritude as a concept was transformed by and survived in various subsequent efforts, through this century, to posit a black aesthetics. Senghor's work traces an influence to the Harlem Renaissance, to Langston Hughes and Richard Wright, and, subsequently to Black Power movements. In the 1980s it was once again addressed, via black musical structures as these related to literary style, in Henry Louis Gates's influential compilation *Black Literature and Literary Theory* (1984) while Gates's own book *The Signifying Monkey* (1988) attempted 'to identify a theory of criticism that is inscribed within the Black vernacular tradition'.

The double problem—how to assert ethnicity and at the same time combat the essentializing imperialist ethnography on which that identity has, all too often, been based—bedevils a great deal of black theory on the subject. There has also been a certain discounting of 'nativism', of whatever kind, in the face of what Vivek Dhareshwar has called 'immigritude'—the 'whole narrative of displacement which has become a normative experience in metropolitan politics' (1989: 143). If 1970s–1980s Latin America saw in its right-wing takeovers one spectacular end of anti-colonial nationalism, clearly it was on a scale nowhere near the experience of Black Africa's own experience, of having to comprehend an earlier 'global' economy of the slave-trade. The descendants of those enslaved, and later immigrants, some of whom emigrated through choice, experienced the end of nationalism within the heartlands of globalized capital, even as they were forced to acknowledge the impossibility of return.

Some of the richest interventions into political theory, and indeed the cutting edge of post-colonial theory itself, have taken place at this particular frontier. Frantz Fanon's work in positing black identity as first and foremost a political one clearly shifted negritude into a different terrain (see notably Fanon 1967). E. K. Braithwaite's emphasis on a pan-African nationalism, alongside his interests in forming a new cultural thrust for creolization (Braithwaite 1984), informed a new effort to understand the phenomenon of racism, especially following the realization that 'by defining "race" and ethnicity as cultural absolutes, blacks themselves and parts of the anti-racist movement risk endorsing the explanatory frameworks and political definitions of the new right' (Gilroy 1987: 13). Gilroy points to the 'social movements which have sprung up in different parts of the world as evidence of African dispersal, imperialism and colonialism' as providing a 'global perspective from the memories of slavery and indenture which are the property of the African diaspora' (156–7).

Perhaps the most useful way of reading the African American and black British theory mentioned would be in its address of nationalism itself, but from the outside, and in the process its transformation of the very terrain on which 'the national' operates as a phenomenon. If, as Gilroy has argued, an effort to understand racism requires a new understanding of class, then, by extension, an effort to understand the conditions of immigrant ethnic, minorities equally requires a new understanding of nation.

At any rate a new area was opened up for theory itself within this broad field when in 1964 the Centre for Cultural Studies was started in Birmingham. Interestingly, black cultural theory and politics were not on the centre's agenda in much of its initial work. The thrust was mainly around culture—the space it occupied on the terrain of a public arena. Ethnography was, however, a key area, anticipating much of what came later to be known as 'ethnic studies', and underpinned the centre's early interest in working-class subcultures. For Cohen (1972) all subcultures correspond to a 'parent' culture, and attempt to work out, express, and resolve, 'albeit magically, the contradictions which remain hidden or unresolved in the parent culture' or which are 'inserted' into the subculture by the parent culture. Placed on the realm of the symbolic, the 'parent culture' could discursively extend into both an understanding of the state—in Britain, crucially the Thatcherite state—as well as the numerous communitarian institutions that constitute, as well as oppose, 'state apparatuses'.

Gilroy's *There Ain't No Black in the Union Jack* (1987) comes out of this tradition, but remains one of the first works to remap the 'parent' symbolic—here the symbolic of racial identity—onto questions of class and nation (in the sense in which British 'patriotic' nationalism crucially depends on mobilizing racial factors), and eventually onto what he calls an 'affirmative' culture of syncretism. This mass upsurge had its component in a 'dimension of diaspora', a 'back to Africa' move, which saw its culmination in the Rastafari, a pan-African, Ethiopianist movement (see Gilroy 1987: 187–92), and inaugurated numerous cultural forms, in dress, music, and the very formation of what Gilroy, quoting Said, calls an 'interpretative community'.

Those outside the debates encapsulated above (which includes myself) are nevertheless aware of some of the impact made by this entire history onto the cinema: notably, in the first phase, the revaluation of first-generation black filmmakers from Africa (Sembene and Souleymane Cissé), and, later, black cinema's efforts to enter both the mass-cultural mainstream (notably Spike Lee) as well as create an independent sector which nevertheless relates to the cultural repositionings that the later theoretical history took (e.g. Charles Burnett in the United States, the Black Audio, Sankofa, and Ceddo collectives in the United Kingdom).

Conclusion

Although Gilroy's later book *The Black Atlantic* (1993) has attempted to address the shift in the space occu-

pied by identity politics—the shift towards imaginary constructs, discourse theory, and the broad terrain of constructing Subjects-as-the-Other of deconstructionism—it is clear that several of the areas I have tried to map in this chapter, quite simply, do not talk to each other. A great deal more work still needs to be done before we can clearly identify 'post-colonial theory' and before—in the words of Spivak—'power, desire and interest' can come together to offer large patterns of what has happened and what is likely to happen.

BIBLIOGRAPHY

Ahmad, Aijaz (1977/1992a), 'Jameson's Rhetoric of Otherness and the "National Allegory"', in *In Theory: Classes, Nations, Literatures* (London: Verso).
—— (1992b), 'Literature among the Signs of our Time', in *In Theory: Classes, Nations, Literatures* (London: Verso).
—— (1996), 'Postcoloniality: What's in a Name?', in Roman de la Campa et al. (eds.), *Late Imperial Culture* (London: Verso).
Anderson, Benedict (1983), *Imagined Communities: Reflections on the Origin and Spread of Nationalism* (London: Verso).
Appaiah, Kwame Anthony (1991/1996), 'Is the Post- in Postmodernism the Post- in Postcolonial?', *Critical Inquiry*, 17 (Winter); repr. in Padmini Monga (ed.), *Contemporary Postcolonial Theory* (London: Arnold).
—— (1992), *In my Father's House: Africa in the Philosophy of Culture* (New York: Oxford University Press).
Armes, Roy (1987), *Third World Film Making and the West* (Berkeley: University of California Press).
Ashcroft, Bill, Gareth Griffiths, and **Helen Tiffin** (1989), *The Empire Writes Back. Theory and Practice in Post-Colonial Literatures* (London: Routledge).
Benjamin, Walter (1973/1979), 'Theses on the Philosophy of History', in *Illuminations*, ed. Hannah Arendt (London: Fontana/Collins).
Bhabha, Homi K. (1987), 'Of Mimicry and Man', in *October* (Boston, Mass.: MIT Press).
—— (1989/1994), 'The Commitment to Theory', in Pines and Willemen (1989); Babha (1994).
—— (1994), *The Location of Culture* (London: Routledge).
Birri, Fernando (1986), 'Acta de Naciniento de la Esquela Internacionale de Cine y TV'.
Braithwaite, E. K. (1984), *History of the Voice: The Development of Nation Language in Anglophone Caribbean Poetry* (London: New Beacon Press).
Buchloh, Benjamin H. D. (1981), 'Figures of Authority, Ciphers of Regression: Notes on the Return of Representation in European Painting', *October*, 16 (Spring), 39–68.

423

Bürger, Peter (1972/1994), *Theory of the Avant-Garde*, trans. Michael Shaw (Minneapolis: University of Minnesota Press).

Burton, Julianne (1983), 'The Politics of Aesthetic Distance: Sao Bernando', *Screen*, 24/2: 30–53.

—— (1985), 'Marginal Cinemas and Mainstream Critical Theory', *Screen*, 26/3–4: 2–21.

Chambers, Iain, and **Lidia Curti** (eds.) (1996), *The Post-Colonial Question: Common Skies, Divided Horizons* (London: Routledge).

Chanan, Michael (ed.) (1983), *Twenty-Five Years of the New Latin American Cinema* (London: British Film Institute and Channel 4).

Chatterjee, Partha (1986), *Nationalist Thought and the Colonial World: A Derivative Discourse* (New Delhi: Oxford University Press).

—— (1994), *The Nation and its Fragments: Colonial and Postcolonial Histories* (New Delhi: Oxford University Press).

Cohen, Phil (1972/1980), 'Subcultural Coflict and Working-Class Community', in Stuart Hall *et al.* (eds.), *Culture, Media, Language* (London: Routledge).

de la Campa, Roman, E. Ann Kaplan, *et al.* (eds.) (1996), *Late Imperial Culture* (London: Verso).

Deocampo, Nick (1985), *Short Film: Emergence of a New Philippine Cinema* (Communication Foundation for Asia).

Dhareshwar, Vivek (1989), 'Towards a Narrative Epistemology of the Postcolonial Predicament', in James Clifford and Vivek Dhareshwar (eds.), *Travelling Theories, Travelling Theorists*, Inscriptions.

—— (1995), 'Postcolonial in the Postmodern; or, The Political after Modernity', *Economic and Political Weekly*, 30/30, 29 July, 104–11.

Diawara, Manthia (1992), *African CInema: Politics and Culture* (Bloomington: Indiana University Press).

Dirlik, Arif (1994), 'The Postcolonial Aura: Third World Criticism in the Age of Global Capitalism', *Critical Inquiry*, 20 (Winter), 328–56.

Fanon, Frantz (1967), *Toward the African Revolution* (Harmondsworth: Pelican Books).

Film Enquiry Committee (1951), (Chairman, S. K. Patil), *Report of the Film Enquiry Committee* (New Delhi: Government of India Press).

Frankenberg, Ruth, and **Lata Mani** (1993), 'Crosscurrents, Crosstalk: Race, "Postcoloniality" and the Politics of Location', *Cultural Studies*, 7/2: 292–310.

Fusco, Coco (ed.), (1987), *Reviewing Histories: Selections from New Latin American Cinema* (Buffalo, NY: Hallwallis Contemporary Arts Center).

Gabriel, Teshome H., (1982), *Third Cinema in the Third World: The Aesthetics of Liberation* (Ann Arbor, Mich.: UMI Research Press).

—— (1983), 'Teaching Third World Cinema', *Screen*, 24/2:

—— (1986), 'Colonialism and "law and Order" Criticism', *Screen*, 27/3–4: 140–7.

Gates, Henry Louis (ed.) (1984), *Black Literature and Literary Theory* (London: Methuen).

—— (1988), *The Signifying Monkey: A Theory of African-American Literary Criticism* (New York: Oxford University Press).

Gellner, Ernest (1983), *Nations and Nationalism* (Oxford: Blackwell).

Gerima, Haile (1989), 'Triangular Cinema, Breaking Toys and Dinknesh vs. Lucy', in Pines and Willemen.

Gilroy, Paul, (1987), 'There Ain't No Black in the Union Jack': The Cultural Politics of Race and Nation (Chicago: University of Chicago Press).

—— (1993), *The Black Atlantic: Modernity and Double Consciousness* (London: Verso).

'Godard on Solanas/Solanas on Godard: An Interview', in Fusco (1987).

Guha, Ranajit (ed.) (1982–9), *Subaltern Studies*, i–vii (New Delhi: Oxford University Press).

***Hall, Stuart** (1996), 'When was "the Post-Colonial"? Thinking at the Limit', in Chambers and Curti (1996).

Harasym, Sarah (ed.) (1990), *Gayatri Chakravorty-Spivak: The Post-Colonial Critic: Interviews, Strategies, Dialogues* (New York: Routledge).

Hulme, Peter (1995), 'Including America', *Ariel*, 25/1.

Huyssen, Andreas (1986), *After the Great Divide: Modernism, Mass Culture, Postmodernism* (Bloomington: Indiana University Press).

Jameson, Fredric (1977/1980), Reflections in Conclusion', in Theodor Adorno *et al.*, *Aesthetics and Politics*, London (trans. Ronald Taylor, Verso 1977).

—— (1986a/1992), 'On Magic Realism in Film', *Critical Inquiry*, 12/2 (Winter); repr. in *Signatures of the Visible* (New York: Routledge).

—— (1986b), 'Third World Literature in the Age of Multinational Capital', *Social Text*, 15 (Fall), 65–88.

—— (ed.) (1993), 'Postmodernism: Center and Periphery', *South Atlantic Quarterly*, 92/3 (Summer), 417–22.

Krauss, Rosalind (1986), *The Originality of the Avant-Garde and Other Modernist Myths* (Cambridge, Mass.: MIT Press).

McClintock, Anne (1992), 'The Angel of Progress: Pitfalls of the Term Post-Colonial', *Social Text*, 31–2: 84–98.

Majid, Anouar (1995–6), 'Can the Postcolonial Critic Speak? Orientalism in the Rushdie Affair', *Cultural Critique*, (Winter), 5–42.

Mongia, Padmini (ed.) (1996), *Contemporary Postcolonial Theory* (London: Arnold).

Mulvey, Laura (1991/1996), 'The Carapace that Failed: Ousmane Sembene's *Xala*', *Fetishism and Curiosity* (London: British Film Institute).

Ngũgĩ wa Thiong'o, (1986) *Decolonizing the Mind: The*

Politics of Language in African Literature (London: James Currey).

O'Hanlon, Rosalind, and David Washbrook (1992), 'After Orientalism: Culture, Criticism and Politics in the Third World', *Comparative Studies in Society and History*, 34/1 (Jan.).

Pandey, Gyanendra (1991), 'In Defence of the Fragment: Writing about Hindu–Muslim Riots in India Today', *Economic and Political Weekly*, 26/11–12, Annual Number, 559–72.

*Pines, Jim, and Paul Willemen (eds.) (1989), *Questions of Third Cinema* (London: British Film Institute).

Prakash, Gyan (1990), 'Writing Post-Orientalist Histories of the Third World: Perspectives from Indian Historiography', *Comparative Studies in Society and History*, 32/2 (Apr.), 383–408.

—— (1992), 'Postcolonial Criticism and Indian Historiography', *Social Text* 31–2: 8–19.

—— (ed.) (1995), *Imperial Histories and Postcolonial Displacements* (Princeton: Princeton University Press).

Prasad, Madhava (1992), 'On the Question of a Theory of (Third World) Literature', *Social Text*, 31–2: 57–93.

Rajadhyaksha, Ashish, and Paul Willemen (eds.) (1994–5), *Encyclopaedia of Indian Cinema* (London: British Film Institute and Oxford University Press).

Said, Edward (1978), *Orientalism* (London: Routledge & Kegan Paul).

Shahani, Kumar (1986), 'Dossier: Kumar Shahani', *Framework*, 30–1: 67–111.

Shohat, Ella (1992), 'Notes on the Post-Colonial', *Social Text*, 31–2: 99–113.

*Solanas, Fernando, and Octavio Getino (1969), 'Towards a Third Cinema', in Fusco (1987).

Soyinka, Wole (1975), 'Neo-Tarzanism: The Poetics of Pseudo-Tradition', *Transitions*, 48.

Spivak, Gayatri Chakravorty (1987), *In Other Worlds: Essays in Cultural Politics* (New York: Methuen).

—— (1988), 'Can the Subaltern Speak?', in Cary Nelson and Lawrence Grossberg (eds.), *Marxism and the Interpretation of Culture* (Urbana: University of Illinois Press).

Wallis, Brian, and Marcia Tucker (eds.) (1984), *Art after Modernism: Rethinking Representation* (New York: New Museum of Contemporary Art).

Willemen, Paul (1989), 'The Third Cinema Question: Notes and Reflections', in Pines and Willemen (1989).

*—— (ed.) (1993), *The Films of Amos Gitai* (London: British Film Institute).

*Williams, Patrick, and Laura Christman (eds.) (1994), *Colonial Discourse and Post-Colonial Theory* (New York: Columbia University Press).

Wollen, Peter (1972/1982), 'Godard and Counter-Cinema: Vent d'est', in Wollen (1982).

—— (1975/1982) 'The Two Avant-Gardes', in Wollen (1982).

—— (1982), *Readings and Writings: Semiotic Counter-Strategies* (London: Verso).

4 | The documentary

John Izod and Richard Kilborn

Looking back on the achievements of a century of moving images, critics often remark on two contrary tendencies. On the one hand, there is the tradition of narrative, or fictional, film in which the primary object is to divert or entertain, and, on the other, there is that of documentary whose main aim, it has been said, is to instruct or inform (Kracauer 1960). Historically this division into fictional and factual modes of filmmaking is seen to be classically exemplified in the work of the early French film pioneers Georges Méliès and the Lumière brothers. While the work of Méliès regularly transported viewers into mythic and fantastical realms (Christie 1994), the main appeal of the actuality of the Lumière brothers lay in the camera's ability to reproduce scenes from everyday life that were instantly recognizable by those who flocked to see them. In the subsequent history of cinema, and later in television, this factual–fictional typology has been main-

tained, even though it is generally recognized that it is over-simplistic, disguising the degree to which these opposing tendencies coexist in practice.

Defining 'documentary'

The term 'documentary' itself seems to have been coined in 1926 by John Grierson, the man usually considered to be the founding father of British documentary. Grierson not only outlined what he saw as the defining features of documentary, but also reflected on the purposes to which documentary could be put. For him, whilst every documentary is bound to present evidence or information about the socio-historical world, it must be more than a quasi-scientific reconstruction of reality. The documentarist must deploy a whole range of creative skills to fashion the 'fragments of reality' into an artefact that has a specific social impact: that is educationally instructive or, in some measure, culturally enlightening. This account must be, in Grierson's phrase, a 'creative treatment of actuality', being aesthetically satisfying while also having a clearly defined social purpose (Hardy 1979: 35–46).

> **The term 'documentary' itself seems to have been coined in 1926 by John Grierson, the man usually considered to be the founding father of British documentary.**

Many critics have regarded Grierson's definition as a useful starting-point for debating the form and function of documentary, but his concept of 'creative treatment' is by no means unproblematic. It attempts to bring together two elements that are not easily reconciled: a commitment to construct an account based on observable reality and, in contrast, the recognition that to produce the desired impact on an audience always requires a good deal of artifice (Nichols 1991). Arising out of this dilemma, there has always been a lively debate amongst documentarists and critics over the legitimacy of certain techniques in the shaping of the documentary account. What indeed is the status of works bearing the documentary label, when so many are structured in much the same way as the fictional works to which they are said to be diametrically opposed? Even some of the short actuality films of the Lumière brothers are marked by conventional storytelling procedures. Furthermore, doesn't the fact that documentaries are made up of 'fragments of reality' which are carefully assembled and edited according to established narrative principles make them an essentially fictional construct? Doesn't the declared or undeclared presence of the documentarist during the recording process mean documentaries are authored pieces much like any other feature film? And do the commercial imperatives, which are so influential in moving-image production, mean that documentaries will always be assessed as much for their entertainment value as for their educational or consciousness-raising potential? Especially in the last few decades, with television's increasing influence on the form that documentary has taken, the debate has remained alive, and ensured that it is impossible to come up with a definition of the genre more watertight than Grierson's.

Recent theoretical work, particularly by Edward Branigan (1992), draws a clear distinction between narrative, as a means used by journalists as well as feature film writers for structuring information, and fiction, as a way of describing the truth-claims of a text. For instance, while it is widely agreed that narrative underlies much documentary, there has been heated controversy over the legitimacy of certain types of dramatic re-enactment (Kilborn 1994b). In the early days of cinema, documentarists were often forced to use dramatic reconstruction. For example, in *Night Mail* (Harry Watt and Basil Wright, GB, 1936) the sequences in which postal workers sort the mail as the train runs through the night were shot on a studio set because the equipment then available was too cumbersome to use on location. Today's generation of filmmakers, with the help of lightweight, go-anywhere cameras, have few such technical problems and dramatic reconstructions tend to be used for different reasons: to re-enact events where camera access has been denied (as is usually the case in the British courts of justice) or to enhance the film's commercial appeal by including a strong dramatic element. Predictably enough, the disagreements have tended to centre on the concern that this blurring of fact and fiction might mislead audiences. Can they distinguish sufficiently well those parts of a work which are based on surmise from those which are more solidly substantiated? Could audiences be duped into taking something to be factual which in fact has its origins in the creative imagination of the drama-documentarist? There is, however, one principal difference between the reconstruction done out of technical necessity and today's drama-documentary that critics often seem to forget: reconstructions in drama-documentaries such as *Who Bombed Birmingham?* (Granada for ITV, 1990) are explicitly signalled as such.

A further issue which has featured prominently in the critical discourse surrounding documentaries centres on questions of realism. Right from the outset documentary's special claim on an audience's attention has been its capacity to provide a seemingly objective window on the world. Much has been made, for instance, of the so-called 'indexical bond' which allows viewers to make a clear connection between on-screen representations and events in the historical world. Whilst there has been widespread acceptance of documentary's referential or indexical qualities, there has

Classic British documentary—*Night Mail* (1936)

been far less agreement about the significance of this defining feature: documentaries may well give us privileged access to empirically observable reality, but this is far from suggesting that they can reveal important truths about that reality (Nichols 1991). Brecht was always keen to remind us, that to capture what is going on beneath the surface of empirically observable reality is far more challenging than accurately to record the surface itself (Brecht 1938/1980). By the same token, documentarists have always had to be careful not to make too grand a claim about how representative of the wider reality is a specific detail they have captured on film.

Critics of documentary have always been aware that all attempts to represent reality carry with them important ideological implications. The photographic realism of the documentary, for instance, can easily conceal the extent to which it often actively constructs a particular view of the world. This view is determined, among other things, by the filmmaker's own preconceptions, by the perspective from which the events are witnessed, and by the structuring principles according to which the material is edited. In other words, documentaries can never be wholly objective; they will always involve a greater or lesser degree of intervention on the part of the documentarist. This is always painfully obvious when one looks at documentaries

from eras gone by. For example, the narration of *Industrial Britain* (GB, 1931) tells us that Robert Flaherty and John Grierson meant to celebrate the craftsmanship of the shop-floor worker. To our ears, however, the fruity accent of the narrator and the heavily value-laden language of the script suggest the patronizing curiosity of the educated middle classes facing an unfamiliar working-class culture.

The very act of documenting an event implies intervention, of course, and there has always been argument about the extent to which the (mere) presence of

> **The photographic realism of the documentary, for instance, can easily conceal the extent to which it often actively constructs a particular view of the world. This view is determined, among other things, by the filmmaker's own preconceptions, by the perspective from which the events are witnessed, and by the structuring principles according to which the material is edited.**

a documentary camera team will influence the course of events. Filming events in the public arena might influence them only minimally, but, where the documentarist is operating in a more confined domestic or institutional setting, the impact of the camera's presence can be quite considerable.

Modes of documentary

While advances in camera and microphone design have made it possible for the documentarist to be less obtrusive than in the past, the intervention issue has remained a matter of intense debate. It might even be said that distinct modes of filmmaking have developed out of the manner in which documentarists indicate their role in the filmmaking process: whether they appear on camera in the presence of their documentary subjects; whether they tell their audience how the documentary material has been gathered; or even whether they go as far as to reflect on other ways in which the project might have been handled.

Discussion of the various modes in which filmmakers might work has been a feature of debates about documentary since the mid-1980s (see Nichols 1991), and for the purposes of critical analysis the idea of modes is attractive as a means of dividing the subject. If we think of documentary as a vast genre as substantial as fiction or journalism, then it is tempting to see the modes as representing the parts of that genre. However, unlike subgenres, they differ from one from another primarily in the manner in which they represent the historical world, and only after that in the nature of their subject-matter. At their most distinctive, the modes are themselves so different in appearance that they make it possible to conceive of a neat formula whereby the many functions that documentary can fulfill are paralleled by a variety of formats in which they can be constructed.

Unfortunately, the matter is not quite so simple. On the one hand, discussion of the modes of filmmaking practice has brought a measure of clarity of thought concerning the various ways in which documentary can construct its discourses and address its audiences; it has thus also drawn attention to the discursive richness of the genre. On the other hand, the debate has given rise to expectations of critical precision where, because of the very nature of the modes, precision is not always to be found. Symptomatic of this is the problem theorists have had in distinguishing one

mode from another. For the fact is that they are no more tidily delineated than the genre in its entirety. Just as we have had to learn to recognize that documentary has permeable boundaries, with fiction on one side and journalism on another, so we have to understand that the modes are equally ill-defined. What is more, some of them (the reflexive one, described below, is an obvious case in point) readily absorb some of the main characteristics of other modes. Therefore, when observers of documentary form refer to its modes, it is probably best to understand them as having in mind the dominant formal characteristics that shape a film.

The evolution into mainstream practice of each of the modes tends to be associated with technological advance, which is usually said to lie in the improvement and miniaturization of sound- and picture-recording equipment. However, most theorists would not regard technology as the sole determining factor; institutional constraints and opportunities are also seen as highly significant in the development of new modes, as becomes clear when we look at the way they are described.

The *expository mode* addresses its audience directly, usually through a narrator who interprets what we see, in effect telling us what we should think of the visual evidence before our eyes. Because the limited sound-recording technology of the 1930s made it easier to dub in an unseen speaker, narration of this type became known as the 'voice-of-God' mode, which describes so well the implicit claim of narrators in this mode to speak with authority. I have already referred to the narration of the film *Industrial Britain*, and it was rare for a documentary of the 1930s and 1940s to be made in any other mode (see Barnouw 1974; Ellis 1989). Television production technology overcame these restrictions on sound long ago, and it is now almost as easy to record the narrator on- as off-screen, but the expository mode is still in use (for example, in almost all natural history and scientific documentaries), but its innate tendency to authoritarianism is softened by using people with gentle voices and by offsetting interviews against the commentary, which seems to give the subjects of the film their own voice.

The *observational* mode, or *direct cinema*, is often referred to as a product of the new technology of the late 1950s, and it is true that without lightweight equipment, large magazines, and audiotape machines with the facility for synchronous sound recording, it would not have been possible to get extended footage of people going about the routine business of their lives. This is the single most obvious characteristic of observational films (Barnouw 1974). However, the more sensitive historians of cinema have noted that even these films, with their claim simply to observe reality as it unfolds, are both the vehicles of a distinctive ideology and the product of institutional pressures and opportunities. Allen and Gomery (1985) show how the philosophical implications of direct cinema fitted the dominant liberal values of the Kennedy era. Indeed, Kennedy himself was ready to allow observational cameras to accompany him on more than one occasion (for example, on the campaign trail in the film *Primary* (D. A. Pennebaker and Richard Leacock, USA, 1960). Where these films provided insights into chronic social problems, it was assumed they would be politically effective: the state would be able to relieve social malaise just so long as it had been recognized. Allen and Gomery also demonstrate how, in its early days at the start of the 1960s, it was hoped that the new format would boost the audience for the US television network ABC, which at the time was trailing its competitors. When it failed to do this, the direct film was dropped from the schedules.

Also dependent on the new equipment of the late 1950s was the *interactive mode*. Partly because it can also use long takes recorded in the field, it is sometimes confused with the direct mode. However, at its most distinct, the mode is characterized by the film crew interacting with the people in front of the lens (see Nichols 1991). In general this will occur via an on-camera interview, but sometimes it can be achieved in the editing process, for instance by constructing the facsimile of a dialogue from fragments of recorded statements by people who have not actually met. In this way the main procedures of the interactive mode resemble those of the journalistic interview, which is why interactive documentary has become routine television practice (Lockerbie 1991). Since it gets round one of the disadvantages of the direct documentary—that the latter can only eavesdrop on what is said in front of the camera—the interactive mode suits that current of television discourse that claims to get the truth from the horse's mouth (as it were). It is a form that familiarity has rendered seemingly natural to viewers; but it too is redolent with cultural associations, including the very idea that 'truth' can be uncovered in this way.

The *reflexive mode* is found where the manner in which the historical world is represented itself becomes the topic of cinematic representation. It makes not only the film's subjects, but also its own formal qualities, the object of questioning and doubt. Such films frequently discourage spectators from accepting that a single point of view is an adequate representation of the whole truth on any topic (see Nichols 1991; Renov 1993). The reflexive mode has aroused greater interest among observers of documentary than among most members of the public. This is probably because reflexive films accommodate theoretical goals of the kind that Brecht or Godard might have advocated for documentary. To a whole generation of critics and theorists weaned in the 1970s on *Screen* and the cultural debates of the left, the reflexive documentary was a concept whose time had come even before it had hit the screen. And, indeed, in its re-visioning of the world, the reflexive documentary often does have a political goal, undermining the certainties of a political leader or a business executive by refusing the visible or epistemological bases upon which certainty is founded. Nick Broomfield's pursuit of Margaret Thatcher, *Tracking down Maggie* (Channel 4, GB, 1994), and Michael Moore's hunt for the Chief Executive of General Motors, *Roger and Me* (USA, 1989), are good examples.

The political dimension of the reflexive project lies partly in the way such films imply that people's memory, perception, and interpretation of events are distorted by the stereotypes (largely screen-based) that circulate in our culture. More emphatically, the deconstructive methods these films deploy undermine realism, which term, as we have seen, is usually taken by documentarists to refer to an unproblematic access to the world through traditional mimetic representation. In reflexive films such as *The Thin Blue Line* (Errol Morris, USA, 1987), the viewer begins to question whether the images and sounds of the text could possibly represent the world adequately, since they are plainly a construction of the filmmakers.

> **In reflexive films such as *The Thin Blue Line* (Errol Morris, USA, 1987), the viewer begins to question whether the images and sounds of the text could possibly represent the world adequately, since they are plainly a construction of the filmmakers.**

The Thin Blue Line (1987)—deconstructive methods used to undermine realism

Whereas the norm in other forms of documentary is to concentrate attention on the filmmaker's encounter with the world in the reflexive mode the encounter between viewer and filmmaker is emphasized. The viewer comes to expect the unexpected, designed not so much to shock or surprise as to raise questions about the film's own status and that of documentary in general (Nichols 1991; Renov 1993). As Lockerbie argues, a text is likely to switch constantly between different forms of representation in a typically Brechtian fashion: 'Snatches of song or dance, clips from other films, sequences of animation, and other film forms, are mixed in with documentary material' (1991: 228).

Categorizing such a large corpus of work according to particular documentary modes, as outlined above, has proved to be a useful starting-point for discussing *some* of documentary's characteristic forms of address.

Nevertheless, it is important to remember that this taxonomy is by no means exhaustive. Throughout the history of documentary, for instance, there has been a clearly discernible strand of work to which one might attach the label *poetic* (Nichols 1991; Loizos 1993). Here the filmmaker will, typically, gather together recorded sights and sounds of the natural or social world and mould them in such a way as to evoke a particular mood or atmosphere. Such documentaries will more often than not eschew the guiding commentary or narration in favour of musical or diegetic sound accompaniment. Often, as in the case of the city symphonies of the 1930s, but also in the more recent work of filmmakers like Werner Herzog, the documentarist will use an incremental montage technique to evoke an emotional rather than intellectual response from the viewer. These poetic accounts clearly bear the marks of a shaping and sensitive intelligence. For similar reasons some critics have suggested that it might be appropriate to establish a further category, that of *authored documentary* to characterize work where the individual creative input, and even personality, of the filmmaker has manifestly become an important factor in determining its appeal (Winston 1995; Crawford and Turton 1992).

In the 1990s in the output of television channels yet other forms of documentary have emerged which may well warrant description as modes, although they have not yet been identified as such in the critical literature. They include the *video diary*, or first-person documentary. It is yet another product of the confluence of new technology (especially the development of high-quality camcorders) and institutional pressure (in this case for novel and comparatively inexpensive programming material). It carries the documentary inwards, being able to do directly things at which other documentaries have to labour. It can do this by revealing an individual's personality both from the inside, through interior monologue in which the filmmaker reflects upon the nature of his or her own life, and also from the outside, via the opinions and actions of others directed towards the filmmaker. A compelling example is Willa Woolston's *My Demons: The Legacy* (Video Diaries, BBC, 1992), in which a journey back to the land of her birth becomes both a recovery of auto-biographical history and a self-administered therapy.

Another emergent mode is that known as *reality programming*, in which television packaging makes the most sophisticated intervention in actuality-based production, as it seeks to highlight the sense of shared experience or lived reality. Such programming uses a wide range of television techniques to enhance the entertainment value of the material. Indeed, many such programmes are entirely devoted to prime-time entertainment bearing a close relationship to tabloid journalism and having no meaningful connection with documentary. But even where they do resemble documentaries, the emphasis is on capturing the vibrancy of real-life events in short packages, each with its unmissable emotional climax. The whole is linked into programme format by a celebrity presenter who typically builds audience anticipation so as to focus it on the sequence of emotional impacts—which arrive regularly every three or four minutes. It follows that each series has its own characteristic and tightly defined themes, and these are usually identified by a dramatic series title: *999* (BBC), *Rescue 911* (CBS), *Crimewatch UK* (BBC), *Cops* (Fox), and *America's most Wanted* (Fox). Reality programming has been introduced to the schedules in response to institutional pressure simply because it is popular and brings large audiences (see Kilborn 1994a).

When we add to these emergent modes another well-established one that has already been mentioned, namely *drama-documentary*, we have to recognize that documentaries exist in many forms, and may often be a hybrid of several of them. They perform multiple functions which tend to change with the passing of the years and as this brief look at their history suggests, the rise and fall of grand new projects accounts in part for the way in which each mode rises to prominence and is superseded by others.

BIBLIOGRAPHY

Allen, Robert, and **Douglas Gomery** (1985), *Film History: Theory and Practice* (New York: Alfred A. Knopf).

Barnouw, Erik (1974), *A History of the Non-Fiction Film* (New York: Oxford University Press).

Bloch, Ernst, et al. (1980), *Aesthetics and Politics* (London: Verso).

Branigan, Edward (1992), *Narrative Comprehension and Film* (London: Routledge).

Brecht, Bertolt (1938), 'Against Georg Lukács', in Bloch et al. (1980).

Christie, Ian (1994), *The Last Machine* (London: British Film Institute).

Crawford, Peter, and **David Turton** (eds.) (1992), *Film as Ethnography* (Manchester: Manchester University Press).

Ellis, Jack C. (1989), *The Documentary Idea* (Englewood Cliffs, NJ: Prentice-Hall).

Hardy, Forsyth (ed.) (1979), *Grierson on Documentary* (London: Faber & Faber).

Kilborn, Richard (1994a), 'How Real can you Get?: Recent Developments in "Reality" Television', *European Journal of Communication*, 9: 421–39.

—— (1994b), 'Drama over Lockerbie: A New Look at the Drama-Documentary Debate', *Historical Journal of Film, Radio and Television*, 14/1: 59–76.

Kracauer, Siegfried (1960), *Theory of Film* (New York: Oxford University Press).

Lockerbie, Ian (1991), 'The Self-Conscious Documentary in Quebec: *L'Emotion Dissonante* and *Passiflora*', in Peter Easingwood et al. (eds.), *Probing Canadian Culture* (Augsburg: AV-Verlag).

Loizos, Peter (1993), *Innovation in Ethnographic Film: From Innocence to Self-Consciousness 1955–1985* (Manchester: Manchester University Press).

Lovell, Alan, and **Jim Hillier** (1972), *Studies in Documentary* (New York: Viking).

***Nichols, Bill** (1991), *Representing Reality: Issues and Concepts in Documentary* (Bloomington: Indiana University Press).

***Renov, Michael** (ed.) (1993), *Theorizing Documentary* (London: Routledge).

Rosenthal, Alan (1988), *New Challenges for Documentary* (Berkeley: University of California Press).

—— (1990), *Writing, Directing and Producing Documentary* (Carbondale: Southern Illinois Press).

Winston, Brian (1995), *Claiming the Real* (London: British Film Institute).

5

The animated film

Michael O'Pray

Definitions and theoretical approaches

The animated film is an enormously wide and heterogeneous category, traditionally understood as film that is shot frame by frame and by which drawings and objects are given the appearance of moving. However, it ranges from Hollywood cartoons to abstract modernist animation, from puppet films to types of special-effects cinema to computer-generated moving imagery, and so on. This promiscuity of forms is bewildering, and unique in cinema and this is one of the main reasons why animation has suffered theoretical and critical neglect for so long. Another is the low status it has derived from its massive use in children's entertainment and in advertising.

Another major and related reason for its neglect is animation's use of a broad array of image-making materials and techniques—drawings, paint, cels, clay, plasticine, puppets and marionettes, dolls, computers, sand, glass, film footage, paper cut-outs, pins, special effects. Inevitably this technical and material eclecticism has marginalized it from current film theory and anlaysis (Kotlarz 1995). For some, the massive introduction of special effects and computer-generated imagery in contemporary mainstream cinema, as in *Robocop* (USA, 1987) and *Terminator II* (USA, 1991), has radically complicated the matter (Cholodenko 1991).

Understandably, animators themselves propose var-

ied definitions, ranging from Norman McLaren's 'the art of movements-that-are-drawn' (Gordon 1977) to Jan Svankmajer's refusal of the term 'animation' (Hames 1995). Definitions are complicated by the differences between two-dimensional animation, primarily identified as drawing animation, and all its derivatives (painting, cel, collage, and so forth), and three-dimensional animation using real objects, puppets, or clay models. A further complication, though one shared with live-action film, is that animation is divided between narrative and non-narrative. The story-telling charm of Disney can be contrasted to the abstract rhythms of the 1920s graphic cinema of Hans Richter and Walter Ruttmann (Lawder 1975), even if the two traditions merge fleetingly in films like Disney's experimental film *Fantasia* (USA, 1940).

Thus the question of the definition of film animation remains acute in so far as its resolution nearly always excludes certain kinds of filmmaking. Crafton (1984), for instance, sees animation as a subspecies of film in general. On the other hand, Cholodenko (1991) understands animation, perhaps unhelpfully, as that which pervades all film as a result of the latter's origins in the 'persistence of vision' of pre-cinematic optical toys and its 'illusion of life'. In contrast, Klein (1993) conceives of the American cartoon as at least primarily a graphic art form.

One of the most sustained and rewarding studies of animation is to be found in the Soviet filmmaker Sergei

Eisenstein's writings on Disney. Written in the 1940s, they focus on the 'protoplasmatic' (O'Pray 1997) of Disney's pre-sound cartoons. Connected with his concept of ecstasy and the primitive notion of an omnipotent fluid 'form' which is pre-imagistic, Eisenstein's 'protoplasmaticism' stresses the versatility of the formal line of the drawing, suggesting that its creation is an expression of the artist's unconscious and its transformational powers are omnipotent in character.

Eastern Europe remains the source of fairly abstract inquiry into animation. For example, Yuri Lotman (1981) suggests that the basic property of animation is the operation of 'signs on signs' so that the animated representation is an image of an image (Yampolsky 1987). In other words, the screen image with its sign system represents the images produced by drawings, cels, puppets, clay models, and so on, and their sign system of dynamic plasticity. The interplay between these two systems lies at the core of any aesthetic understanding of a particular animated film. Endemic to animation is the dominance of the plastic sign system in terms of its versatility, control, and mastery (O'Pray 1997), what Klein (1993) calls the *machina versatilis* of animation.

Roland Barthes's (1982) essay on the painter Giuseppe Arcimboldo suggests that the way in which he deals with levels of meanings—using the natural objects (trees, flowers, books, and so on) that make up a portrait of a face which is also a painting—is similar to animation. So animation could be divided into three systems: (1) that of the means of representation—drawings, cels, clay, objects; (2) that of the representation—Mickey Mouse, a Svankmajerian collage figure, Grommit, and so on; and (3) that of the representational system of film with its close-ups, zooms, pans, edits, superimpositions, sound, and colour.

Studies of computerized imagery with a strong realist aesthetic imitating live action, as in *Toy Story* (USA, 1995), has given it the rather far-fetched characterization of 'postmodernist' for its intertextual referencing (Cholodenko 1991). Digital imaging, totally generated by a computer whilst marketed as animation, mimics the realist aesthetic of mainstream live-action film. The fascination, and perhaps for some confusion, of such films lies in the ambiguity of whether or not they are animation at all. Such an effect is to be likened perhaps to *trompe-l'œil* painting, where we thrill to the virtuosity of the means of representation itself (O'Pray 1997).

The American animated cartoon

Undoubtedly, the major area of serious research has been into the American cartoon (notably Maltin 1987; Klein 1993; Crafton 1984). In particular, this research has been undertaken from the historical perspective of the major cartoon studio systems like Disney (Finch 1973) and Warner Bros. (Schneider 1988; Maltin 1980), emphasizing the animation studio as part of the American film industry complex. However, there have been exceptions, with studies of the role of racism (Kotlarz 1983), genre (Thompson 1976), auteurism (Thompson 1976; Hames 1995), and the political function of Disney (Dorfman and Matellart 1975; Smoodin 1993).

By definition, the American cartoon is grounded in drawing, and this allows it great flexibility so that, through scale and perspective, it can imitate the camera's movements and angles; whereas in object-animation the camera must operate in three-dimensional space with pans, tracks, and zooms, as in live-action narrative cinema. Thus drawing frees animation from the denotative qualities of film and photography. Prior to sound, with its demand for dialogue and therefore more orthodox narrative structures, cartoons were intrinsically graphic, dealing with line, rhythm, and surface (Klein 1993) and thus indebted to comic strips, vaudeville (Crafton 1984), and madcap silent comedies (Klein 1993). Mimicry of the camera was minimal. In many ways this early period of late 1920s Disney, Max Fleischer, and the creator of Felix the Cat, Otto Messmer, reflects to Eisenstein's (1949) notion of the ideogram and the hieroglyphic using the early, more graphically based notion of montage. The introduction of sound established a tendency in cartoons away from a modernist anti-realism, with its stress on the picture plane, and towards a deep-space naturalism-cum-realism.

The arrival of sound undoubtedly led to highly developed plot lines and characterization, which lent themselves to the auteurist approaches and genre analyses found in the literature on the American cartoon. The literal creation and control of particular characters (such as Roadrunner and Bugs Bunny), even within the heavy division of labour of the Hollywood animation studios between the late 1920s and 1950s, made cartoons more amenable to auterist analyses, which have been usefully applied to Tex Avery, Chuck Jones, and others from the Hollywood cartoon classical period (Thompson 1976). In more recent years filmmakers such as Svankmajer have also received auteurist accounts of their work (Hames 1995).

Cartoons especially have been more open to a genre reading (Thompson 1976) although the idea of cartoon *per se* being a genre rather makes the idea of subgenre within it—the chase film, the dotty individual, or whatever—more problematic. In fact the subgenre is most understood in terms of long-standing characters such as Tom and Jerry, Bugs Bunny, and Donald Duck. Animation itself is a type of filmmaking, rather than a genre with its shared thematic and institutional coherence.

The relationship between animation and fairy- and folk-tales has been well recognized and suggests an approach to narrative analysis (Propp 1928) in which narrative functions and elements are identified and relationships between them established. Analysis in terms of paradigmatic and syntagmatic elements and their functions provides a formal basis for cartoon theory. In the case especially of post-1930 Hollywood cartoons, this has been done by Klein (1993) in terms of the nuisance, over-reactor, and controller.

Three-dimensional animation

The revived popularity of object-animation using three-dimensional space, as practised by Svankmajer, the Quay brothers, Aardman, and others, establishes close connections with mainstream film and divides the ontological basis of animation. The animation of actual objects could be understood within the notion of a realist mode and self-generating two-dimensional work within a more semiotic one. However, the most sustained semiotic analyses have been of drawing animation (Yampolsky 1987; Lotman 1981), although semiotics has been applied to puppetry (Jurkowski 1988) and thus by implication to the works of Svankmajer and the Quay brothers.

Loman's (1981) argument that animation is essentially 'an image of an image' and is constituted by signs of signs accompanies discussion of the disquiet of images moving at all. This latter idea can be related to Freud's (1919/1960) concept of the 'uncanny', which has been applied to East European object-animation (O'Pray 1989), which has been associated with psychoanalysis, surrealism, and notions of fantasy (O'Pray 1989; Hammond 1987; Cardinal 1995). 3-D or object-animation has been largely identified with East Euro-

pean traditions, as manifested in the puppet and marionette tradition of Czechoslovakia and Poland, where it has had a strong cultural and historical significance as a part of popular culture and as a political allegorical system (Hames 1995; Holloway 1983; Jurkowski 1988). Jiři Trnka was the most important of these animators. As susceptible to Proppian analysis as Hollywood cartoons, given their siting in European folk-tales and myths, they have at times also been influenced by art movements, especially surrealism in the case of Svankmajer (O'Pray 1995; Cardinal 1995) and Walerian Borowczyck.

Theories of surrealism in recent years (Forster 1993), in which the role of the automaton in surrealist photography has been identified with issues around the 'uncanny', have led to a more psychoanalytical approach. Both Forster (1993) and Todorov (1975) use the surrealist uncanny in their differing theories of fantasy. With its links to castration anxiety and fantasies linked with death through the animation of inanimate objects, the uncanny became a fertile ground for theorizing in animation. The links between the uncanny and surrealism are also strong in the use of mannequins and dolls by such artists as Man Ray and Hans Bellmer (Krauss 1986) and by animators like the Quay brothers and Svankmajer.

That such an approach is largely appropriate to object-animation also suggests that the genre of the fantastic could be applied creatively to certain animation films—possibly three-dimensional films, and not just cartoons *per se*. In the case of the Quay brothers, for instance, who use both live action and object-animation, the distinctions between animation and live-action narrative become blurred. Any analysis of such films is not entirely separable from those applicable to such special-effects films as *The Fly* (USA, 1986), *Edward Scissorhands* (USA, 1990), and *Robocop* (USA, 1987). The profound difference lies in the narrative role of such special-effects animata in most special-effects films (Robocop is a robot) and the juxtaposing and quite transparent use of animated figures in their own right, as found in the films of the Quay brothers. This emphasis on the means of representation as being part of the representation itself seems central to much animation and lends it an uncanny air at times. There seem to be conscious elements of versatility and the marvellous in animation which are not shared in the same way by live-action film. The idea of taking an animated figure (whether cartoon or three-dimensional) for its own sake links with

Jan Svankmajer modelling

notions of psychical omnipotence and control (Freud 1919; O'Pray 1997). Of course, this cannot be generalized over all instances of animation, but it is probably one way of making initial, if tenuous, distinctions.

The fascination of audiences for anthropomorphic models and puppets in recent years (as in Nick Park's *Creature Comforts* (GB, 1989), Tim Burton's *The Nightmare before Christmas* (USA, 1989) and Henry Selick's *James and the Giant Peach* (USA, 1996)), with their elements of satire, social humour, and nightmare, suggests both the influence of Svankmajer and the long-standing tradition of the grotesque and the carnivalesque (Bakhtin 1968; O'Pray 1989) flowing out of caricature, fairy-tales, and newspaper cartoons whereby 'difficult' material finds a cultural space often abetted by the safety-net of humour (Kris 1964).

Avant-garde and abstraction

Paradoxically, the pre-sound cartoons were often more modernist in their acceptance of the screen surface than the so-called abstract graphic cinema of the 1920s of Richter, Ruttmann, Oskar Fischinger, and Viking Eggeling, (Le Grice 1977). Like its cartoon counterparts, it was rarely silent (Eggeling's classic Diagonalsymphonien/*Diagonal Symphony* (Germany, 1925) was an exception). Often using cut-out paper manipulation, it worked with movement of shapes through space, and at times had anthropomorphic tendencies. Marcel Duchamp's *Anemic Cinema* (France, 1925), also used text with obscene visual puns as part of a Dadaesque project. Again the impetus was graphic as opposed to filmic (Sitney 1974). This abstraction was developed by James and John Whitney, who in the 1960s developed a high-technology computer aesthetic in the United States (*Permutations*, USA, 1967).

Len Lye's camera-less, partially hand-painted films of the 1930s (*Colour Box*, GB, 1935; *Trade Tattoo*, GB, 1937) owed much to modernist ideas of collage and abstraction intermixed with ideas culled from 'primitive' Maori art. McLaren's films of this period were also modernist, but with a strong political agit-prop in the case of *Hell Unlimited* (USA, 1936). In the period after the Second World War Robert Breer began his career with similar experiments with shape and space but moved onto anarchic Dadaesque montages of drawings, the result of tracing from live-action film (rotoscoping), object-animation with free-wheeling domestic allusions which owe more perhaps to Émile Cohl and pre-sound cartoons than to a pure modernist aesthetic.

In the case of abstraction in animation, critical approaches are filtered through notions of avant-gardism and modernism within the fine arts in general. Richter's and Ruttmann's work can be seen as responses to abstract painting, using music as an analogy (Lawder 1975). In the case of experimental animators like Breer, there are connections to be made both to the commercial animation film, especially that of the early pioneers Cohl (Crafton 1990) and the Fleischers, and to Dada and surrealism and notions of collage, montage, and modernism. In other words the institutional context of such work is importantly wider than that of mainstream cinema and some of its aims arise from issues in other art forms.

Part of European avant-gardism, but standing closer to notions of art cinema in their psychological exploration and sexual and political radicalism, are the early European animation films of Borowczyk (Pierre 1968), Trnka, and Jan Lenica (Holloway 1983), who used techniques and materials of many kinds, but especially the puppet, to explore themes of sexuality, political allegory, and surrealist symbolism.

Futures

There are many areas within animation studies crying out for serious thought and analysis. One of the dangers of focusing too much on animation as such is that the complexity and imaginative qualities of a particular film can be too easily cut off from other kinds of cinema. The Quay brothers, Burton, and Svankmajer are good examples of filmmakers who straddle many kinds of film—children's animation, art cinema, avant-gardism, and of course mainstream 'entertainment'. Animation's traditional formal and material promiscuity and hybridity are its strength at a time when new technologies like computerization are beginning to saturate the broad spectrum of cinema. To this extent, definition is probably inappropriate; rather, we should be using the Wittgensteinian model of the 'family resemblance'. A film is often simply more than 'animated'; it bears a family resemblance to many other kinds of filmmaking and an analytical approach that is rigorous but broadminded is more likely to produce critical and theoretical analyses that escape reductionism and do justice to the density of the work in hand.

BIBLIOGRAPHY

Afterimage (1987), 13, Special Issue: *Animating the Fantastic*, (Autumn).

Bakhtin, Mikhail (1968/1984), *Rabelais and his World* (Bloomington: Indiana University Press).

Barthes, Roland (1982/1991), 'Arcimboldo; or, Magician and Rhetoriqueur', in *The Responsibility of Forms: Critical Essays on Art, Music and Representation* (Berkeley: University of California Press).

*****Bendazzi, Giannalberto** (1994), *Cartoons: One Hundred Years of Cinema Animation* (London: John Libbey).

Canemaker, John (ed.) (1988), *Storytelling in Animation: The Art of the Animated Image*, 2 vols., ii (Los Angeles: American Film Institute).

Cardinal, Roger (1987), 'Stirrings in the Dust', *Afterimage* (1987).

—— (1995), 'Thinking through Things: The Presence of Objects in the Early Films of Jan Svankmajer', in Hames (1995).

Ceram, C. W. (1965), *Archaeology of the Cinema* (London: Thames & Hudson).

Cholodenko, Alan (ed.) (1991), *The Illusion of Life: Essays on Animation* (Sydney: Power Publications).

Crafton, Donald (1984), *Before Mickey: The Animated Film 1889–1928* (London: MIT Press).

—— (1990), *Émile Cohl, Caricature, and Film* (Princeton: Princeton University Press).

Dorfman, Ariel, and **Armand Mattelart** (1975), *How to Read Donald Duck: Imperialist Ideology in the Disney Comic* (New York: International General).

Eisenstein, Sergei (1949/1977), 'The Cinematographic Principle and the Ideogram', in *Film Form: Essays in Film Theory* (London: Harvest/Harcourt Brace Jovanovich).

—— (1988), *Eisenstein on Disney* (London: Methuen).

Finch, Christopher (1973/1995), *The Art of Walt Disney: From Mickey Mouse to the Magic Kingdoms* (rev. London: Virgin Books).

Forster, Hal (1993), *Compulsive Beauty* (London: MIT Press).

Freud, Sigmund (1913/1985), 'The Uncanny', in *Art and Literature: The Pelican Freud Library* (Harmondsworth: Penguin).

—— (1919/1960), *Totem and Taboo* (London: Routledge & Kegan Paul).

Gordon, Lindsay (1977), *Norman McLaren* (Edinburgh: Scottish Arts Council).

Hames, Peter (ed.) (1995), *Dark Alchemy: The Films of Jan Svankmajer* (Trowbridge: Flicks Books).

Holloway, Ronald (1983), 'The Short Film in Eastern Europe: Art and Politics of Cartoons and Puppets', in David W. Paul (ed.), *Politics, Art and Commitment in the East European Cinema* (London: Macmillan).

Jurkowski, Henry K. (1988), *Aspects of Puppet Theatre* (London: Puppet Centre Trust).

Klein, Norman M. (1993), *Seven Minutes: The Life and Death of the American Animated Cartoon* (London: Verso).

Kotlarz, Irene (1983), 'The Birth of a Notion', *Screen*, 24/2 (Mar.–Apr.) 21–9.

—— (1995), 'In Betweening: An Interview with Irene Kotlarz', *Art History*, 18/1 (Mar.), 24–36.

Krauss, Rosalind (1986), 'Corpus Delicti', in *L'Amour fou: Photography and Surrealism* (London: Arts Council of Great Britain).

Kris, Ernst (1964) in collaboration with Ernst Gombrich, 'The Principles of Caricature', in *Psychoanalytic Explorations in Art* (New York: Schocken Books).

Lawder, Standish (1975), *The Cubist Cinema* (New York: New York University Press).

*Le Grice, Malcolm (1977), *Abstract Film and Beyond* (London: Studio Vista).

Lotman, Yuri (1981), 'On the Language of Animated Cartoons', in *Russian Poetics in Translation*, 8: 36–8.

Maltin, Leonard (1980/1987), *Of Mice and Magic: A History of American Animated Cartoons* (rev. New York: Plume Printing).

Moritz, William (1979), 'Non-Objective Film: The Second Generation', in *Film as Film*, exhibition catalogue (London: Hayward Gallery).

Noake, Roger (1988), *Animation: A Guide to Animated Film Techniques* (London: Macdonald).

O'Pray, Michael (1989), 'Surrealism, Fantasy and the Grotesque: The Cinema of Jan Svankmajer', in James Donald (ed.), *Fantasy and the Cinema* (London: British Film Institute).

—— (1995), 'Jan Svankmajer: A Mannerist Surrealist', in Hames (1995).

—— (1997), 'Eisenstein and Stokes on Disney: Film Animation and Omnipotence', in Pilling (1997).

Peary, Gerald, and Danny (1980), *The American Animated Cartoon: A Critical Anthology* (New York: Dutton).

Pierre, Sylvie (1987), 'The Theatre of Monsieur Borowczyck', *Afterimage* (1987).

Pilling, Jayne (1997a), *Women and Animation: A Compendium* (London: British Film Institute).

—— (1997b), *A Reader in Animation Studies* (Luton: University of Luton Press/John Libbey Media).

Propp, Vladimir (1928/1977), *Morphology of the Folk Tale* (rev. London: University of Texas Press).

Russett, Robert, and Cecile Starr (1976/1988), *Experimental Animation: Origins of a New Art* (New York: Da Capo Press).

Schneider, Steve (1988), *That's all Folks: The Art of Warner Brothers Animation* (New York: Henry Holt).

Sitney, P. Adams (1974/1979) *Visionary Film: The American Avant-Garde 1943–1978* (Oxford: Oxford University Press).

Smoodin, Eric (1993), *Animating Culture: Hollywood Cartoons from the Sound Era* (Oxford: Roundhouse).

Solomon, Charles (ed.) (1987), *The Art of the Animated Image* (Los Angeles: American Film Institute).

Thompson, Kristin (1980), 'Implications of the Cel Animation Technique', in Teresa de Lauretis and Stephen Heath (eds.), *The Cinematic Apparatus* (London: Macmillan).

Thompson, Richard (1976), 'Meep Meep', in Bill Nichols (ed.), *Movies and Methods*, 2 vols., i (London: University of California Press).

Todorov, Tzvetan (1975), *The Fantastic: A Structural Approach to a Literary Genre* (New York: Cornell University Press).

Yampolsky, Mikhail (1987), 'The Space of the Animated Film: Khrzhanovsky's *I Am With You Again* and Norstein's *The Tale of Tales*', *Afterimage* (1987).

6 Issues in European cinema

Ginette Vincendeau

European cinema has always been recognized as aesthetically and culturally important and yet, as a branch of film studies, it was, until recently, underdeveloped. This is a problem of both terminology and concept. Since it has traditionally been defined in terms of 'high art'—as opposed to Hollywood—and of originality and diversity, European cinema has tended either to be reduced to the work of a few auteurs, under the concept of 'European art cinema', or to be split between studies of national cinemas, movements, and individual filmmakers. Only since the early 1990s has it emerged as a topic in its own right, for reasons which I will examine at the end of this chapter. But first I will chart the more established ways in which European cinema has been approached.

European art cinema

The dominant concept in studies of the cinemas of Europe has been that of 'art cinema'. Arising from the avant-garde works of the 1920s, the films of prominent figures such as Jean Renoir, Ingmar Bergman, and Federico Fellini, and the post-war movements of Italian Neo-Realism and the French New Wave, the essence of European cinema has been defined as residing in works that are, to various degrees, aesthetically innovative, socially committed, and humanist in outlook. To these features are often added the auteurist notions of originality and personal vision—all characteristics which define, and promote, European art cinema as fundamentally different from the industrially based and generically coded Hollywood. Although the French critics of the 1950s claimed the possibility of authorship and artistry in Hollywood films—Alfred Hitchcock, Howard Hawks—the sense of art as being the defining characteristic of European film has remained.

In the 1970s and 1980s European art cinema was further defined, as an institutional (Neale 1981) and aesthetic (Bordwell 1979) phenomenon designed to counter Hollywood's invasion of European film markets. European art films, it was claimed, propose a different spectatorial experience—loose, ambiguous narratives, characters in search of meaning rather than action, overt directorial expression, a heightened sense of realism (including depictions of sexuality), and a slower pace— and therefore require a different viewing context. Hence, the films are exhibited in 'art cinemas' and at film festivals and they receive a special kind of critical attention.

> **The dominant concept in studies of the cinemas of Europe has been that of 'art cinema'. Arising from the avant-garde works of the 1920s, the films of prominent figures such as Jean Renoir, Ingmar Bergman, and Federico Fellini, and the post-war movements of Italian Neo-Realism and the French New Wave, the essence of European cinema has been defined as residing in works that are, to various degrees, aesthetically innovative, socially committed, and humanist in outlook.**

While these are observable facts, this approach involves three dangers. One is a flattening-out of differences between individual films and filmmakers. The second is of reducing a vast and diverse European production to what is—or at least has been for many decades—only one section of the market. The third is to reinforce American-centrism: if a variety of diverse practices, some of which pre-date Hollywood, are reduced to an 'alternative', then Hollywood is reinforced as for ever 'the norm'. Ultimately, the notion of European art cinema is a useful polemical and marketing tool and a guide to an aesthetically rich tradition of European filmmaking, but it should be no more than that.

'The national' in European cinema

The cinemas of Europe have traditionally been considered 'national' in a way which Hollywood has rarely

been. For instance, most reference works and film history books (e.g. Cook 1985; Allen and Gomery 1985; Nowell-Smith 1996) classify Hollywood under headings relating to genre, industry, and technological developments, while they subsume European cinemas under 'national cinemas'. In the United Kingdom and the United States this is reflected institutionally in the fact that European cinemas—except the British cinema, which is always in an ambiguous position *vis-à-vis* continental cinema— are often studied within foreign-language departments, as opposed to film and media departments.

Many of the seminal film histories were studies of national European cinemas or of world cinema organized along nationalist lines, especially British (Rotha 1936), French (Bardèche and Brasillach 1935; Sadoul 1953), and German (Kracauer 1947; Eisner 1952). Soviet cinema also attracted attention from an early age, thanks to the writings of its practitioners (Eisenstein 1942, 1949) and to the communist bias of formative French film history (Sadoul 1953). The dominance of these 'major' countries in scholarly studies of European cinema has continued to the present day, with the addition of Italy in the wake of Neo-Realism. The rest of Europe tends to be considered in regions— Central Europe, Nothern Europe—while 'minor' countries remain in isolation if not oblivion: Belgium, Holland, Greece, Portugal, Austria, Switzerland. In this respect, one remarkable development of the 1990s has been the rise of Spanish cinema, attributable to the post-Franco liberalization of the country, but especially, as José Arroyo points out, to the enormous success of director Pedro Almodóvar (Part 3, Chapter 13d).

While European national cinemas are generating a regular flow of books and university courses, the limited availability of subtitled film prints or videos hinders their comprehensive study. In most cases—even in the 'major' countries—only a narrow canon of work is known outside that country. As Ian Christie says of the 1920s, 'the bulk of the mainstream cinema . . . remains little known in comparison with the handful of Soviet, French, and German avant-garde classics that dominate the decade's image' (Part 1, Chapter 7); Simona Monticelli makes a similar comment in relation to Neo-Realism (Part 3, Chapter 8). Truly comprehensive histories of national European cinemas in the English language still remain to be written.

A contributing factor is that, unlike Hollywood (the 'dream factory'), European cinemas, globally and individually, have been treated with little reference to their industrial context. There are complex reasons for this, which include the international promotion of European 'art' cinema, but also the nature of the European film industries. With some notable exceptions—Pathé and Gaumont in early twentieth-century France, UFA in Germany in the 1920s and 1930s, Cinecittà in post-war Italy, the Central and East European countries under socialism—European production has been small-scale, fragmented, and disorganized. Since the 1950s there have been few integrated distribution or exhibition systems, and most studios have worked on a hire basis. Empirical studies of the industry therefore tend to be localized—studies of the Film Europe movement, of the coming of sound, of funding (the latter especially during and since the 1993 GATT negotiations; see Mattelart, Part 3, Chapter 12). There are few large-scale studies of European production, distribution, and exhibition in the English language; two exceptions are Crisp (1993) and especially Finney (1996). Work on audiences is equally underdeveloped and localized (for example, studies of reception in early German cinema and 1950s Britain). Studies of film culture are mostly restricted to the British context (Higson 1993) and the French cinéphile environment (Hillier 1985, 1986; Roud 1983). There is no pan-European study of industrial practices in relation to film aesthetics on the lines of David Bordwell, Janet Staiger, and Kristin Thompson's, *The Classical Hollywood Cinema* (1985). Salt (1983) and Crisp (1993) consider such matters, but are restricted, for the former to a small selection of filmmakers and for the latter to one country. As mentioned earlier, the dominant concept informing studies of the national cinemas of Europe remains that of 'European art cinema', a largely aesthetic category.

The sense of 'the national' has been most pervasive in studies of national cinemas that are concerned with a cultural and social contextualization: Siegfried Kracauer's From *Caligari to Hitler* (1947), Millicent Marcus's *Italian Films in the Light of Neo-Realism* (1986), Alan Williams's *Republic of Images* (1992), Thomas Elsaesser's *New German Cinema* (1989), Susan Hayward's *French National Cinema* (1993), Andrew Higson's *Waving the Flag* (1995), to name a few. Although there has been, over the years, a shift in these studies towards a more self-conscious examination of the concept of 'national cinema' (Hayward, Higson), all take national boundaries as the defining factor of their study. In different ways, their project is to match the

stylistic and representational strategies of a national film production with the cultural, social, and political events and climate of the country from which the films emerge.

While some national surveys have suffered from the problems outlined above—especially the reduced canon on which they are often based—the matching of texts and contexts has been variously productive or reductive. For instance, Daniel Goulding remarks of Central European cinema that there is a tendency among Western critics 'to stress the political messages of the films and to celebrate the most controversial and provocative of them'. Goulding's point can be extended to most studies of national cinemas produced outside their country of origin. As a result of a bias towards art films and/or politically 'subversive' films, the entirety of a national production can be very sketchily examined. For example, it is only recently that the German cinema of the Nazi period has begun to be properly examined (Rentschler 1996). Conversely, as we will see, a few 'privileged moments' in each national cinema continue to dominate public perception.

The difficulties in conceptualizing national film industries are compounded by their international nature. Cinema personnel have always crossed national boundaries: the French Pathé and Gaumont operators went all over Europe, Russians came to Germany and France in the 1920s, Germans to France in the 1930s, and many went back and forth between these countries as well as to Britain and Italy on a regular basis. A more individual form of emigration has continued to take place, with such figures as Luis Buñuel, Jean Vigo, Roman Polanski, Chantal Akerman (Fowler, Part 3, Chapter 13c), while in the post-war period co-production deals became a major element in the reconstruction of national European cinemas. American funding, the increased part taken by television companies since the 1970s, and more recently the role of the European Union (Horrocks 1995), have further problematized the notion of 'national' cinemas in Europe. What determines the national identity of a film when funding, language, setting, topic, cast, and director are increasingly mixed? How can we classify films such as Louis Malle's 1992 film *Damage* (French director, Franco-British cast, English settings), Krzysztof Kieślowski's *Three Colours* trilogy (*Blue*, 1993; *White*, 1993; *Red*, 1994; made by a Polish director with French funds and a Franco-Polish cast), and Lars von Trier's 1996 film *Breaking the Waves* (Danish director, Norwegian–

The 'allegorical medievalism' of *The Seventh Seal* (1957)—European art-house staple and success of the 1950s

European funds, British cast, Scottish setting)? However, despite the fluidity of national boundaries, the majority of European films are perceived as having a clear national identity, especially when it comes to particular movements and filmmakers.

Movements and moments

The selection and canonization of privileged 'moments' in national cinemas is a method derived from art and literary history. It informs the structure of history books, the planning of film courses and art cinema retrospectives, and the spatial organization of film museums, such as the Museum of the Moving Image in London. Based on recent film history surveys and encyclopaedias (Bordwell and Thompson 1979; Cook 1985; Vincendeau 1995; Nowell-Smith 1996), the canon of such movements includes: Soviet cinema,

Weimar cinema and German Expressionism, the British documentary movement, French poetic realism, Italian Neo-Realism (Monticelli, Part 2, chapter 8), the French New Wave (Forbes, Part 2, Chapter 9), New German Cinema (Sieglohr, Part 2, Chapter 10). Others, such as Early Scandinavian cinema, the British and Czech New Waves, and the Polish Cinema of Moral Concern (Goulding, Part 2, Chapter 11) appear as more specialized interests. Recently, pre-Soviet Russian cinema, Nazi cinema, French cinema of the occupation, post-Franco Spanish cinema, French *cinéma beur* (or 'film de banlieue') have emerged as new areas of study and the canon may be enlarged.

The benefits of isolating movements are obvious; they help us make sense of a mass of otherwise unmanageable material and, in so far as scholarship has any impact on distribution, it helps ensure the continued availability of films on video and through television and cinema retrospectives. The analogy with art and literary movements also gave these pockets of European cinema cultural legitimacy and media identity, and it continues to do so in marketing films which do not have the benefit of a well-known auteur (for instance, the French 'films de banlieue' in the wake of *La Haine*, Mathieu Kassovitz, 1995). The drawbacks are equally obvious: the wood of a national cinema becomes invisible behind the trees of a small number of canonical movements. This is true both of the gaps between the movements (what happens between Weimar and New German Cinema?), and of the rest of the production at the time of the movements (how does the French New Wave relate to the mainstream production of its time?). The concept of 'influence' equally pervades film history, which tends to relate subsequent films to an earlier, 'golden' movement—the documentary tradition for British cinema, poetic realism and then the New Wave in France, and so on. Finally, the desire to bracket films together inevitably homogenizes a collection of diverse works. A close study of films belonging to a movement reveals at least as many stylistic and ideological differences as it reveals similarities, a point made by both Sieglohr about New German Cinema and Monticelli about Italian Neo-Realism.

Despite these problematic aspects, the concept of film movements is a useful one, if only because it is so controversial. As critical constructions, European film movements make sense, and yet they are almost without exception rejected or challenged by filmmakers. Furthermore, they are subject to change. The fate of Neo-realism as a critical category first constructed and then deconstructed (Monticelli) is, in this respect, exemplary.

Authorship in European cinema: the canon and how to challenge it

The figure of the director has always been central to European cinema. Powerful directorial figures arose as in Hollywood from the mid-1910s (e.g. Abel Gance, Victor Sjöström), but unlike their American counterparts, decision-making rested primarily with them. Concurrently, early theoretical writing in 1920s France identified the director as the main source of artistic creativity (Abel 1984, 1988), preparing the grounds for the more comprehensive theorization of the *politique des auteurs* in the 1950s (Hillier 1985, 1986). This claimed the director's personal vision as paramount,

transcending the team-work of filmmaking while also unifying a filmmaker's *œuvre* across time, through a body of stylistic and thematic motifs.

Over the decades, a canon of 'great European directors' has arisen, which has fluctuated (as exemplified by the *Sight and Sound* critics' polls made every ten years since 1952), but which has nevertheless established a pantheon. The selective list below, which parodies that published in *Movie* in June 1962, is simply meant to identify the canon as well as ways of challenging it. It is based on critical opinion rather than personal taste (though absolute objectivity is impossible).

The great: Angelopoulos, Antonioni, Bergman, Bresson, Buñuel, Clair, Dreyer, Eisenstein, Fassbinder, Fellini, Godard, Kieślowski, Lang, Murnau, Oliveira, Ophuls, Pabst, Pasolini, Renoir, Resnais, Rohmer, Rossellini, Sjöström, Tarkovsky, Tati, Vertov, Vigo, Visconti, Wajda.

The good: Bardem, Becker, Bertolucci, Blasetti, Carné, Chabrol, De Sica, Dupont, Duvivier, Feyder, Forman, Frears, Grémillon, Herzog, (European) Hitchcock, Ivens, Jancsó, L'Herbier, Loach, Lubitsch, Malle, Mikhalkov, Munk, Passer, Pudovkin, Saura, Stiller, Szabó, Tavernier, Truffaut, Varda, Wenders.

The interesting: Almodóvar, Bava, Borowczyk, Cohl, Demy, Dulac, Ferreri, Feuillade, Franju, Gance, Greenaway, Guitry, Jarman, the Kaurismäki brothers, Kusturica, Leigh, Leone, Makavejev, Marker, Méliès, Melville, Moretti, Pialat, Polanski, Powell and Pressburger, Reisz, Riefensthal, Rivette, Rouch, Ruiz, Schroeter, Svankmajer, Syberberg.

The rest . . .

First of all, the lists are overwhelmingly male, reflecting not so much the male bias of cinema, since European cinema has nurtured the highest number of women directors, but the male bias inherent in ideas of genius. A counter, all-female European canon might read:

The great: Akerman, Chytilová, Dulac, Duras, Mészáros, Muratova, Sanders-Brahms, Varda.

The good: Audry, Balasko, Box, Dorrie, Gogoberidze, Jakubowska, Kaplan, Kurys, Miró, Osten, Serreau, Toye, von Trotta.

The interesting: Breillat, Gorris, Guy, Isserman, Notari, Ottinger, Potter, Sander, Schub, Treut.

They are also significantly art-cinema-oriented. As discussed at the beginning of this chapter, art cinema has dominated critical constructions of European film, and this is reflected in the canon of 'great auteurs'. Yet, European cinema also produced rich traditions of popular films, some of which are identified—at least in their own country—by their director alongside genre and star. Thus the category of the 'popular auteur' is an important one in European cinema, though critically unrecognized. Names in this particular canon would include some 'cross-overs'—e.g. Tavernier, Serreau, Reisz, Almodóvar—as well as mainstream film-makers—Annaud, Attenborough, Balasko, Beineix, Berri, Besson (see Hayward, Part 3, Chapter 13e), Lean, Schünzel, Matarazzo, May, Pagnol, Verneuil—to name a few.

Though the canon is largely international, national variations occur. For example, Sacha Guitry figures under 'interesting', but in France many see him as one of the 'greats'. The canon thus also bears the marks of availability problems for non-English-language films.

Closely allied to the 'masterpiece tradition' (Allen and Gomery 1985), the idea of a canon of great directors, like that of movements, derives from art and literary history. Directors deemed geniuses tower above the production of their country (Ivens for the Netherlands, Wajda for Poland, Jancsó for Hungary) or even world cinema (Bergman, Lang, Fellini, Renoir: see Reader, Part 3, Chapter 13a). Some stand for the entire production of their 'small' country (Angelopoulos for Greece, Bergman for Sweden). Some were celebrated in the pre-war period (Eisenstein, Hitchcock, Sjöström, Renoir), but the critical practice of auteur canons developed mainly in the 1950s and 1960s, in the wake of the *politique des auteurs*, provoking a boom in monographs on individual directors. Subsequently, auteurism has been the most contested critical approach. Throughout the 1970s a severe critique of authorship was conducted, displacing it in favour of the structuralist analysis of narratives and of close textual studies (Cook 1985). At the same time, the critical revaluation of Hollywood and the rise of cultural studies produced a (critical) devaluation of art cinema and European auteurs, and arguably of European cinema altogether.

The 1980s and 1990s saw a 'return to the auteur' for two main reasons. One is the renaissance of film history after the 'theoretical 1970s', which sparked off an interest in neglected areas such as early cinema, and in the process some early cinema auteurs (Crafton 1990). The

other has to do with gender studies. Feminist studies polemically reclaimed the notion of authorship for women and, although this work has been predominantly on American cinema, important studies of European women directors have also come out (Flitterman-Lewis 1990; Portuges 1993). Some established male filmmakers have been reappraised in the light of feminism (Mulvey 1996) and more work of this kind is under way. Similarly, gay studies have generated an interest in gay directors such as Pedro Almodóvar (Smith 1994) and in rereading the work of classic figures such as Marcel Carné (Turk 1989).

The concept of the auteur, like that of movements, has fluctuated in the light of changing critical discourse and increased availability of material. If understood in an industrial, social, and cultural context, as opposed to just as an expression of genius, it can still illuminate areas of European film history that remain unknown—for example, the popular auteurs alluded to above—leading us to the most uncharted terrain of European film studies, that of genre and stardom.

The forgotten categories: genre and stardom

Genre and stardom, the twin foundations of popular cinema, have always existed in European cinema. However, the fact that both operate in an unsystematic way compared to Hollywood, and the unavailability of subtitled versions of much popular European cinema, have created enormous scholarly difficulties. I will briefly sketch out the main trends in popular European genres (concentrating, as a case-study, on heritage cinema) and stardom.

Most European countries have produced national inflexions to universal genres, and in particular comedy, melodrama, horror, and the musical (Dyer and Vincendeau 1992; Vincendeau 1995). The critically ignored genre of pornography should be added to this list. Even the archetypal American western has had European variations, especially in Italy and Germany—though these are numerically small. On the other hand, the other genre thought of as uniquely American, the thriller, has a rich following (and antecedents) in Europe—in Britain and especially in France, where the *policier* is one of the mainstays of post-war cinema (along with comedy). There are many reasons why these genres, which have been—and in France still are—numerically important, are critically virgin territory. One is the art cinema bias. Popular European genres (unless personalized by an auteur, such as Sergio Leone's 'spaghetti' westerns and the comedies of Claude Chabrol and Jacques Tati) simply do not correspond to the international *idea* of European cinema. In addition, national agencies promote art cinema and are somehow embarrassed by their popular films. Ironically perhaps, popular genres require more complex decoding than art cinema, because of their closeness (through language, character's gestures, topical references) to popular culture. Thus the international nature of high culture helps the exportability or art cinema, while the cultural 'noise' around popular films renders them more or less 'inexportable' (Jeancolas 1992). However, the eminent exportability of popular American cinema points to the single most important reason for the lack of export (as opposed to inexportability) of popular European cinema, that is the American monopoly of world distribution circuits in Europe, and the European failure to develop its own (Finney 1996). As the number of European films shown on the world market keeps decreasing (under 2 per cent in the mid-1990s), only two 'genres' of European cinema still travel relatively well: art cinema and heritage films.

European 'heritage' cinema describes popular costume films made in Europe since the 1970s, usually with high production values and often based on a canonical literary source. Typical examples include *Babette's Feast* (Denmark 1987), *Cyrano de Bergerac* (France, 1990), *A Room with a View* (UK, 1985), *Emma* (UK, 1996). As a European genre which exports well, heritage films are worthy of interest. They also raise interesting issues of definition. For instance, how different are they from earlier costume films? How close to the present does a 'heritage' film come? The Second World War? The 1960s? As films that re-present national history and myths to their audience, they have often been rejected by critics as conservative (Higson 1993), but are being re-assessed (Dyer 1995;

> **Ironically perhaps, popular genres require more complex decoding than art cinema, because of their closeness (through language, character's gestures, topical references) to popular culture.**

Higson 1996). Finally, heritage films are classic narrative films which on the whole do not display the self-conscious stylistic marks of European art authorship, and thus provide a good terrain to study classical *European* film style.

Heritage films' high production values include the use of stars; indeed some European stars (Emma Thompson, Gérard Depardieu) are increasingly associated with the genre, which has given them an international profile, where their predecessors traditionally attained international status through Hollywood (Marlene Dietrich, Greta Garbo) or their association with art cinema (Jeanne Moreau, Marcello Mastroianni, Liv Ullman). A few others gained global fame in their own national cinema, among them Max Linder, Jean Gabin, Sophia Loren, Brigitte Bardot (Vincendeau, Part 3, Chapter 13f), Totò, Alain Delon, and Catherine Deneuve. Academic star studies (Dyer 1979, 1987; Gledhill 1991), however, have conceptualized stardom as intrinsically linked to Hollywood. And yet, there are many important European stars beyond those mentioned above who have, in Dyer's formulation, crystallized social and ideological values, have enjoyed enormous popularity in their own country, but are virtually unknown outside. Examples include: Lida Baarová (Czechoslovakia), Annabella, Bourvil, Martine Carol, Micheline Presle, and Louis de Funès (France), Zarah Leander, Willi Fritsch, and Hildegard Knef (Germany), Lola Flores and Sara Montiel (Spain), Gino Cervi and Alberto Sordi (Italy), Paula Wessely (Austria), Regina Linnanheimo (Finland).

The difficulties in studying European stars resemble the difficulties in studying European cinema. They start with the material problem of getting hold of films as well as other resources: letters, press books, popular film journals. On the other hand, these hurdles point to the originality and interest of such studies. There are three other main issues raised by the study of European stars. The first one relates to the fragmentation of the European film industry, making it difficult to identify with precision this dimension of stardom; for example, the construction by the industry of the star's image and the determinants of a 'star vehicle'. Meanwhile, budgets and detailed box-office figures are hard to get, especially for the pre-war period. The second one relates to aesthetics. In mainstream cinema, a study of a particular star needs to be aware of the genre(s) in which (s)he works. So, for instance, a study of Martine Carol needs to have a good understanding of the French costume dramas of the 1950s. As far as auteur

ISSUES IN EUROPEAN CINEMA

cinema is concerned, the most interesting issue is that of the interaction between star and directorial voices. Here the relatively low attention given to European stars is in direct (inverse) relation to the attention lavished on auteurs, who in a sense *are* the stars of European cinema. Another interesting issue is the differential value a star acquires at home as opposed to internationally; for example, Mastroianni was both a popular and art cinema star at home, but only an art cinema star abroad, while Moreau, predominantly an art cinema star, has a consequently much higher reputation outside France than inside. Finally, the greatest impediment, but also the greatest reward, in studying European stars is to gain an understanding of their relationship with social, historical, and ideological values. Here, the most 'inexportable' are potentially the most interesting.

The international canon of European stars is still very narrow, and there is, correspondingly, much scope for innovative and revealing work in this area of film studies.

'European cinema': a new category

As alluded to at the beginning of this chapter, a recent expansion of studies of 'the European' in relation to the cinema has taken place, which can be understood within three contexts. The first is a boom in theoretical and historical studies of national cinema(s) and national identity. The second is the topicality of Europe on the social and political scene and the prominent role now played by the European Union *vis-à-vis* the cinema (Horrocks 1995; Finney 1996). The third relates to the severe difficulties experienced by film industries throughout Europe, due to the fiercer than ever competition from Hollywood since the mid-1980s. This has produced a sense of a beleaguered (perhaps even doomed) cinema, the condition of which needs to be documented.

With the publication of Pierre Sorlin's *European Cinemas, European Societies* (1991), of Duncan Petrie's *Screening Europe* (1992), and of Richard Dyer and my *Popular European Cinema* (1992), an area of academic study emerged. Other books followed, such as my *Encyclopedia of European Cinema* (1995), Wendy Everett's *European Identity in Cinema* (1996), and Angus Finney's *The State of European Cinema* (1996). These books adopt different methodologies: Finney's is an industry study while the others concen-

trate on aesthetics. But while Petrie (1992), Sorlin (1991), and to a large extent Everett (1996) concentrate on auteur films, Dyer and Vincendeau (1992) address popular genres. All, however, share a major concern with the nature of European cultural identity: does it exist as an entity, or is it no more than a patchwork of discrete national identities? There is a tension between a search for common features—'the European'—and a desire to isolate or preserve national specificity. New European cinema studies have reclaimed important pan-European genres and themes, for example heritage cinema and comedy, and the representation of the Second World War. Ultimately, though, national differences keep resurfacing. Even such a systematic attempt at characterizing the European film industry as an entity as Finney's frequently breaks down into national specificities ('the French case', 'the British case' . . .). At the same time, most pan-European statistics (e.g. film production) need to be broken down into national units to be meaningful. Thus scholars and viewers are thrown back on to the rich diversity of national industries, individuals, and films that constitutes European cinema.

BIBLIOGRAPHY

Abel, Richard (1984), *French Cinema: The First Wave 1915–1929* (Princeton: Princeton University Press).
—— (1988) *French Film Theory and Criticism*, 2 vols. (1907–1929, 1930–1939) (Princeton: Princeton University Press).
Allen, Robert C., and **Douglas Gomery** (1985), *Film History: Theory and Practice* (New York: Alfred A. Knopf).
Armes, Roy (1976), *The Ambiguous Image: Narrative Style in Modern European Cinema* (London: Secker & Warburg).
Balski, Grzegorz (1992), *Directory of Eastern European Film-Makers and Films 1945–1991* (Trowbridge: Flicks Books).
Bardèche, Maurice, and **Robert Brasillach** (1935), *Histoire du cinéma* (Paris: Denoël & Steele).
*****Bordwell, David** (1979), 'Art Cinema as a Mode of Film Practice', *Film Criticism*, 4/1: 56–64.
—— and **Kristin Thompson** (1979/1993), *Film Art: An Introduction* (New York: McGraw-Hill).
—— **Kristen Thompson,** and **Janet Staiger** (1985), *The Classical Hollywood Cinema: Film Style and Mode of Production to 1960* (London: Routledge & Kegan Paul).
Cook, Pam (ed.) (1985), *The Cinema Book* (London: British Film Institute).
Cowie, Peter (1992), *Scandinavian Cinema: A Survey of Film and Film-Makers in Denmark, Finland, Iceland, Norway and Sweden* (London: Tantivy Press).

Crafton, Donald (1990), *Émile Cohl, Caricature and Film* (Princeton: Princeton University Press).

Crisp, Colin (1993), *The Classic French Cinema 1930–1960* (Bloomington: Indiana University Press).

Dyer, Richard (1979), *Stars* (London: British Film Institute).

—— (1987) *Heavenly Bodies: Film Stars and Society* (Basingstoke: Macmillan).

—— (1995), 'Heritage Cinema in Europe', in Vincendeau (1995).

*—— and **Ginette Vincendeau** (eds.) (1992), *Popular European Cinema* (London: Routledge).

Eisenstein, Sergel (1942), *The Film Sense*, ed. and trans. Jay Leyda (London: Faber & Faber).

—— (1949), *Film Form*, ed. and trans. Jay Leyda (New York: Harcourt Brace).

Eisner, Lotte (1952/1969), *L'Écran Démoniaque*, trans. Roger Greaves as *The Haunted Screen: Expressionism in the German Cinema and the Influence of Max Reinhardt* (London: Thames & Hudson).

Elsaesser, Thomas (1989), *New German Cinema: A History* (London: British Film Insitutue and Macmillan).

Everett, Wendy (1996), *European Identity in Cinema* (Exeter: Intellect Books).

Finney, Angus (1996), *The State of European Cinema* (London: Cassell).

Flitterman-Lewis, Sandy (1990/1993), *To Desire Differently: Feminism and the French Cinema* (Bloomington: Indiana University Press; repr. New York: Columbia University Press).

Gledhill, Christine (ed.) (1991), *Stardom, Industry of Desire* (London: Routledge).

Goulding, Daniel J. (1989) *Post New Wave Cinema in the Soviet Union and Eastern Europe* (Bloomington: Indiana University Press).

—— (1994), *Five Filmmakers: Tarkovsky, Forman, Polanski, Szabó, Makavejev* (Bloomington: Indiana University Press).

Hayward, Susan (1993), *French National Cinema* (London: Routledge).

Hewitt, Nicholas (ed.) (1989), *The Culture of Reconstruction: European Literature, Thought and Film 1945–1950* (Basingstoke: Macmillan).

Higson, Andrew (1993), 'Re-Presenting the National Past: Nostalgia and Pastiche in the Heritage Film', in Lester Friedman (ed.), British Cinema and Thatcherism (London: University College London Press).

—— (1995), *Waving the Flag: Constructing a National Cinema in Britain* (Oxford: Oxford University Press).

—— (1996), 'The Heritage Film and British Cinema', in Higson (ed.), *Dissolving Views: Key Writings on British Cinema* (London: Cassell).

Hill, John, Martin McCloone, and Paul Hainsworth (eds.) (1994), *Border Crossing: Film in Ireland, Britain and Eur-* ope (Belfast: Institute of Irish Studies; London: British Film Institute).

Hillier, Jim (ed.) (1985), *Cahiers du cinéma*, i: *The 1950s* (London: Routledge & Kegan Paul).

—— (1986), *Cahiers du cinéma*, ii: *The 1960s* (London: Routledge & Kegan Paul).

Horrocks, Simon (1995), 'The European Community and the Cinema', in Vincendeau (1995).

Jeancolas, Jean-Pierre (1992), 'The Inexportable: The Case of French Cinema and Radio in the 1950s', in Dyer and Vincendeau (1992).

Kracauer, Siegfried (1947), *From Caligari to Hitler* (Princeton: Princeton University Press).

Liehm, Mira, and J. Antonin (1977), *The Most Important Art: East European Film after 1945* (Berkeley: University of California Press).

Marcus, Millicent (1986), *Italian Film in the Light of Neo-Realism* (Princeton: Princeton University Press).

Mulvey, Laura (1996) 'The Hole and the Zero', in *Fetishism and Curiosity* (London: British Film Institute).

*Neale, Stephen (1981), 'Art Cinema as Institution', *Screen*, 22/1: 11–39.

Nowell-Smith, Geoffrey (ed.) (1996), *The Oxford History of World Cinema* (Oxford: Oxford University Press).

Petrie, Duncan (1992), *Screening Europe* (London: British Film Institute).

Portuges, Catherine (1993), *Screen Memories: The Hungarian Cinema of Márta Mészáros* (Bloomington: Indiana University Press).

Rentschler, Eric (1996), *The Ministry of Illusion, Nazi Cinema and its Afterlife* (Cambridge, Mass.: Harvard University Press).

Rotha, Paul (1936) *Documentary Film* (London: Faber & Faber).

Roud, Richard (1983), *A Passion for Films: Henri Langlois and the Cinémathèque Française* (London: Secker & Warburg).

Sadoul, Georges (1953), *French Film* (London: Falcon Press).

Salt, Barry (1983), *Film Style and Technology: History and Analysis* (London: Starword).

Smith, Paul Julian (1994), *Desire Unlimited: The Cinema of Pedro Almodóvar* (London: Verso).

*Sorlin, Pierre (1991) *European Cinemas, European Societies* (London: Routledge).

Turk, Edward Baron (1989), *Child of Paradise: Marcel Carné and the Golden Age of French Cinema* (Cambridge, Mass.: Harvard University Press).

*Vincendeau, Ginette (ed.), (1995) *The Encyclopedia of European Cinema* (London: Cassell and British Film Institute).

Williams, Alan (1992), *Republic of Images: A History of French Filmmaking* (Cambridge, Mass.: Harvard University Press).

7

The avant-gardes and European cinema before 1930

Ian Christie

The 1920s golden age of avant-garde film might be said to have culminated in an international conference held at La Sarraz in Switzerland in 1929. Here film-makers from a dozen countries gathered to discuss possible forms of co-operation in production and distribution. They also made a collective film, *Storm over La Sarraz*, which is lost—or perhaps was never completed (Montagu 1968). For, despite its resolutions and plans, La Sarraz left little trace, except the idea of an independent cinema, both avant-garde and international, which would soon fragment and retreat in the face of political confrontation in the 1930s. Its legacy, however, would prove powerful. For when synoptic histories of cinema first began to be written in that decade, a handful of Soviet, French, and German avant-garde classics—the films of Sergei Eisenstein, Dziga Vertov, René Clair, G. W. Pabst, Walter Ruttman—came to occupy a disproportionate space compared with the bulk of the mainstream cinema of this period, an anomaly which has largely persisted.

Although the earliest instances of modernist artists planning and making films were in Russia and Italy in the 1910s, it was in the 1920s that the term 'avant-garde' began to be applied to film, as part of a new kind of discourse about cinema (Elliott 1986; Kirby 1971). What proved crucial was the self-definition of a group of French filmmakers, who were also active as critics and theorists. Louis Delluc and Jean Epstein, together with Abel Gance, Marcel L'Herbier, Germaine Dulac, and Henri Chomette, all subscribed to a preoccupation with film's 'specificity', in order to demonstrate the legitimacy of cinema as an art in its own right. Their films ranged from short experiments, like Chomette's *Five Minutes of Pure Cinema* (1925), to Gance's six-hour epic *Napoléon* (1927), but they shared a common interest in exploring the optical and psychological power of the film image, focusing on the concept of *photogénie* (Willemen 1994). They also spawned a support system of film clubs, specialized cinemas, and magazines, all devoted to the promotion of film as a modern art; and this network soon spread beyond France, creating a sympathetic context for innovative work from elsewhere.

By the end of the 1920s more mainstream critics had institutionalized the avant-garde as a kind of 'R & D' department, present to a greater or lesser degree in most major national schools of filmmaking. Thus Paul Rotha, in his pioneering world survey *The Film till Now* (1930), defended the French avant-garde as 'an excellent grounding for the young film director' (211), providing 'object lessons in cinematic values', which in turn 'should be of the utmost interest to the big-scale director' (227). And when discussing the limitations of British cinema, he noted as a factor that 'there has never been any school of *avant-garde* in England', The critic C. A. Lejeune invoked a similar rationale: 'the value of the experimental film lies less frequently in achievement than in suggestion, in the fact that it precedes mature work' (1931: 205). She also maintained that experimental films could help free movies from their 'one great obsession' with the human figure.

But if the avant-gardes were gaining mainstream acceptance, they had also already come under fire from a number of positions which equally could be— and often are—considered avant-garde. First came the attack of the Soviet left, also composed of filmmaker-critics, and led by Eisenstein. In a polemical reply to a 1926 German article, Eisenstein challenged the claim that Soviet montage films, like all serious cinema, depended on the 'figurative quality of the [individual] shot' (1926: 79). Instead of 'literary' or 'pictorial', shots, Eisenstein argued for the 'director's' or 'compositional' shot, which is conceived as an integral part of the montage sequence; and in doing so he dismissed the work of the French avant-garde as 'children's playthings', which merely exploit 'the photographic possibilities of the apparatus'—in terms similar to those he would also use against his equally polemical Soviet contemporary Dziga Vertov.

Neither Eisenstein nor the other new Soviet filmmakers who emerged after 1924 would have accepted the label 'avant-garde', regarding it as symptomatic of a bourgeois conception of art. Yet they were committed to challenging Soviet audiences' conservatism by means of experiment; and such experiments, as Leonid Trauberg argued, would often not be, at first, 'intelligible to the millions' (1929: 250). This may seem broadly similar to the western 'R & D' concept of an avant-garde, but in fact the Soviet left's refusal of avant-garde status and willingness to 'battle with pub-

lic taste' marked a rejection both of the autonomy of aesthetics and of an implicitly élitist view of art. As Eisenstein and Grigori Alexandrov admitted of *The General Line* (1929), 'while rejecting the glitter of external formal searches, it is inescapably an experiment', but one which they hoped would be, 'however contradictory it may sound . . . *intelligible to the millions*' (Eisenstein and Alexandrov 1929: 257).

Another challenge to the self-declared French avant-garde in the late 1920s came from closer to home. The Surrealist movement, composed initially of writers, although with a growing number of visual artists, declared its opposition to all conventional art in the name of a call to revolt. Surrealist activity, in whatever genre, aimed to provoke, to scandalize, and to seek new forms of self-expression and pleasure. As such, it could easily be seen—and was—as yet another faction within the avant-garde. But Surrealists vigorously rejected this conscription, venting their outrage particularly on avant-garde work which seemed close to Surrealism in its themes, such as Dulac's realization of a scenario by the Surrealist Antonin Artaud, *The Seashell and the Clergyman* (France, 1927), or Epstein's adaptation of Edgar Allan Poe's *The Fall of the House of Usher* (France, 1928). When Luis Buñuel and Salvador Dali followed Surrealist precepts to make one of that movement's first authentic films *Un chien andalou* (France, 1929), they proclaimed a break with the French avant-garde tradition, yet the film's shock tactics and its early success clearly owe much to that same tradition.

The Surrealist and Soviet 'anti-avant-gardes' were to have a lasting influence on the cinema at large, far beyond the relatively short duration of the original movements. Their key films became the 'classics' of the 1920s, when histories of cinema began to be written in the following decade, and have largely remained so ever since. The prestige of their leading figures—Eisenstein, Pudovkin, and Vertov; Buñuel, Dali, and Jean Vigo—became linked to the appeal of Soviet montage's dialectic and of the Surrealist belief in the unconscious as cyphers for Marxism and Freudianism respectively. Thanks in large part to these alliances, film was acquiring a new status, which allowed it to engage with the most serious cultural and political issues of the day.

By 1930 the new film culture spawned by the avant-gardes had produced its own radical film clubs, magazines, distribution networks—and an emerging generation of filmmakers and activists already steeped in

The Surrealist and Soviet 'anti-avant-gardes' were to have a lasting influence on the cinema at large, far beyond the relatively short duration of the original movements. Their key films became the 'classics' of the 1920s, when histories of cinema began to be written in the following decade, and have largely remained so ever since.

the ideologies and debates of the rival avant-gardes. Many of these would become leaders of the documentary movements which were typical of the 1930s: figures like John Grierson, Ivor Montagu, Len Lye, and Humphrey Jennings in Britain, Joris Ivens in the Netherlands, and Henri Storck in Belgium. In effect, documentary became an 'applied' avant-garde, inheriting much of its theory and practice from the avant-gardes of the previous decade, while recasting these in instrumental rhetorics of information, revelation, or mobilization, depending on who, if anyone, was the sponsor (Winston 1995).

The fact that much pioneering cinema history was written under the influence of the early Soviet and/or

Surrealist positions has meant that the received history of film still echoes many of the original battles, and indeed often follows the contours of these highly polemical movements. A good example of this kind of 'engaged' history is an account of the French avant-garde of the 1920s by the Surrealist critic and filmmaker Jacques Brunius, who remained in Britain after the war and was prompted to write his essay by rumours of a new avant-garde emerging in America (Brunius 1948). Brunius stresses how the French avant-garde emerged from a combination of dissatisfaction with existing French cinema at the end of the First World War and the new stimuli of German Expressionism, American comedy, Swedish mysticism, and Soviet montage. He dismisses much of its output as pretentious, but defends the importance of the aesthetic issues it raised and the need to break 'the routine of a developing academicism', which in turn paved the way for French cinema's great achievements in the more accessible genres of satirical comedy and poetic realism in the 1930s.

This long-term dialectical view of the relationship between avant-garde and mainstream marks an advance on the Rotha–Lejeune laboratory view, and introduces an important historial perspective. But the lasting influence of Surrealism on critical opinion was to reinforce antagonism towards any idea of a distinct

Entr'acte (1924)—Dada meets cinema in this cornerstone of the 'historic avant-garde', which was originally commissioned to be shown during the interval of the ballet *Relâche*

avant-garde, replacing this with a wide-ranging selection of films chosen for their largely unintended qualities of *amour fou*, incongruity, *näiveté*, fantasy, and the like—a selection of 'involuntary Surrealist' works by such as Georges Méliès, Louis Feuillade, Charlie Chaplin, F. W. Murnau, but also by Mack Sennett, Tod Browning, Albert Lewin, Joseph H. Lewis, and many lesser names (French Surrealist Group 1951). Against this pantheon, the Surrealists set a list of filmmakers to *avoid*, which included, as well as the entire French avant-garde of the 1920s, Walt Disney, Carl Theodor Dryer, D. W. Griffith, Ernst Lubitsch, Alexander Dovzhenko, and many who would be regarded by others as 'surrealist' (French Surrealist Group 1951). This also featured two particular Surrealist *bêtes noirs*, Fernand Léger and Jean Cocteau, creators of two of the most remarkable and influential avant-garde films of the 1920s, *Ballet mécanique* (France, 1924) and *Le Sang d'un poète* (France, 1930).

Fairness, of course, was not the point. The grounds for rejection of most deliberately avant-garde work were precisely that it *was* deliberate: 'intellectual' or 'literary' were Surrealist terms of abuse. As an exercise in radical revisionism, the post-Second World War Surrealist intervention was to prove influential far beyond the narrow confines of the group, encouraging interest in many areas of genre cinema and establishing a counter-canon (in opposition to the traditional realist histories of cinema) which is still recognizably the basis of much French and French-inspired criticism. But in doing so, it created a strong antagonism against the non-Surrealist avant-garde which long discouraged many from investigating this at first hand. For example, it was not until the feminist film movement of the 1970s began to research forgotten women directors that Germaine Dulac—effectively stigmatized by the Surrealists—was actually shown and reassessed.

What encouraged a widespread renewal of interest in avant-garde film in the 1970s was no doubt in part a search for ancestry or legitimization by a new generation of critics who were also often filmmakers—and avant-garde either by choice or by economic necessity. The sheer variety and vigour of contemporary avant-garde production in the late 1960s and early 1970s resulted not only from a growing radicalization of the European 'new wave' art cinema of Jean-Luc Godard, Jean-Marie Straub, and Danièle Huillet and Dušan Makavejev, but also from the burgeoning American 'underground' of Jonas Mekas, Jack Smith, and Andy Warhol, and also from the Third World, with the challenging agitational work of the Argentinians Fernando Solanas and Octavio Getino, the Cuban Santiago Alvarez, and the mythopoeic cinema of the Brazilian Glauber Rocha; and from the network of filmmakers' co-operatives which sprang up across Europe.

Against this background, a new historiography began to emerge, articulated first in the United States by way of explaining the ancestry of 'new American cinema' (Renan 1968), then in a more balanced form in David Curtis's *Experimental Cinema* (1971), subtitled 'A Fifty Year Evolution' and in a number of works by UK-based filmmakers. Curtis included in his survey, not only the European avant-gardes of the 1920s and the American post-war 'underground', but also numerous examples of creativity and 'personal' filmmaking in the margins of industrial production, such as the Serbian special-effects expert Slavko Vorkapich working in Hollywood during the 1920s and 1930s. Similar trajectories were followed in two 'participant-observer' accounts, by the filmmakers and teachers Stephen Dwoskin and Malcolm Le Grice, which effectively traced a parallel history to that of narrative cinema (Dwoskin 1975; Le Grice 1977). Le Grice, a leader of the structural school of filmmaking and performance in Britain, naturally saw in much of the Cubist and abstract film of the 1920s the ancestry of his own work.

In the midst of this alternative canon-making, another intervention by a critic-filmmaker, Peter Wollen's influential essay 'The Two Avant-Gardes' (1982) sought to mediate between what seemed to be two polarized traditions within the avant-garde, those of artists' film and radicalized art cinema (see Smith, Part 3, Chapter 2, for another treatment of Wollen's argument). Using a semiotic terminology, Wollen argued that any attempt to distinguish these as 'formal' and 'political' was simplistic, since both traditions included what could be considered work on the signifier and on the signified, although to differing degrees in different periods. His declared aim, 'writing as a filmmaker', was in fact to create a sympathetic climate for new work that would draw on both traditions and create a 'third'—or mixed—avant-garde (Wollen 1981).

But Wollen's appeal for a truce and mutual understanding, although influential in terms of reopening theoretical interest in the historical avant-gardes, did not silence debate. In a move intended to counter the recuperation of the avant-garde, Paul Willemen proposed to 'rearrange' Wollen's celebrated two avant-gardes into 'an opposition between avant-garde and modernism' (Willemen 1984/1994: 148). According to this view, the tradition identified by Wollen as concerned with semiotic reduction and reflexiveness is effectively what modernism has become in the twentieth century—a conservative force seeking to preserve art's traditional autonomy by new formal means—while his 'other' avant-garde, which challenges purism and seeks expansion of the semiotic range, is the true avant-garde, constantly posing problems of reference—to politics and to life.

The idea of an avant-garde cannot, by its nature, be static or agreed. It is perhaps best understood as, in the philosophers' term, an essentially contested concept, always open to dispute or redefinition. As recently as 1968 it was possible for the critic Andrew Sarris to introduce his encyclopaedic survey of American cinema in the sound era with an attack on the idea that 'avant-garde movies point the way for commercial movies' (Sarris 1968). On the contrary, Sarris insisted, avant-garde filmmakers have usually been more conservative about technology than their commercial contemporaries. In terms of meaning, he was even more dismissive: 'few avant-garde mannerisms can stand for long the withering gaze of the camera'. After the debates and the rediscoveries of the 1970s and 1980s, such attitudes seem antediluvian. The 'historic' avant-gardes of the 1920s are still being explored; neglected work comes to light; and the known threshold of avant-garde film activity itself is pushed back to the early years of the century, contemporary with the birth of the seminal Futurist and Cubist avant-gardes out of late Symbolism (Christie 1995).

But even as the historiography of the avant-gardes grows more sophisticated, this prompts new debates. The concept of the avant-garde has seemed intrinsically European—perhaps, indeed, a differentiating feature of European cinema in the post-First World War era, when Hollywood began to consolidate its global domination. But does the specificity of individual avant-garde productions and ideologies not also undermine any overarching concept of 'Europe'? Philip Dodd has suggested, in the context of questioning notions of European identity, that perhaps 'we should no longer think of Buñuel and Dali's *Un Chien Andalou* as a European movie but as a part of Catalan modernism' (Dodd 1992). Similar questions of identity could be posed in any number of cases from the historic avant-gardes: *Ballet mécanique* as a cross between American West Coast modernism, via Dudley Murphy, and Léger's late Parisian Cubism; Len Lye bringing Oceanic neo-primitivist influences to bear on his work in Britain in the late 1920s and 1930s; or Vorkapich as part of the exiled Serbian Futurist (Zenithist) diaspora. At issue in all such cases, it would seem, is what force, or value, or even topography, we assign to 'Europe'—that Europe is or was the crucial *site* of avant-garde film is not in question.

> **The concept of the avant-garde has seemed intrinsically European— perhaps, indeed, a differentiating feature of European cinema in the post-First World War era, when Hollywood began to consolidate its global domination.**

However, the most fundamental question, implicit in many recent interventions, is whether it makes sense to continue thinking of *any* film as 'avant-garde', instead of as an 'independent' or an artist's film. To the legendary La Sarraz conference more recent scholarship has added another late 1920s focus for the concept of independent cinema, now conceived more as a process and discourse (which was also how the attenders at La Sarraz saw it). This is the linked publishing and production activity of the Pool group, led by Bryher and Kenneth Macpherson, which published the journal *Close Up* between 1927 and 1932 and produced a pioneering psychoanalytic film, *Borderline*, in 1930 (Cosandey 1985; Christie 1996). Meanwhile, as Walter Benjamin noted in the mid-1930s, 'Dadaism attempted to create by pictorial—and literary—means the effects which the public today seeks in the film' (Benjamin 1936). Certainly many of the aspirations which drove avant-garde art in the first quarter of the twentieth century subsequently found expression in film (and later in other moving-image media), and so escaped the aura of avant-gardism. Thus the avant-garde, in Benjamin's sense and perhaps in Curtis's or Wollen's, is all about us, distinguished only by its artisanal point of production and its attack on preconceptions of a what a film, video, or CD-ROM should be.

BIBLIOGRAPHY

Benjamin, Walter (1936/1978), 'The Work of Art in the Age of Mechanical Reproduction', in *Illuminations* (London: Fontana-Collins).

Brunius, Jacques (1948), 'Rise and Decline of an "Avant-Garde"', in *Penguin Film Review,* v (London: Penguin).

Christie, Ian (1995), 'L'Avant-garde internationale et le cinéma', in E. Toulet (ed.), *Le Cinéma au rendez-vous des arts: France, années 20 et 30* (Paris: Bibliothèque nationale).

—— (1996), 'The Odd Couple', in Phillip Dodd and Ian Christie (eds.), *Spellbound: Art and Film* (London: Hayward Gallery and British Film Institute).

Cosandey, Roland (1985), 'On *Borderline*: Reassessing a Lost Film', *Afterimage*, 12 (Autumn).

Curtis, David (1971), *Experimental Cinema: A Fifty Year Evolution* (London: Studio Vista).

Dodd, P. (1992), 'Introduction to Saturday Morning Session, in Duncan Petrie, (ed.) *Screening Europe: Image and Identity in Contemporary European Cinema* (London: British Film Institute).

Dwoskin, Stephen (1975), *Film Is* (London: Peter Evans).

Eisenstein, Sergei (1926/1988), 'Bela Forgets the Scissors', in Taylor (1988).

—— and Grigori Alexandrov (1929/1988), 'An Experiment Intelligible to the Millions', in Taylor and Christie (1988).

Elliott, David (1986), *New Worlds: Russian Art and Society 1900–1937* (London: Thames & Hudson).

French Surrealist Group (1951/1978), 'Some Surrealist Advice' in Hammond (1978).

Hammond, Paul (ed.) (1978), *The Shadow and its Shadow: Surrealist Writings on Cinema* (London: British Film Institute).

Kirby, Michael (1971), *Futurist Performance* (New York: Dutton).

Le Grice, Malcolm (1977), *Abstract Film and Beyond* (London: Studio Vista).

Lejeune, C. A. (1931), *Cinema* (London: Alexander Maclehose).

Montagu, Ivor (1968), *With Eisenstein in Hollywood* (Berlin: Seven Seas).

Renan, Sheldon (1968), *The Underground Film* (London: Studio Vista).

Rotha, Paul (1930), *The Film till Now* (London: Jonathan Cape).

Sarris, Andrew (1968), *The American Cinema: Directors and Directions* (New York: Dutton).

Taylor, Richard, and Ian Christie (eds.) (1988), *The Film Factory: Russian and Soviet Cinema in Documents* (London: Routledge).

Trauberg, Leonid (1929/1988), 'An Experiment Intelligible to the Millions', in Taylor and Christie (1988).

Willemen, Paul (1984), 'An Avant-Garde for the 80s', *Framework*, 24 (Spring), 53–73; repr. as 'An Avant-Garde for the 90s' in Willemen (1994).

—— (1994), *Looks and Frictions* (London: British Film Institute). See esp. '*Photogénie* and Epstein'.

Winston, Brian (1995), *Claiming the Real: The Documentary Film Revisited* (London: British Film Institute).

Wollen, Peter (1981), 'The Avant-Gardes: Europe and America' *Framework*, 14, (Spring): 9–10.

—— (1982), 'The Two Avant-Gardes', in *Readings and Writings* (London: Verso).

8

Italian post-war cinema and Neo-Realism

Simona Monticelli

Accounts of the history of Italian cinema are dominated by the critical centrality of a cluster of films made between the mid-1940s and the mid-1950s and commonly described as Neo-Realist. The films themselves are relatively few, constituting no more than eighty or ninety over a period in which domestic film production figures were ten times larger. Yet discussion of these films has been substantial and has encompassed a complex range of theoretical, methodological, and historiographical debates.

The bulk of Neo-Realist films were made at a particularly sensitive time in the history of contemporary Italy, as the country emerged from over twenty years of fascist dictatorship (lasting from 1922 to 1943). In the immediate post war years, Neo-Realist films provided an immediate response to the desire to wipe out the material and ideological legacies of fascism. They denounced the horrors of the war and/or dealt with themes central to the agency of Reconstruction such as poverty, unemployment, shortage of housing, and social strife. Moreover, in their social and geographical inclusiveness, they represented a bid to redefine the co-ordinates of national and cultural identity uncontaminated by the legacy of fascism.

Central to this discourse was the construction of fascism itself as the antithesis of truth and authenticity. The realism of films like *Roma città aperta* ('Rome Open City', Roberto Rossellini, 1945), and *Ladri di biciclette* ('Bicycle Thieves', Vittorio De Sica, 1948) was

perceived as a rejection of the distortions of fascist ideology and the culture it had engendered. As such, Neo-Realism was construed as constituting a radial break from the practices and values which had informed film production during the fascist regime. This, in turn, depended upon the almost wholesale condemnation of the Italian cinema produced during the regime which was mostly dismissed as vacuous entertainment (e.g. 'white telephone' comedies) or bougeois formalism (e.g. 'calligraphic style').

Accordingly, Neo-Realist films may be seen to depart quite radically from the conventions and production values of the studio system of the 1930s. Location shooting and use of available light resulted in more naturalistic photography, closer to the documentary than to the studio-made fiction film. In addition, the contemporary topicality of subject-matter, the focus on the lower-class milieux, and the casting of unglamorous minor stars, or even unknown non-professional actors, further distinguished the films from both indigenous studio productions and those of Hollywood. However, although these developments are characterized as entailing a significant break with pre-war Italian cinema and undoubtedly acquired tremendous poignancy in the post-war period, their use was not entirely new.

Worthy artistic experimentations such as *1860* (Alessandro Blasetti, 1933), or fictionalized documentaries such as *La nave bianca* ('The White Ship', Roberto

'A rejection of the distortions of fascist ideology'—*Roma città aperta* (1945)

Rossellini, 1941) had already made use of similar representational strategies, involving real locations and non-professional performers, while, since the silent era, a range of subgenres rooted in regional theatrical traditions had represented popular milieux with their distinct local character. As a result, it is interesting to note that the first film to be credited as Neo-Realist, *Roma città aperta*, can be seen to draw on both these documentary and subgeneric strands. Trained as a documentary filmmaker, director Roberto Rossellini also cast as his leads two actors, Anna Magnani and Aldo Fabrizi, who had made their names on the Roman vaudeville scene and who had previously duetted in popular film comedies such as *Campo de'fiori* (Mario Bonnard, 1943) and *L'ultima carrozzella* (Mario Mattoli, 1943).

What this suggests is that the Neo-Realist corpus does not display the degree of stylistic coherency that would allow for easy categorization (and, indeed, the definition and selection of films seen to represent 'Neo-Realism' has been a matter of some dispute). The evidence of the films themselves is complicated. Some films may be seen to be clearly indebted to popular forms of entertainment and existing film genres. Other films may be more aptly described as 'art cinema'. In some cases, from *Roma città aperta* to *Riso amaro* ('Bitter Rice' Giuseppe De Santis, 1949), it is simply

not possible to make a clear-cut categorization (and, indeed, a part of their novelty consists of the blurring of distinctions between 'art' and 'popular' cinema). The evidence of the films' commercial success is therefore varied, with a few hugely successful hits and a number of disastrous flops. However, on the whole the box-office performance of Neo-Realist films was respectable, albeit uneven.

These difficulties in identifying a clear set of features specific to Neo-Realist cinema are compounded by the persistence of uncertainties over the origins of the term 'Neo-Realism' and its semantic content. What is clear, however, is that the word cannot be traced back to the consciously thought out and publicly circulated manifesto of a movement. On the contrary, the term 'Neo-Realism' is a descriptive category which has evolved through critical discourse. As a result, the meaning and use of the term have been closely linked to developments in the theory and practice of film criticism and historiography.

It seems that the film editor Mario Serandrei was among the first to use the word when, in a letter to director Luchino Visconti, he employed it with reference to *Ossessione* (Luchino Visconti, 1943) (quoted in Fofi and Faldini, 1979). Indeed, because of its use of real locations and uncompromisingly grim portrayal of the provincial fringes of Italian society during fascism,

Ossessione has generally been regarded as a harbinger of post-war Neo-Realism. Serandrei's use of the term was one of a few isolated instances of its occurrence before the end of the war and was possibly the first instance of its use in relation to an Italian film, rather than to literature or to the French films of Marcel Carné and Jean Renoir.

The context in which *Ossessione* was produced and described as a Neo-Realist film, however, raises some interesting historical issues. Throughout the early 1940s Visconti and the screenwriters of *Ossessione*, Giuseppe De Santis, Mario Alicata, and Gianni Puccini, were writing articles for the specialist film journal *Cinema*, edited by Benito Mussolini's son Vittorio. Their articles, some of which are reprinted in Overbey (1978), insisted on the necessity of using realism in the development of a national film language. In doing so, they suggested models from both an indigenous tradition of high cultural literature and painting and from film styles, such as French poetic realism, and even, on occasions, from Hollywood film genres, such as the 1930s gangster film. The strongest emphasis, however, was placed on the power of landscape—and the human presence within it—to act as signifiers of Italian cultural identity.

Significant though these writings were, they do not fully account for the emergence of Neo-Realism, which must be traced to a much wider range of developments in Italian film production and critical discourse from the pre-war to the post-war period. In terms of critical discourse, moreover, the term 'Neo-Realism' did not acquire wide critical currency until the late 1940s, when it was also invested with a new range of meanings. Indeed, during the post-war years, it was the international critical acclaim with which some Italian films were recieved on the fast-growing art-house circuit which was to play a decisive role in shaping the canon of films and authors to which the term 'Neo-Realism' was applied.

> **What is clear, however, is that the word cannot be traced back to the consciously thought out and publicly circulated manifesto of a movement. On the contrary, the term 'Neo-Realism' is a descriptive category which has evolved through critical discourse.**

It was the French critic André Bazin, in particular, who was to express highly influential views regarding the essence of the Neo-Realist phenomenon (Bazin 1971). Bazin's concern with the definition of an ontology of film language, and his belief that genuine film art derives from a phenomenological rather than analytical approach to the real, was strongly linked to his appraisal of Neo-Realism. He particularly valued a number of formal traits found in Rossellini's films such as elliptical narrative structure, the rejection of plot-enhancing detail, unpredictability of character motivation, use of long takes, and the preference for medium and long shots and rejection of close-ups. As a result of Bazin's influence, these formal traits became common terms in the description of the Neo-Realist style. This was not without its problems, however. Indeed, Bazin himself faced some difficulty in reconciling his enthusiasm for Rossellini's phenomenological approach with his own praise for *Ladri di biciclette*, which displayed a much more conventional use of camera style and continuity editing.

Moreover, while Bazin acknowledged the importance of the historical circumstances in which Neo-Realism had emerged, he did not see them as an essential part of its novelty or significance. In contrast, it was precisely a concern with these historical circumstances which structured the debate on Neo-Realism taking place in Italy. There, it was the construction of Neo-Realism as a movement with specifically national roots which defined the parameters of the term's currency in the critical discourse of leftist intellectuals. These writers were particularly concerned with placing Neo-Realism at the very core of the cultural reconstruction of post-war, post-fascist Italy. Indeed, it was in the late 1940s, when the Cold War was beginning and the anti-fascist political front was breaking down, that the most intense period of debate around Neo-Realist cinema took place.

The parties of the left, and in particular the Communist Party (PCI), had been at the forefront of the anti-fascist Resistance; the PCI enjoyed considerable popular support, but soon after the war it was marginalized from the institutional political mainstream occupied by the conservative Christian Democrats (DC). The championing of Neo-Realism on the part of leftist intellectuals was consistent with the aim of reasserting the credentials of the left as the 'true' representative of a genuine national-popular tradition against both the persisting legacies of fascism and overwhelming American influence in the life and politics of the country.

This is not to say, however, that the conceptualizations of Neo-Realism inside and outside Italy were entirely incompatible. For what was shared was an unqualified support for the absolute artistic and moral value of realist aesthetics. The equation of realism with film art and the opposition of realism to the standardized conventions of entertainment film therefore figure prominently in all the writings of this period. There were, none the less, differences and disagreements over the scope and aims of the commitment to realism as well as conflicting concepts of what constituted the 'essence' of the real.

Perhaps the most compelling definition of Neo-Realism in this period remains the one formulated by Cesare Zavattini, the screenwriter who teamed up regularly with Vittorio De Sica to produce such key Neo-Realist works as *Ladri di biciclette* and *Umberto D* (Vittorio De Sica, 1952). Zavattini maintained that the greatest achievement of Neo-Realist cinema was that it brought onto the screen the lives of ordinary people. This contrasted with more conventionally constructed fictions which fascinated their audiences but bore no relation to their experience outside of the cinema. For Zavattini, the aim of Neo-Realism had to be to rediscover, without embellishment or dramatization, the 'dailiness' of people's lives. He argued that the most minute and apparently insignificant detail of these lives was full of poetry as well as the 'echoes and reverberations' of the human condition (Zavattini 1953).

> **For Zavattini, the aim of Neo-Realism had to be to rediscover, without embellishment or dramatization, the 'dailiness' of people's lives. He argued that the most minute and apparently insignificant detail of these lives was full of poetry as well as the 'echoes and reverberations' of the human condition.**

Other critics and filmmakers such as Luigi Chiarini, Giuseppe De Santis, Carlo Lizzani, and the editor of the Marxist journal *Cinema nuovo*, Guido Aristarco, were more explicit in placing the representation of social reality at the very core of the aesthetic and ethical commitments of Neo-Realism. From their perspective, the roots of the phenomenon in the socially progressive ideals of the Resistance represented its innermost essence. Thus, the promotion of a democratic sense of collective identity for the Italian people, and more specifically for the working classes, was considered the primary aim of Neo-Realism.

Writing in the 1950s, Guido Aristarco insisted that, to remain faithful to its original impulse, Neo-Realism had to evolve, making the leap from 'chronicle to history', from 'short story to novel' (Aristarco 1975). Only in making this leap, he argued, would the films produce a thorough understanding of the conflicts and dynamics of social and historical processes. In doing so, Aristarco favoured the novelistic narrative structure and sense of clear character development characteristic of nineteenth-century literary realism. However, as Nowell-Smith (1976–7) observes, Aristarco's choice of artistic models was anachronistic even for the time when he was writing. Moreover, the line adopted by Aristarco and others at *Cinema nuovo* also exemplified a more general failure to take into full account the material modes of production, distribution, and consumption of film texts. This, in turn, had consequences for the way the development of Neo-Realism was critically assessed in the 1950s.

The critical discourse of the 1950s was dominated by a concern with the commercial and political bastardization of Neo-Realism. From the late 1940s onwards, new generic strands of the sentimental comedy (i.e. 'pink Neo-Realism') and melodrama (i.e. 'popular Neo-Realism') were at the forefront of the commercial resurgence of the domestic product. These films incorporated elements of mise-en-scène and thematic motifs from their worthier Neo-Realist predecessors, but they were generally denounced by critics, who saw in them a victory for commercialism and escapism over art and engagement (views which then necessarily reinforced a split between *cinema d'autore* (auteur or art cinema), on the one hand, and genre production, on the other). However, the attachment of many critics to criteria of Neo-Realist purity also complicated the discussion of the films made by those authors who had originally been most closely identified with Neo-Realism.

In diverse ways *Riso amaro*, *Stromboli terra di Dio* ('Stromboli', Roberto Rossellini, 1951), *L'oro di Napoli* ('Gold of Naples', Vittorio De Sica, 1954), *Senso* (Luchino Visconti, 1954), and *La strada* (Federico Fellini, 1954), to name only a few of the most controversial cases, all departed from understood Neo-Realist orthodoxies. Throughout the 1950s Rossellini and Fellini defended the integrity and coherence of their work against what they saw as an imposition of ideological restrictions on the development of a 'new way of seeing' (see Overbey 1978; Bondanella 1978). In 1956, in a letter to Guido Aristarco, André Bazin reiterated this point, arguing that Rossellini and Fellini had remained faithful to the spirit of Neo-Realism in their aesthetic approach to the wholeness of human reality, its ambiguity and resistance to analysis (Bazin 1971). Aristarco, on the other hand, admired the formal accomplishments of the two authors' films, but, in branding them spiritualistic and individualistic, emphatically rejected the idea that they were truly realist or free from ideological considerations.

While these debates revealed differences regarding the relationship between form and content, and between art and ideology, in Neo-Realism there was none the less a shared belief in the value of a realist aesthetic. From the early 1960s onwards, however, a series of challenges were waged against existing definitions of Neo-Realism as an inherently innovative and progressive phenomenon. One of the most serious of these challenges stemmed from the reassessment of the historiography of fascism, the Resistance, and the post-war settlement. The radical left developing on the fringes of the Communist Party mounted a harsh critique of the Resistance politics pursued by the PCI, the culture of Reconstruction, and the ways the legacies of fascism had been negotiated in post-war Italy. It was argued that, far from marking a break with the past regime, the culture of Reconstruction was characterized by long-term continuities in the history of Italian culture and politics, continuities to which fascism had itself accommodated. From this point of view, the idealist and humanist core of bourgeois cultural traditions and the perpetuation of the hegemony were viewed as central facets of the post-war organization of consensus and its continuity with the past.

This critique inevitably queried received ideas about Neo-Realism as an innovative practice springing from the rejection of fascist rhetoric and representing a genuine expression of the national-popular character. Instead, new historiographical perspectives suggested that the genesis of Neo-Realism could be traced in discourses and practices already existing within fascist culture and that it had never really challenged the Establishment, nor its post-war reorganization (see Cannella 1973–4; Rohdie 1981). Salutary though such revisionist work has been, its polemical slant has none the less tempted it towards claims and dismissals that are as monolithic in their character as the accounts which they have sought to challenge.

A further challenge to Neo-Realist orthodoxy, however, has come from the theoretical and methodological development of non-realist, or frankly anti-realist, positions in film criticism (see Easthope, Part 1, Chapter 6). As a result of these developments, it has become increasingly difficult to fasten definitions of Neo-Realist aesthetics to an ontology of film language free from ideological determinations (see Micciché 1975; Williams 1973–4; Bettettini 1975).

A positive consequence of this phase of deconstruction, conducted on the two fronts of previous definitions of Neo-Realism, was to open the study of the films to perspectives no longer concerned with identifying Neo-Realism with some kind of 'essence' which then had to be defended against subsequent developments. On the other hand, the effects of this process have often been disorientating, questioning the very need for, and validity of, a distinct descriptive category of Neo-Realism and rendering its contours both conceptually and historiographically nebulous.

More recent work, however, has reinstated some of Neo-Realism's importance for the study of Italian film history by providing a more detailed and exhaustive picture of the modes of production and consumption of film culture in post-war Italy. An important development in this respect has been the renegotiation of the boundaries between film and cultural studies, which has led to a greater emphasis on the role which film plays in relation to a nation's cultural history. Therefore, outside Italy, the area of Italian studies has provided many fresh insights into the position of Neo-Realist cinema in Italian culture (see Hewitt 1989; Baranski and Lumley 1990; Wagstaff and Duggan 1995). In such work, the impact of Neo-Realism on domestic production has been analysed in relation to the viewing habits of Italian filmgoers in the 1940s and 1950s, the structures and institutions which regulated these habits and defined the scope of viewer's semantic competence. Neo-Realist films have also been studied for their relations with a wider spectrum of discursive and iconographical components of Italian culture. And, within this wider network of references, the question of the breaks and continuities which characterize the development of Neo-Realism has also been re-examined (see Dalle Vacche 1991).

What also emerges from this redefinition of the field of study is the necessity to extend knowledge of Italian cinema to include those filmmaking practices and genres which were marginalized by the sustained focus on the dozen or so films which won international acclaim. This does not mean denying the aesthetic specificity of Neo-Realist cinema. Neo-Realist films did contain a challenging aesthetic project and, to this day, they may still be regarded as one of the generative sources of the national film vocabulary.

> **Paradoxically, the continuing interest of Neo-Realism lies precisely in that it was neither a straightforwardly homogeneous or unitary phenomenon but successfully crossed the boundaries between highbrow and lowbrow, tradition and modernity, engagement and pleasure.**

What the redefinition of the field of study does mean, however, is that it is no longer possible to take for granted the nature of cinematic realism or the ways in which Neo-Realist films have been implicated in often conflicting notions of national and cultural identities. It also suggests the importance of understanding these aesthetic practices in relation to specific historical and production contexts. Paradoxically, the continuing interest of Neo-Realism lies precisely in that it was neither a straightforwardly homogeneous or unitary phenomenon but successfully crossed the boundaries between highbrow and lowbrow, tradition and modernity, engagement and pleasure.

BIBLIOGRAPHY

Aristarco, Guido (ed.) (1975), *Antologia di 'Cinema Nuovo' 1952–1958* (Florence: Guaraldi).

Baranski, Zygmut, and **Robert Lumley** (eds.) (1990), *Culture and Conflict in Postwar Italy* (London: Macmillan).

*****Bazin, André** (1971), *What is Cinema?*, 2 vols. (Berkeley: trans. Hugh Gray, University of California Press).

Bettettini, Gianfranco (1975), 'On Neo-Realism', *Framework*, 2: 9–10.

Bondanella, Peter (ed.) (1978), *Federico Fellini: Essays in Criticism* (Oxford: Oxford University Press).

Cannella, Mario (1973–4), 'Ideology and Aesthetic Hypotheses in the Criticism of Neo-Realism', *Screen*, 4/4 (Winter), 5–60.

Dalle Vacche, Angela (1991), *The Body in the Mirror: Shapes of History in Italian Cinema* (Princeton: Princeton University Press).

Fofi, Goffredo, and **Franca Faldini** (eds.) (1979), *L'avventurosa storia del cinema italiano raccontata dai suoi protagonisti 1935–1959* (Milan: Feltrinelli).

Hewitt, Nicholas (ed.) (1989), *The Culture of Reconstruction: European Literature, Thought and Film* (London: Macmillan).

*****Marcus, Millicent** (1986), *Italian Film in the Light of Neorealism* (Princeton: Princeton University Press).

Micciché, Lino (ed.) (1975), *Il neorealismo cinematografico: atti del Convegno della X mostra internazionale del nuovo cinema* (Venice: Marsilio).

Nowell-Smith, Geoffrey (1976–7), 'Cinema Nuovo and Neo-Realism', *Screen*, 17/4 (Winter), 111–17.

*****Overbey, David** (ed.) (1978). *Springtime in Italy: A Reader on Neorealism* (London: Talisman).

*****Rohdie, Sam** (1981), 'A Note on Italian Cinema during Fascism', *Screen*, 22/4: 87–90.

Wagstaff, Christopher, and **Christopher Duggan** (eds.) (1995), *Italy and the Cold War: Politics, Culture and Society* (Oxford: Berg).

Williams, Christopher (1973–4), 'Bazin on Neo-Realism', *Screen*, 14/4 (Winter).

Zavattini, Cesare (1953), 'Some Ideas on the Cinema', *Sight and Sound*, 23/2 (Oct.) 64–9.

9

The French Nouvelle Vague

Jill Forbes

The history of French cinema in the 1950s and 1960s is marked by three moments of radical change: the Blum–Byrnes trade agreement of 1946, the birth of the Nouvelle Vague in 1959, and the events of May 1968. Each of these had a profound impact on the way cinema developed in France after the Second World War and on the kinds of film made in that country.

French cinema experienced a 'golden age' during the German occupation of 1940–4, when it was protected from foreign competition. As soon as the war ended, however, the backlog of Hollywood's wartime production flooded into France and was enthusiastically received by audiences fascinated by all aspects of American culture. The flow of American imports was regulated by the Blum–Byrnes Agreement (whose cinema clauses were revised in 1948), which set at thirteen the maximum number of weeks during which cinemas could only screen French films, the remainder being free for American and other imports. This quota probably corresponded, more or less, to the production capacity of the French film industry, which had been badly hit by lack of investment during the war and by damage incurred at the Liberation. However, it was widely condemned as failing to protect French interests. Some of the loudest complaints came from the strongly pro-communist film technicians' union, and these naturally intensified with the advent of the Cold War in 1947. The effect of these protests was to reinforce the corporatism of the French industry, and to

ensure that the administrative structures established to control it under the wartime Vichy regime were continued in peacetime. Equally importantly, they persuaded the government of the need to vote a series of measures designed to give financial assistance to French film production and exhibition. These were: the *loi d'aide* of 1948, under which production and exhibition were automatically assisted by a tax on profits and which, perhaps ironically, was largely funded, at first, by the huge success of *Gone with the Wind* (1939); the *fonds de développement*, established in 1953 specifically to support artistically ambitious productions; and the *fonds de soutien*, created in 1959, which provided for *avances sur recettes*, or interest-free loans, allocated on the basis of a project and which were repayable if a film made a profit. In addition to these three domestic measures, a Franco-Italian co-production agreement signed in 1946, and renewed regularly thereafter, allowed the two film industries to pool resources for ambitious co-productions during the 1950s and 1960s.

These measures are not the only indicators of the cultural significance of cinema in France in the 1950s. For all the combatant powers, the war had brought home film's significance as a means of propaganda and as a way of promoting national cohesion. Cinema attendances were extremely high—often because it was the only entertainment available—and they remained high after the war, especially in France, where television was slow to develop. Popular education movements such as Travail et culture, Peuple et culture, and La Ligue de l'enseignement, organized film screenings followed by group discussions led by luminaries such as André Bazin, who also wrote notes for their programmes. Most literary and arts magazines—*La Nouvelle Revue française*, *Les Temps modernes*, *Arts*—devoted space to serious discussion of the cinema and to film reviews. The specialist film press flourished. Alongside *L'Écran français*, which was clandestinely published during the war and emerged afterwards as the most influential of film magazines, the period saw the founding of *La Revue du cinéma* (1946–9), *Cahiers du cinéma* (1951), *Positif* (1952), and *Image et son* (1951). Many cinemas, like the Ursulines and Studio 28 in Paris, ran 'ciné-clubs' where impassioned discussion of films took place, while the Cinémathèque française, under Henri Langlois, offered unparalleled opportunities for eclectic viewing. France was therefore perhaps the first country in which the cinema was taken seriously as an object of study, and although this was conducted in a decidedly 'counter-cultural' manner, outside the universities by individuals who were often either drop-outs from academic life (Bazin, Eric Rohmer, Jean-Luc Godard) or auto-didacts (François Truffaut), the problematic, the rhetoric, and the range of references of their writings—especially those of Godard and Rohmer—pointed to a concerted and provocative attempt to position the cinema within the mainstream of French and European culture. These issues were explicitly addressed in Godard's film *Le Mépris* ('Contempt' 1963), which tells the story of an American producer's attempt to film *The Odyssey* in the Cinecittà studios in Rome, and they have inspired the evident literariness of virtually all of Rohmer's films.

Among those to benefit immediately from the various measures of support was the so-called Left Bank Group of directors of short films, including Alain Resnais, Chris Marker, and Agnès Varda. With *Nuit et brouillard* ('Night and Fog', 1956), *Lettre de Sibérie* ('Letter from Siberia', 1958), and *Du côté de la Côte* ('On the Riviera', 1958) they evolved a highly personal, often politically committed, style of avant-garde documentary filmmaking characterized by a montage of striking images and a poetic voice-over commentary. Similarly, some fifteen productions a year were mounted as a result of the Franco-Italian agreements. Perhaps not surprisingly, the first of these was Christian-Jaque's *La Chartreuse de Parme* (1947), but many important post-war directors—Jean-Pierre Melville,

Max Ophuls, Marcel Carné, Jean Grémillon for the French, Roberto Rossellini, Federico Fellini, Michaelangelo Antonioni for the Italians—benefited from their provisions. In the same way, the *avance sur recettes* system was often instrumental in the 1960s in determining whether or not a film could be made, and assisted many young filmmakers in raising the capital for their productions. It was, in short, crucial in the creation of a lively art cinema movement.

Two distinct trends are to be observed in French 1950s cinema. On the one hand, 'la tradition de qualité' identified in François Truffaut's devastating critique 'Une certaine tendance du cinéma français', published in *Cahiers du cinéma* in 1954; on the other, the so-called *francs-tireurs*, or independents, who belonged to no identifiable school. Following Alexandre Astruc's seminal article 'Naissance d'une nouvelle avant-garde: La caméra style', published in *L'Écran français* in 1948, Truffaut's polemic, rightly considered the manifesto of the Nouvelle Vague, was a plea for an auteur cinema, one in which the director would control the film and in which the film would be the expression of his personal preoccupations. Truffaut's principal targets of criticism were the writers of screenplays who reduce the role of the director to that of 'the chap who puts the frame round the story'. He particularly attacked the 'psychological realism' of Jean Aurenche and Pierre Bost, whose literary adaptations he accused of distorting the original works so as to derive from them an ideology of anticlericalism and anti-militarism, and of inventing scenes to pursue their ideological points. The respect shown for literature throughout Truffaut's films perhaps explains his outrage at Aurenche and Bost's infidelities, but the main purpose of his article is the search for a new kind of realism based on differently conceived authenticity.

Another less immediately obvious target of Truffaut's criticism of the films of Claude Autant-Lara, Christian-Jaque, and Jean Delannoy seems just as important today. The astonishing homogeneity of their films has, more recently, been attributed to the influence of technicians rather than to that of writers. Indeed, veteran filmmaker Louis Daquin somewhat mischievously attributed the *tradition de qualité* to the German Jewish cinematographers and producers who emigrated to France before the war and who trained an entire generation of French technicians. Their perfectionism and the legacy of Expressionism all contributed to the 'glacis de la lumière', the coldly perfect photography which not only gave mainstream French cinema in the 1950s a studio 'look', which is, indeed, impersonal, but ultimately created a *Weltanschauung* in which style was more important than substance.

Although the *tradition de qualité* was dominant in France in the 1950s, it was not exclusively so. Italian Neo-Realism offered a different model of filmmaking which used authentic locations and non-professional actors, marrying fiction and documentary in a manner that was to influence the Nouvelle Vague, while in France itself there were many directors who bucked the trend: Jacques Tati (*Jour de fête*, 1949; *Les Vacances de Monsieur Hulot*, 'Monsier Hulot's Holiday', 1953) and Melville (*Le Silence de la mer*, 1948; *Bob le flambeur*, 'Bob the Gambler', 1956) because they worked outside the studios, writing and producing as well as directing their own films; Robert Bresson and Jean Renoir because they consistently contrived to subvert the studios even while working within them; Ophuls and Jacques Becker because they assumed the legacy and turned it into a self-referential feature of their movies which are often consciously, and sometimes parodically, expressionist.

Despite this, the Nouvelle Vague represented a significant break with the *tradition de qualité* and brought into filmmaking a large number of younger directors. The phrase 'Nouvelle Vague' was coined by the journalist Françoise Giraud, who was conscious of the birth of 'youth culture' at the end of the 1950s and who wrote a series of portraits of young people and their aspirations for the magazine *L'Express*. In the cinema, however, it refers to the group of directors, Truffaut, Godard, Claude Chabrol, Jacques Rivette, and Rohmer, who had all worked as critics for *Cahiers du cinéma* in the 1950s and who, at the end of the decade, began to make films. Their talent was recognized when Truffaut's first feature film, *Les Quatre Cent Coups* ('The 400 Blows', 1959), was awarded the critics' prize at the 1959 Cannes Film Festival, and the Nouvelle Vague quickly became a marketing slogan in the pro-Gaullist press to promote the idea that with the change of regime in 1958 France had been regenerated and rejuvenated.

Although the directors themselves resisted the idea that they belonged to a 'school' or 'wave', since this would have appeared incompatible with their insistence on making highly personal films, it is indisputable that a series of brilliant first and second features was launched in France in the late 1950s and 1960s: Truffaut's *Tirez sur le pianiste* ('Shoot the Pianist', 1960) and *Jules et Jim* (1961); Godard's *À bout de souffle*

('Breathless', 1959), *Une femme est une femme* ('A Woman is a Woman', 1961), *Vivre sa vie* ('My Life to Live', 1962); Chabrol's *Le Beau Serge* ('Bitter Reunion', 1959) and *Les Cousins* ('The Cousins', 1959); Rivette's *Paris nous appartient* ('Paris Belongs to Us', 1960); and Rohmer's *Le Signe du lion* ('The Sign of Leo', 1959). It is also clear that whatever their many individual differences, collectively these films represented a significant break with the *tradition de qualité* and a revolution not just in the way films were made but also in their social and aesthetic significance.

What these Nouvelle Vague directors had in common was an approach to filmmaking which dispensed with the technical hierarchies required by the *tradition de qualité*. Thus the divisions between producer, director, editor, cameraman, actor, writer, and so on became extremely blurred. Unlike, say, Claude Autant-Lara, who prided himself on visualizing the entire film before he commenced shooting it, Nouvelle Vague directors worked from an idea, frequently improvised, served as the producers and writers for one another's films, cast their wives and girlfriends in starring roles, and used their own or one another's apartments instead of sets. The subject-matter of the films changed too in line with Chabrol's belief that 'small subjects' could be every bit as important as 'big subjects' and with Godard's precept that 'we must begin with what we know'. Thus literary adaptation went out of the window, except for Truffaut's *Jules et Jim*, where it is subverted in a self-conscious manner, and, along with it, the facile morality that was the mainstay of Aurenche and Bost's screenplays. Instead, the moral message of Nouvelle Vague films was to be indistinguishable from their aesthetics because, in Godard's famous phrase, 'les travellings sont affaire de morale'.

The central *topos* of a Nouvelle Vague film is the young heterosexual couple and, more generally, relations between young men and women, exemplified in the long, central sequence between Jean Seberg and Jean-Paul Belmondo in *À bout de souffle*, which is set in and on the bed in a hotel room. The stock characters of *tradition de qualité* cinema which derived ultimately from melodrama were therefore swept aside, and with them the actors they had employed. New actors like Jean-Claude Brialy and Jean-Paul Belmondo, Marie Dubois, Jeanne Moreau, and Anna Karina came to the fore. Godard's penchant for using foreign actresses like Anna Karina and Jean Seberg, whose accents were difficult to understand, showed how little importance was now attached to 'mots d'auteur', the so-called witty dialogue deriving from the theatrical tradition. Above all, in a search for a new kind of realism, *Nouvelle Vague* directors gave their films the 'look' of documentaries by shooting in authentic and recognizable locations instead of in the studio, by using faster film with natural light and lighter cameras which were often hand-held, blurring the distinction between fiction and documentary at the same time as abandoning any pretence that the world depicted was not that of a film. They were profoundly influenced by the French school of ethnographic filmmaking represented by Jean Rouch, whose *Moi un noir* (1958) had received public screening. But they were also assisted by their cameramen, Raoul Coutard and Henri Decaë, whose training had not been in the studios but in documentaries, newsreels, and the army film unit.

The preoccupations of the Nouvelle Vague matched those of more clearly avant-garde directors like Resnais or Varda, whose films explicitly interrogate the relationship between fiction and documentary and between naturalism and formalism. But what they additionally brought into their films was a consciousness of the history of the cinema, and especially of Hollywood movies, which, as critics for *Cahiers du cinéma* in the 1950s, they had analysed at length. As Eric Rohmer put it: 'We didn't attend IDHEC [the film school], but we did spend years at the Cinémathèque'. Nouvelle Vague films are studded with references to American genres, American directors, American actors, and American studios, from the dedication to Monogram Pictures at the opening of *À bout de souffle*, the parodies of Howard Hawks in *Une femme est une femme*, the imitation of Hitchcock in Truffaut's *Baisers volés* ('Stolen Kisses', 1968), to the innumerable *mises-en-abîme* which take the fictional characters to the cinema— almost always, as is the case with *The Harder they Fall* in *À bout de souffle*, to see an American movie. At the same time, however, the Nouvelle Vague brought about a revolution in the history of the cinema by abandoning the 'grammar' of Hollywood films. This is most brilliantly illustrated in Godard's appropriately titled *À bout de souffle*, which, instead of the shot–reverse shot and continuity editing in which bodies are carefully positioned in space, eyelines are matched, and the sources of sound are identified, a more elliptical, faster-moving, and apparently inconsequential narrative based on jump cuts and a montage of sound and images profoundly changed film techniques.

The Nouvelle Vague gave a new lease of life to French cinema, which had survived the 1950s with declining audiences, but which, with the spread of television, was about to lose its mass audience for good. Producers like Georges de Beauregard and Pierre Braunberger saw in this new approach to filmmaking not merely a way of making films with lower budgets, or films which could be designated as 'art movies', thus qualifying for the *avance sur recettes*, but also a way of targeting the audience aged 16–25 which did remain faithful to the cinema. They thus financed the production of a large number of first feature films in the 1960s, bringing about a radical rejuvenation of the film industry.

The final moment of radical change to affect the French cinema was, of course, the revolt of May 1968. Filmmakers were involved in a number of ways. In February 1968 many directors had demonstrated in support of Henri Langlois, the director of the Cinémathèque, and against government proposals to take over the organization. During the events themselves, filmmakers held a States-General of the Cinema, a series of meetings intended to set out what the revolutionary role of film might be, what form of state intervention should suport filmmaking, and how films might be distributed to a wider audience. In addition, many filmmakers like Jean-Luc Godard were involved in making so-called *cinétracts*—or film leaflets. These were film records of events in the streets and public buildings that were intended to serve as a counterweight to the strongly pro-Gaullist ORTF television service, which was hostile to the striking students and workers.

One of the most important longer-term effects of May 1968 was to throw into sharp relief the ideology of the Nouvelle Vague. Until that time it was frequently affirmed that the undoubted aesthetic iconoclasm of the Nouvelle Vague directors was matched by political radicalism. This belief was reinforced by the banning of Godard's *Le Petit Soldat*, made in 1960 and not released until 1963, which appeared critical of the war in Algeria, and of Rivette's *La Religieuse*, made in 1966 and not released until 1967, which not only seemed to adumbrate a different sexual politics but was also highly critical of the Catholic church. However, the transformation of politics itself, brought about by the May events, and especially the way in which gender and race joined class as matters of acute political concern, exposed the extremely reactionary nature of the ideology of some Nouvelle Vague films as well as that of the critics who had hailed 'auteur cinema' as a form of art for art's sake. Thus Chabrol's *Le Beau*

Serge and *Les Cousins* were now reread as right-wing anarchist statements, while Truffaut's refusal to engage in politics was taken as an expression of his conservative views.

However, it was the sexual politics of Nouvelle Vague films that occasioned most re-evaluation. Whether encouraged by Truffaut's misogynistic denunciation of the mother figure in *Les Quatre Cents Coups* or of the predatory female in *Tirez sur le pianiste*, Godard's vision of the contemporary spider-woman in *À bout de souffle*, or of prosititution as the general condition of women in virtually all of his pre-1968 films, or Chabrol's thesis, in the pejoratively entitled *Les Bonnes Femmes*, that sexually active women invite rape, it is certain that the events of May and the birth of the women's movement imposed a rereading of this corpus that placed it in a much less favourable ideological light. Later still, the homophobia evident in many of Truffaut's films, but especially *Baisers volés*, and its echo in Godard's *Masculin–féminin*, became a subject of criticism in its own right.

May 1968 also marked the divergence of the careers of Nouvelle Vague directors and revealed how fragile and temporary the apparent homogeneity of the group had been. Truffaut and Chabrol seemed content to rejoin the mainstream, with the former shooting a series of autobiographical essays (*L'Enfant sauvage*, 1970; *La Nuit américaine*, 'Day for Night', 1973; *La Chambre verte*, 1978), whose morbidity has only recently been noted, while the latter embarked on a series of immensely successful bourgeois comedies and thrillers. Godard, on the other hand, took seriously the politics of May 1968 and, in his attempts to make political and feminist films and to experiment with new technologies of production and distribution, helped to expose the ideological assumptions of the Nouvelle Vague aesthetic (see Smith, Part 3, Chapter 2).

More recent interpretations of the Nouvelle Vague, especially of Godard and Truffaut, have been inspired by postmodernism. Taking their cue from Godard's professed admiration for the double narrative of William Faulkner's *The Wild Palms* (and the admiration echoed by the character Patricia in *À bout de souffle*), critics have emphasized the cultural eclecticism of the early works of these directors as well as their disjunctive narratives. Godard, in *À bout de souffle*, *Le Mépris*, and *Pierrot le fou* (1965), Truffaut, in *Tirez sur le pianiste* and, to a degree, in *Jules et Jim*, mix genres and styles, taking elements from both popular culture and high culture, passing rapidly from cartoon strips to Rimbaud, from Romantic music and painting to agitprop. This approach to filmmaking might be understood as the inevitable anxiety of influence generated by French cinema's colonial relationship to Hollywood or as the astonishing aesthetic prescience of great artists who abandoned grand narratives and the unitary point of view before the post-industrial society was invented. The very fact that such films continue to lend themselves to reinterpretation suggests that the Nouvelle Vague has not ceased to exercise an influence on contemporary filmmaking and criticism. Whereas the Nouvelle Vague was traditionally held to have invented the low-budget art film and the director as auteur, it is now seen as having introduced a radical approach to narrative and genre, but to have done this without taking any account of the social transformations that have placed gender and race at the heart of aesthetic concerns.

BIBLIOGRAPHY

Armes, Roy (1985), *French Cinema* (London: Secker & Warburg).

Astruc, Alexander (1949/1968), 'Naissance d'une nouvelle avant-garde: La caméra style', trans. as 'The Birth of a New Avant-Garde: La Caméra-Style', in Peter Graham (ed.), *The New Wave* (London: Secker & Warburg).

Austin, Guy (1996), *Contemporary French Cinema* (Manchester: Manchester University Press).

Forbes, Jill (1992), *The Cinema in France after the New Wave* (London: British Film Institute and Macmillan).

Hayward, Susan (1993), *French National Cinema* (London: Routledge).

*Monaco, James (1976), *The New Wave* (New York: Oxford University Press).

Pauly, Rebecca (1993), *The Transparent Illusion: Image and Ideology in French Text and Film* (New York: Peter Lang).

Truffaut, François (1954/1976), 'Une certain tendance du cinéma français', trans. as 'A Certain Tendency of the French Cinema', in Bill Nichols (ed.), *Movies and Methods*, 2 vols., i (Berkeley: University of California Press).

Williams, Alan (1992), *Republic of Images: A History of French Filmmaking* (Cambridge, Mass.: Harvard University Press).

10 New German Cinema

Ulrike Sieglohr

Critical positions

The non-commercial West German cinema of the 1960s and mid-1970s, which brought to international prominence auteurs such as Rainer Werner Fassbinder, Werner Herzog, and Wim Wenders, is one of the most aesthetically eclectic and politically radical national cinemas of the post-war period. Unlike its predecessors and its influential models—Italian Neo-Realist Cinema, British Free Cinema, and the French New Wave—this national cinema did not constitute a coherent grouping with a unifying style. Consequently film historians, such as Thomas Elsaesser (1989), Eric Rentschler (1984), Timothy Corrigan (1983), and James Franklin (1983), have debated the ways in which these films may be regarded as forming a movement and assessing whether their stylistically very different auteurs have, in fact, anything in common.

Their respective books indicate their different perceptions of the German cinema of this period. Whereas Franklin's book concentrates on individual 'star' directors within a chronological framework and Corrigan's work focuses upon the themes and stylistic approaches of the films in relation to art cinema in general, Rentschler's approach traces generic trends which are discussed as part of the wider German cultural–political environment. Elsaesser's multifaceted book of interlocking essays, however, breaks with these earlier, more linear historical models by emphasizing the discontinuities of German cinema between the 1960s and 1970s and questioning some of the assumptions upon which they were based. He suggests, for example, that aesthetic innovation is often more of an economic necessity than an avant-garde formalist inclination, and that the concept of the self-expressive auteur is better understood as a discursive construction designed to attract media attention rather than the indicator of any creative originating source.

Historical determinants and institutional frameworks

In order to understand what first gave rise to the intellectual formalism of the Young German Cinema in the 1960s, and the subsequently more narratively accessible New German Cinema at the end of the decade, it is necessary to examine the cinema and politics of the 1950s. From the end of the Second World War Germany was an occupied country and America, as one of the occupying powers, indirectly controlled all aspects of the West German cinema industry. This was justified in terms of a denazification process of education-as-entertainment, through which it was intended that German audiences would be shown the error of their ways in narratives of moral example, made by people them-

466

selves only recently denazified. The Cold War, however, brought the denazification process to a premature end, and subsequent American anti-communist policies led to the promotion of only the most conservative film personnel, who tended to be those with a Nazi past. These directors and technicians continued to reproduce—albeit ambiguously—an ideology that had its roots in fascism, and West Germany's post-war commercial cinema generally had little to offer but escapist *Heimat* films—clichéd romances, set in some idyllic, pastoral environment—and apologetic war films. At the same time, the industry faced the prevalence of Hollywood films and the rise of television, which, combined with under-investment, brought it to the brink of collapse by the early 1960s.

The bleak prospects for the commercial cinema meant that the West German government could not help but welcome the young filmmakers' *Oberhausen Manifesto* of 1962 arguing for a subsidized non-commercial cinema. This manifesto was instrumental in bringing about legislative changes in the funding institutions and gave rise to a highly complex framework of state subsidies whereby a national cinema was fostered as a 'high' art form. The first films made under this system became known as Young German Cinema and, while they were thematically varied, they tended to share a narrative and formal austerity. As a result, films like Alexander Kluge's *Abschied von Gestern* ('Yesterday Girl', 1966), Edgar Reitz's *Mahlzeiten* ('Mealtimes', 1967), Danièle Huillet and Jean-Marie Straub's *Nicht versöhnt* ('Not Reconciled', 1965), although acclaimed critically, were virtually ignored by audiences.

The Young German Cinema's intense lobbying and the founding of the grant agency Kuratorium junger deutscher Film in 1965 prepared the institutional framework for the more spectator-friendly New German Cinema, and in the late 1960s a new generation started to make their first feature-length films. In 1968 Herzog directed *Lebenszeichen* ('Signs of Life') and in 1969 Fassbinder made *Liebe ist kälter als der Tod* ('Love is Colder than Death'). It is important to note that the films were made in a climate of political upheaval and of marked anti-Americanism due to US involvement in the Vietnam War. In West Germany and throughout the West the years 1967–8 were marked by student rebellion, extra-parliamentary opposition, and anti-authoritarianism, which in turn produced a surge in what were then considered counter-cultural activities, such as huge rock festivals, 'happenings', and the popularization of psychedelic drugs.

Within this larger context, specific cinematic cultural policies gave radical left-wingers the opportunity to make films. The government felt, as Sheila Johnston (1981–2) argues, that the political radicalism of the young filmmakers could be contained and also exploited in terms of an ideological 'pay-off' which would demonstrate its cultural liberalism. As a result, funding—however inadequate—became available for projects that were to some extent critical of the state. This political dimension of the New German Cinema also became a means for the West German government, particularly under Willy Brandt's chancellorship between 1969 and 1976, to prove its ability and readiness for self-criticism both at home and abroad. Internationally, this cinema became a kind of cultural ambassador (the Goethe Institut, a government-funded agency for promoting German culture abroad, exhibited the majority of these films rather than cinemas) that would bear witness to the liberalization brought about by the Social Democrats.

> **In effect, the New German Cinema functioned in West Germany throughout the 1970s primarily as a public sphere—a forum for debating contemporary issues—rather than within the realm of entertainment.**

At home the New German Cinema found its audiences primarily among students. As Thomas Elsaesser (1989: 155) points out, audience and filmmakers had come together through the events of 1967–8, which had politicized them, and this shared political perspective gained the filmmakers a devoted audience. However, the films never attracted a mass audience and were more often screeened at 'special-interest' events, such as trade union meetings, or feminist conferences, where it was quite common for filmmakers to be present to introduce and discuss their work with the audience. In effect, the New German Cinema functioned in West Germany throughout the 1970s primarily as a public sphere—a forum for debating contemporary issues—rather than within the realm of entertainment. This cultural conception of the New German Cinema therefore distanced it from the market values of both Hollywood and the commercial German cinema.

Themes and formal strategies

West Germany's post-war national identity was shaped by the division of Germany in 1949, the largely unacknowledged historical guilt of the Holocaust, and by US cultural–political imperialism. Anton Kaes (1989) and Eric L. Santner (1990) explore in depth how these factors are articulated in the New German Cinema as a steadily growing preoccupation with history and with what it means to be German. Examples are Hans Jürgen Syberberg's 'German Trilogy' *Ludwig—Requiem für einen jungfräulichen König* ('Ludwig—Requiem for a Virgin King', 1972), *Karl May* (1974), and his highly controversial *Hitler—Ein Film aus Deutschland* ('Our Hitler', 1977), Fassbinder's *Die Ehe der Maria Braun* ('The Marriage of Maria Braun', 1978) and Volker Schlöndorff's *Die Blechtrommel* ('The Tin Drum', 1979). However, an engagement with history is not necessarily articulated as an explicit theme, but conveyed as a diffuse sense of alienation, as in Wenders's *Im Lauf der Zeit* ('Kings of the Road', 1976).

Unlike other national cinemas it is more difficult, if not impossible to identify shared formal characteristics amongst the filmmakers of the New German Cinema, since a diversity of stylistic responses to a common historical situation were its hallmarks. Aesthetic strategies range from the documentary realism of Erwin Keusch and Christian Ziewer, through the biting anarchic satires of Herbert Achternbusch, to the outlandish operatic camp and kitsch of Rosa von Praunheim and Werner Schroeter. However, characteristics which *are* common to most of the films are those that David Bordwell (1985: 206–7) has identified as constitutive of art cinema in general: ambling narratives with a lingering on details and seemingly unimportant events; a stress on mood rather than on actions; and an overall sense of ambiguity.

In the German context, however, stylistic diversity can also be understood as an ideological choice, one arising from a desire to invent a new cinematic language uncontaminated by fascism. A concern with history is therefore not confined to thematic treatment but inscribed, albeit obliquely, in notable features of the mise-en-scène, such as, for example, theatricality, excess, and artifice. Fassbinder's *Katzelmacher* (1969) starts with the aphorism by Yaak Karsunke: 'It's better to make new mistakes than to reproduce old ones unthinkingly'. And, similarly, Wenders (1977/1988: 128) notes the unavailability of a native cinema tradition for him and his peers, and the loss of confidence in German images, stories and myth. 'Never before and

A preoccupation with history: *Ludwig—Requiem für einen jungfräulichen König* (1972)

nowhere else have [images and language] been debased so deeply as vehicles to transmit lies.'

New German Cinema's quest for new anti-illusionist styles was therefore centrally motivated by a desire not to reproduce the mode of representation which had contributed to seducing millions of Germans into Nazism. But anti-illusionism can also be seen as a rather more ambivalent rejection, or negotiation, of the dominant cinema's aesthetics and of the role Hollywood had played in US strategies of cultural domination in West Germany: 'The Yanks have colonized our subconscious' (*Im Lauf der Zeit*).

Finally, the non-commercial look of some of the New German films can be attributed to the funding system itself. Insufficient funding frequently meant that producing a seamless classic narrative was beyond the filmmakers' means, even if that had been their intention, which rarely it was. The very name *Autor* for a filmmaker (and, indeed, *Autorenfilm* for the New German Cinema itself) was, therefore, less the product of retrospective critical evaluation than a conscious cultural strategy to identify filmmakers as working almost artisanally, like traditional artists, and to distinguish them from commercial and industrial filmmakers.

Given these determinants it becomes clear why New German Cinema cannot simply be absorbed into an art cinema framework, for to do so would be at the expense of a specific historical and political understanding of a national cinema. Nevertheless, the New German Cinema derives its international acclaim precisely from being constructed by the critics and by the distributors as a national variant of art cinema.

Women filmmakers

Although the New German Cinema was dominated by male filmmakers, the emergence of the women's movement and the broadly liberal policies employed in film funding provided a limited space for women filmmakers. From the mid-1970s an increasing number of women were competing with the already established male auteurs and had to campaign intensively to receive funding and access to the media. In particular, television offered many first-time filmmakers, and therefore women, a chance. Julia Knight (1992) notes that many women filmmakers had a political commitment to the left and were actively engaged in the women's movement. In this respect, political activism rather than auteurist self-expression may be seen

to be the motivating force for many. An autobiographical example of this tendency is Helke Sander's *Die allseitig reduzierte Persönlichkeit—Redupers* ('Redupers', 1977), which shows the struggle of a single parent and professional photographer. In a number of films the characters—fictional and autobiographical—are used to engage with historical processes from a feminist perspective (see Frieden *et al.* 1993): Jutta Brückner's semi-autobiographical film *Hungerjahre—In einem reichen Land* ('Hunger Years', 1979) depicts growing up in the repressive Adenauer era and Helma Sanders-Brahms's internationally acclaimed, but nationally controversial, autobiographical film *Deutschland, bleiche Mutter* ('Germany Pale Mother', 1980) indicts patriarchy for the rise of fascism and the atrocities of war. Margarethe von Trotta, like Fassbinder, uses melodrama as a powerful device for an engaged political cinema. This approach is already evident in her first solo feature film, *Das zweite Erwachen der Christa Klages* ('The Second Awakening of Christa Klages', 1978), a contemporary tale about a morally justified bank robbery. Unlike many of her peers, Ulrike Ottinger rejected a realist treatment of women's issues, preferring exaggeration, artifice, and parody. Her film *Madame X—Eine Absolute Herrscherin* ('Madame X—An Absolute Ruler', 1978), about a band of female pirates, provoked a mostly hostile response from feminists at the time. Although, the majority of women filmmakers could only produce intermittently low-budget films—and thus remained marginal—von Trotta's and Sanders-Brahms's move towards international art cinema paid off in terms of public recognition and paved the way for other successes in the 1980s.

End of the New German Cinema

Increasingly official support for the New German Cinema became restrictive and conservative as the power of the state was undermined and then seriously threatened by a surge of direct confrontational actions from the Baader-Meinhof group in 1977. It is indicative of the changes in government funding policy that *Deutschland im Herbst* ('Germany in Autumn', 1978)—an almost immediate reaction by some of the most notable leftwing filmmakers (Alf Brustellin, Rainer Werner Fassbinder, Alexander Kluge, Maximiliane Mainka, Edgar Reitz, Katja Ruppé, Hans Peter Cloos, Bernhard Sinkel, and Volker Schlöndorff) to the alleged suicides of 'terrorists' in Stammheim prison—was produced and funded by the collectively owned Filmverlag der Autoren rather than by the government. However, the break-up of the support system was not just one-way and a much wider range of determinants needs to be taken into account, including the effectiveness of vigorous commercial lobbying, and indeed the changing political consciousness of the filmmakers themselves. By the early 1980s New German Cinema had no longer institutional, or ideological, support. Instead, state subsidies and international co-productions gave rise to a much more popular and genre-oriented cinema and, in the process, a political drive and national distinctiveness were lost.

Why should we still be interested?

The New German Cinema matters because it clearly embodies the *Zeitgeist* of a period marked by political utopian ideals and then melancholic disillusionment. It is a cinema which foregrounds the struggle over an embattled national identity in the way in which the filmmakers negotiated the past, not as a heritage to be preserved, but as a site for investigation and excavation, and for reconstructing history as histories and her-stories. It is also important for its institutional framework, which granted access to politically under-represented groups: women, gays and lesbians, and

> It is a cinema which foregrounds the struggle over an embattled national identity in the way in which the filmmakers negotiated the past, not as a heritage to be preserved, but as a site for investigation and excavation, and for reconstructing history as histories and her-stories.

ethnic minorities. Finally, it is still one of the most exciting national cinemas, in so far as this body of work encompasses films which range from romantic excess and spectacular visions to documentary realism. The more films one sees, the more interested one becomes in understanding how these diverse films nevertheless bear witness to a particular period and culture rather than merely expressing the outlook of a few talented auteurs—although they may do that too.

BIBLIOGRAPHY

Bordwell, David (1985), *Narration in the Fiction Film* (London: Methuen).

Corrigan, Timothy (1983/1994), *New German Film: The Displaced Image* (Austin: University of Texas Press).

*****Elsaesser, Thomas** (1989), *New German Cinema: A History* (London: Macmillan and British Film Institute).

Franklin, James (1983/1986), *New German Cinema: From Oberhausen to Hamburg* (London: Columbus Books).

Frieden, Sandra, Richard W. McCormick, Vibekke R. Petersen, and **Laurie Melissa Vogelsang** (eds.) (1983), *Gender and German Cinema: Feminist Interventions*, 2 vols., i: *Gender and Representation in New German Cinema*, ii: *German Film History/German History on Film* (Providence, RI: Berg).

Johnston, Sheila (1981–2), 'A Star is Born: Fassbinder and the New German Cinema', *New German Critique* 24–5 (Fall–Winter), 57–72.

*****Kaes, Anton** (1989), *From Hitler to Heimat: The Return of History as Film* (Cambridge, Mass.: Harvard University Press).

*****Knight, Julia** (1992), *Women and the New German Cinema* (London: Verso).

*****Rentschler, Eric** (1984), *West German Film in the Course of Time* (New York: Redgrave).

Santner, Eric L. (1990), *Stranded Objects: Mourning, Memory, and Film in Postwar Germany* (Ithaca, NY: Cornell University Press).

Wenders, Wim (1977/1988), 'That's Entertainment: Hitler'; repr. in Eric Rentschler (ed.), *West German Filmmakers on Film: Visions and Voices* (London: Holmes & Meier).

11

East Central European cinema: two defining moments

Daniel J. Goulding

The fall of the Berlin Wall and the dramatic collapse of communist regimes in East Central Europe and the former Soviet Union during 1989–91 brought to a close a unique chapter in the history of world cinema. In the four decades or so after the end of the Second World War, an attempt was made to forge national cinemas predicated upon and guided by Marxist-inspired aesthetic, ideological, and political doctrines promulgated and enforced by the state. With the exception of Albania, the communist regimes of East Central Europe (Poland, Hungary, Czechoslovakia, Romania, Bulgaria, and the former East Germany, and Yugoslavia) made a deep and unprecedented commitment in their respective countries to building up the material infrastructure of film production, exhibition, and distribution and in subsidizing the development of film education and film culture. Even in difficult economic times, the annual levels of production of feature films, animated films, experimental, and short films in these countries far exceeded what could be sustained in a commercially oriented industry totally or substantially dependent upon box-office returns. On the other hand, the creation of artistically and socio-culturally significant films was often stymied by shifting party lines and the alternations of periods of freer film creativity with periods of crisis, repression, bureaucratic intervention, and what regime authorities euphemistically termed processes of 'stabilization' or 'normalization'.

Because of the diversity and scope of developments in East Central European national cinemas—with their different rhythms of 'reform' and 'repression', cinematic resurgence and decline, and distinct national histories, literatures, and cultures—it is not possible, in a chapter of this length, to cover all of the key movements and moments since the end of the Second World War that have raised important issues of critical interest to students of film. This chapter will focus instead, on the Czechoslovak New Wave of the 1960s and the Polish Cinema of Moral Concern of the late 1970s and 1980s as being among the most significant defining and paradigmatic moments in the development of post-war East Central European cinema. Both of these moments illustrate struggles common to all of the East Central European national, socialist cinemas in striving for greater freedom, diversity, and socio-cultural and political relevance of artistic film expression.

The struggle for greater artistic freedom was waged on several fronts. First, there was the struggle to free film expression from the dogmatic norms of socialist realism. Articulated by Stalin's supreme aesthetic arbiter Andrei A. Zhdanov in the 1930s, this rigid doctrine was imposed on the emergent socialist cinemas of East Central Europe soon after the end of the Second World War, and it never fully relinquished its grip even into the 1970s and 1980s, especially in the ideologically more conservative regimes of East Germany, Bulgaria,

Romania, and the neo-Stalinist period in Czechoslovakia following the fall of Dubček in 1968. At its most rigid, the doctrine of socialist realism emphasized the strict delineation of good and evil, approved genres, and set character types. It combined socialist orthodoxy with classical patterns of film narrative; i.e. film narrative based on directed logical coherence, rationally presented character motivation, and a predictable 'clockwork' functioning of intentions, causes, and effects. The dogmatic application of socialist realist doctrine in the area of film creation led to films that served the explicit, immediate needs of socialist construction by fostering appropriate attitudes and by depicting reality not as it existed but in terms of its 'revolutionary development'. Films were expected to be didactic and clear-cut, avoiding formal and stylistic innovation and providing assessments of situations that were ultimately 'progressive' and optimistic.

The struggle to free film from the confining tenets of socialist realism initially took the form of expanding the range of permissible film genres and challenging the idealized, optimistic representations of socialist 'reality' called for by socialist realist doctrine. Filmmakers claimed for themselves the right to express a more critical 'realism'—including the right to invoke the darker, ironic, and more alienated side of human, social, and political existence. A more radical struggle involved freeing film from the requirements of 'realistic' representation itself, in favour of wide-ranging modernist experimentation with film form and non-linear narrative structures that directly opposed the prescriptions of socialist realism.

In addition to struggling against the confining dogma of socialist realism, East Central European filmmakers fought to reconnect their national film cultures to world-wide film developments. As they succeeded in doing so, their work was especially influenced by Italian Neo-Realism, the French Nouvelle Vague, and the British school of social realism of the 1960s. Even more important was the effort to reconnect film to the filmmakers' own distinctive national histories, folklore, and literary and cultural traditions. These efforts gained increasing momentum after the death of Stalin in 1953, but did not reach full fruition until the 1960s and 1970s.

On a more pragmatic level, intense efforts were made to free film production, distribution, and exhibition from the Stalinist centralized bureaucratic structures set up after the Second World War. The most radical experiments in decentralization, and the placing of greater control in the hands of filmmakers themselves, was carried out in the former Yugoslavia after Tito's dramatic break with Stalin in 1948. As part of Tito's programme of 'self-management socialism', extensive reforms of the film industry were codified into law in 1956 and continually modified through the 1960s and early 1970s. The 1950s witnessed similar, though less radical, developments in Poland, Hungary, and Czechoslovakia—developments that involved the formation of separate small, specialized studios and the reorganization of large, centralized studios into smaller production units headed by creative teams of filmmakers.

As previously noted, the waxing and waning struggles for greater artistic autonomy and freedom of expression that occurred throughout East Central European cinema are nowhere more dramatically etched than in the two defining moments selected for brief discussion in this chapter: the Czechoslovak New Wave (sometimes called the Czech Film Miracle) of the 1960s, and the Polish Cinema of Moral Concern of the late 1970s and 1980s.

The Czechoslovak New Wave

During the brief period from the beginning of the 1960s to the fall of Dubček in 1968 the former Czechoslovakia produced an astonishing number of internationally significant films of great stylistic diversity and creative range. Along with the many critically acclaimed films that received major awards at prestigious international film festivals and achieved limited art-house circulation, there were a significant number that also succeeded in capturing a much wider domestic and international audience. Among the better known of these critically and commerically successful films were *Loves of a Blonde* ('Lásky jedné plavovlásky', 1965) and *The Firemen's Ball* ('Hoři má panenko', 1967) directed by Miloš Forman: *The Shop on Main Street* ('Obchod na korze', 1965), winner of the 1965 Academy Award for best foreign film, directed by Elmar Klos and Ján Kadár; and *Closely Observed Trains* ('Ostře sledované vlaky', 1966), winner of the 1966 Academy Award for best foreign film, directed by Jiří Menzel.

The surge of creative energy from Czech and Slovak filmmakers in the 1960s was paralleled by modernist 'new wave' tendencies in the neighbouring socialist cinemas of Hungary, Poland, and the former Yugoslavia. All of these film movements were tied, in part, to larger political and economic struggles within their respective countries to move away from Stalinism towards a more 'liberal' interpretation of Marxist socialism. In Czechoslovakia, Alexander Dubček led the forces of reform against the more conservative factions of the Communist Party aligned with President Novotný. Dubček's efforts were crowned with triumph in January 1968 with his elevation to party secretary—a triumph, however, that was remarkably short-lived and quickly turned to defeat when the Soviet tanks rolled into Prague in August of the same year. The fall of Dubček ushered in a harsh period of neo-Stalinism characterized by greatly increased censorship, a draconian purge of the film community, and the reinstatement of strict party control.

In the early 1960s Czechoslovakia was favourably positioned to take a leading role among East Central European socialist states in widening and deepening film expression and making its presence felt in world cinema. First, it shared with Hungary the distinction of possessing a sophisticated film tradition that stretched back to the silent period. Second, it was alone among East Central European socialist states to come through the Second World War with its film infrastructure virtually intact. In fact, the well-equipped labs and studios in Prague were improved even further during the war by the Germans, who planned to make Prague a major producing centre in the Third Reich.

At a much deeper level, there existed a close relationship between filmmakers and the related arts of literature, painting, music and theatre. Especially enriching was the direct collaboration of filmmakers with leading Czech and Slovak writers—including several who had already begun to acquire an international reputation. Among the most important of these were Bohumil Hrabal, Josef Škvorecký, Milan Kundera, Ludvík Aškenazy, Alfonz Bednár, Ladislav Fuks, Ladislav Grosman, František Hrubín, Vladimír Körner, Arnošt Lustig, Sergej Machonin, Vladimír Páral, and Jan Procházka. In addition, a group of talented screenwriters specifically trained and experienced in their craft contributed significantly to some of the most important films of the period, including, among others, Jaroslav Papoušek (all of Miloš Forman and Ivan Passer's films), Antonín Máša (*Everyday Courage*, 'Každý den odvadhu', 1964), Pavel Juráček (*Josef Kilián*, 'Postava k podpíráni', 1963), and Ester Krumbachová (*The Party and the Guests*, 'O slavnosti a hostech', 1966; *Martyrs of Love*, 'Mučedníci lásky', 1967; *Daisies*, 'Sedmik-

rásky', 1966; *Valeri and her Week of Wonders*, 'Valerie a tyden divů', 1969.

The impressive pre-war Czechoslovak literary tradition also exerted a strong influence. Jaroslav Hašek's satirical masterpiece *The Good Soldier Schweick* was a sophisticated model for the ironic, humorous, and satirical portrayal of unheroic protagonists in the Forman–Passer and Menzel films. Franz Kafka's major works, rehabilitated in Czechoslovakia in the early 1960s, inspired dark and mordant filmic explorations into the labyrinthine complexities of psychological and socio-political tyranny and repression. Several of the 'experimental' or 'fantastic' films of the Czechoslovak New Wave explicitly revealed their linkage to the pre-war poetic Surrealist avant-garde and to the writings of Vadislav Vančura and Vítězslav Nezval. Among the most important theatrical influences on the New Wave was Alfred Radok's experimental *Laterna Magika* with its audacious combination of live action and cinematic projections, and the Semafor Theatre of Jiří Suchý and Jiří Šlitr, whose work revealed parallels to the influential pre-war avant garde theatrical works of Jiří Voskovec and Jan Werich.

Paradoxically, the most 'unifying' characteristic of the Czechoslovak New Wave was its very lack of a unifying aesthetic and of any attempt to define itself as a collective movement aimed at achieving consciously articulated goals. Breaking through the stale crust of socialist realist dogma and cultural Stalinism, it openly tolerated and encouraged a variety of aesthetic approaches.

> **Paradoxically, the most 'unifying' characteristic of the Czechoslovak New Wave was its very lack of a unifying aesthetic and of any attempt to define itself as a collective movement aimed at achieving consciously articulated goals. Breaking through the stale crust of socialist realist dogma and cultural Stalinism, it openly tolerated and encouraged a variety of aesthetic approaches.**

Among the most influential stylistic and thematic approaches was the critical realism and the ironic ant-heroic cinéma vérité depictions of 'everyday' reality in the films of Forman, Passer, Menzel, Klos and Kadár; the expressionistic and Kafkaesque film portrayal of Juráček (*Josef Kilian; The End of August at the Hotel Ozone*, 'Konec srpna hotel Ozón', 1966; the dream realism of Jan Němec (*Diamonds of the Night*, 'Démanty noci', 1964; *The Party and the Guests; Martyrs of Love*); the feminist absurdist films of Věra Chytilová (*Daisies; The Fruit of Paradise*, 'Ovoce stromů rajaských jíme', 1969); the stylized fantasy and surrealistic films of Vojtěch Jasný (*Cassandra Cat*, 'Až přijede kocour', 1963; and *All My Good Countrymen*, 'Všichni dobří rodáci', 1969), and Jaromil Jireš (*Valerie and her Week of Wonders*); and the films of lyrical social engagement by Evald Schorm (*Everyday Courage; Return of the Prodigal Son*, 'Návrat ztraceného syna', 1966). The leading New Wave filmmakers, of course, combined several complex stylistic influences in their film works. The above schematic categorization is meant to be suggestive only.

In the initial critical assessments of Czechoslovak New Wave films, some Western critics tended to view them primarily as derivative reflections of major West European film movements—most notably vanguard Italian cinema (Neo-Realism and beyond) and French Nouvelle Vague. More complete analyses, however, both by Czech film writers and critics (Josef Škvorecký and Antonín Liehm) and Western film scholars (David Paul and Peter Hames) illuminated the specifically Czech and Slovak historical, socio-political, cultural, and folkloric influences that stamped the films with originality and depth.

There was also a tendency among some Western film critics to stress the political messages of the films and to celebrate the most controversial and provocative of them as anti-regime and anti-communist 'dissident' films. Such critics were especially intrigued by films that delivered their socio-political critiques with irony, subtle allegorical indirection, and Aesopian language. Milan Kundera was one of several leading figures in contemporary Czechoslovak literature and film to speak out eloquently against such critical reductionism. He lamented the tendency of some Western critics to interpret East Central European art in terms of being pro- or anti-communist in its attitudes. He suggested that if Western critics could not view art coming from Prague, Budapest, or Warsaw 'in any other way than by means of this wretched political code, you murder it, no less brutally than the worst Stalinist dogmatists'. He went on to suggest that the importance of this art does not lie in the fact that it pillories this or that political regime (although it may, in fact, do so with wit and devastating effectiveness) but that, 'on the strength of social and human experience of a kind people here in the West cannot even imagine, it offers new testimony about mankind' (quoted in Hames 1985: 142). Kundera expresses an important insight. The best of the Czechoslovak films transcended the political particularities of the moment to express deeper layers of the unique Czechoslovak historical and cultural experience and such dimensions of human existence as the grotesque, the tragic, the absurd, death, laughter, conscience, and social responsibility.

Some Western leftist critics attempted to measure Czechoslovak New Wave films against contemporary Marxist and neo-Marxist theoretical and aesthetic models in opposition to the distorted, vulgar Marxism of socialist realist dogma. Antonín Liehm and František Daniel have both expressed considerable scepticism regarding the utility of such models. They argue that in East Central Europe, not only did the attempt to apply Marxist models to the active creation of literature and film not succeed, but efforts to elucidate the meaning of arts through a Marxist aesthetic similarly failed to produce worthwhile results (Paul 1983: 149–57). Liehm points to Czechoslovakia's pre-war experience with democratic institutions and cultural humanism as a more valid starting-point for understanding the underlying values expressed in Czechoslovak New Wave films. It is these same democratic and humanistic values that expressed themselves later in the 'Velvet Revolution' of 1989 and in the accomplishment of an orderly and peaceful separation of Czechoslovakia into the Czech Republic and Slovakia in 1993.

The Polish Cinema of Moral Concern

In Poland the richest periods of post-war film expression occurred from the mid-1950s to the early 1960s and again in the mid-1970s and early 1980s. The first, 'New School', period was nourished by a system of decentralized film production 'units' headed by leading film artists, by the steady maturation of the internationally respected Polish film school at Łódź, and by the high artistic, moral, and political status achieved by a gifted community of film directors, scenarists, cinematographers, actors, and other film artists. As in the case of Czechoslovakia and other East Central European cinemas, there was a close relationship of film

Wajda's *Man of Iron* (1981) traces the formation of the Solidarity movement

expression to the deepest and best currents of Polish national literature and the arts as well as to the distinctive shaping influences of Polish history, past and contemporary. Among those shaping historic influences was the Polish Romantic tradition, with its emphasis on nationalism, mysticism, and messianism; the profound consequences of the long years of Polish partition (from the close of the eighteenth century until 1918); the more recent history of war, socialist reconstruction, and cultural Stalinism; and the tradition of the artist as moral agent and participant as well as reflector of socio-cultural and historical forces.

After a comparatively sterile period in the mid-1960s to early 1970s, Polish cinema once again burst onto the world stage in the late 1970s and early 1980s with an impressive outpouring of artistically and socially meaningful films, labelled by the filmmakers themselves as the 'cinema of moral concern'. Andrzej Wajda, who led the way in the first post-war period of Polish film resurgence with his visually sophisticated and emotionally powerful film trilogy of the war years, *A Generation* ('Pokolenie', 1955), *Canal* ('Kanał', 1957) and *Ashes and Diamonds* ('Popioł i diament', 1958), also initiated the 'Cinema of Moral Concern' with his film *Man of Marble* ('Czlowiek z marmaru', 1977), the first film to penetrate the official mythology surrounding the Stalinist years and to expose its propagandistic excesses and grotesqueries. His film *Man of Iron* ('Czlowiek z zelaza', 1981) staked out even bolder territory by mirroring the formation of the Solidarity movement—a film that both reflected and helped to shape its dramatic course.

The new mood of Polish cinema was richly confirmed and enhanced by Krzysztof Zanussi's complex cinematic and philosophical meditations *Camouflage* ('Barwy ochronne', 1976), *Spiral* ('Spirala', 1978), and *The Constant Factor* ('Constans', 1980). These two long-established filmmakers were soon joined by a younger generation of filmmakers (Agnieszka Holland, Krzysztof Kieślowski, Tomasz Zygadło, Piotr Andrejew, Zbigniew Kamiński, Witold Orzechowski, Ryszard Bugajski, Feliks Falk, and others) who rapidly rose to international prominence. Following the crackdown on Solidarity in late 1981, several of these rising talents emigrated to the West, and Polish film production went through a brief period of shock and suspended animation. It was widely assumed by Western film critics that the recently reborn Polish cinema would be strangled in the cradle. Such gloomy prognostications did not take into account the moral and intellectual tough-mindedness of the Polish film community and the unique and complex relationship which existed between the Polish intelligentsia and regime authorities. By 1983–4 Polish filmmakers were once again making artistically interesting films that continued to critique contemporary Polish social and political realities. The films explicitly denounced official corruption, media manipulation, economic failure, social disintegration, lack of political and personal integrity, and the worn-out myths and shabby results of communist ideology and practice—critiques that helped prepare the ground for the eventual fall of communism and the triumph of the Solidarity movement in 1989.

Continuing legacy

The most important defining moments in post-war East Central European cinema have contributed an impressive legacy of critically significant films. They also have raised serious issues concerning the subtle and complex interrelationships of politics, art, and social commitment within a government-subsidized system of film production, distribution, and exhibition. Issues of artistic freedom, censorship, and the economic and ideological determinants of artistic production are brought dramatically to the foreground. Important questions are raised about the various and sometimes conflicting roles of the filmmaker in society: as popular entertainer and celebrity icon; as 'serious'

> **The most important defining moments in post-war East Central European cinema have contributed an impressive legacy of critically significant films. They also have raised serious issues concerning the subtle and complex interrelationships of politics, art, and social commitment within a government-subsidized system of film production, distribution, and exhibition. Issues of artistic freedom, censorship, and the economic and ideological determinants of artistic production are brought dramatically to the foreground.**

artist freed from the dominating influence of box-office success; as propagandist and reinforcer of the established order; or as transgressive provocateur and agent of reform and revolution.

Since the fall of communism in 1989 the cinemas of East Central Europe have been engaged in an often painful and difficult transition towards a mixed system of free enterprise buttressed by modest government subsidies. Whether such a system will result in films that match the artistic and socio-cultural significance of those made during the 'best' moments of the post-war communist past remains to be seen, and to be systematically studied.

BIBLIOGRAPHY

***Goulding, Daniel J.** (ed.) (1989), *Post New Wave Cinema in the Soviet Union and Eastern Europe* (Bloomington: Indiana University Press).

***Hames, Peter** (1985), *The Czechoslovak New Wave* (Berkeley: University of California Press).

Liehm, Antonín J. (1974), *Closely Watched Films: The Czechoslovakian Experience* (White Plains, NY: International Arts and Sciences).

Liehm, Mira, and **Antonín J. Liehm** (1977), *The Most Important Art: Eastern European Film after 1945* (Berkeley: University of California Press).

***Michałek, Bolesław,** and **Frank Turaj** (1988), *The Modern Cinema of Poland* (Bloomington: Indiana University Press).

Paul, David W. (ed.) (1983), *Politics, Art and Commitment in the East European Cinema* (New York: St Martin's Press).

Skvorecky, Josef (1971), *All the Bright Young Men and Women: A Personal History of the Czech Cinema* (Toronto: Peter Martin).

12

European film policy and the response to Hollywood

Armand Mattelart

'Cinema is an art, but it is also an industry', the novelist André Malraux liked to recall in the 1960s, after he had become de Gaulle's Minister for Culture. He had previously used the phrase to round off his *Ésquisse d'une psychologie du cinéma*, published in 1939, and while it must have seemed banal to the Hollywood studio bosses who had, since about 1910, made an industry out of producing films, in the France of the 1960s, this little aphorism was surprisingly bold given the traditional French emphasis upon the 'art' of the film director. Paradoxically, if Malraux's phrase still retains some of its provocative nature, it is not because of the second part but because of the first. The importance of industrialization in the whole process of cultural production, as well as the intimate relationship which links it to the internationalization of markets and products, are now recognized as integral to the shaping of cultures, both present and future. On the other hand, in this conversion to market laws, the idea that cinema is something other than just a product can get lost. In 1993 it was precisely this balance between economics and culture that representatives of the member states of the European Union and those of the United States debated during the final Uruguay Round of negotiations between the members of the General Agreement on Tariffs and Trade (GATT).

Until then, the controversy about the definition and the place of cultural creation in the new commercial order of the world had been lurking just below the surface. When it was debated whether to extend the principles of free exchange to the audiovisual, the problem exploded into the open. 'Creations of the mind cannot simply be assimilated to simple products', was how President Mitterrand expressed it in October 1993. The French position was to call for special treatment of this section of international exchange: a clause entitled 'cultural exception' to exclude the audiovisual from the measures governing the liberalization of commerce in the same way that public health, the environment, and a state's internal security are excluded. After controversies and agitated talks, the parties present decided to exclude 'creations of the mind' from the rules governing other merchandise on 15 December 1993. However, the intensity of the argument obscured the fact that the GATT negotiations were only part of a long history of debates in France, in a wider Europe, and elsewhere about whether or not they needed to protect themselves from an unequal relation of forces in this area. To understand what is really at stake in what is no doubt only the first stage of the 'commercial war of images' on a world-wide level, it is more than ever necessary to trace the genealogy of the problem.

Germany: a pioneer country

The idea that it is essential for a nation-state to safeguard the independence of its production of images appeared for the first time in Europe in the Kaiser's Germany, right in the middle of the First World War, when European companies were losing control of the European film market. Before this, the international film trade was not encumbered by any customs measures or commercial policies specific to this type of production. In 1916–17, however, the German authorities equipped themselves with legal measures to combat the free exchange of films. Thereafter, they exerted a strict control on the importation of foreign films and developed a state policy of constructing a national cinema industry.

Thus, in 1917 the famous Universum-Film-Aktiengesellschaft (UFA) was founded in Berlin thanks to the conjunction of banking groups, the state, and the armed forces, who recognized the role that film could play as a propaganda weapon. The UFA brought together the majority of the existing national businesses, and combined production with distribution and exhibition. The communiqué published on the occasion of the inauguration of the UFA is revealing of the philosophy which inspired its foundation:

We are pleased to note that the general public is increasingly of the opinion that films are not just produced as a diversion for people, but that they must respond to the national educational and economic needs. It is for this reason that it was necessary to give the German film industry a more solid base, particularly in commercial and financial terms, so that when a peace has been concluded, it will be able to compete on an equal footing, both in terms of capital and also in terms of organization, with foreign films whose influence has, until now, been dominating. (Bächling 1947)

This global strategy was in keeping with the philosophy handed down by the economist Friedrich List (1789–1846), one of the spiritual fathers of the *Zollverein* (the customs union) who did not think of the construction of the nation-state and a 'national economy' as separate from an 'educational protectionism', and who was fiercely opposed to the theory of free exchange inspired by the theoreticians of classical economics such as Adam Smith and David Ricardo (Mattelart 1996). Opening up one's national economy to foreign competition is not profitable until it has developed to a level on which it can compete. What resulted was a doctrine which advocated neither total self-sufficiency nor total protectionism, but one which could be varied from case to case depending on the degree of independence achieved by any particular sector of

the industry. As we shall see, this is an argument which was used again by opponents of a totally free market in the debates on the construction of the 'European economy', the ratification of the Maastricht Treaty, and the negotiations between the Twelve and GATT.

The fear of America

During the Great War American cinema took advantage of the gap left by the warring countries in Europe to extend their exportation networks, and in the interwar period they further consolidated their power. At the same time, a number of European countries, in particular France and Britain, organized systems to protect themselves from the influence of Hollywood films in the cinemas. At the end of the Second World War the American government did all that it could to alleviate these restrictions by using the occasion of the Marshall Plan. In the case of France, the Blum–Byrnes Agreement, named after the French representative Leon Blum and the American Secretary of State James Byrnes, was signed in Washington in May 1946 (Guback 1969). In place of an importation quota, this substituted a 'screen' quota which reserved four weeks in every quarter (or 31 per cent) of screen time for French films (compared with 50 per cent before the war) (see Forbes, Part 3, Chapter 9). This meant that the new quota did not allow enough screen time for the full potential of French production to make it into the cinemas. Thus, whereas before the war France produced about 120 films per year, in 1946, it produced ninety-six and, in 1947, only seventy-four.

This new crisis, which extended across various sections of the industry, pushed French actors, directors, and producers, supported by the press, onto the street and obliged the National Assembly to reconsider the agreement. Negotiations with Washington succeeded in altering it, and a new agreement was signed in September 1948. The system of an importation quota was put back in place, backed up with the control of 'screen' time. Of the 186 foreign films which would be allowed to be screened each year, 121 could come from the United States. The reserved 'screen' time for French films was also increased from four to five weeks (or 31 to 38 per cent). These protective measures were accompanied by a policy of actively encouraging film production at home. The Centre national de la cinématographie (CNC) was at the heart of a new support system and one of its roles was to ensure that part of the

479

receipts received in France from foreign films was rein-vested in the national industry.

France, because of this strategy of protection and production of national films, became one of the few countries, not only in Europe but also in the world, to retain a certain pluralism in its cinemas. Jacques Thibau, the director-general for cultural, scientific, and technical relations of the Ministry of Foreign Affairs, remarked in 1982, in a published report on French policy on cultural matters: 'The lesson of these last twenty years in Europe is clear: there can be no national cinema without a policy of aid to the national cinema. This is true for France, Italy, Germany. . . . The example of Great Britain (which made the opposite choice), is very instructive in this respect: a film industry survives, but British cinema has practically disappeared' (Mattelart et al. 1984: 67).

> The lesson of these last twenty years in Europe is clear: there can be no national cinema without a policy of aid to the national cinema.

Unequal exchange and the cultural industries

The 1970s mark a historic turning-point in the understanding of both the industrial mechanisms which govern the production and distribution of films and other audiovisual material and the international imbalance of cultural exchange. A concern to diagnose these problems and to propose policies at both national and international levels first sprung up in Third World countries which chose Unesco, the organization representing the community of nations in matters of culture, communication, education, and science, as its main forum. From 1969 this international institution (presided over at the time by the Frenchman Jean Maheu) debatd the idea of 'one-way communication' which characterized the relationship between developing countries and the others, and which, because of its unilateral nature, was in danger of 'causing problems for the mutual understanding of nations'. In 1977 Mr Maheu's successor, Amadou Mahtad M'Bow from Senegal, ordered a report from an international commission to study the problems of communication. The MacBride Commission's report was published in 1980 and clearly set down the imbalances in the international flow of programmes, films, and other cultural products (MacBride 1980).

A number of factors—such as the intransigence of Reagan's America, which, following free market principles, wanted to impose the argument for the free flow of information at all costs (an argument that would be taken up later during the GATT talks), and a telescoping of the interests of Southern countries who were struggling for national cultural emancipation and the interests of communist bloc countries who knew how to manipulate these legitimate demands to oppose any opening-up of their systems of mass communication—blocked a successful outcome to proposals of a 'new world order of communication and information' (Mattelart 1994).

Despite this, the Unesco debates were the first occasion when concern had been voiced about the unequal exchange of information and images, and these did encourage policies in certain Third World countries for protecting their own cinema market. This was particularly the case in Latin America, where ever since 1967 and 1969, when the first meetings of filmmakers from the Southern continent had been organized at Viña del Mar in Chile, the idea of a 'common market for Latino-American film' had been making headway. In 1977 Embrafilme, the state enterprise for film in Brazil, proposed extending the project to Italy and France and asked its Latin American partners to demand of the various governments a quota policy in favour of national films. In 1985, however, the United States, invoking the drift towards a politicization of the problems of communication, turned their backs on Unesco and were followed shortly after by Mrs Thatcher's Britain. In the 1980s, as a result, the question about the regulation of media networks and exchange slipped into the domain of organizations which were more technical in character (of which GATT was at the forefront).

'Television without Frontiers'

In the 1980s deregulation, the privatization of audiovisual systems, and the increase in the power of the market moved the centre of gravity of both the debates and the players. While the Third World countries, who had supported calls for a 'new world order of communication and information' during the 1970s, deserted the field of debate and rallied around the principle of free exchange of cultural merchandise, Europe was impressing upon its community institutions the question of the unequal exchange of audiovisual material. In June 1984 the EEC published a voluminous report entitled *Television without Frontiers: A Green Paper on the Establishment of the Common Market for Broadcasting especially by Satellite and Cable* and invited the other players in the audiovisual future of Europe to make their opinions known. This was the first shot in the debate that went back and forth between the different authorities in the Community, the government representatives, and the professional organizations concerned. Their aim was to establish a directive on television without borders. The Council of Europe for its part set in motion a convention on the same subject in 1986.

The final version of *Television without Frontiers* was approved by the Twelve on 3 October 1989. Article 4 invites the member countries to reserve the majority of air time for European productions (films and documentaries) 'whenever possible'. A joint declaration from the European Council of Ministers and the Commission specified that this was a 'political obligation'. In other words, the directive was a legally enforceable document, except in the cases of quotas whose non-observation in a certain country could not in practical terms be punished by the European Court of Justice. Article 4 thus had the status of a 'declaration of intention'. The directive also dictated the frequency of commercial breaks and forced television stations to promote independent production and respect the chronology cinema–video–television in their exposure of works. It also recognized the right of each member country to determine for itself the quota of European productions. In France, for example, channels are obliged to broadcast 40 per cent French productions (60 percent European) and must invest a part of their turnover in film production. The Convention on Television without Frontiers elaborated by the Council of Europe and adopted shortly before was hardly different from that approved a few months later in Brussels. Against its will, France gave its support to these two texts. At the last moment Paris advocated more stringent terms for the quotas. Led by the British delegation, those member states most opposed to the imposition of quotas succeeded in persuading a majority of the Twelve to back them against the French proposition, which was supported by Belgium, Luxembourg, and Spain. France wanted to impose a minimum quota of 60 per cent of air-time, excluding the time given over to the news, sporting events, game shows, advertisements, or teletext services.

Over the five years of confrontation it was clear how much the European governments were split rather than brought together by the very notion of culture. Whilst the neo-liberal government delegation from London jumped at the mention of the word 'cultural' when applied to the audiovisual, the French representatives ardently defended a quota system in the name of a 'European cultural identity'. Others thought this identity to be unlocatable. Portugal could not understand why they had to swap the latest successful Brazilian telenovella for a French soap opera like *Chateauvallon*, merely so as to favour European productions. Smaller countries like Belgium openly criticized both sides for ignoring the intercultural power relations in a Europe composed of national and regional communities whose capacity for audiovisual and advertising production was unequal.

However, despite numerous concessions and compromises, the directive was badly received by those working in the audiovisual environment in the United States, and they announced a recourse to GATT almost immediately. According to them, the directive infringed the obligation made on member states not to discriminate against foreign products. The reception worsened in December 1990, a year after its adoption, when the Council of Ministers of the Twelve took a series of decisions with a view to setting a deadline for a European audiovisual industry: the MEDIA programme. Endowed with a budget of some 220 million ECUs spread over the period 1991 to 1995, and overseen in a decentralized way from the large European cities (London, Hamburg, Barcelona, Brussels, Paris), this programme covered teaching, production, and distribution: help for screenplays, documentaries, and cartoons, and aid for distribution and exhibition.

An overwhelming balance sheet deficit

Throughout the 1980s one fact underpinned the strategy of the European Union: the growing commercial domination of the audiovisual market in Europe by the American cinema, television, and video industries. According to the estimates made in 1990 by the Institut de l'audio-visuel et de télécommunications en Europe (IDATE), American revenue in the EEC countries was as high as $US3.719 billion (of which $1.134 billion was earned in cinema, $1.278 billion in television, and $1.307 billion in video) whilst EEC revenue in the United States only reached $247 million: a deficit of $3.472 billion.

External markets were becoming more and more important for the US major studios. In 1988 these large companies earned 41.6 per cent of their turnover abroad; four years later that figure was almost 47 per cent. In 1991 an average of 72 per cent of cinema takings in Europe went to American films. Although France was the only country that managed to save a substantial percentage for its national cinema, even it had to face the growing proportion of American films, which jumped from 31 to 57 per cent between 1979 and 1993. Steven Spielberg's *Jurassic Park* showed, in 1993, how much power the American cinema has: in the United States and Canada the film earned $345 million while in other countries it earned $538 million. Thanks to utilization rights granted to licensed companies (covering 500 firms and 5,000 products), the film generated more than $1 billion in sales. The film cost $60 million dollars to make, whereas the average French film costs $4 million.

By including services in the commercial negotiations for the first time since its creation in 1947, GATT put the transnational exchange of intangible products, including all the products of the cultural industries, up for debate. Until then, the question of regulating this flow had been a purely European one. Henceforth it would be thrown into the contentious problems of worldwide application. At the end of the Second World War the General Agreement on Tariffs and Trade had been signed by twenty-three countries; in 1993 it brought together 107 nations. The problem was that while GATT underlined the necessity of applying the same general rules of the liberalization of international commerce that governed other goods and services to the audiovisual, this would involve the abolition of the different systems installed by Europe and each European country to protect their own audiovisual space such as financial support for cinema at a national and EU level and the fixing of television transmission quotas for fiction of European or national origin. This was the object of the wrestling-match begun in 1993 between the European Union, represented by Leon Brittan (the commissioner for foreign economic relations), and the United States in the person of the American Mickey Kantor, the special representative for commerce from the White House. The mediator was the director-general of GATT, the Irishman Peter

Sutherland, whose brief was to conclude the last phase of the agreement (the Uruguay Round) and to create a new insitition, the World Trade Organization.

In the name of which European cultural identity?

The reason for the scale of the French involvement in the GATT affair is that it has a long tradition of defending national cinema, rooted in a concern both for culture and for the numerous companies in the cinema business who year in, year out, produce between 100 and 120 films, in a sector which has some 70,000 employees. Another important element has been the official fear of seeing French culture lose influence in Europe and throughout the world: a fact which has not escaped African intellectuals and artists given that imported French programmes account for between 23 and 50 per cent of programmes broadcast in French-speaking Africa. This has meant that the way that they have looked at the problem of a threatened cultural identity is very different. Echoing the words of the former French minister of Culture Jack Lang ('Culture and Economy: it's the same struggle'), the Cameroon producer Michael Lobe Ewane summed up the position of African audiovisual workers: '*Dallas* and *The Olive Castle* [a successful French television series]-it's the same struggle!' (*Liberation*, 8 November 1993).

What this suggests is some of the problems involved in mobilizing the concept of 'European culture'. This leitmotif was evident in the appeal, published as a full-page article in the daily newspaper *Le Monde* (18 September 1993) by leading French arts and media organizations when authors and filmmakers gathered in Venice on the initiative of the Fédération européenne des réalisateurs audiovisuels to discuss the GATT question:

A reasonable GATT for a European Culture
. . . Each people benefits from an inalienable right to develop its own culture at the same time as having access to the wealth of other peoples' cultures. They know that in this crisis, which is tearing apart a fin-de-siècle world, it is essential that cinema and other means of audiovisual expression be allowed to contribute to understanding, to a coming together, and to cultural blossoming. The maintaining and reinforcing of a strong cultural identity in the Community is nowadays indispensable if the European construction is to succeed . . . [We wish] European negotiators to demand unconditionally that the rules laid down in the

agreement have no hold over the audiovisual sector in Europe. The clause for a cultural exception, a rule only designed to protect our identities, must be included in the GATT agreement without any concession.

However, the declaration does not indicate that there was unanimity among French filmmakers on this question. Some of them openly demonstrated their reservations and showed how difficult it was to defend the interests of independent creators at the heart of this debate. As the filmmaker Marcel Hanoun was to write later in the newspaper *Libération* (6 March 1995):

'Cultural exception' is the tree that hides the forest of cultural exclusion . . . For some people, 'cultural exception' is only a struggle between markets. For others it is the silent, permanent exploration of the immense field of writing for the audiovisual, the field of research, of innovation, of discovery. . . . The vociferous supporters of the cultural exception cannot and will not accept the alternative of alterity, difference, right here at home in France.

In this respect, we should note the real absence of any probing interrogation into what a 'European cinematographic and audiovisual identity' might or should be.

> We should note the real absence of any probing interrogation into what a 'European cinematographic and audiovisual identity' might or should be.

We should also note another important complication. For, if the professionals—and in particular the organizations of authors, directors, and producers—were at the vanguard of mobilization against the initial GATT plan, the large communications groups claiming to be European, both in France and elsewhere, did not display the same anxieties. Despite the growing sense of confrontation between France and America, French groups such as Canal plus and the Chargeurs réunis were signing agreements with the conglomerate Time Warner with the aim, particularly in the case of the Chargeurs réunis, of creating a cinema network on the European mainland whilst the NBC network took control of the European cable channel Superchannel. As for the broadcaster TF1, the old 'voice of France', which had been privatized in 1986, it was content

merely to reiterate its hostility towards any policy of quotas.

The partners in the European Union, estimating that they did not have the same interests (nor the same conception of culture) to defend as the French, were also reluctant to support the idea of the 'cultural exception' fully and only the Belgian government and those of southern Europe initially rallied behind it. However, when the outcome of negotiations was announced, the cultural sector was successfully excluded from the GATT agreement. There was not long to wait for the reactions of those representing the American film industries. Jack Valenti, president since 1963 of the Motion Picture Association of America, whose statements throughout the previous two years had surprised a number of European directors and producers, made the following statement on the night of the announcement of the verdict:

The greatest negotiations of our age have come to an end. The EEC, our biggest market, leaves us with no cause for hope. . . . Their final offer is, in fact, lamentable . . . These negotiations had nothing to do with culture (unless we are to believe that every television series or game show from Europe considers itself to be the cultural equivalent of a Molière comedy). The only thing that really mattered was money, and what avarice there was! (Valenti, 1993).

Towards the digital super highway: White Paper, Green Paper

Hardly had the GATT problems been concluded than more appeared on the horizon, the great projects for an infrastructure of information networks in Europe. These were 'information superhighways', a deployment of networks for new multi-media services, mixing sound, text, and images, either still or animated. This hybridization of televisions, computers, and telephones signalled the beginning of communication in which the user has the possibility of participating, thanks to intelligent consoles, and plugging into interactive services (films, games, catalogues, video conferences, education, banking, medicine, and so on).

The send-off for these projects was given in the White Paper prepared by Jacques Delors and adopted by the European Union Council of Ministers in December 1993. This official report describes the technological leap as a 'change comparable to the first industrial revolution', and the digital networks are seen as right at the heart of a reorganization of the modes of production and distribution within society, their 'growth', their 'competitiveness', and 'employment' (three terms included in the title of the White Paper). With this, another difference between Europe and America came into play. At least, that is how Jack Valenti understood matters in February 1994: 'The development of satellites, number compression and transmission by telephone will multiply tenfold, a hundred fold, the capacity of a cable network. And not in the year 2000 but tomorrow. Each individual will be able to choose from between 5,000 and 10,000 programmes, and that sort of power will render the very idea of quotas absurd!' (Valenti 1994.) Thus will begin the period of the 'audiovisual superhighway', to take up Mr Valenti's phrase.

It was with these new technological stakes in mind that in April 1994, in the wake of the White Paper, Jacques Delors and João de Deus Pinheiro (the Portuguese commissioner in charge of culture and the audiovisual) presented a Green Paper on the audiovisual. Its title was *Strategy Options to Strengthen the European Programme Industry in the Context of the Audiovisual Policy of the European Union*. Its goal was to construct a well-defined framework and a credible financial basis for European audiovisual businesses in order to exploit the 'potential of the digital revolution' and to prevent the Single Market from becoming solely for American companies. Directly linked to the preoccupations elaborated in the White Paper, there is a promise for the future, to create 2 to 4 million jobs by the year 2000 in a Europe which has 18 million unemployed. Even if the figures that make this report sparkle are, in the eyes of many economists, deceptive, one thing is certain: the spectre of a crisis henceforth projects the discussion about employment (and unemployment) to the heart of the concerns about identity and the relations between 'art' and 'industry'.

On the centenary of the cinema

In 1995 the European Union Council of Ministers for Culture and Communication met to discuss the revision of the 1989 Directive on Television without Frontiers. On this occasion France proposed strengthening the quotas imposed on European channels, hoping to have the clause which obliged stations to transmit a majority of European works 'whenever possible' removed. According to them, the lack of legal clarity in this wording allowed the clause to be abused. The French delegation found itself practically isolated in defending this revision, and most of the European partners refused any rewording that would tighten the existing constraints on television. France's European partners remained dug into their minimalist position.

Also in 1995 the group of the world's most industrialized nations, G7, met in Brussels for a summit on new communications technology, and more specially to discuss information highways. For the first time, representatives from the large American, European, and Japanese firms in the communications sector were invited to a meeting of this type. They stressed the pressing necessity to hasten the deregulation of the telecommunications services and to suppress public monopolies in order to accelerate the development of future electronic arteries. They were all agreed that 'private initiatives must drive the global information society' (Bangemann 1994).

So the G7 representatives parted, recommending a rapid liberalization of telecommunications. Employment and cultural diversity, however, were either excluded from the agenda or treated as marginal issues. A tacit agreement had prompted the seven great industrialized nations not to tackle such questions, which were 'by nature too polemical'. The representatives of Hollywood have also been pragmatic and have avoided any open polemic. They wait for the future deployment of these highways so that they will be proved to have been right about what they still insist on interpreting as a sign of European (and French) chauvinism in the era of 'global' media.

BIBLIOGRAPHY

Bächlin, P. (1947) *Histoire économique du cinéma* (Paris: La Nouvelle Édition).

Bangemann, M. (chairman) (1994), *Europe and the Global Information Society: Recommendations to the European Council* (Brussels: EC).

Delors, J. (1993), *Livre blanc. Croissance, compétitivité et emploi: les défis et les pistes pour entrer dans le vingt et unième siècle* (Brussels: European Economic Community).

European Commission (1984), *Television without Frontiers: A Green Paper on the Establishment of the Common Market for Broadcasting especially by Satellite and Cable*, Com (84) 300 final (Brussels: EC).

—— (1994), *Strategy Options to Strengthen the European Programme Industry in the Context of the Audiovisual Policy of the European Union* (Brussels: EC).

*Guback, T. (1969), *The International Film Industry: Western Europe and America since 1945* (Bloomington: Indiana University Press).

MacBride, S. (1980), *Many Voices, One World* (Paris: Unesco).

Malraux, A. (1939), *Esquisse d'une psychologie du cinéma* (Paris: Nouvelle Revue française).

Mattelart, A. (1994), *Mapping World Communication: War, Progress, Culture*, trans. S. Emanuel and J. Cohen. (Minneapolis: University of Minnesota Press).

—— (1996), *The Invention of Communication*, trans. S. Emanuel (Minneapolis: University of Minnesota Press).

*—— X. Delcourt, and M. Mattelart (1984), *International Image Markets: In Search of a New Perspective*, trans. D. Buxton (London: Comedia and Methuen).

Pinheiro, J. D. (1994), *Green Paper on Audiovisual Policy* (Brussels: EC).

Valenti, J. (1993), 'La CEE tourne le dos à l'évenir', *Le Monde* 16 Dec.

—— (1994), 'Le Concurrence stimule le qualité', *Le Monde*, 15 Feb.

(a) **Jean Renoir**   KEITH READER

Very few filmmakers, paradoxically, arouse so little critical debate, in the negative sense of the term, as Jean Renoir. His two best-known films are *La Grande Illusion* (1937), acclaimed as one of the true masterpieces of humanist cinema, and *La Règle du jeu* ('The rules of the Game', 1939), which consistently vies with *Citizen Kane* (USA, 1941) in *Sight and Sound*'s critics' poll for all-time best film. One major reason for this is Renoir's status as auteur. Leo Braudy writes of how he was 'fascinated to find that each of the films of Jean Renoir stayed whole, establishing its continuity with other films, at the same time that it refused to lose its individual artistic identity' (1977: 17). His iconic status for the French New Wave stems largely from this continuity, often articulated around a number of key themes: the theatre (clearly a metaphor for cinematic mise-en-scène), nature in general and water in particular, the importance of location shooting, and the elusive balance between order and improvisation.

That these thematic continuities should have been perceived across a range of genres that is exceptionally wide for a European art filmmaker—from political drama (*Le Crime de Monsieur Lange*, 1936) to literary adaptation (*La Bête humaine*, 1938), from social farce

(*Boudu sauvé des eaux*, 'Boudu Saved from Drowning', 1932) to near-musical (*French Can-Can*, 1955)—makes Renoir in many respects the archetypal European auteur. This is not, however, to say that his career forms an entirely homogeneous whole, and the major critical debates around his work centre around both its socio-political relevance and the quality and status of the films he made between fleeing to the United States at the outbreak of the Second World War and the end of his filmmaking career in 1969.

'The auteurist obsession with the transhistorical wholeness of art and the artist' (Faulkner 1986: 6–7) long obscured the acute social relevance of Renoir's pre-war work. The propaganda film he made for the French Popular Front, *La Vie est à nous* (1936), was given one of the 'classic' analyses of *Cahiers du cinéma*'s Marxist period (Bonitzer *et al.* 1970), but for the rest he was often seen, by Truffaut and by Beylie (1975) among others, as the timeless humanist *par excellence*. That quality has often been seen as distilled in the remark made by Octave, the character he himself plays in *La Règle du jeu*: 'Everybody has their reasons.' Yet the remark is prefaced by: 'on this earth, there is one thing which is terrible', which is borne out by the violent, and ultimately tragic, social conflicts in the film.

In the wake of the influence of Marxism on film theory, more recent work on Renoir (Serceau 1981; Faulkner 1986; Vincendeau and Reader 1986) has placed much more stress on how his 1930s work is imbued with a savagely satirical socio-political awareness that goes well beyond his whole-hearted but brief commitment to the French Popular Front. *Le Crime de Monsieur Lange* asserts Renoir's commitment to a precarious, but necessary, social solidarity not only through its subject-matter (it is about a workers' publishing co-operative), but, as Bazin (1971) masterfully demonstrates, through the circularity of its mise-en-scène, culminating in the 360° pan around the courtyard immediately before Lange kills the exploitative Batala.

La Grande Illusion's humanist qualities are not in doubt, but to overstress them is to risk obscuring the fact that the film, although set during the First World War, is also a fierce social anatomy of the France that was about to plunge into the Second (see Faulkner 1986: 85–7). From 1939 until his death in 1979, although he returned regularly to film in France, his main residence was in California, and for François Poulle (1969) this isolation from the mainstream of French society has a deleterious effect on his work. The majority of critics, not necessarily for reasons as overtly political as Poulle's, would agree with this, and *La Règle du jeu*'s status as cinematic myth doubtless owes much to its being widely perceived as the summit of Renoir's 'real' career, after which the rest could not but be an anticlimax.

Yet *Le Carrosse d'or* ('The Golden Coach', 1953) was the film whose title Truffaut chose for his production company (Les Films du carrosse), and *Cahiers du cinéma* found no difficulty in getting prominent directors and critics to write favourably about every one of the post-1939 films in their special Renoir issue (July–August 1994). The most stalwart and articulate defender of the later films is Daniel Serceau—one of the first critics to analyse the social importance of the earlier period—for whom they represent a supreme refinement of Renoir's art and the articulation of an ethic of renunciation, beginning with *The River* (1950) (Serceau 1985).

Renoir was also, for André Bazin above all, one of the masters of cinematic realism—a term defined not by plausibility of subject-matter, but by the organic qualities of the mise-en-scène. For Bazin, the fact that 'pan-

ning and lateral dollying became his two main camera techniques' (Bazin 1971/1973: 21) goes beyond stylistic observation to constitute an aesthetic and ontological—even an ethical—judgement. But film theory, in its pomp, systematically eschewed ethics and ontology (though emphatically not judgement), so that, while the importance of Bazin's views was always recognized, they did not influence later critics in the way that might have been expected.

Renoir's own comments on his work, collected in interviews and television programmes, may seem at first sight inconsequential. Yet an observation such as 'realism is not realism at all. It is simply another way of translating nature' (Renoir 1989: 57) has much in common with more overtly theoretical and semiological approaches, and his stress on the importance of material and technological change in art is scarcely consonant with a timeless or transcendental view of his work. Perhaps what almost all commentators would agree is that Renoir's mise-en-scène, his collaborative style of working with actors, his use of the cinematic medium to articulate the coexistence of the comic and the tragic, make him, for all his lack of overt theoretical pretensions, one of the cinema's major innovators.

BIBLIOGRAPHY

*Bazin, André (1971/1973) *Jean Renoir*, trans. W. W. Halsey II and William H. Simon (Paris: Éditions Champ Libre; New York: Simon & Schuster).

Bertin, Célia (1994), *Jean Renoir* (Monaco: Éditions du Rocher).

Beylie, Claude (1975), *Jean Renoir: le spectacle, la vie* (Paris: Éditions Seghers).

Bonitzer, Pascal, Jean-Louis Comolli, Serge Daney, and Jean Narboni (1970), '"La Vie est à nous, film militant', *Cahiers du cinéma*, 218 (Mar.), 44–51.

*Braudy, Leo (1977), *Jean Renoir: The World of his Films* (London: Tobson Books).

*Faulkner, Christopher (1986), *The Social Cinema of Jean Renoir* (Princeton: Princeton University Press).

Poulle, François (1969), *Renoir 1936; ou, Jean Renoir pour rien?* (Paris: Éditions du Cerf).

Renoir, Jean (1989), *Renoir on Renoir* (Cambridge: Cambridge University Press).

Serceau, Daniel (1981), *Jean Renoir, l'insurgé* (Paris: Le Sycomore).

—— (1985) *Jean Renoir: la sagesse du plaisir* (Paris: Éditions du Cerf).

Vincendeau, Ginette, and Keith Reader (eds.) (1986), *La Vie est à nous! French Cinema of the Popular Front 1935–1938* (London: British Film Institute).

(b) Ingmar Bergman CHRIS DARKE

The case of Ingmar Bergman indicates that neither the longevity of a director's career nor the breadth of his influence guarantee his reputation. Although Bergman directed forty films between 1944 and 1982, his critical profile has declined from 1960s auteur cinema supremacy to present-day neglect. The popular memory of Bergman today is a kind of pale parodic photocopy, exemplified by Woody Allen's homages, where the Swedish director is stylistically invoked as a reference for European art cinema *gravitas* and to generate a kind of profundity-by-proxy (acutely analysed by the American critic Jonathan Rosenbaum 1993). But this fate is itself highly revealing of the shifts that have taken place in film criticism since the late 1950s. Indeed, Thomas Elsaesser (1994) has studied the process of Bergman's steady disappearance from the canon, as well as his centrality in defining the outlook of 1960s cinephile.

'The first critical articles I struggled with—as reader and writer—were on Bergman', recalls David Thompson (1994). He was not alone. For many film critics in the late 1950s, and throughout the 1960s, Bergman was the central figure of European art cinema. When writing for *Cahiers du cinéma*, the future French New Wave directors recruited him as an inspirational figure. Bergman's 1953 film *Sommaren med Monika* ('Summer with Monika'), released in Paris in 1957, provoked Jean-Luc Godard's eulogy 'Bergmanorama', in which he claimed that Bergman was the most original filmmaker of the European cinema and a stylistic inspiration (Godard 1958).

In Britain too, where the film magazine *Movie* was reappraising and promoting Hollywood cinema along auteurist lines, critics were cutting their teeth on the emergent European cinema of directors such as Bergman, Michelangelo Antonioni, Alain Resnais, and Godard. This was the heyday of auteur-based criticism, with close textual analysis serving to reveal the continuity of themes and style across the body of a director's work. Exemplary of this critical approach is the work of the British critic Robin Wood (1969), who devoted a book-length study to Bergman's films. Wood's study is a model of the sort of criticism—serious, humanistic, and text-based—that led to Bergman becoming synonymous with the idea of art cinema. With the allegorical medievalism of *The seventh Seal* (1957) and the complex narrative time-schema of *Wild Strawberries* (1957), Bergman's first internationally successful films marked the director as being equally preoccupied with symbolism and psychology and therefore ripe for extensive critical exegesis and interpretation.

The cycle of more intimate 'chamber dramas' including *The Silence* (1963), *Persona* (1966)—one of the key films of the 1960s—and *Cries and Whispers* (1973) saw Bergman's focus narrow but become increasingly refined and austere, concentrating on intimate relationships, family breakdown, and the foregrounding of female characters. If art cinema can be seen to address its audience in such a way that audience identification shifts from characters to author (Cook 1985: 116), these films capitalized on this mode of address in their repeated casting of a troupe of performers, most notably the actresses Ingrid Thulin, Liv Ullmann, and Bibi Andersson, as well as Bergman's preferred actors, Max von Sydow and Gunnar Björnstrand. This family of performers lent Bergman's films an increasingly personal, autobiographical tone—a mode that perhaps reached its peak with *Fanny and Alexander* (1982)—and served to underline the authority of the director's control over his characters. Bergman's fascination with his female characters led Wood to assert: 'If one were to name the cinema's greatest director of women, the automatic response would probably be George Cukor. But on further reflection one might be tempted to retract this and say "No—Ingmar Bergman"' (Wood 1969).

In the 1970s feminist critics began to question the 'greatness' that Wood attributes to the director. In her essay 'Bergman's Portrait of Women: Sexism or Subjective Metaphor' (1979), Birgitta Steene critiques this characterization of Bergman. While she acknowledges that, in his 'chamber dramas', Bergman focused predominantly on female characters, she nevertheless identifies these films as conforming to a conventional artistic male perspective on female subjectivity that identifies femininity with hysteria.

That Bergman was to become the focus of alternative critical tendencies was to be expected, whether that perspective was feminist or one contextualizing the director within his national culture (Bergom-Larsson 1978); that he was unable to remain as central a figure to film studies, or even to film criticism, as Hitchcock is testimony to the way in which a commitment to art cinema was jettisoned in the 1970s, and faith was increasingly placed in an idea of 'the popular'. Bergman might be said to have been both occulted by academic fashions and a victim of his own art cinema success. Whatever the emphasis one chooses to place, it is to the disadvantage of academic film studies that such a crucial European director should remain quite so sidelined.

BIBLIOGRAPHY

Bergom-Larsson, Maria (1978), *Ingmar Bergman and Society* (London: Tantivy).

Cook, Pam (ed.) (1985), *The Cinema Book* (London: British Film Institute).

Elsaesser, Thomas (1994), 'Putting on a Show: The European Art Movie', *Sight and Sound*, 4/4 (Apr.), 22–7.

Godard, Jean-Luc (1958/1972), 'Bergmanorama', *Cahiers du cinéma*, 85 (July), in *Godard on Godard*, trans. Tom Milne, ed. Jean Narboni and Tom Milne (London: Secker & Warburg).

Rosenbaum, Jonathan (1993), 'Notes towards the Devaluation of Woody Allen', in *Placing Movies: The Practice of Film Criticism* (Berkeley: University of California Press).

Steene, Birgitta (1979), 'Bergman's Portrait of Women: Sexism or Subjective Metaphor', in Patricia Erens (ed.), *Sexual Stratagems: The World of Women in Film* (New York: Horizon Press).

Thompson, David (1994), *Biographical Dictionary of Cinema* (London: André Deutsch).

Wood, Robin (1969), *Ingmar Bergman* (London: Studio Vista).

(c) Chantal Akerman CATHY FOWLER

When, in 1981, Peter Wollen revised his initial definition of two avant-gardes, he also suggested that some work straddled the two. One body of work, he suggested, was that of Chantal Akerman, whom Wollen positions at some point between the two avant-garde traditions of New York and Paris. Although Akerman has since moved away from this mid-way position, her work retains that initial sense of hybridity, so that, while her films have a place in discussions of avant-garde cinema, art cinema, and (women's) auteur cinema, they do not fit neatly into any one of these categories.

For Anglo-American film theory, the value of Akerman's early films in the mid-1970s lay in their careful interrogation of film language at a time when film theory itself was trying to come to terms with the workings of the cinematic apparatus and cinema's textual operations. However, what distinguished Akerman's project from that of other 'modernist' directors such as Jean-Luc Godard and Michael Snow was the fact that she interrogated without actually interrupting the fictional world. Instead of a Godardian 'counter-cinema' in which Brechtian strategies ensure the distance and unpleasure necessary for a critical viewing, Akerman offered a different way of seeing and of making meaning. Although each of Akerman's films can be said to have a 'story', it is in the telling of that story that emphasis is shifted from narrative to other aspects such as time, space, ritual, and repetition. The result of this shift of focus is that attention is given to what would normally be considered 'minor' subjects. Thus *Jeanne Dielman, 23 quai du commerce, 1080 Bruxelles* (1975) depicts the quotidian rituals and routine of the eponymous widow over the course of three days, while in *News From Home* (1976), set in New York, we see not the meta-cinematic image, but those parts of the city which have been overlooked.

The 'difference' of Akerman's cinema, though, is primarily located in what can be seen as her stylistic signature. From her early films to her most recent work, Akerman has favoured the use of a low-angle static camera which sees its world through a tableau frame. This static framing is coupled with a denial of camera angles and movements, point-of-view shots and close-ups. Such a style could be read in terms of art cinema's 'objective realism' (Bordwell 1979), in which meaning is made according to the rules of reality rather than those of classical narrative. However, Akerman also enforces a denial of the conventional modes of

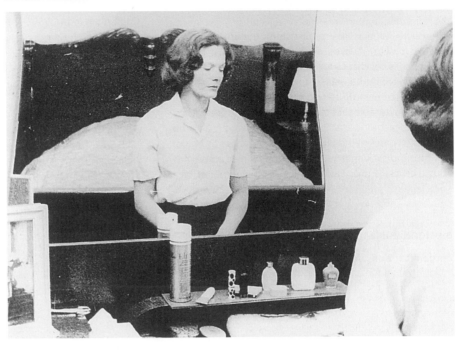

'Feminist film practice' and 'female aesthetic'—*Jeanne Dielman, 23 quai du commerce, 1080 Bruxelles* (1975)

identification and involvement, which lie uneasily within art cinema's mode of address.

Akerman's style is more usually read as promoting a liberation of the gaze: rather than examining the image in terms of narrative information, the spectator is allowed, and indeed encouraged, to let his or her gaze wander within the frame. In *Les Rendez-vous d'Anna* (1979) the lack of expression through camera movement and cutting would at first seem to echo the passive wandering of Anna. However, once the different gaze is in action, new levels of expression and meaning emerge. On one level Akerman's strategies could be seen as a response to Mulvey's call in her famous article 'Visual Pleasure and Narrative Cinema' to 'free the look of the camera into its materiality in time and space' (1975: 18), but on another level this style illustrates the 'cinema of attractions', theorized by Tom Gunning (1986) as one part of early cinema which he suggests finds its way into certain aspects of the avant-garde.

These connections with Mulvey and Gunning also refer us to the two key discourses within which Akerman's work has figured: feminist film theory and debates around avant-garde and alternative filmmaking. Akerman's unmoving camera offered a cinema which was neither ruled by narrative (having other priorities) nor regimented by a voyeuristic impulse. Both of

these aspects proved attractive to film feminism, which was seeking out ways of denying the spectacular objectification of woman which it saw as axiomatic of dominant cinema. *Jeanne Dielman*, released the same year as Mulvey's article, was seized upon as the key illustration of a 'feminist film practice' and 'female aesthetic' (Bergstrom 1977; Kuhn 1982: 173–4). Equally, as Wollen's reference to Akerman proves, her reintroduction of narrative and characters into the avant-garde's otherwise de-humanized world led the way for an alternative practice which would challenge mainstream cinema on its own ground.

If Akerman's denial of identification with characters opens the way for other ways of reading, then one of the strongest of these is via the 'auteur' Akerman. Yet, as with Akerman's use of avant-garde and art cinema strategies, important differences from conventional (read: male) auteur cinema should be noted. Though Akerman would deny any associations with a 'women's' auteur cinema, her films inevitably assert a different desire (which must be expressed through a different form) from the model which originated in the 1950s with *Cahiers du cinéma*.

The task of tracing Akerman's female authorship across all twenty-eight years of her filmmaking has yet to be undertaken, as film theory generally lost interest after her 1970s work. This lack of attention to her more recent work has meant an ignorance of the shifts these films make towards genre (melodrama in *Toute une nuit*, 1982, and the musical in *Golden Eighties*, 1986) and the spectacular elements of cinema. What is more, it has left Akerman associated almost wholly with 1970s discourses around the deconstruction of narrative for formal or political (feminist) purposes.

Other more important questions raised by her films of both the 1970s and later have also been ignored. Thus Akerman's place in French cinema was assured by her move to Paris in the mid-1980s and her subsequent dallying with 'French' subjects, actors, and inter-texts. However, this embracing of France has obscured Akerman's Belgian ties, and work is lacking on her 'Belgianness', whether through her relation to Belgian cinema (which is also relatively critically ignored), her place among a Belgian school of auteurs (other examples being André Delvaux, Jean-Jacques Andrien, and Marion Hänsel), or the ways in which her films explore this identity (specifically through *Toute une nuit*, which is set in Brussels).

Finally, Akerman's reintroduciton of genre, spectacle, and ultimately narrative pleasure into her work is echoed by feminist film theory's sudden fascination with these very same elements. It is here, then, that the critical connection could be renewed, and Akerman's work examined once more for the rigorous interrogation and, most recently, play with film language which it offers.

BIBLIOGRAPHY

Bergstrom, Janet (1977), '*Jeanne Dielman, 23 Quai de Commerce, 1080 Bruxelles* by Chantal Akerman', *Camera Obscura*, 2: 115–21.

Bordwell, David (1979), 'The Art Cinema as Mode of Film Practice', *Film Criticism*, 4/1 (Fall), 56–64.

Gunning, Tom (1986), 'The Cinema of Attractions', *Wide Angle*, 8/3–4 (Fall), 63–77.

Kuhn, Annette (1982), *Women's Pictures* (London: Routledge & Kegan Paul).

Mulvey, Laura (1975), 'Visual Pleasure and Narrative Cinema', *Screen*, 16/3 (Autumn), 6–18.

Wollen, Peter (1981), 'The Avant-Gardes: Europe and America', *Framework* 14: 9–10.

—— (1982), 'The Two Avant-Gardes', in *Readings and Writings* (London: Verso).

(d) Pedro Almodóvar JOSÉ ARROYO

Pedro Almodóvar is the most successful film director of the post-Franco period in Spain and the best-known Spanish film director abroad since Luis Buñuel. His success is such that in Spain it is referred to as the 'Almodóvar phenomenon'. From *Pepi, Luci, Bom, y otras chicas del montón* ('Pepi, Luci, Bom, and Other Girls on the Heap', 1980), his first feature, each of his subsequent films outdid the box-office success of the previous one, a rise that climaxed with *Mujeres al borde de un ataque de nervios* ('Women on the Verge of a Nervous Breakdown', 1988), the most financially successful Spanish film ever. Abroad, Almodóvar's films have also succeeded: the films are international box-office hits; they have garnered excellent reviews and festival prizes; and, in English-language academic film studies, literature on Almodóvar represents a large and disproportionate amount of literature on Spanish film studies in general. Critical discussion of Almodóvar's work has focused on interrelated (though often decontextualized) issues of representation (gender, homosexuality, the nation) and on aesthetics (postmodernism).

Since *Pepi, Luci, Bom, y otras chicas del montón*, Almodóvar's films have centred on a gallery of complex women (housewives, nuns, lawyers, singers, actresses, writers, mothers, and daughters) who seek to fulfil their sometimes socially transgressive emotional and sexual desires: Luci (Eva Siva) is a masochist who wants to get beaten up; Sexilia (Cecilia Roth) in *Laberinto de pasiones* ('Labyrinth of Passion', 1982) is a nymphomaniac; the Mother Superior (Julieta Serrano) in *Entre tinieblas* ('Dark Habits', 1983) is a lesbian drug addict; Maria (Assumpta Serna) in *Matador* (1986) gets turned on by killing her sexual partners during orgasm.

However, these social transgressions are narrated as perfectly moral within the films' terms, and audiences are asked to identify with the transgressor. The women in Almodóvar's films have provided career-making roles for what amounts to a repertory company of actors which includes some of the biggest stars of Spanish cinema (Carmen Maura, Victoria Abril, Verónica Forqué) and some of the most able and appealing supporting players (Chus Lampreave, Maria Barranco, Rossy de Palma).

The male characters in Almodóvar's films are often rooted in the melodramatic clichés of Spanish popular culture: bullfighters, detectives, priests, brutal or adulterous husbands, escaped prisoners, sons dominated by their mothers. Many of the male characters in Almodóvar's films may be interpreted as failed attempts at hegemonic notions of masculinity or a *machista* ideal. For example, in *Matador* the bullfighter (Nacho Martinez) has been gored, the policeman (Eusebio Poncela) is gay, and the youth (Antonio Banderas) faints at the sight of blood. These three archetypes of Spanish machismo are subverted by the story and are also structurally subservient to their female counterparts in the film.

While the representation of men in Almodóvar's films has been largely downplayed if not downright ignored, the representation of women has received a great deal of attention. Women are so associated with Almodóvar's *œuvre* that the repertoire of actresses who appear in his films is often referred to as 'las chicas Almodóvar', a patronizing moniker that highlights their association with Almodóvar while obscuring their distinguished bodies of work in the theatre and in other films. Almodóvar is considered a 'women's director' and his representation of women has generally been lauded. However, the release of *¡Atame!* ('Tie Me Up! Tie Me Down!' 1990), a story of a former porn star who falls in love with her kidnapper, led to accusations of misogyny which have not quite abated. These accusations have been culturally specific. According to Paul Julien Smith, 'English- and German-speaking viewers attack Almodóvar for the "negative" political content of his images and Spanish and French critics absolve those images of any content, displace them wholly into ironic humour or pastiche' (1994: 112). Debates around the representation of gender and sexual orientation in Almodóvar's work have also raised questions about film criticism *per se*: should critics measure these films by 'universal' criteria or should cultural context be taken into account?

The question of sexual orientation has also been a key one in discussions of Almodóvar's work. The director is known to be gay and all of his films up to *La ley del deseo* ('The Law of Desire', 1987) featured homosexual characters. Lesbian characters featured prominently in *Pepi* and *Entre tinieblas*. Gay male characters featured in *Laberinto, ¿Que he hecho yo para merecer esto?* ('What have I Done to Deserve This?', 1984), and *Matador*. *La ley*, up to now the only Almodóvar film to focus on a gay relationship, was a breakthrough for its director. Within Spain it was considered his first 'personal' film, in which subject-matter and what was known about the director's personal life finally coincided, and thus Almodóvar could finally be bestowed auteur status by critics. Outside Spain *La ley*'s publicity addressed a gay audience as well as the traditional art cinema audience for foreign films, and gay culture was instrumental in making of Almodóvar arguably the most popular auteur of 1980s international art-house cinema.

The representation of gender and sexual orientation in Almodóvar's films are of crucial importance in considering how his films came to represent post-Franco Spain at home and abroad. Basically these representations would not have been allowed before censorship was abolished in Spain in 1977. Gender was one of the certainties of Franco's Spain, whereas Almodóvar's films continually highlight its constructedness (as, for example, when he has Bibi Andersson, a well-known Madrid transsexual, play Ada's biological mother in *La ley*, while Carmen Maura plays a transsexual in the same film). However, Almodóvar's films also signified the 'new' Spain in other ways. *Pepi* and *Laberinto* were seen in Spain as almost documents of the Movida madrileña, a diverse group of young underground artists who aimed to test the limits of the new freedoms in various arts. Almodóvar's films stress their 'modernity', i.e. their commonalities with the rest of Europe, and by doing so distance themselves not only from the privations of the Franco years but also from contemporary Spanish cinema, which in the 1980s seemed to be obsessively trawling through those privations. Almodóvar's films are urban, camp, frivolous, sexy, colourful, fun, and free. They epitomize how post-Franco Spain liked to see itself and how it liked to be seen (*La Ley* was the film that most represented Spain in international film festivals in 1987).

Almodóvar's films have lent themselves easily to theories of postmodernism: they can be seen as pastiches, they rely on intertextuality, they de-centre tradi-

'Urban, campy, frivolous, sexy, colourful, fun, and free'—Almodóvar's *Kika* (1993)

tional notions of socio-sexual identity, and, through their uses of television, they seem both to embody and to ironize Jean Baudrillard's notion of the hyper-real. Almodóvar borrows indiscriminately from film history. A case in point is QQue he hecho?, which contains direct reference to, or echoes of Neo-Realism, the caper film, *Carrie*, Luis Buñuel, Billy Wilder, Andy Warhol, and John Waters. Moreover, it is clear that Almodóvar's preferred mode of cinema is the melodramatic. It is a mode that cuts across genre, equally capable of conveying the tragic and the comic, eminently emotional, adept at arousing intense audience identification, and capable of communicating complex psychological processes no matter what the character's gender or sexual orientation.

Almodóvar's signature, and a unique contribution to the movies, is the synthesis of the melodramatic mode with a clash of quotations. This combination allows Almodóvar both a quasi-classical Hollywood narrative structure (which facilitates audience identification) and a very self-conscious narration (which normally pro-

duces a sense of alienation. This results in dialectical moments in which the absurd is imbued with emotional resonance (the mother selling her son to the dentist in QQue he hecho?). In this way the emotional can be checked with cheek without disrupting identification (superimposing a character's crying eyes with the wheels of a car in *La ley*) and camp can be imbued with depth without losing its wit (the transference of emotions that occurs when we see Pepa dubbing Joan Crawford's dialogue from *Johnny Guitar* in *Mejeres*). At his best (QQue he hecho?, *La ley*, *Mujeres*), Almodóvar drills a heart into the postmodern and fills it with an operatic range of feeling.

In Spain critical attention has focused more on Almodóvar's films as a sociological phenomenon (on what their popularity, themes, marketing, design, and characters say about contemporary Spain) than on their artistic merits. Abroad, however, Almodóvar's work has been a rich mine to academics involved in various areas including feminism, Hispanic studies, queer studies, and film studies. Critics and scholars have focused on the consistencies of Almodóvar's *œuvre*: his focus on women, his use of boleros and other sentimental music, the insertion of satirical advertisements in the narrative, the urban setting, the characters' search for pleasure, the themes of passion and desire. There is a tendency to narrate his career in terms of his 'underground' work (*Pepi, Laberinto*), his work for other producers (*Entre tinieblas, ¿Que he hecho?, Matador*), and the work he produced after setting up his own independent company (from *La ley* to the present). The beginning of the last period is seen as the pinnacle of his success (*La ley, Mujeres*) before a gentle but steady decline (*A'tame; Tacones lejanos*, 'High Heels', 1991), *Kika* (1993), and then a resurgence (*La flor de mi secreto*, 'The Flower of my Secret', 1995). With few exceptions (Paul Julien Smith's (1992, 1994, 1996) exemplary work; Vernon and Morris's (1995) excellent collection of essays), foreign critics have tended to ignore the films' industrial and cultural context.

BIBLIOGRAPHY

Abaladejo, Miguel et al. (1988), *Los fantasmas del deseo: a propósito de Pedro Almodóvar* (Madrid: Aula 7).

Besas, Peter (1985), *Behind the Spanish Lens: Spanish Cinema under Fascism and Democracy* (Denver: Arden Press).

Blanco, Francisco (pseud. Boquerini) (1989), *Pedro Almodóvar* (Madrid: Ediciones JC).

García de León, Maria, and Teresa Maldonado (1989), *Pedro Almodóvar: la otra España cañí* (Ciudad Real: Biblioteca de Autores y temas Manchegos).

Higginbotham, Virginia (1988), *Spanish Film under Franco* (Austin: University of Texas Press).

Hopewell, John (1986), *Out of the Past: Spanish Cinema after Franco* (London: British Film Institute).

Kinder, Marsha (1993), *Blood Cinema: The Reconstruction of National Identity in Spain* (Berkeley: University of California Press).

Smith, Paul Julien (1992) *Law of Desire: Questions of Homosexuality in Spanish Writing and Film 1960–1990* (Oxford: Clarendon Press).

—— (1994), *Desire Unlimited: The Cinema of Pedro Almodóvar* (London: Verso).

—— (1996), *Vision Machines: Cinema, Literature and Sexuality in Spain and Cuba 1983–1993* (London: Verso).

Strauss, Frédéric (1996), *Almodóvar on Almodóvar*, trans. Yves Baignères (London; Faber & Faber).

Vernon, Kathleen M., and Barbara Morris (1995), *Post-Franco, Postmodern: The Films of Pedro Almodóvar* (Westport, Conn.: Greenwood Press).

(e) Luc Besson SUSAN HAYWARD

A very anti-establishment director, Besson aims to compete technically with American action films, quoting as his inspiration Sam Peckinpah. His work is visually and sonorifically pulsating and technically brilliant. Dominant themes of loneliness, suffering, and displacement resonate throughout his work. A new moralist of the cinema, in the tradition of Jean Renoir, he exposes the negative connotations of commodity fetishism: consumer goods as signs of death. Against this he opposes his modest protagonists, with their vision of self-fulfilment, the value of which is based in a purely personal aesthetic (for example, the music in *Subway* (1985); deep-sea diving in *Le Grand Bleu* (1988); violence in *Nikita* (1991) and *Léon* ('The Professional', 1994)).

To date Besson has made seven feature films, including *Atlantis* (1991), his homage to the sea; and his most recent film, The Fifth Element (*Le Cinquième Élément*.)

However, this relatively young filmmaker says he will go on to make only ten, partly because, much like Constantin Costa-Gavras, it takes him two years to make a film. With the exception of his first feature film, *Le Dernier Combat* (1983), which was liked by all, Besson's work has been acclaimed by popular film critics in journals like *Première* and dismissed by other, more heavyweight critics in journals like *Cahiers du cinéma* and *Positif*. All of his films, none the less, have been huge successes with audiences of the 1980s and 1990s (which consist mostly of 15- to 35-year-olds) in France and abroad—in the United States and particularly Japan.

Besson lays no claim to being an auteur; indeed, he says he does not make art or culture—he tells stories. And the stories he tells are of individuals who experience great difficulty in adapting to society, who are prevented from achieving their goals because they

494

are in a state of 'dis-ease' with society—a society, Besson claims, that has seriously unbalanced the family and thereby created emotional deprivation in young people. His films are his way of fighting against this, and, given the appeal of his work, it is clear that Besson is a filmmaker who makes films that are perceived as signs of their time.

Besson broke into the film scene very young, aged 17, and, from 1976 to 1982 worked across virtually all the film set jobs: from gofer to casting, and from camera assistant to editing assistant. In these early years he also made advertisements, short films, and promotional films for songs. What emerged from these formative years was a filmmaker of deep convictions, particularly in the domain of cinema technology, as is evidenced by his commitment to CinemaScope, designing special lightweight cameras, and use of the Louma crane. These convictions include a deep-rooted non-conformity. Ever since he founded his own production company, Les Films du loup, to finance his first feature film, Besson has fought against the rules and conventions established by producers and distributors. He now owns a second company, Les films du dauphin. But, more significantly, he has shown, through his own filmmaking practices, the way in which the French film industry can compete with the Americans: by co-financing, and shooting in English, but retaining director's control (in short, by making hybrid films that cut across French and American cultures).

All Besson's films have violence at the core of the narrative. But it is not just a case of 'designer violence'. Violence is inscribed onto the body; the body becomes the site of violence. More significantly still, violence is represented not just through any body but through that of the main protagonist. In other words, the site of representation for violence is the star text. The star embodies a tension that melds violence with fragility, be it Christophe Lambert (*Subway*), Anne Parillaud (*Nikita*), or Jean Reno (*Léon*). Nor is this tension restricted to a particular gender, as the eponymous heroine of *Nikita* makes clear. With Besson's films, the star text, in the end, disappears—either literally or through death. And technology functions as an extension of this violence which leads to their disappearance. Cameras, high-powered, long-distance rifles with telescopic lenses, proliferate in Besson's films; even the superficially non-violent *Le Grand Bleu* abounds with camera technology that probes and investigates. In his films, technology is a two-way system. Cameras function as instruments of investigation

and surveillance, and while the star text may well use them to observe and destroy, they are also used to observe and destroy him or her. Technology stands as a metaphor for the conformity and control and the policing of social norms, all of which are institutionally sanctioned. It is against this that Besson's heroes and heroines revolt—first in the form of aggression against the norms, and secondly in the form of violence against the self.

Besson's protagonists, then, fail or are unwilling to adapt to contemporary society. And this partly manifests itself in their regressive nature. Isabelle Adjani erupts like a petulant teenager in *Subway*; Lambert (in the same film) persists in fulfilling his childhood fantasy of starting a rock band at the expense of completing his Oedipal trajectory. Jean-Marc Barr (*Le Grand Bleu*) tops himself deep-sea diving rather than resume 'normal' life with his child-bearing landlubber partner, Rosanna Arquette. Anne Parillaud (*Nikita*) remains stuck as a woman-child robotic hit-woman, only to disappear, and Jean Reno (alias *Léon*) does much the same as a man-child robotic hit-man. Fathers and mothers are massively absent except in substitute form, and when they are present in a film they are as dysfunctional as the adult-child they are purporting to parent.

As a filmmaker, Besson has been described as neo-baroque, post-New Wave, and postmodern. From both the point of view of style and genre he is indeed all of these. His films are highly stylized bricolage, pastiche, and reproduction, and they cut across genres. *Subway*, for example, is a melodrama, a musical, and a thriller. It is also a remake that is as indebted to Jean Cocteau's *Orphée* (1949) as it is to any American television cop series. In this film ugliness is emptied out and atmospheric shots transform the Paris Métro into an attractive, even seductive, space where anything can and does happen. This, coupled with the interplay between illusion and reality, is high baroque at its best.

In terms of the New Wave and the postmodern, Besson—like his antecedents—does play with genre and film style. He also addresses spectator pleasure derived from the foregrounding of generic elements and visual and aural counterpointing, even to the point of excess. Like the New Wave filmmakers, he is a director-producer who is technology-conscious. But he also harks back to earlier times. In his own practices of team filmmaking, he recalls those of filmmakers in the 1930s. Finally, as much as he is in a tradition of French filmmaking, he is also a ground-breaker in that he has managed to marry Frenchness with internationalism: French films with speed and visual brilliance—what could be termed an American edge—something serious critics may find difficult to countenance.

BIBLIOGRAPHY

Austin, Guy (1996), *Contemporary French Culture* (Manchester: Manchester University Press).
Hayward, Susan (forthcoming), *Luc Besson: Filmmaker* (Manchester: Manchester University Press).

(f) Brigitte Bardot   GINETTE VINCENDEAU

Brigitte Bardot, or 'B.B.', is arguably the French film star best known internationally. As in the case of her contemporary Marilyn Monroe, her fame outlasts the period of her main films, the late 1950s and early 1960s. In the mid-1990s she is still a recognizable icon in several areas of popular culture: film and television, fashion, postcards, music, coffee-table books, and even current affairs, for her involvement in animal rights campaigns. Her extraordinary youthful beauty, 'ideal' body, and powerful sexual aura position her as a traditional object of male desire. At the same time, the bold expression of her desire and rebellious stance make her enduringly fascinating for women, including feminists. Her star persona is thus characterized by a series of dualities and paradoxes: she is both traditional sexual object *and* agent of her own sexuality; she can be seen as modern heroine or retrograde version of femininity. Her international fame needs to be studied as part of contemporary (global) popular culture, while her persona needs to be understood within the specific context of French cinema and French culture of the 1950s.

A European star

After appearing in sixteen films, Brigitte Bardot emerged (at the age of 22) as a star in *Et Dieu . . . créa la femme*, directed in 1956 by her then husband, Roger Vadim. The character of Juliette she plays in this film was instantly perceived as a new and *authentic* type, closely connected to Bardot the real person. As Richard Dyer (1979) has shown, the popularity of stars can be ascribed in large part to the way they crystallize and authenticate social values which the audience can relate to. Bardot in this respect is a powerful example of

stardom, as a woman emblematic of a new—and controversial—type of femininity. A beautiful and charismatic performer who was obsessively photographed and imitated and whose life became the object of intense media scrutiny, she was also a star in the film industry sense of the term.

Bardot became a valuable commodity for the French film industry, in terms of export (in the late 1950s she allegedly earned France more foreign currency than the Renault car factory) more than on the domestic market, where she briefly challenged but did not displace the male hegemony: the top ten French stars of the post-war period have all been men. Thus the phenomenon of her popularity is complex. Her films enjoyed box-office success for a short period of time (1956–65) and low critical status, with the exception of *La Vérité* (1960) and *Le Mépris* ('Contempt', 1963), but her *image* appealed to the public on a massive scale, and became associated with a particular vision of French femininity (she modelled for Marianne, the effigy of the Republic). Virtually all writing on Bardot is interested in her global image and her life rather than her films. This is just as true of Simone de Beauvoir's seminal text (1960), Edgar Morin's sociological study of stars (1957), and Catherine Rihoit's excellent analysis of Bardot's 'myth' (1986) as of the numerous coffee-table books (Crawley 1975; Evans 1972; French 1994), biographies (Roberts 1984; Robinson 1994) and Andy Martin's 'romance' (1996). This is as much to do with the extraordinary vividness of Bardot's image as with the fact that most of her films were mainstream French productions and thus suffer from the common lack of critical interest in popular European cinema (Vincendeau). Bardot's own memoirs (1996) have equally little time for her films.

Following *Et Dieu . . . créa la femme*, a series of films

Brigitte Bardot—'sex kitten', cultural icon, feminist role model?

were made that perpetuated, accommodated, or commented on the image developed in that film. Out of the twenty-eight films she subsequently made, *La Vérité*, *En cas de malheur* ('Love is my Profession', 1958), *Vie privée* (1961), *Babette s'en va-t-en guerre* (1959), *Le Mépris* (1963), and *Viva Maria* (1965) constitute the classic Bardot canon. Bardot can be regarded as the 'author' of these films, from both an industry and a theoretical point of view. All post-1956 Bardot films were marketed on her name (now even films such as *Les Grandes Manœuvres* (1955), in which she played a small part, appear in a video collection of her films marketed in the United Kingdom). They built their narrative entirely around her. *La Vérité*, *Vie privée*, and *Le Mépris* are, in addition, commentaries on her stardom. In the French cinema of the 1950s and early 1960s, with no studio in the American sense to 'groom' her, and a diffuse genre system, a star such as Bardot acquired special importance, as a stable element in an otherwise unregulated industry. However, as French directors commanded more decision-making power than in Hollywood, with a few exceptions (most obviously Jean-Luc Godard) Bardot worked with French directors without a strong authorial agenda. Given Bardot's high 'authorial' role and the lack of attention her films have elicited so far, a thorough study of Bardot's function in French mainstream cinema from the mid-1950s to the mid-1960s would be both original and illuminating.

Bardot emerged at a time when European cinema was trying to take advantage of the weakening of the Hollywood studio system and the end of the Hays Code. Female sexuality was a selling-point not lost on Vadim: 'Of course the success of *Et Dieu . . . créa la femme* came from its sexual frankness . . . That is what distributors, and especially American ones, demanded' (Vadim 1976). The European cinema of the late 1940s and 1950s produced successful stars such as Sophia Loren, Silvana Mangano, and Harriet Andersson, noted for their 'natural' sexuality, compared with the overtly manufactured glamour of Hollywood stars such as Monroe. Bardot in this respect is poised half-way between the blonde glamour of Monroe and Diana Dors in the United Kingdom (she had started her career as a brunette) and the 'earthy' sexuality of Loren and Mangano. Later, she would form a contrast with the more 'intellectual' stars of the New Wave, such as Anna Karina and Jeanne Moreau. Bardot's sexuality was her main asset and the most debated area of her persona.

Sexuality: feminist debates

Bardot epitomizes the attributes and paradoxes of the sex goddess. In her films, the camera systematically highlights her face and body in a suggestive manner; her full, pouting mouth and wild mane of hair are picked up by close-ups, while her breasts, hips, bottom, and legs are emphasized by her poses, clothes, and camera angles in a way which frequently evokes strip-tease or pin-up. Her sexuality and its impact are at the core of the narratives. *Et Dieu . . . créa la femme* and *La Vérité* are exemplary in this respect. Bardot's sexuality is a disruptive force which the community (Saint Tropez, provincial France, even Paris's bohemian Latin Quarter) tries to tame, with difficulty. Here, two paradoxes operate. First, there is a dichotomy between mise-en-scène and narrative. The work of the camera clearly 'objectifies' Bardot: in Laura Mulvey's terms, it emphasizes her 'to-be-looked-at-ness' (Mulvey 1975), and her films offer spectacular moments of display (for example, the mambo sequence at the end of *Et Dieu . . .*). At the same time, the narrative point of view gives the spectator more knowledge of her subjectivity than the characters around her possess; in *La Vérité*, the spectator knows long before the jury that she is 'not guilty'. Secondly, like the *femmes fatales* of American film noir, Bardot dominates her films, but is punished at the end: in *Et Dieu . . .* she is denied the man she desires, in *En cas de malheur*, *La Vérité*, and *Le Mépris* she dies brutally.

Bardot's originality, her 'scandal', however, comes from another, more powerful, paradox. In her films, unlike the more 'reactive' Monroe, she takes active pleasure in her body and expresses her own desire. In Simone de Beauvoir's much-quoted remark, in the sexual game, she is 'the hunter, not the prey' (Beauvoir 1960). This feature underlines the films' narratives— she goes after the men she wants, or from whom she wants things—and her performance: her direct gaze, insolent voice, rebellious or *j'men-foutiste* (careless) poses. This was reinforced by her off-screen promiscuous and non-conformist life-style: many lovers, several husbands, a child whom she rejected, as she confirms in her memoirs (Bardot 1996). Many of her songs reiterated this message, for instance her hit *Sidonie* ('Sidonie has more than one lover'). Sex, however, is a double-edged weapon for women; as de Beauvoir also pointed out, the Bardot persona called forth the most reactionary myth of the 'eternal feminine', a fantasy of an identity reduced to sex. As Vadim ineffably put it, she would be 'the impossible dream of married men'. Following Beauvoir, many feminist commentators have debated this paradox, some celebrating Bardot as a role model or a 'force of nature', others voicing more or less stringent criticism of a misogynistic representation. Among those celebrating Bardot's use of sexuality as empowering are Françoise Audé (1979) and Camille Paglia, speaking on the Channel 4 programme *Without Walls* (1994). Others are more critical, emphasizing the misogyny of the Bardot character (Burch and Sellier 1995) and others again concentrate on the ambivalence of the Bardot persona (Rihoit 1986; Vincendeau 1992) as well as her enduring fascination for feminists (Merck 1994). Ultimately, the irreducibility of the paradox is precisely what makes Bardot fascinating: rather than being either pure male fantasy, or affirmation of women's desire, she is both. The force of her star persona is to reconcile these two antagonistic aspects.

> **The paradox is precisely what makes Bardot fascinating: rather than being either pure male fantasy, or affirmation of women's desire, she is both. The force of her star persona is to reconcile these two antagonistic aspects.**

Bardot was truly a 'shocking' figure whose attitude was ahead of what was permitted to women at the time, illustrated by the passion and hostility she provoked (as detailed in her memoirs; Bardot 1996). Her films were banned in many provincial towns, in France and abroad, and her appeal, like the narrative conflicts of her films, arose simultaneously from her sexual aura and from its repression. It is noticeable that the later films in her career, for example *Si Don Juan était une femme* ('Don Juan was a Woman', 1973), made in a more liberal era, increased the display of her naked body—edging towards soft pornography—but lost audience appeal. She had served her purpose. Bardot's sexual persona was crucially connected to her youth and the era of her youth. While a mature sexuality was evoked, she occupied the territory of the sex kitten in her looks and performance style—her initials 'B.B.' ('bébé' in French) stand in for baby in both senses of infant and young woman. Furthermore, one may,

from a feminist point of view, see the limits of her sexual rebellion in the way it was always pitted against mother figures (usually hostile), but aimed at pleasing father figures. And the image of sexual liberation she proposed was, for women too, a fantasy: in 1950s Catholic France dominant sexual mores—especially outside Paris—were oppressive to women (though lenient to men); contraception and abortion were illegal.

The modernity of Bardot

As central as sexuality was to the Bardot phenomenon, it does not exhaust her novelty or interest. Bardot crystallized the importance and sexiness of youth during the wave of modernization that swept through post-war France, especially from the advent of de Gaulle's Fifth Republic in 1958. Bardot both anticipated and epitomized the rise of youth consumer power. Like James Dean in America, she embodied a notion of youthful rebellion, and her films dramatize generational conflicts. The paradox mentioned earlier in relation to her sexuality, of her triumph over the narrative of her films, and yet fateful endings can be reread as expressing an ambivalence towards modernity, desired yet feared. Here, a thorough examination of all her films would especially yield useful information on France's attitude to modernization.

If Bardot became such a model, if her hairstyle and clothes were widely imitated (Mylène Demongeot and Julie Christie are the most obvious examples), it is because she signalled a new era of fashion and behaviour. Compared with the rigid and expensive *couture* clothes of her mother's generation and previous French stars, such as Michèle Morgan and Edwige Feuillère, Bardot proposed a cheap and easy, yet sexy and glamorous, alternative: the famous gingham dresses, Capri pants, and striped sailors' tops, the working overalls wittily unbuttoned. When, in *Et Dieu . . . créa la femme*, she tells Curt Jurgens's rich woman friend that she bought her dress 'on the market', she symbolically signals the end of *haute couture* and the arrival of *prêt-à-porter*. Her 'unkempt' hairstyle equally makes nonsense of the neat perms of her predecessors, from Martine Carol to Danielle Darrieux, and her contemporaries Monroe and Dors. It is fitting that in the nostalgic 1990s her most prominent heiress is supermodel Claudia Schiffer (in the French cinema, one can look to Vanessa Paradis and Béatrice Dalle as latter-day versions of her uppity young sexual rebels).

But Bardot signalled modernity in more profound and ambivalent ways. Emerging at the time when the cinema started putting characters on the streets, the Bardot heroines took women characters from the domestic sphere into public space. True, these spaces tended to be, like Saint Tropez and central Paris, the playground of the rich. But it is also true that the subversiveness of this move can be measured by the frequency with which she was punished. In the eyes of the judge in *La Vérité*, one of her greatest crimes is being attracted to 'the bright lights and shop windows of the Champs-Élysées'. Another is that she is reading Simone de Beauvoir's *Les Mandarins*.

The key to Bardot's appeal, alongside her looks and sexual aura, was her 'naturalness'. It no doubt corresponds to a genuine desire for innocence, transparency, and freedom—very much a leitmotif in her memoirs—but it is a desire which also sums up her era. In this respect, one needs to explore further the emergence of 'the natural' in late 1950s and early 1960s culture, together with Bardot's 'non-performance' style of performance, her on- and off-screen association with children, animals, and what would now be called 'world music'. I would concur with feminist historian Michelle Perrot (1996), who argues that Bardot represented not so much a new woman as the male desire for that new woman. Furthermore, like all sex goddesses, she must not age, as the caricatures and comments that accompany photographs of her ageing show. However, unlike Monroe and Dors, Bardot did not suffer a tragic death. In her memoirs, which must rank as among the best in the genre, she reveals herself to be in turn exasperating, spoilt, and fully of her (bourgeois) class, but equally shrewd, tough, and extremely funny. She proves that there can be life and fun after the sex goddess. Her image, however, like the one she chose for the cover of her memoirs, is bound to remain eternally young and beautiful.

BIBLIOGRAPHY

Audé, Françoise (1979) *Ciné-modèles, Cinéma d'elles* (Lausanne: L'Age d'homme).

Bardot, Brigitte (1996), *Initiales B.B.: Mémoires* (Paris: Bernard Grasset).

Beauvoir, Simone de (1960), *Brigitte Bardot and the Lolita Syndrome* (London: André Deutsch and Weidenfeld & Nicolson).

Burch, Noël, and **Geneviève Sellier** (1995), *La Drôle de guerre des sexes du cinéma français* (Paris: Nathan).

Crawley, Tony (1975), *Bébé* (LSP books).

Dyer, Richard (1979), *Stars* (London: British Film Institute).

Evans, Peter (1972), *Bardot, Eternal Sex Goddess* (London: Leslie Frewin).

French, Sean (1994), *Bardot* (London: Pavilion Books).

Martin, Andy (1996), *Waiting for Bardot* (London: Faber & Faber).

Merck, Mandy (1994), *Perversions, Deviant Readings* (London: Virago).

Morin, Edgar (1957), *Les Stars* (Paris: Éditions du Seuil).

Mulvey, Laura (1975), 'Visual Pleasure and Narrative Cinema', *Screen*, 16/3: 6–18.

Perrot, Michelle (1996), interviewed on *Brigitte Bardot*, Arte, June.

Rihoit, Catherine (1986), *Brigitte Bardot, un mythe français* (Paris: Livre de poche).

Roberts, Glenys (1984), *Bardot: A Personal Biography* (London: Sidgwick & Jackson).

Robinson, Jeffrey, (1994) *Bardot: Two Lives* (London: Simon & Schuster).

Vadim, Roger (1976), *Memoirs of the Devil* (London: Arrow Books).

Vincendeau, Ginette (1992), 'The Old and the New: Brigitte Bardot in 1950s France', *Paragraph*, 15: 73–96.

14   British cinema

Andrew Higson

In the late 1960s two prominent British film critics complained that British cinema was an 'unknown cinema' (Lovell 1969), 'utterly amorphous, unclassified, unperceived' (Wollen 1969: 115). What Lovell and Wollen had in mind was not that there wasn't a popular film culture, or that audiences didn't watch British films or know how to make sense of them, but that British films had not been written about extensively by the new generation of critics, historians, and scholars. In the late 1960s little serious critical writing engaged with British cinema, past or present, and certainly not on the scale of the strong body of writing about American cinema that already existed. There were no major studies of key British directors, no influential surveys of the most important genres of the British cinema, no

detailed analyses of the output of individual studios. All this has changed in the last couple of decades with numerous publications classifying the history and present configuration of British cinema from the point of view of the dominant critical discourses of academic film studies. It would be misleading, however, to suggest that no serious attempts had been made to classify British cinema before this period.

Over the years various commentators have constructed their preferred versions of British cinema. Inevitably, this has brought competing definitions of British cinema, its strengths, and its weaknesses into the market-place of ideas. In each period, however, certain key ideas have prevailed over others so that it is possible to talk about the dominant critical discourses of the moment. The films which have the greatest prominence in the history books may occasionally be those which fared best at the box-office. But they are just as likely to be those which most met the approval of the prevailing critical discourse, or which captured the imagination of influential critics and intellectuals. The understanding of British cinema promoted by those discourses has been written into the histories of that cinema so that future generations have also been coloured by the same critical judgements. It is only in recent years that a new revisionist history of British cinema has emerged which both attempts to understand why certain films have appealed to particular critics, and goes behind the discourses mobilized by those critics to reassess, or even rediscover, other traditions of filmmaking.

It is in this spirit that I chart the historical development of the critical discourses which have dominated intellectual debate about cinema in Britain. Which are the films, the filmmakers, and the traditions of filmmaking that have been singled out for attention, and why? Why have other films been neglected? And how is British cinema understood as a national cinema, distinct from Hollywood, its main competitor?

The first efforts at writing about British cinema as a specifically national cinema with its own characteristics and sensibility can be found in the specialist film trade press in the 1910s. Already, some of the problems facing later commentators on British cinema dogged the writers of the 1910s. How could British films comprise a national cinema when American films were so popular with British audiences? If British-made films simply copied American styles and stories, could they really be considered British? And if international standards were defined by the films of the emergent Hollywood studio system, how should one evaluate British films which worked according to different standards? Were they to be seen as primitive, because they lagged behind the well-made American film, failing to use what were seen by many as the most up-to-date and appropriate methods for story construction and film style? Or were they to be seen as specifically British (which very often meant English), working over national themes in a distinctively national style?

A number of observers in the 1910s and early 1920s commented on what they saw as just such a national cinema, especially in the work of Cecil Hepworth's company. They focused on the many tasteful and respectable adaptations of canonic British literature which emerged in these years, and on those films which used a particular picturesque version of the English rural landscape for their setting. Perhaps the high point of this tradition of filmmaking, and the critical discourse which valorized it, was Hepworth's final feature film, *Comin' thro' the Rye*, an elegant and slow-moving literary adaptation, which was first released, significantly, during the British Film Weeks of 1923 and 1924 (Higson 1995).

From the perspective of the late 1920s, by which time the critical landscape had changed dramatically, such films, and the discourse which supported them, seemed far too parasitic upon the other more established and respectable arts, and especially literature and theatre. But this particular conception of the quality British film has never been entirely displaced. Tasteful and reverential adaptations of canonic novels or plays, performed by the cream of British theatre-trained actors, have always been able to curry critical favour, most recently in the form of heritage films such as the Merchant–Ivory version of E. M. Forster's *Howards End* (1993) (Higson 1993, 1996a). There are many who feel that this is what British filmmakers do best, even as there are others who feel this has little to do with what they would define as cinema (or the specifically cinematic).

This tension between different ideas of what constitutes good cinema can already be seen in the 1920s. If Hepworth's films dominated critical thinking about British cinema as a national cinema in the early 1920s, the agenda had changed radically by the late 1920s. In the intervening years, a new intellectual film culture had emerged in Britain, around the Film Society, founded in 1925, and specialist publications such as the periodical *Close Up*, which first appeared in 1927, and Paul Rotha's influential *The Film till Now*, first published in 1930. The critical discourses put into circulation in this period had a major impact over the next three decades on the way in which British cinema was understood and written about by those who preferred not to have their film tastes dictated by the box-office.

The prevailing concern was to find a way of treating cinema as an art form in line with the main tenets of modernist thinking. The most significant films from this point of view were those of the emergent European art cinema, and especially German Expressionism, French Impressionism, and Soviet montage cinema. British cinema was berated for failing to develop along the same lines as these film movements, and for remaining too attached to the pre-modernist sensibility of a Hepworth. Rotha and the *Close-Up* critics could perceive no British film movement with a distinctively modernist national style. The exception that proved the rule was the young Alfred Hitchcock, described in *Close-Up* as 'the one man in this country who can think cinema' (Castle 1930: 189). What was admired in Hitchcock's films was the commitment to visual narration, to metaphor and symbolism, to dynamic lighting and camera angles, and to the meaningfulness of editing, the juxtaposition of one shot with another (Ryall 1986).

By the early 1930s a distinctively British film movement was emerging, a movement that was subsequently to be promoted by its supporters as 'Britain's outstanding contribution to the cinema' (Arts Enquiry 1947: 1). This was the documentary movement, associated above all with the name of John Grierson. Interest in the movement was initially assured among intellectuals because of its commitment to a modernist understanding of cinema as an art form, and especially to montage. But it was the commitment to the realist representation of contemporary Britain and of ordinary British people which secured the reputation of the documentary movement as the foundation of a specifically national cinema (Hood 1983; Lovell and Hillier 1972). The documentarists not only made films, but also wrote extensively about their films (e.g. Rotha 1936; Hardy 1946). Their influence on thinking about British cinema can be seen in the extent to which subsequent histories privileged the documentary movement, as if this was the only development of significance in the British cinema of the 1930s.

> **It was the commitment to the realist representation of contemporary Britain and of ordinary British people which secured the reputation of the documentary movement as the foundation of a specifically national cinema.**

The commitment to realism and to the documentary idea persisted into the 1940s, under the peculiar conditions of wartime filmmaking. By now the centre-ground of critical debate had been won by a prominent group of mainly journalistic film reviewers (Ellis 1996) who were familiar with the achievements of the documentary film movement but who felt that the pure

documentary was too austere and needed to be tempered by the more imaginative and populist elements of the narrative feature film. These critics promoted a series of quality British films, from *In which we Serve* (1942) to *This Happy Breed* (1944) and beyond, which, like documentary, dealt with the contemporary lives of ordinary people. They saw in these films the emergence of a distinctively national cinema, in which the nation was represented as a consensual community, with people of different classes, regions, and genders pulling together for the common good (Barr 1977; Higson 1995).

One of the key features of the realist-dominated critical debates of the 1930s and 1940s was an anxiety about popular cinema and what was perceived as a standardized, artistically impoverished, trivial, and escapist mass culture. What was desired was a culturally respectable quality national cinema, which meant in effect a middle-class cinema. The preferred aesthetic was one of social responsibility, restraint, and sincerity, with individual desire subsumed within the communal enterprise. This was in contradistinction to what critics such as Roger Manvell (1944) saw as the irresponsibility of Hollywood's flamboyance, its wish-fulfilling fantasy and escapist individualism. Britain's popular genre filmmaking fared no better. Indeed, it has only been in the last couple of decades that Britain's popular cinema has been taken seriously within critical debate, with previously discredited genres re-evaluated as significant elements of the national cinema.

Take the costume picture, for instance, one of the most popular genres of the 1930s and 1940s. The effort to promote a realist quality national cinema during those years was pulled in two directions when faced with historical drama. On the one hand, such films seemed escapist, since they apparently refused to confront the realities of the present. On the other hand, certain costume pictures, such as Laurence Olivier's Shakespeare adaptations and David Lean's Dickens adaptations of the 1940s, seemed culturally respectable, either because they were adapted from canonic national literature, or because their representations of the past were promoted as authentic—that is, realist—historical re-creations. Either way, the vast majority of often extremely popular period pictures—the Gainsborough costume dramas like *The Wicked Lady* (1945), for instance—were dismissed by the critical consensus as unworthy of serious consideration.

That consensus became increasingly unstable as the

1940s progressed and, between the late 1940s and the mid-1960s, a split began to emerge. On the one hand, there was a continuing commitment to realism. This culminated in the celebration of, first, a series of documentaries made in the mid-1950s, promoted collectively as Free Cinema, and secondly, the 'kitchen sink' dramas made at the turn of the new decade by the same people who had now graduated to feature filmmaking (Hill 1986). From this point of view, films like *Saturday Night and Sunday Morning* (1960) and *This Sporting Life* (1963), about working-class life in provincial England, were seen to have inherited the legacy of the documentary movement of the 1930s and the quality film movement of the 1940s.

On the other hand, there was in this same period, through magazines such as *Sequence* and *Movie*, a renewed critical interest in cinemas outside Britain, from the post-war European art cinemas to Hollywood. What held these interests together was the concern for the idea of the director as author. When critics attached to this auteurist perspective turned their attention to British cinema, they could find almost no signs of the distinctive world-view or the dynamic and consistent style that they associated with the true film author. This was in many ways a return to the critical debates of the late 1920s, with Michael Powell this time the exception that proved the rule. Here was a filmmaker whose career had been virtually destroyed by the realist critics, who were unable to cope with the extravagance and internationalism of his films, and their poetic and often fantastic qualities. But it was precisely these qualities that appealed to *Movie*'s brand of auteurism and that singled out Powell from the rest of British cinema (Christie 1978).

Even so, critical support for Powell is hard to find in the 1960s. By the 1990s the tide had turned completely and, for many commentators, Powell's work between the 1930s and the 1960s, much of it made in collaboration with Emeric Pressburger, is considered among the most significant and interesting in the whole of British cinema history. This critical rehabilitation is a sign of the eclipse of the realist discourse in British film criticism, and the ascendance of auteurism, at least among mainstream film journalists.

As genre cinema has all but disappeared from the production schedules in Britain in the 1980s and 1990s, British cinema has been increasingly promoted in terms of authorship. What the mainstream film journalists have considered significant and distinctive about British cinema in this period has not been a sense of national style, or a coherent movement, or a concern with representing the nation, but the particular styles and world-views of a number of critically successful directors whose allegiance is more to the art-house than to the multiplex mainstream: Nicolas Roeg, Peter Greenaway, Derek Jarman, Stephen Frears, Mike Leigh . . . Even realist filmmakers, like Ken Loach, are now treated as auteurs (see Park 1984).

The other key development in critical discussion of British cinema in the last two decades has been the establishment of film studies as an academic discipline. In such circles, auteurism has played a much weaker, though still significant, role in critical debate about British cinema. That role can be seen in three books written on the edges of the academy in the first half of the 1970s which have since been very influential in academic writing about British cinema (see also Armes 1978). All three emerge from a *Movie*-influenced auteurist perspective, yet all go off in new directions.

Raymond Durgnat's *A Mirror for England* (1970) blends auteurist criticism with a thematic analysis of a whole range of popular British genre films of the late 1940s and 1950s. What is significant about this work is its revisionist concern with both fashionable films and the unfashionable, and the effort to read the films collectively in terms of how they speak to the nation about itself.

Charles Barr's *Ealing Studios* (1977) took a much narrower focus. Like Durgnat, Barr was concerned with how the films of Ealing Studios projected a particular image of the nation. And once again, the consideration of the studio was tinged with an auteurist interest in the work of particular directors, and a developing fascination with the fantastic as much as the realist.

David Pirie's *A Heritage of Horror* (1973) was a study of the British horror film in the post-war period. Like Barr, this involved looking at the work of key studios (notably Hammer) and key directors (notably Terence Fisher) in terms of style and theme. Perhaps the most radical aspect of Pirie's book was the fact that the object of study was one of the popular genres most despised by the adherents of the realist critical discourse which studies such as these were helping to displace.

Over the next two decades, the developments set in train by these three books were followed up with a wealth of writing, much of it emanating from the academy. The greater part of this writing has taken the form

'Poetic' and 'fantastic'—Powell and Pressburger's *A Matter of Life and Death* (1946)

of revisionist historiography, rewriting the history of British cinema from the point of view of new critical perspectives which reject the value judgements of earlier commentators. There have been perhaps three dominant concerns in this historical work: first, a critical reappraisal of the realist tradition; secondly, an attention to films which defy the norms of that tradition; and thirdly, an interest in cinema as institution and in the political economy of the film industry.

A key part of the revisionist enterprise has involved revisiting the films promoted within the realist discourse, examining them in the light of more recent critical debates, particularly in terms of the issues they raise around gender and national identity (e.g. Hill 1983, 1986; Lant 1991; Higson 1995; Dodd and Dodd 1996). At the same time, there has been a concern to foreground the assumptions about realism, about national cinema, and about cultural production which underlie the claims made for these films. The concern thus shifted from whether or not these films were realist to why they seemed realist (and significant) to a particular group of critics. This meant the films and the discourses through which they were valorized were explored in light of their socio-historical conditions of existence. While the conclusions reached often seemed very different from those of Grierson, Manvell, and others, it has been argued that, simply by virtue of attending to the same body of films, those films retain a central place in our understanding of British cinema, at the expense of other, marginalized British film traditions (Cook 1996).

> **A key part of the revisionist enterprise has involved revisiting the films promoted within the realist discourse, examining them in the light of more recent critical debates, particularly in terms of the issues they raise around gender and national identity.**

If one of the concerns of recent academic writing about British cinema has been to reconsider the documentary-realist debate, another has been precisely to bring to critical attention those films which had fallen outside the terms of that debate. This tendency had already been set in motion by Durgnat, Barr, and Pirie,

given their evident interest in the popular and the fantastic. Auteurism has played an important revisionist role here in promoting previously neglected film-makers as significant artists. Ian Christie's (1985) re-evaluation of the work of Powell and Pressburger is the most prominent example of auteurist writing revising the received wisdoms of British film criticism. Even so, it remains attached to a conception of film as an art which leaves little place for the popular. Nevertheless, it is the sustained attempt to find worth in popular but discredited genre filmmaking, and especially horror, comedy, and the woman's film, which has been one of the defining characteristics of academic writing of the last two decades (e.g. Hutchings 1993; Murphy 1989, 1992; Jordan 1983; Medhurst 1986; Petley 1986; Landy 1991; King 1996).

If we return to the popular costume dramas of the 1930s and 1940s, so harshly dismissed by the realist critics, we can find more recent historians arguing that such films are vital to any consideration of British cinema as a national cinema precisely because of their popularity (Richards 1984; Landy 1991; Harper 1994; Cook 1996). Moreover, it is argued, they should not be seen as escapist: very often they confront contemporary fears, anxieties, desires, and pleasures by displacing those concerns into another time and place. And, as Pam Cook (1996) has shown, they have also played a vital role in enabling audiences, especially female audiences, to construct their identities in relation to ideas of the nation, *inter alia*.

On occasion, it seems the popular is valued simply because it is popular, and there is a refusal to confront the problems and complexities of popular films and film culture. On the whole, however, such work provides a powerful antidote to the masculinism and élitism of other traditions of writing about British cinema.

A third tendency in recent work on British cinema has been the move away from textual analysis and evaluation towards an interest in institutions, state policy, censorship, and related issues. This work has been characterized above all by its attention to archival empirical detail, following in the tradition of Rachael Low's now standard multi-volume *History of the British Film* (1948–85). The tendency can be seen at work in John Barnes's excavations of the very early years of British filmmaking (1976, 1983, 1988, 1992), and in Robert Murphy's revisionist surveys of the 1940s and 1960s (1989, 1992). There have also been thoroughgoing investigations of key aspects of the organization of the cinema industry (e.g. Dickinson and Street 1985;

Macnab 1993) and of the systems of censorship of British films (e.g. Richards 1984; Aldgate 1995).

Informing each of these three tendencies in recent writing about British cinema have been a series of often overlapping critical perspectives, including structuralism and post-structuralism, feminism, and cultural history. Thus much of the recent writing about films as texts, whether inside or outside the realist canon, has resisted the assumption (sometimes apparent in more archive-based work) that meanings can effortlessly be read off film texts. They have employed the insights of structuralist and post-structuralist theory to reveal the narrational and ideological complexities of texts and their potential for multiple readings. Such work, however, frequently turns a blind eye to questions of historical reception (e.g. Landy 1991).

> **If we return to the popular costume dramas of the 1930s and 1940s, so harshly dismissed by the realist critics, we can find more recent historians arguing that such films are vital to any consideration of British cinema as a national cinema precisely because of their popularity.**

The influence of feminist perspectives has encouraged an interest in questions of gender, displacing the focus on class in earlier debates about the documentary-realist tradition. This has opened up to investigation a whole array of highly popular films, addressed primarily to a female audience, which had previously escaped the attention of earlier generations of critics.

The turn to cultural history has been equally influential, situating film within a much broader set of historical coordinates. Thus, there have been studies looking at the ways in which popular genre filmmaking draws on already established indigenous cultural traditions (e.g. Ryall 1986; Higson 1995). Others have explored the relationship between prevailing social, political, and economic forces and the cinema which emerged from them (e.g. Chanan 1980; Richards and Aldgate 1983; Hill 1986; Lant 1991). Yet others have examined the formation of popular taste and its impact on the reception of films by audiences (Harper 1994).

It is clearly no longer possible to talk about British cinema as an unknown cinema. It has always been known in some form or other, even if changing critical perspectives mean that the boundaries are constantly being redrawn. The realist discourse promoted a very narrow understanding of British cinema. More recent debates have made it possible to acknowledge the diversity and richness of British filmmaking, from the actualities and gag films at the turn of the century to the Ivor Novello star vehicles of the 1920s, from early Hitchcock to Sally Potter, from the documentary movement to Hammer horror, from Alexander Korda's costume films of the 1930s to *My Beautiful Laundrette* (1985), *Naked* (1993), and *Trainspotting* (1995), from vulgar comedy to the new black British cinema.

Charles Barr (1986a), has suggested what is most exciting about British cinema is not the realist in itself, but the dynamic relation between the real and the fantastic. None the less, it still seems reductive to define a whole film culture in terms of a binary opposition, however productive that opposition may be. The complexity, fluidity, and heterogeneity of British cinema constantly escapes exhaustive analysis. The realist critics could only define the national cinema in terms of an aesthetic of restraint and a thematic of consensual community by ignoring some of the most popular films of the moment, films which often transgressed those very conventions.

Each of the discourses which has dominated British film criticism has had its own axe to grind, its own favoured films, its own version of the national cinema. In the relativism of the 1980s and 1990s, no single discourse predominates over all others. In collections such as Curran and Porter (1983), Barr (1986b), and Higson (1996b), a sense of the diversity of British cinema emerges. If that in itself sounds like a celebration of a national cinema rich enough to diversify but secure within its own boundaries, it is important to remind ourselves that those boundaries are in fact by no means secure. Some of the most 'English' films of the 1930s were made by Alexander Korda, a Hungarian; some of the most 'English' films of the last decade were made by James Ivory, an American. In both cases, they worked with a truly cosmopolitan team of collaborators. If the realist discourse defined British cinema against Hollywood and in terms of a narrow nationalism, it is equally possible to define British cinema in terms of internationalism.

Another avenue of possibilities has been opened up by writers who have attempted to deconstruct the consensual and predominantly Anglo-Saxon English nationalism of British cinema by exploring the differing constructions of 'nationality' in Scottish, Welsh, and Irish cinema (e.g. McArthur 1982; Dick 1990; Berry 1994; Hill *et al.* 1994) and the cinema of the new black Britons (e.g. Mercer 1988; Malik 1996). Such writing—and the filmmaking it discusses—is very much about redrawing the boundaries of national cinema, revising long-established wisdoms about the 'Britishness' of British cinema.

BIBLIOGRAPHY

Aldgate, Anthony (1995), *Censorship and the Permissive Society: British Cinema and Theatre 1955–1965* (Oxford: Clarendon Press).

Armes, Roy (1978), *A Critical History of British Cinema* (London: Secker & Warburg).

Arts Enquiry (1947), *The Factual Film* (London: PEP and Oxford University Press).

Barnes, John (1976), *The Beginnings of the Cinema in Britain* (London: David & Charles).

—— (1983), *The Rise of the Cinema in Britain* (London: Bishopsgate Press).

—— (1988), *Pioneers of the British Cinema* (London: Bishopsgate Press).

—— (1992), *Filming the Boer War* (London: Bishopsgate Press).

Barr, Charles (1977/1993), *Ealing Studios* (London: Cameron & Tayleur and David & Charles; rev. London: Studio Vista).

—— (1986a), 'Introduction: Amnesia and Schizophrenia', in Barr (1986b).

*—— (1986b), *All our Yesterdays: Ninety Years of British Cinema* (London: British Film Institute).

Berry, David (1994), *Wales and Cinema: The First Hundred Years* (London: British Film Institute and University of Wales Press).

Castle, Hugh (1930), 'Attitude and Interlude', *Close Up*, 7/3: 184–90.

Chanan, Michael (1980/1996), *The Dream that Kicks: The Prehistory and Early Years of Cinema in Britain* (London: Routledge).

Christie, Ian (ed.) (1978), *Powell, Pressburger and Others* (London: British Film Institute).

—— (1985/1994), *Arrows of Desire: The Films of Michael Powell and Emeric Pressburger* (London: Waterstone).

Cook, Pam (1996), *Fashioning the Nation: Costume and Identity in British Cinema* (London: British Film Institute).

*Curran, James, and Vincent Porter (eds.) (1983), *British Cinema History* (London: Weidenfeld & Nicolson).

Dick, Eddie (ed.) (1990), *From Limelight to Satellite: A Scottish Film Book* (London: Scottish Film Council and British Film Institute).

Dickinson, Margaret, and Sarah Street (1985), *Cinema and State: The Film Industry and the British Government 1927–1984* (London: British Film Institute).

Dodd, Kathryn, and Philip Dodd (1996), 'Engendering the Nation: British Documentary Film 1930–1939', in Higson (1996b).

Durgnat, Raymond (1970), *A Mirror for England: British Movies from Austerity to Affluence* (London: Faber & Faber).

Ellis, John (1996), 'The Quality Film Adventure: British Critics and the Cinema 1942–1948', in Higson (1996b).

Hardy, Forsyth (ed.) (1946/1979), *Grierson on Documentary* (London: Faber & Faber).

Harper, Sue (1994), *Picturing the Past: The Rise and Fall of the British Costume Film* (London: British Film Institute).

Higson, Andrew (1993), 'Re-Presenting the National Past: Nostalgia and Pastiche in the Heritage Film', in Lester Friedman (ed.), *Fires were Started: British Cinema and Thatcherism* (Minneapolis: University of Minnesota Press; London: UCL Press).

*—— (1995), *Waving the Flag: Constructing a National Cinema in Britain* (Oxford: Clarendon Press).

—— (1996a), 'The Heritage Film and British Cinema', in Higson (1996b).

*—— (ed.) (1996b), *Dissolving Views: Key Writings on British Cinema* (London: Cassell).

Hill, John (1983), 'Working Class Realism and Sexual Reaction: Some Theses on the British "New Wave"', in Curran and Porter (1983).

—— (1986), *Sex, Class and Realism: British Cinema 1956–1963* (London: British Film Institute).

—— Martin, McLoone, and Paul Hainsworth (eds.) (1994), *Border Crossing: Film in Ireland, Britain and Europe* (Belfast: Institute of Irish Studies; London: British Film Institute).

Hood, Stuart (1983), 'The Documentary Film Movement', in Curran and Porter (1983).

Hutchings, Peter (1993), *Hammer and Beyond* (Manchester: Manchester University Press).

Jordan, Marion (1983), 'Carry On . . . Follow that Stereotype', in Curran and Porter (1983).

King, Justine (1996), 'Crossing Thresholds: The Contemporary British Woman's Film', in Higson (1996b).

Landy, Marcia (1991), *British Genres: Cinema and Society 1930–1960* (Princeton: Princeton University Press).

Lant, Antonia (1991), *Blackout: Reinventing Women for Wartime British Cinema* (Princeton: Princeton University Press).

Lovell, Alan (1969), 'British Cinema: The Unknown Cinema', stencilled seminar paper (London: British Film Institute Education Department).

—— and **Jim Hillier** (1972), *Studies in Documentary* (London: Secker & Warburg and BFI).

Low, Rachael (1948–85), *A History of the British Film* (London: George Allen & Unwin): *1896–1906* (with Roger Manvell; 1948); *1906–1914* (1949); *1914–1918* (1950); *1918–1929* (1971); *1929–1939* (*Film Making in 1930s Britain*; 1985).

McArthur, Colin (ed.) (1982), *Scotch Reels: Scotland in Cinema and Television* (London: British Film Institute).

MacNab, Geoffrey (1993), *J. Arthur Rank and the British Film Industry* (London: Routledge).

Malik, Sarita (1996), 'Beyond "The Cinema of Duty"? The Pleasures of Hybridity: Black British Film of the 1980s and 1990s', in Higson (1996b).

Manvell, Roger (1944/1946), *Film* (London: Penguin).

Medhurst, Andy (1986), 'Music Hall and British Cinema', in Barr (1986b).

Mercer, Kobena (ed.) (1988), *Black Film, British Cinema*, ICA Document No. 7 (London: Institute of Contemporary Arts).

Murphy, Robert (1989), *Realism and Tinsel: Cinema and Society in Britain 1939–1948* (London: Routledge).

—— (1992), *Sixties British Cinema* (London: British Film Institute).

Park, James (1984), *Learning to Dream* (London: Faber).

Petley, Julian (1986), 'The Lost Continent', in Barr (1986b).

Pirie, David (1973), *A Heritage of Horror: The English Gothic Cinema 1946–1972* (New York: Avon).

Richards, Jeffrey (1984), *The Age of the Dream Palace: Cinema and Society in Britain 1930–1939* (London: Routledge & Kegan Paul).

—— and **Anthony Aldgate** (1983), *Best of British: Cinema and Society 1930–1970* (Oxford: Blackwell).

Rotha, Paul (1930), *The Film till Now* (London: Jonathan Cape).

—— (1936/1952), *Documentary Film* (London: Faber & Faber).

Ryall, Tom (1986), *Alfred Hitchcock and the British Cinema* (London: Croom Helm).

Wollen, Peter (1969), *Signs and Meaning in the Cinema* (London: Secker & Warburg and British Film Institute).

Ireland and cinema

Martin McLoone

In his *Irish Filmography*, Kevin Rockett makes the point that, of over 2,000 feature films on an Irish theme produced world-wide since the beginnings of the cinema, rather less than 200 have been made in Ireland itself and most of these only in the last fifteen years or so (Rockett 1996). This stark statistic helps to explain much about the nature of the cinema debate in and about Ireland. On the one hand, despite the relative poverty of indigenous film production until the 1980s, Ireland has enjoyed a considerable presence in the cinemas of other cultures, especially that of the United States and the United Kingdom, and Irish men and women have exerted perhaps a disproportionate influence on the development of cinema, again especially in the United States. The result has been that a lot of literature on the cinema and Ireland has been concerned to excavate the contribution of the Irish to the development of the cinema and to write up a 'lost' history, both of the Irish in cinema and of Ireland in cinema.

On the other hand, this considerable presence has drawn the attention of scholars in both the United States and Ireland to the representation of Irishness contained in these 'outsider' views. Debate in Ireland itself, not surprisingly, has focused on the need not only to develop an indigenous film industry but to develop a film culture that is sensitive to the issues of representation and which is prepared to interrogate the nature of any indigenous cinematic response to these domi-

nant images. In this regard, the key academic work continues to be Kevin Rockett, Luke Gibbons, and John Hill's *Cinema and Ireland* (1987), published originally at a crucial point in the development of both an indigenous film industry and the emergence of a recognizable critical film culture. In retrospect, it can now be seen not only that this study achieved a synthesis and development of much work that had preceded it but that it also mapped out the critical agenda for debates that were to follow.

Rockett's historical analysis of film production in Ireland since the earliest days of the cinema encapsulates a number of key themes that continue to have relevance in Ireland today and are echoed in film cultures across the globe: the difficulty of a small and economically weak country in sustaining a consistent level of film production without state support; the need for film lobbyists to mount a cultural as well as an economic argument for such state support; and finally the need for a national film culture to be aware of the dangers inherent in an overly essentialist response to the dominance of more powerful cultures, like Hollywood.

Indeed, Rockett's historical survey considers the effect on the cinema in Ireland of the narrow and restrictive mores of Catholic nationalism in the period down to the 1960s. Censorship, and a negative or defensive attitude to the cinema in general, created a cultural and ideological impediment to the growth of native filmmaking that was as decisive as the lack of economic support. In later writings, Rockett argues that in the censorious and morally constricting culture that emerged in nationalist Ireland, the images that emanated from Hollywood, and which dominated the cinemas of Catholic Ireland from the 1920s to the 1960s, were positively liberating (Rockett 1991). The polemical thrust of this argument has been picked up by other critics (McLoone 1994) and has considerably muddied the debate over what constitutes a national cinema in Ireland—once again a polemic that is familiar to parallel debates in other cultures.

Rockett's later concerns have focused on what he has called 'the cinema of the diaspora'—precisely that large and influential Irish presence in the cinema of the United States in particular (Rockett and Finn 1995; Rockett 1996). His *Irish Filmography* (1996) represents the most comprehensive listing of the field, but the impulse to track and critically engage with this cinematic heritage has long been a concern with film scholars of Hollywood's ethnic representations. Much of this literature has been concerned merely with establishing the Irish contribution as a matter of historical record—as in Liam O'Leary's (1980) study of Dublin-born Rex Ingram, for example—or tracing the emerging cinematic stereotypes embodied in artists of Irish descent, such as James Cagney, Spencer Tracy, and Maureen O'Hara (Clark and Lynch 1980; Slide 1988; Curran 1989). The most interesting explorations of the Irish influence have often been in the context of auteur studies of eminent filmmakers of Irish descent, and the Irishness of John Ford, a preoccupation with many critics, is paradigmatic here (McBride and Wilmington 1974; Ford 1979; Anderson 1981).

The most sustained work on the Irish influence on American cinema is Lee Lourdeaux (1990) and it is here that the purely historical gives way to a deeper concern with questions of ethnicity (a comparative study of Irish and Italian in this case). His analysis of the Irish and Italian presence in Hollywood emphasizes the essentially dialectic relationship between the global and the local, between the universal and the particular, and draws attention to the fact that Hollywood itself is deeply imbued with the cultural influences of many of those indigenous cultures now struggling to find a cinematic presence in its global shadow. Lourdeaux's approach to the question of ethnicity also demonstrates how the cinematic debate about Ireland and Irishness now exists in a wider cultural studies, as much as in a purely film studies, framework. This is a trend

again anticipated in Rockett *et al.*'s *Cinema and Ireland*, in the section written by Gibbons (1987).

Gibbons approaches the cinematic debates about representation and Ireland through a wide-ranging consideration of pre-cinematic and extra-cinematic cultural discourses (eighteenth- and nineteenth-century European romanticism, the melodramas of Dion Boucicault, landscape painting, travel writing, and the myth of the West in Ireland and America are some of his reference-points). Unlike Rockett, whose rejection of nationalism as a motivating impulse behind an indigenous cinema is clear and unequivocal, Gibbons is more concerned to explore the radical edges of nationalism, and of cultural practice in general, precisely to rediscover the 'unapproved roads' that were blocked and the 'unruly and refractory narratives of vernacular history' that were silenced by the hegemony of Catholic nationalism. While clearly rejecting essentialism and sensitive to the materialist nature of cultural production, Gibbons is, none the less, concerned to establish the 'peculiarities' of the Irish cultural experience and to validate those films, indigenous or international, that he sees as laying bare the nature of these peculiarities. Thus a film as influential and as controversial in its depiction of the Irish as John Ford's *The Quiet Man* (1953) is reread in a positive light, its playfulness and internal self-consciousness revealing the 'ability of certain strains of Irish romanticism to conduct a process of self-interrogation, to raise doubts at key moments about their own veracity, which cuts across any tendency to take romantic images as realistic accounts of Irish life' (Gibbons 1987: 200).

This project is amplified in a series of important and influential pieces gathered together in a later publication (Gibbons 1996) where his focus has shifted more to the 'myth of modernization', which he sees, if anything, as a more paralysing hegemony than the nationalist myths which it has attempted to supplant. For Gibbons, tradition is not necessarily always reactionary and modernity is not always progressive and in his rejection of the grand narrative of modernization, his postmodern, post-colonial arguments echo many of the concerns posed by post-colonial theorists of other cultures.

Gibbons is motivated by a desire to theorize the constituents of a national culture, including a national cinema, and as the production of indigenous filmmaking gathered pace in the early 1990s, stimulated by an enlightened government funding policy (the

Irish culture—complexity and contradictions (*Maeve*, 1981)

emergence of which is traced by Rockett 1994), the question of what the parameters of an 'Irish' national cinema might be has become more acute. For example, McLoone agrees with Gibbons that the stark juxtaposition between the local and the global, or the centre and the periphery, is more complex and more dialectical than it is often assumed (McLoone 1990, 1994). In his analysis of recent indigenous filmmaking, he appropriates from postmodern theory the concept of 'critical regionalism' (Frampton 1985) to explain the thematic and filmic concerns of the emerging Irish 'new wave' (for example, the films of Bob Quinn, Joe Comerford, Cathal Black, Pat Murphy, Margo Harkin, and many of the younger directors of short films who emerged in great numbers after 1987). In his analysis, films like Black's *Our Boys* (1980) and *Pigs* (1984),

Comerford's *Reefer and the Model* (1987), Murphy's *Maeve* (1981) and *Ann Devlin* (1984), and Harkin's *Hush-a-Bye Baby* (1989), are seen to appropriate the forms of dominant narrative cinema and not merely to mimic them. The best of recent Irish cinema, therefore, explores indigenous culture, in all its contradictions, with an outsider's eye, but at the same time subjects this outsider's perspective to the peculiar interrogation of the local culture. It is a dialectical *pas de deux* and it achieves the double effect of avoiding a tendency towards essentialism while offering a critical response to the influences of the outside.

Central to McLoone's project is the relationship between the local and the global—in cinematic terms the relationship between indigenous filmmaking and Hollywood. He is concerned that a national cinema (and national cultural policies) should avoid falling between 'a self-defeating essentialism and a self-abusing domination'. But unlike Gibbons's rejection of the myth of modernization, McLoone argues that it is precisely the grand narrative of modernization, as represented in the increasingly global cinema of Hollywood, which has stimulated the great national cinemas of Europe over the last fifty years. Thus for him, Italian Neo-Realism, the French New Wave, New German Cinema, and even the intermittent flurries from Australia, New Zealand, and a host of other cultures not normally associated with sustained film production, can all be described as forms of critical regionalism. The difference in perspective between Gibbons and McLoone, therefore, might be characterized thus: while the latter offers a definition of national cinema as a critical regionalism, the former might propose a notion of 'critical nationalism'.

The concern, however, to theorize and understand what might constitute a national culture and a national cinema in Ireland is considerably complicated by the contested nature of Irish identity in the first place. The important differences of emphasis in the work of Rockett, Gibbons, and McLoone indicates a much wider debate that exists in culture and politics generally (especially in literary and historical studies) about identity in Ireland. The revisionist, anti-revisionist, and postcolonial theoretical positions now being articulated and challenged have been given added urgency by the increasing modernization of the Irish economy and the gathering pace of Europeanization. However, hanging over these sometimes strident and increasingly acrimonious academic debates is the shadow of Northern Ireland, where contested notions of identity have led to civil strife, violence, and over 3,000 deaths in the last thirty years and which, recently, has witnessed increasing sectarian polarization. It is hardly surprising, therefore, that the representation of Northern Ireland has been a major concern for media academics in Ireland generally (Rolston 1990; Butler 1995; Miller 1994) and that the fall-out from the crisis in Northern Ireland has been explored in film and television studies in particular (McLoone 1991, 1996; Hill et al. 1994).

Again, though, the seminal study is in Rockett et al.'s Cinema and Ireland, in the section written by Hill on the cinema's representation of violence in Ireland (Hill (1987). Like his co-authors Rockett and Gibbons, Hill is concerned to place his study in a historical context. He traces the dominant modes of representation in British cinema back to earlier periods of colonial and imperial imagery and locates a central thrust to the image of the Irish that has endured. Violence, he argues, is denied a political or historical context and is represented as a 'manifestation of the Irish character', a tragic flaw inherent in the Irish themselves. Thus, in Hill's analysis, a 'humanist classic' of British cinema, Carol Reed's Odd Man Out (1947), is revisited and reinterpreted in the light of this long tradition of negative imagery. Its refusal to deal directly with the causes of the violence which it portrays and its emphasis on the tragic romanticism of James Mason's gunman-on-the-run have the effect of reinforcing the dominant British view that violence in Ireland is the fault of the Irish themselves. Interestingly enough, Hill applies his analysis to two films made in Ireland by Irish filmmakers—Neil Jordan's Angel (1981) and Pat O'Connor's Cal (1984)—and identifies the same tendency to ignore the historical or socio-political context of the violence in Northern Ireland, as if the dominant mode of representation has become so internalized that it is reproduced unconsciously, even by the Irish themselves.

The reasons for this, though, are matters more of cinematic form than merely failures of perception by individual filmmakers. These formal matters are pursued in more detail in a later piece by Hill, on the political thriller in general and Ken Loach's Hidden Agenda (1990) in particular (Hill 1991). In raising these issues, Hill revisits the debate on film aesthetics and politics that informed much film theory in the 1960s and 1970s and considers again the problems inherent in trying to employ dominant narrative and realist forms in order to explore complex political realities or promote radical politics. The failure of Hidden Agenda to deal with the politics of Northern Ireland (reducing, as it does, complex issues to little more than a conspiracy theory that stretches the viewer's credulity) is, he argues, a failure of form. Interestingly enough, as a solution, Hill canvasses not a film practice based around the modernist avant-garde, which was the argument of radical film theorists in the 1960s and 1970s, but a form of 'third cinema', where matters of form are approached through an engagement with, rather than a rejection of, dominant forms and exhibit a 'sensitivity to place'. In this, he comes close to McLoone's notion of 'critical regionalism', where questions of form are motivated by the encounter of dominant forms with a local cultural agenda. It might be noted here that many of the indigenous films discussed

CRITICAL APPROACHES TO WORLD CINEMA

by all these writers do evince a concern with film aesthetics (perhaps, especially, those of Comerford and Murphy) and that, of the film scholars who have engaged with these films, it is Rockett who has canvassed most clearly for a politically engaged avant-garde, locating in the work of the younger filmmakers, emerging through the short-filmmaking route, a greater formal and political conservatism.

There is one final important point to note about the nature of film scholarship in Ireland. Although the work of the male academics discussed above is deeply informed by feminist criticism, it is perhaps surprising that there has been no concerted feminist intervention itself in Irish film studies. This is all the more surprising given that many of the films produced in Ireland over the years have been made by women and explore the questions of identity through a feminist concern with gender (especially, as in the work of Pat Murphy and Margo Harkin, where the gender issues intersect with the wider politics of Irish nationalism). Both Murphy (in Johnston 1981) and Harkin (1991) have themselves contributed to the film debates in detailed discussions of their filmmaking agenda. And, in the wider cultural ferment in Ireland, women have contributed with growing influence to a whole range of literary, historical, and sociological debates, reflecting the strength of feminist studies generally in Ireland and the importance of gender politics to these wider concerns. However, in strictly film studies terms, there have been relatively few direct feminist interventions.

One of these was an important critique of the gender politics of Neil Jordan's The Crying Game (1992), in which Sarah Edge (1995) has argued that the radical nature of the film's discussion of male gender issues was at the expense of the woman character, and that, consequently, the portrayal of women and nationalism in the film may be seen as positively reactionary. The Crying Game, of course, has engendered a mini academic industry in the United States and has featured as a key text both in queer film theory and in the growing academic field of Irish studies. The final irony, then, of film scholarship in Ireland, and the much larger cultural discourse of which it is a part, is that its concerns with nationality, definitions of Irishness, and identity no longer seem like the archaic lingerings of a pre-modern era, as it has sometimes been characterized. On the contrary, these questions now seem to be at the very cutting edge of contemporary cultural debate.

BIBLIOGRAPHY

Anderson, Lindsay (1981), About John Ford (London: Plexus).

Butler, David (1995), The Trouble with Reporting Northern Ireland: The British State, the Broadcast Media and Non-fictional Representations of the Conflict (Aldershot: Avebury).

Clark, Dennis, and William J. Lynch (1980), 'Hollywood and Hibernia: The Irish in the Movies', in Randall M. Miller (ed.), The Kaleidoscopic Lens: How Hollywood Views Ethnic Groups (Englewood Cliffs, NJ: James S. Ozer).

Curran, Joseph M. (1989), Hibernian Green on the Silver Screen: The Irish and American Movies (Westport, Conn.: Greenwood Press).

Edge, Sarah (1995), '"Women are Trouble, did you know that, Fergus?" Neil Jordan's The Crying Game', Feminist Review, 50 (Summer), 173–86.

Ford, Dan (1979), Pappy: The Life of John Ford (Englewood Cliffs, NJ: Prentice-Hall).

Frampton, Kenneth (1985), 'Towards a Critical Regionalism: Six Points for an Architecture of Resistance', in Hal Foster (ed.), Postmodern Culture (London: Pluto Press).

Gibbons, Luke (1987), 'Romanticism, Realism and Irish Cinema', in Rockett et al. (1987).

—— (1996), Transformations in Irish Culture (Cork: Cork University Press).

Harkin, Margo (1991), 'Broadcasting in a Divided Community', transcript of a talk given at a symposium at the University of Ulster, in McLoone (1991).

Hill, John (1987), 'Images of Violence', in Rockett et al. (1987).

—— (1991), 'Hidden Agenda: Politics and the Thriller', Circa Arts Magazine, 57 (May–June), 36–41.

*—— Martin McLoone, and Paul Hainsworth (eds.) (1994), Border Crossing: Film in Ireland, Britain and Europe (Belfast: Institute of Irish Studies; London: British Film Institute).

Johnston, Claire (1981), 'Maeve: Interview with Pat Murphy', Screen, 22/4: 54–71.

Lourdeaux, Lee (1990), Italian and Irish Filmmakers in America: Ford, Capra, Coppola and Scorsese (Philadelphia: Temple University Press).

McBride, Joseph, and Michael Wilmington (1974), John Ford (London: Secker & Warburg).

McLoone, Martin (1990), 'Lear's Fool, Goya's Dilemma', Circa Arts Magazine, 50 (Mar–Apr.), 54–8.

—— (ed.) (1991), Culture, Identity and Broadcasting in Ireland: Local Issues, Global Perspectives (Belfast: Institute of Irish Studies).

*—— (1994), 'National Cinema and Cultural Identity: Ireland and Europe', in Hill et al. (1994).

—— (ed.) (1996), Broadcasting in a Divided Community: Seventy Years of the BBC in Northern Ireland (Belfast: Institute of Irish Studies).

Miller, David (1994), *Don't Mention the War: Northern Ireland, Propaganda and the Media* (London: Pluto Press).

O'Leary, Liam (1980), *Rex Ingram: Master of the Silent Cinema* (Dublin: Academy Press).

Rockett, Kevin (1987), 'History, Politics and Irish Cinema', in Rockett *et al.* (1987).

—— (1991), 'Aspects of the Los Angelesation of Ireland', *Irish Communications Review*, 1: 20–5.

—— (1994), 'Culture, Industry and Irish Cinema', in Hill *et al.* (1994).

—— (1996), *Irish Filmography* (Dublin: Red Mountain Press).

—— and **Eugene Finn** (1995), *Still Irish: A Century of the Irish in Film* (Dublin: Red Mountain Press).

*—— **Luke Gibbons,** and **John Hill** (1987/1988), *Cinema and Ireland* (Beckenham: Croom Helm; rev. London: Routledge).

Rolston, Bill (ed.) (1990), *The Media and Northern Ireland: Covering the Troubles* (London: Macmillan).

Slide, Anthony (1988), *The Cinema and Ireland* (Jefferson, NC: McFarland).

16 Australian cinema

Elizabeth Jacka

Debates in national cinema

Australian scholars (such as Stern 1995; Creed 1993; Berry 1994; Martin 1993; Jayamanne 1994, 1995; Routt 1992; Brooks 1992; Hodsdon 1992; and Mortimer 1995) have made a significant contribution to the discipline of screen studies and the study of various non-Australian cinemas, most notably those of the United States and various countries in Asia. However, it is undoubtedly in the area of Australian cinema that most work has been done. No other country has such a rich tradition of theorizing national cinema, and it is a pity that the scope and variety of the work is not better known in other places. Of course, this is precisely Australia's dilemma—it is not metropolitan enough to be in the international mainstream of either intellectual or artistic life, and not marginal enough to be exotic. It was the struggle to come to terms with, and find a response to, this intermediate position that produced the original polemic around the need for a national cinema, and the film studies literature that has emerged partly grew up in support of the campaign to institute an Australian film industry and culture.

The growth of a distinctive Australian film studies literature was intimately connected with the re-establishment of the Australian film industry after 1970. Just as government intervention and support was a crucial ingredient in the development of a renewed Australian industry, so it also played a role in fostering an Australian film culture, including the support for critical works which examined the history, politics, and aesthetics of Australian cinema. There has been a fruitful collaboration between writers, both inside and outside the academy, publishers, and government-funded film culture organizations which has led to a large body of work, especially on Australian cinema history.

The first serious critical writing about Australian cinema—the first that had some overt connection with the discipline of film studies that was rapidly emerging in the United Kingdom, Europe, and the United States appeared in the 1970s. However, some of the terms which were to govern writing about Australian film well into the 1980s had been set by a series of influential articles from the 1950s and 1960s. In a 1958 article which has come to be seen as the manifesto for a national film industry, and which is resonantly entitled 'No Daydreams of our Own: The film as National Self-Expression', 'Tom Weir' (actually Tom Fitzgerald, editor of the influential journal *Nation*), wrote:

It is typical of the undeveloped personality of our people that we have practically no indigenous films. Every standard that our impressionable mass audiences imbibe is the standard of an alien culture. Like pre-Chaucerian England, tugged between Italy and France, we are also torn between two dominant cultures, those of America and Britain. No wonder our voices are so thin and so weakly articulated as to be barely audible to visitors when they first step ashore. The daydreams we get from celluloid are not Australian daydreams. Our kingdom is not of this world. (Weir 1985: 144)

Along with the work of other significant writers and campaigners, such as Sylvia Lawson (1965, 1979), this was to set the tone for much of the work on Australian cinema in the 1970s and into the 1980s. It was framed by the idea of a national culture and involved a set of explorations of Australia's complicated colonial and post-colonial relationships with Britain and America, and the influence this had on its film culture.

Indeed, Graeme Turner goes so far as to declare that the revival of the Australian cinema was not only an economic project but that it 'also represented a semi-official project of nation formation' (1994: 202). He argues that, by the end of the 1960s, a developing nationalist mythology in Australia had come to 'recognise film as the most desirable medium for projecting an image of new confidence and maturity seen to mark contemporary Australian culture and society' (Turner 1989: 101). Therefore, both the films of the first few years of the revival and the writing about these films all in some ways engage with this idea of a national project.

This interest in Australian cinema became manifest in the number of histories which had appeared by the beginning of the 1980s. These include the indispensable Pike and Cooper (1981), Shirley and Adams (1983), Tulloch (1981, 1982), Bertrand and Collins (1981), Moran and O'Regan (1989), Moran (1991), and Cunningham (1991), all of which were histories of the pre-1970 period. Histories of the period after 1970 include Dermody and Jacka (1987, 1988a, b), Hinde (1981), and Stratton (1980, 1990). The film historians of the 1980s were almost all part of, or influenced by, the 1970s campaign for government support for a contemporary film industry. This explained their desire to cast the cinema of the past as something to be praised and celebrated; and also motivated their explanations—in terms of the concepts of media or cultural imperialism—of why this cinema had all but disappeared. Such an analysis sees the fragile national culture of countries like Australia as threatened and ultimately conquered by the imperialist invasion from outside, usually from the United States. Some of this early work was undoubtedly flawed conceptually in so far as it did not always avoid posing an essentialist notion of national culture: culture was seen as somehow being

born naturally out of landscape or people and waiting to find expression in words and images, rather than being something syncretic, acquired, and constructed from a complex and politically implicated set of influences. However, much of it was highly sophisticated and, conscious of the traps of essentialism, evolved a nuanced view of Australian culture and film which was able to acknowledge both the local particularities of Australian cinema and its position as the product of a complex set of aesthetic influences and industrial pressures (Lawson 1979; Martin 1988; Tulloch 1982; Cunningham 1991).

> Some of this work was highly sophisticated and, conscious of the traps of essentialism, evolved a nuanced view of Australian culture and film which was able to acknowledge both the local particularities of Australian cinema and its position as the product of a complex set of aesthetic influences and industrial pressures.

Contesting the bush legend

Because there has been such a strong interconnection between Australian cinema studies and the process of recognizing and extending Australia's national culture, the methodologies and approaches used in the study of Australian cinema have been broad and eclectic. Australian film scholars have been less concerned with narrowly conceived formal and aesthetic questions about the film texts produced (though this has not been ignored—see e.g. Tulloch 1982; Dermody and Jacka 1988a) than with reading them symptomatically as both signs of, and producers of, a whole culture.

So, many Australian film writers have fruitfully used a combination of cultural studies, literary criticism, visual art theory, and film studies approaches in their highly sophisticated readings of particular films or film movements. During the 1970s critical work tended to be concerned with promoting an Australian cinema which could be an authentic site on which to articulate the unique Australian experience. There was an anxiety that the cinema was derivative or that it was so constrained by its economic marginality that it could not afford to take thematic or formal risks (see Dermody and Jacka 1987, 1988a). There was also criticism of the limitations of the 'bush legend' as an expression of national identity. During the period leading up to the constitution of Australia as a federated state in 1901, there was a cultural flowering manifested in popular literature, most notably the journal *Bulletin*, which glorified the idea of the 'essential' Australia as a land of 'sunlight, wattle, the bush, the future, freedom, mateship and egalitarianism' (White 1981: 97). This bush legend, however, was criticized for its obvious masculinist and Anglo-Irish bias and remoteness from the experience of contemporary modern urban Australia (see Turner 1986).

As John Tulloch's pioneering account of the Australian cinema of the 1920s shows, the bush legend, and the opposition of city and the bush, was the key structuring narrative device of many of the films of that period (Tulloch 1981). This, in turn, may be linked to a long tradition of finding in landscape the source of an 'authentic' Australian identity. This opposition of city and country is not, of course, unique to Australia; it tends to be a constant theme in all cultures where the dynamic but destructive forces of modernity are in contest with an Arcadian vision of traditional ways of life. However, it takes on a particular colour in frontier societies where the rural landscape has a dual character as either a place of innocence and refuge against the predations of the city or a threatening wilderness inimical to human life.

A number of film scholars have explored the place of landscape in Australian cinema (Turner 1986; Cunningham 1991); but it is in the work of Ross Gibson that it is given its fullest treatment. In his films (for example *Camera Natura*, 1986) and scholarly work, Gibson has examined the way that the Australian continent has been imagined by Europeans in writings of exploration and travel and in the cultural artefacts of the colonial period (Gibson 1984). In an essay which has become an often reprinted classic—'The Nature of a Nation: Landscape in Australian Feature Films'—Gibson uses the perspective developed in this work to look at the rich variety of depictions of the landscape in Australian cinema. Gibson argues that in virtually every plot 'outside city limits', the land is a 'leitmotif and ubiquitous character' (1992: 63). The reason for this, he argues, is that 'non-Aboriginal Australia is a young society, underendowed with myths of "belonging".

The country is still sparsely populated and meagerly historicized. Alienation and the fragility of culture have been the refrains during two hundred years of white Australian images and stories' (64). In another essay, Gibson applies his formidable critical skills to the Mad Max cycle of films, and using a combination of cultural theory, art history, and film studies, sees *Mad Max 2* (1981) and *Mad Max 3* (1985) as both allegories of failure—the continual failure of white explorers to master the land (thus linking to Gibson's interest in landscape films)—and, in their baroque mise-en-scène and editing style (a surprising discovery of a parallel between Mad Max and Tintoretto), a representation of a 'world peopled with signs, figures and emblems, where all objects and beings . . . exchange attributes and properties in a perpetual semantic shift', a condition Gibson sees as common to both late Renaissance Europe and (post)modern Australia.

The ongoing engagement with, and contestation of, the bush version of the Australian legend in Australian films often displayed a distaste for the popular idioms with which Australian films worked, especially when they depended on stylistic traits seen to be derived from Hollywood (see Hinde 1981). However, in the early 1980s work began to appear which challenged these initial positions and which celebrated rather than deplored the necessarily syncretic nature of Australian cinema. Two essays in particular—one by Tom O'Regan, the other by Meaghan Morris—opened up some new directions for Australian film criticism.

In 'The Man from Snowy River [1982] and Australian Popular Culture', O'Regan (1985) argued against those who saw that film as simply crude melodrama, an imitation western, or an opportunistic attempt to appropriate an Australian legend, and traced the complex ways in which the film represented a non-metropolitan Australia and how it intersected with the popular cultural desires of city-based Australians and their diverse set of imaginings about the 'bush'. Meaghan Morris's (1988) article on *Crocodile Dundee* (1986) also saw beyond local critics' distaste for the movie's apparent rerunning of the 'ocker' stereotype and argued that its 'positive-unoriginality' acted as a cunning export allegory, a '*take-over* fantasy of breaking into the circuit of [American] media power', involving both admiration and resistance. She goes on: 'In this admiration, appropriation as positive-unoriginality figures as a means of resolving the practical problems of a peripheral cinema, while reconciling conflicting desires for power and independence: symbolic nationalist victory is declared, but on internationalist (American) grounds' (Morris 1988: 250).

Cinema and post-coloniality

More recently, as theories of 'post-coloniality have developed, there has been an increasing interest in conceptualizing Australia as post-colonial. The relations between Aboriginal and non-Aboriginal Australia have naturally been a major focus of this work. In 1992 Aboriginal scholar Marcia Langton was commissioned by the Australian Film Commission to investigate the politics and aesthetics of filmmaking by and about Aboriginal people from an Aboriginal perspective. The book which resulted (Langton 1993) was a landmark, both because it redressed a gap in the film literature in Australia, but also because it was such a fruitful and creative combination of post-structuralist theory, film studies, and Aboriginal perspectives. As critic Stephen Muecke (1994) argues, it signalled 'the collapse of a long-felt antagonistic opposition between Aboriginal essentialism and non-Aboriginal theory'. For Langton, film and television are the main ways in which non-Aboriginal Australians know about Aborigines and thus their knowledge is always a second-order one (Langton 1993: 33). As a result, the way films construct Aboriginality is of the utmost political concern. She analyses well-known 'Aboriginal' films like Charles Chauvel's *Jedda* (1955), drawing out its colonialist constructions of the 'native' and showing its affinities with long-standing Western traditions as exemplified, for example, in the Tarzan legend. She then goes on to examine Aboriginal filmmaker Tracey Moffat's 'deconstruction' of *Jedda* in her 1989 film *Night Cries*, which depicts the white mother and Aboriginal adopted daughter (played incidentally by Marcia Langton) forty years on. Moffat's film is a highly stylized 'experimental' film, in which the original dependency relation between the white homesteaders and their adopted black child is reversed. As Langton suggests, 'the worst nightmare of the adoptive parents is to end life with the black adoptive child as the only family' (1993: 47).

Tracey Moffat's treatment of the 'Jedda text' is also the subject of an influential article by Laleen Jayamanne. Jayamanne—a Sri Lankan Australian who was educated partly in the United States—brings a combination of intellectual influences, including performance theory, film studies, and visual art theory, to

> More recently, as theories of post-coloniality have developed, there has been an increasing interest in conceptualizing Australia as post-colonial. The relations between Aboriginal and non-Aboriginal Australia have naturally been a major focus of this work.

bear on both her own film work (such as *A Song of Ceylon* (1985), a kind of 'reply' to Basil Wright's celebrated 1937 documentary), and to her film criticism. In her essay on *Night Cries*, Jayamanne (1993) offers a 'Sri Lankan reading' of the film, linking its concerns with the general field of post-colonial studies, but also tracing some of what is specific to the colonial and post-colonial situation in Australia, by linking the visual style of the film to Aboriginal painters (such as Albert Namatjira) who had reappropriated the work of European landscape artists. She uses the film to ruminate on the politics of artistic assimilation, appropriation, hybridization, and decolonization that is involved in Aboriginal cultural production and the challenge to Eurocentric artistic practice (Jayamanne 1993: 83).

Colonialism has also been a rich subject for Australian documentary filmmaking, notably in the work of Denis O'Rourke. His controversial 1991 film *The Good Woman of Bangkok* provoked an extended discussion (see Berry *et al.*, forthcoming) which debated the film's treatment of gender, sexuality, and the colonial subject, the ethics of documentary filmmaking, as well as the way in which O'Rourke positions himself as both author and subject of the film. Apart from this debate about *The Good Woman of Bangkok*, there has been surprisingly little work done in documentary theory and criticism for a country which has contributed so much to the documentary form. There has also been a small but robust Australian avant-garde sector which has produced a considerable body of commentary and theory, mainly in the pages of the leading critical avant-garde journal, published since 1971, *Cantrills Filmnotes*. Film critic Adrian Martin (1989) has written the best general history of Australia's avant-garde.

As already indicated, while the general field of film studies in Australia was heavily influenced by intellectual debates which originated in Europe and the United States (especially the *Screen* tradition, which was

A 'challenge to Eurocentric artistic practice'—Aboriginal film maker Tracey Moffat's *Night Cries* (1989)

dominant in Australian scholarship and teaching from about 1976 to 1984), the more formalist and psycho-analytic frameworks associated with this tradition have not been dominant in the study of Australian film, because they were not found serviceable in the wider study of the interpenetration of cinema and the wider culture. These frameworks, however, have been more relevant to the theory and practice of feminist film in Australia. Taking a lead from early work done in the United States on feminism and cinema (notably the journal *Women and Film*), the feminist debate was vigorously joined in Australia from about 1974 onwards. The work of the *Screen* theorists, especially Laura Mulvey and Claire Johnston, as interpreted by writers like Lesley Stern was extremely influential on both filmmaking and film criticism (Macallan 1995). As in other Western countries in this period, a large body of films made from a feminist perspective was pro-duced (usually with government support), and their

reception was accompanied by intense debate about the politics of feminist filmmaking, most of which was carried on in the pages of film journals and magazines like *Filmnews*, *Cinema Papers*, and less regular and less long-lived newsletters. The history of Australian feminist filmmaking and theory is well covered in Blonski, Creed, and Freiberg (1987) and Collins (1995) and usefully summarized in Sands (1988).

While a number of Australian film writers have made a considerable contribution to the general field of feminist film studies (e.g. Stern 1982; Creed 1993)—and notwithstanding the fact that there is a rich tradi-tion of Australian women's films—there has been remarkably little written on Australian cinema from within the tradition of feminist film studies (apart from Collins 1995). Much general commentary on Australian films, especially that written by women, has a feminist inflexion or notes the role of gender representations in films from various periods, but there has been virtually no sustained treatment of individual women film-makers, nor detailed critical or formal analysis of film texts using the protocols of feminist film theory. The reasons for this have been suggested above: the primary concerns of the Australian cinema and its commentaries have been questions of national identity and, while gender is clearly an essential aspect of the construction of such an identity, the more general questions seem so far to have blocked the development of a strong feminist intellectual tradition in Australian cinema studies. It is, therefore, interesting to note that in a recent Australian collection on feminism and film (Jayamanne 1995) the only writer to engage with Australian film was the only non-Australian contributor!

Conclusion

Australia has produced a significant body of work on its own national cinema. This work has been made possible because of both the institutionalization of screen studies within academia, which occurred in the late 1970s, as well as a significant level of awareness and support from government funding bodies, where a commitment to film culture was seen as an important ingredient for the production and reception of Australian films. Scholarly work on Australian cinema has also been intimately linked to film practice and to the politics of film funding. Many of the theorists were also filmmakers, but futher than that the fragility of the Australian industry vis-à-vis the massive forces of the international audiovisual industry has lent an urgency and a strategic value to much of the writing—an ongoing connection to the struggle to retain a space for local filmmaking in the face of what is perceived to threaten it.

BIBLIOGRAPHY

Berry, Chris (1994), *A Bit on the Side: East–West Topographies of Desire* (Sydney: IMPress).
—— Annette Hamilton, and **Laleen Jayamanne** et al. (forthcoming), *The Good Woman of Bangkok: The Debate* (Sydney: Power Institute of Fine Arts, University of Sydney).
Bertrand, Ina, and **Dianne Collins** (1981), *Government and Film in Australia* (Sydney: Currency Press).
Blonski, Annette, Barbara Creed, and **Freda Freiberg**

(1987), *Don't Shoot Darling: Women's Independent Filmmaking in Australia* (Richmond, Victoria: Greenhouse Publications).
Brooks, Jodi (1992), 'Fascination and the Grotesque: Whatever Happened to Baby Jane?', *Continuum: The Australian Journal of Media and Culture*, 5/2: 225–34.
Collins, Felicity (1995), 'Ties that Bind: The Psyche of Feminist Filmmaking Sydney 1969–89', Ph.D. thesis (Sydney: University of Technology, Sydney).
Creed, Barbara (1993), *The Monstrous-Feminine: Film, Feminism, Psychoanalysis* (London: Routledge).
Cunningham, Stuart (1991), *Featuring Australia: The Cinema of Charles Chauvel* (Sydney: Allen & Unwin).
*__Dermody, Susan,__ and **Elizabeth Jacka** (1987), *The Screening of Australia*, i: *Anatomy of a Film Industry* (Sydney: Currency Press).
*—— (1988a), *The Screening of Australia*, ii: *Anatomy of a National Cinema* (Sydney: Currency Press).
—— (1988b), *The Imaginary Industry: Australian Cinema in the Late Eighties* (North Ryde: Australian Film, Television and Radio School).
Gibson, Ross (1984), *The Diminishing Paradise: Changing Literary Perceptions of Australia* (Sydney: Angus & Robertson).
—— (1992), *South of the West: Postcolonialism and the Narrative Construction of Australia* (Bloomington: Indiana University Press).
Hinde, John (1981), *Other People's Pictures* (Sydney: Australian Broadcasting Commission).
Hodsdon, Barrett (1992), 'The Mystique of *Mise en Scène* Revisited', *Continuum: The Australian Journal of Media and Culture*, 5/2: 68–86.
Jayamanne, Laleen (1993), '"Love me Tender, Love me True, never Let me Go . . .": A Sri Lankan Reading of Tracey Moffatt's *Night Cries—A Rural Tragedy*', in Sneja Gunew and Anna Yeatman (eds.), *Feminism and the Politics of Difference* (Sydney: Allen & Unwin).
—— (1994), 'Postcolonial Gothic: The Narcissistic Wound in Jane Campion's *The Piano*', Department of Fine Arts, University of Sydney.
—— (ed.) (1995), *Kiss me Deadly: Feminism and Cinema for the Moment* (Sydney: Power Institute of Fine Arts, University of Sydney).
Langton, Marcia (1993), '*Well, I Heard it on the Radio and I Saw it on the Television . . .*' (Sydney: Australian Film Commission).
Lawson, Sylvia (1965/1985), 'Not for the Likes of Us', in Moran and O'Regan (1985).
—— (1979) 'Towards Decolonization: Some Problems and Issues for Film History in Australia', *Film Reader 4* (Chicago: Northwestern University).
Macallan, Helen (1995), *Travelling in Circles (The Screen Project 1971–1981)*, Ph.D. thesis, (Sydney: University of Technology).

CRITICAL APPROACHES TO WORLD CINEMA

Martin, A. (1988), 'No Flowers for the Cinephile: The Fates of Cultural Populism 1960–1988', in Paul Foss (ed.), *Islands in the Stream: Myths of Place in Australian Culture* (Sydney: Pluto Press).
—— (1989), 'Indefinite Objects: Independent Film and Video', in Moran and O'Regan (1989).
—— (1993), *Phantasms: The Dreams and Desires at the Heart of our Popular Culture* (Melbourne: McPhee Gribble).
Moran, Albert (1991), *Projecting Australia: Government Film since 1945* (Sydney: Currency Press).
—— and **Tom O'Regan** (eds.) (1985), *An Australian Film Reader* (Sydney: currency Press).
—— —— (eds.) (1989), *The Australian Screen* (Melbourne: Penguin).
Morris, Meaghan (1988), 'Tooth and Claw: Tales of Survival and *Crocodile Dundee*' in *The Pirate's Fiancée: Feminism, Reading, Postmodernism* (London: Verso).
Mortimer, Lorraine (1995), 'The Grim Enchantment of *It's a Wonderful Life*', *Massachusetts Review* 36/4 (Dec.) 656–86.
Muecke, Stephen (1994), 'Narrative and Intervention in Aboriginal Filmmaking and Policy', *Continuum: The Australian Journal of Media and Culture*, 8/2: 248–57.
O'Regan, Tom (1985), 'The Man from Snowy River and Australian Popular Culture', in Moran and O'Regan (1985).
*—— (1996), *Australian National Cinema* (London: Routledge).
Pike, Andrew, and **Ross Cooper** (1981), *Australian Film 1900–1977* (Melbourne: Oxford University Press and Australian Film Institute).
Routt, William (1992), 'L'Évidence', *Continuum: The Australian Journal of Media and Culture*, 5/2: 40–67.

Sands, Kate (1988), 'Women of the Wave', in Scott Murray (ed.), *Back of Beyond: Discovering Australian Film and Television*, catalogue for exhibition held by the Australian Film Commission and the UCLA Film and Television Archive, Sydney (Sydney: Australian Film Commission).
Shirley, Graham, and **Brian Adams** (1983), *Australian Cinema: The First Eighty Years* (Sydney: Angus & Robertson and Currency Press).
Stern, Lesley (1982), 'The Body as Evidence', *Screen*, 23/5: 39–62.
—— (1995), *The Scorsese Connection* (London: British Film Institute).
Stratton, David (1980), *The Last New Wave: The Australian Film Revival* (Sydney: Angus & Robertson).
—— (1990), *The Avocado Plantation: Boom and Bust in the Australian Film Industry* (Sydney: Pan Macmillan).
Tulloch, John (1981), *Legends on the Screen* (Sydney: Currency Press).
—— (1982), *Australian Cinema: Industry, Narrative, Meaning* (Sydney: Allen & Unwin).
*Turner, Graeme** (1986), *National Fictions: Literature, Film and the Construction of Australian Narrative* (Sydney: Allen & Unwin).
—— (1989), 'Art-Directing History: The Period Film', in Moran and O'Regan (1989).
—— (1994), 'The End of the National Project? Australian Cinema in the 1990s', in Wissal Dissayanake (ed.), *Questions of Nationhood and History in Asian Cinema* (Bloomington: University of Indiana Press).
Weir, Tom (1985), 'No Daydreams of our Own: The Film as National Self-Expression', in Moran and O'Regan (1985).
White, Richard (1981), *Inventing Australia: Images and Identity 1688–1980* (Sydney: George Allen & Unwin).

17 Canadian cinema

Will Straw

The academic study of English Canadian film has followed two broad lines of development since its emergence in the 1960s. Each of these is rooted in a form of cultural nationalism, the predominant impulse in postwar English Canadian intellectual culture. One such line of development is that of cultural policy studies, the chronicling of the Canadian state's response to the perceived threat to Canadian national culture represented by the United States. Like Canadian media studies generally, this work is inspired by the political economy of Harold Innis (e.g. 1995), whose theorization of Canada's economic and political dependence, first on Great Britain and, subsequently, on the United States, has been a prominent influence on Canadian scholarship in a variety of fields.

For several decades, the most substantial analyses of Canadian film policy were published in the research appendices which accompanied the reports of government commissions. Such reports still provide the most comprehensive overviews of the Canadian film industry and of state policies directed at this industy. In the last decade, however, communications scholars have undertaken a more highly theorized and comprehensive analysis of the long-term structural problems blocking the development of a Canadian cinema. Dorland (1991), Pendakur (1990), and Magder (1993) have offered analyses, rooted in the traditions of political economy, of that long process whereby Canadian film exhibition and distribution has remained under US control with disastrous effects on levels of investment in a national film industry.

The significant role played by policy studies within English Canadian film scholarship is evidence of a more general privileging of state action within the cultural sphere in Canada. Those involved in film culture in Canada have long reiterated the claim, first made by public-broadcasting activist Gordon Sparling in the 1930s, that Canadians must choose between 'the State and the United States' (cited in Magder 1993: 13). Popular and scholarly histories of Canadian cinema have typically offered a narrative in which a continuous experience of failure, beginning with the earliest arrival of cinema in Canada, is broken only with the heroic emergence of the National Film Board in 1939. A more recent wave of historical scholarship has challenged such accounts, noting the rich (albeit intermittent and unstable) legacy of attempts to found a national industry dating back to the turn of the century (e.g. Morris 1975).

It is partly in terms of the role played by policy studies that divergences between French-language and English-language film studies in Canada become clear. While English-language work has concentrated on the absence of an indigenous feature film industry, and chronicled the economic and political reasons for this absence, histories of French-language, Québécois cinema have displayed a higher degree of triumphalism. (Not all French-language culture within

Canada, it must be noted, is produced within Quebec; nor is the entirety of Quebec culture produced in the French-language.) While, arguably, the dominant barrier to the development of an English Canadian cinema has been imposed by the US industry, Québécois historians have tended to see the historical weakness of their own cinema as rooted in the long-standing underdevelopment of a distinctive francophone culture within Canada and Quebec. The sense that this underdevelopment was overcome in the 1960s and 1970s, as part of what has come to be known as Quebec's Quiet Revolution, allows histories of French-language cinema in Canada to offer a more heroic tone. In the post-war emergence of a Québécois cinema, we may note two paradoxes.

One is that federal institutions, such as the National Film Board and Canadian Broadcasting Corporation, played crucial (if unintended) roles in fostering a sense of nationalist, even separatist, consciousness in Quebec in the post-war period, in large measure by sponsoring and disseminating images of a population and geographical space undergoing a process of rapid modernization. The second is that, despite an even smaller population base than English Canada, francophone Quebec has produced a popular cinema (alongside its art–auteur cinema), one which, while of variable stability, is embedded in a star system, publicity apparatus, and constellation of collective cultural reference-points lacking in English Canada. Prominent examples of this popular cinema include *Mon Oncle Antoine* (Claude Jutra, 1971) and *Les Noces de papier* ('Paper Wedding', Michel Brault, 1989).

The other line of development in the study of English Canadian cinema has had a more direct impact on the development of Canadian film studies itself as a discipline. This is the attempt to define the specificity of English Canadian culture, an enterprise which flourished amidst the surge of interest in the late 1960s and 1970s in defining a national culture. From a present-day perspective, these attempts bear the mark of an all too obvious essentialism, but in seeking to establish the thematic and formal basis of national cultural traditions, Canadian writers were replicating processes observable in other national cultures before them. Margaret Atwood's *Survival* (1972) was perhaps the most influential of the texts produced as part of this project. Through a detailed study of Canadian fiction, poetry, and drama, she concluded that the thematic unity of Canadian literature (in both its English and French language forms) was based on a persistent preoccupation with the notion of survival. Writers on the visual arts were very often drawn to the argument that Canadian artistic practice was marked by a preoccupation with landscape, and with the oppressiveness (as much as the sublime beauty) of nature (e.g. McGregor 1985).

In his influential book *Movies and Mythologies*, Peter Harcourt (1977) found a thematic unity for English Canadian cinema in a crisis of character motivation. Looking at the scattered feature film tradition of the 1960s and early 1970s, and at such works as *Paperback Hero* (Peter Pearson, 1973) or *Rowdyman* (Peter Carter, 1971) for example, he noted that the heroes of Canadian films were typically trapped in a real or emotional adolescence. Later, Geoff Pevere (1992: 36) would write of the stubbornly worrisome character of English Canadian films, regarding this as the appropriate response of one national culture to a powerful neighbour whose cultural artefacts include the constant exhortation to be happy. The sense that English Canadian feature films are typically more elliptical, unresolved, and restrained in narrative and stylistic terms is by now a commonplace within discussions of this cinema. Less frequently addressed is the extent to which these attributes are typical of art-house cinematic practices generally, rather than the necessary expression of a national character.

The project of defining a national film tradition found itself increasingly marginalized within the discipline of film studies, as that discipline settled into the departmental structure of Canadian universities in the late 1970s and early 1980s. The first degree programme in film studies in Canada was offered at York University in Toronto in 1969 (Morris 1991: 97). In Canada, as elsewhere in the English-speaking world, the rise of psychoanalytic, formalist, and ideological forms of analysis displaced, for a time, the question of the specificity of national cinematic practices. Indeed, for several years, there were evident tensions between the hermeneutics of suspicion which dominated film theory and the impulse to validate a national tradition which underlay much work on Canadian cinema. Feminist scholars and critics, writing in such magazines as *Cine Action* and *Borderlines*, were virtually alone in undertaking to address Canadian film practice from the perspective of those forms of analysis developed in such non-Canadian journals as *Screen* adnd *Camera Obscura*. More recently, as cultural theory in its Anglo-American variants has come to take up the question of nationhood, this work has served to revitalize Canadian film studies in important ways (e.g. Acland 1994). Indeed, Canadian studies itself, as a broadly interdisciplinary intellectual enterprise, has in recent years been marked by more sustained and vital diaologue with cultural studies.

For two decades teachers of film studies in Canada have met regularly within the Film Studies Association of Canada (FSAC). While FSAC is a bilingual organization (in spirit, if not in practice), French-language scholars in Quebec are more likely to belong to the Association québécoises des études cinématographiques. The sole academic publication devoted exclusively to film studies work in English Canada is the *Canadian Journal of Film Studies*, founded in 1990. (*Cinémas*, a French-language journal published in Montreal, is, characteristically, glossier and receives wider distribution.) Most of the significant debates over Canadian film have transpired in a cultural space in which the academic world and a broader sphere of intellectual culture overlap. Magazines such as *Cinema Canada* (now defunct), *Take One*, *Cine Action*, and *Point of View*, or periodicals of the political and cultural left, such as *Canadian Forum* and *Borderlines*, have done much to establish a critical tradition around English-Canadian cinema. Indeed, the most important controversy over the future of English Canadian cinema, the so-called 'Cinema we Need' debate, began within non-academic magazines and has since became standard assigned reading for courses in Canadian cinema. (It is collected in Featherling 1988.)

This debate was significant, in part, because it departed from the long-standing notion that a Canadian cinematic sensibility found its most natural expression in documentary forms. Typically, all participants concurred that the appropriate Canadian aesthetic was one which offered an alternative to the hegemony of Hollywood forms, but there was significant disagreement over whether the most effective alternative lay in the traditions of materialist experimental film or in new variations of the narrative feature. Bruce Elder, a prominent Canadian filmmaker himself, argued that only an experimental, non-narrative cinema, focused on the 'present' of perception, might successfully challenge the means–end rationality of US narrative cinema. Among those responding, Peter Harcourt (1985) and Piers Handling (1985) insisted on the need for the links to the social world offered by so-called New Narrative films, a cycle represented by such films as *Sonatine* (Micheline Lanctot, 1983) and *Family Viewing* (Atom Egoyan, 1987).

In a variety of ways, this debate echoed similar debates of a decade earlier within film studies and radical film culture internationally, and it was easy to dismiss arguments in favour of a phenomenological, experimental cinema as outmoded. By the mid-to-late 1980s, however, when the debate over 'The Cinema we Need' erupted, there were good reasons to believe that an indigenous tradition of experimental filmmaking, from the work of Michael Snow through that of Brenda Longfellow, Chris Gallagher, and Bruce Elder himself, offered a firmer foundation for a Canadian film culture than the intermittently successful feature, narrative films held up as an alternative. At the same time, as Kass Banning (1992) has noted, the tendency to dismiss documentary filmmaking as an anachronistic legacy of the Grierson period ignored the importance of documentary film in the development of a feminist film practice in Canada. Such films as *Our Marilyn* (Brenda Longfellow, 1988) and *Speak Body* (Kay Armitage, 1979) rework documentary within new, hybrid forms in which the influence of an indigenous experimental tradition is evident.

As might be expected, the most interesting recent work in Canadian film studies is that which challenges long-established orthodoxies. Nelson (1990) set out to undermine the National Film Board's status as the most powerful expression of our national cultural autonomy, noting the Board's role within the Canadian state's broader acquiescence to the security interests of the United States in the post-war period. More recently, Michael Dorland (1996, forthcoming) has suggested that the endless attempt within Canada to found a national feature film industry is in important ways the history of a 'fetish'. Young countries, he suggests, long for a feature film industry to serve as a sign of their national maturity and legitimacy. The principal effect of this longing, Dorland (forthcoming) argues, 'has not been a film industry *per se*, but elements of a film production infrastructure sufficiently established to support the periodic emergence of discursive formations that produce talk about an imaginary or potential industry'.

Arguably, the 'fetish' of a national feature film industry has withered over the last decade, the effect of three interrelated developments. One of these is the emergence of an English Canadian auteur cinema, evident in the works of such directors as Atom Egoyan (e.g. *Family Viewing* 1987; *Speaking Parts*, 1989; *Calendar*, 1994), Patricia Rozema (*I've Heard the Mermaids Singing*, 1987; *White Room*, 1991), Bruce

McDonald (*Road Kill*, 1989; *Highway 61*, 1991), and William D. MacGillivray (*Stations*, 1983; *Life Classes*, 1987). These works have reinvigorated a critical discourse of auteurist interpretation, just as their success has inspired the acknowledgement that an English Canadian cinema may only ever be an art-house cinema with occasional cross-overs to mainstream success. At the same time, the number of Canadian firms producing speciality television programming has expanded, as part of a broader growth in the international markets for television programmes. A national industry which services these markets (particularly in such genres as animated and children's programming, in which Canadian producers have traditionally done well) has taken shape, offering the levels of employment and return on investment which, it was once hoped, would come from the production of feature films. Finally, Canada is home to an elaborate network of independent film and video co-operatives, an infrastructure nourished by the cultural activism of municipal artistic scenes. Much of the important discourse of and about Canadian film is now to be found in independent short films and videos (and in the critical apparatus which surrounds such works), of which *Sally's Beauty Spot* (Helen Lee, 1990) and *Ten Cents a Dance* (Midi Onodera, 1989) offer noteworthy examples. It is here that the debate over cultural identity has moved from the conventional preoccupation with national specificity to embrace the complexities of identity politics and the shifting status of the nation-state (for an overview, see Marchessault 1995).

BIBLIOGRAPHY

Acland, Charles (1994), 'National Dreams, International Encounters: The Formation of Canadian Film Culture in the 1930s', *Canadian Journal of Film Studies*, 3/1: 3–26.

Atwood, Margaret (1972), *Survival: A Thematic Guide to Canadian Literature* (Toronto: Anansi).

Banning, Kass (1992), 'The Canadian Feminist Hybrid Documentary', *CineAction*, 26–7 (Winter), 108–13.

Dorland, Michael (1991), 'The War Machine: American Culture, Canadian Cultural Sovereignty and Film Policy', *Canadian Journal of Film Studies*, 1/2: 35–48.

—— (1996), 'Policy Rhetorics of an Imaginary Cinema: The Discursive Economy of the Emergence of the Australian and Canadian Feature Film', in Albert Moran (ed.), *Film Policy* (London: Routledge).

—— (forthcoming), *The Three Percent Solution: The Discursive Economy of the Emergence of the Canadian Feature Film 1957–1968* (Toronto: University of Toronto Press).

Featherling, Doug (ed.) (1988), *Documents in Canadian Film* (Peterborough: Broadview Press).

Handling, Piers (1985), 'The Cinema we Need?', *Cinema Canada*, nos. 120–1 (July–Aug.), 29–30.

Harcourt, Peter (1977), *Movies and Mythologies: Towards a National Cinema* (Toronto: Canadian Broadcasting Corporation Publications).

—— (1985), 'Politics or Paranoia?', *Cinema Canada*, nos. 120–1 (July–Aug.), 31–2.

Innis, Harold (1995), *Staples, Markets and Cultural Change: Selected Essays* (Montreal: McGill-Queen's University Press).

McGregor, Gaile (1985), *The Wacousta Syndrome: Explorations in the Canadian Landscape* (Toronto: University of Toronto Press).

Magder, Ted (1993), *Canada's Hollywood: The Canadian State and Feature Films* (Toronto: University of Toronto Press).

Marchessault, Janine (ed.) (1995), *Mirror Machine: Video and Identity* (Toronto: YYZ Books and CRCCII).

Morris, Peter (1975), *Embattled Shadows: A History of Canadian Cinema 1895–1939* (Montreal: McGill-Queen's University Press).

—— (1991), 'From Film Club to Academy: The Beginnings of Film Education in Canada', in Réal La Rochelle (ed.), *Québec/Canada: l'enseignement du cinéma et de l'audiovisuel/The Study of Film and Video* (Condé-sur-Noireau: CinémaAction).

Nelson, Joyce (1990), *The Colonized Eye* (Toronto: Between the Lines).

Pendakur, Manjunath (1990), *Canadian Dreams and American Control: The Political Economy of the Canadian Film Industry* (Toronto: Garamond Press).

Pevere, Geoff (1992), 'On the Brink', *CineAction*, 28 (Spring), 34–8.

18 Issues in world cinema

Wimal Dissanayake

Dadasaheb Phalke, who is generally regarded by Indian film historians as the father of Indian cinema, relates an interesting anecdote (1970). His *Raja Harish-chandra*, released on 3 May 1913, is highlighted by scholars as the first Indian feature film. Phalke tells us that he was inspired to make this film after seeing the movie *The Life of Christ* (USA, 1906) in the America–India Picture Palace in Bombay in 1910. As he was watching the film, he was overwhelmed by both a deep religiosity and an awareness of the potentialities of the art of cinematography. As he watched the life of Christ unfold before his eyes, he thought of the gods Krishna and Ramachandra and wondered how long it would be before Indians would be able to see Indian images of their divinities on screen. In fact, it was not long: three years later Phalke made the first Indian feature film based on the celebrated Indian epic the *Ramayana* (see Rajadhyaksha, Part 3, Chapter 19). However, what this anecdote—and many similar ones by the early filmmakers in Asia, Latin America, and Africa—points to is a series of binaries that underpin

the discourse of cinema in those continents: binaries of Westernization and indigenization, tradition and modernity, the local and the global. Any discussion of these cinemas, and the trajectories of their development, must necessarily address these crucial issues.

However, it is important that we do not lump these cinemas together indiscriminately as 'non-Western'. It is, of course, true that, geographically, they are from the non-Western world (with 'Western' here referring to North America and Europe), and that they share many interests and preoccupations. However, as the following chapters clearly demonstrate, while they may display commonalities of interest, each of the countries, because of its specific social formations and historical conjunctures, has its own distinctive trajectories of cinematic development and concerns.

In the same way, we must also avoid treating non-Western cinemas as expressive of some unchanging 'essence'. Instead, we must see them as sites of discursive contestations, or representational spaces, in which changing social and cultural meanings are

The first Indian feature film,
Raja Harischandra (1913)

generated and fought over. The discursive boundaries of the various societies that constitute the non-Western world are constantly expanding and cannot be accounted for in essentialist terms. Moreover, the film-makers and film commentators (critics as well as scholars) who are at the leading edge of development of the film cultures of their respective societies have been exposed to, and in many cases trained in, Western countries so that their self-positioning in relation to the contours of their specific cultures is understandably complex and multifaceted (see Burton-Carvajal, Part 3, Chapter 25).

The concept of Third Cinema, originally formulated by the Argentinian film directors Fernando Solanas and

> **We must also avoid treating non-Western cinemas as expressive of some unchanging 'essence'. Instead, we must see them as sites of discursive contestations, or representational spaces, in which changing social and cultural meanings are generated and fought over.**

Octavio Getino (1973) and later expanded by film scholars such as Teshome H. Gabriel (1982), addresses a number of issues related to non-Western cinemas. Put simply, one can say that First Cinema refers to mainstream Hollywood cinema, and Second Cinema to European 'art' cinema. In distinguishing it from First and Second Cinemas, proponents of Third Cinema see it as the articulation of a new culture and a vehicle of social transformation (see Burton-Carvajal). Paul Willemen (1989), however, suggests how the manifestos laying out the guiding ideas of Third Cinema give the impression that it was developed by Latin Americans for Latin America and that its wider applicability was added as an afterthought. He also argues that there is a danger in the concept of Third Cinema of homogenizing non-Western cinema and not grappling sufficiently with questions of ethnic and gender divisions as well as the vexed relationship between cinema and nationhood. It is this complicated relationship between nationhood and cinema with which we shall begin.

Nationhood and cinema

Nationhood, as with all other forms of identity, revolves around the question of difference, with how the uniqueness of one nation differs from the uniqueness of other comparable nations. Benedict Anderson (1983) suggests that nationhood may be understood as an 'imagined community', and indicates how nationhood is a cultural artefact of a particular kind. It is imagined, because the members of even the smallest nation can never get to know, or even meet, most of their fellow members; yet in the imagination of each the notion of the nation persists. The nation is also imagined as a community because, regardless of the very real inequities and injustices that exist in society, it is always perceived as deep and horizontal comradeship. It is important, however, to note that Anderson employed the term 'imagined' and not 'imaginary'. 'Imaginary' signifies absence, or nothingness, while 'imagined' foregrounds a nice balance between the real and not the real. The critical weakness of Benedict Anderson's formulaton, however, is that it pays scant attention to materialities and underplays the discontinuities of history. It also minimizes the salience of the political character of nationhood and the role which ethnicity and religion have played in the construction of the nation. Any investigation into the ways in which cinema constructs nationhood, therefore, has to consider these thorny issues of ethnic loyalties, religious affinities, and local patriotism. It must also recognize that the nation also contains within itself diverse local narratives of resistance and memory and therefore take into account the full force of these local and dissenting narratives which are embedded in the larger narrative of the nation.

It is evident that cinema is a very powerful cultural practice and institution which both reflects and inflects the discourse of nationhood. As a result, the concept of national cinema is at the base of many discussions of popular culture in Africa, Asia, the Middle East, and Latin America. It is generally analysed at two interrelated levels: the textual and the industrial (although see Crofts, Part 3, Chapter 1, for a full discussion of the complexities involved in theorizing the concept of 'national cinema'). The textual level involves a focus upon the distinctiveness of a given cinema—whether it be Indonesian or Nigerian, Mexican or Senegalese—in terms of content, style, and indigenous aesthetics. The industrial level involves a focus upon the relationship between cinema and industry, the nature of film production, distribution, and consumption, and the ways in which the ever-present threats from Hollywood are met. However, it should also be noted that the concept of national cinema serves to privilege notions of coherence and unity and to stabilize cultural meanings linked to the perceived uniqueness of a given nation. As I have pointed out (Dissanayake 1994), it is implicated in national myth-making and ideological production and serves to delineate both otherness and legitimate selfhood.

How a nation tells its unifying and legitimizing story about itself to its citizens is crucial in the understanding of nationhood, and after the popularization of cinema as a medium of mass entertainment in Latin America, Asia, the Middle East, and Africa, the role of cinema in this endeavour has come to occupy a significant place (see Rajadhyaksha and Burton-Carvajal, Chapters 19 and 25 below). Benedict Anderson (1983) focused attention on the centrality of print capitalism in giving rise to the idea of the nation and the deep horizontal comradeship it promoted. He observed that newspapers and nationalistic novels were primarily responsible for the creation of a national consciousness. In social circumstances that were antecedent to the establishment of nation-states, newspapers, journals, and fiction served to co-ordinate time and space in a way that enabled the formation of the imagined community that is the nation. In the contemporary world, cinema has assumed the status of a dominant medium of communication, and its role in conjuring up the imagined community among both the literate and illiterate strata of society is both profound and far-reaching. David Harvey (1989) suggests that the way in which cinema works to capture the complex and dynamic relationship between temporality and spatiality is not available to other media, and this becomes a significant issue for non-Western cinemas.

The topos of nationhood becomes significant for another reason as well. Cinema in most countries in Africa, the Middle East, Asia, and Latin America is closely linked to the concept and functioning of the nation-state. Questions of economics—production, distribution, and exhibition—and control of content through overt and covert censorship have much to do with this. For most film producers in Latin American, African, and Asian countries that depend on the patronage of local audiences for returns on their investments, the assistance, intervention, and co-ordination of governments become extremely important (in the form of film corporations, training institutes, script boards, censorship panels, national festivals, and the honouring of filmmakers). It is evident, therefore, that the demands of the economics of film industries and the imperatives of the nation-state are interlinked in complex, and at times disconcertingly intrusive, ways.

Speaking in very broad terms, we can divide films made in Asia, Africa, and South America into three main groups: the popular, the artistic, and the experimental (again, see Crofts, Part 3, Chapter 1, for a further elaboration of these categories). The popular films are commercial by nature and are designed to appeal to the vast mass of moviegoers and to secure the largest profit. The artistic films, while not immune to commercial pressures, are, none the less, driven by 'high art' concerns and tend to be showcased at international film festivals. The experimental films are much smaller in number and much less visible in the filmic landscape; they are committed to the creation of an oppositional cinema characterized by an audacious attempt to interrogate the Establishment and its values. Thus, if we take India as an example, filmmakers such as Raj Kapoor, Manmohan Desai, and Ramesh Sippy represent the popular tradition, directors such as Satyajit Ray and Adoor Gopalakrishnan belong to the 'art' tradition, while some of the work of Kumar Sahani and Mani Kaul may be categorized as experimental (see Rajadhyaksha, Part 3, Chapter 19). What is of interest in terms of the relationship between the nation-state and cinema is that—again in general terms—while popular cinema generally upholds notions of a unified nation, the artistic cinema tends to offer critiques of the nation-state (and its associated economic, social, political, and cultural discourses and institutions) and the experimental cinema characteristically calls into question the hegemonic project of the nation-state and the privileged vocabularies of national narration. Thus, in a large country like India with its numerous languages and religions, films produced in regional languages like Bengali or Malayalam tend to valorize, directly or obliquely, the regional at the expense of the national, thereby revealing certain fissures and fault lines in the national discourse. The artistic and experimental filmmakers seek to draw attention to the ambiguous unities, silenced voices, emergent and oppositional discourses, that occupy the national space, and thereby instigate a de-totalizing project.

For filmmakers in Asia, Africa, and Latin America, the cinematic representation of minorities presents a challenging problem, and this issue is inseparable from the dictates of the nation-state. The putatively homogeneous nature of the nation-state and its legitimizing meta-narratives begin to come under scrutiny as film-

makers attempt to articulate the experiences and lifeworlds of the minorities, whether they be ethnic, religious, linguistic, or caste, who inhabit the national space. Films that thematize the hardships of minorities create a representational space from where the hegemonic discourse of the state can be usefully subverted, and the idea of social and cultural difference emphasized. Indeed, one can see a wholly understandable tension between the idea of the unitary nation and cultural difference in many works of cinema produced in Asian, Latin American, and African countries. This tension is discernible in some of the works of internationally celebrated film directors like Nagisa Oshima of Japan, as well as in the creations of less well-known filmmakers such as Ji Qingchun (China), Park (Korea), and Euthana Mukdasnit (Thailand).

> **Artistic and experimental filmmakers seek to draw attention to the ambiguous unities, silenced voices, emergent and oppositional discourses, that occupy the national space, and thereby instigate a de-totalizing project.**

Film commentators in Latin America and Africa also display such propensities to rethink issues and repose questions. For example, if we take Mexican cinema, we find that in the past the concept of *mexicanidad* (Mexicanness) was privileged in intellectual and aesthetic discussions, and was perceived as a leading *topos* guiding Mexican cinema. Distinguished writers, such as the Nobel laureate Octavio Paz, underlined its significance, and both filmmakers and film critics positively valorized it. However, modern commentators of Mexican cinema now highlight how *mexicanidad*, as it was formulated, was élitist, sexist, and class-bound, and privileged the *criollo* over the *mestizo* and the Indians. Through the interrogation of such concepts as 'Japaneseness' and 'Mexicanness' associated with filmic discourse, scholars are emphasizing the need for the reacquisition of subaltern agency and the repossessing of history. The discursive spaces that they are opening up can have profound consequences in examining afresh the cinemas of the non-West.

The public sphere

This discussion of the interconnections between cinema and nationhood leads to the importance of cinema in the public sphere. From the very beginning, cinemas in South America, Africa, and Asia were involved in the public sphere, addressing important questions related to tradition, Westernization, democracy, the caste system, and cultural identity. The pioneering work of the German social philosopher Jurgen Habermas (1991) has resulted in the widespread interest in the concept of the public sphere which has helped to foreground issues of democratization, public participation, and oppositionality. Others such as Oskar Negt and Alexander Kluge (1993) have built upon Habermas's work and discussed the ability of cinema to provide a site for the contestation of meaning in an increasingly technologically saturated public sphere, where democratic self-realization and community participation have become much more problematic. The question of the public sphere is particularly important in the case of the nations of Asia, Africa, and Latin America. In many of these countries, cinema has always been perceived as playing a social role and continues to be a significant form of mass communication, even in the face of the censorship which many countries—be it Indonesia or the Philippines or Nigeria—impose.

Many examples of the mutual animation of cinema and the public sphere may be provided. In the 1930s Indian filmmakers addressed the issue of untouchability, which continues to be extremely sensitive. In 1946 Akira Kurosawa made *No Regrets for Youth*, which had a profound impact on Japanese society, raising the whole issue of the democratization of society and leaving an indelible mark on later filmmakers such as Oshima, Kei Kumai, and Kazuo Kuroki. Oshima, in his earlier films, made cinema a vital part of the public sphere by raising issues related to the plight of Korean minorities in Japan, capital punishment, and sexuality. The Indian film director Ritwik Ghatak, in his works, sought to focus on important issues related to the Indian public sphere such as the partitioning of India, the plight of the poor, the predicament of the artists, and the nature of mechanization. Many of the most interesting films made in Argentina after 1983, when the country returned to constitutional democracy, textualize the nature, significance, and urgency of re-democratization and the sweeping-aside of fascistic tendencies. African filmmakers like Idrissa Ouedraogo

have sought to make cinema a vital adjunct of the public sphere by raising questions concerning tradition, cultural identity, stereotypes, and misleading Western representations of African society.

However, it is in China where this relationship between cinema and the public sphere can be seen in its most vivid form. The work of the post-1980 group of filmmakers, generally referred to as the Fifth Generation of filmmakers, stirred up a great deal of interest both inside and ouside China (see Reynaud, Part 3, Chapter 20). Many of these films deal with the Cultural Revolution and seek to textualize directly or indirectly the phenomenon of the Cultural Revolution and its effects on the rural population, in particular, through an innovative filmmaking approach characterized by minimal narration, striking camera movements, a stress on spatiality, and disruptive montage. Films such as Chen Kaige's *Yellow Earth* (1984), *King of the Children* (1985), *The Big Parade* (1986), and *Farewell, my Concubine* (1993), Zhang Yimou's *Red Sorghum* (1988) and *To Live* (1994), Tian Zhuangzhuang's *The Horse Thief* (1986) and *The Blue Kite* (1991), to mention but a few titles, all bear testimony to a desire to make cinema an indispensable facet of the public sphere.

Intertextuality

As indicated at the start of this chapter, cinema was an imported art form that quickly became indigenized in the non-Western world. In a similar manner, European–American theories of cinema are impinging ever more strongly on the thought and sensibility of both filmmakers and film critics in Asian, African, and Latin American countries. The impact of European–American film scholarship on the non-Western world raises some fundamental issues related to comparative film study.

Is it possible to broaden the European–American referents that guide Western film theories so as to accommodate the cinematic experiences of the non-Western world? Do those African, Asian, Middle Eastern, and Latin American intellectuals and film scholars who are vigorously antipathetic to these Western theories subscribe to a merely spurious notion of cultural authenticity and purity? What is the nature of the theoretical space from which Asian, Latin American, and African film scholars and theorists speak? Writing in the context of literature, African-born Harvard professor

Kwame Anthony Appiah (1992) argues against both the pseudo-universalism of Eurocentric theorizations which pose as universal and a 'nativism' which nostalgically appeals to an apparently 'pure' and 'authentic' indigeneous culture. As Appiah points out, while 'nativism' may challenge Western norms, the way in which the contest is framed remains unchanged. 'The Western emperor has ordered the natives to exchange their robes for trousers: their act of defiance is to insist on tailoring them from homespun material. Given their arguments, plainly, the cultural nationalists do not go far enough; they are blind to the fact that their nativist demands inhabit a Western architecture' (1992: 60). These remarks also have a relevance for film theory.

It is clear that Eurocentric paradigms cannot take on the mantle of universal templates or they will hamper a deeper understanding and appreciation of cinemas in the non-Western world (see Ukadike, Part 3, Chapter 24). During the last fifteen years or so, following a retheorization of such issues as the nature of cinematic representation, the role of ideology in cultural production, and the importance of female subjectivity in cinema, the genre of melodrama, for example, has been critically rehabilitated in Western film studies. However, melodramas produced in Latin America, Africa, and Asia—and the majority of films made in these regions have been melodramas—cannot be judged in terms of Western conceptualizations of melodrama. Melodrama functions differently in different cultural contexts and the melodramatic traditions evolved in these countries, especially in the theatre, have acquired highly distinctive characteristics. For example, in India, film melodramas bear the cultural inscriptions of folk theatre as well as the Parsee theatre of the nineteenth century. Other analytical tools developed by Western film scholars—such as those relating to point of view, the gaze, and textual subjectivity—may also be seen to have limited application. Paul Willemen (1994), for example, has perceptively demonstrated, in relation to the work of the Israeli filmmaker Amos Gitai, how in his cinemas it is most decidedly not through point-of-view shots that we are mobilized, but through the differences between one point of view and another even within the one shot. The role of the aesthetic inter-texts and cultural contexts, in this respect, are crucial to the understanding of the various non-Western cinemas.

Film is not an isolated art form; it inhabits a common expressive culture fed by tradition, cultural memory, and indigenous modes of symbolic representation.

> **It is clear that Eurocentric paradigms cannot take on the mantle of universal templates or they will hamper a deeper understanding and appreciation of cinemas in the non-Western world.**

Therefore, films and other arts are mutually implicated in the production of meaning and pleasure, and this deserves to be examined more closely. In most African, Latin American, and Asian countries cinema, from the very beginning, has had a symbiotic relationship with the theatre, and continues to do so. Similarly with painting. The complex ways in which traditional arts inspire modern filmmaking would reward further exploration and are vitally connected to what Paul Willemen refers to as the 'orchestration of meaning' in cinema.

Let us, for example, consider the filmmaker Yasujiro Ozu. In his films, stillness and emptiness play a crucial role in the production of meaning. On the surface, if seen through Western eyes, nothing happens. But at a deeper level of emotional and cultural apprehension, much is going on in those stillnesses and emptinesses. This is, of course, connected with traditional Japanese aesthetics. For example, in Japanese manuals of painting it is remarked that emptiness does not occur until the first ink mark is inscribed on the paper, thereby calling attention to the vital interplay between emptiness and inscriptions as co-producers of meaning. In the same way, African filmmakers have made a conscious attempt to draw on the traditional African arts in filmmaking, especially the art of oral storytelling, and the use of dreams, fantasies, narrative detours, and parallelisms in the films of Ousmane Sembene, Haile Gerima, Souleymane Cissé, and Idrissa Ouedraogo demonstrate this link (see Ukadike, Part 3, Chapter 24).

The interconnections between cinema and painting in most Asian countries is a fascinating one. Japanese, Chinese, and Korean filmmakers in the past have tapped the rich resources of painting in framing their shots, creating mise-en-scène, and organizing their visual material, and they continue to do so. For example, in the visual style of films such as Chen Kaige's *Yellow Earth*, one can see the impact of Taoism and traditional Chinese paintings of nature. The towering presence of hills and mountains and the diminutive human beings etched against them, the use of a limited range of colours, natural lighting, and the nonperspectival deployment of space, bear testimony to this fact. Similarly, in the work of Ritwik Ghatak, one perceives an attempt to use creatively and innovatively traditional Indian iconography associated with painting in order to communicate a cinematic experience that is anchored in the past but reaching out to the present.

However, we also need to bear in mind that this is not only a question of aesthetics; there is also an ideological and political aspect to it. For example, in *Yellow Earth*, the extreme long shots, the absence of depth, and the empty spaces that fill the frame can be read as a critique of the Cultural Revolution and its excesses. The supposedly apolitical visuals inscribed in the massive presence of nature therefore make a political statement. Going beyond this reading, as Rey Chow (1995) points out, we need to examine the film in terms of its material makings and rethink the cognitive value of emptiness and blankness. As she rightly observes, in order to make sense of 'space' the viewer would have to 'view' space from a position whose locality would 'see' non-signifying blankness in relation to the representational presence itself. Hence, in order to grasp the complexities of the enunciative positions and spectatorships that characterize non-Western cinemas, texts—and their inter-texts—must be analysed in terms of ideology and politics as well as artistic apprehension.

Any meaningful discussion of the cinemas of the non-Western world would compel us to confront issues of economics, politics, aesthetics, institutions, technology, and cultural discourse in general. What is the nature of the national film industry? What role do governments play, both positive and negative? How are the cinema industries located at the local and the global? How are they dealing with the hegemony of Hollywood? How do filmmakers seek to construct alternative histories and cultural identities? These, and similar issues that merit closer anlaysis, will be dealt with at length in the specific case-studies that follow. What I have sought to do in this introductory chapter is to raise some salient issues related to the cinemas of the non-Western world. As Paul Willemen (1989) observes, what the outstanding filmmakers from Asia, Africa, and Latin America have done is to start from a recognition of the multilayeredness of their own cultural-historical formations, with each layer being shaped by intricate linkages between local as well as international forces. As a consequence, these filmmakers suggest a way of inhabiting one's culture which is neither myopically nationalist nor evasively cosmopolitan. This is the ideal that stands before the filmmakers of the non-Western world.

> **What the outstanding filmmakers from Asia, Africa, and Latin America have done is to start from a recognition of the multilayeredness of their own cultural-historical formations, with each layer being shaped by intricate linkages between local as well as international forces.**

BIBLIOGRAPHY

Anderson, Benedict (1983), *Imagined Communities: Reflections on the Origin and Spread of Nationalism* (London: Verso).

Appiah, Kwame Anthony (1992), *In my Father's House: Africa in the Philosophy of Culture* (Oxford: Oxford University Press).

Chow, Rey (1995), *Primitive Passions: Visibility, Ethnography, and Contemporary Chinese Cinema* (New York: Columbia University Press).

Davis, Darrell William (1996), *Picturing Japaneseness: Monumental Style, National Identity, Japanese Films* (New York: Columbia University Press).

Dissanayake, Wimal (ed.) (1994), *Colonialism and Nationalism in Asian Cinema* (Bloomington: Indiana University Press).

Gabriel, Teshome K. (1982), *Third Cinema in the Third World* (Ann Arbor, Mi.: UMI Research Press).

Habermas, Jurgen (1991), *The Structural Transformation of the Public Sphere: An Inquiry into a Category of Bourgeois Society*, trans. Thomas Burger and Frederick Lawrence (Cambridge, Mass.: MIT Press).

Harvey, David (1989), *The Condition of Postmodernity: An Enquiry into the Origins of Cultural Change* (Oxford: Blackwell).

Negt, Oskar, and **Alexander Kluge** (1993), *Public Sphere and Experience: Towards an Analysis of the Bourgeois and Proletarian Public Sphere* (Minneapolis: University of Minnesota Press).

Phalke: Commemoration Souvenir (1970), (Bombay: Phalke Centenary Celebrations Committee).

Rajadhyaksha, Ashish (1985), 'The Phalke Era: Conflict of Traditional Forms and Modern Techology', *Journal of Arts and Ideas*, nos. 14–15.

CRITICAL APPROACHES TO WORLD CINEMA

Solanas, Fernando E., and Octavio Getino (1973), *Cine: cultura y descolonizacion* (Buenos Aires: Siglo XXI Argentino Editores).

*Willemen, Paul (ed.) (1989), *Questions of Third Cinema* (London: British Film Institute).

—— (1994), *Looks and Frictions: Essays in Cultural Studies and Film Theory* (Bloomington: Indiana University Press).

19

Indian cinema

Ashish Rajadhyaksha

As with the history of modern India itself, the history of the Indian cinema has until recently been written mainly with nationalist intention. India became an independent 'sovereign democratic republic' in 1947, with the transfer of power from the British into the hands of a nationalist ruling élite. In the process, the independent nation-state was heir to a century-old history of engagment with modernity, social reform, and democracy that culminated in something like a seventy-year freedom struggle from colonization. It has been the business of India's most important historians to write, from this vantage-point of political independence, what Gyanendra Pandey calls the 'biography of the nation-state', and from its ensuing contention that

the [Indian political] 'centre' remains the recognised vantage point for a meaningful reconstruction of 'Indian' history, and the 'official' archive . . . the primary source for its construction. By attributing a 'natural' quality to a particular unity, such as 'India', and adopting its 'official' archive as the primary source for historical knowledge . . . the history of India since the early 19th century has tended to become

the biography of the emerging nation-state. It has also become the history in which the story of Partition, and the accompanying Hindu–Muslim and Muslim–Sikh riots . . . is written up as a secondary story . . . one that, for all its consequences miraculously left the course of Indian history unaltered [as] 'India' started firmly . . . and naturally on its secular, democratic, non-violent course. (Pandey 1991)

Part of the history of modern India has been the enormously influential presence of what is now famous as the 'world's largest film industry'. This was one of the legacies of the colonial state that Independence bestowed upon free India and, as with nationalist political history, India's film history has been largely written up from the standpoint of state policy on Indian cinema after 1947, with its efforts to install a respectable 'realist cinema'. A concern with respectability and, occasionally, political usefulness is also evident in critical-theoretical efforts to make sense of Indian cinema in the era of high nationalism.

In recent years, however, there has emerged a body of new writing that is as influenced by what we could call 'post-nationalist' historiography, notably that pioneered by the famed Subaltern Studies collective (see Guha 1982–9), as by new theory in the West, such as cultural studies and post-colonial theory. In the following survey, I shall first briefly outline Indian cinema's own history, asking readers to bear in mind that the periodizations I use are still mainly orthodox ones, the cinematic equivalents of the 'biography of the nation-state'. They are used mainly because newer ones are still not sufficiently common as to be useful for such a brief survey. Then I shall outline an influential critical tradition that I have identified as largely 'nationalist', including important film journalism; and in the final section, I shall provide a brief summary of recent theoretical writing on Indian film.

Indian cinema: a brief history

Virtually all conventional history of Indian cinema begins with the man considered its pioneer: Dhundiraj Govind Phalke (also known as Dadasaheb Phalke). Born in Nasik in 1870, Phalke had had a colourful history an an artist, photographer, and printer before he launched his film career with the mythological *Raja Harishchandra* in 1914 (see Rajadhyaksha 1987). This was the first Indian fiction film we know of, but it was hardly India's first movie. Since 1896 India had had a thriving nascent film industry mainly on the periphery of a vast and well-entrenched theatre industry, including in particular the Parsee theatre and commercial theatrical troupes in its main presidency cities of Bombay, Calcutta (see Mukherjee 1980), and Madras, as well as many other cities (e.g. Lucknow and Lahore).

Part of the history of modern India has been the enormously influential presence of what is now famous as the 'world's largest film industry'. This was one of the legacies of the colonial state that Independence bestowed upon free India and, as with nationalist political history, India's film history has been largely written up from the standpoint of state policy on Indian cinema after 1947, with its efforts to install a respectable 'realist cinema'.

India also had a nearly century-old history of popular visual art, extending into what has come to be called 'Company School' painting (Indian art made for British clients and Indian bureaucracy and aristocracy, named after the East India Company) and further developing at the turn of the century, into bazaar paintings, notably in Calcutta, and art for a growing publishing industry (e.g. woodcut print-making) (see Archer 1953, 1962; Archer 1977). This practice, constituting among other things India's first encounter with Western oil-painting and naturalism—exemplified by the painter Raja Ravi Varma, who started as a portraitist, went on to paint Indian mythological scenes in naturalist style, and finally became a mass producer of religious oleographs and lithographs (see Kapur 1989)—also extended into still photography, which then formed a key bridge into cinema itself.

A great deal of recent writing has investigated the cultural practices of the pre-cinema traditions of popular art, as industry, and politically in its gradual assimilation of nationalist identity, for example Guha-Thakurta's landmark book *The Making of New 'Indian' Art* (1992). This now well-charted territory has not, however, been duplicated by significant research into early Indian cinema before Phalke, although biographical material on other contemporaries, notably Hiralal Sen in Calcutta (who started by filming plays; see Mukherjee 1966) and Nataraja Mudaliar in Madras, is available. Phalke's own undoubtedly influential cinema has, however, been enhanced by two further factors: first, his accompaniment of that cinema with an early effort towards theory, especially Swadeshi (or national-indigenism), which allowed him to claim a political character to his staple genre of the Hindu mythological. The survival of the genre well into recent times (and the new lease of life that television has recently given it) partly explains Phalke's key presence in all nationalist Indian film histories ever since, especially those written up by the film industry itself or on its behalf by 'official' historians. There has, however, been a major recent revival of interest in the silent film, mainly as a result of a restoration project at the National Film Archive of India and the showcasing of surviving silents in the Pordenone Film Festival (see Chabria 1994).

The more concrete historiography of Indian cinema, however, emerges only from the 1920s with the founding of major studios—notably the Kohinoor and Ranjit in Bombay, the New Theatres in Calcutta, the Maharashtra Film Company (Kolhapur), and its famous offshoot, Prabhat, which moved to Poona. These studios, and their famed sound versions—which coalesced mainly into the 'dominant' three: New Theatres, Prabhat, and Bombay Talkies—introduced professional distribution systems, as well as star manufacture, establishing a substantial base for the Indian cinema before the Second World War (by which time audiences for local products already far exceeded those for imported films).

Conventional film histories of this period usually focus on the three studios mentioned above, and its famous film directors—V. Shantaram (Prabhat), the German Franz Osten and his producer Himansu Rai (Bombay Talkies), and the whole stable of directors at New Theatres, notably P. C. Barua and Nitin and Debaki Bose—for having introduced many of the tenets of modernism, 'art' cinema, and respectable nationalism. It is less noticed that even at this time the considerably larger bulk of production already came out of independent production outfits based in Bombay, Calcutta, and Madras, which often reduced the major studios into hirers of studio space. As with Phalke, here too the survival of studio productions from the 'big three' has further reinforced claims regarding the admittedly major cultural influence of these houses.

The Second World War was crucial for perhaps exactly the opposite reason of its impact in the West. The war economy, it has been extensively documented, actually stimulated independently financed industry, and after the war the big studios were overwhelmed by independent financier-producers entering the film industry with mainly short-term benefits in mind.

Three main trends in Indian cinema are evident after the war. First, there is the founding of something like a national, or nation-wide, audience for the Hindi cinema, which benefited from the Partition of India as the former movie industries of Lahore and Karachi, in what became Pakistan, migrated to Bombay. Secondly there is an extension of the 'all-India' aesthetic—of fantasies that often came to be called 'masala' films—into other languages, notably Tamil, Teluga, Bengali, and Marathi, and new production bases in Hyderabad, Bangalore, and Coimbatore, for example. Thirdly, a major political influence came with the founding of the Indian state itself, and the adoption of official measures to discipline the film industry into adhering to new cultural and ideological priorities. This latter initiative led to the government itself entering film production, and to the establishment of an art cinema movement that produced India's best-known filmmaker, Satyajit Ray.

To a great extent the ideological tensions that characterize these three developments decide the priorities of much nationalist film writing and have been analysed notably by Ravi Vasudevan (1993). This period, when several 'all-time hits' by filmmakers like Guru Dutt, Raj Kapoor, Mehboob, and V. Shantaram were made, has also been written up as the 'golden age' of the Indian cinema and in numerous books and essays on the work of Satyajit Ray (notably Das Gupta 1980, 1981).

In the late 1960s direct state action realized some of the recommendations of the 1951 Film Enquiry Committee to 'provide, afford or procure finance or other facilities for the production of films of good standard', by designating new priorities for the Film Finance Corporation (FFC), which helped to launch the famed New Indian Cinema movement. Launched in part by Mrinal Sen's *Bhuvan Shome* (1969) and Mani Kaul's highly experimental *Uski Roti* (1969), the FFC produced both self-consciously avant-garde film—especially the work of Kaul and Kumar Shahani (see Shahani 1986)—as well as what came, with the work especially of Shyam Benegal, to define further an aesthetic of 'state realism'. Emphasizing what is usually interpreted as a romantic realism with a major investment in regional roots (i.e. as against the Hindi cinema's 'rootless' pan-nationalism), the New Cinema helped establish local industries, notably in Kerala, Assam, and Orissa, which were all relatively marginal until the 1970s.

However, this was also the time when the mainstream Hindi cinema transformed itself yet again, in the light of political developments that culminated in the National Emergency declared by Indira Gandhi in 1975, a transformation usually equated with the star who was to dominate Hindi cinema until the present, Amitabh Bachchan. Associated in the 1970s with a vigilante 'angry young man' stereotype, which often appropriated rhetorically the political movements of the peasantry and working classes that had led to the Emergency, the Bachchan phenomenon in many ways encapsulates this turbulent period in Indian history, which only transformed itself in the late 1980s with economic liberalization, the arrival of satellite television, and the founding of Doordarshan, the massive Indian state television infrastructure.

Nationalist film theory: a brief history

In 1948, a year after Independence, Satyajit Ray wrote his influential essay 'What is Wrong with Indian Films?' to launch a now well-entrenched attack on the Indian cinema for its inability to comprehend what is basic to film, namely temporality and movement. 'In India, it would seem that the fundamental concept of a coherent dramatic pattern existing in time was generally misunderstood . . . often by a queer process of reasoning, movement was equated with action and action with melodrama'.

Ray's own cinema, which has conventionally been seen as the point at which Indian cinema's initiatives towards realism, and the mastering of the storytelling idiom, were finally realized, has also provided the post-Independence focus for debates about divisions between realism versus modernism, high art versus low, and, after the avant-garde practice of some New Indian Cinema filmmakers, modernism versus avant-garde (usually mapped onto the two very different legacies of Ray himself as against his equally influential, but less well-known, contemporary Ritwik Ghatak; for Ghatak, see Rajadhyaksha 1982, 1987; Ghatak 1987). One of the key figures embodying the Ray aesthetic is the writer Chidananda Das Gupta, his long-time colleague, with whom Ray launched the seminal Calcutta Film Society in 1947. Das Gupta's important collection of essays, published mainly in film society periodicals like the *Indian Film Review* and *Indian Film Culture*—a crucial forum for educating people into modernist filmmaking and film seeing practices—includes the classic 'The Cultural Basis of Indian Cinema' (1968). In that article Das Gupta argued for the 'all-India film', a genre of the nationalist mass entertainer that played the political function of culturally integrating the country and in that sense performed by default a role that Ray also, with greater self-consciousness, was attempting in his practice. Another key writer from this period, addressing a range of issues from the viewpoint of this modernist divide, was Kobita Sarkar (1975, 1982).

As the question of art cinema merged into that of the specific reformist role of the Indian state in the area of film, there emerged a substantial body of both historical writing (see notably Barnouw and Krishnaswamy (1963), the best-known book on Indian cinema until recently) and writings on film policy, the nature of state funding, questions of censorship, and the role of the reviewer in popular journals. Key roles were played by mass circulation periodicals like *Filmfare* (a fortnightly owned by the *Times of India*) and *Screen* (a film weekly owned by the *Indian Express* group); and by B. K. Karanjia, a film journalist who at different times in his career edited both journals, and was responsible, as chairman of the FFC in the late 1960s for many of the aesthetic decisions and choices made by that organization regarding the New Indian Cinema.

> **Ray's own cinema, which has conventionally been seen as the point at which Indian cinema's initiatives towards realism, and the mastering of the storytelling idiom, were finally realized, has also provided the post-Independence focus for debates about divisions between realism versus modernism, high art versus low, and, after the avant-garde practice of some New Indian Cinema filmmakers, modernism versus avant-garde.**

This body of nationalist film writing also addressed the 'pre-Ray' era through an often evolutionist notion of history which saw filmmakers like Barua, Bimal Roy, and those associated with the left-wing Indian Peoples' Theatre Association as the precursors of what reached fruition with Independence. Much of this earlier 'author' cinema, produced by the major studios, has also been seen in terms of bringing literary respectability to cinema, notably at the New Theatres. This also constitutes a major feature of early critical writing in films of this time (see Jha 1990). Alongside this critical writing are two other influences: the film reviewers and journalists who took upon themselves the responsibility of 'educating' viewers into realism (e.g. Kalki, in Tamil, and the critic with the pseudonym Cynic in Malayalam), and the government reports addressing state intervention (the Film Enquiry Committee Report, 1951), censorship (the Khosla Report on Film Censorship, 1969), and the role of the FFC (Committee on Public Undertakings Report on the Film Finance Corporation, 1976).

Much recent theory on this period has addressed the role of melodrama, rather than realism in its orthodox sense, as having played a pivotal role in the cinematic 'writing of the biography of the nation-state' (see Chakravarty 1993). Both Ravi Vasudevan (1993) and Madhava Prasad (1994) examine melodrama as a system of cohering narratives addressing post-Independence urbanization in particular.

Recent film theory: a brief history

A politically well-researched area in India is the 1970s, when the earlier nationalist definition of the state underwent a series of crises: the emergence of the extreme left Naxalite movement, working-class agitations culminating in the Nav Nirman movements in Bihar and Gujarat and the declaration of an internal Emergency by Indira Gandhi in 1975 (see Frankel 1978).

The later New Indian Cinema in this period also yielded a specifically avant-garde practice in the films, teachings, and writings of Kumar Shahani. A student of Ritwik Ghatak, Shahani's cinema and his body of writing constitutes, alongside the political developments of that decade, the first major shift in the 'national modernist' writing of Indian film history (Shahani 1986). Shahani's work parallels a range of practices in Indian visual art, music, and theatre that systematically sought both formal and ideological alternatives to realism, often reworking pre-colonial practices with the awareness of a historical internationalist avant-garde. The key theories of this time are mainly encapsulated in an influential journal, the *Journal of Arts and Ideas*, founded in the late 1980s. The journal demonstrates at least three phases through which Indian cultural and film theory have gone since the Emergency. The immediate and specifically political crises following the Emergency led to numerous inquiries into an aesthetic that might resurrect the still-valuable nationalist imperative, but on lines other than those which had prevailed in 'official' histories and which were incarnated in official cultural institutions. Geeta Kapur's writings covering this period (Kapur 1990, 1991, 1993) are key markers of this shift towards investigating the history of a specifically Indian, and generally non-Western, modernism. Other important writings from this time, criticizing state formations, include M. S. S. Pandian's landmark book (1992) on the movie megastar and Chief Minister M. G. Ramachandran and his despotic rule even as he became an almost unreachable icon in Tamil Nadu.

The second phase constituted the formal entry of

> Shahani's work parallels a range of practices in Indian visual art, music, and theatre that systematically sought both formal and ideological alternatives to realism, often reworking pre-colonial practices with the awareness of a historical internationalist avant-garde.

post-colonial theory, and with this the reinvestigation of the history of Indian nationalism itself as one that specifically opened up the 'biography of the nation-state'. *Arts and Ideas'* special issue *Careers of Modernity*, edited by Tejaswini Niranjana, goes alongside Niranjana, P. Sudhir, and Vivek Dhareshwar's seminal anthology *Interrogating Modernity* (1993), to form the definitive material on this area. This by-now-substantial body of work has been mainly influenced by the new terrain of analysing nationalist historiography opened up by the Subaltern Studies historians, and notably Partha Chatterjee (1986, 1994). Chatterjee's work is premissed on the Gramscian concept of the passive revolution, in which the state first exists and then constructs the pre-conditions of its existence, which include the terms of normative and designative interpellation of its 'citizen subjects'.

The third, and perhaps most recent, dimension opened up specifically in the realm of film studies in India follows the founding of the first postgraduate department of film studies at Jadavpur University, Calcutta. Apart from Prasad's own thesis (1994) and Vasudevan's writings, recent developments in film studies include the now-famous 'Roja debate', around Mani Rathnam's film, following Niranjana's (1994) essay in the *Economic and Political Weekly*. In late 1995 conferences in film studies in Simla (at the Indian Institute of Advanced Studies), Poona (at the National Film Archive of India), and on cultural studies (organized by the Centre for Studies in Social Sciences) indicate a growing academic acceptance of film studies in orthodox literature, history, and social science departments.

BIBLIOGRAPHY

Archer, Mildred (1977), *Indian Popular Paintings in the India Office Library* (London: HMSO).

Archer, W. G. (1953), *Bazaar Paintings of Calcutta* (London: Victoria and Albert Museum).

—— (1962), *Kalighat Drawings* (Bombay: Marg Publications).

*Barnouw, Eric, and S. Krishnaswamy (1963/1980), *Indian Film* (New York: Columbia University Press; rev. edn. (incl. New Indian Cinema) Oxford: Oxford University Press).

Chabria, Suresh, and Paolo Cherchi Usai (eds.) (1994), *Light of Asia* (National Film Archive of India and Le Giornate del Cinema Muto).

*Chakravarty, Sumita S. (1993), *National Identity in Indian Popular Cinema 1947–1987* (Austin: University of Texas Press).

Chatterjee, Partha (1986), *Nationalist Thought and the Colonial World: A Derivative Discourse* (New Delhi: Oxford University Press).

—— (1994), *The Nation and its Fragments: Colonial and Postcolonial Histories* (New Delhi: Oxford University Press).

Das Gupta, Chidananda (1980), *The Cinema of Satyajit Ray* (New Delhi: Vikas).

—— (1968/1981a), 'The Cultural Basis of the Indian Cinema', in *Talking about Films* (New Delhi: Orient Longman).

—— (ed.) (1981b), *Satyajit Ray* (New Delhi: Directorate of Film Festivals).

Film Enquiry Committee (1951) (Chairman, S. K. Patil), *Report of the Film Enquiry Committee* (New Delhi: Government of India Press).

Frankel, Francine (1978), *India's Political Economy 1947–1977: The Gradual Revolution* (Princeton: Princeton University Press).

Ghatak, Ritwik (1987), *Cinema and I* (Calcutta: Ritwik Memorial Trust and Rupa).

Guha, Ranajit (ed.), *Subaltern Studies*, 1 (1982), 2 (1983), 3 (1984), 4 (1985), 5 (1987), 6 (1989) (New Delhi: Oxford University Press).

Guha-Thakurta, Tapati (1992), *The Making of a New 'Indian' Art: Artists, Aesthetics and Nationalism in Bengal c.1850–1920* (Cambridge: Cambridge University Press).

Gutman, Judith Mara (1982), *Through Indian Eyes: Nineteenth and Early Twentieth Century Still Photography in India* (New York: Oxford University Press and International Centre of Photography).

Jha, Bagishwar (ed.) (1990), *B. N. Sircar* (Calcutta: NFAI and Seagull Books).

Kapur, Geeta (1989), 'Ravi Varma: Representational Dilemmas of a Nineteenth Century Indian Painter', *Journal of Arts and Ideas*, 17–18 (June).

—— (1990), 'Contemporary Cultural Practice: Some Polemical Categories', *Social Scientist*, 18/3 (Mar.).

—— (1991), 'The Place of the Modern in Contemporary Cultural Practice', *Economic and Political Weekly*, 26/49 (7 Dec.).

—— (1993), 'When was Modernism in Indian/Third World Art?', *South Atlantic Quarterly*, 92/3 (Summer).

Mukherjee, Prabhat (1966), *Hiralal Sen: India's First Film-maker* (Calcutta: Cine Central).

Mukherjee, Sushil Kumar (1980), *The Story of the Calcutta Theatres 1753–1980* (Calcutta: K. P. Bagchi).

Niranjana, Tejaswini (1994), 'Integrating whose Nation? Tourists and Terrorists in *Roja*', *Economic and Political Weekly* 24/3 (15 Jan.).

—— P. Sudhir, and Vivek Dhareshwar (1993), *Interrogating Modernity: Culture and Colonialism in India* (Calcutta: Seagull Books).

Pandey, Gyanendra (1991), 'In Defence of the Fragment: Writing about Hindu–Muslim Riots in India Today', *Economic and Political Weekly*, 26/11–12 (Annual).

Pandian, M. S. S. (1992), *The Image Trap: M. G. Ramachandran in Film and Politics* (New Delhi: Sage).

Prasad, Madhava (1994, forthcoming), *The State and Culture: Hindi Cinema in the Passive Revolution*, Ph.D. thesis, University of Pittsburgh (New Delhi: Oxford University Press).

Rajadhyaksha, Ashish (1982), *Ritwik Ghatak: A Return to the Epic* (Bombay: Screen Unit).

—— (1987), 'The Phalke Era: Conflict of Traditional Form and Modern Technology', *Journal of Arts and Ideas*, 14–15 (July–Dec.).

—— and Amrit Gangar (1987), *Ghatak: Arguments/Stories* (Bombay: Screen Unit).

*—— and Paul Willemen (1994–5), *Encyclopaedia of Indian Cinema* (London and New Delhi: British Film Institute and Oxford University Press).

Ray, Satyajit (1948/1976), 'What is Wrong with Indian Films?', in *Our Films, Their Films* (New Delhi: Orient Longman).

Sarkar, Kobita (1975), *Indian Cinema Today* (New Delhi: Sterling).

—— (1982), *You Can't Please All: Film Censorship, the Inside Story* (Bombay: IBH).

Shahani, Kumar (1986), 'Dossier on Kumar Shahani', *Framework*, 30–1.

Vasudevan, Ravi (1993), 'Shifting Codes, Dissolving Identities: The Hindi Social Film of the 1950s as Popular Culture', *Journal of Arts and Ideas*, 23–4.

Popular Hindi cinema

Rosie Thomas from Rosie Thomas, 'Indian Cinema: Pleasures and Popularity', *Screen*, 26/3–4 (May–Aug. 1985), 116–31.

Discussion of Indian popular cinema as 'other' cinema is immediately problematic. There is no disputing that, within the context of First World culture and society, this cinema has always been marginalized, if not ignored completely. It has been defined primarily through its 'otherness' or 'difference' from First World cinema, and consumption of it in the West, whether by Asians or non-Asians, is something of an assertion: one has chosen to view an 'alternative' type of cinema. However, this is a cinema which, in the Indian context, is an overridingly dominant, mainstream form, and is itself opposed by an 'Other': the 'new', 'parallel', 'art' (or often simply 'other') cinema which ranges from the work of Satyajit Ray, Shyam Benegal, and various regional filmmakers, to Mani Kaul's 'avant-garde' or Anand Patwardhan's 'agitational' political practice. In these terms Indian popular cinema is neither alternative nor a minority form. Moreover, in a global context, by virtue of its sheer volume of output, the Indian entertainment cinema still dominates world film production, and its films are distributed throughout large areas of the Third World, where they are frequently consumed more avidly than both Hollywood and indigenous 'alternative' or political cinemas. Such preference suggests that these films are seen to be offering something

positively different from Hollywood, and, in fact, largely because it has always had its own vast distribution markets, Indian cinema has, throughout its long history, evolved as a form which has resisted the cultural imperialism of Hollywood. This is not, of course, to say that it has been 'uninfluenced' by Hollywood: the form has undergone continual change and there has been both inspiration and assimilation from Hollywood and elsewhere, but thematically and structurally, Indian cinema has remained remarkably distinctive.

Bombay filmmakers repeatedly stress that they are aiming to make films which differ in both format and content from Western films, that there is a definite skill to making films for the Indian audience, that this audience has specific needs and expectations, and that to compare Hindi films to those of the West, or of the Indian 'art' cinema is irrelevant.

Compared with the conventions of much Western cinema, Hindi films appear to have patently preposterous narratives, overblown dialogue (frequently evaluated by filmmakers on whether or not it is 'clapworthy'), exaggeratedly stylized acting, and to show disregard for psychological

Making a popular Hindi film—Dev Anand on location in *Lootmaar* (1980)

Popular Hindi cinema continued

characterization, history, geography, and even, sometimes, camera placement rules. (Camera placement rules can be disregarded, particularly in action (fight) scenes, which seem to be allowed something of the non-continuity conventions of song sequences.)

Tolerance of overt fantasy has always been high in Hindi cinema, with little need to anchor the material in what Western conventions might recognize as a discourse of 'realism', and slippage between registers does not have to be marked or rationalized. The most obvious example is the song sequences, which are much less commonly 'justified' within the story (for example, introduced as stage performances by the fictional characters) than in Hollywood musicals. Hindi film songs are usually tightly integrated, through words and mood, within the *flow* of the film—and misguided attempts to doctor Hindi films for Western audiences by cutting out the songs are always fatal. However, the song sequences (often also dream sequences) do permit excesses of fantasy which are more problematic elsewhere in the film, for they specifically allow that continuities of time and place be disregarded, that heroines may change saris between shots and the scenery skip continents between verses, whenever the interests or spectacle or mood require it.

However, this is not to say that 'anything goes': there is a firm sense of 'acceptable realism and logic', beyond which material is rejected as 'unbelievable'. In fact, the criteria of verisimilitude in Hindi cinema appear to refer primarily to a film's skill in manipulating the rules of the film's moral universe, and one is more likely to hear accusations of 'unbelievability' if the codes of, for example, ideal kinship behaviour are ineptly transgressed (i.e. a son kills his mother; or a father knowingly and callously causes his son to suffer), than if the hero is a superman who single-handedly knocks out a dozen burly henchmen and then bursts into song.

It would appear that the spectator-subject of Hindi cinema is positioned rather differently from that of much Western cinema. In fact, even on the most overt level, Indian cinema audience behaviour is distinctive: involvement in the films is intense, and audiences clap, sing, recite familiar dialogue with the actors, throw coins at the screen (in appreciation of spectacle), 'tut-tut' at emotionally moving scenes, cry openly and laugh and jeer knowingly. Moreover, it is expected that audiences will see a film they like several times, and so-called 'repeat value' is deliberately built into a production by the filmmakers, who believe that the keys to this are primarily the stars, music, spectacle, emotion, and dialogue—this last having a greater significance than in Western cinema.

What seems to emerge in Hindi cinema is an emphasis on emotion and spectacle rather than tight narrative, on *how* things will happen rather than *what* will happen next, on a succession of modes rather than linear denouement, on familiarity and repeated viewings rather than 'originality' and novelty, on a moral disordering to be (temporarily) resolved rather than an enigma to be solved. The spectator is addressed and moved through the films primarily via affect, although this is structured and contained by narratives whose power and insistence derives from their very familiarity, coupled with the fact that they are deeply rooted (in the psyche and in traditional mythology).

20

Chinese cinema

Bérénice Reynaud

The rise of critical interest in Chinese cinema

Geopolitical events of the last thirty years have drastically affected Western scholarship on Chinese cinema—including even the transcription of proper names into the Latin alphabet. In the early 1980s the old Wade–Giles system was eventually replaced by the internationally standardized Pinyin developed in the People's Republic of China (PRC). Mao Tse-tung (Mao Tsé-toung in French) became Mao Zedong, and the filmmaker Tsai Chu-sheng (Tsai Tchou-cheng in French) is now spelled Cai Chusheng. Some major texts, such as Jay Leyda's *Dianying* (1972) and Régis Bergeron's first volume (1977), pre-date the adoption of Pinyin, which makes cross-referencing difficult. And, since Western habits contrast with the Chinese custom of placing the family name *before* the given name, some historians prefer to print the family name in capital letters. However, perhaps the major problem confronting scholars working on Chinese cinema is access to films. Deng Xiaoping's open-door policy of the late 1970s has facilitated cultural exchanges, but Chinese cinema largely remains an uncharted sea, even if a few islands have now come into view.

The highly successful screening of Chen Kaige's *Huang tudi* ('The Yellow Earth', 1984) at the 1985 Hong Kong Film Festival (McDougall 1991: 55–114) prompted a new interest in Chinese cinema. While ignored and criticized in the PRC, the film launched the concept of the 'Fifth Generation' at an international level. Specifically, the 'Fifth Generation' denotes filmmakers such as Zhang Yimou, Tian Zhuangzhuang, and Huang Jianxin, who, like Chen Kaige, had entered the Beijing Film Academy in 1978, the year it reopened after the Cultural Revolution. The first Fifth Generation film therefore is actually not *The Yellow Earth*, but Zhang Junzhao's *Yige he bage* ('One and Eight', 1984).

The term 'Fifth Generation' echoes the various 'new wave' movements taking place in the early 1980s in Hong Kong and Taiwan (Browne et al 1994). It is often assumed that the term 'generation' is used to designate the distinct role that each decade's filmmakers have played in the political and aesthetic construction of a national cinema in China. Tony Rayns, however, states that Fifth Generation directors were simply 'the fifth class to graduate from the school's Directing Department' (Rayns, 1991: 104) while, for Chris Berry, the term highlights the stylistic breakthrough between Fifth Generation films and those which preceded them (Berry 1991: 116).

Since 1985 scholarship in the West has focused on a few films and a few directors: in particular, the detailed essays of Esther C. M. Yau (1991) on Chen Kaige's *Yellow Earth* and Wang Yuejin (1991) on Zhang Yimou's *Hong gaoliang* ('Red Sorghum', 1987) as well as Rey Chow (1995) on Chen Kaige's *Yellow Earth* and *Haizi*

Chen Kaige's *The Yellow Earth* (1984) prompted a new interest in Chinese cinema

Wang ('King of the Children', 1987), which all employ the various strategies of textual analysis (psychoanalysis, structuralism, feminist and cultural theory). The work of other filmmakers, both within and without the Fifth Generation, has been much less explored. There are, however, some exceptions: most notably Berry's research on the viewing subject of Chinese cinema, as it is constructed in films from the 1960s and 1980s (Berry 1991a; 1994), Ma Ning's (1994) and Nick Browne's (1994: 40–56) work on Xie Jin's melodramas, and Paul G. Pickowicz's (1994) study of Huang Jianxin's 'post-socialist' films.

Recent scholarship on Fifth Generation films and melodramas of the 1980s has often focused on the construction of sexual difference and the representation of women. Yet, the 'placement' of femininity and masculinity within the Chinese tradition (especially Confucianism) does not coincide with the Western construction of gender, which problematizes the application of cross-cultural analyses. While Esther C. M. Yau makes a brilliant case for the use of Western analysis of a non-Western text (Yau 1991), prompting a debate taken up in particular by Rey Chow (1995), issues of gender are often combined with explorations of other forms of difference in Chinese culture: such as those of insider–outsider and moral–immoral (Ma Ning 1994), yin–yang and class differences (Wang 1991), or ethnic differences (Yau 1994).

The great emphasis of recent scholarship and criticism on Chen and Zhang, often in the form of comparisons between the style of the two directors (Chow 1995: 160–3), has, however, marginalized the contributions of Fifth Generation women filmmakers (Hu Mei, Peng Xiaolian, Li Shaohong, Ning Ying). Two notable exceptions are Berry's text 'Chinese "Women's Cinema"' (1988) and E. Ann Kaplan's feminist analysis of Hu Mei's *Nü'er lou* ('Army Nurse', 1986) (Kaplan 1991*b*).

While Browne's and Berry's essays contextualize Fifth Generation work within the history of Chinese cinema, most texts on recent films consist purely of synchronic analyses. Pickowicz (1993: 295) sees the 'new research on Chinese cinema' as too 'narrowly focused' as a result of the 'absence of a large scholarly literature that covers all the decades of the twentieth century', while Clark (1987: 1) was prompted to write his book by the lack of a 'full-length scholarly study of film in China after 1949'. Apart from Clark's book, the three major contributions to the history of Chinese cinema are those of Leyda (1972), Bergeron (1977, 1983–4), and a French collection that covers Chinese cinema from 1922 to 1984 from a variety of point of views (historical, aesthetic, cultural, theoretical) and includes very comprehensive data on 141 films and 54 filmmakers (Quiquemelle and Passek 1985). Unfortunately these books were completed too early to include the Fifth Generation (although Clark briefly mentions *The Yellow Earth*). The texts dealing with post-1985 Chinese cinema (Berry 1991; Browne 1994; Chow 1995) are collections of essays written at different times without claim to exhaustiveness or a unified point of view.

How Chinese is it?

The interest raised in the West by the Fifth Generation has reopened an old question: is Chinese cinema merely derivative of Western forms, or has it made an original use of the medium? The Chinese detractors of *The Yellow Earth* found its success abroad 'suspect' (McDougall 1991: 102): if foreigners liked the film, it was argued, it was because it presented a 'bad' image of China. Since 1949 foreignness and cosmopolitanism have been associated with an implicit betrayal of Maoist ideology. For Rey Chow (1995: 37–8), the question of the image projected to Western audiences implies the fetishization and commodification of China in a post-colonial circulation of filmic signifiers. Yet, while comparing this presentation of China to the West accomplished by Fifth Generation filmmakers like Chen and Zhang to the state of mind of colonized subjects trying to 'engage with the colonizer's own terms' (38), Chow also finds them guilty of a 'form of

primitive passion that is sinocentrism' (51) and generating the nativist belief that foreign audiences 'cannot understand China . . . the ultimate essence beyond representation' (49–50). The dual nature of Chinese cinema underlines this contradiction: produced by and for Chinese, it also belongs to an international film history through which China and the West have constructed exotic spectacles for each other.

> **The dual nature of Chinese cinema underlines this contradiction: produced by and for Chinese, it also belongs to an international film history through which China and the West have constructed exotic spectacles for each other.**

The 1995 centenary prompted renewed inquiries about the introduction of cinema into China, especially among Hong Kong scholars (Law and Teo 1995); a matter which had previously been investigated by Leyda's (1972) generous and enthusiastic curiosity. However, while the genesis of the filmic images in China's early cinema raises a number of theoretical and epistemological issues, it has mostly been presented by historians as a collection of facts. China discovered cinema when in a state of semi-colonial domination, having had a series of unequal treaties imposed upon it by the Western powers following the two Opium Wars (1840–2 and 1856–60). The first screening of 'electric shadows' took place in Shanghai in 1896, but historians disagree about the system of projection: a Lumière camera (Leyda 1972: 1; Clark 1987: 6, 1988: 176) or Edison's Vitascope (Law and Teo 1995: 33–6). After 1898 Edison cameramen, the American Mutoscope and Biograph company, Pathé Frères, and the French banker Albert Kahn all made documentaries about China. The first images shot by Chinese (1905–8) were scenes from famous Peking operas (Leyda 1972: 10). In 1913 the first two Chinese narrative features were directed in Hong Kong by Li Minwei (*Zhuangzi Tests his Wife*), who had formed the Sino-American Company in partnership with an American businessman, Benjamin Brodsky (Law and Teo 1995: 28), and in Shanghai by Zhang Schichuan (*Nan fu nan qi*, 'An Unfortunate Couple'), an employee of the American-owned Asian Motion Pictures Company. In 1922 both men set up their own studios, and these ranked among the most influential film companies in Hong Kong and Shanghai (He 1985). A combination of Western and local entrepreneurship, Chinese cinema was therefore produced as a hybrid form: in China 'the association of film art with foreignness is overwhelming' (Clark 1988: 176).

The majority of films shown on Chinese screens were imported (mostly from Hollywood), yet in the 1920s and 1930s film companies mushroomed in Shanghai, and a star system developed quickly (He 1985). Ruan Lingyu, 'the Chinese Garbo', who appeared in such classics as Sun Yu's *Xiao wanyi* ('Small Toys', 1933) and Cai Chusheng's *Xin nüxing* ('New Women', 1935) before committing suicide at 25, has retained an enduring fascination among film lovers, historians, and intellectuals (Shu 1985). Analysing *Small Toys*, Pickowicz (1993: 305–8) argues that China's struggle with modernity at the beginning of the twentieth century was largely experienced as a crisis in family values. The cinematic representation of women was already a central question for left-wing filmmakers in the 1930s. As Ma Ning notes, 'because the woman's position is lowest in traditional Chinese society, she has become a metonymic figure for other disadvantaged social groups' (Ma 1994: 22). As a result, before and after 1949, woman was constantly used to signify the necessity of social change, and this may help to explain the recurrence of melodrama in Chinese cinema. Bergeron (1977), who admires the genre in post-revolutionary fictions, dismisses the films of the Republican era for 'their lack of class consciousness'. Other historians and analysts (Leyda, Rayns, Tadao Sato, Li Cheuk-to) emphasize the formal experimentation and political subtlety of pre-revolutionary cinema, and for most historians the 1930s and the post-war years represent two 'golden ages' of pre-revolutionary Chinese cinema (Lau 1985).

Whether they criticize it (Bergeron 1977) or merely report it, historians agree on the paramount influence of Hollywood on Chinese cinema of the 1920s and 1930s. Classic films, such as Shen Xiling's *Shizi jietou* ('Crossroads', 1937) achieved an original combination of forms borrowed from Hollywood and a commentary on China's social reality. Since the Shanghai studios continued to produce silent films until 1935–6, their point of reference, however, was, as Rayns aptly observes, 'the visual expressiveness' and formal experimentation of American *silent* cinema (Rayns 1995: 105). With the advent of the talkies, Hollywood's influence continued to be felt, but cinema also devel-

oped close ties with literature and theatre, a feature that has remained a major characteristic of Chinese cinema until the present day and which has given an emphasis to the screenplay over the mise-en-scène (Clark 1987: 20, 94–5).

In its 'most escapist period' of the 1910s and 1920s (Leyda 1972: 64), cinema, often drawing its inspiration from the popular 'Mandarin Duck and Butterfly' literature, was divorced from the intellectuals. Politicized by the 1931 Japanese invasion, leftist artists and intellectuals subsequently infiltrated the major studios, and some formed underground communist cells, such as the one headed by the screenwriter Xia Yan. A key figure in Chinese cinema, Xia was the first to adapt to the screen a May Fourth literary work, Mao Dun's *Chun can* ('Spring Silkworms', 1933). Started on 4 May 1919 as a protest and mass demonstration regrouping students and intellectuals against the Chinese government's compromising policies towards the Western powers and Japan, the May Fourth movement criticized the stifling effects of Chinese tradition and Confucianism and promoted a democratic, modernized 'new China', that would be patriotic and self-sufficient yet open to foreign ideas. Consequently, May Fourth intellectuals advocated various forms of literary experimentation. While its importance in Chinese intellectual life is a known fact in Chinese studies, Pickowicz (1993) questions the nature of its influence on cinema, as he examines the leftist melodramas of the 1930s and the 1980s. Arguing that May Fourth fiction lost its relevance as protest literature when adapted to the screen after 1949, he does not discuss the films it directly inspired: so the attacks they underwent remain the domain of the historian.

Politics and censorship

In 1949 nine Chinese out of ten had never seen a film; in 1952, 600 million admissions were recorded, and this number continued to grow (2.05 billion admissions in 1957, 25.5 billion in 1982). Party leaders set out to shape cinema, with a Leninist enthusiasm, into a national mass culture for the benefit of the new heroes of the Revolution: soldiers, workers, and peasants. As Mao Zedong implied in his 1942 talks at the Yan'an Conference on Literature and Art (Mao 1980), this meant a break with the May Fourth tradition represented by the urban-educated and Westernized Shanghai filmmakers. The new cultural cadres had been formed after 1936 in Yan'an, where the Communist People's Liberation Army was based. Clark (1987) reads the history of post-1949 cinema as a constant struggle between the Yan'an and Shanghai traditions, with the Party favouring the former. This also reflects a defiance against the foreign origin of the medium, and a drive towards the sinification of cinema.

The Communist Party set out to establish 'a national system for the production, censorship, distribution and projection of films' (Clark 1987: 34) and limit the number of American movies available to Chinese spectators (while simultaneously exposing them to Soviet cinema). After the completion of a few landmark films such as Wang Bin and Shui Ha's *Baimao nü* ('The White-Haired Girl', 1950), political pressure caused production to drop. Sun Yu's *Wu Xun zhuan* ('The Life of Wu Xun', 1950) has been often written about as an example of the early interference of politics into film-making in the PRC (Leyda 1972: 197–8; Bergeron 1983–4: i. 72–84; Clark 1987: 38, 45–54). While the film depicted the protagonist as a generous educator, Maoist attacks denounced him as an opportunist, reformist, and feudal exploiter. The campaign against the film helped speed the nationalization of the Shanghai studios, completed in 1953.

After 1956 the Soviet-inspired commitment to socialist realism was replaced by a demand for the combination of 'revolutionary realism and revolutionary romanticism'. This encouraged filmmakers to seek inspiration in the Chinese past—in particular May Fourth fiction and a modified operatic tradition. In the following decades Chinese cinema developed unevenly. It was expanding, experimenting, and gaining audiences when creativity was encouraged by the Party—such as the 1956–7 'Hundred Flowers' period (during which the slogan 'let a hundred flowers blossom and a hundred schools of thought contend' encouraged people, but especially artists and intellectuals to make suggestions to the Communist Party and even criticize its line), the political relaxation of the early 1960s, and the 'new period' initiated by Deng Xiaoping in 1979; conversely, there were times of heightened censorship during which films were banned, filmmakers persecuted, and production drastically curtailed, such as the 1957 'Anti-Rightist' campaign (during which the people who had taken the freedom of the 'Hundred Flowers' too literally were severely punished) and the Cultural Revolution (1966–78). Following the liberalization of the late 1970s, victims of both campaigns appeared in melodramas of the 1980s (Ma

1994: 15–39, 40–56; Pickowicz 1993: 295–326) and later in a (banned) Fifth Generation film, Tian Zhuangzhuang's *Lan Fengzheng* ('The Blue Kite', 1993).

One of the first targets of the Cultural Revolution was the screenwriter Xia Yan (head of the Film Bureau since 1951). In addition to *Spring Silkworms*, he had, since 1949, written the screen adaptation of two May Fourth stories, Lu Xun's *Zhufu* ('The New Year's Sacrifice', 1956) and Mao Dun's *Linjia puzi* ('The Lin Family Shop', 1959), and endorsed the adaptation of another one, Rou Shi's *Zaochun eryue* ('Early Spring in February', 1963); these films were denounced by the Red Guards, and Xia Yan spent ten years in jail. Despite the key roles many had played in building their national cinema, both before and after 1949 at least thirty filmmakers (including the President of the Filmmakers' Association, Cai Chusheng) died as a result of this persecution. Many more lost their jobs, were tortured, imprisoned, or exiled. Film production dropped dramatically (and later completely halted in 1967–9) and was not restored to its 1965 level until 1978 (Khang 1985: 143; Clark 1987: 187–8).

Because the names of Xia Yan and Cai Chusheng are still unfamiliar in the West, it remains difficult to evaluate the tragedy involved in their imprisonment or death. Leyda completed his book at the onset of the Cultural Revolution, too soon to fully understand and describe it; Bergeron's communist sympathies distract him from an accurate assessment of the damages of Maoist censorship; Clark provides a detailed, well-documented account of the Cultural Revolution years, but his book deals only with the post-1949 era, and its object is therefore *not* to write Chinese film history as a continuum since 1896.

Historians, theoreticians, and critics have therefore inherited a conceptualization of cinema history as a series of political ruptures whose origin is extra-cinematographic. Accordingly, the fetishization of the Fifth Generation, which cultural critics such as Chow denounce, may be seen to result from such a fragmented approach to Chinese film history. Moreover, apart from Rayns's journalistic pieces in *Sight and Sound*, there is no serious essay on the emergence of the 'Sixth Generation' (Zhang Yuan, Wang Xioashuai, He Yi). Zhang Yuan's *Mama* ('Mama', 1990), 'the first Chinese independent film since 1949' according to Rayns, was produced illegally outside the state-run studios. Sixth Generation films are often banned, and depend on international circuits for exposure and/or funding, which raises the old question of how Chinese they are. Articulating a post-Tiananmen Square dilemma, the Sixth Generation is part of a nascent counter-cultural milieu centred in Beijing, which also includes underground rock musicians (such as Cui Jian), visual artists and, significantly, independent videomakers (Wu Wenguang, the 'Structure, Wave, Youth, Cinema Experimental Group') (Reynaud 1996: 253–8).

The Western gaze

If the history of Chinese cinema before and after the Fifth Generation remains a war waged by anonymous soldiers, the name of one filmmaker emerges: Xie Jin. His importance is stressed by Browne (1994), Berry and Clark (1991: 198), Pickowicz (1993: 313), and Ma Ning (1994: 15). He directed melodramas and revolutionary operas before combining both genres in *Wutai jiemei* ('Stage Sisters', 1965), considered his masterpiece but criticized during the Cultural Revolution. He directed a number of successful 'tear-jerkers' in the 1980s, the most famous being *Furongzhen* ('Hibiscus Town', 1987). The first half of his career is a successful example of combining revolutionary realism with revolutionary romanticism, while his work during the 1980s has been used to test and expand Western theories about melo-drama. His work reflects the ruptures used to write the history of Chineses cinema—the Communist takeover, the Cultural Revolution, the aesthetic break of the Fifth Generation (whose members define themselves *against* him)—as well as articulating the tensions between Chinese tradition and Western influence and realism and melodrama.

In his case, melodrama and realism are in a dialec-tical relationship with one another and pose the ques-tion of cross-cultural interpretation. For Catherine Yi-Yu Cho Woo, Bazin-inspired filmic realism 'seems incompatible with traditional Chinese art' (Woo 1991: 21), and Browne cautions that applying 'the category of melodrama' to Chinese cinema 'entails a shift of cultural perspective' (1994: 40). Melodrama's sche-matic, theatrical opposition between good and evil, it is argued, are 'incommensurable' with the aesthetic and ethical categories at work in Chinese society— either in classical painting and poetry, Confucianism, or the post-1949 ideological order. The question Chi-nese film studies will have to face in the next few years, therefore, is how to contain Western theoretical imperialism while simultaneously avoiding the fetishi-zation of the specificity of Chinese culture—the turning

of it into an exotic Other knowable only through the critical analyses of native insiders. The concept of real-ism, when combined with that of authenticity, has often been used to construct or perpetrate an exotic image of China and/or Chinese cinema: it is well known, for example, that the most popular films in the West are those that present Chinese rural landscapes rather than urban scenes. On the other hand, if Wes-tern scholars are to eschew 'nativist' criticism, the way forward is to base their theoretical arguments on an ever-increasing knowledge of Chinese culture, film, and political history.

BIBLIOGRAPHY

Bergeron, Régis (1977), *Le Cinéma chinois*, i: *1905–1949* (Lausanne: Alfred Eibel).
—— (1983–4), *Le Cinéma chinois 1949–1983*, 3 vols. (Paris: L'Harmattan).
Berry, Chris (1982), 'Stereotypes and Ambiguities: An Examination of the Feature Films of the Chinese Cultural Revolution', *Journal of Asian Culture*, 6: 37–72.
—— (1988), 'Chinese "Women's Cinema"', *Camera Obscura*, 18: 4–41.
—— (1991*a*), 'Sexual Difference and the Viewing Subject in *Li Shuanghuang* and *The In-Laws*', in Berry (1991*c*).
—— (1991*b*), 'Market Forces: China's 'Fifth Generation' Faces the Bottom Line', in Berry (1991*c*).
*—— (ed.) (1991*c*), *Perspectives on Chinese Cinema* (London: British Film Institute).
—— (1994), 'Neither One Thing nor Another: Toward a Study of the Viewing Subject in Chinese Cinema in the 1980s', in Browne *et al.* (1994).
—— and **Paul Clark** (1991), 'Appendix 1: Major Directors', in Berry (1991*c*).
Browne, Nick (1994), 'Society and Subjectivity: On the Political Economy of Chinese Melodrama', in Browne *et al.* (1994).
*—— **Paul G. Pickowicz, Vivian Sobchack,** and **Esther Yau** (eds.) (1994), *New Chinese Cinemas: Forms, Identi-ties, Politics* (Cambridge: Cambridge University Press).
Chow, Rey (1995), *Primitive Passions: Visuality, Sexuality, Ethnography, and Contemporary Chinese Cinema* (New York: Columbia University Press).
*Clark, Paul** (1987), *Chinese Cinema: Culture and Politics since 1949* (Cambridge: Cambridge University Press).
—— (1988), 'The Sinification of Cinema: The Foreignness of Film in China', in Wimal Dissanayake (ed.), *Cinema and Cultural Identity: Reflections on Films from Japan, India, and China* (Lanham, Md.: University Press of Amer-ica).
Dissanayake, Wimal (ed.) (1988), *Cinema and Cultural*

Identity: Reflections of Films from Japan, India, and China (Lanham, Md.: University Press of America).

He Xiujun (1985), 'Histoire de la compagnie shanghaienne *Mingxing* et son fondateur Zhang Shickuan', in Quiquemelle and Passek 1985.

Kaplan, E. Ann (1991a), 'Melodrama/Subjectivity/Ideology: The Relevance of Western Melodrama Theories to Recent Chinese Cinema', *East–West Film Journal*, 5/1 (Jan.), 6–27.

—— (1991b), 'Problematising Cross-Cultural Analysis: The Care of Women in the Recent Chinese Cinema', in Berry (1991c).

Khang Budong (1985), 'Convalescence', in Quiquemelle and Passek (1985).

Kwok and **Marie-Claire Quiquemelle** (1986), 'Chinese Cinema and Realism', in John D. H. Downing (ed.), *Film and Politics in the Third World* (Brooklyn: Automedia).

Lau Shing Hon (1985), 'Deux Ages d'or du cinéma chinois: Les années trente et l'après-guerre', in Quiquemelle and Passek (1985).

Law, Kar, and **Stephen Teo** (eds.) (1995), *Early Images of Hong Kong and China: the Nineteenth Hong Kong International Film Festival* (Hong Kong: Urban Council).

Leyda, Jay (1972), *Dianying: An Account of Films and the Film Audience in China* (Cambridge: MIT Press).

McDougall, Bonnie S. (1991), *The Yellow Earth: A Film by Chen Kaige*, with complete trans. of the filmscript (Hong Kong: Chinese University Press).

Ma Ning (1994), 'Spatiality and Subjectivity in Xie Jin's Film Melodrama of the New Period', in Browne *et al.* (1994).

Mao Zedong (1980), *Mao Zedong's 'Talks at the Yan'an Conference on Literature and Art:' A Translation of the 1943 Text with Commentary*, ed. and trans. Bonnie S. McDougall (Ann Arbor: Center for Chinese Studies, University of Michigan).

Pickowicz, Paul G. (1993), 'Melodramatic Representation and the "May Fourth" Tradition of Chinese Cinema', in Ellen Widem and David Der-Wei Wang (eds.), *From May Fourth to June Fourth: Fiction and Film in Twentieth-Century China* (Cambridge: Harvard University Press).

—— (1994), 'Huang Jianxin and the Notion of Post-Socialism', in Browne *et al.* (1994).

Quiquemelle, Marie-Claire, and **Jean-Loup Passek** (eds.) (1985), *Le cinéma chinois* (Paris: Centre national d'art et de culture Georges Pompidou).

Rayns, Tony (ed.) (1985), *More Electric Shadows: Chinese Cinema 1922–1984* (London: British Film Institute).

—— (1991), 'Breakthrough and Setbacks: The Origins of the New Chinese Cinema', in Berry (1991c).

—— (1995), 'Missing Links: Chinese Cinema in Shanghai and Hong Kong from the 1930s to the 1940s', in Law and Teo (1995).

—— and **Scott Meek** (eds.) (1980), *Electric Shadows: Forty-Five Years of Chinese Cinema* (London: British Film Institute).

Reynaud, Bérénice (1994), 'Gong Li and the Glamour of the Chinese Stars', in Pam Cook and Philip Dodd (eds.), *Women and Film: A Sight and Sound Reader* (London: Scarlet Press).

—— (1996), 'New Visions/New Chinas—Video: Art, Documentation and the Chinese Modernity in Question', in Michael Renov and Erika Suderburg (eds.), *Resolutions: Essays on Contemporary Video Practices* (Minneapolis: Minnesota University Press).

Semsel, George S. (ed.) (1987), *Chinese Film: The State of Art in the People's Republic* (New York: Praeger).

—— **Hong Xia,** and **Jianping Hou** (eds.) (1990), *Chinese Film Theory: A Guide to the New Era* (New York: Praeger).

—— **Xihe Chen,** and **Hong Xia** (eds.) (1993), *Film in Contemporary China: Cultural Debates 1979–1989* (Westport, Conn.: Praeger).

Shu Kei (1985), 'La Légende de Ruan Lingyu', in Quiquemelle and Passek (1985).

Yau, Esther C. M. (1989), 'Cultural and Economic Dislocation: Filmic Phantasies of Chinese Women in the 1980s', *Wide Angle*, 11/2: 6–21.

—— (1989/1994), 'Is China the End of Hermeneutics? or, Political and Cultural Usage of Non-Han Women in Mainland Chinese Films', *Discourse*, 11/2: 115–38; repr. in Diane Carson, Linda Dittmar, and Janice R. Welsch (eds.), *Multiple Voices in Feminist Film Criticism* (Minneapolis: University of Minnesota Press).

—— (1991), 'Yellow Earth: Western Analysis and a Non-Western Text', in Berry (1991c).

Wang Yuejin (1989), 'The Cinematic Other and the Cultural Self? De-Centering the Cultural Identity on Cinema', *Wide Angle*, 11/2: 32–9.

—— (1991), 'Red Sorghum: Mixing Memory and Desire', in Berry (1991c).

Woo, Catherine Yi-Yu Cho (1991), 'The Chinese Montage: From Poetry and Painting to the Silver Screen', in Berry (1991c).

21

Hong Kong cinema

(a) Discovery and pre-discovery   STEPHEN TEO

The discovery of Hong Kong cinema in the West essentially began in the 1970s with the importation of kung fu action pot-boilers. Traditionally, the Hong Kong film industry drew its audiences from Taiwan and key Southeast Asian countries like Malaysia and Singapore. But the films of Bruce Lee and director King Hu made non-Chinese audiences in non-traditional markets like Europe and America sit up and take notice for the first time.

This somewhat facile 'discovery' of Hong Kong cinema was supplemented by the rise of the Hong Kong New Wave in 1979. New Wave films such as Ann Hui's *The Secret* (1979) and *The Boat People* (1983), Tsui Hark's *The Butterfly Murders* (1979) and *Dangerous Encounter—1st Kind* (1980), and Allen Fong's *Father and Son* (1981) made Western audiences realize that Hong Kong cinema was more than kung fu and martial arts.

However, it is really the action genres that gained a cult following for Hong Kong cinema, spawning a certain misconception that the strength of the cinema is founded on only one genre, and that its history started in the early 1970s, when Bruce Lee became popular. We can therefore divide the whole history of Hong Kong cinema into two distinct phases: a 'Discovery History' and a 'Pre-Discovery History'.

> It is really the action genres that gained a cult following for Hong Kong cinema, spawning a certain misconception that the strength of the cinema is founded on only one genre, and that its history started in the early 1970s, when Bruce Lee became popular.

The 'Discovery History' is relatively well known since it covers the contemporary development of Hong Kong cinema and may, in fact, be subdivided into a 'Post-Discovery' phase that takes into account the subsequent progress of the Hong Kong New Wave into a 'second wave' in the 1990s. This post-discovery phase covers mature and sophisticated works (such as Stanley Kwan's *Rouge*, 1989 and *Actress*, 1993, Wong Kar-wai's *Days of Being Wild*, 1991, *Chungking Express*, 1994,

550

and *Ashes of Time*, 1994) that are more recognizably art-house-type movies and acknowledged as such by critics in the West.

While it is too much of a generalization to refer to the whole period of the development of Hong Kong cinema from its beginnings up to 1970 as a 'Pre-Discovery History', the fact remains that a large chunk of the history of Hong Kong cinema before the kung fu wave hit Western shores is largely undiscovered and unappreciated. However, Hong Kong critics and scholars have, for the last twenty years, emphasized its importance in a continuing series of thematic studies (published in book-length catalogues) organized by the Hong Kong International Film Festival (see Leung, Part 3, Chapter 21).

The early history

The first production of a fictional film occurred in 1909. *Stealing the Roast Duck* was produced by the Asia Film Company, founded by an American businessman, Benjamin Brodsky, who went on to produce films in Shanghai. The key figure to emerge during this pioneering period was Li Minwei, who founded the Sino-American Film Company (Huamei) with Brodsky, and produced *Zhuang Zi Tests his Wife* (1913), in which Li himself appeared in drag, playing the wife. Li was also a major figure in the founding of two other important companies, China Sun (Minxin) in 1922 and United Photoplay Services (Lianhua) in 1930, that would dominate the fledgling film industries of Hong Kong and Shanghai, the centres of filmmaking in the Chinese-speaking world. In the 1930s, with the arrival of sound, Hong Kong's film industry found a niche as the production centre of Cantonese-dialect movies. Shanghai's Tianyi Company, which produced the first Cantonese-dialect movie *Platinum Dragon* in 1933, relocated to Hong Kong in 1934 to take advantage of the resources there and its distribution markets. It was followed by the establishment of the Grandview Company (Daguan) in 1935, which began to make patriotic films that exploited the Chinese antipathy towards the Japanese, who had embarked on a militarist policy and were slowly eating up Chinese territory.

When full-scale war got under way in 1937, Hong Kong was turned into a production base for 'national defence films'—war films lauding the war effort and exhorting the Chinese populace to rise up against the Japanese. These films, such as Situ Huimin's *March of the Guerrillas* (1938) and Cai Chusheng's *Devils' Paradise* (1939), were made by Shanghai filmmakers who had fled the occupation and voluntarily exiled themselves in the colony, thus initiating the first migratory movement of Shanghai filmmakers into Hong Kong. When Hong Kong itself was occupied by the Japanese in December 1941, the film industry came to a complete stop.

Post-war renaissance

The Hong Kong cinema as we know it today owes its existence to post-war developments. The years between 1946 and 1949 were crucial in laying the foundations for Hong Kong to replace Shanghai as the 'Hollywood of the East'. Once again, Hong Kong was the receiving centre of filmmaking talent fleeing Shanghai. The exodus occurred in two waves. First, immediately after the war, actors and directors who had elected to stay on in Shanghai under Japanese occupation were accused of collaborating with the enemy. These filmmakers, including veteran directors Zhu Shilin, Yue Feng, Bu Wancang, Ma-Xu Weibang, Li Pingqian, and producer Zhang Shankun, took off for Hong Kong.

The Great China Film Company was established in 1946 by mainland interests, and many exiled filmmakers found employment with the company. Great China was virtually the only company making movies in the colony during the immediate post-war years. Its output was mainly Mandarin movies scheduled for release in Shanghai and other major cities in the mainland. China was the main market, but when that market effectively vanished with the communist victory in 1949, the Hong Kong film industry began to rely on overseas Chinese communities in South-east Asia, Taiwan, and other countries around the world for its bread and butter.

The second influx of Shanghai talent into Hong Kong took place in 1947 and 1948 as the civil war raged on the mainland. This time many of the directors were communists or sympathizers fleeing white terror campaigns launched by the Kuomintang government. When the Great China company closed down in 1948, the gap was filled by Yonghua, founded by Li Zuyong, another mainland entrepreneur, and the charismatic producer Zhang Shankun. Yonghua rapidly became the most prestigious company in Hong Kong producing Mandarin movies, beginning with the spectacular epics *Soul of China*, directed by Bu Wancang, and *Sorrows of the Forbidden City*, directed by Zhu Shilin (both released in 1948).

While social conscience dramas such as Li's *A Strange Woman* and *The Awful Truth* (both 1950) and Zhu Shilin's *The Flower Girl* (an adaptation of Maupassant's *Boule de suif*) and *Spoiling the Wedding Day* (both 1951) proved popular in the early 1950s, popular genres such as the comedies and musicals produced by the Motion Picture and General Investment Company (MP and GI) were more successful in the second half of the decade. In 1957 the Shaws, a remarkable family of film entrepreneurs and producers from Shanghai, established a new studio named Shaw Brothers. Its logo, a close copy of the Warner Bros. logo, became one of the dominant symbols of Hong Kong cinema in the next decade.

Like Yonghua before it, the studio built its success on costume pictures such as Li Hanxiang's *The Enchanting Shadow* (1960), *The Love Eterne* (1963), and *The Empress Wu* (1963). In the late 1960s a spate of martial arts sword-fighting movies, mostly directed by Zhang Che (*The One-Armed Swordsman*, 1967, *The Assassin*, 1967, *The Golden Swallow*, 1968), consolidated the Shaws' supremacy in the market. The sword-fighting movies also signalled the rise of the kung fu genre that would dominate the 1970s. Shaw Brothers had tried to sign Bruce Lee to a contract, but Lee made a better deal with a new studio, Golden Harvest, established in 1970 and run by a new-generation studio mogul, Raymond Chow. Chow was the ex-production chief at Shaw Brothers. His departure from Shaws dealt a blow to the studio, and it never fully recovered from the loss and the competition Chow presented with Golden Harvest.

The Cantonese cinema

The 1950s was also the golden age of Cantonese cinema. The film that first won the attention of critics was *Tears of the Pearl River* (1950), made by a left-wing company whose founders included the mainland director Cai Chusheng. The left-wing movement in Cantonese cinema initiated a campaign to inject more social substance and progressive thinking into Cantonese movies. A filmmaking co-operative was formed, which made a multi-episodic film *Kaleidoscope* (1950), with each episode directed by a leading director. However, it was the establishment of the

Union Film Company (Chung-luen) in 1952 that launched Cantonese cinema into a period of creative growth during the next two decades. Some of the greatest classics of Cantonese cinema were made by Union: *In the Face of Demolition* (Lee Sun-fung, 1953), *Father and Son* (Ng Wui, 1954), *Cold Nights* (Lee Sun-fung, 1955), *Parents' Hearts* (Chun Kim, 1955).

Cantonese movies, however, were primarily a popular mass medium, with comedies, opera films martial arts action movies, and melodramas making up the standard genres. About sixteen pictures were released each month, and stars and directors would make several films back to back. Quantity overwhelmed quality and Cantonese movies never got over the image of being a 'fast-food' cinema: cheap, mass-produced, easily consumed and discarded. Cantonese production continued its quantitative push into the 1960s, but in 1965 the market reached saturation-point, sparking off an economic crisis and fall in production which presaged the decline of Cantonese cinema that would come to pass at the end of the decade. Despite the releases of some memorable Cantonese pictures during the 1960s—Lee Sun-fung's father-and-son melodrama *The Orphan* (1960, starring a teenage Bruce Lee) and Lee's reverential costume picture *So Siu-siu* (1962); Chan Lit-bun's gothic martial arts masterpiece *Green-Eyed Demoness* (1967); Chor Yuen's comic parodies *The Black Rose* (1965) and *Young, Unmarried and Pregnant* (1967); and Lung Kong's vivid portrait of a middle-class teenager's fall from social grace, *Teddy Girls* (1969)—Cantonese film production had come to an end by 1973. This decline of the Cantonese cinema has been attributed to various factors, such as the perception that it was outdated, technically inferior, and lacking quality, and thus unable to compete with the more sophisticated Mandarin cinema. However, perhaps a more important factor was the rise of local Cantonese-dialect broadcast television in 1967, which siphoned off audience support from Cantonese movies and allowed Mandarin movies to enjoy predominance (see Leung, Part 3, Chapter 21).

The Cantonese dialect was to make a come-back in Hong Kong cinema in 1973, when Chor Yuen's *The*

> **Cantonese movies never got over the image of being a 'fast-food' cinema: cheap, mass-produced, easily consumed and discarded.**

House of 72 Tenants featured the dialect, spoken by a cast of familiar actors from television and became one of the biggest box-office successes of that year. It was the television comedian Michael Hui who did much to re-establish Cantonese as the lingua franca of Hong Kong screens when he switched to a cinema career with the films *Games Gamblers Play* (1975), *The Last Message* (1975), and *The Private Eyes* (1976).

The cultural significance of Cantonese cinema has been substantial. Cantonese opera film in the 1950s is unimaginable without the distinctive use of Cantonese lyrics, while Cantonese comedies relied upon Cantonese colloquial humour and slang. Cantonese melodrama in the 1950s introduced realism and explored family values against the background of an industrializing and urbanizing society. Cantonese martial arts movies from the 1950s to the 1960s popularized the serial adventure and standardized kung fu as the predominant martial art of Hong Kong movies. Cantonese action movies in the 1960s also contained a fine sense of parody that would lay the foundations of the postmodern humour of later films.

Indeed, the achievements of Cantonese cinema have been recognized by New Wave directors who have evoked old Cantonese movies in their films: Tsui Hark, going back to the tradition of Cantonese martial arts serials in *Once upon a Time in China* (1991); Allen Fong, quoting from Cantonese melodramas which deal with the father-and-son relationship in his 1981 movie *Father and Son*; John Woo, remaking a Cantonese-action-movie-with-a-social-conscience with his *A Better Tomorrow* (1986). What these few examples also highlight is the role of the Cantonese cinema in awakening the new-found identity of the younger generation of directors known as the New Wave.

Generational change

The Hong Kong New Wave was prefigured as far back as 1969 in *The Arch*, a seminal work about the impact of feudalism on a widow in ancient China filmed by a woman director, Tang Shuxuan. With her next film, *China Behind* (1974), Tang condemned the Cultural Revolution before it was fashionable to do so. Experimental New Wave styles embellished standard genres like the martial arts, in Chor Yuen's *The Magic Blade* (1976), and the crime thriller, in Leong Po-chih and Josephine Siao's *Jumping Ash* (1976). These works,

plus those of the comedian Michael Hui, signalled generational change in Hong Kong cinema. The generation that was born after the war and grew up in the 1950s and 1960s now stood at the forefront of the industry. Many of the new filmmakers had studied in film schools abroad. Upon their return to Hong Kong they had gone into television and made drama series, short films, documentaries. Television, which had earlier robbed Cantonese cinema of its audience, now became a training-ground of new talent for the cinema. These talents included Ann Hui, Yim Ho, Tsui Hark, Allen Fong, Alex Cheung, Patrick Tam, all of whom made their film debuts in the years 1979–80.

The New Wave ushered Hong Kong cinema into the modern age, winning international recognition for the industry and a cult following for some of its directors. However, the Hong Kong cinema has always remained true to the tenets of commercialism and popular cinema even in the films made by New Wave directors. The kung fu films of Jackie Chan are perhaps the most representative of commercial Hong Kong cinema at its best.

In the mid-1980s directors began to tackle the question of 1997 (the year of China's take-over of Hong Kong as a Special Administrative Region) in a series of allegorical dramas: Yim Ho's *Homecoming* (1984), Leong Po-chih's *Hong Kong 1941* (1984), and Ann Hui's *Love in a Fallen City* (1984). As the 1980s ended Hong Kong cinema had gained a new sophistication and even more international attention through the films of Stanley Kwan (*Rouge*) and John Woo (*The Killer*, 1989).

In the 1990s Hong Kong cinema entered a period of uncertainty. The 'postmodern' comedies of Stephen Chiau and outlandish martial arts movies (utilizing a gender-bending motif such as the 1992 release *Swordsman II*) secured cult followings. International interest was maintained through the stylish movies of Wong Kar-wai (*Days of being Wild*, *Ashes of Time*), Clara Law (*Autumn Moon*, 1993), and Stanley Kwan (*Actress*). However, since 1993 the film industry has experienced a period of sluggish box-office returns, escalating costs, and shrinking markets (with only 29 million tickets sold in 1994 compared with 44.8 million tickets sold in 1989). As a result, the China market is destined to become especially important for the future Hong Kong film industry given the hand-over of Hong Kong in 1997.

(b) **China and 1997** N. K. LEUNG

In 1997 Hong Kong ceased to be a British colony and became a Special Administrative Region of the People's Republic of China. This political watershed has overshadowed almost all aspects of life in Hong Kong, including its cinema. Indeed, how the relations between Hong Kong and China have been represented in films has been one of the more ostensible themes in the study of Hong Kong cinema since the 1980s. However, it is also possible to look at the way Hong Kong cinema has handled its relationship with China over a longer period, and this will shed light on aspects of the history of film studies of Hong Kong.

Three historical periods may be identified, starting with the most recent. From the 1980s onwards the Hong Kong cinema has been in what might be described as its 'Post-1997 Consciousness' period, a period when the Hong Kong cinema finally caught up with this issue of paramount political importance and began to express, not always overtly, its sentiments on the matter. The period between the late 1960s and the late 1970s represents a kind of 'Mirror Stage' (to borrow a Lacanian phrase) of the Hong Kong cinema, when it only cared to see its own body as its source of pleasure and was oblivious to the ever-present law as symbolized by China. According to this periodization, the whole period of the Hong Kong cinema up to 1966 could be described as its gestation period, during which time it battled with the problems of language, genre, and subjectivity, and, in doing so, indicated the extent to which Hong Kong cinema has seen Hong Kong as the legitimate master of its own fate.

The year 1966, as we know, was the year of the Great Cultural Revolution in China, the reverberations of which would result in a large-scale riot in Hong Kong in 1967 and which indirectly contributed to the student revolt in much of Europe and across America in 1968. Before the revolution, films both in Cantonese (the Chinese dialect spoken in Hong Kong and China's southern province Guangdong) and in Mandarin (China's national 'dialect', commonly spoken by people from the north) were being made. The coexistence of the two languages also reflected the fact that the Hong Kong film industry had been perodically augmented by filmmakers emigrating down south from China, not

only throughout the 1930s and 1940s, but also in the years immediately after China officially established its communist government in 1949. The gradual development of and indigenous film culture in Hong Kong, therefore, was always paralleled by an influx of external, if not alien, cultural elements, resulting in various kinds of tension between the two languages, different literary and cinematic genres, and, most importantly, a Hong Kong and Chinese subjectivity.

Film studies in Hong Kong from the 1940s to the 1960s reflected this state of affairs. Critical studies were mainly concerned with the Hong Kong cinema in its two language versions: either the Cantonese cinema or the Mandarin cinema with, occasionally, some comparisons between the two. Within each language domain, the focus was mainly on genre study (of social realism, melodrama, musicals, and so on) and historical periodization (such as the 'golden' period of the Cantonese or Mandarin cinema and the years before or after the Second World War). The aesthetics employed were derived from literature rather than from film, and the practice of film criticism, with the exception of erratic film publications such as the short-lived *Film Forum* (which appeared from 1947 to 1948), was chiefly in the form of newspaper reviews. Not surprisingly, it was the leftist newspapers in Hong Kong (those that followed the revolutionary politics of mainland China) that carried some of the better-quality film reviews. But, these reviews tended to display traces of early Soviet radical aesthetics (putting politics above all else) and became redundant when the Hong Kong cinema entered its next stage.

The logic of using the year 1966 as a demarcation date seems self-evident. The Great Cultural Revolution of China signified, on a world scale, a peak of social radicalism. However, when Hong Kong recovered from the shocking riots in 1967 and looked forward to a new direction in 1968, its cinema underwent a change. Suddenly, the Cantonese cinema in Hong Kong was proclaimed dead. For the next few years, films were mainly produced in Mandarin. It was as though the people of Hong Kong had lost their voice or the desire to speak in their own language. While other aspects of life in Hong Kong were to embark on an all-out capitalist take-off, its cinema was left to speak in a tone

(Mandarin) which, in the absence of Cantonese, signified an alien Other that was China.

Although the historical approach in film studies would put 1968 or 1969 as the year in which the Cantonese cinema ended, it has found it difficult to offer an explanation for this. However, viewed from the perspective of the Hong Kong–China power relationship, it can be seen that the Hong Kong cinema lost its desire to speak because it sought to forget the 1967 trauma, which was viewed as a Chinese imposition of its fanatical radicalism on an indifferent Hong Kong. The Hong Kong cinema could therefore only speak with its own vioice when it re-emerged as a confident self, as it did in 1972, when the Cantonese cinema came back with a vengeance with director Chu Yuan's box-office hit *The House of 72 Tenants*. In the decade which followed, the Hong Kong cinema pursued a path of pure pleasure and sensuality, leaving politics out of the scene as much as it could, relecting a Hong Kong which seemingly only knew the pursuit of wealth and materialism.

> **Although the historical approach in film studies would put 1968 or 1969 as the year in which the Cantonese cinema ended, it has found it difficult to offer an explanation for this.**

As far as tracing the evolution of film studies in Hong Kong is concerned, other things began to happen in the late 1960s as well. A group of young film critics began to gather around a weekly magazine called the *Chinese Student Weekly*, aimed primarily at college and high-school students, and attempted to write film reviews from a more unorthodox perspective. Helped by the screening of international art films (made available by the budding film club activities at the time) and inspired by new critical approaches in film studies from overseas, particularly the auteurism of Andrew Sarris and the new stream of film writings from England (such as *Movie* and the *Cinema One* series), these film critics sought to bring a fresh and more vigorous approach to the analysis of both Chinese and international films. Although they did not formulate any original theoretical models, the influence they exerted on the film culture of Hong Kong was undeniably huge. Some of them went on to become film directors, such as Patrick Tam (*The Sword*, 1980) and

Shu Kei (*Days without the Sun*, 1989) while some have continued to write to this day, such as Law Kar and Sek Kei, who has now become Hong Kong's most popular film reviewer and critic. There were also other film personalities who initially were either associated with the activities around the group and the weekly publication, such as director John Woo (now working in Hollywood), or grew up under the group's influence, such as director Ann Hui (*The Secret*, 1979; *The Story of Wu Viet*, 1981; *Woman at 40*, 1995). In its own way, the *Chinese Student Weekly* was like the *Cahiers du cinéma* in miniature for the Hong Kong cinema, and marked a turning-point in the evolution of its film studies.

> **In its own way, the *Chinese Student Weekly* was like the *Cahiers du cinéma* in miniature for the Hong Kong cinema, and marked a turning-point in the evolution of its film studies.**

The development of this new film culture, in the context of a commercially buoyant cinema in Hong Kong, provided the setting for the birth of the Hong Kong International Film Festival in 1977. In its second year, the festival started publishing an annual book to go along with its Hong Kong Cinema Retrospective section, which was organized around a different theme each year. This project has not only been breathtaking in its scope of coverage, but has also provided an effective guide to the history of film studies in Hong Kong over the past two decades. Moreover, the key essays of this yearly volume appear in both Chinese and English and thus represent the most useful means for English-speaking readers to find out about the Hong Kong cinema.

While the work done in this area has been impressive, it is also clear from this project that film studies in Hong Kong has not delivered as much as might have been expected. The approaches adopted have largely been the conventional ones of historical periodization and genre study, as some of the early thematic titles indicate: *Cantonese Cinema 1950–1959* for 1978, *Cantonese Cinema 1960–1969* for 1982, *A Study of Hong Kong Martial Arts Film* for 1980, and so on. The project was at its most stimulating when it dealt with *Changes in Hong Kong Society through Cinema* in

A 'sophisticated . . . art-house type movie'?
Chungking Express (1995)

1988 and *The China Factor in Hong Kong Cinema* in 1990, just as the Hong Kong cinema was entering its 'Post-1997 Consciousness' period, described above. Since the 1990s the Hong Kong cinema has shown signs of losing direction, and the themes selected by this project have looked fatigued as well, as *Mandarin Films and Popular Songs from the 1940s to 1960s* for 1993 and *The Restless Breed: Cantonese Stars of the Sixties* for 1996 would indicate. On the whole, a critical project that is grounded in a more in-depth synthesis of Chinese and Western aesthetics, and which faces up to the politics of the Greater China region in an open manner, has yet to be accomplished. Just as the hand-over of Hong Kong in 1997 raises important questions about the future of the Hong Kong film industry (will China open up new audiences for an ailing industry or will Hong Kong filmmakers need to move to China to cultivate a new political and cinematic space), so the future of Hong Kong film studies is likely to depend upon the way these questions are answered.

22 Taiwanese New Cinema

Kuan-Hsing Chen

My central task in this short chapter is to question the very notion of the Taiwan New Cinema (hereafter TNC). I shall argue that the TNC was born out of, and participated in facilitating the nativist movement (by which I mean not only the 'self-rediscovery' movement in the specific case of Taiwan, but a general historical reaction to the end of colonial domination in the colony). However, it has ultimately been taken over by the new nation-building and state-making project and become part of the mechanism of transnational corporations (TNCs of a different kind, known as Hollywood). Indeed, one of the future trends of 'world cinema' will be a move into what I shall term a 'global nativism', a nativism predicated upon the commodification of the implicit dialectic between nationalism and transnationalism.

Throughout this chapter the term 'TNC' refers generally to a range of cinematic practices from the early 1980s to the present. As a sign that gathers together a whole set of activities (including production, film criticism, promotion, consumption), 'TNC' was initially coined by critics and later accepted by a wider population. According to such critics, 'TNC' strictly refers to the alternative cinematic movement, which began with *In our Time* (1982), co-directed by four then younger-generation directors, and ended with *All for Tomorrow* (1986; a military school recruitment advertising clip) co-directed with Chen Kuo-fu by the foremost director of TNC, Hou Hsiao-Hsien. According to this definition,

what has come after that can be termed 'post-TNC'. On the other hand, critics have also recognized that there has been continuity between the 'new' (of the Taiwan New Cinema) and the 'post', and that while the 'new' has lost its original commitment to 'alternative' cinematic practices, the 'post' has none the less inherited its concerns with the cinematic representation of Taiwan's local histories. The question them becomes: how does one position and understand this obsession with 'histories'?

Unlike most Third World countries which mobilized nativism in the movement towards independence and global decolonization after the Second World War, Taiwan's 'self-rediscovery' was blocked by the kuomingtang government (the nationalist party, or KMT). Although it can be argued that the tradition of an 'oppositional' nativist movement began at the end of Japanese occupation, especially immediately after the 28 February 1947 massacre, and was culturally crystallized in the 'homeland' literary movement (*hsiang-t'u wen-hsue yun-dong*) of the 1970s, the drive towards nativism could not develop fully under this authoritarian, semi-colonial regime. The full-blown nativization movement (*ben-tu-hua yun-dong*) did not come about until the late 1970s and early 1980s, when the late President Chiang Ching-kuo, the son of Chiang Kai-shek, began, in recognition of 'no hope of recovering the mainland' (*fan-kung wu-wang*), to nativize (or more accurately, to ethnicize) his political regime, as a strategy for maintaining government legitimacy. (The term to 'ethnicize' is used here deliberately, because, from the point of view of the most deprived population—the aboriginals—the Han people are, and have been, the colonizer, no matter whether they came before or after 1945, when the Japanese handed the regime back to the Han Chinese. In the decade-long nativist-nationalist movement, aboriginals have been excluded and marginalized. They contest the imposed categories classifying 'ethnic' differences as Taiwanese (Tai-wan-jen) or Mainlander (Wai-shen-jen, or people coming from outside the province) between 1945 and the late 1980s, and as 'four main ethnic groups' which include the dominant Min-nan-jen, Hakka (Ker-jia-jen), Wai-shen-jen, and the aborigines, since the late 1980s. For the aboriginals, it is not so much an ethnic as a racial difference between aboriginal and the Han Chinese.)

When the political spaces were opened up and the export-oriented national economy was fully incorporated into the structure of global capital to become an often exaggerated member of the 'four tigers' or NICs (Korea, Hong Kong, Singapore, Taiwan), TNC, along with other forms of cultural practices (literature, music, dancing, painting, academic production, religion, and so on), seized the chance to look back on (or, more accurately, to begin a desperate search for) the historical formation of the 'lost self' from the imaginary location of this geopolitical space—Taiwan rather than China. In this sense, the invention of histories where a new identity could be constructed and struggled over, and which had been suppressed in history textbooks, found a new arena in cinematic writing.

However, this wider social mood and ideological structure of feeling cannot alone explain the birth of TNC: the inner logic of the film industry and the cinematic apparatus have also to be understood. From the mid-1970s onwards Taiwan's film industry lost its battle with Hong Kong, which had gradually become the little Hollywood throughout the region (Lii, forthcoming). The formation of a TNC movement was thus in part an attempt to revive the local film industry. As critic Tung Wa explained in 1986, 'TNC was born in the chaotic situations of demand–supply dysfunction in the local market and defeat in the external market' (1986: 31). Furthermore, with the so-called 'Taiwan Miracle', a consumer society was to take shape in the late 1970s which had diversified and shifted the landscape of cultural tastes in the market. Hence, a new generation of moviegoers demanded something directly connected to their own experiences, a need

to which the older generation of directors had failed to respond. In short, the formation of TNC was historically overdetermined by economic and political forces.

What was new about the TNC since the 1980s in relation to previous cinematic production was essentially this reclamation of the 'real' home space from which to construct the popular memory of people's lives on the island, especially in the post-war era. Moreover, the call for an alternative 'national cinema' by critics was self-consciously placed against Hollywood's 'global expansion' (Tung 1986: 34). As Wu Chi-yen (1993: 7) summarizes it, the newness of the TNC expressed itself on two levels: in the use of historical 'materials . . . from the local and the exploration and creation of new cinematic languages (mise-en-scène, cutting, narrative structure)', in other words the use of the long take, non-linear narrative, and critical social realism. However, whether TNC possesses its own language in the history of world cinema remains a open-ended. Critic Cheng Chund-shing points out that, if there is one, it is a 'parrot' language, imitating and assembling various outside elements. Therefore, the crucial point about TNC is not so much the originality of its aesthetic forms as its strategic ideological function within the wider cultural history of Taiwan and, more precisely, its historical turn on the discovery and construction of the 'Taiwanese self'.

> The crucial point about TNC is not so much the originality of its aesthetic forms as its strategic ideological function within the wider cultural history of Taiwan and, more precisely, its historical turn on the discovery and construction of the 'Taiwanese self'.

There is a general consensus among critics that TNC was born in 1982, when the low-budget film *In our Time*, co-directed by newcomers Edward Yang, Tao Te-chen, Ko I-cheng, and Chang Yi and produced by the state-owned Central Motion Picture Company (CMPC), was released. The success of *In our Time* provided the incentive for the CMPC to produce a second film, *The Sandwich Man* (1983), based on three short stories by Huang Tsuen-ming from the homeland literary movement and co-directed by Hou Hsiao-

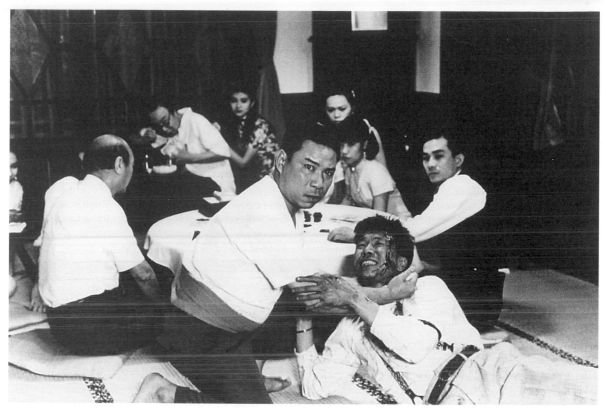

The controversial *City of Sadness* (1989) explores the taboos of ethnic conflict and state violence

hsien, Zeng Zhuang-xiang, and Wang Jen. This borrowing from nativist literature constituted a defining feature of the TNC which was in evidence throughout the 1980s. What can be termed as *Bildungsroman* narrative—expressed in *Ah-Fei* ('Rape Seed', 1983), *The Boys from Fengkuei* (1983), *Growing Up* (1983), *Summer at Grandpa's* (1984), *Dust in the Wind* (1986), *Taipei Story* (1985), *A Time to Live and a Time to Die* (1985), *Banana Paradise* (1989), and *A Brighter Summer Day* (1991)—not only retraced their youth in the memory of the post-war generation, but also charted the trajectories of changing environments, political and economic. In this sense, the TNC's obsession with history signals the end of an era and the beginning of a new one: the move from an agricultural to an industrial society, from poor rural life to the urban centres, from political identification with China to that with Taiwan.

Perhaps because the ethnic background of the directors, as well as those who were in control of the film industry, was largely ethnically Mainlander (Wai-

shen-jen), historical memory did not stretch back to the era of Japanese occupation or earlier, until the appearance of recent films such as *Hills of no Return* (Wang Tong, 1992), *The Puppetmaster* (Hou Hsiao-hsien, 1993), and *A Borrowed Life* (Wu Nien-chen, 1995). With the explosion of identity politics in various forms of social movements (women, labour, aboriginals, older soldiers, lesbians and gays, and youth) from the late 1980s onward, there emerged a set of movies that concerned themselves with the politics of identity such as the critically important *Banana Paradise*, *Two Painters* (1990), *Rebels of the Neon God* (1992), *Dust of Angels* (1992), *The Wedding Banquet* (1993), and *Vive l'amore* (1995). However, unlike Hong Kong cinema, TNC has been predominantly male; indeed, it is difficult to claim the existence of any women's film in TNC.

In retrospect, two rounds of heated debate may be seen to have taken place in the history of TNC: the first surrounding *All for Tomorrow* and the second surrounding *A City of Sadness* (1989). In 1988 the key players of the TNC, including directors Hou Hsiao-hsien and Chen Kuo-fu and scriptwriters Hsiao Yeh and Wu Nien-chen, jointly produced *All for Tomorrow*, an MTV-style promotion film for military school recruitment funded by the Ministry of Defence. This association between TNC and militarism came as a shock to critics, who lamented that what had begun as an alternative cultural movement had been co-opted into the Establishment and announced the death of the TNC (see the articles collected and documented in Mi-chou and Liang 1991: 33–79). Perhaps, the 'death' of TNC as a conscientious intellectual project was inevitable: TNC never operated outside 'the system' (of production, distribution, and consumption) and the Party–state-owned CMPC was its production base. In effect, the launching of the TNC could be read as a generational struggle over power, apparent in the 1987 'Manifesto on Taiwan's Cinema', drafted and signed by this new generation. Once the resources fell into the hands of this new generation, and they learned how to survive within commercial industry, the radicalness of the initial project was inevitably diluted.

By far the most politically controversial debate on history centred around *A City of Sadness*, directed by Hou. Departing from the *Bildungsroman* mode typical of TNC, *A City of Sadness* attempted to deal with the taboos of ethnic conflict and state violence. The film reinvoked the violent 'white horror' (*bai-se kung-bu*) experiences of the 1940s, especially the massacre of 28 February 1947, when some 30,000 people were killed. More than any other film, *A City of Sadness* provoked response from large sections of society. As Mi-chou and Liang (1991, p. xii) put it, the film triggered off a 'sudden explosion' of debate that forced critics to face neglected social and historical problems. Through this emotionally charged film event, the debate confronted a wide range of issues such as historical narration (who has the power to write history, in what directions, and to what ends), the ideological role of cinema, and the system of popular film criticism. It can be argued that TNC's contribution has been precisely its ability to cut into the social fabric in interpellating cultural identities of different constituencies, sparking off the hitherto suppressed collective flow of desire, and offering itself as a sounding-board against which to articulate affective responses.

Ironically, the seemingly taboo film *A City of Sadness* also marked the TNC's entrance into the international circuit. In 1987 martial law had been lifted, but the habit of self-censorship was not broken overnight and, as the 'packager' of the film Tsan Hung-chih

explained, he decided upon a strategy of 'promote expansively overseas, play low key back home' (quoted in Mi-chou 1991: 109), a policy which helped the film to win the Golden Lion award at the 1989 Cannes Film Festival. The success of this strategy also made the producers aware that there was a potential market overseas for its exotic aliennesss. This new discovery (by the local and international industry) marked a shift in the character of TNC, as well as in its financing: *A Brighter Summer Day*, for example, was produced with Japanese investment.

In its concern to join the United Nations (in order to gain bargaining-chips with the Chinese state), the Taiwanese government recognized the value of TNC as registering the name of Taiwan in the American mind. In 1992 the Government Information Office, in charge of international propaganda and local censorship, signed a contract with Warner Bros. to distribute TNC. To facilitate the process further, the diasporic director Lee Ang, who had been living in New York for over a decade, was contracted to make films such as *Pushing Hands* (1991) and later *The Wedding Banquet*, both of which were funded by the Central Studio. It is no accident that the setting for both films was New York, thus permitting the 'transnationalization' of TNC and 'Ang Lee', who has almost achieved the status of national hero since the release of *Sense and Sensibility* (1996). For the state, what matters is not so much the ideological content of the film, but whether it will disseminate the name of Taiwan (and ensure that the world-wide audience is able to distinguish 'Taiwan' from 'Thailand').

In 1993 the crew of *The Wedding Banquet* was warmly received by President Lee Teng-hui, while the movie's homosexual question was of course comple-

> **While national cinema is partly under threat from the rise of the international co-production, there is also an awareness on the part of Hollywood of the importance of the local. This might be characterized as a form of 'global nativism', in which exotic images of natives and national local histories and signs are employed as selling-points in the world cinema.**

tely ignored. From then on, the production of TNC was no longer simply locally oriented (the supposed nativist mode of production), but was also geared to the foreign market, and *The Wedding Banquet* became the first TNC circulated in US theatres. So while national cinema is partly under threat from the rise of the international co-production, there is also an awareness on the part of Hollywood of the importance of the local. This might be characterized as a form of 'global nativism', in which exotic images of natives and national local histories and signs are employed as selling-points in the world cinema. Whether nation-states are in decline, the transnational corporations (the other TNCs) are taking over the world is, of course, a matter for debate. But there is no sign that nationalism is disappearing; quite the contrary, transnationalism and nationalism seem to be bonded together. In this respect, TNC may be seen to be becoming a TNC.

BIBLIOGRAPHY

Chen, Robert R. S. (1993), *The Historical and Cultural Experiences of the Taiwan New Cinema* (Taipei: Wuan-Hsiong).

Lii Ding-tzann (forthcoming), 'A Colonized Empire: Reflections on the Expansion of Hong Kong Film Industry in Asian Countries', in Kuan-Hsing Chen (ed.), *The Trajectories of Cultural Studies: The Decolonization Effects* (London: Routledge).

Mi-chou (1991), 'The Foggy Discourses surrounding *A City of Sadness*: On the Problems of Film Criticism', in Mi-chou and Liang Hsing-hua (1991).

—— and Liang Hsing-hua (eds.) (1991), *The Death of New Cinema: from 'All for Tomorrow' to 'City of Sadness'*, War Machine 3 (Taipei: Tonsan Books).

—— (eds.) (1994), *After/Outside the New Cinema*, War Machine, 13 (Taipei: Tonsan Books).

Nandy, Ashis (1982), *Intimate Enemy: The Loss and Rediscovery of the Self under Colonialism* (India: Oxford University Press).

Tung, Wa (1986), 'Language Law and Color Pen: Notes on the 1985 Taiwan New Cinema', *Film Appreciation Journal*, 22: 29–36.

Wang Fei-ling (1994), *An Unfinished Film Dream: In Memory of Wang Fei-Ling*, ed. Chien Cheng et al. (Taipei: Klim).

Wu, Chi-yen (1993), *Underdeveloped Memories*, War Machine, 8 (Taipei: Tonsan Books).

Wuo, Young-yie (1993), 'Hong Kong, Pig King, Nation: Mainlander's National Identity in "Home Coming" Films', *Chung Wai Literary Monthly*, 22/1: 32–44.

Japanese cinema

Freda Freiberg

In the second half of the Showa imperial era, from the 1950s until the end of the 1980s, the art cinema of Japan exerted a particular fascination over film critics and film scholars in the West. This fascination was maintained through a number of shifts in critical orientations, shifts both in film studies and in attitudes to Japan. This phenomenon, the Western critic's seduction, my own included, is truly worthy of deconstruction, as suggested by Yoshimoto (1993).

Initially, there was the thrill of the first encounter with a strange culture, and one which displayed a highly developed aesthetic consciousness. The exotic settings, costumes, rituals, and performance styles of Akira Kurosawa and Kenji Mizoguchi's *jidai geki* (period films), exhibited at Venice and then other international film festivals in the early 1950s, doubtless appealed to our orientalist fantasies of a mysterious exotic Japan, totally other from the world we knew. (In retrospect, we may recognize a self-orientalizing tactic on the part of the Japanese film industry, in its attempt to break into foreign markets and achieve critical attention overseas, not unlike the successful strategy deployed by Fifth Generation Chinese filmmakers, such as Chen Kaige and Zhang Yimou, in recent times (see Reynaud, Part 3, Chapter 20). For, just as Chinese viewers find the feudal China of Chinese cinema far removed from their experience, and knowledge of Chinese history, so too did Japanese critics question the veracity of Kurosawa and Mizoguchi's feudal Japan and deplore the neglect of films that addressed contemporary Japanese social problems.)

But the masterly film direction—the exquisitely orchestrated long takes and deliciously fluid dissolves of late Mizoguchi, and the dazzling display of dynamic editing techniques by Kurosawa—were also totally seductive. Perhaps this rediscovery of an aesthetic Japan, of Japan as the locus of supreme style, fitted a post-war political agenda to reinstate Japan in the Western alliance against Eastern communism, offsetting the image of a brutal and primitive Japan cultivated by the Allies during the Second World War (Dower 1986). These films also included snatches of 'democratic' and 'pacifist' rhetoric, calculated to make Western audiences believe that the American occupation had succeeded in taming and reforming its former enemy. It was now the Soviet Union and China which were awarded the traits of oriental despotism.

However, the discovery of the Japanese cinema also coincided with the rise of auteurism in film studies, so that the idea of Japanese cinema came to be conflated with the work of a few directors, those who were accorded the status of 'auteurs', true authors. Initially the canon was confined to Mizoguchi and Kurosawa; soon, however, a third name was introduced, that of Yasujiro Ozu, who finally eclipsed the other two both in terms of the number of publications devoted to analysis of his work and in terms of his centrality to theoretical debates about the Japanese cinema. The fact that these three masters emerged from three different company studios (Mizoguchi from Nikkatsu, Ozu from Shochiku, and Kurosawa from Toho) that specialized in three different genres (the melodrama, the home drama (*shomin-geki*), and the period film (*jidai-geki*)) was overlooked; for industrial contexts and genre conventions were deemed barriers to true artistic expression: the true artist transcended them.

> **The discovery of the Japanese cinema also coincided with the rise of auteurism in film studies, so that the idea of Japanese cinema came to be conflated with the work of a few directors, those who were accorded the status of 'auteurs'.**

If the French critics around *Cahiers du cinéma*, many of whom later became leaders of the French New Wave cinema, acclaimed Mizoguchi for his transcendental style, judging him a superior artist to Kurosawa (the filmmaker who had long reigned unrivalled in the United States and the British Commonwealth), as *the* Japanese film artist it was Paul Schrader (1972) in America (another film critic who was to become a writer-director) who located transcendental style in the films of Ozu, alongside those of the Dane Theodor Dreyer and Frenchman Robert Bresson. Prefiguring David Bordwell's (1985) 'parametric' stylists, Schrader's 'transcendental' stylists share a common approach to filmmaking, rather than a common culture. For Schrader, they document, with extreme precision, banal, everyday rituals; introduce disparities and disjunctions which disturb the equilibrium; and finally transcend rather than resolve the disturbances through aesthetic strategies that are imbued with spiritual, religious, and philosophical meaning. In Ozu's case, the transcendence is achieved through his use of 'codas', a montage of still-life shots that partake of the spirit of Zen.

Schrader relates Ozu's spriritual aesthetic to a Zen aesthetic which permeates the Japanese arts in general and is evident in haiku, the tea ceremony, ink painting, Noh drama, and the martial arts. This aesthetic is marked by a creative use of silences and voids (*mu*), and a predominant mood of *mono no aware* (literally, the pathos of things) based on a sorrowing awareness of the transcience and mutability of all living things (*mujo*). Schrader has not been alone in identifying this aesthetic at work in the Japanese cinema. Although she does not specifically identify it with Zen, Japanese American academic Keiko McDonald (1983) finds several major Japanese films of the 1950s—Kon Ichikawa's *Biruma no tategoto* ('The Harp of Burma', 1956), Mizoguchi's *Ugetsu monogatari* ('Tales of Ugetsu', 1953), Kurosawa's *Kumonsu-jo* ('Throne of Blood', 1957), Keisuke Kinoshita's *Nijushi no hitomi* ('Twenty-Four Eyes', 1954) and Ozu's *Tokyo monogatari* ('Tokyo Story', 1953)—imbued with the philosophy of *mujo*, which she describes as a traditional philosophical concept or traditional Japanese attitude to life.

McDonald sees her role as a native informant who can explicate Japanese cinema to the Western viewer not versed in Japanese culture, and, in this respect, she follows Richie rather than Schrader. Donald Richie, who has lived for many years in Japan, and has familiarized himself with Japanese theatre, art and culture, cinema and society, has performed the role of mediator between Japanese cinema and the West, helping to make it accessible to the uninitiated. In both his collaborative work with J. L. Anderson (1959), and his own books, he has functioned as an interpreter of a largely unknown territory—assuming the seductive role of pioneer and explorer. Because there are very few film scholars in the West who can speak and understand Japanese, and who have more than a cursory knowledge of Japanese culture and society, art, and history these few are easily seduced into performing the role of experts with specialist knowledge of Japan and the Japanese, of educators who can open doors to an understanding of Japanese cinema and Japanese culture. Unlike the current situation in Chinese cinema scholarship, there have been few Japanese who write in English, French, or German, or work in the Western academy, who could contest their readings; little Japanese-language material has been translated into English; and the fact that Japan has been an imperial power itself, rather than a direct victim of European imperialism, seemed to exonerate such Western forays into Japanese culture from the charge of cultural imperialism.

In fact, an American tradition of using the Japanese cinema as a mirror of, or door into, Japan and the Japanese has its origins in wartime Washington. Researchers there studied Japanese films, documen-

Tokyo Story (1953)—Ozu's 'narrational playfulness'

tary and fiction, in an effort to understand the Japanese national character, so as to better ensure defeat of the Japanese military forces and a smooth transition to the post-war American occupation. Richie came to Japan with the occupation and remained there to write, among other things, a book on Japanese cinema, subtitled 'Film Style and National Character', for the Japan Travel Bureau in 1961, a work which was revised, expanded, and updated for Doubleday in New York a decade later. Apart from working as film critic for the *Japan Times* and writing book-length studies of the life and films of Kurosawa and Ozu, Richie was also very generous with his time, knowledge, and contacts towards the next generation of Western researchers on Japanese film, who started arriving in Japan in the 1970s. Their debt to Richie is evident, not merely in

their formal acknowledgements of his assistance, and their deference to his opinions, but also in their emulation of his methodology. Both Audie Bock (1978) and Joan Mellen (1976) survey a wide historical field, cover a broad range of directors, mix biographical information with summary accounts of the films, give some attention to film style, but generally concentrate on thematic readings of the work of the surveyed directors. In her introduction, Mellen echoes Richie's description of Japanese cinema as 'the most perfect reflection of a people' (Richie 1961/1971, p. xix): it is, she suggests, 'a mirror into the hearts of a people' (Mellen 1976, p. xxvii). If reflection theory has fallen out of favour, even more questionable, in the light of deconstruction and post-colonial theory, is her statement that '[t]hrough the Japanese film, we, as well as the Japanese, are able to penetrate this society and its history' (Mellen 1976, p. xxvi).

On the other hand, Mellen does offer a new slant in her sustained feminist critique of Ozu and Kurosawa. Unfortunately, her readings of films, unlike Bock's, suffer from the categorical imperative, and a failure to perceive ambiguities and ambivalences. Swept up in the rhetorical mode of a universalist Western feminist film criticism, she is very quick to label a text or a director either feminist or misogynist, pacifist or militarist, feudal or democratic, when these labels may not be appropriate or accurate, given the historical and industrial constraints of the conditions of Japanese film production and reception. On the other hand, the paucity of politically committed criticism in Western writing on Japanese film makes her work seductive: here is a woman daring to criticize some of the acknowledged great masters of the cinema, while praising some others for their commitment to social change and resistance to dominant values. Empowered by feminist ideology, she may be unaware of her privilege as a Western woman, but she confidently cuts through the cant of mysticism and aestheticism that surrounds the reception of Japanese film and directly addresses social issues.

Since Mellen, one of the few Western researchers to investigate the relevance of social issues to Japanese cinema has been David Desser, another American scholar. In his *Eros Plus Massacre* (1988), he undertakes an explication of the New Wave Japanese Cinema of the 1960s in the light of contemporary Japanese social and political issues and debates, supplying the historical context of production and reception, and attributing political motivations to the filmmakers. His stated intention was to balance the neo-formalist bias of contemporary theoretical debates about the Japanese cinema by putting film content and social context back into the picture.

Until the late 1970s the field of Japanese film studies was dominated by film critics and historical researchers, some from inside and others from outside the Japanese studies area. In the late 1970s a crucial shift occurred: film theorists from outside the Japanese studies area entered the terrain. Three major publications were significant in this shift: first, a special issue of *Screen* magazine in 1976, devoted to an analysis of Ozu film texts; secondly, the publication of Noël Burch's *To the Distant Observer* in 1979; and thirdly, the publication of David Bordwell's book on Ozu in 1988.

These projects coincided with the arrival, and rapid expansion, of cinema studies in the Western academy that seemed to demand a greater theoretical, quasi-scientific rigour than had been hitherto practised in film study; detailed close analysis of the construction of film texts (made possible by new technology); and systematic investigations of the relations between cinema and psychoanalysis, sociology, history, linguistics, and aesthetics. Radical intellectuals around *Screen* in London drew upon the exciting work of French structuralist and post-structuralist theorists, as well as Russian Formalists, in their search for a total theory of the cinema and for strategies of film analysis. Theorizations and analyses of mainstream Hollywood cinema led to investigations of alternative cinemas (the Soviet silent cinema; Godard; German Expressionism; primitive cinema; the avant-garde) and here the Japanese cinema was seized upon as another alternative. In the *Screen* issue on Ozu, Branigan (1976) and Thompson and Bordwell (1976) presented the Ozu text as a modernist text. With evidence gleaned from close textual analysis, they argued that, in Ozu's film practice, unlike the Hollywood system, space was prioritized over narrative. They did not argue that Ozu represented the Japanese cinema: it was the author Ozu who posed the difference. But Noël Burch went further and argued that the Japanese cinema as a whole provides a formidable example of a totally other system from the 'institutional mode of representation' (the dominant style of international filmmaking) in prioritizing presentation over representation, decentred composition over centred composition, surface over depth . . .

In his grand master-theory, Burch employed the language of Marxist historiography and French post-structuralism interlarded with bold (and questionable) assertions about the uniqueness of Japanese society, culture, and art, due to national isolation, unoriginality, and uniformity. He traced a history of Japanese cinema, based on its imitation, adaptation, and ultimate transgression of Western codes of filmmaking, illustrating it with close formal analyses of the editing techniques, shot composition, and camera deployments in isolated sequences from a large number of films. He concluded that the classical (pre-American occupation) Japanese cinema displayed a preference for the long shot over the medium shot and close-up; editing codes that draw attention to themselves (showy, excessive editing or exceptionally long takes); non-anthropocentric composition; and other departures from standard Hollywood practice.

Although he included in his argument an extended range of film directors active in the 1930s (Teinosuke Kinugasa, Hiroshi Shimizu, Sadao Yamanaka, Mikio Naruse, Tamizo Ishida, Tomotaka Tasaka, *et al.*, as well as the Big Three), he was prone to ignore or dismiss as un-Japanese or (implicitly) as non-art industrial practice that did not fit his argument. He was just not interested in the popular generic cinema that is not formally aberrant (in relation to dominant codes of Western realism), and that is not art cinema.

Fascination for a profoundly other aesthetic tradition, one not based on Cartesian perspectivalism, links Schrader, Burch, and recent art historians, such as Norman Bryson (1988). However, where this other tradition is other than the Euro-American, its links with other Asian aesthetic traditions (Chinese and Indian) are unexplored. With the rise of the Chinese art cinema, some of the arguments posed about its aesthetic antecedents (Ehrlich and Desser 1994, part 1) give a strong sense of *déjà-vu*. The explication of a Chinese artistic tradition—one with multiple perspectives rather than a fixed one, flat composition rather than composition in depth, even lighting rather than chiaroscuro, and one that allots an active role to emptiness—suggests that the supposedly exceptional 'aesthetic tradition' of Japan was derived from China and not uniquely Japanese. Beyond that, Willemen (1995) has argued for the persistence of a feudal mode of visuality alongside other modes of visuality in the modern cinema generally. In support of his argument, one may note that flat composition, character typology and frontality, and even lighting are attributes of European feudal art, as well as of Ozu's cinema.

Bordwell takes issue with Burch over his notion of a pure Japanese tradition, arguing that Ozu developed a unique set of 'intrinsic norms' (unique in the Japanese cinema as well as the West), which draw on Taisho era popular cultural forms heavily influenced by modern Western culture. In his later work, Bordwell (1988, chs. 2 and 3) explored the historical and industrial, as well as the cultural, context of Ozu's filmmaking career. However, he continues to assert his belief that Ozu's formal strategies make his work exciting and interesting, while dismissing his thematic material as reiterations of trite cultural clichés. In other short papers on Mizoguchi (Bordwell 1983) and the pre-war Japanese cinema (Bordwell 1992: 328–46), Bordwell continues to concentrate on the departures of Japanese directors from Hollywood and European filmmaking norms, identifying a different treatment of deep space in the case of (pre-war) Mizoguchi, and a stylistic preference for the decorative or ornamental flourish in the case of the Japanese cinema generally.

> **Bordwell continues to concentrate on the departures of Japanese directors from Hollywood and European filmmaking norms, identifying a different treatment of deep space in the case of (pre-war) Mizoguchi, and a stylistic preference for the decorative or ornamental flourish in the case of the Japanese cinema generally.**

Even though celebrating Ozu's narrational playfulness, and identifying it as rooted in a love of fun and games, rather than a ponderous aesthetic rigour, Bordwell himself pursues his subject with such exhaustive rigour, with such a welter of (formal) analytic detail, and with such polemical insistence that he kills the charm and fun. Characteristically, too, he refuses to pursue the symptoms of anything beneath the surface. In contrast, French critic Sylvie Pierre (1992) responds to the Ozu films with a sense of wonder and in a spirit of exploration, pursuing various lines of approach. *Inter alia*, she suggests that one could read the lack of serious attention to sex and politics, and prankish humour, and the low-angle shooting style in Ozu's cinema as symptoms of arrested development; his obsession with perceptual games and quasi-electric charging of the living texture of the passing moment and a displacement of eroticism. (Pierre's tentative deployment of psychoanalytic terminology is uncommon in criticism of Japanese film. The only case of a sustained application of (Western feminist) psychoanalytic theory to Japanese film that I am aware of is Robert Cohen's (1992) analysis of Mizoguchi's film *Saikaku Ichidai Onna* ('The Life of Oharu', 1952).

Both Thompson and Bordwell's (1976) and Branigan's (1976) rigorous analyses of the clearly perceptible surface structures of the Ozu text, and Burch's (1979) ambitious argument about the essential difference of the Japanese cinema in general, rely on Barthes's proposition that 'the Japanese text' is pure surface, with no depth—a proposition they have applied literally and metaphorically. Their syntactic, anti-semantic approach has been very seductive to film scholars unfamiliar with Japanese language, culture, history, and politics, because it seems to make these knowledges redundant: since there is no depth to this cinema, there is no need to pursue the matter further. Until now, despite extensive criticism of their approach in book reviews and academic journalism (see esp. Lehman 1987), there have been no substantially developed counter-theories. Two reasons could be proposed for this failure to pursue the matter: the decline of interest in the Japanese cinema, and its replacement, in the later 1980s and 1990s, by the Chinese cinema(s); and the dearth of scholars equally qualified in Japanese studies and film theory.

However, the question of Nagisa Oshima intervened. Stephen Heath 1976, 1977) found his work of paramount interest to questions and debates about subjectivity, politics, and aesthetics, which preoccupied Marxist and Lacanian British film scholars around *Screen* magazine. Oshima, rather than Ozu, offered a breakthrough for the political avant-garde in the West. The translation of Tadao Sato's work (1982), along with Desser's (1988) book on the Japanese New Wave, enabled us to position this work in a Japanese political context. Oshima's agenda shared with the international New Left movement an attack on the doctrinaire Old Left, and a stress on personal and sexual liberation, but also had specifically local targets: the victim mentality and sentimentality of Japanese leftist filmmaking; Japan's legacy of imperialism, militarism, racism, and sexism; the oppression of Koreans by the Japanese state.

One could say that the Big Three (Ozu, Kurosawa, and Mizoguchi) had become the Big Four (the former three plus Oshima), in the West's understanding of Japanese cinema. The industry's reliance on staple genres was acknowledged but usually dismissed with disdain (Anderson and Richie 1959/1982: 315–22; Burch 1979: 151–3). Some spasmodic attention has been given to the yakuza movie (Schrader 1974; Keiko McDonald, in Nolletti and Desser 1992; Mellen 1976: 121–33) and to the samurai film (David Desser, in Nolletti and Desser 145–64), but generally one could say that we are still awaiting the substantial kinds of analysis of the Japanese popular genres that have been undertaken in regard to the popular Hollywood genres. The same could be said of the star system in the Japanese cinema. Since the classical Japanese film industry was, like Hollywood, based on genre specialization (and diversification) and the star system, these absences would seem to be serious gaps.

In their absence, two racy texts on archetypes of Japanese popular culture, written by two knowledgeable non-academics, Buruma (1984) and Barrett (1989), are useful antidotes to the academic preoccupation with art cinema. Both entertaining and informative, these texts trace the continuities and shifts in the dominant archetypes as manifested in a variety of popular media (comic strips, popular literature, theatre, radio, film, oral storytelling), bringing out the rich intertextual texture of Japanese popular culture. More scholarly historical research on pre-war Japanese popular culture has been undertaken by Miriam Silverberg (1993), who gives welcome attention to the mobility of gender and cultural identifications in pre-war Japan, thus breaking down the sharp split between 'them' and 'us' (women and men, Japanese and non-Japanese).

The dominance of Japanese commerce and capital in the international arena in the 1980s produced renewed speculations about Japan's relation to modernity and postmodernity, both within and outside Japan. Film scholars had long been debating whether Ozu, Mizoguchi, or Kurosawa were traditional or modern (terms often conflated with the essentially Japanese and the Westernized, or with the conservative and the progressive). But now, in the light of postcolonial theory, the terms have become problematic. Scott Nygren (1989) has suggested a considerable amount of cross-cultural confusion in their application, in both East and West: in both cases, conservative, traditional norms have been read as 'modern' or 'modernist' in the other context. Yoshimoto (1991) sees the terminology of modernity and postmodernity as unavoidably tainted by imperialism: the non-West by definition cannot be modern. The vaunted postmodernity of Japan, which has supposedly surpassed that of the West, masks the survival of feudal and politically despotic social and cultural forms, and allows them to be rationalized and naturalized as authentic and desirable national differences. Yoshimoto (1993) decries the emphasis of recent scholarship on the problems of cross-cultural analysis, and advocates a return to politically engaged and informed criticism.

BIBLIOGRAPHY

*Anderson, Joseph A., and Donald Richie (1959/1982), *The Japanese Film: Art and Industry* (rev. Princeton: Princeton University Press).

Barrett, Gregory (1989), *Archetypes in Japanese Film: The Socio-political and Religious Significance of the Principal Heroes and Heroines* (Selinsgrove: Susquehanna University Press).

Bock, Audie (1978), *Japanese Film Directors* (Tokyo: Kodansha).

Bordwell, David (1983), 'Mizoguchi and the Evolution of Film Language', in Stephen Heath and Patricia Mellencamp (eds.), *Cinema and Language* (Los Angeles: American Film Institute).

—— (1985), *Narration in the Fiction Film* (London: Methuen).

—— (1988), *Ozu and the Poetics of Cinema* (London: British Film Institute; Princeton University Press).

—— (1992), 'A Cinema of Flourishes: Japanese Decorative Classicism of the Prewar Era', in Nolletti and Desser (1992).

Branigan, Edward (1976), 'The Space of *Equinox Flower*', *Screen*, 17/2 (Summer), 74–105.

Bryson, Norman (1988), 'The Gaze in the Expanded Field', in Hal Foster (ed.), *Vision and Visionality* (Seattle: Bay Press.

*Burch, Noël (1979), *To the Distant Observer: Form and Meaning in the Japanese Cinema* (London: Scolar Press).

—— (1983), 'Approaching Japanese Film', in Stephen Heath and Patricia Mellencamp (eds.), *Cinema and Language* (Los Angeles: American Film Institute).

Buruma, Ian (1984), *A Japanese Mirror: Heroes and Villains of Japanese Culture* (London: Jonathan Cape).

Cohen, Robert (1992), 'Why does Oharu Faint? Mizoguchi's *The Life of Oharu* and Patriarchal Discourse', in Nolletti and Desser (1992).

Desser, David (1988), *Eros plus Massacre: An Introduction to the Japanese New Wave Cinema* (Bloomington: Indiana University Press).

Dower, John (1986), *War without Mercy: Race and Power in the Pacific War* (New York: Pantheon Books).

Ehrlich, Linda C., and David Desser (eds.) (1994), *Cinematic Landscapes: Observations on the Visual Arts and Cinema of China and Japan* (Austin: University of Texas Press).

Freiberg, Freda (1992), 'Genre and Gender in World War II Japanese Feature Films', *Historical Journal of Film, Radio and Television*, 12/3: 245–52.

Heath, Stephen (1981), 'Narrative Space', *Screen*, 17/3 (Autumn), 68–112; repr. in *Questions of Cinema* (Bloomington: Indiana University Press).

—— (1977/1981), 'The Question Oshima', *Wide Angle* 2/1: 48–57; repr. rev. in *Questions of Cinema* (Bloomington: Indiana University Press).

Lehman, Peter (1987), 'The Mysterious Orient, the Crystal Clear Orient, the Non-existent Orient: Dilemmas of Western Scholars of Japanese Film', *Journal of Film and Video*, 39 (Winter), 5–15.

McDonald, Keiko (1983), *Cinema East: A Critical Study of Major Japanese Films* (London: Associated University Presses).

Mellen, Joan (1976), *The Waves at Genji's Door: Japan through its Cinema* (New York: Pantheon Books).

Nolletti, Arthur, and David Desser (eds.) (1992), *Reframing Japanese Cinema: Authorship, Genre, History* (Bloomington: Indiana University Press).

Nygren, Scott (1989), 'Reconsidering Modernism: Japanese Film and the Postmodern Context', *Wide Angle*, 11/3 (July), 6–15.

Pierre, Sylvie (1992), 'Le Monde d'Ozu' ou, L'Empire de la décence', *Trafic*, 4 (Autumn), 68–87.

Richie, Donald (1961/1971), *Japanese Cinema: Film Style and National Character* (rev. expanded New York: Doubleday).

Sato, Tadao (1982), *Currents in Japanese Cinema*, trans. Gregory Barrett (Tokyo: Kodansha International).

Schrader, Paul (1972/1988), *Transcendental Style in Film: Ozu, Bresson, Dreyer* (Berkeley: University of California Press; repr. New York: Da Capo Press).

—— (1974), 'Yakuza-Eiga, a Primer', *Film Comment*, 10/1 (Jan.–Feb.), 8–17.

Silverberg, Miriam (1993), 'Remembering Pearl Harbour, Forgetting Charlie Chaplin and the Case of the Disappearing Western Woman: A Picture Story', *Positions*, 1/11: 24–76.

Thompson, Kristin, and David Bordwell (1976), 'Space and Narrative in The Films of Ozu', *Screen*, 17/2 (Summer), 41–73.

Willemen, Paul (1995), 'Regimes of Subjectivity and Looking', *UTS Review* 1/2 (Oct.), 101–29.

Yoshimoto, Mitsuhiro (1991), 'Melodrama, Postmodernism, and the Japanese Cinema', *East–West Film Journal*, 5/1 (Jan.), 28–55.

—— (1993) 'The Difficulty of being Radical: The Discipline of Film Studies and the Postcolonial World Order', in Masao Miyoshi and H. D. Harootunian (eds.), *Japan in the World* (Durham, NC: Duke University Press).

24 African cinema

N. Frank Ukadike

In recent times scholarly inquiries into African cinema have proliferated. These have involved multidisciplinary perspectives and have resulted in a diversity of both African and non-African perspectives. The major concerns of this academic writing have been the relationship of African cinematic discourse to the 'dominant' modes of representation and the theoretical contexts and frameworks necessary for their understanding. However, the term 'dominant' has also become problematic in so far as it privileges the hierarchical standing of Hollywood and other Western cinemas, in relation to which all other cinemas, including Africa's, are considered to be either different, alternative, or oppositional. This categorization has also posed other important questions such as: Can there be an autonomous African cinema? What makes African cinema different from Hollywood and other Western cinemas? Can African cinema's uniqueness be understood from the perspectives of other cinemas outside the dominant traditions? In order to begin to answer these questions, it is necessary to examine not only the history of African film production but also the critical and theoretical perspectives employed to account for this history and the difference of African film.

Problems of production

African filmmaking is a very recent phenomenon that has, after independence, developed differently in the anglophone, francophone, and lusophone regions. The shifting conditions and changes which have taken place during the colonial and post-independence periods demonstrate that the cinemas were born under unique circumstances not common to other national cinemas. In short, the varied character of African films today reflects a convulated historical pattern of development. An account of their histories must, therefore, identify factors which have led to their growth or retardation, focusing specifically on socio-political, cultural, and economic issues as well as the state practices which have impacted upon the production of films. In terms of creativity, narrative refinement, and quantity of films produced in the continent, it is now possible to speak of genuine growth, but this success is threatened by a number of economic and political factors. As Kenneth Harrow (1996) has argued, 'it is hard to imagine any other aspect of culture so controlled by neo-colonial forces as in African film'—a control as retrogressive in many ways as the outmoded myths which permeate the interpretation of African history and culture.

Indeed, much 'African' film production is scarcely African at all and results from foreign exploitation of African resources, cheap labour, and production facilities in Zimbabwe and Kenya (which are made available to the highest bidder). This situation helps to explain the unfortunate case in Zimbabwe, where films such as *Neria* (Jit, 1993), *Consequences* (1987), and *More*

Time (1992) are marketed as African films when the producers and distributors are foreign. A number of blockbuster foreign films have also been produced in Africa. These include *Out of Africa* (USA, 1985), shot in Kenya, *Gorillas in the Mist* (USA, 1988), shot in Rwanda, *Mr Johnson* (GB, 1990), shot in Nigeria, and most recently, *The Ghost and the Darkness* (USA, 1996), shot in the South African animal reserves. Although shot in Africa, however, these foreign films none the less deny Africans any point of view. In the same way it is difficult to explain the legitimacy of *Cry Freedom* (1987) and *Sarafina* (USA, 1993) being paraded as black South African films, given the time at which they were made.

In order to understand the various factors which have limited the growth of African film, it is therefore necessary to examine Africa's relationship with other producing nations and assess the impact of 'hegemonic foreign' (Cham 1995) tendencies on the situation in Africa today. Hollywood virtually monopolizes sub-Saharan African theatres, along with foreign distributors and exhibitors of Hong Kong, kung fu, and Indian musical melodramas, with the result that very few African films get seen. This problem is exacerbated by the proliferation of satellite television transmitted live across the continent. South Africa is the home base of MNET, the satellite television network that beams foreign cable networks to most African countries. Because it does not give prominence to African films, it has become the worst perpetrator of cultural colonialism inside Africa.

> Hollywood virtually monopolizes sub-Saharan African theatres, along with foreign distributors and exhibitors of Hong Kong, kung fu, and Indian musical melodramas, with the result that very few African films get seen.

In the 1990s this situation of African film worsened, and filmmakers appealed, to no avail, for government intervention as the only way to compel foreign theatre-owners to promote indigenous African films. This has, however, forced the promotion of video production in anglophone Ghana and Nigeria, in particular. What has been the impact of this video boom on the film industries of Ghana and Nigeria? Are we witnessing the demise of celluloid film production in Africa? Is African film history being rewritten with the video revolution? Most middle-class workers in Nigeria and Ghana, for example, have never seen African films (as opposed to the new video films, as they are popularly called) but can mention numerous American films that even US citizens have never seen or heard of. With the advent of video, however, Ghana has been able to cultivate an indigenous film and video culture. So far it is the only country in Africa I know where Hollywood has lost out to African video films.

The United States and Europe have designed strategies to protect their film industries and Africa needs to do the same, especially with regard to economic viability. How can African film practice be encouraged to reach the industrial level? In what ways can effective control of free flow of foreign films and satellite television be channelled to work for the transformation of African film practices? This worked in Europe in the 1920s (and is still working for the United States). Is it applicable to Africa, as we approach the twenty-first century? Burkina Faso has set precedents which should inspire other African countries. A country of about 6.5 million people with meagre economic resources, it organizes, every other year, the world's largest film festival, the Pan-African Festival of Film and Television of Ouagadougou (FESPACO), which it uses to showcase African films. Burkina Faso has also sponsored inter-state co-productions, an initiative which has helped to produce some award-winning films, and runs a film archive in Ouagadougou, which provides an invaluable facility for research on African cinema.

What, then, is African cinema? or toward an African world cinema?

The first question has been addressed in several studies (Diawara 1992; Ukadike 1994; Tomaselli 1993; Pfaff 1986) and in the writings of Teshome H. Gabriel (1982), Clyde Taylor (1985), Mark A. Reid (1985), Mbye B. Cham (1982) and so on. It is interesting that Africa is no longer regarded as the filmic cul-de-sac it was once thought. Over the years African cinema has undergone a radical transformation by widening its scope and offering an expanded definition of the continent's cinemas as work which expresses the diversity and plurality of the cultures of the producing nations. Indeed, the term 'African cinema' may be seen as outdated, now used only for convenience. For it is important to make it clear that the cinema in Tunisia may not have anything in common with the cinema in Cameroon. Each nation's cinema is a loose assortment of films by individual filmmakers of various backgrounds and with different agendas. Their ostensible goals may be the same with regard to the representation of continental issues, but stylistic trends do not mirror the unity that we find in the filmmakers' declamations. Still, some broad trends link all the generations of filmmakers.

As independence paved the way for the acquisition of cinematic know-how and filmmaking infrastructure, it is understandable how, in the pioneering period of the 1960s–1970s, it became the concern of African film practitioners to link the emerging cinema with politics and education and to stress African histories and culture which Euro-American cinemas often caricature. The African cinema of this period is didactic and unabashedly political and denunciative. For example, Ousmane Sembene, widely regarded as the father of African cinema, proclaimed that 'the cinema is the night school of my people'. For him, the film theatre could provide the forum for education unavailable under colonialism.

This also implied the adoption of particular filmmaking strategies. Simply put, the effect of Sembene's ideology can be seen in the narrative style employed in his film *Borom Sarret* (Senegal, 1963), a twenty-minute short which, arguably, initiated the model African film in which the synthesis of fiction and documentary, meticulous attention to detail, and oral narrative technique coalesce into an indigenous aesthetic. This approach suggests new ways of seeing and interpreting African history through cinematic images, and highlights the dichotomy between African cinema and Euro-American cinema, in this case between a social cinema and a commercial cinema orientated towards profit.

As the leading pioneer, Sembene exerted enormous influence on other African filmmakers. However, his narrative style has been neither prescriptive nor binding on other pioneer African filmmakers such as Med Hondo, Souleymane Cissé, Haile Gerima, Safi Faye, and Sarah Maldoror. Although these pioneers differ in their narrative approaches to African issues, they are unanimous in eschewing the dominant notion of a cinema geared towards entertainment. These African filmmakers initiated interrogative narrative patterns by appropriating and subverting 'dominant' conventions, blending them with their own cultural codes (oral narrative art) to create a novel aesthetic formula. Dubbed 'the aesthetics of decolonization', it is this aesthetic, and its difference from Western notions of art, that some critics have argued has invested the language of cinema with new meaning and encouraged new methods of critical orientation.

Although African filmmakers invoke oral tradition as a primary influence, they have appropriated it and applied it in various ways to create paradigms for addressing the broad range of social, political, cultural, and historical issues of Africa. Even among critics of African film practice, oral tradition as a creative matrix has generated controversies and disagreements regarding its application to African films (Akudinobi 1995). Although their styles are diametrically opposed to each other, this use of oral tradition and African film language can be identified and analysed in the films of Ousmane Sembene and Med Hondo. While Sembene's narrative is more linear than Hondo's and imbued with straightforward didacticism (as in *Borrom Sarret*, *Mandabi*, 'The Money Order', 1968, *Xala*, 1974, and *Camp de Thiaroye*, 1987), Hondo's films (*Soleil O*, 1969, and *West Indies*, 1979) are, as Pfaff (1986) suggests, syncopated and eruptive in tone, and reminiscent of the stylistically disruptive tone of black French liberationist literature. The two filmmakers not only share a number of Western influences (such as Italian Neo-Realism, Hollywood, Latin American documentary, and Soviet montage) but are indebted to indigenous oral storytelling techniques as well. Thus, while Western critics have tended to read Hondo's style as avante-garde and Godardian, Africanist discourse has emphasized its links with oral tradition (see Pfaff 1986; Ukadike 1994).

Specific applications of the oral storytelling art abound in African films. In Désiré Écaré's exuberant film *Faces of Women* (Côte d'Ivoire, 1988), music, song, and dance intersperse the narrative. Unlike Western films, where music is used to contradict or complement the visual information, song and dance in *Faces* are narrative components working together to

> *Borom Sarret* (Senegal, 1963), is a twenty-minute short which, arguably, initiated the model African film in which the synthesis of fiction and documentary, meticulous attention to detail, and oral narrative technique coalesce into an indigenous aesthetic.

Senegalese filmmaking—*Xala* (1974)

advance the film's structure and to create continuity between images or what they signify. Moussa Kemoko Diakite's *Naitou* (Guinea, 1982) employs no dialogue—only music and dance—to show how the cultural power of art can be used to tell the tale of a young orphan girl in a polygamous home, who has been badly mistreated by the stepmother who killed her real mother. In *Angano . . . Angano . . . Tales from Madagascar* (Madagascar and France, 1989), Marie-Clemence and Cesar Paes use oral storytelling techniques to demystify dominant documentary film practice. In this film, storytelling is foregrounded as art, and oral tradition becomes the principal actor which renders vivid an eyewitness account of the myths and belief systems of the Malagasy culture. They include tales about the origins of life, rice cultivation, and the

ritual practice of the exhumation of the dead. The images captured are presented without trivializing or folklorizing the ritual as in conventional ethnographic films. Close-ups are judiciously employed, but not the type of psychologizing close-ups used in Jean Rouch's psychodrama *Les Maîtres fous* (1953).

For some critics the quest of Africanizing film language has and is being achieved in the films themselves and has initiated a set of critical assumptions that include a counter-discourse against the 'dominant' aesthetic. If this suggests modification and revision of cinematic discourse and the cinematic canon, what theoretical and critical methodology is applicable? Can the pan-Africanist model intermingle with the European–American model to initiate a new inquiry into the means of signification? Both cinemas require

> **Is the time ripe now for an African film historiography to address the works of exiled filmmakers and situate them within the global concept of African world cinema?**

different critical or theoretical methodologies, or a blend of methodologies, for formulating discourses on their evolution.

South Africa offers another dimension to African film history and the discourse of African cinema. The cinema in South Africa which was once referred to as the cinema of apartheid is now simply known as South African cinema since the country has been admitted to the Organization of African Unity following the demise of apartheid. South Africa is a multiracial society that is unlike many other countries in Africa. Film production in this Southern hemisphere is dominated by South African whites. In the 1995 Pan-African Film and Television Festival of Ouagadougou, the question of who is a South African filmmaker or whether white South African filmmakers fit into this category arose. Although the delegation was predominantly black, it was a white South African 'queer' film that sparked a mass exodus from the theatre where the film was shown. It suggests that homosexuality has not begun to be publicly addressed in Africa as it has been in other societies, or, to put it in another way, African audiences outside South Africa may not yet be prepared for such a cultural shock.

Notable filmmakers who live outside the continent such as Med Hondo, Ngangura Nweze, Jean-Marie Teno, Safi Faye, and Haile Gerima identify their works as African. But how does African historiography position John Akomfrah, a Ghanaian-born filmmaker, or Nigeria's Ngozi Onwurah, whose works are identified with black British film practice? Also, there have been important films set in Africa that deal with African issues in serious terms which have been categorized as African films, even though their makers are diasporan blacks. A few of these filmmakers are Sarah Maldoror (*Sambizanga*, Angola and Congo, 1972), Raoul Peck (*Lumumba*, France and Germany, 1992), and Marie-Clemence Blanc-Paes (the producer of *Angano . . . Angano*). Is the time ripe now for an African film historiography to address the works of exiled filmmakers and situate them within the global concept of African world cinema?

Critical and theoretical concepts

Another perspective from which to view African cinema concerns the critical theories used in their appraisal and appreciation. Until recently, writings on African cinema were dominated by the French. With few exceptions, the approach was Eurocentric and more journalistic than academic. But with the coming of a new breed of critics, such as Françoise Pfaff, Teshome Gabriel, Mbye B. Cham, Mark A. Reid, Clyde Taylor, Keyan Tomaselli, myself and others, critical theories and academic assessment of African cinematic practices have taken new and innovative paths. These new critics have begun to blend what are perceived as dominant theories and criticisms into pan-Africanist discourses which provide new interpretations of the configurations and significations of this new aesthetic. The strategy recalls the Latin American film practices of the 1960s, when filmmakers were not only able to use film as a weapon of liberation but also generated the critical theory that was relevant to the cultural, political, and historical transformations that led to the consideration of alternative (read: indigenous) aesthetics (see Burton-Carvajal, Part 3, Chapter 25).

> **African critics have tended to differ from their Western counterparts, and have argued that it is not adequate to formulate African film discourse only within the critical and theoretical frameworks of European–American contexts.**

In the late 1990s, as the field of African film studies expanded, a plethora of African film theory and criticism began to emerge. This has been beneficial to African cinema, but has also initiated debates regarding the adequacy of critical methodologies. There are two schools of thought—the one advocating the adequacy of Western critical canons, and the other arguing for a reassessment of the canon so that African cinematic discourse should not be merely appended to dominant cinematic discourse. Thus, African critics have tended to differ from their Western counterparts, and have argued that it is not adequate to formulate

African film discourse only within the critical and theoretical frameworks of European–American contexts.

Keyan Tomaselli (1993), for example, has raised concerns regarding imported theories 'grounded in deconstruction and post-Freudian Lacanian psychoanalysis'. He argues that it may be inappropriate to apply such theories, which were developed to explain Westernized subjectivities, for intepreting cultural images of Africa. Thus, Sheila Petty's (1995) analysis of Djibril Mambety's *Hyenas* (Senegal, 1992) shows how Western feminist film theory may not be appropriate in the African film discourse. Similarly, the limitations of psychoanalytically informed feminist readings of African film may also be seen in the case of Sembene's *Xala* (Senegal, 1974), where the cultural meaning of the pestle for pounding food has been interpreted as a phallic symbol and misread to fit Western feminist discourse. In *Xala*, the pestle is used as a metaphor to reinforce the impact of the collusion of African and Western cultures, which contributes to the tearing-apart of El Hadj's life. This is an important cultural motif in the film, for, irrespective of wealth or how well placed in society a person may be, African customs demand that one must respect one's mother-in-law. El Hadj contravenes this simple rule by denying the obligation to take off his Western suit, sit on the wooden chair provided for him, and pound the grain in the mortar. One can therefore understand why an African reader would be amused to see the pestle equated with phallocentrism.

In order to advance the understanding of African film, it is necessary to reformulate film theory and criticism in order to do justice to the specificity of African cinemas and the particular socio-political and cultural situations in which they occur. This does not mean, as Harrow contends, that this would entail that only 'African perspectives are appropriate in the consideration and theorizing of African film' (Harrow 1996). This approach can be seen in the special issue of the journal *Iris* on African cinema, entitled *New Discourses of African Cinema* (Ukadike 1995): the content of this volume is rich and the ways in which contributors have engaged the issues is diverse. The theoretical models employed in the studies represent critical interventions whose orientations range from Western critical paradigms and anthropological reading of film images to pan-Africanist readings of the significance of images. The essays, for example, display a concern to criticize the concepts of tradition and modernity as applied to African films (and surrounding discourses) such as Henri Duparc's *Bal poussière* (Côte d'Ivoire, 1988)

and Jean-Pierre Bekolo's *Quartier Mozart* (Cameroon, 1992). The theory and criticism of the documentary film is also seen to be expanded by such African documentaries as *Afrique je te plumerai* ('Africa, I Will Fleece You', Cameroon, 1992) and *Allah Tantou* ('God's Will', Guinea, 1991). The transposition of an alien story (a play by the Swiss writer Friedrich Dürrenmatt) into an African setting in Djibril Mambety's *Hyenas* is seen to explore the socio-political contradictions of contemporary Africa through an exploratory and hybrid style which compels viewers to re-examine their ways of seeing and reacting to African issues.

The introduction to this special issue also suggests the direction African cinematic discourse should take. It calls for an informed critical dialogue that does not need to be an African-centred discourse, as this would 'imply new forms of hegemony', and 'a retrenchment to the tyranny of a [new] canon'. The articles published therefore, eschew 'monolithic dialogue' even if they do 'signify a monolithic tendency—a tendency which argues for the broadening of investigations' (Ukadike 1995: 4), but not at the expense of the cultural, political, historical, and economic determinants of African film initiatives. The history and discussion of African cinema and of world film should go along this route. Inclusion, not exclusion, is the buzz-word for proliferation of ideas.

BIBLIOGRAPHY

Akudinobi, Jude (1995), 'Tradition/Modernity and the Discourse of African Cinema', *Iris: A Journal of Theory on Image and Sound*, N. Frank Ukadike, ed., 18: 25–37.

Bakari, Imruh, and **Mbye Cham** (eds.) (1996), *African Experiences of Cinema* (London: British Film Institute).

Cham, Mbye B. (1982), 'Ousmane Sembene and the Aesthetics of African Oral Traditions', *Africana Journal*, 13/1 and 4: 24–40.

—— (1995), 'Filming the African Experience', in Gaston Kaboré (ed.), *Africa and the Centenary of Cinema* (Paris: Présence africaine).

*Diawara, Manthia** (1992), *African Cinema: Politics and Culture* (Bloomington: Indiana University Press).

Gabriel, Teshome (1982), *Third Cinema in the Third World: The Aesthetics of Liberation* (Ann Arbor: University of Michigan Research Press).

Harrow, Kenneth (1993), *Critical Arts*, 7/1–2, Special Issue: *African Cinema*.

—— (1996), *Research in African Literatures*, 27/3: 173–7.

*Martin, Michael T.** (ed.) (1995), *Cinemas of the Black Diaspora: Diversity, Dependence and Oppositionality* (Detroit: Wayne State University Press).

Petty, Sheila (1995), 'Whose Nation is it Anyhow? The Politics of Reading African Cinema in the West' in Gaston Kaboré (ed.), *Africa and the Centenary of Cinema* (Paris: Présence africaine).

Pfaff, Françoise (1986), 'Films of Med Hondo: An African Filmmaker in Paris,' *Jump Cut*, 31: 44–6.

Reid, Mark A.(1985), 'Dialogic Modes of Representing Africa's Womanist Film', *African American Review*, 25/2: 375–88.

Taylor, Clyde (1985), 'FESPACO '85 was a Dream Come True', *Black Film Review*, 1/4: 6–9.

Tomaselli, Keyan (1993), African Cinema: Theoretical Perspectives on Some Unresolved Questions', *Critical Arts: A Journal for Cultural Studies*, 7/1–2: 1–10.

*Ukadike, N. Frank (1994), *Black African Cinema* (Berkeley, University of California Press).

—— (ed.) (1995), *Iris: A Journal of Theory on Image and Sound*, 18, Special Issue: *New Discourses of African Cinema*.

Hyenas

Richard Porton from Richard Porton, 'Mambety's *Hyenas*: Between Anti-Colonialism and the Critique of Modernity', *Iris*, 18 (Spring 1995), 95–103.

Hyenas (Senegal 1992) revolves around a wealthy old woman's return to the village where, years before, whe was 'seduced and abandoned' by a man who now seems completely benign. Yet despite the film's apparent embrace of grim determinism, Djbril Diop Mambety strips Friedrich Dürrenmatt's parable of its quasi-theological veneer. The desolate town of Colobane encapsulates many of the contradictions of Senegalese society as both revolutionary hopes and traditional bonds of solidarity erode. With its faded bourgeoisie and rapacious petty bourgeoisie, Colobane serves as a microcosm reflecting Africa's current economic crisis.

Linguère Ramatou, the film's vengeful elderly woman, agitates Colobane's populace to the point of frenzy by promising a future of untold wealth. 'Ramatou is coming back to us . . . richer than the World Bank . . . only the lady can save us' is the townspeople's hopeful exhortation. The local politicians and clergy, immobolized by despair, view Ramatou's largess as the only possible solution to the never-ending cycle of poverty and exploitation. Dramaan Drameh, the amiable shopkeeper who never fails to sip calvados with his eager customers, awaits the eminent *grande dame* with more anticipation than any of the other inhabitants. Ramatou's beneficence eventually turns sour, of course, and the cataclysmic series of events that inevitably bedevil Calobane seem designed to frustrate critics and audiences who might be tempted to indulge themselves with moralistic interpretations.

The film's allegorical structure is directly mediated by the suffering imposed on African countries by 'structural adjustment', the World Bank's attempt to control the internal policies of debtor nations by coercing them to increase exports and seriously curtail social spending, thus insuring misery for the the poor. Given these constricting material realities, a misguided moralist might, for example, see the film merely as an indictment of consumerism, a tract that apparently blames the victims of structural adjustment for their yearnings to enjoy some paltry material pleasures. In the final analysis, however, the film seems more like an intermittently comic dirge than a sermon.

Despite Mambety's occasional rhetorical flourishes—the juxtaposition of a Sony sign and shots of African starvation is one of the flashier examples—the film is far removed from earlier examples of African social realism, whether exemplified by the novels and films of Ousmane Sembene or Safi Faye's synthesis of documentary and autobiography.

Hyenas's overlapping ironies and tragicomic tone shares a kinship with an earlier Mambety film, *Touki-Bouki* (1973). In that film, rather ethnocentrically stereotyped as an African *Breathless* by some critics, the rebellious protagonists hope to escape to France, but their nihilistic exaltation of violence dooms them. The lure of Parisian glamour proves a hollow fantasy, but the film does not promote an artificial recuperation of pre-colonial tradition. Similarly, *Hyenas* presents a bleak sketch of contemporary acquisitiveness, without endorsing, however hesitantly, a return to some sort of Edenic, pre-colonial bliss. In discussing various African films including *Touki-Bouki*, Roy Armes and Lizbeth Malkmus claim, in a vein of dubious essentialism, that the pre-eminent directors 'structure their films around a series of external oppositions (e.g. past/present, tradition/modernity)'. Yet the interest of Mambety's films seems to lie in their concerted attempts to explode this kind of binarism, posing these alternatives not as choices but as self-consuming artefacts.

The gruesome carnivalesque crescendo of *Hyenas* turns out to be a case in point. As the villagers satisfy their cravings for shoes from Burkina Faso and sparkling refrigerators, Ramatou imports an actual carnival to Colobane, with a dazzling Ferris wheel as the fair's centrepiece. If these diversions are meant to pacify the townspeople while Dramaan is made a scapegoat, Ramatou's plan succeeds all too well. Despite his genial manner, we are resigned to accept Dramaan as the man responsible for the millionairess's former life of privation and forced prostitution, yet Ramatou herself does not embody moral probity of any sort. Dramaan's plaintive outburst—'Madam, we hold fast to the principles of our civilization'—evokes more the pain of a self-inflicted wound than the shrillness of a rallying-cry. Unlike the unambiguously affirmative heroines of *Sambizanga (Angola, 1972) and Med Hondo's Sarraounia* (Mauritania, 1986), Ramatou is not an icon of empowerment. She can only offer the mere negative freedom of ruthless demystification.

In the final analysis, therefore, Mambety's thematic tapestry is geared more towards narrative polyphony than a series of sterile oppositions; as in all complex parables, the interpretive work is left to the audience. The film suggests several disparate, if complementary, points of departure: a materialist gloss, as well as a contextualization within African cinema's elaboration of the oral tradition.

In his recent comprehensive survey of African oral literature, Isidore Okpewho demonstrates how contemporary writers

Hyenas continued

such as Ousmane Sembene and Wole Soyinka transform and subvert traditional trickster narratives for the purpose of radical social critique. In works such as *The Road, and Kongi's Harvest, traditional solidarity with victims is transformed into barbed attacks on entrenched power. Hyenas's relationship* to the critical legacy of oral tradition is somewhat different. Mambety's tragicomic stance contains the seeds of social critique, but is not prescriptive or programmatic in the tradition of Soyinka or Sembene. Mambety's approach is abrasively parodic. With a skilful deployment of what Mikhail Bakhtin termed 'double-voiced discourse', *Hyenas* expertly reframes motifs from both the oral tradition and more earnest, hopeful African films. The film could not be characterized as cynical, but this example of good-humoured despair is a far cry from the insurrectionary cinema of years past.

In addition, the film deviates from the simple observational style of recent African films such as *Yaaba* (Burkina Faso, 1987). Unlike that film's unobtrusive lyrical realism, Mambety's film employs a form of rhetoric that unashamedly calls attention to itself. Autonomous shots of hyenas herald the villagers' joyous anticipation of wealth, and stark overhead shots punctuate Dramaan's interrogation by the town's clergy. The rhetorical overlay cannot be viewed as heavy-handed, however, since it is impossible to distil a monolithic credo from the ornate, self-conscious editing style.

Hyenas's carefully modulated syncretism helps to modify—perhaps even undermine—some of the strictures laid down in studiously nationalist works such as *Toward the Decolonization of African Literature*. The Nigerian literary critics who collaborated on this lively polemic provide a derisive account of the condescension endemic to most accounts of African literature, and the 'severance' of contemporary African fiction and poetry from the roots of oral tradition. The authors reserve their choicest epithets for Wole Soyinka; the playwright and novelist who would

eventually win the Nobel Prize is condemned for his capitulation to 'Euro-modernism'. Conversely, other authors are seen as more exemplary representatives of anti-colonialist zeal, and more genuine progenitors of a new African tradition. Ousmane Sembene, for example, is praised as a 'people's *griot*'.

If European modernism and indigenous African modes were irreconcilable polarities, Mambety's cinematic parable would prove unsettling indeed. Mambety is certainly not ashamed to proclaim that 'it is a joy for me to pay tribute to Friedrich Dürrenmatt'. Yet this homage to a modernist European playwright is as politically acute as Sembene's most didactic novels and films and, in paradoxical ways, as attuned to important currents in African tradition as the stories of Amos Tutuola. It could be plausibly asserted that *Hyenas* incorporates a 'double consciousness' that is almost endemic to many African co-productions of recent vintage. While W. E. B. Du Bois's use of the term 'double consciousness' described African Americans' anguished oscillation between black identity and American selfhood, filmmakers like Mambety must delicately balance African identity with a modernist legacy that influenced an earlier generation of African intellectuals, most notably the founders of *Présence africaine* (a journal founded in Paris in 1956).

Several sequences in *Hyenas* can be viewed as sardonic (and subtly parodic) interludes which chronicle the contradictions stemming from Africa's ambivalent embrace of both modernity and literary and cinematic modernism. The fact that *Hyenas* can reject a Manichean traditionalism, while poking fun at the fatuities of modernist Europhiles (despite the fact that the film itself is an example of an idiosyncratic modernism) reveals an unusually sophisticated sensibility. Mambety's film is more a slyly subversive appropriation of Western modernism than a concession to its homogenizing lingua franca. Like the West Indian cricketers celebrated by C. L. R. James in *Beyond a Boundary*, Mambety transforms a petrified Western aesthetic into a vibrantly critical practice.

25

South American cinema

Julianne Burton-Carvajal

Introduction

The bibliography on Latin American cinema has grown exponentially from the 1940s to the present, with the most explosive increase taking place over the past decade. Between 1960 and 1972 the British film journal *Sight and Sound* published only two articles on Latin American film. The 1970s saw some 150 articles (excluding film and book reviews) on related topics published in English, and the 1980s doubled that number. Of the roughly 100 books written on Argentine cinema, to take one example, more than 25 per cent date from the 1990s.

The multiple and sometimes overlapping motives for expanding the bibliography on film in Latin America are not always scholarly. Promotion, commemoration, and the will to register personal testimony have been prevalent alongside more academic impulses. Emphases also differ according to the national-cultural, institutional, and historical contexts of the writers. A survey of the international panorama of books and monographs indicates, perhaps predictably, that commemoration, documentation, and the recuperation of submerged histories dominate the early phases of Latin American publishing (1940s to 1960), promotion and critical assessment the 1970s, scholarly investigation, and historiography the 1980s and 1990s. Critical discourses currently emerging from cultural studies,

queer theory, post-colonial, and post-national (e.g. border, exile, globalization) studies are also leading to a re-examination of consecrated texts and reconceptualizations of the critical object. This chapter, therefore, begins with a consideration of the problems involved in defining and conceptualizing South American cinema followed by an overview of South American filmmaking practices and the issues to which they give rise. These include the relationship between the film medium and processes of social change; the modes most appropriate for the representation of 'national' realities; questions of modes of production and consumption; and the role of the filmmaker in societies characterized by severe inequalities.

Mass, popular, and élite culture

Understanding the historical role and cultural impact of cinema in South or Latin or, more accurately, Indo-Ibero-Afro-America, presupposes a recognition that the film medium has intervened in this multi-ethnic, multilingual, multinational (and increasingly transnational) hemisphere, not simply as a manifestation of mass or popular or high culture but—in varying degrees and at different times—as all three of these. As the first mass art form, film was introduced in most nations and proto-nations of the region within a few years of its 'invention' in 1895, and in the intervening century the creation of—or the impulse to create—a national cinema has been viewed as one of the obligatory indices of both modernity and nationhood.

> **As the first mass art form, film was introduced in most nations and proto-nations of the region within a few years of its 'invention' in 1895, and in the intervening century the creation of—or the impulse to create—a national cinema has been viewed as one of the obligatory indices of both modernity and nationhood.**

No national cinema tradition sustained the goal of replicating Hollywood's studio-based, industrial model of film production, but in the three that came closest to this persistent if impractical aspiration—Mexico, Argentina, and Brazil, in descending order of magnitude—the film medium became the most important register of popular culture, in part through its ability selectively to hegemonize social types, costumes, customs, landscapes, and eventually speech patterns and musical traditions into composites that came to symbolize both the national and the popular. These composites took on a life of their own in the sphere of reception, eliciting reproduction in popular song, speech, dress, social habits, and self-conception. In the case of Mexican cinema more than any other, unrivalled dissemination throughout the Spanish-speaking world and Brazil helps explain why the cultural imaginary invoked was widely embraced as an expression of a shared supranational imaginary. Finally, television's successful conquest of the mass audience has helped make cinema an increasingly élite form of expression. The international success of recent films from Mexico or Brazil, Chile or Bolivia, for example, occurs in a radically altered context, since these films now circulate as part of an international art cinema that is relatively indifferent to national specificity and targets privileged rather than popular audiences.

In no country has the cinema been more central to the deliberate construction of a new, homogenizing national consciousness than in Mexico, especially during the 1930s, when the coming of sound coincided with the consolidation phase of the post-revolutionary regime. Yet Aurelio de los Reyes (1983), historian of the silent period of Mexican film production, argues that the nationalist impulse is inherent in the entire trajectory of Mexican filmmaking, marking the uses to which the fledgling medium was put in the waning years of the dictatorship of Porfirio Díaz (whose overthrow in 1910 inaugurated the Mexican Revolution). It also marks the zeal that prevailed during the subsequent decade, under Venustiano Carranza, to export on film 'the richness, beauty, civilized and useful aspects' (de los Reyes 1983: 228) of national culture to a world already woefully misled by Hollywood's distorted representations of Mexico and Mexicans.

Subsequent to the Second World War in nearly every instance of socio-political transformation towards a more inclusive conceptualization of the nation—the initiation of the Castro regime in Cuba in 1959, peasant and student mobilizations in Brazil prior to the 1964 military coup, student and worker mobilization in Mexico City prior to the Tlatelolco massacre of 1968, the Popular Unity period in Chile (1970–3) and the decade preceding it, the Sandinista regime in Nicaragua (1979–90), the Salvadorean civil war and processes of redemocratizaton in the Southern Cone nations during the 1980s, Bolivia's ethno-democratic resurgence in the mid-1990s—film has been a weapon of choice in the (re)definition of the national project and the enlistment of previously excluded or under-represented national constituencies. Two of these historical conjunctures in particular, Cuban cinema of the 1960s and 1970s and post-dictatorship Argentine cinema of the 1980s, offer exemplary instances of film as the register through which a revised national project can be both formulated and promulgated. The new social movements of the 1980s and 1990s—women's, indigenous, and environmental movements, for example—are also associated with this audiovisual imperative, though their medium of choice is most often video because of its lower costs, greater flexibility, and ease of use.

However, the failure to achieve infranational integration has also been one of the primary symptoms of the incompleteness of the process of nation-building throughout continental Latin America, where people continue to self-identify primarily on the basis of their province or region. The existence of sporadic regional filmmaking traditions should therefore be no less surprising than the attempts to subsume them into a single national tradition often centred in and subordinated to the capital. Sometimes these regional cinematic traditions are associated with individuals; in other instances, a regional production centre has focused the efforts of numerous individuals across one or more generation (e.g. Guadalajara in Mexico and Medellín and Cali in Colombia). Therefore, many Latin American nations demonstrate both 'metropolitan' and 'peripheral' traditions not only in the evolution of commercial filmmaking initiatives but also in oppositional ones.

Nation and anti-nation: the new Latin American cinema movement, artist-intellectuals, and the notion of the popular

The recent focusing of international critical attention on questions of how cinema implicates and expresses the national has made it obvious that all cinemas, even that perennially dominant construct known as Hollywood, are national cinemas. Some, however, have been more transparently—that is, hegemonically—'national' than others. In dependent countries, questions of film and nation-(hood) are incomparably fraught because 'a sense of national powerlessness generates a sisyphean struggle to conquer an elusive "authenticity" (that must be) constructed anew with every generation' (Stam et al. 1995: 395). Haunted by spectres of dependency and cultural colonialism, national cinemas throughout the post-colonial world have been habitually evaluated in terms of their service to national 'consolidation' and 'integration' and later 'development' and 'national liberation'. Both individual and generational creative expression have been subordinated to the larger project of vindicating a national image and/or consolidating a national cinema. In Latin America from the late 1960s to the 1980s a 'continental project', unifiying in its diversity and tied to the larger project of continental revolution, was superimposed upon the mandate to (re)assert the nation in cinematic terms.

Predictably, the nation that film culture has been (self-)mandated to (re)assert has varied according to particular national–historical–political conjunctures. *Utopia Unarmed*, Jorge Castañeda's (1993) analysis of the Latin American left before and after the Cold War, dissects the perennial commitment to nationalism on the part of the many strands of the left alliance.

According to Castañeda, in terms of its power to mobilize and elicit the ultimate sacrifices from Latin American populations, nationalism has no rival in Latin America except for the region's (now waning) devotion to the Catholic Church. The characteristically populist strain that flourished in Latin American nationalisms from the 1930s to the 1950s and occasionally beyond, a strain that reflected 'the unfulfilled Latin American dream of a painless modernity' (1993: 43), conferred upon the artist-intellectual sector the role of representational agent of the national citizenry, and mediator between the latter and the state as well as the extra-national realm. During this period the Latin American nation was understood as being made up of two incompatible populations: the *comprador* élites, a foreign-identified 'anti-nation'; and the people, (re)defined as the true nation. The latter category consisted of the excluded or marginalized masses—socially, economically, racially, ethnically, and often culturally 'other'. Regarded as voiceless and socially invisible, they were perceived to require the intervention of self-appointed mediators to give them voice and visibility. For three decades this shared 'social imaginary' was constitutive of the supraregional and pan-nationalism that the New Latin American Cinema movement both catalysed and reflected.

For roughly the same thirty-year period—from the takeover of Havana by the Fidelistas on 1 January 1959 to the electoral defeat of the Nicaraguan Sandinistas in February 1990—the idea of armed revolution occupied centre-stage in the left's pageant of history while the interpretive filter was provided by dependency theory. The first autochthonous theoretical discourse to emerge from the hemisphere, dependency theory, as characterized by Castañeda, posited the colonial status of the hemisphere, the dysfunctional nature of capitalism in the region due to the impotence and/or treacherousness of the local business classes, the dearth of democratic channels, and the non-viability of any form of non-socialist development (Castañeda 1993: 71). The revolution was to be anti-imperialist, anti-capitalist, and hemispheric; hence it needed hemispherically viable cultural expressions. Film, foremost among these because its massive reception did not require literacy, needed to be dissociated from its origins, both imperialist and capitalist, by emphasizing anti-industrial, artisanal modes of production; original, autochthonous (as opposed to derivative and dependent) modes of expression; and participatory, activating modes of reception.

Motivated by social concern rather than economic ambition, seeking to make films about, for, and with 'the people', filmmakers were artist-intellectuals with an impulse to activism. Socially, and often politically as well, they were part of an alternative élite, almost invariably upper middle class. Though earnest and consequential, their efforts to realign their class affiliation were seldom unproblematic. Bolivian filmmaker Jorge Sanjinés, for example, gives an account of how he and his Grupo Ukamau learned almost too late, that hierarchically individualistic cultural perspectives anchored in inherited class and ethnic privilege, however 'natural' they may seem to those who subscribe to them, are incompatible with any aspiration to a genuinely popular, indigenous-centred cinema. High in the remote Andes, prepared to begin filming *Yawar Mallku* ('Blood of the Condor', 1969), Sanjinés and his La Paz-based crew were mystified by initial resistance from the local community that quickly evolved into open hostility. Faced with the prospect of complete failure, the filmmakers offered to submit to the judgement of the community through the time-honoured *jawaico* ritual, the casting and reading of the coca leaves, and finally secured their support.

Fernando Birri, in a manifesto from the early 1960s, called for a national, realist, and popular cinema, according to which filmmakers should not only re-examine biases inherent to their social and educational level, but also develop effective modes of expression capable of connecting to actual audiences and reception practices. A double challenge is inherent in the dual sense of the word 'popular': of the people and acclaimed by them. The career trajectories of Brazilian Nelson Pereira dos Santos, revered 'father' of Cinema Novo, and the comparatively unsung Venezuelan auteur Román Chalbaud, are exemplary in this regard.

Pereira dos Santos's career has spanned almost five decades and produced seventeen features to date. The quest for resonance with ordinary Brazilians from all walks of life, if occasionally detoured, has never been abandoned. Following the itineraries of several young peanut-vendors, *Rio 40 graus* ('Rio 100 Degrees', 1956) traces the socioeconomic panorama of Brazil's (then) capital city. His second, *Rio zona norte* ('Rio Northern Zone', 1957), enlists melodrama and popular music into new regimes of social sensitivity as it retrospectively pieces together the story of a brilliant Afro-Brazilian samba composer from Rio's most marginal sector who dies without ever getting his due. Commissioned by the British Film Institute and Chan-

nel 4 telelvision to make a feature commemorating the hundredth anniversary of the film medium, Pereira dos Santos brought forth a tribute to and meditation on the popular appeal of the 'old' cinema. His *Cinema das lagrimas* ('Cinema of Tears', 1995) charts a thinly plotted pilgrimage, shared by an ageing director and a young but tragically afflicted critic, through the ecstatic excesses of dozens of Mexican melodramas and one climactic Argentine tear-jerker.

Intriguingly, one of the most successful examples of this impulse to produce a cinema that is both genuinely popular in the dual sense and also socially meaningful occurs outside the radius of the New Latin American Cinema. Venezuelan cinema began sporadically in the 1950s and only emerged as a national-cultural movement in the mid-1970s after reiterated demands for state support finally bore fruit. Of Venezuela's several dozen active feature filmmakers, Román Chalbaud is widely recognized locally as the country's foremost cinematic auteur.

Chalbaud was a pioneer first in theatre and then in television. From the late 1950s his career has alternated between these and film. From his début film, *Caín adolescente* ('Teenage Cain', 1959) to his sixteenth, *Cuchillos de fuego* ('Knives of Fire', 1990), Chalbaud's films have won a large following in Venezuela, helping to create a significant audience for national cinema where none existed before. Almost invariably set and shot in marginal areas of contemporary Caracas, Chalbaud's films enlist a panoply of popular types, invoke recognizably idiosyncratic modes of speech and ritualized belief systems, and employ an affectionate and humorous yet also ironic and mildly allegorical *costumbrismo*. Despite his characteristic social concern, Chalbaud neither embraced nor was embraced by the New Latin American Cinema movement, perhaps in large part because, unlike that cadre, his commitment to the expressive potential and popular appeal of melodrama has never wavered.

Exile, diaspora, international co-productions, and migrations of creative talent

Simple models of 'national' cinema in Latin America are complicated by transatlantic and trans-hemispheric migrations of talent, international co-productions, exile, and diasporic film production (including the rise of 'Latino' cinemas in North America). In most Latin American nations, the first practitioners of the new mode of expression were not nationals but foreigners. Incipient film production in Brazil, Argentina, Mexico, Colombia, and elsewhere enlisted numerous Europeans, primarily Italian, French, and Spanish. In the late 1940s and early 1950s Vera Cruz, São Paulo's infamous attempt to establish a Brazilian MGM, imported its technical talent from Italy and the United States in the late 1940s and early 1950s. The prevalence of co-production strategies in the 1980s and 1990s calls the very concept of national cinema into question. The aspiration to an autonomous national filmmaking tradition is complicated, therefore, not only by the founding presence of Europeans and North Americans, but also by the often sustained nature of this 'foreign' contribution. As Ann Marie Stock (1996) suggests, the concepts of 'migrancy' and border crossings counter the perceived fixedness of critical emphases on national and regional paradigms as well as the associated, and anachronistic, constructs of authenticity and inauthenticity.

> **Simple models of 'national' cinema in Latin America are complicated by transatlantic and trans-hemispheric migrations of talent, international co-productions, exile, and diasporic film production (including the rise of 'Latino' cinemas in North America).**

The results of Irene Castillo de Rodríguez's (1995) research into the Spanish contribution to the visual media in Colombia may not be atypical. Colombia's first feature film, *María* (1920), and its first talking feature, *Flores del Valle* ('Flowers of the Valley', 1940) were both directed by the Spaniard Máximo Calvo. Colombia's first film society was founded in Bogotá in 1949 by the Catalonian Luis Vicens. The country's first socially committed film movement was initiated by José María Arzuaga, a Spaniard who is credited with drawing attention to the incipient problematics of urbanization in *Raíces de piedra* ('Roots of Stone', 1961) and *Pasado meridiano* ('Post-Meridian', 1963). Sergio Cabrera, the most prominent director of the present generation (*Técnicas de duelo*, 'Details of a Duel', 1988; *La estra-*

tegia del caracol, 'The Snail's Strategem', 1993), is a first-generation Colombian of Spanish parentage.

Examples of migrations of talent *within* Ibero-America are rife if infrequently cited, and go back to the 1930s (e.g. Cuban director and producer Ramón Peón's contribution to Mexican cinema in the 1930s or Argentinian director Carlos Hugo Christensen's involvement in both Brazilian and Venezuelan filmmaking from the 1950s onwards). Dolores Del Rio and Carmen Miranda, on the other hand, are the foremost examples of Latin American actresses successfully transplanted from their respective national contexts to Hollywood, where they were (re)cast as ubiquitous pan-ethnic signifiers. Dolores Del Rio had the unique distinction of two consecutive careers. After twenty years in Hollywood she returned to Mexico, on the verge of 40, to undertake a second star trajectory as an emblem of 'authentic' Mexico during the most gilded years of Mexican cinema's 'golden age', beginning in 1943 with *Flor silvestre* and *María Candelaria*.

Co-productions are often perceived as a recent phenomenon, when in fact interhemispheric co-productions were key to maintaining the international reach of the 'old' Mexican cinema during the late 1940s and 1950s. Countless New Latin American Cinema projects depended on more or less formalized international co-production arrangements, from series sponsored by Radio-televisione italiana (RAI) in the 1970s and Televisión española (TVE) in the 1980s to personal interventions like French film-essayist Chris Marker's on behalf of Patricio Guzmán's *Grupo tercer año*. Marker provided film stock for what turned out to be the three-part documentary epic *La batalla de Chile* ('The Battle of Chile', 1975–9), which nevertheless would not have seen the light of day without extensive post-production support from the Cuban national film institute, Instituo cubano del arte y industria cinematográficos (ICAIC). Before the collapse of the Soviet Union and related internal economic pressures curtailed ICAIC's activities, a significant percentage of New Latin American Cinema output was the beneficiary of co-production with Cuba, acknowledged or unacknowledged.

The assumption that co-productions inevitably undermine and even erase national differences has been persuasively challenged by Laura Podalsky's (1994) study of pre-revolutionary Cuban filmmaking from the 1930s to the 1950s. Contrasting national productions with Cuban–Mexican and Cuban–Spanish collaborations, she demonstrates how cross-national co-productions function to mark national differences

The 'formally audacious' epic documentary *Hour of the Furnaces* (1968), a film counterpart to Solanas and Getino's manifesto *Towards a Third Cinema*

rather than occlude them. Podalsky also illustrates how intraregional, cross-national influences can be as explanatory as neo-colonial impositions.

Latin American filmmakers who have developed portions of their careers in involuntary exile include Argentines Fernando Solanas, Gerardo Vallejo, and (Spanish-born) Octavio Getino, collaborators on the epic documentary trilogy *La hora de los hornos* ('The Hour of the Furnaces', 1968) and the theorization of 'third cinema'. After the restitution of democratic rule, all subsequently returned to Argentina, where they remain active on the national film scene. Other leading Argentines whose careers were interrupted by political exile include Fernando Birri, Lautaro Murúa, Leonardo Favio, and countless other leading artists and performers.

Brazil's *enfant terrible* of the Cinema Novo, director and polemicist Glauber Rocha, sought to establish a base in numerous Latin American and European countries in the late 1960s, when the military government's repressive measures were at their height. After filming *Der leone have sept cabezas* ('The Lion has Seven Heads') and *Cabezas cortadas* ('Severed Heads', both 1970) in North Africa and Spain, the *apertura* (opening-up) of the military regime enabled him to return to Brazil and make several additional films including his last, *A idade da terra* ('The Age of Earth', 1980). The Bolivian director Jorge Sanjinés was doing post-production in Italy when a 1971 military coup made his return to his native country imprudent. He dedicated the next several years to tracing an itinerary through the Andes, making collaborative features with the Quechua and Aymara populations of Peru, Ecuador, and Colombia until conditions permitted his return to Bolivia in 1979.

The Chilean case is the most notable example of how a national cinema transcends its own borders in response to historical–political conjunctures, becoming diasporic. The foundations of Chilean film culture prior to Salvador Allende's socialist coalition regime (1970–3) were disjunctive: an ill-fated attempt at government-sponsored commercial production in Santiago under Chile Films (1938–49); a later decade of oppositional activity catalysed by Dutch documentarist Joris Ivens's 1962 visit to Valparaiso and climaxing with the 1973 *coup d'état*. Massive exodus over the subsequent decade resulted in 176 Chilean exile productions made in France, Italy, Spain, Holland, Belgium, Great Britain, Germany, Switzerland, the Soviet Union, Sweden, Finland, Romania, Canada, Cuba, Nicaragua, Mexico, Venezuela, Colombia, and the United States. If exile disperses, *desexilio* (the process of returning home and reintegrating into a national culture that has not remained frozen in time) coalesces. As Zuzana Pick has argued, both processes 'expand conceptual and aesthetic boundaries' and 'contribute to a decentering of views on identity, nationality and difference' (1993: 158).

The inverse instance, one of influx rather than scattering, is demonstrated by Mexico in the 1930s, Cuba in the early 1960s, and Nicaragua in the early 1980s. Newly inaugurated revolutionary regimes in each of these countries placed film among their foremost cultural priorities and struggled to recruit and/or accommodate an influx of international talent and assistance. Though he was never permitted to edit his footage, Sergei Eisenstein's US-financed effort to film *Que viva Mexico!* (1932), an epic of Mexican culture across regions and centuries, was pivotal to both the director's career trajectory and the country's subsequent film aesthetics. A year earlier Fred Zinneman and Paul Strand from the United States had collaborated with Mexican peers on *Redes* ('The Wave', 1931), a documentary-style feature denouncing exploitation in a Vera Cruz fishing community. The following decade, novelist John Steinbeck and director John Ford both engaged in major collaborations with the Mexican director Emilio Fernández. In the Cuban case, Italian Neo-Realist screenwriter Cesare Zavattini and cinematographer Otello Martelli, Mexican producer Manuel Barbachano Ponce, Dutch documentarist Joris Ivens, Soviet director Mikhail Kalatozov and his virtuoso cinematographer Sergei Urusevsky, French New Wave director Agnès Varda and cinéma vérité documentarist Chris Marker, as well as emerging filmmakers Ugo Ulive from Uruguay and Alejandro Saderman from Argentina, all participated in a kind of 'solidarity co-production' with uneven success. Nicaragua's INCINE (the national film insititute during the Sandinista government) has facilitated international co-productions and numerous independent productions by Cubans, Mexicans, Puerto Ricans, Bolivians, Chileans, North Americans, and others.

Finally, both long-standing territorial appropriations and ongoing population displacements have contributed to the production of independent Chicano and Latino cinemas across the United States (e.g. the films of Luis Valdez and Gregorio Nava) and, to a lesser extent, Canada. Zuzana Pick's characterization of the New Latin American Cinema movement as a 'continental project' might also be applied to such cinemas in a resignifying move calculated to underline the successful pan-ethnic, transnational breeching of borders characteristic of this body of audiovisual expression which, as product of and response to the increasing arbitrariness and ineffectiveness of geopolitical bor-

ders, is also, though not unproblematically, 'unified in its diversity'. The concept of transculturation is also helpful in this regard.

The notion of transculturation

The concept of transculturation, first articulated in 1940 by Cuban anthropologist and ethnographer Fernando Ortiz in his study *Contrapunteo cubano del tabaco y azúcar* (1940) and subsequently adapted by Uruguayan literary critic Angel Rama in his 1982 work *Transculturación narrativa en América Latina*, can be usefully applied to the long-standing debate about national cultural autonomy and the denial, dismissal, or disparagement of 'foreign' components. Ortiz proposed the term 'transculturation' as an alternative to the term 'acculturation'. He emphasized that the process of transition from one culture to another entails complex and almost inevitably reciprocal 'transmutations of culture' (1947/1995: 98) in a triple process of new cultural acquisition (acculturation), the uprooting of previous cultural characteristics (deculturation), and the creation of new cultural phenomena (neoculturation) (102–3). Ortiz's 'modest proposal' for a modification in terminology, itself an example of transculturation, is an early and still-generative instance of local theory originating in the periphery.

Rama, writing four decades later, argued that the concept of transculturation 'visibly translated a Latin American perspectivism' (1982: 33) in its explicit recognition, on the one hand, that Cuban culture in particular and Latin American culture in general are the products of permanent, ongoing transcultural dynamics and in its implicit recognition, on the other, of the dynamism and creative agency involved in achieving characteristically original re-elaborations of 'cultural norms, behaviors, beliefs and objects' (34). Rama identified a dual dynamic of transculturation around the potentially overlapping impact of an *external* and an *internal* metropolis. The 'mother country' under a colonial regime and the dominant country in a neo-colonial situation are both external metropolises which relegate the nation as a whole to peripheral status. Within each Latin American nation, however, Rama recognized how the capital often exerts an analogous impact as overly dominant centre *vis-à-vis* the doubly peripheralized 'provinces' (34).

Applying this notion of Latin American cultural production as 'transculturative' to the evolution of cinema in Latin America offers a way of breaking out of national versus foreign, autonomous versus imposed, authentic versus inauthentic dichotomies and their impossible either/or mandate. It suggests how visitor and visited are mutually transformed by their encounter and how exile both reinforces and reinflects national identity. This view of cultural, and film, expression as the transformed and transforming product of ongoing—and to some extent selective and self-renovating—processes of transculturation also appropriately relativizes the perceived novelty of the nowadays much-touted globalization process, which, despite the current intensification of its pace and impact, must be seen as historically rooted in processes that pre-date even the European conquest of the New World.

> **Applying this notion of Latin American cultural production as 'transculturative' to the evolution of cinema in Latin America offers a way of breaking out of national versus foreign, autonomous versus imposed, authentic versus inauthentic dichotomies and their impossible either/or mandate.**

Film historiography and production: industries and artisans

Historiographical debates and dilemmas have been central to the formation of the discourses—political ideological, critical, theoretical, methodological—that circulate in and around the cinematic traditions and practices of the Ibero-American region. These dilemmas have been exacerbated by the fact of dependency in that these histories are always written against other, dominant histories and inflected by political partisanship and ideological inclinations.

Four phases of Ibero-American film history may be identified: the silent period, the consolidation of national cinemas after the introduction of sound, the development of counter-cinemas—most strongly manifest in the 1960s and 1970s but continuing into the 1980s and beyond—and the uneven realignment of commercial and committed cinemas in the face of television and video that characterizes the 1980s and

1990s. Within these later periods two 'moments' stand out. The years 1968–9 saw the release of an inordinate number of landmark political films, all of which challenged both their socio-political context and the film medium itself in radical ways: *Yawar Mallku*, *Terra em transe* ('Land in Anguish', Brazil, Glauber Rocha), *El Chacal de Nahueltoro* ('The Jackal of Nahueltoro', Chile, Miguel Littín), *Memorias del subdesarrollo* ('Memories of Underdevelopment', Cuba, Tomás Gutiérrez Alea), *Lucía* (Cuba, Humberto Solás), and *La hora de los hornos*. A decade and a half later, the years 1984–5 can also be retrospectively seen as a watershed in terms of works that broke new thematic ground and signalled new formal directions. These included three from Argentina: María Luisa Bemberg's *Camila*, Fernando Solanas's *Tangos: el exilio de Gardel* ('Tangos: The Exile of Gardel'), and Luis Puenzós *La historia oficial* ('The Official Version'); three from Brazil: Nelson Pereira dos Santos's *Memorias do carcere* ('Prison Memoirs'), Tizuka Yamasaki's *Patriamada* ('Beloved Country'), Eduardo Coutinho's *Cabra marcado pra morer: vinte anos depois* ('Man Marked to Die: Twenty Years Later'); as well as Jorge Alí Triana's *Tiempo de morir* ('Time to Die', Colombia), Paul Leduc's *Frida: naturaleza viva* (Mexico), and Fina Torres's *Oriana* (Venezuela).

Like other historical subdivisions, these are, of course, heuristic conveniences and remain subject to modification. Of the four, the two intermediate periods—commercially focused cinemas of national consolidation, and subnational–supranational oppositional movements—have been the object of more sustained and systematic historical and critical inquiry than either the silent era or the contemporary 'postnational' moment (Newman 1993).

Each (post-)national tradition also elicits individualized periodization as well. In 1982 Randal Johnson and Robert Stam divided Brazilian Cinema Nôvo into a preparatory phase (1954–60); an initial phase lasting until the military coup (1960–4); a third phase (1964–8), when the 'coup-within-the-coup' severely restricted expressive freedom; and a final tropicalist–allegorical phase (1968–72), after which, they argued, Cinema Nôvo as a movement fragmented into the multiple practices of Brazilian cinema. Paulo Antonio Paranaguá (1993) divided Mexican film history into seven periods. Ana Lopez (1996) identified three generations of exiled Cuban filmmakers. As heuristic conveniences, these and all other historical subdivisions remain subject to future modification.

Throughout these histories, Latin American cinema practices have oscillated between industrial aspirations and artisanal necessities. A significant number of recently rediscovered female film pioneers from the 1920s to the 1940s—Brazil's Carmen Santos and Gilda de Abreu, Mexico's Mimi Derba, Adela Sequeyro, and Matilde Landeta—were involved in attempts to found production companies. Like those of most their male counterparts, their efforts turned out to be ephemeral, their mode of production more artisanal than industrial. Even a country as tiny as Uruguay aspired (futilely) to a national film industry as early as the late 1930s. Chile, which saw its high point of film production in 1925 with fifteen features, made a concerted attempt in the 1940s under Chile Films to produce films for a domestic and export audience, importing talent from elsewhere in the hemisphere. Venezuela's Bolívar Films, founded in 1940, employed a similar trans-hemispheric strategy in the production of eight features between 1949 and the mid-1950s. In the 1960s the appropriateness of the industrial model began to be questioned at the same time that critics began to emphasize the personal stamp of individualized directional expression over formulaic genre pictures with a characteristic studio stamp.

Mexico's major studies were founded over three decades: Chapultepec (later Nacional productora) in 1922, Clasa in 1935, Azteca in 1937, Churubusco in 1944, Tepeyac in 1946, San Angel Inn in 1949. If the fifty features produced in 1938 marked the attainment of industrial stature, the drop to twenty-nine two years later signalled the precariousness of an enterprise that would persistently oscillate between boom and crisis. Major Mexican studios began to be broken up in the 1980s with sell-outs to foreign production companies and reconversion to other uses.

Neither Brazil nor Argentina, Mexico's only potential competitors in the hemisphere, saw sustained studio-based production on the Mexican scale, though at its short-lived high point in 1942, when fifty-six features were produced, Argentina employed 4,000 technicians in thirty studios. Filmmaking, along with other forms of cultural expression, was later chronically curtailed by censorship; despite the notable resurgence of national film production with the return to democratic government in 1983, the massive closing of theatres and decline in audiences has meant that even the most long-lived of the Argentine studios, Argentina Sono Films and Aries, have now disappeared or been reoriented towards distribution or the production of *telenovelas* (televised soap operas).

In Brazil, Rio de Janeiro's Atlântida studios saw their heyday in the 1940s and 1950s with the production of hundreds of carnival-linked *chanchadas*, an autochthonous parodic genre, usually musical, that was as adored by audiences as it was reviled by critics. The last and most spectacular attempt at industrialization on the Hollywood model took place in Brazil in the late 1940s. On the strength of his association with the French avant-garde and British documentary movements, Brazilian-born Alberto Cavalcanti was invited to take the helm of the state-of-the-art Vera Cruz film studio, an ambitious post-Second World War 'import subsitution' venture by São Paulo's powerful Matarazzo investment group. The financial failure of this controversial initiative, which produced eighteen features between 1949 and 1954, generated much rancour and recrimination. According to Maria Rita Galvão, a specialist in the history of São Paulo-based film production, 'Vera Cruz was historically the most complete realization Brazil has known of the film industry myth . . . It implanted a mode of production that, despite its total inappropriateness to the conditions of the national film market, tended to impose itself as a standard to be followed' (Johnson and Stam 1982/1995: 271).

Politicizing *la politique des auteurs*

Reacting against formulaic studio production, a generation formed by the film societies and film study circles that proliferated in many Latin American cities after the Second World War attempted to carve out a space for personalized expression in independent productions. The phenomenon was first registered in Argentina with the generation of the 1960s. Because few of these young Turks succeeded in finding production support for subsequent features in a deteriorating political climate, this generation failed to coalesce into a movement. Its legacy endures in films like Lautaro Murúa's *Alias Gardelito*, David José Kohon's *Tres veces Ana* ('Three Times Ana'), both from 1961, and Rodolfo Kuhn's *Pajarito Gómez* and Leonardo Favio's *Crónica de un niño solo* ('Chronicle of a Boy Alone'), both released in 1965.

Similar conditions existed in Brazil in the late 1950s and early 1960s, but there sporadic and geographically distant attempts to produce another kind of

A 'landmark of political filmmaking'—*Blood of the Condor* (1969), a film that 'touched a national nerve'

cinema did successfully coalesce into the paradigmatic new cinema movement, Cinema Nôvo, characterized by new modes and philosophies of production and a new aesthetics. Various models, selectively appropriated—such as Italian Neo-Realism, the French New Wave, and assorted trends in international documentary—were conjugated into a self-consciously contestatory national imaginary: whether urban or rural, Brazil was best seen from below. The industrial model was now abandoned by choice rather than default.

Invoking the antithesis of the industrial model, Glauber Rocha turned a phrase attributed to Jean-Luc Godard, 'a camera in your hand and an idea in your head,' into a slogan. Endorsing the prevalent trend towards nationalization of the country's natural resources, and echoing the nationalist-developmentalist rhetoric of the period, Rocha (1963) argued that 'Brazilian art forms had to nationalize their modes of expression'. Rocha's invocation of an aesthetics of hunger, and of the violence that hunger engenders (1965b), was translated into signification practices based on scarcity, as anticipated in films like Linduarte Noronha's documentary *Aruanda* (1959) and quintessentially embodied in others like Nelson Pereira dos Santos's feature *Vidas secas* ('Barren Lives', 1963). Yet for all its creative energy, contentious cohesion, and international recognition, Cinema Nôvo, which inspired oppositional film movements throughout Latin America, never succeeded in sustaining the popular response its advocates and practitioners sought because the transformations it cultivated remained incomplete.

Transforming modes of production and consumption

Oppositional Latin American cinema took as its point of departure not only the introduction of new content or the transformation of cinematic forms, but the transformation of the conditions of film production and viewing. Where dominant cinema prioritized exchange value (profit), oppositional filmmakers emphasized use values (social benefits). Where industrializing modes of production turned filmmakers into virtual 'piece-workers' or managers, alternative procedures sought reintegrative participation at all levels of the creative process. Where dominant practices required large amounts of capital and a complex infrastructure with expensive equipment, studio sets, professional actors, polished screenplays, fixed shooting-schedules, and a large crew, oppositional filmmakers opted for simplified, artisanal modes of production using location shooting, non-professional actors or a mix of professionals and non-professionals, improvised scripts, and a less technologically mediated style of filming. These efforts were financed by a variety of means: personal loans, local co-operatives, international co-productions, partial state subsidy, and, in Cuba and Nicaragua, complete state subsidy.

Where the structures and conventions of traditional filmmaking required passive, socially fragmented audiences who did their viewing in the ritualized space of the conventional movie theatre, oppositional filmmakers sought to transform diffusion and reception practices in order to encourage broader audience participation, response, and feedback. Distribution strategies included bringing films to often remote targeted audiences through self-distribution, organized mobile cinema projects, and sustained parallel circuits utilizing community spaces. Reception strategies included organized discussions and debates, the enlistment of indigenous narrators to reprise film content, and stylistic modifications in the films themselves in order to catalyse audience intervention. Cuba's popular prime-time television programme *24 × segune* ('Twenty-Four Frames a Second'), hosted by filmmaker and humorist Enrique Colina, exemplified the commitment to a broadly disseminated, demystificatory film literacy. These transformations in modes of production and consumption reached their apogee in Argentina during the late 1960s and early 1970s with the semi-clandestine production and completely clandestine exhibition of the formally audacious epic documentary *La hora de los hornos* and the Cine de la base group's ambitious clandestine feature *Los traidores* ('The Traitors', Raymundo Gleyzer, 1973).

Practical theories: third and other imperfect cinemas

Through manifestos, founding documents, film festival proclamations, occasional essays, and eventual books, a series of practical theories began to circulate centred on naming oppositional filmmaking practices. First among these was Argentina's Fernando Solanas and Octavio Getino's Third (or guerrilla) Cinema as an alternative to 'First' (industrial) and 'Second' (auteurist) Cinema (1969a). The following year, Cuban Julio García Espinosa called for a rejection of technically perfect cinema modelled on Hollywood in favour of a deliberately imperfect, process-oriented cinema that exposes

and questions genre conventions even as it utilizes them to forge a pleasurable link with audiences. Bolivian Jorge Sanjinés's concept of *une cine junto al pueblo* (a cinema close to the people, 1979), a cinema close to the people, shuns individual close-ups and strives to re-create historical events in long takes with the collaboration of the historical actors, using a dramaturgy compatible with indigenous narrato-logical traditions. Of these, Third Cinema was the concept that enjoyed the widest circulation beyond Latin America, having been promoted, for example, by Zuzana Pick in Canada, Guy Hennebelle in France, Teshome Gabriel in the United States, and Paul Willemen in Great Britain, while within Latin America (the equally imprecise) concept of imperfect cinema generated the most resounding echo.

> The theoretical propositions contained in all these manifestos derive from the concrete practice of attempting to make specific films under specific historical conditions. This is the source of both their strengths and their weaknesses: because these praxis-based theories were eminently conjunctural, bound by history and geography, they proved resistant to transplantation.

Solanas and Getino's 'Towards a Third Cinema' was the most widely circulated of a set of theoretical statements formulated by the pair between 1969 and 1971, though not published until 1973. In 1979, from his Peruvian exile, Octavio Getino published a reappraisal of Third Cinema 'ten years later' (Getino 1982). Stressing the particular national-historical circumstances and concrete cinematic practice that generated the theoretical reflections, as well as the ambivalent social location of its authors as middle-class intellectuals, Getino regretted the group's rhetorical stridency and their animosity towards other militant film groups working in Argentina at the same time, and expressed scepticism regarding the reported diffusion of the Third Cinema concept in Europe, Africa, and North America. The theoretical propositions contained in all these manifestos derive from the concrete practice of attempting to make specific films under specific historical conditions. This is the source of both their strengths and their weaknesses: because these praxis-based theories were eminently conjunctural, bound by history and geography, they proved resistant to transplantation.

With the proliferation of film practices apparent since the 1980s, the advent of new generations less oriented to ideology, the end of filmmaking conceived as collective crusade, and the recogntiion that marginal and mainstream, dominant and oppositional film cultures are inextricably interrelated, the impetus to manifestos has declined. In a kind of counter-manifesto delivered at the 1989 Havana festival, Mexican director Paul Leduc called for a 'cinema of the salamanders' as the only viable successor to the two-principal models of world filmmaking, Hollywood and European (auteur) cinema, both of which have now gone the way of the dinosaurs. This 'salamander cinema' would be characterized by organized collective action on the one hand and the embracing of the new technologies on the other.

Genre, gender, history, documentary, realism, and the rest

Comedy, epic, and melodrama are the three major generic categories of Latin American fictional filmmaking, with the disposition to melodrama powerful enough to subtend the other two. Particular subgenres, often hybridized, began to characterize the major national cinemas of Latin America with the coming of sound and the incorporation of incipiently national musical traditions whose primary outlet for massive diffusion until that time had been radio. These autochthonous subgenres include Argentine tango melodramas, Brazilian *chanchadas* with carnival-inspired plots and celebration of samba, and Mexican cabaret melodramas (*cabareteras*) with their imported Caribbean dance rhythms and signature boleros. The most popular Latin American film of all time—*Allá en el Rancho Grande* ('Over at the Big Ranch', Mexico, Fernando de Fuentes, 1936, remade 1948) inaugurated a national genre, the *comedia ranchera*, a regionally idiosyncratic version of the American western. Epics inspired by history and folk-heroes—the Mexican revolutionary, the Brazilian *cangaçeiro* (backlands rebel), the Argentine gaucho—configured characteristic

national subgenres equally indebted to the Hollywood western.

Another characteristic Latin American subgenre, the street chronicle depicting the lives of indigent children, has its most famous exponent in Luis Bruñuel's *Los olvidados* ('The Young and the Damned', Mexico, 1950). A Venezuelan prototype, *Juan de la calle* ('Juan of the Streets'), directed by Rafael Rivero, appeared nearly a decade earlier, in 1941. Two pioneering Mexican women directors worked in this subgenre in its incipient stages: Adela Sequeyro in *Diablillos del arrabal* ('Little Slum Devils', 1938) and Matilde Landeta in her award-winning screenplay 'Tribunal de menores' ('Juvenile Court'), written in the late 1940s and filmed as *El camino de la vida* under the direction of Alfonso Corona Blake in 1956.

With the rise in the 1960s of alternative filmmaking practices centred around auteurism and more artisanal modes of production, the importance of genre tended to diminish as melodramatic forms were rejected on the grounds of their alleged imperial contamination and escapist (apolitical, ahistorical) orientation. While some new cinema products reworked national generic traditions (Glauber Rocha's *Deus e o diabo na terra do sol*, 'Black God, White Devil', 1963, and *Antonio das Mortes*, 1969, invoked the *cangaçeiro* genre, for example), most directors chose to work 'outside' genre by enlisting history as a documentary presence both stylistically and narratologically.

History and melodrama are two pillars of Latin America cinema that most practitioners and promoters of New Latin American Cinema believed to be at odds with one another and throughout the 1960s and 1970s most of these filmmakers shunned melodrama in order to privilege the historical. Much of the stylistic innovation characteristic of this period was a product of filmmakers' aggressive undermining of conventional dichotomies between documentary and fictional modes of representation, favouring the former in order to insert history into the imaginary construct that is cinema.

This is the case, for example, with three of the best-known Cuban films. Tomás Cutiérrez Alea's *Memorias del subdesarrollo* is a fictional collage composed of fragments in every conceivable documentary register. Sara Gómez's *De cierta manera* ('One Way or Another', 1974, 1979) disrupts its cross-class, interracial love story with pseudo-sociological discourses and reconstructed biographies of social actors. Humberto Solás's *Lucía* puts the experience of women from three key periods at the centre of the epic of Cuban history, using stylistic and subgeneric markers to 'document' the dominant modes of perception characteristic of each era.

Deliberately counter- and anti-epic modes of (re)writing history in cinema are exemplified by Jorge Sanjinés's *El coraje del pueblo* ('The Courage of the People', 1971), Leon Hirszman's *São Bernardo* (Brazil, 1972), Paul Leduc's *Frida: Naturaleza viva* (Mexico, 1984), María Luisa Bemberg's *Miss Mary* (Argentina, 1986) and *Yo, la peor de todas* ('I, the Worst Woman of All', 1990). Significantly, feminine experience lies at the narrative core of each of these films and seems inseparable from the stylistic choices that contribute to their appeal. A gendered reckoning with history, and a reconceptualization of history capable of reckoning with gender, reinvigorated cinematic expression in Latin America from the 1970s not only in the films directed by women that began to appear for the first time in significant numbers, but also in the approaches of their male counterparts. (Cuban director Humberto Solás and Brazilian director Leon Hirszman were among the pioneers of gender-sensitive representation with *Lucía* and *São Bernardo*).

During the 1980s the break-up of the Soviet Union and proliferation of neo-liberal economic policies coincided in Latin America with political redemocratization processes and the disintegration of the utopian vision of revolutionary socialism. A return to the melodramatic mode on the part of Latin American filmmakers (many of them women) coincided with a critical-theoretical reassessment of melodrama, particularly among Euro-American scholars. In films like *Camila* (María Luisa Bemberg, 1984) and *The Official Story* (Luis Puenzó, 1985), both products of post-dictatorship Argentina, melodrama and history are no longer at odds. Political (in)justice is the secular substitute for the absent sacred which, in Peter Brooks's (1991) theorization, is the generative impetus of melodrama. The Brazilian film *Patriamada* (Tizuka Yamasaki, 1984) also recuperates melodrama in order to exceed and subjectivize the documentary-based representations that were the dominant markers of Brazil's analogous moment of political transition.

A suspicion of illusionism characterized the era of heroic militancy. Alfredo Guevara, head of Cuba's ICAIC, described the goal of the Cuban film project as 'demystification of cinema for the entire population', the deliberate dismantling of 'all the mechanisms of cinematic hypnosis' (in Rosen 1972: 53). The empha-sis on asserting the presence of history through the multiple modalities of documentary has been one of the many ways that realist discourses have dominated the Latin American feature film scene. Documentary realism, social realism, critical realism are multiple ways of naming this insistence on reality as made up of external, observable phenomena. The diversifying of the filmmaking ranks that began in the 1970s with the incorporation of female talent on a significant scale and the widespread questioning of political ideologies during the following decade have led to a heightened valuation of subjectivity, fantasy, and emotion, to what B. Ruby Rich has described as a shift from exteriority to interiority (1993: 12).

Magical realism, so prone to hackneyed appropriation, is hardly a credible counterweight to the predominant realist bias. The narrative and stylistic exuberance and rich allegorical layering of Brazilian Tropicalismo, a form of allegorized expressionism generated during the darkest period of the dictatorship in films like Glauber Rocha's *Terra en transe* and Joaquim Pedro de Andrade's *Macunaíma* (1969), is a more viable example of an efficacious counter-modality, as is the oneric subversiveness of Ana Carolina Teixeira Soares's *Das tripas coração* ('Bending over Backwards', 1980). In *Julio comienza en julio* ('Julio Begins in July', Chile, 1978), the first and only feature film released under the seventeen-year Pinochet dictatorship, offers another deconstructive variation. Simultaneously enlisting and undermining realism, director Silvio Caiozzi created cognitive dissonance by combining sepia photography, enlisting and exceeding realism in stylistic terms, and an early twentieth-century mise-en-scène with a hypermodern shooting and editing style.

It must be stressed that documentarists also questioned received wisdom regarding mechanisms of perception, cognition, and socio-political transformation early and often, beginning with the parodic statistics of the opening voice-over of Fernando Birri's foundational social documentary *Tire dié* ('Toss me a Dime', 1958, 1960). In *Hombres de Mal Tiempo* ('Men of Mal Tiempo', Cuba, 1968) Argentine Alejandro Saderman used solarization, negative reversal, slow motion, and other experimental techniques to externalize the subjective 'fiesta of memory' evoked by the reunion of five centenarian veterans of Cuba's war for independence. Numerous documentaries of the Chilean diaspora also use highly subjectivized modes, such as *Por debajo de la mesa* ('Under the Table', Luis Osvaldo García and

Tony Venturi, Canada, 1983), which uses the visual metaphor of a hearing-aid to evoke one illegal immigrant's sense of non-personhood through assumed deafness.

Old and new media in the era of globalization

Examining audiovisual production in terms of the parameters and practices of critical discourse since the transition from dictatorship to democracy in Chile, Gastón Lillo has identified a series of *nudos tensionales* (tensional knots) characteristic of the discourse of the contemporary period: concepts of history, the subject, and identity (national, social, sexual), notions of the people, the national, and the popular (and the national-popular), and the opposition between tradition and modernity (Lillo 1995: 32). As this century dominated by cinema draws to a close, questions regarding the fate of national cinemas in a post-national era and the film medium's prospects for survival in an electronic, globalizing age comes to the fore.

Since its inception, and particularly since the Second World War, the film medium in Latin America has been central to the definition of national and pan-regional identity, to its redefinition in times of crisis, and to the enlistment of generalized support for the national (or transnational) project. As the key components of a mass visual culture, film and television structured the imaginary of modernizing developmentalism and socialized citizens of traditional societies by showing them how to act 'modern' as they migrated to the swelling cities. The mass media (radio, film, and television) were agents and promoters of technological innovation: by socializing consumers into consuming what was expected of them, they helped unify patterns of consumption and behaviour. Today national projects, if they exist at all, must compete with the post-national and transnational realities to which the electronic media, thanks to neo-liberal economics and other globalizing forces, are currently socializing their citizenry.

As film production and consumption have declined by as much as 90 per cent in the principal countries (due to rising production costs, lack of infrastructural reinvestment, massive theatre closings, and changing patterns of cultural consumption), cultural access in the private domestic sphere (via television, video, cable, laser, satellite) has increased proportionately. Collective use of public space and basic forms of sociability and civility have declined as a result, while national identities are being reconfigured transnationally because—despite the increasingly global reach of regional television networks like Brazil's TV Globo and Mexico's Televisa—the forms of culture being consumed derive increasingly from a single extra-national source, the United States. US products dominate Latin American home video and cable markets, where space for national and hemispheric products has been minuscule or non-existent.

Geo-economic realignments since the late 1980s have transformed modes of cinematic consumption to a degree unimaginable only a decade earlier. Ever more costly to produce, a film now has to recover its investment in several media markets, since the theatrical return is no longer sufficient. This is more difficult to achieve in dependent countries given market saturation by US products and limited access to the new technologies.

Reversing the 1970s trend to increased state participation in audiovisual cultural production, the current trend to privatization and transnationalization of film, television, video, and other techno-cultures aggravates communicational dependency. The vacuum created by the dearth of national policies regarding cultural production and new technologies risks allowing the default privatization and mercantilization of everything from scientific research and artistic innovation to the symbolic construction of national history. The increasing de-territorialization of the audiovisual media is minimally counterbalanced by reterritorialization: regional radio and television stations, musical micro-markets, grass-roots video movements, specialized cable broadcasters, the perhaps quixotic efforts of two prominent *cinematecas* at opposite ends of the hemisphere (Caracas and Montevideo) to operate a major commercial theatre dedicated exclusively to screening films from Latin America.

> **Today national projects, if they exist at all, must compete with the post-national and transnational realities to which the electronic media, thanks to neo-liberal economics and other globalizing forces, are currently socializing their citizenry.**

In countries throughout Latin America, filmmakers have united for decades to lobby for national film legislation, meaning that in numerous Latin American countries this is the only cultural sphere with a precedent in policy formation. The European Union's practice of consolidating film, television, and video under the unifying designation 'audiovisual space' correlates with both the increasing technological and aesthetic integration of the three media and their practical integration in the public's habits of consumption. Film's fate is globally tied to television, video, and satellite, and in order to survive and prosper, filmmakers must cast in their lot with their counterparts working in television, video, computer imaging, and other new technologies, guiding the evolution of state policy in the realm of culture and communications and encouraging co-production with television.

What are the implications of the hybridizations that transnationality and globalization produce? How will ethnic, regional, national, and hemispheric identities reconstitute themselves in response to contemporary processes of transcultural hybridization, and what will be the role of the film medium in that process? In '¿Habrá cine latinoamericano en el año 2000?' ('Will there be Latin American Cinema in the Year 2000?') Néstor García Canclini proposes a concept of identity that is 'not simply sociospatial but sociocommunicational' in its simultaneous articulation of local, national, and post-national referents. He sees multi-media and multicontextuality as the two key notions for redefining the social role of film and other communications systems: film will only survive as part of a complex of visual media; constructs of identity will and must evolve as part of an ongoing 'co-production' process (1993: 33).

As the century draws to a close and the silver screen is everywhere upstaged by the computer screen, there is a marked over-production of filmmakers in Latin America. Where no film schools existed until the late 1950s, over thirty have been founded during the past three decades. On the other hand, Latin America boasts 300 million potential image consumers. The voracious expansion of televisual markets and broadcast slots promises to keep the cinema of the past in circulation as well as offering contemporary production a potential outlet that has barely begun to be tapped.

Peruvian novelist and erstwhile politician Mario Vargas Llosa once declared bitterly that the real revolution in Latin America would be the end of revolution. Movies and revolutions have been characteristic if not essential spectacles in the hemisphere since the turn of the century. If the Mexican Revolution, the first such popular uprising, inaugurated the century with a prolonged conflict that produced a vast cinevisual archive, the outbreak of the Zapatista rebellion as the century draws to its close poses both a fitting symmetry and a radical difference. The Cuban Revolution in the 1960s, the Chilean struggle for electoral socialism in the 1970s, the reinauguration of democracy in Brazil and Argentina in the 1980s all privileged cinema, as did the Central American revolutionary movements of the past two decades. As recently as the 1980s Salvador's Sistema Radio Venceremos Film and Television Collective prioritized radio, film, and video as the key communications media. In their cinematic production, they utilized an eclectic synthesis of media (16mm, Super-8, video, black and white interspersed with colour), creating a characteristic 'look' that was both the result of accommodation to practical limitations and an original expressive synthesis. In marked contrast, a decade later the Zapatistas of remote Chiapas went directly to the Internet. Immediacy, portability, minimal cost, and massive global dissemination made this option irresistible. 'Reverting' to the primacy of the written word, and opting to let others gather and disseminate moving images of their movement in whatever formats they choose, the Zapatistas look simultaneously backward and forward in time from their uniquely pre-/postmodern vantage-point.

As the next century unfolds, creators of Latin American audiovisual media could do worse than follow the example of the media-savvy Zapatistas in their selective recombination of traditional and hypermodern elements. The world-wide trend towards ever greater concentration of media technologies and information systems and their subordination to exclusively market forces coexists with its antithesis: the increasing democratization inherent in those same new technologies, along with their actual and potential adaptability to heterogeneous non-commercial uses.

BIBLIOGRAPHY

*Barnard, Timothy, and Peter Rist (eds.) (1996), *South American Cinema: A Critical Filmography 1915–1994* (New York: Garland).

Birri, Fernando, interviewed by Julianne Burton, 'The Roots of Documentary Realism', in Burton (1986).

Brooks, Peter (1991), 'The Melodramatic Imagination', in Marcia Landy (ed.), *Imitations of Life: A Reader in Film* and Television Melodrama (Detroit: Wayne State University Press).

*Burton, Julianne (1986), Cinema and Social Change in Latin America: Conversations with Filmmakers (Austin: University of Texas Press).

—— (1990), The Social Documentary in Latin America (Pittsburgh: University of Pennsylvania Press).

Castañada, Jorge (1993), Utopia Unarmed: The Latin American Left after the Cold War (New York: Knopf).

Castillo de Rodríguez, Irene (1995), 'Cien años de presencia de Espaã en el cine colombiano', Españo en Colombia. Revista de la Embajada de España, 3 (May), 52–3.

Chanan, Michael (1985), The Cuban Image (London: British Film Institute).

Colina, Enrique, and Daniel Díaz (1971), 'Ideología del melodrama en el viejo cine latinoamericano', Cine cubano, 73–5: 14–26.

de los Reyes, Aurelio (1983), Cine y sociedad en México 1896–1930, i: Vivir de sueños 1896–1920 (Mexico City: Universidad nacional autónoma).

Galvão, Maria Rita (1995), 'Vera Cruz: A Brazilian Hollywood', in Johnson and Stam (1982/1995).

García Canclini, Néstor (1993/1997), '¿Habrá cine latinoamericano en el año 2000?', Jornada Semanal, 193 (17 Feb.), 27–33; trans. as 'Will there be a Latin American Cinema in the Year 2000?', in Ann Marie Stock (ed.), Framing Latin American Cinema: Contemporary Critical Directions (Minneapolis: University of Minnesota Press).

García Espinosa, Julio (1970/1983), 'Por un cine imperfecto', trans. as 'Towards an Imperfect Cinema'; Julianne Burton in Michael Chanan (ed.), Twenty-Five Years of the New Latin American Cinema (London: British Film Institute and Channel 4).

—— (1985), 'Meditations on Imperfect Cinema . . . Fifteen Years Later', Screen, 26/3–4: 93–5.

—— (1995), 'Por un cine imperfecto: Veinte años después', in La doble moral del cine (Bogotá: Editorial Voluntad).

Getino, Octavio (1982), A diez anos del 'Hacia un tercer cine' (Mexico: Filmoteca UNAM).

Johnson, Randal (1991), 'The Rise and Fall of Brazilian Cinema 1960–1990', Iris, 13 (Summer), Special Issue: Latin American Cinema, ed. Kathleen Newman, 97–124; repr. Johnson and Stam (1982/1995).

*—— and Robert Stam (eds.) (1982/1995), Brazilian Cinema (New Brunswick, NJ: Associated University Presses; expanded edn. New York: Columbia University Press).

*King, John (1990), Magical Reels: A History of Cinema in Latin America (London: Verso).

Leduc, Paul (1989), 'Dinosaurs and Lizards', in Pat Aufderheide (ed.), Latin American Visions (Philadelphia: International House).

Lillo, Gastón (1995), 'El cine y el contexto político-cultural en el Chile de la posdictadura', Revista canadiense de estudios hispánicos, 10/1, Special Issue: Mundos contemporáneos en el cine español e hispanoamericano, ed. Robert Young, 31–42.

Lopez, Ana M. (1996), 'Memorias of a Home: Mapping the Revolution (and the Making of Exiles?).' Revista canadiense de estudios hispánicos, 10/1, Special Issue: Mundos contemporáneos en el cine español e hispanoamericano, ed. Robert Young, 5–17.

Newman, Kathleen (1993), 'National Cinema after Globalization: Fernando Solanas's Sur and the Exiled Nation', in John King, Ana Lopez, and Manuel Alvarado (eds), Mediating Two Worlds: Cinematic Encounters in the Americas (London: British Film Institute).

Noriega, Chon, and Ana Lopez (eds.) (1996), The Ethnic Eye: Latino Media Arts (Minneapolis: University of Minnesota Press).

—— and Steven Ricci (eds.) (1994), The Mexican Cinema Project (Los Angeles: UCLA Film and Television Archive).

O'Grady, Gerald (ed.) (1994), Nelson Pereira dos Santos: Cinema Novo's 'Spirit of Light' (New York: Film Society of Lincoln Center and Harvard University).

Ortiz, Fernando (1940/1995), 'On the Social Phenomenon of Transculturation and its Importance in Cuba', in Contrapunteo urbano del tabaco y azúcar, trans. Harriet de Onis as Cuban Counterpoint: Tobacco and Sugar (New York: Random House and Vintago).

Paranaguá, Paulo Antonio (1988), 'News from Havana: A Restructuring of the Cuban Cinema', Framework, 35: 88–103.

*Pick, Zuzana (1993), The New Latin American Cinema: A Continental Project (Austin: University of Texas Press).

Podalsky, Laura (1994), 'Negotiating Differences: National Cinemas and Co-Productions in Prerevolutionary Cuba', Velvet Light Trap, 34 (Fall), 59–70.

Rama, Angel (1982), Transculturación narrativa en América Latina (Mexico City: Siglo XXI).

Ramirez Berg, Charles (1992), Cinema of Solitude: A Critical Study of Mexican Film 1967–1983 (Austin: University of Texas Press).

Rich, B. Ruby (1991), 'An/Other View of the New Latin American Cinema', Iris, 13 (Summer), Special Issue: Latin American Cinema, ed. Kathleen Newman, 5–28.

Rocha, Glauber (1963/1965a), Revisão crítica do cinema brasileiro (Rio de Janeiro: Editora civilização brasileira); trans. into Spanish as Revisión crítica del cine brasileiro (Havana: Ediciones ICAIC).

—— (1965b/1995), 'Estética da fome', trans. Randal Johnson and Burnes Hollyman in Johnson and Stam (1995).

Rosen, Marjorie (1972), 'The Cuban Film Fiasco', Saturday Review, 17 June.

Sanjinés, Jorge (1977/1986), 'Cine revolucinario: La experiencia boliviana', trans. as 'Revolutionary Cinema: The Bolivian Experience', in Burton (1986).

Sanjinés, Jorge (1979), *Teoría y práctica de un cine junto al pueblo* (Mexico City: Siglo XXI).

Shohat, Ella, and Robert Stam (1994), *Unthinking Eurocentrism: Multiculturalism and the Media* (London: Routledge).

Solanas, Fernando, and Octavio Getino (1969*a*/1973*a*), 'Hacia un Tercer Cine', trans. as 'Towards a Third Cinema', in Solanas and Getino, *Cine, cultura y descolonización* (Buenos Aires: Siglo XXI).

—— —— (1969*b*), 'La cultura nacional, el cine y *La hora de los hornos*', *Cine cubano*, 56–7 (Mar.).

—— —— (1973*b*), 'Cine militante: una categoría interna del Tercer Cine', in Solanas and Getino, *Cine, cultura y descolonización* (Buenos Aires: Siglo XXI).

Stam, Robert, João Luiz Viera, and Ismail Xavier (1995), 'The Shape of Brazilian Cinema in the Post-Modern Age', in Johnson and Stam (1982).

Stock, Ann Marie (1996), 'Migrancy and the Latin American Cinemascape: Towards a Post-National Critical Praxis', *Revista canadiense de estudios hispánicos*, 10/1 Special Issue: *Mundos contemporáneos en el cine español e hispanoamericano*, ed. Robert Young, 19–30.

Valjalo, David, and Zuzana M. Pick (eds.) (1984), *Literatura chilena*, 8, Special Issue: *10 años de cine chileno 1973–1983*.

Vega, Alicia (1979), *Re-vision del cine chileno* (Santiago: Editorial Aconcagua).

Redefining cinema: film in a changing age

26

Film and changing technologies

Laura Kipnis

The problem in writing this chapter is that by the time you read it, everything will have changed radically, once again. Electronic and digital technologies are having seismic, unsettling effects on the film industry, and film production practices are being transformed and retransformed on practically a monthly basis. Computers are increasingly affecting every stage of production. Traditional filmic processes are disappearing, replaced by new forms of digital image manipulation. Everyone connected with film is waging a valiant struggle to keep up with rapidly changing technologies, trying to make sense of the present, while simultaneously hazarding calculated guesses about the future. Professional organs like *American Cinematographer*, which always viewed encroaching electronic technologies (such as video) with barely contained suspicion, are now suffused with free-floating anxiety, their articles permeated with loss and pathos about film's potentially diminished stature in the digital age. One can hardly help but notice the emotional and at times overwrought language brought to bear on the topic within the world of film production.

The anxiety is not confined to the industry either. At a film studies conference in Chicago in 1996, academic panellists fretted about 'the death of the camera', and 'the end of film'. Academics involved in teaching new technologies routinely speculate about the 'end of narrative', given the various forms of non-linear temporality and interactivity that new digital technologies have made possible. And how is our curriculum supposed to reflect the end of narrative, when we can't even figure out what production technologies to invest in, given that every time you look up, another one is being phased out? And these changes aren't entirely welcome ones. To the great detriment of independent filmmakers, Super-8 film is now virtually extinct (although still making special guest appearances in fieatures like Oliver Stone's *Natural Born Killers* (1994) to signal 'experimentation'), killed off quickly by the introduction of affordable and easy-to-use VHS camcorders *circa* 1985. (On the subject of technological change and uncertainty, let's not even get into the panoply of video formats that have come and gone over the last two decades, and how many carcasses of dead or dying production technologies litter our equipment rooms.)

Even the future of 16mm seems precarious, with support services—labs, sound services, projector-manufacturing—rapidly crumbling. Once Betacam camcorders hit the scene in 1982, news-gathering changed immediately to video, as did industrial and corporate film, as well as much documentary production aimed for broadcast. Eastman Kodak, the world's largest film manufacturer, has been struggling schizophrenically to keep up with these technological changes, shifting corporate strategies virtually from week to week—first moving into videotape, then shoring up film production and fighting to ensure that film would remain the favoured origination medium in image-based mass entertainment, now jumping feet first into digital imaging. Kodak has laid off at least 17,000 employees in the United States and over 30,000 workers abroad since the mid-1980s, in corporate belt-tightening occasioned by a series of bad forecasts about new technologies and heavy world-wide losses. Kodak's Rochester workforce has been downsized—to use the current euphemism—by 40 per cent in the same period. Rochester, NY, had long been something of a company town treated by Kodak like a favourite nephew; more recently the company has vastly retreated from this century-long civic commitment. These changes in technology don't affect filmmakers alone or happen in a social vacuum: they have had sweeping repercussions everywhere, from international markets to local issues like health care for Kodak's retirees—even down to the specifics of the number of hospital charity beds available for the poor in Rochester.

In short, the language of crisis, loss, and uncertainty is endemic to anything connected to film these days. It may be that these are the linguistics of any period of rapid technological transformation, and that at the birth of radio, or of film itself, or the introduction of film sound, or the invention of television and early computers, similar anxieties reigned. Or it may be that digital technology will transform all things, includ-

ing film, beyond recognition and that what we are hearing now are merely small rumblings compared to the thunder of stampeding elephants coming over the horizon.

At the same time as technological changes in film-related industries are having sweeping material effects in terms of jobs and markets, transformations in image-making procedures brought about by digital technologies are spawning complex theoretical questions about the ontological status of the filmic image itself. Can a photograph be considered *evidence* of anything in the digital age, and if not, what does this mean—aesthetically, socially, or juridically? It has now become routine, via the magic of digital manipulation, to see long-dead cult actors like Humphrey Bogart or Jimmy Cagney 'interacting' with live actors in commercials; or to witness 'character replacement'—for *In the Line of Fire* (1993), footage of George and Barbara Bush disembarking from Air Force One was digitally scanned, and actors playing the First Couple were composited into the image. The truth-status of any given image is anyone's guess. Or if there is no 'original' but only endless perfect digital clones, does this have implications for how value and meaning are assigned or experienced? How photographic technologies work and how they make images available to audiences—questions of reception—open onto an array of impossibly large questions about referentiality and indexicality, onto questions about mimesis and realism. Issues of photographic reproducton, as Walter Benjamin has so famously pointed out, are inseparable from even larger issues of modernity, capital, and their respective ideologies. And *will* the new modes of interactivity make linear narrative obsolete? This is certainly a question with ramifications far beyond film studies, as narrative seems to be one of those basic categories of human conceptualization.

Or, taking the long view, are interactivity, non-linearity, and the 'digital revolution' a bit over-hyped, and are we falling into a romantic and narrow technological determinism if we envision that new technologies alone will alter something so indelible as narrative, or vastly change something so much a facet of contemporary culture as film? And is all of this really so new? After all, the mute button on your television remote control is an interactive technology. Non-linear narrative has been a staple of modernist experimentation for most of this century (or since the invention of the unconscious, if you consider dreams a media form). And are computer-generated images so completely different from the use of models, mattes, optical effects, rear projection, and a host of other ways of inventing and manipulating images that have long been staples of cinematic technology? In other words, did the photographic or filmic image ever have any particular relation to truth or evidence to begin with? And does it really matter whether those dinosaurs are miniatures or computer-generated, optically printed or shot against blue screen or digitally composited? *Should* the mode of production of the image change the kinds of theoretical question we ask about it? So, for example, if a filmic image no longer originates in a 'pro-filmic event', but is generated by a computer, does that necessitate revisions in theories about realism and reception? If a character in a film isn't portrayed by an actor acting, but is the result of manipulating scanned images of numerous faces or bodies, for instance, do new theories about identification need to be devised?

But as technological changes are provoking or reprovoking such epistemological uncertainties, let us remember that these revolutionary new technologies are *social* technologies, meaning that their revolutionary potential is limited to the uses that surrounding social institutions and economic forces allow to be made of them. The captains of industry have a lot invested, in all senses of the word, in hooking us on ideologies of continual technological obsolescence and change: if, as in one proposed scenario for the future, movie theatres stop projecting film and convert to screening high-definition television (HDTV) signals beamed in by satellite, some lucky captain of industry and his stockholders stand to make a megafortune on the deal. Or, will HDTV—the latest much-hyped thing—eventually go the way of 3-D film, into the trash-heap of technological also rans with all those cute little cardboard 3-D glasses? And do consumers really *care* about television images with better resolution, or do they care to the tune of the several thousand dollars they'll have to spend to convert to the new system, *if* it ever gets off the ground, which still seems doubtful? Do you? It is estimated that consumers will be forced to spend $75 billion to upgrade old television sets once the conversion to HDTV is complete.

But before you whip out your credit card, keep in mind that much of the fascination with newness and innovation, our beliefs in progress and the necessity of change, have ideological implications and serve specific interests, namely those of capitalism's ongoing necessity for new markets and fresh innovations to keep itself viable. And despite the hype about interactivity and revolution, the centres of cultural influence and power are not likely to change one bit, and neither is the direction of the flow of cultural products, or the move towards global domination of cultural markets by big capital. Rather, digital reproduction will most likely simply aid the penetration of new markets by multinational media conglomerates, creating new delivery systems for not-very-new and hardly-very-different images and information.

So if film studies has been somewhat slow to come to terms with a changing apparatus, or to theorize the shifts in film language and grammar that technological change seems to have so rapidly brought about, the reasons are understandable. As I have tried to indicate, these are impossibly large questions, and unfortunately this article too cannot even begin to attempt to answer them: predicting the future, or revamping film theory, or performing large-scale social analysis, or even offering detailed comparative historical case-studies in previous technological changes are all beyond my scope. Instead, let us call this chapter both a case-study in technological innovation (and particularly in the anxiety of technological innovation), *and* an experiment in how to write about technological innovation from within the midst of the maelstrom, where things are both nebulous and hopping about drastically from one moment to the next, like Silicon Valley techno-nerds on No-Doz and caffeine highballs.

Film and video

But another reason for the hesitation around technological change is that film studies is, to a large extent, premised on an understanding of film *as* a discrete technology. The same understanding permeates the industry's discourse about itself. I would like to suggest that, historically, film has constructed an identity for itself that was maintained by erecting a somewhat fictive separation between itself and neighbouring electronic technologies, and that changes in technology are making this separation increasingly problematic.

One of the ways that film studies has been able to achieve credibility as an academic discipline in the humanities is precisely to distinguish itself from television, to claim (and produce) a more elevated and more high-minded status for itself, that is to distinguish film as art—or 'Film Art' (the title of a well-known introductory film textbook)—from the noisy lower orders of video and television. Perhaps this imperative even factors into which film theories achieve success as paradigms for the field, and which fade away: the emphasis on film as a discrete technology and on cinematic specificity seems to be maintained within the dominant traditions of contemporary film theory, such as apparatus theory (Rosen 1986).

What will be the fate of dominant film studies paradigms in the face of technological shifts that attenuate the distinctions between the film and electronic technologies? It now makes less sense than ever to speak of 'film' as though it were a discrete technology. But, in fact, if you examine the recent history of film technology, it appears that, despite the conventional academic separation of film and television studies, in *practice* film and video have been quite interdependent and increasingly proximate for at least the last twenty years, that is, ever since the introduction of the Rank-Cintel Flying Spot Scanner in 1972. What the Rank-Cintel did was obviate the difference in frame rates between film (24 frames per second) and video (30 frames per second) in film-to-video transfers. You don't really care how—the important point is that this opened the possibility of reinventing the entire method of film post-production and distribution in North America, because now origination medium wouldn't necessarily determine the finishing medium. In other words, something could be shot on film, and edited and finished on videotape, and released on either film *or* video.

The advent of digital non-linear editing (the Avid is the best-known example) has pretty much finished off film editing: even films that are theatrically released on film are almost universally edited electronically (either on tape, or on a non-linear system) before being reconformed on film. And of course film-to-video transfers opened up the possibility of the home rental market, which has had a major transforming effect on all aspects of film financing, production, and viewership, not to mention transforming film studies and education, given the new access and availability of film. The unfortunate casualty has been the 16mm film print business, pretty much dead and buried.

Other major intersections of the two technologies are video assist on film cameras, in which a video tap on the film camera allows the image (or a black-and-white version of it) to be viewed on a television monitor on the film set, instead of waiting for the film to be processed, printed, and returned from the lab the next day. This, as you can imagine, has had a decisive effect on the directorial process, and on film sets. Francis Ford Coppola now directs from an electronically rigged trailer off the set, where he can view the unfolding scene on television monitors, rather than, as was once the practice, from on the set, and in proximity to the actors.

The ever-greater commingling of film and video seems to provoke a certain state of alarm, and indeed acrimony, on the part of the film profession, or so you would infer from the language used to describe the experience. 'Video technology is encroaching on traditional film production techniques from several directions . . . advances in video assist and addressing the dreams—and nightmares—of many directors of photography' (Brandt 1991: 93). Or 'A lot of film shooters and editors come to video with a queasy feeling, a sense that they're about to surrender control of their work.' Film folk get the 'flutters' when they approach video, according to this author, who begs his reader not to conclude that he has been seduced by the 'mindless and endless proliferation of video technology' (Roland 1992: 53–4). So while there is no argument that computer-based random access editing—which is to video editing what word-processing is to typing on a typewriter—is incredibly convenient *and* allows editors increased flexibility and creativity, it is still an experience fraught with risk. According to *American Cinematographer*, 'It's only natural for an experienced professional to feel some trepidation towards new technology, especially in a historically hands-on task like film editing. One [film] editor who recently tried our system for the first time was very, very nervous,' recalls the vice-president of a company manufacturing digital editing systems; 'He actually got a piece of film and attached it to his desk, so he'd still be able to touch film' (Pizzelo 1994: 22). Or, 'Rostock, like most film editors, initially resisted the idea of editing film on tape . . . She still has fond memories of film cutting, however. "There's this whole cosmic thing about wanting to touch the film, which I still miss, and you can't mark tape with a grease pencil"' (Comer 1992: 26–7). Anecdotes of this sort are quite typical of the curiously *emotional* tone of much of the writing about new technologies from within the film profession—as is the somewhat talismanic and weirdly occult status accorded to film in these accounts. And I can personally testify that one quite often *does* hear filmmakers, when discussing the inferiority of video editing to film editing, invoking this loss of 'touching film' as if editing film were a conduit to something deeply personal, even religious, to which punching buttons on a video edit controller can't compete. (For those unfamiliar with the video-editing process, touching tape is *verboten* and you don't physically splice the tape; rather, an electromagnetic signal is transferred from one piece of tape to another, or, in the case of digital editing, onto computer hard drives before being laid off to tape.)

The film-to-tape transfer—also known as the telecine process—and the site of greatest full-body contact between film and electronic technology, becomes, perhaps predictably, a scene of particular fretting and distinction-making. One reason, of course, is that film and video still do have different aspect ratios, one of the problems HDTV is meant to solve. Film has a wider frame than video, and when transferred to video, only the centre of the film frame makes it to your living-room. To compensate, especially on the widest screen film formats, video engineers often add camera movements the director never intended (this is known as 'pan and scan'), by panning to the edges of the film frame itself during the transfer process, thus enabling viewers at least to see any crucial action instead of lopping it off. This is a less than happy solution, but so is 'letter-boxing', in which widescreen films are shown full width, but squeezed down to microscopic size, with bands of black at the top and bottom of the video frame. Most directors, knowing their films are eventually destined for television, simply do not employ the edges of the frame for significant story information, in a routine compliance of aesthetics with commerce—another defeat of film's breadth by video's narrow frame.

It is these resonances and connotations that need to be pointed out, rather than focusing on the obvious material differences between film and video. The more interesting question is one of assigned differences: how does value come to be attached to what are mere distinctions, and how has film's discourse about itself relied on hierarchizing such distinctions into relations of value and merit? Like the penchant for touching film, when you start looking closely at these things, they can start to seem rather odd.

In reading over the last ten years of *American Cinematographer* on the subject of film's relation to electronic technologies, one can't help but notice that the vocabulary brought to bear on the subject—which often relies on metaphors involving the lack of a 'shared language' and corresponding concerns about

'relationships', 'communication problems', and 'incompatibility'—seems oddly reminiscent of the vocabularies associated with other hotbed issues involving cultural confrontations with 'others' like race or immigration, in which language differences also become a way of articulating boundary anxieties. And language issues are also typically a mechanism through which the 'other' is imbricated into a structure in which dissimilarity is redefined as inferiority, and in which cultural differences are rearticulated as hierarchized oppositions. So the fact that, from within film discourse, video didn't speak the right language is significant in its fall from value. It is not simply a *different* technology, it is figured as a social inferior. My point here is not that the film–video opposition has crashing social significance on the order of race or immigration issues, or that we should bring humanistic empathy to bear on video's plight, but that discourses about social technologies can be seen to follow certain conventions of the social and linguistic contexts they inhabit. And I am suggesting that these discursive conventions *have* had significance in both the film profession and film studies, and that current shifts in technologies—in which video and electronic technologies are permeating film far more than ever before (and perhaps eventually displacing it)—are making this more apparent.

Typically, an article in the March 1993 *American Cinematographer* on 'Telecine: The Tools and how to Use Them' (Harrell 1993) focused less on material differences like the 'pan and scan' problem than on the cultural differences—the shared-language problem. Film people just don't know how to talk to telecine operators. The kind of 'close relationship' that exists between a film's director of photography and the film's colourist, that is, between two film professionals from the same world 'is very much a personal relationship'. But, conversely, 'telecine color correction and movie color timing are two different worlds'. The shared 'terminology that has been honed and developed for nearly a hundred years [in film] hasn't yet been fully developed'. And, in that what makes film an *art* is the photographic intent of the film, or what director of photography Conrad Hall calls 'the artistic use of color, grain, sharpness, darkness and motion', the fear is that, left to the mercy of the telecine colourist, this art will be lost. So, 'It is up to the telecine operator to make film *art* work for video *technology*' (my emphasis).

So the language difficulties become a way of erecting an art–technology opposition, and that opposition is one of the most frequent ways that film figures its distinction from, and hierarchizes its relation to, video. I think this is worth a closer look. The typical form this distinction takes is that film is human, sensuous, and creative, while video is dominated by machines, engineers, and technocrats. (Thus the control panels of the telecine colourist are described in the *American Cinematographer* article as looking like 'the cockpit of a 747'.)

To those outside the field, film's aversion to video, or its relegation of video to the sphere of technology, might be seen as merely an instance of what Freud referred to as the narcissism of small differences. Many people can't even tell the difference between something shot on film and something shot on video, particularly on broadcast television, which reduces the appearance of the difference anyway, by squashing the number of lines of resolution (a measurement of the quality of picture information) down to television's bandwidth. (If you are one of those who can't tell them apart, think about news, soap operas, live sports: that's video. Hour-long dramas, movies of the week: that's film. See the difference?) The difference between the look of the two is diminishing with the advent of digital video cameras, which feature controls that allow you to shape the look of the picture to make it resemble film, adding grain, flicker, and diffusion.

But video does look different from film. It is not only its lower resolution: video can't reproduce the same contrast ratio from lights to darks, meaning that it has less range, and gives less detail at either end of the light–dark spectrum. A consequence is that there are certain technical rules about how light your video whites can be and how dark your video blacks can be, and how vast a difference between the two there can be, particularly in broadcast situations. So video is routinely bad-mouthed in film discourses for allowing less latitude to the cinematographer, and thus less creative freedom, and less 'art'. And the fact that television engineers do get the final say about what may or may not be broadcast leads to no end of carping by cinematographers that video is a medium overruled by control-room engineers and soulless technocrats, not artists, because if your blacks are below 7.5 and your whites above 100 on a horrible contraption called a waveform monitor, you may have won an Oscar for cinematography, but your masterpiece won't go on the air.

So when filmmakers approach video, it has usually been with great trepidation about losing their souls in a devil's pact with technology. The arm's-length distan-cing is evident in the jacket copy from a widely used 1985 (that is, pre-digital) American Society of Cinematographers handbook whose project was exactly to forge some heretofore unknown *rapprochement* between film and video via what would have previously been thought an oxymoronic title: *Electronic Cinematography: Achieving Photographic Control over the Video Image*. The jacket reassures the nervous cinematographer:

Here's a book that *uniquely* demystifies video and reveals its creative potential. The authors, who have worked in both film and video, approach electronic cinematography from the point of view of the *cinematographer*, rather than that of the engineer . . . If you are interested in combining the refinements of motion picture film techniques and aesthetics with the technology of video, you will find a wealth of applications . . .

The book requires 'no previous electronics experience', the reader is assured. Once again, film is the realm of aesthetics, video is technology.

But let's get real. Shooting film can *hardly* be considered less technocratic than shooting video, and is actually far *more* technically difficult, requiring precise measurement of light, detailed knowledge of arcane things like sensitometry, and a somewhat overstructured relation to numbers: between film stocks (7287, 5298), film speeds (250, 500 . . .), frame rates, f-stops, lenses, filters, the Kelvin scale (a measurement of colour temperature), footcandles (a measurement of light intensity), and wattage (the power drawn by lights). These hardly seem less 'technological' or more sensuously personal than anything you would encounter on a video shoot.

Perhaps the art–technology distinction starts to seem a little more iffy. Now a hard-core film buff will probably intervene at this point to insist that we talk about the quality of the image, and the 'artfulness' possible with film that simply can't be achieved with video. And video often does look different from film, but that is also largely the result of the uses to which it is put. Video does do a technically less precise job of directly reproducing reality with the same degree of detail and verisimilitude, even though it tends to have a 'harder edge' and a more 'real' look. But this look of 'realness' is, to a great degree, a product of video's historic association with electronic news-gathering, or ENG: it is a convention, not an essence. When videographers want to make video look more like film, they will actually try to fuzz that hard edge somehow: by using diffusion or filtration. Film may tend to look more beautiful, but this is also, to a great degree, a matter of conventions: it is generally lit differently (low-key or arty, as opposed to high-key and functional), and for different purposes.

But the issue is the way in which material distinctions and differences between film and video become expressed as relations of value, and the issue of value is never far away from any discussion of film–video distinctions. One reason may be that, as one filmmaker philosopher put it, 'In shooting on film you're shooting on precious metal, that is, silver. With video technologies, you're shooting on silicon, which is essentially dirt.' It may not be exactly the silver–dirt distinction that lends film its aura of preciousness, but the fact that this makes film costs subject to fluctuations in the silver market. Film *does* cost more to shoot and process. Consequently, video is often shot in situations where money needs to be saved, for example lower-status genres like sitcoms or soap operas, or to advertise lower-status consumer commodities like used cars or down-market furniture, or in live (and thus usually more passing and disposable) programming like news or sports. So it may be that video has come to be associated with cheapness, with the momentary, the real, the quotidian. So it starts to *look* cheap, while film, by contrast, comes away with higher-class status. It starts to look richer, and this, I'd suggest, is a *sub rosa* aspect of the romance about film. And, of course, you only see video on television, for free, in your home, whereas the optimal film-viewing experience is after you have travelled somewhere and paid for your seat. So, in short, the film–video distinction has come to have certain class connotations that are piled on top of the other oppositions already in play: art–technology, silver–dirt, higher genres–lower genres, and cinema–television (even though 75 to 85 per cent of what is broadcast on prime time US television is shot on film).

Film, video, and digital culture

This brings us back to the present, and to the vast changes sweeping the world of production. How exactly do they affect and trouble the status of film? Well, a new generation of digital video cameras has recently been introduced by Sony that is said to rival 35mm film in terms of image quality. New advances in digital cinematography software allow camerapersons to simulate different film stocks on video, by selectively adding graininess or other film characteristics, to boost particular highlights, alter colours, change the overall tonal scale or contrast ratio—all previously activities proprietary to the 'art' of cinematography. The first all-digital live-action filmless movie was shown at last year's Sundance Film Festival, about which *American Cinematographer* wrote, 'The Berlin Wall between film and video may or may not be tumbling down. But if the recent all-digital production of *Mail Bonding* is any indication, there may be some serious cracks in the separation between these two media' (Kaufman 1995: 50). It is interesting to note, though, that three years earlier the magazine's editor had announced breathlessly, 'Cinematography now stands at the crossroads of film, video and computer technologies' (Heuring 1992: 25). The film world still seems unsure, regarding electronic technology, whether the Cold War rages still or *détente* has been achieved: should we pull up the drawbridge or welcome the invaders with cake and punch? Even though video technology has been in bed with film for at least twenty years, the profession, with a certain symptomatic disavowal ('yes I know, but . . .'), seems to keep greeting it anew.

Anxiety and disavowal are typical responses to unwelcome change, but what might also make film particularly prone to a current sense of instability is that, as I have suggested, it had never completely habituated itself to the presence of electronic technologies to begin with, and the technological changes currently under way seriously muck up the distinctions that have traditionally structured film's own discourse about itself. If digital technologies will allow video to rival 35mm film in terms of image quality, positioning electronic technologies to share in 'film art', perhaps it starts to become more apparent that the deeply held conviction that film is art, not technology, is something of a smokescreen for another material issue: that film is, of course, really, a vast business. It is economics, not art, that drives the development of these new technologies and their applications, just as it is economics that has driven the film industry from its inception. It seems fairly clear that one way film has played out its art–commerce ambivalence is by assigning all forms of such crudeness to the realm of video, while clinging to the notion of itself as somehow purer, an 'art form'. Even film academics, who might seem less likely to buy into the art thing in any wholesale way, can regularly be heard disparaging and distancing themselves from television studies. The Society for Cinema Studies,

Digital imaging and box-office success—*Jurassic Park* (1993)

the leading film studies professional organization, has only recently contemplated changing its name to allow some allusion to television.

It may be that film *is* on its last legs. Speculation is currently running high that economic forces will inevitably lead to electronic distribution of theatrical features, and to the demise of projected film. That is because it is ultimately cheaper to distribute electronic images and sound via satellite, fibre optics lines, or another carrier than it is to mass-produce film prints and physically deliver them to theatres. And instant home distribution of first releases by satellite (with pay-per-view by credit card) is even more financially advantageous because producers could recoup on their investments almost immediately. If 60 per cent of revenues are now generated by video distribution a year after a theatrical release, financiers are carrying those debts until the features hit the home viewer. Why wait so long? The most dire scenario for film is that there won't be sufficient economic incentive for film manufacturers to compete, and that there will even ultimately be a transition away from film as an origination medium, as digital cameras achieve greater and greater sophistication.

Whether or not this is the future is anyone's guess. As I said, a general sense of impeding loss permeates much of these discussions. What seems to provoke ambivalence about so much of this technological change is the sense that something 'human' is being lost, or shunted aside. There is a definite loss of older crafts and craft knowledge: film editing is virtually dead, as are special effects crafts like mould-making, casting, modelling, drawing, not to mention optical compositing and effects. Matte painting is on its way out, replaced by computer workstations. One response has been a defiant quasi-Luddite return to older technologies: Tim Burton's *The Nightmare before Christmas* (1993) had a cast entirely composed of puppets, bringing stop-motion photography back from the edge of extinction because many older technologies like stop-motion, according to Ray Harryhausen—one of the big names in traditional special effects—lend a certain strangeness to fantasy films which is lost if you make a film too realistic: 'You lose that dream quality.' Other special effects old-timers compare the cleanliness of computer workstations to 'accounting procedures' (Magrid 1994: 26–8). Perhaps there *is* the loss of something ineffably human in these new technologies. The two big hits of summer 1996, *Independence Day* (which had the largest opening grosses of any film in history) and *Twister*, are both noted for replacing 'star power' with massive computer-generated special effects. New computer software, such as the infamous 'morphing' technique of *Terminator 2* (1991), become the stars of the big new blockbusters, which now tend increasingly to be written around new special effects rather than special effects being used organically to help tell a compelling story.

There has also been much post-*Jurassic Park* (1993) speculation that computer technologies will ultimately replace actors, sets, and locations with digital simulacra; that 'If an actor's too fat to do movie number four, his head can be grafted onto somebody else's body or recreated digitally'. Whether or not this is the wave of the future, *Jurassic Park* did, in fact, feature a computer-generated actor portraying a human: for the final seconds of the shot in which the T-rex devours the attorney Gennaro head first, a computer re-creation of the actor was used (Magrid 1994: 30). Certainly cutting costs by eliminating actors is always an incentive. In *Forrest Gump* (1994) an anti-war protest scene involved a crowd of 200,000; all but 1,000 of them were digital replicants. Spiralling mega-salaries are the largest factor in out-of-control film costs, and film executives are starting to notice that big stars don't necessarily generate big profits.

Forrest Gump was, of course, the breakthrough movie that digitally put words in former presidents' mouths by 'repixillating' their lips, leading to much commentary and concern about the propagandistic or manipulative potential made available by digital technologies, in which every pixel in a frame can be endlessly manipulated and transformed. Says special effects artist Ken Ralston, '*Forrest Gump*'s shots of Hanks interacting with historical figures definitely pushes the outer edges of effects work, dabbling with what were supposed to be photographic documentations of history. When seeing is no longer believing, the concept of photography as proof of anything seems on the verge of extinction. Here's the technology to do really dangerous work.'

Political and cultural theorists have been writing about the loss of a sense of history for some time now. So does a society get the technology it deserves, or technologies that make its own dominant ideologies more visible, more livable? As *American Cinematographer* wrote with some excitement regarding the then revolutionary morphing techniques in *Terminator 2* (you can now buy a similar programme for your home computer for under $100), 'The big news was that the audience accepted an incredible illusion as reality, and they loved it.' Well, it hardly seems like news, following on the heels of Reagan–Thatcherism, that audiences will accept incredible illusions as reality, or that the relationship between technologies and social ideologies has a certain quality of identity.

The task is then, as usual, for independent image-makers to work to utilize these new technologies to create images and contents that *aren't* simply business as usual. Technology needs to be demystified, as do silly manufactured oppositions between this or that technology on the basis of false notions of 'value'. Instead, technology can be utilized to contest the forces of social amnesia, rather than reproducing the industry's incessant bottom-line drive towards newer, bigger, shinier tech. What does it matter if independents produce more 'artistic' but equally tunnel-visioned technological reveries, that is, succumb to experimentation as an end in itself? Too many young film- and videomakers have got caught up in mastering each successive new technology, each new computer-imaging program, and end up producing pretty, technically competent wallpaper. Many of the most talented students seem to be producing the most vapid work, spending endless hours manipulating pixels into submission without stepping back to wonder what for.

Instead, now that it's possible to alter landscapes digitally, perhaps we can think about using these 'revolutionary' technologies as tools to alter social landscapes in more permanent and even more unsettling ways, rather than being seduced into quiescence by the lure of the new.

BIBLIOGRAPHY

Benjamin, Walter (1936/1969), 'The Work of Art in the Age of Mechanical Reproduction', trans. Harry Zohn in *Illuminations* (New York: Schocken Books).

Bordwell, David, and **Kristin Thompson** (1990), *Film Art: An Introduction* (New York: McGraw-Hill).

Brandt, James B. (1991), 'Video Assist: Past, Present and Future', *American Cinematographer*, 72/6 (June), 93–8.

Comer, Brooke (1992), 'Incident at Oglala: Advancing the Art of Editing', *American Cinematographer*, 73/4 (Apr.), 26–32.

Film Art: An Introduction (1990) (New York: McGraw-Hill).

Harrell, Alfred D. (1993), 'Telecine: The Tools and how to Use Them', *American Cinematographer*, 74/3: 61–6.

*****Hayward, Philip,** and **Tana Wollen,** (eds.) (1993), *Future Visions: New Technologies of the Screen* (London: British Film Institute).

Heuring, David (1992), 'When "Post" Becomes the Main Event', *American Cinematographer*, 73/9 (Sept.), 22–3.

Kaufman, Debra (1995), 'Mail Bonding: Foray into Digital Filmmaking', *American Cinematographer*, 76/4 (Apr.) 50–4.

Lister, Martin (ed.) (1995), *The Photographic Image in Digital Culture* (London: Routledge).

Magrid, Ron (1994), 'Exploring the Future of Special Effects', *American Cinematographer*, 75/2 (Feb.), 52–6.

Millennium Film Journal (1995), Special Issue: *Interactivities*, 28 (Spring).

Petro, Patrice (ed.) (1995), *Fugitive Images: From Photography to Video* (Bloomington: Indiana University Press).

Pizzelo, Chris (1994), 'Forecasting the Digital Future', *American Cinematographer*, 73/9 (Mar.), 25–30.

Roland, Fritz (1992), 'Making Peace with Technology', *American Cinematographer*, 73/9 (Sept.), 53–7.

Rosen, Phillip (ed.) (1986), *Narrative, Apparatus, Ideology* (New York: Columbia University Press).

Williams, Raymond (1975), *Television: Technology and Cultural Form* (New York: Schocken Books).

27

Film and television

John Hill

Despite the centenary of cinema in 1995, it has been common in recent years to talk of the decline of cinema, and even its 'death'. A number of factors have underpinned this kind of thinking: the decline in cinema attendances world-wide and a declining variety in film production, the loss of a certain kind of cinematic experience involved with cinemagoing, and a corresponding dimunition of the cultural importance of film. There is certainly a degree of validity in these claims. Although there has been an upturn in a number of countries in recent years as a result of the opening of multiplexes, the global trend in cinemagoing has been downwards. At the same time, there has been a crisis in film production in a number of countries and a growing domination of the world market, outside Asia, by the output of Hollywood. Cinemagoing is no longer the central leisure activity it once was, even for those who attend the cinema, while the composition of the cinema audience has also changed, no longer consisting of the 'mass' of the population, but only a particular—mainly youthful—segment of it.

However, if we take into account the significance of television and video, this situation looks somewhat different. For while cinemagoing has been in decline, the actual watching of films has not, and is probably greater than ever before. This can be seen in the way in which the economics of film, television, and video have become increasingly entwined. Towards the end of the 1960s and the beginning of the 1970s the Hollywood

majors were faced with economic crisis; by the end of the 1980s, however, they were once again restored to financial health. The key factor in this turn-around lay in the ability of the studios to adapt to, and take advantage of, the new video and pay-TV markets, the revenues from which soon outstripped those from theatrical release. Whereas returns from theatrical release (both domestic and foreign) accounted for nearly 76 per cent of studio revenues in 1980, these were only responsible for 32 per cent of revenues in 1990. In contrast, revenues from pay-TV rose over the same period from 4.8 to 9 per cent, while, most dramatically, revenues from video increased from 1 to over 45 per cent (*Screen Finance* 1993: 8). Thus, while cinema admissions over the same period fell in the United States as well as globally, this clearly does not indicate that films were watched less—only that they were increasingly viewed on the small screen (*Screen Digest* 1993: 204–5).

This means that, 100 years on from the first public film screening in 1895, films—whether broadcast or on video—are now more likely to be watched at home on television than in the cinema. But does this matter, and what are the implications of this for an understanding of the current situation of cinema? In order to answer these questions, it may be helpful to examine some of the arguments which have surrounded the development of the increasingly close relationship between film and television and the ways in which this has been perceived as both a loss and a gain.

Economics

As the above suggests, the drive towards a convergence of film and television has been economic. For although film and television have often been seen as clearly distinct (and even as enemies of each other), the relationship between the two has been complex and varied. As William Lafferty has argued, 'contrary to conventional wisdom, the economic relationship between film and television has a lengthy history' (1988: 273). He traces this relationship back to the 1930s, when Hollywood invested in television and radio broadcasting stations and networks as a means of controlling the development of a potential competitor, and also explored the potential of theatre television (see also Gomery 1984). These strategies, however, failed to bear fruit because of the opposition of the Federal Communications Commission, which was already concerned about monopoly tendencies in the film industry. Consequently, it is the 1950s which Lafferty identifies as the period in which a 'symbiotic relation between the film and television industries' was properly sealed (1988: 281). It was at this time that the studios fully opened up their film libraries to television broadcasters and began direct production of programmes specifically for televison, leading to the emergence of the 'made-for-TV movie' in the early 1960s.

In doing so, Peter Kramer argues, the Hollywood majors were involved in a 'dual strategy' (1996: 38). On the one hand, the majors adapted the processes of the old studio system to regular production for the television audience; on the other hand, they sought to 'differentiate' the cinema film from television through investment in special 'blockbuster' movies (characterized by the use of new technological developments, special effects, and spectacle) that would continue to attract audiences into the cinemas. Despite the growing dependence of the big-budget 'event' movie on small-screen media for the generation of revenues, Kramer argues that this is not as contradictory as it might at first seem. For it is precisely 'the lure of the big picture'—the 'grandeur and mystique of cinema'—which he argues provides a major part of a film's appeal for the television and video audience (12).

This 'dual strategy' may also be linked to changing modes of movie consumption. For the majority of people, the actual activity of cinemagoing has become much less regular and more of a 'special' activity than in the heyday of Hollywood's studio system. The social character of the audience has also changed, with the bulk of the moviegoing audience belonging to the 15–24 age-group. In contrast, films on television and video are watched by an older and more socially diverse audience for whom the activity of film viewing is often regular and habitual. Thus, in the case of US telefilms, Laurence Jarvik and Nancy Strickland argue that, despite their low critical status, they often attract audiences well in excess of theatrical releases and that 'the enormous viewership for movies-of-the-week and mini-series parallels the huge regular moviegoing family audience of Hollywood's Golden Age' (1988: 42). However, while much more time is now spent watching films of all kinds on television than in the cinema, questions also remain. As Sylvia Harvey suggests, it is important to consider the significance of the time spent watching films not just in terms of 'quantity' but also in terms of 'quality' (1996: 241). A number of different issues arise in this respect.

Technology

In the first instance, the viewing of film on television or video inevitably involves a drop in technical quality. This has various aspects and includes a certain loss of quality in sound, colour range, and resolution (from 3,500 to 4,000 lines of resolution to 525 lines of resolution in the United States and 625 in Europe). There is also the vexed question of aspect ratio. Whereas the aspect ratio of television is normally 1.33 : 1, films—since the advent of widescreen processes in the 1950s—have characteristically been shot in much more rectangular ratios (such as 1.85 or 2.35 : 1). In order to accommodate films to a television format, 'panning and scanning' techniques (ironically developed by the film industry itself) have been adopted, which lead not only to a loss of much of the original image but also to a degree of 'remaking' of films as well. As a result, and despite the appeal of the 'big picture', filmmakers have increasingly had to acknowledge that television is a film's ultimate destination and stick to 'safe-action' areas when filming. Frank Thompson (1990), for example, indicates the differences between John Boorman's *Point Blank* (1967) and Miloš Forman's *Amadeus* (1984) when seen on television. The latter, he argues, was evidently filmed with television in mind, whereas the former was not. As a result, *Amadeus* still 'works' on television; *Point Blank*, by contrast, looks 'jumbled' and 'sloppy' (1990: 41). However, with the growing acceptability to audiences of 'letter-boxing' (whereby films are shown in their proper aspect ratio), some of the problems associated with panning and scanning are beginning to be overcome.

It is also the case, as Dan Fleming (1996) has argued, that there has been nothing inevitable about television's inability to deal with the widescreen image. The technology has existed for some time to provide widescreen television, with high-definition images and good-quality stereo sound, which, if not necessarily matching the quality of the projected film image, is at least capable of approximating it much more closely. That this has not so far been made widely available has more to do with its economic feasibility than any 'essential' difference between the film and television media. This is also true of what are often taken to be other fundamental differences between film and television. Thus, while film involves the watching of a large screen image in a darkened public space whereas television involves the viewing of a small screen image in a private domestic space, this again is largely a historical contingency, resulting from the economic imperatives of the film and television industries, rather than any inevitable difference. As Kramer (1996) indicates, in its early phase of development, film was initially conceived (by pioneers such as Thomas Edison) as a domestic technology, just as television was in turn conceived, and tested (in the form of theatre television), as a public one.

In the same way, television has often been regarded as basically a 'live' medium which is better suited to relaying the 'live' event than transmitting pre-recorded entertainment, such as film (see Barr 1996). However, while television may have exploited this 'live' quality to great effect in relation to news, sport, and important public events, it does not follow that television is 'essentially' a 'live' medium or that it is this 'live' quality which should shape the direction of drama on television. Robert Vianello, for example, argues in relation to US television in the 1950s that 'The question of "live" versus film formats' was not simply a technological or aesthetic matter but an economic one (1984: 210). 'Live' programming, he argues, gained dominance in the early years of US television not only because it was cheaper to produce than filmed programming, but because it was used to justify the power of the television networks and enforce the dependency of local television stations. By the late 1950s, however, when the conditions that had made 'live' programming an advantageous strategy for the networks began to change, production shifted decisively towards the telefilm. In this respect, the legacy of 'live' drama on television has been read in different ways: as something particular to television which the shift to recorded forms has lost, or as an inhibition upon the aesthetic potential of television which the development of a closer relationship with cinema then overcame (McLoone 1996).

Aesthetics

However, if the influence of film forms on television drama may be seen to have encouraged the demise of 'live' television drama, this influence has not always been seen as leading to drama which is then regarded as properly 'cinematic'. This again has been partly a matter of economics. Made-for-TV films or theatrical films made with television money have often been made more quickly and cheaply than those made by Hollywood and often lack the production values associated with the 'big picture'. However, as McLoone argues, there is also a tendency in this kind of discussion to draw a 'false contrast' between film and television: between the extremes of 'television at its least "adventurous" (aesthetically) and cinema in its big picture, "event" mode' (1996: 81). In this respect, it is often the big Hollywood 'event' movie which is used to define 'cinema' even though the bulk of Hollywood's output during the studio era consisted of much more routine, modestly budgeted productions that lacked the special effects or expensive displays that are now associated with the 'event' movie.

As a result, many US television films can be seen to belong to a tradition of low-budget Hollywood filmmaking, and succeed as cinema despite their television origins. Steven Spielberg's *Duel* (1971) is one of the most celebrated examples of this, but, more recently, John Dahl's *Red Rock West* (1993) and *The Last Seduction* (1994), which were given successful theatrical releases *after* they had been made for, and shown on, cable television, vividly illustrate how television beginnings do not necessarily vitiate against the production of 'proper' cinema (Lyons 1994). Similar examples may also be found in Europe, where television broadcasters have been involved in extensive support of film production. Despite complaints, especially in Britain, that the films which television finances have lacked the cinematic values associated with 'real cinema', it is difficult to identify any shared television influence or 'TV aesthetic' informing such films, especially when it has included work as diverse as that of Federico Fellini, Roberto Rossellini, Ermanno Olmi, and the Taviani brothers in Italy, Rainer Werner Fassbinder, Werner Herzog, and Wim Wenders in Germany, Pedro Almodóvar in Spain, and Peter Greenaway, Derek Jarman, Stephen Frears, Mike Leigh, and Ken Loach in Britain.

However, if it is difficult to isolate clear-cut aesthetic differences between film and television, this is not to say that the way in which film and television have become intertwined has not had aesthetic consequences. Lafferty, for example, argues that although television inherited from film a set of narrative and stylistic conventions, the pressures of time and cost upon television production led to the adoption of new techniques by television which then fed back into film production. He cites, for example, the use of 'non-classical' techniques such as rack-focus, overlapping sound, and, particularly, the zoom which were adopted by television in the interests of speed and cost but subsequently became commonplace in filmmaking practice. Indeed, by the 1970s, Lafferty argues, there had been 'a virtual melding of film and television techniques' (1988: 299). With the advent of video, critics have also argued for more wide-ranging forms of interaction. Timothy Corrigan, for example, argues that the 'distracted' conditions of television and video viewing has encouraged new types of cinematic narration. He indicates how the 'classical' model of film narration has begun to give way to forms of narration in which time is 'wasted' and in which narrative incident and visual display exceed motivational logic (1991: 166). Corrigan, in this respect, identifies some of the features of what has become identified as 'post-classical' cinema in which plots have become looser and more episodic, identification with characters less intense, and the relations between narrative and spectacle less tight-knit than in films of the 'classical' period. In doing so, he is also attributing special significance to the changed viewing conditions of films in so far as such features are connected to the less concentrated manner in which films are likely to be watched on television and video.

Spectatorship

To some extent, it is this interest in spectatorship that has informed some of the more recent writing of film and television. Sylvia Harvey, for example, has sought to differentiate film from television in terms of 'the quality of the viewing experience' and its 'social and public character' (1996: 250). The quality of the viewing experience, she argues, is related not only to the size and density of the film image, but also to the concentrated attention span which it receives in the cinema. Drawing on Bazin's work on the ontology of the photographic image, she calls for a 'recognition of the special, even "sacred" character of the film image', which, she argues, 'derives not from divine authority but from human response' (250). Something of a similar line is taken also by Anne Friedberg, who argues that, with the advent of the video movie, 'the "aura" of the original moment of cinema exhibition also disappears' (1993: 139). There is, however, a slightly paradoxical twist to this argument. For Walter Benjamin (1936), it was precisely the 'mechanical reproducibility' of the mass media, as exemplified by film, which destroyed the 'aura' of traditional art and its attachment to notions of the 'original'. In the age of television and video, however, it is now the film-viewing experience that is seen to possess 'auratic' qualities and provide precisely the experience of the 'original' which, it is argued, the television or video viewing of films now lacks.

In such arguments, it is the concentration and involvement that characterizes watching film in a cinema rather than on television or video which is given emphasis. Television spectatorship, in this respect, is seen to be fundamentally different from cinema spectatorship. Raymond Williams (1974), for example, has defined the key experience of television as one of 'flow', while John Ellis (1982) lays stress on television's dependence on 'segmentalisation'. For both authors, it is the experience of 'watching television' that is considered more important than the watching of individual programmes and, for Ellis, this also involves a particular relationship with the viewer. Thus, unlike the concentrated gaze at the screen expected by cinema, television only invites the 'glance' (163).

It is this 'glance aesthetics' that Corrigan (1991: 31) sees as governing the contemporary viewing of films, while Friedberg (1993: 139–43) discusses the 'spectatorial flânerie' and active relationship to texts permitted by television and video technologies. In both cases, this new form of spectatorship is also linked to changing forms of (postmodern) subjectivity. For Corrigan, the new forms of film reception involve the disappearance of 'a clear and stable viewer' (1991: 2), while, for Friedberg, the new media produce 'a shift-ing, mobile, fluid subjectivity' (1993: 143). However, although it is clear that television and video have allowed a greater control (and interactivity) over the viewing of films, there is also a tendency in such writing to make overly general claims and draw too strong a contrast between 'old' and 'new' forms of viewing. Thus, the watching of films in cinemas is not, and has not been, as concentrated—just as the viewing of film on television and video is not necessarily as inatten-tive—as the oppositions drawn between film and tele-vision viewing sometimes suggest. The conditions characterizing the viewing of films have varied accord-ing to historical and geographical circumstances and, indeed, John Belton suggests how contemporary movie-'going' has echoes of both the peep-show and the nickelodeon era (1994: 342). Moreover, the assumption that the conditions generally taken to be characteristic of cinema spectatorship (large screen, darkness, relative immobility) necessarily 'fix' subjec-tivity in some straightforward way (as in apparatus the-ory) is clearly inadequate for an understanding of the complex ways in which audiences have actually responded to films socially and historically. In the same way, it is not possible simply to 'read off' forms of subjectivity from the technologies of television and video. Subjectivity in this respect is 'produced' not by the media, but by a whole set of social and cultural determinants, which may, nevertheless, include film, television, and video.

Cultural Identity

This emphasis upon subjectivity also overlaps with concerns regarding the role of film in the shaping of social and cultural identities. As we have seen, one contrast between film and television has been to see television as encouraging a more 'privatized' form of film consumption. However, once again, the opposi-tion is not necessarily clear-cut. As Harvey notes, while cinema may offer a shared experience in a social space, it can also be one which is 'intensely private' (1996: 241). And, while watching film on television may be regarded as private, it can also be a shared experience. This is not simply because television viewing often involves a group of some kind (be it family members or friends), but because watching a film as it is broad-cast can involve a sense of collective belonging as well. From this point of view, the simultaneous viewing of a

film by a large audience draws together spectators in a shared experience similar to those provided by other forms of television such as public occasions or epi-sodes of a soap opera.

This also complicates models of television viewing as a relatively undifferentiated 'flow'. While the empha-sis upon 'flow' may have drawn attention to important aspects of television viewing, it has also underesti-mated the role of the independent programme and how it is distinguished from, and often watched sepa-rately from, the overall flow of television (Waller 1988; McLoone 1996). Films on television can be important in this regard precisely because television can make use of a film as an 'event' which breaks up the televisual flow and offers a 'special' experience separated out from the rest of television. In doing so, film can also participate in the 'public sphere' of which television is now a central part. Thus, Jarvick and Strickland defend US TV movies in terms of their 'social function', arguing that, in addition to the provision of entertainment, they constitute 'the town hall of public debate on important historical, social and political issues' (1988: 42)

This is an argument which also has relevance to the relations between film and television outside the Uni-ted States, and especially in Europe. For European television has been much less driven by commercial imperatives than its US counterpart, and the co-opera-tion between film and television which has occurred within European countries has characteristically been linked to public-service values. Thus, while in the Uni-ted States it has been the networks and the commercial pay-TV channels, such as Home Box Office (HBO) and Showtime, that have financed films, in Europe it has been public-service stations (such as ZDF in Germany, RAI in Italy, Channel 4 in Britain, RTVE in Spain, and RTP in Portugal) that have been of crucial importance in sustaining European film production. In the case of France, the government's legal requirement that broadcasters support French film production has ensured that France is the Continent's largest film-producing country.

The importance of television's support for film pro-duction in Europe may be explained by the growing economic might of Hollywood and the problems national cinemas have faced in trying to maintain levels of production. From this point of view, an alliance between film and television has provided not only the most economically prudent form of cinema for European countries, but also the one most likely to offer a culturally distinctive alternative to Hollywood

My Beautiful Laundrette (1985)—a fusion of 'art cinema' and public-service television

norms, by drawing on television's public-service traditions and speaking to their own cultures in ways that
Hollywood films, aimed at a global market, cannot.
Thus, in the case of films supported by Britain's Channel 4—such as *My Beautiful Laundrette* (1985), *Letter
to Brezhnev* (1985), *Riff-Raff* (1990), *The Crying Game*
(1992), and *Naked* (1993)—there has been something
of a fusion between the formal interests of 'art cinema'
and the socio-political concerns of public service television (Hill 1996). The issue in respect of Europe, therefore, is not so much whether it is desirable that
television should support film, but whether it will continue to possess the means to do so. This question has
become especially pertinent in the 1990s, given the
increasingly commercial climate of broadcasting
across Europe, which has made support for film,
because of its cost, increasingly difficult, as the examples of RAI in Italy and RTVE in Spain have demonstrated.

Conclusion

It is now clear that the future of film is inextricably linked
with that of television and video. In this sense, it is an
irreversible development, and there is little point in
lamenting the 'decline' of cinema in its traditional
form. However, this chapter has also suggested that
it is misleading to 'essentialize' the differences
between the two mediums or homogenize the characteristics of each. It has also pointed out that the relationship between film and television is historically and
geographically variable, and, although crucially important, the US experience is but one model of the way in
which film and television have reached an alliance. And
while there may be certain losses involved in the new
relationship between film and television (such as technical quality or type of viewing experience), there have
also been corresponding gains (such as the increased
accessibility of films and the emergence of more

'active' viewing forms). In this respect, cinema is not so much in 'decline' as entering a new historical era.

BIBLIOGRAPHY

Anderson, Christopher (1994), *Hollywood TV: The Studio System in the Fifties* (Austin: University of Texas Press).

Balio, Tino (ed.) (1990), *Hollywood in the Age of Television* (Boston: Unwin Hyman).

Barr, Charles (1996), '"They Think it's all Over": The Dramatic Legacy of Live Television', in Hill and McLoone (1996).

Belton, John (1994), *American Cinema/American Culture* (New York: McGraw-Hill).

Benjamin, Walter (1936/1973), 'The Work of Art in the Age of Mechanical Reproduction', in *Illuminations*, ed. Hannah Arendt and trans. Harry Zohn (London: Collins).

Corrigan, Timothy (1991), *A Cinema without Walls: Movies and Culture after Vietnam* (London: Routledge).

Ellis, John (1982), *Visible Fictions Cinema: Television: Video* (London: Routledge).

Fleming, Dan (1996), 'Dial "M" for Movies: New Technologies, New Relations', in Hill and McLoone (1996).

Friedberg, Anne (1993), *Window Shopping: Cinema and the Postmodern* (Berkeley: University of California Press).

Gomery, Douglas (1984), 'Failed Opportunities: The Integration of the U.S. Motion Picture and Television Industries', *Quarterly Review of Film Studies*, 9/3 (Summer), 219–28.

*****Harvey, Sylvia** (1996), 'What is Cinema? The Sensuous, the Abstract and the Political', in Christopher Williams (ed.), *Cinema: The Beginnings and the Future* (London: University of Westminster Press).

Hill, John (1996), 'British Television and Film: The Making of a Relationship', in Hill and McLoone (eds.), *Big Picture, Small Screen*.

***—— and Martin McLoone** (eds.) (1996), *Big Picture, Small Screen: The Relations between Film and Television* (Luton: John Libbey Media and University of Luton Press).

Hilmes, Michèle (1990), *Hollywood and Broadcasting: From Radio to Cable* (Urbana: University of Illinois Press).

Jarvik, Laurence, and **Nancy Strickland** (1988), 'TV Movies: Better than the Real Thing', *American Film* (Dec.), 41–3, 56.

Kramer, Peter (1996), 'The Lure of the Big Picture: Film, Television and Hollywood', in Hill and McLoone (1996).

*****Lafferty, William** (1988), 'Film and Television', in Gary R. Edgerton (ed.), *Film and the Arts in Symbiosis: A Resource Guide* (New York: Greenwood Press).

Lyons, Donald (1994), 'Genre and Caste in Cableland', *Film Comment*, 30/5 (Sept–Oct.), 2–7.

McLoone, Martin (1996), 'Boxed In? The Aesthetics of Film and Television', in Hill and McLoone (1996).

Screen Digest (1993), 'World Cinema: Falling Screens and Failing Audiences' (Sept.), 201–8.

Screen Finance (1993), 'Studio Film Revenues Set to Grow by 6.9 per cent in 1993' (5 May), 8–13.

Thompson, Frank (1990), 'The Big Squeeze', *American Film* (Feb.), 40–3.

Vianello, Robert (1984), 'The Rise of the Telefilm and the Networks' Hegemony over the Motion Picture Industry', *Quarterly Review of Film Studies*, 9/3 (Summer), 204–18.

Waller, Gregory A. (1988), 'Flow, Genre and the Television Text', *Journal of Popular Film and Television*, 16/1 (Spring), 6-11.

Williams, Raymond (1974), *Television: Technology and Cultural Form* (London: Fontana).

List of Picture and Reading Sources

PICTURES

Unless otherwise stated all photographic material was reproduced courtesy of the Kobal collection. Whilst every effort has been made to identify copyright holders that has not been possible in a few cases. We apologize for any apparent negligence and any omissions brought to our attention will be remedied in any future editions. 1.1 Courtesy of Hyphen Films etc. 1.2 Courtesy of the British Film Institute 1.3 RKO/Goldwyn 1946 1.4 Universal City Studios, Inc. a division of MCA 1956 1.6 Polygram 1.7 Paramount 1.8 Miramax 1994 1.9 Turner Entertainment Co. 1939 1.10 Courtesy of Ian Christie 1.11 Courtesy of Ian Christie 1.12 Metro Goldwyn Mayer Inc. 1932 1.13 Paramount 1.14 De Laurentis and Warner Home Video 1.15 Universal City Studios, Inc. a division of MCA 1934 1.16 and 1.17 © Women Make Movies Inc. 1.18 Universal City Studios, Inc. a division of MCA 1940 1.19 Courtesy of the British Film Institute 1.22 RKO/Goldwyn 1936 1.23 Courtesy of the British Film Institute 1.26 and 1.27 Metro Goldwyn Mayer Inc. 1991 1.29 The Rank Organization Plc 1980 2.2 Courtesy of the British Film Institute 2.5 Courtesy of the British Film Institute 2.7 Universal City Studios, Inc. a division of MCA 2.8 Turner Entertainment Co. 1942 2.9 Warner Brothers 1967 2.10 Lucasfilm 1977 2.11 Universal City Studios, Inc. a division of MCA 1975 2.12 Twentieth Century Fox 1939 2.13 Metro Goldwyn Mayer 1954 2.14 Warner Brothers 1945 2.15 Courtesy of the British Film Institute 2.17 Metro Goldwyn Mayer 1937 2.18 Paramount 1960 3.1 1969 Embra Line 3.2 Les Grand Films Classiques 3.5 British Post Office 3.6 1990 J & M Entertainment Ltd/Miramax Film Corp. 3.7 Courtesy of the British Film Institute 3.8 Svenskfilmindustri 1957 3.9 Courtesy of Ian Christie 3.10 1945 Excelsa Films 3.11 Contemporary Films 1975 3.12 Artificial Eye 1981 3.13 Courtesy of Paradise Films 3.15 Courtesy of the British Film Institute 3.16 The Rank Organization 1946 3.17 Courtesy of the British Film Institute 3.18 Courtesy of the British Film Institute 3.19 Courtesy of the British Film Institute 3.20 Navketan International Films Ltd from collection of Hyphen Films Ltd 3.21 Guangxi Film Studio/Artificial Eye 1984 3.22 Artificial Eye/Courtesy of the Movie Store 3.23 Courtesy of the British Film Institute/ERA International Ltd 3.25 Contemporary Films 1974 3.26 Courtesy of the British Film Institute 3.27 Ukamau Limitada 3.28 Universal Studios and Amblin

READINGS

Robin Wood: 'Written on the Wind' from Robin Wood, *University Vision*, 12, 1974. Peter Wollen: 'Citizen Kane', from 'Introduction to Citizen Kane' in *Film Reader*, 1, 1975. Richard Taylor and Ian Christie: Translation of Viktor Shklovsky's 'Poetry Prose in Cinema' from Richard Taylor and Ian Christie (eds.), *The Film Factory: Russian and Soviet Cinema in Documents 1896–1939* (revised edition, London and New York: Routledge) © Richard Taylor, 1994. John Hill: 'The Political Thriller Debate' from John Hill, 'Finding a Form: Politics and Aesthetics in *Fatherland, Hidden Agenda*, and *Riff-Raff*' in George McKnight (ed.), *Agent of Challenge and Defiance: The Films of Ken Loach* (Trowbridge: Flicks Books, 1997). Mary Anne Doane: 'Rebecca' from Mary Anne Doane, *The Desire to Desire: The Woman's Film of the 1940s*, Basingstoke Macmillan Ltd/Bloomington, Indiana University Press 1987. © Mary Anne Doane. Tania Modleski: 'Rebecca' from *The Women Who Knew Too Much: Hitchcock and Feminist Theory*, Methuen, 1988. Richard Maltby: 'Casablanca' from Richard Maltby, *Harmless Entertainment: Hollywood and the Ideology of Consensus*, Metuchan, NJ: Scarecrow Press 1983. Rick Altman: 'Casablanca' from 'Dickens, Griffith, and Film Theory Today' in *South Atlantic Quarterly*, 88(2) 1989, © 1989 Duke University Press, 1992. Reprinted with permission. Peter Wollen: 'John Ford' from Peter Wollen, *Signs and Meaning in the Cinema*, Secker & Warburg, 1992. Linda Williams: 'Body genres' excerpted from Linda Williams, 'Film Bodies: Gender, Genre and Excess', *Film Quarterly*, 44(4), © 1991 by The Regents of the University of California. Robert B. Ray: 'Hollywood and Ideology' from Robert B. Ray, *A Certain Tendency of the Hollywood Cinema, 1930–1980*, © 1985 Princeton University Press. Reprinted with permission from Princeton University Press. Rosie Thomas: 'Popular Hindi Cinema', from Rosie Thomas, 'Indian Cinema: Pleasures and Popularity', reprinted with permission from *Screen* 26(3–4), 1985. Richard Porton: 'Hyenas' from Richard Porton, 'Mambety's *Hyenas*: Between Anti-Colonialism and the Critique of Modernity' *Iris*, 18, 1995 © Richard Porton.

Index of Selected Names
and Film Titles

INDEX OF SELECTED NAMES AND FILM TITLES